ww.prenhall.com/dessler www.prenhall.com/dessler
ww.prenhall.com/dessler www.prenhall.com/dessler
ww.prenhall.com/dessler www.prenhall.com/dessler
ww.prenhall.com/dessler www.prenhall.com/dessler
ww.prenhall.com/dessler www.prenhall.com/dessler
ww.prenhall.com/dessler www.prenhall.com/dessler
ww.prenhall.com/dessler www.prenhall.com/dessler
ww.prenhall.com/dessler www.prenhall.com/dessler
ww.prenhall.com/dessler www.prenhall.com/dessler
ww.prenhall.com/dessler www.prenhall.com/dessler
ww.prenhall.com/dessler www.prenhall.com/dessler
ww.prenhall.com/dessler www.prenhall.com/dessler
ww.prenhall.com/dessler www.prenhall.com/dessler
ww.prenhall.com/dessler www.prenhall.com/dessler
ww.prenhall.com/dessler www.prenhall.com/dessler
ww.prenhall.com/dessler www.prenhall.com/dessler
ww.prenhall.com/dessler www.prenhall.com/dessler
ww.prenhall.com/dessler www.prenhall.com/dessler
ww.prenhall.com/dessler www.prenhall.com/dessler
ww.prenhall.com/dessler www.prenhall.com/dessler
ww.prenhall.com/dessler www.prenhall.com/dessler
ww.prenhall.com/dessler www.prenhall.com/dessler
ww.prenhall.com/dessler www.prenhall.com/dessler

HUMAN RESOURCE MANAGEMENT

8th Edition

Gary Dessler
Florida International University

Prentice Hall, Upper Saddle River, New Jersey 07458

Senior Editor: Stephanie Johnson
Assistant Editor: Hersch Doby
Editor-in-Chief: Natalie Anderson
Managing Editor (editorial): Jennifer Glennon
Executive Marketing Manager: Michael Campbell
Associate Managing Editor (production): Judy Leale
Permissions Coordinator: Monica Stipanov
Manufacturing Supervisor: Arnold Vila
Senior Manufacturing Manager: Vincent Scelta
Senior Designer: Cheryl Asherman
Design Manager: Patricia Smythe
Interior Design: Donna Wickes
Photo Research Supervisor: Melinda Lee Reo
Image Permission Supervisor: Kay Dellosa
Image Permission Coordinator: Michelina Viscusi
Photo Researcher: Kathy Ringrose
Cover Design: Cheryl Asherman
Cover Illustration: Ron Chan
Composition: UG / GGS Information Services, Inc.

Reprinted with corrections February, 2000
Copyright © 2000, 1997, 1994, 1991, 1988 by Prentice-Hall, Inc.
Upper Saddle River, New Jersey 07458

Library of Congress Cataloging-in-Publication Data

Dessler, Gary,
    Human resource management / Gary Dessler. — 8th ed.
        p.   cm.
    Includes bibliographical references and index.
    ISBN 0-13-014124-0 (hardcover)
    1. Personnel management.   I. Title.
HF5549.D4379   1999
658.3—dc21
                                              99-11243
                                            CIP

Prentice-Hall International (UK) Limited, London
Prentice-Hall of Australia Pty. Limited, Sydney
Prentice-Hall Canada, Inc., Toronto
Prentice-Hall Hispanoamericana, S.A., Mexico
Prentice-Hall of India Private Limited, New Delhi
Prentice-Hall of Japan, Inc., Tokyo
Prentice-Hall (Singapore) Pte. Ltd.
Editora Prentice-Hall do Brasil, Ltda., Rio de Janeiro

Printed in the United States of America

10 9 8 7 6 5 4

Dedicated to my son, Derek

BRIEF CONTENTS

CONTENTS

6   INTERVIEWING CANDIDATES   215

Sidebar (left margin):

▲ **INFORMATION TECHNOLOGY AND HR** Computer-Interactive Performance Test   **184**

▲ **THE HIGH-PERFORMANCE ORGANIZATION** Building Better, Faster, More Competitive Organizations Through HR: Skills Testing   **189**

▲ **SMALL BUSINESS APPLICATIONS** Small Business Testing and Reference Checking   **204**

▲ **INFORMATION TECHNOLOGY AND HR** Computer Applications in Interviewing: The Computer-Aided Interview   **223**

▲ **DIVERSITY COUNTS** Dressing for the Interview   **227**

13 BENEFITS AND SERVICES   475

▲ **THE HIGH-PERFORMANCE ORGANIZATION** Building Better, Faster, More Competitive Organizations Through HR: Worker's Compensation   485

▲ **INFORMATION AND HR TECHNOLOGY** Computers and Benefits Administration   502

▲ **SMALL BUSINESS APPLICATIONS** Benefits and Employees Leasing   503

PREFACE

Human Resource Management provides students in Human Resource Management courses and practicing managers with a complete, comprehensive review of essential personnel management concepts and techniques in a highly readable and understandable form.

This eighth edition has several distinguishing characteristics. While it again focuses almost entirely on essential personnel management topics like job analysis, testing, compensation, and appraisal, **HR and The High-Performance Organization** is introduced as an integrating theme. Globalization, deregulation, and technological advances mean organizations today must be more competitive than ever to survive. Special features in all chapters show how managers can build better, faster, more competitive organizations through human resource management.

As this eighth edition goes to press, I feel even more strongly than I did when the first was published that all managers—not just human resource/personnel managers—need a strong foundation in personnel management concepts and techniques to do their jobs. Because all managers do have personnel-related responsibilities, Human Resource Management is again aimed at all students of management, not just those who will someday carry the title "human resource manager," and our second theme thus continues this book's focus on **practical applications** that help all managers deal with their personnel-related responsibilities. I've added more "how to" topics, such as how to deal with abusive employees (chapter 15) and how small-business owners can establish manual HR systems (in the book's new appendix). Technology is rapidly changing how we all work and learn, and so you'll find there's been a major leap in this book's use of **technology and HR** content and supplements including a new on-line WebCT course. Finally, creating competitive advantage by fostering employee commitment continues as an integrating theme. A few of these themes deserve some elaboration:

THE HIGH-PERFORMANCE ORGANIZATION	The eighth edition emphasizes HR's role in making companies better, faster, and more competitive. I introduce this theme in Chapter 1, and revisit it throughout the remainder of the book, both in the chapters' contents, and in a continuing feature called "**The High-Performance Organization: Building Better, Faster, More Competitive Organizations**

Through HR." Each feature shows how one or more companies are using modern HR practices to build better, faster, and more competitive organizations. For instance, Chapter 4's feature shows how GE and Cisco Systems are responding faster and more competitively by using Internet HR techniques to recruit high-tech workers; Chapter 13's feature illustrates how Weirton Steel Corp. drives down costs with its workers' compensation methods; and Chapter 15's feature shows how Dayton Parts Corp. reduced expenses and boosted performance with a new safety management program. Many of these features are based on actual "best practices" examples compiled by the Best Manufacturing Practices Center of Excellence.

A PRACTICAL APPROACH

This edition continues our emphasis on providing practical applications that all managers—not just those who carry the title of "Human Resource Manager"—can apply in their daily activities. This includes, for instance, how to interview candidates, appraise performance, handle grievances, and avoid safety problems at work. Furthermore, a new set of **skills videos** now provide practical support by showing students what it's like to conduct an interview, give a performance appraisal, and engage in other key managerial activities. These videos are available on VHS and are designed to spark classroom discussion and debate. New experiential exercises for each chapter provide further opportunities for students to learn-by-doing. There's nothing quite like such learning by doing, and the purpose of these new skills videos and exercises is to help students put what they learn into practice.

TECHNOLOGY CONTENT AND SUPPLEMENTARY SUPPORT

If you are reading this preface, you already know that technology is changing how people work. New technologies affect how employees do their jobs, how managers communicate with employees, and the ways in which businesses interact with each other and with customers. This calls for expanded coverage of technology as it relates to HR practices. In addition to the inclusion of dozens of new technology-based text examples, such as how to recruit employees and conduct salary surveys on the Internet, we've achieved this expansion in technology in several ways:

- **New: WebCT On-Line Course.** This eighth edition offers the first fully developed on-line course for HRM.
- **New: HRIS Appendix.** Computer applications, ranging from individual applications for computerized testing and appraisal to integrated HR Information Systems, are increasingly used at work today. You'll therefore find an **all-new appendix** on "Establishing and Computerizing HR Systems." The appendix explains in practical terms how businesses of all sizes can build manual HR systems, and then move to computerized applications and ultimately to integrated HR Information systems.
- **"Information Technology and HR" features.** To illustrate the impact of information technology on some of the specific topics we cover, you'll find Information Technology and HR features in about half the chapters in this new edition. These features focus on topics like using CD-ROM-based training methods (Chapter 7).
- **New: PHLIP/CW Website.** Our seventh edition was one of the first HRM books to offer a dedicated Website that provided Internet exercises and regular content updates. The eighth edition's Website represents a tremendous leap forward, offering the most robust, content-rich Web support available with any HRM text. For details on what the new Dessler Website offers for both students and instruc-

tors, pleas see the description of the "PHLIP/CW Site" below under "Ancillary Support Materials" (p. xxvii).

New: *Chapter Opening Vignettes*

Each chapter opens with a very brief and pointed example from a real business, and focuses on the strategic role of HR in achieving high performance within an organization.

New: *The High-Performance Organization*

In every chapter of this edition, you'll find a new feature showcasing businesses that are using innovative HR practices to build better, faster, more competitive organizations.

Global HRM

Global issues are emphasized in the text in two ways. First, you'll find "Global HRM" features integrated into many chapters. These illustrate global HR applications, such as for training employees to go abroad, formulating salary plans for expatriates, dealing with labor unions in other countries, and other important topics. Second, you'll find a comprehensive chapter on international HR practices (Chapter 16). This provides in-depth coverage of the international aspects of HR selection, training, compensation management, inter-country differences in personnel laws and requirements, and more.

New: *HRIS Appendix*

As noted previously, this edition contains a new, practical, hands-on appendix, describing how managers from the smallest to the largest companies can develop and implement manual and computerized human resource information systems.

New: *We've Downsized from 18 to 16 Chapters*

Responding to reviewers' suggestions, we've made this book easier to use by shortening it to 16 chapters. We accomplished this by merging career management and guaranteed fair treatment into a single chapter and by merging training and management development in to another single chapter. Chapter 7 is now titled, "Training and Developing Employees," while Chapter 10 is titled, "Managing Careers and Fair Treatment."

New Chapter: *Managing Organizational Renewal (Chapter 8)*

The seventh edition's Chapter 9 (titled, "Managing Quality and Productivity") has been reoriented and completely revised. This new chapter emphasizes topics like teams, organizational change, and re-engineering to focus on HR's role in managing organizational renewal to make companies better, faster, and more competitive.

New and Revised: *Application Exercises*

Reviewers asked for more resources to aid and encourage experiential learning, and we've responded by strengthening the end of chapter exercises. In each chapter you'll find:

- **A set of 3 to 4 individual and group activities** can be used in class or in study groups outside of class. Notes for each activity are provided in the instructor's manual.

- **Experiential exercises** are a new addition at the end of each chapter. These help students apply their knowledge in an interactive group situation. Notes for these exercises are provided in the instructor's manual.
- **Case incidents**—brief cases usually based on practices in real organizations. They ask students to answer questions about how they would deal with the situation faced by the people in each incident. Suggested answers and discussion points are provided in the instructor's manual.
- **New application cases** are longer, more in-depth, and are featured at the end of each chapter. These cases provide the basis for class discussion or for written assignments.
- **New skills videos** provide practical opportunities for students to watch dramatizations of actual HR activities like a job interview or performance appraisal. Students can then respond to and critique the practices they've observed in the videos.
- **New Small Business 2000 Videos** give real-world examples of HR in small businesses. These are highlighted in various chapters.
- To accomodate the new cases and exercises, the seventh edition's Carter Cleaning Company cases are now available in the instructor's and student's manuals and on our Web site.

Small Business Applications

Managers in small and mid-sized businesses face some unique challenges in managing human resources. The eighth edition continues our use of a special small business feature that's found in about half of the chapters. Each Small Business Application illustrates to readers how that chapter's material can be and is applied in a small-business context.

Information Technology and HR

We continue to include "Information Technology and HR" boxes in about half the chapters to show technology applications related to that chapter or topic. In addition, as noted above, we've added a new appendix on HR information systems; this provides a more comprehensive and in-depth coverage of HR technology topics, such as how to find and use computerized HR applications for training and appraisal, and the pros and cons of implementing human resource information systems.

Diversity Counts

As the U.S. workforce becomes more diverse and as businesses become more global, managers need to develop skills for managing diverse populations. You'll therefore find expanded coverage of diversity management in Chapter 2 and "Diversity Counts" boxes in about half the chapters of this edition. These boxes provide examples and tips for managing diversity, such as comparing males and females in a discipline situation, gender issues in dressing for interviews, and the impact of bias in performance appraisals.

New Content: Research Insights

These are short, relevant snapshots showing how recent research studies illustrate important HR activities such as performance appraisal. You'll find one or two per chapter.

Chapter Summaries

Each chapter contains a point-by-point chapter summary that students can use to quickly refresh their memories and to get an overview of what they've read in that chapter.

Discussion Questions

Each chapter has a set of discussion questions that can be used as the basis for class discussion.

Ancillary Support Materials

We want to make teaching and learning HRM from this book a successful experience. We therefore designed each of the supplemental resources to be integrated with the textbook and to add value.

1. **Instructor's Manual**—this has been expanded to offer more extensive lecture notes, extra examples for classroom use, and clear suggestions for integrating all aspects of the teaching package (such as transparency acetates, PowerPoint slides, and the PHLIP/CW Website);

2. **Test Item File**—We've expanded this supplement to offer a greater number and variety of test questions. We've also organized the test questions according to sections within chapters, in case you don't want to test on all sections in that chapter. The questions also indicate the difficulty level—easy, moderate, and challenging.

3. **Prentice Hall Custom Test for Windows** is a state-of-the-art test generation software program that gives you flexibility to customize tests to suit your course needs. Its user-friendly, powerful test-creation features also mean that you can develop tailor-made tests quickly and efficiently without error. You also have the option of entering your exams traditionally or on-line, evaluating and tracking student results, and analyzing the success of the exam.

4. **Color Transparencies and Electronic PowerPoint Slides** give you visual aids for classrooms of any size. We offer PowerPoint slides and color transparencies covering the major concepts of each chapter.

5. **Student Study Guide.** A new study guide offers students the opportunity to review and test themselves on concepts from the text.

6. The **Video Package** offers two different options for enhanced learning:

   ■ *New:* **Skills Videos**—Six videos (one for each part of the text) offer dramatizations that highlight an HR skill related to that part. They allow students to see what it's like to conduct an interview, give a performance appraisal, deal with sexual harassment issues, and more. The videos provide excellent starting points for classroom discussion and debate. These videos are available on VHS for classroom presentation.

   ■ *New:* **Company Videos**—Additional videos focus on the HR practices at small and medium-size companies. These videos are from the *Small Business 2000* series (as seen on PBS). Video notes are found in the Instructor's Manual, and offer a summary of each video with discussion points and suggested responses.

7. **New: WebCT On-Line Course**—This eighth edition offers the first fully developed on-line course for HRM.

8. **PHLIP Website (www.prenhall.com/dessler)**—Developed by Professor Dan Cooper at Marist College, PHLIP provides academic support for faculty and student using this text. PHLIP is divided into a **Student Page** and a **Faculty Page**. The **Faculty Page** helps professors prepare lectures, integrate technology into the classroom, and enhance in- and out-of-class learning with industry examples as

current as today's world news. The **Student Page** supports students through an Interactive Study Guide, Current Events Cases, Exercises, Study Skills, and Writing and Research Assistance. Features include:

- *For Instructors (Faculty Page):*
  Text-specific **Faculty Resources** including downloadable supplements (Instructor's Manual, Technology Resource Manual, and PowerPoint presentations) and on-line faculty support for the Student Page (including additional cases, articles, links, and suggested answers to the questions posted on the Student Page).

- **Faculty Lounge** featuring generic faculty resources:
  - *Talk to the Team* is a moderated and password-protected conference and chat room system designed to allow faculty the opportunity to ask questions, make suggestions, and explore new teaching ideas.
  - *Teaching Archive* features teaching resources submitted by instructors throughout the world, and includes tips, techniques, academic papers, and Sample Syllabi for traditional classroom presentations, and for integrating technology in and out of the classroom.
  - *Help with Computers* provides tips and links to tutorials to help you master spreadsheets, word processing, and/or presentation software.
  - *Internet Skills* offers beginners and advanced advice, tips, and tutorials for using the Internet.

- *For Students (Student Page):*
  Student Study Hall helps develop student's study skills through the following resources:
  - **Ask the Tutor** serves as Virtual Office Hours, allowing students to post questions or comments to the threaded message board, and receive responses from both the PHLIP faculty and the entire learning community. This feature is monitored by Professor Dan Cooper to maintain quality.
  - **Writing Center** provides links to on-line dictionaries, writing tutors, style and grammar guides, and additional tools to help students develop their writing skills.
  - **Study Skills Center** helps student develop better study skills.
  - **Career Center** encourages students to investigate potential employers, get career information and advice, view sample resumes, and even apply for jobs on-line.
  - **Research Center** provides tips and resources that make it easy to harness the power of the Internet as a research tool through tutorials and descriptive links to virtual libraries and a wealth of search engines.

- **Current Events Articles and Exercises**—Each chapter offers numerous current events to keep your class up to date. Each current event is a summary and analysis of a current news event, written by our PHLIP faculty provider, and supported Web links to the text, discussion questions, group activities, background/historical information, a glossary, a bibliography, and links to the related news sources. Whenever possible, there is a link to the original article itself. New current events are added every 2 weeks (past current events remain on the site until they are not longer useful or valid).

- **Interactive Study Guide** offers multiple-choice and true/false questions for every chapter of this text. Students submit responses to the server, which scores them and provides immediate feedback, including additional help and page references linked to the text. Test scores can be sent to as many as four e-mail addresses.

- **Internet Resources** provide links to helpful Web sites, complete with an "Info" button that offers the professors and students a description of each site.

ACKNOWLEDG-MENTS

While I am of course solely responsible for the content in *Human Resource Management,* I want to thank several people for their professional assistance. This includes first, the faculty who reviewed this edition: Edwin Arnold, *Auburn University (Montgomery);* Mary Connerley, *Virginia Polytechnic Institute & State University;* Ken Digby, *Fayetteville (NC) Technical Community College;* Gordon Meyer, *Canisius College;* Mary Ellen Rosetti, *Hudson Valley (NY) Community College;* Tom Tudor, *Winthrop University;* Ken Wallace, *Craven (NC) Community College;* Sandy J. Wayne, *University of Illinois at Chicago;* Kenneth M. York, Oakland University; and a special thanks to George Puia of *Indiana State University* who contributed experiential exercises, case incidents, case applications, and the Small Business 2000 video notes.

I would also like to thank Jay Hochstetler, George Puia, Tom Patterson, Anne Cowden, Mary Gowan, and Dan Cooper for their conscientious and complete work on the supplementary package, under the direction of Hersch Doby, and to express my gratitude to professor John E. Oliver of Valdosta State University for allowing me to use "Distributing the Raise Pool," and "Empowerment Through Assignment Flexibility."

At Prentice Hall I am grateful for the support and dedicated assistance of Stephanie Johnson, Natalie Anderson, Judy Leale, Jennifer Glennon, and Elisa Adams in creating this book.

My son Derek has been an enormous source of pride and, as usual, my best source of advice on managing people, and my wife Claudia has provided support and encouragement.

Gary Dessler

THE STRATEGIC ROLE OF HUMAN RESOURCE MANAGEMENT

When Mead Corporation installed new computers in its Escanaba, Michigan plant, it wisely built their design and installation around the needs of the plant's employees. Other companies have installed sophisticated computerized factory machines as part of a strategy to be better, faster, and more competitive but haven't been so wise, or so successful. Many of these installations have failed to cut costs, and studies have uncovered a surprising reason. As one expert put it, "the flexibility of the plants depended much more on people than on any technical factor." It turned out that the only way these companies could take advantage of their newly computerized plants was by instituting the human resource management planning, recruiting, selecting, training, and pay practices that would create a dedicated and committed workforce.[1] ▲

Behavioral Objectives

When you finish studying this chapter, you should be able to:

- ▲ *Answer* the question, "What is Human Resource Management?"
- ▲ *Discuss* the components of the changing environment of Human Resource Management.
- ▲ *Present* examples of the new management practices that are changing Human Resource Management.
- ▲ *Give* examples of Human Resource Management's role as a strategic business partner.

Chapter Outline

- ▲ Human Resource Management at Work
- ▲ The Changing Environment of Human Resource Management
- ▲ Tomorrow's HR Today
- ▲ Strategic Planning and HR Management
- ▲ The Plan of This Book

<table>
<tr><td>

HUMAN
RESOURCE
MANAGEMENT
AT WORK

</td><td>

What Is Human Resource Management?

Most experts agree that there are five basic functions all managers perform: planning, organizing, staffing, leading, and controlling. In total, these functions represent the **management process**. Some of the specific activities involved in each function include:

</td></tr>
</table>

management process

The five basic functions of planning, organizing, staffing, leading, and controlling.

Planning. Establishing goals and standards; developing rules and procedures; developing plans and forecasting—predicting or projecting some future occurrence.

Organizing. Giving each subordinate a specific task; establishing departments; delegating authority to subordinates; establishing channels of authority and communication; coordinating the work of subordinates.

Staffing. Deciding what type of people should be hired; recruiting prospective employees; selecting employees; setting performance standards; compensating employees; evaluating performance; counseling employees; training and developing employees.

Leading. Getting others to get the job done; maintaining morale; motivating subordinates.

Controlling. Setting standards such as sales quotas, quality standards, or production levels; checking to see how actual performance compares with these standards; taking corrective action as needed.

In this book we are going to focus on one of these functions, the *staffing*, or, (as it's usually called today,) *human resource (HR)* or *personnel management* function. **Human resource management** refers to the practices and policies you need to carry out the people or personnel aspects of your management job. These include:

human resource management

The policies and practices one needs to carry out the "people" or human resource aspects of a management position, including recruiting, screening, training, rewarding, and appraising.

- *Conducting job analyses* (determining the nature of each employee's job)
- *Planning labor needs* and *recruiting* job candidates
- *Selecting* job candidates
- *Orienting* and *training* new employees
- *Managing wages and salaries* (determining how to compensate employees)
- *Providing incentives and benefits*
- *Appraising performance*
- *Communicating* (interviewing, counseling, disciplining)
- *Training and developing*
- *Building employee commitment*

And what a manager should know about:

- Equal opportunity and affirmative action
- Employee health and safety
- Grievances and labor relations

Why Is HR Management Important to All Managers?

Why are these concepts and techniques important to all managers? Perhaps it's easier to answer this question by listing some of the personnel mistakes you don't want to make while managing. For example, you don't want to:

- Hire the wrong person for the job
- Experience high turnover

- Find your people not doing their best
- Waste time with useless interviews
- Have your company taken to court because of your discriminatory actions
- Have your company cited under federal occupational safety laws for unsafe practices
- Have some of your employees think their salaries are unfair and inequitable relative to others in the organization
- Allow a lack of training to undermine your department's effectiveness
- Commit any unfair labor practices

Carefully studying this book can help you avoid mistakes like these, but avoiding mistakes is certainly not the only reason for studying it. More important, doing so can help ensure that you get results—through others. Remember you could do everything else right as a manager—lay brilliant plans, draw clear organization charts, set up modern assembly lines, and use sophisticated accounting controls—but still fail as a manager (by hiring the wrong people or by not motivating subordinates, for instance). On the other hand, many managers—whether presidents, generals, governors, or supervisors—have been successful even with inadequate plans, organization, or controls. They were successful because they had the knack for hiring the right people for the right jobs and motivating, appraising, and developing them. Remember as you read this book that getting results is the bottom line of managing, and that, as a manager, you will have to get those results through people. As one company president summed up:

> For many years it has been said that capital is the bottleneck for a developing industry. I don't think this any longer holds true. I think it's the work force and the company's inability to recruit and maintain a good work force that does constitute the bottleneck for production. I don't know of any major project backed by good ideas, vigor, and enthusiasm that has been stopped by a shortage of cash. I do know of industries whose growth has been partly stopped or hampered because they can't maintain an efficient and enthusiastic labor force, and I think this will hold true even more in the future. . . . [2]

That statement is especially true today. A decade of globalization, deregulation, and technical advances has vastly increased the degree of competitiveness most organizations face today. Companies today must therefore be better, faster, and more competitive just to survive, let alone thrive; and they need committed employees to achieve such competitiveness. In this chapter and in the rest of this book we will see how HR management can help companies and their managers achieve this.

Line and Staff Aspects of HRM

All managers are, in a sense, HR managers, since they all get involved in activities like recruiting, interviewing, selecting, and training. Yet most firms also have a human resource department with its own human resource manager. How do the duties of this HR manager and his or her staff relate to "line" managers' human resource duties? Let's answer this question, starting with a short definition of *line* versus *staff* authority.

Line Versus Staff Authority

authority
The right to make decisions, direct others' work, and give orders.

line manager
A manager who is authorized to direct the work of subordinates and responsible for accomplishing the organization's goals.

Authority is the right to make decisions, to direct the work of others, and to give orders. In management, we usually distinguish between line authority and staff authority.

Line managers are authorized to direct the work of subordinates—they're always someone's boss. In addition, line managers are in charge of accomplishing the organization's basic goals. (Hotel managers and the managers for production and sales are generally line managers, for example.) In addition to direct responsibility for accomplishing the organization's basic goals, they also have the authority to direct the work of their subordinates. **Staff managers**, on the other hand, are authorized to assist and advise line managers in accomplishing their basic goals. HR managers are generally staff managers. They are responsible for advising line managers in areas like recruiting, hiring, and compensation.

Line Managers' Human Resource Management Responsibilities

According to one expert, "The direct handling of people is, and always has been, an integral part of every line manager's responsibility, from president down to the lowest-level supervisor."[3]

For example, one major company outlines its line supervisors' responsibilities for effective human resource management under the following general headings:

1. *Placing* the right person on the right job
2. *Starting* new employees in the organization (orientation)
3. *Training* employees for jobs that are new to them
4. *Improving the job performance* of each person
5. *Gaining creative cooperation* and developing smooth working relationships
6. *Interpreting* the company's policies and procedures
7. *Controlling labor costs*
8. *Developing* the abilities of each person
9. *Creating and maintaining department morale*
10. *Protecting* employees' health and physical condition

In small organizations, line managers may carry out all these personnel duties unassisted. But as the organization grows, they need the assistance, specialized knowledge, and advice of a separate human resource staff.[4]

Human Resource Department's HR Management Responsibilities

The human resource department provides this specialized assistance.[5] In doing so, the HR manager carries out three distinct functions:

   1.   **A line function.** First, the HR manager performs a line function by directing the activities of the people in his or her own department and in service areas (like the plant cafeteria). In other words, he or she exerts **line authority** within the personnel department. HR managers are also likely to exert **implied authority**. Why? Because line managers know the HR manager often has access to top management in personnel areas like testing and affirmative action. As a result, HR managers' "suggestions" are often seen as "orders from top-side." This implied authority carries even more weight with supervisors troubled by human resource/personnel problems.

   2.   **A coordinative function.** HR managers also function as coordinators of personnel activities, a duty often referred to as **functional control**. Here the HR manager and department act as "the right arm of the top executive to assure him [or her] that HR objectives, policies, and procedures (concerning, for example, occupational safety and health) that have been approved and adopted are being consistently carried out by line managers."[6]

   3.   **Staff (service) functions.** Serving and advising line managers is the "bread and butter" of the HR manager's job. For example, HR assists in the hiring, training, evaluating, rewarding, counseling, promoting, and firing of employees. It also administers the

various benefit programs (health and accident insurance, retirement, vacation, and so on). It assists line managers in their attempts to comply with equal employment and occupational safety laws. And it plays an important role with respect to grievances and labor relations.[7] As part of these service activities, HR also carries out an "innovator" role by providing "up to date information on current trends and new methods of solving problems."[8] For example, there is interest today in instituting reengineering programs and in providing career planning for employees. HR managers stay on top of such trends and help their organizations implement these programs.

In assisting line managers, though, HR can't forget its **employee advocacy** role. Among other things this means HR must take responsibility for clearly defining how management should be treating employees, make sure employees have the mechanisms required to contest unfair practices, and represent the interests of employees within the framework of its primary obligation to senior management.[9]

employee advocacy

HR must take responsibility for clearly defining how management should be treating employees, make sure employees have the mechanisms required to contest unfair practices, and represent the interests of employees within the framework of its primary obligation to senior management.

A summary of the HR positions you might find in a large company is presented in the organization chart in Figure 1-1 (page 6). As you can see, HR positions include compensation and benefits manager, employment and recruiting supervisor, training specialist, employee relations executive, safety supervisor, and industrial nurse. Examples of job duties include:

Recruiters. Maintain contact within the community and perhaps travel extensively to search for qualified job applicants.

Equal Employment Opportunity (EEO) Representatives or Affirmative Action Coordinators. Investigate and resolve EEO grievances, examine organizational practices for potential violations, and compile and submit EEO reports.

Job Analysts. Collect and examine detailed information about job duties to prepare job descriptions.

Compensation Managers. Develop compensation plans and handle the employee benefits program.

Training Specialists. Responsible for planning, organizing, and directing training activities.

Labor Relations Specialists. Advise management on all aspects of union-management relations.[10]

Cooperative Line and Staff Human Resource Management: An Example

Exactly which HR management activities are carried out by line managers and staff managers? There's no single division of line and staff responsibilities that could be applied across the board in all organizations. But to show you what such a division might look like, see Figure 1-2 (page 7).[11] This shows some HR responsibilities of line managers and staff managers in five areas: *recruitment and selection, training and development, compensation, labor relation,* and *employee security and safety.*

For example, in the area of *recruiting and hiring* it's the line manager's responsibility to specify the qualifications employees need to fill specific positions. Then the HR staff takes over. They develop sources of qualified applicants and conduct initial screening interviews. They administer the appropriate tests. Then they refer the best applicants to the supervisor (line manager), who interviews and selects the ones he or she wants.

The need for cooperation between line and staff managers in accomplishing these tasks is well illustrated by a recent survey, and the results are highlighted in Table 1-1 (pages 8–9). As you can see, HR management in real companies is always a joint line–staff

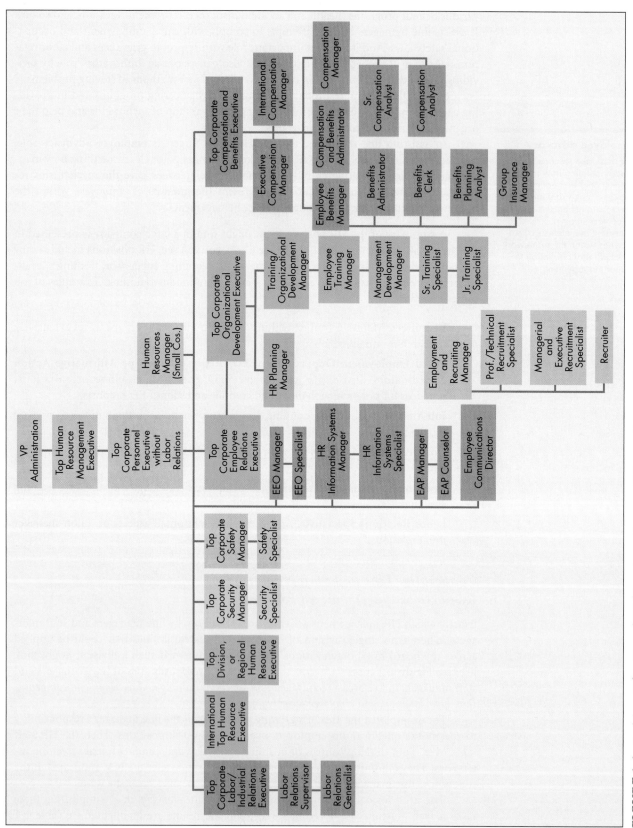

FIGURE 1-1   *Positions Often Found Within a Large Personnel/Human Resource Department*

	DEPARTMENT SUPERVISORS' (LINE) ACTIVITIES	PERSONNEL SPECIALISTS' (STAFF) ACTIVITIES
I Recruitment and Selection	Assist job analyst by listing specific duties and responsibilities of the job in question Explain to HR future staffing needs and sorts of people needed to be hired. Describe "human requirements" of job so HR can develop selection tests. Interview candidates and make final selection decisions.	Write job description and job specification based on input from department supervisor. Develop personnel plans showing promotable employees. Develop sources of qualified applicants and engage in recruiting activities aimed at developing a pool of qualified applicants. Conduct initial screening interviews and refer feasible candidates to department supervisor.
II Training and Development	Orient employees regarding the company and job, and instruct and train new employees. Evaluate and recommend managers for developmental activities. Provide the leadership and empowerment that builds effective work teams. Use the firm's appraisal forms to appraise employee performance. Assess subordinates' career progress and advise them regarding career options.	Prepare training materials and orientation documents and outlines. Advise CEO regarding development plan for managers based on CEO's stated vision of firm's future needs. Serve as resource for providing information regarding how to institute and operate quality improvement programs and team-building efforts. Develop performance appraisal tools and maintain records of appraisals.
III Compensation	Assist HR by providing information regarding the nature and relative worth of each job, to serve as the basis for compensation decisions. Decide on the nature and amounts of incentives to be paid to subordinates. Decide on the package of benefits and services the firm is to pay.	Conduct job evaluation procedures aimed at determining relative worth of each job in the firm. Conduct salary surveys to determine how other firms are paying the same or similar positions. Serve as a resource in advising line management regarding financial incentives and pay plan alternatives. Develop, in consultation with line management, the firm's benefits and services packages including health care options and pensions.
IV Labor Relations	Establish the day-to-day climate of mutual respect and trust needed to maintain healthy labor-management relations. Consistently apply the terms of the labor agreement. Ensure that the firm's grievance process is functioning in a manner consistent with the labor agreement and make final decisions on grievances after investigating same. Work with HR in negotiating the collective bargaining agreement.	Diagnose underlying causes of labor discontent with an eye toward anticipating the sorts of morale and other problems that may lead to unionization efforts. Train line managers regarding the interpretation of contract terms and the legal pitfalls to be avoided during the union organizing effort. Advise managers regarding how to handle grievances and assist all parties in reaching agreements regarding grievances.
V Employee Security and Safety	Keep the lines of communication open between employees and managers so employees are kept abreast of important company matters and have a variety of vehicles they can use to express concerns and gripes. Make sure employees are guaranteed fair treatment as it relates to discipline, dismissals, and job security. Continually direct employees in the consistent application of safe work habits. Prepare accident reports promptly and accurately.	Advise line management regarding the communication techniques that can be used to encourage upward and downward communication. Develop a guaranteed fair treatment process and train line managers in its use. Analyze jobs to develop safe practice rules and advise on design of safety apparatus such as machinery guards. Promptly investigate accidents, analyze causes, make recommendations for accident prevention, and submit necessary forms to Occupational Safety and Health Administration.

FIGURE 1-2 *Selected Activities Illustrating Division of HR Responsibility Between Line and Staff*

TABLE 1-1 Human Resource Activities and Responsibilities

ACTIVITY	RESPONSIBILITY FOR THE ACTIVITY IS ASSIGNED TO:		
	HR DEPT. ONLY	HR & OTHER DEPT(S)	OTHER DEPT(S) ONLY
Employment and recruiting			
Employment interviews	31%	65%	3%
Recruiting (other than college recruiting)	70	29	1
Temporary labor coordination	67	28	4
Pre-employment testing (except drug tests)	87	11	2
College recruiting	76	21	2
Training and development			
Orientation of new employees	61	37	1
Supervisory training/management development	45	48	7
Performance appraisal, management	36	52	12
Performance appraisal, nonmanagement	33	55	12
Skills training, nonmanagement	24	55	21
Tuition aid/scholarships	77	17	6
Career planning/development	46	49	5
Productivity/quality enhancement programs	12	55	33
Compensation			
Wage/salary administration	77	20	3
Job descriptions	61	38	1
Job evaluation	67	29	4
Payroll administration	29	29	42
Job analysis	70	29	1
Executive compensation	52	27	22
Incentive pay plans	44	45	11
Benefits			
Vacation/leave policies and administration	78	22	1
Insurance benefits administration	86	10	4
Unemployment compensation	82	13	5
Pension/retirement plan administration	76	16	9
Flexible spending account administration	83	10	7
Cafeteria benefits plan administration	85	9	6
Profit sharing plan administration	57	27	16
Stock plan administration	45	28	27
Employee services			
Recreation/social programs	41%	45%	14%
Employee assistance plan/counseling	83	12	5
Relocation services	76	18	6
Preretirement counseling/retirement planning	85	9	6
Outplacement services	88	8	3
Employee and community relations			
Disciplinary procedures	44	55	2
Complaint procedures	57	41	2
Exit interviews	86	13	1
Award/recognition programs	67	30	3
EEO compliance/affirmative action programs	87	11	1
Employee communications/publications	41	46	13
Community relations/contribution programs	29	43	28
Suggestion systems	53	37	9
Attitude surveys	73	23	4
Union/labor relations	59	37	4
Personnel records			
Personnel recordkeeping	86	14	—
Promotion/transfer/separation processing	72	27	1
Human resource information systems	68	29	3
Health and safety			
Workers' compensation administration	74	17	9
Safety training	31	42	27

ACTIVITY	RESPONSIBILITY FOR THE ACTIVITY IS ASSIGNED TO:		
	HR DEPT. ONLY	HR & OTHER DEPT(S)	OTHER DEPT(S) ONLY
Safety inspections/OSHA compliance	29	40	31
Drug testing	80	16	5
Health/wellness program	77	17	6
Strategic planning			
Human resource forecasting/planning	63	34	3
Organization development	37	56	7
Mergers and acquisitions	42	47	11
International personnel/HR administration	59	33	9

Source: Adapted from *BNA Bulletin to Management,* "SHRM-BNA Survey No. 63: Human Resource Activities, Budgets, & Staffs, 1997–1998," pp. 2–3.

coordinated effort. Most activities (including interviewing, supervisory training, and performance appraisal) are divided jointly between line and staff (HR) managers.

The bottom line is that HR management is an integral part of every manager's job. Whether you're a first-line supervisor, middle manager, or president; or whether you're a production manager, sales manager, office manager, hospital administrator, county manager (or HR manager!), getting results through committed people is the name of the game. And to do this, you'll need a good working knowledge of the human resource management concepts and techniques in this book.

THE CHANGING ENVIRONMENT OF HUMAN RESOURCE MANAGEMENT

Most changes in this world don't take place in a vacuum—artists and poets create their works in response to the times in which they live, wars emerge out of economic and political pressures, and companies change their structures in response to the need to follow their customers overseas, for instance.

Therefore, to better understand HR's role in organizations today, it's useful to understand how companies themselves are changing and the trends that are causing these changes to occur. Perhaps most importantly, organizations today are under intense pressure to be better, faster, and more competitive—HMOs are squeezing more productivity out of hospitals, companies like Citigroup are merging and downsizing, and universities are working hard to boost enrollments and faculty productivity. Why is this the case? Globalization, technical advances, and deregulation are three of the trends accounting for these competitive pressures. Other trends include diversity and other workforce changes; we'll look more closely at these trends on the next few pages.

Globalization

globalization

The tendency of firms to extend their sales or manufacturing to new markets abroad.

Globalization refers to the tendency of firms to extend their sales or manufacturing to new markets abroad, and, for businesses everywhere, the rate of globalization in the past few years has been nothing short of phenomenal. For example, the total value of U.S. imports and exports jumped from $907 billion in 1991 to $1.4 trillion in 1996.[12] Production is being globalized, too, as manufacturers around the world put manufacturing facilities where they will be most advantageous. Today's Toyota Camry is produced in Georgetown, Kentucky, with almost 80% U.S.-made parts, while GM's Pontiac LeMans contains almost two-thirds foreign-made parts.[13]

Such globalization has vastly increased global competition. Throughout the world, firms that formerly competed only with local firms—from airlines to automakers to banks—now face an onslaught of foreign competitors. Today, as a result, Ford and GM have huge market shares in Europe, while firms like Deutche Bank and Daimler—through its merger with Chrysler—have a powerful presence in the U.S. today. As one international business expert puts it, "the bottom line is that the growing integration of the world economy into a single, huge marketplace is increasing the intensity of competition in a wide range of manufacturing and service industries."[14]

Globalization also means that more U.S. firms are transferring operations abroad, not just to seek cheaper labor, but to tap what *Fortune* magazine calls "a vast new supply of skilled labor around the world."[15] Even today, most multinational firms set up manufacturing plants abroad partly to establish beachheads in promising markets and partly to utilize that country's professionals and engineers. For example, Asea Brown Boveri (a $30-billion-a-year Swiss/Swedish builder of transportation and electric generation systems) already has 25,000 new employees in former Communist countries and has thus shifted many jobs from Western to Eastern Europe. And Levi Strauss—once a leading "made in the USA" advocate—closed most of its remaining U.S. plants in 1999, shifting more production overseas. From boosting the productivity of a global labor force to formulating compensation policies for expatriate employees, managing globalization and its effects on competitiveness will thus be a major HR challenge in the next few years.

Technological Advances

Similarly, technology has been forcing—and enabling—firms to become more competitive. For example, Inter-Design of Ohio sells plastic clocks, refrigerator magnets, soap dishes, and similar products. Its president explains the impact of information technology—merging communications with computers—this way. "In the seventies we went to the Post Office to pick up our orders. In the early 80s, we put in an 800 number. In the late 80s, we got a fax machine. In 1991, pressured by Target [stores], we added electronic data interchange." Now, more than half of Inter-Design's orders arrive via modem, straight

Computer-aided design and manufacturing processes are revolutionizing work in dozens of industries. These techniques require better trained and more highly committed employees.

into company computers. Inter-Design's errors in order entry and shipping have all but disappeared, while some of its less technologically adept competitors have fallen by the wayside.[16]

Technology is also changing the nature of work. For example, telecommunications already makes it relatively easy for many to work at home, and the use of computer-aided design/computer-aided manufacturing (CAD/CAM) systems plus robotics is booming. Manufacturing advances like these will eliminate many blue-collar jobs, replacing them with more highly skilled jobs, and these new workers will require a degree of training and commitment that their parents probably never dreamed of. As a result, to remain competitive, jobs and organization charts will have to be redesigned, new incentive and compensation plans instituted, new job descriptions written, and new employee selection, evaluation, and training programs instituted—all with the help of HR management.

Deregulation

Being better, faster, and more competitive is also more important because for many industries the comfortable protection provided by government regulations has been stripped away. For example in the United States (and in many other industrialized countries such as England, France, and Japan), industries from airlines to banks to utilities must now compete nationally and internationally without the protection of government-regulated prices and entry tariffs.

One big consequence has been the sudden and dramatic opening of various markets to competition. MCI/Worldcom and other long distance phone companies have entered the previously protected monopoly of AT&T, and startups from Kiwi Air to Morris Air compete head-to-head with industry giants like Delta and American, for instance. No less significant has been the impact that deregulation—and the resulting new competition—has had on prices, requiring these firms to get and stay "lean and mean." Prices for hundreds of services from airline tickets to long-distance calls have dropped dramatically, often to below what they were 10 years ago, which means companies must get their costs down too.

Trends in the Nature of Work

Globalization, deregulation, and technology are also changing the nature of jobs and work. For one thing, there has been a pronounced shift from manufacturing jobs to service jobs in North America and Western Europe. Today over two-thirds of the U.S. workforce is employed in producing and delivering services, not products. In fact, the manufacturing workforce declined over 12% since the 1980s. Of the 21 million or so new jobs added to the U.S. economy through the 1990s, many will be part-time, and virtually all will be in services industries such as fast foods, retailing, consulting, teaching, and legal work. These service jobs will in turn require new types of "knowledge" workers, new HR management methods to manage them and a new focus on human capital.[17]

Human capital refers to the knowledge, education, training, skills, and expertise of a firm's workers, and it's more important than it has ever been before.[18] One reason is the rise in service jobs: Service jobs like consulting put a bigger premium on worker education and knowledge than do traditional manufacturing jobs. Another is the fact that even factory jobs are becoming more demanding. For one thing, factory jobs in steel, auto, rubber, and textiles are being replaced by "knowledge-intensive high tech manufacturing in such industries as aerospace, computers, telecommunications, home electronics, pharmaceuticals, and medical instruments,"[19] and even heavy manufacturing jobs are becoming more high tech. At Alcoa Aluminum's Davenport, Iowa plant, a computer stands at each workpost to help each employee control his or her machines. As *Fortune* magazine recently put it, "practically every package delivery, bank teller, retail clerk, telephone operator, and bill collector in America works with a computer [today]."[20] Jobs today thus demand a level of expertise far beyond that required of most workers 20 or 30 years ago. Human capital is thus quickly replacing machines as the basis for most firms' success.

The challenge for managers is that such workers can't be managed as were their parents. As one expert put this, "the center of gravity in employment is moving fast from manual and clerical workers to knowledge workers, who resist the command and control model that business took from the military 100 years ago."[21] In other words, workers like these can't just be ordered around and closely monitored. New HR systems and skills will be required to select, train, and motivate such employees and to win their their commitment. Implementing them won't be easy: Insecurity and shorter job tenure are diminishing employee commitment today, in the opinion of some experts.[22]

Workforce Diversity

Workforce diversity is another major work-related trend. Specifically, the workforce is becoming more diverse as women, minority-group members, and older workers flood the workforce.[23] Diversity has been defined as "any attribute that humans are likely to use to tell themselves, 'that person is different from me'" and thus includes such factors as race, sex, age, values, and cultural norms.[24]

Examples abound: women represented 42.1% of the civilian U.S. labor force in 1979, 46% in 1994, and they are expected to represent 47.8% by the year 2005.[25] Related to this, about two-thirds of all single mothers (separated, divorced, widowed, or never married) are in the labor force today, as are almost 45% of mothers with children under three years old. The human resource department will increasingly be called upon to help companies accommodate these employees, with new child care and maternity leave provisions, and with basic skills training where such training is required.

Changes in racial composition will be even more dramatic. For example, between 1992 and 2005 people classified as Asian and other (including Native Americans) in the workforce will jump by just over 81%. The number of Hispanics in the civilian labor force will jump by almost 64% in the next 10 years, so that Hispanics will represent 11% of the civilian labor force in 2005, up from 8% in 1992.[26]

Jody Hatch is the vice president for human resources at Whole Foods Markets, Inc. in Austin (TX). In this position she is responsible for developing recruiting and retention strategies, developing human resource policies, and designing payroll, benefits, and incentive programs for the nearly 15,000 "team members" of this highly decentralized firm.

The labor force is getting older, too. The median age of the labor force in 1979 was 34.7 years. This has risen continuously since then to 37.8 years in 1995, and is projected to be 40.5 years in 2005.[27] (This is due mostly to the aging of the baby-boom generation, those born between 1946 and 1964, since baby boomers now comprise just over half the U.S. labor force).[28] Employees will also likely remain in the workforce well past the age at which their parents retired, due to Social Security and Medicare funding shortfalls and the termination of traditional benefit plans by many employers.[29]

Increased diversity will provide many challenges for HR management.[30] As the workforce ages, for instance, employers will have to grapple with higher health care costs and pension contributions. At the same time today's "Generation Xers," (born between 1963 and 1981) reportedly often crave more of the benefits such as free time and "flex-time" than their baby-boom parents ever did.[31] With more females in the workforce, an upswing in the number of dual-career couples will force more employers to establish child care facilities on or near company premises and to accommodate the travel, scheduling, and moving needs of dual-career employees.

Creating unanimity from a diverse workforce may also turn out to be a considerable challenge for HR. As several experts recently put it, there are "two fundamental and inconsistent realities operating today with regard to diversity. One is that organizations claim they seek to maximize diversity in the work place, and maximize the capabilities of such a diverse workforce. The other is that traditional human resources systems will not allow diversity, only similarity."[32] What they mean is that employers traditionally hire, appraise, and promote people who fit their image of what employees should believe and act like, and there's a corresponding tendency to screen out those who don't "fit."[33] Establishing HR programs that don't just pay lip service to diversity may thus be a challenge for many employers.[34]

Legal Trends Affecting Human Resource Management

Other trends are shaping HR management as well. For example, as we will see in this book, many laws continue to be passed, which effectively limit managers' actions. For example, equal employment opportunity laws bar discrimination on the basis of race, age, disability, religion, sex, or national origin. Mandated health benefits, occupational safety and health requirements, and union-management relations laws are among the other legal constraints managers must deal with, generally with the assistance of HR management.[35]

TOMORROW'S HR TODAY

New Management Practices

In turn, trends like these are changing the way firms are managed, and this is summarized in Figure 1-3. Organizations today must grapple with revolutionary trends—accelerating product and technological change, globalized competition, deregulation, demographic changes, and trends toward a service society and the information age. These trends have dramatically increased the degree of competition in virtually all industries, while forcing firms to cope with unprecedented product innovation and technological change. Companies in such an environment either become competitive high-performers or they die.

The quest to be more competitive has led many firms to change how they are organized and managed. For example:

The traditional, pyramid-shaped organization is going out of style.[36] At firms like AT&T, the new way of organizing stresses cross-functional teams and boosting interdepartmental communications. There is a corresponding de-emphasis on "sticking to the chain of command" to get decisions made. At General Electric, Chairman Jack Welch talks

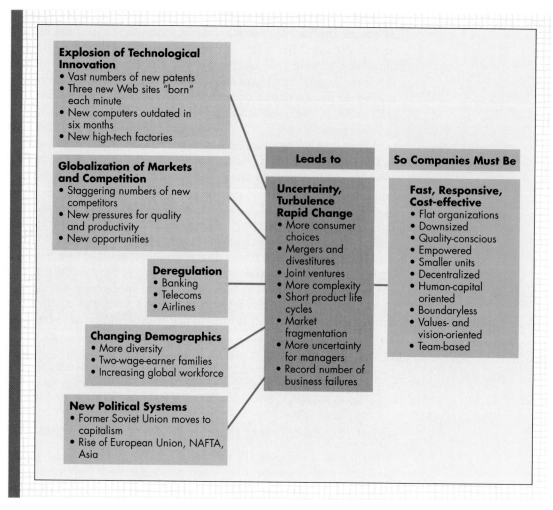

FIGURE 1-3 *Fundamental Changes Facing Managers*

of the *boundaryless organization,* in which employees do not identify with separate departments but instead interact with whomever they must to get the job done.

Employees are being empowered. Some experts argue that today's organization should put the customer on top, and emphasize that every move the company makes should be toward satisfying the customer's needs. Management must therefore *empower* its front-line employees—the front desk clerks at the hotel, the cabin attendants on the Delta plane, and the assemblers at Saturn—to see that they have what they need to serve the customers.

Flatter organizations are becoming the norm. Instead of the pyramid-shaped organization with 7 to 10 or more layers of management, flat organizations with just 3 or 4 levels will prevail. Many companies (including AT&T and General Electric) have already cut the management layers from a dozen to 6 or fewer.[37] Because the remaining managers have more people reporting to them, they will be less able to meddle in the work of their subordinates.

Work is increasingly organized around teams and processes rather than specialized functions. On the plant floor, a worker does not just have the job of installing the same door handle over and over again. He or she belongs to a multifunction team, one that manages its own budget and controls the quality of its own work.

General Electric's CEO Jack Welch. In his 17-year tenure at the helm of GE, Welch has attracted, developed, and retained many talented people who have helped him achieve enormous business success. He knows the value of cultivating their loyalty and does so by maintaining direct communication with many of his managers and running constant training and motivational programs at which he is often the featured speaker.

The bases of power are changing. In the new organization, says professor Rosabeth Moss Kanter, position, title, and authority are no longer adequate tools for managers to rely on to get their jobs done.[38] Instead, "success depends increasingly on tapping into sources of good ideas, on figuring out whose collaboration is needed to act on those ideas, and on working with both to produce results. In short, the new managerial work implies very different ways of obtaining and using power."[39]

Managers today must build commitment. Building a better, larger, more competitive organization means that eliciting employees' commitment and self-control is more important than ever before. GE's Jack Welch put it this way, "The only way I see to get more productivity is by getting people involved and excited about their jobs. You can't afford to have anyone walk through a gate of a factory or into an office who is not giving 120%."[40] The following feature shows how one company accomplished this.

THE HIGH-PERFORMANCE ORGANIZATION

Building Better, Faster, More Competitive Organizations Through HR

Asea Brown Boveri shows how one firm is putting changes like these into practice. The Zurich-based electrical equipment maker is an example of a firm that "disorganized itself to compete in the fast-moving global market of the next ten years."[41] ABB did four things to make itself superresponsive: it organized around mini-units, empowered its workers, flattened its hierarchy, and eliminated central staff. How did ABB do it?

First, within two years of taking over this $30-billion firm, Chairman Percy Barnevik "de-organized" its 215,000 employees into 5,000 minicompanies, each averaging only about 50 workers each.[42] For example, the ABB hydropower unit in Finland is a highly customer-focused little business, one in which employees' efforts are all centered on its local (Finnish) customers. Each of ABB's 50-person units is run by its own manager and three or four lieutenants. Such small units are very manageable. It's a lot easier to keep track of what everyone is doing when there are only 50 people than when there are 1,000, let alone 5,000 or 10,000.

Second, to speed decision making, employees in the 5,000 minicompanies were empowered. The employees now have the authority to make most of their own business decisions without checking first with top management. For example, if a customer has a complaint about a $50,000 machine, a minicompany employee can approve a replacement on the spot, rather than having to wait for reviews by several levels of management. (What does such employee empowerment mean for HR? For one thing, it means that ABB's 5,000 businesses must be staffed, as management expert Tom Peters put it, by "high-performing team members," highly skilled employees with the capacity and commitment to make those big decisions.)

Third, ABB's 215,000-employee organization was "de-layered". It has only three management levels (compared to the seven or eight a comparably sized company might have). There is a 13-member top-management executive committee based in Zurich. Below this is a 250-member executive level that includes country managers and executives in charge of groups of businesses. Below this is a third level, consisting of the 5,000 mini-company managers and their management teams. The firm thus flattened the hierarchy, or chain of command. By slicing out layers of management and letting lower-level employees make their own on-the-spot decisions, ABB allows its employees to respond more quickly to customers' needs and competitors' moves. But, of course, ABB needs the sort of employees who can make such decisions.

Fourth, since decision making was pushed down to front-line ABB employees, ABB could eliminate most headquarters staff advisors. For example, when he acquired Finland's Stromberg Company, Barnevik reduced its headquarters staff from 880 to 25. Similarly, he reduced German ABB headquarters in Mannheim from 1,600 to 100.

Responsiveness and increased competitiveness is the net effect of such reorganization—a lean, flat organization staffed with highly committed employees who are organized into small, empowered teams, each able to respond quickly to competitors' moves and customers' needs with no need to wait for approval from headquarters. In turn, ABB became a high-performing organization in part through HR methods that allowed it to attract, train, and motivate a committed team of empowered employees.

The Changing Role of HR Management: People and Performance

Not surprisingly, the role of HR management is also changing, to help companies achieve such structural and cultural changes. Indeed, HR has actually gone through several changes. In the early 1900s personnel people first took over hiring and firing from supervisors, ran the payroll department, and administered benefit plans. The job consisted largely of ensuring that procedures were followed. As technology in such areas as testing and interviewing began to emerge, the personnel department began to play an expanded role in employee selection, training, and promotion.[43]

The emergence of union legislation in the 1930s led to a second phase in personnel management and a new emphasis on protecting the firm in its interaction with unions. The discrimination legislation of the 1960s and 1970s triggered a third phase. Because of the large penalties that lawsuits could bring to a company, effective personnel practices became more important. In this phase (as in the second), personnel continued to provide expertise in areas like recruitment, screening, and training, albeit in a more expanded role. Notice, though, that whether dealing with unions or equal employment, personnel gained status as much for what it could do to protect the organization as for the positive contribution it made to the firm's effectiveness.

Today, personnel is speeding through a fourth phase, and its role is shifting from protector and screener to strategic partner and change agent. The metamorphosis of *personnel* into *human resource management* reflects a fact of corporate life today: In today's flattened, downsized, and high-performing organizations, highly trained and committed employees—not machines—are often the firm's competitive key.

Indeed, managers today recognize that employees are the key. For example, GE's Jack Welch—who since 1991 has driven his firm's market value from barely $60 billion to over $300 billion—says his biggest achievement is the people he hires and cultivates. "This place runs by its great people . . . the biggest accomplishment I've had is to find people. An army of them. They are all better than most. They are big hitters, and they seem to thrive here."[44]

A recent Price Waterhouse survey of 377 CEOs from the world's 2,000 largest companies shows that GE's emphasis on employees isn't unique. The results are summarized in Figure 1-4. Notice that about half of the CEOs said they spend a "great deal" of time "reshaping corporate culture and employee behavior," even more time than they spend "monitoring corporate financial information." Another study found that 70% of companies with above-average financial performance considered employee development a critical factor in corporate success; they therefore emphasize HR programs such as leadership training to help build competitive advantage by developing their human capital.[45] Consider some other examples of how HR helps make companies better, faster, and more competitive.

HR and Employee Commitment

HR can impact employees' performance in many ways. For example, Toyota Motor Manufacturing in Georgetown, Kentucky knows that employee commitment—an employee's identification with and agreement to pursue the company's or the unit's mission—is essential when so many jobs involve high-tech work and teamwork. HR can be crucial here. For example, two-way communications foster commitment, and firms like Federal Express and Toyota have installed HR programs that guarantee two-way communications and fair treatment of all employees' grievances and disciplinary concerns.[46] High-commitment firms also tend to engage in employee development practices, which aim to ensure that employees can use all their skills and gifts at work. HR is also crucial here, for in-

FIGURE 1-4

What Has the CEO's Attention

Source: AMA International, September 1998, p. 12.

WHAT HAS THE CEOs ATTENTION?
The issues of culture and behavioral change have surged to the forefront of CEO consciousness, as revealed in a Price Waterhouse survey of 377 CEOs from the world's 2,000 largest companies.
The CEOs identified the amount of personal attention they ascribe to various actions. What follows are the percentages that said they spend a "great deal" of time on four aspects of the job. The first two items and the fourth are fairly predictable, but the third suggests a real shift in CEOs thinking.

ACTION	ALL CEOs	U.S. & CANADA	EUROPE & ASIA
Setting vision and strategy	66%	67%	65%
Exploring M&As	51%	51%	51%
Reshaping corporate culture and employee behavior	47%	48%	45%
Monitoring corporate financial information	45%	47%	43%

stance, in establishing career-oriented performance appraisal procedures and effective training and development practices. We'll present other examples in this book of how HR fosters employee commitment.

HR and Performance

HR can help improve a firm's performance in other ways. In the U.S. government, for instance, researchers found that using personnel screening tests to select high-potential computer programmers produced savings of millions of dollars per year. For many firms, instituting tough head-count controls is the first line of attack on lowering labor costs. The HR department generally plays the central role in planning and implementing corporate downsizings, like those at IBM and Citigroup, and then taking steps to maintain the morale of the remaining employees. At employers like pharmaceuticals firm Merck & Company, HR helps employees adapt to the increased pressures in their downsized departments by helping them learn to prioritize tasks and reduce job stress.[47]

HR AND SERVICE   Employee behavior is especially important in the performance of service firms like banks and retail establishments. If a customer is confronted by a salesperson who is tactless, unprepared to discuss the pros and cons of the different products, or (even worse) downright discourteous, all the firm's other efforts will have been wasted. Service firms have little to sell but their good service. That makes them very dependent on their employees' attitudes and motivation—and on HR management.

HR therefore plays a crucial role in service companies,[48] as a recent study of service firms illustrates. The study found that HR practices such as facilitating employees' career progress, and providing orientation/socialization programs for new employees improved employees' customer service as well as the overall quality of that service from the customers' point of view.[49] The philosophy behind this idea was summed up by Fred Smith, the chairman and founder of Federal Express as "people-service-profits." In other words, use HR to build employee commitment and morale; employees will then provide excellent customer service, which in turn will generate profits.

HR AND RESPONSIVENESS   In making companies better and more competitive, HR can also help make companies faster—more responsive to product and technological innovations, and competitors' moves. For example, downsizing, flattening the pyramid, empowering employees, and organizing around teams—all HR jobs—are aimed at improving communications and making it easier for decisions to be made, so the company can respond more quickly to its customers' needs and its competitors' challenges. At Levi Strauss, for instance, HR helped create the firm's new team-based alternative manufacturing system. This system ties employees' compensation incentives to team goals and, along with Levi's new flexible-hours program, helps inject more flexibility into the firm's production process.[50] We'll see many other examples throughout this book of how HR practices can help to boost a firm's responsiveness.

RESEARCH INSIGHT   That HR practices can improve a firm's performance is not just intuitively attractive—it is supported by the research evidence.

One recent study used a sample of senior HR managers from 1,050 banks. Information was obtained regarding seven HR practices at the banks: internal career opportunities, training, results-oriented appraisals, profit sharing, employment security, participation, and job descriptions. Performance was measured on two financial measures important to banks: return on average assets, and return on equity.[51] The researchers found that "the results of these analyses show that differences in HR practices are associated with rather large differences (approximately 30%) in financial performance."[52]

For example, having three HR practices—profit sharing, results-oriented appraisals, and employment security—had relatively strong relationships with the banks' performance; these three practices influenced the performance of all the banks, across the board. Several of the other HR practices (such as whether or not there was employee participation, and internal career opportunities) were related to performance of some banks but not others.

Similar evidence of the HR–performance link has been found in other industries, such as in a recent study of 97 manufacturing plants in the metal-working industry.[53] This second also found, however that it's not enough to indiscrimantly apply the same HR practice to every situation. Instead, how you design the HR practice has to fit the company's strategy and what the company wants to achieve. We'll look at some examples later in this chapter.[54]

In summary, as two researchers recently put it, "The most fundamental implication is that the choice of HR systems can have an economically significant effect on firm performance. Research is just beginning to establish the plausible range of these effects, but early work indicates that reasonable changes in an HR system can affect a firm's market value by $15,000–45,000 per employee and can affect the probability of survival for a new firm by as much as 22%."[55]

HR and Corporate Strategy

Perhaps the most striking change in HR's role today is its growing involvement in developing and implementing the company's strategy. Strategy—the company's plan for how it will balance its internal strengths and weaknesses with external opportunities and threats in order to maintain a competitive advantage—was traditionally a job mostly for the firm's operating (line) managers. Thus, the president and his or her staff might decide to enter new markets, drop product lines, or embark on a five-year cost-cutting plan. Then he or she would more or less leave the personnel implications of that plan (hiring or firing new workers, hiring outplacement firms for those fired, and so on) to be carried out by HR management.

Today things have changed. Strategies increasingly depend on strengthening organizational competitiveness and on building committed work teams, and these put HR in a central role. We've seen that in a fast-changing, globally competitive and quality-oriented industrial environment, it's often the firm's employees—its human resources—who provide the competitive key. It is thus now increasingly common to involve HR in the earliest stages of developing and implementing the firm's strategic plan, rather than to let HR react to it. Let's look more closely at HR's strategic role.

STRATEGIC PLANNING AND HR MANAGEMENT

The Nature of Strategic Planning

Managers engage in three levels of strategic decision making for their firms.[56] This is summarized in Figure 1-5. Many firms, such as Time Warner consist of several businesses such as Warner music, Warner Pictures, and Turner Networks. They therefore need a *corporate-level strategy*. A company's corporate-level strategy identifies the portfolio of businesses that, in total, will comprise the organization, and the ways in which these businesses will relate to each other.

At the next level down, each of these businesses (such as Warner Music) is then guided by a *business-level/competitive strategy*. A competitive strategy identifies how to build and strengthen the business's long-term competitive position in the marketplace.[57] It identifies, for instance, how Warner Music will compete with Sony, or how Wal-Mart will compete with Kmart.

FIGURE 1-5

Relationships Among Strategies in Multiple-Business Firms

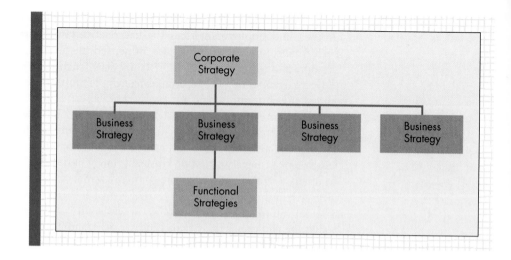

Finally, each business will in turn be comprised of departments, such as manufacturing, sales, and human resource management. Functional strategies identify the basic courses of action that each of the business's departments will pursue in order to help the business attain its competitive goals.

Although companies pursue three levels of strategies, the term *strategic planning* is usually reserved for the company's corporate level, organizationwide strategic planning process. Specifically, strategic planning outlines the type of business the firm will be, given the firm's external opportunities and threats and its internal threats and weaknesses. Deciding whether Mom and Pop's Supermarket will compete with Enormous Markets head-to-head by building similar superstores or instead will continue with small local gourmet markets is a typical strategic-planning problem.

The manager's strategic plan will ideally seek to balance two sets of forces—the firm's external opportunities and threats, and its internal strengths and weaknesses. For example, IBM bought the Lotus software firm in part to acquire the Lotus Notes networking programs. Sensing the opportunities and threats presented by the Internet's growing popularity and by IBM's relative lack of expertise in networking software, IBM Chairman Louis Gerstner decided to diversify by buying Lotus. He thereby positioned IBM to compete more effectively with other systems used to link or network companies and individuals.

In any case, the three levels of strategic decision making should be interrelated and mutually supportive. For example, consider IBM's Lotus acquisition. At the corporate organizationwide level, the acquisition represents an attempt to reposition the giant corporation to compete more effectively in the business of networking computers. However, having decided to acquire Lotus, Gerstner then had to make a business-level strategic decision regarding how to organize IBM's new networking business and in particular how to compete with other firms making similar products. In this case John Manzi, Lotus's head, proposed to Gerstner that Lotus merge with IBM's other software divisions with Manzi in charge; Gerstner rejected this suggestion, deciding to keep Lotus and its Lotus Notes software separate and to let Manzi leave the firm.

Corporate and business-level strategic decisions like these in turn help determine what IBM's functional strategies should be. For example, IBM's push into networking has production strategy implications, since it may require phasing out several hardware manufacturing facilities and consolidating the firm's network program design facilities into fewer locations. Similarly, IBM's marketing and sales efforts may have to be increasingly organized around a networking sales effort. The HR function will also have to accomplish its share. There will be facilities to be closed, new ones to be staffed, and new network program designers to be recruited and hired, for instance.[58]

BUILDING COMPETITIVE ADVANTAGE   Companies try to achieve competitive advantages for each business they are in. A **competitive advantage** can be defined as any factor that allow an organization to differentiate its product or service from those of its competitors to increase market share.[59]

competitive advantage

Any factors that allow an organization to differentiate its product or service from those of its competitors to increase market share.

cost leadership

The enterprise aims to become the low-cost leader in an industry.

differentiation

A firm seeks to be unique in its industry along dimensions that are widely valued by buyers.

There are several ways to achieve competitive advantage. One, **cost leadership**, means that the enterprise aims to become *the* low-cost leader in an industry. For example, Wal-Mart is an industry cost leader; it maintains its competitive advantage through its satellite-based distribution system, and the fact that it generally keeps store location costs to a minimum by placing most stores on low-cost land outside small to medium-sized southern towns.

Differentiation is a second example of a competitive strategy. In a differentiation strategy, a firm seeks to be unique in its industry along dimensions that are widely valued by buyers.[60] Thus, Apple stresses its computers' usability, and Mercedes Benz stresses reliability and quality. Like Mercedes Benz, firms can usually charge a premium price if they successfully stake out their claim to being substantially different from their competitors in some coveted way.

HUMAN RESOURCES AS A COMPETITIVE ADVANTAGE   We've seen that in today's competitive global marketplace, maintaining a competitive advantage puts a premium on having a committed and competent workforce. Low-cost, high-quality cars like Toyotas and Saturns aren't just a product of sophisticated automated machines. Instead they're a result of committed employees all working hard to produce the best cars that they can at the lowest possible cost. Here's how one expert put it:

> In a growing number of organizations human resources are now viewed as a source of competitive advantage. There is greater recognition that distinctive competencies are obtained through highly developed employee skills, distinctive organizational cultures, management processes, and systems. This is in contrast to the traditional emphasis on transferable resources such as equipment . . . Increasingly, it is being recognized that competitive advantage can be obtained with a high quality work force that enables organizations to compete on the basis of market responsiveness, product and service quality, differentiated products, and technological innovation.[61]

Strategic Human Resource Management

The fact that employees today can be a competitive advantage has led to the growth of a new field known as strategic human resource management.[62] *Strategic human resource management* has been defined as "the linking of HRM with strategic goals and objectives in order to improve business performance and develop organizational cultures that foster innovation and flexibility."[63] Put another way, it is "the pattern of planned human resource deployments and activities intended to enable an organization to achieve its goals."[64] Strategic HR means accepting the HR function as a strategic partner in both the formulation of the company's strategies, as well as in the implementation of those strategies through HR activities such as recruiting, selecting, training, and rewarding personnel.

The term *HR strategies* refers to the specific HR courses of action the company uses to achieve its aims. Thus, one of Federal Express's main aims is to achieve superior levels of customer service and high profitability through a highly committed workforce. Its overall HR strategy is thus aimed at building a committed workforce, preferably in a nonunion environment.[65] The specific components of FedEx's-HR strategy follow from that basic aim: To use various mechanisms to build healthy two-way communications; to screen out potential managers whose values are not people oriented; to provide highly competitive salaries and pay-for-performance incentives; to guarantee to the greatest extent possible fair treatment and employee security for all employees; and to institute various promotion-from-within activities aimed at giving employees every opportunity to fully utilize their skills and gifts at work.

Figure 1-6 illustrates the interplay between HR strategy and the company's business plans and results. Ideally, HR and top management work together to formulate the company's overall business strategy; that strategy then provides the framework within which HR activities such as recruiting and appraising must be crafted. If this is done successfully, it should produce the employee competencies and behaviors that in turn should help the business implement its strategies and realize its goals.[66] Let's turn to a closer look at HR's role as a strategic partner.

FIGURE 1-6

Key Components of the HR Strategy Model

Source: Adapted from *HRMagazine*, March 1998, p. 101.

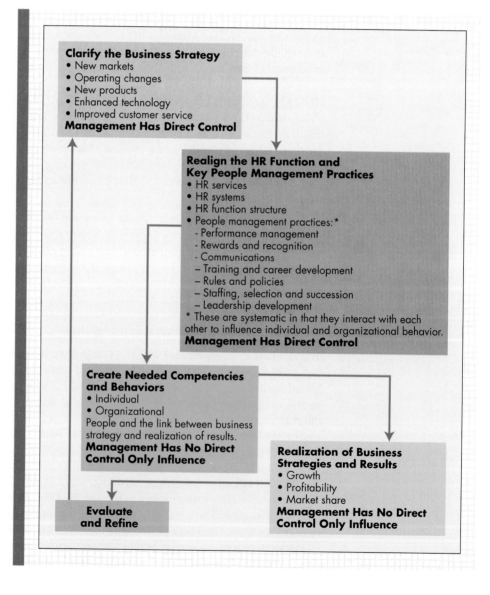

Clarify the Business Strategy
- New markets
- Operating changes
- New products
- Enhanced technology
- Improved customer service

Management Has Direct Control

Realign the HR Function and Key People Management Practices
- HR services
- HR systems
- HR function structure
- People management practices:*
  - Performance management
  - Rewards and recognition
  - Communications
  - Training and career development
  - Rules and policies
  - Staffing, selection and succession
  - Leadership development

* These are systematic in that they interact with each other to influence individual and organizational behavior.

Management Has Direct Control

Create Needed Competencies and Behaviors
- Individual
- Organizational

People and the link between business strategy and realization of results.

Management Has No Direct Control Only Influence

Realization of Business Strategies and Results
- Growth
- Profitability
- Market share

Management Has No Direct Control Only Influence

Evaluate and Refine

HR's Role As a Strategic Partner

HR's long history as a staff or advisory function has left it with a somewhat impoverished reputation—some still tend to view it as less than it is. For example, one view is that HR is strictly operational and that HR activities are not strategic at all.[67] According to this line of reasoning, HR activities simply, "involve putting out small fires—ensuring that people are paid on the right day; the job advertisement meets the newspaper deadline; a suitable supervisor is recruited for the night shift by the time it goes ahead; and the same manager remembers to observe due process before sacking the new rep who didn't work out."[68]

A second, more sophisticated (but perhaps no more accurate) view of HR is that its role is simply to "fit" the company's strategy. In this view HR's strategic role is to adapt individual HR practices (recruiting, rewarding, and so on) to fit specific corporate and competitive strategies. By this view, top management crafts a corporate strategy—such as to buy Lotus—and then HR is told to create the HR programs required to successfully implement that corporate strategy.[69] As two strategic planning experts have argued, "the human resources management system must be tailored to the demands of business strategy."[70] The idea here is that "for any particular organizational strategy, there is purportedly a matching human resource strategy."[71]

A third view of HR management is that it is an equal partner in the strategic planning process. Here HR management's role is not just to tailor its activities to the demands of business strategy, nor, certainly, just to carry out operational day-to-day tasks like ensuring that employees are paid. Instead, by this third view, the need to forge a company's workforce into a competitive advantage means that human resource management must be an equal partner in both the formulation and the implementation of the company's organizationwide and competitive strategies.[72]

Is it realistic to see HR managers as equal partners in both the formulation and implementation of a firm's strategic plans? One study of top HR managers in New Zealand is probably typical and suggests that the answer is "yes and no."[73] By their own descriptions, most of these managers were "more intimately involved with the implementation of strategic change and with the recruitment and development of key staff, notably managers" than with actually formulating the firm's strategic plans.[74] Yet even in this sample there was a tendency for these HR executives to increasingly take a broader focus on the business as a whole and on its wider environment.[75] HR managers therefore both traditionally and today seem to have their greatest strategic impact on the implementation of a company's plans; however, the opportunity and necessity is there for their involvement in strategy formulation as well.

HR'S ROLE IN FORMULATING STRATEGY   Formulating a company's overall strategic plan requires identifying, analyzing, and balancing two sets of forces—the company's *external opportunities and threats* on the one hand, and its *internal strengths and weaknesses* on the other.

This is one area in which strategic HR can play a role. For example, HR management can play a role in what strategic planners call *environmental scanning*, identifying and analyzing external opportunities and threats that may be crucial to the company's success. For example, both United Airlines and American Airlines considered and then rejected the opportunity to acquire USAir, a smaller and relatively weak airline. While both American and United had several reasons for rejecting a bid, HR considerations loomed large. Specifically, both American and United had doubts about their abilities to successfully negotiate new labor agreements with USAir's employees, and both felt the problems of assimilating them might be too great.

HR management can also supply *competitive intelligence* that may be useful as the company formulates its strategic plans. Details regarding new incentive plans being used by competitors, opinion survey data from employees that provide information about customer complaints, and information about pending legislation like labor laws or mandatory health insurance are some examples. Furthermore:

> *From public information and legitimate recruiting and interview activities, you ought to be able to construct organization charts, staffing levels and group missions for the various organizational components of each of your major competitors. Your knowledge of how brands are sorted among sales divisions and who reports to whom can give important clues as to a competitor's strategic priorities. You may even know the track record and characteristic behavior of the executives.*[76]

HR also participates in the strategy formulation process by supplying information regarding the company's internal strengths and weaknesses. For example, IBM's decision to buy Lotus was probably prompted in part by IBM's conclusion that its own human resources were inadequate for the firm to reposition itself as an industry leader in networking systems, or at least to do so quickly enough. Similarly, about two months after Wells Fargo acquired Crocker National [Bank] Corporation, it surveyed 1500 Crocker employees to ensure that Wells Fargo would discover any morale problems as quickly as possible.

Some firms even build their strategies around an HR-based competitive advantage. For example, in the process of automating its factories, farm equipment manufacturer John Deere developed a workforce that was exceptionally talented and expert in factory automation. This in turn prompted the firm to establish a new-technology division to offer automation services to other companies.[77] As another example, the accounting and consulting firm Arthur Andersen developed unique human resource capabilities in training. The firm's Illinois training facility is so sophisticated that it provides the firm with a competitive advantage, enabling it to provide fast, uniform training in house and so "react quickly to the changing demands of its clients."[78]

HR'S ROLE IN EXECUTING STRATEGY   Strategy execution has traditionally been the "bread and butter" of HR's strategy role. For example, Federal Express's competitive strategy is to differentiate itself from its competitors by offering superior customer service and guaranteed on-time deliveries. Since the same basic technologies are available to UPS, DHL, and FedEx's other competitors, it's FedEx's workforce—its human resource—who necessarily provide FedEx with a crucial competitive advantage. This puts a premium on FedEx's HR processes, as discussed earlier, and on the firm's ability to create a highly committed, competent, and customer-oriented workforce.[79]

HR management supports strategic implementation in other ways. For example, HR is involved in the execution of most firms' downsizing and restructuring strategies, through outplacing employees, instituting pay-for-performance plans, reducing health care costs, and retraining employees. For example, when Wells Fargo subsequently went on to also acquire First Interstate Bancorp, HR played a strategic role in merging two "wildly divergent" cultures and in dealing with the uncertainty and initial shock that rippled through both organizations when the merger was announced.[80]

HR PRACTICES: IS THERE A "ONE BEST WAY?"   The idea that HR can help top management execute its strategy raises an interesting question, namely, Is there a set of universal "HR best practices" (such as a particular way to appraise or compensate employees) that have been shown to be applicable for a wide range of companies and strategies, or is it mandatory to design the HR practice to fit each company's strategy? This question has been the subject of much debate, and while there's no definitive answer yet, some conclusions can be drawn.

First, studies do suggest that there are some broad general HR principles or philosophies that seem to be universally applicable to all or most companies. As noted earlier (in the study of banks), for instance, profit sharing, results-oriented appraisals, and employment security have been found to have strong relationships with measures of organizational performance in a range of situations.[81] Similarly, for all companies aiming to globalize, HR departments that (1) foster informal relationships between employees with the aim of fostering worldwide communication, (2) develop global executives through international assignments, (3) have people with international experience in key global HR management positions, and (4) have a global HR person on the initial business strategy team when entering new markets all seem more effective.[82]

On the other hand, as two researchers say, "There appears to be no best practice magic bullet", except to organize a firm's HR system to fit its strategy and to "support the firm's operating and strategic initiatives."[83] Some broad HR practices (such as holding special training sessions to foster informal relationships between employees so as to improve worldwide communications) may be widely applicable, at least to most global companies. However, indiscriminately dropping a practice into your firm just because it worked well in another can be unwise. For example, "systematic efforts to enhance the skill levels of employees are especially important to firms trying to compete on quality."[84] Similarly (in the bank study above), whether or not the banks benefitted from HR practices such as employee participation, results-oriented appraisals, and internal career opportunities depended on the type of bank and what it was trying to achieve strategically (i.e., cut costs, boost quality, expand geographically, or some other).[85]

For current and future managers, the best advice therefore seems to be to learn as much as possible about the HR practices we'll discuss in the following chapters, and then design a practice that's consistent with what your company wants to achieve. The corollary is that flexibility is advisable, since any HR practice (such as your firm's compensation plan) will have to change as competitive conditions require that your firm's strategy change.[86]

THE STRATEGIC FUTURE OF THE HR DEPARTMENT   Ironically, while the need for HR is obviously booming, the future of the HR department itself sometimes seems in doubt. One study showed a decline of 18% in HR expenditures per employee, which were down from $1,418 in 1980 to $1,153 per full-time employee in 1995.[87] The average ratio of HR staff per 100 employees was up slightly between 1996 and 1997 but appears to be flattening. "HR staffing relative to total employment still may be growing more conservative," one survey concludes.[88] Human resource departments will again face downsizing and "reengineering", says one expert, "as they face pressure from senior management to add value to the organization or have their functions contracted out."[89]

The belt tightening in HR seems to reflect several causes—reengineering, downsizing, and outsourcing. At Sears, Roebuck and Company, for instance, reengineering/reorganizing of the HR department resulted in slashing the corporate HR department from 700 to about 200 employees. HR responsibilities that had previously been dispersed at 32 U.S. locations were consolidated in one Atlanta office, as part of this downsizing.[90]

Outsourcing is having an impact, too. For example, a recent survey by the American Management Association found that 77% of the 619 surveyed employers said they currently outsourced one or more HR activities such as temporary staffing, recruiting, benefits administration, payroll, or training.[91] Cost reduction was the most commonly cited explanation.[92]

What can HR departments do to keep themselves from getting "outsourced" out of existence?[93] For one thing, says one expert, the HR department needs to focus more on activities that clearly add value to the company's bottom line—activities such as strategic planning, change management, corporate culture transition, and development of human capital.[94]

Another HR expert—Professor David Ulrich of the University of Michigan—believes that "HR can help deliver organizational excellence in four main ways."[95] First, HR's role as a strategic partner needs to be enhanced. For example, "if strategy implementation requires, say, a team-based organizational structure, HR would be responsible for bringing state-of-the-art approaches for creating this structure to senior management's attention."[96] Second, HR "should become an expert in the way work is organized and executed, delivering administrative efficiency to ensure that costs are reduced while quality is maintained."[97] Third, with employee behavior increasingly the key to competitive advantage, HR "should become a champion for employees, vigorously representing their concerns to senior management and at the same time working to increase . . . employees' commitment to the organization and their ability to deliver results."[98] Fourth, HR needs to ensure the organization has the capacity to embrace and capitalize on change,[99] for instance by making sure that "broad vision statements get transformed into specific behaviors."[100] As the tasks they face grow more complex, the HR field is also becoming more professionalized. Thus, thousands of HR professionals have already passed one or both of the HR professional certification exams offered by the Human Resource Certification Institute (703-548-3440, or hrci@shrm.org). The two levels of the exams test the professionals' knowledge in all aspects of HR, including management practices, staffing, HR development, compensation, labor relations, and health and safety. Those successfully completing all requirements earn the right to be designated PHR or SPHR.

In summary, trends including globalization, deregulation, and technological innovation are creating the need for better, faster, more competitive organizations. Employee behavior and performance is often the key to gaining a competitive advantage under such conditions. HR is in a unique position to help create better, faster more competitive organizations through its influence on employees' behavior. Research findings show that effective HR management does translate into higher productivity and market value.[101] In this book we'll look more closely at how HR accomplishes this.

THE PLAN OF THIS BOOK

This book is built around two themes. The first theme is that HR management is the responsibility of every manager—not just those in the HR department. Throughout this book, you'll therefore find an emphasis on practical material that you as a manager will need to carry out your day-to-day management responsibilities. The second theme is that, given the need to build a more competitive organization around highly committed employees, HR programs should help make organizations better, faster, and more competitive. You'll also therefore find many examples and highlighted features showing how HR activities are making companies better, faster, and more competitive, as well as illustrations of how HR can help foster employee commitment. Here is a brief overview of the chapters to come:

Chapter 2: Equal Opportunity and the Law. What you'll need to know about equal opportunity laws as they relate to human resource management activities such as interviewing, selecting employees, and evaluating performance appraisal.

PART II: RECRUITMENT AND PLACEMENT

Chapter 3: Job Analysis. How to analyze a job; how to determine the human resource requirements of the job, as well as its specific duties and responsibilities.

Chapter 4: Personnel Planning and Recruiting. Determining what sorts of people need to be hired; recruiting them.

Chapter 5: Employee Testing and Selection. Techniques like testing you can use to ensure that you're hiring the right people.

Chapter 6: Interviewing Job Candidates. How to interview candidates to help ensure that you hire the right person for the right job.

PART III: TRAINING AND DEVELOPMENT

Chapter 7: Training and Development. Providing the training necessary to ensure that your employees have the knowledge and skills needed to accomplish their tasks; concepts and techniques for developing more capable employees, managers, and organizations.

Chapter 8: Managing Organizational Renewal. HR techniques such as quality improvement programs and team building that firms use to help them manage quality and productivity.

Chapter 9: Appraising Performance. Techniques for appraising performance.

Chapter 10: Managing Careers and Fair Treatment. Techniques such as career planning and promotion from within; firms use these to help ensure employees can achieve their potential and be treated fairly.

PART IV: COMPENSATION

Chapter 11: Establishing Pay Plans. How to develop equitable pay plans for your employees.

Chapter 12: Pay-for-Performance and Financial Incentives. Pay-for-performance plans such as financial incentives, merit pay, and incentives that help tie performance to pay.

Chapter 13: Benefits and Services. Providing benefits that make it clear the firm views its employees as long-term investments and is concerned with their welfare—such as stock ownership plans, pensions, and health plans.

PART V: EMPLOYEE SECURITY AND SAFETY

Chapter 14: Labor Relations and Collective Bargaining. Concepts and techniques concerning the relations between unions and management, including the union-organizing campaign; negotiating and agreeing upon a collective bargaining agreement between unions and management and then managing the agreement via the grievance process.

Chapter 15: Employee Safety and Health. The causes of accidents, how to make the workplace safe, and laws governing your responsibilities in regard to employee safety and health.

PART VI: INTERNATIONAL HRM

Chapter 16: Managing Human Resources in an International Arena. The growing importance of international business, and HR's role in managing the personnel side of multinational operations.

We invite you to visit the Dessler page on the Prentice Hall Web site at **www.prenhall.com/dessler** for our on-line study guide, Internet exercises, current events, links to related Web sites, and more.

SUMMARY

1. There are basic functions all managers perform—planning, organizing, staffing, leading, and controlling. These represent what is often called the *management process.*

2. Staffing, personnel management, or human resource management is the function focused on in this book. It includes activities like recruiting, selecting, training, compensating, appraising, and developing.

3. HR management is a part of every manager's responsibilities. These HR responsibilities include placing the right person in the right job, and then orienting, training, and compensating to improve his or her job performance.

4. The HR manager and his or her department carry out three main functions. First, the manager exerts *line authority* in his or her unit and implied authority elsewhere in the organization. He or she exerts a *coordinative function* to ensure that the organization's HR objectives and policies are coordinated and implemented. And he or she provides various *staff services* to line management; for example, the HR manager or department assists in the hiring, training, evaluating, rewarding, promoting, and disciplining of employees at all levels.

5. Trends such as globalization, technological advances, and deregulation mean that companies must be better, faster, and more competitive to survive and thrive today. Other important trends include growing workforce diversity, and changes in the nature of work such as the movement toward a service society and a growing emphasis on education and human capital.

6. Trends like globalization and technological innovation are changing the way firms are managed. For example, the traditional pyramid-shaped organization is flattening, employees are being empowered to make more decisions; work is increasingly organized around teams and processes; the bases of power are changing; and managers today must build commitment. Changes like these mean that organizations must depend more on self-disciplined and committed employees. HR activities can have measurable effects on a company's bottom line, and on making a company better, faster, and more competitive.

7. HR management should be involved in both the formulation and the implementation of a company's strategies, given the need for the firm to galvanize employees into a competitive advantage.

8. We defined strategic human resource management as "the linking of HRM with strategic goals and objectives in order to improve business performance and develop organizational cultures that foster innovation and flexibility." HR is a strategic partner, in that HRM works with other top managers to formulate the company's strategy as well as to execute it.

KEY TERMS

management process 2	staff manager 4	globalization 9
human resource management 2	line authority 4	competitive advantage 21
authority 3	implied authority 4	cost leadership 21
line manager 3	functional control 4	differentiation 21
	employee advocacy 5	

DISCUSSION QUESTIONS

1. Explain what HR management is and how it relates to the management process.

2. Give several examples of how HR management concepts and techniques can be of use to all managers.

3. Compare and contrast the work of line and staff managers; give examples of each.

4. Why is it important for a company to make its human resources into a competitive advantage? How can HR contribute to doing so?

5. What is meant by strategic human resource management and what exactly is HR's role in the strategic planning process?

1. Working individually or in groups, develop several lists showing how trends like workforce diversity, technological trends, globalization, and changes in the nature of work have affected the college or university you are attending now.

2. Working individually or in groups, develop a list of examples showing how the new management practices discussed in this chapter (worker empowerment, flatter organizations, and so on) have or have not been implemented to some extent in the college or university you are now attending, or in the organization for which you work.

3. Working individually or in groups, interview an HR manager; based on that interview write a short presentation regarding HR's role today in building a more responsive organization.

EXPERIENTIAL EXERCISE

HRM As a Strategic Partner in Strategic Planning

You are part of a strategic planning task force at your university. The HR department wishes to identify changes that are taking place in the workforce and how they will affect the human resource needs of the university. The team has identified a set of critical issues in the external business environment. What role should HR play (if any) in responding to these critical issues?

CRITICAL ISSUE	EFFECT ON EXISTING EMPLOYEES	POTENTIAL HR ROLE(S)
(Example) 1. Distance learning technology	*(Example)* Need for better computer skills	*(Example)* Provide greater technical training
2. Government reductions in funding to higher education		
3. Greater workforce diversity		
4. More international students		
5. High percentage of faculty to retire over next decade		
6. Local large business is developing its own corporate university		

Directions:
Divide the class into teams of three to four students. Ask each team to develop a response to two items on the list (each team should work on a different set of items). Bring the teams together to share their results. When the teams have had time to discuss their responses, consider the following questions:

1. Which environmental change would have the greatest impact on the human resource needs of the university?

2. What environmental change will be the most difficult for your HR group to manage?

3. Overall, how will this combination of changes affect your organization?

CASE INCIDENT

Jack Nelson's Problem

As a new member of the board of directors for a local bank, Jack Nelson was being introduced to all the employees in the home office. When he was introduced to Ruth Johnson, he was curious about her work and asked people in her office what her machine did. Johnson replied that she really did not know what the machine was called or what it did. She explained that she had only been working there for two months. She did, however, know precisely how to operate the machine. According to her supervisor, she was an excellent employee.

At one of the branch offices, the supervisor in charge spoke to Nelson confidentially, telling him that "something was wrong," but she didn't know what. For one thing, she explained, employee turnover was too high, and no sooner had one employee been put on the job than another one resigned. With customers to see and loans to be made, she explained, she had little time to work with the new employees as they came and went.

All branch supervisors hired their own employees without communication with the home office or other branches. When an opening developed, the supervisor tried to find a suitable employee to replace the worker who had quit.

After touring the 22 branches and finding similar problems in many of them, Nelson wondered what the home office should do or what action he should take. The banking firm was generally regarded as a well-run institution that had grown from 27 to 191 employees during the past eight years. The more he thought about the matter, the more puzzled Nelson became. He couldn't quite put his finger on the problem, and he didn't know whether to report his findings to the president.

■ QUESTIONS

1. What do you think is causing some of the problems in the bank home office and branches?
2. Do you think setting up an HR unit in the main office would help?
3. What specific functions should an HR unit carry out? What HR functions would then be carried out by supervisors and other line managers?

Source: From *Supervision in Action,* 4/e by Claude S. George, © 1985. Adapted by permission of Prentice-Hall, Inc., Upper Saddle River, NJ.

Case Application

TURNOVER IN THE BANK

The Conservative State Savings Bank was a medium-sized bank located in a large southern city. A sizeable unit of the bank's operation was the check processing department. The employees in this department, who served as checkreader operators, were all women between the ages of eighteen and forty. The women feed checks into the check readers and manually input any "defective checks" into a computerized proofing system. The machines were the latest models and were spaced approximately 3 to 4 feet apart. There were about thirty check-reader operators; the other departmental employees were clerks and word and data processors who were

connected with the check-collection process. In total, about forty women worked together in the same large room. There were four supervisors in the department, all of whom were women. These supervisors reported to Jennifer Szorba, a middle-level manager who had several other departments under her responsibility.

The bank had been experiencing an annual turnover rate in the check processing department of about 40%. This turnover rate had been steadily rising over the previous few years despite efforts by management to stem the trend. With turnover of this magnitude, efficiency had been greatly reduced.

Identifying the Problem

Juanita Nelson, a young staff employee in the human resources department, was assigned by Marvin Vanderber, Vice President for Operations of the bank, to investigate the situation. Top management hoped that Nelson might obtain better insights into the problems that existed in the check processing department and suggest ways of dealing with them.

As a first step, Juanita Nelson decided to choose a sample of former departmental employees who, for various reasons, had either left the bank voluntarily or who had been discharged within the preceding six months. She hoped to interview these ex-employees and to encourage them to speak objectively about their past jobs. Nelson selected a sample of ten former employees, but she was able to interview only six of them. (See Figure 1-7 for additional information concerning each former employee who was interviewed.) The remaining had either changed addresses or were not available because of circumstances or personal reasons.

Interview Information

The types of questions Juanita Nelson asked during the interviews were meant to allow the former employees ample freedom to discuss their situations. By prearranged appointments, she interviewed these women either in their homes or at a nearby restaurant.

JANE CALDWELL According to bank personnel records, Jane Caldwell had resigned from her job "to remain at home." Caldwell stated that she had liked her job for the first two and one-half years of the three years of her employment. The thing she disliked most was that she had become totally bored with the routine of her job, and she felt that there was no hope of ever moving to a different department. On several occasions, she had mentioned to her supervisor her desire to get out of the check processing department, but Caldwell felt that her supervisor did not take her seriously. This was the major complaint she had concerning this supervisor.

According to Caldwell, one of her sources of difficulty had been that she was receiving a considerably higher salary than most of the employees in the department. Some of her co-workers knew about her higher salary and resented the fact that they were not paid as well. In fact, every time Caldwell received a raise, it seemed as if everyone knew about it before she was notified. Caldwell did not know how the others found out about her pay raises, but she alluded to the possibility that the departmental supervisors had let the information escape.

Pertaining to the bank's overall attitude toward its employees, Jane Caldwell believed that the bank regarded her as a number. She felt that the supervisors were too busy to help when problems came up. As a result, she felt that most of the employees in the department had very low morale and were concerned only with "putting in their time" and receiving a regular raise. None of them had more than the minimum amount of pride or loyalty toward their employer. When Caldwell was first employed, there seemed to be some hope and competition for advancement. But now she felt that only a few employees—"the ones who only worked hard when the boss was looking"—competed, and only to appear that they did a good job. And, she added, since there was no real competition, the jobs became exceptionally boring.

FIGURE 1-7 Interviewee Backgrounds

EMPLOYEE	AGE	RACE	MARITAL STATUS	PERIOD OF EMPLOYMENT	MONTHLY RATE OF PAY	STATED REASON FOR LEAVING BANK
Jane Caldwell	24	W	M	3 years	$1,665	RESIGNED: to stay home
Alice Wendell	20	W	M	1 year	$1,255	RESIGNED: to seek employment closer to home
Bernice Ritchey	32	B	M	1 year	$1,550	RESIGNED: pregnancy
Ruth Mentler	22	W	M	3 years	$1,470	RESIGNED: pregnancy
Gloria Sheetz	19	B	S	1 year	$1,255	RESIGNED: unsatisfactory attendance
Linda Ligon	19	W	S	2 years	$1,340	RESIGNED: unsatisfactory attendance

(continued)

ALICE WENDELL   Alice Wendell had told her supervisor that she was resigning "to seek other employment closer to home." However, her interview with Juanita Nelson seemed to suggest other motivations. Wendell stated that she had "hated" her job. Work schedules were a major reason for her dissatisfaction. The daily schedule was from 8 A.M. to 5 P.M., but during the afternoons, no scheduled break time was allowed. Further, Saturday work was required every third weekend. As far as the supervisors were concerned, they were not particularly helpful. In fact, on several occasions when Wendell had gone to her supervisor for help, she felt as if the supervisor gave her any kind of answer just "to get me off her back." Wendell thought that the departmental supervisors generally favored a few of the employees and that they were uninterested in helping the others. As a result, these "favored employees" were the ones who received the more frequent raises, even when they did not deserve them.

When asked about her impressions of the bank's overall attitude toward employees, Alice Wendell said that the employees "were nothing but numbers like in the computers." However, she inserted at this point an exception to her statement. Wendell had been told by one of her supervisors that she should contribute to an annual community charity fund. The supervisor implied that she had to give to this fund or her job might be in jeopardy. Wendell resented this type of coercion, and she said that only when the bank had something to gain was it aware of employees as individuals.

BERNICE RITCHEY   Bernice Ritchey left the employment of the bank for maternity reasons. However, she, too, had some interesting comments to make in her interview. Ritchey had enjoyed her job except for the "tensions" it created and the Saturday work. Her opinion was that the supervisors were the greatest cause of discontent within the department and were responsible for most of the problems. Ritchey stated that the supervisors tended to unduly criticize employees and that they constantly made the employees feel inferior and uneasy. When asked about pay for her job, Bernice Ritchey claimed that while the bank's pay scale had risen somewhat, it was still very low and some of the new incoming employees received higher wages by comparison to the older ones. The result was that the new and inexperienced person could come in at virtually the same salary as those who had been at the bank for several years. This brought about resentment. Further, Ritchey felt that although the bank claimed that raises were based mainly on merit, an employee could do the best job possible and yet go unnoticed and not rewarded. She asserted

that the bank always put itself first, and any concern for the well-being of the employees was of low priority. Since only a few of the departmental employees looked for advancement, most of them just did their routine jobs with little pride and without commitment.

RUTH MENTLER   Ruth Mentler was another case of resignation for maternity reasons. However, she, too, had not been happy with her job. She disliked the Saturday shifts, although she realized that someone had to do the work. In her opinion, the supervisors were usually too busy to take an interest in complaints or problems the employees might have. When a supervisor did offer assistance, it was always "my way or no way." Ruth Mentler thought that the supervisors had too much to do to give individual attention to employees. Most of Mentler's comments were similar to the first three interviewees' statements regarding attitudes of the employees and the bank's attitudes toward the employees. Mentler also mentioned that the situation on pay raises was common knowledge and a source of considerable discontent.

GLORIA SHEETZ   Gloria Sheetz had resigned her position at the bank, but she actually was "forced" into this since she had knowledge of the fact that the bank planned "to let me go" due to alleged unsatisfactory attendance. Sheetz stated that she, too, disliked the long hours which often arose. Someone had to stay until the work was finished each evening, and, in many cases, this meant considerable overtime. The uncertainty of hours made the job "unbearable" to Gloria. When she tried to make suggestions that she felt might help conditions within the department, she was told by her supervisor that it was not her role to suggest changes. Sheetz said she could not remember ever hearing a supervisor compliment an employee, even when an employee was doing more than what she was told to do. It was only when someone committed an error that the employee heard from a supervisor.

Gloria Sheetz acknowledged that the bank's physical working conditions were good in general. The other employees were enjoyable to work with, but the supervisors in the department were the greatest source of employee dissatisfaction. The supervisors, she felt, were out to make themselves look good to their manager at the expense of the employees. As an example, she cited the incident concerning the "forced contributions" to the charitable fund. In Gloria's opinion, the supervisors wanted it to look as if there had been 100% cooperation of the employees relative to giving. Most of the time, "We were treated like dirt under the supervisors' feet," as far as Gloria was concerned. Quite frequently, supervisors had told various employees that their attitudes were "poor." She had suggested to a human resources staff person that the bank should give the supervisors training in human relations, rather than just training them to be competent on the technical aspects of the job. This suggestion was ignored.

Gloria Sheetz felt that a union was needed for this department of the bank. However, one day when she and some of her co-workers were discussing the merits of unions, a supervisor overheard the discussion. The supervisor proceeded to tell them that if management ever discovered that any of them had responded to a union's attempt to organize the bank, they would lose their jobs. Gloria also mentioned the matter of pay-raise information "leaking" throughout the department. She felt that this was another cause of resentment within the department.

LINDA LIGON Linda Ligon "resigned" for reasons similar to those of Gloria Sheetz. Ligon also disliked her job, saying that employees in the check processing department were treated as if they were located in the bank's "ghetto." She added, "It is the lowest department in the bank, and even those in other departments consider it as such."

As far as Linda was concerned, the worst problem was the supervision. She was even afraid to approach her supervisor, who never issued compliments, just

complaints. Right before she left the bank, Linda was told that her attitude was bad. This only made matters worse. Linda felt that the reason her supervisor thought her attitude was bad was because she merely tried to be "honest" with the supervisors. Ligon said that she wasn't reluctant to speak her mind, and she often complained when she felt it was necessary.

After reflecting on these interviews, Juanita Nelson pondered what actions and/or recommendations she should make to higher management of Conservative State Savings Bank. She wondered if she should first interview the supervisors for their opinions, or whether this would primarily be a waste of time, with the supervisors only attempting to blame the employees for the department's shortcomings.

■ QUESTIONS

1. What would you do now if you were Juanita Nelson? Why?
2. What HR functions (selection, training, appraisal, pay, etc.) would be relevant in explaining the apparent problems at the bank? How might each be modified to improve the situation?

Source: Raymond L. Hilgert and Cyril C. Ling, *Cases and Experiential Exercises in Human Resource Management* (Upper Saddle River, NJ: Prentice Hall, 1996), pp. 12–16.

NOTES

1. David Upton, "What Really Makes Factories Flexible?" *Harvard Business Review* (July–August 1995), p. 75.

2. Quoted in Fred K. Foulkes, "The Expanding Role of the Personnel Function," *Harvard Business Review* (March–April 1975), pp. 71–84. See also Warren Wilhelm, "HR Can Make the U.S. a Global Leader," *Personnel Journal* (May 1993), p. 280.

3. See Robert Saltonstall, "Who's Who in Personnel Administration," *Harvard Business Review*, Vol. 33 (July–August 1955), pp. 75–83, reprinted in Paul Pigors, Charles Meyers, and F. P. Maim, *Management of Human Resources* (New York: McGraw-Hill, 1969), pp. 61–73.

4. For a description of this see, for example, *BNA Bulletin to Management*, "SHRM-BNA Survey #63: Human Resource Activities, Budgets, & Staffs, 1997–98," (June 18, 1998), pp. 10–12.

5. For a detailed discussion of the responsibilities and duties of the human resource department, see Mary Zippo, "Personal Activi-

ties: Where the Dollars Went in 1979," *Personnel*, Vol. 57 (March–April 1980), pp. 61–67; and "ASPABNA Survey No. 49, Personnel Activities, Budgets, and Staffs: 1985–1986," *BNA Bulletin to Management*, June 5, 1986.

6. Saltonstall, "Who's Who," p. 65.

7. Fred K. Foulkes and Henry Morgan, "Organizing and Staffing the Personnel Function," *Harvard Business Review*, Vol. 56 (May–June 1977), p. 146.

8. Ibid., p. 149.

9. "Employee Advocacy Remains HR Priority," *BNA Bulletin to Management*, September 26, 1996, p. 312.

10. U.S. Department of Labor, Bureau of Labor Statistics, *Occupational Outlook Handbook*, Bulletin 2250, 1986–1987 Edition, pp. 45–47.

11. Saltonstall, "Who's Who," pp. 68–69.

12. *The World Almanac and Book of Facts*, 1998 (K-III Reference Corporation, Mahwah, NJ: 1998), p. 207.

13. Charles W. Hill, *International Business* (Burr Ridge, IL: McGraw-Hill, 1994), p. 6.

14. Ibid., p. 9.

15. Bryan O'Reilly, "Your New Global Workforce," *Fortune*, December 14, 1992, pp. 52–66.

16. Thomas Stewart, "Welcome to the Revolution," *Fortune*, December 13, 1993, p. 68.

17. Rachel Moskowitz and Drew Warwick, "The 1994–2005 Job Outlook in Brief," *Occupational Outlook Quarterly*, Vol. 40, no. 1 (Spring 1996), pp. 2–41. See also Mahlon Apgar, IV, "The Alternative Workplace: Changing Where and How People Work," *Harvard Business Review* (May–June 1998), pp. 121–136.

18. Richard Crawford, *In the Era of Human Capital* (New York: Harper, 1991), p. 10.

19. Ibid., p. 26.

20. O'Reilly, "Your New Global Workforce," p. 63.

21. Peter Drucker, "The Coming of the New Organization," *Harvard Business Review* (January–February 1988), p. 45. See also Richard Cappelli, "Rethinking the Nature of Work: A Look at the Research Evidence," *Compensation & Benefits Review* (July/August 1997), pp. 50–59.

22. "Major Changes Redefine the Modern Workplace," *BNA Bulletin to Management*, July 3, 1997, p. 209.

23. Gerald Ferris, Dwight Frink, and M. Carmen Galang, "Diversity in the Workplace: The Human Resources Management Challenge," *Human Resource Planning*, Vol. 16, no. 1, pp. 41–51.

24. Ibid., p. 42.

25. Howard Fullerton, Jr., "Another Look at the Labor Force," *Monthly Labor Review* (November 1993), pp. 31–40; "The American Workforce, 1994–2005," *BNA Bulletin to Management*, January 4, 1996, pp. 4–5.

26. "Immigrants in the Workforce," *BNA Bulletin to Management Datagraph*, August 15, 1996, pp. 260–261.

27. Ibid., p. 38.

28. Ibid., p. 37.

29. "Workforce Becoming Older, Better Educated," *BNA Bulletin to Management*, October 17, 1996, pp. 332–333.

30. Except as noted, this section is based on Charles Greer, *Strategy and Human Resources* (Upper Saddle River, NJ: Prentice-Hall, 1995), pp. 49–52.

31. Gillian Flynn, "Xers vs. Boomers: Teamwork or Trouble?" *Personnel Journal* (November 1996), pp. 86–89.

32. Ferris et al., "Diversity in the Workplace," p. 43.

33. Ibid.

34. For related discussions see, for example, Felice Schwartz, "Women in American Business: The Demographic Imperative," *Business and the Contemporary World* (Summer 1993), pp. 10–19; Karen Stephenson and Valdis Krebs, "A More Accurate Way to Measure Diversity," *Personnel Journal* (October 1993), pp. 66–74.

35. For a discussion, see "Special Survey Report: Legal Oversight of the HR Department," *BNA Bulletin to Management*, February 2, 1995, pp. 1–12.

36. These are based on Walter Kiechel, III, "How We Will Work in the Year 2000," *Fortune*, May 17, 1993, p. 79.

37. Bryan Dumaine, "What the Leaders of Tomorrow See," *Fortune*, July 3, 1989, p. 58.

38. Rosabeth Moss Kanter, "The New Managerial Work," *Harvard Business Review* (November–December 1989), p. 88.

39. Ibid.

40. Thomas A. Steward, "How GE Keeps Those Ideas Coming," *Fortune*, August 12, 1991, p. 42.

41. Tom Peters, *Liberation Management* (New York: Alfred Knopf, 1992), p. 9.

42. Ibid.

43. This discussion is based on Gary Dessler, *Management Fundamentals* (Reston, VA: Reston, 1977), p. 2; William Berliner and William McClarney, *Management Practice and Training* (Burr Ridge, IL: McGraw-Hill, 1974), p. 11.

44. John A. Byrne, "Jack," *Business Week*, June 8, 1998, p. 105.

45. "Human Capital Critical to Success," *Management Review* (November 1998), p. 9.

46. Commerce Clearing House, "HR Role: Maximize the Competitive Advantage of People," *Ideas and Trends in Personnel*, August 5, 1992, p. 121.

47. Charlene Marmer Solomon, "Working Smarter: How HR Can Help," *Personnel Journal*, June 1993, pp. 54–64.

48. See, for example, Benjamin Schneider and David Bowen, "The Service Organization: Human Resources Management is Crucial," *Organizational Dynamics*, Vol. 21, no. 4, 1993, pp. 39–52.

49. Schneider and Bowen, "The Service Organization."

50. Jennifer Laabs, "HR's Vital Role at Levi Strauss," *Personnel Journal* (December 1992) p. 37.

51. John Delery and D. Harold Doty, "Modes of Theorizing in Strategic Human Resource Management: Tests of Universalistic, Contingency, and Configurational Performance Predictions," *Academy of Management Journal*, Vol. 39, no. 4 (1996), pp. 802–835.

52. Ibid., p. 825.

53. Mark Youndt, Scott Snell, James Dean, Jr., and David Lepak, "Human Resource Management, Manufacturing Strategy, and Firm Performance," *Academy of Management Journal*, Vol. 39, no. 4 (1996), pp. 836–866.

54. Ibid., p. 858.

55. Brian Becker and Barry Gerhart, "The Impact of Human Resource Management on Organizational Performance: Progress and Prospects," *Academy of Management Journal*, Vol. 39, no. 4 (1996), pp. 796–797.

56. Patrick Gunnigle and Sara Moore, "Linking Business Strategy and Human Resource Management: Issues and Implications," *Personnel Review*, Vol. 23, no. 1 (1994), pp. 63–84.

57. Arthur Thompson and A. J. Strickland, *Strategic Management* (Burr Ridge, IL: McGraw-Hill, 1992), p. 38.

58. For a description of the need for an effective and integrated strategy see, for example, Erhard Valentin, "Anatomy of a Fatal Business Strategy," *Journal of Management Studies*, Vol. 31, no. 3 (May 1994), pp. 359–382.

59. Gunnigle and Moore, "Linking Business Strategy," p. 64.

60. Michael Porter, *Competitive Strategy* (New York: The Free Press, 1980), p. 14.

61. Greer, *Strategy and Human Resources*, p. 105.

62. For a discussion see, for example, Jay Galbraith, "Positioning Human Resource as a Value-Adding Function: The Case of

Rockwell International," *Human Resource Management*, Vol. 31, no. 4 (Winter 1992), pp. 287–300; and Augustine Lado and Mary Wilson, "Human Resource Systems and Sustained Competitive Advantage: A Competency-Based Perspective," *Academy of Management Review*, Vol. 19, no. 4 (1994), pp. 699–727.

63. Catherine Truss and Lynda Gratton, "Strategic Human Resource Management: A Conceptual Approach," *The International Journal of Human Resource Management*, Vol. 5, no. 3 (September 1994), p. 663.

64. P. Wright and G. McMahan, "Theoretical Perspectives for Strategic Human Resource Management," *Journal of Management*, Vol. 18, no. 2 (1992), p. 292.

65. While still largely nonunionized, FedEx's pilots did vote to join the Airline Pilots Union in 1995.

66. This is based on Timothy Galpin and Patrick Murray, "Connect Human Resource Strategy to the Business Plan," *HRMagazine* (March 1997), pp. 99–104.

67. For a discussion, see Peter Boxall, "Placing HR Strategy at the Heart of Business Success," *Personnel Management*, Vol. 26, no. 7 (July 1994), pp. 32–34.

68. Ibid., p. 32.

69. Randall Schuler, "Human Resource Management Choices and Organizational Strategy," in Randall Schuler, S. A. Youngblood, and V. L. Huber (editors), *Readings in Personnel and Human Resource Management* (3rd edition) (St. Paul, MN: West, 1988).

70. For a discussion, see Catherine Truss and Lynda Gratton, "Strategic Human Resource Management," pp. 670–671.

71. Ibid., p. 670.

72. For a discussion see, for example, Randall Schuler, Peter Dowling, and Helen DeCieri, "An Integrative Framework of Strategic International Human Resource Management," *Journal of Management*, Vol. 19, no. 2 (1993), pp. 419–459; Vida Scarpello, "New Paradigm Approaches to Strategic Human Resource Management," *Group and Organization Management*, Vol. 19, no. 2 (June 1994), pp. 160–164; and Sharon Peck, "Exploring the Link Between Organizational Strategy and the Employment Relationship: The Role of Human Resources Policies," *Journal of Management Studies*, Vol. 31, no. 5 (September 1994), pp. 715–736.

73. Jeremy Hunt and Peter Boxall, "Are Top Human Resource Specialists 'Strategic Partners'? Self-Perceptions of a Corporate Elite," *The International Journal of Human Resource Management*, Vol. 9, no. 5 (October 1998), pp. 767–781.

74. Ibid., p. 778.

75. Ibid., p. 779.

76. William Henn, "What the Strategist Asks From Human Resources," *Human Resource Planning*, Vol. 8, no. 4 (1985), p. 195; quoted in Greer, *Strategy and Human Resources*, pp. 117–118.

77. Ibid., p. 105.

78. Ibid., p. 117.

79. Schuler and Jackson point out that the competitive strategies of innovation, quality enhancement, and cost reduction suggest different role behaviors and that different human resource practices are, therefore, needed to support these three types of competitive strategies. See Randall Schuler and Susan Jackson, "Link-

ing Competitive Strategies with Human Resource Management Practices," *Academy of Management Executive*, Vol. 1, no. 3 (1987), pp. 207–219.

80. Samuel Greengard, "You're Next! There's No Escaping Merger Mania!" *Workforce*, April 1997, pp. 52–62.

81. Delery and Doty, "Modes of Theorizing," p. 825.

82. Linda Stroh and Paula Caligiuri, "Strategic Human Resources: A New Source for Competitive Advantage in the Global Arena," *The International Journal of Human Resource Management*, Vol. 9, no. 1 (February 1998), pp. 1–17.

83. Brian Becker and Barry Gerhart, "The Impact of Human Resource Management on Organizational Performance: Progress and Prospects," *Academy of Management Journal*, Vol. 39, no. 4 (1996), p. 797.

84. Youndt, Snell, Dean, and Lepak, "Human Resource Management," p. 858.

85. Delery and Doty, "Modes of Theorizing," p. 825.

86. Brenda Richey and Stefan Wally, "Strategic Human Resource Strategies for Transnationals in Europe," *Human Resource Management Review*, Vol. 8, no. 1 (1998), pp. 93–94.

87. "Shrinkage of HR Examined," *BNA Bulletin to Management*, August 3, 1995, p. 248.

88. "SHRM-BNA Survey No. 62—Human Resource Activities, Budgets, and Staffs: 1996–97," *BNA Bulletin to Management*, June 25, 1997, p. 1.

89. "Human Resource Departments Fight for Their Future," *BNA Bulletin to Management*, January 25, 1996, p. 25.

90. Ibid.

91. "Outsourcing Gains Attention," *BNA Bulletin to Management*, June 5, 1997, pp. 180–181.

92. Ibid.

93. "HR's Value Measured in Terms of Strategy, CFO Says," *BNA Bulletin to Management*, April 10, 1997, p. 113.

94. "The Shifting Role of HR Departments," *BNA Bulletin to Management*, May 16, 1996, p. 1. For similar comments see, for example, Michael Donahue, "Do Your Human Resources Add Value?" *Management Accounting* (June 1996), pp. 47–48; "HR Faces Challenge of Adding Value," *BNA Bulletin to Management*, April 24, 1997, p. 136; and Bernard Tyson, "Kaiser's HR Services Get a Shot in the Arm," *Personnel Journal* (September 1996), pp. 87–90.

95. Dave Ulrich, "A New Mandate for Human Resources," *Harvard Business Review* (January-February 1998), pp. 124–134.

96. Ibid., p. 129.

97. Ibid., p. 125.

98. Ibid., p. 125.

99. Ibid., p. 125.

100. Ibid., p. 130.

101. Mark Huselid, Susan Jackson, and Randall Schuler, "Technical and Strategic Human Resource Management Effectiveness as Determinants of Firm Performance," *Academy of Management Journal*, Vol. 40, no. 1 (1997), pp. 171–188.

2

EQUAL OPPORTUNITY AND THE LAW

Hardly a day goes by without news reports of Equal Opportunity-related lawsuits at work: State Farm agrees to pay $157 million to 814 women who were unlawfully denied entry-level sales agent positions by the company;[1] Astra USA, Inc. agrees to pay almost $10 million to settle sexual harassment charges and fires its CEO for alleged complicity in the scandal;[2] senior-level Texaco, Inc. executives are tape-recorded allegedly making disparaging remarks about minority employees while discussing a class action discrimination suit brought by those employees;[3] and Home Depot USA agrees to pay $65 million and change its HR practices to settle a class action suit that alleged discrimination against women in hiring for sales and management positions at its West Coast Division stores.[4] Claims like these can derail any firm's strategy, by diverting valuable management attention, by hampering the firm's efforts to hire a first-class staff, and, of course, by undermining the firm's ability to maintain a committed workforce. ▲

Behavioral Objectives

When you finish studying this chapter, you should be able to:

▲ *Summarize* the basic Equal Employment Opportunity laws regarding age, race, sex, national origin, religion, and handicap discrimination.

▲ *Explain* the basic defenses against discrimination allegations.

▲ *Present* a summary of what employers can and cannot do with respect to illegal recruitment, selection, and promotion and layoff practices.

▲ *Explain* how to set up an affirmative action program.

Chapter Outline

INTRODUCTION   The number of employment discrimination cases brought to America's federal courts recently doubled in three years, to 23,000 in 1996, and the number of attorneys specializing in the field has tripled since 1990.[5] No wonder almost 40% of employers responding to one survey report they now carry employment practices liability insurance,[6] and that understanding equal employment law is crucial for all managers today.

State Farm's alleged equal employment errors help illustrate the personnel problems these laws aim to prevent. The basic problem at State Farm was that the hiring managers weren't asking, "Can these women do the job?" Instead, they were applying subjective criteria unrelated to job performance. For example, some women were told that it might be unsafe for them to make sales calls at night, although the evidence showed that women could do so safely. This let managers illegally reject women applicants for jobs for which they were actually qualified. In this chapter we'll look more closely at the equal employment opportunity laws with which employers are required to comply.

EQUAL EMPLOYMENT OPPORTUNITY 1964–1991

Background

Legislation barring discrimination against members of minority groups in the United States is certainly nothing new. For example, the Fifth Amendment to the U.S. Constitution (ratified in 1791) states that "no person shall be deprived of life, liberty, or property, without due process of the law." The Thirteenth Amendment (ratified in 1865) outlawed slavery and has been held by the courts to bar racial discrimination. The Fourteenth Amendment (ratified in 1868) makes it illegal for any state to "make or enforce any law which shall abridge the privileges and immunities of citizens of the United States," and the courts have generally viewed this law as barring discrimination on the basis of sex or national origin, as well as race. Section 1981 of Title 42 of the U.S. Code, passed over 100 years ago as the Civil Rights Act of 1866, gives all persons the same right to make and enforce contracts and to benefit from the laws of the land.[7] Other laws as well as various court decisions made discrimination against minorities illegal as early as the turn of the century—at least in theory.[8]

But as a practical matter, Congress and various presidents were reluctant to take dramatic action on equal employment issues until the early 1960s. At that point, "they were finally prompted to act primarily as a result of civil unrest among the minorities and women" who eventually became protected by the new equal rights legislation and the agencies created to implement and enforce it.[9]

Title VII of the 1964 Civil Rights Act

Title VII of the 1964 Civil Rights Act

The section of the act that says an employer cannot discriminate on the basis of race, color, religion, sex, or national origin with respect to employment.

WHAT THE LAW SAYS   **Title VII of the 1964 Civil Rights Act** was one of the first of these new laws. Title VII (as amended by the 1972 Equal Employment Opportunity Act) states that an employer cannot discriminate on the basis of race, color, religion, sex, or national origin. Specifically, it states that it shall be an unlawful employment practice for an employer:[10]

(1) To fail or refuse to hire or to discharge an individual or otherwise to discriminate against any individual with respect to his/her compensation, terms, conditions, or privileges of employment, because of such individual's race, color, religion, sex, or national origin.
(2) To limit, segregate, or classify his/her employees or applicants for employment in any way that would deprive or tend to deprive any individual of employment opportunities or otherwise adversely affect his/her status as an employee, because of such individual's race, color, religion, sex, or national origin.

WHO DOES TITLE VII COVER? Title VII of the Civil Rights Act bars discrimination on the part of most employers, including all public or private employers of 15 or more persons. In addition, it covers all private and public educational institutions, the federal government, and state and local governments. Public and private employment agencies are also barred from failing or refusing to refer for employment any individual because of race, color, religion, sex, or national origin. Labor unions with 15 or more members are barred from excluding, expelling, or classifying their membership because of race, color, religion, sex, or national origin. Joint labor-management committees established for selecting workers for apprenticeships and training similarly cannot discriminate against individuals.

Equal Employment Opportunity Commission (EEOC)

The commission, created by Title VII, is empowered to investigate job discrimination complaints and sue on behalf of complainants.

THE EEOC. EEOC stands for **Equal Employment Opportunity Commission,** which was instituted by Title VII. The EEOC consists of five members who are appointed by the president with the advice and consent of the Senate; each member serves a five year term.

Establishing the EEOC greatly enhanced the federal government's ability to enforce equal employment opportunity laws. The EEOC receives and investigates job discrimination complaints from aggrieved individuals. When it finds reasonable cause that the charges are justified, it attempts (through conciliation) to reach an agreement eliminating all aspects of the discrimination. If this conciliation fails, the EEOC has the power to go directly to court to enforce the law. Under the Equal Employment Opportunity Act of 1972, discrimination charges may be filed by the EEOC on behalf of an aggrieved individual, as well as by the individuals themselves. This procedure is explained in more detail later in this chapter.

Executive Orders

affirmative action

Steps that are taken for the purpose of eliminating the present effects of past discrimination.

Office of Federal Contract Compliance Programs (OFCCP)

This office is responsible for implementing the executive orders and ensuring compliance of federal contractors.

Under executive orders issued in the Johnson administration, employers who do business with the U.S. government have an obligation beyond that imposed by Title VII to refrain from employment discrimination. Executive Orders 11246 and 11375 don't just ban discrimination, they require that contractors take **affirmative action** to ensure equal employment opportunity (we will explain affirmative action later). All firms with contracts over $50,000 and 50 or more employees must develop and implement such programs. The orders also state a policy against employment discrimination based on age or physical handicap, in addition to race, color, religion, sex, or national origin. These orders also established the **Office of Federal Contract Compliance Programs (OFCCP)**. It is responsible for implementing the executive orders and ensuring the compliance of federal contractors. For example, it recently reached a settlement involving Triad International Management Company, an aviation contractor, which agreed to pay over $240,000 to settle claims that women and blacks were subjected to a "perversely hostile work environment," including racial slurs.[11]

Equal Pay Act of 1963

Equal Pay Act of 1963

The act requiring equal pay for equal work, regardless of sex.

The **Equal Pay Act of 1963** (amended in 1972) made it unlawful to discriminate in pay on the basis of sex when jobs involve equal work, equivalent skills, effort, and responsibility, and are performed under similar working conditions. However, differences in pay do not violate the act if the difference is based on a seniority system, a merit system, a system that measures earnings by quantity or quality of production, or a differential based on any factor other than sex.

Age Discrimination in Employment Act of 1967

Age Discrimination in Employment Act of 1967

The act prohibiting arbitrary age discrimination and specifically protecting individuals over 40 years old.

The **Age Discrimination in Employment Act of 1967 (ADEA)** made it unlawful to discriminate against employees or applicants for employment who are between 40 and 65 years of age. A 1973 Supreme Court ruling held that most states and local agencies, when acting in the role of employer, must also adhere to provisions of the act that protect workers from age discrimination. Subsequent actions by Congress have eliminated the age cap, effectively ending most mandatory retirement.

One-fifth of the court actions filed by the EEOC recently were ADEA cases. (Another 30% were sex discrimination cases.) This act is a "favored statute" among employees and lawyers because it allows jury trials and double damages to those proving "willful" discrimination.[12]

Vocational Rehabilitation Act of 1973

Vocational Rehabilitation Act of 1973

The act requiring certain federal contractors to take affirmative action for disabled persons.

The **Vocational Rehabilitation Act of 1973** required employers with federal contracts over $2,500 to take affirmative action for the employment of handicapped persons. The act does not require that an unqualified person be hired. It does require an employer to take steps to accommodate a handicapped worker unless doing so imposes an undue hardship on the employer.[13] A federal district court recently held that compensatory damages (a payment for "future pecuniary losses, emotional pain, suffering, inconvenience, mental anguish, loss of enjoyment of life, and other nonpecuniary losses") are available under the 1973 rehabilitation act.[14]

LEGAL ASPECTS OF AIDS AT WORK   The Vocational Rehabilitation Act took on added prominence because of a ruling that suggested it could be used to prohibit discrimination against people with AIDS.

In any case, the EEOC's position today is that the Americans with Disabilities Act (discussed later) prohibits discriminating against people with AIDS. Furthermore, numerous state laws now protect people with AIDS from discrimination. The guidelines issued by the Labor Department's Office of Federal Contract Compliance Programs also require that AIDS-type diseases be treated according to the provisions of the Rehabilitation Act.[16] The bottom line for most employers is that discriminating against people with AIDS would be viewed as unlawful.[17]

Vietnam Era Veterans' Readjustment Assistance Act of 1974

Vietnam Era Veterans' Readjustment Act of 1974

An act requiring that employers with government contracts take affirmative action to hire disabled veterans.

The provisions of the **Vietnam Era Veterans' Readjustment Act of 1974** require that employers with government contracts of $10,000 or more take affirmative action to employ and advance disabled veterans and qualified veterans of the Vietnam era. The act is administered by the OFCCP.[18]

Pregnancy Discrimination Act of 1978

Pregnancy Discrimination Act (PDA)

An amendment to Title VII of the Civil Rights Act that prohibits sex discrimination based on "pregnancy, childbirth, or related medical conditions."

Congress passed the **Pregnancy Discrimination Act (PDA)** in 1978 as an amendment to the Civil Rights Act of 1964, Title VII. The act broadened the definition of sex discrimination to encompass pregnancy, childbirth, or related medical conditions. It prohibits using these to discriminate in hiring, promotion, suspension, or discharge, or any other term or condition of employment.[19] Basically, the act says that if an employer offers its employees disability coverage, then pregnancy and childbirth must be treated like any other disability and must be included in the plan as a covered condition.[20] The U.S. Supreme Court ruled in *California Federal Savings and Loan Association v. Guerra* that if an employer offers no disability leave to any of its employees it can (but need not necessarily) grant pregnancy leave to a woman who requests it when disabled for pregnancy, childbirth, or a related medical condition, although men get no comparable benefits.[21]

Federal Agency Guidelines

The federal agencies charged with ensuring compliance with the aforementioned laws and executive orders issue their own implementing guidelines. The overall purpose of these **federal agency guidelines** is to specify the procedures these agencies recommend employers follow in complying with the equal opportunity laws.

UNIFORM GUIDELINES ON EMPLOYEE SELECTION PROCEDURES   Detailed guidelines to be used by employers were approved by the EEOC, Civil Service Commission, Department of Labor, and Department of Justice.[22] These uniform guidelines supersede earlier guidelines developed by the EEOC alone. They set forth "highly recommended" procedures regarding such matters as employee selection, record keeping, preemployment inquiries, and affirmative action programs. As an example, the guidelines specify that any employment selection devices (including but not limited to written tests) that screen out disproportionate numbers of women or minorities must be validated. The guidelines also explain in detail how an employer can validate a selection device. (This procedure will be explained in chapter 5.) For its part, the OFCCP has its own Manual of Guidelines.[23]

The American Psychological Association has published the latest Standards for Educational and Psychological Testing, and many experts expect that this document, which represents a consensus among testing authorities, "will be used in court to help judges resolve disagreements about the quality of . . . validity studies that arise during litigation."[24]

EEOC GUIDELINES   The EEOC and other agencies also periodically issue updated guidelines clarifying and revising their positions on matters such as national origin discrimination and sexual harassment.[25] For instance, the EEOC issued guidelines on the 1991 Civil Rights Act, the Americans with Disabilities Act, and sexual harassment; the Department of Labor issued guidelines on immigration; and the Office of Federal Contract Compliance Programs issued a compliance manual dealing in part with "glass ceiling" audits—audits of firms that have subtle barriers to promotion for minorities.[26]

Historically, these guidelines have fleshed out the procedures to be used in complying with equal employment laws. For example, the EEOC published guidelines that further explained and revised the agency's position on age discrimination.[27] Recall that the Age Discrimination in Employment Act of 1967 (as amended) prohibited employers from discriminating against persons over 40 years old merely because of age. Subsequent EEOC guidelines stated that it was unlawful to discriminate in hiring (or in any way) by giving preference because of age to individuals within the 40-plus age bracket. Thus, if two people apply for the same job, one 45 and the other 55, you may not lawfully turn down the 55-year-old candidate because of his or her age and expect to defend yourself by saying that you hired someone over 40.[28]

Sexual Harassment

The President Clinton–Paula Jones lawsuit drew wide public attention to the question of sexual harassment. The EEOC's guidelines on **sexual harassment** state that employers have an affirmative duty to maintain a workplace free of sexual harassment and intimidation.[29] Harassment on the basis of sex is a violation of Title VII when such conduct has the purpose or effect of substantially interfering with a person's work performance or creating an intimidating, hostile, or offensive work environment. The Civil Rights Act of 1991 (discussed later) added teeth to this. It permits victims of intentional discrimination, including sexual harassment, to have jury trials and to collect compensatory damages for pain and suffering and punitive damages in cases where the employer acted with "malice or

In the context of sexual harassment, the courts may decide a hostile environment exists even if no direct threats or promises are made in exchange for sexual behavior.

reckless indifference" to the individual's rights.[30] The Federal Violence Against Women Act of 1994 provides another avenue women can use to seek relief for violent sexual harassment. It provides that a person "who commits a crime of violence motivated by gender and thus deprives another" of her rights shall be liable to the party injured. In 1998 a female administrative assistant successfully sued under this Act when an officer of her corporate employer became verbally abusive and his requests for sex became "increasingly threatening."[31]

The EEOC guidelines define sexual harassment as "unwelcome sexual advances, requests for sexual favors, and other verbal or physical conduct of a sexual nature that takes place under any of the following conditions":[32]

> *(1) Submission to such conduct is made either explicitly or implicitly a term or condition of an individual's employment.*
> *(2) Submission to or rejection of such conduct by an individual is used as the basis for employment decisions affecting such individual.*
> *(3) Such conduct has the purpose or effect of unreasonably interfering with an individual's work performance or creating an intimidating, hostile, or offensive work environment.*

Based on a recent U.S. Supreme Court decision, sexual harassment does not apply just to relations between males and females; employees can file discrimination suits claiming sexual harassment by people of their own gender.[33] In this particular case a worker on an offshore oil rig claimed that his male supervisors restrained him several times while another worker harassed him, and that he ultimately had to quit out of fear of being raped.

Experts suggest that the EEOC and the courts will ask two basic questions when determining whether or not a company is liable for sexual harassment:

1. Did the company know or should it have known that harassment was taking place?
2. Did the company take any action to stop the harassment?[34]

There are three main ways an employee can prove sexual harassment.

QUID PRO QUO   The most direct is to prove that rejecting a supervisor's advances adversely affected the employee's tangible benefits, like raises or promotions. For example, in one case the employee was able to show that continued job success and advancement were dependent on her agreeing to the sexual demands of her supervisors. And she showed that after an initial complaint to her employer she was subjected to adverse performance evaluations, disciplinary layoffs, and other adverse actions.[35]

HOSTILE ENVIRONMENT CREATED BY SUPERVISORS   Showing that the harassment had tangible consequences (such as demotion) is not always necessary. For example, in one case the court found that a male supervisor's sexual harassment had substantially affected a female employee's emotional and psychological ability to the point that she felt she had to quit her job. Therefore, even though no direct threats or promises were made in exchange for sexual advances, the fact that the advances interfered with the woman's performance and created an offensive work environment were enough to prove that sexual harassment had occurred. On the other hand, the courts will not interpret as sexual harassment a sexual relationship that arises during the course of employment but that does not have substantial effect on that employment.[36]

HOSTILE ENVIRONMENT CREATED BY COWORKERS OR NONEMPLOYEES   The advances do not have to be made by the person's supervisor to qualify as sexual harassment. An employee's coworkers (or even the employer's customers) can cause the employer to be held responsible for sexual harassment. The EEOC guidelines state that an employer is liable for the sexually harassing acts of its nonsupervisory employees if the employer knew or should have known of the harassing conduct.

Case law is quickly accumulating regarding employers' responsibilities for sexual harassment by clients, customers, and suppliers. The gist of these decisions is that employers are often held responsible for sexual harassment by clients, customers, and suppliers if the employers' managers knew or reasonably should have known about the harassing behavior.

The U.S. Supreme Court's first decision on sexual harassment was *Meritor Savings Bank, FSB v. Vinson,* decided in June 1986. In this case there were three sexual harassment issues before the Court:

> *(1) Whether a hostile work environment (where hostility is due to the victim's sex) in which the victim does not suffer any economic injury violates Title VII,*
> *(2) whether an employee's voluntary participation in sexual acts with a manager constitutes a valid defense for an employer to a Title VII complaint, and*
> *(3) whether an employer is liable for the conduct of supervisors or coworkers when the employer is unaware of that conduct.[38]*

The Court's ruling broadly endorsed the EEOC guidelines (issues 1 and 2), but the majority on a 5 to 4 split vote declined to issue a definitive ruling on employers' automatic liability (issue 3). However, the clear message of the decision was that employers should establish accessible and meaningful complaint procedures for employee claims of sexual harassment.

WHAT THE EMPLOYER SHOULD DO   Two 1998 U.S. Supreme Court 7–2 decisions clarified the law on sexual harassment and particularly on employers' responsibilities under the statutes. The decisions will make some harassment lawsuits against employers easier to win, while limiting the exposure of those employers who take steps to have anti-harassment policies in place.

In the first, *Burlington Industries v. Ellerth,* the employee accused her supervisor of "quid pro quo" harassment. She said she was propositioned by her boss, and threatened with demotion if she did not respond. The threats were not carried out and she was in fact

Meritor Savings Bank, FSB v. Vinson

U.S. Supreme Court's first decision on sexual harassment holding that existence of a hostile environment even without economic hardship is sufficient to prove harassment, even if participation was voluntary.

promoted. In the second, *Faragher v. City of Boca Raton*, the employee accused the employer of condoning a hostile work environment; she said she quit her lifeguard job after repeated taunts from other lifeguards. The Court ruled in favor of the employees in both cases.

The Court's decisions have several important consequences for employers. They make it clear that in a "quid pro quo" case it is *not* necessary for the employee to have suffered a tangible job action (like being demoted) to win the case. And, the Court spelled out a defense employers can use when confronted with a harassment suit; the employer must show it took "reasonable care" to prevent and promptly correct any sexually harassing behavior, and that the employee unreasonably failed to take advantage of the employer's policy.

Therefore, how can an employer help minimize its liability for such suits? To show reasonable care, it is crucial that the employer have a policy against sexual harassment, including a publicized and effective complaint procedure that all employees are aware of and can take advantage of. Furthermore, if the employer knew (or should reasonably have known) that the harassment was occurring, it should take immediate steps to stop it.

Based on these and previous decisions, employers can take steps to minimize liability if a sexual harassment claim is filed against the organization and to prevent such claims from arising in the first place:

1. Take all complaints about harassment seriously. As one sexual harassment manual for managers and supervisors advises, "When confronted with sexual harassment complaints or when sexual conduct is observed in the workplace, the best reaction is to address the complaint or stop the conduct."[39]

2. Issue a strong policy statement condemning such behavior. The policy should include a workable definition of sexual harassment, spell out possible actions against those who harass others, and make it clear that retaliatory action against an employee who makes charges will not be tolerated. An example, presented in Figure 2–1, states, for example, that "such behavior may result in . . . dismissal."

3. Inform all employees about the policy prohibiting sexual harassment and of their rights under the policy.

4. Develop a complaint procedure.

5. Establish a management response system that includes an immediate reaction and investigation by senior management. The likelihood of employer liability is lessened considerably when the employer's response is "adequate" and "reasonably calculated to prevent future harassment."[40]

6. Begin management training sessions with supervisors and managers to increase their own awareness of the issues.

7. Discipline managers and employees involved in sexual harassment.

8. Keep thorough records of complaints, investigations, and actions taken.

FIGURE 2-1

Sample Sexual Harassment Policy

Source: Adapted from *Sexual Harassment Manual for Managers and Supervisors,* Commerce Clearing House, Inc., October 1991, p. 46.

> The company's position is that sexual harassment is a form of misconduct that undermines the integrity of the employment relationship. No employee—either male or female—should be subject to unsolicited and unwelcome sexual overtures or conduct, either verbal or physical. Sexual harassment does not refer to occasional compliments of a socially accepted nature. It refers to behavior that is not welcome, that is personally offensive, that debilitates morale, and that, therefore, interferes with work effectiveness. Such behavior may result in disciplinary action up to and including dismissal.

9. Conduct exit interviews that uncover any complaints and that acknowledge by signature the reasons for leaving.
10. Republish the sexual harassment policy periodically.
11. Encourage upward communication through periodic written attitude surveys, hot lines, suggestion boxes, and other feedback procedures to discover employees' feelings concerning any evidence of sexual harassment and to keep management informed.[41]

These steps are consistent with the EEOC's new proposed workplace harassment guidelines. These guidelines state that once the employer knows or should have known of harassing conduct, the employer is expected to take immediate corrective action, even if the offending party is a nonemployee.[43]

WHAT THE EMPLOYEE CAN DO   An employee—whether male or female—who believes he or she has been sexually harassed can also take several steps to address the problem.

The steps to take are based in part on how courts define sexual harassment. For example, "hostile environment" sexual harassment generally means the workplace was permeated with discriminatory intimidation, and ridicule, and that the insult was sufficiently severe or pervasive to alter the conditions of employment. Courts therefore look at such things as whether the questionable conduct is frequent or severe; whether it is physically threatening or humiliating, or a mere offensive utterance; and whether it unreasonably interferes with an employee's work performance.[43] In turn, whether or not an employee subjectively perceived the work environment as abusive is reflected by such things as whether she or he welcomed the conduct, or immediately made it clear that the conduct was unwelcome, undesirable, or offensive.[44] The steps an employee can take thus include:

1. File a verbal contemporaneous complaint or protest with the harasser and the harasser's boss stating that the unwanted overtures should cease because the conduct is unwelcome;
2. Write a letter to the accused. This may be a polite, low-key letter that does three things: provides a detailed statement of the facts as the writer sees them; describes his or her feelings and what damage the writer thinks has been done; and states that he or she would like to request that the future relationship be on a purely professional basis. This letter should be delivered in person, with a witness if necessary;
3. If the unwelcome conduct does not cease, file a report regarding the unwelcome conduct and unsuccessful efforts to get it to stop with the harasser's manager and/or to the human resource director verbally and in writing;
4. If the letters and appeals to the employer do not suffice, the accuser should turn to the local office of the EEOC to file the necessary claim;
5. The employee can also consult an attorney about suing the harasser for assault and battery, intentional infliction of emotional distress, and injunctive relief and to recover compensatory and punitive damages if the harassment is of a serious nature.

Selected Early Court Decisions Regarding Equal Employment Opportunity

Several court decisions between 1964 and 1991 helped to create the interpretative foundation for EEO laws such as Title VII.

Griggs v. The Duke Power Company

Case heard by the Supreme Court in which the plaintiff argued that his employer's requirement that coal handlers be high school graduates was unfairly discriminatory. In finding for the plaintiff, the Court ruled that discrimination need not be overt to be illegal, that employment practices must be related to job performance, and that the burden of proof is on the employer to show that hiring standards are job related.

protected class

Persons such as minorities and women protected by equal opportunity laws including Title VII.

GRIGGS V. DUKE POWER COMPANY *Griggs* was a landmark case, since the Supreme Court used it to define unfair discrimination. In this case, a suit was brought against the Duke Power Company on behalf of Willie Griggs, an applicant for a job as a coal handler. The company required its coal handlers to be high school graduates. Griggs claimed this requirement was illegally discriminatory because it wasn't related to success on the job and because it resulted in more blacks than whites being rejected for these jobs.

Griggs won the case. The decision of the Court was unanimous, and in his written opinion Chief Justice Burger laid out three crucial guidelines affecting equal employment legislation. First, the Court ruled that discrimination on the part of the employer need not be overt; in other words, the employer does not have to be shown to have intentionally discriminated against the employee or applicant; it need only be shown that discrimination did take place. Second, the court held that an employment practice (in this case requiring the high school degree) must be shown to be job related if it has an unequal impact on members of a **protected class.** In the words of Justice Burger,

The act proscribes not only overt discrimination but also practices that are fair in form, but discriminatory in operation. The touchstone is business necessity. If an employment practice which operates to exclude Negroes cannot be shown to be related to job performance the practice is prohibited.[45]

Chief Justice Burger's opinion also clearly placed the burden of proof on the employer to show that the hiring practice is job related. Thus, the employer must show that the employment practice (in this case, requiring a high school degree) is needed to perform the job satisfactorily if it has adverse or disparate impact on (*un*intentionally discriminates against) members of a protected class. In summary, the *Griggs* case established the following principles:

1. A test must be job related. For example, if verbal ability is not required to perform the job's main functions, one should not test for it;
2. An employer's intent not to discriminate is irrelevant;[46]
3. If a practice is "fair in form but discriminatory in operation," it will not be upheld by the courts;
4. *Business necessity* is the defense for any existing program that has adverse impact. Business necessity was not defined by the *Griggs* court;
5. Title VII does not forbid testing, only tests that do not measure the link between the person's performance on the test and job performance;
6. A test must measure the person for the job and not the person in the abstract.[47]

Albemarle Paper Company v. Moody

Supreme Court case in which it was ruled that the validity of job tests must be documented and that employee performance standards must be unambiguous.

ALBEMARLE PAPER COMPANY V. MOODY In the *Griggs* case, the Supreme Court decided a screening tool (like a test) had to be job related or valid, in that performance on the test must be related to performance on the job. The *Albemarle* case is important because here the Court provided more details regarding how an employer should validate its screening tools—in other words, how it should prove that the test or other screening tools are related to or predict performance on the job.[48] In the *Albemarle* case the Court emphasized that if a test is to be used to screen candidates for a job, then the nature of that job—its specific duties and responsibilities—must first be carefully analyzed and documented. Similarly, the Court ruled that the performance standards for employees on the job in question should be clear and unambiguous, so the employer could intelligently identify which employees were performing better than others.

In arriving at its decision, the Court also cited the EEOC guidelines concerning acceptable selection procedures and made these guidelines the "law of the land."[49] Specifically, the Court's ruling had the effect of establishing the detailed EEOC (now federal) guidelines on validation as the procedures for validating employment practices.[50]

Equal Employment Opportunity 1989–1991: A Shifting Supreme Court

After more or less championing the cause of minorities and women in the workplace for three decades, in a series of decisions in 1989 the Supreme Court signaled a shift toward a narrower scope for civil rights protection. Various factors including the addition of several legal conservatives to the Supreme Court caused the change. But, whatever the factors were, the results were quite dramatic, as in the following cases.

PRICE WATERHOUSE V. HOPKINS   The background of this case is as follows:[51] In 1982, the plaintiff, a woman, was proposed for partnership in the Price Waterhouse accounting firm. At the time, the firm had 662 partners, of whom seven were women. In 1982, 88 candidates were proposed for partnership, but only one—the employee who sued—was a woman. Of the 88, 47 became partners, 21 were rejected, and 20 were "held" for further consideration the following year. The employee who sued had brought $25 million in business with the State Department into the firm—but her promotion was held for further consideration. She responded by resigning and bringing suit under Title VII.

At the trial, it was found that both lawful and unlawful factors had contributed to her being passed over. She showed that her sex had been an unlawful factor in her denial of promotion, while the employer showed that "abrasiveness" had been a lawful factor. She won her case and won on appeal, but the U.S. Supreme Court eventually (on May 1, 1989) reversed the U.S. Court of Appeals. The Supreme Court found she would have been passed over anyway due to her "abrasiveness,"[52] and so found the firm's actions were not illegally discriminatory.

Wards Cove v. Atonio

U.S. Supreme Court decision that makes it difficult to prove a case of unlawful discrimination against an employer.

WARDS COVE PACKING COMPANY V. ATONIO   In *Wards Cove Packing Company v. Atonio,* the Supreme Court acted in a case of alleged racial discrimination in Alaskan salmon canneries.[53] The facts of the case are as follows: Unskilled jobs in the canneries were held mostly by nonwhite Alaskans. Higher-paid noncannery jobs (carpenters, accountants, etc.) were mostly held by white employees who were recruited in the Seattle area. Cannery and noncannery workers were housed and fed separately. Predominantly white noncannery workers were assigned to more desirable, better-insulated bunkhouses. The racial minorities at the canneries sued, claiming that the employment practices at the canneries discriminated and also had the effect of blocking them from getting the higher-paying jobs. Decisions at the lower courts were mixed; the U.S. Supreme Court's ruling favored the employer.

Breaking with a precedent set in *Griggs v. Duke Power Company,* the Supreme Court said the employees (not the employer) had the burden of showing any disparity was caused by the employers disputed practice. Recall that in *Griggs v. Duke Power Company* the Supreme Court had defined what was meant by unfair discrimination; it also placed the burden of proof on the employer to show that the hiring practice in question is job related when it adversely impacts members of a protected class.[54] After the *Griggs* case, proving that you were illegally discriminated against often meant just showing statistically, for example, that one classification of jobs was primarily held by whites while a second less-attractive classification was held mostly by nonwhites. With this statistical case made, the burden of proof shifts to the employer to prove that its employment practices served a necessary business purpose—a defense that became known as the business necessity defense. Mounting a defense in such a case was often so expensive that many employers didn't try.

Wards Cove basically changed all that. After *Wards Cove* the employee/plaintiff had the burden of proving that the statistical imbalance was caused by an employment policy or practice of the employer.[55]

EQUAL EMPLOYMENT OPPORTUNITY 1991–PRESENT

Civil Rights Act of 1991 (CRA 1991)

It places burden of proof back on employers and permits compensatory and punitive damages.

The Civil Rights Act of 1991

Supreme Court rulings such as *Wards Cove* and *Price Waterhouse* had the effect of limiting the protection of women and minority groups under equal employment laws; this prompted Congress to pass a new Civil Rights Act in 1991. The **Civil Rights Act of 1991 (CRA 1991)** was then signed into law by President Bush in November 1991. The basic effect of CRA 1991 was to reverse several U.S. Supreme Court decisions including *Wards Cove,* and several others. But the effect was not just to roll back the clock to where it stood prior to these Supreme Court decisions. The effect was to add additional legislation that makes it even more important that employers and their managers and supervisors adhere to both the spirit and the letter of EEO law. We can summarize the act's main provisions as follows.

BURDEN OF PROOF (WARDS COVE)   On the burden of proof, the Civil Rights Act of 1991 basically turns the EEO clock back to where it was prior to *Wards Cove.* With the passage of CRA 1991, the burden today is once again on employers to show that the practice (such as a test) is required as a business necessity.

MONEY DAMAGES   Section 102 of the new Civil Rights Act provides that an employee who is claiming intentional discrimination (disparate treatment) can ask for (1) compensatory damages and (2) punitive damages, if it can be shown the employer engaged in discrimination "with malice or reckless indifference to the federally protected rights of an aggrieved individual."[56]

This is a marked change from the conditions that prevailed up until 1991. Victims of intentional discrimination who had not suffered financial loss and who sued under Title VII could not then sue for compensatory or punitive damages. All they could expect was to have their jobs reinstated (or be awarded a particular job). They were also eligible for back pay, attorney's fees, and court costs.

MIXED MOTIVES (PRICE WATERHOUSE)   The Civil Rights Act of 1991 states that

> *An unlawful employment practice is established when the complaining party demonstrates that race, color, religion, sex, or national origin was a motivating factor for any employment practice, even though other factors also motivated the practice.*[57]

In other words, under the new Civil Rights Act, an employer can no longer avoid liability by proving it would have taken the same action even without the discriminatory motive.[58]

PROOF OF DISCRIMINATION   This Civil Rights Act could actually make it a bit more difficult for minorities to prove discrimination. This section says that test scores cannot be "adjusted" to "alter the results of employment related tests on the basis of race, color, religion, sex, or national origin." Up to now, some employers might have allowed minority applicants who scored, say, 80 on a test to be employed, while nonminority applicants had to score 90. Such adjustments are no longer permitted under CRA 1991.[59]

GLOBAL HRM

■ Enforcing the 1991 Civil Rights Act Abroad

The 1991 Civil Rights Act marked a substantial change in the geographic applicability of equal rights legislation. Congressional legislation generally only applies within U.S. territorial borders unless specifically stated otherwise.[60] However, CRA 1991 specifically expanded coverage by amending the definition of "employee" in Title VII to mean a U.S. citizen employed in a foreign country by a U.S.-owned or U.S.-controlled company.[61] At least theoretically, therefore, U.S. citizens now working overseas for U.S. companies enjoy the same equal employment opportunity protection as those working within U.S. borders.[62]

Two factors limit the wholesale application of CRA 1991 to U.S. employees abroad, however. First, the civil rights protections are not universal or automatic, since there are numerous exclusions. For example, an employer need not comply with Title VII if compliance would cause the employer to violate the law of the host country. (For instance, some foreign countries have statutes prohibiting the employment of women in management positions.)

A more vexing problem is the practical difficulty of enforcing CRA 1991 abroad. For example, the EEOC investigator's first duty in an extraterritorial case is to analyze the finances and organizational structure of the employer, but in practice few, if any investigators are trained for this duty and no precise standards exist for such investigations.[63] Similarly, one expert argues that U.S. courts "will be little help in overseas investigations, because few foreign nations cooperate with the intrusive enforcement of U.S. civil law."[64] It is possible, therefore, that in this case CRA 1991's bark will be considerably worse than its bite and that, as one expert says, "Congress' well-meaning effort to leave no American uncovered by U.S. antidiscrimination law will not have its intended effect."[65]

The Americans with Disabilities Act

In July 1990 President Bush signed into law the **Americans with Disabilities Act (ADA).** Title I of the act prohibits employment discrimination against the disabled.[66] The employment provisions of the ADA went into effect in July 1992. Since that time employers with 25 or more workers have been prohibited from discriminating against qualified individuals with disabilities with regard to applications, hiring, discharge, compensation, advancement, training, or other terms, conditions, or privileges of employment.[67] The act now covers employers with only 15 or more employees. The Americans with Disabilities Act was enacted to reduce or eliminate serious problems of discrimination against disabled individuals. The act prohibits employers from discriminating against qualified disabled individuals. It also says employers must make "reasonable accommodations" for physical or mental limitations unless doing so imposes an "undue hardship" on the business.

The definitions of the act's pivotal terms are important in understanding its impact. For example, specific disabilities aren't listed; instead, the EEOC's implementing regulations regarding ADA provide that an individual is disabled when he or she has a physical or mental impairment that substantially limits one or more major life activities. They also provide that an impairment includes any physiological disorder or condition, cosmetic disfigurement, or anatomical loss affecting one or more of several body systems, or any mental or psychological disorder.[68] On the other hand, the act does set forth certain conditions that are not to be regarded as disabilities, including homosexuality, bisexuality, voyeurism, compulsive gambling, pyromania, and certain disorders resulting from the current illegal use of drugs.[69]

Simply being disabled doesn't qualify someone for a job, of course. Instead, the act prohibits discrimination against qualified individuals, those who, with (or without) a reasonable accommodation, can carry out the essential functions of the job. That means that the individual must have the requisite skills, educational background, and experience to do the essential functions of the position. A job function is essential when, for instance, it is the reason the position exists, or because the function is so highly specialized that the person doing the job is hired for his or her expertise or ability to perform that particular function.

New tools for the disabled include voice synthesizers that can read Internet text out loud to the blind and special pointers that allow people to "type" who otherwise could not use a keyboard. Shown here is Rich Walsh, executive director of the Resource Center for the Handicapped, a vocational training institute for people with physical disabilities in Seattle, Washington.

If the individual can't perform the job as currently structured, the employer is required to make a "reasonable accommodation" unless doing so would present an "undue hardship." Reasonable accommodation might include redesigning the job, modifying work schedules, or modifying or acquiring equipment or other devices to assist the person in performing the job. For example, an employee with a bad back who worked as a Wal-Mart Store door greeter asked Wal-Mart if she could sit on a stool while on duty; the employer rejected her request. She sued, but the federal district court agreed with Wal-Mart that the door greeters must act in an "aggressively hospitable manner," which can't be done sitting on a stool.[70]

Attorneys, employers, and the courts are still working through the question of what "reasonable accommodations" really means. One expert recently noted that, "three federal appeals courts have held that for it to be a reasonable accommodation, the employee must show that the costs of the accommodation do not outweigh the benefit."[71]

Many employers have successfully done so. In one case, a social worker threatened to throw her co-worker out a window and to "kick her [butt]," and continued her tirade after returning from a 10-day suspension. After being transferred to another job she was diagnosed as paranoic; after telling her supervisor several times she was "ready to kill her" she was fired. She sued under ADA and her case was dismissed because although she had a debilitating mental illness ADA does not require retention of employees who make threats.[72] In another case a virtually blind correctional officer lost her ADA case after she was fired for being unable to carry out essential job functions like counting inmates, inspecting for contraband, and searching for escaped prisoners.[73] On the other hand, another decision reflects the importance that must be placed on preemployment inquiries under ADA. A one-armed man was awarded $157,500 after suing Wal-Mart Stores when he was rejected for a stocker's job. The problem in this case was that during his interview he was asked, "What current or past medical problems might limit your ability to do the job?" The ADA prohibits such inquiries (although employers generally are allowed to ask if the applicant can carry out specific essential job functions).[74]

EMPLOYER OBLIGATIONS   The ADA imposes certain legal obligations on employers:[75]

1. An employer must not deny a job to a disabled individual if the person is qualified and able to perform the essential functions of the job; if the person is otherwise qualified but unable to perform an essential function, the employer must make a reasonable accommodation unless doing so would result in undue hardship. HIV-positive individuals are generally considered ADA disabled, whether or not they are symptomatic.[76]

2. Employers are not required to lower existing performance standards or stop using tests for a job as long as those standards or tests are job related and uniformly applied to all employees and candidates for that job.

3. As mentioned above, employers may not make preemployment inquiries about a person's disability. However, employers may ask questions about the person's ability to perform specific essential job functions; similarly, preemployment medical exams or medical histories may not be required, but employers may condition job offers on the results of a postoffer medical exam. Under the new EEOC ADA guidelines, "disability-related" questions are illegal and cannot be asked at the initial interview stage or until the employee is actually hired. For example, the EEOC says it is illegal to ask: "Do you have AIDS? Have you ever filed for workers' compensation? What prescription drugs are you currently taking? Have you ever been treated for mental health problems? How much alcohol do you drink each week?"

Much the same applies to medical exams, even for current employees. In one case, for instance, a Chicago police officer was ordered to take a blood test to determine if the level of Prozac his physician said he was taking would seriously impair his ability to do his job. At the time the officer had not engaged in any behavior that suggested any performance problems. The court therefore said the blood test was not job related and violated the ADA's prohibition against inquiries into the nature or severity of an individual's disability.[77]

On the other hand, an employer can legally ask questions such as, "Can you perform the functions of this job with or without reasonable accommodation? Please describe or demonstrate how you would perform these functions. Can you meet the attendance requirements of the job? Do you have the required licenses to perform these jobs?"[78]

4. Employers should review job application forms, interview procedures, and job descriptions. For example, employers may not ask applicants questions about their health, disabilities, medical histories, or previous workers' compensation claims.[79]

5. The ADA does not require employers to have job descriptions but it's probably advisable to do so. As one expert writes, "In virtually any ADA legal action, a critical question will be, what are the essential functions of the position involved? . . . If, for example, a disabled employee is terminated because he or she cannot perform a particular function, in the absence of a job description that includes such function it will be difficult to convince a court that the function truly was an essential part of the job."[80]

ADA IN PRACTICE The types of disabilities alleged in ADA charges have been somewhat surprising. It hasn't been common conditions associated with "disability" like vision, hearing, or mobility impairments that represented most charges. Instead, back impairments accounted for about 20% of all ADA charges filed. However, what reportedly caught many employers and the EEOC by surprise was the prevalence of charges alleging mental impairments: Such impairments constituted almost 10% of all charges filed during the first 14 months of the act's enforcement, making it the second largest classification of disabilities named in ADA charges.[81]

The Equal Opportunity Employment Commission recently set forth its position on how the Americans with Disabilities Act of 1990 applies to individuals with psychiatric disorders. Under the guidelines, "mental impairment" includes "any mental or psychological disorder, such as . . . emotional or mental illness." Examples include major depression, anxiety disorders, panic disorders, obsessive-compulsive disorder, and personality disorders. Traits like irritability, chronic lateness, and poor judgment are not, in themselves, mental impairments, although they may be linked to mental impairments and therefore indicate a situation that may come under the protection of the ADA. The guidelines basically say that employers have to be alert to the possibility that traits normally regarded as undesirable (such as chronic lateness, hostility to co-workers, or poor judgment) may be linked to mental impairments and therefore covered by the ADA. Reasonable accommodation, says the EEOC, might then include providing room dividers, partitions, or other barriers between work spaces to accommodate individuals who have disability-related limitations, say, in concentration. Allowing someone who has difficulty concentrating due to his or her disability to take detailed notes during client presentations (even though company policy discourages employees from doing so) is another example.

State and Local Equal Employment Opportunity Laws

In addition to the federal laws, all states and many local governments also prohibit employment discrimination.

In most cases the effect of the state and local laws is to further restrict employers regarding their treatment of job applicants and employees. In many cases, state equal employment opportunity laws cover employers (like those with fewer than 15 employees) who are not covered by federal legislation.[83] Similarly, some local governments extend the protection of age discrimination laws to young people as well, barring discrimination not only of those over 40, but those over 17 as well; here, for instance, it would be illegal to advertise for "mature" applicants, because that might discourage some teenagers from applying. The point is that a wide range of actions by many employers that might be legal under federal laws are illegal under state and local laws.[83]

Antibias laws recently passed by several states provide some insight into the more limiting nature of state EEO laws. In Arizona, for instance, the Arizona Civil Rights Act was amended so that sexual harassment claims can now be brought against employers with as few as one employee. In Massachusetts the state's Fair Employment Practice Act now requires employers to adopt policies against sexual harassment and encourages employers to conduct sexual harassment employee training. In both New York and New Jersey genetic testing is now generally barred, as is discrimination based on genetic information.[84]

State and local equal employment opportunity agencies (often called Human Resources Commissions, Commissions on Human Relations, or Fair Employment Commissions) play a role in the equal employment compliance process. When the EEOC receives a discrimination charge, it usually defers it for a limited time to the state and local agencies that have comparable jurisdiction. If satisfactory remedies are not achieved, the charges are then referred back to the EEOC for resolution.

Summary

Selected equal employment opportunity laws, actions, executive orders, and agency guidelines are summarized in Table 2–1, on page 52.

DEFENSES AGAINST DISCRIMINATION ALLEGATIONS

adverse impact
The overall impact of employer practices that result in significantly higher percentages of members of minorities and other protected groups being rejected for employment, placement, or promotion.

What Is Adverse Impact?

Adverse impact plays a central role in discriminatory practice allegations. Under the Civil Rights Act of 1991, a person who believes he or she has been unintentionally discriminated against need only establish a prima facie case of discrimination. This means showing that the employer's selection procedures did have an adverse impact on a protected minority group. Adverse impact "refers to the total employment process that results in a substantially different rate of hiring, promotions, or other employment decisions which works to the disadvantage of members of a minority or other protected group."[85]

What does this mean? If a minority or other protected group applicant for the job feels he or she has been discriminated against, the applicant need only show that the selection procedures resulted in an adverse impact on his or her minority group. (For example,

TABLE 2-1 Summary of Important Equal Employment Opportunity Actions

ACTION	WHAT IT DOES
Title VII of 1964 Civil Rights Act, as amended	Bars discrimination because of race, color, religion, sex, or national origin; instituted EEOC
Executive orders	Prohibit employment discrimination by employers with federal contracts of more than $10,000 (and their subcontractors); establish office of federal compliance; require affirmative action programs
Federal agency guidelines	Indicate policy covering discrimination based on sex, national origin, and religion, as well as employee selection procedures; for example, require validation of tests
Supreme Court decisions: *Griggs* v. *Duke Power Co.*, *Albemarle* v. *Moody*	Rule that job requirements must be related to job success; that discrimination need not be overt to be proved; that the burden of proof is on the employer to prove the qualification is valid
Equal Pay Act of 1963	Requires equal pay for men and women for performing similar work
Age Discrimination in Employment Act of 1967	Prohibits discriminating against a person 40 or over in any area of employment because of age
State and local laws	Often cover organizations too small to be covered by federal laws
Vocational Rehabilitation Act of 1973	Requires affirmative action to employ and promote qualified handicapped persons and prohibits discrimination against handicapped persons
Pregnancy Discrimination Act of 1978	Prohibits discrimination in employment against pregnant women, or related conditions
Vietnam Era Veterans' Readjustment Assistance Act of 1974	Requires affirmative action in employment for veterans of the Vietnam war era
Ward Cove v. *Atonio*	Made it more difficult to prove a case of unlawful discrimination against an employer
Price Waterhouse v. *Hopkins*	Unlawful actions may not be discriminatory if lawful actions would have resulted in the same personnel decision.
Americans with Disabilities Act of 1990	Strengthens the need for most employers to make reasonble accommodations for disabled employees at work; prohibits discrimination
Civil Rights Act of 1991	Reverses *Wards Cove*, *Price Waterhouse*, and other decisions; places burden of proof back on employer and permits compensatory and punitive money damages for discrimination

Note: The actual laws (and others) can be accessed at: http://www.legal.gsa.gov/legal(#1)fed.htm.

if 80% of the white applicants passed the test, but only 20% of the black applicants passed, a black applicant has a prima facie case proving adverse impact.) Then, the employee has proved his or her point, and the burden of proof shifts to the employer. It becomes the employer's task to prove that its test, application blank, interview, or the like is a valid predictor of performance on the job (and that it was applied fairly and equitably to both minorities and nonminorities).

How Can Adverse Impact Be Proved?

It is actually not too difficult for an applicant to show that one of an employer's procedures (such as a selection test) has an adverse impact on a protected group. Four basic approaches can be used.

1. *Disparate Rejection Rates.* This means comparing the rejection rates for a minority group and another group (usually the remaining nonminority applicants). For example, ask "Is there a disparity between the percentage of blacks among those applying for a particular position and the percentage of blacks among those hired for the position?" Or, "Do proportionately more blacks than whites fail the written examination we give to all applicants?" If the answer to either question is yes, you and your firm could be faced with a lawsuit.

disparate rejection rates

One test for adverse impact in which it can be demonstrated that there is a discrepancy between rates of rejection of members of a protected group and of others.

Federal agencies have adopted a formula to determine when **disparate rejection rates** actually exist. Their guidelines state that "a selection rate for any racial, ethnic or sex group which is less than 4/5 or 80% of the rate for the group with the highest rate will generally be regarded as evidence of adverse impact, while a greater than 4/5 rate will generally not be regarded as evidence of adverse impact." For example, suppose 90% of male applicants are hired, but only 60% of female applicants are hired. Then, since 60% is less than four-fifths of 90%, adverse impact exists as far as these federal agencies are concerned.[86]

restricted policy

Another test for adverse impact, involving demonstration that an employer's hiring practices exclude a protected group, whether intentionally or not.

2. *Restricted Policy.* The **restricted policy** approach means demonstrating that the employer has intentionally or unintentionally been using a hiring policy to exclude members of a protected group. Here the problem is usually obvious. For example, policies have been unearthed against hiring bartenders under six feet tall. Evidence of restricted policies such as these (against women) is enough to prove adverse impact and to expose an employer to litigation.

3. *Population Comparisons.* This approach compares (1) the percentage of Hispanic (or black or other minority/protected group) and white workers in the organization with (2) the percentage of the corresponding groups in the labor market, where labor market is usually defined as the U.S. Census data for that Standard Metropolitan Statistical Area. For some jobs, such as manual laborer or secretary, it makes sense to compare the percentage of minority employees with the percentage of minorities in the surrounding community, since these employees will in fact be drawn from the surrounding community. However, for some jobs, such as engineers, the surrounding community may not be the relevant labor market, since recruiting may be nationwide or even global. Determining whether an employer has enough black engineers might thus involve determining the number of black engineers available nationwide rather than just in the surrounding community. Defining the relevant labor market is a crucial task here.

4. *McDonnell-Douglas Test.* This approach (which grew out of a case at the former McDonnell-Douglas Corporation) shows that the applicant was qualified but was rejected by the employer, who then continued seeking applicants for the position. It is used in situations of intentional disparate treatment rather than unintentional disparate impact (for which approaches 1–3 above are used). Here the rejected protected-class candidate uses the following guidelines as set forth by the U.S. Supreme Court: (a) that he or she belongs to a protected class; (b) that he or she applied and was qualified for a job in which the employer was seeking applicants; (c) that, despite this qualification, he or she was rejected; and (d) that, after his or her rejection, the position remained open and the employer continued to seek applications from persons of the complainant's qualifications. If all these conditions are met, then a prima facie case of disparate treatment is established. At that point the employer is required to articulate a legitimate nondiscriminatory reason for its action and to produce evidence but not prove that it acted on the basis of such a reason. If it meets this relatively easy standard, the plaintiff then has the burden of proving that the employer's articulated reason is merely a pretext for engaging in unlawful discrimination.

BRINGING A CASE OF DISCRIMINATION: SUMMARY   Assume that an employer turns down a member of a protected group for a job based on a test score (although it could have been based on some other employment practice such as interview questions or application blank responses). Further assume that the person believes that he or she was discriminated against due to being in a protected class and decides to sue the employer.

All he or she basically must do is show that the employer's test had an adverse impact on members of his or her minority group, and there are four approaches that could be used to show that such adverse impact exists—disparate rejection rates, restricted policy, population comparisons, and the McDonnell-Douglas test. Once the person has shown the existence of adverse impact to the satisfaction of the court, the burden of proof shifts to the employer who then has to defend against the charges of discrimination.

There are then basically two defenses that the employer can use: the bona fide occupational qualification (BFOQ) defense and the business necessity defense. Either can be used to justify an employment practice that has been shown to have an adverse impact on the members of a minority group.[87]

Bona Fide Occupational Qualification

bona fide occupational qualification (BFOQ)

Requirement that an employee be of a certain religion, sex, or national origin where that is reasonably necessary to the organization's normal operation. Specified by the 1964 Civil Rights Act.

One approach an employer can use to defend itself against charges of discrimination is to claim that the employment practice is a **bona fide occupational qualification (BFOQ)** for performing the job. Specifically, Title VII provides that "it should not be an unlawful employment practice for an employer to hire an employee . . . on the basis of religion, sex, or national origin in those certain instances where religion, sex, or national origin is a bona fide occupational qualification reasonably necessary to the normal operation of that particular business or enterprise." BFOQ is a statutory exception to the equal employment opportunity laws that allows employers to discriminate in certain very specific instances. The BFOQ exception is usually interpreted narrowly by the courts. As a practical matter, it is used primarily (but not exclusively) as a defense against charges of intentional discrimination based on age. BFOQ is essentially a defense to a disparate treatment case based upon direct evidence of intentional discrimination and not to disparate impact (unintentional) discrimination.

AGE AS A BFOQ   The Age Discrimination in Employment Act (ADEA) does permit disparate treatment in those instances when age is a BFOQ. For example, age is a BFOQ when federal requirements impose a compulsory age limit, such as when the Federal Aviation Agency sets a ceiling of age 64 for pilots. Actors required for youthful or elderly roles or persons used to advertise or promote the sales of products designed for youthful or elderly consumers suggest other instances when age may be a BFOQ. As another example, a bus line's maximum-age hiring policy for bus drivers has been held to be a BFOQ by the courts. The court said that the essence of the business was safe transportation of passengers, and given that, the employer could strive to employ the most qualified persons available.[88]

It is unlawful to discriminate against job applicants over 40 years of age. Their skills and experience are often a boon to hiring firms.

Yet Supreme Court decisions such as *Western Airlines, Inc. v. Criswell* seem to be narrowing BFOQ exceptions under ADEA. In this case the Court held that the airline could not impose a mandatory retirement age (of 60) for flight engineers, even though they could for pilots. In 1998 the U.S. Supreme Court declined to review the FAA's blanket rule that airline pilots must retire at 60.[89]

In April of 1996 the U.S. Supreme Court also answered a question that has confused employers and employees since passage of the ADEA: Specifically, does an employer discriminate if it replaces an employee who is over 40 years old with another who is younger but also over 40? The answer in general is "yes." In its April 1996 decision in *O'Connor v. Consolidated Coin Caterers Corp.*, the court held that an employee who is over 40 may sue for discrimination if he or she is replaced by a "significantly younger" employee, even if the replacement is also over 40. They didn't specify what they meant by significantly younger, but did seem to suggest that just 3 or 4 years would be insignificant. In O'Connor's case, he was replaced by someone 16 years younger.

There has been a dramatic increase in the number of employment-related age discrimination complaints filed with state and federal agencies over the past few years. Reasons for this include increasing numbers of older workers, increasingly militant older workers, corporate downsizings, and the prospect of collecting double damages (as plaintiffs can do under the Age Discrimination in Employment Act).[90]

Employer defenses against ADEA claims usually fall into one of two categories: BFOQ or FOA (factors other than age). Employers using the BFOQ defense admit their personnel decisions were based on age but seek to justify them by showing that the decisions were reasonably necessary to normal business operations. (As an airline that insists a pilot maximum-age requirement is necessary for the safe transportation of its passengers.) An employer who raises the FOA defense generally argues that its actions were "reasonable" based on some business factor other than age, such as the terminated person's poor performance.

RELIGION AS A BFOQ   Religion may be a BFOQ in the case of religious organizations or societies that require employees to share their particular religion. For example, religion may be a BFOQ when hiring persons to teach in a denominational school. Similarly, practices such as Saturday work rules that adversely affect certain religious groups are excusable if the employer "is unable to reasonably accommodate . . . without undue hardship."[91] In this and in all cases, however, the BFOQ defense is construed very narrowly by the courts.

GENDER AS A BFOQ   It is difficult today to claim that gender is a BFOQ for most jobs for which employers are recruiting. For example, gender is not accepted as a BFOQ for positions just because they require overtime or the lifting of heavy objects. Gender is not a BFOQ for parole and probation officers, nor, of course, is gender a BFOQ for flight attendants.[92] Courts have said that it is illegal to apply a "no marriage" rule to female flight attendants and not to male employees, even though one airline claimed the rule was justified as a BFOQ due to customer preference. On the other hand, gender may be a BFOQ for positions requiring specific physical characteristics necessarily possessed by one sex. These include positions like actor, model, and restroom attendant.

NATIONAL ORIGIN AS A BFOQ   In some cases a person's country of national origin may be a BFOQ. For example, an employer who is running the Chinese pavilion at a fair might claim that Chinese heritage is a BFOQ for persons to be selected as pavilion employees to deal with the public.

Business Necessity

business necessity

Justification for an otherwise discriminatory employment practice, provided there is an overriding legitimate business purpose.

The **business necessity** defense basically requires showing that there is an overriding business purpose for the discriminatory practice and that the practice is therefore acceptable.

It's not easy proving that a practice is required for "business necessity."[93] The Supreme Court has made it clear that business necessity does not encompass such matters as avoiding inconvenience, annoyance, or expense to the employer. The Second Circuit Court of Appeals held that business necessity means an "irresistible demand," and that to be retained the practice "must not only directly foster safety and efficiency" but also be essential to these goals.[94] Similarly, another court held that:

> The test is whether there exists an overriding legitimate business purpose such that the practice is necessary to the safe and efficient operation of a business; thus, the business purpose must be sufficiently compelling to override any racial impact; and the challenged practice must effectively carry out the business purpose it is alleged to serve.[95]

Thus, to repeat, it is not easy to prove that a practice is required for business necessity. For example, an employer can't generally discharge employees whose wages have been garnished merely because garnishment (requiring the employer to divert part of the person's wages to pay his or her debts) creates an inconvenience. On the other hand, the business necessity defense has been used successfully. For instance, in *Spurlock v. United Airlines*, a minority candidate sued United Airlines, stating that its requirements that pilot candidates have 500 flight hours and college degrees were unfairly discriminatory. The court agreed that these requirements did have an adverse impact on members of the person's minority group. However, the court held that in light of the cost of the training program and the tremendous human and economic risks involved in hiring unqualified candidates, the selection standards were required by business necessity and were job related.[96]

In general, when a job requires a small amount of skill and training, the courts scrutinize closely any preemployment standards or criteria that discriminate against minorities. The employer in such instances has a heavy burden to demonstrate that the practices are job related. However, there is a correspondingly lighter burden when the job requires a high degree of skill and when the economic and human risks in hiring an unqualified applicant are great.[97]

Attempts by employers to show that their selection tests or other employment practices are valid represent one example of the business necessity defense. Here the employer is required to show that the test or other practice is job related, in other words, that it is a valid predictor of performance on the job. Where such validity can be established, the courts have often supported the use of the test or other employment practice as a business necessity. Used in this context, the word *validity* basically means the degree to which the test or other employment practice is related to or predicts performance on the job; validation will be discussed in chapter 5.

Other Considerations in Discriminatory Practice Defenses

There are three other points to stress in regard to defending against charges of discrimination. First, good intentions are no excuse. As the Supreme Court held in the *Griggs* case,

> Good intent or absence of discriminatory intent does not redeem procedures or testing mechanisms that operate as built-in headwinds for minority groups and are unrelated to measuring job capability.[98]

Second, employers cannot count on hiding behind collective bargaining agreements (for instance, by claiming that the discriminatory practice is required by a union agreement). Courts have often held that equal employment opportunity laws take precedence over the rights embodied in a labor contract. This isn't iron clad, however. For example, the U.S. Supreme Court, in its *Stotts* decision, held that a court cannot require retention of black employees hired under a court's consent decree in preference to higher-seniority white employees who were protected by a bona fide seniority system. Its unclear whether this decision also extends to personnel decisions not governed by seniority systems.[99]

Finally, remember that although a defense is often the most sensible response to charges of discrimination, it is not the only response. When confronted with the fact that one or more of your personnel practices is discriminatory, you can react by agreeing to eliminate the illegal practice and (when required) by compensating the people you discriminated against.

ILLUSTRATIVE DISCRIMINATORY EMPLOYMENT PRACTICES	

A Note on What You Can and Cannot Do

Before proceeding, we should clarify what federal fair employment laws allow (and do not allow) you to say and do. Federal laws like Title VII usually don't expressly ban preemployment questions about an applicant's race, color, religion, sex, or national origin. In other words, "with the exception of personnel policies calling for outright discrimination against the members of some protected group, it is not really the intrinsic nature of an employer's personnel policies or practices that the courts object to. Instead, it is the result of applying a policy or practice in a particular way or in a particular context that leads to an adverse impact on some protected group."[100] For example, it is not illegal to ask a job candidate about her marital status (although at first glance such a question might seem discriminatory). In reality, you can ask such a question as long as you can show either that you do not discriminate or that the practice can be defended as a BFOQ or business necessity.

But, in practice, there are two good reasons why most employers avoid such questionable practices. First, although federal law may not bar asking such questions, many state and local laws do. Second, the EEOC has said that it will disapprove of such practices (as asking women their marital status or applicants their age). Therefore, just asking such questions may draw the attention of the EEOC and other regulatory agencies.

Inquiries and practices like those summarized on the next few pages are thus usually not illegal per se. They are "problem questions" because they tend to identify an applicant as a member of a protected group or to adversely affect members of a protected group. They become illegal if it can be shown that they are used to screen out a greater proportion of a protected group's applicants and that the employer cannot prove the practice is required as a BFOQ or a business necessity. Thus, if you are sure that your hiring practices are legal in your municipality and that they do not adversely affect the members of a protected group—that, for example, you hire the same proportion of female applicants as male—then you may choose to continue asking such problem questions. Similarly, if you are convinced that an employment practice (such as a question about age) is required as a BFOQ or business necessity, you may choose to continue using it. However, as these questions will draw the attention of regulatory agencies, most employers do eliminate them. At a minimum, they delay asking them until after the applicant has been hired, when the questions might be useful for, say, insurance purposes.

We can now turn to a listing of some of the specific discriminatory personnel management practices you should avoid.[101]

Recruitment

WORD OF MOUTH   You cannot rely upon word-of-mouth dissemination of information about job opportunities when your workforce is all (or substantially all) white or all members of some other class such as all female, all Hispanic, and so on. Doing so might reduce the likelihood that others will become aware of the jobs and thus apply for them.

MISLEADING INFORMATION It is unlawful to give false or misleading information to members of any group or to fail or refuse to advise them of work opportunities and the procedures for obtaining them.

HELP WANTED ADS "Help wanted—male" and "Help wanted—female" advertising classifications are violations of laws forbidding sex discrimination in employment unless gender is a bona fide occupational qualification for the job advertised.[102] Also you cannot advertise in any way that suggests that applicants are being discriminated against because of their age. For example, you cannot advertise for a "young" man or woman.

Selection Standards

EDUCATIONAL REQUIREMENTS An educational requirement may be held illegal when (1) it can be shown that minority groups are less likely to possess the educational qualifications (such as a high school degree) and (2) such qualifications are also not job related. For example, in the *Griggs v. Duke Power* case, a high school diploma was found both unnecessary for job performance and discriminatory against blacks. In other cases, a public school board was found to have unlawfully discriminated against blacks by requiring a master's degree (and specific scores on Graduate Record Examinations) that had not been validated as predictors of job performance. A requirement for a college degree for management trainee positions was found to be unfairly discriminatory against blacks in another case.

TESTS According to former Chief Justice Burger,

> Nothing in the [Title VII] act precludes the use of testing or measuring procedures; obviously they are useful. What Congress has forbidden is giving these devices and mechanisms controlling force unless they are demonstrating a reasonable measure of job performance.

Tests that disproportionately screen out minorities or women and are not job related are deemed unlawful by the courts. But remember that a test or other selection standard that screens out a disproportionate number of minorities or women is not by itself sufficient to prove that the test unfairly discriminates. It must also be shown that the tests or other screening devices are not job related.

PREFERENCE TO RELATIVES You cannot give preference to relatives of your current employees with respect to employment opportunities if your current employees are substantially nonminority.

HEIGHT, WEIGHT, AND PHYSICAL CHARACTERISTICS Requirements for physical characteristics (such as height and weight) that can have an adverse impact upon certain ethnic groups or women are unlawful unless they can be shown to be job related. For example, one company required that a person weigh a minimum of 150 pounds for positions on its assembly lines. This requirement was held to discriminate unfairly against women. Under the Americans with Disabilities Act, you also cannot ask applicants about physical or mental disabilities.

ARREST RECORDS You cannot ask about or use a person's arrest record to disqualify him or her automatically for a position, since there is always a presumption of innocence until proven guilty. In addition, (1) arrest records in general have not been shown valid for predicting job performance and (2) a higher proportion of minorities than whites have been arrested. Thus, disqualifying applicants based on arrest records automatically has an adverse impact on minorities. Unless security clearance is necessary, you cannot ask an applicant whether he or she has ever been arrested or spent time in jail. However, you can ask about conviction records and then determine on a case-by-case basis whether the facts concerning any conviction justify refusal to employ an applicant in a particular position.

DISCHARGE DUE TO GARNISHMENT   A disproportionately higher number of minorities are subjected to garnishment procedures (where creditors make a claim to a portion of the person's wages). Therefore, firing a minority member whose salary has been garnished is illegal, unless you can show some overriding business necessity.

Sample Discriminatory Promotion, Transfer, and Layoff Practices

Fair employment laws protect not just job applicants but current employees as well.[103] The Equal Pay Act requires that equal wages be paid for substantially similar work performed by both men and women. Similarly, Title VII prohibits discrimination in compensation regardless of race, national origin, religion, or sex. With respect to promotions, terminations, and disciplinary actions, standards for determining when a person will be promoted, terminated, or disciplined should also be the same for all employees. Therefore, any employment practices regarding pay, promotion, termination, discipline, or benefits that (1) are applied differently to different classes of persons; (2) have the effect of adversely affecting members of a protected group; and (3) cannot be shown to be required as a BFOQ or business necessity may be held to be illegally discriminatory.

PERSONAL APPEARANCE REGULATIONS AND TITLE VII   Employees have filed suits against employers' dress and appearance codes under Title VII, usually claiming sex discrimination but sometimes claiming racial discrimination as well. A sampling of what has been ruled to be acceptable or unacceptable personal appearance codes follows.[104]

Dress   In general, employers do not violate Title VII's ban on sex bias by requiring all employees to dress conservatively. For example, a supervisor's suggestion that a female attorney tone down her attire was permissible when the firm consistently sought to maintain a conservative dress style and men were also counseled on the conservativeness of their dress.

Grooming   Minor gender-related differences in personal appearance are usually deemed lawful when they reflect customary codes of grooming. For example, short hair requirements for men but not for women probably wouldn't constitute sex bias under Title VII, nor would letting women but not men wear earrings.

Hair   Hair styles, beards, sideburns, and mustaches have come under scrutiny by the courts. Here again the courts usually rule in favor of the employers. For example, employer rules against facial hair do not constitute sex discrimination because they discriminate only between clean-shaven and bearded men, a type of discrimination not qualified as sex bias under Title VII. In many cases the courts have also rejected arguments that grooming regulations such as prohibitions against cornrow hair styles are racially biased in that they infringe on black employees' expression of cultural identification. In one case involving American Airlines, for example, the court decided (in favor of American) that a braided hair style is a characteristic easily changed and not worn exclusively or even predominantly by black people.

Uniforms   When it comes to discriminatory uniforms and suggestive attire, however, courts have frequently sided with the employee. For example, a bank's dress policy requiring female employees to wear prescribed uniforms consisting of five basic color-coordinated items but requiring male employees only to wear "appropriate business attire" is an example of a discriminatory policy. Similarly, requiring female salesclerks to wear smocks while male clerks were allowed to wear business attire, or female technologists to wear white or pastel-colored uniforms while male technologists could wear white lab coats over street clothing was ruled discriminatory. And requiring female employees (such as waitresses) to wear sexually suggestive attire as a condition of employment has also been ruled as violating Title VII in many cases.[105]

THE EEOC ENFORCEMENT PROCESS

Processing a Charge

There are several steps involved in filing and processing an employment discrimination charge with the EEOC.[106] Under CRA 1991, the charge itself must generally be filed within two years after the alleged unlawful practice took place. It must be filed in writing and under oath, by (or on behalf of) either the person claiming to be aggrieved or a member of the EEOC who has reasonable cause to believe that a violation occurred. In practice, the Supreme Court has approved the EEOC's practice of accepting a charge, orally referring it to the state or local agency on behalf of the charging party, and then, if the matter has not been cleared up, beginning to process it upon the expiration of a deferral period without requiring the filing of a new charge.[107] In practice, then, a person's charge to the EEOC is often first deferred to the relevant state or local regulatory agency; if the latter waives jurisdiction or cannot obtain a satisfactory solution to the charge, it is referred back to the EEOC. (Note that if the EEOC does not sue on behalf of the charging party it must issue that person a Notice of Right to Sue irrespective of whether it finds "cause" or "no cause" to believe that unlawful discrimination occurred. The charging party must file a lawsuit in federal district court within 90 days of receipt of that Notice of Right to Sue.)

After a charge has been filed (or the state or local deferral period has ended), the EEOC has 10 days to serve notice of the charge on the employer. The EEOC then investigates the charge to determine whether there is reasonable cause to believe it is true; it is expected to make this determination within 120 days. If no reasonable cause is found, the EEOC must dismiss the charge, in which case the person who filed the charge has 90 days to file a suit on his or her own behalf. If reasonable cause for the charge is found, the EEOC must attempt to conciliate. If this conciliation is not satisfactory, it may bring a civil suit in a federal district court, or issue a Notice of Right to Sue to the person who filed the charge. Figure 2–2 summarizes important questions an employer should ask after receiving notice from the EEOC that a bias complaint has been filed. The questions include, for example, "To what protected group does the worker belong?" and "Is the employee protected by more than one statute?"[108] The EEOC now approves the use of "testers"—individuals who pose as applicants to test a firm's equal employment procedures. Employers thus must be even more careful in devising interview procedures and training recruiters.[109]

Conciliation Proceedings

Under Title VII, the EEOC has 30 days to work out a conciliation agreement between the parties before bringing a suit. The EEOC conciliator first meets with the employee to determine what remedy would be satisfactory and then tries to persuade the employer to accept the remedy. If accepted by both parties, a conciliation agreement is reached, signed, and submitted to the EEOC for approval. If the EEOC is unable to obtain an acceptable conciliation agreement within 30 days after finding there is reasonable cause to believe that dis-

1. To what protected group does the worker belong? Is the employee protected by more than one statute?
2. Would the action complained of have been taken if the worker were not a member of a protected group? Is the action having an adverse impact on other members of a protected group?
3. Is the employee's charge of discrimination subject to attack because it was not filed on time, according to the applicable law?
4. In the case of a sexual harassment claim, are there offensive posters or calendars on display in the workplace?
5. Do the employee's personnel records demonstrate discriminatory treatment in the form of unjustified warnings and reprimands?
6. In reviewing the nature of the action complained of, can it be characterized as disparate impact or disparate treatment? Can it be characterized as an individual complaint or a class action?
7. What are the company's probable defenses and rebuttal?
8. Who are the decision makers involved in the employment action, and what would be their effectiveness as potential witnesses?
9. What are the prospects for a settlement of the case that would be satisfactory to all involved?

FIGURE 2-2   *Questions to Ask When an Employer Receives Notice That a Bias Complaint Has Been Filed*

Source: Gail J. Wright, assistant counsel for the NAACP's Legal Defense and Education Fund, quoted in Bureau of National Affairs, *Fair Employment Practices*, January 7, 1988, p. 3.

crimination occurred, it may sue the employer in a federal district court. The EEOC is now also experimenting with using outside mediators to settle claims in selected cities.[110]

About 88,000 charges of alleged discrimination are filed annually with the EEOC.[111] Of these, about 36% were based on race; 27% on gender; 23% on age; 17% on disability; 8.5% on national origin; 1.6% on religion; and 1.5% on equal pay.[112]

In the past few years the EEOC seems to be getting more efficient. In 1998 the EEOC reported that its backlog of pending cases had dropped from about 81,000 to about 65,000 during the previous fiscal year, for instance. And much of the money they obtain for plaintiffs is obtained without litigation; in other words during the preliminary, administrative, and conciliation process before the cases even go to the EEOC general counsel's office for litigation. In fiscal year 1997, for instance, the EEOC reportedly obtained about $178 million for plaintiffs, up from about $145 million the year before. The amount they obtained from litigation also rose dramatically, doubling to almost $112 million. Figures like these—especially, the $178 million obtained without even suing the employer—underscores the need to understand how to respond to a discrimination charge and deal with the EEOC.[113]

How to Respond to Employment Discrimination Charges

There are several things to keep in mind when confronted by a charge of illegal employment discrimination; some of the more important can be summarized as follows:[114]

INVESTIGATING THE CHARGE   First, remember that EEOC investigators are not judges and aren't empowered to act as courts; they cannot make findings of discrimination on their own but can merely make recommendations. If the EEOC eventually determines that an employer may be in violation of a law, its only recourse is to file a suit or issue a Notice of Right to Sue to the person who filed the charge.

Some experts advise meeting with the employee who made the complaint to determine all relevant issues. For example, ask: What happened? Who was involved? When did the incident take place? Was the employee's ability to work affected? Were there any witnesses? Then, prepare a written statement summarizing the complaints, facts, dates, and issues involved and request that the employee sign and date this.[115]

As far as documents are concerned, it may often be in the employer's best interests to cooperate (or appear cooperative). However, remember that the EEOC can only ask for, not demand, the submission of documents.[116] The EEOC can ask employers to submit documents and ask for the appearance and testimony of witnesses under oath. However, it cannot compel employers to comply. If an employer feels that the EEOC has overstepped its authority and refuses to cooperate, the commission's only recourse is to obtain a court subpoena. The feature on page 65 shows one firm controls its document costs.

It may also be in the employer's best interest to give the EEOC a position statement based on its own investigation of the matter. One congressional investigation found that at least in the EEOC's Chicago office, EEOC investigators were writing up cases based solely on the position statement filed by the employer because the EEOC is under such internal pressure to resolve cases. According to one management attorney, employers' position statements should contain words to the effect that "We understand that a charge of discrimination has been filed against this establishment and this statement is to inform the agency that the company has a policy against discrimination and would not discriminate in the manner charged in the complaint." The statement should be supported by some statistical analysis of the workforce, copies of any documents that support the employer's position, or an explanation of any legitimate business justification for the employment decision that is the subject of the complaint.[117]

If a predetermination settlement isn't reached, the EEOC will completely investigate the charge, and here there are three major principles an employer should follow. First, it should ensure that there is information in the EEOC's file demonstrating lack of merit of the charge; often the best way to do that is not by answering the EEOC's questionnaire but by providing a detailed statement describing the firm's defense in its best and most persuasive light.

Second, the employer should limit the information supplied as narrowly as possible to only those issues raised in the charge itself. For example, if the charge only alleges sex discrimination, the firm should not respond unwittingly to the EEOC's request for a breakdown of employees by age and sex. Releasing too much information just invites more probing by the EEOC, says one expert.[118] Third, the employer should seek as much information as possible about the charging party's claim in order to ensure it understands the claim and its ramifications.

THE FACT-FINDING CONFERENCE   Problems can arise in the EEOC's fact-finding conferences. According to the commission, these conferences are to be informal meetings held early in the investigatory process, aimed at defining issues and determining if there is a basis for negotiation. According to one expert, however, the EEOC's emphasis here is often on settlement. Its investigators therefore use the conferences to find weak spots in each party's respective position so that they can use this information as leverage to push for a settlement.

If an employer wants a settlement, the fact-finding conference can be a good forum at which to negotiate, but there are three big problems to watch out for. First, the only official record maintained is the notes taken by the EEOC investigator, and the parties cannot have access to them to rectify mistakes or clarify facts. Second, the employer can bring an attorney but the EEOC often "seems to go out of its way to tell employers that an attorney's presence is unnecessary."[119] Third, these conferences are often arranged soon after a charge is filed, before the employer has been fully informed of the charges and facts of the case.

An employer should thoroughly prepare witnesses who are going to testify at a fact-finding conference, especially supervisors, because their statements can be considered admissions against the employer's interest. Therefore, before appearing, they need to be aware of the legal significance of the facts they will present and of the possible claims that the charging party and other witnesses may make.

The EEOC's Determination and the Attempted Conciliation

If the fact-finding conference does not solve the matter, the EEOC's investigator will determine whether there is reason to believe ("cause") or not to believe ("no cause") that discrimination may have taken place, and there are several things to keep in mind here. First, the investigator's recommendation is often the determining factor in whether the EEOC finds cause, so it is usually best to be courteous and cooperative (within limits). Second, if there is a finding of cause, review the finding very carefully; make sure that inaccuracies are pointed out in writing to the EEOC. Use this letter to again try to convince the EEOC, the charging party, and the charging party's attorney that the charge is without merit in spite of the finding. Finally, keep in mind that even with a no-cause finding, the charging party will still be issued a right to sue letter by the EEOC and have 90 days from receipt of the letter to bring a private lawsuit.

If the EEOC issues a cause finding, it has (as noted above) 30 days to work out a conciliation agreement between the parties. Some experts argue against conciliating. First, the EEOC often views conciliation not as a compromise but as complete relief to the charging party. Second, "if you have properly investigated and evaluated the case previously, there may be no real advantage in settling at this stage. It is more than likely (based on the statistics) that no suit will be filed by the EEOC."[120] Furthermore, even if a lawsuit is later filed by either the EEOC or the charging party, the employer can consider settling after receiving the complaint.

Avoiding Discrimination Lawsuits Through Dispute Resolution

Employment discrimination claims constitute the largest number of civil suits filed annually in federal courts. As a result, some firms are establishing internal dispute resolution procedures similar to the following one at Aetna Life and Casualty Company.

STEP 1   First the employee discusses the problem with a supervisor, who may consult other members of the management team who might have handled similar problems.

STEP 2   The employee may contact a divisional personnel consultant for a case review if he or she is dissatisfied with the results of the first step. The employee is then informed and advised on plausible alternatives.

STEP 3   If the employee believes that company policy is not being followed, he or she may then request a corporate-level review of the case, and a corporate consultant will review the case with management. The employee is then notified of the decision in writing.

STEP 4   Finally, a senior management review committee may be asked to review the case. At Aetna the committee itself comprises the senior vice president of the employees' division as well as the vice presidents of corporate personnel and corporate public involvement.[121]

Mandatory Arbitration of Employment Discrimination Claims

Litigation is not necessarily the only alternative when it comes to resolving employment discrimination claims: Arbitration is another. The U.S. Supreme Court's decisions in *Gilmer v. Interstate/Johnson Lane Corp.* and similar cases "have made it clear that employment discrimination plaintiffs may be compelled to arbitrate their claims under some circumstances."[122] In *Gilmer* the Supreme Court held that an agreement entered into between a stockbroker and the stock exchange providing for mandatory arbitration of all employment-related disputes can require arbitration of claims arising under the Federal Age Discrimination in Employment Act (ADEA).

It is still not clear how widely the *Gilmer* decision will affect employment discrimination claims. On the one hand, there seems little doubt that within the securities industry, any employee who executed a similar registration document containing an arbitration agreement may be compelled to arbitrate ADEA claims arising out of his or her employment.[123] The extent of its impact outside the securities industry is not so clear.[124]

However, in light of the fact that compulsory arbitration may come to be viewed as an acceptable alternative to litigation by many courts, the following practical suggestions are in order:[125]

> *Employers should review immediately all employment discrimination filed against them in state and federal courts to determine whether they involve an employee subject to a registration agreement similar to the one signed by Mr. Gilmer, or some other type of agreement to arbitrate. They should then decide whether to move to compel arbitration of the claim.[126]*
>
> *Employers "may wish to consider inserting a mandatory arbitration clause in their employment applications or employee handbooks."[127]*
>
> *To protect such a process against appeal, the employer should institute steps to protect against arbitrator bias; allow the arbitrator to afford a claimant broad relief (including reinstatement); and allow for a reasonable amount of pre-hearing discovery (fact-finding).*

Arbitration can be an attractive alternative to costly litigation but is not necessarily a panacea. For example, arbitrators are not necessarily lawyers and may ignore prevailing law. Furthermore, the grounds for appealing arbitration awards are extremely narrow.[128] However, given the fact that even winning a discrimination lawsuit can cost an employer over $100,000 in attorney's fees and defense costs, it is an alternative worth considering.[129]

More employers are therefore switching to compulsory mandatory arbitration.[130] For example, after a long and expensive equal employment lawsuit, Rockwell International implemented a grievance procedure that provides for binding arbitration at the last step. Initially, Rockwell's 970 executives had to sign a mutual agreement to arbitrate employment disputes as a condition of participation in an executive stock plan. The program (called, as is traditional, an alternative dispute resolution or ADR program) was later extended to cover all nonunion employees at some locations. New hires at Rockwell must also sign the agreement to arbitrate as a condition of employment, and current employees must sign it to be promoted or transferred.[131] ADR plans appear to be becoming more popular, although the EEOC recently reasserted its long-standing opposition to such mandatory arbitration of workplace bias claims.[132] With or without ADR, handling EEOC claims can be expensive, as the High-Performance feature on page 65 illustrates.

DIVERSITY MANAGEMENT AND AFFIRMATIVE ACTION PROGRAMS

To some extent the goals of equitable and fair treatment driving equal employment legislation are being overtaken by demographic changes and globalization of markets. Today, as we've seen, white males no longer dominate the labor force, and women and minorities will represent the lion's share of labor force growth over the foreseeable future. Furthermore, globalization of markets increasingly requires employers to hire minority members with the cultural and language skills to deal with far-flung customers.

THE HIGH-PERFORMANCE ORGANIZATION

*Building Better, Faster, More Competitive Organizations
Through HR: A Paperless EEO Complaint Process*

■ Rhode Island Arsenal—Rock Island, IL

Rock Island Arsenal (RIA) has implemented and demonstrated a new computer system designed to automate the processing of EEO complaints. The system is called the Paperless EEO Complaint System. Typical EEO complaints include files which are complex and can contain hundreds or thousands of pages. The data is sensitive and must be protected. Case files must be available for review at various levels in a company, and must be forwarded to the Equal Employment Opportunity Commission for hearings. Many complaints could be in process at any given time. Labor and resources that must be dedicated to manually handling these tasks must be diverted from other activities and can thereby undermine a firm's competitiveness.

Prior to this system, EEO complaints were processed using a time consuming and costly paper document system. Documents were created manually, stored in cabinets, and transferred by mail. Postage and copying costs were high, and security was a problem. Under the old paper system, it was relatively common for case file documents to be lost or misfiled.

In order to safeguard and reduce the time and cost of handling EEO case files, RIA purchased a computerized system that electronically creates, maintains, and transfers EEO case files. The system was designed by RBP Associates of Landover, MD. The cost of the system in 1994 was approximately $25,000. The system is compatible with the Army's Equal Employment Opportunity Management and Analysis System that has been used within the Army Materiel Command for the past ten years. The new system runs on a Pentium-based PC and has a 40-page per minute scanner, and provides secure transmission over the Internet and encryption on CD-ROM.

The Paperless EEO System eliminates reproduction and misfiled or misplaced documents. It provides increased accessibility, greater security, and reduced overall processing costs. Processing a typical file by the old paper system could cost $100–200. The new system reduced overall processing costs by nearly 70%. It has been recognized as an important business process improvement by the Army Materiel Command, and is being evaluated for future use by other agencies and Army installations.

As a result, companies today are increasingly striving for racial, ethnic, and sexual workforce balance, "not because of legal imperatives, but as a matter of enlightened economic self-interest."[133] Increasingly, in other words, more and more employers are coming to the realization that they have to actively recruit and maintain a diverse workforce in order to tap the changing demographics in this country. And, they want to take advantage of the contributions that a diverse workforce can make toward customer goodwill, marketing, and other functional areas of the business.

While there's no unanimity about what diversity means, there's considerable agreement about diversity's components. For example, in one study a majority of the respondents listed race, gender, culture, national origin, handicap, age, and religion as diversity components. In other words, these comprised the demographic building blocks that represent diversity at work, and that people often think of when they ask what diversity means to employers.[134]

Managing Diversity

Managing diversity means maximizing diversity's potential advantages while minimizing the potential barriers—such as prejudices and bias—that can undermine the functioning of a diverse workforce. And, it means—as the accompanying IBM advertisement shows (Figure 2-3)—using various programs with the aim of showing that the firm welcomes and values individual differences, so as to help the firm attract and retain "the best and most talented individuals."

In practice, *diversity management* involves both compulsory and voluntary management actions. First, there are (as we've seen in this chapter) many legally mandated actions employers must take to minimize discrimination at work. However, while such compulsory actions can reduce the more blatant diversity barriers, blending a diverse workforce into a close-knit and thriving community also requires employers to take other steps. Based on his review of research studies, one diversity expert concludes that five sets of voluntary organizational activities are at the heart of any diversity management program. These can be summarized as follows:

> *Provide strong leadership.* Companies that have exemplary reputations in managing diversity are typically led by chief executives who champion the cause of diversity. Such leaders include John Houghton of Corning and David Kearns, the former chairman of Xerox Corporation. Leadership in this case means, for instance, taking a strong personal stand on the need for change and becoming a role model for the behaviors required for the change.

> *Research: Assess the situation.* The company must assess the current state of affairs with respect to diversity management. For example, this might entail administering surveys to measure employees' current attitudes and perceptions toward different cultural groups within the company.

> *Provide diversity training and education.* One expert says that "the most commonly utilized starting point for . . . managing diversity is some type of employee education program."[135]

> *Change culture and management systems.* Ideally, education programs should be combined with other concrete steps aimed at changing the organization's culture and management systems. For example, the performance appraisal procedure might be changed to emphasize that supervisors will henceforth be appraised based partly on their success in reducing inter-group conflicts.

> *Evaluate the managing diversity program.* For example, do the employee attitude surveys now indicate any improvement in employees' attitudes toward diversity?

Boosting Workforce Diversity

As we'll see throughout this book, employers use various means to boost workforce diversity. Baxter Healthcare Corporation's program provides one good example. Baxter starts with a stated philosophical position ("Baxter International believes that a multi-cultural employee population is essential to the company's leadership in healthcare around the world").

Next, Baxter takes concrete steps to foster diversity at work. For example they evaluate diversity program efforts, recruit minority members to the board of directors, and interact with representative minority groups and networks. Diversity training is another

FIGURE 2-3
IBM Values Diversity

It has long made sense to us at IBM to welcome and value individual differences. We prove this commitment to our workforce every day. Programs such as employee networking groups, child/elder care, domestic partner benefits and flexible work hours help us attract and retain the best and most talented individuals. And in our diverse marketplace, that's always good business. To learn more, just visit our Web site at www.ibm.com/diversity

IBM.

Solutions for a small planet™

concrete activity. It aims to sensitize all employees to the need to value differences, build self-esteem, and generally create a more smoothly functioning and hospitable environment for the firm's diverse workforce.

Some employers have also tried to better manage diversity through voluntary affirmative action programs. As explained later, affirmative action means employers make an extra effort to hire and promote those in protected (female or minority) groups. Recently, as noted, the aim often has been to voluntarily enhance the employment opportunities of women and minorities (in contrast to the involuntary affirmative action programs a number of courts have imposed on some employers since enactment of the 1964 Civil Rights Act).

Ironically, however, such voluntary affirmative action programs may now conflict with sections of the Civil Rights Act of 1991.[136] CRA 1991 amended Title VII of the 1964 Civil Rights Act to add language that provides:

Except as otherwise provided in this title, an unlawful employment practice is established when the complaining party demonstrates that race, color, religion, sex, or national origin was a motivating factor for any employment practice, even though other factors also motivated the practice.[137]

Two experts have written that "read literally, this new statutory restriction appears to bar employers from giving any consideration whatsoever to an individual's status as a racial or ethnic minority or as a woman when making an employment decision."[138] At the present time, this does not seem to be much of a problem, at least as long as employers emphasize the external recruitment and internal development of better-qualified minority and female employees, "while basing employment decisions on legitimate criteria. . . ."[139] However, employers will have to take care that in achieving the desirable goal of workforce diversity they do not inadvertently "step over the line of permissible diversity management into the realm of unlawful affirmative action (i.e., reverse discrimination)."[140]

Affirmative action may also backfire. For example, nonbeneficiaries may react negatively when they feel such programs result in them being treated unfairly.[141] Even beneficiaries may react boldly. In one study the perception that subjects had benefited from affirmative-action-based preferential selection resulted in them giving themselves unfavorable self-evaluations.[142] In spite of this, such voluntary programs are often advisable. And, in any case, they are sometimes mandated by the courts to remedy the effects of blatant past discrimination by employers.

Equal Employment Opportunity Versus Affirmative Action

Equal employment opportunity aims to ensure that anyone, regardless of race, color, sex, religion, national origin, or age, has an equal chance for a job based on his or her qualifications.

Affirmative action goes beyond equal employment opportunity by requiring the employer to make an extra effort to hire and promote those in the protected group. Affirmative action thus includes specific actions (in recruitment, hiring, promotions, and compensation) that are designed to eliminate the present effects of past discrimination. According to the EEOC, the most important measure of an affirmative action program is its results. The program should result in "measurable, yearly improvements in hiring, training, and promotion of minorities and females" in all parts of the organization.

Steps in an Affirmative Action Program

According to the EEOC, in an affirmative action program the employer ideally takes eight steps:

1. Issues a written equal employment policy indicating that it is an equal employment opportunity employer, as well as a statement indicating the employer's commitment to affirmative action.
2. Appoints a top official with responsibility and authority to direct and implement the program.
3. Publicizes the equal employment policy and affirmative action commitment.
4. Surveys present minority and female employment by department and job classification to determine locations where affirmative action programs are especially desirable (see Figure 2–4).
5. Develops goals and timetables to improve utilization of minorities, males, and females in each area where utilization has been identified.
6. Develops and implements specific programs to achieve these goals. According to the EEOC, this is the heart of the affirmative action program. Here the employer

Job Group 47 Title	Incumb #	Males #	Males %	Female #	Female %	Minority #	Minority %	Asian #	Asian %	Black #	Black %	Hispanics #	Hispanics %	American Indian #	American Indian %	White #	White %
Data Pro. Control Spec.	2			2	100.00	1	50.00					1	50.00			1	50.00
Computer Operator	5	5	100.00			4	80.00	1	20.00	2	40.00	1	20.00			1	20.00
Computer Repair Tech.	1	1	100.00			1	100.00					1	100.00				
Computer Programmer	2			2	100.00	1	50.00					1	50.00			1	50.00
Photographer	3	2	66.67	1	33.33	1	33.33					1	33.33			2	66.67
Graphic Artist	2	2	100.00			2	100.00					2	100.00				
Library Tech. Asst.	11	2	18.18	9	81.82	9	81.82			3	27.27	6	54.55			2	18.18
Laboratory Technician	1			1	100.00	1	100.00					1	100.00				
TOTALS	27	12	44.44	15	55.56	20	74.07	1	3.70	5	18.52	14	51.85			7	25.95

Date of Survey *1997–1998*

FIGURE 2-4   *Sample Affirmative Action Report. EEO Category: Technical/Paraprofessional*

has to review its entire personnel management system (including recruitment, selection, promotion, compensation, and disciplining) to identify barriers to equal employment opportunity and to make needed changes.

7. Establishes an internal audit and reporting system to monitor and evaluate progress in each aspect of the program.
8. Develops support for the affirmative action program, both inside the company (among supervisors, for instance) and outside the company in the community.[143]

Affirmative Action: Two Basic Strategies

good faith effort strategy

Employment strategy aimed at changing practices that have contributed in the past to excluding or underutilizing protected groups.

quota strategy

Employment strategy aimed at mandating the same results as the good faith effort strategy through specific hiring and promotion restrictions.

When designing an affirmative action plan, employers can choose either of two basic strategies to pursue—the **good faith effort strategy** or the **quota strategy**—each with its own risks.[144] The first emphasizes identifying and eliminating the obstacles to hiring and promoting women and minorities on the assumption that eliminating these obstacles will result in increased utilization of women and minorities. The quota strategy, on the other hand, mandates bottom-line results by instituting hiring and promotion restrictions.

GOOD FAITH EFFORT STRATEGY   This strategy is aimed at changing the practices that have contributed to the exclusion or underutilization of minority groups or females. Specific actions here might include placing advertisements where they can reach target groups, supporting day care services and flexible working hours for women with small children, and establishing a training program to enable minority-group members to better compete for entry-level jobs. The assumption is that if existing obstacles are identified and eliminated, the desired results (improved utilization of minority members and women) will follow. The risk is that if the desired results are not achieved (in terms of hiring or promoting more minorities or women), the employer must convince the EEO that (1) a reasonable effort to hire or promote more protected individuals has taken place and (2) that failure to do so resulted from factors outside the employer's control.

QUOTA STRATEGY   Whereas the good faith strategy attempts to get results by eliminating obstacles, the quota strategy aims at mandating results through hiring and promotion restrictions. With the quota strategy, "desirable" hiring goals are treated operationally as required employment quotas.

reverse discrimination

Claim that due to affirmative action quota systems, white males are discriminated against.

The courts have been grappling with the role of quotas in hiring, and particularly with claims by white males of **reverse discrimination** (discriminating against male non-minority persons). A series of cases has addressed these issues without a uniform answer emerging. For example in *Bakke v. The Regents of the University of California* (1978), white student Allen Bakke had been denied admission to the University of California at Davis Medical School, allegedly because of the school's affirmative action quota system, which required that a specific number of openings go to minority applicants. In a 5 to 4 vote, the Court struck down the school's policy that made race the only factor in considering applications for a certain number of class openings and thus allowed Bakke to be admitted.

However, subsequent U.S. Supreme Court cases have continued to address these issues and clarify the scope and intent of affirmative action. For example:

Wygant v. Jackson Board of Education (1986): The Court struck down a mechanism in a collective bargaining agreement that gave preferential treatment to minority teachers in the event of a layoff.[145]

Local 28 Sheet Metal Workers v. EEOC (1986): The Court ruled that Title VII empowers a court to order a union to use quotas to overcome "egregious discrimination" and that the quota may benefit even individuals who were not themselves victims of past unlawful union discrimination.[146]

International Association of Firefighters v. The City of Cleveland (1986): The Court upheld a consent decree that reserved a specific number of promotions for minority firefighters and established percentage goals for minority promotions.[147]

U.S. v. Paradise (1987): The Court ruled that the lower courts can impose racial quotas to address the most serious cases of racial discrimination.[148]

Johnson v. Transportation Agency, Santa Clara County (1987): Public and private employers may voluntarily adopt hiring and promotion goals to benefit minorities and women. This ruling limited claims of reverse discrimination by white males.[149]

On November 3, 1997, the U.S. Supreme Court declined to hear a challenge to California's new law (Proposition 209) banning race or sex-based preferences in contracting, public hiring, and school admission. According to a report in *The New York Times*, "Supporters of the measure promptly hailed the (U.S. Supreme) Court's action as paving the way for adoption of similar prohibitions around the nation, like a ballot measure to be voted on in Houston on Tuesday." As one Proposition 209 supporter put it, "Today's ruling sends a green light to citizens of other states who can now act to end racial preference."

The U.S. Supreme Court never got to decide one highly publicized reverse bias case that many believed could have undermined affirmative action programs. In November 1997, Sharon Taxman, a white schoolteacher who had challenged her layoff by the Board of Education of Piscataway, New Jersey, as due to reverse discrimination accepted a $433,500 settlement. She had claimed reverse bias, basing her case on the allegation that she was laid off while a black school teacher with the same seniority was retained. The U.S. Court of Appeals for the Third Circuit had sided with Taxman, and the Supreme Court had granted review. About three-quarters of her settlement was paid by the Black Leadership Forum, a coalition of several minority Civil Rights groups who reportedly feared "that the case could overturn affirmative action precedent set over the past 20 years. . . ."[150]

A PRACTICAL APPROACH   According to one writer, these legal uncertainties suggest that the good faith effort strategy is often preferable to the quota strategy.[151] An employer might reasonably ask, therefore, "What specific actions should I take to be able to show that I have in fact made a good faith effort?"

One study helps answer this question. Questionnaires were sent to EEOC compliance officers who were asked to rate about 30 possible actions on their importance in evaluating the compliance effort of a hypothetical company. This company was described as having determined that minorities were underutilized in several blue-collar and white-collar jobs. The compliance officers were then asked to indicate the possible tactics or actions they thought the employer could take in order to show evidence of an acceptable good faith effort affirmative action program. The results of this study showed that there were six main areas for action:

1. Increasing the minority or female applicant flow.
2. Demonstrating top-management support for the equal employment policy, for instance by appointing a high-ranking EEO administrator.
3. Demonstrating equal employment commitment to the local community, for instance by providing in-house remedial training.
4. Keeping employees informed about the specifics of the affirmative action program.
5. Broadening the work skills of incumbent employees.
6. Institutionalizing the equal employment policy to encourage supervisors' support of it for instance by making it part of their performance appraisals.

 We invite you to visit the Dessler page on the Prentice Hall Web site at **www.prenhall.com/dessler** for our on-line study guide, Internet exercises, current events, links to related Web sites, and more.

SUMMARY

1. Legislation barring discrimination is nothing new. For example, the Fifth Amendment to the U.S. Constitution (ratified in 1791) states that no person shall be deprived of life, liberty, or property without due process of law.
2. New legislation barring employment discrimination included Title VII of the 1964 Civil Rights Act (as amended), which bars discrimination because of race, color, religion, sex, or national origin; various executive orders; federal guidelines (covering procedures for validating employee selection tools, etc.); the Equal Pay Act of 1963; and the Age Discrimination in Employment Act of 1967. In addition, various court decisions (such as *Griggs v. Duke Power Company*) and state and local laws bar various aspects of discrimination.
3. The EEOC was created by Title VII of the Civil Rights Act. It is empowered to try conciliating discrimination complaints, but if this fails, the EEOC has the power to go directly to court to enforce the law.
4. The Civil Rights Act of 1991 had the effect of revising several Supreme Court equal employment decisions and "rolling back the clock." It placed the burden of proof back on employers, said postemployment decisions were covered by the 1866 Civil Rights Act, held that a nondiscriminatory reason was insufficient to let an employer avoid liability for an action that also had a discriminatory motive, and said that Title VII applied to U.S. employees of U.S. firms overseas. It also now permits compensatory and punitive damages, as well as jury trials.
5. The Americans with Disabilities Act prohibits employment discrimination against the disabled. Specifically, qualified persons cannot be discriminated against if the firm can make reasonable accommodations without undue hardship on the business.
6. A person who feels he or she has been discriminated against by a personnel procedure or decision must prove either that he or she was subjected to unlawful disparate treatment (intentional discrimination) or that the procedure in question has a disparate impact (unintentional discrimination) upon members of his or her protected class. Disparate treatment can be proven under the *McDonnell-Douglas* standards, while

disparate impact proof can involve disparate rejection rates, restrictive policies, or population comparisons. Once a prima facie case of disparate treatment is established, an employer must produce evidence that its decision was based upon legitimate nondiscriminatory reasons. If the employer does that, the person claiming discrimination must prove the employer's reasons are just a pretext for letting the company discriminate. Once a prima facie case of disparate impact has been established, the employer must produce evidence that the allegedly discriminatory practice or procedure is job related and is based upon a substantial business reason. If it does so, the employee must prove a less-discriminatory alternative existed that would have been equally effective in achieving the employer's legitimate objectives or disprove the employer's justification for disparate impact.

7. Various specific discriminatory human resource management practices that an employer should avoid were discussed.

(a) In recruitment. An employer usually should not rely on word-of-mouth advertising or give false or misleading information to minority-group members. Also (usually), do not specify the desired gender in advertising or in any way suggest that applicants might be discriminated against.

(b) In selection. Avoid using any educational or other requirements where (1) it can be shown that minority-group members are less likely to possess the qualification and (2) such a requirement is also not job related. Tests that disproportionately screen out minorities and women and that are not job related are deemed unlawful by the courts. Do not give preference to relatives of current employees (when most are nonminority) or specify physical characteristics unless it can be proved they are needed for job performance. Similarly, a person's arrest record should not be used to disqualify him or her automatically for a position, nor should a person be fired whose salary has been garnished. Remember that you can use various tests and standards, but must prove that they are job related or show that they are not used to discriminate against protected groups.

8. In practice, a person's charge to the EEOC is often first referred to a local agency. When it does proceed, and if it finds reasonable cause to believe that discrimination occurred, EEOC has 30 days to try to work out a conciliation. Important points for the employer to remember include (a) EEOC investigators can only make recommendations, (b) you cannot be compelled to submit documents without a court order, and (c) you may limit the information you do submit. Also make sure you clearly document your position (as the employer).

9. There are two basic defenses an employer can use in the event of a discriminatory practice allegation. One is business necessity. Attempts to show that tests or other selection standards are valid is one example of this defense. Bona fide occupational qualification is the second defense. This is applied when, for example, religion, national origin, or gender is a bona fide requirement of the job (such as for actors or actresses). An employer's "good intentions" and/or a collective bargaining agreement are not defenses. (A third defense is that the decision was made on the basis of legitimate nondiscriminatory reasons [such as poor performance] having nothing to do with the prohibited discrimination alleged.)

10. Eight steps in an affirmative action program (based on suggestions from the EEOC) are (1) issue a written equal employment policy, (2) appoint a top official, (3) publicize policy, (4) survey present minority and female employment, (5) develop goals and timetables, (6) develop and implement specific programs to achieve goals, (7) establish an internal audit and reporting system, and (8) develop support of in-house and community programs.

DISCUSSION QUESTIONS

1. What are the main EEO laws and court decisions and what do they say?
2. What important precedents were set by the *Griggs v. Duke Power Company* case? The *Albemarle v. Moody* case?
3. What is adverse impact? How can it be proven?

INDIVIDUAL AND GROUP ACTIVITIES

1. Assume you are a supervisor on an assembly line; you are responsible for hiring subordinates, supervising them, and recommending them for promotion. Working individually or in groups, compile a list of discriminatory management practices you should avoid.
2. Working individually or in groups, discuss how you would set up an affirmative action program.
3. Compare and contrast the issues presented in *Bakke* with new court rulings on affirmative action. Working individually or in groups, discuss the current direction of affirmative action as a policy in light of the *Johnson* ruling.
4. Explain the defenses and exceptions to discriminatory practice allegations.
5. What is the difference between affirmative action and equal employment opportunity?
6. Explain how the Civil Rights Act of 1991 "turned back the clock" on equal employment Supreme Court cases decided from 1989 to 1991.

EXPERIENTIAL EXERCISE

Too Informal?

Dan Jones had run his textile plant in a midsize Southern town for many years without a whiff of trouble with the EEOC. He did not take formal steps to avoid making EEO-type mistakes; just the opposite. In fact, a professor from a local college had once told him to be

(continued)

(continued from page 163)
more careful about how applicants were recruited and screened and employees were treated. However, Jones's philosophy was "if it ain't broke, don't fix it," and because he'd never had any complaints, he assumed that his screening process wasn't "broke."

For many years Jones had no problems. If he needed a new employee, he simply asked his current employees (most of whom were Hispanic) if they had any friends who were looking for jobs. Sometimes he would also ask the local state employment office to list the open jobs and send over some candidates. He then had his sewing supervisor and plant manager (both also Hispanic) interview the applicants. No tests or other background checks were carried out, in part, said Jones, because, "most of these applicants are friends and relatives of my current employees, and they wouldn't send me any lemons."

Now Jones is being served with a formal notice from the county's Equal Rights Commission. It seems that of the 20 or so non-Hispanic applicants sent to Jones's firm last year from the state employment office, none had received a job offer. In fact, Jones's supervisor had not even returned the follow-up card to the employment office to verify that each applicant had shown up and been interviewed. Jones

was starting to wonder if his HR process was too informal.

Purpose The purpose of this exercise is to provide practice in analyzing and applying knowledge of equal opportunity legislation to a realistic problem.

Required Understanding Be thoroughly familiar with the material presented in this chapter. In addition, read "Too Informal?" the case on which this experiential exercise is based.

How to Set Up the Exercise/Instructions

1. Divide the class into groups of four or five students.
2. Each group should develop answers to the following questions:
   a. How could the EEOC prove *adverse impact*?
   b. Cite specific discriminatory personnel practices at Dan Jones's company.
   c. How could Jones's company defend itself against the allegations of discriminatory practice?
3. If time permits, a spokesperson from each group can present his or her group's findings. Would it make sense for this company to try to defend itself against the discrimination allegations?

CASE INCIDENT
A Case of Racial Discrimination?

John Peters (not his real name) was a 44-year-old cardiologist on the staff of a teaching hospital in a large city in the southeastern United States. Happily married with two teenage children, he had served with distinction for many years at this same hospital, and in fact served his residency there after graduating from Columbia University's medical school.

Alana Anderson (not her real name) was an attractive African American registered nurse on the staff at the same hospital with Peters. Unmarried and without children, she lived in a hospital-owned apartment on the hospital grounds and diligently devoted almost all her time to her work at the hospital or to taking additional coursework to further improve her already excellent nursing skills.

The hospital's chief administrator, Gary Chapman, took enormous pride in what he called the extraordinary professionalism of the doctors, nurses, and other staff members at his hospital. Although he took a number of rudimentary steps to guard against blatant violations of equal employment opportunity laws, he believed that most of the professionals on his staff were so highly trained and committed to the highest professional standards that "they would always do the right thing," as he put it.

Chapman was therefore upset to receive a phone call from Peters, informing him that Anderson had (in Peters's eyes) "developed an unwholesome personal attraction" to him and was bombarding the doctor with Valentine's Day cards, affectionate personal notes, and phone calls—often to the doctor's home. Concerned about hospital decorum and the possibility that Peters was being sexually harassed, Chapman met privately with Anderson, explained that Peters was very uncomfortable with the personal attention she was showing to him, and asked that she please not continue to exhibit her show of affection for the doctor.

Chapman assumed that the matter was over. Several weeks later, when Anderson resigned her position at the hospital, Chapman didn't think much of it. He was therefore shocked and dismayed to receive a registered letter from a local attorney, informing him that both the hospital and Peters and Chapman personally were being sued by Anderson for racial discrimination: Her claim was that Chapman, in their private meeting, had told her, "We don't think it's right for people of different

races to pursue each other romantically at this hospital." According to the lawyer, his preliminary research had unearthed several other alleged incidents at the hospital that apparently supported the idea that racial discrimination at the hospital was widespread.

■ QUESTIONS

1. What do you think of the way Chapman handled the accusations from Peters and his conversation with Anderson? How would you have handled them?

2. Do you think Peters had the basis for a sexual harassment claim against Anderson? Why or why not?

3. What would you do now if you were Chapman to avoid further incidents of this type?

Case Application   ALL IN THE FAMILY

Louis Minardi, age fifty-four, was president and chief operating officer of Minardi Bakery, Inc. Minardi Bakers was begun almost twenty-four years ago by Louis Minardi, who built the enterprise from one to seventy-five employees through hard work and a dedication to customer satisfaction. Minardi had learned the bakery business when, for financial reasons, he was forced to leave high school and go to work in a local bakery. Even though he would have liked to finish high school, providing financial support for his family was more important to him. With the unexpected death of his father, Louis Minardi was expected to help his mother make ends meet for the two of them and three younger children. Louis often told people that those very hard times brought the family together and that "Close family ties are all that really matter."

Minardi Bakery was one of the finest bakeries in the local area. It had an excellent reputation for quality baked goods and customer service. Both retail and wholesale customers seemed to be very satisfied, and the organization was profitable. Employees were a happy and cohesive group, and they seemed to derive considerable satisfaction from social interaction both on and off the job. The employees had organized company-sponsored softball and bowling teams, and they often went out together to unwind after work. Much of this

cohesiveness was attributable to Minardi's human resource policy of internal recruiting. As the organization grew, personnel requirements were met primarily from referrals from current employees. Minardi often would say that the company is "just one big happy family."

A problem, however, had recently developed. Louis Minardi had just received notice from the regional office of the Equal Employment Opportunity Commission (EEOC) that the firm was being investigated on charges of employment discrimination. Takia Wilson, a twenty-two-year-old African American female, who had applied for a supervisory position at Minardi Bakery about a month and a half ago, had charged that she was denied the job because of her race and gender.

Louis Minardi reflected on the events leading to this problem. Takia Wilson had seen an advertisement in the local newspaper that indicated that Minardi Bakery was seeking to fill a supervisory position (see Figure 2-5). Takia had recently graduated from a local community college with a two-year degree in business management. For the past four years, she had been working in a women's apparel shop; during the last two years, she was assistant manager. Takia had received good performance reviews. She provided Mr. Minardi with letters of recommendation that indicated she was a highly motivated and

(continued)

Figure 2-5
Employment Advertisement

> ***SUPERVISORY***
>
> Minardi Bakery is looking for an energetic and highly motivated person to assume a front-line supervisory position. Ability to get along with others essential. Past supervisory experience or technical training required.
>
> Call: Louis Minardi
>   Minardi Bakery
>   732-555-3456

productive employee in her current position. During her four years of employment at the apparel shop, Takia received recognition for her ability to deal effectively with customers. In her position as assistant manager, she was praised for her skills in supervising sales associates.

After reading the discrimination charge, Louis commented to Harry Bruns, his production manager: "Yeah, I remember her. I just didn't think that she would fit in here." The position was later filled by Nick Pitino, a nephew of a supervisor at Minardi who had worked in the bakery during the summer months throughout high school and college. Although Nick Pitino did not have supervisory experience, he did have knowledge of the business, and Minardi had been able to assess Pitino's abilities during the six summers he was employed at the bakery.

Takia Wilson had called the telephone number in the advertisement and scheduled an interview with Mr. Minardi. When she arrived at the bakery, she was given an application form to fill out (see Figure 2-6). Upon completing the application form, she was granted an interview with Minardi. During the interview, he asked Takia about her work experience at the "dress shop." The interview process was interrupted several times by telephone calls and company personnel who needed Mr. Minardi's advice. During the interview, Louis Minardi asked Takia if she, or her boyfriend, would mind if she had to work the late shift. Takia responded that the late shift would present no problems; in fact, she often worked nights at the apparel shop. A major concern Mr. Minardi expressed during the interview was Takia's ability to supervise men. He told her that she would have to supervise the work of eight men, most of whom were older than Takia and who had worked in the bakery on average seven to ten years. Minardi said that he was concerned that Takia did not have previous experience supervising men. Takia told him that she had supervised the work of six part-time women in the apparel shop. Takia Wilson also mentioned to Mr. Minardi that she had taken a number of supervision courses in her

studies at the community college and that these courses had prepared her to deal with any problems she would encounter at the bakery. Takia reiterated that even though she had no direct supervisory experience with men nor experience in the bakery business, she would be willing to work very hard to learn the business and to get along with everyone.

Louis Minardi ended the interview by stating that he would "let her know his decision in about a week or so." After two weeks had passed, Takia Wilson called Mr. Minardi to ask about his decision. He told her that the position had been filled by someone else. When pressed about his decision, Minardi responded that a young man had been hired becuse of his experience and education. "He will probably fit in here better since he has a four-year degree and has worked here before," were the words used by Minardi. He thanked Takia for her application and wished her luck in finding a position. As he put the telephone receiver down, he felt that he would never see Takia Wilson again.

Louis Minardi recognized that he had to respond to Takia Wilson's and the EEOC's charges of employment discrimination.

■ QUESTIONS:

1. Where did Louis Minardi go wrong? What specific laws and guidelines discussed in this chapter (if any) did he violate?

2. Present a short report detailing a system and set of procedures he should use from now on to avoid these problems in the future.

3. What should he do now with respect to the EEOC charges? What can he expect now in terms of EEOC procedures.

This case was prepared by Charles A. Rarick, Ph.D., Associate Professor and Director of Management at Transylvania University in Lexington, Kentucky. All names are disguised. Used by permission.

MINARDI BAKERY
APPLICATION FOR EMPLOYMENT

Name _____   Date _____

Address _____
             Street   City   State   Zip

Telephone Number _____   Date of Birth _____

Social Security Number _____   Age _____

Education   _____ Grade School
                 School Name   Dates

              _____ High School
                 School Name   Dates

              _____ Other School
                 School Name   Dates

Work Experience   Employer   Position   Dates

_____

_____

_____

Do you smoke?   _____ Yes   _____ No

Do you owe money?   _____ Yes   _____ No

Have you ever been arrested?   _____ Yes   _____ No

Who do you know that works at Minardi Bakery? _____

I hereby affirm that my answers are true and correct to the best of my knowledge.

Signed _____   Date _____

Figure 2-6

NOTES

1. Commerce Clearing House, *Ideas and Trends in Personnel*, May 13, 1992, p. 73.

2. Julia Flynn, "Astra: It's Not Over Yet," *Business Week*, February 23, 1998, pp. 50–51.

3. Shari Caudron, "A Discrimination Mistake," *Workforce*, March 1997, pp. 59–66.

4. Bureau of National Affairs, "$65 Million Sex Bias Settlement," *Fair Employment Practices*, October 2, 1997, p. 120.

5. "You'll Be Hearing From My Lawyer," *The Economist*, June 21, 1997, p. 67.

6. "Employee Lawsuits Spur New Insurance Coverage," *BNA Bulletin to Management*, June 5, 1997, p. 177.

7. "Section 1981 Covers Racial Discrimination in Hiring and Promotion, But No Other Situation," Commerce Clearing House, *Human Resources Management*, June 28, 1989, p. 116.

8. Portions of this chapter are based on or quoted from *Principles of Employment Discrimination Law*, International Association of Official Human Rights Agencies, Washington, D.C. In addition, see W. Clay Hamner and Frank Schmidt, *Contemporary Problems in Personnel*, rev. ed. (Chicago: St. Clair Press, 1977), Chapter 3. Employment discrimination law is a changing field, and the appropriateness of the rules, guidelines, and conclusions in this book may also be affected by factors unique to the employer's operation. They should, therefore, be reviewed by the employer's attorney before implementation.

9. James Higgins, "A Manager's Guide to the Equal Employment Opportunity Law," *Personnel Journal*, Vol. 55, no. 8 (August, 1976), p. 406.

10. The Equal Employment Opportunity Act of 1972, Sub-Committee on Labor or the Committee of Labor and Public Welfare, United States Senate, March 1972, p. 3. In general, it is not discrimination but unfair discrimination against a person merely because of that person's race, age, sex, national origin, or religion that is forbidden by federal statutes. In the federal government's Uniform employee Selection Guidelines, "unfair" discrimination is defined as follows: "unfairness is demonstrated through a showing that members of a particular interest group perform better or poorer on the job than their scores on the selection procedure (test, etc.) would indicate through comparison with how members of the other group performed." For a discussion of the meaning of fairness, see James Ledvinka, "The Statistical Definition of Fairness in the Federal Selection Guidelines and Its Implications for Minority Employment," *Personnel Psychology*, Vol. 32 (August 1979), pp. 551–562. In summary, a selection device (like a test) may discriminate, say, between low and high performers. However, it is unfair discrimination that is illegal, discrimination that is based solely on the person's race, age, sex, national origin, or religion.

11. "OFCCP Lists Egregious Bias Cases," *BNA Fair Employment Practices*, November 28, 1996, p. 139.

12. Bureau of National Affairs, *Fair Employment Practices*, October 8, 1992, p. 117.

13. Note that under the Rehabilitation Act, the law strictly speaking applied only to a particular "program" of the employer. In March 1988 Congress passed the Civil Rights Restoration Act of 1987, overturning this interpretation. Now, with few exceptions, any institution, organization, corporation, state agency, or municipality using federal funding in any of its programs must abide by the section of the act prohibiting discriminating against handicapped individuals. See bureau of National Affairs, "Federal Law Mandates Affirmative Action for Handicapped," *Fair Employment Practices*, March 30, 1989, p. 42.

14. *Tanberg v. Weld County Sheriff*, SUDA Colo, No. 91-B-248, 3/18/92.

15. Steven Fox, "Employment Provisions of the Rehabilitation Act," *Personnel Journal*, Vol. 66, no. 10 (October 1987), p. 140.

16. Bureau of National Affairs, "Guidelines on AIDS," *Fair Employment Practices*, March 30, 1989, p. 39.

17. David B. Ritter and Ronald Turner, "AIDS: Employer Concerns and Options," *Labor Law Journal*, Vol. 38, no. 2 (February 1987), pp. 67–83.

18. Howard J. Anderson and Michael D. Levin-Epstein, *Primer of Equal Employment Opportunity*, 2nd ed. (Washington, DC: Bureau of National Affairs, 1982), p. 507; and Commerce Clearing House, "Federal Contractors Must File VETS-100 by March 31," *Ideas and Trends*, February 23, 1988, p. 32.

19. Ann Harriman, *Women/Men Management* (New York: Praeger, 1985), pp. 66–68.

20. Commerce Clearing House, "Pregnancy Leave," *Ideas and Trends*, January 23, 1987, p. 10.

21. Bureau of National Affairs, "High Court Upholds Pregnancy Law," *Fair Employment Practices*, January 22, 1987, p. 7; Betty Sonthard Murphy, Wayne E. Barlow, and D. Diane Hatch, "Manager's Newsfront: U.S. Supreme Court Approves Preferential Treatment for Pregnancy," *Personnel Journal*, Vol. 66, no. 3 (March 1987), p. 18.

22. Thomas Dhanens, "Implications of the New EEOC Guidelines," *Personnel*, Vol. 56 (September-October 1979), pp. 32–39.

23. Bureau of National Affairs, "First Two Chapters of Long-Awaited Manual Released by OFCCP," *Fair Employment Practices*, January 5, 1989, p. 6.

24. Lawrence S. Kleiman and Robert Faley, "The Applications of Professional and Legal Guidelines for Court Decisions Involving Criterion-Related Validity: A Review and Analysis," *Personnel Psychology*, Vol. 38, no. 4 (Winter 1985), pp. 803–833.

25. Oscar A. Ornati and Margaret J. Eisen, "Are You Complying with EEOC's New Rules on National Origin Discrimination?" *Personnel*, Vol. 58 (March-April 1981), pp. 12–20; Paul S. Greenlaw and John P. Kohl, "National Origin Discrimination and the New EEOC Guidelines," *Personnel Journal*, Vol. 60, no. 8 (August 1981), pp. 634–636.

26. Barbara Berish Brown, "Guidance and Regs from EEOC, OFCCP, and INS," *Employment Relations Today* (Spring 1992), pp. 81–86; Morgan Hodgson and Ronald Cooper, EEOC Issues proposed Guidelines and guidance Memorandum," *Employment Relations Today* (Winter 1993/94), pp. 455–459; "EEOC Issues Disability Guidance," *BNA Fair Employment Practices*, March 23, 1995, p. 31.

27. Paul S. Greenlaw and John P. Kohl, "Age Discrimination and Employment Guidelines," *Personnel Journal*, Vol. 61, no. 3 (March 1982), pp. 224–228.

28. 29 CFR 1625.2(a) quoted in Greenlaw and Kohl, "Age Discrimination."

29. Patricia Linenberger and Timothy Keaveny, "Sexual Harassment: The Employer's Legal Obligations," *Personnel*, Vol. 58 (November-December 1981), pp. 60–68.

30. Larry Drake and Rachel Moskowitz, "Your Rights in the Workplace," *Occupational Outlook Quarterly* (Summer 1997), pp. 19–20.

31. *Mattison v. Click Corp. Of America*, DC Epa#97-cv-2736, 1/27/98; discussed in "Preventing Sexual Harassment: Helpful Advice and Another Reason," *BNA Fair Employment Practices*, February 19, 1998, p. 21.

32. Mary Rowe, "Dealing with Sexual Harassment," *Harvard Business Review*, Vol. 61 (May-June 1981), pp. 42–46.

33. Edward Felsenthal, "Justices' Ruling Further Defines Sex Harassment," *Wall Street Journal*, March 5, 1998, pp. B1, B5.

34. Commerce Clearing House, *Sexual Harassment Manual for Managers and Supervisors* (Chicago: Commerce Clearing House, Inc., 1991), pp. 28–29.

35. Robert H. Faley, "Sexual Harassment: Critical Review of Legal Cases with General Principles and Preventive Measures," *Personnel Psychology*, Vol. 35, no. 3 (Autumn 1982), pp. 590–591; Bureau of National Affairs, "In Terms of Sexual Harassment, What Makes an Environment 'Hostile'?" *Fair Employment Practices*, June 1988, p. 78.

36. Patricia Linenberger and Timothy Keaveny, "Sexual Harassment: The Employee's Legal Obligations," *Personnel*, Vol. 58 (November-December 1981), p. 64.

37. Jerome Watson, "Employer Liability for the Sexually Harassing Actions of its Customers," *Employee Relations Law Journal*, Vol. 19, no. 3 (Winter 1993/1994), pp. 227–237; see also Robert Alberts and Lorne Seidman, "Sexual Harassment by Clients, Customers, and Suppliers: How Employers Should Handle an Emerging Legal Problem," *Employee Relations Law Journal*, Vol. 20, no. 1 (Summer 1994), pp. 85–100.

38. Michael W. Sculnick, "The Supreme Court 1985–86 EEO Decisions: A Review," *Employment Relations Today*, Vol. 13, no. 3 (Fall 1986), pp. 197–206; *Brown* v. *City of Guthrie*, 22FEP Cases 1627, 1980. See also Terry Morehead Dworkin, "Harassment in the 1990s," *Business Horizons* (March-April 1993), pp. 52–58; Robert Robinson et al., "Sexual Harassment in the Workplace: A Review of the Legal Rights and Responsibilities of All Parties," *Public Personnel Management*, Vol. 22, no. 1 (Spring 1993), pp. 123–135; and Donald Petersen and Douglas Massengill, "Sexual Harassment Cases Five Years After *Meritor Savings Bank* v. *Vinson*," *Employee Relations Law Journal*, Vol. 18, no. 3 (Winter 1992–93), pp. 489–515.

39. Commerce Clearing House, *Sexual Harassment Manual*, p. 8.

40. "Adequate Response Bars Liability," *BNA Fair Employment Practices*, June 26, 1997, p. 74.

41. Frederick L. Sullivan, "Sexual Harassment: The Supreme Court Ruling," *Personnel*, Vol. 65, no. 12 (December 1986), pp. 42–44. Also see the following for additional information on sexual harassment: Jonathan S. Monat and Angel Gomez, "Decisional Standards Used by Arbitrators in Sexual Harassment Cases," *Labor Law Journal*, Vol. 37, no. 10 (October 1985), pp. 712–718;

George M. Sullivan and William H. Nowlin, "Critical New Aspects of Sexual Harassment Law," *Labor Law Journal*, Vol. 37, no. 9 (September 1986), pp. 617–623.

42. Hodgson and Cooper, "EEOC Issues Proposed Guidelines and Guidance Memorandum," p. 456.

43. See the discussion in "Examining Unwelcome Conduct in a Sexual Harassment Claim," *BNA Fair Employment Practices*, October 19, 1995, p. 124.

44. Ibid.

45. *Griggs v. Duke Power Company*, 3FEP Cases 175.

46. This is applicable only to Title VII and CRA 91; other statutes require intent.

47. This is paraphrased from and/or quoted from Kenneth L. Sovereign, *Personnel Law*, 3rd ed. (Upper Saddle River, NJ: Prentice-Hall, 1994), p. 48.

48. James Ledvinka, *Federal Regulation of Personnel and Human Resources Management* (Boston: Kent, 1982), p. 41.

49. 10FEP cases 1881.

50. James Ledvinka and Lyle Schoenfeldt, "Legal Development in Employment Testing: Albemarle and Beyond," *Personnel Psychology*, Vol. 31, no. 1 (Spring 1978), pp. 1–13. It should be noted that the Court, in its *Albemarle* opinion, made one important modification regarding the EEOC guidelines. The guidelines required that employers using tests that screened out disproportionate numbers of minorities or women had to validate those tests—prove that they did in fact predict performance on the job—and further had to prove that there was no other alternative screening device the employer could use that did not screen out disproportionate numbers of minorities and women. This second requirement proved a virtually impossible burden for employers. Up through the *Griggs* decision, it was not enough to just validate the test; instead, the employer also had to show that some other tests or screening tools were not available that were (1) also valid but that (2) did not screen out a disproportionate number of minorities or women. In the *Albemarle* case the Court held that the burden of proof was no longer on the employer to show that there was no suitable alternative screening device available. Instead, the burden for that was now on the charging party (the person allegedly discriminated against) to show that a suitable alternative is available. Ledvinka and Schoenfeldt, "Legal Development," p. 4; Gary Lubben, Dwayne Thompson, and Charles Klasson, "Performance Appraisal: The Legal Implications of Title VII," *Personnel* (May/June 1980).

51. This was quoted from Commerce Clearing House, "Supreme Court Releases First 'Mixed Motives' Decision Under Title VII," *Ideas and Trends*, May 17, 1989, p. 82.

52. Ibid., p. 82.

53. "High Court Makes Race, Sex Bias in Work Place Tougher to Prove," *The Miami Herald*, June 6, 1989, p. 4A.

54. Commerce Clearing House, "The Supreme Court Explains How Statistics Are to Be Used in Fair Employment Suits," *Ideas and Trends*, June 14, 1989, p. 109.

55. Based on Ibid.

56. Commerce Clearing House, "House and Senate Pass Civil Rights Compromise by Wide Margin," *Ideas and Trends in Personnel*, November 13, 1991, p. 179.

57. Commerce Clearing House, "House and Senate Pass Civil Rights Compromise," p. 182.

58. Mark Kobata, "The Civil Rights Act of 1991," *Personnel Journal* (March 1992), p. 48.

59. For a discussion, see Commerce Clearing House, *Ideas and Trends in Personnel*, November 13, 1991, p. 182. See also Glen Nager and Edward Bilich, "The Civil Rights Act of 1991 Going Forward," *Employee Relations Law Journal*, Vol. 21, no. 2 (Autumn 1994), pp. 237–251.

60. Patricia Feltes, Robert Robinson, and Ross Fink, "American Female Expatriates and the Civil Rights Act of 1991: Balancing Legal and Business Interests," *Business Horizons* (March-April 1993), pp. 82–85.

61. Ibid., p. 84.

62. Title VII does not apply to foreign operations not owned or controlled by a U.S. employer, however.

63. This is based on Gregory Baxter, "Over There: Enforcing the 1991 Civil Rights Act Abroad," *Employee Relations Law Journal*, Vol. 19, no. 2 (Autumn 1993), pp. 257–266.

64. Ibid., p. 265.

65. Ibid.

66. Elliot H. Shaller and Dean Rosen, "A Guide to the EEOC's Final Regulations on the Americans with Disabilities Act," *Employee Relations*, Vol. 17, no. 3 (Winter 1991/92), pp. 405–430.

67. Bureau of National Affairs, "ADA: Simple Common Sense Principles," *Fair Employment Practices*, June 4, 1992, p. 63.

68. Shaller and Rosen, "A Guide to the EEOC's Final Regulations," p. 408.

69. Ibid., p. 409.

70. "No Sitting for Store Greeter," *BNA Fair Employment Practices*, December 14, 1995, p. 150.

71. "Reasonable Accommodation Issues in the Workplace," *BNA Fair Employment Practices*, June 12, 1997, p. 69.

72. *Palmer v. Circuit Court of Cook County, Illinois*, c7#95–3659–6/26/97; reviewed in "No Accommodation for Violent Employee," *BNA Fair Employment Practices*, July 10, 1997, p. 79.

73. *Miller v. Illinois Department of Corrections*, CA7, 1997, 6ad cases 678; reviewed in "Courts Define Parameters of the Americans with Disabilities Act," BNA *Fair Employment Practices*, March 20, 1997, p. 34.

74. *EEOC v. Wal-Mart Stores*, DC NMEX, 95–1199, 2/21/97; reviewed in *BNA Fair Employment Practices*, March 6, 1997, p. 30.

75. These are adapted from Wayne Barlow and Edward Hane, "A Practical Guide to the Americans with Disabilities Act," *Personnel Journal*, Vol. 72 (June 1992), p. 59.

76. "Tips for Employers with Asymptomatic HIV-Positive Employees," *BNA Fair Employment Practices*, November 27, 1997, p. 141.

77. *Krocka v. Bransfield*, DC NI11, #95C627, 6/24/97; reviewed in "Test for Prozac Violates ADA," *BNA Fair Employment Practices*, August 7, 1997, p. 91.

78. "EEOC Explains Legal Boundaries of Job Questions under ADA," *BNA Fair Employment Practices*, June 2, 1994, p. 63.

79. Elliot Shaller, "Reasonable Accommodation Under the Americans with Disabilities Act: What Does It Mean," *Employee Relations Law Journal*, Vol. 16, no. 4 (Spring 1991), pp. 445–446.

80. Ibid., p. 446. See also Michael Esposito, "Are You 100 Percent ADA-compliant?" *Management Review* (February 1993), pp. 27–29; and William R. Tracey, "Auditing ADA Compliance," *HR Magazine* (October 1994), pp. 88–90.

81. Ibid., p. 502.

82. James Ledvinka and Robert Gatewood, "EEO Issues with Preemployment Inquiries," *Personnel Administrator*, Vol. 22, no. 2 (February 1977), pp. 22–26.

83. These are based on Bureau of National Affairs, "A Wrap-up of State Legislation: 1988 Anti-bias Laws Focus on Aids," *Fair Employment Practices*, January 5, 1989, pp. 3–4.

84. "1996 State Anti-Bias Laws Focus on Harassment, Genetic Testing," *BNA Fair Employment Practices*, January 9, 1997, pp. 1–3.

85. John Klinfelter and James Thompkins, "Adverse Impact in Employment Selection," *Public Personnel Management* (May-June 1976), pp. 199–204.

86. H. John Bernardin, Richard Beatty, and Walter Jensin, "The New Uniform Guidelines on Employee Selection Procedures in the Context of University Personnel Decisions," *Personnel Psychology*, Vol. 33 (Summer 1980), pp. 301–316.

87. International Association of Official Human Rights Agencies, Principles of Employment Discrimination Law; James M. Higgins, "A Manager's Guide to the Equal Opportunity Laws," *Personnel*, Vol. 55 (August 1976); James Ledvinka, *Federal Regulation*.

88. *Usery v. Tamiami Trail Tours*, 12FEP cases 1233; see also Anderson and Levine-Epstein, *Primer of Equal Employment Opportunity*, p. 57.

89. *Professional Pilots Federation v. Federal Aviation Administration*, U.S. SUP CT #97–1267, cert. denied 5/18/98.

90. *Benjamin v. United Merchants and Manufacturers*, CA2, 1989, 49FEP cases 1020, discussed in Bureau of National Affairs, *Fair Employment Practices*, May 25, 1989, p. 61; Bureau of National Affairs, *Fair Employment Practices*, February 18, 1988, p. 19.

91. Ledvinka, *Federal Regulation*, p. 82. For a further discussion of religious and other types of accommodation and what they involve see, for example, Bureau of National Affairs, *Fair Employment Practices*, January 21, 1988, pp. 9–10; Bureau of National Affairs, *Fair Employment Practices*, April 14, 1988, pp. 45–46; and James G. Frierson, "Religion in the Work Place," *Personnel Journal*, Vol. 67, no. 7 (July 1988), pp. 60–67.

92. Ledvinka, *Federal Regulation*.

93. Anderson and Levin-Epstein, *Primer of Equal Employment Opportunity*, pp. 13–14.

94. *U.S. v. Bethlehem Steel Company*, 3FEP cases 589.

95. *Robinson v. Lorillard Corporation*, 3FEP cases 653.

96. *Spurlock v. United Airlines*, 5FEP cases 17.

97. Anderson and Levin-Epstein, *Primer of Equal Employment Opportunity*, p. 14.

98. Quoted in Wayne Cascio, *Applied Psychology in Personnel Management* (Reston, VA: Reston, 1978), p. 25.

99. *Firefighters Local 1784 v. Stotts* (BNA, April 14, 1985).

100. Ledvinka and Gatewood, "EEO Issues with Preemployment Inquiries," pp. 22–26.

101. Ibid.

102. Anderson and Levin-Epstein, *Primer of Equal Opportunity*, p. 27.

103. This is based on Anderson, Ibid., pp. 93–97.

104. This is based on Bureau of National Affairs, *Fair Employment Practices*, April 13, 1989, pp. 45–47.

105. Eric Matusewitch, "Tailor Your Dress Codes," *Personnel Journal*, Vol. 68, no. 2 (February 1989), pp. 86–91.

106. Even during President Reagan's administration—often viewed as a not particularly supportive period for equal rights enforcement in the United States—an EEOC press release dated June 13, 1988

says it filed 527 court actions during fiscal year 1987, "setting an agency record for legal activity and maintaining its high level of enforcement on behalf of persons discriminated against in the work place." The release continues: "A record high 430 lawsuits were filed on the merits of discrimination charges in fiscal 1987, topping the previous record of 427 direct suits and interventions filed in fiscal 1986. Cases filed under Title VII of the 1964 Civil Rights Act totaled 69 and 12 filings, respectively. Twenty-nine cases were filed concurrently under Title VII and ADEA or Title VII and EPA. Agency investigative subpoena enforcement actions totaled 97, slightly below the 99 filed in fiscal 1986." Furthermore, in fiscal 1987, "The commission resolved more cases of discrimination through litigation than ever before: 460 as compared to 386 in fiscal 1986, the previous record number of resolutions. Direct suits and interventions accounted for 357 of the resolutions and there were 103 subpoena enforcement actions." EEOC news release dated June 13, 1988, and titled "EEOC Continues Record Enforcement Pace in Fiscal Year 1987." Quoted in Commerce Clearing House, *Ideas and Trends*, June 28, 1988, pp. 101–102.

107. If the charge was filed initially with a state or local agency within 180 days after the alleged unlawful practice occurred, the charge may then be filed with the EEOC within 30 days after the practice occurred or within 30 days after the person received notice that the state or local agency has ended its proceedings.

108. Paul S. Greenlaw, "Reverse Discrimination: The Supreme Court's Dilemma," *Personnel Journal*, Vol. 67, no. 1 (January 1988), pp. 84–89.

109. John Wymer, III and Deborah Sudbury, "Employment Discrimination 'Testers'—Will Your Hiring Practices 'Pass'?" *Employee Relations Law Journal*, Vol. 17, no. 4 (Spring 1992), pp. 623–633.

110. Bureau of National Affairs, *Fair Employment Practices*, May 21, 1992, p. 59.

111. "Backlog of Pending EEOC Cases," *BNA Fair Employment Practices*, June 16, 1994, p. 67.

112. "Record Number of EEOC Charges Filed in Fiscal Year 1993," *BNA Fair Employment Practices*, January 27, 1994, p. 9.

113. "EEOC Reaps Record Benefits," *BNA Fair Employment Practices*, April 2, 1998, p. 37.

114. Robert H. Sheahan, "Responding to Employment Discrimination Charges," *Personnel Journal*, Vol. 60, no. 3 (March 1981), pp. 217–220; Wayne Baham, "Learn to Deal with Agency Investigations," *Personnel Journal*, Vol. 67, no. 9 (September 1988), pp. 104–107.

115. "Conducting Effective Investigations of Employee Bias Complaints," *BNA Fair Employment Practices*, July 13, 1995, p. 81.

116. Note, however, that there are certain general guidelines regarding the archival data your firm must periodically compile. See E. Bryan Kennedy, "Archival Data Must Be Accurate," *Personnel Journal*, Vol. 6, no. 11 (November 1988), pp. 108–111.

117. Based on Commerce Clearing House, *Ideas and Trends*, January 23, 1987, pp. 14–15.

118. "Tips for Employers on Dealing with EEOC Investigations," *BNA Fair Employment Practices*, October 31, 1996, p. 130.

119. Ibid., p. 219.

120. Ibid., p. 220.

121. Quoted from Bureau of National Affairs, *Fair Employment Practices*, February 9, 1984, p. 4.

122. Stuart Bonpey and Michael Pappas, "Is There a Better Way? Compulsory Arbitration of Employment Discrimination Claims After Gilmer," *Employee Relations Law Journal*, Vol. 19, no. 3 (Winter 1993–94), pp. 197–216.

123. Ibid., p. 200.

124. Ibid., p. 201.

125. These are based on Ibid., pp. 210–211.

126. Ibid., p. 210.

127. Ibid.

128. Ibid., p. 211.

129. "Preventing Costly Employment Discrimination Lawsuits," *BNA Fair Employment Practices*, September 8, 1994, p. 105.

130. "Preventing Costly Employment Discrimination Lawsuits," *BNA Fair Employment Practices*, September 9, 1994, p. 105.

131. David Nye, "When the Fired Fight Back," *Across-the-Board* (June 1995), pp. 31–34.

132. "EEOC Opposes Mandatory Arbitration," *BNA Fair Employment Practices*, July 24, 1997, p. 85.

133. James Coil, III and Charles Rice, "Managing Work-Force Diversity in the 90s: The Impact of the Civil Rights Act of 1991," *Employee Relations Law Journal*, Vol. 18, no. 4 (Spring 1993), pp. 547–565.

134. Michael Carrell and Everett Mann, "Defining Work Force Diversity in Public Sector Organizations," *Public Personnel Management*, Vol. 24, no. 1 (Spring 1995), pp. 99–111.

135. Taylor Cox, Jr., *Cultural Diversity in Organizations: Theory, Research and Practice* (San Francisco: Berrett- Koehler, 1993), p. 236.

136. Coil and Rice, "Managing Work-Force Diversity in the 90s," p. 548.

137. Ibid.

138. Ibid.

139. Ibid., pp. 562–563.

140. Ibid., p. 563.

141. Madeline Heilman, Winston McCullough, and David Gilbert, "The Other Side of Affirmative Action: Reactions of Nonbeneficiaries to Sex-Based Preferential Selection," *Journal of Applied Psychology*, Vol. 81, no. 4 (1996), pp. 346–357.

142. Ibid., p. 346.

143. U.S. Equal Employment Opportunity Commission, Affirmative Action and Equal Employment (Washington, DC: January 1974); Antonio Handler Chayes, "Make Your Equal Opportunity Program Court Proof," *Harvard Business Review* (September 1974), pp. 81–89.

144. This discussion is based on Kenneth Marino, "Conducting an Internal Compliance Review of Affirmative Action," *Personnel*, Vol. 59 (March-April 1980), pp. 24–34.

145. See Michael W. Sculnick, "The Supreme Court 1985–86 EEO Decisions: A Review," *Employment Relations Today*, Vol. 13, no. 3 (Fall 1986).

146. Ibid.

147. Ibid.

148. Ibid.

149. Aric Press and Ann McDaniel, "A Woman's Day in Court," *Newsweek*, April 6, 1987, pp. 58–59.

150. "Reverse Bias Case Settles," *BNA Fair Employment Practices*, November 27, 1997, p. 139.

151. Marino, "Conducting an Internal Compliance Review;" Lawrence Kleiman and Robert Faley, "Voluntary Affirmative Action and Preferential Treatment: Legal and Research Implications," *Personnel Psychology*, Vol. 42, no. 3 (Autumn 1988), pp. 481–496.

VIDEO CASE

SKILLS LIVE!

PART I
A CASE OF SEXUAL HARASSMENT

This first video, "A Case of Sexual Harassment," introduces some of the staff members at Quicktakes Video, a small television production company that produces short films and videos for various corporate and entrepreneurial clients. Quicktakes is owned by Hal Boylston, who manages most of the administrative tasks for the firm, and Karen Jarvis, who functions as the director of sales, managing the salespeople and bringing new clients to the firm.

The firm employs 40 people, among them script writers, producers, union actors (known in the business as "talent"), salespeople, editors, and support staff including clerical workers and accounting professionals. Its mission is fairly specialized, but you'll see in the video segments that its staff must deal with the same strategic, legal, and personal issues that people typically face in many work environments. The experiences of Quicktakes' employees will demonstrate why it's important for everyone to have basic human resource skills, whether the company has a formal Human Resource Department or not. (Quicktakes does not.) Quicktakes' products—customer videos—require the input and expertise of many different kinds of media professionals, so a good deal of the work that gets done is a team effort. Good human resource skills are important to foster teamwork, too.

Although Quicktakes is small, it does consider itself a global operation thanks to a small office it maintains in London to manage a growing European market. We'll meet the occupant of the London office in a later segment.

Part 1 presents Kim, Quicktakes' chief writer, and Brad, a successful Quicktakes salesperson. We'll also meet Hal Boylston and observe how he interacts with each of these employees when a conflict arises between them.

While you watch the video, keep in mind that, as you saw in Chapter 2, the Equal Employment Opportunity Commission (EEOC) charges employers with an affirmative duty to maintain a workplace free of sexual harassment and intimidation. Harassment on the basis of sex is a violation of Title VII (of the 1964 Civil Rights Act) when its purpose or effect is to substantially interfere with a person's work performance or to create a hostile work environment. Of particular concern to Hal should be the law's provision that an employer is liable for the sexually harassing acts of its nonsupervisory (or supervisory) employees if it knew or should have known about them.

QUESTIONS

1. Does it appear that Brad might have sexually harassed Kim? Why or why not?
2. If Kim believes she has been sexually harassed, how should she react now? Is there anything she should do that she has not done?
3. Hal has made at least one mistake already. What was it, and how can he correct it? How will that help him resolve the difference between Brad's and Kim's accounts of the reason for their disagreement?
4. Does the quality of Kim's work have any bearing on the eventual resolution?
5. In trying to resolve the issue, what weight should Hal give to Brad's skill at bringing in new business to the firm?

3

JOB ANALYSIS

erging Universal Music and Polygram meant more than just combining the likes of artists Erykah Badu, Marilyn Manson, Sheryl Crow, and U2. For months prior to the merger, consultants from Boston Consulting Group pored over the two companies' job descriptions, seeking ways to implement the cost-cutting strategy of the merged company's new owner, Seagram, Inc. Seagram knew that to make the merger work, savings of hundreds of millions of dollars per year would have to be obtained, in part by combining and consolidating jobs. One big task the BCG consultants therefore faced was analyzing what each person in each company was doing, and then developing new assignments—new jobs—for the people who remained, so that the merged goliath could work more efficiently. ▲

Behavioral Objectives

When you finish studying this chapter, you should be able to:

▲ *Describe* the basic methods of collecting job analysis information.
▲ *Conduct* a job analysis.
▲ *Write* a job description.
▲ *Explain* the purpose of a job specification and a procedure for developing one.

Chapter Outline

▲ The Nature of Job Analysis
▲ Methods of Collecting Job Analysis Information
▲ Writing Job Descriptions
▲ Writing Job Specifications
▲ Job Analysis in a "Jobless" World

THE NATURE OF
JOB ANALYSIS

job analysis

The procedure for determining the duties and skill requirements of a job and the kind of person who should be hired for it.

job description

A list of a job's duties, responsibilities, reporting relationships, working conditions, and supervisory responsibilities—one product of a job analysis.

job specification

A list of a job's "human requirements," that is, the requisite education, skills, personality, and so on—another product of a job analysis.

Job Analysis Defined

Organizations like Universal consist of positions that have to be staffed. **Job analysis** is the procedure through which you determine the duties of these positions and the characteristics of the people who should be hired for them.[1] The analysis produces information on job requirements; this information is then used for developing **job descriptions** (a list of what the job entails) and **job specifications** (a list of a job's human requirements, or what kind of people to hire for the job).

Like The Boston Consulting Group Consultants, a supervisor or HR specialist normally aims to collect one or more of the following types of information via the job analysis.[2]

Work activities. Information is usually collected about the actual work activities performed, such as cleaning, selling, teaching, or painting. Such a list may also indicate how, why, and when the worker performs each activity.

Human behaviors. Information about human behaviors like sensing, communicating, deciding, and writing may also be collected. Included here would be information regarding job demands such as lifting weights or walking long distances.

Machines, tools, equipment, and work aids used. Information is gathered regarding products made, materials processed, knowledge dealt with or applied (such as finance or law), and services rendered (such as counseling or repairing).

Performance standards. Information is also collected about performance standards (in terms of quantity or quality levels for each job duty, for instance). These standards will be the basis on which the employee will be evaluated.

Job context. Included here is information about such matters as physical working conditions, work schedule, and the organizational and social context—for instance, the number of people with whom the employee would normally interact. Information regarding incentives for doing the job might also be included here.

Human requirements. Finally, information is usually compiled regarding human requirements of the job, such as job-related knowledge or skills (education, training, work experience) and required personal attributes (aptitudes, physical characteristics, personality, interests).

Uses of Job Analysis Information

As summarized in Figure 3-1, job analysis information is the basis for several interrelated HR management activities, as follows.

RECRUITMENT AND SELECTION   For example, job analysis provides information about what the job entails and what human characteristics are required to carry out these activities. This description and job specification information is then used to decide what sort of people to recruit and hire.

COMPENSATION   Job analysis information is also essential for estimating the value of and appropriate compensation for each job. This is because compensation (such as salary and bonus) usually depends on such things as the job's required skill and education level, safety hazards, and degree of responsibility—all factors that are assessed through job analysis. We'll also see that many employers group jobs into classes (like Secretary III and IV). Job analysis provides the information for determining the relative worth of each job so that each job can be accurately classified.

PERFORMANCE APPRAISAL   A performance appraisal compares each employee's actual performance with his or her performance standards. It is often through job analysis

FIGURE 3-1

Uses of Job Analysis Information

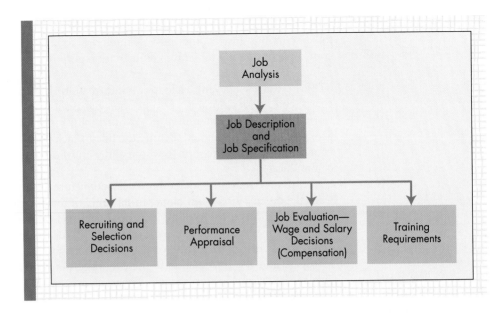

that experts determine the standards to be achieved and the specific activities to be performed.

TRAINING   Job analysis information is also used for designing training and development programs, because the analysis and resulting job description show the skills—and therefore the training—that are required.

ENSURE COMPLETE ASSIGNMENT OF DUTIES   Job analysis can also help discover unassigned duties. For example, in analyzing the job of your company's production manager, you may find she reports herself as being responsible for two dozen or so duties including planning weekly production schedules and purchasing raw materials. Missing, however, is any reference to managing raw material or finished goods inventories. On further investigation you find that none of the other manufacturing people is responsible for inventory management either. Your job analysis (based not just on what employees report as their duties, but on what you know these duties should be) has identified a duty to be assigned. Missing duties like this are often uncovered through job analysis. Job analysis thus plays a role in remedying the sort of problems that would arise if, for example, no one were assigned to manage inventories.

As you can see, job analysis plays a central role in HR management. This fact is acknowledged by the U.S. Federal Agencies Uniform Guidelines on Employee Selection, which stipulate that job analysis is a crucial step in validating all major personnel activities.[3] Employers must be able to show that their screening tools and appraisals are actually related to performance on the job in question. Doing this, of course, requires knowing what the job entails—which in turn requires a competent job analysis.

Steps in Job Analysis

There are six steps in doing a job analysis, as follows.

STEP 1   Identify the use to which the information will be put, since this will determine the data you collect and how you collect them. Some data collection techniques—like interviewing the employee and asking what the job entails—are good for writing job descriptions and selecting employees for the job. Other job analysis techniques (like the position analysis questionnaire described later) do not provide qualitative information for job descriptions. Instead, they provide numerical ratings for each job; these can be used to compare jobs to one another for compensation purposes.

STEP 2   Review relevant background information such as organization charts, process charts, and job descriptions.[4] *Organization charts* show the organizationwide division of work; how the job in question relates to other jobs; and where the job fits in the overall organization. The chart should identify the title of each position and, by means of its interconnecting lines, who reports to whom and with whom the job incumbent is expected to communicate.

A *process chart* provides a more detailed picture of the work flow than is obtainable from the organization chart alone. In its simplest form, a process chart (like the one in Figure 3-2) shows the flow of inputs to and outputs from the job being analyzed. (In Figure 3-2 the inventory control clerk is expected to receive inventory from suppliers; take requests for inventory from the two plant managers; provide requested inventory to these managers; and give information to these managers on the status of in-stock inventories.) Finally, the existing *job description*, if there is one, usually provides a starting point for building the revised job description.

STEP 3   Select representative positions to be analyzed. This is done when many similar jobs are to be analyzed, and it is too time consuming, for instance, to analyze the jobs of all assembly workers.

STEP 4   Next actually analyze the job, by collecting data on job activities, required employee behaviors, working conditions, and human traits and abilities needed to perform the job. For this step, use one or more of the job analysis methods explained later in this chapter.

STEP 5   Review the information with job incumbents. The job analysis information should be verified with the worker performing the job and with his or her immediate supervisor. This will help to confirm that the information is factually correct and complete. This review step can also help gain the employee's acceptance of the job analysis data and conclusions, by giving that person a chance to review and modify your description of his or her job activities.

FIGURE 3-2

Process Chart for Analyzing a Job's Work Flow

Source: Richard J. Henderson, *Compensation Management: Rewarding Performance*, 2nd ed., 1985, p. 158. Reprinted by permission of Prentice Hall, Upper Saddle River, NJ.

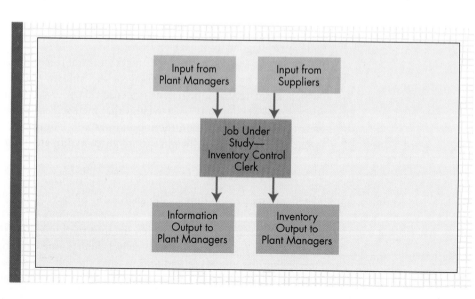

STEP 6   Develop a job description and job specification. A job description and a job specification are usually two concrete products of the job analysis. The *job description* (to repeat) is a written statement that describes the activities and responsibilities of the job, as well as important features of the job, such as working conditions and safety hazards. The *job specification* summarizes the personal qualities, traits, skills, and background required for getting the job done; it may be either in a separate document or on the same document as the job description.

METHODS OF COLLECTING JOB ANALYSIS INFORMATION

Introduction

There are various ways to collect information on the duties, responsibilities, and activities of the job, and we'll discuss the most important ones in this section. In practice, you could use any one of them or combine the techniques that best fit your purpose. Thus, an interview might be appropriate for creating a job description, whereas the position analysis questionnaire that we'll discuss is more appropriate for determining the worth of a job for compensation purposes.

Conducting the job analysis usually involves a joint effort by an HR specialist, the worker, and the worker's supervisor. The HR specialist (perhaps an HR manager, job analyst, or consultant) might observe and analyze the job and then develop a job description and specification. The supervisor and worker will also get involved, perhaps by filling out questionnaires listing the subordinate's activities. The supervisor and worker may then review and verify the job analyst's conclusions regarding the job's activities and duties. Popular methods for collecting job analysis information are discussed next.

The Interview

Three types of interviews are used to collect job analysis data—individual interviews with each employee, group interviews with groups of employees having the same job, and supervisor interviews with one or more supervisors who are thoroughly knowledgeable about the job being analyzed. The group interview is used when a large number of employees are performing similar or identical work, and it can be a quick and inexpensive way to learn about the job. As a rule, the workers' immediate supervisor would attend the group session; if not, you should interview the supervisor separately to get that person's perspective on the job's duties and responsibilities.

The job analysis process begins when the analyst collects information from the worker and supervisor about the nature of the work and the specific tasks to be done.

Whichever interview you use, the interviewee should fully understand the reason for the interview, since there's a tendency for such interviews to be viewed-rightly or wrongly as "efficiency evaluations." When they are, interviewees may not be willing to describe the jobs accurately.

PROS AND CONS   The interview is probably the most widely used method for determining a job's duties and responsibilities, and its wide use reflects its advantages. Most important, interviewing allows the worker to report activities and behaviors that might not otherwise come to light. For example, important activities that occur only occasionally, or informal communication (between, say, a production supervisor and the sales manager) that would not be obvious from the organization chart could be unearthed by a skilled interviewer. The interview also provides an opportunity to explain the need for and functions of the job analysis. And, it can let the employee vent frustrations or views that might otherwise go unnoticed by management. Interviews are also relatively simple and quick ways to collect information.

The major problem with interviews is distortion of information, whether due to outright falsification or honest misunderstandings.[5] Job analysis is often a prelude to changing a job's pay rate. Employees, therefore, sometimes (legitimately) view them as efficiency evaluations that may affect their pay. They may then tend to exaggerate certain responsibilities while minimizing others. Obtaining valid information can thus be a slow process, and it's useful to get multiple inputs.

TYPICAL QUESTIONS   Despite their drawbacks, interviews are widely used. Some typical interview questions include:

What is the job being performed?

What are the major duties of your position? What exactly do you do?

What physical locations do you work in?

What are the education, experience, skill, and (where applicable) certification and licensing requirements?

What activities do you participate in?

What are the job's responsibilities and duties?

What are the basic accountabilities or performance standards that typify your work?

What are your responsibilities? What are the environmental and working conditions involved?

What are the job's physical demands? The emotional and mental demands?

What are the health and safety conditions?

Are you exposed to any hazards or unusual working conditions?

Most fruitful interviews follow a structured or checklist format. One such *job analysis questionnaire* is presented in Figure 3-3. It includes a series of detailed questions regarding such matters as the general purpose of the job; supervisory responsibilities; job duties; and education, experience, and skills required. A list like this can also be used by a job analyst who collects information by personally observing the work being done or by administering it as a questionnaire, two methods that will be explained shortly.[6]

INTERVIEW GUIDELINES   There are several things to keep in mind when conducting a job analysis interview. First, the job analyst and supervisor should work together. Identify the workers who know the most about the job, as well as those who might be expected to be the most objective in describing their duties and responsibilities.

FIGURE 3-3

Job Analysis Questionnaire for Developing Job Descriptions

A questionnaire like this one can be used to interview job incumbents or may be filled out by them.

Source: Douglas Bartley, *Job Evaluation: Wage and Salary Administration* (Reading, MA: Addison-Wesley Publishing Company, 1981), pp. 101–103.

JOB QUESTIONNAIRE
KANE MANUFACTURING COMPANY

NAME _____   JOB TITLE _____

DEPARTMENT _____   JOB NUMBER _____

SUPERVISOR'S NAME _____   SUPERVISOR'S TITLE _____

1. *SUMMARY OF DUTIES*: State in your own words briefly your main duties. If you are responsible for filling out reports/records, also complete Section 8.

2. *SPECIAL QUALIFICATIONS*: List any licenses, permits, certifications, etc. required to perform duties assigned to your position.

3. *EQUIPMENT*: List any equipment, machines, or tools (e.g., typewriter, calculator, motor vehicles, lathes, fork lifts, drill presses, etc.) you normally operate as a part of your position's duties.

        MACHINE   *AVERAGE NO. HOURS PER WEEK*

4. *REGULAR DUTIES*: In general terms, describe duties you regularly perform. Please list these duties in descending order of importance and percent of time spent on them per month. List as many duties as possible and attach additional sheets, if necessary.

5. *CONTACTS*: Does your job require any contacts with other department personnel, other departments, outside companies or agencies? If yes, please define the duties requiring contacts and *how often*.

6. *SUPERVISION*: Does your position have supervisory responsibilities? ( ) Yes ( ) No. If yes, please fill out a *Supplemental Position Description Questionnaire for Supervisors* and attach it to this form. If you have responsibility for the work of others but do not directly supervise them, please explain.

7. *DECISION MAKING*: Please explain the decisions you make while performing the regular duties of your job.

(continued)

(continued from page 89)

(a) What would be the probable result of your making (a) poor judgment(s) or decision(s), or (b) improper actions?

_____

_____

8. *RESPONSIBILITY FOR RECORDS:* List the reports and files you are required to prepare or maintain. State, in general, for whom each report is intended.

(a)   *REPORT*   *INTENDED FOR*

_____

_____

(b)   *FILES MAINTAINED*

_____

_____

9. *FREQUENCY OF SUPERVISION:* How frequently must you confer with your supervisor or other personnel in making decisions or in determining the proper course of action to be taken?

(   ) Frequently   (   ) Occasionally   (   ) Seldom   (   ) Never

10. *WORKING CONDITIONS:* Please describe the conditions under which you work— inside, outside, air conditioned area, etc. Be sure to list any disagreeable or unusual working conditions.

_____

_____

11. *JOB REQUIREMENTS:* Please indicate the minimum requirements you believe are neccessary to perform satisfactorily in your position.

(a) Education:
Minimum schooling _____
Number of years _____
Specialization or major _____

(b) Experience:
Type _____
Number of years _____

(c) Special training:

TYPE   *NUMBER OF YEARS*

_____

_____

(d) Special Skills:
Typing: _____ w.p.m.   Shorthand _____ w.p.m.
Other: _____

12. *ADDITIONAL INFORMATION:* Please provide additional information, not included in any of the previous items, which you feel would be important in a description of your position.

_____

_____

_____

EMPLOYEE'S SIGNATURE _____   DATE: _____

Second, establish rapport quickly with the interviewee by knowing the person's name, speaking in easily understood language, briefly reviewing the purpose of the interview, and explaining how the person came to be chosen for the interview.

Third, follow a structured guide or checklist, one that lists questions and provides space for answers. This ensures that you'll identify crucial questions ahead of time and that all interviewers (if there are more than one) cover all the required questions. However, make sure to also give the worker some leeway in answering questions and provide some open-ended questions like, "Was there anything we didn't cover with our questions?"

Fourth, when duties are not performed in a regular manner—for instance, when the worker doesn't perform the same job over and over again many times a day—you should ask the worker to list his or her duties *in order of importance* and *frequency* of occurrence. This will ensure that crucial activities that occur infrequently—like a nurse's occasional emergency room duties—aren't overlooked.

Finally, after completing the interview, review and verify the data. This is normally done by reviewing the information with the worker's immediate supervisor and with the interviewee.

Questionnaires

Having employees fill out questionnaires to describe their job-related duties and responsibilities is another good way to obtain job analysis information.

The main thing to decide here is how structured the questionnaire should be and what questions to include. Some questionnaires are very structured checklists. Each employee is presented with an inventory of perhaps hundreds of specific duties or tasks (such as "change and splice wire"). He or she is asked to indicate whether or not he or she performs each task and, if so, how much time is normally spent on each. At the other extreme, the questionnaire can be open ended and simply ask the employee to "describe the major duties of your job." In practice, the best questionnaire often falls between these two extremes. As illustrated in Figure 3-3, a typical job analysis questionnaire might have several open-ended questions (such as "state your main job duties") as well as structured questions (concerning, for instance, previous experience required).

Whether structured or unstructured, questionnaires have both pros and cons. A questionnaire is a quick and efficient way to obtain information from a large number of employees; it's less costly than interviewing hundreds of workers, for instance. However, developing the questionnaire and testing it (perhaps by making sure the workers understand the questions) can be expensive and time consuming.

Observation

Direct observation is especially useful when jobs consist mainly of observable physical activity. Jobs like those of janitor, assembly-line worker, and accounting clerk are examples. On the other hand, observation is usually not appropriate when the job entails a lot of unmeasurable mental activity (lawyer, design engineer). Nor is it useful if the employee engages in important activities that might occur only occasionally, such as a nurse who handles emergencies. And *reactivity*—the worker's changing what he or she normally does because you are watching—can also be a problem.

Direct observation and interviewing are often used together. One approach is to observe the worker on the job during a complete work cycle. (The cycle is the time it takes to complete the job; it could be a minute for an assembly-line worker or an hour, a day, or longer for complex jobs.) Here you take notes of all the job activities you observe. Then, after accumulating as much information as possible, you interview the workers. The person is asked to clarify points not understood and explain what other activities he or she performs that you didn't observe. You can also observe and interview simultaneously, while the worker performs his or her job.

Participant Diary/Logs

Another approach is to ask workers to keep a **diary/log** or list of what they do during the day. For every activity he or she engages in, the employee records the activity (along with the time) in a log. This can produce a very complete picture of the job, especially when supplemented with subsequent interviews with the worker and his or her supervisor. The employee might, of course, try to exaggerate some activities and underplay others. However, the detailed, chronological nature of the log tends to mediate against this.

Some firms today take a high-tech approach to diary/logs. They give employees pocket dictating machines and pagers. Then, at random times during the day they page the workers, who dictate what they are doing at that time. This approach can avoid one pitfall of the traditional diary/log method, namely relying on the worker to remember what he or she did when the log is filled out at the end of the day.

Interviews, questionnaires, observations, and diary/logs are the most popular methods for gathering job analysis data. They all provide realistic information about what job incumbents actually do. They can thus be used for developing job descriptions and job specifications.

U.S. Civil Service Procedure

The U.S. Civil Service Commission job analysis technique provides a standardized procedure by which different jobs can be compared and classified. With this method the information is compiled on a *job analysis record sheet*. Here, as shown in Figure 3-4, identifying information (like job title) and a brief summary of the job are listed first. Next the analyst lists the job's specific tasks in order of importance. Then, *for each task*, the analyst specifies the:

1. Knowledge required (for example, the facts or principles the worker must be acquainted with to do his or her job).
2. Skills required (for example, the skills needed to operate machines or vehicles).
3. Abilities required (for example, mathematical, reasoning, problem-solving, or interpersonal abilities).
4. Physical activities involved (for example, pulling, pushing, or carrying).
5. Any special environmental conditions (cramped quarters, vibration, inadequate ventilation, noise, or moving objects).
6. Typical work incidents (for example, performing under stress in emergencies, working with people beyond giving and receiving instructions, or performing repetitive work).
7. Worker interests areas (the preferences the worker should have for activities dealing with things and objects, or the communication of data, or dealing with people, for example).[7]

In Figure 3-4, for example, the first task listed for a "welfare eligibility examiner" is "decide (determine) eligibility of applicant in order to complete client's application for food stamps using regulatory policies as guide." Beneath this task are listed the analyst's conclusions concerning the knowledge a welfare eligibility examiner is required to have; any special skills or abilities; types of physical activities involved in this task; special environmental conditions; typical work incidents; and the sorts of interests that would corre-

JOB ANALYSIS RECORD SHEET

IDENTIFYING INFORMATION

        Name of Incumbent: A. Adler
        Organization/Unit: Welfare Services
        Title: Welfare Eligibility Examiner
        Date: 11/12/98
        Interviewer: E. Jones

BRIEF SUMMARY OF JOB

Conducts interviews, completes applications, determines eligibility, provides information to community sources regarding food stamp program; refers noneligible food stamp applicants to other applicable community resource agencies.

TASKS*

1. Decide (determine) eligibility of applicant in order to complete client's application for food stamps using regulatory policies as guide.

   Knowledge Required
   —Knowledge of contents and meaning of items on standard application form
   —Knowledge of Social-Health Services food stamp regulatory policies
   —Knowledge of statutes relating to Social-Health Services food stamp program

   Skills Required
   —None

   Abilities Required
   —Ability to read and understand complex instructions such as regulatory policies
   —Ability to read and understand a variety of procedural instructions, written and oral, and convert these to proper actions
   —Ability to use simple arithmetic: addition and subtraction
   —Ability to translate requirements into language appropriate to laymen

   Physical Activities
   —Sedentary

   Environmental Conditions
   —None

   Typical Work Incidents
   —Working with people beyond giving and receiving instructions

   Interest Areas
   —Communication of data
   —Business contact with people
   —Working for the presumed good of people

2. Decides upon, describes, and explains other agencies available for client to contact in order to assist and refer client to appropriate community resource using worker's knowledge of resources available and knowledge of client's needs.

   Knowledge Required
   —Knowledge of functions of various assistance agencies
   —Knowledge of community resources available and their locations
   —Knowledge of referral procedures

   Skills Required
   —None

   Abilities Required
   —Ability to extract (discern) persons' needs from oral discussion
   —Ability to give simple oral and written instructions to persons

   Physical Activities
   —Sedentary

   Environmental Conditions
   —None

   Typical Work Incidents
   —Working with people beyond giving and receiving instructions

   Interest Areas
   —Communication of data
   —Business contact with people
   —Abstract and creative problem solving
   —Working for the presumed good of people

*This job might typically involve five or six tasks. For *each* task, list the knowledge, skill abilities, physical activities, environmental conditions, typical work incidents, and interest areas.

FIGURE 3-4 *Portion of a Completed Civil Service Job Analysis Record Sheet*

spond to this task. The analyst would typically use his or her own knowledge of the job as well as information obtained through interviews, observations, logs, or questionnaires in completing the job analysis record sheet.

Almost any job can be broken into its component tasks, each of which can then be analyzed in terms of knowledge required, skills required, and so forth. The Civil Service procedure thus provides a standardized method by which different jobs can be compared and classified. In other words, the knowledge, skills, and abilities required to perform, say, an assistant fire chief's job can be compared with those required to perform a librarian's job. If the requirements are similar, the jobs might be classified together for, say, pay purposes.

Quantitative Job Analysis Techniques

Although most employers use interviews, questionnaires, observations, or diary/logs for collecting job analysis data, there are many times when these narrative approaches are not appropriate. For example, when your aim is to assign a quantitative value to each job so the jobs can be compared for pay purposes, a more quantitative job analysis approach may be best. The position analysis questionnaire, the Department of Labor approach, and functional job analysis are three popular quantitative methods.

position analysis questionnaire (PAQ)

A questionnaire used to collect quantifiable data concerning the duties and responsibilities of various jobs.

POSITION ANALYSIS QUESTIONNAIRE   The **position analysis questionnaire (PAQ)** is a very structured job analysis questionnaire.[8] The PAQ itself is filled in by a job analyst, a person who should already be acquainted with the particular job to be analyzed. The PAQ contains 194 items, each of which (such as "written materials") represent a basic element that may or may not play an important role in the job. The job analyst decides whether each item plays a role on the job and, if so, to what extent. In Figure 3-5, for example, "written materials" received a rating of 4, indicating that written materials (like books, reports, and office notes) play a considerable role in this job.

The advantage of the PAQ is that it provides a quantitative score or profile of any job in terms of how that job rates on five basic job activities: (1) having decision-making/communications/social responsibilities, (2) performing skilled activities, (3) being physically active, (4) operating vehicles/equipment, and (5) processing information. The PAQ's real strength is thus in classifying jobs. In other words, it lets you assign a quantitative score to each job based on its decision-making, skilled activities, physical activity, vehicle/equipment operation, and information-processing characteristics. You can therefore use the PAQ results to compare jobs relative to one another,[9] and can then assign pay levels for each job.[10]

Department of Labor job analysis

Standardized method for rating, classifying, and comparing virtually every kind of job based on data, people, and things.

DEPARTMENT OF LABOR (DOL) PROCEDURE   The U.S. **Department of Labor (DOL)** procedure also aims to provide a standardized method by which different jobs can be quantitatively rated, classified, and compared. The heart of this type of analysis is a rating of each job in terms of what an employee does with respect to data, people, and things.

The basic procedure is as follows: As illustrated in Table 3-1 (page 96), a set of basic activities called *worker functions* describes what a worker can do with respect to data, people, and things. With respect to data, for instance, the basic functions include synthesizing, coordinating, and copying. With respect to people, they include mentoring, negotiating, and supervising. With respect to things, the basic functions include manipulating, tending, and handling. Note also that each worker function has been assigned an importance level. Thus, "coordinating" is 1, whereas "copying" is 5. If you were analyzing the job of a receptionist/clerk, for example, you might label the job 5, 6, 7, which would represent copying data, speaking-signaling people, and handling things. On the other hand, a

FIGURE 3-5

Portions of a Completed Page from the Position Analysis Questionnaire

Source: E. J. McCormick, P. R. Jeanneret, and R. D. Mecham, *Position Analysis Questionnaire.* Copyright 1989 by *Purdue Research Foundation,* West Lafayette, IN. Reprinted with permission.

INFORMATION INPUT

1 INFORMATION INPUT

	Extent of Use (U)
NA	Does not apply
1	Nominal/very infrequent
2	Occasional
3	Moderate
4	Considerable
5	Very substantial

1.1 Sources of Job Information

Rate each of the following items in terms of the extent to which it is used by the worker as a source of information in performing his job.

1.1.1 Visual Sources of Job Information

1 | 4 | Written materials (books, reports, office notes, articles, job instructions, signs, etc.)

2 | 2 | Quantitative materials (materials which deal with quantities or amounts, such as graphs, accounts, specifications, tables of numbers, etc.)

3 | 1 | Pictorial materials (pictures or picturelike materials used as *sources* of information, for example, drawings, blueprints, diagrams, maps, tracings, photographic films, x-ray films, TV pictures, etc.)

4 | 1 | Patterns/related devices (templates, stencils, patterns, etc., used as *sources* of information when *observed* during use; do *not* include here materials described in item 3 above)

5 | 2 | Visual displays (dials, gauges, signal lights, radarscopes, speedometers, clocks, etc.)

6 | 5 | Measuring devices (rulers, calipers, tire pressure gauges, scales, thickness gauges, pipettes, thermometers, protractors, etc., used to obtain visual information about physical measurements; do *not* include here devices described in item 5 above)

7 | 4 | Mechanical devices (tools, equipment, machinery, and other mechanical devices which are *sources* of information when *observed* during use or operation)

8 | 3 | Materials in process (parts, materials, objects, etc., which are *sources* of information when being modified, worked on, or otherwise processed, such as bread dough being mixed, workpiece being turned in a lathe, fabric being cut, shoe being resoled, etc.)

9 | 4 | Materials *not* in process (parts, materials, objects, etc., not in the process of being changed or modified, which are *sources* of information when being inspected, handled, packaged, distributed, or selected, etc., such as items or materials in inventory, storage, or distribution channels, items being inspected, etc.)

10 | 3 | Features of nature (landscapes, fields, geological samples, vegetation, cloud formations, and other features of nature which are observed or inspected to provide information)

11 | 2 | Man-made features of environment (structures, buildings, dams, highways, bridges, docks, railroads, and other "man-made" or altered aspects of the indoor or outdoor environment which are *observed* or *inspected* to provide job information; do not consider equipment, machines, etc., that an individual uses in his work, as covered by item 7)

Note: The 194 PAQ elements are grouped into six dimensions. This exhibits 11 of the "information input" questions or elements. Other PAQ pages contain questions regarding mental processes, work output, relationships with others, job context, and other job characteristics.

---

psychiatric aide in a hospital might be coded 1, 7, 5 in relation to data, people, and things. In practice, each task that the worker performed would be analyzed in terms of data, people, and things. Then the highest combination (say 4, 6, 5) would be used to identify the job, since this is the highest level that a job incumbent would be expected to attain.

As illustrated in Figure 3-6, the summary produced from the DOL procedure contains several types of information. The job title, in this case dough mixer in a bakery, is listed first. Also listed are the industry in which this job is found and the industry's stan-

TABLE 3-1 Basic Department of Labor Worker Functions

	DATA	PEOPLE	THINGS
Basic Activities	0 Synthesizing 1 Coordinating 2 Analyzing 3 Compiling 4 Computing 5 Copying 6 Comparing	0 Mentoring 1 Negotiating 2 Instructing 3 Supervising 4 Diverting 5 Persuading 6 Speaking—signaling 7 Serving 8 Taking instructions—helping	0 Setting up 1 Precision working 2 Operating—controlling 3 Driving—operating 4 Manipulating 5 Tending 6 Feeding—offbearing 7 Handling

Note: Determine employee's job "score" on data, people, and things by observing his or her job and determining, for each of the three categories, which of the basic functions illustrates the person's job. "0" is high, "6," "8," and "7" are lows in each column.

dard industrial classification code. There is a one- or two-sentence summary of the job, and the worker function ratings for data, people, and things (in this case 5, 6, 2). This indicates that in terms of difficulty level, a dough mixer in a bakery is expected to copy data, speak-signal with people, and operate-control with respect to things. Finally, the human requirements of the job are specified, for instance, in terms of training time required, apti-

FIGURE 3-6

Sample Report Based on Department of Labor Job Analysis Technique

JOB ANALYSIS SCHEDULE

1. Established Job Title _____ DOUGH MIXER _____

2. Ind. Assign _____ (bake prod.) _____

3. SIC Code(s) and Title(s) _____ 2051 Bread and other bakery products _____

4. JOB SUMMARY:

Operates mixing machine to mix ingredients for straight and sponge (yeast) doughs according to established formulas, directs other workers in fermentation of dough, and curls dough into pieces with hand cutter.

5. WORK PERFORMED RATINGS:

Worker Functions	D Data	P People	(T) Things
	5	6	2

Work Field _____ Cooking, Food Preparing _____

6. WORKER TRAITS RATING: (To be filled in by analyst)

Training time required
Aptitudes
Temperaments
Interests
Physical Demands
Environment Conditions

tudes, and temperaments. As you can see, each job analyzed ends up with a numerical score (such as 5, 6, 2). All jobs with similar scores can thus be grouped together and paid the same, even if one job is dough mixer and another mechanics helper.

functional job analysis

A method for classifying jobs similar to the Department of Labor job analysis but additionally taking into account the extent to which instructions, reasoning, judgment, and verbal facility are necessary for performing job tasks.

FUNCTIONAL JOB ANALYSIS   **Functional job analysis** is based on the DOL method but differs in two ways.[11] First, functional job analysis rates the job not just on data, people, and things, but also on four other dimensions: the extent to which specific instructions are necessary to perform the task; the extent to which reasoning and judgment are required to perform the task; the mathematical ability required to perform the task; and the verbal and language facilities required to perform the task. Second, functional job analysis also identifies performance standards and training requirements. Functional Job Analysis therefore lets you answer the question, "To do this task and meet these standards, what training does the worker require?"

Figure 3-7 illustrates a completed functional job analysis summary sheet. In this case the job is that of grader (a type of heavy-equipment operator employed in road building). As illustrated, the functional job analysis specifies things, data, people, instructions, reasoning, math, and language ratings. The summary sheet also lists the main tasks in the job, performance standards, and training required.

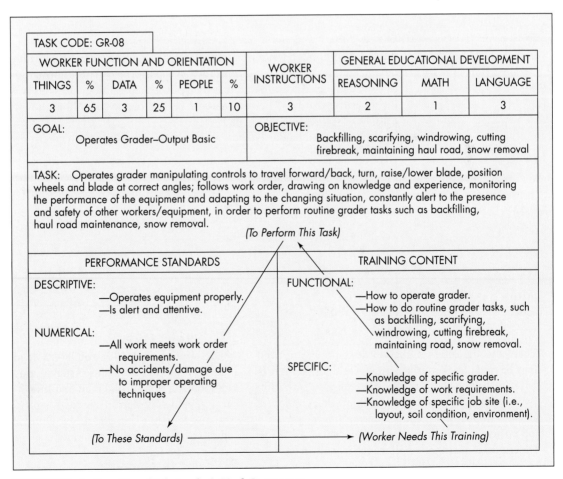

FIGURE 3-7 *Functional Job Analysis Task Statement*

Source: Howard Olson, Sidney A. Fine, David C. Myers, and Margarette C. Jennings, "The Use of Functional Job Analysis in Establishing Performance for Heavy Equipment Operators," *Personnel Psychology,* Summer 1981, p. 354.

Getting Multiple Perspectives Is Advisable

We've seen on the last few pages that there are many ways to obtain job analysis information. The information may be obtained from individual workers or from groups; from supervisors; or from the observations of job analysts, for instance. Several tools including interviews, observations, or questionnaires of one sort or another can also be used. Most firms tend to focus on using one basic approach—like having the job analyst do interviews with current job incumbents.

RESEARCH INSIGHT   Yet a recent study suggests that using just one source may not be a good thing.[12] The fact that human judgment is subject to potential sources of inaccuracy is fairly well known. For example, group members often feel forced to go along with the consensus of the group; or an employee may be careless about how he or she completes a questionnaire. What this means is that collecting job analysis data from just interviews, or just observations, for instance, may lead to inaccurate conclusions. It's better to take steps to help "cancel out" or avoid such inaccuracies by using several sources.[13] For example: Collect job analysis data from several types of respondents—groups, individuals, observation, supervisors, and analyst—where possible; make sure the questions and surveys are clear and understandable to the respondent; and, if possible, observe and question respondents early in the job analysis process to help catch such problems while it's still early enough to rectify them.

| WRITING JOB DESCRIPTIONS | A job description is a written statement of what the jobholder actually does, *how* he or she does it, and under what conditions the job is performed. This information is in turn used to write a job specification that lists the knowledge, abilities, and skills needed to perform the job satisfactorily. (The Information Technology feature shows how the Internet can help.) |

There is no standard format you must use in writing a job description, but most descriptions contain sections on:

1. Job identification
2. Job summary
3. Responsibilities and duties
4. Authority of incumbent

INFORMATION TECHNOLOGY AND HR

Thanks to the Internet, the job description you need may be just a few keystrokes away. For example, *Workforce* magazine has a Website called Post-A-Job (www.workforceonline.com/postajob/) that employers can use to post job openings on the Internet. To aid job posters, the site has a page called "Write Your Job Descriptions Online." Following it will take you to a site called Descriptions Now! Direct, at www. jobdescription.com. Here you'll be able to choose (for a fee) the job title you're interested in, pull up the relevant job description, and then fine-tune it, if you wish.

The description in Figure 3-8 on page 100—in this case for a Marketing Manager—provides an example. As you can see, the description is quite complete and includes such essential elements as Summary, Duties, and the human qualifications for the job.

5. Standards of performance
6. Working conditions
7. Job specifications

Examples of job descriptions are presented in Figures 3-8 and 3-9 on pages 100–101.

Job Identification

As in Figure 3-8, the job identification section contains several types of information.[14] The *job title* specifies the title of the job, such as supervisor of data processing operations, marketing manager, or inventory control clerk. Job titles and descriptions should be kept current, and the Department of Labor's *Dictionary of Occupational Titles* can be useful in this regard. It lists titles for thousands of jobs (as well as lists of job duties for each). The *job status* section permits quick identification of the exempt or nonexempt status of the job. (Under the Fair Labor Standards Act certain positions, primarily administrative and professional, are exempt from the act's overtime and minimum wage provisions.) The date refers to the date the job description was actually written, and "prepared by" indicates the person who wrote it. There is also space to indicate who approved the description and perhaps a space that shows the location of the job in terms of its plant/division and department/section. The immediate supervisor's title is sometimes shown in the identification section, as is information regarding the job's salary and/or pay scale. There might also be a grade/level space that indicates the grade or level of the job if there is such a category; for example, a firm may classify programmers as programmer II, programmer III, and so on.

Job Summary

The *job summary* should describe the general nature of the job, listing only its major functions or activities. Thus (in Figure 3-8), the marketing manager "Plans, directs, and coordinates the marketing of the organizations products and/or services." For the job of materials manager, the summary might state that the "materials manager purchases economically, regulates deliveries of, stores, and distributes all material necessary on the production line." For the job of mailroom supervisor, "the mailroom supervisor receives, sorts, and delivers all incoming mail properly, and he or she handles all outgoing mail including the accurate and timely posting of such mail."[15]

Try to avoid including a general statement like "performs other assignments as required." Including such a statement can give supervisors more flexibility in assigning duties. However, some experts state unequivocally that "one item frequently found that should *never* be included in a job description is a 'cop-out clause' like 'other duties, as assigned'"[16] since this leaves open the nature of the job—and the people needed to staff it.

Relationships

There is occasionally a relationships statement (not in the example), which shows the jobholder's relationship with others inside and outside the organization, and might look like this for a human resource manager:[17]

Reports to: vice president of employee relations.

Supervises: human resource clerk, test administrator, labor relations director, and one secretary.

Works with: all department managers and executive management.

Outside the company: employment agencies, executive recruiting firms, union representatives, state and federal employment offices, and various vendors.[18]

OLEC CORP.
Job Description

Job Title:	Marketing Manager
Department:	Marketing
Reports To:	President
FLSA Status:	Non Exempt
Prepared By:	Michael George
Prepared Date:	April 1, 1997
Approved By:	Ian Alexander
Approved Date:	April 15, 1997

SUMMARY

Plans, directs, and coordinates the marketing of the organization's products and/or services by performing the following duties personally or through subordinate supervisors.

ESSENTIAL DUTIES AND RESPONSIBILITIES include the following. Other duties may be assigned.

Establishes marketing goals to ensure share of market and profitability of products and/or services.

Develops and executes marketing plans and programs, both short and long range, to ensure the profit growth and expansion of company products and/or services.

Researches, analyzes, and monitors financial, technological, and demographic factors so that market opportunities may be capitalized on and the effects of competitive activity may be minimized.

Plans and oversees the organization's advertising and promotion acitivities including print, electronic, and direct mail outlets.

Communicates with outside advertising agencies on ongoing campaigns.

Works with writers and artists and oversees copywriting, design, layout, pasteup, and production of promotional materials.

Develops and recommends pricing strategy for the organization which will result in the greatest share of the market over the long run.

Achieves satisfactory profit/loss ratio and share of market performance in relation to pre-set standards and to general and specific trends within the industry and the economy.

Ensures effective control of marketing results and that corrective action takes place to be certain that the achievement of marketing objectives are within designated budgets.

Evaluates market reactions to advertising programs, merchandising policy, and product packaging and formulation to ensure the timely adjustment of marketing strategy and plans to meet changing market and competitive conditions.

Recommends changes in basic structure and organization of marketing group to ensure the effective fulfillment of objectives assigned to it and provide the flexibiltiy to move swiftly in relation to marketing problems and opportunities.

Conducts marketing surveys on current and new product concepts.

Prepares marketing activity reports.

SUPERVISORY RESPONSIBILITIES

Manages three subordinate supervisors who supervise a total of five employees in the Marketing Department. Is responsible for the overall direction, coordination, and evaluation of this unit. Also directly supervises two non-supervisory employees. Carries out supervisory responsibilities in accordance with the organization's policies and applicable laws. Responsibilites include interviewing, hiring, and training employees; planning, assigning, and directing work; appraising performance; rewarding and disciplining employees; addressing complaints and resolving problems.

QUALIFICATIONS

To perform this job successfully, an individual must be able to perform each essential duty satisfactorily. The requirements listed below are representative of the knowledge, skill, and/or ability required. Reasonable accommodations may be made to enable individuals with disabilities to perform the essential functions.

EDUCATION and/or EXPERIENCE

Master's degree (M.A.) or equivalent; or four to ten years related experience and/or training; or equivalent combination of education and experience.

LANGUAGE SKILLS

Ability to read, analyze, and interpret common scientific and technical journals, financial reports, and legal documents. Ability to respond to common inquiries or complaints from customers, regulatory agencies, or members of the business community. Ability to write speeches and articles for publication that conform to prescribed style and format. Ability to efffectively present information to top management, public groups, and/or boards of directors.

MATHEMATICAL SKILLS

Ability to apply advanced mathematical concepts such as exponents, logarithms, quadratic equations, and permutations. Ability to apply mathematical operations to such tasks as frequency distribution, determination of test reliability and validity, analysis of variance, correlation techniques, sampling theory, and factor analysis.

REASONING ABILITY

Ability to define problems, collect data, establish facts, and draw valid conclusions. Ability to interpret an extensive variety of technical instructions in mathematical or diagram form.

FIGURE 3-8 *Sample Job Description*

**166.117–018   MANAGER, PERSONNEL (profess. & kin.) alternate titles:
                 manager, human resources**

Plans and carries out policies relating to all phases of personnel activity: Recruits, interviews, and selects employees to fill vacant positions. Plans and conducts new employee orientation to foster positive attitude toward company goals. Keeps record of insurance coverage, pension plan, and personnel transactions, such as hires, promotions, transfers, and terminations. Investigates accidents and prepares reports for insurance carrier. Conducts wage survey within labor market to determine competitive wage rate. Prepares budget of personnel operations. Meets with shop stewards and supervisors to resolve grievances. Writes separation notices for employees separating with cause and conducts exit interviews to determine reasons behind separations. Prepares reports and recommends procedures to reduce absenteeism and turnover. Represents company at personnel-related hearings and investigations. Contracts with outside suppliers to provide employee services, such as canteen, transportation, or relocation service. May prepare budget of personnel operations, using computer terminal. May administer manual and dexterity tests to applicants. May supervise clerical workers. May keep records of hired employee characteristics for governmental reporting purposes. May negotiate collective bargaining agreement with BUSINESS REPRESENTATIVE, LABOR UNION (profess. & kin.) *187.167–018. GOE: 11.05.02 STRENGTH: S GED: R5 M5 L5 SVP: 8 DLU: 88*

FIGURE 3-9   *"Personnel Manager" Description from* Dictionary of Occupational Titles

Source: *Dictionary of Occupational Titles,* 4th ed. (Washington, DC: U.S. Department of Labor, Employment Training Administration, U.S. Employment Service, 1991.

Responsibilities and Duties

This section presents a list of the job's major responsibilities and duties. As in Figure 3-8, each of the job's major duties should be listed separately and described in a few sentences. In the figure, for instance, the duties include "establishes marketing goals to ensure share of market . . .," "develops and executes marketing plans and programs," "communicates with outside advertising agencies," and "develops and recommends pricing strategy." Typical duties for other jobs might include maintaining balanced and controlled inventories, making accurate postings to accounts payable, maintaining favorable purchase price variances, and repairing production line tools and equipment.

You can use the Department of Labor's *Dictionary of Occupational Titles* here for itemizing the job's duties and responsibilities. As shown in Figure 3-9, for example, the dictionary lists a human resource manager's specific duties and responsibilities. These include "plans and carries out policies relating to all phases of personnel activity"; "recruits, interviews, and selects employees to fill vacant positions"; and "conducts wage surveys within labor markets to determine competitive wage rate."

This section should also define the limits of the jobholder's authority, including his or her decision-making authority, direct supervision of other personnel, and budgetary limitations. For example, the jobholder might have authority to approve purchase requests up to $5,000, grant time off or leaves of absence, discipline department personnel, recommend salary increases, and interview and hire new employees.[19]

Standards of Performance

Some job descriptions contain a standards of performance section. This states the standards the employee is expected to achieve under each of the job description's main duties and responsibilities.

Setting standards is never an easy matter. However, most managers soon learn that just telling subordinates to "do their best" doesn't provide enough guidance to ensure top performance. One straightforward way of setting standards is to finish the statement: "I will be completely satisfied with your work when . . ." This sentence, if completed for each duty listed in the job description, should result in a usable set of performance standards.[20] Some examples would include the following:

Duty: Accurately Posting Accounts Payable

1. All invoices received are posted within the same working day.
2. All invoices are routed to proper department managers for approval no later than the day following receipt.
3. An average of no more than three posting errors per month occurs.
4. Posting ledger is balanced by the end of the third working day of each month.

Duty: Meeting Daily Production Schedule

1. Work group produces no less than 426 units per working day.
2. No more than an average of 2% of units is rejected at the next workstation.
3. Work is completed with no more than an average of 5% overtime per week.

Working Conditions and Physical Environment

The job description may also list the general working conditions involved on the job. These might include things like noise level, hazardous conditions, or heat.

Job Description Guidelines

Here are some final guidelines for writing up your job descriptions:[21]

Be clear. The job description should portray the work of the position so well that the duties are clear without reference to other job descriptions.

Indicate scope of authority. In defining the position, be sure to indicate the scope and nature of the work by using phrases such as "for the department" or "as requested by the manager." Include all important relationships.

Be specific. Select the most specific words to show (1) the kind of work, (2) the degree of complexity, (3) the degree of skill required, (4) the extent to which problems are standardized, (5) the extent of the worker's responsibility for each phase of the work, and (6) the degree and type of accountability. Use action words, such as *analyze, gather, assemble, plan, devise, infer, deliver, maintain, supervise,* and *recommend.* Positions at the lower levels of organization generally have the most detailed duties or tasks, while higher-level positions deal with broader aspects.

Be brief. Short, accurate statements usually accomplish the purpose best.

Recheck. Finally, to check whether the description fulfills the basic requirements, ask yourself, "Will a new employee understand the job if he or she reads the job description?"

WRITING JOB DESCRIPTIONS THAT COMPLY WITH THE ADA   As explained in Chapter 2, the Americans with Disabilities Act (ADA) was enacted to reduce or eliminate serious problems of discrimination against disabled individuals. Under the ADA, the individual must have the requisite skills, educational background, and experience to perform the job's essential functions. A job function is essential when it is the reason the position exists or when the function is so specialized that the person doing the job is hired for his or her expertise or ability to perform that particular function. If the disabled individual can't perform the job as currently structured, the employer is required to make a "reasonable accommodation," unless doing so would present an "undue hardship."

As we said earlier, the ADA does not require employers to have job descriptions, but it's probably advisable to do so. Virtually all ADA legal actions will revolve around the question, "What are the essential functions of the job?" Without a job description that lists such functions, it will be hard to convince a court that the functions were essential to the job. The corollary is that the essential functions can't just be listed on the description but should be clearly identified as essential.

IDENTIFYING ESSENTIAL JOB FUNCTIONS   *Essential job functions* are those job duties that employees must be able to perform, with or without reasonable accommodation.[22] Questions to be considered in determining whether a function is essential include:

1. Does the position exist to perform that function?[23]
2. Are employees in the position actually required to perform the function?[24]
3. Is there a limited number of other employees available to perform the function, or among whom can the performance of the function be distributed?
4. What is the degree of expertise or skill required to perform the function?
5. What is the actual work experience of present or past employees in the job?
6. What is the amount of time an individual actually spends performing the function?
7. What are the consequences of not requiring the performance of a function?

SMALL BUSINESS APPLICATIONS

■ A Practical Job Analysis Approach

Without their own job analysts or (in many cases) their own HR managers, many small-business owners face two hurdles when conducting job analyses and writing job descriptions. First they often need a more streamlined approach than those provided by questionnaires like the one shown in Figure 3-3. Second, there is always the reasonable fear that in writing up their job descriptions they will overlook duties that should be assigned to subordinates, or assign duties not usually associated with such positions. What they need is an encyclopedia listing all the possible positions they might encounter, including a detailed listing of the duties normally assigned to these positions. Such an "encyclopedia" exists—the *Dictionary of Occupational Titles* briefly mentioned earlier. The practical approach to job analysis for small-business owners, presented next, is built around this invaluable reference. (Starting in 1999 an on-line version, o*net, will be phased in. Check www. doleta.gov/programs/onet/. Other computerized packages for developing job descriptions are discussed in our HR systems appendix, on pages 645–652).

STEP 1. DECIDE ON A PLAN.

Start by developing at least the broad outlines of a corporate plan. What do you expect your sales revenue to be next year, and in the next few years? What products do you intend to emphasize? What areas or departments in your company do you think will have to be expanded, reduced, or consolidated, given where you plan to go with your firm over the next few years? What kinds of new positions do you think you'll need in order to accomplish your strategic plans?

STEP 2. DEVELOP AN ORGANIZATION CHART.

Given your plan, the next step should be to develop an organization chart for your firm. Draw a chart showing who reports to the president and to each of his or her subordinates. Then complete the chart by showing who reports to each of the other managers and supervisors in the firm. Start by drawing up the organization chart as it is now. Then, depending upon how far in advance you're planning, produce a chart showing how you'd like your chart to look in the immediate future (say, in two months) and perhaps two or three other charts showing how you'd like your organization to evolve over the next two or three years.

STEP 3. USE A JOB ANALYSIS/DESCRIPTION QUESTIONNAIRE.

Next, use a job analysis questionnaire to determine what the job entails. You can use one of the more comprehensive job analysis questionnaires (see Figure 3-3, for instance) to collect job analysis data. A simpler and often satisfactory alternative is to use the job description questionnaire presented in Figure 3-10. Fill in the information called for (using the procedure outlined later) and ask the supervisors or the employees themselves to list their job duties (on the bottom of the page), breaking them into daily duties, periodic duties, and duties performed at irregular intervals. A sample of how one of these duties should be described (Figure 3-11) can be distributed to supervisors and/or employees.

STEP 4. OBTAIN THE DICTIONARY OF OCCUPATIONAL TITLES.

Next, obtain standardized examples of the job descriptions you will need from the *Dictionary of Occupational Titles* (DOT).

The best way to learn how to use the *Dictionary of Occupational Titles* is to buy a copy and begin using it. The dictionary is available for about $40.00 from the Superintendent of Documents, Government Printing Office, Washington, DC 20402-9325. (Call the information desk at 202/783-3238 to verify prices and order your manuals.)

STEP 5. CHOOSE APPROPRIATE DEFINITIONS AND PUT THEM ON INDEX CARDS.

Next, for each of your departments, choose from the DOT job titles and job descriptions that you believe might be appropriate for your own enterprise.

For example, suppose you want to develop job descriptions for the employees in the retail sales department of your store. You leaf through occupational code numbers in the DOT starting with 0, 1, or 2 (since these include all professional, technical, and managerial occupations as well as clerical and sales occupations). On page 134 (see Figure 3-12) you find that category 185 refers to "Wholesale and Retail Trade Managers and Officials," and you find here "Manager, Department Store" (185.117–010) and "Fashion Coordinator" (185.157–010). Moving on, on page 208 you find that category 261 refers to "Sales Occupations—Apparel," and here you find "Salesperson, Children's Wear" (261.357–046), "Salesperson, Men's Clothing" (261.357–050), and "Salesperson, Women's Wear" (261.357–038). On the off chance that you may have inadvertently left out some titles that might be appropriate, you leaf through the alphabetical index of occupational titles under "Retail Trade Industry" occupations toward the back of the manual and stumble across "Assistant Buyer, Retail Trade" (162.157–022). You decide you should pick up several aspects of that job's duties as well. Make copies of each of the pertinent descriptions and glue them to index cards. You now have a comprehensive set of the management-related jobs typically found in a retail sales department and can rearrange them on your chart and consolidate positions until you have a division of work that you believe will work for you. This will help to ensure that you've considered the full range of retail sales management

FIGURE 3-10
Job Description Questionnaire

**Background Data
for Job Description**

Job Title _____   Department _____

Job Number _____   Written by _____

Today's Date _____   Applicable DOT Codes _____

I. Applicable DOT Definition(s):

II. Job Summary:
(List the more important or regularly performed tasks)

III. Reports To:

IV. Supervises: _____

V. Job Duties: _____
*(Briefly describe, for each duty, what employee does and, if possible, how
employee does it. Show in parentheses at end of each duty the approximate
percentage of time devoted to duty.)*

A. Daily Duties:

B. Periodic Duties:
(Indicate whether weekly, monthly, quarterly, etc.)

C. Duties Performed at Irregular Intervals:

FIGURE 3-11
Background Data for Examples

Example of Job Title: Customer Service Clerk

Example of Job Summary: Answers inquiries and gives directions to customers, authorizes cashing of customers' checks, records and returns lost charge cards, sorts and reviews new credit applications, works at customer-service desk in department store.

Example of One Job Duty: Authorizes cashing of checks: authorizes cashing of personal or payroll checks (up to a specified amount) by customers desiring to make payment by check. Requests identification, such as driver's license, from customers, and examines check to verify date, amount, signature, and endorsement. Initials check and sends customer to cashier.

184.167–290

lizing knowledge of railroad maintenance regulations: Analyzes production reports, work schedules, and freight car repair list to determine efficient utilization of human resources, and recommends to superiors increasing, reducing, or shifting human resources as necessary to complete work requirements. Fills out daily worksheets identifying defective freight cars, necessary repairs, and priority of repairs for use of subordinate supervisors. Notifies YARD MANAGER (r.r. trans.) 184.167–278 to close tracks on which freight trains are being inspected to other rail traffic. Coordinates dispatching of wreck crews and heavy equipment to wreck site within yard and assigned geographic area. Contacts private contractors to rent equipment needed at wreck site. Informs consignees of damaged freight cars and obtains permission to transfer loads when necessary. Observes work in yard and repair shop to determine that areas are clean and free of hazards. Serves on committees to investigate causes of wrecks. Conducts investigations to determine cause of accidental worker injuries. Submits written reports of findings to superiors.
GEO: 05.02.02 STRENGTH: L GED: R4 M3 L3 SVP: 7 DLU: 86

184.167–290 SUPERVISOR, COMMUNICATIONS-AND-SIGNALS (r.r. trans.)

Directs and coordinates, through subordinate supervisory personnel, activities of workers engaged in installing, maintaining, and testing communications and signaling equipment within specified jurisdiction of railroad: Reviews reports that describe handling of communications and signal irregularities to discern whether deployment of personnel and maintenance procedures followed administrative and labor regulations. Discusses causes of irregularities with supervisor who directed repairs to suggest changes in inspection or maintenance techniques that would prevent recurrence of irregularities, utilizing knowledge of communication and signal functioning. Writes summary of reports indicating worker overtime involved and nature of equipment malfunctions and routes reports to superior. Confers with company engineers regarding major repairs or installation projects in communication and signal system to stay apprised of changes within system. Confers with supervisors throughout projects to provide technical assistance and to ensure availability of equipment needed to complete project.
GOE: 11.11.03 STRENGTH: L GED: R4 M4 L4 SVP: 8 DLU: 86

184.167–294 SUPERVISOR, TRAIN OPERATIONS (r.r. trans.)

Directs and coordinates activities of personnel engaged in scheduling and routing trains and engines in specified railroad territory: Observes record entries and monitors railroad radio communications and lights on train location panelboard to oversee train and engine movements along specified territory of railroad. Confers with railroad dispatchers to determine scheduling of trains and engines. Directs delays of train departures upon notification of substandard track conditions. Coordinates train movements to utilize train crews efficiently to schedule engines to arrive at service locations when due for maintenance and to maximize use of local trains versus special work trains. Scrutinizes train schedules and advises specified personnel of availability of tracks for scheduled repair and maintenance. Issues directives to subordinates to coordinate movement of expedited, late, or special railroad trains, using information received through railroad information network.
GOE: 05.02.02 STRENGTH: L GED: R4 M3 L4 SVP: 8 DLU: 86

184.267–010 FREIGHT-TRAFFIC CONSULTANT (business ser.) alternate titles: transportation consultant

Advises industries, business firms, and individuals concerning methods of preparation of freight for shipment, rates to be applied, and mode of transportation to be used: Consults with client regarding packing procedures and inspects packed or crated goods for conformance to shipping specifications to prevent damage, delay, or penalties. Selects mode of transportation, such as air, water, railroad, or truck without regard to highter rates when speed is necessary. Confers with shipping brokers concerning export and imports papers, docking facilities, or packing and marking procedures. Files claims with insurance company for losses, damages, and overcharges of freight shipments.
GOE: 11.05.02 STRENGTH: S GED: R5 M4 L4 SVP: 8 DLU: 77

184.387–010 WHARFINGER (water trans.)

Compiles reports, such as dockage, demurrage, wharfage, and storage, to ensure that shipping companies are assessed specified harbor fees: Compares information on statements, records, and reports with ship's manifest to determine that weight, measurement, and classification of commodities are in accordance with tariff. Calculates tariff assessment from ship's manifest to ensure that charges are correct. Prepares and submits reports. Inspects sheds and wharves to determine need for repair. Arranges for temporary connection of water and electrical services from wharves. Reads service meters to determine charges to be made.
GEO: 07.02.04 STRENGTH: L GED: R3 M3 L2 SVP: 5 DLU: 77

185 WHOLESALE AND RETAIL TRADE MANAGERS AND OFFICIALS

This group includes managerial occupations concerned with selling merchandise to retailers; to industrial, commercial, institutional or professional users; or to other wholesalers; or acting as agents in buying merchandise for or selling merchandise to such persons or companies.

185.117–010 MANAGER, DEPARTMENT STORE (retail trade)

Directs and coordinates, through subordinate managerial personnel, activities of department store selling lines of merchandise in specialized departments: Formulates pricing policies for sale of merchandise, or implements policies set forth by merchandising board. Coordinates activities of nonmerchandising departments as purchasing,

credit, accounting, and advertising with merchandising departments to obtain optimum efficiency of operations with minimum costs in order to maximize profits. Develops and implements, through subordinate managerial personnel, policies and procedures for store and departmental operations and customer personnel and community relations. Negotiates or approves contracts negotiated with suppliers of merchandise, or with other establishments providing security, maintenance, or cleaning services. Reviews operating and financial statements and departmental sales records to determine merchandising activities that require additional sales promotion, clearance sales, or other sales procedures in order to turn over merchandise and achieve profitability of store operations and merchandising objectives.
GEO: 11.05.02 STRENGTH: S GED: R5 M4 L5 SVP: 8 DLU: 77

185.11–014 AREA SUPERVISOR, RETAIL CHAIN STORE (retail trade) alternate titles: operations manager

Directs and coordinates activities of subordinate managerial personnel involved in operating retail chain stores in assigned area: Interviews and selects individuals to fill managerial vacancies. Maintains employment records for each manager. Terminates employment of store managers whose performance does not meet company standards. Directs, through subordinate managerial personnel, compliance of workers with established company policies, procedures, and standards, such as safekeeping of company funds and property, personnel and grievance practices, and adherence to policies governing acceptance and processing of customer credit card charges. Inspects premises of assigned area stores to ensure that adequate security exists and that physical facilities comply with safety and environmental codes and ordinances. Reviews operational records and reports of store managers to project sales and to determine store profitability. Coordinates sales and promotional activities of store managers. Analyzes marketing potential of new and existing store locations and recommends additional sites or deletion of existing area stores. Negotiates with vendors to enter into contracts for merchandise and determines allocations to each store manager.
GOE: 11.11.05 STRENGTH: L GED: R4 M3 L4 SVP: 7 DLU: 86

185.137–010 MANAGER, FAST FOOD SERVICES (retail trade; wholesale tr.)

Manages franchised or independent fast food or wholesale prepared food establishment: Directs, coordinates, and participates in preparation of, and cooking, wrapping or packing types of food served or prepared by establishment collecting of monies from in-house or take-out customers, or assembling food orders for wholesale customers. Coordinates activities of workers engaged in keeping business records, collecting and paying accounts, ordering or purchasing supplies, and delivery of foodstuffs to wholesale or retail customers. Interviews, hires, and trains personnel. May contact prospective wholesale customers, such as mobile food vendors, vending machine operators, bar and tavern owners, and institutional personnel, to promote sale of prepared foods, such as doughnuts, sandwiches, and specialty food items. May establish delivery routes and schedules for supplying wholesale customers. Workers may be known according to type or name of franchised establishment or type of prepared foodstuff retailed or wholesaled.
GOE: 11.11.04 STRENGTH: L GED: R4 M4 L4 SVP: 5 DLU: 81

185.157–010 FASHION COORDINATOR (retail trade) alternate titles: fashion stylist

Promotes new fashions and coordinates promotional activities, such as fashion shows, to induce consumer acceptance: Studies fashion and trade journals, travels to garment centers, attends fashion shows, and visits manufacturers and merchandise markets to obtain information on fashion trends. Consults with buying personnel to gain advice regarding type of fashions store will purchase and feature for season. Advises publicity and display departments of merchandise to be publicized. Selects garments and accessories to be shown at fashion shows. Provides information on current fashions, style trends, and use of accessories. May contract with models, musicians, caterers, and other personnel to manage staging of shows. May conduct teenage fashion shows and direct activities of store-sponsored club for teenage girls.
GOE: 11.09.01 STRENGTH: L GED: R5 M4 L5 SVP: 7 DLU: 77

185.157–014 SUPERVISOR OF SALES (business ser.)

Coordinates and publicizes tobacco marketing activities within specified area: Visits tobacco growers, buyers, and auction warehouses to cultivate interest and goodwill. Develops publicity for tobacco industry. Investigates and confirms eligibility of buyers. Collects membership dues for tobacco Board of Trade. Schedules tobacco auction dates. Records quantity and purchase price of tobacco sold daily, and prepares reports specified by board. May prepare report of marketing activities for state and federal agencies. May review and verify reports for individual warehouses. May examine quality and growth of tobacco in fields of individual growers and inform buyers of results.
GOE: 11.09.01 STRENGTH: L GED: R4 M4 L4 SVP: 7 DLU: 77

185.157–018 WHOLESALER II (wholesale tr.)

Exports domestic merchandise to foreign merchants and consumers and imports foreign merchandise for sale to domestic merchants or consumers: Arranges for purchase and transportation of imports through company representatives abroad and sells imports to local customers. Sells domestic goods, materials, or products to representatives of foreign companies. May be required.

FIGURE 3-12 *Page from* Dictionary of Occupational Titles

Source: Dictionary of Occupational Titles (Washington, DC: U.S. Department of Labor, 1991), p. 134.

jobs that might be pertinent for your enterprise. It also helps to ensure that no important retail-management duties are inadvertently omitted.

STEP 6. PUT APPROPRIATE DOT SUMMARIES ON THE TOP OF YOUR JOB DESCRIPTION FORM.

Next write a job description for the job you want done. To facilitate this, write the corresponding DOT codes and DOT definitions under "Applicable DOT Definitions" in the Job Description Form in Figure 3-10. Particularly when (as is usually the case) only one or two DOT definitions apply to the job description you are writing, the DOT definition will give your own definition a firm foundation. It will provide a standardized list and constant reminder of the specific duties that should be included in your own definition. Including the DOT codes and definitions will also facilitate your conversations with the state job service, should you use them to help find employees for your open positions.

STEP 7. COMPLETE YOUR JOB DESCRIPTION.

Finally, in Figure 3-10, write an appropriate job summary for the job under consideration. Then use the job analysis information obtained in step 3 together with the information gleaned from the DOT to create a complete listing of the tasks and duties of each of your jobs.

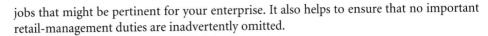

WRITING JOB SPECIFICATIONS

The job specification takes the job description and answers the question, "What human traits and experience are required to do this job well?" It shows what kind of person to recruit and for what qualities that person should be tested. The job specification may be a separate section on the job description or a separate document entirely. Often—as in Figure 3-8—it is presented as part of the job description.[25]

Specifications for Trained Versus Untrained Personnel

Writing job specifications for trained employees is relatively straightforward. For example, suppose you want to fill a position for a trained bookkeeper (or trained counselor or programmer). In cases like these, your job specifications might focus mostly on traits like length of previous service, quality of relevant training, and previous job performance. Thus, it's usually not too difficult to determine the human requirements for placing already trained people on a job.

But the problems are more complex when you're filling jobs with untrained people (with the intention of training them on the job). Here you must specify qualities such as physical traits, personality, interests, or sensory skills that imply some potential for performing the job or for having the ability to be trained for the job.

For example, suppose the job requires detailed manipulation in a circuit board assembly line. Here you might want to ensure the person scores high on a test of finger dexterity. Your goal, in other words, is to identify those personal traits—those human requirements—that validly predict which candidate would do well on the job and which would not. Identifying these human requirements for a job is accomplished either through a subjective, judgmental approach or through statistical analysis.

Job Specifications Based on Judgment

The judgmental approach is based on the educated guesses of people like supervisors and human resource managers. The basic procedure here is to ask, "What does it take in terms of education, intelligence, training, and the like to do this job well?"

The job specifications for already-trained candidates, such as the customer service operator shown here, should clearly indicate which skills, like computer literacy, are job requirements.

The *Dictionary of Occupational Titles* can be useful here. For jobs in the dictionary, job analysts and vocational counselors have made judgments regarding each job's human requirements. Each of these human requirements or traits has been rated and assigned a letter as follows: G (intelligence), V (verbal), N (numerical), S (spatial), P (perception), Q (clerical perception), K (motor coordination), F (finger dexterity), M (manual dexterity), E (eye-hand-foot coordination), and C (color discrimination). The ratings reflect the amount of each trait or ability possessed by people with different performance levels currently working on the job, based on the experts' judgments. Each has also been rated on the extent to which the job involves dealing with Data, People, and Things. Thus an accountant might rate high on Data, and a mechanic rate higher on dealing with Things.

Common sense should be applied when compiling a list of the job's human requirements. Certainly job-specific human traits like those unearthed through job analysis—traits such as manual dexterity and educational level—are important. However, don't ignore the fact that there are also work behaviors that may apply to almost any job one could think of (although they might not normally surface through a job analysis).

RESEARCH INSIGHT   A recent study is a case in point. The researcher obtained supervisor ratings and other information from over 18,000 employees in 42 different hourly entry-level jobs in predominantly retail settings.[26] Regardless of the job, here are the work behaviors (with examples) that he found to be "generic"—in other words, that seem to be important across the board, to all jobs, regardless of the job:

Job-Related Behavior	*Some Examples*
Industriousness	Keeps working even when other employees are standing around talking; takes the initiative to find another task when finished with regular work.
Thoroughness	Cleans equipment thoroughly creating a more attractive display; notices merchandise out of place and returns it to the proper area.
Schedule flexibility	Accepts schedule changes when necessary; offers to stay late when the store is extremely busy.

Attendance	Arrives at work on time; maintains good attendance.
Off-task behavior (reverse)	Uses store phones to make personal unauthorized calls; conducts personal business during work time; lets joking friends be a distraction and interruption to work.
Unruliness (reverse)	Threatens to bully another employee; refuses to take routine orders from supervisors; not cooperate with other employees.
Theft (reverse)	(As a cashier) Under-rings the price of merchandise for a friend; cheats on reporting time worked; allows nonemployees in unauthorized areas.
Drug misuse (reverse)	Drinks alcohol or takes drugs on company property; comes to work under the influence of alcohol or drugs.

Job Specifications Based on Statistical Analysis

Basing a job specification on statistical analysis is the more defensible approach, but also the more difficult. Basically, the aim is to statistically determine the relationship between (1) some predictor or human trait such as height, intelligence, or finger dexterity and (2) some indicator or criterion of job effectiveness (such as performance as rated by the supervisor). The procedure has five steps: (1) analyze the job and decide how to measure job performance; (2) select personal traits like finger dexterity that you believe should predict successful performance; (3) test candidates for these traits; (4) measure these candidates' subsequent job performance; and (5) statistically analyze the relationship between the human trait (finger dexterity) and job performance. Your objective is to determine whether the former predicts the latter. In this way, the human requirements for performing the job can be statistically ascertained.

This method is more defensible than the judgmental approach, because equal rights legislation forbids using traits that you can't prove distinguish between high and low job performers. Hiring standards that discriminate on the basis of sex, race, religion, national origin, or age may have to be shown to predict job performance; this generally requires a statistical validation study.

Personality-related Job Requirements. A new job analysis survey form may make it easier for managers to identify the personality traits required for a job's performance. Called the *Personality-Related Position Requirements Form* (PPRF), it helps a job analyst identify personality traits that a job's incumbents should have. This is important; most job analysis techniques typically do a better job of unearthing the human aptitudes and skills—like manual dexterity—that a job requires.[27] The PPRF helps identify potential personality-related traits that may be important for the job. A statistical analysis can then be used to assess the relevance of these personality traits.

The form uses questionnaire items to assess the relevance of basic personality dimensions such as agreeableness, conscientiousness, and emotional stability to the job. This is accomplished by asking whether specific items—such as "adapt easily to changes in work procedures"—are "not required," "helpful," or "essential" for performing the job.

JOB ANALYSIS IN A "JOBLESS" WORLD

Introduction

A job is generally defined as a set of closely related activities carried out for pay, but over the past few years the concept of job has been changing quite dramatically. As one observer recently put it:

The modern world is on the verge of another huge leap in creativity and productivity, but the job is not going to be part of tomorrow's economic reality. There still is and will always be enormous amounts of work to do, but it is not going to be contained in the familiar envelopes we call jobs. In fact, many organizations are today well along the path toward being "de-jobbed."[28]

From Specialized to Enlarged Jobs

The term *job* as we know it today is largely an outgrowth of the industrial revolution's efficiency demands. As the substitution of machine power for people power became more widespread, experts including Adam Smith and Frederick Taylor wrote glowingly of the positive correlation between specialization and efficiency.[29] The popularity of specialized, short-cycle jobs soared—at least among management experts and managers.

By the mid-1900s other writers were reacting to what they viewed as the "dehumanizing" aspects of pigeonholing workers into highly repetitive and specialized jobs; many proposed solutions. *Job enlargement* means assigning workers additional same-level activities, thus increasing the number of activities they perform. Thus, if the work was assembling chairs, the worker who previously only bolted the seat to the legs might take on the additional tasks of assembling the legs and attaching the back as well. *Job rotation* means systematically moving workers from one job to another. Thus, on an assembly line, a worker might spend an hour fitting doors, the next hour installing headlamps, and so on.

Similarly, psychologist Frederick Herzberg argued that the best way to motivate workers is to build opportunities for challenge and achievement into their jobs via job enrichment. *Job enrichment* means redesigning jobs in a way that increases the opportunities for the worker to experience feelings of responsibility, achievement, growth, and recognition by doing the job well. Five ways to do this are:

1. *Form natural work groups.* Here the job is changed so that each person is responsible for or "owns" an identifiable body of work. For example, instead of doing work for all departments, the typist in a typing pool becomes responsible for doing all the work for one or two departments.

2. *Combine tasks.* For example, one person assembles a product from start to finish, replacing a system in which several separate operations are performed by different people.

3. *Establish client relationships.* Here the worker has contact as often as possible with the consumer of the product.

4. *Vertical loading.* The worker plans and controls his or her own job instead of having it controlled by outsiders. For example, the worker sets his or her own schedule, does his or her own troubleshooting, decides when to start and stop working, and so on.

5. *Open feedback channels.* Finally, the company implements more and better ways for the worker to get quick feedback on his or her performance.[30]

Whether specialized, enlarged, or enriched, however, workers still generally have had specific jobs to do, and these jobs required job descriptions. In many firms today, jobs are becoming more amorphous, more difficult to define. In other words, the trend is toward *de-jobbing* many companies.

Why Companies Are Becoming De-jobbed: The Need for Competitiveness

De-jobbing is ultimately a result of the changes taking place in business today. Organizations need to grapple with revolutionary forces—accelerating product and technological change, globalized competition, deregulation, political instability, demographic changes,

When employees work on teams, as they do at Saturn's auto factory, job descriptions tend to be very broad because everyone on the team shares a set of common tasks.

and trends toward a service society and the information age. Forces like these have dramatically increased the need for firms to be responsive, flexible, and capable of competing in a global marketplace.

The organizational methods firms use to foster such competitiveness have helped to blur the meaning of *job* as a well-defined and clearly delineated set of responsibilities. Here is a sampling of how these methods have contributed to this blurring.

FLATTER ORGANIZATIONS   Instead of traditional pyramid-shaped organizations with seven or more management layers, flat organizations with just three or four levels are becoming more prevalent. Many firms (including AT&T, ABB, and General Electric) have already cut their management layers from a dozen to six or fewer. As the remaining managers are left with more people reporting to them, they can supervise them less, so the jobs of subordinates end up bigger in terms of both breadth and depth of responsibilities.

WORK TEAMS   Work itself is increasingly organized around teams and processes rather than around specialized functions. For example, at Chesebrough-Ponds USA, a subsidiary of Unilever United States, Inc., a traditional pyramidal organization was replaced with multiskilled, cross-functional, and self-directed teams that now run the plant's four product areas. Hourly employees make employee assignments, schedule overtime, establish production times and changeovers, and even handle cost control, requisitions, and work orders. They also are solely responsible for quality control under the plant's continuous quality improvement.[31] In an organization like this, employees' jobs change daily; the effort to avoid having employees view their jobs as a limited and specific set of responsibilities is thus intentional.

THE BOUNDARYLESS ORGANIZATION   A *boundaryless organization* is one in which widespread use of teams and similar structural mechanisms means that the boundaries that typically separate organizational functions (like sales and production) and hierarchical levels are reduced and made more permeable.[32] Boundaryless organizations foster responsiveness by encouraging employees to rid themselves of the "It's not my job" attitudes that typically create walls between one employee's area and another's. Instead the focus is on defining the job at hand in terms of the overall best interests of the organization, thereby further de-jobbing the company.

REENGINEERING   *Reengineering* is defined as "the fundamental rethinking and radical redesign of business processes to achieve dramatic improvements in critical, contemporary measures of performance, such as cost, quality, service, and speed."[33] In their book *Reengineering the Corporation*, Michael Hammer and James Champy argue that the principles that shaped the structure and management of business for hundreds of years—like highly specialized divisions of work—should be retired. Instead the firm should emphasize combining tasks into integrated, unspecialized processes that are then carried out by committed employees.

Reengineering is achieved in several ways. Specialized jobs are combined into one so that formerly distinct jobs are integrated and compressed into enlarged, enriched ones.[34] A necessary correlate of combining jobs is that workers make more decisions, since each person's responsibilities are generally broader and deeper after reengineering; supervisory checks and controls are reduced and, indeed, committed employees largely control their own efforts. Finally, workers become collectively responsible for overall results rather than being individually responsible for just their own tasks. As a result, their jobs change dramatically. "They share joint responsibility with their team members for performing the whole process, not just a small piece of it. They not only use a broader range of skills from day to day, they have to be thinking of a far greater picture."[35] Most importantly, "while not every member of the team will be doing exactly the same work . . . the lines between [the workers' jobs] blur." And to that extent reengineering also contributes to de-jobbing the enterprise.

THE FUTURE OF JOB DESCRIPTIONS   Most firms today continue to utilize job descriptions and to rely on jobs as traditionally defined. However, it's clear that more and more firms are moving toward new organizational configurations, ones built around jobs that are broad and that may change every day. As one writer has said, "In such a situation people no longer take their cues from a job description or a supervisor's instructions. Signals come from the changing demands of the project. Workers learn to focus their individual efforts and collective resources on the work that needs doing, changing as that changes. Managers lose their 'jobs,' too. . . ."[36] The high-performance organization feature that follows describes some practical HR implications.

THE HIGH-PERFORMANCE ORGANIZATION

Building Better, Faster, More Competitive Organizations Through HR: Modern Job Analysis Methods

■ British Petroleum, Exploration Division

JOB ANALYSIS, HR, AND THE DE-JOBBED COMPANY

Because job descriptions are (deservedly) so well ingrained in the way that most companies operate, it's unlikely that most firms could (or should) do without them, at least for now. But, for the growing number of firms that are shifting to HR systems that don't use job descriptions, what replaces them?

In one firm—British Petroleum's exploration division—the need for flatter organizations and empowered employees inspired management to replace job descriptions with matrices listing skills and skill levels.[37] Senior management wanted to shift employees' attention from a job description/"that's not my job" mentality to one that would motivate them to obtain the new skills they needed to accomplish their broader responsibilities.

The solution was a skills matrix like that shown in Figure 3-13. Skills matrices were created for various jobs within two classes of employees, those on a management track and those whose aims lay elsewhere (such as to stay in engineering). For each job or job family (such as

H	H	H	H	H	H	H
G	G	G	G	G	G	G
F	F	F	F	F	F	F
E	E	E	**E**	E	E	E
D	D	D	D	**D**	**D**	D
C	**C**	C	C	C	C	**C**
B	B	**B**	B	B	B	B
A	A	A	A	A	A	A
Technical Expertise	**Business Awareness**	**Communication and Interpersonal**	**Decision Making and Initiative**	**Leadership and Guidance**	**Planning and Organizational Ability**	**Problem Solving**

FIGURE 3-13 *The Skills Matrix for One Job at BP*
The rose boxes indicate the minimum level of skill required for the job.

drilling manager), a matrix was prepared. As in Figure 3-13, it identified (1) the basic skills needed for that job and (2) the minimum level of each skill required for that job or job family.

Such a matrix shifts employees' focus. The emphasis is no longer on a job description's listing of specific job duties. Instead the focus is on developing the new skills needed for the employees' broader, empowered, and often relatively undefined responsibilities.

The skills matrix approach has prompted other HR changes in BP's exploration division. For example, the matrices provide a constant reminder of what skills employees must improve, and the firm's new skill-based pay plan awards raises based on skills improvement. Similarly, performance appraisals now focus more on employee skills, and training emphasizes developing broad skills like leadership and planning—ones that are applicable across a wide range of responsibilities and jobs.

Broader HR issues are also involved when firms de-job. For one thing, "you must find people who can work well without the cue system of job descriptions."[38] This puts a premium on hiring people with the skills and values to handle empowered jobs. As two reengineering experts put it:

> For multi-dimensional and changing jobs, companies don't need people to fill a slot, because the slot will be only roughly defined. Companies need people who can figure out what the job takes and do it, people who can create the slot that fits them. Moreover, the slot will keep changing.[39]

There's also a shift from training to education, in other words, from teaching employees the "how" of the job to increasing their insight and understanding regarding its "why." In a rapidly changing industrial environment the demands for flexibility and responsiveness mean that it's impossible to hire people "who already know everything they're ever going to need to know. . . ."[40] Here continuing education over the course of the employees' organizational career becomes the norm.

We invite you to visit the Dessler page on the Prentice Hall Web site at **www.prenhall.com/dessler** for our on-line study guide, Internet exercises, current events, links to related Web sites, and more.

SUMMARY

1. Developing an organization structure results in jobs that have to be staffed. Job analysis is the procedure through which you find out (1) what the job entails and (2) what kinds of people should be hired for the job. It involves six steps: (1) determine the use of the job analysis information, (2) collect background information, (3) select the positions to be analyzed, (4) collect job analysis data, (5) review information with participants, and (6) develop a job description and job specification.

2. There are five basic techniques one can use to gather job analysis data: interviews, direct observation, questionnaires, participant logs, and the U.S. Civil Service Procedure. These are good for developing job descriptions and specifications. The Department of Labor, functional job analysis, and PAQ approaches result in quantitative ratings of each job and are therefore useful for classifying jobs for pay purposes.

3. The job description should portray the work of the position so well that the duties are clear without reference to other job descriptions. Always ask, "Will the new employee understand the job if he or she reads the job description?"

4. The job specification takes the job description and answers the question, "What human traits and experience are necessary to do this job well?" It tells what kind of person to recruit and for what qualities that person should be tested. Job specifications are usually based on the educated guesses of managers; however, a more accurate statistical approach to developing job specifications can also be used.

5. Job analysis is in many ways the first personnel activity that affects commitment and performance. Most people can't perform a job when they don't have the ability and skills to do the job. It is through job analysis that you determine what the job entails and what skills and abilities you should look for in job candidates.

6. Use the *Dictionary of Occupational Titles* to help write job descriptions. Find and reproduce the DOT descriptions that relate to the job you're describing. Then use those DOT descriptions to "anchor" your own description and particularly to suggest duties to be included.

7. De-jobbing is ultimately a product of the rapid changes taking place in business today. As firms try to speed decision making by taking steps like reengineering, individual jobs are becoming broader and much less specialized. Increasingly, firms don't want employees to feel limited by a specific set of responsibilities like those listed in a job description. As a result, more employees are deemphasizing detailed job descriptions, often substituting brief job summaries, perhaps combined with summaries of the skills required for the position.

KEY TERMS

job analysis 84	diary/log 92	Department of Labor job
job description 84	position analysis	analysis 94
job specification 84	questionnaire (PAQ) 94	functional job analysis 97

DISCUSSION QUESTIONS

1. What items are typically included in the job description? What items are not shown?
2. What is job analysis? How can you make use of the information it provides?
3. We discussed several methods for collecting job analysis data—questionnaires, the position analysis questionnaire, and so on. Compare and contrast these methods, explaining what each is useful for and listing the pros and cons of each.

4. Describe the types of information typically found in a job specification.

5. Explain how you would conduct a job analysis.

6. Do you think companies can really do without detailed job descriptions? Why or why not?

7. Since the president's job in a firm is by nature broader than a factory worker's, is there less need for a job description for the president? Why or why not?

INDIVIDUAL AND GROUP ACTIVITIES

1. Working individually or in groups, obtain copies of job descriptions for clerical positions at the college or university where you study, or the firm where you work. What types of information do they contain? Do they give you enough information to explain what the job involves and how to do it? How would you improve on the description?

2. Working individually or in groups, use the job analysis questionnaire in this chapter to develop a job description for your professor in this class. Based on that, use your judgment to develop a job specification. Compare your conclusions with those of other students or groups. Were there any significant differences? What do you think accounted for the differences?

3. Working individually or in groups, obtain a copy of the DOT from your library. Choose any two positions and compare the jobs' Data-People-Things ratings. (These are the 4th, 5th, and 6th digits of the job's DOT number; ratings are explained at the end of the DOT.) Do the ratings make sense based on what you know about the jobs? Why or why not?

EXPERIENTIAL EXERCISE

Purpose: The purpose of this exercise is to give you experience in developing a job description, by developing one for your instructor.

Required Understanding: You should understand the mechanics of job analysis and be thoroughly familiar with the job analysis questionnaire. Figure 3-14 and the job description questionnaire Figure 3-15.

How to Set up the Exercise/Instructions: Set up groups of four to six students for this exercise. As in all exercises in this book, the groups should be separated and should not converse with each other. Half the groups in the class will develop the job description using the job analysis questionnaire, and the other half of the groups will develop it using the job description questionnaire. Each student should review his or her questionnaire (as appropriate) before joining his or her group.

1. Each group should do a job analysis of the instructor's job; half the groups (to repeat) will use the job

analysis questionnaire for this purpose, and half will use the job description questionnaire.

2. Based on this information, each group will develop its own job description and job specification for the instructor.

3. Next, each group should choose a partner group, one that developed the job description and job specification using the alternate method. (A group that used the job analysis questionnaire should be paired with a group that used the job description questionnaire.)

4. Finally, within each of these new combined groups, compare and criticize each of the two sets of job descriptions and job specifications. Did each job analysis method provide different types of information? Which seems superior? Does one seem more advantageous for some types of jobs than others?

(continued)

JOB QUESTIONNAIRE
KANE MANUFACTURING COMPANY

NAME _____   JOB TITLE _____

DEPARTMENT _____   JOB NUMBER _____

SUPERVISOR'S NAME _____   SUPERVISOR'S TITLE_____

1. *SUMMARY OF DUTIES:* State in your own words briefly your main duties. If you are responsible for filling out reports/records, also complete Section 8.

    _____
    _____

2. *SPECIAL QUALIFICATIONS:* List any licenses, permits, certifications, etc. required to perform duties assigned to your position.

    _____
    _____

3. *EQUIPMENT:* List any equipment, machines, or tools (e.g., typewriter, calculator, motor vehicles, lathes, fork lifts, drill presses, etc.) you normally operate as a part of your position's duties.

    MACHINE   *AVERAGE NO. HOURS PER WEEK*
    _____
    _____
    _____

4. *REGULAR DUTIES:* In general terms, describe duties you regularly perform. Please list these duties in descending order of importance and percent of time spent on them per month. List as many duties as possible and attach additional sheets, if necessary.

    _____
    _____

5. *CONTACTS:* Does your job require any contacts with other department personnel, other departments, outside companies or agencies? If yes, please define the duties requiring contacts and how often.

    _____
    _____

6. *SUPERVISION:* Does your position have supervisory responsibilities? ( ) Yes ( ) No. If yes, please fill out a Supplemental Position Description Questionnaire for Supervisors and attach it to this form. If you have responsibility for the work of others but do not directly supervise them, please explain.

    _____
    _____

7. *DECISION MAKING:* Please explain the decisions you make while performing the regular duties of your job.

    _____
    _____
    _____

FIGURE 3-14 *Job Analysis Questionnaire for Developing Job Descriptions*

Source: From *Job Evaluation: Wage and Salary Administration* by Douglas Bartley. Reprinted by permission of the author.

(a) What would be the probable result of your making (a) poor judgment(s) or decision(s), or (b) improper actions?

_____

_____

8. *RESPONSIBILITY FOR RECORDS:* List the reports and files you are required to prepare or maintain. State, in general, for whom each report is intended.

(a)   *REPORT*   *INTENDED FOR*

_____

_____

(b)   *FILES MAINTAINED*

_____

_____

9. *FREQUENCY OF SUPERVISION:* How frequently must you confer with your supervisor or other personnel in making decisions or in determining the proper course of action to be taken?

( )Frequently   ( )Occasionally   ( )Seldom   ( )Never

10. *WORKING CONDITIONS:* Please describe the conditions under which you work— inside, outside, air conditioned area, etc. Be sure to list any disagreeable or unusual working conditions.

_____

_____

11. *JOB REQUIREMENTS:* Please indicate the minimum requirements you believe are necessary to perform satisfactorily in your position.

(a) Education:
Minimum schooling _____
Number of years _____
Specialization or major _____

(b) Experience:
Type_____
Number of years _____

(c) Special training:

         TYPE   *NUMBER OF YEARS*

_____

_____

(d) Special Skills:
Typing: _____w.p.m.   Shorthand_____w.p.m.
Other: _____

12. *ADDITIONAL INFORMATION:* Please provide additional information, not included in any of the previous items, which you feel would be important in a description of your position.

_____

_____

EMPLOYEE'S SIGNATURE _____   DATE:_____

FIGURE 3-14 *(continued)*

(continued from page 117)

BACKGROUND DATA
FOR JOB DESCRIPTION

Job Title _____   Department _____

Job Number _____   Written by _____

Today's Date _____   Applicable DOT codes _____

   I.   Applicable DOT Definition(s):

   II.   Job Summary:
        (*List the more important or regularly performed tasks*)

   III.   Reports to:

   IV.   Supervises:

   V.   Job Duties: _____
        (*Briefly describe, for each duty, what employee does and, if possible, how employee does it. Show in parentheses at end of each duty the approximate percentage of time devoted to duty.*)

   A.   Daily Duties:

   B.   Periodic Duties:
        (*Indicate whether weekly, monthly, quarterly, etc.*)

   C.   Duties Performed at Irregular Intervals:

FIGURE 3-15 *Job Description Questionnaire*

CASE INCIDENT   Hurricane Bonnie

In August 1998 Hurricane Bonnie hit North Carolina and the Optima Air Filter Company. Many employees' homes were devastated and the firm found that it had to hire almost three completely new crews, one for each of its shifts. The problem was that the "old timers" had known their jobs so well that no one had ever bothered to draw up job descriptions for them. When about 30 new employees began taking their posts, there was general confusion about what they should do and how they should do it.

The hurricane quickly became old news to the firm's out-of-state customers who wanted filters, not excuses. Phil Mann, the firm's president, was at his wits' end. He had about 30 new employees—10 old-timers, and his original factory supervisor, Maybelline. He decided to meet with Linda Lowe, a consultant from the local university's business school, who immediately had the old-timers fill out a job questionnaire that listed all their duties. Arguments ensued almost at once because both Phil and Maybelline thought the old-timers were exaggerating to make themselves look more important, and the old-timers insisted that the list faithfully reflected their duties. Meanwhile, the customers clamored for their filters.

■ **QUESTIONS**

1. Should Phil and Linda ignore the old-timers' protests and write up the job descriptions as they see fit? Why? Why not? How would you go about resolving the differences?

2. How would you have conducted the job analysis?

Case Application   DOES YOUR SECRETARY RANK HIGHER THAN MINE?

It wasn't until Fay Jacobs retired from her post as secretary to the CEO that anyone in Dublin Candy's human resource department realized how much variation there was in the compensation the company's secretaries earned. Elizabeth Linnell, compensation specialist, decided it was time to prepare an updated analysis of the secretarial position as it existed at Dublin.

It was easy to see why there were no consistent standards for secretarial pay. With the advance of office-automation technology, managers' differing styles of delegation, and secretaries' varying degrees of willingness to take on increasing managerial responsibilities, the job had assumed a wide variety of profiles throughout the secretary's level of pay. It would be difficult now to determine whether ant two people with the same job title were actually doing the same job.

Elizabeth decided to use an objective method of culling information about the secretarial role, in order to be prepared for resistance to change and the reluctance of those who might want to protect their status and pay. She developed a questionnaire that she planned to distribute to each member of Dublin's secretarial staff and their managers, in the course of a brief explanatory interview. The interviews, she hoped, would give her a chance to dispel any secretary's fears that the analysis was meant to cut jobs, reduce salaries, or lower the grade level of the position.

Before finalizing the questionnaire, Elizabeth shared it with a small group of secretaries in her own department. Based on their input she made some modifications, such as adding questions about the use of office technology and its impact on the job.

The questionnaire now covered nearly every aspect of the secretarial role, from processing m,ail to making travel arrangements to editing and preparing

(continued)

company correspondence, budgets, and reports. The questions also captured information about how much time was spent on each activity and how much supervision each task required. Elizabeth hoped that in addition to establishing common standards on which Dublin could base a more equitable pay structure, the survey would also allow the human resource staff to assess training needs, examine the distribution of work, and determine accurate specifications for hiring and for developing employment tests to be used in the future.

Just before Elizabeth gave out the questionnaires, however, she got a phone call from Garrett Fried, vice president of sales. Garrett had heard about the upcoming analysis and was very upset. He claimed to be worried about how much time his secretary would have to take away from her work in order to meet with Elizabeth and fill out the questionnaire, and he also expressed concern that she might feel her job was threatened and start looking for another position elsewhere. Elizabeth agreed to meet with Garrett to discuss his reservations, but as he thanked her and hung up he added, "You know, Elizabeth, I sure wouldn't want to see *my* secre-

tary rated at a lower grade level than the vice president of operations' secretary!"

■ QUESTIONS

1. What do you think is the real problem from Garrett's point of view?
2. How should Elizabeth address each of the concerns he expressed?
3. What can Elizabeth do to prepare herself for any resistance to the analysis from the secretaries themselves?
4. Given current advances in office technology such as sophisticated spreadsheet programs, voice mail systems, and e-mail, as well as the elimination of many middle-management positions through corporate downsizings, secretaries in many forms are taking on quasi-management tasks. How can Elizabeth account, in her job analysis, for the degrees to which individual secretaries at Dublin are doing so?

NOTES

1. For a good, discussion of job analysis, see James Clifford, "Job Analysis: Why Do It, and How Should It be Done?" *Public Personnel Management*, Vol. 23, no. 2 (Summer 1994), pp. 321–340.
2. Ernest J. McCormick, "Job and Task Analysis," in Marvin D. Dunnette, ed., *Handbook of Industrial and Organizational Psychology* (Chicago: Rand McNally, 1976), pp. 651–696.
3. James Clifford, "Manage Work Better to Better Manage Human Resources: A Comparative Study of Two Approaches to Job Analysis," *Public Personnel Management* (Spring 1996), pp. 89–102.
4. Richard Henderson, *Compensation Management: Rewarding Performance* (Upper Saddle River, NJ: Prentice Hall, 1994), pp. 139–150. See also Patrick W. Wright and Kenneth Wesley, "How to Choose the Kind of Job Analysis You Really Need," *Personnel*, Vol. 62, no. 5 (May 1985), pp. 51–55; C. J. Cranny and Michael E. Doherty, "Importance Ratings in Job Analysis: Note on the Misinterpretation of Factor Analyses," *Journal of Applied Psychology* (May 1988), pp. 320–322.
5. Wayne Cascio, *Applied Psychology in Personnel Management* (Reston, VA: Reston, 1978), p. 140. See also Michael Lundell et al., "Relationships Between Organizational Content and Job Analysis Task Ratings," *Journal of Applied Psychology*, Vol. 83, no. 5, 1998, pp. 769–776.
6. See Henderson, *Compensation Management*, pp. 148–152.
7. A complete explanation and definition of each of these seven attributes (knowledge, skills, abilities, etc.) can be found in U.S. Civil Service Commission, *Job Analysis* (Washington, DC: U.S. Government Printing Office), December 1976.
8. Note that the PAQ (and other quantitative techniques) can also be used for job evaluation, which is explained in chapter 12.
9. Again we will see that *job evaluation* is the process through which jobs are compared to one another and their values determined. Although usually viewed as a job analysis technique, the PAQ is, in practice, actually as much or more of a job evaluation technique and could therefore be discussed in either this chapter or in chapter 12. For a discussion of how to use PAQ for classifying jobs, see Edwin Cornelius III, Theodore Carron, and Marianne Collins, "Job Analysis Models and Job Classifications," *Personnel Psychology*, Vol. 32 (Winter 1979), pp. 693–708. See also Edwin Cornelius III, Frank Schmidt, and Theodore Carron, "Job Classification Approaches and the Implementation of Validity Generalization Results," *Personnel Psychology*, Vol. 37, no. 2 (Summer 1984), pp. 247–260.
10. Jack Smith and Milton Hakel, "Comparisons Among Data Sources, Response Bias, and Reliability and Validity of a Structured Job Analysis Questionnaire," *Personnel Psychology*, Vol. 32 (Winter

1979), pp. 677–692. See also Edwin Cornelius III, Angelo DeNisi, and Allyn Blencoe, "Expert and Naive Raters Using the PAQ: Does It Matter?" *Personnel Psychology*, Vol. 37, no. 3 (Autumn 1984), pp. 453–464; Lee Friedman and Robert Harvey, "Can Raters with Reduced Job Description Information Provide Accurate Position Analysis Questionnaires (PAQ) Ratings?" *Personnel Psychology*, Vol. 34 (Winter 1986), pp. 779–789; and Robert J. Harvey et al., "Dimensionality of the Job Element Inventory, A Simplified Worker-Oriented Job Analysis Questionnaire," *Journal of Applied Psychology* (November 1988), pp. 639–646; Stephanie Butler and Robert Harvey, "A Comparison of Holistic Versus Decomposed Rating of Position Analysis Questionnaire Work Dimensions," *Personnel Psychology*, (Winter 1988), pp. 761–772.

11. This discussion is based on Howard Olson et al., "The Use of Functional Job Analysis in Establishing Performance Standards for Heavy Equipment Operators," *Personnel Psychology*, Vol. 34 (Summer 1981), pp. 351–364.

12. Frederick P. Morgeson and Michael A. Campion, "Social and Cognitive Sources of Potential Inaccuracy in Job Analysis," *Journal of Applied Psychology*, Vol. 82, no. 5 (1997), pp. 627–655.

13. Ibid., p. 648.

14. Regarding this discussion, see Henderson, *Compensation Management*, pp. 175–184. See also Louisa Wah, "The Alphabet Soup of Job Titles," *Management Review*, Vol. 87, no. 6, pp. 40–43.

15. James Evered, "How to Write a Good Job Description," *Supervisory Management* (April 1981), pp. 14–19; Roger J. Plachy, "Writing Job Descriptions That Get Results," *Personnel* (October 1987), pp. 56–58. See also Matthew Mariani, "Replace with a Database," *Occupational Outlook Quarterly*, Vol. 43, no. 1, (Spring 1999), pp. 2–9.

16. Ibid., p. 16.

17. This discussion is based on Ibid.

18. Ibid., p. 16.

19. Ibid., p. 17.

20. Ibid., p. 18.

21. Ernest Dale, *Organizations* (New York: American Management Association, 1967).

22. Deborah Kearney, *Reasonable Accommodations: Job Descriptions in the Age of ADA, OSHA, and Workers Comp* (New York: Van Nostrand Reinhold, 1994), p. 9.

23. Ibid. Unless otherwise noted, numbers 1 and 3 through 8 are based on or quoted from Kearney.

24. Michael Esposito, "There's More to Writing Job Descriptions Than Complying with the ADA," *Employment Relations Today* (Autumn 1992), p. 279. See also Richard Morfopoulos and William Roth, "Job Analysis and the Americans with Disabilities Act," *Business Horizons*, Vol. 39, no. 6 (November 1996), pp. 68–72; and Kristin Mitchell, George Alliger, and Richard Morfopoulos, "Toward an ADA-Appropriate Job Analysis," *Human Resource Management Review*, Vol. 7, no. 1 (Spring 1997), pp. 5–16.

25. Based on Ernest J. McCormick and Joseph Tiffin, *Industrial Psychology* (Upper Saddle River, NJ: Prentice Hall, 1974), pp. 56–61.

26. Steven Hunt, "Generic Work Behavior: An Investigation into the Dimensions of Entry-level, Hourly Job Performance," *Personnel Psychology*, Vol. 49 (1996), pp. 51–83.

27. Patrick H. Raymark, Mark J. Schmidt, and Robert M. Guion, "Identifying Potentially Useful Personality Constructs for Employee Selection," *Personnel Psychology*, Vol. 50 (1997), pp. 723–736.

28. William Bridges, "The End of the Job," *Fortune*, September 19, 1994, p. 64.

29. For example, Charles Babbage listed six reasons for making jobs as specialized as possible: There is less time required for learning; there is less waste of material during the training period; there is less time lost in switching from task to task; proficiency increases with practice; hiring is made more efficient; and parts become uniform and interchangeable. Charles Babbage, *On the Economy of Machinery and Manufacturers* (London: Charles Knight, 1832), pp. 169–172; reprinted in Joseph Litterer, *Organizations* (New York: John Wiley & Sons, 1969), pp. 73–75.

30. J. Richard Hackman and Greg Oldham, "Motivation Through the Design of Work: Test of a Theory," *Organizational Behavior and Human Performance*, Vol. 16, no. 2 (August 1976), pp. 250–279.

31. William H. Miller, "Chesebrough-Ponds At a Glance," *Industry Week*, October 19, 1992, pp. 14–15. For an interesting discussion of the need to move from an "it's not by job" mentality from the point of view of an employee, see Kathy Shaw, "It's Not in My Job Description," *CMA Magazine* (June 1994), p. 42.

32. Larry Hirschhorn and Thomas Gilmore, "The New Boundaries of the Boundaryless' Company, *Harvard Business Review* (May–June 1992), pp. 104–108. For another point of view, see George Stack, Jr., and Jill Black, "The Myth of the Horizontal Organization," *Canadian Business Review* (Winter 1994), pp. 28–31.

33. Michael Hammer and James Champy, *Reengineering the Corporation* (New York: Harper Business, 1993), p. 32.

34. Ibid., p. 51.

35. Ibid., p. 68.

36. William Bridges, "The End of the Job," p. 68.

37. Milan Moravec and Robert Tucker, "Job Descriptions for the 21st Century," *Personnel Journal* (June 1992), pp. 37–44.

38. William Bridges, "The End of the Job," p. 68. See also Gilbert Siegel, "Job Analysis in the TQM Environment," *Public Personnel Management*, Vol. 25, no. 4 (Winter 1997), pp. 485–494.

39. Hammer and Champy, *Reengineering the Corporation*, p. 72.

40. Ibid.

4

PERSONNEL PLANNING AND RECRUITING

The enormous losses incurred by the hedge fund Long Term Capital did more than drain capital from U.S. firms like Merrill Lynch. Switzerland's UBS Bank—one of the world's largest—sustained big losses too, while facing the prospect of an imminent Asian recession. The bank's first response was to fire its chairman and several top executives. But now, with cutbacks required in Asia too, it needed a strategy to address how to downsize its far-flung operations and cut costs. All its personnel plans had to be revised as UBS faced a new, more competitive, global financial terrain. ▲

Behavioral Objectives

When you finish studying this chapter, you should be able to:

- ▲ *Explain* the process of forecasting personnel requirements.
- ▲ *Discuss* the pros and cons of eight methods used for recruiting job candidates.
- ▲ *Describe* how to develop an application form.
- ▲ *Explain* how to use application forms to predict job performance.

Chapter Outline

- ▲ The Recruitment and Selection Process
- ▲ Employment Planning and Forecasting
- ▲ Recruiting Job Candidates
- ▲ Developing and Using Application Forms

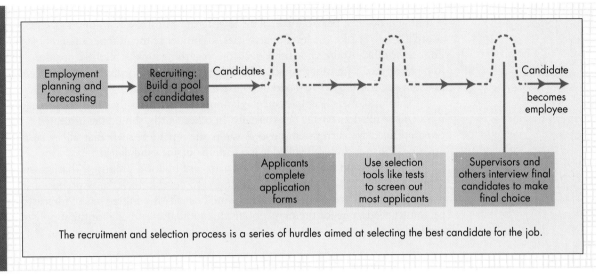

FIGURE 4-1 *Steps in Recruitment and Selection Process*

THE RECRUITMENT AND SELECTION PROCESS

Personnel planning is the first step in the recruiting and selecting process. The recruiting and selecting process itself can best be envisioned as a series of hurdles, as in Figure 4-1:

1. Do employment planning and forecasting to determine the duties of the position to be filled.
2. Build a pool of candidates for these jobs by recruiting internal or external candidates.
3. Have the applicants fill out application forms and perhaps undergo an initial screening interview.
4. Utilize various selection techniques such as tests, background investigations, and physical exams to identify viable job candidates.
5. Send one or more viable job candidates to the supervisor responsible for the job.
6. Have the candidate(s) go through one or more selection interviews with the supervisor and other relevant parties for the purpose of finally determining to which candidate(s) an offer should be made.

Recruiting and selecting is the subject of this and the next two chapters. In this chapter we'll focus on employment *planning and forecasting* (in other words, on how to determine what positions are to be filled) and on *recruiting* techniques. Chapter 5 focuses on *employee selection techniques*, including tests, background checks, and physical exams. Finally, Chapter 6 is devoted to a discussion of the selection technique that is by far the most widely used, namely, *interviewing job candidates*.

EMPLOYMENT PLANNING AND FORECASTING

As at UBS, *employment* or *personnel planning* is the process of formulating plans to fill or eliminate future openings, based on an analysis of the positions that are expected to be open and needed and whether these will be filled by inside or outside candidates. Employment planning, therefore, refers to planning regarding any or all the firm's future positions, from maintenance clerk to CEO. However, most firms use the term *succession planning* to refer to the process of planning how the company's most important executive positions will be filled.

In any case, employment planning is an integral part of a firm's strategic and HR planning processes. For example, plans to enter new businesses, to build new plants, or—as at UBS—to reduce the level of activities, all influence the number of and types of positions to be filled. At the same time, decisions regarding how to fill these positions will have to be integrated with other aspects of the firm's HR plans, for instance, with plans for appraising and training current and new employees.

The fundamental employment planning decision will be whether projected positions will be filled internally or externally. In other words, should the projected open positions be filled by current employees? Or is the situation such that all or some of the openings must or should be filled by recruiting outside candidates?

Like any good plans, employment plans are built on premises—basic assumptions about the future. The purpose of *forecasting* is to develop these basic premises. If you are planning for employment requirements, you'll usually need three sets of forecasts: one for personnel needs, one for the supply of inside candidates, and one for the supply of outside candidates.

How to Forecast Personnel Needs

There are several things to consider when forecasting personnel needs.[1] From a practical point of view, the expected demand for your product or service is paramount.[2] Thus, sales are generally estimated first. Then the staff required to achieve this volume of output is estimated. In addition, you will also have to consider several other things, such as:

1. *Projected turnover* (as a result of resignations or terminations)
2. *Quality and skills* of your employees (in relation to what you see as the changing needs of your organization)
3. *Decisions* to upgrade the quality of products of services or enter into new markets
4. *Technological and other changes* resulting in increased productivity
5. The *financial resources* available to your department

There are several ways to predict future employment needs. They include the following:

trend analysis
Study of a firm's past employment needs over a period of years to predict future needs.

TREND ANALYSIS   With **trend analysis** you study your firm's employment levels over the last five years or so to predict future needs. Thus, you might compute the number of employees in your firm at the end of each of the last five years, or perhaps the number in each subgroup (like salespeople, production people, secretarial, and administrative) at the end of each of those years. The purpose is to identify employment trends you think might continue into the future. Trend analysis is valuable as an initial estimate, but employment levels rarely depend solely on the passage of time. Other factors (like changes in sales volume and productivity) will also affect your future staffing needs.

ratio analysis
A forecasting technique for determining future staff needs by using ratios between sales volume and number of employees needed.

RATIO ANALYSIS   Another approach, **ratio analysis,** means making forecasts based on the ratio between (1) some causal factor (like sales volume) and (2) number of employees required (for instance, number of salespeople). For example, suppose you find that a salesperson traditionally generates $500,000 in sales. Then, if the sales revenue–salespeople ratio remains the same, you would require six new salespeople next year (each of whom produces an extra $500,000 in sales) to produce the hoped-for extra $3 million in sales.

Like trend analysis, ratio analysis assumes that productivity remains about the same—for instance, that each salesperson can't be motivated to produce much more than $500,000 in sales each. If sales productivity were to increase or decrease, then the ratio of sales to salespeople would change. A forecast based on historical ratios would then no longer be as accurate.

scatter plot

A graphical method used to help identify the relationship between two variables.

THE SCATTER PLOT   A **scatter plot** is another option. You can use scatter plots to determine whether two factors—a measure of business activity and your staffing levels—are related. If they are, then if you can forecast the measure of business activity you should also be able to estimate your personnel requirements.

For example, assume a 500-bed hospital expects to expand to 1,200 beds over the next five years.[3] The director of nursing and the human resource director want to forecast the requirement for registered nurses. The human resource director decides to determine the relationship between size of hospital (in terms of number of beds) and number of nurses required. She calls five similar hospitals of various sizes and gets the following figures:

Size of Hospital (Number of Beds)	Number of Registered Nurses
200	240
300	260
400	470
500	500
600	620
700	660
800	820
900	860

One way to determine the relationship between size of hospital and number of nurses is to draw a scatter plot as illustrated in Figure 4-2. Hospital size is shown on the horizontal axis. Number of nurses is shown on the vertical axis. If the two factors are related, then the points will tend to fall along a straight line, as they do here. If you then carefully draw in a line to minimize the distances between the line and each one of the plotted points, you will be able to estimate the number of nurses that will be needed for each given hospital size. Thus, for a 1,200-bed hospital, the human resource director would assume that she needs about 1,210 nurses.

FIGURE 4-2

Determining the Relationship Between Hospital Size and Number of Nurses

Note: After fitting the line, you can extrapolate—project—how many employees you'll need, given your projected volume.

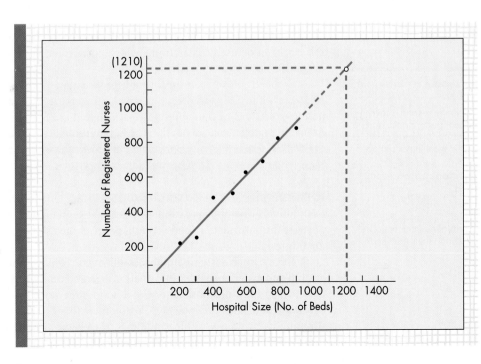

USING COMPUTERS TO FORECAST PERSONNEL REQUIREMENTS   Employers also use computer programs to forecast personnel requirements.[4] Typical data needed include direct labor hours required to produce one unit of product (a measure of productivity), and three sales projections—minimum, maximum, and probable—for the product line in question. Based on such data, a typical program generates figures on average staff levels required to meet product demands, as well as separate **computerized forecasts** for direct labor (such as assembly workers, indirect staff (such as secretaries), and exempt staff (such as executives).

With such systems, employers can quickly translate projected productivity and sales levels into forecasts of personnel needs, while estimating the effects of various productivity and sales levels on personnel requirements.[5]

MANAGERIAL JUDGMENT   Whichever forecasting approach you use, managerial judgment will play a big role. It's rare that any historical trend, ratio, or relationship will continue unchanged into the future. Judgment is thus needed to modify the forecast based on factors—such as projected turnover or a desire to enter new markets—you believe will change in the future.

Forecasting the Supply of Inside Candidates

The personnel demand forecast only provides half the staffing equation by answering the question, "How many employees will we need?" Next, the supply—both internal and external—must be estimated.

A qualification inventory can facilitate forecasting the supply of internal candidates. **Qualifications inventories** contain data on things like each employee's performance record, educational background, and promotability, compiled either manually or in a computerized system.

MANUAL SYSTEMS AND REPLACEMENT CHARTS   There are several types of manual systems used to track employees' qualifications. In the personnel inventory and development record shown in Figure 4-3, information is compiled about each employee and then recorded on the inventory. The information includes education, company-sponsored courses taken, career and development interests, languages, and skills. Information like this can then be used to determine which current employees are available for promotion or transfer to projected open positions.

Some employers use **personnel replacement charts** (Figure 4-4 on page 128) to keep track of inside candidates for their most important positions. These show the present performance and promotability for each potential replacement for important positions. As an alternative, you can develop a **position replacement card**. Here you make up a card for each position, showing possible replacements as well as present performance, promotion potential, and training required by each possible candidate.

COMPUTERIZED INFORMATION SYSTEMS   Qualifications inventories on hundreds or thousands of employees cannot be adequately maintained manually. Many firms computerize this information, and a number of packaged systems are available for accomplishing this task.[6]

In one such system, employees fill out a 12-page booklet to describe their background and experience. This information is stored on disk. When a manager needs a qualified person for a position, he or she describes the position (for instance, in terms of the education and skills it entails) and then enters this information into the computer. After scanning its bank of possible candidates, the program presents the manager with a computer printout of qualified candidates.

---

computerized forecast

The determination of future staff needs by projecting a firm's sales, volume of production, and personnel required to maintain this volume of output, using computers and software packages.

---

qualifications inventories

Manual or computerized systematic records listing employees' education, career and development interests, languages, special skills, and so on to be used in forecasting inside candidates for promotion.

---

personnel replacement charts

Company records showing present performance and promotability of inside candidates for the most important positions.

position replacement card

A card prepared for each position in a company to show possible replacement candidates and their qualifications.

PERSONNEL INVENTORY AND DEVELOPMENT RECORD | Date: month, year

Department	Area or sub-department	Branch or section	Location

Company service date (month, day, year)	Birthdate (month, day, year)	Marital status	Job title

Education | Degree, year obtained, college, and major field of study

Grade school	High school
6 7 8	9 10 11 12 13

College
1   2   3   4   5

Courses (company sponsored)

Type of course	Subject or course	Year	Type of course	Subject or course	Year

Career and development interests

Are you interested in an alternative type of work?	Yes ☐ No ☐	Would you accept transfer to another division?	Yes ☐ No ☐	Would you accept lateral moves for further development?	Yes ☐ No ☐

If yes, specifically what type?	Comment on any qualifying circumstances	Photo

What type of training do you believe you require to:	A) Improve your skills and performance in your present position. B) Improve your experience and abilities for advancement.	

		Last name
		First name

What other assignments do you believe you are qualified to perform now?

languages	Written		Spoken		Middle name
	☐	☐	☐	☐	SS Number
	☐	☐	☐	☐	

Societies and organizations   Memberships in community organizations, etc., within last five years, indicate name of association and office held, if any

Skills

Type of skill	Certification, if any	Type of skill	Certification, if any

Other significant work experience, and/or military service. (Omit repetitive experiences)

	Location	From yr.	To yr.	

Comments: Other significant experience, recreational activities, hobbies, interests, or personal data.

FIGURE 4-3 *Personnel Inventory Form Appropriate for Manual Storage and Retrieval*

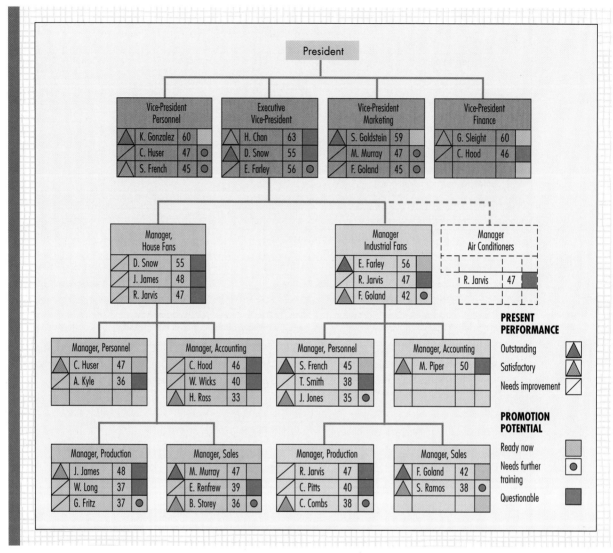

FIGURE 4-4 *Management Personnel Replacement Chart*

According to one expert, the basic ingredients of a computerized human resource skills inventory should include the following:

Work experience codes: a list of work experience descriptors, titles, or codes describing jobs within the company so that the individual's present, previous, and desired jobs can be coded.

Product knowledge: the employee's level of familiarity with the employer's product lines or services as an indication of where the person might be transferred or promoted.

Industry experience: the person's industry experiences, because for certain positions knowledge of key related industries is very useful.

Formal education: the name of each postsecondary educational institution attended, the field of study, degree granted, and year granted.

Training courses: those taken or conducted by the employee and, possibly, training courses taught by outside agents like the American Management Association.

Foreign language skills: degree of proficiency in language other than the employee's native tongue.

Relocation limitations: the employee's willingness to relocate and the locales to which he or she would prefer to go.

Career interests: work experience codes to indicate what the employee would like to be doing for the employer in the future. Space can be provided for a brief priority of choices, and a code should be included indicating whether the employee's main qualification for the work he or she wants to do is experience, knowledge, or interests.

Performance appraisals: updated periodically to indicate the employee's achievement on each dimension appraised (leadership ability, motivation, communication skills, and so on) along with a summary of the employee's strengths and deficiencies.[7]

The data elements in a human resources information system could number 100 or more. For example, one major vendor of a mainframe personnel/payroll package reportedly used by over 2,000 companies suggests the 140 elements shown in Table 4-1. Notice that these elements range from home address to driver's license number, weight, salary, sick leave used, skills, and veteran status.[8]

Skills are often included in these types of data banks. Including "training courses completed" might only show what the employee is trained to do, not what he or she has actually shown he or she can do. Including skills such as "remove boiler casings and doors" (number of times performed, date last performed, time spent) lets you use your computer to zero in on which employees are competent to accomplish the task that must be done. You can even include a skill level in the data bank, perhaps ranging from skill level 1 (can lead or instruct others), to level 2 (can perform the job with minimal supervision), level 3 (has some experience: can assist experienced workers), and level 4 (has not had opportunity to work on this job).[9]

THE MATTER OF PRIVACY   Several developments have intensified the HR manager's need to better control the data stored in the company's personnel data banks. First, as you can see in Table 4-1, there is a great deal of employee information in most employers' data banks. Second, the expansion of end-user computing capabilities offers greater opportunities for more people to have access to these data.[10] Third, legislation, such as the Federal Privacy Act of 1974 and the New York Personal Privacy Act of 1985, gives some employees legal rights regarding who has access to information about their work history and job performance.

Balancing the employer's legitimate right to make this information available to those in the organization who need it with the employees' right to privacy isn't easy. One approach is to use the access matrices incorporated in the software of many database management systems. Basically, these matrices define the rights of users (specified by name, rank, or functional identification) to have various kinds of access (such as "read only" or "write only") to each data element contained on the database. Thus, the computer programmers who are charged with the job of inputting data regarding employees might be authorized only to write information into the database, while those in accounting are authorized to read a limited range of information such as the person's address, phone number, social security number, and pension status. The human resource director, on the other hand, might be authorized to both read and write all items when interacting with the database.

TABLE 4-1 Typical Data Elements in a Human Resources Information System

Address (work)	Garnishments	Salary change type
Address (home)	Grievance (type)	Salary
Birthdate	Grievance (outcome)	Salary range
Birthplace	Grievance (filing date)	Schools attended
Child support deductions	Handicap status	Service date
Citizenship	Health plan coverage	Service branch
Claim pending (description)	Health plan (no. dependents)	Service discharge type
Claim pending (outcome)	Injury date	Service ending rank
Claim pending (court)	Injury type	Service discharge date
Claim pending (date)	Job location	Sex
Date on current job	Job preference	Sick leave used
Department	Job position number	Sick leave available
Dependent (sex)	Job title	Skill function (type)
Dependent (number of)	Job location	Skill sub-function (type)
Dependent (relationship)	Leave of absence start date	Skill (number of years)
Dependent (birthdate)	Leave of absence end date	Skill (proficiency level)
Dependent (name)	Leave of absence type	Skill (date last used)
Discipline (appeal date)	Life insurance coverage	Skill (location)
Discipline (type of charge)	Marital status	Skill (supervisory)
Discipline (appeal outcome)	Marriage date	Social Security number
Discipline (date of charge)	Medical exam (date)	Spouse's employment
Discipline (outcome)	Medical exam (restrictions)	Spouse's date of death
Discipline (hearing date)	Medical exam (blood type)	Spouse's name
Division	Medical exam (outcome)	Spouse's birthdate
Driver's license (number)	Miscellaneous deductions	Spouse's sex
Driver's license (state)	Name	Spouse's social security number
Driver's license (exp. date)	Organizational property	Start date
Education in progress (date)	Pay status	Stock plan membership
Education in progress (type)	Pension plan membership	Supervisor's name
Educational degree (date)	Performance rating	Supervisor's work address
Educational degree (type)	Performance increase($)	Supervisor's work phone
Educational minor (minor)	Performance increase (%)	Supervisor's title
Educational level attained	Phone number (work)	Termination date
Educational field (major)	Phone number (home)	Termination reason
EEO-I code	Prior service (term. date)	Training schools attended
Emergency contact (phone)	Prior service (hire date)	Training schools (date)
Emergency contact (name)	Prior service (term. reason)	Training schools (field)
Emergency contact (relation)	Professional license (type)	Training schools completed
Emergency contact (address)	Professional license (date)	Transfer date
Employee weight	Race	Transfer reason
Employee number	Rehire code	Union code
Employee code	Religious preference	Union deductions
Employee status	Salary points	United Way deductions
Employee height	Salary (previous)	Vacation leave available
Employee date of death	Salary change date	Vacation leave used
Federal job code	Salary change reason	Veteran status
Full-time/part-time code		

Source: Donald Harris, "A Matter of Privacy: Managing Personal Data in Company Computers," *Personnel* (February 1987), p. 37.

Internal Sources of Candidates

Although recruiting may bring to mind employment agencies and classified ads, current employees are sometimes your best source of recruits.

Filling open positions with inside candidates has several advantages. Employees see that competence is rewarded, and morale and performance may thus be enhanced. Having already been with your firm for some time, inside candidates may be more committed to company goals and less likely to leave. Promotion from within can boost employee commitment and provide managers a longer-term perspective when making business decisions. It may also be safer to promote employees from within, since you're likely to have a more accurate assessment of the person's skills than you would otherwise. Inside candidates may also require less orientation and training than outsiders.

Yet hiring from within can also backfire. Employees who apply for jobs and don't get them may become discontented; informing unsuccessful applicants as to why they were rejected and what remedial actions they might take to be more successful in the future is thus essential.[11] Similarly, many employers require managers to post job openings and interview all inside candidates. Yet the manager often knows ahead of time exactly whom he or she wants to hire, and requiring the person to interview a stream of unsuspecting inside candidates is therefore a waste of time for all concerned. Groups are sometimes not as satisfied when their new boss is appointed from within their own ranks as when he or she is a newcomer; sometimes, for instance, it is difficult for the insider to shake off the reputation of being "one of the gang."[12]

Inbreeding is another drawback. When all managers have been brought up through the ranks, there may be a tendency to maintain the status quo, when an innovative and new direction is needed. Balancing the benefits of morale and loyalty with the drawback of inbreeding is thus a challenge.

To be effective, promotion from within requires using job posting, personnel records, and skill banks.[13] **Job posting** means publicizing the open job to employees (often by literally posting it on bulletin boards) and listing its attributes like qualifications, supervisor, working schedule, and pay rate (as in Figure 4-5). Some union contracts require job posting to ensure that union members get first choice of new and better positions. Yet, job posting can also be a good practice even in nonunion firms, if it facilitates the transfer and promotion of qualified inside candidates. (However, posting is often not used when promotion to a supervisory position is involved, since management often prefers to select personnel promotion to management levels.)[14] *Personnel records* are also useful here. An examination of personnel records (including application forms) may uncover employees who are working in jobs below their educational or skill levels. It may also reveal persons who have potential for further training or those who already have the right background for the open jobs in question. *Computerized systems* discussed previously can help to ensure that qualified inside candidates are identified and considered for the opening. Some firms also develop skill banks that list current employees who have specific skills. For example, under "aerospace engineers," the names of all persons with this experience or training are listed. If you need an engineer in unit A, and the skill bank shows a person with those skills in unit B, that person may be approached about transferring to unit A, although he or she is not now using the aerospace skills.

job posting

Publicizing an open job to employees (often by literally posting it on bulletin boards) and listing its attributes, like qualifications, supervisor, working schedule and pay rate.

HIRING EMPLOYEES—THE SECOND TIME AROUND   Until recently it was often considered unusual to rehire former employees—particularly those who'd left voluntarily "for greener pastures." Voluntarily leaving was often seen as a form of betrayal; and problems ranging from disloyalty to bad morale were often expected of those who'd been involuntarily let go.[15]

FIGURE 4-5

Job Posting Form

Source: Bureau of National Affairs, Inc., *Recruiting and Selection Procedures* (Washington, DC, 1988), p. 35.

NO. ____

POSTED: _____
CLOSING: _____

There is a full-time position available for a _____ in the _____ Department. This position is/is not open to outside candidates.

PAY SCALE

Minimum	Midpoint	Maximum
$ ____	$ ____	$ ____

or
SALARIED

DUTIES
See attached job description.

REQUIRED SKILLS AND ABILITIES
(Must possess all the following skills and abilities to be considered for this position.)
1. Demonstrated successful performance at past/present positions including:
   – ability to perform tasks in a complete and accurate manner
   – demonstrated timeliness and follow-through on duties and assignments
   – ability to work well with other people
   – ability to communicate effectively
   – reliability and good attendance
   – good organizational skills
   – problem solving attitude and approach
   – positive work attitude: enthusiastic, confident, outgoing, helpful, committed
2.

DESIRED SKILLS AND ABILITIES
(These skills and abilities will make a candidate more competitive.)

Application procedure FOR _____ EMPLOYEES is as follows:

1. Apply by phoning _____, on ext. ____ , by 3:00 p.m. _____

2. Ensure that a completed Internal Job Application and up-to-date resume/application is delivered to _____ by the same date.
Applicants will be pre-screened according to the above qualifications.
Selection will be made by the _____ .
   is an equal opportunity employer.
0255M/1

Today—thanks partly to high turnover in some high-tech occupations and partly to several years of low unemployment—rehiring former employees seems to be coming back into style. For example, AT&T now routinely reemploys former workers, and in 1996 it rehired more than 130 employees it had previously let go.[16]

Rehiring former employees has its pros and cons. On the plus side your former employees are known quantities (more or less), and are already familiar with your company's culture, style, and ways of doing things. On the other hand, employees who were let go may return with less than positive attitudes. And hiring former employees who left for greener pastures back into better positions may signal your current employees that the best way to get ahead is to leave the firm.

In any event, there are several preventive measures you can take to reduce the chances for adverse reactions.[17] For example, once rehired employees have been back on the job for a certain period of time, credit them with the years of service they had accumulated before they left; this may have a positive impact on benefits such as vacation time, and thereby on their morale. In addition, carefully inquire about what they did during the layoff and how they feel about returning to the firm: "You don't want someone coming back who feels they've been mistreated," said one manager.[18]

SUCCESSION PLANNING   Forecasting the availability of inside or outside candidates is particularly important in succession planning. In a nutshell, succession planning simply refers to the plans a company makes to fill its most important executive positions. In practice, however, the process often involves a fairly complicated series of steps. For example, potential successors for top management might be routed through the top jobs at several key divisions as well as overseas, and they might be sent through the Harvard Business School's Advanced Management Program. As a result, a more comprehensive definition of succession planning is that it is "the process of ensuring a suitable supply of successors for current and future senior or key jobs arising from business strategy, so that the careers of individuals can be planned and managed to optimize the organization's needs and the individuals' aspirations."[19] Succession planning includes these activities:

Analysis of the demand for managers and professionals by company level, function, and skill

Audit of existing executives and projection of likely future supply from internal and external sources

Planning of individual career paths based on objective estimates of future needs and drawing on reliable performance appraisals and assessments of potential

Career counseling undertaken in the context of a realistic understanding of the future needs of the firm, as well as those of the individual

Accelerated promotions, with development targeted against the future needs of the business

Performance-related training and development to prepare individuals for future roles as well as current responsibilities

Planned strategic recruitment not only to fill short-term needs but also to provide people for development to meet future needs

The actual activities by which openings are filled[20]

Forecasting the Supply of Outside Candidates

If there are not enough inside candidates to fill anticipated openings, or you want to go outside for another reason, you will probably focus next on projecting supplies of outside candidates—those not currently employed by your organization. This may require forecasting general economic conditions, local market conditions, and **occupational market conditions.**

The first step is to forecast general economic conditions and the expected prevailing rate of unemployment. Usually, the lower the rate of unemployment, the more difficult it will be to recruit personnel.

There is a wealth of published economic forecast information you can use. For example, in December of each year, *Business Week* magazine presents its economic forecast for the following year; each week it presents a snapshot of the economy on its "Outlook" page. *Fortune* magazine has a monthly forecast for the coming year. Many banks publish periodic analyses and forecasts of the economy. Each December the Prudential Insurance

occupational market conditions

The Bureau of Labor Statistics of the U.S. Department of Labor publishes projections of labor supply and demand for various occupations, as do other agencies.

Company publishes an economic forecast for the coming year. The U.S. Council of Economic Advisors prepares Economic Indicators each month showing the trend to date of various economic indicators. The regional branches of the Federal Reserve also publish economic reports monthly.

Local labor market conditions are also important. For example, the buildup of computer and semiconductor companies resulted in relatively low unemployment recently in cities like Seattle, quite aside from general economic conditions in the rest of the country.

Finally, you may want to forecast the availability of potential job candidates in specific occupations (engineers, drill press operators, accountants, and so on) for which you will be recruiting. Recently, for instance, there has been an undersupply of computer specialists and nurses.

Forecasts for various occupations are available from many sources. For example, the Bureau of Labor Statistics of the U.S. Department of Labor publishes annual projections in the *Monthly Labor Review*. The National Science Foundation regularly forecasts labor market conditions in the science and technology fields. Other agencies providing occupational forecasts include the Public Health Service, the U.S. Employment Service, and the Office of Education.

RECRUITING JOB CANDIDATES

Once you have been authorized to fill a position, the next step is to develop an applicant pool, using internal recruiting and one or more of the recruitment sources described next. Recruiting is important because the more applicants you have the more selective you can be in your hiring. If only two candidates apply for two openings, you may have little choice but to hire them. But if 10 or 20 applicants appear, you can use techniques like interviews and tests to screen out all but the best.

Effective recruiting is increasingly important today, for several reasons. First, the U.S. unemployment rate declined each year for five years through 1996; this led some experts to refer to the current recruiting situation as one of "evaporated employee sources."[21] Related to this, many believe that today's "Generation X" employees (those born between 1963 and 1977) are less inclined to build long-term employment relationships than were their predecessors.[22] High average turnover rates for some occupations is another problem; the average annual turnover rate for high-tech employees was recently 14.5%, according to one study.[23]

Finding the right inducements for attracting and hiring employees—and especially "Generation X" employees—can therefore be quite a problem.[24] For example, in 1996, about 47,000 jobs opened up worldwide for computer animators, but only 14,000 graduated from art school. With a little experience, these people can therefore earn $100,000 a year.[25] Similarly, $10,000 to $20,000 signing bonuses were often common for MBA students in the mid-to-late 1990s.[26]

Aggressively recruiting job candidates has therefore become very important today. "Poaching workers is fair game" reads one HR newsletter's headline, and some new recruiting jargon is even being used. Luring workers away from other high-tech firms is affectionately called "nerd wrestling," for instance.[27]

Some employers use a recruiting yield pyramid to calculate the number of applicants they must generate to hire the required number of new employees. In Figure 4-6, the company knows 50 new entry-level accountants must be hired next year. From experience, the firm also knows the ratio of offers made to actual new hires is 2 to 1; about half the people to whom offers are made accept them. Similarly, the firm knows that the ratio of candidates interviewed to offers made is 3 to 2, while the ratio of candidates invited for interviews to candidates actually interviewed has been 4 to 3. Finally, the firm knows that the ratio of new leads generated to candidates actually invited has been 6 to 1; in other

FIGURE 4-6
Recruiting Yield Pyramid

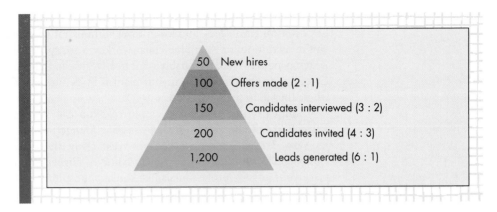

words, of six leads that come in from the firm's advertising, college recruiting, and other recruiting efforts, only one applicant in six typically is invited to come for an interview. Given these ratios, the firm knows it must generate 1,200 leads to be able to invite 200 viable candidates to its offices for interviews. The firm will then get to interview about 150 of those invited, and from these it will make 100 offers. Of those 100 offers, half (or 50 new CPAs) will be hired.

RESEARCH INSIGHT   However, it's not just recruiting but effective recruiting that's important. For example, consider the results of this study of college recruiter effectiveness.[28] Subjects were 41 graduating students from four colleges (arts and sciences, engineering, industrial relations, and business) of a northeastern university. The students were questioned twice during their spring semester, once just after they'd had their first round of interviews with employers and once after their second round of interviews.

The quality of a firm's recruiting process had a big impact on candidates' opinions of the firm. For example, when asked after the initial job interview why they thought a particular company might be a good fit, all 41 mentioned the nature of the job; however, 12 also mentioned the impression made by the recruiters themselves, and 9 said the comments of friends and acquaintances affected their impressions. Unfortunately, the reverse was also true. When asked why they judged some firms as bad fits, 39 mentioned the nature of the job, but 23 said they'd been turned off by recruiters. For example, some were dressed "sloppily"; others were "barely literate"; some were rude; and some made offensively sexist comments. All these recruiters, needless to say, were ineffectual recruiters for their firms.

LINE AND STAFF COOPERATION   In recruitment, line and staff cooperation is essential. The HR manager who recruits and initially screens for the vacant job is seldom the one responsible for supervising its performance. He or she must therefore know exactly what the job entails, and this, in turn, means speaking with the supervisor involved. For example, the HR person might want to know something about the behavioral style of the supervisor and the members of the work group. Is it a tough group to get along with, for instance? He or she might also want to visit the work site and review the job description with the supervisor to ensure that the job has not changed since the description was written and to obtain any additional insight into the skills and talents the new worker will need.

Advertising as a Source of Candidates

To use help wanted ads successfully, you need to address two issues: the media to be used and the ad's construction.[29] The selection of the best medium—be it the local paper, the *Wall Street Journal*, TV, or a technical journal—depends on the type of positions for which you're recruiting. Your local newspaper is usually the best source for blue-collar help, clerical employees, and lower-level administrative employees. On the other hand, if you're recruiting for even blue-collar workers with special skills—such as in fixing textile weaving looms—you'd probably want to advertise in the heart of the textile industry—the Carolinas or Georgia—even if your plant is in Tennessee. The point is to target your ads where they'll do the most good.

Similarly, for specialized employees, you can advertise in trade and professional journals like the *American Psychologist, Sales Management, Chemical Engineering, Electronics News, Travel Trade,* and *Women's Wear Daily.* In publications like *American Banker, Hospital Administration,* and the *Chronicle of Higher Education,* you would most likely place your ads for professionals like bankers, hospital administrators, or educators. One drawback to this type of trade paper advertising is the long lead time that is usually required; there may be a month or more between insertion of the ad and publication of the journal or specialized paper, for instance. Yet ads remain good sources, and ads like the one in Figure 4-7 continue to appear.

Help wanted ads in papers like the *Wall Street Journal* and *International Herald Tribune* can be good sources of middle- or senior-management personnel. The *Wall Street Journal,* for instance, has several regional editions so that the entire country or the appropriate geographic area can be targeted for coverage.

Most firms use newspaper ads, but other media are used too. Table 4-2 on page 138 summarizes when to use various media. For example, radio is best when multiple jobs are involved, such as when staffing a new facility.

PRINCIPLES OF HELP WANTED ADVERTISING   The construction of the ad is important. Experienced advertisers use a four-point guide called AIDA (attention, interest, desire, action) to construct their ads. First, you must attract attention to the ad. Figure 4-8 on page 139 shows an ad from one paper's classified section. Why does this ad attract attention? Note that closely printed ads would be lost, while one like this with wide borders or a lot of empty space stand out. For this reason, key positions are often advertised in separate display ads.

Develop interest in the job. As in Figure 4-9 on page 140, interest may be created by the nature of the job itself, such as "you'll thrive on challenging work." Sometimes other aspects of the job, such as its location, can be used to create interest.

Create desire by amplifying the job's interest factors plus extras such as job satisfaction, career development, travel, or similar advantages. Write the ad with the target audience in mind. For example, nearby graduate schools appeal to engineers and professional people.

Finally, the ad should prompt action. In almost every ad you'll find a statement like "call today," "write today for more information," or "go to your nearest travel agent and sign up for the trip." The help wanted ad shown in Figure 4-10 on page 141 is a good example of an action prompt.

The increased internationalization of the U.S. economy has created many opportunities for companies to do business all over the world. Figure 4-11 on page 142 provides an example of the use of ads for these broader opportunities.

Constructing the ad (as discussed above) is important, but so is complying with the various equal employment laws. After over 30 years of living with EEO laws, we might imagine that by now most employers are familiar with the sorts of things they can't generally put in ads (such as "man wanted," or "young woman preferred"). Yet the results of one recent study on illegal recruitment advertisement suggests that questionable or illegal ads still do slip into recruitment advertising, so this is apparently still an area in which more caution is required.[30]

FIGURE 4-7
*Managerial
Help Wanted Ad*

Introduce Yourself to an Industry Leader.

SUPERIOR PRODUCTS, INNOVATIVE MARKETING PROGRAMS AND UNPARALLELED CUSTOMER SERVICE HELP MAKE FIDELITY INVESTMENTS® ONE OF THE NATION'S TOP FINANCIAL SERVICES ORGANIZATIONS. BEHIND OUR SUCCESS ARE HIGHLY-SKILLED AND COMMITTED INDIVIDUALS WHOSE EXPERTISE AND DRIVE ARE POSITIONING FIDELITY FOR UNPRECEDENTED GROWTH IN THE 1990S. IF YOU SHARE OUR ETHIC AND VISION, PLEASE CONSIDER THE FOLLOWING OPENING:

SENIOR STAFFING MANAGER

Fidelity Investments has an opening for an experienced staffing specialist to manage the employment function for the Fidelity Institutional and Brokerage businesses. Responsibilities include working with H.R. generalists and business managers to identify future staffing needs, develop candidate pools and creative sourcing strategies, and filling varied professional openings. Candidates must have at least 10 years' responsible business and/or H.R. experience with a focus on high volume, professional-level recruiting and experience in the brokerage and/or mutual fund/institutional financial services industries.

Fidelity offers exceptional benefits for exceptional people, including health/dental insurance, tuition reimbursement, profit sharing and a 401(k) plan. Send your resume to:

HOW TO GET YOUR CAREER OUT OF THE BOX

Introduce Yourself to Fidelity.
WRITE.
NOW.

FIDELITY INVESTMENTS, HUMAN RESOURCES, 82 DEVONSHIRE ST., DEPT. SSM, MAIL ZONE I7A, BOSTON, MA 02109
An equal opportunity employer, M/F/D/V.

Employment Agencies as a Source of Candidates

There are three types of employment agencies: (1) public agencies operated by federal, state, or local governments; (2) agencies associated with nonprofit organizations; and (3) privately owned agencies.[31]

Every state has a public, state-run employment service agency. These agencies are supported by the U.S. Department of Labor, in part through grants and in part through other assistance—such as a nationwide computerized job bank to which all state employ-

TABLE 4-2 Advantages and Disadvantages of Some Major Types of Media

TYPE OF MEDIUM	ADVANTAGES	DISADVANTAGES	WHEN TO USE
Newspapers	Short deadlines. Ad size flexibility. Circulation concentrated in specific geographic areas. Classified sections well organized for easy access by active job seekers.	Easy for prospects to ignore. Considerable competitive clutter. Circulation not specialized— you must pay for great amount of unwanted readers. Poor printing quality.	When you want to limit recruiting to a specific area. When sufficient numbers of prospects are clustered in a specific area. When enough prospects are reading help wanted ads to fill hiring needs.
Magazines	Specialized magazines reach pinpointed occupation categories. Ad size flexibility. High-quality printing. Prestigious editorial environment. Long life—prospects keep magazines and reread them.	Wide geographic circulation— usually cannot be used to limit recruiting to specific area. Long lead time for ad placement.	When job is specialized. When time and geographic limitations are not of utmost importance. When involved in ongoing recruiting programs.
Radio and television	Difficult to ignore. Can reach prospects who are not actively looking for a job better than newspapers and magazines. Can be limited to specific geographic areas. Creatively flexible. Can dramatize employment story more effectively than printed ads. Little competitive recruitment clutter.	Only brief, uncomplicated messages are possible. Lack of permanence; prospect cannot refer back to it. (Repeated airings necessary to make impression.) Creation and production of commercials—particularly TV— can be time-consuming and costly. Lack of specialinterest selectivity; paying for waste circulation.	In competitive situations when not enough prospects are reading your printed ads. When there are multiple job openings and there are enough prospects in specific geographic area. When a large impact is needed quickly. A "blitz" campaign can saturate an area in two weeks or less. Useful to call attention to printed ads.
"Point-of-purchase" (promotional materials at recruiting location)	Calls attention to employment story at a time when prospects can take some type of immediate action. Creative flexibility.	Limited usefulness; prospects must visit a recruiting location before it can be effective.	Posters, banners, brochures, audiovisual presentations at special events such as job fairs, open houses, conventions, as part of an employee referral program, at placement offices, or whenever prospects visit at organization facilities.

Source: Adapted from Bernard S. Hodes, "Planning for Recruitment Advertising: Part II," *Personnel Journal*, Vol. 28, no. 5 (June 1983), p. 499. Reprinted with the permission of *Personnel Journal*, Costa Mesa, CA. All rights reserved.

ment offices are connected. The National Job Bank enables an agency counselor in one state to advise job applicants about available jobs not just in their local area but in other geographical areas as well.

The services provided by the state agencies are increasing, along with the effectiveness of what used to be "the unemployment office." An important source of both blue-collar and white-collar workers, some employers' experience with these agencies has been mixed. For one thing, applicants for unemployment insurance are required to register with these agencies and to make themselves available for job interviews. A fraction of these people are not interested in getting back to work; employers can therefore end up with applicants who have little or no real desire to obtain immediate employment. And, fairly or not, some of these local agencies are probably viewed as somewhat lethargic in their efforts to fill area employers' jobs.

Today, however, these agencies' usefulness is on the rise. Beyond just filling jobs, for instance, counselors will visit an employer's work site, review the employer's job requirements, and even assist the employer in writing job descriptions. And some states, like Illinois and Wisconsin, are turning their local state employment service agencies into "one-stop" shops. Under this concept, say managers from Illinois' Department of Employment Security," employers and jobseekers now access, under a single roof, a broader array of employment security, workforce-development, and business-support programs. Services

FIGURE 4-8

A Help Wanted Ad That Draws Attention

available to employers include recruitment services, tax credit information, employee training programs and access to the latest local and national labor market information."[32]

Other employment agencies are associated with nonprofit organizations. For example, most professional and technical societies have units that help their members find jobs. Similarly, many public welfare agencies try to place people who are in special categories, such as those who are physically disabled or are war veterans.

Private employment agencies are important sources of clerical, white-collar, and managerial personnel. Such agencies charge fees for each applicant they place. These fees are usually set by state law and are posted in their offices. Whether the employer or the candidate pays the fee is mostly determined by market conditions. However, the trend has been toward "fee-paid jobs" in which the employer pays the fees. The assumption is that the most qualified candidates are presently employed and would not be as willing to switch jobs if they had to pay the fees themselves. Many private agencies now offer temporary help service and provide secretarial, clerical, or semiskilled labor on a short-term basis. These agencies can be useful in helping you cope with peak loads and fill in for vacationing employees; we'll return to such "temp" agencies later in this chapter.

Some specific reasons you might want to turn to an agency include the following:

1. Your firm does not have its own HR department and is not geared to do recruiting and screening.
2. Your firm has found it difficult in the past to generate a pool of qualified applicants.
3. A particular opening must be filled quickly.
4. There is a perceived need to attract a greater number of minority or female applicants.
5. The recruitment effort is aimed at reaching individuals who are currently employed and who might feel more comfortable dealing with employment agencies rather than competing companies.

FIGURE 4-9

A Help Wanted Ad That Creates Interest

Group Health Underwriters

WE NEED AN UNDERWRITER WHO'S AN OVERACHIEVER.

To keep pace with our rapidly expanding account base, we're looking for ambitious self starters to join the Employee Benefit Group in our Orinda office. The kind of pro's with proven records and super analytical skills.

If this sounds like you, consider joining The Travelers, a $46 billion insurance and financial services leader.

To qualify, you need at least 3 years of group health underwriting experience where you've gained a solid knowledge of employee benefits coverages. You must also have excellent communications and interpersonal skills.

In return, you'll thrive on challenging work in a dynamic environment. We've recently combined our New Business and Customer Relations Groups, creating a leaner, more aggressive force. As part of this new unit, you'll have broad exposure and career growth opportunities. Plus receive a highly competitive salary and benefits package.

So, if you're an overachiever, join The Travelers. And enjoy a career that's a cut above the rest.

Send your resume, with salary requirements, to: Sonia Mielnik, The Travelers Companies, 30-CR, SF426L1, One Tower Square, Hartford, CT 06183-7060.

TheTravelers

You're better off under the Umbrella.℠

Home Office: The Travelers Companies, Hartford, Connecticut. An Equal Opportunity Employer.

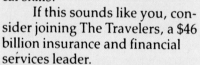

There are other reasons to use an employment agency for some or all of your recruiting needs.[33] Employment agencies' promotional ads in the *Wall Street Journal* list these advantages in terms like "cut down on your interviews," "interview only the right people," and "have recruiting specialists save you time by finding, interviewing, and selecting only the most qualified candidates for your final hiring process."

On the other hand, employment agencies are no panacea. For example, an employment agency prescreens applicants for your job, but this advantage can also backfire.[34] The employment agency's screening may let poor applicants bypass the preliminary stages of

FIGURE 4-10

A Help Wanted Ad with a Call to Action

Source: BSA Advertising, San Mateo, CA

We Can Take You Places.

Kaiser Permanente Medical Care Program is one of the largest Health Maintenance Organizations in the nation. We offer highly skilled professionals who are committed to those in need of quality medical care to consider these excellent opportunities and experience health care at its best.

We reward our people with competitive salaries, comprehensive benefits, educational programs and the ability to transfer between facilities without losing seniority. Kaiser Permanente is proud to be an equal opportunity employer.

Hayward

For these positions in our Hayward Medical Center please apply Monday-Thursday, 10am-1pm to **Personnel Department, 27400 Hesperian Blvd., Hayward, CA 94545** or call **Ellen Gutstadt at (415) 784-4258.**

Staff Nurses

ER: Nights & On-Call   **ICU/CCU:** Evenings & Nights
L&D: Nights   **Med/Surg:** Nights
ICN: All shifts available   **Float:** All shifts available

Employee Health Service Nurse Practitioner: Requires 5 years of adult practitioner experience and a Master's degree.

Adult Nurse Practitioner: Requires 2 years of experience and a Master's degree.

OB Supervisor: A Bachelors degree, strong clinical and management skills combined with a clinical speciality are necessary to supervise our active tertiary, L&D, Gyn and perinatal units. RN licensure and 3 years of labor and delivery are required. MS degree preferred.

Advice Nurse: Two years of recent Med/Surg experience. Part-time and on-call positions available.

OR Nurses: Day and evening positions available with 6 months experience and a current CA RN license.

Night Shift Supervisor: To work 3 nights per week, Bachelors degree preferred.

We are also accepting applications for:
New Graduate Program:
Re-entry Program:

KAISER PERMANENTE
Medical Care Program

your own selection process. Unqualified applicants may thus go directly to the supervisors responsible for the hiring, who may in turn naively hire them. Such errors show up in high turnover and absenteeism rates, morale problems, and low quality and productivity. Similarly, potentially successful minority and nonminority applicants may be blocked from entering your applicant pool by improper testing and screening at the employment agency. To help avoid such problems, two experts suggest the following:

FIGURE 4-11

A Help Wanted Ad in International Management

1. Give the agency an accurate and complete job description. The better the employment agency understands the job or jobs to be filled, the greater the likelihood that a reasonable pool of applicants will be generated.
2. Specify the devices or tools that the employment agency should use in screening potential applicants. Tests, application blanks, and interviews should be a proven part of the employer's selection process. At the very least, you should know which devices the agency uses and consider their relevance to the selection process. Any subjective decision-making procedures used by the agency would be of particular concern.
3. Where possible, periodically review data on candidates accepted or rejected by your firm, and by the agency. This will serve as a check on the screening process and provide valuable information if there is a legal challenge to the fairness of the selection process.
4. If feasible, develop a long-term relationship with one or two agencies. It may also be advantageous to designate one person to serve as the liaison between the employer and agency. Similarly, try to have a specific contact on the agency's staff to coordinate your recruiting needs.

There are several things you can do to select the best agency for your needs. Checking with other managers or HR people will reveal the agencies that have been the most effective at filling the sorts of positions you want to have filled. Another approach is to review seven or eight back issues of the Sunday classified ads in your library to find the agencies that consistently handle the positions you want. This will help narrow the field.

Once you've narrowed the field, here are some questions you should ask in order to decide which agency is best for your firm. What is the background of the agency's staff? What are the levels of their education and experience and their ages? Do they have the qualifications to understand the sorts of jobs for which you are recruiting? What is their reputation in the community and with the Better Business Bureau?

USING TEMPORARY HELP AGENCIES   Many employers today supplement their permanent employee base by hiring contingent or temporary workers, often through special temporary help agencies. Also defined as part-time or just-in-time workers, the contingent workforce is big and growing (recently accounting for about 20% of all new jobs created in the U.S.) and is broadly defined as workers who don't have permanent jobs.[35]

Contingent staffing owes its growing popularity to several things. For one thing, corporate downsizing seems to be driving up the number of temp workers that firms employ. For example, while DuPont says it has cut its workforce by 47,000 in the past few years, it also estimates that only 70% of those workers actually stopped working for the company: the remaining 30%—about 14,000 workers—returned in some temporary capacity, or as vendors or contractors.[36] Historically, employers have also always used "temps" to fill in for the days or weeks that permanent employees were out sick or on vacation. Today's desire for ever-higher productivity also contributes to temp workers' growing popularity. In general, as one expert puts it, "Productivity is measured in terms of output per hour paid for," and "if employees are paid only when they're working as contingent workers are, overall productivity increases."[37] Employers also find that by tapping temporary help agencies, they can save the time and expense of personally recruiting and training new workers, as well as the expenses involved in personnel documentation (such as filing payroll taxes and maintaining absence records).[38]

As a result, the contingent workforce is no longer limited to clerical or maintenance staff. In one recent year almost 100,000 people found temporary work in engineering, science, or management support occupations, for instance.[39] In fact, growing numbers of firms use temporary workers as short-term chief financial officers, or even chief executive officers. It's estimated that 60% of the total U.S. temporary payroll is nonclerical and includes "CEOs, human resources directors, computer systems analysts, accountants, doctors, and nurses."[40]

The benefits of contingent staffers don't come without a price. They may be more productive and less expensive to recruit and train, but contingent workers hired through temporary agencies generally cost employers 20% to 50% more than comparable permanent workers (per hour or per week) since the agency gets a fee. Furthermore, "people have a psychological reference point to their place of employment. Once you put them in the contingent category, you're saying they're expendable."[41] One would also assume that such expendable workers are less likely to exhibit the benefits of loyalty that many employers expect from their permanent workers. This problem is exacerbated by the fact that while "additional income" is the top reason individuals give for becoming temporary employees, the second most important reason is "as a way to get a full-time job." To the extent that a temp finds his or her hopes dashed, the ties that bind employer and employee are even more tenuous.[42] Low unemployment is also restricting the temp services, recruiting efforts, which could possibly lead to some temp agencies becoming less selective in the people they send out to employers.[43]

In order to make such employment relationships as fruitful as possible, anyone recruiting temps should understand their main concerns. In one survey, six key concerns emerged:[44]

1. Temporary workers are discouraged by the dehumanizing and impersonal way that they are treated on the job.
2. Temporary workers feel insecure about their employment and are pessimistic about the future.
3. Temporary workers worry about their lack of insurance and pension benefits.
4. Temporary workers claim that employers fail to provide an accurate picture of their job assignments and in particular about whether temporary assignments are likely to become full-time positions.
5. Temporary workers feel underemployed, particularly those trying to return to the full-time labor market.
6. Temporary workers feel a generalized anger toward the corporate world and its values; participants repeatedly expressed feelings of alienation and disenchantment.

Given such concerns, what can employers do to boost the likelihood that relationships with temporary workers will be mutually beneficial? Here are six guidelines:[45]

1. Provide honest information to both temp agencies and temp workers about the length of the job assignment.
2. Implement personnel policies that ensure fair and respectful treatment of temporary workers. (For example, in one instance claims of sexual harassment by an employer's supervisors were not addressed by the firm because the temps were not its legal employees. Nor were the claims addressed by the temporary agency because the perpetrators were not the agency's employees.)
3. Use independent contractors (people who—like consultants—work for themselves rather than for the company) and permanent part-time employees to complement the conventional temporary agency workforce. Especially where you require a highly skilled and committed workforce, using permanent part-timers and independent contractors may provide a level of trained expertise and loyalty that exceeds that of employees from temporary agencies. These people are likely to be more familiar with your company's procedures and more committed to its goals than temporary workers.
4. Before hiring temporary workers, consider their potential impact on regular full-time employees. For example, any apparent exploitation or mistreatment of contingent workers may have a corrosive effect on permanent workers' morale.
5. Provide the necessary training and orientation for temporary workers. For example, one survey's comments included, "If you are expected to hit the ground running, that should be specified when requesting a temp from the agency." "[Organizations] need to be more specific in their instructions to temps. Give them the [correct] tools and materials to do their jobs."
6. Beware of legal snares in your payroll decisions. In particular, the IRS has been paying special attention to jobs such as sales rep and janitor. Although such jobs are often contracted out, some employers may be categorizing their permanent workers incorrectly as independent contractors to avoid paying withholding taxes and social security taxes.[46] In other words, the employer should be careful not to use a contingent workforce classification such as "independent contractor" as a means for illegally avoiding paying the taxes to which permanent employees are usually entitled.

Given the increased use of contingent workers, it's not surprising that one survey reported over 84% of employers use temp agencies, and their use is on the rise.[47]

The nature of the temporary-help relationship means employers must address some special issues when dealing with such agencies. Of course, putting time and effort into meeting with several and choosing the one that's best for you is important. But you must also ensure that basic policy and procedures are in place, including:[48]

Invoicing   Get a sample copy of the company's invoice. Make sure you understand the invoicing procedure and that it fits your company's needs.

Time Sheets   Also get a sample time sheet. With temps, the time sheet that is signed by the worker's supervisor is usually in effect an agreement to pay the agency's fees rather than simply a verification of hours worked.

Temp-to-Perm Policy   Specifically, what is the policy if the client wants to permanently hire one of the service's temps? Most services prefer to keep the temp on their payroll for a specific waiting period before moving the person to the client's payroll (at no extra cost).

Recruitment of and Benefits for Temp Employees   Find out how the temp service plans to recruit employees and what sorts of benefits it pays.

Inside Staff   Learn as much as you can about how the temp service's staff (such as the people who interview applicants) match skills to position requirements and place and dispatch the temp work force.

Dress Code   Clearly indicate the appropriate attire at each of your offices or plants.

Equal Employment Opportunity Statement   You should get a document from the temp service stating that it is not discriminating when filling temp orders.

Job Description Information   Set up a procedure whereby you can be reasonably sure that the temp service completely understands the nature of the job to be filled and the sort of person, in terms of skills and so forth, you want to fill it.

Some firms today employ so many temporary workers that they hire temporary agencies to manage their temporary workforces. New York-based MasterCard, for instance, has a temporary workforce of 200 to 400 workers on any given day, and retained Manpower, Inc., a large temporary staffing agency, to coordinate the hiring, training, and paperwork of new temporary workers. The temporary employment agency may even assign on-site supervisors to the employer to manage the manpower-related duties involved in managing the temporary employees.[49] Some temp agencies are even opening in shopping malls. Olsten Staffing Services, for instance, has opened centers in six locations to offer mall tenants assistance in areas such as job postings, temporary employment, candidate screening and interviewing, background checks, reliability and integrity testing, and training. They're even thinking of adding a squad of trained temporary staff in each mall to fill in for mall tenants during short-term gaps, such as when a tenant's employee needs to be out of town briefly.[50]

Alternative Staffing Techniques

Temporary employees and temp agencies represent one example of what HR professionals call "alternative staffing"—basically, the use of nontraditional recruitment sources. The use of alternative staffing sources is widespread and growing; the most recent Bureau of Labor Statistics data indicates that about 1 of 10 U.S. employees is employed in an alternative working arrangement.[51]

Common alternative staffing options include traditional temporary help (as discussed above), as well as long-term temporary assignments and "payrolling"—having the employer identify specific people it wants to hire and then referring them to a staffing firm, which employs them and assigns them to work at the company. Short descriptions of alternative staffing options are presented in Figure 4-12.

DEFINITIONS

Common Alternative Staffing Options

Today's alternative staffing options are flexible and creative enough to meet myriad needs of employers.

1. Traditional temporary help. In the traditional scenario, a person is recruited, tested, screened and employed by a temporary help firm. The temporary firm assigns people to work at clients' sites, generally to support or supplement the workforce to cover employee absences, temporary skill shortages, special assignments or projects of finite duration. Temporary employees may be obtained from many different services simultaneously. Some temporary help firms specialize in particular industries or specific types of personnel.

2. Long-term temporary assignments. Many companies now use temporary employees to supplement their regular workforce on an ongoing basis, rather than simply as short-term replacements. The overall size of the temporary workforce ebbs and flows depending on workload, thus enhancing the stability of the employer's core group of regular employees.

3. Master vendor arrangements. In these arrangements—sometimes referred to as an on-site program or vendor-on-premises—one staffing firm supplies all needed temporary employees, which consolidates billing and invoicing, and streamlines administration.

Generally, the master vendor will assign one or more of its employees to work on the client's premises to coordinate all job orders, orient new temporaries, oversee scheduling, compile reports and statistics on temp usage, and perform other administrative tasks.

Master vendors often engage staffing-firm subcontractors (secondary suppliers) to help meet the client's supplemental staffing needs. In such cases, the on-site coordinator serves as liaison with those firms.

4. In-house temporary employees. These are people employed directly on the company's payroll on an explicit temporary basis. Sometimes referred to as "floaters," they typically rotate among departments, depending on work requirements. In-house temporaries are not usually eligible for benefits programs.

5. Payrolling. In payrolling, the company needing help identifies specific people and refers them to a staffing firm, which employs them and assigns them to work at the company. The staffing firm oversees the pre-employment process, administers the payroll, retains employment records, provides workers' compensation coverage, absorbs unemployment costs if the person is laid off, and locates replacements when necessary, usually for a lower cost than that charged for traditional temporary employees.

6. Part-time employees. Employees scheduled to work less than a regular work week on an ongoing basis may be on the company's payroll or assigned through a temporary service. Their eligibility for benefits depends on various factors, in-

cluding the number of hours worked and the terms of the company's benefits plans.

7. Independent contractors. Self-employed individuals whose services are engaged on a contract basis are hired to perform specialized tasks generally requiring a high level of independence, judgment, skill and discretion. Independent contractors are compensated on a contract or fee basis, are issued Form 1099s, and are free to render services to other organizations. People who work as independent contractors must genuinely satisfy the legal criteria for that status, or the employer may be held liable for payroll taxes, benefits and other payments.

8. Contract technical workers. Highly skilled technical workers—often professionals such as engineers, electronic data processing specialists or database architects—are supplied for long-term projects under contract between the company and a technical services firm. These professionals often travel or work on projects far from their homes, and may have multi-year or indefinite assignments.

9. Employee leasing. A company may transfer all employees, substantially all employees, or sometimes just the employees at a discrete facility or site, to the payroll of an employee leasing firm or Professional Employer Organization (PEO) in an explicit joint-employment relationship. The PEO then leases the workers back to the client company and administers the payroll, provides benefits and benefits administration, maintains personnel records, and performs most of the functions normally handled by an HR department.

10. Outsourcing or managed services. In these arrangements, an independent company with expertise in operating a specific function contracts with a client company to take full operational responsibility for performing that function, rather than just supplying personnel. Companies usually outsource functions peripheral to their core business—security, landscaping or food services—but the range of functions companies are outsourcing is increasing. Some companies have outsourced the task of managing their alternative staffing programs.

11. Temp-to-perm programs. These employees are hired on a temporary basis—generally through a temporary help firm—with the understanding that if they perform competently for a specific period they will receive offers of regular employment.

12. Temp-to-lease programs. In these arrangements, a company contracts with two (usually affiliated) staffing firms, generally a temporary service and a PEO. The temporary service recruits, screens, interviews, tests and assigns its employees as long-term temporaries at the client company. After a negotiated period of satisfactory employment, the temporary employee is "promoted" to leased employee status and transferred to the PEO's payroll, becoming eligible for specific benefits through the PEO.

FIGURE 4-12 *Common Alternative Staffing Options*

Source: Thomas Greble, "A Leading Role for HR in Alternative Staffing," *HR Magazine*, February 1997, pp. 100–101.

Executive Recruiters as a Source of Candidates

Executive recruiters (also called headhunters) are special employment agencies retained by employers to seek out top-management talent for their clients. They fill jobs in the $50,000 and up category, although $70,000 is often the lower limit. The percentage of your firm's positions filled by these services might be small. However, these jobs would include your most crucial executive and technical positions. For executive positions, headhunters may be your only source of candidates. Their fees are always paid by the employer.

Two trends—technology, and specialization—are changing the executive search business. Top firms traditionally took up to seven months to complete a big search, much of that time spent shuffling chores between headhunters and researchers who need to dig up the initial "long list" of candidates;[52] this often takes too long in today's fast-moving environment. Most of these firms are therefore establishing Internet-linked computerized databases the aim of which, according to one senior recruiter, is "to create a long list by pushing a button."[53] Recruiter Korn/Ferry launched a new Internet service called Futurestep to draw more managerial applicants into its files; in turn, it has teamed up with the *Wall Street Journal*, which runs a career Website of its own.[54]

Executive recruiters are also becoming more specialized, and the large ones are creating new businesses aimed specifically at specialized functions or industries. For example, recruiter LAI Ward Howell recently launched a new business specializing in financial executives, with bases in London and New York.[55]

Headhunters can be quite useful. They have many contacts and are especially adept at contacting qualified candidates who are employed and not actively looking to change jobs. They can also keep your firm's name confidential until late into the search process. The recruiter can save top management time by doing the preliminary work of advertising for the position and screening what could turn out to be hundreds of applicants. The recruiter's fee might actually turn out to be insignificant compared to the cost of the executive time saved.

But there are some pitfalls. As an employer, it is essential for you to explain completely what sort of candidate is required—and why. Some recruiters are also more salespeople than professionals. They may be more interested in persuading you to hire a candidate than in finding one who will really do the job. Recruiters also claim that what their clients say they want is often not really accurate. Therefore, be prepared for some in-depth dissecting of your request. In choosing a recruiter, guidelines include:[56]

1. *Make sure the firm is capable of conducting a thorough search.* Under the code of the Association of Executive Recruiting Consultants, a headhunter cannot approach the executive talent of a former client for a vacancy with a new client for a period of two years after completing a search for the former client. Since former clients are off limits to the recruiter for a period of two years, the recruiter must make a search from a constantly diminishing market. Particularly for the largest executive recruiting firms, it could turn out to be very difficult to deliver a top-notch candidate, since the best potential candidates may already be working for the recruiter's former clients.

2. *Meet the individual who will be handling your assignment.* The person handling your search will determine the fate of the search. If this person hasn't the ability to seek out top candidates aggressively and sell them on your firm, it is unlikely you will get to see them. Beware of the fact that in wooing you as a new client, the search firm will send its best salesperson, someone with a record of successfully signing new clients. However, this is usually not the person who will be doing the actual search.

3. *Ask how much the search firm charges.* There are several things to keep in mind here. Search firm fees range from 25% to 35% of the guaranteed annual income of the position being filled. They are often payable one-third as a retainer at the outset, one-third at the end of 30 days, and one-third after 60 days, and they are not necessarily paid on a contingency basis only. Often a fee is payable whether or not the search is terminated for any reason. The out-of-pocket expenses are extra and could run to 10% to 20% of the fee itself, and sometimes more.

4. *Choose a recruiter you can trust.* This is essential because this person will find not only your firm's strengths, but its weaknesses too. It is therefore important that you find someone you can trust with what may be privileged information.

5. *Talk to some of their clients.* Finally, ask to be given the names of two or three companies for whom the search firm has recently completed assignments. Ask such questions as: Did the recruiter's appraisal of the candidate seem accurate? Did the firm really conduct a search, or was the job simply filled from their files? And were time and care taken in developing the job specifications?[57]

As a job candidate, keep several things in mind when dealing with executive search firms. Most of these firms pay little heed to unsolicited resumes, preferring instead to ferret out their own candidates. Some firms have also been known to present an unpromising candidate to a client simply to make their other one or two proposed candidates look that much better. Some eager clients may also jump the gun, checking your references and undermining your present position prematurely. Also remember that executive recruiters and their clients are usually more impressed with candidates who are obviously "not looking" for a job, and that overeagerness to take the job can be a candidate's downfall.[58]

SMALL BUSINESS APPLICATIONS

There comes a time in the life of most small businesses when it dawns on the owner that his or her managers are incapable of taking the company into the realm of expanded sales. A decision must then be made regarding what kinds of people to hire from outside and how this hiring should take place. Should the owner decide what type of person to hire and recruit this person himself or herself? Or should an outside expert be brought in to help with the search?

USING EXECUTIVE RECRUITERS

The heads of most large firms often won't think twice about hiring executive search firms to conduct their search. However, small companies' owners (with their relatively limited funds) will hesitate before committing to a fee that could reach $20,000 to $30,000 (with expenses) for a $60,000 to $70,000 marketing manager. As a small-business owner, however, you should keep in mind that this sort of thinking can be shortsighted when you consider what your options actually are.

Engaging in a search like this by yourself is not at all like looking for secretaries, supervisors, or data entry clerks. When you are looking to hire a key executive to help you run your firm, chances are you are not going to find your candidate by placing ads or using most of the other traditional approaches. For one thing, the person you seek is probably already employed and is probably not reading the want ads, if he or she does happen to glance at the ads, chances are the person is happy enough not to take the effort to embark on a job search with you.

In other words, what you'll end up with is a drawerful of resumes of people who are, for one reason or another, out of work, unhappy with their work, or unsuited for your job. It is then going to fall on you to try to find several gems in this group of resumes, by devoting the time to interview and assess these applicants yourself.

There are thus two problems with conducting these kinds of executive searches yourself. First, as a nonexpert, you may not even know where to begin. You won't know where to place or how to write the ads; you won't know where to search, who to contact, or how to do the sort of job that needs to be done to interview people in order to screen out the laggards and misfits who may well appear on the surface to be viable candidates. You also won't know enough to really do the kind of background checking that a position at this level requires. Second, this process is going to be extremely time consuming and will divert your attention from other duties. Many business owners find that when they consider the opportunity costs (of not making sales calls, for instance) involved with doing their own searches, they are not saving any money at all.

In any event, if you do decide to do the job yourself, consider retaining the services of an industrial psychologist. He or she will be able to spend four or five hours assessing the problem-solving ability, personality, interests, and energy level of the two or three candidates in which you are most interested. Although you certainly don't want the psychologist to make the decision for you, the input can provide an additional perspective on the candidates.

College Recruiting as a Source of Candidates

College recruiting—sending an employer's representatives to college campuses to prescreen applicants and create an applicant pool from that college's graduating class—is an important source of management trainees, promotable candidates, and professional and technical employees. One recent study of 251 staffing professionals concluded, for instance, that about 38% of all externally filled jobs requiring a college degree were filled by new college graduates (the percentage for just entry-level jobs requiring a college degree filled by new grads would probably be much higher).[59]

There are two main problems with on-campus recruiting. First, it is relatively expensive and time consuming for the recruiters. One study from the 1980s estimated the average cost of campus recruiting at 16% of the total human resource budget for Fortune 500 firms. (Most of this money was spent on recruiters' salaries and travel.)[60] Schedules must be set well in advance, company brochures printed, records of interviews kept, and much recruiting time spent on campus. Second, as mentioned earlier, recruiters themselves are sometimes ineffective, or worse. Some recruiters are unprepared, show little interest in the candidate, and act superior. Many recruiters also don't effectively screen their student candidates. For example, students' physical attractiveness often outweighs other more valid traits and skills.[61] Some recruiters also tend to assign females to "female-type" jobs and males to "male-type" jobs.[62] Such findings underscore the need to train recruiters before sending them to the campus.[63]

You have two goals as a campus recruiter. Your main role is screening, which means determining whether a candidate is worthy of further consideration. Exactly which traits you look for will depend on your specific recruiting needs. However, the report presented in Figure 4-13 is typical. Traits to assess include motivation, communication skills, education, appearance, and attitude.[64]

CAMPUS INTERVIEW REPORT

Name _____ Anticipated Graduation Date _____

Current Address _____
    If different than placement form

Position Applied For _____
_____

If Applicable (Use Comment Section if necessary)

    Drivers License   Yes _____ No _____

    Any special considerations affecting your availability for relocation?
_____

_____

    Are you willing to travel? _____ If so, what % of time _____
_____

EVALUATION	Outstanding	Above Average	Average	Below Average
Education: Courses relevant to job? Does performance in class indicate good potential for work?	_____	_____	_____	_____
Appearance: Was applicant neat and dressed appropriately?	_____	_____	_____	_____
Communication Skills: Was applicant mentally alert? Did he or she express ideas clearly?	_____	_____	_____	_____
Motivation: Does applicant have high energy level? Are his or her interests compatible with job?	_____	_____	_____	_____
Attitude: Did applicant appear to be pleasant, people-oriented?	_____	_____	_____	_____

COMMENTS: (Use back of sheet if necessary)
_____
_____
_____

Given Application   Yes _____ No _____ Received Transcript Release Authorization _____

Recommendations Invite _____ Reject _____

Interviewed by: _____ Date: _____

Campus _____

FIGURE 4-13 *Campus Applicant Interview Report*

Source: Adapted from Joseph J. Famularo, *Handbook of Personnel Forms, Records, and Reports* (New York: McGraw-Hill Book Company, 1982), p. 70.

TABLE 4-3 Factors in Selecting College Recruiters

RECRUITING ASPECT	STRENGTH (1–7)
Identification of high-quality applicants	5.8
Professionalism of recruiters	5.6
Filling all vacancies	5.5
Generating the right number of applicants	5.5
High performance of new recruits	5.4
High retention of new recruits	5.3
High job acceptance rates	5.0
Administrative procedures	4.7
Turn-around times	4.5
Planning and goal setting	4.5
Meeting EEO/AA targets	4.4
Program evaluation	4.3
Cost control	4.2

Source: Reprinted with permission from the March 1987 issue of *Personnel Administrator.*
Copyright 1987. The American Society for Personnel Administration, 606 North Washington
Street, Alexandria, VA 23314.

While your main function is to find and screen good candidates, your other aim is
to attract them to your firm. A sincere and informal attitude, respect for the applicant as
an individual, and prompt follow-up letters can help you to sell the employer to the interviewee.

Recruiters and schools must be carefully chosen. As summarized in Table 4-3, employers choose college recruiters on the basis of who can do the best job of identifying top
applicants and filling vacancies. Factors in selecting schools in which to recruit include the
school's reputation and the performance of previous hires from that source (see Table 4-4).

Good applicants are generally invited to the employer's office or plant for an on-site
visit, and there are several ways to make sure this visit is fruitful.[65] The invitation letter
should be warm and friendly but businesslike, and the person should be given a choice of

TABLE 4-4 Factors in Selecting Schools in Which to Recruit

TOPIC	IMPORTANCE (1–7*)
Reputation in critical skill areas	6.5
General school reputation	5.8
Performance of previous hires from the school	5.7
Location	5.1
Reputation of faculty in critical skill areas	5.1
Previous job offer and acceptance rates	4.6
Past practice	4.5
Number of potential recruits	4.5
Ability to meet EEO targets	4.3
Cost	3.9
Familiarity with faculty members	3.8
SAT or GRE scores	3.0
Alma mater of CEO or other executives	3.0

*7 is high; 1 is low.
Source: Reprinted with permission from the March 1987 issue of *Personnel Administrator.* Copyright 1987,
The American Society for Personnel Administration, 606 North Washington Street, Alexandria, VA 22314.

dates to visit the company. Somebody should be assigned to meet the applicant and act as host, preferably meeting the person at the airport or at his or her hotel. A package describing the applicant's schedule as well as other information regarding the employer—such as annual reports and description of benefits—should be waiting for the applicant at the hotel. The interviews should be carefully planned and the schedule adhered to. Interruptions should be avoided; the candidate should have the undivided attention of each person with whom he or she interviews. Luncheon should be arranged at the plant or at a nearby restaurant or club, preferably hosted by one or more other recently hired graduates with whom the applicant may feel more at ease. An offer, if any, should be made as soon as possible, preferably at the time of the visit. If this is not possible, the candidate should be told when to expect a decision. If an offer is made, keep in mind that the applicant may have other offers too. Frequent follow-ups to "find out how the decision process is going" or to "ask if there are any other questions" may help to tilt the applicant in your favor.

INTERNSHIPS   Many college students get their jobs through college internships, a recruiting approach that has grown dramatically in recent years. Today, it's estimated that almost three-quarters of all college students take part in an internship before they graduate, compared to one in 36 in 1980, for instance.[66]

Internships can be win-win situations for both students and employers. For students, it may mean being able to hone business skills, check out potential employers, and learn more about their likes (and dislikes) when it comes to choosing careers. And employers, of course, can use the interns to make useful contributions while they're being evaluated as possible full-time employees.

Referrals and Walk-Ins as a Source of Candidates

"Employee referrals" campaigns are another option. Announcements of openings and requests for referrals are made in the organization's bulletin and posted on wall boards; prizes are offered for referrals that culminate in hirings.

Employee referral programs have their pros and cons. Current employees can and usually will provide accurate information about the job applicants they are referring, especially since they're often putting their own reputations on the line by recommending them.[67] The new employees may also come with a more realistic picture of what working in the firm is really like after speaking with their friends who are currently employed there. Referrals may also result in higher-quality candidates, insofar as employees are reluctant to refer less-qualified candidates. But the success of the campaign depends a lot on your employees' morale.[68] And the campaign can backfire if an employee's referral is rejected and the employee becomes dissatisfied. Using referrals exclusively may also turn out to be discriminatory if most of your current employees (and their referrals) are male or white.

Employee referral programs are increasingly popular. Of the firms responding to one survey, 40% said they use an employee referral system and hire about 15% of their employees through such referrals. A cash award for referring hired candidates is the most common referral incentive. Large firms reportedly spent about $34,000 annually on their referral programs (including cash payments for candidates), medium companies spent about $17,000, and small ones with fewer than 500 employees spent about $3,600. The cost per hire, however, was uniformly low; average per hire expenses were only $388, far below the cost of an employment service.[69] Recruiting high-tech employees (remember "nerd rustling"?) is especially amenable to employee referrals programs. While high-tech sources like the Internet are still widely used for recruiting high-tech workers, some high-tech experts contend that the most effective recruiting method is to encourage existing employees to refer qualified friends and colleagues for high-tech jobs; awards for referrals can go as high as $5,000 for a new hire in such programs.[70]

Particularly for hourly workers, walk-ins—direct applications made at your office—are a major source of applicants and can even be encouraged by posting "for hire" signs on your property. All walk-ins should be treated courteously and diplomatically, for the sake of both the employer's community reputation and the applicant's self-esteem. Many employers thus give every walk-in a brief interview with someone in the HR office, even if it is only to get information on the applicant "in case a position should be open in the future." Good business practice also requires that all letters of inquiry from applicants be answered promptly and courteously.

Recruiting on the Internet

As in Figure 4-14, a large and growing proportion of employers recruit on the Internet. In one survey, 32% of the survey's 203 respondents said they were using the Internet as a primary recruitment source, up from 20% in 1996.[71] Not surprisingly, computer-related positions were the most common jobs filled through Internet postings (accounting for 59% of the workers hired) followed by technical (39%), engineering (29%), consulting (21%), sales (15%), management (14%), marketing (14%), accounting (10%), as well as various other job classifications.[72]

As explained in Chapter 3 (Job Analysis) a multitude of Internet job-placement and recruiting sources are available today. For example the personnel journal *Workforce* has a website (www.workforceonline.com/postajob/) that will take you to various sites including "best Internet recruiter," general recruitment Websites, college recruitment Websites, and specific industry recruitment Websites, and also let you place your own help wanted ad on-line through the *Workforce* on-line Website Figure 4-15. Similarly, Yahoo (http://employment.yahoo.com/) is just one of the other possible ways to place and access employment classified ads.

Employers are using Internet recruiting in various ways. One Boston-based recruiting firm posts job descriptions on its World Wide Web page.[73] NEC Electronics, Inc.,

FIGURE 4-14

Employment Services on a Company's Web Site

Progressive Corp. is just one of many firms that posts a recruiting page on its Web site. Such pages often include a means for job applicants to e-mail their resumes and research what it would be like to work at the firm.

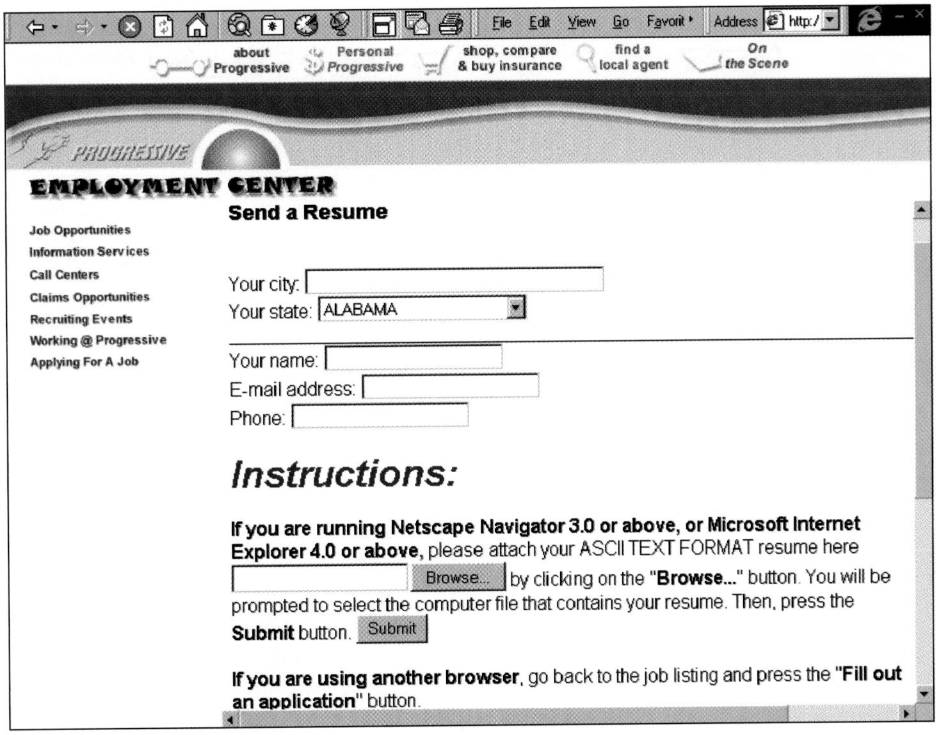

I magine recruitment ads that are less expensive than traditional media...that reach a computer literate, innovative candidate pool...and can be accessed 24-hours a day, from anywhere. Post-a-Job helps you get your jobs ads out, and the resumes in.

Place a Help Wanted Ad Online

Job Ad Price: $150   Duration: 8 weeks

Workture Online users are eligible to receive a free listing in the JobOptions Employer Database for up to 12 months. Click here to e-mail tom@joboptions.com and provide your name, company, address, state, zip code, phone number, site URL and business/industry.

Member Price: $195   Duration: 60 days

With over a million resumes in our database, Monster.com has the tools, technology and expertise to help you hire smart people more intelligently. 1-800-MONSTER.

Job Ad Price: $160   Duration: 30 days

Post your job online with CareerMosaic. As an employer, you can use this online service to post your job openings in our database which currently receives over 200,000 queries every day.

FIGURE 4-15   *Many Web Site Services Permit Employers to Post Their Open Positions, in This Case for a Fee*

Unisys Corp., and LSI Logicorp have all posted Internet-based "cyber fairs" to recruit for applicants.[74] A Minneapolis-based computer firm uses the Internet to search for temporary workers with extensive knowledge of Microsoft Excel.[75] Cisco systems, Inc., has a Website with the Cisco employment Opportunities page, which offers links to such things as hot jobs—job descriptions for hard-to-fill positions; Cisco culture—a look at Cisco work life; Cisco College—internships and mentoring program information; and jobs—job listings.[76]

Employers list several advantages of Internet recruiting. Internet recruiting is, first, cost-effective. Newspapers may charge employers from $50 to $100 to several thousand dollars for print ads; job listings on the Internet may cost as little as $10 apiece, one expert points out.[77] The newspaper ad might also have a life span of perhaps 10 days, while the Internet ad may keep attracting applications for 30 days or more.[78] Internet recruiting can also be more timely; responses to electronic job listings may come the day the ad is posted, whereas responses to newspaper want ads can take a week to reach an employer (although inserting a fax-response number can provide timely responses here, too).

Some firms have been phenomenally successful using Internet recruiting. For example, when Boeing Company had to hire 13,000 employees fast, they opened their recruiting Website. Only 200 resumes were received the first month, but within three months 19,000 resumes had arrived, and in six months, 50,000.[79]

Yet, some employers cite just such a flood of responses as a possible downside of Internet recruiting. The problem is that the relative ease of responding to Internet ads may encourage clearly unqualified jobseekers to apply; furthermore, the nature of the Internet is that applications may arrive from geographic areas that are unrealistically far away. On the whole, though, more applicants are usually better than fewer when it comes to recruiting, and more companies are using their computers to scan, digitize, and process applicant resumes automatically.[80]

THE HIGH-PERFORMANCE ORGANIZATION

Building Better, Faster, More Competitive
Organizations Through HR: Recruiting Tech Workers

■ GE Medical Systems

When it comes to effective recruiting, the rubber really hits the road, as they say, when it comes to recruiting high-tech workers. Turnover amongst these in-demand elites is reportedly around 17%, and according to the Information Technology Association of America about 1 out of 10 information technology jobs in the United States is going begging, for instance.[81]

The techy-recruiting methods used by one industry leader—GE Medical—illustrates how best practices can be brought to the job of recruiting. GE Medical Systems hires about 500 technical workers a year to invent and make sophisticated medical devices such as CT scanners and magnetic resonance images. Since GE Medical must compete for talent with the likes of Intel, Microsoft, and Cisco Systems, it's interesting that in 1997 GE Medical managed to cut its cost of hiring by 17%, reduced time to fill the positions by 20 to 30%, and cut in half the percentage of new hires who don't work out.[82]

GE Medical accomplished this by applying the sorts of best-practices management techniques that have made its parent, General Electric Corporation, such a profit power-house. According to one of its managers, the firm decided to "benchmark off procurement and supplier management initiatives in other areas of the business. We know everything about acquiring wires and screws and boards and computers."[83] What GE Medical did was apply those same techniques to the job of high-tech recruiting.

For example, GE Medical draws up a "multigenerational staffing plan" to go with each of its product's multiyear product plan. That way, management can predict two or three years out more precisely what sorts of specific needs (such as for "absolute algorithm" experts) they're going to have to hire and train for.

GE Medical has also applied some of its manufacturing purchasing techniques to its dealings with recruiters and colleges. For example, it called a meeting several years ago and told a score of recruiters that it would work with only the 10 best of them. To measure "best" they created measurements inspired by manufacturing techniques, such as the percentage of resumes that result in interviews, and the percentage of interviews that lead to offers.

Applying a more benchmarks-oriented approach also worked with college recruiting. When GE Medical's chief recruiter analyzed the recruiting system and found that former summer interns are twice as likely to accept the job offer as other candidates, GE Medical tripled the size of the interns program. (And, to make sure they don't spend their time photocopying files, interns are given special challenging group and team projects.)

Similarly, GE's corporate-wide quality control program enabled GE Medical to discover how effective current employees are as references for new high-tech employees. Overall, for instance, just 1% of applicants whose resumes come into GE Medical are even called for an interview, while 10% of employee referrals result not just in interviews but in actual hires.

As a result, GE Medical has now taken steps that have led to doubling the number of employee referrals. For example, it simplified the referral forms, eliminated bureaucratic submission procedures, and added a small goody like a Sears gift certificate simply for referring a qualified candidate. And, they upped the ante—$2,000 if someone referred is hired, and $3,000 if he or she is a software engineer.

DIVERSITY COUNTS

Recruiting Single Parents

About two-thirds of all single parents are in the work force today, and this group thus represents an important source of candidates.

Formulating an intelligent program for attracting single parents should begin with understanding the considerable problems that they often encounter in balancing work and family life.[84] In one recent survey, working single parents (the majority of whom were single mothers) stated that their work responsibilities interfered significantly with their family life. They described as a no-win situation the challenge of having to do a good job at work and being a good parent, and many expressed disappointment at feeling like failures in both endeavors. To quote from the survey's report:

> Many described falling into bed exhausted at midnight without even minimal time for themselves. They reported rushing through every activity and constantly feeling pressured to keep on going and do more. Vacations, which can be a time to rejuvenate, were often

used for children's appointments or to handle unexpected emergencies. Also personal sick time or excused days off were often needed to care for sick children. As one mother noted, "I don't have enough sick days to get sick."[85]

The respondents generally viewed themselves as having "less support, less personal time, more stress and greater difficulty balancing job and home life" than other working parents.[86] However, most were hesitant to dwell on their single-parent status at work for fear that such a disclosure would affect their jobs adversely. Thirty-five percent of the single mothers reported feeling that it was more difficult for them to achieve a proper work-family balance compared with 10% of the dual-earner mothers.[87] Some single mothers reported that they were treated differently than their male colleagues at work. For example, "When a single mother asks if she can go to her child's school play, she is seen as not committed to her job and often not allowed to go, while a male single parent is more

---

Firms are finding that former welfare recipients make good hires. "It's no different from hiring any entry-level person," says Scott Simons, president of Laser Labs, Inc. in Philadelphia, who has successfully hired several such workers.

Recruiting a More Diverse Workforce

Recruiting a diverse workforce is not just socially responsible: It's a necessity, given the rapid growth of minority and female candidates. Therefore, smart employers have to actively recruit a more diverse workforce. This means taking special steps to recruit older workers, minorities, and women. The Diversity Counts box describes one approach.

OLDER WORKERS AS A SOURCE OF CANDIDATES   More employers are looking to older workers as a source of recruits, and there are several reasons for this. For one thing (because of buyouts and early retirements), many workers have retired early and are ready and willing to reenter the job market.[92] Furthermore, over the next 10 or 15 years the number of annual retirees will double to approximately four million, and "there will be, I guarantee it, many millions of boomers who will have to work beyond age 65 because they simply haven't saved enough money to retire," says a demographer.[93] And, fewer 18- to 25-year-olds are entering the workforce;[94] this has caused many employers to "harness America's gray power" by encouraging retirement-age employees not to leave, or by actively recruiting employees who are at or beyond retirement age.[95]

Is it practical in terms of productivity to keep older workers on? The answer seems unequivocally to be "yes."[96] Age-related changes in physical ability, cognitive performance, and personality have little effect on workers' output except in the most physically

often told 'Sure. It's just great that you are so interested in your children.'"[88]

Given such concerns, the first step in attracting (and keeping) single mothers is to make the workplace as "user friendly" for single mothers as is practical. Organizing regular, ongoing support groups and other forums at which single parents can share their concerns is a good way to provide the support that may be otherwise lacking. Furthermore, although many firms have instituted programs aimed at becoming more family friendly, these may not be extensive enough, particularly for single parents. For example, through *flextime* many employers already give employees a little flexibility (such as one-hour windows at the beginning or end of the day) around which to build their workdays. The problem is that "for some single mothers, this flexibility can help but it may not be sufficient to really make a difference in their ability to juggle work and family schedules."[89] In addition to increased flexibility, employers can and should train their supervisors to have an increased awareness of and sensitivity to the sorts of challenges single parents face. As two researchers concluded:

Very often, the relationships which the single mother has with her supervisor and coworkers is a significant factor influencing whether the single-parent employee perceives the work environment to be supportive.[90]

For their part, single parents reentering the workforce can turn to various agencies for support. For example, displaced homemakers—individuals who reenter the workforce after a long period out of work or who are forced to work due to hardship—can call the Displaced Homemakers Network (202-628-6767) for advice in obtaining training and placement.[91] Women entering or reentering the workforce can also call Women Work! the National Network for Women's Employment in Washington, DC, for referrals to local training programs and information about financial aid options, child support, and health insurance. The toll-free number is 1-800-235-2732.

demanding tasks.[97] Similarly, creative and intellectual achievements do not decline with age and absenteeism drops as age increases. Older workers also usually display more company loyalty than youthful workers, tend to be more satisfied with their jobs and supervision, and can be trained or retrained as effectively as anyone.

Recruiting and attracting older workers involves any or all the sources described earlier (advertising, employment agencies, and so forth), but with one big difference. Recruiting and attracting older workers generally requires a comprehensive HR retiree effort before the recruiting begins, in part because older workers can be hard to find.[98] The aim is to make the company an attractive place in which the older worker can work. Specifically:

Examine your personnel policies. Make sure policies and procedures do not discourage recruitment of seniors or encourage valuable older people to leave. For example, paying limited benefits to part-time workers, promoting early retirement, or not offering flexible schedules can impede older worker recruitment and/or retention.

Develop flexible work options. For example, at Wrigley Company, workers over 65 can progressively shorten their work schedules; another company uses "minishifts" to accommodate those interested in working less than full time.[99]

Create or redesign suitable jobs. At Xerox, unionized hourly workers over 55 with 15 years of service and those over 50 with 20 years of service can bid on jobs at lower stress and lower pay levels if they so desire.

Offer flexible benefit plans. For example, older employees often put more emphasis on longer vacations or on continued accrual of pension credits than do younger workers.

RECRUITING MINORITIES AND WOMEN   The same prescriptions that apply to recruiting older workers also apply to recruiting minorities and women. In other words, employers must formulate comprehensive plans for attracting minorities and women, plans that may include reevaluating personnel policies, developing flexible work options, redesigning jobs, and offering flexible benefit plans. To paraphrase the expert quoted earlier, to recruit minorities and women employers must tailor their way of thinking and institute HR practices that make the firm attractive.

There are many specific things an employer can do to become more attractive to minorities. To the extent that many minority applicants may not meet the educational or experience standards for a job, many companies (including Aetna Life & Casualty) offer remedial training in basic arithmetic and writing.[100] Diversity data banks or nonspecialized minority-focused recruiting publications are another option. For example, Hispan Data provides recruiters at companies like McDonald's access to a computerized data bank; it costs a candidate $5.00 to be included.[101] Checking with your own minority employees can also be useful. For example, about 32% of job seekers of Hispanic origin cited "check with friends or relatives" as a strategy when looking for jobs.[102]

WELFARE-TO-WORK   Employers are also implementing various "welfare-to-work" programs for attracting and assimilating former welfare recipients as new employees. In 1996 President Clinton signed the Personal Responsibility and Welfare Reconciliation Act of 1996, an act that prompted many employers to implement these types of programs. (The act required 25% of people receiving welfare assistance to be either working or involved in a work-training program by September 30, 1997, with the percentage rising each year to 50% by September 30, 2002.)[103]

The key to a welfare-to-work program's success seems to be the employer's "pre-training" assimilation and socialization program, during which participants receive counseling and basic skills training spread over several weeks.[104] For example, Marriott International has hired 600 welfare recipients under its "Pathways to Independence" program. The heart of the program is a six week pre-employment training program teaching work and "life" skills designed to rebuild workers' self-esteem and instill positive attitudes about work.[105] Programs like Marriott's have reportedly been successful—for instance, 77% of the welfare recipients hired by the company are reportedly still on board.[106] On the other hand, other companies report difficulty in hiring and assimilating people previously on welfare, in part because they sometimes lack basic work skills such as reporting for work on time, working in teams, and "taking orders without losing their temper."[107]

Some Other Recruiting Sources

More employers are also turning to relatively nontraditional sources of applicants.[108] For example, moonlighters have often been shunned by employers on the assumption that workers with full-time jobs at other firms might not have the required commitment to a second employer to do their jobs responsibly. Yet more employers are finding that moonlighters usually take second jobs because they must, and that commitment to their second employer is thus high enough for good job performance. Advertising aimed at groups such as teachers, police officers, retail clerks, and firefighters can be a good source of such employees, particularly if you can provide flexible work hours.

Other options include retired or exiting military personnel who often bring with them excellent skills. Testimonials from former military personnel who have joined your firm and ads with slogans such as "Join Our Team" can help attract these individuals. Disabled individuals are a most underused pool of labor. State rehabilitation agencies, Projects With Industry (write to the U.S. Department of Education, 330 C Street, S.W., Switzer Building, Washington, DC 20202), and the U.S. Veterans' Administration can be helpful in identifying such candidates.

Recruiting Methods Used

The type of job generally determines what recruiting source is used. For managerial positions, 80% of employers in one survey used newspaper ads, 75% used private employment agencies, and 65% relied on employee referrals. For professional and technical jobs, 75% used college recruiting, 75% also used ads in newspapers and technical journals, and 70% used private employment agencies. For recruiting sales personnel, 80% of the firms used newspaper ads, 75% used referrals, and 65% also used private employment agencies. For office and plant personnel, on the other hand, referrals and walk-ins were relied on by 90% of the firms, while 80% of the firms used newspaper ads and 70% used public employment agencies.[109]

GLOBAL HRM

The Global Talent Search

As companies expand across national borders, they must increasingly tap overseas recruiting sources.[110] For example, Gillette International has an international graduate training program aimed at identifying and developing foreign nationals. Gillette subsidiaries overseas hire outstanding business students from top local universities. These foreign nationals are then trained for six months at the Gillette facility in their home countries. Some are selected to then spend 18 months being trained at the firm's Boston headquarters in areas such as finance and marketing. Those who pass muster are offered entry-level management positions at Gillette facilities in their home countries.

Coca-Cola also actively recruits foreign nationals. In addition to recruiting students abroad, it looks for foreign students studying in well-known international business programs like those at the University of South Carolina, UCLA, and the American Graduate School of International Management in Arizona.

Increasingly today when employers hire "global" employees they're not just hiring employees who will be sent to work abroad. While it's true that for many corporations "international recruitment is synonymous with expatriate selection,"[111] HR professionals recognize today that with business increasingly being multinational, "every employee needs to have a certain level of global awareness. . . ."[112]

As a result, many employers want their recruiters to look for evidence of global awareness early in the interview process. For example, at the U.S. headquarters of Tetra PAK, Inc., the personnel manager reportedly looks for expatriate potential every time she makes a hire: "We don't often go out and search for someone to go abroad next year . . . but when we recruit, we always look for candidates who have global potential. We're interested in people who eventually could relocate internationally and handle that adjustment well."[113] International experience (including internships and considerable travel abroad) as well as language proficiency are two of the things employers like this would look for.

Global recruiting isn't a one-way street, by the way—in other words, you're not just looking for local talent to send abroad, but possibly for talent from abroad that you can bring here. For example, many U.S. companies are reportedly looking in the United Kingdom, Germany, and Western Europe for high-tech employees to fill jobs that are going begging in the U.S.[114] New technology can be very useful in that regard. For example, the Internet, fax, and video conferencing can make the recruiting process easier by enabling you to place ads more easily and then do at least your initial screening while the candidate is still abroad.[115]

DEVELOPING AND USING APPLICATION FORMS

application form

The form that provides information on education, prior work record, and skills.

Purpose of Application Forms

Once you have a pool of applicants the selection process can begin, and for most employers the **application form** is the first step in this process. (Some firms first require a brief, prescreening interview.) The application form is a good way to quickly collect verifiable and therefore fairly accurate historical data from the candidate. It usually includes information about such areas as education, prior work history, and hobbies.

A filled-in form provides four types of information.[116] First, you can make judgments on substantive matters, such as "Does the applicant have the education and experience to do the job?" Second, you can draw conclusions about the applicant's previous progress and growth, a trait that is especially important for management candidates. Third, you can also draw tentative conclusions regarding the applicant's stability based on previous work record. (Here, however, you have to be careful not to assume that an unusual number of job changes necessarily reflects on the applicant's ability; for example, the person's last two employers may have had to lay off large numbers of employees.) Fourth, you may be able to use the data in the application to predict which candidates will succeed on the job and which will not, which we cover later.

In practice, most organizations need several application forms. For technical and managerial personnel, for example, the form may require detailed answers to questions concerning the applicant's education and so on. The form for hourly factory workers might focus on the tools and equipment the applicant has used and the like.

Equal Opportunity and Application Forms

Employers should carefully review their application forms to ensure they comply with equal employment laws. Questions concerning race, religion, age, sex, or national origin are generally not illegal per se under federal laws, but are illegal under certain state laws. However, they are viewed with disfavor by the EEOC, and the burden of proof will always be on the employer to prove that the potentially discriminatory items are both related to success or failure on the job and are not unfairly discriminatory. For example, you generally can request photographs prior to employment and even ask such potentially discriminatory questions as, "Have you ever been arrested?" The problem is that an unsuccessful applicant might establish a prima facie case of discrimination by demonstrating that the item produces an adverse impact. The burden of proof would then shift to you to show that the item is a valid predictor of job performance and that it is applied fairly to all applicants—that, for instance, you check arrest records of all applicants, not just minority applicants.

Unfortunately, many employers' application forms are highly questionable. A study of 50 actual application forms revealed 17 types of questions containing possible violations of federal regulations.[117] Many of the items should probably have been left out. These included questions regarding maiden name or name used previously, height and weight, age, religion, race or color, national origin, and sex. In addition, several more subtle types of potentially discriminatory questions often crept into the forms:

Education. One common violation on many of the applications was a question on the dates of attendance and graduation from various schools—academic, vocational, or professional. This question may be illegal in that it may reflect the applicant's age.

Arrest records. The courts have usually held that employers violate Title VII by disqualifying applicants from employment because of an arrest record. This item has an adverse impact on minorities and in most cases cannot be shown to be justified by business necessity.

Notify in case of emergency. It is generally legal to require the name, address, and phone number of a person who can be notified in case of emergency. However, asking the relationship of this person could indicate the applicant's marital status or lineage. In any event, information such as this can just as well be requested after the offer has been made and accepted.

Membership in organizations. Many forms ask the applicant to list memberships in clubs, organizations, or societies along with offices held. However, employers should add instructions not to include organizations that would reveal race, religion, physical handicaps, marital status, or ancestry. Those not adding such a clause may be indirectly asking for the applicant's race or religion, for instance, and would thus be guilty of making an unlawful inquiry.

Physical handicaps. It is usually illegal to require the listing of an applicant's physical handicaps, defects, or past illnesses unless the application blank specifically asks only for those that "may interfere with your job performance." Similarly, it is generally illegal to ask whether the applicant has ever received worker's compensation for a previous injury or illness.

Marital status. In general, the application should not ask whether an applicant is single, married, divorced, separated, or living with anyone, or the names and ages of the applicant's spouse or children. Similarly, it may be shown to be discriminatory to ask a woman for her husband's occupation and then reject the woman because, say, her husband is in the military and therefore subject to frequent relocation.

Housing. Asking whether an applicant owns, rents, or leases a house may also be discriminatory. It can adversely affect minority groups and is difficult to justify on grounds of business necessity.

Figure 4-16 presents one employer's approach to collecting application form information—the employment application for Chapman Academy.

Several guidelines should be kept in mind. The "Positions Held" section should request detailed information on each prior employer, including name of supervisor and his or her telephone number, and whether or not the employment was involuntarily terminated—all essential for following up with your reference-checking. Also, in signing the application, the applicant should certify his or her understanding of several things: that falsified statements may be cause for dismissal; that investigation of credit and employment and driving record is authorized; that a medical examination may be required; that drug screening tests may be required; and that employment is for no definite period of time.

MANDATORY DISPUTE RESOLUTION   While the EEOC is generally opposed to the idea, more employers are requiring applicants to sign mandatory alternative dispute resolution forms as part of the applicant process. For example, the employment application package for Circuit City requires applicants to agree to arbitrate certain legal disputes re-

EMPLOYMENT APPLICATION

As an equal opportunity employer, the firm does not discriminate in hiring or in terms and conditions of employment because of an individual's race, creed, color, sex, age, religion, disability or natural origin. The firm only hires individuals authorized for employment in the United States.

___/___/___
Date of Application

Position Applying for: _____

Schedule Desired: ( ) Full time   ( ) Temporary
                    ( ) Part time

PERSONAL INFORMATION

Last Name	First Name	Middle Name	Are you authorized for employment in the U.S.? ( ) Yes ( ) No
Present Street Address	City	State	Zip	How long have you lived there? Yrs. Mo.
Previous Street Address	City	State	Zip	How long did you live there? Yrs. Mo.
Home Phone Number	Social Security Number	If you are under 18 years of age, state your age:	

EDUCATION

Type of School	Name and Location of School	Degree/Area of Study	Number of Years Attended	Graduated (Check One)
HIGH SCHOOL	Name / City State			Yes ☐ No ☐
JUNIOR COLLEGE	Name / City State			Yes ☐ No ☐
COLLEGE	Name / City State			Yes ☐ No ☐
GRADUATE SCHOOL	Name / City State			Yes ☐ No ☐
OTHER	Name / City State			Yes ☐ No ☐

ACADEMIC AND PROFESSIONAL ACTIVITIES AND ACHIEVEMENTS

Academic and Professional Activities and Achievements, Awards, Publications or Technical-Professional Societies. Indicate type or name. Exclude organizations which indicate race, creed, color, sex, age, religion, handicap or national origin of its members.	Date Awarded

SKILLS

Skills applicable to position applied for

PERSON TO CONTACT IN CASE OF EMERGENCY

This information is to facilitate contact in the event of an emergency and is not used in the selection process.

Full Name	Address	Phone	Relationship to you?
Place of Employment	Address	Phone	

15-10.22227 Rev. 5/92

GC 7520

FIGURE 4-16 *Chapman Academy Application Form*

lated to their application for employment or employment with the company (including, for instance, those relating to the Age Discrimination in Employment Act); Circuit City will not consider the application unless this agreement is signed.[118]

While mandatory arbitration is on the rise, it is also under attack.[119] Courts, federal agencies, and even the organizations providing arbitration are increasingly concerned that too many employees' rights are stripped away by mandatory binding arbitration (*volun-*

EMPLOYMENT HISTORY

List employment starting with your most recent position. Account for any time during this period that you were unemployed by stating the nature of your activities. If you have less than four places of employment, include personal references to be contacted. May we contact your present employer?
( ) Yes ( ) No

DATES	NAME AND ADDRESS OF EMPLOYER	POSITION HELD AND SUPERVISOR	LIST MAJOR DUTIES	WAGES	REASON FOR LEAVING
FROM: / MO. YR.	NAME	YOUR JOB TITLE		STARTING	
	ADDRESS				
TO: / MO. YR.		SUPERVISOR		FINAL	
	PHONE				
FROM: / MO. YR.	NAME	YOUR JOB TITLE		STARTING	
	ADDRESS				
TO: / MO. YR.		SUPERVISOR		FINAL	
	PHONE				
FROM: / MO. YR.	NAME	YOUR JOB TITLE		STARTING	
	ADDRESS				
TO: / MO. YR.		SUPERVISOR		FINAL	
	PHONE				
FROM: / MO. YR.	NAME	YOUR JOB TITLE		STARTING	
	ADDRESS				
TO: / MO. YR.		SUPERVISOR		FINAL	
	PHONE				

MISCELLANEOUS

Is there any additional information involving a change of your name or assumed name that will permit us to check your work record?
If yes, please explain.

Have you ever been employed by The Firm or any of its divisions or subsidiaries before? ☐ Yes ☐ No

If yes, Please indicate:	When	Where	Position

List Names of Friends or Relatives now employed by The Firm.

Have you ever been convicted of a crime? ☐ Yes ☐ No   If yes, please explain:

PLEASE READ THIS STATEMENT CAREFULLY

I hereby affirm that the information given by me on this application for employment is complete and accurate. I understand that any falsification or ommission will be immediate grounds for dismissal. I authorize a thorough investigation to be made in connection with this application concerning my character general reputation, employment and education background, and criminal record, whichever may be applicable. I understand what this investigation may include and I hereby authorize the release of documents, and personal interviews with third parties, such as prior employers, family members, business associates, financial sources, friends, neighbors or others with whom I am acquainted. I further understand that I have the right to make a written request within a reasonable period of time for a complete and accurate disclosure of the nature and scope of the investigation.

It is understood that, as a condition of initial or continued employment, I agree to submit to such lawful examinations, medical, substance abuse, or other, as may be required by the compnay. The company will pay the reasonable cost of any such examination which may be required.

If I am hired, I agree that my employment and compensation can be terminated with or without cause and without notice, at any time, at the option of the firm or myself. I understand that no store manager or other representative of the firm other than a Vice-President, and in writing, has the authority to enter into any agreement for employment for any specified period of time, or to make any agreement contrary to the foregoing.

I have read and affirm as my own the above statements.

_____ Signature   _____ Date

APPLICANTS IN THE STATE OF MARYLAND ONLY

Under Maryland law an employer may not require or demand any applicant for employment or prospective employment or any employee to submit to or take a polygraph, lie detector or similar test or examination as a condition of employment or continued employment. Any employer who violates this provision is guilty of a misdemeanor and subject to a fine not to exceed $100.

_____ Signature   _____ Date

APPLICANTS IN THE STATE OF MASSACHUSETTS ONLY

It is unlawful in Massachusetts to require or administer a lie detector test as a condition of employment or continued employment. An employer who violates this law shall be subject to criminal penalties and civil liability.

_____ Signature   _____ Date

FIGURE 4-16 *(continued)*

tary arbitration is not under attack). In fact, in May 1997, a Maryland federal court ruled that Circuit City, Inc., could not force its arbitration program on a job applicant in a case there. In an indication of where the matter is probably heading, many companies that supply arbitrators are refusing to do so unless the employers have ADR policies that are fair to the aggrieved employees—for instance, in terms of giving them an equal right to representation and factual investigation.[120]

Using Application Forms to Predict Job Performance

Some firms use application forms to predict which candidates will be successful and which will not, in much the same way that employers use tests for screening. They do this by conducting statistical studies to find the relationship between (1) responses on the application form and (2) measures of success on the job. Some examples follow.

USING APPLICATION FORMS TO PREDICT JOB TENURE   One study was aimed at reducing turnover at a large insurance company. At the time of the study the company was experiencing a 48% turnover rate among its clerical personnel. This meant that for every two employees hired at the same time, there was about a 50–50 chance that one would not remain with the company 12 months or longer.

This study was done as follows: The researcher obtained the application forms of about 160 clerical employees of the company from the firm's personnel files. The researcher then split the application forms into two categories—long-tenure and short-tenure employees. The researcher found that some responses on the application form were highly related to job tenure. The researcher was thereby able to use the company's application forms to predict which of the firm's new applicants would stay on the job and which would not.

The study helped the firm comply with its equal employment opportunity responsibilities. For example, some of the items on the application form (like marital status) could be viewed as potentially discriminatory. In this case the researcher was able to prove that these items did predict success or failure on the job (long tenure versus short tenure). There was thus a business necessity reason for asking them.[121] (Whether or not an employer would want to risk asking such "red flag" questions is another matter.)

USING APPLICATION FORMS TO PREDICT EMPLOYEE THEFT   Employee theft and pilferage are serious problems that employers find difficult to deal with. Losses range up to $16 billion per year, but useful tests aimed at predicting stealing tend to be in-depth tests of personality and are difficult and time consuming to administer and evaluate.

One solution is to use the application form to predict which applicants have a higher likelihood of stealing. One researcher carried out studies for both a mass merchandiser and a supermarket in Detroit. He found that responses to some application form items (like "does not own automobile" and "not living with parents") were highly related to whether or not the employee was subsequently caught stealing. The researcher was therefore able to identify potential thieves before they were hired (although, again, at the risk of asking "red flag" questions).[122]

The biographical data or biodata items you choose (such as "does not own automobile" or "not living at home" should be chosen with two caveats in mind. First, of course, equal employment law will obviously limit the sorts of items you'll want to use.

You may also want to avoid using items that are perceived as invasive. In one study, for instance, items such as "dollar sales achieved," "received cash bonus for good job," and "GPA in math" were perceived by subjects as less invasive than were others such as "frequently attends religious services," "birth order," and "frequent dates as senior in high school." Basically, items that were seen as more verifiable, more transparent in purpose, and more impersonal were seen as less invasive. The subjects expressing concerns were concerned for various reasons including: fear of stigmatization, concern about having to recall traumatic events, and questions of intimacy and religion. Some other items scoring high on invasiveness included, for your information: age sexually active; frequency of head/stomach aches; elders' heart disease; observes specific holidays; mugged; miscarriage; and attempted suicide.[123]

We invite you to visit the Dessler page on the Prentice Hall Web site at **www.prenhall.com/dessler** for our on-line study guide, Internet exercises, current events, links to related Web sites, and more.

SUMMARY

1. Developing personnel plans requires three forecasts: one for *personnel requirements*, one for the *supply of outside candidates*, and one for the *supply of inside candidates*. To predict the need for personnel, first project the demand for the product or service. Next project the volume of production required to meet these estimates; finally, relate personnel needs to these production estimates.

2. Once personnel needs are projected, the next step is to build up a pool of qualified applicants. We discussed several sources of candidates, including internal sources (or promotion from within), advertising, employment agencies, executive recruiters, college recruiting, the Internet, and referrals and walk-ins. Remember that it is unlawful to discriminate against any individual with respect to employment because of race, color, religion, sex, national origin, or age (unless religion, sex, or origin are bona fide occupational qualifications).

3. The initial selection screening in most organizations begins with an application form. Most managers use these just to obtain background data. However, you can use application form data to make predictions about the applicant's future performance. For example, application forms have been used to predict job tenure, job success, and employee theft.

4. Personnel planning and recruiting directly affect employee commitment because commitment depends on hiring employees who have the potential to do the job; the more qualified applicants you have, the higher your selection standards can be. Selection usually begins with effective testing and interviewing, to which we turn in Chapter 5.

KEY TERMS

trend analysis   124
ratio analysis   124
scatter plot   125
computerized forecast   126

qualifications inventories   126
personnel replacement charts   126
position replacement cards   126

job posting   131
occupational market conditions   133
application form   160

DISCUSSION QUESTIONS

1. Compare and contrast five sources of job candidates.
2. What types of information can an application form provide?
3. Discuss how equal employment laws apply to personnel planning and recruiting activities.

INDIVIDUAL AND GROUP ACTIVITIES

1. Working individually or in groups, develop an application form for the position Marketing Manager as described in the sample job description in Figure 3-8, Chapter 3. Compare the application forms produced by different individuals or groups. Are there any items that should be dropped due to EEOC restrictions? Are there any items you would add to make your application form more complete?

2. Working individually or in groups, bring to class several classified and display ads from this Sunday's help wanted ads. Analyze the effectiveness of these ads using the guidelines discussed in this chapter.

3. Working individually or in groups, obtain a recent copy of the *Monthly Labor Review* or *Occupational Outlook Quarterly*, both published by the U.S. Bureau of Labor Statistics. Based on information in either of these publications, develop a forecast for the next five years of occupational market conditions for various occupations such as accountant, nurse, and engineer.

4. Working individually or in groups, visit the local office of your state employment agency. Come back to class prepared to discuss the following questions: What types of jobs seemed to be available through this agency, predominantly? To what extent do you think this particular agency would be a good source of professional, technical, and/or managerial applicants? What sort of paperwork are applicants to the state agency required to complete before their applications are processed by the agency? What other opinions did you form about the state agency?

5. Working individually or in groups, review help wanted ads placed over the last few Sundays by local employment agencies. Do some employment agencies seem to specialize in some types of jobs? If you were an HR manager seeking a relationship with an employment agency for each of the following types of jobs, which local agencies would you turn to first, based on their help wanted ad history: engineers; secretaries; data processing clerks; accountants; factory workers?

6. Working individually or in groups, interview an HR manager to determine the specific actions his or her company is taking to recruit a more diverse workforce. Back in class, compare the activities of the different employers.

EXPERIENTIAL EXERCISE

Forecasting Personnel Requirements

Park General Hospital is a primary-care hospital in a growing suburban population center. It has been working hard to improve its cost efficiency in patient care. The CEO has asked you (the HR director) to develop a forecast of nursing needs for the next 2 years. You have been provided a forecast of admittance trends showing the number of patients who stay overnight and the number of patients per nurse, a productivity measure that Park Hospital has begun to use. You also have a forecast productivity target of 3.3 patients per nurse 2 years from now.

Admittance Trends

	NUMBER OF OVERNIGHT PATIENTS/MONTH	NUMBER OF NURSES	PATIENTS PER NURSE
Three years ago	1700	590	2.9
Two years ago	1800	600	3
Last year	1900	610	3.1
Next year's forecast	2000		3.2 (forecast)
Year after next	2100		3.3 (forecast)

You also have been provided information on the turnover rate among nursing staff. That information is provided below.

Turnover rate:

	THREE YEARS AGO	TWO YEARS AGO	LAST YEAR	THIS YEAR
Nurses that retired	20	20	20	20
Nurses that quit	20	25	30	35
Nurses discharged	5	5	5	5
Total Turnover	45	50	55	60

Working in small teams, develop a forecast of personnel needs for the hospital by answering the following questions.

1. Based on admittance trends, what number of nurses do you estimate Park General Hospital will need over the next 2 years?
2. Based on turnover forecasts, how many nurses do you estimate Park General will need to replace in the next 2 years?

3. Given your answers to items 1 and 2, how many nurses does your department need to recruit?

Compare the answers of each of the groups. In the process of developing your forecast did your group see any trends that concerned you as HR professionals?

CASE INCIDENT

A Tight Labor Market for Cleaners

While most of the publicity about "tight" labor markets usually revolves around systems engineers, Website designers, and chemical engineers, some of the tightest markets are often found in some surprising places. For example, if you were to ask Jennifer Carter, the head of her family's six-store chain of dry-cleaning stores what the main problem was in running their firm, the answer would be quick and short: hiring good people. The typical dry cleaning store is heavily dependent on hiring good managers, clean air spotters, and pressers. Employees generally have no more than a high-school education (many have less) and the market is very competitive. Over a typical weekend literally dozens of want ads for cleaner-spotters or pressers can be found in area newspapers. These people are generally paid about $8 an hour, and they change jobs frequently.

Why so much difficulty finding good help? The work is hot and uncomfortable; the hours are often long; the pay is often the same or less than the typical applicant could earn working in an air-conditioned environment, and the fringe benefits are usually nonexistent, unless you count getting your clothes cleaned for free.

Complicating the problem is the fact that Jennifer and other cleaners are usually faced with the continuing task of recruiting and hiring qualified workers out of a pool of individuals that are almost nomadic in their propensity to move around. The turnover in her stores and the stores of many of their competitors is often 400% per year. The problem, Jennifer says, is maddening: "On the one hand, the quality of our service depends directly on the skills of the cleaner-spotters,

(continued)

(continued from page 165)

pressers, and counter staff. People come to us for our ability to return their clothes to them spotless and crisply pressed. On the other hand, profit margins are thin and we've got to keep our stores running, so I'm happy just to be able to round up enough live applicants to be able to keep my stores fully manned."

■ QUESTIONS

1. Provide a detailed list of recommendations concerning how Jennifer should go about increasing the number of acceptable job applicants, so that her company need no longer hire just about anyone who walks in the door. Specifically, your recommendation should include:

   a. Completely worded classified ads

   b. Recommendations concerning any other recruiting strategies you would suggest they use.

2. What practical suggestions could you make that might help reduce turnover and make the stores a more attractive place in which to work, thereby reduce recruiting problems?

Case Application FINDING PEOPLE WHO ARE PASSIONATE ABOUT WHAT THEY DO

Trilogy Software Inc., of Austin, TX, is one of the fastest growing software companies in the industry, with current earnings in the $100 million to $200 million range. It prides itself on its unique and unorthodox culture. Many of its approaches to business practice are unusual, but in Trilogy's fast-changing and highly competitive environment they seem to work.

There is no dress code and employees make their own hours, often very long. They tend to socialize together (the average age is 26), both in the office's well-stocked kitchen and on company-sponsored events and trips to places like local dance clubs and retreats in Las Vegas and Hawaii. An in-house jargon has developed, and the shared history of the 8-year-old firm has taken on the status of legend. Responsibility is heavy and comes early, with a "just do it now" attitude that dispenses with long apprenticeships. New recruits are given a few weeks of intensive training, known as Trilogy University and described by participants as "more like boot camp than business school." Information is delivered as if with "a fire hose," and new employees are expected to commit their expertise and vitality to everything they do. Jeff Daniel, director of college recruiting and only 28 himself, admits the intense and unconventional firm is not the employer for everybody. "But it's definitely an environment where people who are passionate about what they do can thrive."

The firm employs about 700 such passionate people. Trilogy's managers know the rapid growth they seek depends on having a staff of the best people they can find, quickly trained and given broad responsibility and freedom as soon as possible. Founder and CEO Joe Liemandt says, "At a software company, people are everything. You can't build the next great software company, which is what we're trying to do here, unless you're totally committed to that. Of course, the leaders at every company say, 'People are everything.' But they don't act on it."

Trilogy makes finding the right people a companywide mission. Recruiters actively pursue the freshest if least experienced people in the job market, scouring college career fairs and computer science departments for talented overachievers with ambition and entrepreneurial instincts. Top managers conduct the first rounds of interviews, letting prospects know they will be pushed to achieve but will be well rewarded. Employees take top recruits and their significant others out on the town when they fly into Austin for the standard 3-day preliminary visit. A typical day might begin with grueling interviews but ends with mountain biking, Roller Blading, or laser tag. Leimandt has been known to fly out to meet and woo hot prospects who couldn't make the trip.

In 1998 Trilogy reviewed 15,000 resumes, conducted 4,000 on-campus interviews, flew 850 prospects in for interviews, and hired 262 college graduates who account for over a third of its current employees. The cost per hire was $13,000; Jeff Daniel believes it was worth every penny.

■ QUESTIONS

1. Identify some of the established selection techniques that underlie Trilogy's unconventional approach to attracting talent.

2. What particular elements of Trilogy's culture most likely appeal to the kind of employees it seeks? How does it convey those elements to job prospects?

3. Would Trilogy be an appealing employer for you? Why or why not? If not, what would it take for you to accept a job offer from Trilogy?

Source: Chuck Salter, "Insanity, Inc.," *Fast Company*, January 1999, pp. 101–108.

NOTES

1. Herbert G. Heneman, Jr., and George Seitzer, "Manpower Planning and Forecasting in the Firm: An Exploratory Probe," in Elmer Burack and James Walker, *Manpower Planning and Programming* (Boston: Allyn & Bacon, 1972), pp. 102–120; Sheldon Zedeck and Milton Blood, "Selection and Placement," from *Foundations of Behavioral Science Research in Organizations* (Monterey, CA: Brooks/Cole, 1974), in J. Richard Hackman, Edward Lawler III, and Lyman Porter, *Perspectives on Behavior in Organizations* (New York: McGraw-Hill, 1977), pp. 103–119. For a discussion of equal employment implications of workforce planning, see James Ledvinka, "Technical Implications of Equal Employment Law for Manpower Planning," *Personnel Psychology*, Vol. 28 (Autumn 1975).

2. Roger Hawk, *The Recruitment Function* (New York: American Management Association, 1967). See also Paul Pakchar, "Effective Manpower Planning," *Personnel Journal*, Vol. 62, no. 10 (October 1983), pp. 826–830.

3. Based on an idea in Elmer H. Burack and Robert D. Smith, *Personnel Management: A Human Resource Systems Approach* (St. Paul, MN: West, 1977), pp. 134–135. Reprinted by permission. Copyright 1977 by West Publishing Co. All rights reserved.

4. Glenn Bassett, "Elements of Manpower Forecasting and Scheduling," *Human Resource Management*, Vol. 12, no. 3 (Fall 1973), pp. 35–43, reprinted in Richard Peterson, Lane Tracy, and Allan Cabelly, *Systematic Management of Human Resources* (Reading, MA: Addison-Wesley, 1979), pp. 135–146.

5. For an example of a computerized system in use at Citibank, see Paul Sheiber, "A Simple Selection System Called 'Job Match,'" *Personnel Journal*, Vol. 58, no. 1 (January 1979), pp. 26–54.

6. For discussions of skill inventories, see, for example, John Lawrie, "Skill Inventories: Pack for the Future," *Personnel Journal* (March 1987), pp. 127–130; John Lawrie, "Skill Inventories: A Developmental Process," *Personnel Journal* (October 1987), pp. 108–110.

7. Alfred Walker, "Management Selection Systems That Meet the Challenge of the 80's," *Personnel Journal*, Vol. 60, no. 10 (October 1981), pp. 775–780.

8. Donald Harris, "A Matter of Privacy: Managing Personnel Data in Computers," *Personnel* (February 1987), pp. 334–39.

9. Amiel Sharon, "Skills Bank Tracks Talent, Not Training," *Personnel Journal* (June 1988), pp. 44–49.

10. This section is based on Harris, "A Matter of Privacy."

11. David Dahl and Patrick Pinto, "Job Posting, an Industry Survey," *Personnel Journal*, Vol. 56, no. 1 (January 1977), pp. 40–41.

12. Jeffrey Daum, "Internal Promotion—Psychological Asset or Debit? A Study of the Effects of Leader Origin," *Organizational Behavior and Human Performance*, Vol. 13 (1975), pp. 404–413.

13. Arthur R. Pell, *Recruiting and Selecting Personnel* (New York: Regents, 1969), pp. 10–12.

14. Ibid., p. 11.

15. See "Hiring Workers the Second Time Around," *BNA Bulletin to Management*, January 30, 1997, p. 40.

16. Ibid.

17. Ibid.

18. Ibid.

19. This is a modification of a definition found in Peter Wallum, "A Broader View of Succession Planning," *Personnel Management* (September 1993), p. 45.

20. Ibid., pp. 43–44.

21. Shari Caudron, "Low Unemployment Is Causing a Staffing Draught," *Personnel Journal* (November 1996), pp. 59–67.

22. "Tight Labor Markets Bring New Paradigm," *BNA Bulletin to Management*, October 23, 1997, p. 344.

23. "High-Stakes Recruiting in High-Tech," *BNA Bulletin to Management*, February 12, 1998, p. 48.

24. See, for example, Nina Munk, "Organization Man," *Fortune*, March 16, 1998, pp. 63–82.

25. Ibid., p. 65.

26. Ibid.

27. "High Stakes Recruiting in High-Tech," *BNA Bulletin to Management*, February 12, 1998, p. 48.

28. Sara Rynes, Robert Breta, Jr., and Barry Gerhart, "The Importance of Recruitment in Job Choice: A Different Way of Looking," *Personnel Psychology*, Vol. 44, no. 3 (Autumn 1991), pp. 487–521.

29. Pell, *Recruiting and Selecting Personnel*, pp. 16–34. See also Barbara Hunger, "How to Choose a Recruitment Advertising Agency," *Personnel Journal*, Vol. 64, no. 2 (December 1985), pp. 60–62. For an excellent review of ads, see Margaret Magnus, *Personnel Journal*, Vols. 64 and 65, no. 8 (August 1985 and 1986); and Bob Martin, "Recruitment Ad Ventures," *Personnel Journal*, Vol. 66 (August 1987), pp. 46–63. For a discussion of how behavior can influence the initial attraction to an advertisement, see Tom Redman and Brian Matthews, "Advertising for Effective Managerial Recruitment," *Journal of General Management*, Vol. 18, no. 2 (Winter 1992), pp. 29–42.

30. John Kohl, David Stephens, and Jen-Chieh Chang, "Illegal Recruitment Advertising: A Ten Year Retrospect," *Employee Responsibilities and Rights*, Vol. 10, no. 3 (September 1977), pp. 213–224.

31. Pell, *Recruiting and Selecting Personnel*, pp. 34–42.

32. Lynn Doherty and E. Norman Sims, "Quick, Easy Recruitment Help—From a State?" *Workforce* (May 1998), p. 36.

33. Stephen Rubenfeld and Michael Crino, "Are Employment Agencies Jeopardizing Your Selection Process?" *Personnel*, Vol. 58 (September–October 1981), pp. 70–77.

34. Ibid.

35. Allison Thomson, "The Contingent Work Force," *Occupational Outlook Quarterly* (Spring 1995), p. 45.

36. Amy Kover, "Manufacturing's Hidden Asset: Temp Workers," *Fortune*, November 10, 1997, pp. 28–29.

37. One Bureau of Labor Statistics study suggests that temporary employees produce the equivalent of two or more hours of work per day more than their permanent counterparts. For a discussion, see Shari Caudron, "Contingent Workforce Spurs HR Planning," *Personnel Journal* (July 1994), p. 54.

38. Thomson, "The Contingent Workforce," p. 47.

39. Ibid., p. 47.

40. Brenda Paik Sunoo, "From Santa to CEO—Temps Play all Rolls," *Personnel Journal* (April 1996), pp. 34–44.

41. Caudron, "Contingent Workforce Spurs HR Planning," p. 60.

42. Ibid., p. 56.

43. Linda Davidson, "The Temp Pool Is Shrinking," *Personnel Journal* (April 1997), pp. 72–79.

44. Daniel Feldman, Helen Doerpinghaus, and William Turnley, "Managing Temporary Workers: A Permanent HRM Challenge," *Organizational Dynamics*, Vol. 23, no. 2 (Fall 1994), pp. 49.

45. Except as noted, the following are based on or quoted from Feldman et al., Ibid., pp. 58–60.

46. Barbara Ettorre, "The Contingency Work Force Moves Mainstream," *Management Review*, p. 15.

47. Bureau of National Affairs, "Part-Time and Other Alternative Staffing Practices," *Bulletin to Management*, June 23, 1988, pp. 1–10.

48. This is based on or quoted from Nancy Howe, "Match Temp Services to Your Needs," *Personnel Journal* (March 1989), pp. 45–51.

49. "Temps Get a Boss of Their Own," *BNA Bulletin to Management*, November 7, 1996, p. 30.

50. "The Newest Shop in the Mall: An Employment Center," *BNA Bulletin to Management*, May 14, 1998, p. 145.

51. Thomas Greble, "A Leading Role for HR in Alternative Staffing," *HR Magazine* (February 1997), p. 100.

52. "Search and Destroy," *The Economist*, June 27, 1998, p. 63.

53. Ibid.

54. Ibid.

55. Ibid.

56. John Wareham, *Secrets of a Corporate Headhunter* (New York: Playboy Press, 1981), pp. 213–225; Chip McCreary, "Get the Most out of Search Firms," *Workforce*, Vol. 76 (August 1997), pp. S28–S30.

57. Pell, *Recruiting and Selecting Personnel*, pp. 56–63; David L. Chicci and Carl Knapp, "College Recruitment from Start to Finish," *Personnel Journal*, Vol. 50, no. 8 (August 1980), pp. 653–657.

58. Allen J. Cox, *Confessions of a Corporate Headhunter* (New York: Trident Press, 1973).

59. Sara Rynes, Marc Orlitzky, and Robert Bretz, Jr., "Experienced Hiring versus College Recruiting: Practices and Emerging Trends," *Personnel Psychology*, Vol. 50 (1997), pp. 309–339.

60. Cynthia Kay Stevens, "Effects of Pre-Interview Beliefs on Applicants' Reactions to Campus Interviews," *Academy of Management Journal*, Vol. 40, no. 4 (1997), pp. 947–966.

61. Robert Dipboye, Howard Fronkin, and Ken Wiback, "Relative Importance of Applicant Sex, Attractiveness, and Scholastic Standing in Evaluation of Job Applicant Resumes," *Journal of Applied Psychology*, Vol. 61 (1975), pp. 39–48. See also Laura M. Graves, "College Recruitment: Removing the Personal Bias from Selection Decisions," *Personnel* (March 1989), pp. 48–52.

62. Ibid., pp. 39–48. See also, "A Measure of the HR Recruitment Function: The 1994 College Relations and Recruitment Survey," *Journal of Career Planning and Employment*, Vol. 55, no. 3 (Spring 1995), pp. 37–49.

63. Ibid. See also, "College Recruiting," in *Personnel* (May–June 1980). For a study of how applicant sex can impact recruiters' evaluations, see, for example, Laura Graves and Gary Powell, "The Affect of Sex Similarity on Recruiters' Evaluations of Actual Applicants: A Test of the Similarity-Attraction Paradigm," *Personnel Psychology*, Vol. 48, no. 1 (Spring 1995), pp. 85–98.

64. See, for example, Richard Becker, "Ten Common Mistakes to College Recruiting—or How to Try Without Really Succeeding," *Personnel*, Vol. 52, no. 2 (March–April 1975), pp. 19–28. See also Sara Rynes and John Boudreau, "College Recruiting in Large Organizations: Practice, Evaluation, and Research Implications," *Personnel Psychology*, Vol. 39 (Winter 1986), pp. 729–757.

65. Pell, *Recruiting and Selecting Personnel*, pp. 62–63.

66. "Internships Provide Workplace Snapshot," *BNA Bulletin to Management*, May 22, 1997, p. 168.

67. "Employee Referrals Improve Hiring," *BNA Bulletin to Management*, March 13, 1997, p. 88.

68. Ibid., p. 13.

69. The study on employment referrals was published by Bernard Hodes Advertising, Dept. 100, 555 Madison Avenue, NY, NY 10022. See also Allan Halcrow, "Employees Are Your Best Recruiters," *Personnel Journal* (November 1988), pp. 41–49. See also Andy Hargerstock and Hank Engel, "Six Ways to Boost Employee Referral Programs," *HR Magazine*, Vol. 39, no. 12 (December 1994), pp. 72ff.

70. "High-Stakes Recruiting in High-Tech," *BNA Bulletin to Management*, February 12, 1998, p. 48.

71. "Internet Recruitment Survey," *BNA Bulletin to Management*, May 22, 1997, pp. 164–165.

72. Ibid.

73. Elaine Appleton, "Recruiting on the Internet," *Datamation* (August 1995), p. 39.

74. Julia King, "Job Networking," *Enterprise Networking*, January 26, 1995.

75. Brenda Paik Sunoo, "Thumbs Up for Staffing Websites," *Workforce* (October 1997), pp. 67–73.

76. Gillian Flynn, "Cisco turns the Internet Inside (and) Out," *Personnel Journal* (October 1996), pp. 28–34.

77. "Internet Recruiting Holds Promise," *BNA Bulletin to Management*, July 17, 1997, p. 232.

78. Ibid.

79. "Internet Recruiting Takes Off," *BNA Bulletin to Management*, February 20, 1997, p. 64.

80. Laura Romei, "Human Resource Management Systems Keep Computers Humming," *Managing Office Technology* (November 1994), p. 45.

81. Thomas Stewart, "In Search of Elusive Tech Workers," *Fortune*, February 16, 1998, pp. 171–172.

82. Ibid., p. 171.

83. Ibid.

84. Unless otherwise noted, this section is based on Judith Casey and Marcie Pitt-Catsouphes, "Employed Single Mothers: Balancing Job and Home Life," *Employee Assistance Quarterly*, Vol. 9, no. 3/4 (1994), pp. 37–53.

85. Ibid., p. 42.

86. Ibid., p. 44.

87. Ibid., p. 45.

88. Ibid., p. 43.

89. Ibid., p. 48.

90. Ibid., p. 48.

91. See Robert W. Wendover, "Smart Hiring," *B & E Review* (July–September 1990), pp. 6–15.

92. "Retirees Increasingly Reentering the Workforce," *BNA Bulletin to Management*, January 16, 1997, p. 17.

93. Diane Cyr, "Lost and Found—Retired Employees," *Personnel Journal* (November 1996), p. 41.

94. Harold E. Johnson, "Older Workers Help Meet Employment Needs," *Personnel Journal* (May 1988), pp. 100–105.

95. This is based on Robert W. Goddard, "How to Harness America's Gray Power," *Personnel Journal* (May 1987), pp. 33–40.

96. Glenn McEvoy and Wayne Cascio, "Cumulative Evidence of the Relationship Between Employee Age and Job Performance," *Journal of Applied Psychology*, Vol. 74, no. 1 (February 1989), pp. 11–17.

97. Goddard, "How to Harness America's Gray Power," p. 33.

98. "Older Workers Valued but Hard to Find, Employers Say," *BNA Bulletin to Management*, April 30, 1998, p. 129–134.

99. For this and other examples here, see Goddard, "How to Harness America's Gray Power."

100. Elizabeth Blackarczyk, "Recruiters Challenged by Economy, Shortages," *HR News* (February 1990), p. 84. Diversity management programs may also make a firm more attractive to job candidates. See, for example, Margaret Williams and Talya Bauer, "The Effect of Managing Diversity Policy on Organizational Attractiveness," *Group & Organization Management*, Vol. 19, no. 3 (September 1994), pp. 295–308.

101. Jennifer Koch, "Finding Qualified Hispanic Candidates," *Recruitment Today*, Vol. 3, no. 2 (Spring 1990), p. 35.

102. This compares with 21.5% for black jobseekers and 23.9% for white jobseekers. Michelle Harrison Ports, "Trends in Job Search Methods, 1970–72," *Monthly Labor Review* (October 1993), p. 64.

103. Bill Leonard, "Welfare Reform: A New Deal for HR," *HR Magazine* (March 1997), pp. 78–86; Jennifer Laabs, "Welfare Law: HR's Role in Employment," *Workforce* (January 1998), pp. 30–39.

104. Herbert Greenberg, "A Hidden Source of Talent," *HR Magazine* (March 1997), pp. 88–91.

105. "Welfare-to-Work: No Easy Chore," *BNA Bulletin to Management*, February 13, 1997, p. 56.

106. Ibid.

107. Ibid.

108. The remainder of this paragraph is based on Robert W. Wendover, "Smart Hiring," *B & E Review* (July–September 1990), pp. 6–15.

109. *Recruiting Practices*, Personnel Policy Forum, Survey No. 462 (Washington, DC: Bureau of National Affairs, August 1979), p. 114; reprinted in Stephen P. Robbins, *Personnel: The Management of Human Resources* (Upper Saddle River, NJ: Prentice Hall, 1982), p. 115. For another view of this see Phillip Swaroff, Alan Bass, and Lizabeth Barclay, "Recruiting Sources: Another Look," *Journal of Applied Psychology*, Vol. 70, no. 4 (1985), pp. 720–728. See also David Caldwell and W. Austin Stivey, "The Relationship Between Recruiting Source and Employee Success: An Analysis by Race," *Personnel Psychology*, Vol. 36, no. 1 (Spring 1983), pp. 67–72.

110. This is based on Jennifer Laabs, "The Global Talent Search," *Personnel Journal* (August 1991), pp. 38–42.

111. Shannon Peters Talbott, "Building a Global Workforce Starts with Recruitment," *Personnel Journal* (March 1996), pp. 9–11.

112. Ibid.

113. Ibid.

114. Jennifer Laabs, "Recruiting in the Global Village," *Workforce* (April 1998), pp. 30–33.

115. Ibid.

116. Pell, *Recruiting and Selecting Personnel*, pp. 96–98. See also Wayne Cascio, "Accuracy of Verifiable Biographical Information Blank Responses," *Journal of Applied Psychology*, Vol. 60 (December 1975), for a discussion of accuracy of bio data.

117. Richard Lowell and Jay Deloach, "Equal Employment Opportunity: Are You Overlooking the Application Form?" *Personnel*, Vol. 59 (July–August 1982), pp. 49–55.

118. Circuit City Stores, Inc., Employment Packet, January 1997.

119. De'Ann Weimer and Stephanie Anderson Forest, "Forced Into Arbitration? Not Anymore," *Business Week*, March 16, 1998, pp. 66, 68.

120. Ibid.

121. Wayne Cascio, "Turnover, Biographical Data, and Fair Employment," *Journal of Applied Psychology*, Vol. 61 (October 1976).

122. Richard Rosenbaum, "Predictability of Employee Theft Using Weighted Application Blanks," *Journal of Applied Psychology*, Vol. 61 (1976), pp. 94–98.

123. Fred Mael, Mary Connerley, and Ray Morath, "None of Your Business: Parameters of Biodata Invasiveness," *Personnel Psychology*, Vol. 49 (1996), pp. 613–650.

5

EMPLOYEE TESTING AND SELECTION

When they set up their firm's new vehicle plant in Alabama, Daimler Chrysler executives knew employee screening would be crucial. Mercedes was known the world over for its strategy of building perhaps the world's highest-quality cars. But that meant the Americans hired for the new plant would need the skills, intelligence, and quality orientation required to fulfill Mercedes' quality commitment. Employee testing and selection would be crucial. ▲

Behavioral Objectives

When you finish studying this chapter, you should be able to:

▲ *Describe* the overall selection process and explain why it is important.
▲ *Define* basic testing concepts including validity and reliability.
▲ *Discuss* at least four types of personnel tests.
▲ *Explain* the pros and cons of background investigations, reference checks, and preemployment information services.

Chapter Outline

▲ The Selection Process
▲ Basic Testing Concepts
▲ Ethical, Legal, and Fairness Questions in Testing
▲ Types of Tests
▲ Work Samples and Simulations
▲ Other Selection Techniques

THE SELECTION PROCESS

With a pool of completed applications, your next step is to select the best person for the job. This usually means whittling down the applicant pool by using the screening tools explained in this chapter, including tests, assessment centers, and background and reference checks. The prospective supervisor can then interview several viable candidates and decide who to hire. We'll turn to interviewing in Chapter 6.[1]

Why Careful Selection Is Important

Selecting the right employees is important for three main reasons. First, your own performance always depends in part on your subordinates'. Employees with the right skills and attributes will do a better job for you and the company. Employees without these skills or who are abrasive or obstructionist won't perform effectively, and your own performance and the firm's will suffer. The time to screen out such undesirables is before they are in the door, not after.

Effective screening is also important because it's costly to recruit and hire employees. Hiring and training even a clerk can cost $5,000 or more in fees and supervisory time. The total cost of hiring a manager could easily be 10 times as high, once search fees, interviewing time, reference checking, and travel and moving expenses are tallied.

LEGAL IMPLICATIONS AND NEGLIGENT HIRING   Careful selection is also important because of the legal implications of incompetent hiring. For one thing (as we saw in Chapter 2), EEO legislation and court decisions require you to systematically evaluate your selection procedure's effectiveness to ensure that you are not unfairly discriminating against any protected group. Furthermore, courts are increasingly finding employers liable when employees with criminal records or other problems take advantage of access to customers' homes or other similar opportunities to commit crimes. Hiring workers with such backgrounds without proper safeguards is called *negligent hiring*.[2]

Several cases illustrate this problem. In one, *Ponticas v. K.M.S. Investments*, an apartment manager with a passkey entered a woman's apartment and assaulted her. Negligence by the owner and by the operator of the apartment complex in not properly checking the manager's background before hiring him was found to be the cause of the woman's personal injury. In another case, *Henley v. Prince Georges County*, an employee who turned out to have a criminal background murdered a young boy; management, aware of the man's prior murder conviction, was held liable.

The recent increase in negligent hiring cases underscores the need for employers to carefully think through what the human requirements really are when doing a job analysis.[3] For example, "'non-rapist' is unlikely to appear as a required knowledge, skill, or ability in a job analysis of a repair person. Yet, it is that type of requirement that has been the focus of many negligent hiring suits."[4] On the other hand, it could be discriminatory to conclude that candidates with, say, conviction records are automatically not right for certain jobs. In other words, the fear of negligent hiring must be balanced with EEO concerns. Steps to take to protect against negligent hiring claims include:[5]

Carefully scrutinize all information supplied by the applicant on his or her employment application. For example, look for unexplained gaps in employment.

Obtain the applicant's written authorization for reference checks from prospective employees, and check former employers' references as carefully as possible.

Save all records and information you obtain about the applicant during each stage of the selection process.

Reject applicants who make false statements of material facts in the application or who have records of conviction for offenses directly related and important to the positions in question.

Keep in mind the need to balance the applicant's privacy rights with others' "need to know," especially when damaging information is discovered.

Take immediate disciplinary action if problems develop.

BASIC TESTING CONCEPTS

Validity

A test is basically a sample of a person's behavior, but some tests are more clearly representative of the behavior being sampled than others. A typing test, for example, clearly corresponds to some on-the-job behavior, in this case typing. At the other extreme, there may be no apparent relationship between the items on the test and the behavior. This is the case with projective personality tests, for example. In the Thematic Apperception Test illustrated in Figure 5-1, the person is asked to explain how he or she interprets the blurred picture. That interpretation is then used to draw conclusions about the person's personality and behavior. In such tests, it is much harder to "prove" that the tests are measuring what they are purported to measure—that they're *valid*.

Test validity answers the question, "Does this test measure what it's supposed to measure?"[6] With respect to employee selection tests, the term *validity* often refers to evidence that the test is job related, in other words, that performance on the test is a valid predictor of subsequent performance on the job. A selection test must be valid since, without proof of its validity, there is no logical or legally permissible reason to continue using it to screen job applicants. In employment testing, there are two main ways to demonstrate a test's validity, **criterion validity** and **content validity**. A third, construct validity, is used less often.[7]

CRITERION VALIDITY   Demonstrating *criterion validity* means demonstrating that those who do well on the test also do well on the job, and that those who do poorly on the test do poorly on the job.[8] Thus, the test has validity to the extent that the people with higher test scores perform better on the job. In psychological measurement, a *predictor* is

test validity

The accuracy with which a test, interview, and so on measures what it purports to measure or fulfills the function it was designed to fill.

criterion validity

A type of validity based on showing that scores on the test (*predictors*) are related to job performance (*criterion*).

content validity

A test that is *content valid* is one in which the test contains a fair sample of the tasks and skills actually needed for the job in question.

FIGURE 5-1

Sample Picture from Thematic Apperception Test

How do you interpret this picture?

the measurement (in this case, the test score) that you are trying to relate to a *criterion*, like performance on the job. The term *criterion validity* comes from that terminology.

CONTENT VALIDITY   The *content validity* of a test is demonstrated by showing that the test constitutes a fair sample of the content of the job.[9] The basic procedure here is to identify job tasks and behaviors that are critical to performance, and then randomly select a sample of those tasks and behaviors to be tested. A typing test used to hire a typist is an example. If the content of the typing test is a representative sample of the typist's job, then the test is probably content valid.

Demonstrating content validity sounds easier than it is in practice. Demonstrating that the tasks the person performs on the test are in fact a comprehensive and random sample of the tasks performed on the job, and demonstrating that the conditions under which the test is taken resemble the work situation, are not always easy. For many jobs, other evidence of a test's validity—such as its criterion validity—must therefore be demonstrated as well.

Reliability

reliability
The characteristic that refers to the consistency of scores obtained by the same person when retested with the identical or equivalent tests.

Reliability is a test's second important characteristic and refers to its consistency. It is "the consistency of scores obtained by the same person when retested with the identical tests or with an equivalent form of a test."[10] A test's reliability is very important; if a person scored 90 on an intelligence test on a Monday and 130 when retested on Tuesday, you probably wouldn't have much faith in the test.

There are several ways to estimate a test's consistency or reliability. You could administer the same test to the same people at two different points in time, comparing their test scores at time 2 with their scores at time 1; this would be a *retest estimate*. Or you could administer a test and then administer what experts believe to be an equivalent test at a later date; this would be an *equivalent form* estimate. The SAT exam is an example.

A test's *internal consistency* is another measure of its reliability. For example, suppose you have 10 items on a test of vocational interests, which are supposed to measure in various ways the person's interest in working out-of-doors. You administer the test and then statistically analyze the degree to which responses to these 10 items vary together. This would provide a measure of the internal reliability of the test and is referred to as an internal comparison estimate. Internal consistency is one reason you often find questions that apparently are repetitive on some test questionnaires.

SOURCES OF UNRELIABILITY   What could cause a test to be unreliable? Imagine for a moment that you are asked to take a test in, say, economics, and then you retake an equivalent test one month later. You find that your score changes dramatically.

There are at least four main sources of error that might explain this anomaly. First, the questions may do a poor job of sampling the material; for example, test 1 focuses more on Chapters 1, 3, 5, and 7, while test 2 focuses more on Chapters 2, 4, 5, and 8. Similarly, one or more of the questions may not do a good job of measuring what it is supposed to measure—such as your knowledge of, say, indifference curves. Second, there may be errors due to chance response tendencies. For example, the test itself is so boring or hard or inconsequential that you give up and start answering questions at random. (Highly personal questions on a psychological test might elicit the same response.) Third, there might be errors due to changes in the testing conditions; for instance, the room next month may be very noisy. And, finally, there could be changes in the person taking the test—in this case, you may have studied more, or forgotten more, or your mood may have changed. In any event you can see that many factors can affect a test's consistency, its reliability. (Additional aspects of reliability and validity are discussed in this chapter's Internet appendix.)

How to Validate a Test

What makes a test like the Graduate Record Examination useful for college admissions directors? What makes a mechanical comprehension test useful for a manager trying to hire a machinist?

The answer to both questions is usually that people's scores on these tests have been shown to be predictive of how they perform. Thus, other things being equal, students who score high on the graduate admissions tests also do better in graduate school. Applicants who score higher on the mechanical comprehension test perform better as machinists.

In order for any selection test to be useful, an employer should be fairly sure that scores on the test are related in a predictable way to performance on the job. In other words, it is imperative that you *validate* the test before using it, by ensuring that test scores are a good predictor of some criterion like job performance. In other words, you must demonstrate the test's criterion validity, to use the phrase from earlier in this chapter. This validation process usually requires the expertise of an industrial psychologist and is coordinated by the HR department. Line management's role is to clearly describe the job and its requirements, so that the human requirements of the job and the job's performance standards are clear to the psychologist. The validation process consists of five steps.

STEP 1. ANALYZE THE JOB   Your first step is to analyze the job and write job descriptions and job specifications. Here specify the human traits and skills you believe are required for adequate job performance. For example, must an applicant be aggressive? Is shorthand required? Must the person be able to assemble small, detailed components? These requirements become your predictors. These are the human traits and skills you believe to be predictive of success on the job. In this first step, you also have to define what you mean by "success on the job," because it is this success for which you want predictors. The standards of success are called *criteria*. You could focus on production-related criteria (quantity, quality, and so on), personnel data (absenteeism, length of service, and so on), or judgments (of worker performance by persons like supervisors). For an assembler's job, predictors to be tested for might include manual dexterity and patience. Criteria that you would hope to predict with your test might include quantity produced per hour and number of rejects produced per hour.

Some employers make the mistake of carefully choosing predictors (such as manual dexterity), while virtually ignoring the question of which performance criteria are best. An illustrative study involved 212 employees of a gas utility company. In this study, the researchers found a significant relationship between the test battery that was used as a predictor and two performance criteria—supervisor ratings of performance and objective productivity indices. However, there was virtually no relationship between the same test battery and an objective quality index or employee self-ratings.[11]

STEP 2. CHOOSE YOUR TESTS   Next choose tests that you think measure the attributes (predictors) important for job success. This choice is usually based on experience, previous research, and "best guesses," and you usually won't start off with just one test. Instead you choose several tests, combining them into a *test battery* aimed at measuring a variety of possible predictors, such as aggressiveness, extroversion, and numerical ability.

What tests are available and where do you get them? The best advice here is probably to use the services of a professional, such as a licensed industrial psychologist, given the sorts of EEO and ethical issues we've alluded to.

However, numerous test publishing services are available. Some—such as Psychological Assessment Resources, Inc. in Odessa, Florida—publish and distribute numerous tests, some of which are basically available to any purchasers, but many of which are available only to qualified buyers (such as those with degrees in psychology or counseling).

Other companies publish employment tests that are generally available to anyone, without qualification. For example, Wonderlic Personnel Test, Inc. not only publishes a well-known intellectual capacity test, but also other tests including technical skills tests (illustrated in Figure 5-2), as well as aptitude test batteries, interest inventories, and reliability inventories. G. Neil Companies of Sunrise, Florida, similarly makes available a variety of employment testing materials including, for example, a clerical skills test, telemarketing ability test, service ability test, management ability test, team skills test, and sales abilities test. Again, though, don't let the widespread availability of personnel tests blind you to the need for ensuring that they're used in a manner consistent with equal employment laws and in a manner that is ethical and protects the test taker's privacy. We'll return to this point in a moment.

STEP 3. ADMINISTER TEST   Next administer the selected test(s) to employees. You have two choices here. First, you can administer the tests to employees presently on the job. You then would compare their test scores with their current performance; this is called *concurrent validation*. Its main advantage is that data on performance are readily available. The disadvantage is that the current employees may not be representative of new applicants (who of course are really the ones for which you are interested in developing a screening test). Current employees have already received on-the-job training and have been screened by your existing selection techniques.[12]

Predictive validation is the more dependable way to validate a test. Here the test is administered to applicants before they are hired. Then these applicants are hired using only existing selection techniques, not the results of the new tests you are developing. After they have been on the job for some time, you measure their performance and compare it to their earlier test scores. You can then determine whether their performance on the test could have been used to predict their subsequent job performance. In the case of an assembler's job, the ideal situation would be to administer, say, the Crawford Small Parts Dexterity Test (see page 184) to all applicants. Then ignore the test results and hire assemblers as you usually do. Perhaps six months later, measure your new assemblers' performance (quantity produced per hour, number of rejects per hour) and compare this performance to their Crawford test scores (see step 4).

STEP 4. RELATE YOUR TEST SCORES AND CRITERIA   The next step is to determine whether there is a significant relationship between scores (the predictor) and performance

FIGURE 5-2
NOCIT™ Technical Skills Test
Wonderlic 1998 catalog, p. 7.
Used with permission.

(the criterion). The usual way to do this is to determine the statistical relationship between (1) scores on the test and (2) performance through correlation analysis, which shows the degree of statistical relationship.

If performance on the test and on the job are correlated, you can develop an **expectancy chart**. This presents graphically the relationship between test scores and job performance. To do this, split the employees into, say, five groups according to their test scores, with those scoring the highest fifth on the test, the second highest fifth, and so on. Then compute the percentage of high job performers in each of these five test score groups and present the data in an expectancy chart like that in Figure 5-3. This shows the likelihood of an employee being rated a high performer if he or she scores in each of these five test score groups. Thus, a person scoring in the top fifth of the test has a 97% chance of being rated a high performer, while one scoring in the lowest fifth has only a 20% chance of being rated a high performer.[13]

STEP 5. CROSS-VALIDATE AND REVALIDATE   Before putting the test into use, you may want to check it by *cross-validating,* by again performing steps 3 and 4 on a new sample of employees. At a minimum, an expert should revalidate the test periodically.

The procedure you would use to demonstrate content validity differs from that used to demonstrate criterion validity as described in steps 1 through 5. Content validity tends to emphasize judgment. Here a careful job analysis is carried out to identify the work behaviors required. Then a sample of those behaviors is combined into a test that should then be content valid. A typing and shorthand test for a secretary would be an example. The fact that the test is a comprehensive sample of actual, observable, on-the-job behaviors is what lends the test its content validity. Criterion validity is determined through the five-step procedure previously described.

expectancy chart

A graph showing the relationship between test scores and job performance for a large group of people.

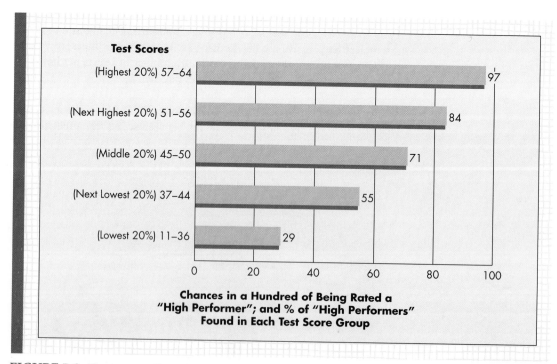

FIGURE 5-3 *Expectancy Chart*

Note: This expectancy chart shows the relation between scores made on the Minnesota Paper Form Board and rated success of junior drafts persons. Example: Those who score between 37 and 44 have a 55% chance of being rated above average and those scoring between 57 and 64 have a 97% chance.

Testing Guidelines

Basic guidelines[14] for setting up a testing program include:[15]

1. *Use tests as supplements.* Do not use tests as your only selection technique; instead use them to supplement other techniques like interviews and background checks. Tests are not infallible. Even in the best of cases the test score usually accounts for only about 25% of the variation in the measure of performance. In addition, tests are often better at telling you which candidates will fail than which will succeed.

2. *Validate the tests.* Validating the test in your own organization is the optimal strategy. However, the fact that the same tests have been proven valid in similar organizations—called validity generalization—is usually adequate.

3. *Analyze all your current hiring and promotion standards.* Ask questions such as, "What proportion of minority and nonminority applicants are being rejected at each stage of the hiring process?" and "Why am I using this standard—what does it mean in terms of actual behavior on the job?" Remember that the burden of proof is always on you to prove that the predictor (such as intelligence) is related to success or failure on the job.

4. *Keep accurate records.* It is important to keep accurate records of why each applicant was rejected. For purposes of the Equal Employment Opportunity Commission, a general note such as "not sufficiently well qualified" would not be enough. As objectively as possible, state why the candidate was rejected. Remember that your reasons for rejecting the candidate may be subject to validation at a later date.

5. *Begin your validation program now.* If you don't currently use tests, or if you use tests that haven't been validated, begin your (preferably predictive) validation study now. Administer the tests to applicants, hire the applicants without referring to the test scores, and at a later date correlate their test scores with their performance on the job.

6. *Use a certified psychologist.* The development, validation, and use of selection standards (including tests) generally require the assistance of a qualified psychologist. Most states require that persons who offer psychological services to the public be certified or licensed. Most industrial and organizational psychologists hold a Ph.D. degree (the bachelor's degree is never sufficient). A potential consultant should be able to provide evidence of similar work and experience in the area of test validation. And the consultant should demonstrate familiarity with existing federal and state laws and regulations applicable to equal rights.

7. *Test conditions are important.* Administer your tests in areas that are reasonably private, quiet, well lighted, and ventilated, and make sure all applicants take the tests under the same test conditions. Once completed, test results should be held in the strictest confidence and be given only to individuals who have a legitimate need for the information and who also have the ability to understand and interpret the scores.

ETHICAL, LEGAL, AND FAIRNESS QUESTIONS IN TESTING

Equal Employment Opportunity Aspects of Testing

We've seen that various federal and state laws bar discrimination with respect to race, color, age, religion, sex, disability, and national origin.[16] With respect to testing, these laws boil down to this: You must be able to (1) *prove* that your tests were related to success or failure on the job (validity), and (2) *prove* that your tests didn't unfairly discriminate against either minority or nonminority subgroups. The burden of proof rests with you; you are presumed guilty until proven innocent and must demonstrate the validity and selection fairness of the allegedly discriminatory item. Yet, it's likely that relatively few employers are validating their tests. The main reason is that compliance can be expensive. For instance, you have to do a validation study, develop a good performance appraisal method, and do a thorough job analysis.

You can't avoid EEO laws just by avoiding tests. EEO guidelines and laws and the burden of proving job relatedness apply to any screening or selection devices, including interviews, applications, and references. In other words, you could be asked to prove the validity and fairness of *any* screening or selection tool that has been shown to have an adverse impact on a protected group.[17] Additional aspects of test unfairness are discussed in the Internet appendix to this chapter.

YOUR ALTERNATIVES   Let's review where we are at this point. Assume that you've used a test and that a rejected minority candidate has demonstrated adverse impact to the satisfaction of a court. How might the person have done this? One way was to show that the selection rate for, say, the applicant's racial group was less than four-fifths that for the group with the highest selection rate. Thus, if 90% of white applicants passed the test but only 60% of blacks passed, then (since 60% is less than four-fifths of 90%) adverse impact exists.

You would then have three alternatives. One is to choose an alternative selection procedure that does not have an adverse impact. In other words, you could choose a different test or selection procedure that does not adversely affect minorities or women.[18]

The second alternative is to show that the test is valid, in other words, that it is a valid predictor of performance on the job. Ideally, you would do this by conducting your own validation study. Under certain circumstances you may also try to show the validity of the test by using information about the test's validity collected elsewhere.[19] In any event, the plaintiff would then have to prove that your explanation for using the test is inadequate.

A third alternative—in this case aimed at avoiding adverse impact rather than responding to it—is to monitor the selection test to see whether it has disparate impact. If so, you would then have to determine if the test is valid. In the absence of disparate rejection rates it's generally permissible to use selection devices that may not be valid or otherwise job related—but why would you want to?

INDIVIDUAL RIGHTS OF TEST TAKERS AND TEST SECURITY   Test takers have certain rights to privacy and information under the American Psychological Association's standard for educational and psychological tests.[20] They have the right to the confidentiality of the test results and the right to informed consent regarding the use of these results. Second, they have the right to expect that only people qualified to interpret the scores will have access to them or that sufficient information will accompany the scores to ensure their appropriate interpretation. Third, they have the right to expect that the test is equally fair to all test takers in the sense of being equally familiar: in other words, no person taking the tests should have prior information concerning the questions or answers.[21]

RESEARCH INSIGHT   What determines if the selection process is viewed as fair?[22] Following good test practices—providing adequate time for the test, a quiet test-taking environment, privacy, and so on—is important.[23] Beyond that, the "obviousness" of the link between (1) the selection procedure and (2) performing the job (its "face validity") is important too. In one study 259 college students from France and the United States rated the "favorability" of 10 selection procedures and then indicated what prompted them to rate some procedures as more favorable than others.[24] In this study the "perceived face validity of the selection procedure was the strongest correlate of favorability reactions among both samples."[25] For example, reactions were highly favorable toward interviews and work sample tests, and moderately favorable toward biographical information and written ability tests. Favorability reactions were neutral toward personality and honesty tests, and negative toward graphology. In this study face validity was the most important but not the sole determinant of students' reactions to the selection procedures. Other strong predictors of favorable reactions on the part of students included beliefs that the employer had the right to obtain information with a particular technique, and the extent to which the procedure is widely used in industry.

THE ISSUE OF PRIVACY   In addition to the APA's standard regarding test privacy and security, certain other protections regarding an employee's right to privacy are embedded in U.S. law.

At the federal level, there are few restrictions on an employer's right to disseminate information about employees either inside or outside the company. The U.S. Constitution does not expressly provide for the right to privacy, but certain U.S. Supreme Court decisions do protect individuals from intrusive governmental action in a variety of contexts.[26] For example, if you are a federal employee or (in many jurisdictions) a state or local government employee, there are limits on disclosure of personnel information to other individuals or agencies within or outside the agency.[27] Although not applicable to employees of private firms, the Federal Privacy Act illustrates the sorts of informational privacy issues legislatures are concerned about. The act (1) requires that an agency maintain only such information as is relevant and necessary to accomplish its purpose; (2) requires to the greatest extent practical that the information come directly from the individual; (3) establishes safeguards to ensure the security and confidentiality of records; and (4) gives federal employees the right to inspect personnel files and limits the disclosure of personnel information without an employee's consent.[28]

The common law of torts also provides limited protection against disclosing information about employees to people outside the company. The most well known application here involves defamation (either libel or slander). If your employer or former employer discloses information that is false and defamatory and that causes you serious injury, you may be able to sue for defamation of character.[29] In general, though, this is easier said than done. Employers (in providing, say, a recommendation) generally cannot be sued for defamation unless the employee can show "malice" (that is, ill will, culpable recklessness, or disregard of the employee's rights) and this is usually hard to prove.[30] An employer may also be sued for interference with business or prospective business relations if it willfully provides information to another for the purpose of harming a former employee. In addition, you should not disclose to another company that a former employee had filed a charge of discrimination or a lawsuit alleging discrimination or other labor law violation, since that has been held to constitute unlawful retaliation.

Common law as it applies to invasion of privacy has been formally recognized in various forms in some states. Such cases usually revolve around "public disclosure of private facts," wherein employees sue employers for disclosing to a large number of people true but embarrassing private facts about the employee. (For example, your personnel file may contain private information regarding your health, test results, or job performance you may not want disclosed outside the firm.) In invasion-of-privacy suits, truth is no defense. One case involved a supervisor in a shouting match with an employee. The supervisor yelled out that the employee's wife had been having sexual relations with certain people. Both the employee and his wife sued the employer for invasion of privacy. The jury found that the employer was liable for invasion of the couple's privacy and awarded damages to both of them, as well as damages for the couple's additional claim that the supervisor's conduct amounted to an intentional infliction of emotional distress.[31] The point is that in these increasingly litigious times more discretion is required than some employers have shown in the past.

Some guidelines to follow here include:

1. Train your supervisors.[32] Employers should meet with everyone from front-line supervisors through middle and upper management. Emphasize the importance of confidentiality with regard to information about employees.

2. Adopt a policy (particularly in areas like drug testing) that only those who "need to know" will share the information. For example, if an employee has been rehabilitated after a period of drug use and that information is not relevant to the employee's functioning in the workplace, then his or her new supervisor may not "need to know."

3. If you know that for some reason the information to be elicited via testing will *not* be kept confidential, you may limit your liability by disclosing that fact prior to testing. For example, if employees who test positive on a drug test are going to be required to use the company's employee assistance program, that should be explained before the tests are given. Similarly, if supervisors are routinely going to be asked to participate in the rehabilitation phase, then employees should understand that their supervisors will become involved if they test positive.

Using Tests at Work

Tests are widely used by employers today. For example, about 45% of 1,085 companies surveyed by the American Management Association in 1998 tested applicants for basic skills (defined as the ability to read instructions, write reports, and do arithmetic at a level adequate to perform common workplace tasks).[33] Test publishers also report strong growth over the past few years. For example, one Chicago-based company that publishes integrity tests and a customer service test said the number of employers on its client list had doubled between 1992 and 1997 and now numbers in the "thousands."[34] Another survey by the American Management Association recently concluded that 38.6% of the companies it surveyed said they performed psychological testing on job applicants, ranging from tests of the applicants' cognitive abilities to "honesty testing."[35] If you want to see what such tests are like, try the short test in Figure 5-4 to see how prone you might be to on-the-job accidents.

TYPES OF TESTS

We can conveniently classify a test according to whether it measures cognitive (mental) abilities, motor and physical abilities, personality and interests, or achievement.[36]

Tests of Cognitive Abilities

Cognitive tests include tests of general reasoning ability (intelligence) and tests of specific mental abilities like memory and inductive reasoning.

INTELLIGENCE TESTS Intelligence (IQ) tests are tests of general intellectual abilities. They measure not a single "intelligence" trait, but rather a range of abilities including memory, vocabulary, verbal fluency, and numerical ability.

Originally, IQ (intelligence quotient) was literally a quotient. The procedure was to divide a child's mental age (as measured by the intelligence test) by his or her chronological age, and then multiply the results by 100. Thus, if an 8-year-old child answered questions as a 10-year-old might, his or her IQ would be 10 divided by 8, times 100, or 125.

For adults, of course, the notion of mental age divided by chronological age wouldn't make sense. For example, we wouldn't necessarily expect a 30-year-old individ-

FIGURE 5-4

Sample Test

Source: Courtesy of NYT Permissions.

CHECK YES OR NO	YES	NO

1. You like a lot of excitement in your life.

_____

2. An employee who takes it easy at work is cheating on the employer.

_____

3. You are a cautious person.

_____

4. In the past three years you have found yourself in a shouting match at school or work.

_____

5. You like to drive fast just for fun.

_____

Analysis: According to John Kamp, an industrial psychologist, applicants who answered no, yes, yes, no, no to questions 1, 2, 3, 4, and 5 are statistically likely to be absent less often, to have fewer on the job injuries, and, if the job involves driving, to have fewer on the job driving accidents. Actual scores on the test are based on answers to 130 questions.

ual to be more intelligent than a 25-year-old one. Therefore, an adult's IQ score is actually a *derived* score. It reflects the extent to which the person is above or below the "average" adult's intelligence score.

Intelligence is often measured with individually administered tests such as the Stanford-Binet Test or the Wechsler Test. Other IQ tests such as the Wonderlic can be administered to groups of people.

SPECIFIC COGNITIVE ABILITIES   There are also measures of specific mental abilities, such as inductive and deductive reasoning, verbal comprehension, memory, and numerical ability.

Tests in this category are often called aptitude tests, since they purport to measure the applicant's aptitudes for the job in question. For example, consider the test of mechanical comprehension illustrated in Figure 5-5. It tests the applicant's understanding of basic mechanical principles. It may therefore reflect a person's aptitude for jobs—like that of machinist or engineer—that require mechanical comprehension. Other tests of mechanical aptitude include the Mechanical Reasoning Test and the SRA Test of Mechanical Aptitude.

Tests of Motor and Physical Abilities

There are many *motor abilities* you might want to measure. These include finger dexterity, manual dexterity, speed of arm movement, and reaction time. The Crawford Small Parts Dexterity Test as illustrated in Figure 5-6 is an example. It measures the speed and accuracy of simple judgment as well as the speed of finger, hand, and arm movements. Other tests include the Stromberg Dexterity Test, the Minnesota Rate of Manipulation Test, and the Purdue Peg Board.

Test of physical abilities may also be required.[37] Physical abilities include static strength (such as lifting weights), dynamic strength (like pull-ups), body coordination (as in jumping rope), and stamina.[38]

FIGURE 5-5

Two Problems from the Test of Mechanical Comprehension

Source: Reproduced by permission. Copyright 1967, 1969 by The Psychological Corporation, New York, NY. All rights reserved. Author's note: 1969 is latest copyright on this test, which is still the main one used for this purpose.

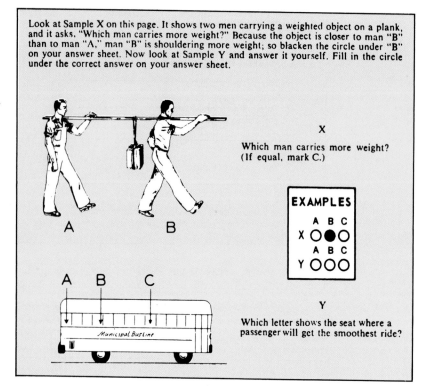

Look at Sample **X** on this page. It shows two men carrying a weighted object on a plank, and it asks, "Which man carries more weight?" Because the object is closer to man "B" than to man "A," man "B" is shouldering more weight; so blacken the circle under "B" on your answer sheet. Now look at Sample Y and answer it yourself. Fill in the circle under the correct answer on your answer sheet.

A   B

X

Which man carries more weight? (If equal, mark C.)

EXAMPLES

A B C
X ○ ● ○
A B C
Y ○ ○ ○

A   B   C

Municipal Busline

Y

Which letter shows the seat where a passenger will get the smoothest ride?

Measuring Personality and Interests

A person's cognitive and physical abilities alone seldom explain his or her job performance. Other factors like the person's motivation and interpersonal skills are important too. Personality and interests inventories are sometimes used as predictors of such intangibles.

FIGURE 5-6

Crawford Small Parts Dexterity Test

Source: The Psychological Corporation.

Personality tests can measure basic aspects of an applicant's personality, such as introversion, stability, and motivation. Many of these tests are *projective*. Here an ambiguous stimulus like an ink blot or clouded picture is presented to the person taking the test. He or she is then asked to interpret or react to it. Since the pictures are ambiguous, the person's interpretation must come from within—he or she supposedly *projects* into the picture his or her own emotional attitudes about life. Thus, a security-oriented person might describe the woman in Figure 5-1 as "my mother worrying about what I'll do if I lose my job." Examples of personality tests (which are more properly called personality inventories) include the Thematic Apperception Test, the Guilford-Zimmerman Temperament Survey, and the Minnesota Multiphasic Personality Inventory. The Guilford-Zimmerman survey measures personality traits like emotional stability versus moodiness and friendliness versus criticalness. The Minnesota Multiphasic Personality Inventory taps traits like hypochondria and paranoia.

Personality tests—particularly the projective type—are the most difficult tests to evaluate and use. An expert must analyze the test taker's interpretations and reactions and infer from them his or her personality. The usefulness of such tests for selection rests on the assumption that you can find a relationship between a measurable personality trait (like introversion) and success on the job.[39]

The difficulties notwithstanding, recent studies confirm that personality tests can help companies hire more effective workers. For example, industrial psychologists often emphasize the "big five" personality dimensions as they apply to personnel testing: extroversion, emotional stability, agreeableness, conscientiousness, and openness to experience.[40] One study focused on the extent to which these five personality dimensions predicted performance (for instance, in terms of job and training proficiency) for professionals, police officers, managers, sales workers, and skilled/semiskilled workers. *Conscientiousness* showed a consistent relationship with all job performance criteria for all the occupations. *Extroversion* was a valid predictor of performance for managers and sales employees—the two occupations involving the most social interaction. Both *openness* to experience and *extroversion* predicted training proficiency for all occupations.[41] Another study with a sample of 89 university employees concluded that absenteeism was inversely related to extroversion and conscientiousness.[42]

A third study confirms the potential usefulness of personality tests while underscoring the importance of job analysis. The researchers analyzed personnel testing studies and concluded that the predictive power of a personality test can be quite high.[43] However, they also found that the full potential of personality testing will be realized only when careful job analysis becomes the "standard practice for determining which traits are relevant to predicting performance on a given job. . . ."[44] In summary, personality tests can help employers predict which candidates will succeed on the job and which will not. However, the job analysis and validation study must be carefully executed.

Being personal in nature, personality tests should also always be used with some caution, but this is particularly the case where your focus is specifically on aberrant behavior. One report concluded that psychological tests can help determine whether an employee's erratic behavior will pose a threat to workplace safety. However, they can also create legal problems for employers—for instance, if rejected candidates claim the results are false, or that they violate the Americans with Disabilities Act or employees' privacy.[45]

Interest inventories compare one's interests with those of people in various occupations. Thus, a person who takes the *Strong-Campbell Inventory* would receive a report comparing his or her interests to those of people already in occupations such as accounting, engineering, management, or medical technology.

Interest inventories have many uses. One example is career planning, since a person will likely do better on jobs that involve activities in which he or she is interested. These tests can also be useful as selection tools. Clearly, if you can select people whose interests are roughly the same as those of successful incumbents in the jobs for which you are recruiting, it is more likely that the applicants will be successful on their new jobs.[46]

Achievement Tests

An achievement test is basically a measure of what a person has learned. Most of the tests you take in school are thus achievement tests. They measure your "job knowledge" in areas like economics, marketing, or personnel.

Achievement tests are also widely used in employment screening. For example, the Purdue Test for Machinists and Machine Operators tests the job knowledge of experienced machinists with questions like, "What is meant by 'tolerance'?" Other tests are available for electricians, welders, carpenters, and so forth. In addition to job knowledge, achievement tests measure the applicant's abilities; a typing test is one example. The use of computers in testing is illustrated in the "Information Technology and HR" box below.

WORK SAMPLES AND SIMULATIONS

work samples

Actual job tasks used in testing applicants' performance.

work sampling technique

A testing method based on measuring performance on actual basic job tasks.

Work samples and simulations (like the assessment centers described in this section) can be considered tests. However, they differ from most of the tests we've discussed because they focus on measuring job performance directly.[47] Personality and interests inventories, on the other hand, aim to predict job performance by measuring traits like extroversion or interests.

Work Sampling for Employee Selection

RATIONALE FOR WORK SAMPLING The **work sampling technique** measures how a candidate actually performs some of (a sample of) the job's basic tasks.[48]

There are several advantages to work sampling. Since you are measuring actual on-the-job tasks, it is harder for the applicant to fake answers. The work sample itself is more

---

INFORMATION TECHNOLOGY AND HR

Computer-Interactive Performance Tests

Computerized testing today is increasingly replacing conventional paper-and-pencil and manual tests. For example, a computerized testing procedure was developed for the selection of clerical personnel in a large manufacturing company.[49] In this case eight test components were constructed to represent actual work performed by secretarial personnel, such as maintaining and developing databases and spreadsheets, answering the telephone and filing, and handling travel arrangements. For the word processing test, applicants were given three minutes (monitored by the computer) to type as much of a letter as possible; the computer recorded and corrected the manuscript. For the

travel expense form completion task, the applicant had to access the database file, use some of the information in it to compute quarterly expenses, and transfer this information to the travel expense form. Other tests successfully computerized include numerical ability tests, reading comprehension tests, and a clerical comparing and checking test.[50]

Yet the cost of creating the computerized test needs to be weighed against its effectiveness. In one study the computerized test meant improved test security but no improvement in required testing time. The test's reliability and validity were found to be similar to those of a conventional test.[51]

clearly relevant to the job you are recruiting for, so in terms of fair employment you may be on safer grounds. The content of the work sample—the actual tasks the person must perform—is not as likely to be unfair to minorities as is a personnel test that inadvertently emphasizes middle-class concepts and values.[52] Work sampling does not delve into the applicant's personality or psyche, so there's almost no chance of its being viewed as an invasion of privacy. Well-designed work samples also exhibit better validity than do tests designed to predict performance.

DEVELOPING A WORK SAMPLING PROCEDURE The basic procedure[53] is to choose several tasks crucial to performing the job in question and test applicants on each. Their performance on each task is monitored by an observer who indicates on a checklist how well the applicant performs. Here is an example.

In developing a work sampling test for maintenance mechanics, experts first list all the possible tasks (like "install pulleys and belts" and "install and align a motor") that maintenance mechanics would be required to perform. For each task, the experts list the frequency of performance on the task and the task's relative importance to the overall job of maintenance mechanic. Thus, four crucial tasks might be installing pulleys and belts, disassembling and installing a gear box, installing and aligning a motor, and pressing a bushing into a sprocket.

Next these four tasks are broken down into the steps needed to complete them. Each step, of course, could be performed in a slightly different way. Since some approaches were better than others, the experts gave a different weight to different approaches.

This is illustrated in Figure 5-7, which shows one of the steps required for installing pulleys and belts—"checks key before installing." As listed on the checklist, different possible approaches here include checking the key against (1) the shaft, (2) the pulley, or (3) neither. Weights reflecting the worth of each of these approaches are shown on the right of the figure. The applicant would perform the task, and the test administration would check off the approach used.

Finally, the work sampling test is validated by determining the relationship between the applicants' scores on the work samples and their actual performance on the job. Then, once it is shown that the work sample is a valid predictor of job success, the employer can begin using it for selection.

Management Assessment Centers

management assessment centers

A situation in which management candidates are asked to make decisions in hypothetical situations and are scored on their performance. It usually also involves testing and the use of management games.

In a two- to three-day **management assessment center**, 10 to 12 management candidates perform realistic management tasks (like making presentations) under the observation of expert appraisers; each candidate's management potential is thereby *assessed* or appraised. The center itself may be a plain conference room; but it is often a special room with a one-way mirror to facilitate unobtrusive observations. Examples of the simulated exercises included in a typical assessment center are as follows:

The in-basket. With this exercise, the candidate is faced with an accumulation of reports, memos, notes of incoming phone calls, letters, and other materials collected

Interactive employment tests administered on the computer are becoming more popular as screening devices at many firms.

CHECKS KEY BEFORE INSTALLING AGAINST:		
_____ shaft	score	3
_____ pulley	score	3
_____ neither	score	1

FIGURE 5-7 *Example of a Work Sampling Question*
This is one step in installing pulleys and belts.

in the in-basket of the simulated job he or she is to take over. The candidate is asked to take appropriate action on each of these materials. For example, he or she must write letters, notes, or agendas for meetings. The results of the candidate's actions are then reviewed by the trained evaluators.

The leaderless group discussion. A leaderless group is given a discussion question and told to arrive at a group decision. The raters then evaluate each group member's interpersonal skills, acceptance by the group, leadership ability, and individual influence.

Management games. Participants engage in realistic problem solving, usually as members of two or more simulated companies that are competing in the marketplace. Decisions might have to be made about matters such as how to advertise and manufacture and how much inventory to keep in stock.

Individual presentations. A participant's communication skills and persuasiveness are evaluated by having the person make an oral presentation of the assigned topic.

Objective tests. All types of paper-and-pencil tests of personality, mental ability, interests, and achievements might also be a part of an assessment center.

The interview. Most centers also require an interview between at least one of the expert assessors and each participant. Here the latter's current interests, background, past performance, and motivation are assessed.

ASSESSMENT CENTERS IN PRACTICE   A recent survey provides a perspective on assessment center practices in the United States.[54] It was found that assessment centers are usually used for selection, promotion, and development purposes. Supervisor recommendations usually play a big role in choosing center participants. Line managers usually act as assessors and typically arrive at their ratings of participants through a consensus process.

Studies indicate that assessment centers that sample actual, realistic job behavior can be effective selection tools.[55] Yet, studies also raise an important question regarding one of the assessment center's main disadvantages—its high cost.[56] The question is whether a center can do its job less expensively than other selection techniques, and here the evidence is not clear. At least one study suggests that the assessment center approach is financially efficient.[57] One study, however, concluded that a straightforward review of the participants' personnel files did as good a job of predicting which participants would succeed as did their assessment center evaluations.[58] Perhaps the best approach is to combine the two. In one study, for instance, a combination of the assessment center and an evaluation of the candidate's records was a relatively good predictor.

Video-Based Situational Testing

Assessment centers are examples of situational tests; in situational tests, examinees are presented with situations representative of the job for which he or she is applying, and his or her responses to these hypothetical situations are evaluated.[59]

The use of video-based tests is one situational testing alternative gaining more attention today (others include work sampling, discussed above, and situational interviews, discussed in Chapter 6.)[60] In the typical video-based test several video scenarios are presented, each followed by a multiple-choice question. For example, a scenario might depict an incumbent handling a typical situation on the job. At a critical moment the scenario ends and the examinee is asked to choose from among several alternative courses of action. An example of a typical video-based scenario/judgment question, about one minute long, follows:

A manager is upset about the condition of the department and takes it out on one of the department's employees.

Manager: Well, I'm glad you're here.

Associate: Oh? Why is that?

Manager: Look at this place, that's why! I take a day off and come back to find the department in a mess. You should know better.

Associate: But, I didn't work late last night.

Manager: Maybe not. But there have been plenty of times before when you've left this department in a mess.

(The scenario stops here.)

If you were this associate, what would you do?

A) Let the other associates responsible for the mess know that you had to take the heat.

B) Straighten up the department, and try to reason with the manager later.

C) Suggest to the manager that he talk to the other associates who made the mess.

D) Take it up with the manager's boss.[61]

While the evidence is somewhat mixed, the results of two recent studies suggest that video-based situational tests can be a useful tool for selecting employees.[62]

The Miniature Job Training and Evaluation Approach

In this approach, the candidate is trained to perform a sample of the job's tasks; his or her ability to perform these tasks is then measured. The approach assumes that a person who can demonstrate the ability to learn and perform the sample of tasks will be able to learn and perform the job itself.

The technique can be useful. One study focused on Navy recruits who had been deemed unacceptable candidates for various naval schools based on their performance on traditional tests. The recruits participated in several miniature job-training and evaluation situations. In one, recruits were taught how to read a simplified plot diagram of the positions of two ships, their headings, and speed and how to extrapolate the new position of each ship and evaluate the danger of collision. Seamen who normally would have been barred from this training based on their initial test scores were found to be competent to pursue it, as a result of their performance in the mini training session.

The approach has pros and cons. It is "content relevant," since it tests applicants with an actual sample of the job rather than just with paper-and-pencil tests. This direct approach may be more acceptable (and more fair) to disadvantaged applicants than the usual paper-and-pencil tests. On the other hand, its emphases individual instruction during training, so this approach is also a relatively expensive screening method.[63]

THE HIGH-PERFORMANCE ORGANIZATION

Building Better, Faster, More Competitive Organizations Through HR: Skills Testing

■ Texas Instruments Semiconductor Group (TISG), Midland, TX

The Texas Instruments Semiconductor Group, Midland, Texas, facility has an intensive assessment/training program it calls its Skills Upgrade Program. TISG hired HR Strategies (a human resource consulting firm) to conduct a job analysis for all operator and technician job classes. From the job analysis results, HR Strategies were able to determine what knowledge and skills were required to perform the operator and technician jobs. Then skills tests in the areas of reading and math were developed to address the functional skills required. Two separate sets of tests were established—one set to be used for the purpose of hiring new people and one set to be used for assessing the skills of incumbents.

Next TISG contracted with Sylvan Learning to establish and maintain an on-site training program. Sylvan provides individualized training in the areas of reading comprehension and math. Math skills taught include computation, reasoning, graph comprehension, measurement, and for technicians, statistics.

After employees have mastered the foundational skills, they are ready for job-specific training. For operators, this training comes from trainers in the facility's training unit or from other qualified employee operators. Operators go through a three-phase process to become qualified for a job. They are given a job knowledge test, audited over time for their particular operation, and then submit material they have processed for a material sample audit. No operator may perform a job that he/she has not been qualified to perform. Operators are re-evaluated over their primary job every six months.

Source: Copyright 1998, Best Manufacturing Practices Center of Excellence.

OTHER
SELECTION
TECHNIQUES

Background Investigations and Reference Checks

USE   Most employers try to check and verify the job applicant's background information and references. Some estimate that about 95% of U.S. corporations now employ such background checks,[64] with the vast majority probably using telephone inquiries. The remainder use background sources like commercial credit-checking agencies and reference letters.

Background checks can be quite comprehensive. As *Fortune* magazine recently noted, if you haven't changed jobs in the past few years you're in for a rude surprise:

> *Chances are, your new employer will delve into your driving record, check for criminal charges or convictions, survey your creditworthiness, examine whether you've been sued or have run afoul of the IRS, and sometimes even query co-workers and neighbors about your reputation. Your educational history, past employment, and references listed on your resume are in for fierce scrutiny.[65]*

While that description may overstate the situation somewhat, it does appear that background investigations and reference checks are used more extensively today.

There are two key reasons for conducting preemployment reference and/or checks—to verify the accuracy of factual information previously provided by the applicant and to discover damaging background information such as criminal records and suspended driver's licenses.[66] Lying on one's application is apparently not unusual. For example, BellSouth's security director estimates that between 15% and 20% of applicants conceal a dark secret. As he says, "It's not uncommon to find someone who applies and looks good, and then you do a little digging and you start to see all sorts of criminal history."[67]

The most commonly verified background areas are legal eligibility for employment (in compliance with immigration laws), dates of prior employment, military service (including discharge status), education, and identification (including date of birth and address).[68]

The recent growth in the phenomenon of youth gangs infiltrating corporate America provides one of many examples why employers should carefully check references.[69] The FBI estimates that more than 400,000 gang members live and work in 700 cities nationwide, and some say this number is just the tip of the iceberg.[70]

Even relatively sophisticated companies fall prey to gang member employees, in part because they haven't conducted proper background and reference checks. In Chicago, for instance, a major pharmaceutical firm discovered it had hired gang members in mail delivery and computer repair. The crooks in turn were stealing close to a million dollars a year in computer parts and then using the mail department to ship them to a nearby computer store they happened to own.[71] Thorough background checks might have unearthed these people's backgrounds.

The actual background investigation/reference check can take many forms. Most employers at least try to verify an applicant's current position and salary with his or her current employer by telephone (assuming doing so was cleared with the candidate). Others call the applicant's current and previous supervisors to try to discover more about the person's motivation, technical competence, and ability to work with others (we'll see below that many employers have policies against providing such information). Some employers get background reports from commercial credit-rating companies. The latter can provide information about an applicant's credit standing, indebtedness, reputation, character, and lifestyle. Some employers ask for written references; Figure 5-8 shows a form used for this purpose.

(COMPANY LETTERHEAD)

To Whom it May Concern:

☐ has been employed by us

_____ ☐ has applied for employment

and given the following information covering employment in your organization. We have been authorized to communicate with you for verification and such reference information as you care to give us.

(Please check if correct or change if incorrect)

Employment dates: _____ _____

Position: _____ _____

Last earning rate: $ _____ per _____ _____

Reason for leaving: _____ _____

Is applicant eligible for rehire _____

_____
Your signature

_____
Title

On the back of this letter we would appreciate any helpful comments you care to make, and will respect your confidence in this matter. The enclosed duplicate is for your own files.

Sincerely yours,

_____
Personnel Department

FIGURE 5-8

Reference Check Form

Source: Steven Mitchell Sack, *The Hiring and Firing Book: A Complete Legal Guide for Employers*, New York: Legal Strategies, Inc., October 1993.

EFFECTIVENESS Handled correctly, the background check can be useful. It is an inexpensive and straightforward way to verify factual information about the applicant, such as current and previous job titles, current salary range, dates of employment, and educational background.

However, reference checking can backfire. Laws like the Fair Credit Reporting Act of 1970 increase the likelihood that rejected applicants will successfully demand access to the background information that was compiled; they may then bring suit against both the source of that information and the recruiting employer. (In one case, a man was awarded $56,000 after being turned down for a job because, among other things, he was called a "character" by a former employer.) From a practical point of view, it is not always easy for a reference to prove that the bad reference given the applicant was warranted. The rejected applicant thus has various legal remedies, including suing the reference for defamation of character.[72] Such a possibility is often enough to cause former employers to limit their bad (or any) comments.

It is not just the fear of legal reprisal that can undermine a reference. Many supervisors don't want to diminish a former employee's chances for a job; others might prefer giving an incompetent employee good reviews if it will get rid of him or her. Even when checking references via the phone, therefore, you have to be careful to ask the right questions and try to judge whether the reference's answers are evasive and, if so, why.

HR managers don't seem to view reference letters as very useful. In one study, 12% replied that reference letters were "highly valuable," 43% call them "somewhat valuable," and 30% viewed them as having "little value," or (6%) "no value." Asked whether they preferred written or telephone references, 72% favored the telephone reference, because it allows a more candid assessment and provides a more interpersonal exchange. Not having a written record is also an appealing feature. In fact, reference letters ranked lowest—seventh out of seven—when rated by these human resource officers as selection tools. Ranked from top to bottom, these tools were, by the way: interview, application form, academic record, oral referral, aptitude and achievement tests, psychological tests, and finally, reference letters.[73]

GIVING EMPLOYMENT REFERENCES: KNOW THE LAW There are also some caveats to follow when supplying employment references on former employees. Federal laws that affect references are the Privacy Act of 1974, the Fair Credit Reporting Act of 1970, the Family Education Rights and Privacy Act of 1974 (and Buckley Amendment of 1974), and the Freedom of Information Act of 1966. These laws give individuals in general and students (The Buckley Amendment) the right to know the nature and substance of information in their credit files and files with government agencies, and (under the Privacy Act), to review records pertaining to them from any private business that contracts with a federal agency. It is therefore quite possible that your comments may be shown to the person you are describing. Furthermore common law, and in particular the tort of defamation, applies to any information you supply. Communication is defamatory if it is false and tends to harm the reputation of another by lowering the person in the estimation of the community or by deterring other persons from associating or dealing with him or her.

Suggested guidelines for defensible references are summarized in Figure 5-9. Guidelines include "Don't volunteer information," "Avoid vague statements," and "Do not answer trap questions such as 'Would you rehire this person?'" In practice, many firms have a policy of not providing any information about former employees except for their dates of employment, last salary, and position titles.[74]

Being sued for defamation is increasingly a concern for employers. In one case, four employees were terminated for "gross insubordination" after disobeying a supervisor's request to review their allegedly fabricated expense account reports. The jury found that the employees' expense reports were actually honest. The employees then argued that al-

FIGURE 5-9

Guidelines for Defensible References

Source: Mary F. Cook, *Human Resources Director's Handbook* (Upper Saddle River, NJ: Prentice Hall, 1984), p. 93.

1. Don't volunteer information. Respond only to specific company or institutional inquiries and requests. Before responding, telephone the inquirer to check on the validity of the request.
2. Direct all communication only to persons who have a specific interest in that information.
3. State in the message that the information you are providing is confidential and should be treated as such. Use qualifying statements such as "providing information that was requested"; "relating this information only because it was requested"; or "providing information that is to be used for professional purposes only." Sentences such as these imply that information was not presented for the purpose of hurting or damaging a person's reputation.
4. Obtain written consent from the employee or student, if possible.
5. Provide only reference data that relates and pertains to the job and job performance in question.
6. Avoid vague statements such as: "He was an average student"; " She was careless at times"; "He displayed an inability to work with others."
7. Document all released information. Use specific statements such as: "Mr. _____ received a grade of C—an average grade"; "Ms. _____ made an average of two bookkeeping errors each week"; or "This spring, four members of the work team wrote letters asking not to be placed on the shift with Mr. _____."
8. Clearly label all subjective statements based on personal opinions and feelings. Say "I believe . . ." whenever making a statement that is not fact.
9. When providing a negative or potentially negative statement, add the reason or reasons why, or specify the incidents that led you to this opinion.
10. Do not answer trap questions such as "Would you rehire this person?"
11. Avoid answering questions that are asked "off the record."

though their employer didn't publicize the defamatory expense account matter to others, the employer should have known that the employees would have to admit the (slanderous) reason for their firing when explaining and defending themselves to future employers. The court agreed and upheld jury awards totaling more than a million dollars to these employees. In another case a manager who claimed he was wrongly accused of stealing from his former employer won $1.25 million in a slander suit.[75] Perhaps this explains why in one survey only 11% of respondents said the information they get about a candidate's violent or "bizarre" behavior is adequate. Fifty-four percent of the respondents specifically indicate that they get inadequate information in this area. Of eleven types of information sought in background checks, only three were ranked by a majority of respondents as ones for which they received adequate information. Dates of employment (96%); eligibility for rehire (65%); and job qualifications (56%). With regard to salary history, reasons for leaving a previous job, work habits, personality traits, human relations skills, special skills or knowledge, and employability, "fewer than half of HR managers responding to the survey said they were able to obtain adequate information."[76]

MAKING BACKGROUND AND REFERENCE CHECKS MORE USEFUL   So, what is the prospective employer to do? Is there any way to obtain more useful information?

There are several things you can do. First, include on your application form a statement to be signed by the applicant explicitly authorizing you to do a background check. For example, include a statement such as

I hereby certify that the facts set forth in the above employment application are true and complete to the best of my knowledge. I understand that falsified statements or misrepresentation of information on this application or omission of any information sought may be cause for dismissal, if employed, or may lead to refusal to make an offer and/or to withdrawal of an offer. I also authorize investigation of credit, employment record, driving record, and, once a job offer is made or during employment, worker's compensation background if required.

Second (since telephone references apparently produce more candid assessments), it's probably best to rely more on telephone references than on written ones. Similarly, remember that you can probably count on getting more accurate information regarding dates of employment, eligibility for rehire, and job qualifications than other background information (such as reasons for leaving a previous job).

Persistence and your sensitivity to potential "red flags" can also improve your results. For example, if the former employer hesitates or seems to qualify his or her answer when you ask, "Would you rehire?" don't just go on to your next question. Instead, try to unearth what the applicant did to give the former employer pause.

There are also a number of local investigation firms that can facilitate your background check. For example, one in South Florida advertises that for under $50 they'll do a criminal history report, motor vehicle/driver's record report, and (after the person is hired) a history of worker's compensation claims report, plus a confirmation of identify, name, and social security number.

Another good idea is to use a structured form as in Figure 5-10. The form helps to ensure that you don't overlook important questions. Another suggestion is to use the references offered by the applicant as merely a source for other references who may know of the applicant's performance. Thus, you might ask each of the applicant's references, "Could you please give me the name of another person who might be familiar with the applicant's performance?" In that way, you begin getting information from references who may be more objective, because they weren't referred directly by the applicant.

Also, conduct a thorough reference "audit" rather than just a reference check.[77] For example, contact at least two superiors, two peers, and two subordinates from each job previously held by the candidate. You should thereby find that a more reliable picture of the candidate is gradually formed. Of course, more and more employers do have policies prohibiting employees (outside HR) from providing reference information. And it is always risky to ask candidates to self-select the references. However, such audits can lead to a more accurate picture of your candidate than will the usual poking around that most reference checks often entail.

For former employers, not disclosing relevant information can be dangerous, too. In one Florida case an employee was fired for allegedly bringing a handgun to work. After he was then fired by his subsequent employer—for absenteeism—he returned to the second company and shot a supervisor as well as the HR director and three other people before taking his own life. The injured parties and the relatives of the employees killed sued the original employer, who had provided the employee with a clean letter of recommendation; the letter stated his departure was not related to job performance, allegedly because that first employer didn't want to make the employee angry over his firing.

PREEMPLOYMENT INFORMATION SERVICES   Computer databases have made it easier to check background information about candidates. There was a time when the only source of background information was the information a candidate provided on the application form and (in some cases) what the employer could obtain through the use of private investigators. Today so-called preemployment information services use databases to accumulate mounds of information about matters such as worker's compensation histories, credit histories, and conviction records. Employers are increasingly turning to these information services in order to make the right selection decision. You can place a call today and obtain data on a person's credit, driving, workers' compensation, and criminal records, for instance.

Yet there are two reasons to use caution when delving into an applicant's criminal, credit, and worker's compensation histories.[78] First (as discussed in Chapter 2), various equal employment laws discourage or prohibit the use of such information in employee screening. For example, under the 1990 Americans with Disabilities Act (ADA) employers are prohibited from making preemployment inquiries into the existence, nature, or severity of a disability. Therefore, a request, prior to offering the person a job, for information

FIGURE 5-10

Structured Telephone or Personal Interview Form

Source: Adapted by permission of the publisher from *Book of Employment Forms*, American Management Association.

TELEPHONE OR PERSONAL INTERVIEW

☐ FORMER EMPLOYER
☐ CHARACTER REFERENCE

COMPANY _____   ADDRESS _____   PHONE _____

NAME OF PERSON _____   POSITION _____
CONTACTED _____   OR TITLE _____

1. I WISH TO VERIFY SOME FACTS GIVEN BY
   (MISS, MRS. MS.)
   MR.
   WHO IS APPLYING FOR EMPLOYMENT WITH OUR FIRM.
   WHAT WERE THE DATES OF HIS/HER EMPLOYMENT BY
   YOUR COMPANY?   FROM ____ 19 ____ TO ____ 19 ____

2. WHAT WAS THE NATURE OF HIS/HER JOB?   AT START _____

   AT LEAVING _____

3. HE/SHE STATES THAT HE/SHE WAS EARNING $ _____ PER _____
   WHEN HE/SHE LEFT. IS THAT CORRECT?   YES ____ NO ____ $ ____

4. WHAT DID HIS/HER SUPERIORS THINK OF HIM/HER? _____

   WHAT DID HIS/HER SUBORDINATES THINK OF HIM/HER? _____

5. DID HE/SHE HAVE SUPERVISORY RESPONSIBILITY?   YES ____ NO ____

   (IF YES) HOW DID HE/SHE CARRY IT OUT? _____

6. HOW HARD DID HE/SHE WORK? _____

7. HOW DID HE/SHE GET ALONG WITH OTHERS? _____

8. HOW WAS HIS/HER ATTENDANCE RECORD?   PUNCTUALITY? _____

9. WHAT WERE HIS/HER REASONS FOR LEAVING? _____

10. WOULD YOU REHIRE HIM/HER? (IF NO) WHY?   YES ____ NO ____

11. DID HE/SHE HAVE ANY DOMESTIC, FINANCIAL OR
    PERSONAL TROUBLE WHICH INTERFERED WITH
    HIS/HER WORK?   YES ____ NO ____

12. DID HE/SHE DRINK OR GAMBLE TO EXCESS?   YES ____ NO ____

13. WHAT ARE HIS/HER STRONG POINTS? _____

14. WHAT ARE HIS/HER WEAK POINTS? _____

REMARKS: _____

---

about a candidate's previous worker's compensation claims would likely be viewed as unlawful. Similarly, making employment decisions based on someone's arrest record would likely be viewed as unfairly discriminatory, since some minorities suffer relatively high arrest rates, and an arrest doesn't mean the person is guilty. (Use of conviction information for particular jobs—for instance, where security is involved—would be less problematical.) The EEOC has also held that a poor credit history should not, by itself, preclude a person from getting a job.

And, it's not just federal employment laws that suggest prudence; many states ban the use of such information as well. For example, in New York State, "It is unlawful for an employer to inquire into or act on information about an arrest not resulting in conviction unless such use is permitted by law. It is unlawful to discriminate against an applicant for licensing or employment because the person has been convicted of one or more criminal offenses or because of a finding of a lack of 'good moral character' based on the conviction."[79] New York also requires employers to notify an applicant before requesting a consumer report. Under the Federal Fair Credit Reporting Act, employers that take adverse employment actions based on a consumer report must follow two rules. First, they must advise the employee or candidate of the fact that he or she was turned down based on the consumer report and the name and address of the consumer reporting agency must be supplied. Second, the employer may not obtain a consumer report from a reporting agency under false pretenses.[80]

To bring the problem into perspective, consider the debate about use of a new antitheft national database that was recently established. *Theftnet* is a database being tested by several large retailers including Home Depot and JC Penney Company. The database contains the names of workers across the country who have either been prosecuted for theft or who have signed admissions statements with former employers.[81] On its face, using a database like Theftnet should be straightforward, focusing as it does on convictions or written admissions.

Yet in practice, utilizing such a database raises several serious issues. For example, one attorney says supplying information to the database could make an employer liable for defamation and retaliation claims unless it has "clear proof" of an employee's guilt.[82] Similarly, employees who have signed admissions statements may in fact be guilty, but may also have signed for unrelated reasons such as coercion or promises by the employer. One attorney goes so far as to contend that a database like this could pose an incalculable risk of harm to employees.[83] Employers tapping into such a database therefore have to balance the pros and cons, consider the legal issues involved before using the database, ensure they have "clear proof" of an employee's guilt, and use the information from the database as only one part of the background checking process.

Some suggestions for collecting background information include the following:

1. Check all applicable state laws.
2. Check beyond applicable state laws and review the impact of federal equal employment laws.
3. Remember the Federal Fair Credit Reporting Act.
4. Do not obtain information that will not be used.
5. Remember that using arrest information will be highly suspect.
6. Avoid blanket policies (such as "we have no one with a record of worker's compensation claims").
7. Use information that is specific and job related.
8. Keep information confidential and up to date.
9. Never authorize an unreasonable investigation.[84]

The Polygraph and Honesty Testing

Some firms still use the polygraph for honesty testing, even though current law prevents most employers engaged in interstate commerce from using lie detector tests either for preemployment screening or during the course of employment. The polygraph (or "lie detector") machine is a device that measures physiological changes like increased perspiration. The assumption is that such changes reflect changes in the emotional stress that accompanies lying. The usual procedure is for an applicant or current employee to be attached to the machine with painless electronic probes. He or she is then asked a series of neutral questions by the polygraph expert. These questions might, for instance, confirm that the person's name is John Smith and that he is currently residing in New York.

Once the person's emotional reaction to giving truthful answers to neutral questions has been ascertained, questions like "Have you ever stolen anything without paying for it?" "Do you use drugs?" or "Have you ever committed a crime?" can be asked. In theory, at least, the expert can then determine with some accuracy whether or not the applicant is lying.

Complaints about offensiveness plus grave doubts about the polygraph's accuracy culminated in the Employee Polygraph Protection Act being signed into law in 1988. With a few exceptions the law prohibits employers from conducting polygraph examinations of all job applicants and most employees. (Also prohibited under this law are other mechanical or electrical devices that attempt to measure honesty or dishonesty, including psychological stress evaluators and voice stress analyzers. Paper-and-pencil tests and chemical testing [as for drugs] are not prohibited under federal laws.)[85] Local, state, or federal government employers can continue to use polygraph exams under the law but many local and state government employers are further restricted under a number of state laws. Other employers that can use polygraph tests include industries with national defense or security contracts; certain businesses with nuclear power-related contracts with the Department of Energy; businesses and consultants with access to highly classified information, as well as those with counterintelligence-related contracts with the FBI or Department of Justice; and private businesses that are (1) hiring private security personnel, (2) hiring persons with access to drugs, or (3) doing ongoing investigations involving economic loss or injury to an employer's business, such as a theft (see Figure 5-11 on page 198).

Even in the case of ongoing investigations of theft, the employer's right to use polygraphs is quite limited under the 1988 Act. To administer a polygraph test during an ongoing investigation an employer must meet four standards. First, the employer must show that it suffered an economic loss or injury. Second, it must show that the employee in question had access to the property. Third, asking the employee to take the polygraph must be based on a reasonable suspicion. Finally, the employee who is asked to take the test must be notified of the details of the investigation before the test as well as the questions to be asked on the polygraph test itself.

A sample case underscores the importance of adhering to the Polygraph Protection Act's four standards.[86] A doctor reported $200 missing from his hospital locker. The hospital questioned workers who had access to the locker room and searched their lockers. Each employee was told there might be a lie detector test and only one expressed reluctance. The hospital fired that employee based on its "strong suspicion" that he was the culprit. The employee then successfully sued the hospital under the Employee Polygraph Protection Act; he showed that the employer hadn't, as required, proven that the loss was a loss to the business, since the theft from the doctor's locker didn't affect the "business of patient care." He also showed the hospital had failed to follow several procedures under the Act. The bottom line is that the polygraph can still be used by employers under limited conditions, but the Act's four standards must be adhered to.

PAPER-AND-PENCIL TESTS   The virtual elimination of the polygraph as a screening device has triggered a burgeoning market for other types of honesty testing devices; there is now a range of these from which to choose. Paper-and-pencil honesty tests are psychological tests designed to predict job applicants' proneness to dishonesty and other forms of counterproductivity.[87] Most of these tests measure attitudes regarding things like tolerance of others who steal, acceptance of rationalizations for theft, and admission of theft-related activities. Tests include the Phase II profile, owned by Wackenhut Corporation of

NOTICE

EMPLOYEE POLYGRAPH PROTECTION ACT

The Employee Polygraph Protection Act prohibits most private employers from using lie detector tests either for pre-employment screening or during the course of employment.

PROHIBITIONS

Employers are generally prohibited from requiring or requesting any employee or job applicant to take a lie detector test, and from discharging, disciplining, or discriminating against an employee or prospective employee for refusing to take a test or for exercising other rights under the Act.

EXEMPTIONS*

Federal, State and local governments are not affected by the law. Also, the law does not apply to tests given by the Federal Government to certain private individuals engaged in national security-related activities.

The Act permits *polygraph* (a kind of lie detector) tests to be administered in the private sector, subject to restrictions, to certain prospective employees of security service firms (armored car, alarm, and guard), and of pharmaceutical manufacturers, distributors and dispensers.

The Act also permits polygraph testing, subject to restrictions, of certain employees of private firms who are reasonably suspected of involvement in a workplace incident (theft, embezzlement, etc.) that resulted in economic loss to the employer.

EXAMINEE RIGHTS

Where polygraph tests are permitted, they are subject to numerous strict standards concerning the conduct and length of the test. Examinees have a number of specific rights, including the right to a written notice before testing, the right to refuse or discontinue a test, and the right not to have test results disclosed to unauthorized persons.

ENFORCEMENT

The Secretary of Labor may bring court actions to restrain violations and assess civil penalties up to $10,000 against violators. Employees or job applicants may also bring their own court actions.

ADDITIONAL INFORMATION

Additional information may be obtained, and complaints of violations may be filed, at local offices of the Wage and Hour Division, which are listed in the telephone directory under U.S. Government, Department of Labor, Employment Standards Administration.

THE LAW REQUIRES EMPLOYERS TO DISPLAY THIS POSTER WHERE EMPLOYEES AND JOB APPLICANTS CAN READILY SEE IT.

*The law does not preempt any provision of any State or local law or any collective bargaining agreement which is more restrictive with respect to lie detector tests.

U.S. DEPARTMENT OF LABOR

EMPLOYMENT STANDARDS ADMINISTRATION

Wage and Hour Division
Washington, D.C. 20210

* U.S GPO 1991-0-522-762

WH Publication 1462
September 1988

FIGURE 5-11 *Employee Polygraph Notice*

Coral Gables, Florida, which provides security services to employers. Similar tests are published by London House, Incorporated, and Stanton Corporation.[88]

While concerns were initially raised by psychologists concerning the proliferation of paper-and-pencil honesty tests, several recent studies support the validity of these selection tools.[89] One study focused on 111 employees hired by a major retail convenience store chain to work at convenience store or gas station outlet counters.[90] "Shrinkage" was estimated to equal 3% of sales, and internal theft was believed to account for much of this. The researchers found that scores on an honesty test successfully predicted theft in this study, as measured by termination for theft. One large-scale review of the use of such tests for measuring honesty, integrity, conscientiousness, dependability, trustworthiness, and reliability recently concluded that the "pattern of findings" regarding the usefulness of such tests "continues to be consistently positive.[91]

RESEARCH INSIGHT   Paper-and-pencil honesty testing may also help companies predict white-collar crime.[92] Subjects in one study included 329 federal prison inmates incarcerated for white-collar crime and 344 individuals from several midwestern firms employed in white-collar positions. Three instruments were administered, including the California Psychological Inventory (a personality inventory), the Employment Inventory (a second personality inventory), and a biodata scale. The researchers concluded that "there are large and measurable psychological differences between white-collar offenders and nonoffenders . . ." and that it was possible to construct a personality-based integrity test to differentiate between the two.[93]

WHAT YOU CAN DO   Given all this, what can an employer do to detect dishonesty? In practice, detecting dishonest candidates involves not tests but a comprehensive screening procedure including reference checking and interviews, too. One expert suggests the following steps:

Ask blunt questions.[94] Within the bounds of legality, you can ask very direct questions in the face-to-face interview. For example, says this expert, there is nothing wrong with asking the applicant, "Have you ever stolen anything from an employer?" Other questions to ask include, "Have you recently held jobs other than those listed on your application?" "Have you ever been fired or asked to leave a job?" "What reasons would past supervisors give if they were asked why they let you go?" "Have past employers ever disciplined you or warned you about absences or lateness?" "Is any information on your application misrepresented or falsified?"

Listen, rather than talk. Specifically, allow the applicant to do the talking so you can learn as much as possible about the person.

Ask for a credit check. Include a clause in your application form that gives you the right to conduct certain background checks on the applicant including credit checks and motor vehicle reports.

Check all references. Rigorously pursue employment and personal references.

Consider a paper-and-pencil test. Consider utilizing paper-and-pencil honesty tests and psychological tests as a part of your honesty screening program.

Test for drugs. Devise a drug-testing program and give each applicant a copy of the policy.

Conduct searches. Establish a search-and-seizure policy. Give each applicant a copy of the policy and require each to return a signed copy. Basically, the policy should state that all lockers, desks, and similar property remain the property of the company and may be inspected routinely.

AN EXAMPLE OF AN HONESTY SCREENING PROGRAM   The Adolf Coors company scrapped polygraph testing of job applicants and substituted a three-step program.

The steps include urinalysis, a paper-and-pencil honesty test, and a reference check. First, Coors uses an outside lab to conduct the urinalysis test. Next applicants take a Stanton Corporation paper-and-pencil survey of 83 questions on attitudes toward honesty and theft. The survey company provides Coors with a written report that categorizes applicants by levels of risk. For example, low-risk individuals are those who have never been involved in any extensive thefts, while marginal-risk applicants might be tempted to steal if they felt they wouldn't be caught. Finally, applicant references and background checks are performed by a company called Equifax Services. They involve contacting previous employers and educational institutions attended.[95]

A CAUTION There are several reasons to use caution with any honesty testing program. First, as noted earlier, doubts have been expressed regarding how valid many paper-and-pencil honesty testing instruments are. Second, one could argue that a rejection (let alone an incorrect rejection) for dishonesty carries more stigma than a rejection for, say, poor mechanical comprehension or even poor sociability. It's true that others may never know just why you rejected the candidate. However, the subject, having just taken and "failed" what may be a fairly obvious "honesty test," may leave the premises feeling that his or her treatment was less than proper. Third, questions and tests in this area pose serious invasion-of-privacy issues, delving as they do into areas such as how you feel about stealing, or whether you have ever stolen anything. There are also local legal constraints to beware of. For instance, Massachusetts and Rhode Island both limit the use of paper-and-pencil honesty tests. Until more widespread evaluations are done, these tests should thus be used cautiously and certainly only as supplements to other techniques like reference checking.

Graphology

The use of graphology (handwriting analysis) is based on the assumption that the writer's basic personality traits will be expressed in his or her handwriting.[96] Handwriting analysis thus has some resemblance to projective personality tests.

In graphology, the handwriting analyst studies an applicant's handwriting and signature in order to discover the person's needs, desires, and psychological makeup.[97] According to the graphologist, the writing in Figure 5-12 exemplifies "uneven pressure, poor rhythm, and uneven baselines." The variation of light and dark lines shows a "lack of control" and is "one strong indicator of the writer's inner disturbance."

While many scientists doubt the validity of handwriting analysis, some writers estimate that over 1,000 U.S. companies use handwriting analysis to assess applicants for cer-

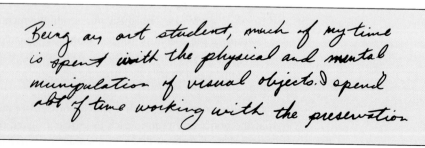

FIGURE 5-12 *Handwriting Exhibit Used by Graphologist*

Source: Reproduced with permission from Kathryn Sackhein, *Handwriting Analysis and the Employee Selection Process* (New York: Quorum Books, 1990), p. 45.

tain strategic positions.[98] And classified sections of international periodicals like the *Economist* still run ads from graphologists offering to aid in an employer's selection process. Yet, in practice, the validity of handwriting analysis is questionable, to say the least.[99] In general, the evidence suggests that graphology does not predict job performance.[100]

Physical Examination

Once an offer is made and a person hired, a medical exam is usually the next step in the selection process (although it may also take place after the new employee starts work).[101]

There are five main reasons for requiring preemployment medical exams. The exam can be used to determine that the applicant qualifies for the *physical requirements* of the position and to discover any *medical limitations* that should be taken into account in placing the applicant. The exam will also establish a *record and baseline* of the applicant's health for the purpose of future insurance or compensation claims. The examination can, by identifying health problems, also reduce *absenteeism and accidents* and, of course, detect *communicable diseases* that may be unknown to the applicant. The exam is usually performed by the employer's medical department in the largest organizations. Smaller employers retain the services of consulting physicians to perform such exams, which are almost always paid for by the employer. In any case remember that under the Americans with Disabilities Act, a person with a disability can't be rejected for the job if he or she is otherwise qualified and if the person could perform the essential job functions with reasonable accommodation. Under the ADA, a medical exam is permitted during the period between the job offer and commencement of work only if such exams are standard practice for all applicants for that job category.[102]

Drug Screening

Drug abuse is a serious problem at work. Counselors at the Cocaine National Help Line polled callers of the 800-Cocaine hot line and found that 75% admitted to occasional cocaine use at work, 69% said that they regularly worked under the influence of a drug, and 25% recorded daily use at work. A study of long-distance truck drivers found that over 62% reported using drugs at least occasionally.[103] The U.S. Chamber of Commerce estimates that employee drug and alcohol use costs U.S. employers over $60 billion each year in reduced productivity, increased accidents, increased sick benefits, and higher worker's compensation claims.[104]

More and more employers therefore conduct drug screenings. The most common practice is to test job candidates just before they are formally hired. Many also test current employees when there is reason to believe the person has been using drugs after a work accident, in the presence of obvious behavioral symptoms, or in the face of chronic lateness or high absenteeism. Some firms routinely administer drug tests on a random basis or periodic basis, while others require drug tests when an employee is transferred or promoted to a new position.[105]

None of these tests are foolproof. 96% of employers who test use urine sampling,[106] but some of these tests can't distinguish between legal and illegal substances—for example, Advil and Nuprin can produce positive results for marijuana. Other employers find such tests are too personal, and turn instead to hair follicle testing. The method, radioimmunoassay of hair (RIAH), requires a small sample of hair, which is analyzed to detect prior ingestion of illicit drugs.[107] Yet classified ads in some alternative newspapers advertise chemicals that can be added to specimens or rubbed on the scalp to fool the test.

Drug testing also raises ethical issues.[108] Unlike breathalizer tests for alcohol like those given roadside to inebriated drivers, urine and blood tests for drugs only indicate whether drug residues are present; they can't measure impairment or, for that matter, habituation or addiction. [109] Without strong evidence linking blood or urine drug levels to impairment, some argue that testing is not justifiable on the grounds of boosting workplace safety.[110] Many feel that the testing procedures themselves are degrading and intrusive. Others argue that one's use of drugs during leisure hours might have little or no relevance to the job itself.[111]

Drug testing also raises legal issues.[112] As one attorney has written, "It is not uncommon for employees to claim that drug tests violate their rights to privacy under common law or, in some states, a state statutory or constitutional provision."[113] Hair follicle testing is less intrusive than urinalysis but can actually produce more extensive personal information. (For example, a three-inch hair segment will record six months of drug use).

Several federal laws are relevant for workplace drug testing. Under the Americans with Disabilities Act, a former drug user (one who no longer uses illegal drugs and has successfully completed or is participating in a rehabilitation program) would probably be considered a qualified applicant with a disability.[114] Under the Drug Free Workplace Act of 1988, federal contractors must maintain a workplace free from illegal drugs. While this doesn't require contractors to conduct drug testing or rehabilitate their affected employees, many do. Under the U.S. Department of Transportation workplace regulations, firms with over 50 eligible employees in transportation industries must also now conduct alcohol testing on workers with sensitive or safety-related jobs. These include mass transit workers, air traffic controllers, train crews, and school bus drivers.[115] Other laws, including the Federal Rehabilitation Act of 1973 and various state laws, give protection to rehabilitating drug users or to those who have a physical or mental addiction.[116]

What should you do when a job candidate tests positive? Most companies will not hire such candidates, and a few will immediately fire current employees who test positive.[117] For example, 120 of the 123 companies responding to the question, "If test results are positive, what action do you take?" indicated that applicants testing positive are not hired. Current employees have more legal recourse if dismissed and must therefore be told the reason for their dismissal if dismissed for a positive drug test.[118]

But, particularly where safety-sensitive jobs are concerned, courts appear to side with employers. In one recent case, for instance, the U.S. Court of Appeals for the First Circuit (which includes Maine, Massachusetts, New Hampshire, Rhode Island, and Puerto Rico) ruled that Exxon acted properly in firing a truck driver who failed a drug test. Exxon corporation's drug-free workplace program included random testing of employees in safety-sensitive jobs. In this case the employee drove a tractor trailer carrying 12,000 gallons of flammable motor fuel and tested positive for cocaine; Exxon discharged him. The union representing the employee challenged the firing, an arbitrator reduced the penalty to a two-month suspension, and the appeals court reversed the arbitrator's decision and ruled that the employer acted properly in firing the truck driver, given the circumstances.[119]

Testing, Selection, and Organizational Performance

Just how useful is it for a firm to use testing and selection tools like those described previously? The evidence suggests that a well-designed program can improve performance and a firm's bottom line.

First, there is considerable anecdotal evidence. A typical selection program was implemented at Franciscan Health System of Dayton.[120] This firm, which operates two skilled-nursing care facilities and one acute care facility in Dayton, Ohio, faced several problems, including turnover of 146% per year. This dramatic turnover, mostly occurring during the first six to eight months of employment, was in turn adversely affecting the company's productivity and quality of care.

Working with a consultant, the company devised a nursing assistant test battery. This consisted of three tests: (1) an employment inventory aimed at identifying people who show conscientious work behaviors; (2) a personality survey aimed at identifying candidates who are more people oriented and more likely to interact positively with others; and (3) a job preferences inventory that looks for a match between actual job conditions and people's preferences for those job conditions.

The company reports that its testing program has been very successful. Turnover rates dropped to 71% annually one year after instituting the test battery, and to 51% within two years of its implementation. In total the company reports saving more than $300,000 annually due to reduced turnover and higher overall employee productivity among nursing assistants.[121] More formal studies similarly support the potential link between testing and performance.[122]

Just how useful is that most popular screening tool, students' grades? Based on the research, several conclusions are warranted.[123] First, "the answer to the question of whether grades predict job performance appears to be yes."[124] The overall observed correlation was modest but still suggested that using grades as a predictor of performance can be useful. Furthermore, undergraduate grades seem to be a better predictor of performance than were one's doctoral grades (possibly because the work of Ph.D.s and M.D.s is harder to measure). On the other hand, while useful, grades are not as valid as other selection measures. For example, they don't seem to be as useful as scores on cognitive ability tests or on structured employment interviews (which we'll discuss in the following chapter).[125]

Complying with the Immigration Law

Under the Immigration Reform and Control Act of 1986, employees hired in the United States have to prove they are eligible to be employed in the United States. A person does not have to be a U.S. citizen to be employed under this Act. However, employers should ask a person who is about to be hired whether he or she is a U.S. citizen or an alien lawfully authorized to work in the United States. To comply with this law, the employers should follow the following procedures.[126]

1. Hire only citizens and aliens lawfully authorized to work in the United States.
2. Continue to advise all new job applicants of your policy to such effect.
3. Require all new employees to complete and sign the verification form designated by the Immigration and Naturalization Service (INS) to certify that they are eligible for employment.
4. Examine documentation presented by new employees, record information about the documents on the verification form, and sign the form.
5. Retain the form for three years or for one year past the employment of the individual, whichever is longer.
6. If requested, present the form for inspection by INS or Department of Labor Officers. No reporting is required.

There are two basic ways prospective employees can prove their eligibility for employment. One is to show a document such as a U.S. passport or alien registration card with photograph that proves both the person's identity and employment eligibility. However, many prospective employees won't have either of these documents. Therefore, the other way to verify employment eligibility is to see a document that proves the person's identity, along with a document showing the person's employment eligibility, such as a work permit.

Congress tried to clarify and simplify the worker verification process by passing the Illegal Immigration Reform and Immigrant Responsibility Act of 1996. The Act mandated simplifying the verification process and reducing the number of documents allowed for employment verification 29 to 6.[127] However, as of recently, the Immigration and Naturalization Service has not issued firm guidelines on how to implement the Act. For the time being, employers should therefore keep using the existing the I–9 form.[128]

Employees cannot and should not use the so-called I–9 Employment Eligibility Verification form to discriminate in any way based on race or country of national origin. For example, the requirement to verify eligibility does not provide any basis to reject an applicant just because he or she is a foreigner, or not a U.S. citizen, or an alien residing in the United States, as long as that person can prove his or her identity and employment eligibility.

SMALL BUSINESS APPLICATIONS

■ Small Business Testing and Reference Checking

Just because a company is small doesn't mean it shouldn't engage in personnel testing. Quite the opposite: Hiring one or two mistakes may not be a big problem for a very large firm, but could cause chaos in a small operation.

Although used by large firms too, a number of tests are so easy to administer they are particularly good for smaller firms. One is the Wonderlic Personnel Test. This easy-to-use test measures general mental ability. In the form of a four-page booklet, it takes less than 15 minutes to administer. You first read the instructions and then time the candidate as he or she works through the 50 problems on the two inside sheets. The person's test can then be scored by totaling the number of correct answers. You compare the person's score to the minimum scores recommended for various occupations (Figure 5-13) to determine whether the person achieved the minimally acceptable score for the type of job in question.

A test like this can be useful for helping to identify people who are not up to the task of doing the job. However, you have to be careful not to misuse it. In the past, for instance, unnecessarily high cutoff scores were required by some employers for some jobs, a tactic that in effect unfairly discriminated against the members of certain minority groups. Similarly , it would probably not be either fair or wise to choose between two candidates who both exceeded the minimum score for a job by choosing the one with the higher score. Remember also that people of lower ability but higher motivation will often outperform those with higher ability but less motivation. Therefore, tests like the Wonderlic are only useful as supplements to a comprehensive screening program. The Wonderlic is available to employers, business owners, and human resource directors with or without previous training in personnel testing.[129]

The Predictive Index is another example of a test that is used by large companies but is equally valuable for small ones because of its ease of administration and interpretation. The index measures personality traits, drives, and behaviors that are work related—in particular, dominance (ranging from submissive to arrogant), extroversion (ranging from withdrawn to gregarious), patience (ranging from volatile to lethargic), and blame avoidance (ranging from sloppy to perfectionist). The Predictive Index test is a two-sided sheet on which candidates or current employees check off the words that best describe them

FIGURE 5-13

Minimum Scores on Wonderlic Personnel Test for Various Occupations

Source: Wonderlic Personnel Test Manual (Northfield, IL: E. F. Wonderlic & Associates, Inc., 1998), p. 14.

Position	No. of Questions Answered Correctly in 12 minutes
Chemist	31
Engineer, Electrical	30
Manager, General	30
Administrator	29
Computer Programmer	29
Adjuster, Claims	28
Librarian	27
Manager, Trainee	27
Writer, News	26
Office, General	24
Sales, General	24
Cashier	24
Secretary	24
Drafter	23
Bank Teller	22
Clerk, Order	22
Foreman	22
Clerical, General	21
Police, Patrol Officer	21
Receptionist	21
Typist	21
Labor, Unskilled	20
Mechanic, Helper	19
Maintenance	18
Guard, Security	17
Nurse's Aide	17
Assembler	16
Packer	15
Warehouse Person	15
Maid/Matron	11

See the Tables presented in this Manual. "Test Scores by Position Applied For" and "Minimum Occupational Scores for The Wonderlic Personnel Test," for additional data on established scores.

(such as "helpful" or "persistent"). The test is then easily scored at your office with the use of a scoring template.

The Predictive Index provides valuable information about the candidate. For example, for a job that you know involves painstaking attention to details, you'd want to think twice about a candidate who rates toward the careless end of the range. For an exceedingly boring job, you'd no doubt lean toward the more patient candidates. Each candidate taking the Predictive Index will probably have his or her own unique pattern of responses. However, the Predictive Index program includes 15 standard patterns that are typical of many of the patterns you will see. For example, there is the "social interest" pattern, representing a person who is generally unselfish, congenial, persuasive, patient, and fairly unassuming. This is a person who'd be good with people and a good personnel interviewer, for instance.

Computerized testing programs like those described earlier in this chapter can be especially useful for small employers. For example, when hiring office help smaller employers typically depend on informal tests of typing and filing. A better way to proceed is to use a program like the Minnesota Clerical Assessment Battery published by Assessment Systems Corp. This program runs on a PC. It includes a typing test, proofreading test, filing test, business vocabulary test, business math test, and clerical knowledge test. It is therefore useful for evaluating the knowledge and skills of various office positions, including secretary, clerk-typist, bookkeeper, and filing clerk. Because it is computerized, administration and scoring are simplified and each test can be adapted to the particular position being applied for.[130]

REFERENCE CHECKING POLICIES

The small-business owner needs to be particularly careful about checking references and offering references on former employees. Checking references is important because, as noted earlier, while one or two hiring mistakes may not be disastrous for a very large firm, it could cause chaos in a small one. In fact, the most common employer mistake that leads to liability for negligent hiring is inadequately investigating an applicant's background.[131] Furthermore, the more frequently employers check references, the less likely they experience problems of absenteeism, tardiness, and poor work quality.[132] Therefore, it's important for small-business owners to check backgrounds carefully.

It would also seem that small-business owners should be more careful before volunteering reference information about former employees. As noted earlier in this chapter, suits claiming defamation are a growing employment menace; in fact, according to one survey published in the late 1980s, one-third of all slander and libel cases were brought by former employees against employers for statements made to prospective employers.[133] The more astonishing statistic is that the ex-employee-plaintiffs won in 77% of the cases, with average damages amounting to $166,094.[134]

What's particularly disturbing about findings like these is that small-business owners seem to be more willing than large ones to volunteer information about former employees. In one survey, for instance, 90% of small businesses were "very" willing to offer such reference information, compared with only 20% of larger firms. Small firms were also relatively more willing than large firms to share information about employee arrests. (Remember that employment inquiries about an applicant's arrest record are illegal under Title VII of the Civil Rights Act, because the practice unfairly and adversely affects certain minority groups.)[135]

In any event, the evidence suggests that small-business owners are much less cautious about the information they provide about former employees. Perhaps this reflects the absence of specialized HR staff. Whatever the cause, small-business owners would do well to ensure that:

> All employment references come from one person in the firm who is knowledgeable about the legal risks involving defamation.

> Reference information is generally limited to the ex-employee's years of employment, wage or salary, job title, and superior at the time of termination.

> References are based on facts and never on hearsay.

> References are only provided based upon a signed and written request from an employer and a written request and release from liability from the former employee.

> Verbal references are avoided.[136]

We invite you to visit the Dessler page on the Prentice Hall Web site at **www.prenhall.com/dessler** for our on-line study guide, Internet exercises, current events, links to related Web sites, and more.

1. In this chapter we discussed several techniques for screening and selecting job candidates; the first was testing.

2. Test validity answers the question, "What does this test measure?" We discussed criterion validity and content validity. Criterion validity means demonstrating that those who do well on the test do well on the job; content validity is demonstrated by showing that the test constitutes a fair sample of the content of the job.

3. As used by psychologists, the term *reliability* always means consistency. One way to measure reliability is to administer the same (or equivalent) tests to the same people at two different points in time. Or you could focus on internal consistency, comparing the responses to roughly equivalent items on the same test.

4. There are many types of personnel tests in use, including intelligence tests, tests of physical skills, tests of achievement, aptitude tests, interest inventories, and personality tests.

5. For a selection test to be useful, scores should be predictably related to performance on the job; you must *validate* the test. This requires five steps: (1) analyze the job, (2) choose your tests, (3) administer the test, (4) relate test scores and criteria, and (5) cross-validate and validate the test.

6. Under equal rights legislation, an employer may have to be able to prove that his or her tests are predictive of success or failure on the job. This usually requires a predictive validation study, although other means of validation are often acceptable.

7. Some basic testing guidelines include (a) use tests as supplements, (b) validate the tests for appropriate jobs, (c) analyze all current hiring and promotion standards, (d) beware of certain tests, (e) use a certified psychologist, and (f) maintain good test conditions.

8. The work sampling selection technique is based on "the assumption that the best indicator of future performance is past performance." Here you use the applicant's actual performance on the same (or very similar) job to predict his or her future job performance. The steps are (a) analyze applicant's previous work experience, (b) have experts list component tasks for the open job, (c) select crucial tasks as work sample measures, (d) break down these tasks into steps, (e) test the applicant, and (f) relate the applicant's work sample score to his or her performance on the job.

9. Management assessment centers are another screening device and expose applicants to a series of real-life exercises. Performance is observed and assessed by experts, who then check their assessments by observing the participants when they are back at their jobs. Examples of "real-life" exercises include a simulated business game, an in-basket exercise, and group discussions.

10. Even though most people prefer not to give bad references, most companies still carry out some sort of reference check on their candidates. These can be useful in raising red flags, and structured questionnaires can improve the usefulness of the responses you receive.

11. Other selection tools include the polygraph, honesty tests, and graphology. While graphology appears to have little predictive value, honesty tests have been used with success although they (and polygraphs) must be used with an eye toward the legal and ethical issues involved.

test validity   174
criterion validity   174
content validity   174

reliability   175
expectancy chart   178
work samples   186

work sampling technique   186

management assessment center   187

DISCUSSION QUESTIONS

1. Explain what is meant by reliability and validity. What is the difference between them? In what respects are they similar?
2. Explain how you would go about validating a test. How can this information be useful to a manager?
3. Explain why you think a certified psychologist who is specially trained in test construction should (or should not) always be used by a company developing a personnel test battery.
4. Explain how you would use work sampling for employee selection.
5. Give some examples of how interest inventories could be used to improve employee selection. In doing so, suggest several examples of occupational interests that you believe might predict success in various occupations including college professor, accountant, and computer programmer.
6. Why is it important to conduct preemployment background investigations? How would you go about doing so?
7. Explain how you would get around the problem of former employers being unwilling to give bad references on their former employees.

INDIVIDUAL AND GROUP ACTIVITIES

1. Write a short essay discussing some of the ethical and legal considerations in testing.
2. Working individually or in groups, develop a test for the Marketing Manager job description that was presented in Chapter 3, Figure 3-8.
3. Working individually or in groups, contact the publisher of a standardized test such as the Scholastic Assessment Test and obtain from them written information regarding the test's validity and reliability. Present a short report in class discussing what the test is supposed to measure and the degree to which you think the test does what it is supposed to do, based on the reported validity and reliability scores.

EXPERIENTIAL EXERCISE

The Reference Check:

You received the following fax concerning a reference for a former employee.

The fax reads:

To the HR manager at your company,

One of your former employees, Mark (Last-name) has applied for a supervisory position with our company. As a matter of policy, we rigorously review the background of any candidate to make sure they can meet high standards. As one HR professional to another, you know how expensive it can be to hire an unqualified or troublesome employee. That's why I am asking for your help. Could you please fax back a response to the following questions concerning the applicant?

1. Date hired and date employment ended:
2. Last salary:
3. Reasons for termination—circle all that apply: (left for more money), (left—didn't like company or job), (left voluntarily—no reason given), (terminated).
4. Did candidate have good personal relationships with his boss? Coworkers? Subordinates?

5. Name one thing this employee did well.

6. Name one thing about this employee you felt needed improvement.

7. Did you ever hear anything about the employee that troubled you, or warranted further investigation?

8. If the employee had stayed with the company would they have been promoted or received raises?

9. Would you rehire this employee?

Directions:

Divide the class into an even number of teams, each with three to four members. The even numbered teams should develop a list of all the reasons the HR manager should provide detailed responses to all the questions on the fax. The odd numbered teams should list all the reasons the HR managers should only respond to question one. After 10 minutes, ask a representative of the first team to list their reasons. Continue with each team.

After you have collected each team's feedback, discuss as a class the following two questions:

Class Discussion Questions

1. What are the most important issues raised by this inquiry?

2. How should the HR manager respond to this inquiry?

CASE INCIDENT   The Tough Screener

Everyone who knows Fred Rosen knows he is a very tough owner when it comes to screening applicants for jobs in his firm. His company, located in a large northeastern city, provides financial planning advice to wealthy clients and, related to that, sells insurance and sets up pension plans for individuals and businesses. His firm's clients range from professionals such as doctors and lawyers to business owners, who are fairly sophisticated in financial matters and very busy people. They expect accurate advice provided in a clear and expeditious manner. It is safe to say that Rosen's firm can be no better than its financial advisors.

Rosen has always been described as somewhat autocratic. The need to be very selective in whom he hires has led him to be extraordinarily careful about how he screens his job applicants. Some of his methods are probably beyond reproach. For example, he requires every applicant to provide a list of names and phone numbers for at least five people the applicant worked with at each previous employer to be used as references. The resulting reference check is time consuming but effective.

On the other hand, given current legislation including the Civil Rights Act of 1991 and the Americans With Disabilities Act, some of his other "tough screening" methods could be problematical. Rosen requires that all applicants take a purported honesty test, which he found in the catalog of an office supply store. He also believes it is extremely important to check every viable applicant's credit history and worker's compensation history in order to screen out what he refers to as "potential undesirables." Unknown to his applicants, he runs a credit check on each of them and also retains the services of a firm that checks worker's compensation and driving violation histories.

■ QUESTIONS

1. What specific legal problems do you think Rosen can run into as a result of his firm's current screening methods? What steps would you suggest he take to eliminate these problems?

2. Given what you know about Rosen's business, write a two-page proposal describing an employee testing and selection program that you would recommend for his firm. Say a few words about the sorts of tests, if any, you would recommend and the application-blank questions you would ask, as well as other methods including drug screening and reference checking.

Case Application

Carter Cleaning Company

Honesty Testing

Jennifer Carter, president of the Carter Cleaning Centers, and her father have what the latter describes as an easy but hard job when it comes to screening job applicants. It is easy because for two important jobs—the people who actually do the pressing and those who do the cleaning–spotting—the applicants are easily screened with about 20 minutes of on-the-job testing. As with typists, as Jennifer points out, "applicants either know how to press clothes fast enough or how to use cleaning chemicals and machines, or they don't and we find out very quickly by just trying them out on the job."

On the other hand, applicant screening for the stores can also be frustratingly hard because of the nature of qualities that Jennifer would like to screen for. Two of the most critical problems facing her company are employee turnover and employee honesty. As mentioned previously, Jennifer and her father sorely need to implement practices that will reduce the rate of employee turnover. If there is a way to do this through employee testing and screening techniques, Jennifer would like to know about it because of the management time and money that are now being wasted by the never-ending need to recruit and hire new employees. Of even greater concern to Jennifer and her father is the need to institute new practices to screen out those employees who may be predisposed to steal from the company.

Employee theft is an enormous problem for the Carter Cleaning Centers, and one that is not just limited to employees who handle the cash. For example, the cleaner–spotter and/or the presser often open the store themselves without a manager present to get the day's work started, and it is not unusual to have one or more of these people steal supplies or "run a route." Running a route means that an employee canvasses his or her neighborhood to pick up people's clothes for cleaning and then secretly cleans and presses them in the Carter store, using the company's supplies, gas, and power. It would also not be unusual for an unsupervised person (or his or her supervisor, for that matter) to accept a one-hour rush order for cleaning or laundering, quickly clean and press the item, and return it to the customer for payment without making out a proper ticket for the item posting the sale. The money, of course, goes into the person's pocket instead of into the cash register.

The more serious problem concerns the store manager and the counter workers who actually have to handle the cash. According to Jack Carter, "you would not believe the creativity employees use to get around the management controls we set up to cut down on employee theft." As one extreme example of this felonious creativity, Jack tells the following story: "To cut down on the amount of money my employees were stealing, I had a small sign painted and placed in front of all our cash registers. The sign said: "Your entire order free if we don't give you a cash register receipt when you pay. Call 962-0734." It was my intention with this sign to force all our cash-handling employees to place their receipts into the cash register where they would be recorded for my accountants. After all, if all the cash that comes in is recorded in the cash register, then we should have a much better handle on stealing in our stores, right? Well, one of our managers found a diabolical way around this. I came into the store one night and noticed that the cash register that this particular manager was using just didn't look right although the sign was dutifully placed in front of it. It turned out that every afternoon at about 5:00 p.m. when the other employees left, this character would pull his own cash register out of a box that he hid underneath our supplies. Customers coming in would notice the sign and of course the fact that he was meticulous in ringing up every sale. But unknown to them and us, for about five months the sales that came in for about an hour every day went into his cash register, not mine. It took us that long to figure out where our cash for that store was going."

■ QUESTIONS

1. What would be the advantages and disadvantages to Jennifer's company of routinely administering honesty tests to all its employees?

2. Specifically, what other screening techniques could the company use to screen out theft-prone employees, and how exactly could these be used?

3. How should her company terminate employees caught stealing and what kind of procedure should be set up for handling reference calls about these employees when they go to other companies looking for jobs?

NOTES

1. For brief overviews of this process see, for example, Philip Schofield, "Improving the Candidate Job-Match," *Personnel Management*, Vol. 25, no. 2 (February 1993), p. 69, and Clive Fletcher, "Testing Times for the World of Psychometrics,"*Personnel Management* (December 1993), pp. 46–50.

2. See, for example, Ann Marie Ryan and Marja Lasek, "Negligent Hiring and Defamation: Areas of Liability Related to Pre-employment Inquiries," *Personnel Psychology*, Vol. 44, no. 2 (Summer 1991), pp. 293–319.

3. *Ibid.*

4. *Ibid.*

5. Steven Mitchell Sack, "Fifteen Steps to Protecting Against the Risk of Negligent Hiring Claims," *Employment Relations Today* (August 1993), pp. 313–320.

6. Leona Tyler, *Tests and Measurements* (Upper Saddle River, NJ: Prentice Hall, 1971), p. 25. More technically, "validity refers to the degree of confidence one can have in inferences drawn from scores, considering the whole process by which the scores are obtained. Stated differently, validity refers to the confidence one has in the meaning attached to scores." (See Robert Guion, "Changing Views for Personnel Selection Research," *Personnel Psychology*, Vol. 40, no. 2 (Summer 1987), p. 208.

7. As indicated, a third way to demonstrate a test's validity is *construct validity*. A construct is a trait such as intelligence. Therefore, to take a simple example, if intelligence is important to the position of engineer, a test that measures intelligence would have construct validity for that position. To prove construct validity, an employer has to prove that the test actually measures the construct and that the construct is in turn required for the job. Federal agency guidelines make it difficult to prove construct validity, however, and as a result few employers use this approach as a means of satisfying the federal guidelines. See James Ledvinka, *Federal Regulation of Personnel and Human Resource Management* (Boston: Kent, 1982), p. 113.

8. Bureau of National Affairs, *Primer of Equal Employment Opportunity* (Washington, DC: BNA, 1978), p. 18. In practice, proving in court the criterion-related validity of paper-and-pencil tests has been difficult.

9. Ledvinka, *Federal Regulations*, p. 111.

10. Anne Anastasi, *Psychological Patterns* (New York: Macmillan, 1968), reprinted in W. Clay Hamner and Frank Schmidt, *Contemporary Problems in Personnel* (Chicago: St. Claire Press, 1974), pp. 102–109. Discussion of reliability based on Marvin Dunnette, *Personnel Selection and Placement* (Belmont, CA: Wadsworth Publishing Company, Inc., 1966), pp. 29–30.

11. Calvin Hoffman, Barry Nathan, and Lisa Holden, "A Comparison of Validation Criteria: Objective versus Subjective Performance Measures and Self-versus Supervisory Ratings," *Personnel Psychology*, Vol. 44 (1991), pp. 601–619.

12. Based on J. Tiffin and E. J. McCormick, *Industrial Psychology* (Upper Saddle River, NJ: Prentice Hall, 1965), pp. 104–105; C. H. Lawshe and M. J. Balma, *Principles of Personnel Testing*, 2nd ed. (New York: McGraw-Hill, 1966).

13. Experts sometimes have to develop separate expectancy charts and cutting points for minorities and nonminorities if the validation studied indicate that high performers from either group (minority or nonminority) score lower (or higher) on the test. See our discussion of differential validity in the appendix to this chapter. For a good discussion of how to evaluate a selection test, see Raymond Berger and Donna Tucker, "How to Evaluate a Selection Test," *Personnel Journal*, Vol. 66, no. 6 (February 1987), pp. 88–91.

14. See, for example, Floyd L. Ruch, "The Impact on Employment Procedures of the Supreme Court Decisions in the Duke Power Case," *Personnel Journal*, Vol. 50, no. 4 (October 1971), pp. 777–783; Hubert Field, Gerald Bagley, and Susan Bagley, "Employment Test Validation for Minority and Non-minority Production Workers," *Personnel Psychology*, Vol. 30, no. 1 (Spring 1977), pp. 37–46; Ledvinka, *Federal Regulations*, p. 110.

15. See Ruch, "The Impact on Employment Procedures," pp. 777–783, in Hamner and Schmidt, *Contemporary Problems in Personnel*, pp. 117–123; Dale Beach, *Personnel* (New York: Macmillan, 1970); Field, Bagley, and Bagley, "Employing Test Validation for Minority and Non-minority Production Workers," pp. 37–46; M. K. Distefano, Jr., Margaret Pryer, and Stella Craig, "Predictive Validity of General Ability Tests with Black and White Psychiatric Attendants," *Personnel Psychology*, Vol. 29, no. 2 (Summer 1976). Also see the Winter 1976 issue of *Personnel Psychology*, Vol. 32, no. 4. See also James Norborg, "A Warning Regarding the Simplified Approach to the Evaluation of Test Fairness and Employee Selection Procedures," *Personnel Psychology*, Vol. 37, no. 3 (Autumn 1984), pp. 483–486; Charles Johnson, Lawrence Messe, and William Crano, "Predicting Job Performance of Low Income Workers: The Work Opinion Questionnaire," *Personnel Psychology*, Vol. 37, no. 2 (Summer 1984), pp. 291–299; Frank Schmidt, Benjamin Ocasio, Joseph Hillery, and John Hunter," Further Within-Setting Empirical Tests of the Situational Specificity Hypothesis in Personnel Selection," *Personnel Psychology*, Vol. 38, no. 3 (Autumn 1985), pp. 509–524.

16. Prentice Hall, "PH/ASPA Survey: Employee Testing Procedures—Where Are They Headed?" *Personnel Management: Policies and Practices*, April 22, 1975, described in James Ledvinka and Lyle Schoenfeldt, "Legal Developments in Employment Testing: Albemarle," *Personnel Psychology*, Vol. 31, no. 1 (Spring 1978), p. 9.

17. Ledvinka and Schoenfeldt, "Legal Developments," p. 9. See also Robert Wood and Helen Bearon, "Psychological Testing Free from Prejudice," *Personnel Management* (December 1992), pp. 34–37; and Travis Gibbs and Matt Riggs, "Reducing Bias in Personnel Selection Decisions: Positive Effects of Attention to Irrelevant Information," *Psychological Reports*, Vol. 74 (1994), pp. 19–26.

18. Ledvinka, *Federal Regulations*, p. 109.

19. Douglas Baker and David Terpstra, "Employee Selection: Must Every Job Be Validated?" *Personnel Journal*, Vol. 61 (August 1982), pp. 602–605.

20. This is based on Marilyn Quaintance, "Test Security: Foundations of Public Merit Systems," *Personnel Psychology*, Vol. 33, no. 1 (Spring 1980), pp. 25–32.

21. William Roskind, "DECO Versus NLRB, and the Consequences of Open Testing in Industry," *Personnel Psychology*, Vol. 33, no. 1 (Spring 1980), pp. 3–9; and James Ledvinka, Val Markos, and Robert Ladd, "Long-Range Impact of 'Fair Selection' Standards on

Minority Employment," *Journal of Applied Psychology*, Vol. 67, no. 1 (February 1982), pp. 18–36.

22. Mark Schmit and Ann Marie Ryan, "Applicant Withdrawal: The Role of Test-Taking Attitudes and Racial Differences," *Personnel Psychology*, Vol. 50 (1997), pp. 855–876.

23. Robert Ployhart and Ann Marie Ryan, "Applicants' Reactions to the Fairness of Selection Procedures: The Effects of Positive Rule Violations and Time of Measurement," *Journal of Applied Psychology*, Vol. 83, no. 1 (1998), pp. 3–16.

24. Dirk Steiner and Stephen Gilliland, "Fairness Reactions to Personnel Selection Techniques in France and the United States," *Journal of Applied Psychology*, Vol. 81, no. 2 (1996), pp. 134–141.

25. *Ibid.*, p. 134.

26. Susan Mendelsohn and Katheryn Morrison, "The Right to Privacy at the Work Place," Part I: "Employee Searchers," *Personnel* (July 1988), p. 20.

27. Wayne Outten and Noah A. Kinigstein, *The Rights of Employees* (New York: Bantam Books, 1984), pp. 53–54.

28. Mendelson and Morrison, "The Right to Privacy in the Work Place," p. 22.

29. Outten and Kinigstein, *The Rights of Employees*, pp. 54–55.

30. *Ibid.*, p. 55.

31. *Kehr v. Consolidated Freightways of Delaware*, Docket No. 86–2126, July 15, 1987, U.S. Seventh Circuit Court of Appeals. Discussed in Commerce Clearing House, *Ideas and Trends*, October 16, 1987, p. 165.

32. For a discussion of these see Commerce Clearing House, *Ideas and Trends*, October 16, 1987, pp. 165–166.

33. "Workplace Testing and Monitoring," *Management Review* (October 1998), pp. 31–42.

34. Constance Hays, "Trying to Get a Job? Check Yes or No," *The New York Times*, November 18, 1997, p. C4.

35. *Ibid.*

36. Except as noted, this is based largely on Laurence Siegel and Irving Lane, *Personnel and Organizational Psychology* (Burr Ridge, IL: McGraw-Hill, 1982), pp. 170–185. See also Tyler, *Tests and Measurements*, pp. 38–79; and Lawshe and Balma, *Principles of Personnel Testing*, pp. 83–160.

37. See, for example, Richard Reilly, Sheldon Zedeck, and Mary Tenopyr, "Validity and Fairness of Physical Ability Tests for Predicting Performance in Craft Jobs," *Journal of Applied Psychology*, Vol. 64, no. 3 (June 1970), pp. 262–274. See also Barten Daniel, "Strength and Endurance Testing," *Personnel Journal* (June 1987), pp. 112–122.

38. Results of meta-analyses in one recent study indicated that isometric strength tests were valid predictors of both supervisory ratings of physical performance, and performance on work simulations. See Barry R. Blakley, Miguel Quinones, Marnie Swerdlin Crawford, and I. Ann Jago, "The Validity of Isometric Strength Tests," *Personnel Psychology*, Vol. 47 (1994), pp. 247–274.

39. If you read note 7, you will see that this approach calls for construct validation which, as was pointed out, is extremely difficult to demonstrate.

40. See, for example, Douglas Cellar, et al., "Comparison of Factor Structures and Criterion-Related Validity Coefficients for Two Measures of Personality Based on the Five Factor Model," *Journal of Applied Psychology*, Vol. 81, no. 6 (1996), pp. 694–704; and Jesus Salgado, "The Five Factor Model of Personality and Job Performance in the European Community," *Journal of Applied Psychology*, Vol. 82, no. 1 (1997), pp. 30–43.

41. Murray Barrick and Michael Mount, "The Big Five Personality Dimensions and Job Performance: A Meta-Analysis," *Personnel Psychology*, Vol. 44, no. 1 (Spring 1991), pp. 1–26.

42. Timothy Judge, Joseph Martocchio, and Carl Thoresen, "Five-Factor Model of Personality and Employee Absence," *Journal of Applied Psychology*, Vol. 82, no. 5 (1997), pp. 745–755.

43. Robert Tett, Douglas Jackson, and Mitchell Rothstein, "Personality Measures as Predictors of Job Performance: A Meta-Analytic Review," *Personnel Psychology*, Vol. 44 (1991), p. 732. For a related study see Patrick Raymark, Mark Schmit, and Robert Guion, "Identifying Potentially Useful Personality Constructs for Employee Selection," *Personnel Psychology*, Vol. 50, no. 3 (Fall 1997), pp. 723–736, and Cynthia Fischer and Gregory Boyle, "Personality and Employee Selection: Credibility Regained," *Asia Pacific Journal of HRM*, Vol. 35, no. 2 (1997), pp. 26–40.

44. *Ibid.*

45. See, "Can Testing Prevent Violence?" *BNA Bulletin to Management*, November 28, 1996, p. 384.

46. For a study describing how matching (1) task and working condition preferences of applicants with (2) actual job and working conditions can be achieved, see Ronald Ash, Edward Levine, and Steven Edgell, "Study of a Matching Approach: The Impact of Ethnicity," *Journal of Applied Psychology*, Vol. 64, no. 1 (February 1979), pp. 35–41. For a discussion of how a standard clerical test can be used to screen applicants who will have to use video displays, see Edward Silver and Corwin Bennett, "Modification of the Minnesota Clerical Test to Predict Performance on Video Display Terminals," *Journal of Applied Psychology*, Vol. 72, no. 1 (February 1987), pp. 153–155.

47. Marvin D. Dunnette and W. D. Borman, "Personnel Selection and Classification Systems," *Annual Review of Psychology*, Vol. 30 (1979), pp. 477–525, quoted in Siegel and Lane, *Personnel and Organizational Psychology*, pp. 182–183.

48. Paul Wernamont and John T. Campbell, "Signs, Samples, and Criteria," *Journal of Applied Psychology*, Vol. 52 (1968), pp. 372–376; James Campion, "Work Sampling for Personnel Selection," *Journal of Applied Psychology*, Vol. 56 (1972), pp. 40–44, reprinted in Hamner and Schmidt, *Contemporary Problems in Personnel*, pp. 168–180; Sidney Gael, Donald Grant, and Richard Ritchie, "Employment Test Validation for Minority and Nonminority Clerks with Work Sample Criteria," *Journal of Applied Psychology*, Vol. 60, no. 4 (August 1974); Frank Schmidt and others, "Job Sample vs. Paper and Pencil Trades and Technical Test: Adverse Impact and Examinee Attitudes," *Personnel Psychology*, Vol. 30, no. 7 (Summer 1977), pp. 187–198.

49. Neal Schmitt, et al., "Computer-Based Testing Applied to Selection of Secretarial Candidates," *Personnel Psychology*, Vol. 46 (1991), pp. 149–165.

50. Randall Overton, et al., "The Pen-Based Computer as an Alternative Platform for Test Administration," *Personnel Psychology*, Vol. 49 (1996), pp. 455–464.

51. *Ibid.*

52. See, for example, George Burgnoli, James Campion, and Jeffrey Bisen, "Racial Bias in the Use of Work Samples for Personnel Selection," *Journal of Applied Psychology*, Vol. 64, no. 2 (April 1979), pp. 119–123.

53. Siegel and Lane, *Personnel and Organizational Psychology*, pp. 182–183.

54. Annette Spychalski, Miguel Quinones, Barbara Gaugler, and Katja Pohley, "A Survey of Assessment Center Practices in Organizations

in the United States," *Personnel Psychology*, Vol. 50, no. 1 (Spring 1997), pp. 71–90.

55. Steven Norton, "The Empirical and Content Validity of Assessment Centers Versus Traditional Methods of Predicting Management Success," *Academy of Management Review*, Vol. 20 (July 1977), pp. 442–453. Interestingly, a recent review concludes that assessment centers do predict managerial success, but after an extensive review, "we also assert that we do not know why they work." Richard Klimoski and Mary Brickner, "Why Do Assessment Centers Work? The Puzzle of Assessment Center Validity," *Personnel Psychology*, Vol. 40, no. 2 (Summer 1987), pp. 243–260.

56. Wayne F. Cascio and Val Silbey, "Utility of the Assessment Center as a Selection Device," *Journal of Applied Psychology*, Vol. 64, no. 4 (April 1979), pp. 107–118. See also Paul R. Sackett, "Assessment Centers and Content Validity: Some Neglected Issues," *Personnel Psychology*, Vol. 40 (Spring 1981), pp. 55–64.

57. David Groce, "A Behavioral Consistency Approach to Decision Making in Employment Selection," *Personnel Psychology*, Vol. 34, no. 1 (Spring 1981), pp. 55–64.

58. For an alternative to assessment centers, see Donald Brush and Lyle Schoenfeldt, "Identifying Managerial Potential: An Alternative Assessment Center," *Personnel*, Vol. 57 (May–June 1980), pp. 72–73.

59. Jeff Weekley and Casey Jones, "Video-Based Situational Testing," *Personnel Psychology*, Vol. 50 (1997), p. 25.

60. *Ibid.*, p. 26.

61. *Ibid.*, p. 30.

62. *Ibid.*, p. 46.

63. Arthur Cosiegel, "The Miniature Job Training and Evaluation Approach: Traditional Findings," *Personnel Psychology*, Vol. 36, no. 1 (Spring 1983), pp. 41–56.

64. Edward Robinson, "Beware—Job Seekers Have No Secrets," *Fortune*, December 29, 1997, p. 285.

65. *Ibid.*, p. 285.

66. Seymour Adler, "Verifying a Job Candidate's Background: The State of Practice in a Vital Human Resources Activity," *Review of Business*, Vol. 15, no. 2 (Winter 1993), pp. 3–8.

67. Robinson, "Beware," p. 285.

68. Seymour Adler, "Verifying a Job Candidate's Background: The State of Practice in a Vital Human Resources Activity," *Review of Business*, Vol. 15, no. 2 (Winter 1993), p. 6.

69. This is based on Samuel Greengard, "Have Gangs Invaded Your Workplace?" *Personnel Journal* (February 1996), pp. 47–57.

70. *Ibid.*, p. 47.

71. *Ibid.*, pp. 47–48.

72. For additional information, see Lawrence E. Dube, Jr., "Employment References and the Law," *Personnel Journal*, Vol. 65, no. 2 (February 1986), pp. 87–91. See also Mickey Veich, "Uncover the Resume Ruse," *Security Management* (October 1994), pp. 75–76.

73. Thomas von der Embse and Rodney Wyse, "Those Reference Letters: How Useful Are They?" *Personnel*, Vol. 62, no. 1 (January 1985), pp. 42–46.

74. James Bell, James Castagnera, and Jane Patterson Yong, "Employment References: Do You Know the Law?" *Personnel Journal*, Vol. 63, no. 2 (February 1984) pp. 32–36. In order to demonstrate defamation, several elements must be present: (a) the defamatory statement must have been communicated to another party; (b) the statement must be a false statement of fact; © injury to reputation

must have occurred; and (d) the employer must not be protected under qualified or absolute privilege. For a discussion see Ryan and Lasek, "Negligent Hiring and Defamation," p. 307. See also James Burns, Jr., "Employment References: Is There a Better Way?" *Employee Relations Law Journal*, Vol. 23, no. 2 (Fall 1997), pp. 157–168.

75. "Jury Awards Manager Accused of Theft $1.25 Million," *BNA Bulletin to Management*, March 27, 1997, p. 97.

76. "Reference Checks Hit Wall of Silence," *BNA Bulletin to Management*, July 6, 1995, p. 216.

77. See Howard M. Fischer, "Select the Right Executive," *Personnel Journal*, April 1989, pp. 110–114.

78. Jeffrey M. Hahn, "Pre-Employment Information Services: Employers Beware?" *Employee Relations Law Journal*, Vol. 17, no. 1 (Summer 1991), pp. 45–69.

79. "State-by-State Review: Laws and Regulations on Access to and Use of Criminal Records," *BNA Bulletin to Management*, June 20, 1996, p. 13.

80. *Ibid.*, p. 51.

81. "Database Helps Employers Screen Applicants for Theft," *BNA Bulletin to Management*, June 12, 1997, p. 186.

82. *Ibid.*, p. 191.

83. *Ibid.*

84. Based in Part on Hahn, "Pre-employment Information Services," pp. 64–66.

85. James Frierson, "New Polygraph Tests Limits," *Personnel Journal* (December 1988), pp. 84–89.

86. This is based on "When Can Workers Refuse Lie Detector Tests?" *BNA Bulletin to Management*, March 9, 1995, p. 73, and is based on the case Lyle Z. Mercy Hospital Anderson, DCS Ohio, 1995, 10 IER cases 401.

87. John Jones and William Terris, "Post-Polygraph Selection Techniques," *Recruitment Today* (May–June 1989), pp. 25–31.

88. Norma Fritz, "In Focus: Honest Answers—Post Polygraph," *Personnel* (April 1989), p. 8.

89. For a discussion of the earlier caveats see, for example, Kevin Murphy, "Detecting Infrequent Deception," *Journal of Applied Psychology*, Vol. 72, no. 4 (November 1987), pp. 611–614.

90. John Bernardin and Donna Cooke, "Validity of an Honesty Test in Predicting Theft Among Convenience Store Employees," *Academy of Management Journal*, Vol. 36, no. 5 (1993), pp. 1097–1108.

91. Paul Sackett and James Wanek, "New Developments in the Use of Measures of Honesty, Integrity, Conscientiousness, Dependability, Trustworthiness, and Reliability for Personnel Selection," *Personnel Psychology*, Vol. 49 (1996), p. 821.

92. The following is based on Judith Collins and Frank Schmidt, "Personality, Integrity, and White Collar Crime: A Construct Validity Study," *Personnel Psychology*, Vol. 46 (1993), pp. 295–311.

93. *Ibid.* For a description of another approach see, for example, Peter Bullard, "Pre-Employment Screening to Weed Out 'Bad Apples,'" *Nursing Homes* (June 1994), pp. 29–31.

94. These are based on Commerce Clearing House, *Ideas and Trends*, December 29, 1998, pp. 222–223. See also Bureau of National Affairs, "Divining Integrity Through Interview," *Bulletin to Management*, June 4, 1987, p. 184.

95. This example is based on *BNA Bulletin to Management*, February 26, 1987, p. 65.

96. See, for example, "Corporate Lie Detectors Under Fire," *Business Week*, January 13, 1973. For a discussion of how to improve the

validity of the polygraph test, see Robert Forman and Clark Mc-Cauley, "Validity of a Positive Control Polygraph Test Using the Field to Practice Model," *Journal of Applied Psychology*, Vol. 71, no. 4 (November 1986), pp. 691–698.

97. Ulrich Sonnemann, *Handwriting Analysis as a Psychodiagnostic Tool* (New York: Grune & Stratton, 1950), pp. 144–145.

98. One empirical study resulted in the conclusion that "we find ourselves compelled to conclude that it is graphology, rather than just our small sample of graphologists, that is invalid." These researchers conclude that when graphology does seem to "work," it does so because the graphologist is reading a spontaneously written autobiography of the candidate and is thereby obtaining biographical information about the candidate from that essay. See Gershon Ben-Shakhar, Maya Bar-Hillel, Yoram Bilu, Edor Ben-Abba, and Anat Flug," Can Graphology Predict Occupational Success? Two Empirical Studies and Some Methodological Ruminations," *Journal of Applied Psychology*, Vol. 71, no. 4 (November 1986), pp. 645–653.

99. *Ibid.*

100. See updated graphology research.

101. Joseph Famularo, *Handbook of Modern Personnel Administration* (New York: McGraw-Hill, 1972), pp. 12–17, 18.

102. Mick Haus, "Pre-Employment Physicals and the ADA," *Safety and Health* (February 1992), pp. 64–65.

103. B. Guinn, "Job Satisfaction, Counterproductive Behavior, and Circumstantial Drug Use Among Long Distance Truckers," *The Journal of Psychoactive Drugs*, Vol. 15, no. 3 (1983), pp. 185–188; discussed in Scott MacDonald, Samantha Wells, and Richard Fry, "The Limitations of Drug Screening in the Workplace," *International Labor Review*, Vol. 132, no. 1 (1993), p. 99.

104. Ian Miners, Nick Nykodym, and Diane Samerdyke-Traband, "Put Drug Detection to the Test," *Personnel Journal*, Vol. 66, no. 8 (August 1987), pp. 191–197.

105. MacDonald, Wells, and Fry, "The Limitations of Drug Screening in the Workplace," p. 98. Not all agree that drug testing is worthwhile. See, for example, Mark Karper, Clifford Donn, and Marie Lyndaker, "Drug Testing in the Transportation Industry: The Maritime Case," *Employee Responsibilities and Rights*, Vol. 71, no. 3 (September 1994), pp. 219–233.

106. Eric Rolfe Greenberg, "Workplace Testing: Who's Testing Whom?" *Personnel* (May 1989), pp. 39–45.

107. Chris Berka and Courtney Poignand, "Hair Follicle Testing—An Alternative to Urinalysis for Drug Abuse Screening," *Employee Relations Today* (Winter 1991–1992) pp. 405–409.

108. MacDonald et al., "The Limitations of Drug Screening," pp. 102–104.

109. R. J. McCunney, "Drug Testing: Technical Complications of a Complex Social Issue," in *American Journal of Industrial Medicine*, Vol. 15, no. 5 (1989) pp. 589–600; discussed in MacDonald et al., "The Limitations of Drug Screening," p. 102.

110. MacDonald et al., "The Limitations Drug Screening," p. 103.

111. For a discussion of this see Ibid, pp. 105–106.

112. This is based on Ann M. O'Neill, "Legal Issues Presented by Hair Follicle Testing," *Employee Relations Today* (Winter 1991–1992), pp. 411–415.

113. *Ibid.*, p. 411.

114. *Ibid.*. p. 413.

115. Richard Lisko, "A Manager's Guide to Drug Testing," *Security Management*, Vol. 38, no. 8 (August 1994), p. 92.

116. For an additional perspective on drug testing as it applies to public agencies and unions see, for example, Nancy C. O'Neill, "Drug Testing in Public Agencies: Are Personnel Directors Doing Things Right?" *Public Personnel Management*, Vol. 19, no. 4 (Winter 1990), pp. 391–397; Michael H. LeRoy, "The Presence of Drug Testing in the Workplace and Union Member Attitudes," *Labor Studies Journal* (Fall 1991), pp. 33–42. For another approach see, for example, Darold Barnum and John Gleason, "The Credibility of Drug Tests: A Multi-Stage Bayesian Analysis," *Industrial and Labor Relations Review*, Vol. 47, no. 4 (July 1994), pp. 610–621.

117. Eric Rolfe Greenberg, "Workplace Testing: Results of a New AMA Survey," *Personnel* (April 1988), p. 40.

118. Michael A. McDaniel, "Does Pre-Employment Drug Use Predict on the Job Suitability?" *Personnel Psychology*, Vol. 41, no. 4 (Winter 1988), pp. 717–729.

119. *Exxon Corp. v. Esso Workers Union, Inc.*, CA1#96–2241, 7/8/97; discussed in *BNA Bulletin to Management*, August 7, 1997, p. 249.

120. This is based on Mark Thomas and Harry Brull, "Tests Improve Hiring Decisions at Franciscan," *Personnel Journal* (November 1993), pp. 89–92.

121. For another view see, for example, Raymond Berger and Donna Tucker, "Recruitment: How to Evaluate a Selection Test," *Personnel Journal New Product News* (March 1994), pp. 2, 3.

122. David E. Terpstra and Elizabeth Rozell, "The Relationship of Staffing Practices to Organizational Level Measures of Performance," *Personnel Psychology*, Vol. 46 (1993), pp. 27–48.

123. Philip Roth, et al., "Meta-Analyzing the Relationship Between Grades and Job Performance," *Journal of Applied Psychology*, Vol. 81, no. 5 (1996), pp. 548–556.

124. *Ibid.*, p. 553.

125. *Ibid.*

126. These are quoted from Commerce Clearing House, *Ideas and Trends*, May 1, 1987, pp. 70–71.

127. "Worker Verification Changes Come Slowly," *BNA Bulletin to Management*, May 29, 1997, p. 176.

128. "I–9 Form and Document Revisions Still Up in the Air," *BNA Bulletin to Management*, October 9, 1997, p. 322.

129. For information about ordering the Wonderlic, contact E. F. Wonderlic and Associates, Inc., 820 Frontage Rd., Northfield, IL 60093. Their phone number is 312-446-8900.

130. Reach Assessment Systems Corporation at 2233 University Avenue, Suite 440, St. Paul, MN 55114, 612-647-9220.

131. See James Fenton, Jr., and Kay Lawnmore, "Employment Reference Checking, Firm Size, and Defamation Liability," *Journal of Small Business Management* (October 1992), pp. 88–95.

132. *Ibid.*, p. 88.

133. *Ibid.*

134. Scott Agnew, "Special Research—False Arrest, Libel and Slander," Jury Verdict Research, Inc., 1988, Solon, OH; referenced in *Ibid.*, p. 88.

135. *Ibid.*, p. 91.

136. These are based on or quoted from Fenton and Larrimore, "Employment Reference Checking," p. 94. Employers may have a "qualified privilege" for truthful references given in good faith with no malice, and truth is an absolute defense to defamation claims. However, as a practical matter, small-business owners may not have the resources or time to devote to defending themselves against even baseless defamation claims.

6

INTERVIEWING CANDIDATES

Since emerging from bankruptcy protection in 1998, Barney's new owners were trying hard to make the store chain succeed. The pricey flagship store on New York's Madison Avenue particularly needed a new strategy: customer complaints ranged from "haughty sales clerks" to "they won't serve me if I don't look like a million bucks." The new strategy—an emphasis on helpful and friendly customer service. The method used to implement the new strategy—customer service training for the staff, and a new focus in its hiring interviews on courtesy, personableness, and friendliness. ▲

Behavioral Objectives

When you finish studying this chapter, you should be able to:

- ▲ *Describe* several basic types of interviews.
- ▲ *Explain* the factors and problems that can undermine an interview's usefulness and techniques for eliminating them.
- ▲ *List* important "guidelines for interviewers."
- ▲ *Explain* how to develop a structured or situational interview.
- ▲ *Discuss* how to improve your performance as an interviewer.

Chapter Outline

- ▲ Basic Features of Interviews
- ▲ What Factors Can Undermine an Interview's Usefulness?
- ▲ Designing and Conducting the Effective Interview

BASIC FEATURES OF INTERVIEWS

An *interview* is a procedure designed to obtain information from a person's oral responses to oral inquiries; a *selection interview*, which we'll focus on in this chapter, is "a selection procedure designed to predict future job performance on the basis of applicants' oral responses to oral inquiries."[1]

Since the interview is only one of several selection procedures, you could reasonably ask, "Why devote a whole chapter to one selection tool?" The answer is that the interview is by far the most widely used personnel selection procedure. Estimates of the proportion of organizations using interviews for selection range from 70% for some types of interviews,[2] to one study of 852 employers that found that 99% of them used interviews for employee selection.[3] The point is that while not all companies use selection tools like tests, assessment centers, and even reference checks, it would be highly unusual for a manager not to interview a prospective employee; interviewing is thus an indispensable management tool.

As we'll see below, historically the interview was criticized as having low validity.[4] However, more recent reviews have been more favorable and an interview—assuming it is conducted properly—can be "a much better predictor of performance than previously thought and is comparable with many other selection techniques."[5]

Types of Interviews

The seven main types of interviews used at work—structured, nonstructured, situational, sequential, panel, stress, and appraisal—can each be classified in one or more of four ways, according to (1) how structured they are, (2) their purpose, (3) their "content"—the types of questions they contain, and (4) the way they are administered.

nondirective interview

An unstructured conversational-style interview. The interviewer pursues points of interest as they come up in response to questions.

directive interview

An interview following a set sequence of questions.

STRUCTURED VS. UNSTRUCTURED INTERVIEWS   First, interviews can be classified according to the degree to which they are structured. In an **unstructured or nondirective type of interview** you ask questions as they come to mind. There is generally no set format to follow, so the interview can take various directions. While questions can be specified in advance, they usually are not, and there is seldom a formalized guide for scoring the quality of each answer. Interviewees for the same job thus may or may not be asked the same or similar questions. Furthermore, the lack of structure allows the interviewer to ask follow-up questions, based on the candidate's last statement, and to pursue points of interest as they develop.

On the other hand, in the **structured or directive interview** the questions and acceptable responses are specified in advance and the responses are rated for appropriateness of content.[6] McMurray's *patterned interview* was one early example. Here the interviewer followed a printed form to ask a series of questions such as "What kind of a car do you own?" Comments printed beneath the questions (such as "Will he or she be able to use his or her car if necessary?") then guide the interviewer in evaluating the acceptability of the answers. Another question on the patterned interview form might be "How was the person's present job obtained?" The evaluative comment would then be "Has he or she shown self-reliance in getting his or her jobs?"

In practice, not all structured interviews go so far as to specify acceptable answers. For example, Figure 6-1 shows a relatively structured interview guide that stops short of specifying the types of answers to watch for. Indeed (as we'll explain in more detail below) there are numerous ways to enhance the structure of an interview, many of which have nothing to do with using structured interview guides like the one in Figure 6-1. Basing the questions on a job analysis, consciously limiting follow-up questioning (to make sure all interviewees are asked only the same questions), using a larger number of questions, and prohibiting questions from candidates until after the interview are some other "structuring" examples.[7]

FIGURE 6-1

Structured Interview Guide

Copyright 1992 The Dartnell Corporation, Chicago, IL. Adopted with permission.

APPLICANT INTERVIEW GUIDE

To the interviewer: This Applicant Interview Guide is intended to assist in employee selection and placement. If it is used for all applicants for a position, it will help you to compare them, and it will provide more objective information than you will obtain from unstructured interviews.

Because this is a general guide, all of the items may not apply in every instance. Skip those that are not applicable and add questions appropriate to the specific position. Space for additional questions will be found at the end of the form.

Federal law prohibits discrimination in employment on the basis of sex, race, color, national origin, religion, disability, and in most instances, age. The law of most states also ban some or all of the above types of discrimination in employment as well as discrimination based on marital status or ancestry. Interviewers should take care to avoid any questions that suggest that an employment decision will be made on the basis of any such factors.

Job Interest

Name _____ Position applied for _____

What do you think the job (position) involves? _____

Why do you want the job (position)? _____

Why are you qualified for it? _____

What would your salary requirements be? _____

What do you know about our company? _____

Why do you want to work for us? _____

Current Work Status

Are you now employed? _____ Yes _____ No. If not, how long have you been unemployed? _____

Why are you unemployed? _____

If you are working, why are you applying for this position? _____

When would you be available to start work with us? _____

Work Experience

(Start with the applicant's current or last position and work back. All periods of time should be accounted for. Go back at least 12 years, depending upon the applicant's age. Military service should be treated as a job.)

Current or last
employer _____ Address _____

Dates of employment: from _____ to _____

Current or last job title _____

What are (were) your duties? _____

Have you held the same job throughout your employment with that company? _____ Yes _____ No. If not,

describe the various jobs you have had with that employer, how long you held each of them, and the main

duties of each. _____

What was your starting salary? _____ What are you earning now? _____ Comments _____

_____

Name of your last or current supervisor _____

What did you like most about that job? _____

What did you like least about it? _____

Why are you thinking of leaving? _____

   Why are you leaving right now? _____

   Interviewer's comments or observations _____

_____

(continued)

FIGURE 6-1
continued

What did you do before you took your last job? _____

    Where were you employed? _____

    Location _____ Job title _____

    Duties _____

    Did you hold the same job throughout your employment with that company? _____ Yes _____ No. If not,

    describe the jobs you held, when you held them and the duties of each. _____

    _____

    What was your starting salary? _____ What was your final salary? _____

    Name of your last supervisor _____

    May we contact that company? _____ Yes _____ No

    What did you like most about that job? _____

    What did you like least about that job? _____

    Why did you leave that job? _____

    Would you consider working there again? _____

    Interviewer: If there is any gap between the various periods of employment, the applicant should be asked

    about them. _____

    Interviewer's comments or observations _____

    _____

What did you do prior to the job with that company? _____

What other jobs or experience have you had? Describe them briefly and explain the general duties of each.

_____

Have you been unemployed at any time in the last five years? _____ Yes _____ No. What efforts did you make

to find work? _____

What other experience or training do you have that would help qualify you for the job applied for? Explain how

and where you obtained this experience or training. _____

Educational Background

What education or training do you have that would help you in the job for which you have applied? _____

_____

Describe any formal education you have had. (Interviewer may substitute technical training, if relevant.) _____

_____

Off-Job Activities

What do you do in your off-hours? ___ Part-time job ___ Athletics ___ Spectator sports ___ Clubs ___ Other

Please explain. _____

Interviewer's Specific Questions

Interviewer: Add any questions to the particular job for which you are interviewing, leaving space for brief answers.

(Be careful to avoid questions which may be viewed as discriminatory.)

_____

_____

_____

Personal

Would you be willing to relocate? _____ Yes _____ No

Are you willing to travel? _____ Yes _____ No

(continued)

FIGURE 6-1
continued

What is the maximum amount of time you would consider traveling? _____

_____

Are you able to work overtime? _____

What about working on weekends? _____

Self-Assessment

What do you feel are your strong points? _____

_____

What do you feel are your weak points? _____

_____

Interviewer: Compare the applicant's responses with the information furnished on the application for employment.

Clear up any discrepancies. _____

_____

Before the applicant leaves, the interviewer should provide basic information about the organization and the job opening, if this has not already been done. The applicant should be given information on the work location, work hours, the wage or salary, type of remuneration (salary or salary plus bonus, etc.), and other factors that may affect the applicant's interest in the job.

Interviewer's Impressions

Rate each characteristic from 1 to 4, with 1 being the highest rating and 4 being the lowest.

Personal Characteristics	1	2	3	4	Comments
Personal appearance					
Poise, manner					
Speech					
Cooperation with interviewer					
Job-related Characteristics					
Experience for this job					
Knowledge of job					
Interpersonal relationships					
Effectiveness					

Overall rating for job

1	2	3	4	5
___ Superior	___ Above Average	___ Average	___ Marginal	___ Unsatisfactory
	(well qualified)	(qualified)	(barely qualified)	

Comments or remarks _____

_____

_____

Interviewer _____ Date _____

Structured and nonstructured interviews each have their pros and cons. In structured interviews all applicants are generally asked all the same required questions by all interviewers; structured interviews are therefore generally more reliable and valid. Structured interviews can also help interviewers who may be less comfortable interviewing to ask questions and conduct more useful interviews. Standardizing the administration of the interview also increases consistency across candidates, enhances job relatedness, reduces overall subjectivity (and thus the potential for bias), and may, as a result, "enhance the ability to withstand legal challenge."[8] On the other hand, structured interviews don't always leave the flexibility to pursue points of interest as they develop.

THE PURPOSE OF THE INTERVIEW   Employment-related interviews can also be classified according to their purpose. Thus, as noted earlier, a *selection interview* is a type of interview designed to predict future job performance on the basis of applicants' oral responses to oral inquiries. A **stress interview** is a special type of selection interview in which the applicant is made uncomfortable by a series of sometimes rude questions. The aim of the stress interview is supposedly to help identify sensitive applicants and those with low or high stress tolerance.

In the typical stress interview, the applicant is made uncomfortable by being put on the defensive by a series of frank and often discourteous questions from the interviewer. The interviewer might first probe for weaknesses in the applicant's background, such as a job that the applicant left under questionable circumstances. Having identified these, the interviewer can then focus on them, hoping to get the candidate to lose his or her composure. Thus, a candidate for customer relations manager who obligingly mentions having had four jobs in the past 2 years might be told that frequent job changes reflect irresponsible and immature behavior. If the applicant then responds with a reasonable explanation of why the job changes were necessary, another topic might be pursued. On the other hand, if the formerly tranquil applicant reacts explosively with anger and disbelief, this might be taken as a symptom of low tolerance for stress.

The stress approach can be a good way to identify hypersensitive applicants who might be expected to overreact to mild criticism with anger and abuse. On the other hand, the stress interview's invasive and ethically questionable nature demands that the interviewer be both skilled in its use and sure that a thick skin and an ability to handle stress are really required for the job. This is definitely not an approach for amateur interrogators or for those without the skills to keep the interview under control.

Interviews serve two more purposes in the employment context. An **appraisal interview** is a discussion following a performance appraisal in which supervisor and employee discuss the employee's rating and possible remedial actions. When an employee leaves a firm for any reason, an exit interview is often conducted. An *exit interview*, usually conducted by the HR department, aims at eliciting information about the job or related matters that might give the employer a better insight into what is right or wrong about the company. Many of the techniques explained in this chapter apply equally well to appraisal and exit interviews. However, a complete explanation of these interviews will be postponed until Chapters 9 and 10, respectively, so we can concentrate here on selection interviews.

THE INTERVIEW'S CONTENT: THE TYPES OF QUESTIONS   Interviews can also be classified according to the nature or "content" of their questions. A **situational type of interview** is one in which the questions focus on the individual's ability to project what his or her behavior would be in a given situation.[9] For example, a candidate for a supervisor's position may be asked how he or she would respond to a subordinate coming to work late 3 days in a row. The interview can be both *structured and situational* with predetermined questions requiring the candidate to project what his or her behavior would be. In a structured situational interview, the applicant could be evaluated, say, on his or her choice between letting the subordinate off with a warning versus suspending the subordinate for 1 week.

Job-related interviews are those in which the interviewer tries to deduce what the applicant's on-the-job performance will be, based on his or her answers to questions about past behaviors. The questions here are not situational, in that they don't revolve around hypothetical situations or scenarios. Instead, job-related questions (such as

---

stress interview

An interview in which the applicant is made uncomfortable by a series of often rude questions. This technique helps identify hypersensitive applicants and those with low or high stress tolerance.

appraisal interview

A discussion following a performance appraisal in which supervisor and employee discuss the employee's rating and possible remedial actions.

situational interview

A series of job-related questions which focuses on how the candidate would behave in a given situation.

job-related interview

A series of job-related questions which focuses on relevant past job-related behaviors.

"Which courses did you like best in business school?") are asked in order to draw conclusions about, say, the candidate's ability to handle the financial aspects of the job to be filled.

The behavioral interview is gaining in popularity.[10] In a *behavioral interview* a situation is described and interviewees are asked how they have behaved *in the past* in such a situation.[11] Thus, while situational interviews ask interviewees to describe how they *would* react to a situation today or tomorrow, the behavioral interview asks interviewees to describe how they *did* react to situations in the past.[12]

Finally, *psychological interviews* are interviews conducted by a psychologist in which questions are intended to assess personal traits such as dependability.[13]

The interview may use situational, job-related, or behavioral questions and be either structured or unstructured. Psychological interviews generally have a significant unstructured element.

structured sequential interview

An interview in which the applicant is interviewed sequentially by several persons and each rates the applicant on a standard form.

panel interview

An interview in which a group of interviewers questions the applicant.

ADMINISTERING THE INTERVIEW   Interviews can also be classified based on how they are administered: one-on-one or by a panel of interviewers; sequentially or all at once; and computerized or personally. For example, most interviews are administered *one-on-one*. As the name implies, two people meet alone and one interviews the other by seeking oral responses to oral inquiries. Most selection processes are also sequential. In a *sequential interview* the applicant is interviewed by several persons in sequence before a selection decision is made. In an *unstructured sequential interview* each interviewer may look at the applicant from his or her own point of view, ask different questions, and form an independent opinion of the candidate. On the other hand, in a **structured sequential interview,** each interviewer rates the candidate on a standard evaluation form, and the ratings are compared before the hiring decision is made.[14]

The **panel interview** means the candidate is interviewed simultaneously by a group (or panel) of interviewers (rather than sequentially). The group structure has several advantages. A sequential interview often has candidates cover basically the same ground over and over again with each interviewer. The panel interview, on the other hand, allows each interviewer to pick up on the candidate's answers, much as reporters do in press conferences. This approach may elicit deeper and more meaningful responses than are normally produced by a series of one-on-one interviews. On the other

Panel interviewers can be useful in allowing each interviewer to follow up on the candidate's answers.

hand, some candidates find panel interviews more stressful, and they may actually inhibit responses. An even more stressful variant is the *mass interview*. In a mass interview several candidates are interviewed simultaneously by a panel. Here the panel poses a problem to be solved and then sits back and watches which candidate takes the lead in formulating an answer.

Increasingly, interviews aren't administered by people at all but are computerized. A *computerized selection interview* is one in which a job candidate's oral and/or computerized responses are obtained in response to computerized oral, visual, or written questions and/or situations. The basic idea is generally to present the applicant with a series of questions regarding his or her background, experience, education, skills, knowledge, and work attitudes—specific questions that relate to the job for which the person has applied.[15]

In a typical computerized interview the questions are presented in a multiple-choice format, one at a time, and the applicant is expected to respond to the questions on the computer screen by pressing a key corresponding to his or her desired response. For example, a sample interview question for a person applying for a job as a retail store clerk might be:[16]

How would your supervisor rate your customer service skills?

A. Outstanding

B. Above average

C. Average

D. Below average

E. Poor

Questions on a computerized interview like this come in rapid sequence and require concentration on the applicant's part.[17] The typical computerized interview then measures the response time to each question. A delay in answering certain questions such as "Can you be trusted?" can flag a potential problem.

Computer-aided interviews are generally used to reject totally unacceptable candidates and to select those who will move on to a face-to-face interview. For example, at Pic'n Pay stores, a chain of 915 self-service shoe stores headquartered in North Carolina, job applicants are given an 800 number to dial for the computerized interview and can take the interview at any Touch-Tone phone. The Pic'n Pay interview involves 100 questions and lasts about 10 minutes, with applicants pressing 1 for "yes" and 0 for "no." In Pic'n Pay's case, every applicant then gets a follow-up live telephone interview from one of six dedicated interviewers located at Pic'n Pay headquarters.

Computer-aided interviews can be very advantageous. Systems like those now on-line at Pic'n Pay and Great Western Bank of California substantially reduce the amount of time managers devote to interviewing what often turn out to be unacceptable candidates.[18] Applicants are reportedly more honest with computers than they would be with people, presumably because computers are not judgmental.[19] The computer can also be sneaky; if an applicant takes longer than average to answer a question like, "Have you ever been caught stealing?" he or she may be summarily screened out or at least questioned more deeply in that area by a human interviewer. Several of the interpersonal interview problems we'll discuss later in this chapter, such as making a snap judgment about the interviewee based on his or her appearance, are also obviously avoided with this nonpersonal interviewing approach.[20] On the other hand, the mechanical nature of computer-aided interviews can leave applicants with the impression that the prospective employer is rather impersonal. A description of a relatively sophisticated actual computer-aided interview is presented in the Information Technology and HR box on the next page.

INFORMATION TECHNOLOGY AND HR

Computer Applications in Interviewing: The Computer-Aided Interview

When Bonnie Dunn, 20 years old, tried out for a teller's job at Great Western Bank in Chatsworth, California, she faced a lineup of tough customers.[21]

One young woman sputtered contradictory instructions about depositing a check and then blew her top when the transaction wasn't handled fast enough. Another customer had an even shorter fuse, "You people are unbelievably slow," he said.

Both tough customers appeared on a computer screen, as part of a 20-minute automated job interview. Ms. Dunn was seated in front of a PC, responding via a color touch screen and a microphone. She was tested on making change and on sales skills, as well as keeping cool in tense situations.

When applicants sit down facing the computer at Great Western's bank branches, they hear it say, "Welcome to the interactive assessment aid." The computer doesn't understand what applicants say at that point, although it records their comments to be evaluated later. To begin the interview, applicants touch a label on the screen, eliciting an ominous foreword: "We'll be keeping track of how long it takes you and how many mistakes you make. Accuracy is more important than speed."

First, the computer tests the applicant on money skills, asking him or her to cash a check for $192.18, in-cluding at least three five-dollar bills and two dollars in quarters. Then, when an angry customer appears on the screen, candidates are expected to grab the microphone and mollify him. Later a bank official who listens to the recorded interviews give applicants five points for maintaining a friendly tone of voice, plus up to 15 points for apologizing, promising to solve the customer's problem, and, taking a cue from the screen, suggesting that in the future he use the bank's deposit-only line.

The touchy young woman on the screen is tougher. Speaking rapidly, she says she wants to cash a $150 check, get $40 in cash, and put $65 in savings and the rest in checking. As an applicant struggles to sort that out, she quickly adds, "No, it has to be $50 in checking because I just wrote a check this morning." If the applicant then touches a label on the screen that says "?" the woman fumes, "How many times do I have to tell you?"

Great Western reports that its computer-aided interviewing system has been successful. Not only has it dramatically reduced the amount of useless interviewing of unacceptable candidates, but candidates hired by the program were reportedly 26% less likely to quit or be fired within 90 days of hiring. (This is partly because the computer shows applicants what the job really involves, something a candidate might be reluctant to ask a person for fear of appearing negative.)

How Useful Are Interviews?

For many years, the ironic thing about interviews is that while used by virtually all employers, the earlier research gave selection interviews low marks in terms of reliability and validity. However, today (as noted above), studies affirm that the interview is "generally a much better predictor of performance than previously thought and is comparable with many other selection techniques."[22] The key, however, seems to be that this is true "especially if (and often only if) [the interview] is structured."[23] Generally speaking, the research evidence suggests that structured interviews have reported validities about twice those of unstructured interviews.[24] In other words, the key to an interview's usefulness is the manner in which it is administered, including (most importantly) the degree to which it is structured. In conclusion:

> With respect to predicting job performance, situational interviews yield a higher mean validity than do job-related (or behavioral) interviews, which in turn yield a higher mean validity than do psychological interviews.[25]
>
> Structured interviews, regardless of content, are more valid than unstructured interviews for predicting job performance.[26]

Interviewing and the Law: Employment Discrimination "Testers"

As with any selection procedure, interviews must adhere to EEOC requirements. Use caution, for instance, with any questions concerning, for instance, candidates' marital status, child care arrangements, ethnic background, and worker's compensation history. Also try to structure the interview, as this makes it easier to validate it.

The increasing use of employment discrimination testers has made such care even more important. As defined by the EEOC, testers are "individuals who apply for employment which they do not intend to accept, for the sole purpose of uncovering unlawful discriminatory hiring practices."[27] Although they're not really seeking employment, testers have legal standing, both with the courts[28] and with the EEOC.[29]

A case filed in 1991 illustrates the usual tester approach. A private, nonprofit civil rights advocacy group sent four university students—two white, two black—to an employment agency supposedly in pursuit of a job. Although the testers were given backgrounds and training to make them appear almost indistinguishable from each other in terms of qualifications, the white applicants and black applicants were allegedly treated quite differently. For example, both white applicants were given interviews and offered jobs, while the two black testers got neither interviews nor job offers.[30] A study by the Urban Institute suggests that such unequal treatment is "entrenched and widespread."[31]

An employer's best strategy is to be actively nondiscriminatory. However, a prudent employer will also take steps in planning the interview process and conducting the actual interviews to ensure that its interviewers avoid tester claims. For example:[32]

1. Caution interviewers that testers may be posing as applicants.
2. Train interviewers to make careful notes during and after the interview, to substantiate differences among applicants and to record responses to questions and other items of interest not on the applicant's resume or application.
3. Have applicants execute a statement acknowledging that they are applying for the job out of a sincere interest in the job and for no other purpose. Signing that and later returning with a claim as a "tester" could constitute evidence of deceit if there is a lawsuit.
4. Remember that testers often enter the employment process with phony resumes and fabricated qualifications, thus emphasizing the importance of carefully checking references.

WHAT FACTORS CAN UNDERMINE AN INTERVIEW'S USEFULNESS?

Several things can undermine an interview's usefulness. We explain these next, since knowledge of the mistakes is the first step in avoiding them. In the following section we'll then discuss how to avoid the mistakes.

Snap Judgments

One of the most consistent findings in the interviewing literature is that interviewers tend to jump to conclusions—make snap judgments—about candidates during the first few minutes of the interview or even before the interview begins, based on test scores or resume data. For example, one study showed that interviewers' access to candidates' test scores biased the interviewer's ultimate assessment of the candidate.[33] In another study the interview results on a candidate were related to the decision about hiring only when the candidate also had low passing scores on a selection test. For candidates with high test scores, the interview results were not related to the interviewers' decisions.[34] Another re-

First impressions are hard to correct, so it is important to be appropriately groomed and dressed for any job interview.

searcher estimated that in 85% of the cases interviewers had made up their minds about candidates before the interview began on the basis of applicants' application forms and personal appearance.

Findings like these underscore that it's important for a candidate to start off on the right foot with the interviewer. For better or worse, interviewers usually make up their minds about candidates during the first few minutes of the interview, and prolonging the interview past this point usually adds little to change their decisions.

Negative Emphasis

Jumping to conclusions is especially troublesome when the information the interviewer has about the candidate is negative. For example, one study found that interviewers who previously received unfavorable reference letters about applicants gave the applicants less credit for past successes and held them more personally responsible for past failures after the interview. Furthermore, the interviewers' final decisions to accept or reject applicants were always tied to what they expected of the applicants based on the references, quite aside from their interview performance.[35]

In other words, interviewers seem to have a consistent negative bias. They are generally more influenced by unfavorable than favorable information about the candidate. And their impressions are much more likely to change from favorable to unfavorable than from unfavorable to favorable. A common interviewing mistake is to make the interview itself mostly a search for negative information. In a sense, therefore, most interviews are probably loaded against the applicant. An applicant who is initially highly rated could easily end up with a low rating, given the fact that unfavorable information tends to carry more weight in the interview. An interviewee who starts out with a poor rating will find it hard to overcome that first bad impression during the interview.[36]

Misunderstanding the Job

Interviewers who don't know precisely what the job entails and what sort of candidate is best suited for it usually make their decisions based on incorrect stereotypes about what a good applicant is. They then erroneously match interviewees with their incorrect stereotypes. On the other hand, interviewers who have a clear understanding of what the job entails hold interviews that are more useful. In one study, 30 professional interviewers were used.[37] Half were given just a brief description of the jobs for which they were recruiting. Specifically, they were told the "eight applicants here represented by their application blanks are applying for the position of secretary." In contrast, the other 15 interviewers were given much more explicit job information.

> *The eight applicants . . . are applying for the position of executive secretary. The requirements are typing speed of 60 words per minute, stenography speed of 100 words per minute, dictaphone use and bilingual ability in either French, German, or Spanish. . . .*

More job knowledge translated into better interviews. The 15 interviewers who had more job information generally agreed among themselves about each candidate's potential, while those without complete job information did not. The latter also did not discriminate as well among applicants and tended to give them all high ratings.

Pressure to Hire

Pressure to hire also undermines an interview's usefulness. In one study a group of managers was told to assume that they were behind in their recruiting quota. A second group was told that they were ahead of their quota. Those "behind" evaluated the same recruits much more highly than did those "ahead."[38]

Candidate-Order (Contrast) Error

candidate-order error

An error of judgment on the part of the interviewer due to interviewing one or more very good or very bad candidates just before the interview in question.

Candidate-order (or "contrast") error means that the order in which you see applicants affects how you rate them. In one study, manages were asked to evaluate a candidate who was "just average" after first evaluating several "unfavorable" candidates. The average candidate was evaluated more favorably than he might otherwise have been since, in contrast to the unfavorable candidates, the average one looked better than he actually was. In some studies, only a small part of the applicant's rating was based on his or her actual potential. Most of the rating was based on the effect of having followed very favorable or unfavorable candidates.[39]

Influence of Nonverbal Behavior

Interviewers are influenced by the applicant's nonverbal behavior. For example, applicants who demonstrate more eye contact, head moving, smiling, and other similar nonverbal behavior are rated higher. These nonverbal behaviors often account for more than 80% of the applicant's rating.[40] In one study, 52 HR specialists reviewed videotaped job interviews in which the applicants' verbal content was identical. However, the interviewees' nonverbal behavior differed markedly. Those in one group had been instructed to exhibit minimal eye contact, a low energy level, and low voice modulation. The interviewees in a second group demonstrated the opposite behavior. Of the 26 personnel specialists who saw the high eye contact, high energy level candidate, 23 would have invited him or her for a second interview. None who saw the low eye contact, low energy level candidate would have recommended a second interview.[41] It would seem that an otherwise inferior interviewee who is trained to "act right" may well be appraised more highly than a more competent applicant lacking nonverbal interviewing skills.

What may be happening is that, accurately or not, interviewers infer the interviewee's personality from the way he or she acts in the interview. In one recent study 99 graduating college seniors completed questionnaires both before and after their job interviews and then reported their success in generating follow-up job interviews and job offers; the questionnaires included measures of personality, among other things.[42] The interviewee's personality, particularly his or her level of extroversion, had a pronounced influence on whether or not he or she received follow-up interviews and job offers. In part, this seems to be because "interviewers draw inferences about the applicant's personality based on the applicant's behavior during the interview."[43]

An applicant's attractiveness and gender also play a role.[44] In general, studies of attractiveness find that individuals ascribe more favorable traits and more successful life outcomes to attractive people.[45] And a study of gender reportedly found that "even when female managers exhibited the same career advancing behaviors as male managers, they still earned less money and were offered fewer career-progressing transfer opportunities."[46] In one recent study, subjects were asked to evaluate candidates for promotability based on photographs. Men were perceived to be more suitable for hire and more likely to advance to a next executive level than were equally qualified women, and more attractive candidates, especially men, were preferred over less attractive ones.[47] Yet another study suggested that in some cases more attractive women may actually be less likely to be offered managerial positions than were less attractive women, possibly because the interviewers erroneously equated attractiveness with femininity and femininity with nonmanagerial jobs.[48] The Diversity Counts feature provides another example.

Race can also play a role, depending on how the interview is conducted. In one study, the interviewees appeared before three interview panels—panels in which the racial composition was primarily black (75% black, 25% white), racially balanced (50% black, 50% white), or primarily white (75% white, 25% black).[49] On the primarily black panels, black and white raters judged black and white candidates similarly. In the primarily white panels or in those where blacks and whites were equally represented, white candidates were rated higher by white interviewers, while black candidates were rated higher by black interviewers.

The structure of the interview also influences the extent to which race plays a role. One review of 31 prior studies, for instance, concluded that structured interviews produced less of a difference between minority and white interviewees on average than did unstructured interviews.[50] The differences between minority and white interviewees also tended to be higher when there was a greater proportion of a minority in the applicant pool.[51]

Findings like these suggest several things. With respect to nonverbal behavior (such as eye contact), one implication is that even inferior candidates who are trained to "act

DIVERSITY COUNTS

Dressing for the Interview

It will not surprise many women to hear that the way they dress can alter interviewers' selection decisions. In one study, 77 HR managers attending a conference evaluated videotapes of women interviewing for management positions. The women were dressed in one of four styles: a light beige dress in a soft fabric (style 1), a bright aqua suit with a short belted jacked (style 2), a beige tailored suit with a blazer jacket (style 3), and "the most masculine" outfit, a dark navy tailored suit and a white blouse with an angular collar (style 4). A comparison of the hiring recommendations associated with each style suggests that, up to a point, the more masculine the style, the more favorable the hiring recommendations were. Specifically, applicants received more favorable hiring recommendations as style masculinity increased from style 1 to style 3. However, applicants wearing style 4 (the most masculine style) were turned down. We might surmise the outfit was considered "too masculine" by the interviewers. The findings may not apply to every individual. However, for what it's worth, the researchers suggest that it might be better for women to risk dressing "too masculine" than "too feminine" when applying for management jobs.[52]

right" in interviews will often be appraised more highly than will more competent applicants without the right nonverbal interviewing skills; interviewers should thus work hard to look beyond the behavior to who the person is and what he or she is saying. Second, demographic and physical attributes may influence your interview decisions. Because such attributes are generally irrelevant to job performance, interviewers need to anticipate the potential impact of such biases and guard against letting them influence their ratings.

Telegraphing

Some interviewers are so anxious to fill a job that they help the applicant respond correctly to their questions by *telegraphing* the expected answers.[53] An obvious example might be a question like: "This job calls for handling a lot of stress. You can do that, can't you?"

The telegraphing isn't always so obvious. For example, an interviewers' favorable first impression of a candidate (from examining application blanks and test scores) tends to result in a more positive interview style by the interviewer. This can translate into sending subtle cues (like a smile) regarding what answer is being sought.[54]

Too Much/Too Little Talking

Providing too much—or too little—guidance is another common mistake. Some interviewers let the applicant dominate the interview to the point where few substantive questions can be pursued. At the other extreme, some interviewers stifle the applicant by talking so much that the interviewee hasn't sufficient time to answer questions.[55]

What the interviewer talks about is important, of course. For example, realistic job previews provide interviewees with balanced pictures of what working for the firm will be like while not shying away from emphasizing the negative aspects of the job. In one recent laboratory study, the subjects who got negative information about the job were less inclined to pursue it, and the highest quality applicants seemed to be even less inclined to pursue it.[56] On the other hand, if realistic job previews can minimize the problem of hiring candidates who subsequently get discouraged and leave, they may not be all bad.[57]

Furthermore, what the interviewer talks about (and how much he or she talks) seems to depend in part on the purpose of the selection interview and the extent to which the interviewer was trained. For example, recruitment-oriented interviewers talked 50% more, volunteered twice as much information, and asked half as many questions as did interviewers who were focused more on screening or on both screening and recruiting.[58] And, trained interviewers used more of their allotted time for asking questions in the interviews.[59]

Playing District Attorney or Psychologist

Since the interviewer often plays the role of gatekeeper in determining whether or not the interviewee gets a job, there's sometimes a tendency to misuse power by playing district attorney or psychologist. For example, although it's smart to be alert for inconsistencies in applicants' responses, it's important to guard against turning the interview into a game of "gotcha" in which the interviewer derives pleasure from ferreting out and pouncing on interviewees' inconsistencies. Similarly, some interviewers play psychologist, probing for hidden meanings in everything the applicants say.[60]

DESIGNING AND CONDUCTING THE EFFECTIVE INTERVIEW

Problems like those just discussed can be avoided by designing and conducting an effective interview. In particular, structuring or *standardizing* the interview can be useful, in that it reduces the possibility that problems such as bias, jumping to conclusions, and too much talking, for instance, can occur.

The Structured Interview

Since *structured interviews* are usually the most valid interviews for predicting job performance, conducting an effective interview ideally starts with designing a structured situational interview, a *series of hypothetical job-oriented questions with predetermined answers that are consistently asked of all applicants for a particular job.*[61] Usually a committee of persons familiar with the job develop situational and job-knowledge questions based on the actual job duties. They then reach consensus on what are and are not acceptable answers to these questions. The actual procedure consists of five steps, as follows:[62]

STEP 1. JOB ANALYSIS   First, write a description of the job in the form of a list of job duties, required knowledge, skills, abilities, and other worker qualifications.

STEP 2. EVALUATE THE JOB DUTY INFORMATION   Next, rate each job duty on its importance to job success and on the amount of time required to perform it compared to other tasks. The aim here is to identify the main duties of the job.

STEP 3. DEVELOP INTERVIEW QUESTIONS   The employees who list and evaluate the job duties then develop interview questions. The interview questions are based on the listing of job duties, with more interview questions generated for the more important duties.

A situational interview may actually contain situational, job-knowledge, and "willingness" questions (although the situational questions tend to be the most valid). *Situational questions* pose a hypothetical job situation, such as "What would you do if the machine suddenly began heating up?" *Job-knowledge questions* assess knowledge essential to job performance that must be known before entering the job. These often deal with technical aspects of a job (such as "What is a ratchet wrench?"). *Willingness questions* gauge the applicant's willingness and motivation to do repetitive physical work, to travel, to relocate, and so forth.

The employees who develop the questions generally state the questions in terms of critical incidents that reflect especially good or poor performance. For example, a situational question based on a critical incident that could be asked of a supervisory candidate is as follows:

> *Your spouse and two teenage children are sick in bed with a cold. There are no relatives or friends available to look in on them. Your shift starts in three hours. What would you do in this situation?*

STEP 4. DEVELOP BENCHMARK ANSWERS   Next, develop answers and a five-point rating scale for each question, with specific answers developed for good (a 5 rating), marginal (a 3 rating), and poor (a 1 rating). For example, consider the preceding situational question where the spouse and children are sick. Each member of the team that developed the questions should write good, marginal, and poor answers based on "things you have actually heard said in an interview by people who subsequently were considered good, marginal, or poor as the case may be on the job." After a group discussion, consensus is reached on the answers to use as 5, 3, and 1 benchmarks for each scenario. Three benchmarks for the example question might be "I'd stay home— my spouse and family come first" (1); "I'd phone my supervisor and explain my situation" (3); and "Since they only have colds, I'd come to work" (5).

STEP 5. APPOINT INTERVIEW PANEL AND IMPLEMENT   These types of interviews are generally conducted by a panel, rather than sequentially. The panel should consist of three to six members, preferably the same employees who participated in writing the interviews and answers. Panel members may also be supervisors of the job to be filled, the job incumbent, peers, and HR representatives. The same panel members should interview all candidates for the job.[63]

Before the interview, the job duties, questions, and benchmark answers are distributed to the panel members and reviewed. Next the panel interview is conducted, usually in a quiet, comfortable, nonstressful atmosphere. Ideally, one member of the panel is designated to introduce the applicant to the panel and to ask all questions of all applicants in this and succeeding interviews to ensure consistency. However, all panel members record and rate the applicant's answers on the rating scale sheet, by indicating where the candidate's answer to each question falls relative to the ideal poor, marginal or good answers. At the end of the interview, each applicant is directed to someone who explains the follow-up procedures and answers any questions the applicant has.[64]

Guidelines for Conducting an Interview

Not all employers will have the time or inclination to create structured situational interviews as part of their screening processes. However, even without going through such a process, there is a good deal you can do to ensure the interview is conducted more effectively.

STRUCTURE THE INTERVIEW Structure in this sense means enhancing the interview by taking steps that increase the standardization of the interview or otherwise assist the interviewer in determining what questions to ask and/or how to evaluate responses.[65] Two recent studies described several ways to standardize or increase the structure of an interview.[66] The important point is that "any interview could be easily enhanced by using at least some of these components."[67] Actions you can take to enhance the interview's structure include:[68]

1. Base interview questions on a job analysis. There are several advantages to doing so. It may prevent interviewers from basing questions on inaccurate beliefs about the job's requirements. And, it has been shown to reduce the likelihood of bias, because the questions inherently focus more on the job, thus limiting the interviewer's discretion to "read" things into the answer.

2. Use objective, specific, and behaviorally-oriented questions and criteria for evaluating the interviewee's responses. Doing so can reduce the overall subjectivity of the process and thereby the interpretation required and the bias that such interpretation may breed. (Sample questions are shown in Figure 6-2.)

3. Train interviewers. Training may also improve the job relatedness of the interview and the interviewer's objectivity. For example, review EEO laws with prospective interviewers and train them to avoid irrelevant or potentially discriminatory questions. Also train them to base their ratings on job-related information and, for instance, to avoid stereotyping minority candidates.

4. Use the same questions with all candidates. When it comes to asking the same questions, interviewers have four choices: ask the exact same questions of each candidate in the exact same order; ask primarily the same questions but allow some flexibility to pursue interesting lines of discussion; don't provide specific questions but provide outlines of topics to cover; and leave interviewers free to ask whatever questions they deem appropriate.[69] In this case, the prescription seems to be "the more standardized, the better." Using the same questions with all candidates can reduce bias "because of the obvious fairness of giving all the candidates the exact same opportunity," and limit many sources of potential bias in the interview.[70]

5. Use rating scales to rate interviewees' answers. For example, this might involve providing, for each question, a range of possible sample answers and a quantitative rating for each. Rating scales can reduce bias and increase the interview's reliability by ensuring that all interviewers are basically using the same criteria.

6. Use multiple interviewers or panel interviews. This can reduce bias by cancelling out one or two interviewers' idiosyncratic opinions and by bringing more points of view to bear before the hiring decision is made.

7. Use better questions. Questions are better that are more objective and work oriented (regardless of whether or not you conduct a job analysis). Examples of different types of structured questions are presented in Figure 6-2. One example is "What factors should you consider in developing a television advertising campaign?" Interview questions like these are not only more job related but reduce the subjectivity of the interview and therefore the chance for bias. On the other hand, questions on opinions and attitudes, goals and aspirations, and self-descriptions and self-evaluations "are sufficiently ambiguous to allow candidates to present their credentials in an overly favorable manner or avoid revealing weaknesses. They focus on poorly defined traits with uncertain links to job performance."[71]

PLAN THE INTERVIEW   Prior to the interview, review the candidate's application and resume, and note any areas that are vague or that may indicate strengths or weaknesses. Review the job specification and plan to start the interview with a clear picture of the traits of an ideal candidate.

If possible, use a structured form. Interviews based on structured guides like those in Figures 6-1 (pages 217–219), and 6-3 (page 232) usually result in the best interviews.[72] At a minimum, write out your questions prior to the interview.

FIGURE 6-2

Examples of Questions That Provide Structure

Source: Campion, Palmer, and Campion, "A Review of Structure in the Selection Interview," *Personnel Psychology*, 1997, p. 668.

EXAMPLES OF DIFFERENT TYPES OF STRUCTURED INTERVIEW QUESTIONS

Situational Questions:

1. Suppose a co-worker was not following standard work procedures. The co-worker was more experienced than you and claimed the new procedure was better. Would you use the new procedure?

2. Suppose you were giving a sales presentation and a difficult technical question arose that you could not answer. What would you do?

Past Behavior Questions:

3. Based on your past work experience, what is the most significant action you have ever taken to help out a co-worker?

4. Can you provide an example of a specific instance where you developed a sales presentation that was highly effective?

Background Questions:

5. What work experiences, training, or other qualifications do you have for working in a teamwork environment?

6. What experience have you had with direct point-of-purchase sales?

Job Knowledge Questions:

7. What steps would you follow to conduct a brainstorming session with a group of employees on safety?

8. What factors should you consider when developing a television advertising campaign?

Note: So that direct comparisons can be made, an example is presented to assess both teamwork (1, 3, 5, and 7) and sales attributes (2, 4, 6, and 8) for each type of question.

CANDIDATE RECORD   NAP 100 (10/77)

CANDIDATE NUMBER   NAME (LAST NAME FIRST)   COLLEGE NAME   COLLEGE CODE

I ☐☐☐ U 921 ☐☐☐☐☐☐☐☐☐☐☐☐☐☐☐☐☐☐☐☐   ☐☐☐
(1-7)   (8-27)   (28-30)

INTERVIEWER NUMBER

☐☐☐☐ 0 ☐☐☐
(33-40)
INTERVIEWER NAME

SOURCE (41)   RACE (42)   SEX (43)   DEGREE (53)   AVERAGE (A = 4.0)   CLASS STANDING (58-59)
Campus ☐ C   White ☐ W   Male ☐ M   Bachelors ☐ B   Overall ☐☐ (54-55)   Top 10% ☐ 10
Walk-In ☐ W   Black ☐ B   Female ☐ F   Masters ☐ M   Top 25% ☐ 25
Intern ☐ I   Asian ☐ A   Init.   Law ☐ L   Acctg ☐☐ (56-57)   Top Half ☐ 50
Agency ☐ A   Hispanic ☐ H   Cont.   Majors   Bottom Half ☐ 75
Native Am. ☐ NA   Date ☐☐☐☐☐☐ (46-51)

CAMPUS INTERVIEW EVALUATIONS

ATTITUDE – MOTIVATION – GOALS
POOR ☐   AVERAGE ☐   GOOD ☐   OUTSTANDING ☐
(POSITIVE, COOPERATIVE, ENERGETIC, MOTIVATED, SUCCESSFUL, GOAL-ORIENTED)
COMMENTS:

COMMUNICATIONS SKILLS-PERSONALITY-SALES ABILITY
POOR ☐   AVERAGE ☐   GOOD ☐   OUTSTANDING ☐
(ARTICULATE, LISTENS, ENTHUSIASTIC, LIKEABLE, POISED, TACTFUL, ACCEPTED, CONVINCING)
COMMENTS:

EXECUTIVE PRESENCE – DEAL WITH TOP PEOPLE
POOR ☐   AVERAGE ☐   GOOD ☐   OUTSTANDING ☐
(IMPRESSIVE, STANDS OUT, A WINNER, REMEMBERED, LEVELHEADED, AT EASE, AWARE)
COMMENTS:

INTELLECTUAL ABILITIES
POOR ☐   AVERAGE ☐   GOOD ☐   OUTSTANDING ☐
(INSIGHTFUL, CREATIVE, CURIOUS, IMAGINATIVE, UNDERSTANDS, REASONS, INTELLIGENT, SCHOLARLY)
COMMENTS:

JUDGMENT – DECISION MAKING ABILITY
POOR ☐   AVERAGE ☐   GOOD ☐   OUTSTANDING ☐
(MATURE, SEASONED, INDEPENDENT, COMMON SENSE, CERTAIN, DETERMINED, LOGICAL)
COMMENTS:

LEADERSHIP
POOR ☐   AVERAGE ☐   GOOD ☐   OUTSTANDING ☐
(SELF-CONFIDENT, TAKES CHARGE, EFFECTIVE RESPECTED, MANAGEMENT MINDED, GRASPS AUTHORITY)
COMMENTS:

CAMPUS INTERVIEW SUMMARY

INVITE (Circle)	AREA OF INTEREST	(Circle)	SEMESTER HRS.	OFFICES PREFERRED:	SUMMARY COMMENTS: _____
YES NO	AUDIT	TAX	Acct'g. ___	No. 1 ___	
DATE AVAILABLE	MCS	ABC	Audit ___	No. 2 ___	
	OTHER		Tax ___	No. 3 ___	

FIGURE 6-3 Structured Interview Form for College Applicants

The interview should take place in a private room where telephone calls are not accepted and interruptions can be minimized.

Also, plan to delay your decision. Interviewers often make snap judgments even before they see the candidate—on the basis of his or her application form, for instance—or during the first few minutes of the interview. Plan on keeping a record of the interview, and review this record after the interview. Make your decision then.[73]

ESTABLISH RAPPORT   The main reason for the interview is to find out about the applicant. To do this, start by putting the person at ease. Greet the candidate and start the interview by asking a noncontroversial question—perhaps about the weather or the traffic conditions that day. As a rule, all applicants—even unsolicited drop-ins—should receive friendly, courteous treatment, not only on humanitarian grounds but because your reputation is on the line.

Be aware of the applicant's status. For example, if you are interviewing someone who is unemployed, he or she may be exceptionally nervous and you may want to take additional steps to relax the person.[74]

ASK QUESTIONS   Try to follow your structured interview guide or the questions you wrote out ahead of time. A menu of additional questions is presented in Figure 6-4.

Some suggestions for actually asking questions include: Try to emphasize structured job-oriented questions (as in Figure 6-2 on page 231); avoid questions that can be answered "yes" or "no"; don't put words in the applicant's mouth or telegraph the desired answer, for instance, by nodding or smiling when the right answer is given; don't interrogate the applicant as if the person is a criminal, and don't be patronizing, sarcastic, or inattentive; don't monopolize the interview by rambling or let the applicant dominate the interview so you can't ask all your questions; do ask open-ended questions; listen to the candidate to encourage him or her to express thoughts fully; and draw out the applicant's opinions and feelings by repeating the person's last comment as a question (such as "You didn't like your last job?")

When you ask for general statements of a candidate's accomplishments, also ask for examples.[75] Thus, if the candidate lists specific strengths or weaknesses, follow up with "What are specific examples that demonstrate each of your strengths?"

CLOSE THE INTERVIEW   Toward the close of the interview, leave time to answer any questions the candidate may have and, if appropriate, to advocate your firm to the candidate.

Try to end all interviews on a positive note. The applicant should be told whether there is an interest and, if so, what the next step will be. Similarly, rejections should be made diplomatically, for instance, with a statement like "Although your background is impressive, there are other candidates whose experience is closer to our requirements." If the applicant is still being considered but a decision can't be reached at once, say this. If your policy is to inform candidates of their status in writing, do so within a few days of the interview.

REVIEW THE INTERVIEW   Once the candidate leaves, review your interview notes, fill in the structured interview guide (if you used one and if this was not done during the interview), and review the interview while it's fresh in your mind. Whether or not note taking during the interview is necessary, by the way, seems to depend on the interviewer's personal preferences. In one recent series of three studies, whether or not the interviewers took notes didn't seem to have much appreciable affect on the validity of the interview, al-

FIGURE 6-4

Some Questions to Ask Interviewees

Source: H. Lee Rust, *Job Search, The Complete Manual for Job Seekers* (New York: AMACOM, 1991), pp. 232–233.

1. Did you bring a résumé?
2. What salary do you expect to receive?
3. What was your salary in your last job?
4. Why do you want to change jobs or why did you leave your last job?
5. What do you identify as your most significant accomplishment in your last job?
6. How many hours do you normally work per week?
7. What did you like and dislike about your last job?
8. How did you get along with your superiors and subordinates?
9. Can you be demanding of your subordinates?
10. How would you evaluate the company you were with last?
11. What were its competitive strengths and weaknessess?
12. What best qualifies you for the available position?
13. How long will it take you to start making a significant contribution?
14. How do you feel about our company—its size, industry, and competitive position?
15. What interests you most about the available position?
16. How would you structure this job or organize your department?
17. What control or financial data would you want and why?
18. How would you establish your primary inside and outside lines of communication?
19. What would you like to tell me about yourself?
20. Were you a good student?
21. Have you kept up in your field? How?
22. What do you do in your spare time?
23. What are your career goals for the next five years?
24. What are your greatest strengths and weaknesses?
25. What is your job potential?
26. What steps are you taking to help achieve your goals?
27. Do you want to own your own business?
28. How long will you stay with us?
29. What did your father do? Your mother?
30. What do your brothers and sisters do?
31. Have you ever worked on a group project and, if so, what role did you play?
32. Do you participate in civic affairs?
33. What professional associations do you belong to?
34. What is your credit standing?
35. What are your personal likes and dislikes?
36. How do you spend a typical day?
37. Would you describe your family as a close one?
38. How aggressive are you?
39. What motivates you to work?
40. Is money a strong incentive for you?
41. Do you prefer line or staff work?
42. Would you rather work alone or in a team?
43. What do you look for when hiring people?
44. Have you ever fired anyone?
45. Can you get along with union members and their leaders?
46. What do you think of the current economic and political situation?
47. How will government policy affect our industry or your job?
48. Will you sign a noncompete agreement or employment contract?
49. Why should we hire you?
50. Do you want the job?

though overall, when note taking was voluntary, the note taker made more valid ratings than did the non-note takers.[76] For those who prefer to take notes the main caveat seems to be to do so in a way that does not interfere with the flow of the interview or lead to recording irrelevant information.[77]

Remember that snap judgments and negative emphasis are two common interviewing mistakes. Reviewing the interview shortly after the candidate has left can help you minimize these two problems. Some employers find videotaping interviews can be an effective way to review the top candidates.[78]

SMALL BUSINESS APPLICATIONS

Interview Procedures

Many of the points discussed in this chapter can be combined into a practical interview procedure for a small business. Such a procedure is especially useful when time and resources are scarce, when HR specialists aren't available, and when a quick way to organize the interview process is required. The procedure consists of four steps as follows:[79]

1. Develop behavioral specifications for the job.
2. Determine what basic factors to probe for.
3. Use an interview plan.
4. Match the candidate to the job.

DEVELOP BEHAVIORAL SPECIFICATIONS

Even a small business can specify the kind of person who would be best for the job. A quick way to do so is to focus on four basic types of behaviors—*knowledge and experience, motivation, intellectual capacity,* and *personality,* and to ask the following questions:

- *Knowledge-Experience Factor.* What must the candidate know to perform the job? What experience is absolutely necessary to perform the job?
- *Motivation Factor.* What should the person like doing to enjoy this job? Is there anything the person should not dislike? Are there any essential goals or aspirations the person should have? Are there any unusual energy demands on the job?
- *Intellectual Factor.* Are there any specific intellectual aptitudes required (mathematical, mechanical, and so on)? How complex are the problems to be solved? What must a person be able to demonstrate he or she can do intellectually? How should the person solve problems (cautiously, deductively, and so on)?
- *Personality Factor.* What are the critical personality qualities needed for success on the job (ability to withstand boredom, decisiveness, stability, and so on)? How must the job incumbent handle stress, pressure, and criticism? What kind of interpersonal behavior is required in the job up the line, at peer level, down the line, and outside the firm with customers?

SPECIFIC FACTORS TO PROBE IN THE INTERVIEW

Next, use a combination of situational questions, plus open-ended questions like those in Figure 6-4, to probe the candidate's suitability for the job. For example:

- *Intellectual Factor.* Here probe such things as complexity of tasks the person has performed, grades in school, test results (including scholastic aptitude tests, and so on), and how the person organizes his or her thoughts and communicates.
- *Motivation Factor.* Probe such areas as the person's likes and dislikes (for each thing done, what he or she liked or disliked about it), the person's aspirations (including the validity of each goal in terms of the person's reasoning about why he or she chose it), and the person's energy level, perhaps by asking what he or she does on, say, a "typical Tuesday."

■ *Personality Factor.* Probe by looking for self-defeating patterns of behavior (aggressiveness, compulsive fidgeting, and so on) and by exploring the person's past interpersonal relationships. Here ask questions about the person's past interactions (working in a group at school, working with fraternity brothers or sorority sisters, leading the work team on the last job, and so on). Also try to judge the person's behavior in the interview itself—is the candidate personable? Shy? Outgoing?

USE AN INTERVIEW PLAN

You should also devise and use an interview plan to guide the interview. According to John Drake, significant areas to cover include the candidate's:[80]

- College experiences
- Work experiences—summer, part-time
- Work experience—full-time (one by one)
- Goals and ambitions
- Reactions to the job you are interviewing for
- Self-assessments (by the candidate of his or her strengths and weaknesses)
- Military experiences
- Present outside activities

Follow your plan, perhaps starting with an open-ended question for each topic, such as "Could you tell me about what you did when you were in high school?" Keep in mind that you are trying to elicit information about four main traits—intelligence, motivation, personality, and knowledge and experience. You can then accumulate the information as the person answers. Particular areas that you want to follow up on can usually be pursued by asking such questions as "Could you elaborate on that, please?"

MATCH CANDIDATE TO THE JOB

After following the interview plan and probing for the four factors, you should now be able to summarize the candidate's general strengths and limitations and to draw conclusions about the person's intellectual capacity, knowledge/experience, motivation, and personality. You should then compare your conclusions to both the job description and the list of behavioral specifications developed earlier. This should provide a rational basis for matching the candidate to the job—one based on an analysis of the traits and aptitudes actually required.

THE HIGH-PERFORMANCE ORGANIZATION

Building Better, Faster, More Competitive
Organizations Through HR: A Total Selection Program

■ Hiring for Commitment at Toyota

Progressive companies like Toyota and Federal Express put enormous effort into combining interviews and other screening procedures like those covered in the last few chapters into *total selection programs* designed to find the best people.[81]

For example, as summarized in Figure 6-5, Toyota's hiring process takes about 20 hours and six phases, spread over 5 or 6 days. The Kentucky Department of Employment

THE PROCESS

Phase I   Orientation/Application
Fill out an application and view a video of the Toyota work environment and selection system process (1 hour)
Objective: To explain the job and collect information about work experiences and skills
Conducted: Kentucky Department of Employment Services

Phase II   Technical Skills Assessment
Pencil/Paper tests
General knowledge test (2 hours)
Tool & die or general maintenance test (6 hours)[1]
Objective: To assess technical knowledge and potential
Conducted: Kentucky Department of Employment Services

Phase III   Interpersonal Skills Assessment
Group and individual problem-solving activities (4 hours)
Production assembly simulation (5 hours)[2]
Objective: To assess interpersonal and decision-making skills
Conducted: Toyota Motor Manufacturing

Phase IV   Toyota Assessment
Group interview and evaluation (1 hour)
Objective: To discuss achievements and accomplishments
Conducted: Toyota Motor Manufacturing

Phase V   Health Assessment
Physical exam and drug/alcohol tests (2½ hours)
Objective: To determine physical fitness
Conducted: Scott County General Hospital and University of Kentucky Medical Center

Phase VI   On-the-Job Observation
Observation and coaching on the job after being hired (6 months)
Objective: To assess job performance and develop skills
Conducted: Toyota Motor Manufacturing

[1] Skilled trades only
[2] Production only

FIGURE 6-5 *Summary of Toyota Hiring Process*

Source: Based on Toyota Motor Manufacturing USA Inc. documents

Services conducts the initial prescreening of Phase I. Here applicants fill out application forms summarizing their work experience and skills and view a video describing Toyota's work environment and selection system. This takes about an hour and gives applicants a realistic preview of work at Toyota and of the hiring process's extensiveness. Many applicants simply drop out at this stage.

Phase II is aimed at assessing the applicant's technical knowledge and potential and in Toyota's case is also conducted by the Kentucky Department of Employment Services. Here applicants take the U.S. Employment Services' General Aptitude Test Battery (GATB), which helps identify problem-solving skills and learning potential, as well as occupational preferences. Skilled trades applicants (experienced mechanics, for example) also take a 6-hour tool and die or general maintenance test. Kentucky Employment Services scores all tests and submits the files to Toyota.

In Phase III Toyota takes over the screening. The aim here is to assess applicants' interpersonal and decision-making skills. All applicants participate in four hours of group and individual problem-solving and discussion activities in the firm's assessment center. This is a separate location where applicants engage in exercises under the observation of Toyota screening experts. In a typical group exercise, participants playing company employees constitute a team responsible for choosing new features for next year's car. The individual problem-solving exercises are aimed at assessing each applicant's problem-solving ability in terms of facets such as insight, flexibility, and creativity.

Also in Phase III, production line assembly candidates participate in a 5-hour production assembly simulation. In one of these, candidates play the roles of the management and workforce of a firm that makes electrical circuits. During a series of planning and manufacturing periods, the team must decide which circuits should be manufactured and how to effectively assign people, materials, and money to produce them.

A 1-hour group interview constitutes Phase IV. Here groups of candidates discuss their accomplishments with Toyota interviewers. This phase helps give the Toyota assessors a more complete picture of what drives each candidate in terms of what each is proudest of and most interested in. Phase IV also gives Toyota another opportunity to watch its candidates interact with each other in groups. Those who successfully complete Phase IV (and are tentatively tapped as Toyota employees) then undergo 2½ hours of physical and drug/alcohol tests at area hospitals (Phase V). Finally, Phase IV involves closely monitoring, observing, and coaching the new employees on the job to assess their job performance and to develop their skills during their first 6 months at work.

WHAT TOYOTA IS LOOKING FOR IN ITS EMPLOYEES

Toyota's total selection process helps to illustrate how selection can translate into improved performance. Toyota is looking, first, for interpersonal skills, due to the firm's emphasis on team interaction. Similarly, the whole thrust of Toyota's production process is to improve job processes through worker commitment to top quality, and so reasoning and problem-solving skills are also crucial human requirements. This emphasis on kaizen—on having the workers improve the system—helps explain Toyota's emphasis on hiring an intelligent, educated workforce. The GATB and problem-solving simulations have helped produce such a workforce. "Those who did the best in their education did the best in the simulations," said one HR officer.

Quality is one of Toyota's central values, and so the firm also seeks a history of quality commitment in the people it hires. This is one reason for the group interview that focuses on one's proudest accomplishments.

Toyota's production system is based on consensus decision making, job rotation, and flexible career paths. These require open-minded, flexible team players, not dogmatists. Toyota's selection process (with its decision-making and problem-solving exercises) also helps identify such people.

BASIC FEATURES OF TOYOTA'S SELECTION SYSTEM

1. Select not just for skills but for values. Whether it's excellence, kaizen/continuous improvement, integrity, or some other, value-based hiring begins with clarifying what those values are. Then hire employees who exhibit commitment to these values.

2. Commit the time and effort for an exhaustive screening process. Eight to 10 hours of interviewing even for entry-level employees is not unusual, and firms like Toyota will spend 20 hours or more with someone before deciding to hire. Many are rejected.

3. Match the candidates' values and skills with the needs of the firm. Teamwork, kaizen, and flexibility are central values at Toyota, so problem-solving skills, interpersonal skills, and commitment to quality are crucial human requirements.

4. Self-selection is an important screening practice at most of these firms. In some firms this just means realistic previews. At others, practices such as long probationary periods in entry-level jobs help screen out those who don't fit. And in firms like these the screening process itself demands a sacrifice of employees—the time and effort are always extensive.

We invite you to visit the Dessler page on the Prentice Hall Web site at **www.prenhall.com/dessler** for our on-line study guide, Internet exercises, current events, links to related Web sites, and more.

SUMMARY

1. There are several basic types of interviews—situational, nondirective, structured, sequential, panel, stress, and appraisal interviews. All interviews can be classified according to content, structure, purpose, and method of administration.

2. Several factors and problems can undermine the usefulness of an interview. These are making premature decisions, letting unfavorable information predominate, not knowing the requirements of the job, being under pressure to hire, not allowing for the candidate-order effect, and sending visual cues to telegraph enthusiasm.

3. The five steps in the interview include: plan, establish rapport, question the candidate, close the interview, and review the data.

4. Guidelines for interviewers include: Use a structured guide, know the requirements of the job, focus on traits you can more accurately evaluate (like motivation), let the interviewee do most of the talking, delay your decision until after the interview, and remember the EEOC requirements.

5. The steps in a structured or situational interview are: job analysis, evaluate the job duty information, develop interview questions with critical incidents, develop benchmark answers, appoint an interview committee, and implement.

6. As an interviewee, keep in mind that interviewers tend to make premature decisions and let unfavorable information predominate; your appearance and enthusiasm are important; you should get the interviewer to talk; it is important to prepare before walking in—get to know the job and the problems the interviewer wants solved; and you should stress your enthusiasm and motivation to work, and how your accomplishments match your interviewer's needs. (See the following appendix.)

7. A quick procedure for conducting an interview is to develop behavioral specifications; determine the basic intellectual, motivational, personality, and experience factors to probe for; use an interview plan; and then match the individual to the job. The procedure is especially useful in small firms without HR groups, but can be used in large firms as well.

8. Value-based hiring can contribute to building employee commitment. It assumes that management has clarified the values it cherishes (such as quality at Toyota), spends adequate time in the selection process, and provides for realistic previews.

KEY TERMS

nondirective interview 216
directive interview 216
stress interview 220
appraisal interview 220
situational interview 220
job-related interview 220
structured sequential interview 221
panel interview 221
candidate-order error 226

DISCUSSION QUESTIONS

1. Explain the four basic ways in which interviews can be classified.

2. Briefly describe each of the following possible types of interviews: unstructured panel interviews, structured sequential interviews; job-related structured interviews.

3. For what sorts of jobs do you think computerized interviews are most appropriate? Why?

4. Why do you think "situational interviews yield a higher mean validity than do job-related or behavioral interviews, which in turn yield a higher mean validity than do psychological interviews?"

5. Similarly, how do you explain the fact that structured interviews, regardless of content, are more valid than unstructured interviews for predicting job performance?
6. Briefly discuss and give examples of at least five common interviewing mistakes. What recommendations would you give for avoiding these interviewing mistakes?
7. Explain why you think that it is (or is not) important to select candidates based on their values, as well as on usual selection criteria such as skills and experience.

INDIVIDUAL AND GROUP ACTIVITIES

1. Give a short presentation entitled "How to be Effective as an Interviewee."
2. Working individually or in groups, develop a structured situational interview for hiring someone to teach a college-level course in human resource management.
3. Working individually or in groups, use the interview process described in this chapter's Small Business Applications feature to explain how you would interview a candidate for the job of President of the United States.

EXPERIENTIAL EXERCISE

Purpose   The purposes of this exercise are:

1. To give you practice in developing a structured interview form, and
2. To give you practice in using this form.

Required Understanding   The reader should be familiar with the interviewing problems we discussed, and with the example of the structured interview form presented in Figure 6-1.

How to Set Up the Exercise/Instructions

1. Set up groups of four or five students. One student will be the "interviewee," while the other students in the group will develop the structured interview form and, as a group, interview the interviewee.
2. Instructions for the interviewee: Please do not read the exercise beyond this point (you can leave the room for a few minutes).
3. Instructions for the interviewers: You may be a president or vice president but in any case you have to interview a candidate for marketing manager about an hour from now. Each of you knows you'd be best off using a structured interview form to guide the interview, so you're now meeting for about half an hour to develop such a

form, based in part on the job descriptions presented in Chapter 3. (Hint: Start by listing the most relevant abilities and then rate these in importance on a five-point scale. They use the high-rated abilities on your interview form.)

4. As soon as you have completed your structured interview form, call in your interviewee and explain that he or she is a candidate for the job and that the president, the vice president (whom the candidate will report to if hired), and perhaps one or more others will interview him or her as a group. You may tell the interviewee what his or her job summary calls for.

Next, interview the candidate, with each interviewer separately keeping notes on his or her own copy of the group's structured interview form. Each interviewer can take turns asking questions.

After the interview, discuss the following questions in the group. Based on each interviewer's notes, how similar were your perceptions of the candidate's responses? Did you all agree on the candidate's potential for the job? Did the candidate ask good questions of his or her interviewers? Did any of the interviewers find themselves jumping to conclusions about the candidate?

CASE INCIDENT
The Out-of-Control Interview

Maria Fernandez is a bright, popular, and well-informed mechanical engineer who graduated with an engineering degree from State University in June 1998. During the spring preceding her graduation she went out on many job interviews, most of which she thought were courteous and reasonably useful in giving both her and the prospective employer a good impression of where each of them stood on matters of importance to both of them. It was, therefore, with great anticipation that she looked forward to an interview with the one firm in which she most wanted to work, Apex Environmental. She had always had a strong interest in cleaning up the environment and firmly believed that the best use of her training and skills lay in working for a firm like Apex, where she thought she could have a successful career while making the world a better place.

The interview, however, was a disaster. Maria walked into a room in which five men, including the president of the company, two vice presidents, the marketing director, and another engineer, began throwing questions at her that she felt were aimed primarily at tripping her up rather than finding out what she could offer through her engineering skills. The questions ranged from unnecessarily discourteous ("Why would you take a job as a waitress in college if you're such an intelligent person?) to irrelevant and sexist ("Are you planning on settling down and starting a family any time soon?). Then, after the interview, she met with two of the gentlemen individually (including the president) and the discussions focused almost exclusively on her technical expertise. She thought that these later discussions went fairly well. However, given the apparent aimlessness and even mean-spiritedness of the panel interview, she was astonished when several days later she got a job offer from the firm.

The offer forced her to consider several matters. From her point of view, the job itself was perfect—she liked what she would be doing, the industry, and the firm's location. And, in fact, the president had been quite courteous in subsequent discussions, as had been the other members of the management team. She was left wondering whether the panel interview had been intentionally tense to see how she'd stand up under pressure, and, if so, why they would do such a thing.

■ QUESTIONS

1. How would you explain the nature of the panel interview Maria had to endure? Specifically, do you think it reflected a well-thought-out interviewing strategy on the part of the firm or carelessness on the part of the firm's management? If it was carelessness, what would you do to improve the interview process at Apex Environmental?

2. Would you take the job offer if you were Maria? If you're not sure, is there any additional information that would help you make your decision, and if so, what is it?

3. The job of applications engineer for which Maria was applying requires: (1) excellent technical skills with respect to mechanical engineering; (2) a commitment to working in the area of pollution control; (3) the ability to deal well and confidently with customers who have engineering problems; (4) a willingness to travel worldwide; and (5) a very intelligent and well-balanced personality. What questions would you ask when interviewing applicants for the job?

Case Application
THE LOST INTERVIEW

Rosa Delillo was tired. It was Friday afternoon, and she had spent the better part of the day interviewing candidates for the position of editorial assistant. Because the new assistant would work for both Rosa and her fellow editor, Keith Harrington, the two colleagues had con-

(continued)

(continued from page 439)

ducted the interviews together. They agreed on the basic requirements of the position—knowledge of Word and Excel, good phone manners, organizational skill, and initiative and an interest in publishing. Rosa thought an older person would make a steady and reliable worker, while Keith preferred a younger assistant whose ambition "would motivate better performance on the job." They had not had a chance to work out a compromise on this point before the candidates began to arrive.

After seeing the first three candidates with Keith, Rosa now faced the prospect of interviewing the last candidate alone. Keith had gone home early, feeling ill.

Rosa had prepared for the interviews carefully, writing down several questions she planned to ask. In fact, between her preparations and the fact that two of the interviews had run longer than planned, she was falling behind in her work and feeling anxious about missing an important deadline. She looked over her notes from this morning's two long interviews and realized with dismay that she had written down almost nothing about either candidate. Keith had done most of the talking. Rosa wondered whether he had prepared any questions; he hadn't asked any that she could recall.

At least the third interview had been shorter, but again Rosa felt she had learned little that she needed to know about the applicant. He'd given the briefest possible answers to her prepared questions, and neither she nor Keith had been able to get him to say very much about himself other than the bare facts of his resume.

Rosa began to wonder whether her questions were the problem. She took her list out and was just looking it over again when her phone rang. The receptionist was sending the final candidate in to see her.

Rosa hung up and looked at her first question. It read, "What did you like least about your last job?"

■ QUESTIONS

1. Is Rosa's fourth interview likely to be more successful than the first three? Why or why not?

2. Do you see any flaws in Rosa's preparations for the interview process? In Keith's?

3. What could Rosa and Keith do differently, both individually and as a team?

APPENDIX 6-1

■ Guidelines for Interviewees

Before you get into a position where you have to do interviewing, you will probably have to navigate some interviews yourself. Here are some hints for excelling in your interview.

The first thing to understand is that interviews are used primarily to help employers determine what you are like as a person.[82] In other words, information regarding how you get along with other people and your desire to work is of prime importance in the interview; your skills and technical expertise are often best assessed through tests and a study of your educational and work history. Interviewers will look first for crisp, articulate answers. Specifically, whether you respond concisely, cooperate fully in answering questions, state personal opinions when relevant, and keep to the subject at hand are by far the most important elements in influencing the interviewer's decision.

There are seven things to do to get that extra edge in the interview.

1. *Preparation is essential.* Before the interview, learn all you can about the employer, the job, and the people doing the recruiting. At the library, look through business periodicals to find out what is happening in the employer's field. Who is the competition? How are they doing? Try to unearth the employer's problems. Be ready to explain why you think you would be able to solve such problems, citing some of your *specific accomplishments* to make your case.

2. *Uncover the interviewer's real needs.* Spend as little time as possible answering your interviewer's first questions and as much time as possible getting him or her to describe his or her needs. Determine what the person is expecting accomplish, and the type of person he or she

feels is needed. Use open-ended questions here such as, "Could you tell me more about that?"

3. *Relate yourself to the interviewer's needs.* Once you know the type of person your interviewer is looking for and the sorts of problems he or she wants solved, you are in a good position to describe your own accomplishments *in terms of the interviewer's needs.* Start by saying something like, "One of the problem areas you've said is important to you is similar to a problem I once faced." Then state the problem, describe your solution, and reveal the results.[83]

4. *Think before answering.*[84] Answering a question should be a three-step process: Pause—Think—Speak. *Pause* to make sure you understand what the interviewer is driving at, *think* about how to structure your answer, and then *speak.* In your answer, try to emphasize how hiring you will help the interviewer solve his or her problem.

5. *Remember that appearance and enthusiasm are important.* Appropriate clothing, good grooming, a firm handshake, and the appearance of controlled energy are important.

6. *Make a good first impression.* Remember, studies show that in most cases interviewers make up their minds about the applicant during the early minutes of the interview. A good first impression may turn to bad during the interview, but it is unlikely. Bad first impressions are almost impossible to overcome. One expert suggests paying attention to the following key interviewing considerations.

1. Appropriate clothing
2. Good grooming
3. A firm handshake
4. The appearance of controlled energy
5. Pertinent humor and readiness to smile
6. A genuine interest in the employer's operation and alert attention when the interviewer speaks
7. Pride in past performance
8. An understanding of the employer's needs and a desire to serve them
9. The display of sound ideas
10. Ability to take control when employers fall down on the interviewing job

Sample questions you can ask are presented in Figure 6-6. They include "Would you mind describing the job for me?" and "Could you tell me about the people who would be reporting to me?"

FIGURE 6-6 *Interview Questions to Ask*

Source: H. Lee Rust, *Job Search: The Complete Manual for Job Seekers* (New York: AMACOM, 1991), pp. 234–235.

1. What is the first problem that needs attention of the person you hire?
2. What other problems need attention now?
3. What has been done about any of these to date?
4. How has this job been performed in the past?
5. Why is it now vacant?
6. Do you have a written job description for this position?
7. What are its major responsibilities?
8. What authority would I have? How would you define its scope?
9. What are the company's five-year sales and profit projections?
10. What needs to be done to reach these projections?
11. What are the company's major strengths and weaknesses?
12. What are its strengths and weaknesses in production?
13. What are its strengths and weaknesses in its products or its competitive position?
14. Whom do you identify as your major competitors?
15. What are their strengths and weaknesses?
16. How do you view the future for your industry?
17. Do you have any plans for new products or acquisitions?
18. Might this company be sold or acquired?
19. What is the company's current financial strength?
20. What can you tell me about the individual to whom I would report?
21. What can you tell me about other persons in key positions?
22. What can you tell me about the subordinates I would have?
23. How would you define your management philosophy?
24. Are employees afforded an opportunity for continuing education?
25. What are you looking for in the person who will fill this job?

7. Remember that your *nonverbal behavior* may broadcast more about you than the verbal content of what you say. Here maintaining eye contact is very important. In addition, speak with enthusiasm, nod agreement, and remember to take a moment to frame your answer (pause, think, speak) so that you sound articulate and fluent.

NOTES

1. Michael McDaniel, et al., "The Validity of Employment Interviews: A Comprehensive Review and Meta-analysis," *Journal of Applied Psychology*, Vol. 79, no. 4 (1994), p. 599. See also Laura Graves and Ronald Karren, "The Employee Selection Interview: A Fresh Look at an Old Problem," *Human Resource Management*, Vol. 35, no. 2 (Summer 1996), pp. 163–180.

2. R. L. Dipboye, *Selection Interviews: Process Perspectives* (Cincinnati: Southwestern Publishing Co., 1992).

3. L. Ulrich and D. Trumbo, "The Selection Interview Since 1949," *Psychological Bulletin*, Vol. 63 (1965), pp. 100–116, quoted in Michael McDaniel, et al., "The Validity of Employment Interviews," p. 599.

4. Laura Gollub Williamson, et al., "Employment Interview on Trial: Linking Interview Structure with Litigation Outcomes," *Journal of Applied Psychology*, Vol. 82, no. 6 (1997), p. 900.

5. Alan Huffcutt, et al., "A Meta-Analytic Investigation of Cognitive Ability in Employment Interview Evaluations: Moderating Characteristics and Implications for Incremental Validity," *Journal of Applied Psychology*, Vol. 81, no. 5 (1996), p. 459.

6. McDaniel, et al., "The Validity of Employment Interviews," p. 602.

7. Michael Campion, David Palmer, and James Campion, "A Review of Structure in the Selection Interview," *Personnel Psychology*, Vol. 50 (1997), pp. 655–702.

8. Laura Gollub Williamson, et al., "Employment Interview on Trial," p. 908.

9. Ibid., p. 601.

10. See, for example, T. Janz, "The Patterned Behavioral Description Interview: The Best Profit of the Future in the Past," in eds. R. W. Eder and G. R. Ferris, *The Employment Interview: Theory, Research, and Practice* (Newbury Park, CA: Sage, 1989), pp. 158–168.

11. McDaniel, et al., "The Validity of Employment Interviews," p. 601.

12. See Philip Roth and Jeffrey McMillan, "The Behavior Description Interview," *The CPA Journal* (December 1993), pp. 76–79.

13. See A. M. Ryan and P. R. Sackett, "Exploratory Study of Individual Assessment Practices: Interrater Reliability and Judgments of Assessor Effectiveness," *Journal of Applied Psychology*, Vol. 74 (1989), pp. 568–579, cited in McDaniel, et al., "The Validity of Employment Interviews," p. 601.

14. Arthur Pell, *Recruiting and Selecting Personnel* (New York: Regents, 1969), p. 119.

15. Douglas Rodgers, "Computer-Aided Interviewing Overcomes First Impressions," *Personnel Journal* (April 1987), pp. 148–152; see also Linda Thornburg, "Computer-Assited Interviewing Shortens Hiring Cycle," *HR Magazine*, Vol. 43, no. 2, February 1998, p. 73ff.

16. Ibid.

17. Gary Robins, "Dial-an-Interview," *Stores* (June 1994), pp. 34–35.

18. William Bulkeley, "Replaced by Technology: Job Interviews," *The Wall Street Journal*, August 22, 1994, pp. B1 and B7.

19. Ibid.

20. For additional information on computer-aided interviewing's benefits, see, for example, Christopher Martin and Denise Nagao, "Some Effects of Computerized Interviewing on Job Applicant Responses," *Journal of Applied Psychology*, Vol. 74, no. 1 (February 1989), pp. 72–80.

21. This is quoted from or paraphrased from William Bulkeley, "Replaced by Technology," pp. B1 and B7.

22. Huffcutt, et al., "A Meta-Analytic Investigation of Cognitive Ability in Employment Interview Evaluations," p. 459.

23. Laura Gollub Williamson, "Employment Interview on Trial," p. 900.

24. Ibid.

25. This validity discussion and these findings are based on McDaniel, et al., "The Validity of Employment Interviews," pp. 607–610; the validities for situational, job-related, and psychological interviews were (.50), (.39), and (.29), respectively.

26. Mean validities were structured (.44) and unstructured (.33). The researchers note that in this case even the unstructured interviews were relatively structured suggesting that "the validity of most unstructured interviews used in practice may be lower than the validity found in this study." Ibid., p. 609.

27. This is based on John F. Wymer III and Deborah A. Subdury, "Employment Discrimination: 'Testers'—Will Your Hiring Practices 'Pass'?" *Employee Relations Law Journal*, Vol. 17, no. 4 (Spring 1992), pp. 623–633. Ibid., pp. 624–625.

28. See for example *Lea v. Cone Mills Corp.*, 438 F2d 86 (1971).

29. Bureau of National Affairs, *Daily Labor Report*, December 5, 1990 at D-1.

30. Wymer and Sudbury, "Employment Discrimination," p. 629.

31. Urban Institute, *Opportunities Denied, Opportunities Diminished: Discrimination in Hiring*.

32. Adapted from Wymer and Sudbury, "Employment Discrimination," pp. 631–632.

33. McDaniel, et al., "The Validity of Employment Interviews," p. 608.

34. Anthony Dalessio and Todd Silverhart, "Combining Biodata Test and Interview Information: Predicting Decisions and Performance Criteria," *Personnel Psychology*, Vol. 47 (1994), p. 313.

35. S. W. Constantin, "An Investigation of Information Favorability in the Employment Interview," *Journal of Applied Psychology*, Vol. 61 (1976), pp. 743–749. It should be noted that a number of the studies discussed in this chapter involve having interviewers evaluate interviews based on written transcripts (rather than face to face)

and that a study suggests that this procedure may not be equivalent to having interviewers interview applicants directly. See Charles Gorman, William Grover, and Michael Doherty, "Can We Learn Anything about Interviewing Real People from 'Interviews' of Paper People? A Study of the External Validity Paradigm," *Organizational Behavior and Human Performance*, Vol. 22, no. 2 (October 1978), pp. 165–192. See also John Binning, et al., "Effects of Pre-interview Impressions on Questioning Strategies in Same and Opposite Sex Employment Interviews," *Journal of Applied Psychology*, Vol. 73, no. 1 (February 1988), pp. 30–37; and Sebastiano Fisicaro, "A Reexamination of the Relation Between Halo Error and Accuracy," *Journal of Applied Psychology*, Vol. 73, no. 2 (May 1988), pp. 239–246.

36. David Tucker and Patricia Rowe, "Relationship Between Expectancy, Casual Attribution, and Final Hiring Decisions in the Employment Interview," *Journal of Applied Psychology*, Vol. 64, no. 1 (February 1979), pp. 27–34. See also Robert Dipboye, Gail Fontenelle, and Kathleen Garner, "Effect of Previewing the Application on Interview Process and Outcomes," *Journal of Applied Psychology*, Vol. 69, no. 1 (February 1984), pp. 118–128.

37. Don Langdale and Joseph Weitz, "Estimating the Influence of Job Information on Interviewer Agreement," *Journal of Applied Psychology*, Vol. 57 (1973), pp. 23–27; for a review of how to determine the human requirements of a job, see Anthony W. Simmons, "Selection Interviewing," *Employment Relations Today* (Winter 1991), pp. 305–309.

38. R. E. Carlson, "Selection Interview Decisions: The Effects of Interviewer Experience, Relative Quota Situation, and Applicant Sample on Interview Decisions," *Personnel Psychology*, Vol. 20 (1967), pp. 259–280.

39. R. E. Carlson, "Effects of Applicant Sample on Ratings of Valid Information in an Employment Setting," *Journal of Applied Psychology*, Vol. 20 (1967), pp. 259–280.

40. See Arvey and Campion, "The Employment Interview," p. 305.

41. T. V. McGovern and H. E. Tinsley, "Interviewer Evaluations of Interviewees' Nonverbal Behavior," *Journal of Vocational Behavior*, Vol. 13 (1978), pp. 163–171. See also Keith Rasmussen, Jr., "Nonverbal Behavior, Verbal Behavior, Resume Credentials, and Selection Interview Outcomes," *Journal of Applied Psychology*, Vol. 60, no. 4 (1984), pp. 551–556; Robert Gifford, Cheuk Fan Ng, and Margaret Wilkinson, "Nonverbal Cues in the Employment Interview: Links Between Applicant Qualities and Interviewer Judgments," *Journal of Applied Psychology*, Vol. 70, no. 4 (1985), pp. 729–736; Scott T. Fleishmann, "The Messages of Body Language in Job Interviews," *Employee Relations*, Vol. 18, no. 2 (Summer 1991), pp. 161–166.

42. David Caldwell and Jerry Burger, "Personality Characteristics of Job Applicants and Success in Screening Interviews," *Personnel Psychology*, Vol. 51 (1998), pp. 119–136.

43. Ibid., p. 130.

44. See, for example, Madelaine Heilmann and Lewis Saruwatari, "When Beauty Is Beastly: The Effects of Appearance and Sex on Evaluation of Job Applicants for Managerial and Nonmanagerial Jobs," *Organizational Behavior and Human Performance*, Vol. 23 (June 1979), pp. 360–372; and Cynthia Marlowe, Sondra Schneider, and Carnot Nelson, "Gender and Attractiveness Biases in Hiring Decisions: Are More Experienced Managers Less Biased?" *Journal of Applied Psychology*, Vol. 81, no. 1 (1996), pp. 11–21.

45. Marlowe, et al., "Gender and Attractiveness Biases," p. 11.

46. Ibid.

47. Ibid., p. 18.

48. Heilmann and Saruwatari, "When Beauty Is Beastly,"

49. Amelia J. Prewett-Livingston, et al., "Effects of Race on Interview Ratings in a Situational Panel Interview," *Journal of Applied Psychology*, Vol. 81, no. 2 (1996), pp. 178–186.

50. Alan Huffcutt and Philip Roth, "Racial Group Differences in Employment Interview Evaluations," *Journal of Applied Psychology*, Vol. 83, no. 2 (1998), pp. 179–189.

51. Ibid., p. 179.

52. Sandra Forsythe, Mary Frances Drake, and Charles Cox, "Influence of Applicants' Dress on Interviewers' Selection Decisions," *Journal of Applied Psychology*, Vol. 70, no. 2 (1985), pp. 374–378.

53. Arthur Pell, "Nine Interviewing Pitfalls," *Managers* (January 1994), p. 20.

54. Thomas Dougherty, Daniel Turban, and John Callender, "Confirming First Impressions in the Employment Interview: A Field Study of Interviewer Behavior," *Journal of Applied Psychology*, Vol. 79, no. 5 (1994), p. 663.

55. See Pell, "Nine Interviewing Pitfalls," p. 29; Parth Sarathi, "Making Selection Interviews Effective," *Management and Labor Studies*, Vol. 18, no. 1 (1993), pp. 5–7.

56. Robert Bretz, Jr. and Timothy Judge, "Realistic Job Previews: A Test of the Adverse Self-Selection Hypothesis," *Journal of Applied Psychology*, Vol. 83, no. 2 (1998), pp. 330–337.

57. See, for example, A. M. Saks, W. H. Wiesner, and R. J. Summers, "Effects of Job Previews on Self-Selection and Job Choice," *Journal of Vocational Behavior*, Vol. 44 (1994), pp. 297–316.

58. Cynthia Kay Stevens, "Antecedents of Interview Interactions, Interviewers' Ratings, and Applicants' Reaction," *Personnel Psychology*, Vol. 51 (1998), p. 55.

59. Ibid., p. 81.

60. Pell, "Nine Interviewing Pitfalls," p. 30.

61. This section based on Pursell, Campion, and Gaylord, "Structured Interviewing," and Latham, et al., "The Situational Interview." See also Michael A. Campion, Elliott Pursell, and Barbara Brown, "Structured Interviewing," pp. 25–42; and Weekley and Gier, "Reliability and Validity of the Situational Interview," pp. 484–487.

62. See also Phillip Lowry, "The Structured Interview: An Alternative to the Assessment Center?" *Public Personnel Management*, Vol. 23, no. 2 (Summer 1994), pp. 201–215. See also Steven Maurer, "The Potential of the Situational Interview: Existing Research and Unresolved Issues," *Human Resource Management Review*, Vol. 7, no. 2 (Summer 1997), p. 185–201.

63. Pursell et al., "Structured Interviewing," p. 910.

64. From a speech by industrial psychologist Paul Green and contained in Bureau of National Affairs, *Bulletin to Management*, June 20, 1985, pp. 2–3.

65. Laura Gollub Williamson, et al., "Employment Interview on Trial," p. 901.

66. Ibid.; Michael Campion, David Palmer, and James Campion, "A Review of Structure in the Selection Interview," *Personnel Psychology*, Vol. 50 (1997), pp. 655–702.

67. Ibid., p. 690.

68. Unless otherwise specified, the following are based on Laura Gollub Williamson, et al., "Employment Interview on Trial," pp. 901–902.

69. Campion, Palmer, and Campion, "A Review of Structure," pp. 662–663.

70. Williamson, et al., "Employment Interview on Trial," p. 901.

71. Campion, Palmer, and Campion, "A Review of Structure," p. 668.

72. Carlson, "Selection Interview Decisions," pp. 259–280.

73. William Tullar, Terry Mullins, and Sharon Caldwell, "Effects of Interview Length and Applicant Quality on Interview Decision, Time," *Journal of Applied Psychology*, Vol. 64 (December 1979), pp. 669–674. See also Tracy McDonald and Milton Hakel, "Effects of Applicants' Race, Sex, Suitability, and Answers on Interviewers' Questioning Strategy and Ratings," *Personnel Psychology*, Vol. 38, no. 2 (Summer 1985), pp. 321–334; see also David Caldwell and Jerry Burger, "Personality Characteristics of Job Applicants and Success in Screening Interviews" *Personnel Psychology*, Vol. 51, no. 1, Spring 1998, pp. 119–136

74. Edwin Walley, "Successful Interviewing Techniques," *The CPA Journal* (September 1993), p. 70.

75. Pamela Kaul, "Interviewing Is Your Business," *Association Management* (November 1992), p. 29.

76. Jennifer Burnett, Chenche Fan, Stephan Motowidlo, and Tim DeGroot, "Interview Notes and Validity," *Personnel Psychology*, Vol. 51 (1998), pp. 375–396.

77. Ibid., p. 395.

78. Robin Rimmer Hurst, "Video Interviewing. Take One!" *HR Magazine*, Vol. 41, no. 11 (November 1996), pp. 100–104.

79. This is based on John Drake, *Interviewing for Managers: A Complete Guide to Employment Interviewing* (New York: AMACOM, 1982).

80. Ibid.

81. Based on Gary Dessler, *Winning Commitment* (New York: McGraw-Hill Book Company, 1993). Similarly, see Glenn Bassett, "From Job Fit to Cultural Compatibility: Evaluating Worker Skills and Temperament in the 90s," *Optimum, The Journal of Public Sector Management*, Vol. 25, no. 2 (Summer 1994), pp. 11–17.

82. James Hollandsworth, Jr., et al., "Relative Contributions of Verbal, Articulative, and Nonverbal Communication to Employment Decisions in the Job Interview Setting," *Personnel Psychology*, Vol. 32 (Summer 1979), pp. 359–367. See also Sara Rynes and Howard Miller, "Recruiter and Job Influences on Candidates for Employment," *Journal of Applied Psychology*, Vol. 68, no. 1 (1983), pp. 147–154.

83. Richard Payne, *How to Get a Better Job Quickly* (New York: New American Library, 1979).

84. J. C. Hollandsworth, R. C. Ladinski, and J. H. Russel, "Use of Social Skills Training in the Treatment of Extreme-Anxiety of Deficient Verbal Skills," *Journal of Applied Psychology*, Vol. 11 (1979), pp. 259–269; see also Carolyn Hirschman, "Playing the High-Stakes Hiring Game," *HR Magazine*, Vol. 43, no. 4, March 1998, pp. 80–89.

VIDEO CASE

PART II
INTERVIEWING JOB CANDIDATES

JOB INTERVIEWS ARE AMONG THE MOST STRESSFUL SITUATIONS MOST OF US FACE AT WORK. WHILE WE NORMALLY ONLY THINK OF HOW "ON THE SPOT" WE FEEL AS JOB APPLICANTS, REMEMBER THAT THE INTERVIEWER, TOO, CAN BE UNDER STRESS. AS YOU KNOW FROM READING CHAPTER 6, INTERVIEWERS ARE SUBJECT TO PRESSURE TO HIRE, CONTRAST ERROR, NEGATIVE EMPHASIS, POOR KNOWLEDGE OF THE JOB TO BE FILLED, THE TENDENCY TO USE SNAP JUDGMENTS, TELEGRAPHING, OR AMATEUR PSYCHOLOGY. IT IS ALSO SURPRISINGLY EASY TO TALK TOO MUCH OR TOO LITTLE. ALL THESE PITFALLS CAN AFFECT THE OUTCOME OF THE INTERVIEW, MAKING IT IMPORTANT FOR THE INTERVIEWER TO BE AWARE OF AND AVOID THEM.

Structured interviews, with their prepared situational, willingness, and job knowledge questions, are designed to assist interviewers in reaching objective conclusions about candidates. Recall that all three types of questions are hypothetical job-oriented questions with predetermined answers that are consistently asked of all applicants for the job. When applicants' answers are compared, the result is usually an unbiased basis for comparing their job skills, willingness and motivation to work, and quality of judgment and decision-making skill.

You may already have interview experience, on either side of the desk. Have you ever interviewed for a job and been nervous and anxious to make a good impression? You may have worried about saying too much or too little, or you may have felt unprepared for the questions you were asked.

While you might at first identify with Quicktakes' new job applicant, Mary Byrns, you should also try to see the situation in the video from Hal's point of view. He's looking for a new producer, and in a small company such as Quicktakes it is difficult to invest a great deal of time in training new employees who have little or no experience. Hal therefore needs someone who can get off to a quick start and maintain a high degree of self-motivation. Try to evaluate Mary's potential as a self-starter based on her behavior in the interview.

Be prepared, too, to evaluate Hal's interviewing skills. Since there is no Human Resource Department at Quicktakes, Hal, like managers at many small-to-medium-sized firms, has the responsibility both for screening job candidates and for making the final hiring decision. How well does he put Mary at ease, and how does he react to her volunteering information about herself? Does he make any interviewing errors?

QUESTIONS

1. Did Hal conduct a structured interview? Justify your answer.

2. Hal has rated Mary "a strong candidate for the job." How do you think he arrived at this conclusion? Do you agree with his assessment? Why or why not?

3. What other facts about Mary's background and experience do you think Hal should have before he makes a decision about whether to hire her? (Assume that her resume provides a brief job history and basic personal data.) How should Hal go about finding this information?

4. What should Mary know about Quicktakes before she decides whether to accept any offer that Hal may make? How can she find this out?

5. How could Hal have better prepared himself for the interview? How could Mary?

TRAINING AND DEVELOPING EMPLOYEES

7

As global competition in the automotive components industry rose, Illinois-based Borg-Warner knew it required a new strategy. Adopting new automated manufacturing processes and equipment would certainly boost the firm's competitiveness. But that strategy also required new worker skills—workers would have to participate as team members, play an active role in the plant's quality efforts, and adapt to the new technologies. Thus, a massive training and development effort emphasizing teamwork, basic literacy, and charting statistical data had to support the firm's new strategy. ▲

Behavioral Objectives

After studying this chapter, you should be able to:

▲ *Describe* the basic training process.
▲ *Explain* the nature of at least five training techniques.
▲ *Discuss* what management development is and why it's important.
▲ *Describe* the five on- and off-the-job development techniques.
▲ *Explain* why training evaluation is important and how it is best accomplished.

Chapter Outline

▲ Orienting Employees
▲ The Training Process
▲ Training Techniques
▲ Training for Special Purposes
▲ Managerial Development and Training Techniques
▲ Evaluating the Training Effort

Once employees have been recruited and selected, the next step is orientation and training. This involves providing them with the information and skills they need to successfully perform their jobs.

ORIENTING EMPLOYEES

employee orientation

A procedure for providing new employees with basic background information about the firm.

Employee orientation provides new employees with basic background information they need to perform their jobs satisfactorily, such as information about company rules. Orientation is actually part of the employer's new-employee socialization process. *Socialization* is the ongoing process of instilling in all employees the prevailing attitudes, standards, values, and patterns of behavior that are expected by the organization and its departments.[1]

Orientation programs range from brief, informal introductions to lengthy, formal programs. In either, new employees usually get a handbook or printed materials that cover things like working hours, performance reviews, getting on the payroll, and vacations, as well as a tour of the facilities. As illustrated in Figure 7-1, other handbook information typically includes employee benefits, personnel policies, the employee's daily routine, company organization and operations, and safety measures and regulations.[2] (There is the real possibility that courts will find your employee handbook's contents represent a contract with the employee. Therefore, disclaimers should be included that make it clear that statements of company policies, benefits, and regulations do not constitute the terms and conditions of an employment contract either expressed or implied. Also, think twice before including statements in your handbook such as "No employee will be fired without just cause" or statements that imply or state that employees have tenure; these could be viewed as legal and binding commitments.)

The first part of the orientation is usually performed by the HR specialist, who explains such matters as working hours and vacations. The employee is then introduced to his or her new supervisor. The latter continues the orientation by explaining the exact nature of the job, introducing the person to his or her new colleagues, familiarizing the new employee with the workplace, and hopefully helping to reduce the new person's first day jitters.

As in most human endeavors, not all new hires react to the orientation process in exactly the same way. In one study, for instance, people with a relatively high desire to control and master their environment sought more information, socialized more, networked more with interdepartmental colleagues, and tried to put a more positive frame around their situations than did those with a lower desire for control.[3] It therefore seems that supervisors should be vigilant and follow up and encourage new employees to engage in those activities that will enable each to "learn the ropes" and become productive as quickly as possible.

THE TRAINING PROCESS

training

The process of teaching new employees the basic skills they need to perform their jobs.

Introduction

Training refers to the methods used to give new or present employees the skills they need to perform their jobs. Training might thus mean showing a machinist how to operate his new machine, a new salesperson how to sell her firm's product, or a new supervisor how to interview and appraise employees.

Training's focus has broadened in the past few years. Training used to focus mostly on teaching technical skills, such as training assemblers to solder wires or teachers to devise lesson plans.[4] However, technical training like that is no longer sufficient. For one thing, in the past decade employers have had to adapt to rapid technological changes, improve product and service quality, and boost productivity to stay competitive.[5] Improving quality may in turn require remedial-education training (since quality-improvement programs require employees who can produce charts and graphs and analyze data).[6] Similarly, employees today need skills (and thus training) in team building, decision making,

Orientation Checklist
(Small southern manufacturing company)

HOURLY & SALARIED EMPLOYEE ORIENTATION GUIDE CHECKLIST
NOTE: ALL APPROPRIATE INFORMATION MUST BE DISCUSSED WITH EACH NEW EMPLOYEE

SUPERVISOR: This form is to be used as a guide for the orientation of new employees in your department.

In order to avoid duplication of instruction the information indicated below has been given to the employee by the Personnel Department.

PERSONNEL DEPARTMENT

EEO BOOKLET		ABSENCES - TARDINESS	
INSURANCE PROGRAM BOOKLET		VETERANS' RE-EMPLOYMENT RIGHTS & RESERVE STATUS	
SALARY CONTINUANCE INSURANCE BOOKLET		UNITED FUND	
SAFETY BOOKLET		VACATIONS	
PENSION PLAN BOOKLET		JURY DUTY	
EMPLOYEE HANDBOOK/LABOR AGREEMENT/RULES BOOKLET		SICK BENEFITS – A & S – LIMITATIONS, ETC.	
MATCHING GIFTS		LEAVE OF ABSENCE - MATERNITY - MEDICAL, ETC.	
EDUCATIONAL ASSISTANCE PROGRAM		SERVICE AWARDS	
PATENT AGREEMENT		VISITORS	
I.D. CARD		HOLIDAYS	
CREDIT UNION		FOOD SERVICES	
STOCK PURCHASE PLAN		FIRST AID & REQUIREMENTS OF REPORTING INJURY	
SAVINGS BOND PLAN		DIFFICULTIES, COMPLAINTS, DISCRIMINATION & GRIEVANCE PROCED.	
PROBATIONARY PERIOD		MILL TOUR	
PAY, SALARY, PROMOTIONS AND TRANSFERS		TERMINATION NOTICE AND PAY ESP. VACATION ALLOWANCE (VOLUNTARY RESIGNATION)	
TRANSPORTATION			
TIME SHEET		INTRODUCTION TO GUARDS	
PERSONAL RECORDS		(OTHERS)	
BULLETIN BOARDS			
PERSONAL MAIL			
PARKING FACILITIES			

SIGNATURE OF EMPLOYEE:	WITNESS:		DATE

SUPERVISOR: The following is a check list of information necessary to orient the new employee to the job in your department. Please check off each point as you discuss it with the employee and return to the Personnel Department within three days following employee placement on the job:

INTRODUCTION TO FELLOW EMPLOYEES		HOURS OF WORK - OVERTIME - CALL IN PROCEDURES	
TOUR OF DEPARTMENT		REST, LUNCH PERIODS	
EXPLANATION OF NEW EMPLOYEES JOB, RESPONSIBILITIES AND PERFORMANCE EVALUATIONS		SUPPLY PROCEDURE	
		LINE OF AUTHORITY	
LAVATORY			
PHONE CALLS - PERSONAL/COMPANY			

SIGNATURE OF SUPERVISOR:		DATE

I have received a copy of the appropriate materials listed above and have had explained to me the information outlined. I understand this information concerning my employment with (Company name). Also, in case of voluntary separation (resignation) I understand the Company's policy, that in order to be eligible for any due vacation allowance, I must give my supervisor at least two weeks' notice in writing prior to my last day of work.

SIGNATURE OF EMPLOYEE:	WITNESS:		DATE

FIGURE 7-1 *Overview of Orientation Program*

Source: Handbook of Modern Personnel Administration by Joseph Famularo. Copyright 1985, McGraw-Hill Book Company. Used with permission of McGraw-Hill, Inc.

and communication, as well as technological and computer skills (such as desktop publishing and computer-aided design and manufacturing).[7] And as competition demands better service, employees increasingly require customer-service training for the tools and abilities required to service customers.

New training demands like these help explain why the training business is booming. In one recent survey about 84% of employees reportedly received some type of formal training while with their current employers.[8] On average, employees annually received about 45 hours of training, about one-third of which was formal, and two-thirds informal training.[9] In another study, 41% of surveyed firms reported that their training budgets increased between 1995 and 1996, and would increase again for 1997.[10]

Unfortunately, a "training gap" exists and may be widening. While some companies—IBM, Xerox, Texas Instruments, and Motorola for instance—devoted 5% to 10% of their payroll dollars to training activities, the average training investment by U.S. firms (while large in dollar terms) is less than 2% of payroll.[11] Experts estimate that between 42% and 90% of U.S. workers need further training to get them up to speed.[12]

The Five-Step Training and Development Process

We can conveniently think of training programs as consisting of five steps, as summarized in Figure 7-2. The purpose of *needs analysis* is to identify the specific job performance skills needed, to analyze the skills and needs of the prospective trainees, and to develop specific, measurable knowledge and performance objectives. (Here make sure that the performance deficiency is amenable to training rather than caused by, say, poor morale

FIGURE 7-2

The Five Steps in the Training and Development Process

Source: These are adapted from Mary D. Carolan, "Today's Training Basics: Some New Golden Rules," *HR Focus* (April 1993), p. 18.

1. NEEDS ANALYSIS

- Identify specific job performance skills needed to improve performance and productivity.
- Analyze the audience to ensure that the program will be suited to their specific levels of education, experience, and skills, as well as their attitudes and personal motivations.
- Use research to develop specific measurable knowledge and performance objectives.

2. INSTRUCTIONAL DESIGN

- Gather instructional objectives, methods, media, description of and sequence of content, examples, exercises, and activities. Organize them into a curriculum that supports adult learning theory and provides a blueprint for program development.
- Make sure all materials, such as video scripts, leaders' guides, and participants' workbooks, complement each other, are written clearly, and blend into unified training geared directly to the stated learning objectives.
- Carefully and professionally handle all program elements—whether reproduced on paper, film, or tape—to guarantee quality and effectiveness.

3. VALIDATION

- Introduce and validate the training before a representative audience. Base final revisions on pilot results to ensure program effectiveness.

4. IMPLEMENTATION

- When applicable, boost success with a train-the-trainer workshop that focuses on presentation knowledge and skills in addition to training content.

5. EVALUATION AND FOLLOW-UP

- Assess program success according to:
  REACTION—Document that learners' immediate reactions to the training.
  LEARNING—Use feedback devices or pre- and posttests to measure what learners have actually learned.
  BEHAVIOR—Note supervisors' reactions to learners' performance following completion of the training. This is one way to measure the degree to which learners apply new skills and knowledge to their jobs.
  RESULTS—Determine the level of improvement in job performance and assess needed maintenance.

due to low salaries.) In the second, *instructional design* step, the actual content of the training program is compiled and produced including workbooks, exercises, and activities. Next, there may be a third *validation* step in which the bugs are worked out of the training program by presenting it to a small representative audience. Fourth, the training program is *implemented,* using techniques like those discussed in this chapter (such as on-the-job training and programmed learning). Fifth, there should be an *evaluation* and follow-up step in which the program's successes or failures are assessed.

Most employers probably don't, and needn't, create their own training materials, since there are many prepackaged materials already available. For example, many companies, including American Media, Inc. of West Des Moines, Iowa, offer training packages. These include training leader's guide, self-study book, and video for improving skills in areas such as customer service, documenting discipline, and appraising performance (see, for example, Figure 7-3).

FIGURE 7-3

American Media Inc. Brochure

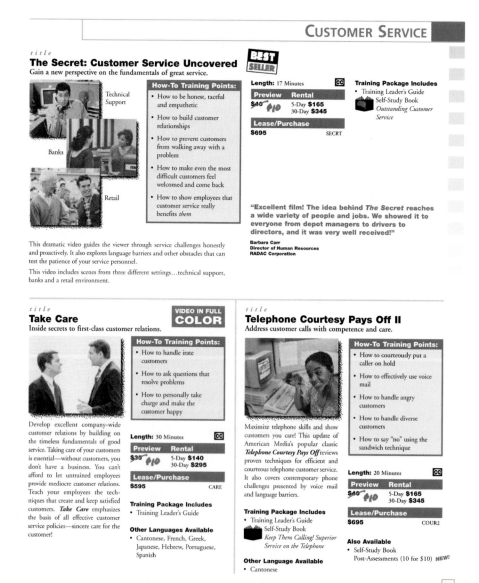

Training and Learning

Training is essentially a learning process. We should therefore start with a quick review of how people learn. First, keep in mind that it's easier for trainees to understand and remember material that is meaningful.[13] Therefore:

1. At the start of training, provide the trainees with a bird's-eye view of the material to be presented. Knowing the overall picture facilitates learning.
2. Use a variety of familiar examples when presenting material.
3. Organize the material so that it is presented in a logical manner and in meaningful units.
4. Try to use terms and concepts that are already familiar to trainees.
5. Use as many visual aids as possible.

Second, make sure it is easy to transfer new skills and behaviors from the training site to the job site:[14]

1. Maximize the similarity between the training situation and the work situation.
2. Provide adequate training practice.
3. Label or identify each feature of the machine and/or step in the process.

Third, motivate the trainee:[15]

1. People learn best by doing. Try to provide as much realistic practice as possible.
2. Trainees learn best when correct responses are immediately reinforced, perhaps with a quick "well done."
3. Trainees learn best at their own pace. If possible, let trainees pace themselves.

RESEARCH INSIGHT   Fourth, effectively prepare the trainees. Recent research evidence shows that the trainee's pretraining preparation is a crucial step in the training process. For example,

1. Create a perceived need for training in the minds of participants.[16] In one study pilots who had experienced pretraining accident-related negative events subsequently learned more from an accident-reduction training program than did those experiencing fewer pretraining negative experiences.[17] You can similarly illustrate the need for the training in other training situations. Creating a perceived need for the training in the minds of the training participants is thus a sensible first step to take before the formal training even begins.
2. Direct the trainees' attention to important aspects of the job they should be aware of. For example, in training customer service representatives about how to quickly handle incoming calls, first alert them to the different types of calls they will encounter and how to recognize such calls.[18]
3. Provide preparatory information to help set the trainees' expectations about the events and consequences of actions that are likely to occur in the training environment and (eventually) on the job. For example, trainees learning to become first-line supervisors might face stressful conditions, high workload, and difficult subordinates. Studies suggest you can reduce the negative impact of such events by preparing trainees ahead of time, by letting them know what might occur.[19]

Legal Aspects of Training

Equal employment laws are quite relevant to designing and implementing training programs.[20] For example, selecting relatively few women or minorities to be trained may eventually require you to show that your admissions procedures are valid—that they predict performance in the training program or on the job for which the person is being trained. For example, it could turn out that the reading level of your training manuals is too high for many minority trainees, and that they are thus doing poorly in the program quite aside from their aptitude for the jobs for which they are being trained.

Negligent training is another potential legal pitfall. *Negligent training* occurs when an employer fails to train adequately, and an employee subsequently harms a third party.[21] Courts will find the employer liable in cases of negligent training, particularly when the employer's business or service is oriented toward serving the public.[22] Precautions to take include:

1. Confirm claims of skill and experience for all applicants.[23]
2. Reduce the risks of harm by extensively training any employees who work with dangerous equipment, materials, or processes.
3. Ensure that the training includes procedures to protect third-parties' health and safety (including that of other employees).
4. Evaluate the training activity to determine its effectiveness in reducing negligence risks.

Training Needs Analysis

The first step in training is to determine what training, if any, is required. Your main task in assessing the training needs of new employees is to determine what the job entails and to break it down into subtasks, each of which is then taught to the new employee. Assessing the training needs of *current* employees can be more complex, since you have the added task of deciding whether or not training is the solution. For example, performance may be down because the standards aren't clear or because the person isn't motivated.

task analysis

A detailed study of a job to identify the skills required so that an appropriate training program may be instituted.

performance analysis

Verifying that there is a performance deficiency and determining whether that deficiency should be rectified through training or through some other means (such as transferring the employee).

Task analysis and **performance analysis** are two main ways to identify training needs. About 19% of employers reporting in one survey said they used *task analysis*—an analysis of the job's requirements—to determine the training required.[24] Task analysis is especially appropriate for determining the training needs of employees who are new to their jobs. *Performance analysis* appraises the performance of current employees to determine whether training could reduce performance problems like excess scrap or low output. Other techniques used to identify training needs include supervisors' reports, personnel records, management requests, observations, tests of job knowledge, and questionnaire surveys.[25]

Whichever technique is used—task analysis, performance analysis, or some other—employee input is essential. It's often true that no one knows as much about the job as the people actually doing it and so soliciting employee input is usually wise.[26]

Task Analysis: Assessing the Training Needs of New Employees

Task analysis is used to determine the training needs of employees who are new to their jobs. Particularly with lower-level workers, it is common to hire inexperienced personnel and train them.[27] Here your aim is to develop the skills and knowledge required for effective performance, and so the training is usually based on task analysis. This is a detailed study of the job to determine what specific skills—like soldering (in the case of an assembly worker) or interviewing (in the case of a supervisor)—the job requires.

Job descriptions and job specifications are helpful here. These list the job's specific duties and skills and provide the basic reference point in determining the training required for performing the job.

TASK ANALYSIS RECORD FORM   Some employers supplement the current job description and specification with a task analysis record form. This consolidates information regarding the job's required tasks and skills in a form that's especially helpful for determining training requirements. As illustrated in Table 7-1, a Task Analysis Record Form contains six types of information: *Column 1, Task List*—Here the job's main tasks and subtasks are listed. *Column 2, How Often Performed*—Here you indicate the frequency with which the task and subtasks are performed. *Column 3, Quantity, Quality Standards*—Here indicate the standards of performance for each task and subtask, in measurable

TABLE 7-1   Task Analysis Record Form

TASK LIST	WHEN AND HOW OFTEN PERFORMED	QUANTITY AND QUALITY OF PERFORMANCE	CONDITIONS UNDER WHICH PERFORMED	SKILLS OR KNOWLEDGE REQUIRED	WHERE BEST LEARNED
1. Operate paper cutter	4 times per day		Noisy pressroom: distractions		
1.1 Start motor					
1.2 Set cutting distance		±tolerance of 0.007 in.		Read gauge	On the job
1.3 Place paper on cutting table		Must be completely even to prevent uneven cut		Lift paper correctly	On the job
1.4 Push paper up to cutter				Must be even	On the job
1.5 Grasp safety release with left hand		100% of time, for safety		Essential for safety	On the job but practice first with no distractions
1.6 Grasp cutter release with right hand				Must keep both hands on releases	On the job but practice first with no distractions
1.7 Simultaneously pull safety release with left hand and cutter release with right hand					
1.8 Wait for cutter to retract		100% of time, for safety		Must keep both hands on releases	On the job but practice first with no distractions
1.9 Retract paper				Wait till cutter retracts	On the job but practice first with no distractions
1.10 Shut off		100% of time, for safety			On the job but practice first with no distractions
2. Operate printing press					
2.1 Start motor					

Note: Task analysis record form showing some of tasks and subtasks performed by a printing press operator.

terms like "± tolerance of 0.007 in.," or "within two days of receiving the order." *Column 4, Performance Conditions*—Here indicate the conditions under which the tasks and subtasks are to be performed. *Column 5, Skills Required*—This is the heart of the task analysis form. Here you list the skills or knowledge required for each of the tasks and subtasks, specifying exactly what knowledge or skills you must teach the trainee. Thus, for the subtask "set cutting distance," the person must be taught how to read the gauge. And, *Column 6, Where Best Learned*—Here (based, for instance, on safety considerations), you indicate whether the task is learned best on or off the job.

Performance Analysis: Determining the Training Needs of Current Employees

Performance analysis means verifying that there is a significant performance deficiency and determining whether that deficiency should be rectified through training or through some other means (such as transferring the employee). The first step is to appraise the employee's performance, since to improve it, you must first compare the person's current performance to what it should be. Examples of specific performance deficiencies follow:

> "I expect each salesperson to make ten new contacts per week, but John averages only six."
>
> "Other plants our size average no more than two serious accidents per month; we're averaging five."

Distinguishing between *can't do* and *won't do* problems is the heart of performance analysis. First, determine whether it's a *can't do* problem and, if so, its specific causes—the employees don't know what to do or what your standards are; there are obstacles in the system such as lack of tools or supplies; job aids are needed, such as color-coded wires that show assemblers which wire goes where or electronic Performance Support Systems that provide employees with on-screen, computerized, step-by-step instructions—for example, on how to respond to a caller's request; poor selection results in hiring people who haven't the skills to do the job; or training is inadequate. On the other hand, it might be a *won't do* problem. Here employees *could* do a good job if they wanted to. If so, perhaps the reward system might be changed, perhaps by installing an incentive system. Once the needs analysis is complete, objectives can be set: These should specify what the Trainee should be able to accomplish upon completing the training program.

THE HIGH-PERFORMANCE ORGANIZATION

Building Better, Faster, More Competitive Organizations Through HR: An Employee Testing and Training Program

■ Sacramento Manufacturing and Services Division—Sacramento, CA

SMSD has implemented a new employee testing and training program. It is designed to train employees in those areas specifically required for their jobs, prepare them for ISO 9000 compliance, and also foster pride and morale. The program has been in operation since 1992.

The employee training and testing program was established to ensure that employees have the knowledge required for their respective job series classifications. It was also intended to give employees the ability to compete for workload, improve morale, and instill pride in quality of workmanship. The program is based on the Air Force Management Occupational Templates which provide the knowledge and skill requirements for each job classification. Tests are developed by subject matter experts on each of the subjects listed in the AFM Occupational Templates. Employees are scheduled to take tests required for their specific job series, and are given credit for full qualification in the subjects for which they receive passing grades. A training matrix has been developed to show training requirements based on test results. Employees are scheduled for training based on individual needs, priorities, and work schedules.

The process was developed in consultation with the union, which supports the concept and helps facilitate its implementation. SMSD has seen positive effects from this program and acknowledges the need to do the training assessment and training program as early as possible in an employee's career. Other lessons learned include establishing a policy to identify training needs at the time of employment and the importance of considering employee training in long-range plans.

Over 70% of the division has completed the training program, producing a significantly improved and effective work force. Employees are now trained only on those subjects they need, to conserve time and resources. Employees also have greater confidence in their ability to perform their jobs. Productivity and morale have improved markedly and employees now have more options and feel better prepared to face the uncertainties of base closure and privatization.

Source: Copyright 1998, Best Manufacturing Practices Center of Excellence.

TRAINING TECHNIQUES

on-the-job training (OJT)
Training a person to learn a job while working at it.

On-the-Job Training

On-the-job training (OJT) means having a person learn a job by actually performing it. Virtually every employee, from mailroom clerk to company president, gets some on-the-job training when he or she joins a firm. In many companies, OJT is the only type of training available. It usually involves assigning new employees to experienced workers or supervisors who then do the actual training.[28]

There are several types of on-the-job training. The most familiar is the coaching or understudy method. Here the employee is trained by an experienced worker or the trainee's supervisor. At lower levels trainees may acquire skills for, say, running a machine, by observing the supervisor. But this technique is also widely used at top-management levels. The position of assistant is often used to train and develop the company's future top managers, for instance. Job rotation, in which an employee (usually a management trainee) moves from job to job at planned intervals, is another OJT technique. Special assignments similarly give lower-level executives firsthand experience in working on actual problems.

OJT has several advantages. It is relatively inexpensive; trainees learn while producing; and there is no need for expensive off-job facilities like classrooms or programmed learning devices. The method also facilitates learning, since trainees learn by actually doing the job and get quick feedback about the correctness of their performance.

However, there are several trainer-related factors to keep in mind when designing OJT programs.[29] The trainers themselves should be carefully trained and given the necessary training materials. (Often, instead, an experienced worker is simply told to "go train John.") Experienced workers who are chosen as trainers should be thoroughly trained in the proper methods of instruction—in particular the principles of learning and perhaps the step-by-step job instruction technique that we address next.

On-the-job training is usually an effective way to learn because it can be structured and concrete. Here a supervisor teaches an employee how to use a drum forming machine.

STEP 1: PREPARATION OF THE LEARNER

1. Put the learner at ease—relieve the tension.
2. Explain why he or she is being taught.
3. Create interest, encourage questions, find out what the learner already knows about his or her job or other jobs.
4. Explain the why of the whole job and relate it to some job the worker already knows.
5. Place the learner as close to the normal working position as possible.
6. Familiarize the worker with the equipment, materials, tools, and trade terms.

STEP 2: PRESENTATION OF THE OPERATION

1. Explain quantity and quality requirements.
2. Go through the job at the normal work pace.
3. Go through the job at a slow pace several times, explaining each step. Between operations, explain the difficult parts, or those in which errors are likely to be made.
4. Again go through the job at a slow pace several times; explain the key points.
5. Have the learner explain the steps as you go through the job at a slow pace.

STEP 3: PERFORMANCE TRYOUT

1. Have the learner go through the job several times, slowly, explaining each step to you. Correct mistakes and, if necessary, do some of the complicated steps the first few times.
2. You, the trainer, run the job at the normal pace.
3. Have the learner do the job, gradually building up skill and speed.
4. As soon as the learner demonstrates ability to do the job, let the work begin, but don't abandon him or her.

STEP 4: FOLLOW-UP

1. Designate to whom the learner should go for help if he or she needs it.
2. Gradually decrease supervision, checking work from time to time against quality and quantity standards.
3. Correct faulty work patterns that begin to creep into the work, and do it before they become a habit. Show why the learned method is superior.
4. Compliment good work; encourage the worker until he or she is able to meet the quality/quantity standards.

Apprenticeship Training

More employers are going "back to the future" by implementing apprenticeship training programs, an approach that began in the Middle Ages. Apprenticeship training is a structured process by which individuals become skilled workers through a combination of classroom instruction and on-the-job training. It is widely used to train individuals for many occupations including electrician and plumber.[30]

Apprenticeship training basically involves having the learner/apprentice study under the tutelage of a master craftsman.[31] In Germany, for instance, students ages 15 to 18 often divide their time between classroom instruction in vocational schools and part-time work under the master craftsman. The apprenticeship lasts about 3 years and ends with a certification examination.

Several U.S. facilities are successfully using this approach. For example, the Siemens Stromberg-Carlson plant in Florida has apprenticeships for adults and high school students for jobs such as electronics technicians:

> Adults work on the factory floor, receive classroom instruction at Seminole Community College, and also study at the plant's hands-on apprenticeship lab. Graduates receive Associates Degrees in telecommunications and electronics engineering. High school students spend two afternoons per week at the apprenticeship lab.[32]

Informal Learning

About two-thirds of industrial training isn't "formal" at all, but rather results from day-to-day unplanned interactions between the new worker and his or her colleagues.[33] Informal learning may be defined as "any learning that occurs in which the learning process isn't determined or designed by the organization."[34]

Although informal learning isn't predetermined or predesigned by the organization, there's still quite a bit you can do to make sure such learning takes place. Most of the steps are surprisingly simple. For example, Siemens Power Transmission and Distribution in Raleigh, North Carolina, places tools in cafeteria areas to take advantage of the work-related brainstorming going on there amidst the usual social banter.[35] Other companies have installed high round tables so people can perch on stools or can stand during impromptu meetings. Even something as simple as installing white boards and keeping them stocked with markers for quick shift change notes can facilitate informal learning.

Job Instruction Training

job instruction training (JIT)

Listing of each job's basic tasks, along with key points in order to provide step-by-step training for employees.

Many jobs consist of a logical sequence of steps and are best taught step-by-step. This step-by-step process is called **job instruction training (JIT)**. To begin, list all necessary steps in the job, each in its proper sequence. Alongside each step also list a corresponding "key point" (if any). The steps show *what* is to be done, whereas the key points show *how* it's to be done—and why. Here is an example of a job instruction training sheet for teaching a trainee how to operate a large motorized paper cutter.

Steps	Key Points
1. Start motor	None
2. Set cutting distance	Carefully read scale—to prevent wrong-sized cut
3. Place paper on cutting table	Make sure paper is even—to prevent uneven cut
4. Push paper up to cutter	Make sure paper is tight—to prevent uneven cut
5. Grasp safety release with left hand	Do not release left hand—to prevent hand from being caught in cutter
6. Grasp cutter release with right hand	Do not release right hand—to prevent hand from being caught in cutter
7. Simultaneously pull cutter and safety releases	Keep both hands on corresponding releases—to avoid hands being on cutting table
8. Wait for cutter to retract	Keep both hands on releases—to avoid having hands on cutting table
9. Retract paper	Make sure cutter is retracted; keep both hands away from releases
10. Shut off motor	None

Lectures

Lecturing has several advantages. It is a quick and simple way to provide knowledge to large groups of trainees, as when the sales force must be taught the special features of a new product. While written material like books and manuals could be used instead, they may involve considerable printing expense, and they don't permit the give and take of questioning that lectures do.

Some useful guidelines for presenting your lecture follow:[36]

Give your listeners signals to help them follow your ideas. For instance, if you have a list of items, start by saying something like "There are four reasons why the sales reports are necessary. . . . The first . . . the second. . . ."

Don't start out on the wrong foot. For instance, don't open with an irrelevant joke or story or by saying something like, "I really don't know why I was asked to speak here today."

Keep your conclusions short. Just summarize your main point or points in one or two succinct sentences.

Be alert to your audience. Watch body language for negative signals like fidgeting and crossed arms.

Maintain eye contact with the trainees in the program. At a minimum you should look at each section of the audience during your presentation.

Make sure everyone in the room can hear. Use a mike or talk loudly enough so that you can be heard by people in the last row and if necessary repeat questions that you get from trainees from the front of the room before you answer.

Control your hands. Get in the habit of leaving them hanging naturally at your sides rather than letting them drift to your face, then your pockets, then your back, and so on. Putting your hands near your face can block your voice projection and also give the impression that you lack confidence in what you are saying.

Talk from notes rather than from a script. Write out clear, legible notes on large index cards and then use these as an outline rather than memorizing your whole presentation.

Eliminate bad habits. Beware of distracting your listeners by jiggling coins in your pocket or pulling on an earlobe.

Practice. If you have the time, make sure to rehearse under conditions similar to those under which you will actually give your presentation.

Programmed Learning

programmed learning
A systematic method for teaching job skills involving presenting questions or facts, allowing the person to respond, and giving the learner immediate feedback on the accuracy of his or her answers.

Whether the programmed instruction device is a textbook or a computer, **programmed learning** consists of three functions:

1. Presenting questions, facts, or problems to the learner
2. Allowing the person to respond
3. Providing feedback on the accuracy of his or her answers

A page from a programmed instruction book for learning calculus is presented in Figure 7-4. Note how facts and questions are presented. The learner can then respond, and the book gives feedback on the accuracy of his or her answers.

FIGURE 7-4

A Page from a Programmed Textbook

Source: David Kleppner and Norman Ramsey, *Quick Calculus.* © Copyright 1985 by John Wiley & Sons, Inc. Reprinted by permission.

Sec. 2   Graphs

17   The most direct way to plot the graph of a function $y = f(x)$ is to make a table of reasonably spaced values of x and of the corresponding values of $y = f(x)$. Then each pair of values (x,y) can be represented by a point as in the previous frame. A graph of the function is obtained by connecting the points with a smooth curve. Of course, the points on the curve may be only approximate. If we want an accurate plot we just have to be very careful and use many points. (On the other hand, crude plots are pretty good for most purposes.)

Go to 18.

18   As an example, here is a plot of the function $y = 3x^2$. A table of values of x and y is shown and these points are indicated on the graph.

x	y
−3	27
−2	12
−1	3
0	0
1	3
2	12
3	27

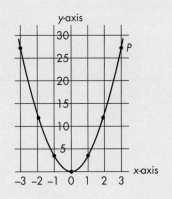

To test yourself, encircle below the pair of coordinates that corresponds to the point P indicated in the figure.

[(3,27) | (27,3) | none of these]

Check your answer. If correct, go on to 19. If incorrect study frame 16 once again and then go to 19.

The main advantage of programmed learning is that it reduces training time by about one-third.[37] In terms of the principles of learning listed earlier, programmed instruction can also facilitate learning, because it lets trainees learn at their own pace, provides immediate feedback, and (from the learner's point of view) reduces the risk of error. On the other hand, trainees do not learn much more from programmed learning than they would from a traditional textbook. Therefore, the cost of developing the manuals and/or software for programmed instruction has to be weighed against the accelerated but not improved learning that should occur.

Audiovisual Techniques

Audiovisual techniques like films, video conferencing, audiotapes, and videotapes can be very effective and are widely used.[38] The Ford Motor Company uses films in its dealer training sessions to simulate problems and sample reactions to various customer complaints, for example.

Audiovisuals are more expensive than conventional lectures but offer some advantages. Consider using them in the following situations.

1. *When there is a need to illustrate how a certain sequence should be followed over time*, such as when teaching wire soldering or telephone repair. The stop action, instant replay, or fast- or slow-motion capabilities of audiovisuals can be useful.

2. *When there is a need to expose trainees to events not easily demonstrable in live lectures*, such as a visual tour of a factory or open-heart surgery.

3. *When the training is going to be used organizationwide* and it is too costly to move the trainers from place to place.

TELETRAINING   Companies today are also using *teletraining*, through which a trainer in a central location can train groups of employees at remote locations via television hookups.[39] For example, AMP Incorporated uses satellites to train its engineers and technicians at 165 sites in the United States and 27 other countries. (The firm makes electrical and electronic connection devices.) To reduce costs for one training program, AMP supplied the program content. PBS affiliate WITF, Channel 33 of Harrisburg, Pennsylvania, supplied the equipment and expertise required to broadcast the training program to five AMP facilities in North America.[40] Macy's, the New York-based retailer, recently established the "Macy's Satellite Network," in part to provide training to the firm's 59,000 employees around the country.[41]

In a low-tech twist to televised teletraining, some firms are successfully using the telephone. For example, Cadillac has what it calls the Craftsman's League, which is a training, testing, and motivational program for Cadillac dealers' mechanics. Employees receive Cadillac materials and service manuals regarding factory-approved service procedures and ongoing technical changes. Then, four times a year, technicians must take a phone exam on any one of eight categories including, for instance, paint repair, electrical, and mechanical.[42]

Honda America Corp. began by using satellite technology to train engineers and now uses it for many other types of employee training as well. For example, its Ohio-based subsidiary purchases seminars from the National Technological University, a provider of satellite education that uses courses from various universities and specialized teaching organizations.[43] The price per course varies, but averages $200 to $250 per employee per seminar so that "it is much more cost effective to keep workers at home and not pay for them to travel," as one of the firm's training managers puts it.

VIDEOCONFERENCE DISTANCE LEARNING   *Videoconferencing* is an increasingly popular way to train employees who are geographically separated from each other—or from the trainer. It has been defined as "a means of joining two or more distant groups using a combination of audio and visual equipment."[44] Videoconferencing allows people in one location to communicate live with people in another city or country or with groups in several other cities.[45] The communication links are established by sending specially compressed audio and video signals over telephone lines or via satellite. Keypad systems allow for audience interactivity; for instance, in a program at Texas Instruments the key-pad system lets instructors call on trainees to confirm they are learning.[46]

Given that videoconferencing is by nature visual, interactive, and remote, there are several things to keep in mind before getting up in front of the camera. For example, because the training is remote, it's particularly important to prepare a training guide ahead of time, specifically a manual the learners can use to keep track of the points that the trainer is making, and a script for the presenter to follow. A sampling of other hints would include:

Avoid bright, flashy jewelry or heavily patterned clothing.[47]

Arrive at least 20 minutes early.

Test all equipment you will be using.

Adjust lights (if necessary and if possible); put lighting in front of participants to avoid shadows.

Have all participants introduce themselves.

Avoid focusing just on one group at one remote site (if there are several) and avoid presenting just to the video camera and not to the in-house participants.

Project your voice and speak clearly; particularly if people at the remote site have a different native language, keep yours free of jargon and needlessly complex words.

Remember that excessive physical movement will cause distortion of the video image where compressed telephone transmission is being used.

vestibule or **simulated training**

Training employees on special off-the-job equipment, as in airplane pilot training, whereby training costs and hazards can be reduced.

Vestibule or Simulated Training

Vestibule or **simulated training** is a technique in which trainees learn on the actual or simulated equipment they will use on the job but are actually trained off-the job. Therefore, it aims to obtain the advantages of on-the-job training without actually putting the trainee on the job. Vestibule training is virtually a necessity when it is too costly or danger-

Vestibule training simulates flight conditions for astronauts at NASA headquarters.

ous to train employees on the job. Putting new assembly-line workers right to work could slow production, for instance, and when safety is a concern—as with pilots—vestibule training may be the only practical alternative.

Simulated training may just take place in a separate room with the equipment the trainees will actually be using on the job. However, it often involves the use of equipment simulators. In pilot training, for instance, the main advantages of flight simulators are as follows.[48]

Safety. Crews can practice hazardous flight maneuvers in a safe, controlled environment.

Learning efficiency. The absence of the conflicting air traffic and radio chatter that exists in real flight situations allows for total concentration on the business of learning how to fly the craft.

Cost savings. The cost of flying a flight simulator is only a fraction of the cost of flying an aircraft. This includes savings on maintenance costs, pilot cost, fuel cost, and the cost of not having the aircraft in regular service.

Computer-Based Training

In computer-based training the trainee uses a computer-based system to interactively increase his or her knowledge or skills. Vestibule or simulated training doesn't necessarily have to rely on computerization. However, computer-based training usually involves presenting trainees with computerized simulations and the use of multimedia including videotapes to help the trainee learn how to do the job.[49]

Teaching methods at many inhouse development centers include multimedia presentations and other uses of communications technology such as videotape and computer simulations.

For example, a computer-based training (CBT) program enables a major pacific Northwest employer to do a better job of training interviewers to conduct correct and legally defensible interviews.[50] Trainees start with a computer screen that shows the "applicant's" completed employment application, as well as information about the nature of the job. The trainee then begins a simulated interview by typing in questions, which are answered by a videotaped model acting as the applicant and whose responses to a multitude of questions have been programmed into the computer. Some items require followup questions, and as each question is answered the trainee records his or her evaluation of the applicant's answer and makes a decision about the person's suitability for the position. At the end of the session the computer tells the trainee where he or she went wrong (perhaps in asking discriminatory questions, for instance) and offers further instructional material to correct these mistakes.[51]

CBT programs can be beneficial. Studies show that interactive technologies reduce learning time by an average of 50%.[52] They can also be very cost effective once designed and produced; Federal Express reportedly expects to save more than $100 million by using an interactive system for employee training.[53] Other advantages include instructional consistency (computers, unlike human trainers, don't have good days and bad days), mastery of learning (if the trainee doesn't learn it, he or she generally can't move on to the next step in the CBT), increased retention, and increased trainee motivation (resulting from the responsive feedback of the CBT program).

Training Via CD-ROM and the Internet

Training on the Internet is already a reality, and many firms are already using the Internet to offer at least some of their training programs.

At the present time, many Internet training programs are (not surprisingly) aimed at teaching Internet users how to use the Internet. Roadmap is one example and is the brainchild of an undergraduate student at the University of Alabama.[54] The course is a bit like a correspondence course that lands in users' e-mail boxes, one new lesson a day for about four weeks. The program uses what's known as Listserve Software to simultaneously distribute the lessons to around 20,000 "trainees" per month. Trainees get to work through each new lesson; some lessons include assignments that send trainers off into the outer reaches of the Internet to practice what they've learned about using the Internet and to retrieve information pertinent to the course. In one variant on this theme the creator of another Internet training program not only delivers courses to the e-mail recipient trainees but also assigns students to discussion groups, so participants "not only learn something, they'll probably meet some new people."[55]

Many firms already use their proprietary internal internets (or "intranets") to facilitate computer-based training. For example, Silicon Graphics transferred many of its training materials into CD-ROMs. However, since not every desktop computer had a CD-ROM player, many employees couldn't access the training program. Silicon Graphics is therefore replacing the CD-ROM distribution method with distribution of training materials via its intranet. "Now employees can access the programs whenever they want. Distribution costs are zero, and if the company wants to make a change to the program, it can do so at a central location."[56]

As a result of such benefits, technology-based learning is booming. Management Recruiters International (MRI) uses the firm's desktop "ConferView" system (see the accompanying photo) to train hundreds of employees—each in their individual offices—simultaneously.[57] Value Rent-a-Car—instead of sending new rental sales agents to week-long classroom-based training courses—now provides them with interactive, multimedia-based training programs utilizing CD-ROMs. These will help them learn the car rental process by walking them through various procedures such as how to operate the rental computer system.[58] Polls suggest such training technology will continue to grow in popularity. For example, one poll of 1,911 trainers found that almost 83% plan to increase their use of multimedia/CD-ROMs, 81% their use of the Internet, and 80% their use of computer-based training.[59]

RESEARCH INSIGHT   Studies are beginning to focus on teaching effectiveness in technology-based distance learning programs to see what teachers can do to be more effective in these kinds of environments. The results of one such study suggest the following:[60]

1. Provide camera and technology layouts that ensure instructors can maintain eye contact with both local and remote audiences.

Doug Donkin, an instructor for Management Recruiters International (MRI), uses the firms ConferView system to conduct MRI University training. ConferView is one type of videoconferencing technology that allows companies to train hundreds of employees simultaneously.
Source: Courtesy of Management Recruiters International, Inc.

2. Encourage instructors to use the variety of media available (CD-ROMS, graphs, videotapes, and so forth).

3. Train instructors not to focus on the technology at the expense of students.

4. Of course, try to emphasize technology that is reliable and of high quality (little delay in audio and video signals is particularly important).

5. Train instructors in how to effectively use the technology and in the importance of a participative style of teaching.

6. Provide an adequate technical support staff.

Research comparing the effectiveness of educational television or interactive video to face-to-face instruction has found little or no differences in student achievement.[61] The preliminary evidence, at least, seems to suggest that technology-supported and particularly video-based training can be effective.[62] However, this assumes that the technology is effective, and that the instructors are (as previously explained) specially trained to utilize it for maximum impact.

COMPUTER-BASED TRAINING   Much of the content for programs like these is produced by specialist multimedia software houses like Graphic Media of Portland, Oregon. They produce not only custom-produced titles but also generic programs like a $999 package for teaching safety in the white-collar workplace. Custom training and development program titles can cost $60,000 to $100,000 per hour of production to produce. That may be a big expense for a smaller firm, but for larger organizations it might be minimal compared with the usual development program costs such as hiring professional trainers and spending money on travel, food, and lodging to bring employees together for training sessions. As the editor and publisher of the Multimedia Training Newsletter in Sunnyville, California, puts it, "Anyone who is involved in training more than 200 people needs to investigate or implement this technology."[63]

Several more examples can illustrate the inroads that technology is making into training and development. After a major downsizing and merger, GTE decided it had to make its training programs more cost effective, and now expects 50% of its training programs to be technology-based.[64] In one program, for instance, GTE's training staff had to train thousands of GTE workers in the use of the firm's new order-processing system. GTE's training staff developed a computer program to simulate the order-entry system, complete with sample customer names, addresses, and requests for service. In this case, the computer-assisted instruction (CAI) eliminated the need for instructors to be available to answer questions during the training, and enabled the employees to learn at their own pace. To facilitate the training, GTE uses its internal intranet to provide ongoing and constantly updated training and to facilitate interaction between each of the computer-based trainees' computers and the firm's central computers.

SMALL BUSINESS APPLICATIONS

■ Training

Because so much is riding on a relatively few employees, it is important that smaller firms carefully train their employees. The concepts and techniques explained in this chapter should enable you to do so. In addition, here is a practical procedure you can use to develop your training program.

STEP 1. SET TRAINING OBJECTIVES

First, write down your training objectives. For example, your objective might be to reduce scrap, or to get new employees up to speed within 2 weeks.

STEP 2. WRITE A DETAILED JOB DESCRIPTION

A detailed job description is the heart of any training program. It should list the daily and periodic tasks of each job, along with a summary of the steps in each task. Thus, for the job presented in Table 7-1, a main task is "operate paper cutter." The press operator's job description should thus explain how the paper cutter should be operated, including steps such as start motor, set cutting distance, and place paper on cutting table. In other words, the detailed job description should list what is to be done as well as how to do it.

STEP 3. DEVELOP AN ABBREVIATED TASK ANALYSIS RECORD FORM

For practical purposes, the small-business owner can use an abbreviated Task Analysis Record Form (Table 7-1) containing just four columns. In the first, list *tasks* (including what is to be performed in terms of each of the main tasks, and the steps involved in each task). In column B, list *performance standards* (in terms of quantity, quality, accuracy, and so on). In column C, list *trainable skills* required, things the employee must know or do to perform the task. This column provides you with specific skills (such as "Keep both hands on releases") that you want to stress. In the fourth column, list *aptitudes required*. These are the human aptitudes (such as mechanical comprehension, tolerance for boredom, and so on) that the employee should have to be trainable for the task and for which the employee can be screened ahead of time.

STEP 4. DEVELOP A JOB INSTRUCTION SHEET

Next develop a job instruction sheet for the job. As explained on page 260, a job instruction training sheet shows the steps in each task as well as key points for each.

STEP 5. PREPARE TRAINING PROGRAM FOR THE JOB

At a minimum, your training program should include the job description, abbreviated Task Analysis Record Form, and job instruction sheet, all collected in a trainer's manual. The latter should also contain a summary of the training program's objectives, the three forms mentioned earlier, and a listing of the trainable skills required for the trainee. A separate manual might then consist of an introduction to the job, an explanation of how the job fits with other jobs in the plant or office, a job description, and a job instruction sheet.

You also have to make a decision regarding which media to use in your training program. A simple but effective on-the-job training program using current employees or supervisors as trainers requires only the materials we just described. However, it could turn out that the nature of the job or the number of trainees requires producing or purchasing special audio or visual tapes or films, a slide presentation, or more extensive printed materials.

Many smaller companies are saving on training expenses by entering into cooperative agreements with other firms in their geographic areas. If one firm has eight employees who need time-management training and one down the street has a similar need, together they can hire a training supplier to teach a full class of 16 participants, thus sharing the trainer's costs.[65]

TRAINING FOR SPECIAL PURPOSES   Increasingly today training does more than prepare employees to perform their jobs effectively. Training for special purposes—dealing with AIDs and adjusting to diversity, for instance—is required too. A sampling of such special-purpose training programs follows.

Literacy Training Techniques

Functional illiteracy—inability to handle basic reading, writing, and arithmetic—is a serious problem at work. For example, a survey of 316 employers concluded that about 43% of all new hires required basic skill improvements, as did 37% of current employees.[66] This reflects, in part, the changing nature of workers' jobs. Today's emphasis on teamwork and quality requires employees to have a level of analytical skills that's impossible to attain without the ability to adequately read, write, and understand numbers. As the U.S. economy shifts from goods to services, there is a corresponding need for workers who are more skilled, more literate, and better able to perform at least basic arithmetic skills.

Employers are responding to this problem in two main ways. First, companies are testing prospective employees' basic skills. Of the 1,085 companies that responded to an American Management Association (AMA) survey on workplace testing, for instance, 39% indicated they conduct basic skills testing.[67] In 85% of the responding companies, job applicants who are deficient in basic skills are refused employment. At about 3% of the other companies, current employees and candidates for promotion are tested (and often rejected) on their literacy scores.

The second response is to institute basic skills and literacy programs. The Life Skills Program implemented at the Bellwood plant of Borg-Warner Automotive, Inc. is one example. Based on test scores, employee participants were chosen and placed into three classes of 15 students each. Two trainers were retained from a local training company. Each session was planned for a maximum of 200 hours. However, employees could leave when they reached a predetermined skill level, so that some were in the program for only 40 hours while others stayed the entire course.[68] Classes are held 5 days a week, 2 hours a day, with classes scheduled so that 1 hour was during the employee's personal time and the second was on company time.

Another simple approach is to have supervisors focus on basic skills by giving employees writing and speaking exercises. After the exercise has been completed, the supervisor can provide personal feedback.[69]

AIDS Education

Many of the estimated 1 million Americans infected with the AIDS virus are in the workforce, and this creates anxiety for many noninfected employees and a dilemma for their employers. On the one hand, infected individuals must be allowed to remain on their jobs, for both moral and legal reasons. On the other hand, the infected person's coworkers often require training to reduce anxieties and maximize the chances that the employees will be able to work together as a team.

Many firms therefore institute AIDS education programs. The program instituted in the Wellesley, Massachusetts, office of Sun Life of Canada, a life insurance company, is typical.[70] Groups of 20 to 30 employees attended 90-minute seminars. In addition to providing detailed information about AIDS, the seminars offered a forum for discussion and questions. Management employees attended 3-hour seminars in groups of 10 to 12 people. The seminars covered additional AIDS-related issues, including the need for confidentiality, the potential impact of discrimination laws, and the company's AIDS policy.

There was reportedly little resistance to holding or attending these seminars, in part because the reasons for them were widely communicated in the company's newsletters. Some management employees initially expressed skepticism about devoting so many hours to AIDS education, but after their sessions most reportedly felt differently. Based on pre- and postseminar questionnaires, the company believes that the seminars were useful in getting employees to learn the facts about AIDS, clearing up misconceptions, and helping to put the personal concerns of many employees to rest.

GLOBAL HRM

■ Training for International Business

As more firms find themselves competing in a global marketplace, they've increasingly had to implement special global training programs. The reasons for doing so range from avoiding lost business due to cultural insensitivity to improving job satisfaction and retention of overseas staff, to enabling a newly assigned employee to communicate with his or her colleagues abroad.[71]

Many global training programs are prepackaged. They are sold by vendors to employers who must train one or more of their employees prior to overseas assignments. A sampling of the programs can help illustrate the wide range of programs available as well as what global training programs actually look like. Sample programs include:[72]

- *The Cultural Awareness Program*: A 1-day cultural awareness training program that looks at U.S. and cross-cultural values and assumptions concerning communication and identity.
- *Executive Etiquette for Global Transactions*: This prepares managers for conducting business globally by training them in the differing etiquette requirements in countries abroad.
- *Cross-Cultural Technology Transfer*: This shows trainees how cultural values affect one's perceptions of technology and technical learning.
- *International Protocol and Presentation*: This shows trainees the correct way to handle people with tact and diplomacy in countries around the world.
- *Cross-Cultural Training and Orientation*: Topics include cross-cultural communication and business skills, practical approaches to managing culture shock and adjusting one's lifestyle, stress management, daily life in the host country, spouse's and family's concerns, area studies, and repatriation procedures.
- *Business Basics for the Foreign Executive*: This covers negotiating cross-culturally, working with U.S. clients, making presentations, writing for U.S. business, and using the phone in the United States.
- *Language Programs*: Various vendors supply language specialists whose services include translation, interpretation, cross-cultural training, and consulting on language-related needs.
- *Language Training*: Training programs here provide language training delivered by certified instructors, usually determined by the learner's needs rather than by the requirements of a predetermined curriculum or textbook.

Diversity Training

With an increasingly diverse workforce, more firms are implementing diversity training programs. As an HR officer for one firm put it, "We're trying to create a better sensitivity among our supervisors about the issues and challenges women and minorities face in pursuing their careers."[73] Diversity training creates better cross-cultural sensitivity among supervisors and nonsupervisors with the aim of creating more harmonious working relationships among a firm's employees.

Diversity training is no panacea, and a poorly conceived program can backfire. Potential negative outcomes include "the possibility of posttraining participant discomfort, reinforcement of group stereotypes, perceived disenfranchisement or backlash by white males, and even lawsuits based on managers' exposure of stereotypical beliefs blurted out during 'awareness raising' sessions."[74]

Strictly speaking, it's probably more accurate to talk about diversity-based training programs than about "diversity training." According to one survey of HR directors, programs aimed at reducing diversity-based problems included (from most used to least used): improving interpersonal skills; understanding/valuing cultural differences; improving technical skills; socializing employees into corporate culture; reducing stress; indoctrinating new workers into U.S. work ethic; mentoring; improving English proficiency; improving basic math skills; and improving bilingual skills for English-speaking employees.[75]

A supervisory training program at Kinney Shoe Corp. provides an example.[76] The firm conducts 8-hour "valuing diversity" seminars for store managers. They show, for instance, how people from various cultures react differently to workplace situations. It works by presenting a number of hypothetical situations. For example, one situation illustrates the fact that a Native American worker might be embarrassed by public praise from his or her supervisor.

Customer Service Training

Today almost two-thirds of U.S. workers are in customer service (rather than manufacturing) jobs, and more and more companies are finding it necessary to compete based on the quality of their service. It's no longer enough, for instance, to offer a clean room at a decent price when a customer checks into a Hilton. To stay competitive, employers like Hilton find they must provide total customer service, from courteous bellhops to easy parking to speedy checkouts.

Many companies are therefore implementing customer service training programs. The basic aim is to train all employees to treat the company's customers in a courteous and hospitable manner.

Customer service training at Alamo Rent-a-Car, called the "Best Friends" program,[77] consisted of a 5-day orientation/customer service training program. First, employees were familiarized with Alamo's history, its growth and expansion, and the company's expectations regarding customer service and the firm's work ethics. The program then shifted to customer service training. This included segments on the importance of exceptional customer service and how to define it, illustrative examples, and the specific employee skills needed to deliver such fine service.

Results suggest the training program was effective. While other factors may have contributed to the improvements, sales complaints were down 15% from the year before training commenced. Similarly, rudeness complaints were down 50% from pretraining levels. The firm's business transactions jumped by 30% in one year.

Training for Teamwork and Empowerment

Most firms find that teamwork doesn't just happen; instead employees must be trained to be good team members. For instance, Toyota devotes dozens of hours to training new employees to listen to each other and to cooperate. Short exercises are used to illustrate examples of good and bad teamwork and to mold new employees' attitudes regarding good teamwork.

Some firms use outdoor training such as Outward Bound programs to build teamwork.[78] Outdoor training usually involves taking a firm's management team out into rugged, mountainous terrain. There they learn team spirit and cooperation and the need to trust and rely on each other by overcoming physical obstacles. As one participant put it, "Every time I climbed over a rock, I needed someone's help."[79] An example of one activity is the "trust fall." Here an employee has to slowly lean back and fall backward from a height of, say, 10 feet into the waiting arms of 5 or 10 team members. The idea is to build trust, particularly trust in one's colleagues.[80]

Not all employees are eager to (or should) participate in such activities. Outward Bound has potential participants fill out extensive medical evaluations to make sure participants can safely engage in risky outdoor activities. Others feel that the outdoor activities are too contrived to be applicable back at work.

Empowering employees (either individually or as teams) also usually requires extensive training. For example, many companies, like Saturn, today use work teams to analyze job-related problems and come up with solutions. Much of the approximately 320 hours of training new Saturn employees receive therefore, aims to develop the problem-solving and analysis skills required to help to empower the work team—in this case, to analyze and solve problems. Training employees to use basic statistical analysis and accounting is an example.

Providing Employees with Lifelong Learning

In today's downsized high performance organizations employers must depend on their first-line employees—those actually building the Saturn cars, or greeting the hotel guests—to recognize new opportunities, identify problems, and react quickly with analyses and recommendations. This requires a continuous upgrade in employees' skills. Providing continuing training from basic remedial skills to advanced decision-making techniques throughout employees' careers is known as lifelong learning.

The program at one Canadian Honeywell manufacturing plant provides an example.[81] This plant called its lifelong learning program the Honeywell-Scarborough Learning for Life Initiative. It was "a concerted effort to upgrade skill and education levels so that employees can meet workplace challenges with confidence."[82]

Honeywell's Lifelong Learning Initiative had several features. It began with adult basic education. Here the company, in partnership with the employees' union, offered courses in English as a second language, basic literacy, numeracy, and computer literacy.

Next the factory formed a partnership with a local community college. Through that partnership Honeywell provides college-level courses to all factory employees—hourly, professional, and managerial—giving them the opportunity to earn college diplomas and certificates.[83] This includes a 15-hour "skills for success" program designed to refresh adults in the study habits required to succeed academically. All courses take place at the factory immediately after work.

In addition, job-related training is provided for 2 hours every other week. These sessions focus on skills specifically important to the job, "such as the principles of just-in-time inventory systems, team effectiveness, interpersonal communication skills, conflict resolution, problem solving and dealing with a diverse work force."[84]

MANAGERIAL DEVELOPMENT AND TRAINING TECHNIQUES

management development

Any attempt to improve current or future management performance by imparting knowledge, changing attitudes, or increasing skills.

succession planning

A process through which senior-level openings are planned for and eventually filled.

job rotation

A management training technique that involves moving a trainee from department to department to broaden his or her experience and identify strong and weak points.

What Is Management Development?

Management development is any attempt to improve managerial performance by imparting knowledge, changing attitudes, or increasing skills. The ultimate aim of such development programs is, of course, to enhance the future performance of the organization itself. For this reason, the general management development process consists of (1) assessing the company's needs (for instance, to fill future executive openings, or to boost competitiveness), (2) appraising the managers' performance, and then (3) developing the managers (and future managers) themselves.

Some development programs are companywide and involve all or most new (or potential) management recruits. Thus, new college graduates may join Enormous Corp. and become part of the companywide management development program. Here they may be rotated through a preprogrammed series of departmental assignments and educational experiences; the aims are identifying their management potential and providing the breadth of experience (in, say, production and finance) that will make the new managers more valuable in their first "real" assignment as group leaders. Superior candidates may then be slotted onto a "fast track," a development program that prepares them more quickly to assume senior-level commands.

On the other hand, the management development program may be aimed at filling a specific position, such as CEO, perhaps with one of two potential candidates. When an executive position is to be filled, the process is usually called **succession planning**. Succession planning refers to the process through which senior-level openings are planned for and eventually filled. (See the Diversity Counts box for an interesting perspective.)

Such a succession program typically takes place in stages. First, an organization projection is made: here you anticipate your department's management needs based on factors like planned expansion or contraction. Next the HR department reviews its management skills inventory to identify the management talent now employed. These inventories, you may recall, contain data on things like educational and work experience, career preferences, and performance appraisals. Next management replacement charts are drawn. These summarize potential candidates for each management slot, as well as each person's development needs. As shown in Figure 7-5, the development needs for a future division vice president might include job rotation (to obtain more experience in the firm's finance and production divisions), executive development programs (to provide training in strategic planning), and assignment for 2 weeks to the employer's in-house management development center.[85]

Managerial on-the-Job Training

On-the-job training is not just for nonmanagers; it's a popular manager development method too. Important techniques include job rotation, the coaching/understudy approach, and action learning.

JOB ROTATION **Job rotation** means moving management trainees from department to department to broaden their understanding of all parts of the business.[86] The trainee—often a recent college graduate—may spend several months in each department; this helps not only broaden his or her experience, but also discover the jobs he or she prefers. The person may just be an observer in each department but more commonly gets fully involved in its operations. The trainee thus learns the department's business by actually doing it, whether it involves sales, production, finance, or some other function.

There are several ways to improve a rotation program's success.[87] The program should be tailored to the needs, interests, and capabilities of the individual trainee, and not be a standard sequence that all trainees take. The length of time the trainee stays in a job should be determined by how fast he or she is learning. And, the managers to whom

FIGURE 7-5

Management Replacement Chart Showing Development Needs of Future Divisional Vice President

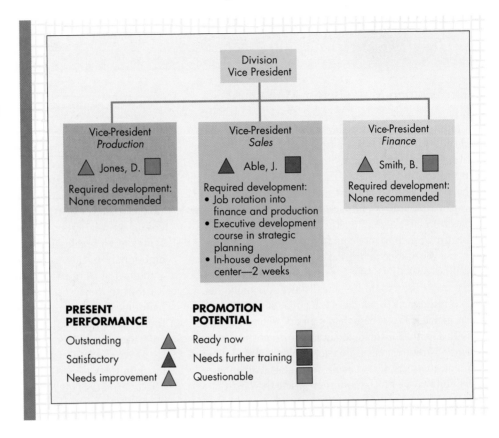

these people are assigned should be specially trained to provide feedback and to monitor performance in an interested and competent way.

The Goodyear Tire and Rubber Company's training program for college graduates is a good example.[88] Each trainee's program is tailored to match his or her experience, education, and vocational preference. Programs vary from 6 to 15 months, beginning with 3 weeks in an orientation program to make the trainees thoroughly acquainted with Goodyear. (Here they study the organization's structure, company objectives, and basic manufacturing processes and participate in informal meetings with top company officials.) After an additional month of factory orientation, trainees discuss their career interests with top-level managers and select up to six assignments in special departments, each of which lasts about 1 month. (For example, a chemical engineering graduate might rotate through departments for fabric development, chemical materials development research, central process engineering, process development, and chemical production.) Trainees then select specific job assignments as the starting point of their careers.

COACHING/UNDERSTUDY APPROACH   In the *coaching/understudy approach*, the trainee works directly with a senior manager or with the person he or she is to replace; the latter is in truth responsible for the trainee's coaching. Normally, the understudy relieves the executive of certain responsibilities, thereby giving the trainee a chance to learn the job.[89] This helps ensure that the employer will have trained managers to assume key positions when such positions are vacated due to retirement, promotions, transfers, or terminations.

ACTION LEARNING   **Action learning** gives managers and other employees released time to work full-time on projects, analyzing and solving problems in departments other than their own.[90] The trainees meet periodically in four- or five-person project groups to

action learning

A training technique by which management trainees are allowed to work full time analyzing and solving problems in other departments.

DIVERSITY COUNTS

Do Women Make Better Managers?

Employees often talk today about the need to "shatter the glass ceiling"—the transparent but often impermeable barrier that many women face in trying to move up to top management. The glass ceiling is not a real barrier, of course, but instead the practical net effect of various prejudices and lack of networking opportunities women face that together make it hard or impossible for women to move up to top management jobs.

While it certainly makes sense to shatter the glass ceiling for equity's sake, research suggests there may be another reason to do so—the distinct possibility that, as two researchers conclude, women may simply make better managers these days than men do.[91] Their basic point is that with the trend today toward high-involvement work teams, consensus decision making, and empowerment, the sorts of leadership styles that women already exhibit may be much more appropriate than men's.

Their conclusion is, of course, based on the assumption that female managers' leadership styles are different than males, and based on their research that appears to be the case. Specifically, their findings indicate that women scored significantly higher than men on all measures of transformational leadership. Transformational leaders "move followers to go beyond their self-interest to concerns for their group or organization. They help followers develop to higher levels of potential. Such leaders diagnose the needs of their followers and then elevate those needs to initiate and promote development. They align followers around a common purpose, mission, or vision. They provide a sense of purpose and future orientation ..." The women scored higher than the men did on such traditional measures of transformational leadership as encouraging followers to question their old way of doing things or to break with the past, providing simplified emotional appeals to increase awareness and understanding of mutually desired goals and providing learning opportunities to employees. On the other hand, male managers were more likely to be "transactional" type leaders, basically by commending followers if they complied or disciplining them if they failed.

Why exactly the male and female managers differed on these leadership measures is not entirely clear. The researchers conclude that the more "plausible explanation for the observed differences regarding transformational leadership ratings may lie in the tendencies of women to be more nurturing, interested in others, and more socially sensitive."[92] In any case, insofar as it may be such transformational leadership behaviors that are increasingly appropriate in organizations today, it could be that female managers have an edge in exhibiting the sorts of leadership style that "comprises the most appropriate leadership behaviors to develop followers to achieve their highest levels of potential" today.[93]

discuss their findings. With action learning several trainees may work together as a project group, or compare notes and discuss each other's projects.

Pacific Gas & Electric Company (PG&E) uses an approach it calls Action-Forum Process.[94] The idea of the Action-Forum Process is to focus on smaller issues that the employees themselves know the most about, and the program has reportedly been a success. In 3 years PG&E hosted almost 80 Action-Forum and saved more than $270 million as a result of them.[95]

The Action-Forum Process itself has three phases: (1) a "framework" phase of 6 to 8 weeks, which is basically an intense planning period during which the team involved tightens and defines an issue to be worked on (which was previously suggested by a PG&E employee); (2) the Action-Forum itself—2 to 3 days at PG&E's learning center discussing the issue and developing recommendations; and (3) accountability sessions. (The accountability sessions mean that the Action-Forum teams meet with the leadership group at 30, 60, and 90 days to review the status of their action plans and to make any necessary changes in them.)

Managerial Off-the-Job Training and Development Techniques

There are also a variety of primarily off-the-job techniques.

case study method

A development method in which the manager is presented with a written description of an organizational problem to diagnose and solve.

THE CASE STUDY METHOD   As most everyone knows, the **case study method** presents a trainee with a written description of an organizational problem. The person then analyzes the case in private, diagnoses the problem, and presents his or her findings and solutions in a discussion with other trainees.[96]

There are several things you can do to make this approach more effective. If possible, the cases should be actual situations from the trainees' own firms. (This will help ensure that trainees understand the background of the case and make it easier for them to transfer what they learn to their own jobs and situations). Argyris also contends that instructors have to guard against dominating the case analysis and make sure that they remain more a catalyst or coach. Finally, they should carefully prepare the case discussion and let the students discuss the case in small groups before class.[97]

management game

A development technique in which teams of managers compete with one another by making computerized decisions regarding realistic but simulated companies.

MANAGEMENT GAMES   Computerized **management games** are popular and are often CD-ROM based. Trainees are divided into five- or six-person companies, each of which competes with the others in a simulated marketplace. For example, each group may be allowed to decide (1) how much to spend on advertising, (2) how much to produce, (3) how much inventory to maintain, and (4) how many of which product to produce. Usually the game itself compresses a 2 or 3-year period into days, weeks, or months. As in the real world, each company usually can't see what decisions (such as to boost advertising) the other firms have made, although these decisions do affect their own sales.[98]

Management games can be good development tools. People learn best by getting involved in the activity itself, and the games can be useful for gaining such involvement. They help trainees develop their problem-solving skills, as well as to focus their attention on the need for planning rather than on just putting out fires. The companies also usually elect their own officers and organizations; they can thus develop leadership skills and foster cooperation and teamwork.

OUTSIDE SEMINARS   There is also a wealth of special seminars and conferences offered aimed at developing managers. For example, the American Management Association provides thousands of courses in areas ranging from accounting and controls to assertiveness training, basic financial skills, information systems, project management, purchasing management, and total quality management.[99]

A typical course is outlined in Figure 7-6. As you can see, it is titled "Management Skills and Techniques for New Supervisors," and covers topics like "Building Your Communication Skills," "The Supervisor's Role in Training and Development," and "Motivation: Understanding How to Influence Your Staff." Many of the American Management Association's courses (as well as those provided by other vendors) can also be presented on-site at the employer's place of business if, for instance, 10 or more employees are enrolled. Many of these programs offer nondegree credit continuing education units (CEUs) for course completion.

UNIVERSITY-RELATED PROGRAMS   In addition to the familiar academic courses and programs, many universities also provide continuing education programs in leadership, supervision, and the like. As with the AMA, these range from 1- to 4-day programs to executive development programs lasting 1 to 4 months.

The Advanced Management Program of the Graduate School of Business Administration at Harvard University is one example. As illustrated in Figure 7-7, each class in this

Management Skills and Techniques for New Supervisors

Three days of intense training in the management skills that supervisors count on.

Your first days on the job as supervisor may be the most critical time of your career. Here's your chance to learn how to lead, communicate and manage successfully. You'll leave this seminar with the tools you need to select appropriate management strategies, coach employees, manage your time, and more!

Who Should Attend

New supervisors who must learn proven management techniques to help them succeed on the job and make a smooth transition from staff member to supervisor.

How You Will Benefit

◆ Make the transition from worker to supervisor
◆ Communicate ideas effectively
◆ Develop a flexible management approach
◆ Build your staff for maximum productivity
◆ Protect employees and the organization when legal issues arise
◆ Understand the conceptual, interpersonal and technical levels of the supervisor's function

◆ Get organized and stay that way
◆ Write and conduct a sample performance evaluation
◆ Motivate your staff to achieve full potential

What You Will Cover

◆ How to establish yourself as a supervisor. Understanding the four basic management functions
◆ Developing an appropriate and flexible management style
◆ Building your communication skills for the year 2000 and beyond; Active listening, effective questioning, and harmonious nonverbal communication
◆ The supervisor's role in training and development
◆ Motivation: Understanding how to influence your staff and maintain employee motivation in today's changing organizations
◆ How to coach for success: Diagnosing your coaching skills...demonstrating effective feedback delivery...learning the benefits of constructive criticism
◆ Your legal responsibilities as a supervisor regarding EEO, Affirmative Action, ADA, and FMLA...legal aspects of hiring and terminating employees
◆ How to prepare for and conduct performance evaluation interviews

FIGURE 7-6 *Management Skills and Techniques for New Supervisors*

Source: Reprinted with permission from the American Management Association Catalog, 4/12/98, p. 4.

Turning insight into opportunity.
The Harvard Business School.

Harvard Business School Executive Education offers dynamic and thought-provoking study in a wide spectrum of disciplines. These intensive programs are specifically designed to provide you with the fresh perspectives and strategic focus needed to improve the performance of your company.

In 1996, the Harvard Business School offers more than twenty courses that run from two and one-half days to eleven weeks. Two programs will be of particular interest to CEOs, their direct reports, and senior-level executives:

Advanced Management Program is for senior-level general managers with more than 15 years experience. The program fosters a greater appreciation of complex business challenges and new strategies to change and lead organizations in today's global marketplace.

Program for Management Development is designed for new general managers as well as senior-level functional managers in succession for a general management role. This course helps executives improve their overall effi-

ciency, develop a new framework for problem-solving, and expand their range of responsibility.

Join your colleagues in the learning experience that has had measurable impact on companies and corporations around the world for more than fifty years. Then see the results for yourself. Explore the opportunities with Executive Education at the Harvard Business School.

1-800-HBS-5577 EXT. 426
CALL OR E-MAIL

Internet: executive_education@hbs.edu
Web address: http://www.exed.hbs.edu/
For more information, brochures, and applications, please contact us today. Space is limited. Outside the U.S. call 617-495-6555 ext. 426.

 Harvard Business School

Executive Education

The Harvard Business School is an affirmative action/equal opportunity institution.

FIGURE 7-7 *Ad for Harvard Executive Training Programs*
Source: Used with permission of the Harvard Business School Executive Education Program.

program consists of a group of experienced managers from all regions of the world. The program uses cases and lectures to provide top-level management talent with the latest management skills, as well as with practice in analyzing complex organizational problems.

Employers are also increasingly granting technical and professional employees extended *sabbaticals*—periods of time off—for attending a college or university to pursue a higher degree or to upgrade skills. For example, Lucent Corporation has a program that includes a tuition refund and released time for up to 1 year of on-campus study.

Universities and corporations are also cooperating in video-linked classroom education. For example, the School of Business and Public Administration at California State University, Sacramento, and a Hewlett-Packard facility in Roseville, California, are video linked. This allows for courses from campuses to be video linked with an employer's sites via telephone and other communication lines.

role playing

A training technique in which trainees act out the parts of people in a realistic management situation.

ROLE PLAYING   The aim of **role playing** is to create a realistic situation and then have the trainees assume the parts (or roles) of specific persons in that situation.[100]

One such role from a famous role-playing exercise called the New Truck Dilemma is presented in Figure 7-8. When combined with the general instructions for the role-playing exercise, roles like these for all of the participants can trigger a spirited discussion among the role players, particularly when they all throw themselves into the roles. The idea of the exercise is to solve the problem at hand and thereby develop trainees' skills in areas like leadership and delegating. For example, a supervisor could experiment with both a considerate and autocratic leadership style, whereas in the real world the person might not have this harmless way of experimenting. According to Maier, role-playing also trains a person to be aware of and sensitive to the feelings of others.[101]

Role-playing has some drawbacks. Some trainees feel that role-playing is childish, while others who have had a bad experience with it are reluctant to participate at all.

behavior modeling

A training technique in which trainees are first shown good management techniques in a film, are then asked to play roles in a simulated situation, and are then given feedback and praise by their supervisor.

BEHAVIOR MODELING   **Behavior modeling** involves (1) showing trainees the right (or "model") way of doing something, (2) letting each person practice the right way to do it, and then (3) providing feedback regarding each trainee's performance.[102] It has been used, for example, to:

1. Train first-line supervisors to handle common supervisor-employee interactions better. This includes giving recognition, disciplining, introducing changes, and improving poor performance.
2. Train middle managers to better handle interpersonal situations, for example, performance problems and undesirable work habits.
3. Train employees and their supervisors to take and give criticism, ask and give help, and establish mutual trust and respect.

FIGURE 7-8

Typical Role in a Role-Playing Exercise

Source: Normal R. F. Maier and Gertrude Casselman Verser, *Psychology in Industrial Organizations*, 5th ed., p. 190. Copyright 1982 by Houghton Mifflin Company. Used by permission of the publishers.

WALT MARSHALL—SUPERVISOR OF REPAIR CREW

You are the head of a crew of telephone maintenance workers, each of whom drives a small service truck to and from the various jobs. Every so often you get a new truck to exchange for an old one, and you have the problem of deciding which of your crew members you should give the new truck. Often there are hard feelings, since each seems to feel entitled to the new truck, so you have a tough time being fair. As a matter of fact, it usually turns out that whatever you decide is considered wrong by most of the crew. You now have to face the issue again because a new truck, a Chevrolet, has just been allocated to you for assignment.

In order to handle this problem you have decided to put the decision up to the crew. You will tell them about the new truck and will put the problem in terms of what would be the fairest way to assign the truck. Do not take a position yourself, because you want to do what they think is most fair.

The basic behavior modeling procedure can be outlined as follows:

1. *Modeling.* First, trainees watch films or videotapes that show model persons behaving effectively in a problem situation. In other words, trainees are shown the right way to behave in a simulated but realistic situation. The film might thus show a supervisor effectively disciplining a subordinate, if teaching how to discipline is the aim of the training program.

2. *Role playing.* Next the trainees are given roles to play in a simulated situation; here they practice and rehearse the effective behaviors demonstrated by the models.

3. *Social reinforcement.* The trainer provides reinforcement in the form of praise and constructive feedback based on how the trainee performs in the role-playing situation.

4. *Transfer of training.* Finally, trainees are encouraged to apply their new skills when they are back on their jobs.

The results of at least one study suggests that behavioral modeling can be a very effective training technique.[103] Participants in this study were 160 members of a Naval construction battalion based in Gulfport, Mississippi. In this program, trainees were trained to use new computer work stations. Three training techniques were used: conventional instruction (primarily, a lecture and slide-show in a conventional classroom setting); computer-assisted (here students were trained by receiving a manual at the beginning of the session, as well as the diskette needed to work through exercises at their new work stations); and behavior modeling.

Measures of learning and skill development were highest for behavior modeling, followed by the computer-assisted training, and then by conventional instruction. However there's considerable evidence that different people have different preferred learning styles.[104] Assuming that everyone will necessarily do better with any specific training technique is therefore probably erroneous; for instance, some trainees probably would excel in the individualized and self-paced environment of computer-assisted learning while others wouldn't.

in-house development centers

A company-based method for exposing prospective managers to realistic exercises to develop improved management skills.

IN-HOUSE DEVELOPMENT CENTERS   Some employers have **in-house development centers.** These centers usually combine classroom learning (lectures and seminars, for instance) with other techniques like assessment centers, in-basket exercises, and role-playing to help develop employees and other managers.

For example, *Fortune* magazine calls General Electric's Crotonville, NY, Management Development Institute, the Harvard of corporate America. The firm's 160-page catalog offers a wide array of management development courses. These range from entry-level programs in manufacturing and sales to a course for English majors called "Everything You Always Wanted to Know About Finance," as well as advanced management training.[105]

In practice, in-house development centers such as this needn't produce all (or most) of their own training and development programs. In fact, employers are increasingly partnering with academic institutions and other training and development program providers in order to create a package of programs and materials that are appropriate to the needs of their own employees. What some of them are creating, in effect, are virtual corporate universities, providing in-house courses and programs from partner educational institutions.[106]

EXECUTIVE DEVELOPMENT IN GLOBAL COMPANIES   Selecting and developing executives to run the employer's overseas operations presents management with a dilemma. One expert cites "an alarmingly high failure rate when executives are relocated overseas." This failure rate is usually caused by inappropriate selection and poor preplacement development.[107] Yet in an increasingly globalized economy, employers must develop managers for overseas assignments despite these difficulties.

Many companies, including Dow, Colgate-Palmolive, and Ciba-Geigy, have developed and implemented successful international executive relocation programs. In addition to the general requirements for successful executive development programs previously listed, preparing and training executives for overseas assignments should also include the following considerations:

1. Choose international-assignment candidates whose educational backgrounds and experiences are appropriate for overseas assignments. The person who has already accumulated a track record of successfully adapting to foreign cultures (perhaps through overseas college studies and summer internships) will more likely succeed as an international transferee.

2. Choose those whose personalities and family situations can withstand the cultural changes they will encounter in their new environments. When many of these executives fail, it is not because these individuals couldn't adapt but because their spouses or children were unhappy in their new foreign setting.

3. Brief candidates fully and clearly on all relocation policies, including moving expenses, salary differentials, and benefits such as paid schooling for the employees' children.

4. Give executives and their families comprehensive training in their new company's culture and language. At Dow Chemical, for instance, orientation begins with a briefing session, during which the transfer policy is explained in detail to the relocating executive. He or she is also given a briefing package compiled by the receiving area containing important information about local matters, such as shopping and housing. In addition, an advisor, who is often the spouse of a recently returned expatriate, will visit the transferee and his or her spouse to explain what sort of emotional issues they are likely to face in the early stages of the move—such as feeling remote from relatives, for instance. The option of attending a 2-week language and cultural orientation program offered by a school like Berlitz is also extended.

5. Provide all relocating executives with a mentor to monitor their overseas careers and to help them secure appropriate jobs with the company when they repatriate. At Dow, for instance, this person is usually a high-level supervisor in the expatriate's functional area. The overseas assignee keeps his or her mentor up to date on his or her activities. Similarly, the mentor monitors the expatriate's career while he or she is overseas.

6. Establish a repatriation program that helps returning executives and their families readjust to their professional and personal lives in their home country. At Dow, for instance, as much as a year in advance of the expatriate's scheduled return, his or her new job is arranged by the person's mentor.[108]

EVALUATING THE TRAINING EFFORT

A recent review of the best training practices in 300 "improvement-driven" companies provides an insight into the management practices associated with effective training programs.[109] Among other things, high-performance organizations: emphasize a strong connection between training and business strategy; utilize group-ware (such as lotus notes) for enabling trainees to interact during training; and ensure that in-house development managers work closely with and partner with plant managers to identify training and development needs.

After trainees complete their training (or perhaps at planned intervals during the training), the program should be evaluated to see how well its objectives have been met and whether or not a better method exists for doing so. Thus, if assemblers should be able to solder a junction in 30 seconds, or a Xerox technician repair a machine in 30 minutes, then the program's effectiveness should be measured based on whether or not these objectives are met.

There is little doubt that training and development can be effective. For example, while it may not be just the training, Xerox retrained over 110,000 employees worldwide in the early 1980s and soon regained market share in its industry. General Motors is another firm that used training to help recapture market share.[110] Formal studies of training programs also substantiate the potential positive impact of such programs. A study conducted in the early 1990s concluded that "firms that establish workplace education programs and reorganize work, report noticeable improvements in their workers' abilities and the quality of their products."[111] Another study found that businesses operating below their expected labor productivity levels had significant increases in productivity growth after implementing new employee training programs.[112] A recent evaluation of their total quality leadership program by the Department of the Navy similarly led them to conclude that training can produce fundamental changes in the way organizations perform.[113]

There are two basic issues to address when evaluating a training program. The first is the design of the evaluation study and, in particular, whether controlled experimentation will be used. The second is the training effect to be measured.

Controlled experimentation is the best method to use in evaluating a training program. In a controlled experiment, both a training group and a control group (that receives no training) are used. Data (for instance, on quantity of production or quality of soldered junctions) should be obtained both before and after the training effort in the group exposed to training and before and after a corresponding work period in the control group. In this way it is possible to determine the extent to which any change in performance in the training group resulted from the training itself rather than from some organization-wide change like a raise in pay; we assume the latter would have affected employees in both groups equally. This approach is feasible and is sometimes used.[114] In terms of current practices, however, one survey found that something less than half the companies responding attempted to obtain before-and-after measures from trainees; the number of organizations using control groups was negligible.[115] One expert suggests at least using an evaluation form like the one shown in Figure 7-9 to evaluate the training program.[116]

controlled experimentation

Formal methods for testing the effectiveness of a training program, preferably with before-and-after tests and a control group.

Training Effects to Measure

Four basic categories of training outcomes can be measured:

1. *Reaction.* First, evaluate trainees' reactions to the program. Did they like the program? Did they think it worthwhile?
2. *Learning.* Second, you can test the trainees to determine whether they learned the principles, skills, and facts they were supposed to learn.
3. *Behavior.* Next ask whether the trainees' behavior on the job changed because of the training program. For example, are employees in the store's complaint department more courteous toward disgruntled customers than previously?
4. *Results.* Last, but probably most importantly, ask: "What final results were achieved in terms of the training objectives previously set? Did the number of customer complaints about employees drop? Did the reject rate improve? Did scrappage cost decrease? Was turnover reduced? Are production quotas now being met?" and so forth. Improved results are, of course, especially important. The training program may succeed in terms of the reactions from trainees, increased learning, and even changes in behavior. But if the desired results are not achieved, then in the final analysis, the training has not achieved its goals. If so, the problem may lie in the training program. Remember, however, that the results may be inadequate because the problem was not amenable to training in the first place.

FIGURE 7-9

A Sample Outside Training Evaluation Form

Purpose: The following items assess the overall value of this training experience:

1. Did you find the quality of this program to be (select one):

   Poor _____   Fair _____   Average _____   Good _____   Outstanding _____

2. Do you feel that this program was worthwhile in terms of its cost and your time away from normal job duties?

   Yes _____   No _____   Undecided _____

3. Would you recommend this program to your peers?

   Yes _____   No _____   Undecided _____

4. Rate the program for the following qualities

	Poor				Outstanding
	1	2	3	4	5
a. Practical value					
b. Thoroughness					
c. New ideas gained					
d. Helpful to self-development					
e. Relevance to your job					
f. Efficient use of time					
g. Maintaining your interest					
h. Clear, understandable					

   Comments:

5. Check the degree to which the kinds of follow-up to this workshop listed here would be useful:

	Necessary	Desirable	Unnecessary
a. Talking with workshop members to share experiences in applying ideas			
b. Opportunity to consult with trainer if a problem arises			
c. Advanced workshop in this area			
d. Briefing for my superiors on what I've learned here			
e. Other			

While these four basic categories are understandable and widely used, there are several things to keep in mind when using them to measure training effects. First, there are usually only modest correlations among the four types of training criteria; in other words, scoring "high" on learning doesn't necessarily mean that behavior or results will also score "high," and the converse is true as well. Similarly, studies show that "reaction" measures (such as "How did you like the program?") can't be used as surrogates for other training effects (such as learning, behavior, or results). Getting trainees' reactions—often the measurement of choice when training is evaluated—may thus provide some insight into how they liked the program, but probably won't provide much insight into what they learned or how they'll behave once they're back on the job.[117]

We invite you to visit the Dessler page on the Prentice Hall Web site at **www.prenhall.com/dessler** for our on-line study guide, Internet exercises, current events, links to related Web sites, and more.

SUMMARY

1. The training process consists of five steps: needs analysis; instructional design; validation; implementation; and evaluation.

2. Some principles of learning theory include: Make the material meaningful (by providing a bird's-eye view and familiar examples, organizing the material, splitting it into meaningful chunks, and using familiar terms and visual aids); make provision for transfer of training; and try to motivate your trainee.

3. Job instruction training is useful for training on jobs that consist of a logical sequence of steps. Vestibule training combines the advantages of on- and off-the-job training.

4. On-the-job training is a third basic training technique. It might take the form of the understudy method, job rotation, or special assignments and committees. In any case, it should have four steps: preparing the learner, presenting the operation (or nature of the job), doing performance tryouts, and following up. Other training methods include audiovisual techniques, lectures, and computer-assisted instruction.

5. There are various training techniques for special purposes. These include customer service training, diversity training, AIDS training, and training for global assignments.

6. Management development is aimed at preparing employees for future jobs with the organization or at solving organizationwide problems concerning, for instance, inadequate interdepartmental communication.

7. Managerial on-the-job training methods include job rotation, coaching, and action learning. Basic off-the-job techniques include case studies, management games, outside seminars, university-related programs, role playing, behavior modeling, and in-house development centers.

8. In gauging the effectiveness of a training program there are four categories of outcomes you can measure: reacting, learning, behavior, and results. In some cases where training seems to have failed, it may be because training was not the appropriate solution.

KEY TERMS

employee orientation 249	vestibule or simulated training 263	case study method 275
training 249		management game 275
task analysis 254	management development 272	role playing 278
performance analysis 254		behavior modeling 278
on-the-job training 257	succession planning 272	in-house development center 279
job instruction training (JIT) 259	job rotation 272	controlled experimentation 281
programmed learning 261	action learning 273	

DISCUSSION QUESTIONS

1. "A well-thought-out orientation program is especially important for employees (like recent graduates) who have had little or no work experience." Explain why you agree or disagree with this statement.

2. You're the supervisor of a group of employees whose task is to assemble tuning devices that go into radios. You find that quality is not what it should be and that many of your group's tuning devices have to be brought back and reworked; your own boss says that "You'd better start doing a better job of training your workers."
   a. What are some of the "staffing" factors that could be contributing to this problem?
   b. Explain how you would go about assessing whether it is in fact a training problem.

3. Explain how you would apply our principles of learning in developing a lecture, say, on orientation and training.

4. John Santos is an undergraduate business student majoring in accounting. He has just failed the first accounting course, Accounting 101, and is understandably upset. Explain how you would use performance analysis to identify what, if any, are John's training needs.

5. What are some typical on-the-job training techniques? What do you think are some of the main drawbacks of relying on informal on-the-job training for breaking new employees into their jobs?

6. This chapter points out that one reason for implementing special global training programs is the need to avoid business losses "due to cultural insensitivity." What sort of cultural insensitivity do you think is referred to and how might that translate into lost business? What sort of training program would you recommend to avoid such cultural insensitivity?

7. This chapter presents several examples of how diversity training can backfire such as "the possibility of posttraining participant discomfort." How serious do you think potential negative outcomes like these are and what would you do as an HR manager to avoid them?

8. How does the involvement approach to attitude surveys differ from simply administering surveys and returning the results to top management?

9. Compare and contrast three organizational development techniques.

10. Describe the pros and cons of five management development methods.

11. Discuss the key alternatives in a typical off-the-job management development program.

12. Do you think job rotation is a good method to use for developing management trainees? Why or why not?

INDIVIDUAL AND GROUP ACTIVITIES

1. Pick out some task with which you are familiar—mowing the lawn or tuning a car—and develop a job instruction training sheet for it.

2. You are to give a short lecture on the subject "Guidelines to Keep in Mind When Presenting a Lecture." Give a 5- or 10-minute lecture on the subject making sure, of course, to follow the guidelines as enumerated in this chapter.

3. Working individually or in groups, you are to develop a short programmed learning program on the subject "Guidelines for Giving a More Effective Lecture." Use the example in Figure 7-4 and any other information you may have available to develop your programmed learning program.

4. Working individually or in groups, contact a provider of management development seminars such as the American Management Association. Obtain copies of their recent listings of seminar offerings. At what levels of managers do they aim their seminar offerings? What seems to be the most popular types of development programs? Why do you think that's the case?

5. Working individually or in groups, develop a series of concrete examples to illustrate how a professor teaching human resource management could use at least eight of the management development techniques described in this chapter in teaching his or her HR course.

6. Check with several local community colleges to determine what if any apprenticeship programs they are partners in.

EXPERIENTIAL EXERCISE

Purpose The purpose of this exercise is to give you practice in developing a training program.

Required Understanding You should be thoroughly familiar with the training methods we discussed in this chapter, including job instruction training, vestibule training, and on-the-job training. Because you'll be developing a training program for directory assistance operators you should read the following description of a directory assistance operator's duties:

Customers contact directory assistance operators to obtain the telephone numbers of persons whose numbers are not yet listed, whose listings have changed, or whose numbers are unknown to the customer. These operators check the requested number via computerized video display, which then transmits the numbers to the customers. If more than one number is requested, the operator reports the first number, and the system then transmits the second to the caller. A number must be found quickly so that the customer is not kept waiting. It is often necessary to check various spellings of the same name, since customers frequently give incorrect spellings.

Next, read this: Imagine you are the supervisor of about 10 directory assistance operators in a small regional phone company that has no formal training program for new operators. Since you get one or two new operators every few months you think it would raise efficiency for you to develop a "new directory assistance operator's training program" for your own use in your department. Consider what such a program would consist of before proceeding to your assigned group.

How to Set Up the Exercise   Divide the class into groups of four or five students.

INSTRUCTIONS

In keeping with the procedure we discussed for setting up a training program, your group should, at a minimum, go through the following steps:

1. List the duties and responsibilities of the job (of directory assistance operator) using the description provided above.

2. List some assumed standards of work performance for the job.

3. Within your group, develop some assumptions about what parts of the job give new employees the most trouble (you'd normally be able to do this based on your experience as the operators' supervisor).

4. Determine what kind of training is needed to overcome these differences.

5. Develop a "new directory assistance operator's training package." In this you'll provide two things: (1) a one-page outline showing the type(s) of training each new operator in your unit will go through (for example, you might indicate that the first two hours on the job will involve the new operator observing existing operators; then four hours of lectures, etc.) and (2) expand on exactly what each training technique will involve. For example, if you are going to use job instruction training, show the steps to be included; if you're going to use lectures, provide an outline of what you'll discuss; etc.

If time permits, a spokesperson from each group can put his or her group's training program outline on the board, and the class can discuss the relative merits of each group's proposal.

CASE INCIDENT

Reinventing the Wheel at Apex Door Company

Jim Delaney, president of Apex Door, has a problem. No matter how often he tells his employees how to do their jobs, they invariably "decide to do it their way," as he puts it, and arguments ensue between Jim, the employee, and the employee's supervisor. One example is the door-design department, where the designers are expected to work with the architects to design doors that meet the specifications. While it's not "rocket science," as Jim puts it, the designers invariably make mistakes— such as designing in too much steel—a problem that can cost Apex tens of thousands of wasted dollars, once you consider the number of doors in, say, a 30-story office tower.

The order processing department is another example. Jim has a very specific and detailed way he wants

(continued)

(continued from page 285)
the order written up, but most of the order clerks don't understand how to actually use the multipage order form, and simply improvise when it comes to a detailed question such as whether to classify the customer as "industrial" or "commercial."

The current training process is as follows. None of the jobs have training manuals per se, although several have somewhat out-of-date job descriptions. The training for new people is all on the job. Usually the person leaving the company trains the new person during the 1- or 2-week overlap period, but if there's no overlap, the new person is trained as well as possible by other employees who have filled in occasionally on the job in the past. The training is basically the same throughout the company, for machinists, secretaries, assemblers, and accounting clerks, for example.

■ QUESTIONS

1. What do you think of Apex's training process? Could it help to explain why employees "do things their way" and if so, how?

2. What role do job descriptions play in training?

3. Explain in detail what you would do to improve the training process at Apex. Make sure to provide specific suggestions, please.

Case Application

A TRAINING AND DEVELOPMENT PROBLEM AT SUMERSON MANUFACTURING

You began working for Sumerson Manufacturing Company as a human resource department trainee a few days after receiving your M.B.A. degree with a major in management from a large midwestern university. After a one-year training program, you served two years as assistant director of training and development in one of Sumerson's machining and assembly plants. You then were promoted to plant director of training and development, in which capacity you served for approximately four years. This assignment ended when you were transferred to corporate headquarters as staff assistant to the corporate director of training and development. The corporate director is scheduled for retirement in six months. You hope to become the next corporate director of training and development, but you know that this depends largely on how well you handle your next major assignment.

Sumerson is planning to open a new plant in sixteen months. The new plant is going to hire approximately one thousand employees. However, only one of eight production lines is to go into operation when the plant opens. The other seven production lines will be phased in over a period of three years from the date of the plant opening. Construction of the new plant has just started in a town of ten thousand people eighteen miles south of Memphis, Tennessee. The plant will be very similar to the plant in which you previously had been director of training and development. You have been asked by the corporate vice president of human resources and your boss to submit a plan for recruiting, selecting, and training the personnel for the new plant. You have been given four months in which to do the job. Four hundred and fifty new employees must be hired and trained prior to the plant opening date.

Top management has made the decision that forty-nine members of management from Sumerson's other twenty-one plants are to be transferred to fill all second- and higher-level management positions. For most of these managers, this will be a promotion. Also, many nonmanagement employees in the company will be offered jobs in the new plant, but few are expected to accept. All front-line management, such as lead persons and supervisors, must be trained by Sumerson, not hired "off the street" as supervisors.

You are not sure what you should do, because this is the first time the company has ever built and staffed a new plant. There is no past experience on which to draw. You have decided that you have two separate but related problems:

■ QUESTIONS

1. How to hire and train an entire staff of new employees below the second level of management in one year and have them ready to open the new plant; and

2. How to procure and train the balance of the thousand employees needed to staff the plant by the projected full-operations date. What is your plan?

This exercise was prepared by Professor James C. Hodgetts of the Fogelman College of Business and Economics of the University of Memphis. The name of the company is disguised. Used by permission.

NOTES

1. For a recent discussion of socialization see, for example, Georgia Chao et al., "Organizational Socialization: Its Content and Consequences," *Journal of Applied Psychology*, Vol. 79, no. 5 (1994), pp. 730–743.

2. Joseph Famularo, *Handbook of Modern Personnel Administration* (New York: McGraw-Hill, 1972), pp. 237–238. See also Ronald Smith, "Employee Orientation: Ten Steps to Success," *Personnel Journal*, Vol. 63, no. 12 (December 1984), pp. 46–49.

3. Susan Ashford and Jay Stewart Black, "Proactivity During Organizational Entry: The Role of Desire for Control," *Journal of Applied Psychology*, Vol. 81, no. 2 (1996), pp. 199–214.

4. See, for example, Carolyn Wiley, "Training for the 90s: How Leading Companies Focus on Quality Improvement, Technological Change, and Customer Service," *Employment Relations Today* (Spring 1993), p. 80.

5. See, for example, our discussion in Chapter 1. Also see Ibid., p. 80.

6. The following is based on Ibid., pp. 81–82.

7. Harley Frazis, Diane Herz, and Michael Horrigan, "Employer-Provided Training: Results from a New Survey," *Monthly Labor Review* (May 1995), pp. 3–17.

8. *BNA Bulletin to Management*, "Employee Training," January 23, 1997, pp. 28–29.

9. Ibid.

10. *BNA Bulletin to Management*, "Training Receives Renewed Emphasis," October 31, 1996, p. 352.

11. Anthony F. Carnevale, "America and the New Economy," *Training and Development Journal*, Vol. 44, no. 11 (November 1990) pp. 31ff. See also Richard Saggers, "Training Climbs the Corporate Agenda," *Personnel Management*, Vol. 26, no. 7 (July 1994), pp. 40–45.

12. Ibid.; "The Training Gap," *Training and Development Journal* (March 1991), p. 9. Terri Bergman, "Training: The Case for Increased Investment," *Employment Relations Today*, Vol. 21, no. 4 (Winter 1994), pp. 381–391.

13. Based on Kenneth Wexley and Gary Yukl, *Organizational Behavior and Personnel Psychology* (Burr Ridge, IL: McGraw-Hill, 1977), pp. 289–295; E. J. McCormick and J. Tiffin, *Industrial Psychology* (Upper Saddle River NJ: Prentice Hall, 1974), pp. 232–240.

14. Wexley and Yukl, *Organizational Behavior*, pp. 289–295.

15. R. E. Silverman, *Learning Theory Applied to Training* (Reading, MA: Addison-Wesley, 1970), Chapter 8; McCormick and Tiffin, *Industrial Psychology*, pp. 239–240.

16. Kimberly A. Smith-Jentsch, et al., "Can Pre-Training Experiences Explain Individual Differences in Learning?" *Journal of Applied Psychology*, Vol. 81, no. 1 (1996), pp. 110–116.

17. Ibid.

18. Janice A. Cannon-Bowers, et al., "A Framework for Understanding Pre-Practice Conditions and Their Impact on Learning," *Personnel Psychology*, Vol. 51 (1998) pp. 291–320.

19. Ibid., p. 305.

20. This is based on Kenneth Wexley and Gary Latham, *Developing and Training Human Resources in Organizations* (Glenview, IL: Scott, Foresman, 1981), pp. 22–27. Note that these legal aspects apply equally to technical training and management development. See also Ron Zemke, "What is Technical Training, Anyway?" *Training*, Vol. 23, no. 7 (July 1986), pp. 18–22. See also Bureau of National Affairs, "Sexual Harassment: Training Tips," *Fair Employment Practices*, June 25, 1987, p. 84.

21. Kenneth Sovereign, *Personnel Law* (Upper Saddle River, NJ: Prentice Hall, 1994), pp. 165–166.

22. *Ibid.*, pp. 165–166; J. Fenton, William Ruud, and J. Kimbell, "Negligent Training Suits: A Recent Entry into the Corporate Employment Negligence Arena," *Labor Law Journal*, Vol. 42, June 1991, p. 351.

23. These are based on Sovereign, *Personnel Law*, pp. 165–166.

24. Bureau of National Affairs, *Training Employees, Personnel Policies Forum, Survey 88* (Washington, DC: November 1965), p. 5. For further discussion of conducting a needs analysis, see Kenneth Nowack, "A True Training Needs Analysis," *Training and Development Journal* (April 1991), pp. 69–73.

25. B. M. Bass and J. A. Vaughan, "Assessing Training Needs," in Craig Schneier and Richard Beatty, *Personnel Administration Today* (Reading, MA: Addison-Wesley, 1978), p. 311. See also Ronald Ash and Edward Leving, "Job Applicant Training and Work Experience Evaluation: An Empirical Comparison of Four Methods," *Journal of Applied Psychology*, Vol. 70, no. 3 (1985), pp. 572–576; John Lawrie, "Break the Training Ritual," *Personnel*

Journal, Vol. 67, no. 4 (April 1988), pp. 95–97; and Theodore Lewis and David Bjorkquist, "Needs Assessment—A Critical Reappraisal," *Performance Improvement Quarterly*, Vol. 5, no. 4 (1992), pp. 33–54; Sasha Cohen, "EPSS to Go," *Training and Development*, Vol. 52, no. 3, (March 1998), pp. 54–57.

26. See, for example, Gean Freeman, "Human Resources Planning—Training Needs Analysis," *Human Resources Planning*, Vol. 39, no. 3 (Fall 1993), pp. 32–34.

27. McCormick and Tiffin, *Industrial Psychology*, p. 245. See also James C. Georges, "The Hard Realities of Soft Skills Training," *Personnel Journal*, Vol. 68, no. 4 (April 1989), pp. 40–45; Robert H. Buckham, "Applying Role Analysis in the Workplace," *Personnel*, Vol. 64, no. 2 (February 1987), pp. 63–65; and J. Kevin Ford and Raymond Noe, "Self-Assessed Training Needs: The Effects of Attitudes towards Training, Management Level, and Function," *Personnel Psychology*, Vol. 40, no. 1 (Spring 1987), pp. 39–54.

28. Wexley and Latham, *Developing and Training*, p. 107.

29. Ibid., pp. 107–112. Four steps in on-the-job training based on William Berliner and William McLarney, *Management Practice and Training* (Burr Ridge, IL: McGraw-Hill, 1974), pp. 442–443. See also Robert Sullivan and Donald Miklas, "On-the-Job Training that Works," *Training and Development Journal*, Vol. 39, no. 5 (May 1985), pp. 118–120, and Stephen B. Wehrenberg, "Supervisors as Trainees: The Long-Term Gains of OJT," *Personnel Journal*, Vol. 66, no. 4 (April 1987), pp. 48–51.

30. Harley Frazis, Diane Herz, and Michael Horrigan, "Employer-Provided Training: Results From a New Survey," *Monthly Labor Review* (May 1995), p. 4.

31. "German Training Model Imported," *BNA Bulletin to Management*, December 19, 1996, p. 408.

32. Ibid.

33. Nancy Day, "Informal Learning Gets Results," *Work Force* (June 1998), p. 31.

34. Ibid., p. 31.

35. Ibid., p. 32.

36. Donald F. Michalak and Edwin G. Yager, *Making the Training Process Work* (New York: Harper & Row, 1979), pp. 108–111. See also Richard Wiegand, "Can All Your Trainees Hear You?" *Training and Development Journal*, Vol. 41, no. 8 (August 1987), pp. 38–43.

37. G. N. Nash, J. P. Muczyk, and F. L. Vettori, "The Role and Practical Effectiveness of Programmed Instruction," *Personnel Psychology*, Vol. 24 (1971), pp. 397–418.

38. Wexley and Latham, *Developing and Training*, pp. 131–133. See also Teri O. Grady and Mike Matthews, "Video . . . Through the Eyes of the Trainee," *Training*, Vol. 24, no. 7 (July 1987), pp. 57–62. For a description of the use of computer-based multimedia training, see Erica Schroeder, "Training Takes Off, Using Multimedia," *PC Week*, August 29, 1994, pp. 33–34.

39. Mary Boone and Susan Schulman, "Teletraining: A High-Tech Alternative," *Personnel*, Vol. 62, no. 5 (May 1985), pp. 4–9. See also Ron Zemke, "The Rediscovery of Video Teleconferencing," *Training*, Vol. 23, no. 9 (September 1986), pp. 28–36; and Carol Haig, "Clinics Fill Training Niche," *Personnel Journal*, Vol. 66, no. 9 (September 1987), pp. 134–140.

40. Joseph Giusti, David Baker, and Peter Braybash, "Satellites Dish out Global Training," *Personnel Journal* (June 1991), pp. 80–84.

41. "Macy's Goes 'On Air' to Inform Employees," *BNA Bulletin to Management*, May 15, 1997, p. 160.

42. "Cadillac Offers a Top-of-the-Line Training Program," *Personnel Journal* (February 1996), p. 25 (no author).

43. "Personnel Shop Talk," *BNA Bulletin to Management*, February 12, 1998, p. 46.

44. Michael Emery and Margaret Schubert, "A Trainer's Guide to Videoconferencing," *Training* (June 1993), p. 60.

45. Ibid., p. 60.

46. "Employer to Learn the Benefits of Distance Learning," *BNA Bulletin to Management*, April 25, 1996, p. 130.

47. These are based on or quoted from Emery and Schubert, "A Trainer's Guide to Videoconferencing," p. 61.

48. Wexley and Latham, *Developing and Training*, p. 141. See also Raymond Wlozkowski, "Simulation," *Training and Development Journal*, Vol. 39, no. 6 (June 1985), pp. 38–43.

49. See, for example, Tim Falconer, "No More Pencils, No More Books!" *Canadian Banker* (March/April 1994), pp. 21–25.

50. Ralph E. Ganger, "Training: Computer-Based Training Works," *Personnel Journal*, Vol. 73, no. 11 (November 1994), pp. 51–52. See also Anat Arkin, "Computing: The Future Means of Training?" *Personnel Management*, Vol. 26, no. 86 (August 1994), pp. 36–40.

51. For another example see Mickey Williamson, "High-Tech Training," *byte* (December 1994), pp. 74–89.

52. These are summarized in Rockley Miller, "New Training Looms," *Hotel and Motel Management*, April 4, 1994, pp. 26, 30.

53. Ibid., p. 26.

54. Bob Filipezak, "Trainers on the Net," *Training* (December 1994), pp. 42–51.

55. Ibid., p. 50.

56. Larry Stevens, "The Internet: Your Newest Training Tool?" *Personnel Journal* (July 1996), pp. 27–31.

57. Shari Caudron, "Your Learning Technology Primer," *Personnel Journal* (June 1996), pp. 120–136.

58. Ibid., p. 130.

59. Ibid., p. 122.

60. Jane Webster and Peter Hackley, "Teaching Effectiveness in Technology—Mediated Distance Learning," *Academy of Management Journal*, Vol. 40, no. 6 (1997), pp. 1282–1309.

61. C. D. Wetzel, P. H. Radtke, and H. W. Stern, *Instructional Effectiveness of Video Media* (Hillsdale, NJ: Erlbaum, 1994).

62. J. Storck and L. Sproull, "Through a Glass Darkly: What Do People Learn in Video Conferences?" *Human Communication Research*, Vol. 22 (1995), pp. 197–219.

63. Charles Bermant, "For the Latest in Corporate Training, Try A CD-ROM," *New York Times*, October 16, 1995, p. C5.

64. Karl Rayl, "GTE's Training Goes High-Tech," *Workforce* (April 1998), pp. 36–40.

65. Bob Filipczak, "Training Consortia: How They Work, How They Don't," *Training* (August 1994), pp. 51–57.

66. "Skill Deficiencies Pose Increasing Problems," *BNA Bulletin to Management*, October 26, 1995, pp. 337–338.

67. This is based on Ellen Sherman, "Back to Basics to Improve Skills," *Personnel* (July 1989), pp. 22–26.

68. Valerie Frazee, "Workers Learn to Walk so They Can Run," *Personnel Journal* (May 1996), pp. 115–120.

69. Nancy Lynn Bernardon, "Let's Erase Illiteracy from the Workplace," *Personnel* (January 1989), p. 92.

70. Jeffrey Mello, "AIDS Education in the Work Place," *Training and Development Journal* (December 1990), pp. 65–70.

71. This is based on Sylvia Odenwald, "A Guide for Global Training," *Training and Development* (July 1993), pp. 22–31.

72. For a full description of these programs as well as the names of the vendors, see Ibid., pp. 24–27.

73. See Joyce Santora, "Kinney Shoes Steps Into Diversity," *Personnel Journal* (September 1991), p. 74.

74. Sara Rynes and Benson Rosen, "What Makes Diversity Programs Work?" *HR Magazine* (October 1994), p. 64. See also Thomas Diamante and Leo Giglio, "Managing a Diverse Workforce: Training as a Cultural Intervention Strategy," *Leadership & Organization Development Journal*, Vol. 15, no. 2 (1994), pp. 13–17.

75. Willie Hopkins, Karen Sterkel-Powell, and Shirley Hopkins, "Training Priorities for a Diverse Workforce," *Public Personnel Management*, Vol. 23, no. 3 (Fall 1994), p. 433.

76. Santora, "Kinney Shoes Steps Into Diversity," pp. 72–77.

77. Joyce Santora, "Alamo's Drive for Customer Service," *Personnel Journal*, April 1991, pp. 42–44.

78. This is based on Jennifer Laabs, "Team Training Goes Outdoors," *Personnel Journal* (June 1991), pp. 56–63.

79. Ibid., p. 56. See also Shari Caudron, "Teamwork Takes Work," *Personnel Journal*, Vol. 73, no. 2, (February 1994), pp. 41–49.

80. Heidi Campbell, "Adventures in Teamland," *Personnel Journal* (May 1996), pp. 56–62.

81. This is based on Norman Nopper, "Reinventing the Factory with Lifelong Learning," *Training* (May 1993), pp. 55–57.

82. Ibid., p. 56.

83. Ibid.

84. Ibid., p. 57. For another example, see Kevin Kelly and Peter Burrows, "Motorola: Training for the Millennium," *Business Week*, March 28, 1994, pp. 158–160, and "Some Nuts and Bolts of Lifelong Learning," *Training* (March 1994), p. 30 (no author cited).

85. For discussions of the steps in succession planning see, for example, Kenneth Nowack, "The Secrets of Succession," *Training and Development* (November 1994), pp. 49–55, and Donald Brookes, "In Management Succession: Who Moves Up?" *Human Resources* (January/February 1995), pp. 11–13.

86. Dale Yoder et al., *Handbook of Personnel Management and Labor Relations* (New York: McGraw-Hill, 1958), pp. 10–27; for a recent review, see William Rothwell, H. C. Kazanas, and Daria Haines, "Issues and Practices in Management Job Rotation Programs as Perceived by HRD Professionals," *Performance Improvement Quarterly*, Vol. 5, no. 1 (1992), pp. 49–69.

87. Kenneth Wexley and Gary Latham, *Developing and Training Resources in Organizations* (Glenview, IL: Scott, Foresman, 1981), p. 118.

88. Ibid., pp. 118–119.

89. Ibid., p. 207.

90. This is based on Nancy Fox, "Action Learning Comes to Industry," *Harvard Business Review*, Vol. 56 (September–October 1977), pp. 158–168; see also Nancy Dixon, "Action Learning," *Performance Improvement Quarterly*, Vol. 11, no. 1 (1998), pp. 44–58.

91. Gillian Flynn, "Thinktanks Power Up Employees," *Personnel Journal* (June 1996), pp. 100–108.

92. Ibid., p. 101.

93. Wexley and Latham, *Developing and Training Resources in Organizations*, p. 193.

94. Chris Argyris, "Some Limitations of the Case Method: Experiences in a Management Development Program," *Academy of Management Review*, Vol. 5, no. 2 (1980), pp. 291–298.

95. Bernard Bass and Bruce Avolio, "Shatter the Glass Ceiling,: Women May Make Better Managers," *Human Resource Management*, Vol. 33, no. 4 (Winter 1994), pp. 549–560.

96. Ibid., p. 556.

97. Ibid., p. 558.

98. For a discussion of management games and also other noncomputerized training and development simulations, see Charlene Marmer Solomon, "Simulation Training Builds Teams Through Experience," *Personnel Journal* (June 1993), pp. 100–109; Kim Slack, "Training for the Real Thing," *Training and Development* (May 1993), pp. 79–89; Bruce Lierman, "How to Develop a Training Simulation," *Training and Development* (February 1994), pp. 50–52.

99. American Management Association, *Catalog of Seminars: April–December, 1998.*

100. John Hinrichs, "Personnel Testing," in Marvin Dunnette, ed., *Handbook of Industrial and Organizational Psychology* (Chicago: Rand McNally, 1976), p. 855.

101. Norman Maier, Allen Solem, and Ayesha Maier, *The Role Play Technique* (San Diego, CA: University Associates, 1975), pp. 2–3. See also David Swink, "Role-Play Your Way to Learning," *Training and Development* (May 1993) pp. 91–97; Alan Test, "Why I Do Not Like to Role Play," *The American Salesman* (August 1994), pp. 7–20.

102. This section is based on Allen Kraut, "Developing Managerial Skill via Modeling Techniques: Some Positive Research Findings—A Symposium," *Personnel Psychology*, Vol. 29, no. 3 (Autumn 1976), pp. 325–361.

103. Steven Simon and Jon Werner, "Computer Training Through Behavioral Modeling, Self-Paced, and Instructional Approaches: A Field Experiment," *Journal of Applied Psychology*, Vol. 81, no. 6 (1996), pp. 648–659.

104. Ibid., p. 657.

105. Thomas Stewart, "How GE Keeps Those Ideas Coming," *Fortune*, August 12, 1991, p. 43.

106. Martha Peak, "Go Corporate U!" *Management Review*, Vol. 86, no. 2 (February 1997), pp. 33–37.

107. Paul Blocklyn, "Developing the International Executive," *Personnel* (March 1989), pp. 44–47. See also T. S. Chan, "Developing International Managers: A Partnership Approach," *Journal of Management Development*, Vol. 13, no. 3 (1994), pp. 38–46.

108. This section is based on Ibid. See also "Developing Global Executives," *BNA Bulletin to Management*, Vol. 44, no. 10 March 11, 1993, pp. 73–74.

109. This is based on Karen Vander Linde, "Seven Ways to Make Your Training Department One of the Best," *Training and Development Journal*, Vol. 51, no. 8 (August 1997), pp. 20–28.

110. Carolyn Wiley, "Training for the 90s," p. 79.

111. Laurie Bassi, "Upgrading the U.S. Workplace: Do Reorganization & Education Help?" *Monthly Labor Review* (May 1995), pp. 37–47.

112. Ann Bartol, "Productivity Gains from the Implementation of Employee Training Programs," *Industrial Relations*, Vol. 33, no. 4 (October 1994), pp. 411–425.

113. Pamela Kidder and Janice Rouiller, "Evaluating the Success of a Large-Scale Training Effort," *National Productivity Review*, Vol. 16, no. 2 (1997), pp. 79–89.

114. See, for example, Charlie Morrow, M. Quintin Jarrett, and Melvin Rupinski, "An Investigation of the Effect and Economic Utility of Corporate-Wide Training," *Personnel Psychology*, Vol. 50 (1997) pp. 91–119.

115. R. E. Catalano and D. L. Kirkpatrick, "Evaluating Training Programs—The State of the Art," *Training and Development Journal*, Vol. 22, no. 5 (May 1968), pp. 2–9. See also J. Kevin Ford and Steven Wroten, "Introducing New Methods for Conducting Training Evaluation and for Linking Training Evaluation to Program Redesign," *Personnel Psychology*, Vol. 37, no. 4 (Winter 1984), pp. 651–666. See also Basil Paquet et al., "The Bottom Line," *Training and Development Journal*, Vol. 41, no. 5 (May 1987), pp. 27–33; Harold E. Fisher and Ronald Weinberg, "Make Training Accountable: Assess Its Impact," *Personnel Journal*, Vol. 67, no. 1 (January 1988), pp. 73–75; and Timothy Baldwin and J. Kevin Ford, "Transfer of Training: A Review and Directions for Future Research," *Personnel Psychology*, Vol. 41, no. 1 (Spring 1988), pp. 63–105. Anthony Montebello and Maurine Haga, "To Justify Training, Test, Test Again," *Personnel Journal*, Vol. 73, no. 1 (January 1994), pp. 83–87. See also John Barron et al., "How Well Do We Measure Training?" *Journal of Labor Economics*, Vol. 15, no. 3 (July 1997), pp. 507–528.

116. Donald Kirkpatrick, "Effective Supervisory Training and Development," Part 3: "Outside Programs," *Personnel*, Vol. 62, no. 2 (February 1985), pp. 39–42. See also James Bell and Deborah Kerr, "Measuring Training Results: Key to Managerial Commitment," *Training and Development Journal*, Vol. 41, no. 1 (January 1987), pp. 70–73. Among the reasons training might not pay off on the job are a mismatching of courses and trainee's needs, supervisory slip-ups (with supervisors signing up trainees and then forgetting to have them attend the sessions when the training session is actually given), and no help applying skills on the job. For a discussion, see Ruth Colvin Clark, "Nine Ways to Make Training Pay Off on the Job," *Training*, Vol. 23, no. 11 (November 1986), pp. 83–87. See also Herman Birnbrauer, "Troubleshooting Your Training Program," *Training and Development Journal*, Vol. 41, no. 9 (September 1987), pp. 18–20; George Bickerstaffe, "Measuring the Gains from Training," *Personnel Management* (November 1993), pp. 48–51; Jim Spoor, "You Can Quantify Training Dollars and Program Value," *HR Focus* (May 1993), p. 3; Jack Trynor, "Is Training a Good Investment?" *Financial Analyst Journal* (September–October 1994), pp. 6–8; and Sarah Dolliver, "The Missing Link: Evaluating Training Programs," *Supervision* (November 1994), pp. 10–12.

117. This is based on George Alliger, Scott Tannenbaum, Winston Bennett, Jr., Holly Traver, and Allison Shotland, "A Meta-Analysis of the Relations Among Training Criteria," *Personnel Psychology*, Vol. 50 (1997) pp. 341–358; see also Robert Rowden, "A Practical Guide to Assessing the Value of Training in Your Company," *Employment Relatives Today*, Vol. 25, no. 2 (Summer 1998), pp. 65–73.

8

MANAGING ORGANIZATIONAL RENEWAL

Immediately after it settled a nationwide strike with the auto workers in 1998, General Motors—the largest corporation in the world—announced a series of massive organizational changes: company-owned suppliers like Delphi were to be spun off; the car divisions' separate marketing staffs were to be consolidated under one head; and dozens of auto plants would be shut or replaced by state-of-the-art high-technology-based facilities.

Strategic changes like these would require intense support from the company's human resource staff. Thousands of employees at former GM subsidiaries would have to be outplaced, and their benefits arranged for; the firm's giant personnel planning systems would have to be combed to find the employees to be promoted, moved, or dismissed; new job descriptions prepared for the newly centralized marketing staff; and massive selection and training programs installed to staff the new high-tech factories. ▲

To some, the idea that HR should be a "strategic partner" may seem a little theoretical, but not to the leaders of companies like GM. Today, around the world, firms including GM, MCI, Worldcom, Sony, and AT&T are undergoing organizational change and renewal to become more competitive. And, as at GM, probably no function is more involved in these changes than is HR. In this chapter we'll turn to the process and techniques of organizational change and renewal and to HR's vital role in that process. We'll start with the overall process of organizational change, and then cover four more specific renewal efforts: total quality programs; team-based organizations; reengineering; and flexible work schedules.

MANAGING ORGANIZATIONAL CHANGE AND DEVELOPMENT	## What to Change? HR's Role

You've just taken over as CEO of a troubled company; what aspects of that company can you change? There are several, including its strategy, culture, structure, tasks, technologies, and the attitudes and skills of its people. All such changes will require the support and expert advice of the HR department.

strategic change

A change in a company's strategy, mission, and vision.

STRATEGIC CHANGE   Organizational change often starts with **strategic change,** a change in the firm's strategy, mission, and vision. Strategic change may then require other changes, for instance, in the firm's, production technology, structure, and culture.

The strategic change initiated at Fuji-Xerox by President Yotaro Kobayashi provides an example.[1] In response to declining market share, a dearth of new products, and increasing customer complaints, Kobayashi and his team formulated a new vision for the firm. It was called the New Xerox Movement and was aimed at transforming Fuji-Xerox into a more cost-conscious, competitive, quality-control-based company.[2]

cultural change

A change in a company's shared values and aims.

CULTURAL CHANGE   As at Fuji, implementing a strategic change often requires changing the culture, the firm's shared values and aims. Fuji-Xerox took several steps to implement such **cultural change.** For example, it created a new set of "heroes," individuals and teams who were publicly congratulated whenever their behavior reflected Fuji's new values of quality, teamwork, and customer focus.

HR plays an important role in changing culture. For example, one expert advocates five "primary embedding mechanisms" to change a company's culture, each of which requires HR's support and advice:[3]

1. *Make it clear to your employees what you pay attention to, measure, and control.* For example, direct the attention of your employees toward controlling costs or serving customers if those are the values you want to emphasize.

2. *React appropriately to critical incidents and organizational crises.* For example, if you want to emphasize the value that "we're all in this together," don't react to declining profits by laying off operating employees and middle managers, leaving your top managers intact.

3. *Deliberately role model, teach, and coach the values you want to emphasize.* For example, Wal-Mart founder Sam Walton embodied the values of "hard work, honesty, neighborliness, and thrift" that he wanted Wal-Mart employees to follow. Although he was one of the richest men in the world, he drove a pickup truck, a preference he explained by asking, "If I drove a Rolls Royce, what would I do with my dog?"

4. *Communicate your priorities by the way you allocate rewards and status.* Leaders communicate their priorities and values by the way they award pay raises and

promotions. For example, when the top management at General Foods decided several years ago to reorient its strategy from cost to diversification and sales growth, the HR department revised the compensation system so as to link bonuses to sales volume (rather than just increased earnings as in the past).

5. *Make your HR procedures and criteria consistent with the values you espouse.* When he became Chairperson and CEO of IBM, Louis Gerstner brought in a new top management team—including a new HR head—whose values were consistent with shaking up IBM's traditionally bureaucratic and politicized culture. They then revised IBM's HR policies and procedures; for example, new incentive plans, promotion and appraisal criteria, and dismissal policies were instituted to support IBM's new performance-oriented strategies.

structural change

The reorganizing-redesigning of an organization's departmentalization, coordination, span of control, reporting relationships, or centralization of decision making.

technological change

Modifications to the work methods an organization uses to accomplish its tasks.

organizational development interventions

HR-based techniques aimed at changing employees' attitudes, values, and behavior.

STRUCTURAL CHANGE   Reorganizing-redesigning the organization's departmentalization, coordination, span of control, reporting relationships, or centralization of decision making is a relatively direct and quick method for changing an organization. At GE, for instance, Jack Welch collapsed the firm's management structure from nine layers to as few as four, reduced 29 pay levels to 5 broad bands, and reorganized 350 different product lines and business units into 13 big businesses.[4]

HR plays a role in such **structural change**. As at GE, downsizings require performance reviews to decide who stays and who goes and an outplacement effort; reorganizing requires personnel planning, selection, and job analysis; and flattening the organization may require consolidating pay levels into fewer, broader bands.

TASK REDESIGN   The tasks and authority assigned to individuals and teams within the organization are often changed as well. For example, traditional assembly-line jobs were abolished at Saturn. Instead, the work is now organized around work teams.

TECHNOLOGICAL CHANGE   **Technological changes** are modifications to the work methods the organization uses to accomplish its tasks. They may include new production technologies, new selection and screening procedures, and new performance appraisal techniques, for instance. The compensation plans and appraisal systems instituted by Fuji-Xerox illustrate HR-based technological changes, in this case implemented to support cultural and strategic changes.

CHANGES IN PEOPLE, ATTITUDES AND SKILLS   Sometimes the employees themselves must change.[5] As explained in Chapter 7 (Training and Development) techniques such as lectures, conferences, and on-the-job training are often used to provide new or present employees with the skills they need to perform their jobs adequately. HR-based **organizational development interventions** (discussed later in this chapter) are aimed at changing employees' attitudes, values, and behavior.

William Bossidy succeeded in changing the values and culture at Allied Signal by organizing meetings with employees, instituting new training programs, and changing compensation plans.

A 10-Step Process for Leading Organizational Change

Actually implementing and leading an organizational change can be a tricky matter, even for a CEO with lots of clout. The change may be complex and require dozens or even hundreds of managers and supervisors to do their parts; resistance may be considerable; and the change may have to be accomplished while the company continues to serve its customer base.

Psychologist Kurt Lewin formulated the classic explanation of how to implement a change. To Lewin, all behavior in organizations was a product of two kinds of forces—those striving to maintain the status quo and those pushing for change. Implementing change thus meant either reducing the forces for the status quo or building up the forces for change. Lewin's process consisted of these three steps:

1. *Unfreezing.* Unfreezing means reducing the forces that are striving to maintain the status quo, usually by presenting a provocative problem or event to get people to recognize the need for change and to search for new solutions.

2. *Moving.* Lewin's second step aims to shift or alter the behavior of the individuals in the departments or organization in which the changes are to take place. Moving means developing new behaviors, values, and attitudes, sometimes through organizational structure changes and sometimes through the sorts of HR-based organizational change and development techniques explained later in this chapter.

3. *Refreezing.* Lewin assumed that organizations tended to revert to their former ways of doing things unless the changes were reinforced. This reinforcement is accomplished by refreezing the organization into its new state of equilibrium. Lewin advocated instituting new systems and procedures (such as compensation plans and appraisal processes) to support and maintain the changes that were made.

Based on several recent large-scale organizational renewal projects, a more detailed listing of the steps involved in such a process may be summarized as follows:

1.   Establish a Sense of Urgency[6] Once they become aware of the need to change, most leaders start by creating a sense of urgency. When he took over electronics giant Philips, CEO Jan Timmer knew that to rouse his top managers out of their status quo thinking, he had to create a sense of urgency; he did this by presenting his top managers with a (ficticious) press announcement describing Phillip's bankruptcy.

2.   Mobilize Commitment to Change through Joint Diagnosis of Business Problems Having established a sense of urgency, many leaders then create one or more task forces to diagnose the business problems. Such teams can produce a shared understanding of what can and must be improved and thereby mobilize the commitment of those who must actually implement the change.

3.   Create a Guiding Coalition Major transformations—such as Bill Gates accomplished in the mid-1990's by transforming Microsoft into an Internet-oriented company—are sometimes associated with just one highly visible leader, but no leader can really implement any such change alone. Many therefore create a guiding coalition of influential people, who act as missionaries and implementers. Such a coalition should include people who individually have the influence to lead such a change. And, it's essential the group works together as a team.

4.   Develop a Shared Vision To transform an organization, a new vision is usually required, "a general statement of the organization's intended direction that evokes emotional feelings in organization members." For example, when Barry Gibbons became CEO of a drifting Spec's Music, its employees, owners, and bankers—all its stakeholders—required a vision of a renewed Spec's around which they could rally. Gibbons's vision of a leaner Spec's offering a diversified blend of concerts and retail music helped to provide the sense of direction they all required.

5.   Communicate the Vision Change expert John Kotter says that "the real power of a vision is unleashed only when most of those involved in an enterprise or activity have a common understanding of its goals and directions."[7] In fact, fostering support for the new vision is virtually impossible unless the vision has been effectively communicated. The key elements in effectively communicating a vision include:[8]

- *Keep it simple.* Eliminate all jargon and wasted words. Here is an example of a good statement of vision: "We are going to become faster than anyone else in our industry at satisfying customer needs."
- *Use multiple forums.* Try to use every channel possible—big meetings and small, memos and newspapers, formal and informal interaction—to spread the word.
- *Use repetition.* Ideas sink in deeply only after they have been heard many times.
- *Lead by example.* "Walk your talk" so that your behaviors and decisions are consistent with the vision you espouse.

6. Enable Employees to Facilitate the Change By now employees understand the vision and want to make it a reality, but may feel inadequate. Perhaps a lack of skills stands in the way; or policies, procedures and the organization chart make it difficult to act; or some bosses may actual discourage those actions aimed at implementing the company's new vision. It's the company's job to see to it that such barriers are removed.

Doing so requires considerable HR assistance. When he took over as CEO of Sony and its loss-making movie studios, Nobuyuki Idei proceeded, "in a most un-Japanese way," to sweep the old studio executives out of office and to install a newly recruited team led by industry veterans, with a mandate to fix Sony's movie business.[9] At Allied Signal, CEO Lawrence Bossidy put every one of his 80,000 people through quality training. He also created geographic "councils" (for instance, for Asia) so that employees from Allied divisions who were undertaking initiatives in those areas could get together, share market intelligence, and compare notes.[10]

7. Generate Short-Term Wins Transforming a company can take time, but employees need reinforcement periodically. That's why building in "short term wins" is important.[11] For example, the guiding coalition in one company intentionally set its sights on producing one highly visible and successful new product about 20 months after the start of the organizational change effort.[12] The new product was selected in part because they knew its introduction was doable.

8. Consolidate Gains and Produce More Change The company can then use the credibility from such short-term wins to change all the systems, structures, and policies that don't fit well with the company's new vision. And, managers can continue to produce more change by hiring and promoting new people; by identifying certain employees to champion the continuing change; and by providing additional opportunities for short-term wins by employees.[13]

9. Anchor the New Ways of Doing Things in the Company's Culture Most organizational changes require a corresponding change in employees' shared values. For example, a "team-based, quality-oriented, adaptable organization" is not going to happen if the values employees share still emphasize selfishness, mediocrity, and bureaucratic behavior.

We've already noted how to lead a change in organizational culture. In brief, it means crystallizing values that are consistent with your vision for the company and then modeling teaching, and communicating the values you want your employees to share.

10. Monitor Progress and Adjust the Vision as Required Progress then must be monitored. Thus one firm appointed an oversight team to monitor its new team-based organization and self-managing teams.

AN EXAMPLE   The following shows how one firm implemented this process, within its HR group. Responding to a change in the parent firms strategy, the HR redesign process at Philadelphia-based PECO Energy began with a *visioning event.* The purpose of this 3-day meeting was to develop the vision for HR and to determine the principles that should guide the redesign activities over the next 5 months. It was critical at the outset to make sure all key stakeholders in the effort agreed on the direction HR needed to take. After agreeing on the vision, participants nominated five "critical" processes (such as employee selection) to be recreated to support the group's new vision.

Next, the core team held "town hall" meetings with all employees, communicating the new vision, mission, and principles and receiving feedback that could be incorporated into it's second session. The second event, a *process design/redesign event,* was then conducted one month later. During this 2 day session the five critical HR processes identified at the first session were reinvented or created. Among the processes redesigned were: selection and placement, policy development and deployment, workforce planning and job pricing. During this second session participants also determined that employees needed to take more responsibility for their career planning. At this stage consulting HR experts from other companies offered ideas, and PECO's own computer experts provided technological recommendations, for implementing, for instance, the new selection process.

Having redesigned how those five basic processes would be redesigned, management had to then rethink the distribution of HR's jobs. During a third session, the *organizational design event,* PECO employees focused on determining where the HR work would be done in the future. During these 2 days, much of HRs routine work was transferred to line employees and managers.

The final *implementation event,* was designed to review the implementation plan, validate the steps required to make the transition, and ensure the continued sponsorship and alignment of employees and managers companywide. This session introduced the new leadership team of human resources for PECO and laid the plans to sustain the effort over the next 4 to 6 months.[14]

Using Organizational Development to Change Organizations

organizational development (OD)

A method aimed at changing the attitudes, values, and beliefs of employees so that employees can improve the organization.

WHAT IS ORGANIZATIONAL DEVELOPMENT?   **Organizational development (OD)** is a special approach to organizational change in which the employees themselves formulate the change that's required and implement it, often with the assistance of a trained consultant. Particularly in large companies the OD process (including hiring of facilitators) is almost always handled through HR, whose staff has the special knowledge and networks required to implement this approach. As an approach to changing organizations, OD has several distinguishing characteristics:

1. It is usually based on *action research*, which means collecting data about a group, department, or organization and then feeding the data back to the employees so they can analyze it and develop hypotheses about what the problems in the unit might be.

2. It applies behavioral science knowledge for the purpose of improving the organization's effectiveness.

3. It changes the attitudes, values, and beliefs of employees so that the employees themselves can identify and implement the technical, procedural, structural, or other changes needed to improve the company's functioning.

4. It changes the organization in a particular direction—toward improved problem solving, responsiveness, quality of work, and effectiveness.[15]

TYPES OF OD APPLICATIONS   The number and variety of OD applications (also called OD interventions or techniques) have increased substantially over the past few years. OD got its start with what were called *human process interventions.* These were generally aimed at enabling employees to develop a better understanding of their own and others' behaviors to improve that behavior for the benefit of organization.

Today, as illustrated in Table 8-1, a much wider range of applications is available. Indeed, the once-clear lines between OD and other types or organizational change efforts (such as reorganizing) are starting to blur. This is happening because OD practitioners have become increasingly involved not just in changing participants' behaviors but also in directly altering the firm's structure, practices, strategy, and culture.

There are four types of OD applications: human process, technostructural, human resource management, and strategic applications. All are based on getting the employees themselves to collect the required data and to create and implement the solutions.

sensitivity training
A method for increasing employees' insights into their own behavior by candid discussions in groups led by special trainers.

Human Process Applications   Human process OD techniques generally aim first at improving employees' human relations skills. The goal is to give employees the insight and skills required to analyze their own and others' behavior more effectively, so they can then solve interpersonal and intergroup problems. **Sensitivity training** is perhaps the most widely used technique in this category.

TABLE 8-1 Examples of OD Interventions and the Organizational Levels They Affect

INTERVENTIONS	PRIMARY ORGANIZATIONAL LEVEL AFFECTED		
	INDIVIDUAL	GROUP	ORGANIZATION
Human Process			
T-Groups	X	X	
Process consultation		X	
Third-party intervention	X	X	
Team building		X	
Organizational confrontation meeting		X	X
Intergroup relations		X	X
Technostructural			
Formal structural change			X
Differentiation and integration			X
Cooperative union–management projects	X	X	X
Quality circles	X	X	
Total quality management		X	X
Work design	X	X	
Human Resource Management			
Goal setting	X	X	
Performance appraisal	X	X	
Reward systems	X	X	X
Career planning and development	X		
Managing workforce diversity	X		
Employee wellness	X		
Strategic			
Integrated strategic management			X
Culture change			X
Strategic change			X
Self-designing organizations		X	X

Sensitivity Training Sensitivity, laboratory, or t-group training (the *t* is for training) was one of the earliest OD techniques; although its use has diminished, it is still found today. Sensitivity training's basic aim is to increase the participant's insight into his or her own behavior and the behavior of others by encouraging an open expression of feelings in the trainer-guided t-group. Typically, 10 to 15 people meet, usually away from the job, and no activities or discussion topics are planned. The focus is on the here and now (specifically, the feelings and emotions of the members in the group). Participants are encouraged to portray themselves as they are in the group rather than in terms of past experiences or future problems. The t-group's success depends largely on the feedback process and in particular on participants' willingness to tell one another how their behavior is being perceived. A climate of "psychological safety" is therefore necessary if participants are to feel safe enough to reveal themselves, to expose their feelings, to drop their defenses, and to try out new ways of interacting.[16]

T-group training is obviously quite personal in nature, so it's not surprising that it's a controversial technique the use of which has diminished markedly since its heyday 20 years ago. The personal nature of such training suggests that participation should be voluntary; some therefore view t-group training as unethical because participation "suggested" by one's superior cannot be considered strictly voluntary.[17] Others argue that it can actually be a dangerous exercise if led by an inadequately prepared trainer.

team building

Improving the effectiveness of teams such as corporate officers and division directors through use of consultants, interviews, and team-building meetings.

Team Building The characteristic OD stress on action research is perhaps most evident in **team building**, which refers to the following process of improving team effectiveness. Data concerning the team's performance are collected and then fed back to the members of the group. The participants examine, explain, and analyze the data and develop specific action plans or solutions for solving the team's problems. This is another example of a human process OD application.

According to experts French and Bell, the typical team-building meeting begins with the consultant interviewing each of the group members and the leader prior to the meeting.[18] They are all asked what their problems are, how they think the group functions, and what obstacles are keeping the group from performing better. The consultant might then categorize the interview data into themes and present the themes to the group at the beginning of the meeting. (Themes like lack of time or lack of cohesion might be culled from such statements as "I don't have enough time to get my job done" or "I can't get any cooperation around here.") The themes are ranked by the group in terms of their importance, and the most important ones become the agenda for the meeting. The group then explores and discusses the issues, examines the underlying causes of the problems, and begins working on some solutions.

confrontation meetings

A method for clarifying and bringing into the open intergroup misconceptions and problems so that they can be resolved.

Other human process interventions aim to bring about intergroup or organization-wide changes. Organizational **confrontation meetings** can help clarify and bring into the open intergroup misconceptions and problems so that they can be resolved. The basic approach here is that the participants themselves provide the input (such as "here's how you make me feel") for the meeting; they then confront and thrash out misperceptions in an effort to reduce tensions.

survey research

A method that involves surveying employees' attitudes and providing feedback to the work groups as a basis for problem analysis and action planning.

Survey research, another human process OD technique, requires that employees throughout the organization fill out attitude surveys. The data are then used as feedback to the work groups as a basis for problem analysis and action planning. In general, such surveys are a convenient method for unfreezing an organization's management and employees by providing a comparative, graphic illustration of the fact that the organization does have problems that should be solved.[19] Employee attitude surveys' continuing popularity reflects the fact that:

> There is validity in employee reports of their experiences and these reports can be very useful as diagnoses of the degree to which a new strategy is being implemented and the degree to which policies and practices are related to the achievement of strategic goals like customer satisfaction and customer attention.[20]

Technostructural Interventions   OD practitioners are also increasingly involved in changing the structures, methods, and job designs of firms. Compared with human process interventions, these *technostructural interventions* (as well as the human resource management interventions and strategic interventions described in the following sections) generally focus more directly on productivity improvement and efficiency.

OD practitioners use a variety of technostructural interventions. For example, in a *formal structure* change program the employees collect data on the company's existing organizational structures; they then jointly redesign and implement a new one, usually answering to HR.

Human Resource Management Applications   OD practitioners increasingly use action research to enable employees to analyze and change their firm's personnel practices. Targets of change here might include the firm's performance appraisal system and reward system, as well as installing diversity programs.

Strategic Applications   Among the newest OD applications are *strategic interventions*, organizationwide programs aimed at achieving a fit between a firm's strategy, structure, culture, and external environment.

Integrated strategic management is one example of how OD can be used to create or change a strategy. This intervention consists of four steps:

1. *Analyze current strategy and organizational design.* Managers and other employees analyze the firm's current strategy, as well as its organizational design.
2. *Choose a desired strategy and organizational design.* Based on the OD consultant-assisted analysis, senior management formulates a strategic vision, objectives, and plan and an organizational structure for implementing them.
3. *Design a strategic change plan.* The group designs a strategic change plan, which "is an action plan for moving the organization from its current strategy and organizational design to the desired future strategy and design."[21] The plan explains how the strategic change will be implemented, including specific activities as well as the costs and budgets associated with them.
4. *Implement the strategic change plan.* The final step is actually implementing the strategic change plan and measuring and reviewing the results of the change activities to ensure that they are proceeding as planned.[22]

INSTITUTING TOTAL QUALITY MANAGEMENT PROGRAMS

What Is Quality?

Quality can be defined as the totality of features and characteristics of a product or service that bears on its ability to satisfy given needs. To put this another way, "quality measures how well a product or service meets customer needs."[23] The basic consideration is thus always the extent to which the product or service meets the customer's expectations.

Quality standards today are international. Doing business in Europe often means the firm must show it complies with **ISO 9000,** the quality standards of the European Community (EC). If required to do so by a customer, the vendor would have to prove that its quality manuals, procedures, and job instructions all comply with the ISO 9000 standards.

As this suggests, improving quality is a necessity to companies all over the world. Globalization of competition has done more than just force firms to become more efficient; it has raised the quality bar too, by forcing competitors in industries ranging from

ISO 9000
The written standards for quality management and assurance of the International Organization for Standardization.

cars to computers to phone service to meet and exceed the quality of the firms with which they compete. HR plays a central role in improving product and service quality, as we'll see in this section.

Total Quality Management Programs

total quality management (TQM)

A type of program aimed at maximizing customer satisfaction through continuous improvements.

Malcolm Baldridge Award

An award created by the U.S. Department of Commerce to recognize quality efforts of U.S. companies.

Total quality management (TQM) programs are organizationwide programs aimed at maximizing customer satisfaction through continuous improvements.[24] In the United States, this approach often goes by the name *continuous improvement, zero defects*, or *six sigma* (a reference the statistical unlikelihood of having a defect); in Japan it's known as *Kaizen*.[25]

To recognize quality efforts the U.S. Department of Commerce created the **Malcolm Baldrige Award**. The award is named after a former Secretary of Commerce, who died while in office. Most U.S. manufacturing firms, service firms, and small businesses are eligible to apply for the Baldrige. Winners have included Motorola, Inc., Federal Express, Cadillac Motor Car Company, and Xerox Business Products and Systems.

IMPLEMENTING TQM AT FLORIDA POWER & LIGHT   Miami-based Florida Power & Light Company (FPL), Florida's largest utility, was the first company outside Japan to win the Deming Prize, which is similar to America's Baldrige Award. Awarded annually (and since 1986 outside Japan), the prize recognizes outstanding achievement in quality control management. The steps FPL took to win the award help to illustrate the activities involved in implementing comprehensive companywide total quality management programs and the role of HR management in doing so.

FPL's quality improvement program contained three main components or phases: policy deployment, quality improvement teams, and quality in daily work.

Policy Deployment   Policy deployment is the process through which the company focuses its resources on achieving customer satisfaction. Policy deployment provides direction. At FPL, the policy deployment process began by determining what FPL customers wanted and then compiling these needs in a customer needs table. Specifically, annual surveys were made of customer needs, and these were then summarized and prioritized into five or six main customer needs categories. These drive the corporate agenda—the plans regarding specifically where the company's employees should focus their quality-improvement efforts. At FPL, the needs emerging from the customer needs assessment included:

- Improve public confidence in safety programs.
- Reduce the number of complaints to the Florida Public Service Commission.
- Improve the reliability of electric service.
- Continue to emphasize safe, reliable, and efficient operation of nuclear plants.
- Strengthen fossil fuel plant reliability and availability.

Such needs are then translated into more measurable goals, such as "increase fossil plant availability to about 95% of total time." Measurable objectives like these, which FPL refers to as *policies*, are then distributed to all FPL employees via the *Annual Guide to Corporate Excellence*. This publication folds out into a wall chart, and, as the company puts it, "Hung in offices throughout FPL, it reminds one and all to check whether their QI teams and daily work are contributing to the corporate vision."[26] It is through policy deployment that the measurable quality objectives (or policies) of FPL are deployed throughout the company and it's facilities, thus giving this process its name.

Quality Improvement Teams   At FPL and many other firms, most total quality efforts rely on quality improvement teams—groups of specially trained employees who meet at work for an hour or so once each week to spot and solve quality programs at work. FPL used several types of teams: functional teams, cross-functional teams, task teams, and lead teams (about 1,700 teams altogether). **Functional teams** are composed of volunteers who typically work together as natural work units on a daily basis. They generally choose their own problems and meet 1 hour each week. The basic aim here is to involve first-line employees in improving their daily work activities to enhance the quality of their work life and to develop their skills. **Cross-functional teams** are ongoing teams that are formed to address problems that cut across organizational boundaries. *Task team* members are appointed from one or more departments to work on specific high-priority assigned problems. When the problem is solved, the task team is disbanded.

Finally, **lead teams** are headed by a vice president or other manager and serve as steering committees for all the teams that operate in their areas. It is the lead team, for instance, that decides how employees are assigned to serve on various teams and establishes guidelines regarding frequency and duration of team meetings.

The basic policies (such as "improve reliability of service") produced by the policy deployment process provide the framework within which the quality improvement teams work. The teams then generally select their own problem topics (called themes) to study, but certain topics are off limits. (These include the company's union agreement, absenteeism, pay, salaries, promotions, the apprenticeship program, and general safety rules produced by a joint safety committee).

Team members must be trained, and this is one area in which HR has a major impact. For example, Team Member Training is a 2-day program focusing on special techniques such as statistical quality control and group decision-making techniques such as brainstorming.

About a thousand quality improvement recommendations are presented per year. For example, one team discovered that it was bird droppings, not inclement weather, that causes some of FPL's high-voltage lines to short out so often.

Quality in Daily Work   In addition to policy deployment and quality improvement teams, FPL encourages *quality in daily work* (QIDW). Individual employees are urged to identify their customers and their needs, keeping in mind that "customers" may be external or internal (that is, inside the company). The basic thrust of QIDW is to encourage individual employees to apply a quality improvement approach to their individual jobs.

Human Resource Management and the Quality Improvement Effort

LESSONS FROM FPL   How can HR contribute to a company's quality improvement efforts? Some HR guidelines based on FPL's experience would include:

- Make sure all teams work within a policy—deployment process to ensure their efforts are consistent with the firm's goals.
- Do not institute quality improvement teams as separate, parallel organization structures. Simply trying to superimpose such teams outside the normal chain of command elicited resistance from supervisors, many of whom made comments like "I don't know what these people are doing—they're not helping me do my job."[27] The teams should, to the greatest extent possible, be composed of natural work units.
- Do not treat the quality improvement program as if it has an end. It is important to emphasize that it is really a systematic and continuing way of doing business, one that has no end.

---

functional team

A quality improvement team composed of volunteers who typically work together as natural work units.

cross-functional team

A quality improvement team formed to address problems that cut across organizational boundaries.

lead team

A quality improvement team headed by a vice president or other manager that serves as a steering committee for all the teams that operate in its area.

- Recognize that training is essential. Quality improvement is successful largely because training continually upgrades the problem analysis and statistics skills of even first-line employees. This training is crucial both to provide the required analytical skills and also to emphasize the firm's commitment to the program.

- Give employees the skills they need to analyze and solve problems; then get them to analyze and solve the problem; and finally follow up on their suggestions.

- Remember that whether or not the company achieves it's quality goals is important but almost secondary. The new employee values that emerge are the heart of the program.

- Don't focus exclusively on "boosting productivity" or assume that emphasizing quality means that productivity will necessarily fall. In fact, FPL and other companies have often found that as quality rises, so does productivity.

- Recognize effort and encourage employees. A main benefit of such a program is the sense of satisfaction it can foster in employees. This results from encouraging employees to identify and devise countermeasures against problems and from giving them the tools and leeway required to get this job done. In fact, when FPL asked their employees what they wanted most, they didn't say "more money." They said they wanted their suggestions implemented and supervisors to recognize their efforts.

- Reward individuals and team efforts in a concrete manner, not necessarily just with money but with rewards like merchandise or pins.

- Remember that the first steps need to be taken by top management: "From the board of directors to every supervisor, management must adopt the principles and language of quality, follow the processes, set examples and guide others. A substantial commitment is necessary for employee education, and for awareness and recognition programs. These programs require reallocation of budgets and personnel, and will take time to produce results but will be worth it."[28]

HR'S ROLE IN WINNING THE BALDRIGE AWARD HR similarly plays a big role in meeting the Malcolm Baldrige Quality Award. As in Figure 8-1, Baldrige applicants are evaluated by a board consisting of quality experts. The experts examine seven basic areas: *senior executive leadership* (top management's symbolic commitment to quality); *information and analysis* (an adequate system for collecting statistical data on matters such as product or service quality); *strategic quality planning* (the adequacy of the firm's planning process and how key quality requirements are integrated into the firm's overall business planning process); *management of quality* (for example, rather than viewing design, production, and sales as separate entities, top firms usually recognize the integrated nature of their work so that the departments work together); *quality and operational results* (to show the firm is achieving continuous improvement in critical operational areas, such as in service quality levels); and *customer focus and satisfaction* (wherein the examiners look for objective, validated data regarding the applicant's success in satisfying the customer).

As part of this process, the applicant's human resource development and management is also evaluated. Specifically, judges evaluate the firm's achievements with respect to developing its employees potential to pursue the firm's quality objectives. In practical terms, examiners focus in this category on the extent to which HR management and related techniques (such as enrichment, empowerment, training, and career development) are used to tap each employee's potential. For example, judges expect that employees should be trained to use problem-solving tools and group decision-making skills.

HR AND ISO 9000 HR practices are also an integral part of companies' efforts to achieve ISO 9000 certification. ISO 9000 refers to the International Organization for Standardization's basic written standards for quality management and assurance.[29] Certifica-

FIGURE 8-1

Baldrige Award Criteria Framework

Senior executive leadership is the "driver" of total quality management, with each of the other six elements, or Baldrige Categories, playing a crucial role.

Source: U.S. Department of Commerce, 1992.

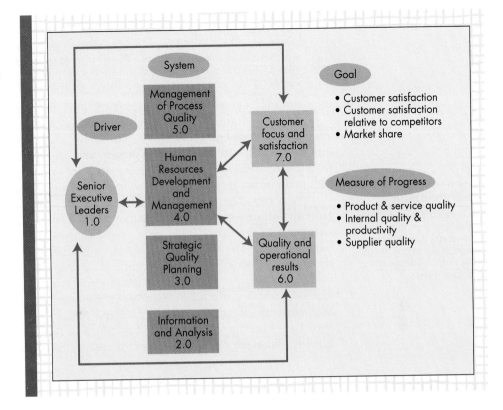

tion usually requires a five-step process: ISO assessment (reviewing the company's quality systems and procedures); quality assurance and policy manual preparation (compiling the specific quality-oriented techniques and policies to be followed); training of employees in ISO 9000; documentation of work instructions (documenting each new work procedure, for instance); and registration audit (having the quality system reviewed by a special "registrar" who audits the company's quality efforts).

Employee training and related HR activities such as selection thus play an important role in gaining ISO 9000 certification. For example, in one instance:

> *Perhaps the most serious problem was that even though a number of people were doing excellent work, they were simply unaware of the physical procedures they were following. Informal on-the-job training that was prevalent in the division was the culprit.*[30]

Training for ISO 9000 would typically cover, for instance, the quality vocabulary associated with ISO 9000, and the requirements embedded in each ISO 9000 standard section.[31]

CREATING TEAM-BASED ORGANIZATIONS

Companies today are also increasingly transforming themselves into team-based organizations; HR plays a big role in creating such team-based organizations and in ensuring they function effectively.

The Nature of Self-Directed Teams and Worker Empowerment

Many years ago psychologist Rensis Likert formulated the classic explanation of cohesive work teams. As he put it,

The most important source of satisfaction for this desire is the response we get from the people we are close to, in whom we are interested, and whose approval and support we are eager to have. The face-to-face groups with whom we spend the bulk of our time are, consequently, the most important to us. [Therefore,] management will make full use of the potential capacities of its human resources only when each person in an organization is a member of one or more effectively functioning work groups that have a high degree of group loyalty.[32]

For many firms today the ideal situation, as Likert predicted, is to organize work around small close-knit teams whose goals are high and whose aims are the same as the firm's. Firms like Saturn, Toyota, Corning, and others are increasingly organizing the work around small self-contained teams, which are variously labeled self-managed teams, high-performance teams, or autonomous work groups or, simply, superteams.[33]

Whatever they're called, **self-directed teams** have much in common. Each team generally performs sets of naturally interdependent tasks (such as all the steps required to assemble a Saturn door). They all use consensus decision making to choose their own team members, solve job-related problems, design their own jobs, and schedule their own break time. And their jobs are always enriched, in that they perform many of the tasks formerly done by supervisors, such as dealing with vendors and monitoring quality. Self-directed teams are also highly trained—to solve problems, to design jobs, to interview candidates, and to understand financial reports. They are, therefore, generally empowered: They have the training and ability as well as the broad authority to get their jobs done. The following *High-Performing Organization* feature illustrates this.

self-directed team

A work team that uses consensus decision making to choose its own team members, solve job-related problems, design its own jobs, and schedule its own break time.

THE HIGH-PERFORMANCE ORGANIZATION

Building Better, Faster, More Competitive Organizations Through HR: Product Improvement Teams

■ Kaiser Electronics—San Jose, CA

Product Improvement Teams at Kaiser Electronics identify and correct problems affecting performance, cost, schedule, and customer satisfaction. They improve engineering and manufacturing processes to reduce cycle times and defects per unit. Teams are formed for specific product lines and establish and maintain individual missions, visions, goals, and working styles. Prior to 1992, production cross-functional teams did not exist, and all defect control and product improvement activities were directed by production and engineering managers using weekly project meetings. The system was reactive rather than proactive, and its ineffectiveness led directly to the development of the product improvement team process.

When a team is now established, a 7-day team-building event is conducted to launch the team and develop its mission and vision. Each team has a sponsor and a trained team leader. The teams have learned that they need to meet frequently, normally five times per week. These working meetings are designed and planned with a specific purpose and expected outcome, and are conducted quickly and efficiently. The teams develop and apply their own improvement strategies. For example, one team that works on F-18 jet displays uses a two-pronged strategy by acting on all production failures as well as on all failures reported by its customer, McDonnell Douglas. All failures and corrective actions are tracked in a database and reported monthly to McDonnell Douglas and the Navy.

Training plays a big role. Pareto charts—special graphs that show defects and their frequencies—are used to identify the most frequent sources of problems, while Kaiser Electronics' Root Cause Problem Solving (RCPS) Roadmap Process is a basic tool in determining root causes and implementing corrective action. Special "metrics and progress charts" are prominently displayed on story boards in the plant. Overall, this process is useful for focusing on and achieving continuous incremental improvements. The focus is moving failure detection upstream, earlier in the process, for less costly, earlier defect detection. That way defects are addressed immediately as they occur.

Kaiser Electronics' Product Improvement teams have been effective. From November 1991 to June 1994, one F-18 display team reduced failures per unit under test by 85% and failures per unit shipped by 78%. It was awarded the highest level supplier rating (Gold) in both Quality and Delivery by its customer McDonnell Douglas.

Lessons learned by product improvement teams have led to improved company design guides and handbooks and to improved calibration maintenance schedules and procedures. Product improvement teams also contributed to the development of such tools as the process improvement story board, team libraries, and special reports used by all teams at Kaiser Electronics.

Source: Copyright 1998, Best Manufacturing Practices Center of Excellence.

Due to successes such as this, the use of work teams is now widespread throughout the U.S. For example, one study concluded that 82% of all U.S. firms have organized at least some of their employees in work groups identified as teams. Thirty-five percent of all U.S. organizations also have at least one team classified as self-directed or semiautonomous (which generally means that the team supervises itself).[34] Teams like these are examples of employee involvement programs. An *employee involvement program* is any formal program that lets employees participate in formulating important work decisions or in supervising all or part of their own work activities.[35]

Managers rank such programs as their biggest productivity boosters. For example, the editors of *National Productivity Review* found that "increased employee involvement in the generation and implementation of ideas was ranked the highest priority productivity improvement action by the respondents." Employee involvement "was similarly ranked number one as the top cause of improvement over the past two years at these firms." (The other eight causes of improvement, in descending order, were quality pro-

Individuals in most work teams such as this one at a paper mill have a high commitment to the group and its work goals, due in part to their shared experiences.

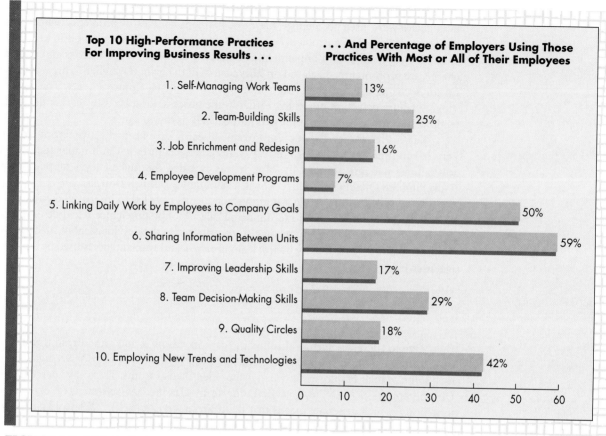

FIGURE 8-2 *BNA Bulletin to Management, June 11, 1998, p. 181.*

Source: Data from Development Dimensions International.

grams, improved process methods, top management, equipment, technology, training, computers, and automation.)

In another study, self-managing teams were listed as "most valuable" in a survey of CEOs, who were asked how their firms' used 39 "high-performance" practices.[36] Yet (see Figure 8-2) only about 13% of the CEOs said they actually used such teams (although 25% said they did make use of "team-building skills)."

GLOBAL HRM

■ Extending Participative Decision Making Abroad

While self-directed teams may be effective in the U.S., the approach doesn't necessarily apply as well abroad. There are deep and often irreconcilable cross-cultural differences in values and attitudes from country to country, so that techniques that work in one country may actually backfire in another.

The findings of one recent study illustrate this problem very well.[37] The study examined how one U.S. multinational manufacturing company tried to implement participative decision making in its European subsidiaries, and how managers and employees in three European countries reacted to the company's efforts.

The company was hoping to implement participative decision-making programs in Europe that were similar to ones that had been successful in the United States; however it got unexpected reactions from the European employees. For example, most Dutch managers felt that the U.S. efforts to improve participation by instituting work teams could actually hurt performance and motivation, because the program failed to take individual differences into account. Several Dutch managers "stated that the type of programmatic, formalized efforts favored by the American parent would not allow managers to encourage participation in ways and at a pace that was consistent with their own styles or the needs of their subordinates."[38] In other words, it forced the Dutch managers to be too participative, too soon.

British managers had similar reservations about implementing the "American approach" to team-based participative management. In their case, they were concerned that the program ignored individual differences in managerial styles and employee abilities. The British managers seemed threatened by the decision-making authority the new work teams would receive.

Interestingly, most of the Spanish managers endorsed the idea of self-directed work teams and said it could work in the Spanish plant. But the Spanish managers' stated beliefs were actually a bit misleading: In fact, Spanish managers reported lower levels of participation among subordinates than did their Dutch and U.S. counterparts. In other words, the actual resulting participation was lower—not higher—in the Spanish plants than elsewhere in Europe, although the managers were relatively enthusiastic about participative management.

Results such as these illustrate that U.S. managers have different values and perspectives on employee participation than do their counterparts in Britain, Holland, and Spain. Therefore, before exporting HR programs like self-directed work teams, HR managers should try to achieve three basic goals:[39]

1. If appropriate, build trust by communicating to local managers that previous corporate HR efforts may have reflected culturally specific beliefs that do not always fit local needs, and that the parent company is committed to developing locally-sensitive policies.

2. Become more aware of the local cultural traditions that may affect attitudes toward participation in decision making.

3. Develop a working partnership with local HR executives to create blended strategies for employee participation, ones that fit the local culture while offering something of value to the corporation as a whole. In effect, this will require joint decision making between U.S. HR executives and their foreign counterparts.

How HR Helps to Build Productive Teams

Building productive teams requires careful selection, training, and motivation, all HR-related activities. HR-related guidelines for building effective teams include:[40]

Establish urgent, demanding performance standards. All team members should believe the team has urgent and worthwhile purposes, and they need to know what their performance standards are.

Select members for skill and skill potential. Select team members for their existing skills and for their potential to learn new ones.

Train leaders to "coach" not "boss". Self-directed work teams are empowered—they have the authority, tools, and information to manage themselves. HR must thus ensure that team leaders know their jobs are not to boss but to support and to coach.

Challenge the group regularly with fresh facts and information. New information (such as on how the company is doing) helps a team to understand the challenges it and the company faces. Having HR supply such information thereby helps the team shape its common purpose, set clearer goals, and improve its approach.

Exploit the power of positive feedback, recognition, and reward. There are many ways HR can arrange to have team performance recognized and rewarded. For example, have a senior executive speak directly to the team about the urgency of its mission and use special awards to recognize the team's contributions.

Choose people who like teamwork. Companies like Toyota recruit and select employees who have a history of preferring to work in teams and of being good team members. Loners and antisocial types don't usually make good team members.

Train, train, train. Perhaps HR's major role here is to ensure team members have the training required to do their jobs. Training should cover topics such as the philosophy of doing work through teams, how teams make decisions, interpersonal and communications skills for team members, and the technical skills that team members will need to perform their jobs.

Cross-train for flexibility. Members of most teams also need cross-training, to learn the jobs of fellow team members either informally or through scheduled rotating assignments. This can help reduce disruptions due to absenteeism and can boost flexibility, since all team members are always ready to fill in when needed.

HR's Role as a Strategic Partner in Creating Teams: An Example

The recent experience of Wisconsin-based Signicast Corp. helps illustrate HR's role in creating a team-based organization. The firm produces metal parts from what's known as the investment casting process: wax molds are used to create ceramic molds which in turn are used to cast the metal parts. In 1992, the company decided to expand by building a new, highly automated plant about 25 miles away. But it discovered that "in the real world, new automation technology requires a new kind of employee . . . ." The firm's HR group therefore played a crucial role in the design, staffing, and start-up of the firm's new facility—and strategy.[41]

HR's involvement began at the plant design stage. It invited employees from the existing facility to participate in several planning and design meetings; here their suggestions on matters ranging from how to design a new piece of equipment, to the work flow in the new plant were solicited: "Employees would come up with suggestions; we'd implement them, and bring them back to [employees] for confirmation."[42]

As the new plant began to take shape HR's task was to select and train a new kind of workforce. While the firm's original plant would continue to operate, the new automated plant would produce parts almost five times faster than the old plant, and this would leave no time for rework or errors. The new plant's employees would therefore have to have more responsibility, and in many ways be more highly trained and carefully selected than were their counterparts at the old facility.

The new plant's selection standards were thus tighter. At the old plant, no specific prior experience was sought, and the only hiring requirements were for a high school diploma and a good work ethic. The 135 employees at the new plant would require the same high school degree and work ethic plus team orientation, good trainability, good communication skills, and a willingness to do varied jobs over a 12-hour shift.[43]

HR's role as a strategic partner in the building of this new plant was apparent in other ways, too. For example, HR had to help create a cross-training program, so that employees could do each other's jobs and be rotated amongst jobs, so as not to become bored or tired during their 12-hour shifts.[44] And, a new compensation plan was designed that paid workers not just for performance but also for knowledge and for the number of new jobs at which they became competent.

HR AND BUSINESS PROCESS REENGINEERING

business process reengineering (BPR)

The redesign of business processes to achieve improvements in such measures of performance as cost, quality, service, and speed.

What Is Business Process Reengineering?

Michael Hammer and James Champy, the fathers of reengineering, define reengineering as "The fundamental rethinking and radical redesign of business processes to achieve dramatic improvements in critical, contemporary measures of performance such as cost, quality, service, and speed."[45] One of **business process reengineering**'s **(BPR)** basic assumptions is that the traditional way of organizing departments and processes around very specialized tasks is inherently duplicative, wasteful, and unresponsive to the firm's customers. In reengineering a company and its departments and processes, the reengineers, therefore, need to ask themselves: "Why do we do *what* we do?" and "Why do we do it *the way* we do?"

AN EXAMPLE   One reengineering effort took place at IBM Credit Corporation, the IBM unit that finances the computers, software, and services sold by IBM. Before reengineering, the credit-checking and approval process took several weeks. (A process is a collection of activities with a clear customer goal. For example, the "credit checking" process is the sequence of activities that takes a credit request as its input and sees the request go through a sequence of steps until the approval or rejection goes to the customer.) A salesperson would call in to get credit for a prospective customer. A sequence of steps was then carried out by individual workers, each of whom logged in the request, carted the request upstairs to the credit department, entered the information into a computer system, checked the credit, and dispatched it to the next link in the chain.

When this process was assessed, IBM Credit made a monumental discovery. Specifically, if the person who got the financing request walked it through all the stages personally and at each stage did what needed to be done, the whole process took only 90 minutes rather than a week or more! Reengineering the process in this case involved substituting several generalists for all the specialists and letting a generalist do all the tasks for a request, rather than having the process carried out like a relay race.[46]

This IBM example illustrates some of the basic characteristics of business process reengineering. In business process reengineering several jobs are combined into one so that an assembly-line process is replaced by generalists who carry out all the tasks themselves. Another reengineering characteristic is, therefore, that workers make more decisions. For example, each of the new generalists at IBM Credit had to be solely responsible for deciding on a potential client's creditworthiness. Related to this checks and controls are reduced; instead, there's more emphasis on carefully selecting and training the new generalist. Reengineered processes also tend to take a "case manager" approach to dealing with customers, in that each customer ends up with a single point of contact when checking on the status of an order or request.[47]

HR's Role in Reengineering Processes

Two years after the concepts and techniques of reengineering were introduced, it was obvious that something was lacking. In their quest to focus on reorganizing the work and eliminating unneeded duplicative operations, many reengineered companies had neglected to also institute new HR practices; as a result, the firms had failed to win the commitment of their managers and employees to their new reengineered jobs.[48] Today, experts therefore understand that HR plays a crucial role in successfully implementing a reengineering effort. Following are some aspects of HR's role.

BUILDING COMMITMENT TO REENGINEERING   As one expert says, "[Reengineering is] about an ongoing, never-ending commitment to doing things better."[49] Therefore, a key to reengineering is winning people's commitment to the changes and what those changes mean. HR can play a big role in winning such commitment, for instance by hiring employees with the right values, by providing the right incentives, and by installing effective two-way communications practices.

HR AND TEAM BUILDING   Business process reengineering generally means reorganizing from functional departments to process-oriented teams (such as the teams of employees working together to process the IBM credit requests). We've seen in this chapter that HR plays a central role in making such teams more effective, for instance by providing carefully selected "team players" and the required technical training.

HR'S ROLE IN CHANGING THE NATURE OF THE WORK   With reengineering, jobs generally change from specialized tasks to multidimensional generalist work. Not only is each worker responsible for a broader, more enriched job, but the new process team members "share joint responsibility with their team members for performing the whole process, not just a small piece of it."[50] What this means is that each worker needs to be capable of using a much broader range of skills from day to day; HR is crucial here for hiring high-potential employees and providing them with the training and development they require.

HR'S ROLE IN MOVING FROM CONTROLLED TO EMPOWERED JOBS   As in the IBM Credit example, people working in a reengineered setting are necessarily empowered to perform a broader set of tasks with relatively little supervision.[51] This means that HR in reengineered companies must stress values in selection.[52] As two experts put it,

> It is no longer enough merely to look at prospective employees' education, training, and skills; their character becomes an issue as well. Are they self-starting? Do they have self-discipline? Are they motivated to do what it takes to please a customer?[53]

HR'S ROLE IN MOVING FROM TRAINING TO EDUCATION   Hammer and Champy say that in companies that reengineer, the emphasis necessarily shifts from training to education. In other words, it's no longer enough to give employees training that shows them "how" to do the job—such as how to turn the bolt on the left front fender. Instead the new generalist team members need education. They need the insight and understanding of how to analyze and solve problems and improve processes continuously, and must thus understand not just the "how" of the job, but the "why" of it.[54]

INSTITUTING FLEXIBLE WORK ARRANGEMENTS

Renewing an organization doesn't always require a massive transformation. At many companies, a change as (relatively) simple as installing flexible hours can sometimes provide a good start. Since it's generally HR that designs and institutes such plans, in this last section we'll focus on various flexible scheduling alternatives.

Flextime

flextime

A plan whereby employees build their workday around a core of midday hours.

There are various types of flexible work scheduling arrangements. For example, **flextime** is a plan whereby employees' flexible workdays are built around a core of midday hours, such as 11 a.m. to 2 p.m. It is called flextime because workers determine their own flexible starting and stopping hours. For example, they may opt to work from 7 a.m. to 3 p.m. or from 11 a.m. to 7 p.m. Well over 15% of the U.S. workforce is on a flextime schedule, not counting professionals, managers, and self-employed persons who customarily set their own work hours anyway.[55]

FLEXTIME IN PRACTICE   In practice, most employers who use flextime give employees only limited freedom regarding the hours they work. Most employers still try to hold fairly close to the traditional 9 a.m. to 5 p.m. workday. For example, in 67% of the companies employees can't start work before 7 a.m., and in almost all firms employees must not clock in before 6 a.m. Similarly, in about half the firms, employees can't start work later than 9 a.m., and employees in about 40% of the firms must be in by 10 a.m. Therefore, the effect of flextime for most employees is to give them about 1 hour leeway before 9 a.m. or after 5 p.m. About 15% of the employers made 9 a.m. to 3 p.m. their core period, while another 28% made their core period 9 a.m. to 4 p.m.

FLEXTIME'S PROS AND CONS   Some flextime programs have been quite successful.[56] Because less time is lost due to tardiness, the ratio of worker-hours worked to worker-hours paid (a measure of productivity) increases. Flextime can also reduce absenteeism and cut down on sick leave being used for personal matters. The hours actually worked seem to be more productive, and there is less slowing down toward the end of the workday. Workers tend to leave early when work is slack and work later when it is heavy. The use of flextime seems to increase employees' receptiveness to changes in other procedures. It also tends to reduce the distinction between managers and workers and requires more delegation of authority by supervisors.

There are some disadvantages. Flextime is complicated to administer and may be impossible to implement where large groups of workers must work interdependently.[57] It also requires time clocks or other time records, which can be disadvantageous to workers.

In any event, flextime seems to work. Surveys covering 445 employers (including drug companies, banks, electronics firms, and government agencies) indicate that the percentage of employees reporting flextime-driven productivity increases ranges from 5% to 10% in some firms to about 95% in one airline. On the whole, about 45% of employees involved in flextime programs report that the program has resulted in improved productivity.[58] The failure rate of flextime is also remarkably low, reportedly 8%, according to one study.[59]

CONDITIONS FOR SUCCESS   There are several ways to make a flextime program more successful.[60] First, management resistance—particularly at the supervisory level and particularly before the program is actually tried—has torpedoed several programs before they become operational, so supervisory indoctrination programs are important prerequisites to success. Second, flextime is usually more successful with clerical, professional, and managerial jobs, and less so with factory jobs (the nature of which tends to demand interdependence among workers). Third, experience indicates that the greater the flexibility of a flextime program, the greater the benefits the program can produce (although the disadvantages, of course, multiply as well). Fourth, the way the program is installed is important; a flextime project director to oversee all aspects of the program should be appointed, and frequent meetings should take place between supervisors and employees to allay their fears and clear up misunderstandings. A pilot study, say, in one department, is advisable.[61]

Flextime may be especially valuable for the employer when the group must share limited resources. For example, some computer programmers spend as much as two-thirds of their time waiting to make computer runs. As one researcher concludes, "because flextime expands the amount of time that the computer is available to the programmer, this allows its usage to be spread over more hours, and the time in queues to make runs and get output back is reduced."[62]

Three-and Four-Day Workweeks

four-day workweek
An arrangement that allows employees to work four ten-hour days instead of the more usual five eight-hour days.

Other employers have switched to a **four-day workweek**. Here employees work four 10-hour days instead of the more usual five 8-hour days.

ADVANTAGES   Compressed workweek plans have been fairly successful, as they have several advantages. Productivity seems to increase due to fewer startups and shutdowns. Workers are more willing to work some evenings and Saturdays as part of these plans. According to one study, 80% of the firms on such plans reported the plan "improves business results"; three-fifths said that production was up and almost two-fifths reported costs were down. Half the firms also reported higher profits. Even the four-day firms not reporting positive results reported that cost and profit factors at least remained the same. One study found the four-day workweek generally reduced paid overtime and absenteeism, and improved efficiency. Furthermore, the workers also gain; there is a 20% reduction in commuter trips and an additional day off per week. Additional savings (for example, in child-care expenses) may also occur.[63]

A recent review of three-day, 38-hour workweeks concluded that compressed workweek schedules have significant positive and long-lasting effects if handled properly. Regardless of individual differences in jobs and backgrounds, those employees experiencing the 3 day–38 hour schedules reacted favorably to it, particularly if they had been involved in the decision to implement the program and their jobs had been enriched by the schedule change. Fatigue did not appear to be a problem in this particular survey.[64]

DISADVANTAGES   There are also disadvantages, some of them potentially quite severe. Tardiness, for example, may become a problem. Of more concern is the fact that fatigue was cited by several firms as a drawback of four-day workweeks. (Note that fatigue was a main reason for adopting 8-hour days in the first place.)

Other Flexible Work Arrangements

job sharing
A concept that allows two or more people to share a single full-time job.

Employers are taking other steps to accommodate their employees' scheduling needs. **Job sharing** is a concept that allows two or more people to share a single full-time job. For example, two people may share a 40-hour-per-week job, with one working mornings and the other working afternoons. About 105 of the firms questioned in one survey indicated that they allow for job sharing.[65] *Work sharing* refers to a temporary reduction in work hours by a group of employees during economic hard times as a way of preventing layoffs; thus 400 employees may all agree to work (and get paid for) only 35 hours per week in order to avoid having the firm lay off 30 workers. *Flexiplace,* in which employees are allowed or encouraged to work at home or in a satellite office closer to home, is another example of a flexible work arrangement that is becoming more popular today.

Telecommuting
A work arrangement in which employees work at remote locations, usually at home, using video displays, computers, and other telecommunications equipment to carry out their responsibilities.

Telecommuting is another option. Here employees work at home, usually with video displays, and use telephone lines to transmit letters, data, and completed work to the home office. For example, Best Western Hotels in Phoenix is using the residents of the Arizona Center for Women, a minimum-security prison, as a telecommuting office staff.

It is estimated that 7 million workers in the United States are telecommuting today in various jobs from lawyer to clerk to computer expert.[66]

Still other employers, especially in Europe, are switching to a plan they call **flexyears.** Under this plan, employees can choose (at 6-month intervals) the number of hours they want to work each month over the next year. A full-timer, for instance, might be able to work up to 173 hours a month. In a typical flexyear arrangement, an employee who wants to average 110 hours a month might work 150 hours in January (when the children are at school and the company needs extra help to cope with January sales). In February, the employee may work only 70 hours because he or she wants to, say, go skiing.[67]

Flexyears

A work arrangement under which employees can choose (at six-month intervals) the number of hours they want to work each month over the next year.

We invite you to visit the Dessler page on the Prentice Hall Web site at **www.prenhall.com/dessler** for our on-line study guide, Internet exercises, current events, links to related Web sites, and more.

SUMMARY

1. Managers in their leadership roles can focus on various change targets. They can change the strategy, culture, structure, tasks, technologies, or attitudes and skills of the people in the organization.

2. The hardest part of leading change is overcoming resistance to change. This resistance stems from various sources: habit, resource limitations, threats to power and influence, fear of the unknown, and altering employees' "personal compacts." Methods for dealing with resistance include education and communication, facilitation and support, participation and involvement, negotiation and agreement, manipulation, and coercion.

3. A 10-step process for actually leading organizational change would include establishing a sense of urgency; mobilizing commitment to change through joint diagnosis of business problems; creating a guiding coalition; developing a shared vision; communicating the vision; removing barriers to the change and empowering employees; generating short-term wins; consolidating gains and producing more change; anchoring the new ways of doing things in the company's culture; and monitoring progress and adjusting the vision as required.

4. Organizational development is a special approach to organizational change that basically involves letting the employees themselves formulate and implement the change that's required, often with the assistance of a trained consultant. Types of OD applications include human process applications, technostructural interventions, human resource management applications, and strategic applications.

5. Quality measures how well a product or service meets customer needs. Quality standards today are international, as shown by the introduction of ISO 9000. Improving quality has become necessary to companies all over the world.

6. Total quality management programs are organizationwide programs that aim to integrate all business functions including design, planning, production, distribution and service, with the aim of maximizing customer service through continuous improvement.

7. Self-directed work teams are becoming increasingly popular in organizations today. Many firms are organizing work around self-contained teams, which are sometimes called self-managing teams, high-performance teams, autonomous work groups, and even superteams. These teams are trained to solve problems, design jobs, interview and hire candidates, and understand financial reports.

8. Reengineering is the fundamental rethinking and radical redesign of business processes to achieve dramatic improvements in critical, contemporary measures of performance,

such as cost, quality, service, and speed. HR contributes to reengineering processes by its effect on: building commitment to reengineering; team building; changing the nature of work; empowering jobs; moving from training to education; and shifting focus from activities to results.

9. Flextime is a plan whereby employees' flexible workdays are built around a core of midday hours, such as 11 a.m. to 2 p.m. It seems to improve employee attitudes and morale, increase production, and decrease tardiness. Flextime and other flexible work arrangements are aimed in part at tapping employees' needs to be treated as responsible human beings, and to that extent they boost employee commitment.

KEY TERMS

strategic change   292
cultural change   292
structural change   293
technological change   293
organizational development interventions   293
organizational development (OD)   296
sensitivity training   297
team building   298
confrontation meetings   298
survey research   298
ISO 9000   299
total quality management (TQM)   300
Malcolm Baldrige Award   300
functional teams   301
cross-functional teams   301
lead teams   301
self-directed teams   304
business process reengineering (BPR)   309
flextime   311
four-day workweek   312
job sharing   312
telecommuting   312
flexyears   313

DISCUSSION QUESTIONS

1. There are several ways a company can initiate change, some of which are strategic change, cultural change, structural change, and technological change. Define three types of change and explain how they can help an organization change for the better.
2. What steps would you take to institute self-directed work teams?
3. Explain the pros and cons of flextime and the four-day workweek.

INDIVIDUAL AND GROUP ACTIVITIES

1. Working individually or in groups, develop an organizational change program for improving service in an area of your university or college that you feel is in need of improvement.
2. Define "reengineering." Working individually or in groups, develop a brief example of how you would reengineer a familiar process such as class enrollment at the start of a semester.

EXPERIENTIAL EXERCISE

Unfreezing an Organization

The first step in developing planned change is finding and reducing the forces that favor the status quo. Imagine that you are a consultant to a large machine manufacturing business. After the first day of meetings, you have met and talked with a number of different stakeholders. Before your next meeting with the client, you want to complete the following table:

STAKEHOLDER	A WHY MIGHT THIS GROUP SUPPORT THE STATUS QUO RATHER THAN CHANGE?	B HOW MIGHT WE HELP THEM RECOGNIZE THE NEED FOR CHANGE?
1. Factory workers—All manufacturing employees belong to a union.		
2. Clerical workers—most of the clerical workers have been with your organization for over a decade.		
3. Sales force—The sales force is compensated entirely by salary.		
4. Top management team—the top management team has been in place for 6 years without a major change in membership		

Directions:

Have each student individually write their responses to the questions in column "A." Divide the class into teams of four to five students. Each team should:

1. Have its team members describe their response for stakeholder number 1, factory workers.

2. Decide which response(s) seem most likely.

3. Have the team identify two possible responses (Column B) for every stakeholder issue raised.

4. Repeat the first three steps for each stakeholder group.

Once the teams have completed their work, have them report their suggestions back to the class.

CASE INCIDENT

"We're Getting Nowhere Fast"

Martin Star, president and founder of Star Valve Co. knows his little company has a problem. Star Valve designs and manufactures sophisticated valves used to control the flow of liquids and gases through pollution control systems in chemical plants. While many of Star's products are real innovations, the company hasn't grown appreciably in the 5 years prior to 1999.

It was not for lack of trying. Star had replaced the head of his accounting, manufacturing, and sales departments in the prior 5 years, and had recently begun a search for a new sales manager for Europe. And yet by almost any criterion—productivity, sales growth, profit margins, or profits, for instance—the company had ei-

ther not made headway in the 5-year period or was actually somewhat behind.

The company is highly labour-intensive. Star Valve is basically an engineering firm. Of its 100 or so employees, about 15 are engineers involved in designing valves in response to customers' requests, about 35 work in the plant in various semiskilled or skill machining-type jobs, and the rest are managers or office employees.

Of particular concern to Mr. Star, aside from the financial results, is the fact that quality is beginning to

(continued)

(continued from page 513)

diminish, as measured by complaints from several long-term customers. Employees also seem to be increasingly ignoring the administrative structure of the firm, such as the network of policies, procedures, and checklists that the company traditionally uses to ensure, for instance, that when a request for a proposal comes in the engineers ask all the required questions. Mr. Star recently met with several members of his board of directors, seeking their advice. "I don't know what the problem is," he said "all I know is that we're getting nowhere fast."

■ QUESTIONS

1. Which organizational change and development techniques discussed in Chapter 8 would you recommend Mr. Star use to try to determine what exactly the problems are at the company? Please be specific.

2. Given the admittedly limited information in the incident, would you recommend that Star implement a team-based organization? Why? Why not?

3. Do you think it would be helpful for Star to implement a total quality management program? Be prepared to tell Mr. Star what the pros and cons of implementing such a program in his company might be.

Case Application

IS THE HONEYMOON OVER AT FLAT ROCK?

It began in the 1980's with great promise: Mazda Motor Corp. was going to build an assembly plant in Flat Rock, Michigan—just outside Detroit—that would eventually provide thousands of high-paying and secure jobs. By 1990, however, conditions had seriously deteriorated and Mazda's honeymoon with Flat Rock seemed to have come to an end. Four top U.S. managers had quit the company since 1988, and Japanese executives had taken the senior posts. The company was on its fourth director of labor relations since hiring began in 1986. Unionized workers were boycotting Mazda's suggestion box, a cornerstone of Japanese-style management. Workers complained of job stress and increased injuries, and absenteeism was running approximately 10%, which was higher than in other Japanese plants in the United States. But let's start at the beginning, when Mazda began the task of staffing its new plant.

All job candidates applying at Flat Rock for assembly jobs went through a five-step screening process that was specifically designed to assess interpersonal skills, aptitude for teamwork, planning skills, and flexibility. This screening process encompassed a lot more than taking a paper-and-pencil test, enduring a few interviews, and providing references. At Mazda, applicants also had to perform tasks that simulated jobs that they might do on the actual factory floor. For example, applicants might bolt fenders onto a car or attach hoses in a simulated engine compartment. This helped Mazda's management to match workers' abilities with specific job requirements, and it also provided applicants with a realistic preview of what they were getting into.

For the initial work force, 10,000 of 100,000 candidates passed the five-step screening process. Of these, only 1,300 were hired. The cost of screening each one of these new employees was about $13,000 per worker.

But new hires didn't just report to the factory floor and join a work team. First, they had to undergo detailed training. That started with a three-week hodgepodge of sessions in which they learned about interpersonal relations, charting quality, stimulating creativity, and the like. This was followed by three days devoted to learning Mazda's philosophy of increasing efficiency through continual improvement. After this basic training came job-specific training. Line workers, for example, spent five to seven more weeks picking up specific technical skills, then another three or four weeks being supervised on the assembly line.

Why did Mazda go to all this expense and effort? The company wanted literate, versatile employees who would accept the company's emphasis on teamwork, loyalty, efficiency, and quality. Moreover, it wanted to weed out any troublemakers. What Mazda got was a work force better educated and nearly a generation younger than the old-line auto workers at most Big Three plants. Mazda also wanted smooth relations with its workers. So it invited the United Auto Workers to organize the plant's employees before operations began. What went wrong? How could all this preparatory work have resulted in a disgruntled work force? The following highlights a few of the causes.

The high turnover among U.S. managers created instability. U.S. managers complained about being left out of the information network. Major decisions were controlled by Mazda executives in Japan or local Japanese superiors. Each morning, for instance, U.S. managers got a "laundry list" from their Japanese "advisor" telling them just what they were supposed to do that day.

Workers' complaints were numerous. They said that the Japanese managers didn't listen to them. They criticized the company's policy for continuous improvement, claiming that this translated into a never-ending push to cut the number of worker-hours spent building each car. To support their argument, they pointed out that U.S. plants use 15% to 20% more workers to produce a similar number of cars. Workers said that even Mazda's team system, which is supposed to give employees more authority and flexibility, is a gimmick. Power was gradually taken away from team leaders; flexibility was a one-way street that management used to control workers; and the team system encouraged workers to pressure each other to keep up the rapid pace.

Japanese executives at Flat Rock responded by publicly lambasting workers for lacking dedication. As to high turnover in the management ranks, Japanese executives admit that Mazda's practice of making decisions by consensus often gives the appearance of keeping authority away from its U.S. executives. But Japanese executives can also claim that the U.S. workers have just not adapted to Mazda's way of doing business. In spite of worker complaints, management can proudly point to the fact that independent experts give Flat Rock's cars high marks for quality; every bit as high, in fact, as those built in Japan. However the problems at the Flat Rock plant took their toll, and several years ago Ford Motor Corp took a half ownership in the plant, and installed several of its own executives to run it. One of the new owner's first moves was to reduce the plant's workforce.

◼ QUESTIONS

1. What do you think accounts for the fact that with all the plant's emphasis on teamwork and on total quality the personnel problems were still so serious?

2. As the consultant to the new Ford plant manager, outline a detailed plan (based in large part on the contents in this chapter) for transforming the culture at Flat Rock and for making the plant more productive.

Source: Stephen Robbins, *Organizational Behavior* (Upper Saddle River NJ: Prentice Hall, 1993), pp. 593–595. Based on W. J. Hampton, "How Does Japan Inc. Pick Its American Workers?," *Business Week*, October 3, 1988, pp. 84–88; G. A. Patterson, "Mazda-UAW's Michigan Honeymoon Is Over," *The Wall Street Journal*, April 17, 1990, p. B1; and J. J. Fucini and S. Fucini, *Working for the Japanese* (New York: Free Press, 1990). "Ford Accord with Mazda Is Completed; US Automaker Given Half Interest in Plant", *New York Times*. July 2, 1992, pp C3, D4; "Ford, Mazda Cutting Back at Flat Rock Facility," *Ward's Auto World*, July 1995, p. 10; Ted Evanoff, "Michigan Ford-Mazda Plant to Roll out New Ford Vehicle Next Year," Knight-Ridder/Tribune Business News, April 20, 1997, p. 420.

NOTES

1. Based on David Nadler and Michael Tushman, "Beyond the Charismatic Leader: Leadership and Organizational Change," *California Management Review* (Winter 1990), pp. 77–97.

2. Ibid., 78. See also Guvenc G. Alpander and Carroll R. Lee, "Culture, Strategy and Teamwork: The Keys to Organizational Change," *Journal of Management Development*, Vol. 14, no. 8 (1995), pp. 4–18; and Benjamin Schneider, Arthur P. Brief, and Richard A. Guzzo, "Creating a Climate and Culture for Sustainable Organizational Change," *Organizational Dynamics*, Vol. 24, no. 4 (Spring 1996), pp. 7–19.

3. Edgar Schein, *Organizational Culture and Leadership* (San Francisco: Jossey-Bass, 1985), pp. 224–237; and Peter Wright, Mark Kroll, and John Parnell, *Strategic Management Concepts* (Upper Saddle River, NJ: Prentice Hall, 1996), pp. 233–236.

4. Stewart Thomas, "G. E. Keeps Those Ideas Coming," *Fortune*, August 12, 1991, p. 42.

5. Roger Harrison, "Choosing the Depth of Organization Intervention," *Journal of Applied Behavioral Science*, Vol. 2 (April–May–June, 1970), pp. 181–202; see also Aslaug Mikkelsen and Per Oystein, "Learning from Parallel Organizational Development Efforts in Two Public Sector Settings: Findings from Research in Norway," *Public Personnel Administration*, Vol. 18, no. 1 (Spring 1998) pp. 5–22.

6. The ten steps are based on Michael Beer, Russell Eisenstat, and Burt Spector, "Why Change Programs Don't Produce Change," *Harvard*

Business Review (November–December 1990), pp. 158–166; Thomas Cummings and Christopher Worley, *Organization Development and Change* (Minneapolis: West Publishing Company, 1993); John P. Kotter, "Leading Change: Why Transformation Efforts Fail," *Harvard Business Review* (March–April 1995), pp. 59–66; and John P. Kotter, *Leading Change* (Boston: Harvard Business School Press, 1996).

7. Ibid., p. 85.

8. Ibid., pp. 90–91.

9. Kathryn Harris, "Mr. Sony Confronts Hollywood," *Fortune*, Vol. 23 (December 1996), p. 36.

10. Noel Tichy and Ram Charan, "The CEO as Coach: An Interview with Allied Signal's Lawrence A. Bossidy," *Harvard Business Review* (March–April 1995), p. 77.

11. This is based on Kotter, "Leading Change: Why Transformation Efforts Fail," pp. 60–61.

12. Ibid., p. 65.

13. Beer, Eisenstat, and Spector, "Why Change Programs Don't Produce Change," p. 164.

14. *Workforce*, September 1997, p. 99.

15. Cummings and Worley, *Organization Development*, p. 3.

16. Based on J. T. Campbell and M. D. Dunnette, "Effectiveness of T-Group Experiences in Managerial Training and Development," *Psychological Bulletin*, Vol. 7 (1968), pp. 73–104; reprinted in W. E. Scott and L. L. Cummings, *Readings in Organizational Behavior and Human Performance* (Burr Ridge, IL: McGraw-Hill, 1973), p. 571.

17. Robert J. House, *Management Development* (Ann Arbor, MI: Bureau of Industrial Relations, University of Michigan, 1967), p. 71; Louis White and Kevin Wooten, "Ethical Dilemmas in Various Stages of Organizational Development," *Academy of Management Review*, Vol. 8, no. 4 (1983), pp. 690–697.

18. Wendell French and Cecil Bell, Jr., *Organization Development* (Upper Saddle River, NJ: Prentice Hall, 1995), pp. 171–193.

19. Benjamin Schneider, Steven Ashworth, A. Catherine Higgs, and Linda Carr, "Design Validity, and Use of Straegically Focused Employee Attitude Surveys," *Personnel Psychology*, Vol. 49 (1996), pp. 695–705.

20. Ibid., p. 74.

21. Cummings and Worley, *Organization Development*, p. 501.

22. For a description of how to make OD a part of organizational strategy, see Aubrey Mendelow and S. Jay Liebowitz, "Difficulties in Making OD a Part of Organizational Strategy," *Human Resource Planning*, Vol. 12, no. 4 (1995), pp. 317–329.

23. James Evans et al., *Applied Production and Operations Management* (St. Paul, MN: West Publishing Co., 1984), p. 39.

24. Based in part on Joel E. Ross, *Total Quality Management: Text, Cases and Readings* (Delray Beach, FL: St. Lucie Press, 1993), p. 1.

25. Barry Render and Jay Heizer, *Principles of Operations Management* (Upper Saddle River, NJ: Prentice Hall, 1997), p. 96.

26. "Building a Quality Improvement Program at Florida Power & Light," *Target* (Fall 1988), p. 6.

27. Private conversation with Wayne Brunetti, Executive Vice President, Florida Power & Light Company.

28. "Building a Quality Improvement Program at Florida Power & Light," p. 8.

29. Rob Murakami, "How to Implement ISO 9000," *CMA Magazine* (March 1994), p. 18.

30. Sidney Emmons, "ISO 9000 on a Shoestring," *Quality Progress* (May 1994), p. 50; see also Darren McCabe and Adrian Wilkinson, "The Rise and Fall of TQM: The Vision, Meaning, and Operation of Change," *Industrial Relations Journal*, Vol. 29, no. 1 (March 1998) pp. 18–29.

31. Rob Murakami, "How to Implement ISO 9000," p. 19.

32. Rensis Likert, *New Patterns of Management* (New York: McGraw-Hill, 1961), p. 104.

33. See, for example, Brian Dumaine, "Who Needs a Boss?" *Fortune*, May 7, 1990, p. 52; David Hames, "Productivity-Enhancing Work Innovations: Remedies for What Ails Hospitals?" *Hospital & Health Services Administration*, Vol. 36, no. 4 (Winter 1991), pp. 551–552; see also Shari Caudron, "Are Self-Directed Teams Right for Your Company?" *Personnel Journal* (December 1993), pp. 76–84 and Kenneth Hultman, "It's a Team Effort," *Training and Development Journal*, Vol. 52, no. 2 (February 1998) pp. 12–13.

34. Jack Gordon, "Work Teams: How Far Have They Come?" *Training* (October 1992), pp. 60–65.

35. For employee involvement survey data, see Lee Towe, "Survey Finds Employee Involvement a Priority for Necessary Innovation," *National Productivity Review*, Vol. 9, no. 1 (Winter 1989–90), pp. 3–15.

36. "Despite Effectiveness, Empowerment Efforts Far From Universal," *BNA Bulletin to Management*, June 11, 1998, p. 181.

37. This is based on Dean McFarlin, Paul Sweeney, and John Cotton, "Attitudes Toward Employee Participation in Decision-making: A Comparison of European and American Managers in a United States Multinational Company," *Human Resource Management*, Vol. 31, no. 4 (Winter 1992), pp. 363–383.

38. Ibid., p. 371.

39. These are quoted from Ibid., p. 379.

40. Gary Dessler, *Management: Leading People and Organizations in the 21st Century* (Upper Saddle River, NJ: Prentice Hall, 1998), pp. 476–478.

41. Ben Nagler, "Recasting Employees into Teams," *Workforce* (January 1998), pp. 101–106.

42. Ibid., p. 102.

43. Ibid., p. 103.

44. Ibid.

45. Michael Hammer and James Champy, *Reengineering the Corporation* (New York: Harper Business, 1994), p. 32.

46. Ibid., pp. 36–38.

47. For other examples, see David Allen and Robert Nafius, "Dreaming and Doing: Reengineering GTE Telephone Operations," *Planning Review* (March/April 1993), pp. 28–31; D. Brian Harrison and Maurice Pratt, "A Methodology for Reengineering Businesses," *Planning Review* (March/April 1993), pp. 6–11.

48. Hugh Willmott, "Business Process Reengineering and Human Resource Management," *Personnel Review*, Vol. 3, no. 3 (May 1994), p. 34.

49. James Champy, *Reengineering Management* (New York: Harper Business, 1995), p. 104.

50. Hammer and Champy, *Reengineering the Corporation*, p. 68.

51. Ibid., p. 70.

52. Ibid., p. 71.

53. Ibid.

54. Ibid.

55. Donald Peterson, "Flextime in the United States: The Lessons of Experience," *Personnel*, Vol. 57 (January–February 1980), pp. 21–37; *1987 AMS Flexible Work Survey* (Willow Grove, PA: Administrative Management Society, 1987); Commerce Clearing House, "ASPA/CCH Survey on Alternative Work Schedules," June 26, 1987; Bureau of National Affairs, "Flexible Work Schedules," *Bulletin to Management*, September 3, 1992, pp. 276–277.

56. Peterson, "Flextime in the United States," p. 22.

57. Stanely Nollen, "Does Flextime Improve Productivity?" *Harvard Business Review*, Vol. 56 (September–October 1977), pp. 12–22; Karen Kush and Linda Stroh, "Flextime: Myth or Reality?" *Business Horizons* (September–October 1994), pp. 51–55.

58. Ibid.

59. Stanley Nollen and Virginia Martin, *Alternative Work Schedules Part One: Flextime* (New York: AMACOM, 1978), p. 44.

60. Peterson, "Flextime in the United States," pp. 29–31.

61. Another problem is that some employers let workers "bank" extra hours by working, say, 45 hours one week so they need work only 35 hours the next week. The problem is that in the 45-hour week the employees should, strictly speaking, be paid an overtime rate for the extra 5 hours worked. Some employers handle this problem by letting hours worked vary from day to day but requiring each week to be a 40-hour week. Others are experimenting with letting workers accumulate hours and be paid overtime if necessary. See J. C. Swart, "Flextime's Debit and Credit Option," *Personnel Journal*, Vol. 58 (January–February 1979), pp. 10–12.

62. David Ralston, David Gustafson, and William Anthony, "Employees May Love Flextime, But What Does It Do to the Organization's Productivity?" *Journal of Applied Psychology*, Vol. 70, no. 2 (1985), pp. 272–279.

63. Herbert Northrup, "The Twelve Hour Shift in the North American Mini-steel Industry," *Journal of Labor Research*, Vol. 12, no. 2 (Summer 1991), pp. 261–278; Charlene Marmer Solomon, "24-hour Employees," *Personnel Journal*, Vol. 70, no. 8 (August 1991), pp. 56ff.

64. Janina Latack and Lawrence Foster, "Implementation of Compressed Work Schedules: Participation and Job Redesign as Critical Factors for Employee Acceptance," *Personnel Psychology*, Vol. 38, no. 1 (Spring 1985), pp. 75–92. Interestingly, one way to determine how your employees will react to a 4/40 or flextime work schedule apparently is to ask them ahead of time. One study suggests that these will be the reactions that emerge 3 to 6 months after commencement of the program. See Randall B. Dunham, Jon L. Pierce, and Maria B. Castanea, "Alternative Work Schedules: Two Field Quasi-Experiments," *Personnel Psychology*, Vol. 40, no. 2 (Summer 1987), pp. 215–242; see also Patrick Bolle, "Part-Time Work: Solution or Trap?," *International Labour Review*, Vol. 136, no. 4 (Winter 1997) pp. 557–579.

65. Commerce Clearing House, *Ideas and Trends*, February 26, 1982, p. 61; Charlene Marmer Solomon, "Job Sharing: One Job, Double Headache?" *Personnel Journal* (September 1994), pp. 88–96.

66. "These Top Executives Work Where They Play," *Business Week*, October 27, 1986, p. 132; see also Jenny McCune, "Telecommuting Revisited," *Management Review*, Vol. 87, no. 2 (February 1998) pp. 10–16.

67. "After Flexible Hours, Now It's Flexiyear," *International Management* (March 1982), pp. 31–32.

9

APPRAISING PERFORMANCE

S tar Valve Company makes pollution-control valves used to control noxious gases and liquids in the chemical processing industry. For years its products were protected by patents, so the firm could focus on developing small volumes of highly sophisticated high-cost valves. As its patents ran out, top management knew it had to focus strategically on rapid expansion of sales volume, both in the United States and abroad. Martin Star, the firm's owner, strongly believed that, "You get what you measure." Having decided to focus on building sales, he therefore believed he had to create a new performance appraisal system. He wanted one that would direct his employees' attention to the standards that were important to the firm today, such as boosting sales and improving market share. ▲

Behavioral Objectives

When you finish studying this chapter, you should be able to:

▲ *Explain* why it is important to effectively appraise performance.

▲ *Describe* eight performance appraisal methods and the pros and cons of each.

▲ *Discuss* the major problems inhibiting effective performance appraisals.

▲ *Conduct* a more effective appraisal interview.

Chapter Outline

▲ The Appraisal Process
▲ Appraisal Methods
▲ Appraising Performance: Problems and Solutions
▲ The Appraisal Interview
▲ Performance Appraisal in Practice
▲ The Role of Appraisals in Managing Performance

THE APPRAISAL PROCESS

Performance appraisal is defined as evaluating an employee's current or past performance relative to his or her performance standards. The appraisal process therefore involves: (1) setting work standards; (2) assessing the employee's actual performance relative to these standards; and (3) providing feedback to the employee with the aim of motivating that person to eliminate performance deficiencies or to continue to perform above par.

You've probably already had experience with performance appraisals. For example, some colleges ask students to rank instructors on scales like the one in Figure 9-1. Do you think this is an effective scale? Do you see any way to improve it? These are two of the questions you should be better able to answer by the end of this chapter.

FIGURE 9-1

Classroom Teaching Appraisal by Students

Source: Richard I. Miller, *Evaluating Faculty for Promotion and Tenure* (San Francisco: Jossey-Bass Publishers, 1987), pp. 164–165. Copyright © 1987 Jossey-Base, Inc., Publishers. All rights reserved. Reprinted with permission.

Evaluating Faculty for Promotion and Tenure
Classroom Teaching Appraisal by Students

Teacher _____   Course _____

Term _____   Academic Year _____

Thoughtful student appraisal can help improve teaching effectiveness. This questionnaire is designed for that purpose, and your assistance is appreciated. Please do not sign your name.

Use the back of this form for any further comments you might want to express; use numbers 10, 11, and 12 for any additional questions that you might like to add.

Directions: Rate your teacher on each item, giving the highest scores for exceptional performances and the lowest scores for very poor performances. Place in the blank space before each statement the rating that most closely expresses your view.

Excep-tional		Moderately Good				Very Poor	Don't Know
7	6	5	4	3	2	1	X

_____ 1. How do you rate the agreement between course objectives and lesson assignments?

_____ 2. How do you rate the planning, organization, and use of class periods?

_____ 3. Are the teaching methods and techniques employed by the teacher appropriate and effective?

_____ 4. How do you rate the competence of the instructor in the subject?

_____ 5. How do you rate the interest of the teacher in the subject?

_____ 6. Does the teacher stimulate and challenge you to think and to question?

_____ 7. Does he or she welcome differing points of view?

_____ 8. Does the teacher have a personal interest in helping you in and out of class?

_____ 9. How would you rate the fairness and effectiveness of the grading policies and procedures of the teacher?

_____ 10. _____

Faculty Evaluation Rating Forms

_____ 11. _____

_____ 12. _____

_____ 13. Considering all the above items, what is your overall rating of this teacher?

_____ 14. How would you rate this teacher in comparison with all others you have had in the college or university?

Why appraise performance?[1] There are four reasons. First, appraisals provide information upon which promotion and salary decisions can be made. Second, they provide an opportunity for you and your subordinate to review the subordinate's work-related behavior. This in turn lets both of you develop a plan for correcting any deficiencies the appraisal might have unearthed, and reinforce the things being done right. Third, the appraisal is part of the firm's career-planning process, because it provides an opportunity to review the person's career plans in light of his or her exhibited strengths and weaknesses. Finally (and in keeping with reasons 1 through 3 above), appraisals can, as we'll see, help you better manage and improve your organization's performance.

The Supervisor's Role in Appraisal

Appraising performance is a crucial supervisory skill. The supervisor—not HR—usually does the actual appraising, and a supervisor who rates his or her employees too high or low is doing a disservice to them, to the company, and to him- or herself as well. Supervisors must therefore be familiar with basic appraisal techniques, understand and avoid problems that can cripple appraisals, and know how to conduct appraisals fairly.

The HR department serves a policy-making and advisory role. In one survey, for example, about 80% of the firms responding said the HR department provides advice and assistance regarding the appraisal tool to use, but leaves final decisions on appraisal procedures to operating division heads; in the rest of the firms the personnel office prepares detailed forms and procedures and insists that all departments use them.[2] HR is responsible as well for training supervisors to improve their appraisal skills. Finally, HR is also responsible for monitoring the appraisal system's use and, particularly, for ensuring that the format and criteria being measured comply with EEO laws and don't become outdated. In one survey, half the employers were in the process of revising their appraisal programs, while others were conducting reviews to see how well their programs were working.[3]

Steps in Appraising Performance

The performance appraisal process contains three steps: define the job, appraise performance, and provide feedback. *Defining the job* means making sure that you and your subordinate agree on his or her duties and job standards. *Appraising performance* means com-

The best performance appraisal systems, as we'll see, are those in which the supervisor or manager makes an ongoing effort to coach and monitor employees, instead of leaving evaluation to the last minute.

paring your subordinate's actual performance to the standards that have been set; this usually involves some type of rating form. Third, performance appraisal usually requires one or more *feedback sessions.* Here the subordinate's performance and progress are discussed and plans are made for any development that is required.

PERFORMANCE APPRAISAL PROBLEMS   When appraisals fail, they do so for reasons that parallel these three steps—defining the job, appraising performance, and providing feedback. Some fail because subordinates are not told ahead of time exactly what is expected of them in terms of good performance. Others fail because of problems with the forms or procedures used to actually appraise the performance; a lenient supervisor might rate all subordinates "high," for instance, although many are actually unsatisfactory. Still other problems arise during the interview-feedback session; these include arguing and poor communication. Let's look first at defining the job.

How to Clarify What Performance You Expect

Effective appraisals begin with defining the job and its standards; however, the job description often isn't sufficient to clarify what you want your subordinates to do, because most are written not for specific jobs but for groups of jobs. All sales managers in the firm might have the same job description, for instance. However, as a sales manager's boss, you may have specific ideas about what you expect *your* sales manager to do. For example, the job description may list duties such as "supervise sales force" and "be responsible for all phases of marketing the division's products." However, you may expect your sales manager to personally sell at least $600,000 worth of products per year by handling the division's two largest accounts; to keep the sales force happy; and to keep customers away from the executives (including you.)[4]

To operationalize these expectations, set measurable standards for each. The "personal selling" activity can be measured in terms of how many dollars of sales the manager is to generate personally. "Keeping the sales force happy" might be measured in terms of turnover (on the assumption that less than 10% of the sales force will quit in any given year if morale is high). "Keeping customers away from executives" can be measured with a standard of no more than 10 customer complaints per year. In general, employees should always know ahead of time how and on what basis they will be appraised.

APPRAISAL METHODS

The appraisal itself is generally conducted using a predetermined and formal method like one or more of those described in this section.

Graphic Rating Scale Method

graphic rating scale
A scale that lists a number of traits and a range of performance for each. The employee is then rated by identifying the score that best describes his or her level of performance for each trait.

The **graphic rating scale** is the simplest and most popular technique for appraising performance. Figure 9-2 shows a typical rating scale. It lists traits (such as quality and reliability) and a range of performance values (from unsatisfactory to outstanding) for each trait. The supervisor rates each subordinate by circling or checking the score that best describes his or her performance for each trait. The assigned values for the traits are then totaled.

Instead of appraising generic traits or factors (such as quality and quantity), many firms specify the duties to be appraised. For example, review Figure 9-3.[5] It shows an appraisal form for the position of administrative secretary. In this case the job's five main sets of duties have been taken from the job description and prioritized. Importance ratings are thus indicated as percentages at the top of each of the five categories (key boarding, reception, and so on). There is also space on the form for comments and for evaluation of general performance attributes like reporting for work on time and observing work rules.

Performance Appraisal

Employee Name _____ Title _____

Department _____ Employee Payroll Number _____

Reason for Review: ☐ Annual   ☐ Promotion   ☐ Unsatisfactory Performance

☐ Merit   ☐ End Probation Period   ☐ Other _____

Date employee began present position _____ / _____ / _____

Date of last appraisal _____ / _____ / _____   Scheduled appraisal date _____ / _____ / _____

Instructions: Carefully evaluate employee's work performance in relation to current job requirements. Check rating box to indicate the employee's performance. Indicate N/A if not applicable. Assign points for each rating within the scale and indicate in the corresponding points box. Points will be totaled and averaged for an overall performance score.

RATING IDENTIFICATION

O—Outstanding—Performance is exceptional in all areas and is recognizable as being far superior to others.

V—Very Good—Results clearly exceed most position requirements. Performance is of high quality and is achieved on a consistent basis.

G—Good—Competent and dependable level of performance. Meets performance standards of the job.

I—Improvement Needed—Performance is deficient in certain areas. Improvement is necessary.

U—Unsatisfactory—Results are generally unacceptable and require immediate improvement. No merit increase should be granted to individuals with this rating.

N—Not Rated—Not applicable or too soon to rate.

GENERAL FACTORS	RATING SCALE	SUPPORTIVE DETAILS OR COMMENTS
1. Quality—The accuracy, thoroughness and acceptability of work performed.	O ☐ 100–90 V ☐ 90–80 G ☐ 80–70 I ☐ 70–60 U ☐ below 60 Points	
2. Productivity—The quantity and efficiency of work produced in a specified period of time.	O ☐ 100–90 V ☐ 90–80 G ☐ 80–70 I ☐ 70–60 U ☐ below 60 Points	
3. Job Knowledge—The practical/technical skills and information used on the job.	O ☐ 100–90 V ☐ 90–80 G ☐ 80–70 I ☐ 70–60 U ☐ below 60 Points	
4. Reliability—The extent to which an employee can be relied upon regarding task completion and follow up.	O ☐ 100–90 V ☐ 90–80 G ☐ 80–70 I ☐ 70–60 U ☐ below 60 Points	
5. Availability—The extent to which an employee is punctual, observes prescribed work break/meal periods and the overall attendance record.	O ☐ 100–90 V ☐ 90–80 G ☐ 80–70 I ☐ 70–60 U ☐ below 60 Points	
6. Independence—The extent of work performed with little or no supervision.	O ☐ 100–90 V ☐ 90–80 G ☐ 80–70 I ☐ 70–60 U ☐ below 60 Points	

FIGURE 9-2 *One Page of a Two-Page Graphic Rating Scale with Space for Comments*

Name _____	Rating Scale Key
Position _____	1 Fails to meet job requirements
Rating period from _____ to _____	2 Essentially meets job requirements
Rater name _____	3 Fully meets job requirements
Rater title _____	4 Meets job requirements with distinction
Department _____	5 Exceeds job requirements

Part II: Rating Scales for Task Areas

Position: Administrative Secretary
   Duties and Responsibilities

A. Keyboarding   PCT. (30%)   RATING: 1 ☐   2 ☐   3 ☐   4 ☐   5 ☐

Producing accurate typewritten documents in the proper format at 60wpm from a variety of sources, including oral dictation: From oral dictation, dictating machine, shorthand notes or standard formats, transcribes correspondence for general manager: transcribes minutes of meetings; types notices, agendas, schedules, and other internal material; types surveys for trade associations; compiles and types operating reports and other reports, including text and tables; types copy for trade magazines and newspapers; composes and types letters, memoranda, copy and other documents as needed or on request.

Comments

B. Reception   PCT. (25%)   RATING: 1 ☐   2 ☐   3 ☐   4 ☐   5 ☐

Receiving and recording initial contacts in person or on the telephone and courteously assisting callers or visitors: Answers incoming telephone calls, takes message, provides information or routes call to appropriate individual; greets visitors, provides information or directs to appropriate office or individual; acts as hostess and provides incidental services to visitors in waiting status; operates automatic answering service; maintains log of callers and visitors to cooperative.

Comments

C. Scheduling   PCT. (20%)   RATING: 1 ☐   2 ☐   3 ☐   4 ☐   5 ☐

Managing calendar efficiently including arranging appointments, meetings, travel and similar activities; maintains calendar and makes appointments for general manager, board members and other staff; prepares requests for reimbursement for official travel; assists with arrangements of annual meeting; makes arrangements for in-service training meetings, including rooms, coffee breaks and food service when necessary; schedules use of organizational facilities; arranges lodging, travel and fees for outside speakers and consultants.

Comments

D. Filing and records managment   PCT. (15%)   RATING: 1 ☐   2 ☐   3 ☐   4 ☐   5 ☐

Creating and maintaining appropriate filing systems and promptly locating and retrieving needed material upon request: Develops space allocation plan and filing system for correspondence, minutes, reports, regulations and related material; places material into proper location in file; searches for and retrieves material from files; culls, files and removes material to central location or destroys as needed; maintains and preserves vital records; organizes data from file search into usable format.

Comments

E. General office service   PCT. (10%)   RATING: 1 ☐   2 ☐   3 ☐   4 ☐   5 ☐

Performing related office duties in accordance with acceptable practice and prescribed procedures; processes mail through postage meter, records readings and posts; opens and distributes incoming mail; makes copies of documents; maintains petty cash fund; clips articles from papers and magazines related to the organization; maintains bulletin board; performs other job duties as assigned.

Comments

FIGURE 9-3 *Sample Performance Appraisal Form for Actual Duties*

Source: James Buford, Jr., Bettye Burkhalter, and Grover Jacobs, "Link Job Description to Performance Appraisals," *Personnel Journal* (June 1988), pp. 135–136.

alternation ranking method

Ranking employees from best to worst on a particular trait, choosing highest, then lowest, until all are ranked.

Alternation Ranking Method

Ranking employees from best to worst on a trait or traits is another method for evaluating employees. Since it is usually easier to distinguish between the worst and best employees than just rank them, an **alternation ranking method** is most popular. First, list all subor-

Part III: Performance Appraisal Form

Does the employee report for and remain at work as required?   ☐ yes ☐ no   If no, please explain.
Does the employee follow instructions and observe work rules?   ☐ yes ☐ no   If no, please explain.
Does the employee get along and cooperate with co-workers on the job?   ☐ yes ☐ no   If no, please explain.
Does the employee have the knowledges, skills, abilities and other qualifications needed for successful job performance?   ☐ yes ☐ no   If no, please explain.
Describe any specific actions employee needs to take to improve job performance.
Summarize this employee's overall job performance as determined in your joint discussion.

Part IV: Signatures

This report is based on my observation and knowledge of both the employee and the job.

My signature indicates that I have reviewed this appraisal. It does not mean that I agree with the results.

_____   _____
Supervisor   Date

_____   _____
Reviewer   Date   Employee   Date

FIGURE 9-3 *Sample Performance Appraisal Form for Actual Duties (continued)*

dinates to be rated, and then cross out the names of any not known well enough to rank. Then, on a form such as that in Figure 9-4, indicate the employee who is the highest on the characteristic being measured and also the one who is the lowest. Then choose the next highest and the next lowest, alternating between highest and lowest until all employees to be rated have been ranked.

FIGURE 9-4

Alternation Ranking Scale

ALTERNATION RANKING SCALE

For the Trait: _____

For the trait you are measuring, list all the employees you want to rank. Put the highest-ranking employee's name on line 1. Put the lowest-ranking employee's name on line 20. Then list the next highest ranking on line 2, the next lowest ranking on line 19, and so on. Continue until all names are on the scale.

Highest-ranking employee

1. _____		11. _____
2. _____		12. _____
3. _____		13. _____
4. _____		14. _____
5. _____		15. _____
6. _____		16. _____
7. _____		17. _____
8. _____		18. _____
9. _____		19. _____
10. _____		20. _____

Lowest-ranking employee

Paired Comparison Method

paired comparison method

Ranking employees by making a chart of all possible pairs of the employees for each trait and indicating which is the better employee of the pair.

The **paired comparison method** helps make the ranking method more precise. For every trait (quantity of work, quality of work, and so on), every subordinate is paired with and compared to every other subordinate.

Suppose there are five employees to be rated. In the paired comparison method you make a chart, as in Figure 9-5, of all possible pairs of employees *for each trait*. Then for each trait indicate (with a + or −) who is the better employee of the pair. Next the number of times an employee is rated better is added up. In Figure 9-5, employee Maria ranked highest (has the most + marks) for quality of work, whereas Art was ranked highest for creativity.

Forced Distribution Method

forced distribution method

Similar to grading on a curve; predetermined percentages of ratees are placed in various performance categories.

The **forced distribution method** is similar to grading on a curve. With this method, predetermined percentages of ratees are placed in performance categories. For example, you may decide to distribute employees as follows:

15% high performers

20% high-average performers

30% average performers

20% low-average performers

15% low performers

(although the proportions in each category need not be symmetrical). As at school, forced distribution means not everyone can get an "A", and that one's performance is always

FIGURE 9-5

Ranking Employees by the Paired Comparison Method

Note: + means "better than," − means "worse than." For each chart, add up the number of +'s in each column to get the highest-ranked employee.

FOR THE TRAIT "QUALITY OF WORK"					
	Employee Rated:				
As Compared to:	A Art	B Maria	C Chuck	D Diane	E José
A Art		+	+	−	−
B Maria	−		−	−	−
C Chuck	−	+		+	−
D Diane	+	+	−		+
E José	+	+	+	−	

Maria Ranks Highest Here

FOR THE TRAIT "CREATIVITY"					
	Employee Rated:				
As Compared to:	A Art	B Maria	C Chuck	D Diane	E José
A Art		−	−	−	−
B Maria	+		−	+	+
C Chuck	+	+		−	+
D Diane	+	−	+		−
E José	+	−	−	+	

Art Ranks Highest Here

rated relative to one's peers. One practical way to do this is to write each employee's name on a separate index card. Then, for each trait being appraised (quality of work, creativity, and so on), place the employee's card in one of the appropriate performance categories.

AN EXAMPLE   Merck and Company, with about 31,000 employees, has used forced distribution for all exempt employees who receive merit pay increases based on their performance ratings.

Merck's reason for using forced distribution is informative.[6] It was instituted when the firm found that 80% of its exempt employees were receiving ratings of four and above on the five-point scale. In other words, employees who had significant accomplishments were getting only slightly higher ratings than were those who did a good but not an extraordinary job. As a result, neither the performance appraisal system nor the merit pay plan had the effects on motivation that Merck wanted. The new program's purpose was to provide for greater differentiation among employees, so outstanding employees could be identified.

At Merck, all exempt employees now receive an annual performance appraisal in December. They meet with their supervisors to review their accomplishments for the year (relative to previously established goals) and receive one of five ratings: EX (exceptional), WD (with distinction), HS (high Merck standard), RI (room for improvement), and NA (not acceptable).

Predetermined percentages of a manager's subordinates must fall in each of the five categories. For example, 5% of the department's employees can receive EX ratings, 15% can receive WD ratings, and the vast majority—70%—should fall in the "high Merck standard" middle level of the range. In other words, this system forces the supervisor to identify no more than 20% of his or her exempt employees as above average when compared with their Merck peers.

The program is working well because Merck has worked hard to overcome forced distribution's inherent problems. For example, it's not realistic to force a manager with only four or five employees to distribute them into five classes. Therefore, Merck uses a roll-up system. Here several departments in the same division are reviewed together for the purpose of meeting the percentage distribution requirements of the rating system. (At each roll-up meeting, the supervisor can argue for two of the employees receiving an EX rating.) The big problem, however, was getting employees who viewed themselves as high achievers to understand that getting an HS (high Merck standard) doesn't equate to getting a "C" on a report card.

At Merck (or when rating college students, for that matter), there is always the question of whether the person's absolute or relative performance should be appraised. On balance however, Merck's relative performance approach has been successful, particularly in helping Merck identify high achievers and reward them.

Critical Incident Method

critical incident method
Keeping a record of uncommonly good or undesirable examples of an employee's work-related behavior and reviewing it with the employee at predetermined times.

With the **critical incident method,** the supervisor keeps a log of desirable or undesirable examples or incidents of each subordinate's work-related behavior. Then every 6 months or so, the supervisor and subordinate meet and discuss the latter's performance using the specific incidents as examples.

This method has several advantages. It provides you with specific hard examples of good and poor performance for explaining the appraisal. It ensures that you think about the subordinate's appraisal all during the year because the incidents must be accumulated; therefore, the rating does not just reflect the employee's most recent performance (we'll return to this important point below). Keeping a running list of critical incidents should also provide concrete examples of what specifically your subordinate can do to eliminate any performance deficiencies. However, this method is not too useful by itself for comparing employees or for making salary decisions.

You can adapt the critical incident method to the specific job expectations laid out for the subordinate at the beginning of the year. Thus, in the example presented in Table 9-1, one of the assistant plant manager's continuing duties was to supervise procurement and to minimize inventory costs. The critical incident shows that the assistant plant manager let inventory storage costs rise 15%; this provides a specific example of what performance must be improved in the future.

Narrative Forms

Some employers use narrative forms to evaluate personnel. For example, Figure 9-6 presents part of the Performance Improvement Plan used by one multinational company to evaluate the progress and development of its exempt employees. As you can see, the person's supervisor is asked (1) to rate the employee's performance for each performance factor or skill such as Planning, and (2) to write down critical examples and an improvement plan designed to aid the employee in understanding where his or her performance was good or bad, and for improving that performance. A summary performance appraisal discussion then focuses on problem solving.[7]

TABLE 9-1 Examples of Critical Incidents for an Assistant Plant Manager

CONTINUING DUTIES	TARGETS	CRITICAL INCIDENTS
Schedule production for plant	Full utilization of personnel and machinery in plant; orders delivered on time	Instituted new production scheduling system; decreased late orders by 10% last month; increased machine utilization in plant by 20% last month
Supervise procurement of raw materials and inventory control	Minimize inventory costs while keeping adequate supplies on hand	Let inventory storage costs rise 15% last month; overordered parts "A" and "B" by 20%; underordered part "C" by 30%
Supervise machinery maintenance	No shutdowns due to faulty machinery	Instituted new preventative maintenance system for plant; prevented a machine breakdown by discovering faulty part

FIGURE 9-6

Performance Improvement Plan

Source: Joseph J. Famularo, *Handbook of Personnel Forms, Records, and Reports* (New York: McGraw-Hill, 1982), pp. 216–219.

PERFORMANCE IMPROVEMENT PLAN

Name _____   Date _____

Position Title _____   Dept./Div. _____

I. Purpose and Objective

This form and process is designed to assist the supervisor in analyzing *how* an employee is performing his or her work, that is, the individual skills and knowledge they use in performing their job responsibilities. The primary objective for you in completing this Performance Analysis and subsequent discussions with the employee is to help the person improve.

II. Steps in the Process

A. Performance Factors and Skills—The individual skills and performance factors represent the major abilities that are required of most employees to perform their jobs. After reading the description of each factor, assign a rating of the employee's skill proficiency using the following guide:

S—Strength
SA—Satisfactory
N—Needs Improvement
NA—Not Applicable

Space is provided at the end of this form to write out performance factors/skills which you may consider to be important and are not found on this form. We suggest, however, that you avoid adding personality traits that do not influence performance.

B. Performance Analysis and Examples—This section is provided for you to support your judgment with specific *performance related* examples of observed behavior. These examples should be stated in terms of what the employee did or said (in completing a task or project) as it relates to the performance factor.

C. Improvement Plan—Specific actions should be listed in this section that will be taken to assist the employee in those areas that require performance improvement. It is suggested that supervisor and subordinate develop this plan jointly in a discussion session. These actions should focus on activities, tasks, training, expanded job duties, etc., that will afford the employee an opportunity to develop the needed skill. The written Improvement Plan should also state *who* is responsible for completing each step, a *timetable* for completion and a *feedback/followup* process that will monitor the progress.

D. Discussion with the Employee—The performance rating and analysis of each factor or skill must be discussed with the employee. The principal focus of this meeting should be on problem solving, i.e., to stimulate the employee to think about the probable causes of the skill or knowledge deficiency and to generate ideas on how to bring about performance improvement in these areas. Working together, supervisor and employee should examine the cause of each deficiency and then jointly develop and agree upon a logical course of action for improvement. The Improvement Plan should be realistic, written down, and followed up in future sessions.

Performance Factors/Skills	Performance Analysis & Examples	Improvement Plan
PLANNING—Forecasting, setting objectives, establishing strategies and courses of action, budeting, scheduling, programming, and outlining procedures.		
ORGANIZING—Grouping of activities to achieve results, delegating, staffing, and using available resources.		

Performance Factors/Skills	Performance Analysis & Examples	Improvement Plan
DIRECTING—Ability to guide and supervise. Stresses the processes of motivating, communicating, and leading.		
CONTROLLING— Developing performance standards, measuring results, and taking corrective action.		
DEVELOPING PEOPLE— Evaluating performance and potential, providing training and development, coaching and counseling and resolving personnel problems.		
PROBLEM ANALYSIS— Determining pertinent data, differentiating significant from less significant facts, defining interrelationships, and arriving at sound practical solutions.		
DECISION-MAKING— Evaluating and selecting among alternative courses of action quickly and accurately.		

Behaviorally Anchored Rating Scales

behaviorally anchored rating scale (BARS)

An appraisal method that aims at combining the benefits of narrative critical incidents and quantified ratings by anchoring a quantified scale with specific narrative examples of good and poor performance.

A **behaviorally anchored rating scale (BARS)** combines the benefits of narratives, critical incidents, and quantified ratings (such as graphic rating scales) by anchoring a quantified scale with specific behavioral examples of good or poor performance, as in Figure 9-7. Its proponents claim that it provides better, more equitable appraisals than do the other tools we discussed.[8]

Developing a BARS typically requires five steps:[9]

1. *Generate critical incidents.* Persons who know the job being appraised (jobholders and/or supervisors) are asked to describe specific illustrations (critical incidents) of effective and ineffective performance.

FIGURE 9-7

Example of a Behaviorally Anchored Rating Scale for the Dimension Salesmanship Skill.

Source: Walter C. Borman, *Behavior Based Rating Scales* in Ronald A. Berk (Ed.) *Performance Assessment: Methods & Applications* (Baltimore: The Johns Hopkins University Press, 1986), p. 103.

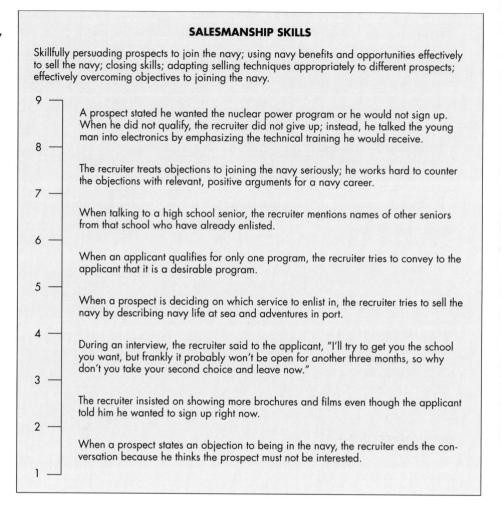

SALESMANSHIP SKILLS

Skillfully persuading prospects to join the navy; using navy benefits and opportunities effectively to sell the navy; closing skills; adapting selling techniques appropriately to different prospects; effectively overcoming objectives to joining the navy.

9 —

A prospect stated he wanted the nuclear power program or he would not sign up. When he did not qualify, the recruiter did not give up; instead, he talked the young man into electronics by emphasizing the technical training he would receive.

8 —

The recruiter treats objections to joining the navy seriously; he works hard to counter the objections with relevant, positive arguments for a navy career.

7 —

When talking to a high school senior, the recruiter mentions names of other seniors from that school who have already enlisted.

6 —

When an applicant qualifies for only one program, the recruiter tries to convey to the applicant that it is a desirable program.

5 —

When a prospect is deciding on which service to enlist in, the recruiter tries to sell the navy by describing navy life at sea and adventures in port.

4 —

During an interview, the recruiter said to the applicant, "I'll try to get you the school you want, but frankly it probably won't be open for another three months, so why don't you take your second choice and leave now."

3 —

The recruiter insisted on showing more brochures and films even though the applicant told him he wanted to sign up right now.

2 —

When a prospect states an objection to being in the navy, the recruiter ends the conversation because he thinks the prospect must not be interested.

1 —

2. *Develop performance dimensions.* These people then cluster the incidents into a smaller set of performance dimensions (say, 5 or 10). Each cluster (dimension) such as "conscientiousness" is then defined.

3. *Reallocate incidents.* Another group of people who also know the job then reallocate the original critical incidents. They are given the clusters' definitions and the critical incidents and are asked to reassign each incident to the cluster they think it fits best. Typically, a critical incident is retained if some percentage (usually 50% to 80%) of this second group assigns it to the same cluster as did the group in step 2.

4. *Scale the incidents.* This second group is generally asked to rate the behavior described in the incident as to how effectively or ineffectively it represents performance on the appropriate dimension (seven- or nine-point scales are typical).

5. *Develop final instrument.* A subset of the incidents (usually six or seven per cluster) is used as *behavioral anchors* for each dimension.

EXAMPLE Three researchers developed a BARS for grocery checkout clerks working in a large Western grocery chain.[10] They collected a number of critical incidents and then clustered them into eight performance dimensions:

Knowledge and Judgment

Conscientiousness

Skill in Human Relations

Skill in Operation of Register

Skill in Bagging

Organizational Ability of Checkstand Work

Skill in Monetary Transactions

Observational Ability

They then developed a behaviorally anchored rating scale for one of these dimensions, "knowledge and judgment." Similar to Figure 9-7, it contained a scale (ranging from 1 to 9) for rating performance from "extremely poor" to "extremely good." Notice how the typical BARS is behaviorally anchored with specific critical incidents. Thus, in the supermarket example, there was a specific critical incident ("by knowing the price of items, this checker would be expected to look for mismarked and unmarked items"); this helped anchor or specify what was meant by "extremely good" performance. Similarly, there are other critical incident anchors along the performance scale.

ADVANTAGES   Developing a BARS can be more time consuming than developing other appraisal tools, such as graphic rating scales. But BARS may also have important advantages:[11]

1. *A more accurate gauge.* People who know the job and its requirements better than anyone else develop the BARS. The result should therefore be a good gauge of performance on the job.

2. *Clearer standards.* The critical incidents along the scale help to clarify what is meant by extremely good performance, average performance, and so forth.

3. *Feedback.* The critical incidents may be more useful in providing feedback to appraisees than simply informing them of their performance rating and not providing specific behavioral examples.

4. *Independent dimensions.* Systematically clustering the critical incidents into five or six performance dimensions (such as "knowledge and judgment") should help to make the dimensions more independent of one another. For example, a rater should be less likely to rate an employee high on all dimensions simply because he or she was rated high in "conscientiousness."

5. *Consistency.*[12] BARS evaluations also seem to be relatively consistent and reliable in that different raters' appraisals of the same person tend to be similar.

The Management by Objectives (MBO) Method

management by objectives (MBO)

Involves setting specific measurable goals with each employee and then periodically reviewing the progress made.

Stripped to its essentials, **management by objectives (MBO)** requires the manager to set specific measurable goals with each employee and then periodically discuss his or her progress toward these goals. You could engage in a modest MBO program with subordinates by jointly setting goals and periodically providing feedback. However, the term *MBO* almost always refers to a comprehensive, organizationwide goal-setting and appraisal program that consists of six main steps:

1. *Set the organization's goals.* Establish an organizationwide plan for next year and set goals.

2. *Set departmental goals.* Here department heads and their superiors jointly set goals for their departments.

One of the foundations of a good Management by Objectives program is open communication, which fosters employee commitment to the objectives and goals.

3. *Discuss departmental goals.* Department heads discuss the department's goals with all subordinates in the department (often at a departmentwide meeting) and ask them to develop their own individual goals; in other words, how can each employee contribute to the department's attaining its goals?

4. *Define expected results* (set individual goals). Here department heads and their subordinates set short-term performance targets.

5. *Performance reviews: Measure the results.* Department heads compare the actual performance of each employee with expected results.

6. *Provide feedback.* Department heads hold periodic performance review meetings with subordinates to discuss and evaluate the latters' progress in achieving expected results.

PROBLEMS TO AVOID   There are three problems in using MBO. Setting unclear, unmeasurable objectives is the main one. An objective such as "will do a better job of training" is useless. On the other hand, "will have four subordinates promoted during the year" is a measurable objective.

Second, MBO is time-consuming. Taking the time to set objectives, to measure progress, and to provide feedback can take several hours per employee per year, over and above the time you already spend doing each person's appraisal.

Third, setting objectives with the subordinate sometimes turns into a tug of war, with you pushing for higher quotas and the subordinate pushing for lower ones. Knowing the job and the person's ability is thus important. To motivate performance, the objectives must be fair and attainable. The more you know about the job and the person's ability, the more confident you can be about the standards you set.

Mixing the Methods

Most firms combine several appraisal techniques. An example is shown in Figure 9-8. This presents a form used to appraise the performance of managers in a large airline. Note that it is basically a graphic rating scale with descriptive phrases included to define the traits being

MAJOR PERFORMANCE STRENGTHS/WEAKNESSES

Read the definitions of each management factor below and choose the ranking that most accurately describes the employee. If, after reading the definition, it is determined that the skill area was not demonstrated because of the nature of the employee's position, indicate as Non-Applicable (N/A). Your evaluation on each of the management factors below should relate directly to the employee's actual performance on the job.

PLANNING SKILL—Degree to which incumbent:
  –Assessed and established priorities of result area.
  –Designed realistic short- and long-range plans.
  –Formulated feasible timetables.
  –Anticipated possible problems and obstacles toward reaching required results.

Ranking Code	(CHECK ONE)	
1	Far exceeds requirements	
4	Usually meets requirements	
3	Fully meets requirements	
2	Usually exceeds requirements	
5	Fails to meet requirements	

Comments: _____

ORGANIZING SKILL—Degree to which incumbent:
  –Grouped activities for optimal use of personnel and material resources in order to achieve goals.
  –Clearly defined responsibilities and authority limits of subordinates.
  –Minimized confusion and inefficiencies in work operations.

Ranking Code	(CHECK ONE)	
3	Fully meets requirements	
2	Usually exceeds requirements	
5	Fails to meet requirements	
1	Far exceeds requirements	
4	Usually meets requirements	

Comments: _____

CONTROLLING SKILL—Degree to which incumbent:
  –Established appropriate procedures to be kept informed of subordinate's work progress.
  –Identifed deviations in work goal progress.
  –Adjusted to deviations in work to ensure that established goals were met.

Ranking Code	(CHECK ONE)	
5	Fails to meet requirements	
4	Usually meets requirements	
3	Fully meets requirements	
2	Usually exceeds requirements	
1	Far exceeds requirements	

Comments: _____

FIGURE 9-8 *One Page from a Typical Management Appraisal Form*

INFORMATION TECHNOLOGY AND HR

Computerized Performance Appraisals and Electronic Performance Monitoring

More employers are turning to computerized performance appraisal systems today, generally with good results. Several relatively inexpensive performance appraisal software programs are on the market, including Employee Appraiser (Austin-Haynes, $129), Review Writer (Avontos, $129), and Performance Now (Knowledgepoint, $169). All three enable managers to log notes on their subordinates during the year and to rate employees on a series of performance traits. The program then generates written text to support each part of the appraisal.[13]

Employee Appraiser illustrates how computerized appraisals are used.[14] It presents the user with a menu of more than a dozen evaluation dimensions, including dependability, initiative, communication, decision making, leadership, judgment, and planning and productivity. Within each dimension are various performance factors, again presented in menu form.

For example, under "communication" are separate factors for writing, verbal communication, receptivity to feedback and criticism, listening skills, ability to focus on the desired results, keeping others informed, and openness.

Once the user clicks on a factor, he or she is presented with a relatively sophisticated version of a graphic rating scale. However, instead of using numbers, Employee Appraiser uses behaviorally anchored examples. For example, for verbal communication there are six choices, ranging from "presents ideas clearly" to "lacks structure." Once the manager picks the phrase that most accurately describes the worker, Employee Appraiser generates sample text. For example, if Juan's boss chooses "is sometimes unclear," the program might generate the following text: "Juan usually presents his ideas clearly and concisely. However, he sometimes uses terminology that is unclear to oth-

measured. However, there is also a section for comments below each trait. This lets the rater jot down several critical incidents. The quantifiable rating aspect permits comparisons of employees and is therefore useful for making salary, transfer, and promotion decisions. The critical incidents provide specific examples of good and poor performance.[17]

Some firms utilize computerized approaches, as in the computer feature above.

Technology has updated the appraisal process. New software programs enable employees to check their own performance against prescribed criteria.

ers. He would be more effective in his communications if he used less jargon and fewer technical terms."

By the time the manager has moved through all the performance categories and subfactors, Employee Appraiser has generated a detailed written performance report. The program's built-in text editor or another word processing program can then be used to modify the report and add or delete comments and details.

Electronic Performance Monitoring (EPM) is another example of how information technology can facilitate appraising employees. EPM may be defined as having supervisors monitor through electronic means the amount of computerized data an employee is processing per day, and thereby his or her performance.[15] As two researchers note, "organizations now use computer networks, sophisticated telephone systems, and both wireless audio and video links to monitor and record the work activities of employees." It's estimated that as many as 26 million U.S. workers have their performance monitored electronically, a fact which has already triggered a proliferation of Congressional legislation aimed at, for instance, requiring that employees receive precise notification of when they will be monitored.

The results of one study suggest two things about electronically monitoring employee's performance. First, "participants [employees] with the ability to delay or prevent electronic performance monitoring indicated higher feelings of personal control and demonstrated superior task performance." In other words, give employees some control over how and when they're monitored.[16] If you can't, then the findings also suggest that you *not* let them know when they're actually being monitored. The participants who knew exactly when they were being monitored actually expressed lower feelings of personal control than did those who were not told when they were being monitored.

APPRAISING PERFORMANCE: PROBLEMS AND SOLUTIONS

Few of the things a manager does are fraught with more peril than appraising subordinates' performance. Employees in general tend to be overly optimistic about what their ratings will be and also know that their raises, career progress, and peace of mind may well hinge on how they are rated. This alone should make it somewhat difficult to rate performance; even more problematical, however, are the numerous technical problems that can cast serious doubt on just how fair the whole process is. In this section we therefore turn to some of the main appraisal problems and how to solve them, as well as to several other pertinent appraisal issues.

Dealing with Rating Scale Appraisal Problems

Most employers still depend on graphic-type rating scales to appraise performance, but these scales are especially subject to several appraisal problems. Specifically, five main problems can undermine appraisal tools such as graphic rating scales: unclear standards, halo effect, central tendency, leniency or strictness, and bias.

unclear performance standards

An appraisal scale that is too open to interpretation; instead include descriptive phrases that define each trait and what is meant by standards like "good" or "unsatisfactory."

UNCLEAR STANDARDS   The problem of **unclear standards** is illustrated in Table 9-2. Although the graphic rating scale seems objective, it would probably result in unfair appraisals because the traits and degrees of merit are open to interpretation. For example, different supervisors would probably define "good" performance, "fair" performance, and so on differently. The same is true of traits such as "quality of work" or "creativity."

There are several ways to rectify this problem. The best way is to develop and include descriptive phrases that define each trait, as in Figure 9-2. There the form specified

TABLE 9-2 A Graphic Rating Scale with Unclear Standards

	EXCELLENT	GOOD	FAIR	POOR
Quality of work				
Quantity of work				
Creativity				
Integrity				

Note: For example, what exactly is meant by "good," "quantity of work," and so forth?

what was meant by "outstanding," "superior," and "good" quality of work. This specificity results in appraisals that are more consistent and more easily explained.

halo effect

In performance appraisal, the problem that occurs when a supervisor's rating of a subordinate on one trait biases the rating of that person on other traits.

HALO EFFECT   **Halo effect** has been defined as "the influence of a rater's general impression on ratings of specific ratee qualities."[18] In practice it might mean, for instance, that your rating of a subordinate on one major trait (such as "gets along with others") biases how you rate that person on other traits (such as "quantity of work"). This problem often occurs with employees who are especially friendly (or unfriendly) toward the supervisor. For example, an unfriendly employee will often be rated unsatisfactory for all traits rather than just for the trait "gets along well with others." Being aware of this problem is a major step toward avoiding it. Supervisory training can also alleviate the problem.[19]

central tendency

A tendency to rate all employees the same way, such as rating them all average.

CENTRAL TENDENCY   Many supervisors have a **central tendency** when filling in rating scales. For example, if the rating scale ranges from 1 to 7, they tend to avoid the highs (6 and 7) and lows (1 and 2) and rate most of their people between 3 and 5. If you use a graphic rating scale, this central tendency could mean that all employees are simply rated "average." Such a restriction can distort the evaluations, making them less useful for promotion, salary, or counseling purposes. Ranking employees instead of using a graphic rating scale can avoid this central tendency problem, because all employees must be ranked and thus can't all be rated average.

strictness/leniency

The problem that occurs when a supervisor has a tendency to rate all subordinates either high or low.

LENIENCY OR STRICTNESS   Some supervisors tend to rate all their subordinates consistently high (or low), just as some instructors are notoriously high graders and others are not. This **strictness/leniency** problem is especially serious with graphic rating scales, because supervisors aren't necessarily required to avoid giving all their employees high (or low) ratings. On the other hand, if you must rank subordinates, you are forced to distinguish between high and low performers. Thus, strictness/leniency is not a problem with the ranking or forced distribution approaches.

In fact, if a graphic rating scale must be used, it may be a good idea to impose a distribution of performance—that, say, about 10% of your people should be rated "excellent," 20% "good," and so forth. In other words, try to get a spread (unless, of course, you are sure all your people really do fall into just one or two categories).

Leniency may result from the purpose of the appraisal, as well as from the inherent leniency of the person doing the appraising. Personnel psychologists have long hypothesized that performance appraisal ratings obtained for administrative purposes (such as pay raises or promotions) would be more lenient than ratings aimed for feedback or employee development purposes.[20] Two researchers recently investigated this hypothesis, reviewing 22 studies of performance appraisal leniency. They concluded that: "performance appraisal ratings obtained for administrative purposes were nearly one-third of a standard deviation larger than those obtained for research or employee development purposes."[21]

Their results suggest that supervisors tend to be more lenient when appraising employees for personnel actions that have concrete outcomes for the employee—things like pay raises or promotions. On the other hand, they tend to be less lenient when the purpose of the appraisal is counseling the employee, providing feedback, correcting performance deficiencies, and other such employee development purposes, a fact the supervisor should keep in mind.

BIAS   Individual differences among ratees in terms of characteristics like age, race, and sex can affect their ratings, often quite apart from each ratee's actual performance.[22] In one study, for instance, researchers found a systematic tendency to evaluate older ratees (over 60 years of age) lower on "performance capacity" and "potential for development" than younger employees.[23]

A study of registered nurses provides an interesting picture of how age can distort evaluations. For nurses 30 to 39 years old, they and their supervisors each rated the nurses' performance virtually the same. In the 21 to 29 category, supervisors actually rated nurses higher than the nurses rated themselves. However, for the 40 to 61 nurse age category, the supervisors rated nurses' performance lower than the nurses rated their own performance. One interpretation is that supervisors are tougher in appraising older subordinates. Specifically, they don't give them as much credit for their success, while attributing any low performance to their lack of ability.[24]

The rater's and ratee's race can also affect the rating a person receives. One recent study was based on performance ratings received from over 20,000 bosses, 50,000 peers, and 40,000 subordinates.[25] The findings illustrate the interplay between the race of the rater and ratee. Researchers concluded that black raters rated black ratees higher than white ratees; that white bosses (but not white subordinates) assigned more favorable ratings to white ratees than to black ratees; and that black raters assigned higher ratings than did whites, regardless of the race of the ratees.[26] Such results sound a cautionary signal for employers; since over 90% of appraisal programs ask the immediate boss to take sole responsibility for appraisals, and since most bosses are white, black managers are likely to find their career progress is largely in white managers' hands, so that "black managers who are rated by white bosses may advance at a lower rate than black managers who are rated by black bosses."[27]

However, the research findings are not entirely consistent, in that the **bias** is not necessarily always against the minorities or women. In another study, for instance, low-performing blacks were often rated significantly higher than were low-performing whites. Similarly, high-performing females were often rated significantly higher than were high-performing males.[28]

RESEARCH INSIGHT   A recent study illustrates how bias can consciously or subconsciously influence the way one person appraises another. In this study, researchers sought to determine the extent to which pregnancy is a source of bias in performance appraisals.[29] The subjects consisted of a sample of 220 undergraduate students between the ages of 17 and 43 attending a Midwestern university.

Two videotapes were prepared of a female "employee" participating in several employment exercises. Each video showed three 5-minute scenarios in which this "employee" interacted with another woman. For example, she acted as a customer representative to deal with an irate customer, tried to sell a computer system to a potential customer, and dealt with a problem subordinate. In each case the performance level of the "employee" was designed to be average or slightly above average. The "employee" was the same in both videotapes and the videotapes were identical except for one difference. The first videotape was made in the "employee's" 9th month of pregnancy, while the second tape was made about 5 months later. The aim of the study was to investigate whether or not the "employee's" pregnancy influenced the performance appraisal rating she received for dealing with the irate customer, selling the computer system, and dealing with the problem subordinate.

Several groups of student raters watched either the "pregnant" or "not pregnant" tape. They rated the "employee" on a five-point graphic rating scale for individual characteristics such as "ability to do the job," "dependability," and "physical mannerisms." For each characteristic the employee was rated from "very poor" (1) to "excellent" (5).

The results of this study suggest that pregnant women may face additional workplace discrimination above and beyond any gender bias that may already exist against women in general. Despite having been exposed to otherwise identical behavior by the same female "employee," the student raters of this study "with a remarkably high degree of consistency" assigned lower performance ratings to a pregnant woman as opposed to a nonpregnant one.[30] Furthermore, men raters seemed more susceptible to negative influence than did women. Given the fact that most employees still report to male supervisors and that supervisory ratings are often the determinant of one's advancement, the researchers conclude that any bias that exists could make it even harder for women to have both children and careers. One implication is that raters must be forewarned of such problems and trained to use objectivity in rating subordinates.

An employee's previous performance can also affect how his or her current performance is perceived.[31] The actual error can take several forms. The rater may systematically overestimate improvement by a poor worker or a decline by a good worker, for instance. In some situations—especially when the behavior change is more gradual—the rater may simply be insensitive to improvement or decline. In any case, the bottom line is to rate performance objectively. Try to block out the influence of factors such as previous performance, age, or race.

How to Avoid Appraisal Problems

There are at least four ways to minimize the impact of appraisal problems such as bias and central tendency. First, be sure to understand the problems as just discussed and the suggestions (like clarifying standards) given for each of them. Understanding the problem can help you avoid it.

Second, choose the right appraisal tool. Each tool, such as the graphic rating scale or critical incident method, has its own advantages and disadvantages. For example, the ranking method avoids central tendency but can cause ill feelings when employees' performances are in fact all "high", and the ranking and forced distribution methods both provide relative—not absolute—ratings (Table 9-3).

Third, train supervisors to eliminate rating errors such as halo, leniency, and central tendency.[32] In a typical training program, raters are shown a videotape of jobs being performed and are asked to rate the worker. Ratings made by each participant are then placed on a flip chart, and the various errors (such as leniency and halo) are explained. Typically, the trainer gives the correct rating and then illustrates the rating errors the participants made.[33]

Rater training is no panacea for reducing rating errors or for improving appraisal accuracy. In practice, several factors including the extent to which pay is tied to performance ratings, union pressure, employee turnover, time constraints, and the need to justify ratings may be more important than training. This means that improving appraisal accuracy calls not just for training but also for reducing outside factors such as union pressure and time constraints.[34]

A fourth solution—*diary keeping*—has been proposed and is worth the effort. A recent study illustrates this.[35] The study involved 112 first-line supervisors from various manufacturing plants of a large multinational electronics firm. A number of these supervisors attended a special training program. The program discussed the role of critical inci-

TABLE 9-3 Important Similarities and Differences, and Advantages and Disadvantages of Appraisal Tools

TOOL	SIMILARITIES/DIFFERENCES	ADVANTAGES	DISADVANTAGES
Graphic rating scale	These are both absolute scales aimed at measuring an employee's *absolute* performance based on objective criteria as listed on the scales.	Simple to use; provides a quantitative rating for each employee.	Standards may be unclear; halo effect, central tendency, leniency, bias can also be problems.
BARS		Provides behavioral "anchors." BARS is very accurate.	Difficult to develop.
Alternation ranking	These are both methods for judging the *relative* performance of employees relative to each other, but still based on objective criteria.	Simple to use (but not as simple as graphic rating scales). Avoids central tendency and other problems of rating scales.	Can cause disagreements among employees and may be unfair if all employees *are*, in fact, excellent.
Forced distribution method		End up with a predetermined number of people in each group.	Appraisal results depend on the adequacy of your original choice of cutoff points.
Critical incident method	These are both more subjective, narrative methods for appraising performance, generally based, however, on the employee's absolute performance.	Helps specify what is "right" and "wrong" about the employee's performance; forces supervisor to evaluate subordinates on an ongoing basis.	Difficult to rate or rank employees relative to one another.
MBO		Tied to jointly agreed-upon performance objectives.	Time consuming.

dents and how these incidents could be compiled in a diary or incident file to be used later as a reference for a subordinate's performance appraisal.[36] The initial training was followed by a practice session. This in turn was followed by a feedback and group discussion session aimed at reinforcing the importance of writing descriptive statements and recording both positive and negative incidents.[37] The conclusion of this and similar studies is that you can reduce the adverse effects of appraisal problems by having raters carefully write down positive and negative critical incidents as they occur during the period to be appraised. Maintaining such behavioral records instead of relying on long-term memories is definitely the preferred approach.[38]

Yet even diary-keeping isn't fool-proof. In one study raters were required to keep a diary, but, contrary to predictions, the diary keeping actually undermined the performance appraisal's objectiveness.[39] What could account for such apparently bizarre findings? One possibility is that managers may develop positive or negative feelings toward ratees based on the performance they observe. For instance, they may develop more positive feelings toward subordinates who perform their jobs better. The managers may then seek out and record incidents in their diaries that are consistent with how they feel about the ratees. In any case, it's apparent that even diary-keeping is no guarantee of objectivity and that as a rater you must always keep the cognitive nature of the appraisal process in mind.

Indeed, most of the appraisal problems we've discussed reflect the fact that performance appraisal is essentially a cognitive, decision-making process. At the risk of oversimplifying a complicated topic, the rater brings to the task of appraising subordinates a bundle of biases, inclinations, and decision-making shortcuts; the appraisal thus is bound to be a product (or a victim, some might conclude) of the rater's biases and inclinations.[40] Being familiar with the potential problems, choosing the right appraisal tool, training supervisors, and keeping a diary can help diminish some of the errors that might therefore crop up.

Legal and Ethical Issues in Performance Appraisal

Appraisal plays a central role in equal employment compliance. Since passage of Title VII, courts have addressed various issues (including promotion, layoff, and compensation decisions) in which performance appraisals play a significant role.[41] Courts have often found that the inadequacies of the employer's appraisal system were at the root of an illegal discriminatory action.[42]

An illustrative case covered layoff decisions. Here the court held that the firm had violated Title VII when it laid off several Hispanic-surnamed employees on the basis of poor performance ratings.[43] The court concluded that the practice was illegal because:

1. The appraisals were based on subjective supervisory observations.
2. The appraisals were not administered and scored in a standardized fashion.
3. Two of the three supervisory evaluators did not have daily contact with the employees being evaluated.

However, subjectivity and inadequate standardization are not the only potential EEO-type problems. To the extent that a supervisor unreasonably rates everyone toward the high (or low), allows the halo effect, exhibits personal bias, or relies solely on more recent events, courts have and will view the appraisal and subsequent personnel decision as indefensible.[44]

Finally, remember that as in most human endeavors, being legal doesn't always equal being ethical, yet ethics should be the bedrock of a performance appraisal. In fact most managers (and college students) understand that an appraiser or professor can "stick to the rules" and conduct a lawful review of one's performance but still fail to provide an honest assessment. As one commentator puts it:

> The overall objective of high-ethics performance reviews should be to provide an honest assessment of performance and to mutually develop a plan to improve the individual's effectiveness. That requires that we tell people where they stand and that we be straight with them.[45]

And, of course, it's exactly this type of honest and fruitful appraisal—not merely a legal one—that managers should shoot for. Guidelines for developing a legally defensible appraisal process include the following:[46]

1. Conduct a job analysis to ascertain the criteria and standards (such as "timely project completion") required for successful job performance.
2. Incorporate these criteria and standards into a rating instrument. (Note that while the professional literature recommends rating instruments that are tied to specific job behaviors, that is, BARS, courts routinely accept less sophisticated approaches such as graphic rating scales.)
3. Use clearly defined individual dimensions of job performance (like "quantity" or "quality") rather than undefined, global measures of job performance (like "overall performance").
4. Communicate performance standards to employees and to those rating them, in writing.
5. When using graphic rating scales, avoid abstract trait names (for example, "loyalty," "honesty") unless they can be defined in terms of observable behaviors.
6. Employ subjective supervisory ratings (essays, for instance) as only one component of the overall appraisal process.
7. Train supervisors to use the rating instrument properly. Give instructions on how to apply performance appraisal standards ("outstanding," and so on) when

making judgments. In 6 of 10 cases decided against the employer, the plaintiffs were able to show that subjective standards had been applied unevenly to minority and majority employees.[47] If formal rater training is not possible, at least provide raters with written instruction for using the rating scale for evaluating personnel.

8. Allow appraisers substantial daily contact with the employee being evaluated.

9. Base appraisals on separate evaluations of each of the job's performance dimensions. In particular, use of a single overall rating of performance or ranking of employees on a similar global standard is not acceptable to the courts,[48] which often characterize such systems as vague. Courts generally require that separate ratings along each performance dimension be combined through some formal weighting system to yield a summary score.

10. Whenever possible, have more than one appraiser conduct the appraisal and conduct all such appraisals independently. This process can help to cancel out individual errors and biases.

11. One appraiser should never have absolute authority to determine a personnel action. This is one reason why a multiple raters' procedure is becoming more popular.

12. Include an employee appeal process. Employees should have the opportunity to review and make comments, written or verbal, about their appraisals before they become final, and should have a formal appeals process through which to appeal their ratings.

13. Document all information and reasons bearing on any personnel decision. In fact, three experts assert that "without exception, courts condemn informal performance evaluation practices that eschew documentation."[49]

14. Where appropriate, provide corrective guidance to assist poor performers in improving their performance. Courts look favorably on this practice.

If your appraisal-based equal employment case gets to court, which of the above guidelines would be the most important in forming a judge's opinion? Of course each case is different, but a recent review of almost 300 U.S. court decisions from 1980 to 1995 concerning performance appraisal is informative.[50] The results suggest that issues reflecting fairness and due process were the most important to judges' decisions. In particular, performing a job analysis, providing raters with written instructions, permitting employee review of results, and obtaining agreement among raters were the four appraisal practices that seemed to have the most consistent impact across the board in all or most of the judicial decisions. The courts placed little emphasis on whether or not the employer's performance appraisal tools and/or process were formally validated.[51]

Who Should Do the Appraising?

Who should actually rate an employee's performance? Several options exist.

APPRAISAL BY THE IMMEDIATE SUPERVISOR   Supervisors' ratings still are the heart of most appraisal systems. Getting a supervisor's appraisal is relatively easy and also makes a great deal of sense. The supervisor should be—and usually is—in the best position to observe and evaluate the subordinate's performance, and is responsible for that person's performance.

USING PEER APPRAISALS   The appraisal of an employee by peers can be effective in predicting future management success. From a study of military officers, for example, we know that peer ratings were quite accurate in predicting which officers would be promoted and which would not.[52] In another study that involved more than 200 industrial managers, peer ratings were similarly useful in predicting who would be promoted.[53] One potential problem is *logrolling*. Here all the peers simply get together to rate each other highly.

With more firms using self-managing teams, peer or team appraisals are becoming more popular. At Digital Equipment Corporation, for example, (now part of Compaq Computer) an employee due for an appraisal chooses an appraisal chairperson each year. This person then selects one supervisor and three other peers to evaluate the employee's work.[54]

RATING COMMITTEES   Many employers use rating committees to evaluate employees. These committees are usually composed of the employee's immediate supervisor and three or four other supervisors.

Using multiple raters can be advantageous. While there may be a discrepancy in the ratings made by individual supervisors, the composite ratings tend to be more reliable, fair, and valid.[55] Several raters can help cancel out problems like bias and the halo effect on the part of individual raters. Furthermore, when there *are* differences in raters' ratings, they usually stem from the fact that raters at different levels often observe different facets of an employee's performance; the appraisal ought to reflect these differences.[56] Even when a committee is not used, it is common to have the appraisal reviewed by the manager immediately above the one who makes the appraisal. This was found to be standard practice in 16 of the 18 companies surveyed in one study.[57] Rating committees are also advantageous insofar as supervisory ratings appear to have higher interrater reliability or consistency than do ratings obtained from several peers.[58]

SELF-RATINGS   Employees' self-ratings of performance are also sometimes used (usually in conjunction with supervisors' ratings). The basic problem with these is that employees usually rate themselves higher than they are rated by supervisors or peers.[59] In one study, for example, it was found that when asked to rate their own job performances, 40% of the employees in jobs of all types placed themselves in the top 10% ("one of the best"), while virtually all remaining employees rated themselves either in the top 25% ("well above average"), or at least in the top 50% ("above average"). Usually no more than 1% or 2% will place themselves in a below-average category, and then almost invariably in the top below-average category. However, one recent study concludes that individuals do not necessarily always have such positive illusions about their own performance, although in rating the performance of their groups, group members did consistently give their group unrealistically high performance ratings in this study.[60]

Supervisors requesting self-appraisals should therefore know that their appraisals and the employees' self-appraisals may accentuate appraiser-appraisee differences, and rigidify positions.[61] Furthermore, even if self-appraisals are not formally requested, each employee will enter the performance review meeting with his or her own self-appraisal in mind, and this will usually be higher than the supervisor's rating.

APPRAISAL BY SUBORDINATES   More firms today let subordinates anonymously evaluate their supervisors' performance, a process many call *upward feedback*.[62] When conducted throughout the firm, the process helps top managers diagnose management styles, identify potential "people" problems, and take corrective action with individual managers as required. Such subordinate ratings are especially valuable when used for developmental rather than evaluative purposes.[63] Managers who receive feedback from subordinates who identify themselves view the upward appraisal process more positively than do managers who receive anonymous feedback; however, subordinates (not surprisingly) are more comfortable giving anonymous responses, and those who have to identify themselves tend to provide inflated ratings.[64]

AN EXAMPLE   Federal Express uses an upward appraisal system called Survey Feedback Action (SFA). SFA has three phases. First, the survey itself (a standard, anonymous form) is given each year to every employee. It contains items designed to gather information about those things that help and hinder employees in their work environment. Sample items include: I can tell my manager what I think; my manager tells me what is expected; my manager listens to my concerns; my manager keeps me informed; upper management listens to ideas from my level; FedEx does a good job for our customers; in my environment we use safe work practices; and I am paid fairly for this kind of work. Results of the survey for a work group are then compiled and returned to the manager. To ensure anonymity the smaller units do *not* receive their own results. Instead their results are folded in with those of several other similar work units until a department of 20 or 25 people obtains the overall group's results.

A feedback session between the manager and his or her work group is the second phase. The session's goal is to identify specific concerns or problems, examine specific causes for these problems, and devise action plans to correct the problems. Managers are therefore trained to ask probing questions. For example, suppose a low-scoring survey item was, "I feel to tell my manager what I think." Managers are trained to ask their groups questions such as "What constrains you?" (specific behaviors); and "What do I do that makes you feel that I'm not interested?"

The feedback meeting should lead to a third, "action plan" phase. The plan itself is a list of actions that the manager will take to address employees' concerns and boost results. Managers thus get an action-planning worksheet containing four columns: (1) What is the concern? (2) What's your analysis? (3) What's the cause? (4) What should be done?

RESEARCH INSIGHT   How effective is upward feedback from subordinates to their supervisors in terms of improving the supervisor's behavior? Considerably, to judge from the research evidence. One study examined data for 92 managers who were rated by one or more subordinates in each of four administrations of an upward feedback survey over 2½ years.[65] Managers were based in North America, Europe, Asia/Pacific, the Caribbean, and Central/South America. The subordinates were asked to rate themselves and their managers in surveys that consisted of 33 behavioral statements. The feedback to the managers also contained results from previous administrations of the survey so they could track their performance over time.[66]

According to the researchers, "managers whose initial level of performance (defined as the average rating from subordinates) was low improved between administrations one and two, and sustained this improvement two years later."[67] Interestingly, the results also suggest that it's not necessarily the specific feedback that caused the performance improvement, since low performing managers seemed to improve over time even if they didn't receive any feedback. Instead, learning what the critical supervisory behaviors were (as a result of themselves filling out the appraisal surveys), plus knowing they might be appraised may have been enough to result in the improved supervisory behaviors. In a sense, therefore, it's the existence of the formal upward feedback program rather than the actual feedback itself that may signal and motivate supervisors to get their behaviors in line with what they should be.

360-DEGREE FEEDBACK   Many firms have expanded the idea of upward feedback into what they call 360-degree feedback; here performance information is collected "all around" an employee, from his or her supervisors, subordinates, peers, and internal or external customers.[68] According to one recent study, 29% of the responding employers already use 360-degree feedback (also called "multisource assessment"), and another 11% had plans to implement it shortly.[69] The feedback is generally used for training and development, rather than for pay increases. [70]

Most 360-degree feedback systems contain several common features. Appropriate parties—peers, supervisors, subordinates, and customers, for instance—complete survey questionnaires on an individual. The questionnaires can take many forms but often include supervisory skill items such as "returns phone calls promptly," "listens well," or, as at FedEx, "[my manager] keeps me informed."[71] Computerized systems then compile all this feedback into individualized reports that are presented to the person being rated. The ratees are often the only ones who get these completed reports. They then meet with their own supervisors and sometimes with their subordinates and share the information they feel is pertinent for the purpose of developing a self-improvement plan.[72] The following High-Performance feature provides an example.

THE HIGH-PERFORMANCE ORGANIZATION

Building Better, Faster, More
Competitive Organizations Through HR: The
360-Degree Performance Management System

■ Rock Island Arsenal—Rock Island, IL

In 1995, RIA instituted the 360-Degree Performance Management System (360 DPMS). Prior to this, RIA relied exclusively on the Total Army Performance Evaluation system (TAPES). TAPES is a supervisor/employee review process that is based on a uni-source evaluation. The shift to 360 DPMS was made to make the evaluation process more accurately reflect the employee's performance by measuring behavioral attributes like team support or workload sharing. Although TAPES is used to comply with administrative requirements, the unique aspect is that one input for it is the 360 DPMS.

The 360 DPMS procedure began with a labor/management team selecting and defining the feedback criteria. The categories formulated include technical support; practical support; technical competence; efficient use of time; communication; initiative; flexibility; customer service; working relationships; and process and self-improvement.

Next, the employee selects the raters from people who are most familiar with the employee's work. This group can include team members, customers, supervisor, team leader, subordinates, and self. A survey is then conducted from which reports are created and analyzed. The final analysis is a concise report that summarizes the ratings of the different categories, and is used to commend or modify the employee's behavior.

The benefits of the 360 DPMS are reportedly that it is fair, simple, and trustworthy. With so many raters, the employee is evaluated from a multidimensional perspective. Being easy to fill out quickly, the survey has a cost savings through reduced labor requirements. An additional benefit is that the number of complaints concerning the evaluation process has decreased because the potential negative feelings related to the supervisor having total control over the subordinate is eliminated.

Source: Copyright 1998, Best Manufacturing Practices Center of Excellence.

THE APPRAISAL INTERVIEW

Types of Interviews

An appraisal typically culminates in an **appraisal interview**. This is an interview in which the supervisor and subordinate review the appraisal and make plans to remedy deficiencies and reinforce strengths. Interviews like these are potentially uncomfortable, since few

appraisal interview
An interview in which the supervisor and subordinate review the appraisal and make plans to remedy deficiencies and reinforce strengths.

people like to receive—or give—negative feedback.[73] Adequate preparation and effective implementation are therefore essential.

There are three basic types of appraisal interviews, each with its own objectives:

Appraisal Interview Type	*Appraisal Interview Objective*
(1) Performance is satisfactory— Employee is promotable	(1) Make development plans
(2) Satisfactory—Not promotable	(2) Maintain performance
(3) Unsatisfactory—Correctable	(3) Plan correction

If the employee is unsatisfactory and the situation uncorrectable, there is usually no need for any appraisal interview. Either the person's poor performance is tolerated for now, or he or she is dismissed.

SATISFACTORY—PROMOTABLE   Here the person's performance is satisfactory and there is a promotion ahead. This is the easiest of the three appraisal interviews. Your objective is to discuss the person's career plans and to develop a specific action plan for the educational and professional development the person needs to move to the next job.

SATISFACTORY—NOT PROMOTABLE   This interview is for employees whose performance is satisfactory but for whom promotion is not possible. Perhaps there is no more room in the company. Some employees are also happy where they are and don't want a promotion.[74] Your objective here is not to improve or develop the person but to maintain satisfactory performance.

This is not easy. The best option is usually to find incentives that are important to the person and enough to maintain satisfactory performance. These might include extra time off, a small bonus, additional authority to handle a slightly enlarged job, and reinforcement, perhaps in the form of an occasional "Well done!"

UNSATISFACTORY—CORRECTABLE   When the person's performance is unsatisfactory but correctable, the interview objective is to lay out an action plan (as explained below) for correcting the unsatisfactory performance.

How to Prepare for the Appraisal Interview

There are three things to do in preparation for the interview.[75] First, assemble the data. Study the person's job description, compare the employee's performance to the standards, and review the files of the employee's previous appraisals. Next prepare the employee. Give your employees at least a week's notice to review their work, read over their job descriptions, analyze problems, and gather their questions and comments. Finally, choose the time and place. Find a mutually agreeable time for the interview and allow enough time for the entire interview. Interviews with lower-level personnel like clerical workers and maintenance staff should take no more than an hour. Appraising management employees often takes two or three hours. Be sure the interview is done in a private place where you won't be interrupted by phone calls or visitors.

How to Conduct the Interview

There are four things to keep in mind here:[76]

1. *Be direct and specific.* Talk in terms of objective work data. Use examples such as absences, tardiness, quality records, inspection reports, scrap or waste, orders processed, productivity records, material used or consumed, timeliness of tasks

or projects, control or reduction of costs, numbers of errors, costs compared to budgets, customers' comments, product returns, order processing time, inventory level and accuracy, accident reports, and so on.

2. *Don't get personal.* Don't say, "You're too slow in producing those reports." Instead try to compare the person's performance to a standard ("These reports should normally be done within 10 days"). Similarly, don't compare the person's performance to that of other people ("He's quicker than you are").

3. *Encourage the person to talk.* Stop and listen to what the person is saying; ask open-ended questions such as "What do you think we can do to improve the situation?" Use a command such as "Go on," or "Tell me more." Restate the person's last point as a question, such as "You don't think you can get the job done?"

4. *Don't tiptoe around.* Don't get personal, but do make sure the person leaves knowing specifically what he or she is doing right and doing wrong. Give specific examples; make sure the person understands; and get agreement before he or she leaves on how things will be improved, and by when. Develop an action plan showing steps and expected results, as in Figure 9-9.

HOW TO HANDLE A DEFENSIVE SUBORDINATE   Defenses are an important and familiar aspect of our lives. When a person is accused of poor performance, the first reaction will sometimes be denial. By denying the fault, the person avoids having to question his or her own competence. Others react to criticism with anger and aggression. This helps them let off steam and postpones confronting the immediate problem until they are able to cope with it. Still others react to criticism by retreating into a shell.

In any event, understanding and dealing with defensiveness is an important appraisal skill. In his book *Effective Psychology for Managers*, psychologist Mortimer Feinberg suggests the following:

1. *Recognize that defensive behavior is normal.*

2. *Never attack a person's defenses.* Don't try to "explain someone to themselves" by saying things like, "You know the real reason you're using that excuse is that you

FIGURE 9-9

Example of an Action Plan

ACTION PLAN

Date: May 18, 1999

For: John, Assistant Plant Manager
Problem: Parts inventory too high
Objective: Reduce plant parts inventory by 10% in June

Action Steps	When	Expected Results
Determine average monthly parts inventory	6/2	Established a base from which to measure progress
Review ordering quantities and parts usage	6/15	Identify overstock items
Ship excess parts to regional warehouse and scrap obsolete parts	6/20	Clear stock space
Set new ordering quantities for all parts	6/25	Avoid future overstocking
Check records to measure where we are now	7/1	See how close we are to objective

can't bear to be blamed for anything." Instead try to concentrate on the act itself ("sales are down") rather than on the person ("you're not selling enough").

3. *Postpone action.* Sometimes it is best to do nothing at all. People frequently react to sudden threats by instinctively hiding behind their "masks." But, given sufficient time, a more rational reaction takes over.

4. *Recognize your own limitations.* Don't expect to be able to solve every problem that comes up, especially the human ones. More important, remember that a supervisor should not try to be a psychologist. Offering your people understanding is one thing; trying to deal with deep psychological problems is another matter entirely.

HOW TO CRITICIZE A SUBORDINATE   When criticism is required, it should be done in a manner that lets the person maintain his or her dignity and sense of worth. Specifically, criticism should be done in private and should be done constructively. Provide examples of critical incidents and specific suggestions of what could be done and why. Avoid once-a-year "critical broadsides" by giving feedback on a daily basis, so that at the formal review there are no surprises. Never say the person is "always" wrong (since no one is ever "always" wrong or right). Finally, criticism should be objective and free of any personal biases on your part.

HOW TO ENSURE THAT THE APPRAISAL INTERVIEW LEADS TO IMPROVED PERFORMANCE   You should clear up job-related problems and set improvement goals and a schedule for achieving them. In one study the researchers found that whether or not subordinates expressed satisfaction with their appraisal interview depended mostly on three factors: (1) not feeling threatened during the interview; (2) having an opportunity to present their ideas and feelings and to influence the course of the interview; and (3) having a helpful and constructive supervisor conduct the interview.[77]

However, you don't just want subordinates to be satisfied with their appraisal interviews. Your main aim is to get them to improve their subsequent performance. Here researchers found that *clearing up job-related problems* with the appraisee and *setting measurable performance targets and a schedule for achieving them*—an action plan—were the actions that consistently led to improved performance.

HOW TO HANDLE A FORMAL WRITTEN WARNING   There will be times when an employee's performance is so poor that a formal written warning is required. Such written warnings serve two purposes: (1) They may serve to shake your employee out of his or her bad habits, and (2) they can help you defend your rating of the employee both to your own boss and (if needed) to the courts. Thus, written warnings should identify the standards under which the employee is judged, make it clear that the employee was aware of the standard, specify any violation of the standard, and show the employee had an opportunity to correct his or her behavior.

PERFORMANCE APPRAISAL IN PRACTICE	How do most employers actually appraise performance? A survey of current practice suggests the following.[78]

Almost all companies responding do have formal appraisal programs. About 93% of smaller organizations (those with fewer than 500 employees) have such programs. About 97% of large organizations have them.

Rating scales are by far the most widely used appraisal technique. About 62% of small organizations use rating scales, 20% use essays, and about 19% use MBO.

Among large organizations, 51% use rating scales, just over 23% use essays, and about 17% use MBO.

However, those using ratings as the main appraisal technique typically also require narrative comments to justify ratings, to describe employee strengths and weaknesses, and to document development plans.[79] Those using essays as the main appraisal technique usually require an overall quantitative performance rating to facilitate employee comparisons for compensation decisions.

Ninety-two percent of appraisals are made by the employee's immediate supervisor. These appraisals are in turn reviewed by the appraiser's supervisor in 74% of the responding organizations.

Only about 7% of the organizations use self-appraisal in any part of the overall appraisal process.

Virtually all employees (99%) are informed of the results of their appraisals. Overall, about 77% are given a chance to respond with written comments on their appraisals.

In 69% of the companies, appraisals are done annually.

Instructions are important: 82% of employers provide written instructions for appraisers, and 60% provide training.

THE ROLE OF APPRAISALS IN MANAGING PERFORMANCE

Appraisals, of course, provide the information upon which promotion and salary decisions are made and the basis upon which to discuss the employee's performance in the hopes of reinforcing desirable behaviors and eliminating undesirable ones. Increasingly, though, HR specialists are emphasizing appraisal's related role as a central player in what they call performance management. *Performance management* may be defined as the whole process impacting how well an employee performs.[80] Performance management may therefore encompass goal setting, worker selection and placement, performance appraisal, compensation, training and development, and career management—in other words, all those parts of the HR process impacting how well an employee performs.[81]

It's therefore useful to close this chapter by looking more closely at appraisal's role as a component in a company's performance management system. Indeed, appraisals should play a crucial performance management role, by providing a concrete basis for an analysis of an employee's work-related performance, and of the steps to be taken to maintain or change it. Let's look more closely at how appraisals can be used to better manage employee performance.

Do Appraisals Really Help To Improve Performance?

Ironically, many experts feel that traditional appraisals don't improve performance and may actually backfire. They argue that most performance appraisal systems neither motivate employees nor guide their development.[82] Furthermore, "they cause conflict between supervisors and subordinates and lead to dysfunctional behaviors."[83] The traits measured are often personal in nature and "Who likes the idea of being evaluated on his or her: honesty, integrity, teamwork, compassion, cooperation [objectivity] . . .?"[84]

As a result, proponents of total quality management programs (including the late W. Edwards Deming), generally argue for eliminating performance appraisals.[85] They believe the organization is a system of interrelated parts and that an employee's performance is more a function of factors like training, communication, tools, and supervision than of his or her own motivation.[86] They also argue that performance appraisals can have unanticipated consequences. (For example, employees might make themselves look better in terms of customer service by continually badgering customers to send in letters of support.) Deming particularly argued against forced distribution appraisal systems due to their potential for undermining teamwork.[87] Traditional appraisals therefore had no role in the performance management process for most of these experts.

Indeed, criticisms like these seem to have some merit. In one study of almost 300 managers from midwestern companies, 32% rated their performance appraisals as "very ineffective," while only 4% rated them "effective to a large extent."[88] Another survey of 181 manufacturing and service organizations concluded that 11% had stopped using annual appraisals, while 25% more planned to discontinue them within 2 years.[89] There's thus not much doubt that most appraisals are viewed with trepidation if not disdain.

Yet while these criticisms have merit, it's not practical to eliminate performance appraisals. Managers still need some way to review subordinates' work-related behavior. And, although Deming reportedly hated performance reviews, "he really didn't offer any concrete solution to the problem or an alternative, other than to just pay everybody the same salary."[90] The solution instead is to use performance appraisal methods that make the appraisal a useful part of the performance management process in today's team-oriented and quality-oriented environments. Avoiding the more glaring appraisal problems, as described in this chapter, is one way to do this. Others suggest taking a TQM-based approach to appraising, an approach to which we now turn.

TQM-Based Appraisals for Managing Performance

Total quality management (TQM) programs are organizationwide programs that integrate all functions and processes of the business so that design, planning, production, distribution, and field service are aimed at maximizing customer satisfaction through continuous improvement.[91] Deming, an early proponent, said such programs are built on several principles including: Cease dependence on inspection to achieve quality; aim for continuous improvement; institute extensive training on the job; drive out fear so that everyone may work effectively for the company; break down barriers between departments; eliminate work standards (quotas) on the factory floor; remove barriers that rob employees of their right to pride of workmanship (in particular, abolish the annual merit rating and all forms of management by objectives); and institute a vigorous program of education and self-improvement.[92]

TQM principles like these can be applied to designing TQM-based appraisals, ones designed to improve an employee's performance by being part of an integrated performance management process. The aim of performance management in TQM-oriented companies is to establish systems that encourage employees to become committed partners in the tasks of boosting quality and performance. Employees here aren't just "told what to do". Instead they are relied upon to make suggestions, improve performance, and generally act like owners of the business. According to proponents, performance appraisals in TQM environments therefore don't force managers to give questionable feedback; instead they facilitate open, job-related discussions between the supervisor and the employee.[93] The characteristics of such a TQM-based performance management-oriented appraisal would include:

> An appraisal scale that contains relatively few performance-level categories and avoids a forced distribution.[94]

Objective ways to measure results, avoiding subjective criteria such as teamwork and integrity.[95]

A way to determine whether any performance deficiency is a result of (1) employee motivation, (2) inadequate training, or (3) factors (like poor supervision) that are outside the employee's control.

360-degree feedback from a number of different sources, not just supervisors but internal and possibly external "customers" of the employee as well.[96]

Adequate samples of work behavior—"regular observations of their staff members' work behaviors and performance."[97]

An atmosphere of partnership and constructive advice.[98]

A thorough analysis of key external and internal customers' needs and expectations on which to base performance appraisal standards. (For example, if accurately completing the sales slip is important for the accounting department, then the retail sales clerk should be appraised in part on this dimension).

A form for implementing such a TQM-oriented performance management appraisal is shown in Figure 9-10. As you can see, it consists of a performance contract specifying customer expectations and performance goals, as well as an internal customer feedback form.[99]

PERFORMANCE CONTRACT

Within the next year, I understand that our organization's objectives are _____
_____
and that the goals of our department are _____. I also
understand that our work unit goals are _____.

My key internal customers are _____ and their
work needs and expectations are
_____.

To make my contribution toward attaining the goals stated above, I understand that I am expected to do the following:

My individual performance goals are _____.

My goals for improving work methods (process) are _____.

My goals for improving specific interpersonal work behaviors when I interact with the following
_____ are _____.

I believe these goals are acceptable and attainable. I also understand that I will be evaluated by multiple appraisal sources (supervisor, peers, internal, and, if appropriate, external customers).

Compensation for my work performance will be based on whether my performance was (1) outstanding, (2) fully competent, or (3) unsatisfactory. I understand that the following forms of compensation will be considered: (1) merit award for my individual performance goal attainment, (2) enhancement and utilization of my skills, (3) my work unit's or team's performance (gainsharing), and (4) our organization's performance (profit sharing).

_____   _____
Your signature   Supervisor's signature

FIGURE 9-10 *Performance Contract and Internal Customer Feedback Forms*

Source: David Antonioni, "Improving the Performance Management Process Before Discontinuing Performance Appraisals," *Compensation and Benefits Review* (May–June 1994), pp. 33, 34.

INTERNAL CUSTOMER FEEDBACK

As an internal customer of (name) _____ , please give him/her feedback regarding his/her work performance and work behaviors. After you have completed this form, send it to _____ . Your responses will be tabulated and then discussed with the individual.

To what extent did this individual meet your expectations of work quality in the areas you indicate as important:

	Exceeds	Meets	Doesn't Meet
1. Accuracy of the work you received			
2. Timeliness of the work you received			
3. Dependability of the work you received			
4. Sharing relevant information to help you do your work more efficiently			

In terms of your interactions with this person, please feel free to comment on any of the following:

1. The type of errors and the amount of rework

2. The nature of any work delays

3. Collaborative efforts to improve work or business processes

4. Interpersonal work behaviors

Please list any *new* expectations that you have regarding the work you receive from this person.

Thank you for completing this feedback form. A follow-up interview with you may be established to discuss the feedback, and if necessary, improvement goals and an action plan will be developed.

FIGURE 9-10 *Performance Contract and Internal Customer Feedback Forms*
                   (continued)

We invite you to visit the Dessler page on the Prentice Hall Web site at **www.prenhall.com/dessler** for our on-line study guide, Internet exercises, current events, links to related Web sites, and more.

SUMMARY

1. People want and need feedback regarding how they are doing, and appraisal provides an opportunity for you to give them that feedback.

2. Before the appraisal, make sure to clarify the performance you expect so that the employee knows what he or she should be shooting for. Ask "What do I really expect this person to do?"

3. Performance appraisal tools include the graphic rating scale, alternation ranking method, forced distribution method, BARS, MBO, and critical incident method.

4. Appraisal problems to beware of include unclear standards, halo effect, central tendency, leniency or strictness problems, and bias.

5. Most subordinates probably want a specific explanation or examples regarding why they were appraised high or low, and for this, compiling a record of positive and negative critical incidents can be useful. Even if your firm requires that you summarize the appraisal in a form like a graphic rating scale, a list of critical incidents can be useful when the time comes to discuss the appraisal with your subordinate.

6. The subordinate should view the appraisal as a fair one, and in this regard there are four things to do: Evaluate his or her performance frequently; make sure you are familiar with the person's performance; make sure there is an agreement between you and your subordinate concerning his or her job duties; and finally, solicit the person's help when you formulate plans for eliminating performance weaknesses.

7. There are three types of appraisal interviews. When performance is unsatisfactory but correctable, the objective is to lay out an action plan for correcting performance. For employees whose performance is satisfactory but for whom promotion is not possible, the objective is to maintain satisfactory performance. Finally, the satisfactory—promotable interview has as its main objective to discuss the person's career plans and to develop a specific action plan for the educational and professional development the person needs to move on to the next job.

8. To prepare for the appraisal interview, assemble the data, prepare the employee, and choose the time and place.

9. To bring about constructive change in your subordinate's behavior, get the person to talk in the interview. Use open-ended questions, state questions in terms of a problem, use a command question, use questions to try to understand the feelings underlying what the person is saying, and restate the person's last point as a question. On the other hand, don't do all the talking, don't use restrictive questions, don't be judgmental, don't give free advice, and don't get involved with name calling, ridicule, or sarcasm.

10. The best way to handle a defensive subordinate is to proceed very carefully. Specifically, recognize that defensive behavior is normal, never attack a person's defenses, postpone actions, and recognize your own limitations.

11. The most important thing you should aim to accomplish is to clear up job-related problems and set improvement goals and a schedule for achieving them.

12. Appraisals should also ideally serve a role in managing performance by providing a concrete and non-threatening basis for an analysis of an employer's work-related performance. Creating more effective appraisals as described in this chapter is one way to accomplish this. Others suggest also taking a TQM-based approach. Characteristics of such an approach include: making the appraisal scale as broadly descriptive as possible so that it contains relatively few performance categories and avoids a forced distribution; measure results objectively; specifically identifies if the performance deficiency is a result of motivation, training, or factors outside the employee's control; uses 360-degree feedback; includes adequate samples of work behavior; addresses problems in an atmosphere of partnership and constructive advice; and bases performance standards on an analysis of key external and internal customers' needs and expectations.

KEY TERMS

graphic rating scale 323
alternation ranking method 325
paired comparison method 327
forced distribution method 327

critical incident method 329
behaviorally anchored rating scale (BARS) 331
management by objectives (MBO) 333

unclear performance standards 337
halo effect 338
central tendency 338
strictness/leniency 338
bias 339
appraisal interviews 347

DISCUSSION QUESTIONS

1. Discuss the pros and cons of at least four performance appraisal tools.
2. Explain how you would use the alternation ranking method, the paired comparison method, and the forced distribution method.
3. Explain in your own words how you would go about developing a behaviorally anchored rating scale.
4. Explain the problems to be avoided in appraising performance.
5. Discuss the pros and cons of using different potential raters to appraise a person's performance.
6. Explain the four types of appraisal interview objectives and how they affect the way you manage the interview.
7. Explain how to conduct an appraisal interview.
8. Answer the question, "How would you get the interviewee to talk during an appraisal interview?"

INDIVIDUAL AND GROUP ACTIVITIES

1. Working individually or in groups, develop a graphic rating scale for the following jobs: secretary, engineer, directory assistance operator.
2. Working individually or in groups, evaluate the rating scale in Table 9-2. Discuss ways to improve it.
3. Working individually or in groups, develop, over the period of a week, a set of critical incidents covering the classroom performance of one of your instructors.

EXPERIENTIAL EXERCISE

Purpose: The purpose of this exercise is to give you practice in developing and using a performance appraisal form.

Required Understanding: You are going to develop a performance appraisal form for an instructor and should therefore be thoroughly familiar with the discussion of performance appraisals in this chapter.

How to Set Up the Exercise: Divide the class into groups of four or five students.

1. First, based on what you now know about performance appraisal, do you think Figure 9-10 (a reproduction of Figure 9-1) is an effective scale for appraising instructors? Why? Why not?

2. Next, your group should develop its own tool for appraising the performance of an instructor. Decide which of the appraisal tools (graphic rating scales, alternation ranking, and so on) you are going to use and then design the instrument itself.

3. Next, have a spokesperson from each group put his or her group's appraisal tool on the board. How similar are the tools? Do they all measure about the same factors? Which factor appears most often? Which do you think is the most effective tool on the board?

FIGURE 9-10

Department Teaching Appraisal Form

Source: Richard I. Miller, *Evaluating Faculty for Promotion and Tenure* (San Francisco: Jossey-Base Publishers, 1987), pp. 164–165. Copyright © 1987 Jossey-Bass, Inc., Publishers. All rights reserved. Reprinted with permission.

Evaluating Faculty for Promotion and Tenure

Classroom Teaching Appraisal by Students

Teacher _____ Course _____

Term _____ Academic Year _____

Thoughtful student appraisal can help improve teaching effectiveness. This questionnaire is designed for that purpose, and your assistance is appreciated. Please do not sign your name.

Use the back of this form for any further comments you might want to express; use numbers 10, 11, and 12 for any additional questions that you might like to add.

Directions: Rate your teacher on each item, giving the highest scores for exceptional performances and the lowest scores for very poor performances. Place in the blank space before each statement the rating that most closely expresses your view.

Excep- tional		Moderately Good				Very Poor	Don't Know
7	6	5	4	3	2	1	X

_____ 1. How do you rate the agreement between course objectives and lesson assignments?

_____ 2. How do you rate the planning, organization, and use of class periods?

_____ 3. Are the teaching methods and techniques employed by the teacher appropriate and effective?

_____ 4. How do you rate the competence of the instructor in the subject?

_____ 5. How do you rate the interest of the teacher in the subject?

_____ 6. Does the teacher stimulate and challenge you to think and to question?

_____ 7. Does he or she welcome differing points of view?

_____ 8. Does the teacher have a personal interest in helping you in and out of class?

_____ 9. How would you rate the fairness and effectiveness of the grading policies and procedures of the teacher?

_____ 10. _____

Faculty Evaluation Rating Forms

_____ 11. _____

_____ 12. _____

_____ 13. Considering all the above items, what is your overall rating of this teacher?

_____ 14. How would you rate this teacher in comparison with all others you have had in the college or university?

CASE INCIDENT

Back with a Vengeance

Conducting an effective appraisal is always important. However, an appraisal can have life-and-death impli- cations when you're dealing with unstable employees, particularly those who must be dismissed. An employee of a U.S. Postal Service station was recently terminated. The employee came back and shot and killed several managers who had been instrumental in the former employee's dismissal. It turned out this person had a history as a troublemaker and that many clues regarding his unstable nature over many years had been ignored.

■ QUESTIONS

1. Could a company with an effective appraisal process have missed so many signals of instability over several years? Why or why not?
2. What safeguards would you build into your appraisal process to avoid missing such potentially tragic signs of instability and danger?
3. What would you do if confronted during an appraisal interview by someone who began making threats regarding his or her use of firearms?

Case Application

APPRAISING THE SECRETARIES AT SWEETWATER U

Rob Winchester, newly appointed vice president for administrative affairs at Sweetwater State University, faced a tough problem shortly after his university career began. Three weeks after he came on board in September, Sweetwater's president, Rob's boss, told Rob that one of his first tasks was to improve the appraisal system used to evaluate secretarial and clerical performance at Sweetwater U. Apparently, the main difficulty was that the performance appraisal was traditionally tied directly to salary increases given at the end of the year. So most administrators were less than accurate when they used the graphic rating forms that were the basis of the clerical staff evaluation. In fact, what usually happened was that each administrator simply rated his or her clerk or secretary as "excellent." This cleared the way for all support staff to receive a maximum pay increase every year.

But the current university budget simply did not include enough money to fund another "maximum" annual increase for every staffer. Furthermore, Sweetwater's president felt that the custom of providing invalid feedback to each secretary on his or her year's performance was not productive, so he had asked the new vice president to revise the system. In October, Rob sent a memo to all administrators telling them that in the future no more than half the secretaries reporting to any particular administrator could be appraised as "excellent." This move, in effect, forced each supervisor to begin ranking his or her secretaries for quality of performance. The vice president's memo met widespread resistance immediately—from administrators, who were

afraid that many of their secretaries would begin leaving for more lucrative jobs in private industry, and from secretaries, who felt that the new system was unfair and reduced each secretary's chance of receiving a maximum salary increase. A handful of secretaries had begun quietly picketing outside the president's home on the university campus. The picketing, caustic remarks by disgruntled administrators, and rumors of an impending slowdown by the secretaries (there were about 250 on campus) made Rob Winchester wonder whether he had made the right decision by setting up forced ranking. He knew, however, that there were a few performance appraisal experts in the School of Business, so he decided to set up an appointment with them to discuss the matter.

He met with them the next morning. He explained the situation as he had found it: The present appraisal system had been set up when the university first opened 10 years earlier, and the appraisal form had been developed primarily by a committee of secretaries. Under that system, Sweetwater's administrators filled out forms similar to the one shown in Table 9.2. This once-a-year appraisal (in March) had run into problems almost immediately, since it was apparent from the start that administrators varied widely in their interpretations of job standards, as well as in how conscientiously they filled out the forms and supervised their secretaries. Moreover, at the end of the first year it became obvious to everyone that each secretary's salary increase was tied directly to the March appraisal. For example, those rated "excellent" received the maximum increases, those rated "good" received smaller increases, and those given neither rating received only the standard across-the-board cost-of-living increase. Since universities in general—and Sweetwater U in particular—have paid secretaries somewhat lower salaries than those prevailing in private industry, some secretaries left in a huff that first year. From that time on most administrators simply rated all secretaries excellent in order to reduce staff turnover, thus ensuring each a maximum increase. In the process, they also avoided the hard feelings aroused by the significant performance differences otherwise highlighted by administrators.

Two Sweetwater experts agreed to consider the problem, and in two weeks they came back to the vice president with the following recommendations. First, the form used to rate the secretaries was grossly insufficient. It was unclear what "excellent" or "quality of work" meant, for example. They recommended instead a form like that in Figure 9.2. In addition, they recommended that the vice president rescind his earlier memo and no longer attempt to force university administrators arbitrarily to rate at least half their secretaries as something less than excellent. The two consultants pointed out that this was, in fact, an unfair procedure since it was quite possible that any particular administrator might have staffers who were all or virtually all excellent—or conceivably, although less likely, all below standard. The experts said that the way to get all the administrators to take the appraisal process more seriously was to stop tying it to salary increases. In other words, they recommended that every administrator fill out a form like that in Figure 9.2 for each secretary at least once a year and then use this form as the basis of a counseling session. Salary increases would have to be made on some basis other than the performance appraisal, so that administrators would no longer hesitate to fill out the rating forms honestly.

Rob thanked the two experts and went back to his office to ponder their recommendations. Some of the recommendations (such as substituting the new rating form for the old) seemed to make sense. Nevertheless, he still had serious doubts as to the efficacy of any graphic rating form, particularly if he were to decide in favor of his original forced ranking approach. The experts' second recommendation—to stop tying the appraisals to automatic salary increases—made sense but raised at least one very practical problem: If salary increases were not to be based on performance appraisals, on what were they to be based? He began wondering whether the experts' recommendations weren't simply based on ivory tower theorizing.

■ QUESTIONS

1. Do you think that the experts' recommendations will be sufficient to get most of the administrators to fill out the rating forms properly? Why? Why not? What additional actions (if any) do you think will be necessary?

2. Do you think that Vice President Winchester would be better off dropping graphic rating forms, substituting instead one of the other techniques we discussed in this chapter such as a ranking method? Why?

3. What performance appraisal system would you develop for the secretaries if you were Bob Winchester? Defend your answer.

NOTES

1. Kenneth Teel, "Performance Appraisal: Current Trends, Persistent Process," *Personnel Journal* (April 1980), pp. 296–301. See also Christina Banks and Kevin Murphy, "Toward Narrowing the Research-Practice Gap in Performance Appraisals," *Personnel Psychology*, Vol. 38, no. 2 (Summer 1985), pp. 335–346. For a description of how to implement an improved performance appraisal system, see, for example, Ted Cocheu, "Performance Appraisal: A Case in Point," *Personnel Journal*, Vol. 65, no. 9 (September 1986), pp. 48–53; William H. Wagel, "Performance Appraisal with a Difference," *Personnel*, Vol. 64, no. 2 (February 1987), pp. 4–6; Jeanette Cleveland et al., "Multiple Uses of Performance Appraisal: Prevalence and Correlates," *Journal of Applied Psychology*, Vol. 74, no. 1 (February 1989), pp. 130–135; Ian Carlton and Martyn Sloman,

"Performance Appraisal in Practice," *Human Resource Management Journal*, Vol. 2, no. 3 (Spring 1992), pp. 80–94.

2. Teel, "Performance Appraisal," p. 301. For a good explanation of why sole reliance on appraisal by supervisors may not be a good idea, see Keki Bhote, "Boss Performance Appraisal: A Metric Whose Time Has Gone," *Employment Relations Today*, Vol. 21, no. 1 (Spring 1994), pp. 1–9.

3. Ibid. See also Martin Friedman, "Ten Steps to Objective Appraisals," *Personnel Journal*, Vol. 65, no. 6 (June 1986).

4. For a recent discussion see Gary English, "Tuning Up for Performance Management," *Training and Development Journal* (April 1991), pp. 56–60.

5. This is based on James Buford, Jr., Bettye Burkhalter, and Grover Jacobs, "Link Job Descriptions to Performance Appraisals," *Personnel Journal* (June 1988), pp. 132–140.

6. This is based on Commerce Clearing House, "Merck's New Performance Appraisal/Merit Pay System Is Based on Bell-Shaped Distribution," *Ideas and Trends*, May 17, 1989, pp. 88–90.

7. Commerce Clearing House Editorial Staff, "Performance Appraisal: What Three Companies Are Doing," Chicago, 1985. See also Richard Girard, "Are Performance Appraisals Passe?" *Personnel Journal*, Vol. 67, no. 8 (August 1988), pp. 89–90, which explains how companies can appraise performance using incidents instead of formal performance appraisals.

8. See, for example, Timothy Keaveny and Anthony McGann, "A Comparison of Behavioral Expectation Scales and Graphic Rating Scales," *Journal of Applied Psychology*, Vol. 60 (1975), pp. 695–703. See also John Ivancevich, "A Longitudinal Study of Behavioral Expectation Scales: Attitudes and Performance," *Journal of Applied Psychology*, Vol. 30, no. 3 (Autumn 1986), pp. 619–628.

9. Based on Donald Schwab, Herbert Heneman, III, and Thomas DeCotiis, "Behaviorally Anchored Scales: A Review of the Literature, *Personnel Psychology*, Vol. 28 (1975), pp. 549–562. For a discussion, see Also Uco Wiersma and Gary Latham, "The Practicality of Behavioral Observation Scales, Behavioral Expectations Scales, and Trait Scales," *Personnel Psychology*, Vol. 30, no. 3 (Autumn 1986), pp. 619–628.

10. Lawrence Fogli, Charles Hulin, and Milton Blood, "Development of First Level Behavioral Job Criteria," *Journal of Applied Psychology*, Vol. 55 (1971), pp. 3–8. See also Terry Dickenson and Peter Fellinger, "A Comparison of the Behaviorally Anchored Rating and Fixed Standard Scale Formats," *Journal of Applied Psychology* (April 1980), pp. 147–154.

11. Keaveny and McGann, "A Comparison of Behavioral Expectation Scales, pp. 695–703; Schwab, Heneman, and DeCotiis, "Behaviorally Anchored Rating Scales"; and James Goodale and Ronald Burke, "Behaviorally Based Rating Scales Need Not Be Job Specific," *Journal of Applied Psychology*, Vol. 60 (June 1975).

12. Wayne Cascio and Enzo Valenzi, "Behaviorally Anchored Rating Scales: Effects of Education and Job Experience of Raters and Ratees," *Journal of Applied Psychology*, Vol. 62, no. 3 (1977), pp. 278–282. See also Gary P. Latham and Kenneth Wexley, "Behavioral Observation Scales for Performance Appraisal Purposes," *Personnel Psychology*, Vol. 30, no. 2 (Summer 1977), pp. 255–268; H. John Bernardin, Kenneth M. Alvares, and C. J. Cranny, "A Recomparison of Behavioral Expectation Scales to Summated Scales," *Journal of Applied Psychology*, Vol. 61, no. 5 (October 1976), p. 564; Frank E. Saal and Frank J. Landy, "The Mixed Standard Rating Scale: An Evaluation," *Organizational Behavior and Human Performance*, Vol. 18, no. 1 (February 1977), pp. 19–35; Frank J. Landy et al., "Behaviorally Anchored Scales for Rating the Performance of Police Officers," *Journal of Applied Psychology*, Vol. 61, no. 6 (December 1976), pp. 750–758; and Kevin R. Murphy and Joseph Constans, "Behavioral Anchors as a Source of Bias in Rating," *Journal of Applied Psychology*, Vol. 72, no. 4 (November 1987), pp. 573–577.

13. Edward C. Baig, "So You Hate Rating Your Workers?" *Business Week*, August 22, 1994, p. 14.

14. This is based on Peter H. Lewis, "A New Way to Rate Employee Performance More Effectively," *The New York Times*, December 19, 1993, p. 10. Employee Appraiser was developed by the Austin-Hayne Corporation of San Mateo, California.

15. Jeffrey Stanton and Janet Barnes-Farrell, "Effects of Electronic Performance Monitoring on Personal Control, Task Satisfaction, and Task Performance," *Journal of Applied Psychology*, Vol. 81, no. 6 (1996), p. 738.

16. Ibid., p. 738.

17. See Martin Levy, "Almost-Perfect Performance Appraisals," *Personnel Journal*, Vol. 68, no. 4 (April 1989), pp. 76–83, for a good example of how one company fine tuned its form for individual performance.

18. Andrew Solomonson and Charles Lance, "Examination of the Relationship Between True Halo and Halo Effort in Performance Ratings," *Journal of Applied Psychology*, Vol. 82, no. 5 (1997), pp. 665–674.

19. Teel, "Performance Appraisal," p. 298.

20. I. M. Jawahar and Charles Williams, "Where All The Children Are Above Average: The Performance Appraisal Purpose Affect," *Personnel Psychology*, Vol. 50 (1997), p. 905.

21. Ibid., p. 921.

22. For a discussion of this see, for example, Wayne Cascio, *Applied Psychology in Personnel Management* (Reston, VA: Reston Publishing, 1978), pp. 337–341.

23. B. Rosen and T. H. Gerdee, "The Nature of Job Related Age Stereotypes," *Journal of Applied Psychology*, Vol. 61 (1976), pp. 180–183.

24. Gerald Ferris, Valerie Yates, David Gilmour, and Kendrith Rowland, "The Influence of Subordinate Age on Performance Ratings and Casual Attributions," *Personnel Psychology*, Vol. 38, no. 3 (Autumn 1985), pp. 545–557. As another example, see Gregory Dobbins and Jeanne Russell, "The Biasing Effects of Subordinate Likeableness on Leader's Responses to Poor Performers: A Laboratory and Field Study," *Personnel Psychology*, Vol. 39, no. 4 (Winter 1986), pp. 759–778. See also Michael E. Benedict and Edward Levine, "Delay and Distortion: Passive Influences on Performance Appraisal Effectiveness," *Journal of Applied Psychology*, Vol. 73, no. 3 (August 1988), pp. 507–514, and James Smither et al., "Effect of Prior Performance Information on Ratings of Present Performance: Contrast Versus Assimilation Revisited," *Journal of Applied Psychology*, Vol. 73, no. 3 (August 1988), pp. 487–496.

25. Michael Mount, et al., "Rater-Ratee Race Effects in Developmental Performance Ratings of Managers," *Personnel Psychology*, Vol. 50 (1997), pp. 51–69.

26. Ibid., see in particular, page 62.

27. Ibid., p. 63. The researchers note, however, that since the true performance of the black managers was unknown, "it is not possible to determine whether ratings made by black bosses overstate performance, whether ratings made by white bosses understate performance, or both."

28. William Bigoness, "Effect of Applicant's Sex, Race, and Performance on Employer's Performance Ratings: Some Additional Findings," *Journal of Applied Psychology*, Vol. 61 (February 1976); Duane Thompson and Toni Thompson, "Task-Based Performance Appraisal for Blue-Collar Jobs: Evaluation of Race and Sex Effects," *Journal of Applied Psychology*, Vol. 70, no. 4 (1985), pp. 747–753.

29. Jane Halpert, Midge Wilson, and Julia Hickman, "Pregnancy as a Source of Bias in Performance Appraisals," *Journal of Organizational Behavior*, Vol. 14 (1993), pp. 649–663.

30. Ibid., p. 655.

31. Kevin Murphy, William Balzer, Maura Lockhart, and Elaine Eisenman, "Effects of Previous Performance on Evaluations of Present

Performance," *Journal of Applied Psychology*, Vol. 70, no. 1 (1985), pp. 72–84. See also Kevin Williams, Angelo DeNisi, Bruce Meglino, and Thomas Cafferty, "Initial Decisions and Subsequent Performance Ratings," *Journal of Applied Psychology*, Vol. 71, no. 2 (May 1986), pp. 189–195.

32. W. C. Borman, "Effects of Instruction to Avoid Halo Error in Reliability and Validity of Performance Evaluation Ratings," *Journal of Applied Psychology*, Vol. 65 (1975), pp. 556–560; Borman points out that since no control group (a group of managers who did not undergo training) was available, it is possible that the observed effects were not due to the short five-minute training experience. G. P. Latham, K. N. Wexley, and E. D. Pursell, "Training Managers to Minimize Rating Errors in the Observation of Behavior," *Journal of Applied Psychology*, Vol. 60 (1975), pp. 550–555; John Ivancevich, "Longitudinal Study of the Effects of Rater Training on Psychometric Error in Ratings," *Journal of Applied Psychology*, Vol. 64 (1979), pp. 502–508. For a related discussion, see, for example, Bryan Davis and Michael Mount, "Effectiveness of Performance Appraisal Training Using Computer Assistance Instruction and Behavior Modeling," *Personnel Psychology*, Vol. 37 (Fall 1984), pp. 439–452.

33. Walter Borman, "Format and Training Effects on Rating Accuracy and Rater Errors," *Journal of Applied Psychology*, Vol. 64 (August 1979), pp. 410–412, and Jerry Hedge and Michael Cavanaugh, "Improving the Accuracy of Performance Evaluations: Comparison of Three Methods of Performance Appraiser Training," *Journal of Applied Psychology*, Vol. 73, no. 1 (February 1988), pp. 68–73.

34. Dennis Warnke and Robert Billings, "Comparison of Training Methods for Improving the Psychometric Quality of Experimental and Administrative Performance Ratings," *Journal of Applied Psychology*, Vol. 64 (April 1979), pp. 124–131. See also Timothy Athey and Robert McIntyre, "Effect of Rater Training on Rater Accuracy: Levels of Processing Theory and Social Facilitation Theory Perspectives," *Journal of Applied Psychology*, Vol. 72, no. 4 (November 1987), pp. 567–572.

35. Angelo DeNisi and Lawrence Peters, "Organization of Information in Memory and the Performance Appraisal Process: Evidence from the Field," *Journal of Applied Psychology*, Vol. 81, no. 6 (1996), pp. 717–737.

36. Ibid., p. 722.

37. Ibid., p. 722.

38. Juan Sanchez and Philip DeLaTorre, "A Second Look at the Relationship Between Rating and Behavioral Accuracy in Performance Appraisal," *Journal of Applied Psychology*, Vol. 81, no. 1 (1996), p. 7.

39. Arup Varna, et al., "Interpersonal Affect and Performance Appraisal: A Field Study," *Personnel Psychology*, Vol. 49 (1996), pp. 341–360.

40. DeNisi and Peters, op cit. pp. 733–734.

41. This is based on Gary Lubben, Duane Tompason, and Charles Klasson, "Performance Appraisal: The Legal Implications of Title VII," *Personnel* (May–June 1980), pp. 11–21. See also Larry Axline, "Ethical Considerations of Performance Appraisals," *Management Review*, Vol. 83, no. 3 (March 1994), p. 62.

42. Shelley Burchett and Kenneth DeMeuse, "Performance Appraisal and the Law," *Personnel*, Vol. 62, no. 7 (July 1985), pp. 34–35.

43. See also Ian Carlson and Martyn Sloman, "Performance Appraisal in Practice," *Human Resource Management*, Vol. 2, no. 3 (Spring 1992), pp. 80–94.

44. This is based on Kenneth L. Sovereign, *Personnel Law* (Upper Saddle River, NJ: Prentice Hall, 1994), pp. 113–114; and David Rosen, "Appraisals Can Make—or Break—Your Court Case," *Personnel Journal* (November 1992), pp. 113–118.

45. Larry Axline, "Ethical Considerations of Performance Appraisals," *Management Review* (March 1994), p. 62.

46. Wayne Cascio and H. John Bernardin, "Implications of Performance Appraisal Litigation for Personnel Decisions," *Personnel Psychology* (Summer 1981), pp. 211–212, and Gerald Barrett and Mary Kernan, "Performance Appraisal and Terminations: A Review of Court Decisions since *Brito v. Zia* with Implications for Personnel Practices," *Personnel Psychology*, Vol. 40, no. 3 (Autumn 1987), pp. 489–504.

47. Barrett and Kernan, "Performance Appraisal and Terminations," p. 501.

48. James Austin, Peter Villanova, and Hugh Hindman, "Legal Requirements and Technical Guidelines Involved in Implementing Performance Appraisal Systems," in Ferris and Buckley, *Human Resources Management*, 3rd edition (Upper Saddle River, NJ: Prentice Hall, 1996), pp. 271–288.

49. Ibid., p. 282.

50. Jon Werner and Mark Bolino, "Explaining U.S. Courts of Appeals' Decisions Involving Performance Appraisal: Accuracy, Fairness, and Validation," *Personnel Psychology*, Vol. 50 (1997), pp. 1–24.

51. Ibid., p. 19.

52. R. G. Downey, F. F. Medland, and L. G. Yates, "Evaluation of a Peer Rating System for Predicting Subsequent Promotion of Senior Military Officers," *Journal of Applied Psychology*, Vol. 61 (April 1976); and Glenn McEvoy and Paul Buller, "User Acceptance of Peer Appraisals in an Industrial Setting," *Personnel Psychology*, Vol. 40, no. 4 (Winter 1987), pp. 785–798. See also Julie Barclay and Lynn Harland, "Peer Performance Appraisals: The Impact of Rater Competence, Rater Location, and Rating Correctability on Fairness Perceptions," *Group and Organization Management*, Vol. 20, no. 1 (March 1995), pp. 39–60.

53. Allan Kraut, "Prediction of Managerial Success by Peer and Training Staff Ratings," *Journal of Applied Psychology*, Vol. 60 (February 1975). See also Michael Mount, "Psychometric Properties of Subordinate Ratings of Managerial Performance," *Personnel Psychology*, Vol. 37, no. 4 (Winter 1984), pp. 687–702.

54. Carol Norman and Robert Zawacki, "Team Appraisals—Team Approach," *Personnel Journal* (September 1991), pp. 101–103.

55. Robert Libby and Robert Blashfield, "Performance of a Composite as a Function of the Number of Judges," *Organizational Behavior and Human Performance*, Vol. 21 (April 1978), pp. 121–129; Walter Borman, "Exploring Upper Limits of Reliability and Validity in Job Performance Ratings," *Journal of Applied Psychology*, Vol. 63 (April 1978), pp. 135–144; M. M. Harris and J. Schaubroeck, "A Meta-Analysis of Self-Supervisor, Self-Peer, and Peer-Supervisor Ratings," *Personnel Psychology*, Vol. 41 (1988), pp. 43–62.

56. Walter C. Borman, "The Rating of Individuals in Organizations: An Alternate Approach," *Organizational Behavior and Human Performance*, Vol. 12 (1974), pp. 105–124.

57. Teel, "Performance Appraisal," p. 301.

58. Chockalingam Viswesvaran, Denize Ones, and Frank Schmidt, "Comparative Analysis of the Reliability of Job Performance Ratings," *Journal of Applied Psychology*, Vol. 81, no. 5 (1996), pp. 557–574.

59. George Thornton, III, "Psychometric Properties of Self-appraisal of Job Performance," *Personnel Psychology*, Vol. 33 (Summer 1980), p. 265; Cathy Anderson, Jack Warner, and Cassie Spencer, "Inflation Bias in Self-Assessment Evaluations: Implications for Valid Employee Selection," *Journal of Applied Psychology*, Vol. 69, no. 4

(November 1984), pp. 574–580. See also Shaul Fox and Vossi Dinur, "Validity of Self-Assessment: A Field Evaluation," *Personnel Psychology*, Vol. 41, no. 3 (Autumn 1988), pp. 581–592; and John W. Lawrie, "Your Performance: Appraise It Yourself!" *Personnel*, Vol. 66, no. 1 (January 1989), pp. 21–33, a good explanation of how self-appraisals can be used at work.

60. Forest Jourden and Chip Heath, "The Evaluation Gap in Performance Perceptions: Illusory Perceptions of Groups and Individuals," *Journal of Applied Psychology*, Vol. 81, no. 4 (August 1996), pp. 369–379.

61. Herbert Myer, "Self-Appraisal of Job Performance," *Personnel Psychology*, Vol. 33 (Summer 1980), pp. 291–293; Robert Holzbach, "Rater Bias in Performance Ratings: Superior, Self, and Peer Ratings," *Journal of Applied Psychology*, Vol. 63, no. 5 (October 1978), pp. 579–588. Herbert C. Heneman, III, "Comparison of Self and Superior Ratings of Managerial Performance," *Journal of Applied Psychology*, Vol. 59 (1974), pp. 638–642; Richard J. Klimoski and Manuel London, "Role of the Rater in Performance Appraisal," *Journal of Applied Psychology*, Vol. 59 (1974), pp. 445–451; Hubert S. Field and William H. Holley, "Subordinates' Characteristics, Supervisors' Ratings, and Decisions to Discuss Appraisal Results," *Academy of Management Journal*, Vol. 20, no. 2 (1977), pp. 215–221. See also Robert Steel and Nestor Ovalle, II, "Self-Appraisal Based Upon Supervisory Feedback," *Personnel Psychology*, Vol. 37, no. 4 (Winter 1984), pp. 667–685; Gloria Shapiro and Gary Dessler, "Are Self-Appraisals More Realistic Among Professionals or Non-professionals in Health Care?" *Public Personnel Management*, Vol. 14 (Fall 1985), pp. 285–291; James Russell and Dorothy Goode, "An Analysis of Managers' Reactions to Their Own Performance Appraisal Feedback," *Journal of Applied Psychology*, Vol. 73, no. 1 (February 1988), pp. 63–67; and Harris and Schaubroeck, "A Meta-Analysis of Self-Supervisor, Self-Peer, and Peer-Supervisor Ratings," pp. 42–62.

62. Manuel London and Arthur Wohlers, "Agreement Between Subordinates and Self-Ratings in Upward Feedback," *Personnel Psychology*, Vol. 47 (1994), pp. 349–355.

63. Ibid., p. 376.

64. David Antonioni, "The Effects of Feedback Accountability on Upward Appraisal Ratings," *Personnel Psychology*, Vol. 47 (1994), pp. 349–355.

65. Richard Reilly, James Smither, and Nicholas Vasilopoulos, "A Longitudinal Study of Upward Feedback," *Personnel Psychology*, Vol. 49 (1996), pp. 599–612.

66. Ibid., p. 602.

67. Ibid., p. 599.

68. Kenneth Nowack, "360-Degree Feedback: The Whole Story," *Training and Development* (January 1993), p. 69. For a description of some of the problems involved in implementing 360-degree feedback see Matthew Budman, "The Rating Game," *Across the Board*, Vol. 31, no. 2 (February 1994), pp. 35–38.

69. "360-degree Feedback on the Rise, Survey Finds," *BNA Bulletin to Management*, January 23, 1997, p. 31.

70. Katherine Romano, "Fear of Feedback," *Management Review* (December 1993), p. 39.

71. Ibid.

72. See, for instance, Gerry Rich, "Group Reviews—Are You Up To It?" *CMA Magazine* (March 1993), p. 5.

73. Donald Fedor and Charles Parsons, "What Is Effective Performance Feedback?" in Gerald Ferris and M. Ronald Buckley, *Human Re-*

sources Management, 3rd edition (Upper Saddle River, NJ: Prentice Hall, 1996), pp. 265–270.

74. Johnson, *The Appraisal Interview Guide*, Chapter 9.

75. Judy Block, *Performance Appraisal on the Job: Making It Work* (New York: Executive Enterprises Publications, 1981), pp. 58–62. See also Terry Lowe, "Eight Ways to Ruin a Performance Review," *Personnel Journal*, Vol. 65, no. 1 (January 1986).

76. Block, *Performance Appraisal on the Job.*

77. Ronald Burke, William Weitzel, and Tamara Weis, "Characteristics of Effective Employee Performance Review and Development Interviews: Replication and Extension," *Personnel Psychology*, Vol. 31 (Winter 1978), pp. 903–919. See also Joane Pearce and Lyman Porter, "Employee Response to Formal Performance Appraisal Feedback," *Journal of Applied Psychology*, Vol. 71, no. 2 (May 1986), pp. 211–218.

78. Allan Locher and Kenneth Teel, "Appraisal Trends," *Personnel Journal*, September 1988, pp. 139–145. This paper describes a survey sent to 1,459 organizations belonging to the Personnel and Industrial Relations Association of Southern California; 324 companies responded.

79. Ibid., p. 140.

80. Allan Mohrman, Jr., and Susan Albers-Mormon, "Performance Management Is Running the Business," *Compensation and Benefits Review* (July–August 1995), p. 69.

81. Ibid.

82. Edward E. Lawler, III, "Performance Management: The Next Generation," *Compensation and Benefits Review* (May–June 1994), p. 16.

83. Ibid., p. 16.

84. Dr. M. Michael Markowich, "Response: We Can Make Performance Appraisals Work," *Compensation and Benefits Review* (May–June 1995), p. 25.

85. See, for example, Greg Boudreaux, "Response: What TWM Says About Performance Appraisal," *Compensation and Benefits Review* (May–June 1994), pp. 20–24.

86. Ibid., p. 21.

87. See, for example, Lawler, "Performance Management: The Next Generation," p. 17.

88. David Antonioni, "Improve the Management Process Before Discontinuing Performance Appraisals," *Compensation and Benefits Review* (May–June 1994), p. 29.

89. Ibid.

90. Boudreaux, "Response: What TQM Says About Performance Appraisal," p. 23.

91. Based in part on Joel E. Ross, *Total Quality Management: Text, Cases and Readings* (Delray Beach, FL: Saint Lucie Press, 1993), p. 1.

92. Ibid., pp. 2–3, 35–36.

93. Boudreaux, "Response: What TQM Says About Performance Appraisal," p. 23.

94. Lawler, "Performance Management: The Next Generation," p. 17.

95. Markowich, "Response: We Can Make Performance Appraisals Work," p. 26.

96. Antonioni, "Improve the Management Process Before Discontinuing Performance Appraisals," p. 30.

97. Ibid.

98. Ibid.

99. See also Clive Fletcher, "Appraisal: An Idea Whose Time Has Gone?" *Personnel Management* (September 1993), pp. 34–37.

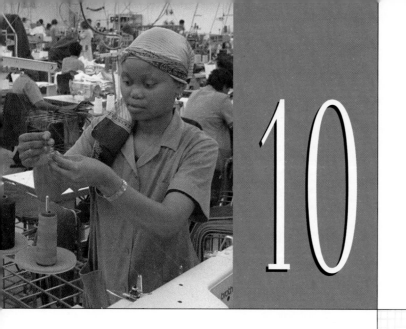

10

MANAGING
CAREERS AND
FAIR TREATMENT

When Levi Strauss announced it was shutting most of its U.S. factories as part of a cost-cutting strategy, many were surprised at how well the dismissed workers were treated. But the company's CEO believed that his company's long-term strategy was best served by treating all his employees fairly, in part because by doing so the remaining employees would be more committed to doing their best to support the company. ▲

Behavioral Objectives

When you finish studying this chapter, you should be able to:

▲ *Discuss* the manager's and employer's role in the career management process.

▲ *Explain* how you would make a new subordinate's first assignment more meaningful.

▲ *Discuss* how to more effectively manage promotions and transfers.

▲ *Explain* in detail techniques for building two-way communications in organizations.

▲ *Discuss* how you would discipline employees.

▲ *Define* wrongful discharge and explain its importance.

▲ *Explain* how to dismiss an employee.

THE BASICS OF CAREER MANAGEMENT

Many people look back on their careers—on the progression of occupational positions they've had—with satisfaction, knowing that what they might have achieved they did achieve, and that their career hopes were fulfilled. Others are less fortunate and feel that (at least career-wise) their potential was not realized.

Unfortunately (or fortunately, as the case may be) careers today are usually not what they were several years ago. "Careers were traditionally viewed as an upward, linear progression in one or two firms or as stable employment within a profession."[1] Today, instead, someone's career is more likely to be "driven by the person, not the organization [and] reinvented by the person from time to time, as the person and the environment change."[2] Some even suggest that tomorrow's career won't be so much a gradual mountain climb as much as a series of short hills or learning stages, as the person switches from job to job and from firm to firm. (Thus the sales rep, laid off by a publishing firm that's just merged may reinvent her career for the next few years as a security analyst specializing in media companies, or as an account executive at a brokerage firm.)[3]

What does this mean for HR? For one thing, the psychological contract between employers and workers has changed. Yesterday, employees "exchanged loyalty for job security."[4] Today, "employees instead exchange performance for the sort of training and learning and development that will allow them to remain marketable."[5] This in turn means that the somewhat uni-directional nature of HR activities like selection and training is starting to change; in addition to serving the company's needs, these activities must now be designed so that the employees' long-run interests are served, and that, in particular, the employee is encouraged to grow and realize his or her full potential. Table 10-1 summarizes how activities such as training and appraisal can be used to provide more of such a **career planning and development** focus.

career planning and development

The deliberate process through which a person becomes aware of personal career-related attributes and the life-long series of stages that contribute to his or her career fulfillment.

Roles in Career Development

As summarized in Table 10-2, the individual, the manager, and the employer all have roles in the individual's career development. Ultimately the individual must accept responsibility for his or her own career; assess his or her own interests, skills, and values; and generally take those steps that must be taken to ensure a happy and fulfilling career. You'll find techniques to help you do so in Appendix B, "Managing Your Career," on page 653.

TABLE 10-1 HR Traditional versus Career Development Focus

ACTIVITY	TRADITIONAL FOCUS	CAREER DEVELOPMENT FOCUS
Human resource planning	Analyzes jobs, skills, tasks—present and future. Projects needs. Uses statistical data.	Adds information about individual interests, preferences, and the like to data. Provides career path information.
Training and development	Provides opportunities for learning skills, information, and attitudes related to job.	Adds individual growth orientation.
Performance appraisal	Rating and/or rewards.	Adds development plans and individual goal setting.
Recruiting and placement	Matching organization's needs with qualified individuals.	Matches individual and jobs based on a number of variables including employees' career interests.
Compensation and benefits	Rewards for time, productivity, talent, and so on.	Adds non-job-related activities to be rewarded, such as United Way leadership positions.

Source: Adapted from Fred L. Otte and Peggy G. Hutcheson, *Helping Employees Manage Careers* (Englewood Cliffs, NJ: Prentice-Hall, 1992), p. 10.

TABLE 10-2 Roles in Career Development

Individual
- Accept responsibility for your own career.
- Assess your interests, skills, and values.
- Seek out career information and resources.
- Establish goals and career plans.
- Utilize development opportunities.
- Talk with your manager about your career.
- Follow through on realistic career plans.

Manager
- Provide timely performance feedback.
- Provide developmental assignments and support.
- Participate in career development discussions.
- Support employee development plans.

Organization
- Communicate mission, policies, and procedures.
- Provide training and development opportunities.
- Provide career information and career programs.
- Offer a variety of career options.

Source: Fred L. Otte and Peggy G. Hutcheson, *Helping Employees Manage Careers* (Upper Saddle River, NJ: Prentice-Hall, 1992), p. 56.

The person's manager plays a role, too. For example, the manager will have to provide timely and objective performance feedback, offer developmental assignments and support, and participate in career oriented appraisals, for instance.

Finally, the employer through its policies and systems also plays a career development role. For example, it will have to provide career-oriented training and development opportunities, offer career management programs, and establish career-oriented appraisal and job-posting policies. Some specific employer career-oriented actions would include:

reality shock

Results of a period that may occur at the initial career entry when the new employee's high job expectations confront the reality of a boring, unchallenging job.

AVOID REALITY SHOCK   **Reality shock** refers to what occurs at initial career entry when a new employee's high job expectations confront the reality of a boring, unchallenging job. Perhaps at no other stage in a person's career is it more important for the employer to be career development-oriented than when a person is recruited, hired, and gets a first assignment and boss. For the employee, this is a period during which he or she has to develop a sense of confidence, learn to get along with the first boss and with coworkers, learn how to accept responsibility, and gain an insight into his or her talents, needs, and values as they relate to initial career goals. In other words, this is (or should be) a period of *reality testing* during which his or her initial hopes and goals first confront the reality of organizational life and of the person's talents and needs.

For many first-time workers, this turns out to be a period in which their often naive expectations first confront the realities of organizational life. The young MBA or CPA, for example, might come to the first job seeking a challenging, exciting assignment in which to apply the new techniques learned in school and to prove his or her abilities and gain a promotion. In reality, however, the trainee is often turned off—by being relegated to an unimportant low-risk job where he or she "can't cause any trouble while being tried out"; by the harsh realities of interdepartmental conflict and politicking; or by a boss who is neither rewarded for nor trained in the unique mentoring tasks required to properly supervise new employees.[6]

PROVIDE CHALLENGING INITIAL JOBS   One thing employer's can do is provide new employees with challenging first jobs. In one study of young managers at AT&T, for example, the researchers found that the more challenging a person's job was in his or her first year with the company, the more effective and successful the person was even 5 or 6 years later.[7] Based on his own research, Douglas Hall contends that challenging initial jobs provide "one of the most powerful yet uncomplicated means of aiding the career development of new employees."[8] In most organizations, however, providing such jobs seems more the exception than the rule. In one survey of research and development organizations, for example, only 1 of 22 companies had a formal policy of giving challenging first assignments.[9] This imbalance, says one expert, is an example of "glaring mismanagement" when one considers the effort and money invested in recruiting, hiring, and training new employees.[10]

Some firms "front-load" the job challenge by giving new employees considerable responsibility. At Saturn and Toyota even assembly workers are assigned at once to self-managing teams of highly skilled and motivated colleagues where they must quickly learn to be productive team members. At Goldman Sachs young professionals are expected to contribute at once, and immediately find themselves on teams deeply involved in challenging projects.[11]

PROVIDE REALISTIC JOB PREVIEWS IN RECRUITING   Providing recruits with realistic previews that describe both the attractions and also possible pitfalls of the job can help minimize reality shock and improve long-term performance. Schein points out that one of the biggest problems recruits and employers encounter during the interview is getting accurate information in a "climate of mutual selling."[12] The recruiter (anxious to hook good candidates) and the candidate (anxious to present as favorable an impression as possible) often give and receive unrealistic information during the interview. The result is that the interviewer may not form a clear picture of the candidate's career goals, while at the same time the candidate forms an unrealistically favorable image of the organization.[13]

BE DEMANDING   There is often a "Pygmalion effect"[14] in the relationship between a new employee and his or her boss.[15] In other words, the more you expect and the more confident and supportive you are of your new employees, the better they will perform. Therefore, as two experts put it, "Don't assign a new employee to a 'dead wood,' undemanding, or unsupportive supervisor."[16] Instead choose specially trained, high-performing, supportive supervisors who can set high standards for new employees during their critical exploratory first year.

PROVIDE PERIODIC JOB ROTATION AND JOB PATHING   The best way new employees can test themselves and crystallize their career anchors is to try out a variety of challenging jobs. By rotating to jobs in various specializations—from financial analysis to production to human resource, for example—the employee gets an opportunity to assess his or her aptitudes and preferences. At the same time, the organization gets a manager with a broader multifunctional view of the organization.[17] One extension of this is called *job pathing*, which means selecting carefully sequenced job assignments.[18]

DO CAREER-ORIENTED PERFORMANCE APPRAISALS   Edgar Schein says that supervisors must understand that valid performance appraisal information is in the long run more important than protecting the short-term interests of one's immediate subordinates.[19] Therefore, he says, supervisors need concrete information regarding the employee's potential career path—information, in other words, about the nature of the future work for which he or she is appraising the subordinate, or which the subordinate desires.[20]

PROVIDE CAREER PLANNING WORKSHOPS AND CAREER PLANNING WORK-BOOKS Employers also should take steps to increase their employees' involvement and expertise in planning and developing their own careers. One option here is to organize periodic career planning workshops. A *career planning workshop* has been defined as "a planned learning event in which participants are expected to be actively involved, completing career planning exercises and inventories and participating in career skills practice sessions."[21]

Figure 10-1 provides an illustrative agenda for a two-day career planning workshop. Such workshops usually contain a self-assessment activity in which individual employees actively analyze their own career interests, skills, and career aspirations. There is then an environmental assessment phase in which relevant information about the company and its career options and staffing needs is presented. Finally, a career planning workshop typically concludes with goal setting and action planning in which the individual sets career goals and creates a career plan.

PROVIDE MENTORING OPPORTUNITIES Mentoring can be defined as "the use of an experienced individual [the mentor] to teach and train someone [the protégeé] with less knowledge in a given area."[22] Organizational mentoring may be formal or informal. Informally, of course, middle- and senior-level managers will often voluntarily take up-and-coming employees under their wings not only to train them but to give career advice and to help them steer around political pitfalls. Particularly where the interest is in creating mentoring relationships for minority employees, informal means such as creating diverse work teams, and increasing the opportunities for networking and interactions among diverse groups of potential proteges and mentors can increase the opportunities for mentoring relationships to emerge.[23]

However, many employers also have formal mentoring programs. Here employers encourage mentoring relationships to take place and may in fact pair proteges with potential mentors. Training—perhaps in the form of instructional manuals—may be provided to facilitate the mentoring process. This can aid both mentor and protege in understanding their respective responsibilities in the mentoring relationship.

MANAGING PROMOTIONS AND TRANSFERS	*Making Promotion Decisions*

For some people "career" is still all but synonomous with "promotion" although (as noted earlier) such upward movement is becoming less the norm in todays downsized companies. Yet promotions often do take place, of course, and so employers must decide on what basis to promote employees.

DECISION 1: IS SENIORITY OR COMPETENCE THE RULE? Probably the most important decision is whether promotion will be based on seniority or competence, or some combinations of the two.

From the point of view of motivation, promotion based on competence is best. However, your ability to use competence as a sole criterion depends on several things, most notably whether or not your firm is unionized or governed by civil service requirements. Union agreements often contain a clause that emphasizes seniority in promotions, such as: "In the advancement of employees to higher paid jobs when ability, merit, and capacity are equal, employees with the highest seniority will be given preference."[24] And many public sector organizations are still governed by civil service regulations that emphasize seniority rather than competence as the basis for promotion.[25]

People of color tend to experience relatively less career progress in organizations, but that's not necessarily the result of decision makers' racist sentiments.[26] Instead, sec-

Before the program—Two weeks prior to the workshop participants receive a letter confirming their participation in the program and package of work to be completed before coming to the workshop. The exercises in this package include skills inventory, values identification, life accomplishments inventory, and a reading describing career direction options.

Day 1

8:30–10:00   Introduction and Overview of Career Planning

Welcome and Introduction to Program

    Welcome by general manager
    Overview of agenda and outcomes
    Participant Introductions (Statements of expectations for the program)

Overview of Career Development

    Company's philosophy
    Why career planning is needed
    What career planning is and is not
    Career planning model

10:00–Noon   Self-Assessment: Part 1

Individual Self-Assessment: Values

    Values card sort exercise
    Reconciling with values pre-work
    Introduce career planning summary work sheet

Individual Self-Assessment: Skills

    Motivated skills exercise
    Examining life accomplishments (synthesize exercise with pre-work)
    Identifying accomplishment themes
    Preferred work skills (from pre-work inventory)
    Fill in career planning summary work sheet

1:00–3:30   Self Assessment: Part 2

Individual Self-Assessment: Career Anchors

    Career anchoring pattern exercise
    Small group discussions
    Fill in career planning summary work sheet

Individual Self-Assessment Preferences

    What success means to me
    Skills, knowledge, personal qualities
    Fill in career planning summary work sheet

Individual Self-Assessment: Career Path Pattern

    Synthesize with direction options from pre-work
    Fill in career planning summary work sheet

3:30–4:30   Environmental Assessment

Information About the Company

Goals, growth areas, expectations, turnover, competition for jobs, skills for the future

Fill in career planning summary work sheet

Personal career profile

Reality test, how you see self at this point by sharing in group

Day 2

8:30–10:00 Goal Setting

Warm-Up Exercise

Review of where we've been and where we're going

Setting goals—where do I want to be?

Creating an ideal future

Future skills and accomplishments

Desired lifestyle

Life and career goals

10:15–1:30 Environmental Assessment: Part 2

Career resources in the company

Introduce support services and hand out information

Marketing yourself—what it takes to achieve your goals here

Describe resource people who will be with the group for lunch and brainstorm questions/issues to be discussed

Lunch with resource people

Review lunch discussions

1:30–4:30   Developing career action plans

Making Career Decisions

Identifying long-range alternatives

Identifying short-range alternatives

Improving career decisions

Decision styles and ways to enhance them

Creating your career plan

Reconciling your goals with options

Next career steps

Development action plan

Contingency planning

Making It Happen—Making Commitments to Next Steps

Summary and Adjourn

FIGURE 10-1   *Sample Agenda—Two-Day Career Planning Workshop*

Source: Fred L. Otte and Peggy Hutcheson, *Helping Employees Manage Careers* (Upper Saddle River, NJ: Prentice Hall, 1992), pp. 22–23.

ondary factors—such as having few people of color employed in the hiring department and the fact that the people of color applying for promotions had more work experience and were therefore (ironically) seen as plateaued are often the determining factors.[27] Yet (see the Diversity Box, below) it would seem that whether it's bias or some other reason, questionable hurdles like these should be ferreted out and eliminated.

DECISION 2: HOW IS COMPETENCE MEASURED?   If promotion is to be based on competence, how will competence be defined and measured? Defining and measuring past performance is a fairly straightforward matter: The job is defined, standards are set, and one or more appraisal tools are used to record the employee's performance. But promotion also requires predicting the person's potential; thus, you must have a valid procedure for predicting a candidate's future performance.

Most employers simply use prior performance as a guide and assume that based on the person's prior performance he or she will perform well on the new job. This is the simplest procedure to use. Others use tests or assessment centers to evaluate promotable employees[28] and to identify those with executive potential.[29]

DECISION 3: IS THE PROCESS FORMAL OR INFORMAL?   Many employers still depend on an informal promotion process. Here open positions are often kept secret. Promotion decisions are made instead by key managers from among employees who, for one reason or another, have impressed them.[30] One problem here is that the criteria for promotion, and how promotion decisions are made remains something of a mystery; the link between performance and promotion is thus cut, and the effectiveness of promotion as a reward is thereby diminished.

Many employers therefore establish formal, published promotion policies and procedures. Here employees are generally provided with a formal promotion policy statement

DIVERSITY COUNTS

In Promotion and Career Management

Women still don't make it to the top of the career ladder in numbers that are proportional to their numbers in U.S. industry. For example, while women constitute 40% of the workforce, they hold less than 2% of top-management positions.[33]

Many explanations have been suggested.[34] Blatant or subtle discrimination, including the belief that "women belong at home and are not committed to careers,"[35] inhibits many managers from taking women as seriously as men. The "old boy network" of informal friendships forged over lunch, at social events, at club meetings, and on the golf course is usually not open to women, although it's often here that promotional decisions are made. A woman who tries to act like "one of the boys" is often considered "too hard or too cold hearted," so that "women aspiring to executive positions have to stay within narrow bands of acceptable behavior. Here they may exhibit only certain traditional masculine and feminine qualities, and walking this fine line represents one of the most difficult tasks for executive women."[36] Unlike many men, women are also often forced to make the "career versus family" decision, since the responsibilities of raising the children and managing the household still falls disproportionately on women. A dearth of women mentors also makes it more difficult for women to find the role models and protectors they need to help them guide their careers.

Women and their managers and employers can take several steps to enhance promotional and career

that describes the criteria by which promotions are awarded. Formal systems often include a job-posting policy. This states that open positions and their requirements will be posted and circulated to all employees. As explained in Chapter 4, many employers also maintain detailed qualification briefs on employees, and use replacement charts and computerized employee information systems.

DECISION 4: VERTICAL, HORIZONTAL, OR OTHER?   Employers are increasingly having to deal with how to "promote" employees in an era of delayering and downsizings.

Several options are available. Some firms, such as the exploration division of British Petroleum, create two parallel career paths, one for managers and another for "individual contributors" such as engineers. In that way individual contributors, such as highly accomplished engineers, can move up to nonsupervisory but still more senior positions such as "senior engineer." These jobs have most of the perks and financial rewards attached to management-track positions at that level.[31]

Another option is to move the person horizontally or even within the same job he or she currently holds. Horizontally, for instance, a production employee might be moved to HR to give him or her an opportunity to develop new skills and test and challenge aptitudes. And, in a sense, "promotions" are possible even when leaving the person in the same job; for example, some job enrichment is usually possible, and the firm can provide training to increase the opportunity for assuming increased responsibility.[32]

Handling Transfers

REASONS FOR TRANSFERS   A transfer is a move from one job to another, usually with no change in salary or grade. Employees may seek transfers for personal enrichment, for more interesting jobs, for greater convenience—better hours, location of work, and so

prospects. Perhaps the most important is to vigorously focus on taking the career interests of female employees seriously; in other words, the first step in stripping away the barriers that have impeded women's progress is to accept that there are problems that must be addressed. Employers must then ensure that in all aspects of promotion and career management—from HR and succession planning to career-oriented performance appraisals to selection for training—the process is objective and not subject to hidden biases. Instituting more flexible career tracks so that women who need to take off for several years to raise a family can do so and then resume their careers is also advisable.

Beyond that experts suggest several things the employee herself can do:[37]

- Be able and capable: Learn and understand your business.
- Be seen as able and capable: Do not let your abilities be discounted or ignored.
- Find a mentor and engage in networking.
- Train yourself beyond the job and increase your career assets so you will be available when a good job opportunity arises.
- Know what you want and prepare to balance and prioritize your life.[38]

on—or for jobs offering greater possibilities for advancement.[39] Employers may transfer a worker to vacate a position where he or she is no longer needed, to fill one where he or she is needed, or more generally to find a better fit for the employee within the firm. Many firms today are trying to boost productivity by consolidating positions. Transfers here are a way to give employees who might have nowhere else to go but out a chance for another assignment and, perhaps, some personal growth.

EFFECT ON FAMILY LIFE   Many firms have had policies of routinely transferring employees from locale to locale, either to give their employees more exposure to a wide range of jobs or to fill open positions with trained employees. Such easy-transfer policies have fallen into disfavor, however. This is partly because of the cost of relocating employees (paying moving expenses, buying back the employee's current home, and perhaps financing his or her next home, for instance) and partly because it was assumed that frequent transfers had a bad effect on an employee's family life.

One study suggests that the latter argument, at least, is without merit.[40] The major finding was that there were few differences between mobile and stable families. Few families in the mobile group believed moving was easy. However, they were as satisfied with all aspects of their lives (except social relationships—making friends at work, for instance) as were stable families. Yet, this study notwithstanding, there is no doubt that employees do resist geographical transfers more today than they did even a few years ago.[41]

Career Management and Commitment

The continuing waves of mergers and downsizings have undermined the traditional psychological contract between employer and employee, and thereby complicated the task of fostering employee commitment. The problem is this: how do you maintain employee commitment—an employee's identification with and agreement to pursue the company's or the unit's mission—if the employee can't be sure he or she will even have a job there at the end of the year? How do you get employees to keep the company's best interests at heart if the company doesn't seem to care about what's good for the employee?

One way is to give employees an opportunity to self-actualize and to develop their potential. Doing so forsters commitment—most employees appreciate and respond well to having their potential and skills enhanced; and to knowing that (if the day should come) they'll be more marketable. Examples of career-enhancing steps employers can take follow.

DEVELOPMENTAL ACTIVITIES   Providing the educational and training resources required to help employees identify and develop their promotion and career potential is important. At Ben & Jerry's, promotional development is encouraged through programs of

Career counseling is an important part of employee development at all stages of a person's career and should be an ongoing process for the manager.

career planning, company internships, and tuition assistance. Ben & Jerry's employees are encouraged to attend a sequence of eight 4-hour career planning seminars, the aim of which is to help employees think about and plan their careers. Employees who have completed the seminars and want to learn about other jobs within the firm can then spend 2 or 3 days interning at another company job, on paid time. The firm offers up to 90% funding for tuition reimbursement for up to three courses per year. It also provides many classes, seminars, counseling and tutoring, both on company premises and off. These include: college courses taught by the Community College of Vermont and including one-on-one tutoring; computer classes, in which employees can earn a certificate from Ben & Jerry's information services group; adult basic education tutoring and high school diploma program; management development counseling one-on-one, by invitation and request; professional development classes and seminars; and financial planning seminars and individual counseling.

The career development program at Saturn is similarly comprehensive. A career growth workshop uses vocational guidance tools (including a skills assessment disk and other career gap analysis tools) to help employees identify career-related skills and the development needs they require. This workshop, according to one employee, "helps you assess yourself, and takes 4 to 6 hours. You use it for developing your own career potential. The career disk identifies your weaknesses and strengths: you assess yourself, and then your team assesses you."[42] Tuition reimbursement and other development aids are then available to help employees develop the skills they need to get ahead.

Career development programs like these can't guarantee an employee will be promoted, of course. However they do help guarantee that all employees have the opportunity to formulate realistic views of their career abilities, interests, and options. They help ensure that all employees have an equal opportunity to make themselves promotable at their firms. They make it easier for employees to choose and make lateral moves, ones that let them broaden and challenge themselves, and, if needed, to compete for jobs at other firms. And, they provide a continuing opportunity for each employee to grow, by learning new subjects and meeting new challenges, and thereby foster commitment. Here is how one Saturn assembler put it:

> I'm an assembler now, and was a team leader for two-and-a-half years. My goal is to move into our people-systems [HR] unit. I know things are tight now, but I know that the philosophy here is that the firm will look out for me—they want people to be all they can be. I know here I'll go as far as I can go; that's one reason I'm so committed to Saturn.[43]

CAREER-ORIENTED APPRAISALS   Career-oriented firms also stress career-oriented appraisals; they don't just assess past performance. Instead the supervisor and the employee are charged with linking the latter's past performance, career preferences, and developmental needs in a formal career plan.

JC Penney is a good example here. As illustrated in Figure 10-2, its Management Appraisal form requires both a "promotability recommendation" and "projections for associate development."

Here is how it works. Prior to the annual appraisal the associate and his or her manager review Penney's Management Career Grid (Figure 10-3). The grid itemizes all supervisory positions at JC Penney (grouped by operations jobs, merchandise jobs, personnel jobs, and general management jobs) and includes specific job titles such as "regional catalog sales manager," "cosmetic market coordinator," "regional training coordinator," and "project manager, public affairs." The firm also provides a "work activities scan sheet." This basically contains thumbnail job descriptions for all the grid's jobs.

The Management Career Grid also identifies typical promotional routes. As the instructions indicate: "When projecting the next assignment for a management associate,

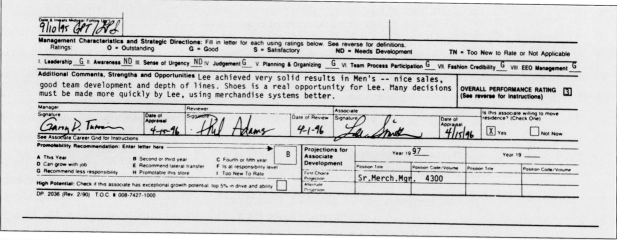

FIGURE 10-2 *Portion of JC Penney's Appraisal Form*

Note: Career oriented appraisal

you should consider not only merchandise positions but also operations and personnel positions as well as general management positions."

Promotional projections can cross these four groups, as well as up one or two job levels. Thus, a senior merchandising manager might be projected for promotion to either assistant buyer or general merchandise manager. ("Assistant buyer" is classified as a general management job at Penney's, since buying is done centrally. The potential general merchandise manager job is a merchandise group job, two levels above the person's current senior merchandising manager position.)

CAREER RECORDS/JOBS POSTING SYSTEMS The basic purpose of career records/jobs posting systems is to ensure that the career goals and skills of inside candidates are matched openly, fairly, and effectively with promotional opportunities. For example,

> *Consider Goldman Sach's Internal Placement Center (IPC).[44] Its aim is to offer Goldman Sachs employees interested in pursuing career opportunities in different areas of the firm the resources to locate and apply for job openings. The IPC also makes it simpler for managers to consider qualified internal candidates when filling open positions, and furnishes managers with information about openings that could provide career development opportunities for their employees.[45]*

The IPC process contains five steps. First, the hiring manager can choose to conduct an internal, external, or combined (internal and external) search, but "an internal or combined search is strongly encouraged."[46] Next the manager and recruiter fill out a job description form for the open position. The form includes job title, department and manager, a description of the position's responsibilities and duties, and a summary of qualifications required for the position. Third, listings of current job opportunities are posted in the Internal Placement Center and in the reception area on each floor. Fourth, any employee interested in applying for an open position submits an IPC application and current résumé to the Internal Placement Center.

Finally, the IPC coordinator and the recruiter assess each applicant's qualifications. Within 2 weeks after submitting his or her application, the employee is informed by the IPC coordinator at his or her home address about the status of the application. (This is the case whether or not the employee is selected to be interviewed for a position.) Those chosen as candidates then start their interviews.

Instructions and Use of Grid for Making Associate Projections of Development

1) Promotability—Enter the appropriate Promotability letter in the box provided. If the answer to Promotability is D, F, or I, leave the "High Potential" and "Projections for Associate Development" sections blank.

2) High Potential—The High Potential box should be checked if this associate has exceptional growth potential—is within the top 5 percent in drive and ability. Please keep in mind that appraisal ratings and high potential ratings while related reflect two distinct judgments—performance in current assignment versus exceptional potential for growth. A "1" rated associate, is not necessarily high potential or vice versa.

| | | **FIELD MANAGEMENT** | |
| **OPERATIONS** | | **MERCHANDISE** | |
Position Title/Volume	Code	Position Title/Volume	Code
Regional Operations Manager	1002	Manager of Geographic Markets	1017
		Manager of Business Planning	1025
		District Manager	1121
		Store Manager 30+ D.S	0109
		Entity Store Manager	0110
		Store Manager 22–30 D.S.	0108
		Store Manager 15–22 D.S.	0107
		Regional Business Planning Manager	1026
		Store Manager 10–15 D.S.	0106
		Store Manager Under 10 D.S.	0105
Regional Catalog Sales Center Manager	1150	Regional Merchandiser/Geographic Markets	1146
Regional Programs Manager	1100		
Regional Systems Manager	1027		
		Store Manager 5–10 S.L.	0104
Regional Catalog Sales Manager	1139	Business Planning Manager	**40( )0
District Operations Manager	2290	District Special Events & Publicity Manager	2800
District Operations/Personnel Manager	2310	Store Merchandise & Marketing Manager	4260
Regional Loss Prevention Manager	4804		
Operations Manager 30+ D.S.	1329	Store Manager 3–5 S.L.	0103
District Merchandise Systems Coordinator	2330	General Merchandising Manager 30+ D.S.	4299
D.L.D.C. Manager	3750	General Merchandising Manager 22–30 D.S.	4298
Operations Manager 25–30 D.S.	1328	Store Manager 1–3 S.L.	0102
		Regional Visual Merchandising Mgr—Geo. Mkts.	1085
		Regional Visual Merchandising Mgr—Metro Mkts.	1092
Regional Loss Prevention Representative	4805		
Regional Styling Salon Sales Manager	1109	General Merchandising Manager 15–22 D.S.	4297
Regional Maintenance Manager	1165	General Merchandising Manager 10–15 D.S.	4296
Regional Telecommunications Manager	1028	General Merchandising Manager under 10 D.S.	4295
District Loss Prevention Manager	5620	Store Manager under 1 S.L.	0101
		Multiple Unit D.L.D.C. Merchandiser	4450
Operations/Personnel Manager 10–25 D.S.	5356	D.L.D.C. Merchandiser	3760
D.L.D.C. Operations Manager	4930	District Merchandise Publicity Coordinator	5580
Systems Implementation & Training Manager	1130	Special Lines Market Coordinator	2340
Catalog Sales Center Manager	1010	District Visual Merchandising Manager	5630
Sales Support Manager	3210	Cosmetic Market Coordinator	0700
		Visual Merchandising Manager	4650
		Senior Merchandising Manager	4300
		Department Sales Manager	3460
		Shoe Department Manager	5590
		Cosmetic Manager	0710
(Functional Title) Manager	4980	Merchandising Manager	4310
		Fine Jewelry Manager	3360
		Multi Store Fine Jewelry Manager	4470
		Fine Jewelry Merchandiser	3370
		Shoe Department Merchandiser	5600
		Cosmetic Merchandiser	0720
		Merchandising Manager Trainee	4330

FIGURE 10-3 *Portion of JC Penney's Management Career Grid*

MANAGING FAIR
TREATMENT

Introduction: The Building Blocks of Fairness

Why treat employees fairly? Two researchers writing in *Harvard Business Review* recently answered that question this way:

> *Never has the idea of fair process been more important for managers than it is today. Fair process turns out to be a powerful management tool for companies struggling to make the transition from a production-based to a knowledge-based company, in which value creation depends increasingly on ideas and innovation. Fair process profoundly influences attitudes and behaviors critical to high performance. It builds trust and unlocks ideas. With it, managers can achieve even the most painful and difficult goals while gaining the voluntary cooperation of the employees affected. Without fair process, even outcomes that employees might favor can be difficult to achieve.[47]*

Treating employees fairly makes sense for other reasons, too. An increasingly litigious workforce makes it important that employers have disciplinary and discharge procedures that will survive the scrutiny of arbitrators and the courts. Second, one study found that employees who perceived they were being treated fairly by the company were more likely to take those discretionary actions that companies need today to remain flexible and responsive to unforeseen occurrences.[48]

Some of the things that motivate managers to be fair may (or may not) be a little surprising. For one thing, the old saying about "the squeaky wheel gets the grease" seems to be true. The aim of one study was to investigate the extent to which assertiveness on the subordinate's part influenced the fairness by which he or she was treated by the supervisor.[49] The findings suggested that the individuals who communicated assertively were more likely to be treated fairly by the decision maker."[50] Employees shouldn't have to be assertive to be treated fairly, however. Actions HR can take to create a more just environment at work are as follows.

Build Two-Way Communications

Fairness generally requires two-way communications. Whether you are an irate customer, student, or employee, having the other person listen to what you're saying and perhaps explain the situation will help signal that you've been treated fairly. For example, two researchers found that three things contributed to perceived fairness in various business settings: *engagement* (involving individuals in the decisions that affect them by asking for their input and allowing them to refute the merits of one another's ideas and assumptions); *explanation* (ensuring that everyone involved and affected should understand why final decisions are made as they are and of the thinking that underlies the decisions); and *expectation clarity* (making sure everyone knows up front by what standards they will be judged and the penalties for failure).[51] Managers in firms such as FedEx and Saturn have therefore established programs such as those described next to foster such communications.

speak up! programs

Communications programs that allow employees to register questions, concerns, and complaints about work-related matters.

"SPEAK-UP!" PROGRAMS   **Speak-up! programs** aim to encourage upward communications. In other words, they encourage employees to speak up about concerns that run the gamut from malfunctioning vending machines to unlit parking lots to a manager spending too much of the department's money on travel.

Toyota Motor Manufacturing company in Lexington, Kentucky. The hot line is the main upward communication channel.[52] Its purpose is to provide Toyota employees with an anonymous way to bring questions or problems to the company's attention. The hot line is available 24 hours per day. Employees are instructed to pick up any phone, dial the hot line extension (the number is posted on the plant bulletin boards), and deliver their messages to the recorder. Toyota guarantees that all hot line inquiries will be reviewed by the HR management and thoroughly investigated.

opinion surveys

Communication devices that use questionnaires to regularly ask employees their opinions about the company, management, and work life.

WHAT'S YOUR OPINION?   Many firms also administer periodic anonymous **opinion surveys**. For example, the FedEx Survey Feedback Action (SFA) program (discussed in Chapter 9) includes an anonymous survey that allows employees to express feelings about the company and their managers. Each manager then has an opportunity to discuss the anonymous department results with his or her subordinates, and thus design a blueprint for improving work group commitment. Sample questions include:

- I can tell my manager what I think.
- My manager listens to my concerns.
- Upper management listens to ideas from my level.
- FedEx does a good job for the customers.
- In my environment we use safe work practices.
- I am paid fairly for this kind of work.

top-down programs

Communications activities including in-house television centers, frequent roundtable discussions, and in-house newsletters that provide continuing opportunities for the firm to let all employees be updated on important matters regarding the firm.

TOP-DOWN PROGRAMS   Firms such as Saturn use several **top-down programs** to get information to all employees. The company provides information continuously via the internal television network, and via financial documents. They also have 'town hall' meetings once per month, with perhaps 500 to 700 people attending.

THE HIGH-PERFORMANCE ORGANIZATION

Building Better, Faster, More Competitive Organizations Through HR: Communications

- ### Communicating Financial Information at Gateway Marriott

The Crystal Gateway Marriott Hotel distributes financial information to all associates (employees) in an easily understood format during quarterly associate meetings. This communication of financial results is well received, and the associates feel involved and informed. This information sharing effort has enhanced employee awareness and increased the ability to manage financial issues in the business, as the associates now have a shared understanding and purpose.

Preliminary profit and loss statements for each operating department are prepared for each reporting period and given to the respective department heads for review and concurrence. These reports are easily understood and are first reviewed by the manager and one of the accounting personnel. Critique meetings are then held among management personnel after each reporting period for a Lessons Learned session and for evaluation of the final report results. These Sessions focus on improvement and learning, as opposed to "why did something happen and who is at fault."

Source: Copyright 1998, Best Manufacturing Practices Center of Excellence.

discipline

A procedure that corrects or punishes a subordinate because a rule or procedure has been violated.

Emphasize Fairness in Disciplining

The purpose of **discipline** is to encourage employees to behave sensibly at work (where *sensible* is defined as adhering to rules and regulations). In an organization, rules and regulations serve about the same purpose that laws do in society; discipline is called for when one of these rules or regulations is violated.[53] Fairness in this case is based on three foundations—rules and regulations, a system of progressive penalties, and an appeals process.

A set of clear rules and regulations is first. These rules address issues such as theft, destruction of company property, drinking on the job, and insubordination. Examples of rules include:

> *Poor performance is not acceptable.* Each employee is expected to perform his or her work properly and efficiently and to meet established standards of quality.
>
> *Alcohol liquor and drugs do not mix with work.* The use of either during working hours and reporting for work under the influence of either are both strictly prohibited.
>
> *The vending of anything in the plant without authorization is not allowed, nor is gambling in any form permitted.*

The purpose of these rules is to inform employees ahead of time what is and is not acceptable behavior. Employees must be told, preferably in writing, what is not permitted. This is usually done during the employee's orientation. The rules and regulations are usually listed in the employee orientation handbook.

A system of progressive penalties is a second foundation of effective discipline. Penalties may range from oral warnings to written warnings to suspension from the job to discharge. The severity of the penalty is usually a function of the type of offense and the number of times the offense has occurred. For example, most companies issue warnings for the first unexcused lateness. However, for a fourth offense, discharge is the more usual disciplinary action.

Finally, an appeals process should be part of the disciplinary process; this helps to ensure that discipline is meted out fairly and is equitable. Discipline guidelines—such as "make sure the evidence fits the charge"—are summarized in Figure 10-4.

DISCIPLINE WITHOUT PUNISHMENT   Traditional discipline has two major potential flaws. First, no one ever feels good about being punished (although fairness guidelines like those previously mentioned can take the edge off this). A second shortcoming is that forcing your rules on employees may gain their short-term compliance, but not their cooperation when you are not around to enforce the rules.

Discipline without punishment (or nonpunitive discipline) is aimed at avoiding these disciplinary problems. This is accomplished by gaining the employees' acceptance of your rules and by reducing the punitive nature of the discipline itself. In summary:[54]

1. *Issue an oral reminder.* As a supervisor, your goal here is to get the employee to agree to solve the problem.

2. *Should another incident arise within 6 weeks, issue the employee a formal written reminder, a copy of which is placed in the personnel file.* In addition, privately hold a second discussion with the employee, again without any threats.

3. *Give a paid one-day "decision-making leave."* If another incident occurs after the written warning in the next 6 weeks or so, the employee is told to take a 1-day leave with pay to stay home and consider whether or not the job is right for him or her and whether he or she wants to abide by the company's rules. When the employee returns to work, he or she meets with you and gives you a decision regarding whether he or she will follow the rules.

4. *If no further incidents occur in the next year or so, the 1-day paid suspension is purged from the person's file.* If the behavior is repeated, dismissal (see later discussion) is required.[55]

FIGURE 10-4
Discipline Guidelines

Discipline Guidelines

- Make sure the evidence supports the charge of employee wrongdoing. In one study, "the employer's evidence did not support the charge of employee wrongdoing" was the reason arbitrators gave most often for reinstating discharged employees or for reducing disciplinary suspensions.
- Ensure that the employees' due process rights are protected. Arbitrators normally reverse discharges and suspensions that are imposed in a manner that violates basic notions of fairness of employee due process procedures. For example, follow established progressive discipline procedures, and don't deny the employee an opportunity to tell his or her side of the story.
- The discipline should be in line with the way management usually responds to similar incidents.
- Adequately warn the employee of the disciplinary consequences of his or her alleged misconduct.
- The rule that allegedly was violated should be "reasonably related" to the efficient and safe operation of the particular work environment. Employees, in other words, are usually allowed by arbitrators to question the reason behind any rule or order.
- Management must fairly and adequately investigate the matter before administering discipline.
- The investigation should produce substantial evidence of misconduct.
- Applicable rules, orders, or penalities should be applied evenhandedly and without discrimination.
- The penalty should be reasonably related to the misconduct and to the employee's past work history.
- Maintain the employee's right to counsel. All union employees have the right to bring help when they are called in for an interview that they reasonably believe might result in disciplinary action.
- Don't rob your subordinate of his or her dignity. Discipline your subordinate in private (unless he or she requests counsel).
- Remember that the burden of proof is on you. In U.S. society, a person is always considered innocent until proven guilty.
- Get the facts. Don't base your decision on hearsay evidence or on your general impression.
- Don't act while angry. Very few people can be objective and sensible when they are angry.

The process must of course be changed in exceptional circumstances. Criminal behavior or in-plant fighting might be grounds for immediate dismissal, for instance. And if several incidents occurred at very close intervals, step 2—the written warning—might be skipped.

Manage Employee Privacy

Electronic monitoring and searches of employees have become quite widespread. For example, in a survey of 906 companies by the American Management Association, 35% said they've recorded employees' telephone calls or voice mail, checked computer files and electronic mail, or videotaped employees' performance.[56] In another survey, 35% of organizations with e-mail systems reported accessing employee e-mail for business necessity or security.[57]

Trespassing electronically is easier than most people think. One review noted, for instance, that today's electronic systems "provide the tools to collect data and monitor the workplace with dazzling efficiency," and that "at the touch of a button, it's possible to view e-mail messages employees send to one another, listen to voice mail or telephone conversations, and actually see what's on their monitors while they're sitting at their computer terminals."[58] Several years ago, a Pillsbury Company regional manager was fired after his supposedly private e-mail message making threatening comments about supervisors was intercepted.[59]

FIGURE 10-5

Sample Telephone Monitoring Acknowledgment Statement

Reprinted with permission from *Bulletin to Management* (*BNA Policy and Practice Series*), Vol. 48, No. 14, Part II, p. 7 (April 3, 1997). Copyright 1997 by The Bureau of National Affairs, Inc.

I understand that my telephone communications will be monitored periodically by my supervisor and other [Company] management staff. I understand that the purpose of this monitoring is to improve:

- The quality of customer service provided to policyholders and prospective customers
- My product knowledge and presentation skills

_____

Signature   Date

_____

Print Name   Department

Electronic eavesdropping is legal—at least to a point. For example, federal law and most states' laws allow employers to monitor their employees' phone calls "in the ordinary course of business," according to one legal expert, but they must stop listening once it becomes clear that a conversation is personal rather than business related.[60] E-mail service can also apparently be (and is) intercepted under federal law when it is to protect the property rights of the provider.[61] However, just to be safe, more employers today are issuing e-mail and on-line service usage policies which, for instance, forewarn employees that those systems are intended to be used for business purposes only. They are also having employees sign e-mail monitoring and telephone monitoring acknowledgement statements like the one in Figure 10-5. One reason for explicit policy statements is the risk that employers may be held liable for illegal acts committed by their employees via e-mail. For example, messages sent by supervisors that contain sexual innuendo or ones defaming an employee can cause problems for the employer if the employer hasn't taken steps to prohibit such e-mail system misuse.[62]

Videotaping in the workplace seems to call for more legal caution. In one case, the U.S. Court of Appeals for the First Circuit ruled that an employer's continuous video surveillance of employees in an office setting did not constitute an unconstitutional invasion of privacy.[63] Yet, a Boston employer recently had to pay over $200,000 to five workers it secretly videotaped in an employee locker room, after they sued in state court.[64]

MANAGING DISMISSALS

dismissal

Involuntary termination of an employee's employment with the firm.

termination at will

The idea, based in law, that the employment relationship can be terminated at will by either the employer or the employee for any reason.

In terms of discipline, **dismissal** is the most drastic step you can take against an employee and one to be taken with deliberate care.[65] Specifically, the dismissal should be just in that sufficient cause exists for it. Furthermore, the dismissal should occur only after all reasonable steps to rehabilitate or salvage the employee have failed. However, there are undoubtedly times when dismissal is required, perhaps at once, and in these instances it should be carried out forthrightly.[66]

Can employees always be dismissed? For more than 100 years the prevailing rule in the United States has been that without a contract, either the employer or the employee can **terminate at will** the employment relationship. In other words, the employee could resign for any reason, at will, and the employer could similarly dismiss an employee for any reason, at will. Today, however, dismissed employees are increasingly taking their cases to court, and in many cases employers are finding that they no longer have a blanket right to fire. Instead, federal EEO and other laws and various state laws and court rulings (based on "public policy" exceptions, or on the fact that employee handbooks are implied contracts, for instance) increasingly limit management's right to dismiss employees at will.

Termination interviews are among the most difficult tasks managers face, but there are guidelines for making them less painful for both parties.

Grounds for Dismissal

There are four bases for dismissal: unsatisfactory performance, misconduct, lack of qualifications for the job, and changed requirements (or elimination) of the job. *Unsatisfactory performance* may be defined as a persistent failure to perform assigned duties or to meet prescribed standards on the job.[67] Specific reasons include excessive absenteeism, tardiness, a persistent failure to meet normal job requirements, or an adverse attitude toward the company, supervisor, or fellow employees. *Misconduct* can be defined as deliberate and willful violation of the employer's rules and may include stealing, rowdy behavior, and insubordination.

Lack of qualifications for the job is defined as an employee's inability to do the assigned work although he or she is diligent. Because in this case the employee may be trying to do the job, it is especially important that every effort be made to salvage him or her—perhaps by assigning the employee to another job or training the person. *Changed requirements of the job* may be defined as an employee's incapability of doing the work assigned after the nature of the job has been changed. Similarly, an employee may have to be dismissed when his or her job is eliminated. Again, the employee may be industrious, so every effort should be made to retrain or transfer this person, if possible.

Insubordination, a form of misconduct, is sometimes the grounds for dismissal, although it may be relatively difficult to prove. Stealing, chronic tardiness, and poor-quality work are fairly obvious grounds for dismissal, but insubordination is sometimes harder to translate into words. To that end, it may be useful to remember that some acts are or should be considered insubordinate whenever and wherever they occur. These include, for instance:

1. Direct disregard of the boss's authority. At sea, this is called mutiny.
2. Flat out disobedience of, or refusal to obey, the boss's orders—particularly in front of others.
3. Deliberate defiance of clearly stated company policies, rules, regulations, and procedures.
4. Public criticism of the boss. Contradicting or arguing with him or her is also negative and inappropriate.

insubordination

Willful disregard or disobedience of the boss's authority or legitimate orders; criticizing the boss in public.

5. Blatant disregard of the boss's reasonable instructions.

6. Contemptuous display of disrespect; making insolent comments, for example; and, more important, portraying these feelings in the attitude shown while on the job.

7. Disregard for the chain of command, shown by going around the immediate supervisor or manager with a complaint, suggestion, or political maneuver. Although the employee may be right, that may not be enough to save him or her from the charges of insubordination.

8. Participation in (or leadership of) an effort to undermine and remove the boss from power.[68]

Several things can help guarantee the perceived fairness of any dismissal.[69] For example (particularly where there was some doubt about the just cause of the dismissal) a more formal and restrictive disciplinary procedure, and a more neutral appeal system both reduced managers' willingness to attempt dismissals.[70]

Who actually does the dismissing is important, too. One study focused on the R&D facility of a large division of a U.S. corporation.[71] Survivors who were informed of the impending layoff by their managers viewed the fairness of the entire dismissal procedure as much fairer than did those who were informed by, say, a representative of the HR department. The prelayoff quality of the relationship between the employee and the manager understandably had some effect on whether or not the employee preferred to get the news from the manager. But, based on this study, at least, one has to question the wisdom of centralizing responsibility for communicating changes like these in the HR department, particularly where the relationship between the employees and their supervising manager has been good.[72]

Avoiding Wrongful Discharge Suits

wrongful discharge

An employee dismissal that does not comply with the law or does not comply with the contractual arrangement stated or implied by the firm via its employment application forms, employee manuals, or other promises.

Wrongful discharge occurs when an employee's dismissal violates the law or the contractual arrangements stated or implied by the firm via its employment application forms, employee manuals, or other promises. The time to protect against such suits is before mistakes have been made and suits have been filed.

Avoiding wrongful discharge suits requires a two-pronged strategy. First is to institute employment policies and dispute resolution procedures (such as those outlined in this chapter) that make employees feel that they are treated fairly.[73] People who are fired and who walk away feeling they've been embarrassed, stripped of their dignity, or treated unfairly financially (for instance, in terms of severance pay) are more likely to seek retribution in the courts. There is probably no way to make a termination pleasant, but an employer's first line of defense is to at least make sure it's viewed as fair.

The second way to avoid wrongful discharge suits is to do the preparatory work—starting with the employment application—that will help avoid such suits before they get started. Steps to take include the following:

Have applicants sign the *employment application* and make sure it contains a clearly worded statement that employment is for no fixed term and that the employer can terminate at any time. In addition, the statement should inform the job candidate that "nothing on this application can be changed."

Review your *employee manual* to look for and delete statements that could prejudice your defense in a wrongful discharge case. For example, delete any reference to the fact that "employees can be terminated only for just cause" (unless you really mean that). Also consider not outlining progressive discipline procedures in the manual since you may be obligated to stick with the rules and follow the steps exactly or be sued for failing to do so. Similarly, references to probationary periods or permanent employment may be unwise because they imply a permanence you may not really mean to imply. Never limit the right to discharge or list specific reasons for discharge.[74] Always add a sentence or paragraph that reserves for the employer the right to make changes to the handbook in the future, and always include a waiver statement in the front of the handbook that asserts the company hires only at will.[75] An acknowledgment form like the one in Figure 10-6 can be useful in underscoring the fact that the handbook is not a contract and that employment-at-will remains in force.[76]

Make sure that no one in a position of authority makes promises you do not intend to keep, such as by saying, "If you do your job here, you can't get fired."

Have clear written rules listing infractions that may require discipline and discharge, and then make sure to adhere to the rules. Generally, employees must be given an opportunity to correct unacceptable behavior, and you should be careful not to single out any one person.

FIGURE 10-6

TJP Inc. Employee Handbook Acknowledgment Form

TJP INC. EMPLOYEE HANDBOOK ACKNOWLEDGMENT FORM

This employee handbook has been given to _____

on (date) _____

by _____ (title) _____

Employee's effective starting date _____

Employee's pay period _____

Employee's hours and workweek are _____

Welcome to TJP Inc. Below are a list of your benefits with their effective date:

Benefit		Effective Date
Hospitalization _____		_____
Life insurance _____		_____
Retirement _____		_____
Vacation _____		_____
Sick leave _____		_____
Holidays _____		_____
Personal days _____		_____
Bereavement _____		_____
Worker's compensation _____		_____
Social Security _____		_____

Your first performance appraisal will be on _____ _____

I understand that my employee handbook is for informational purposes only and that I am to read and refer to the employee handbook for information on employment work rules and company policies. TJP Inc. may modify, revoke, suspend or terminate any and all policies, rules, procedures and benefits at any time without prior notice to company employees. This handbook and its statements do not create a contract between TJP Inc. and its employees. This handbook and its statements do not affect in any way the employment-at-will relationship between TJP Inc.and its employees.

(Employee's signature) _____

(Date) _____

If a rule is broken, get the worker's side of the story in front of witnesses, and preferably get it signed. Then make sure to check out the story, getting both sides of the issue.

Be sure that employees are evaluated at least annually. If an employee is showing evidence of incompetence, give that person a warning and provide a chance to improve. All evaluations should be put in writing and signed by the employee.[77]

Keep careful records of all actions such as employee evaluations, warnings or notices; memos outlining how improvement should be accomplished; and so on. Keep all efforts at counseling or discipline confidential to avoid defamation charges.[78]

Make sure that the company's policy about probationary periods is clear and that employees cannot infer that once they are past the probationary period their jobs are "safe."[79]

Remember that there are a number of public policy issues often used by the courts to protect employees from arbitrary discharge. In the past, in various jurisdictions, these have included whistle-blowing, garnishment for anyone's indebtedness, complaining or testifying about equal pay or wage/hour law violations, and filing a worker's compensation claim.[80]

Before taking any irreversible steps, review the person's personnel file. For example, long-seniority employees may merit more opportunities to correct their actions than newly hired workers.

Finally, consider "buying-out" a wrongful discharge claim with settlement pay. Do not stand in the way of a terminated employee's future employment, since a person with a new job is less likely to bring a lawsuit against the former employer than someone who remains unemployed.[81]

If humanitarianism and wrongful discharge suits aren't enough to encourage you to be fair in dismissing, consider this. A recent study found that managers run double the risk of suffering a heart attack during the week after they fire an employee.[82] Between 1989 and 1994, physicians interviewed 791 working people who had just undergone heart attacks, to find out what might have triggered them. The researchers concluded that the stress associated with firing someone doubled the usual risk of a heart attack for the person doing the firing, during the week following the dismissal.

The Termination Interview

Dismissing an employee is one of the most difficult tasks you can face at work.[83] The dismissed employee, even if warned many times in the past, may still react with disbelief or even violence. Guidelines for the **termination interview** itself are as follows:

1. *Plan the interview carefully.* According to experts at Hay Associates, this includes:
   - Make sure the employee keeps the appointment time.
   - Never inform an employee over the phone.
   - Allow 10 minutes as sufficient time for the interview.
   - Use a neutral site, never your own office.
   - Have employee agreements, the human resource file, and a release announcement (internal and external) prepared in advance.
   - Be available at a time after the interview in case questions or problems arise.
   - Have phone numbers ready for medical or security emergencies.
2. *Get to the point.* Do not beat around the bush by talking about the weather or making other small talk. As soon as the employee enters the meeting room, give the person a moment to get comfortable and then inform him or her of your decision.

termination interview

The interview in which an employee is informed of the fact that he or she has been dismissed.

3. *Describe the situation.* Briefly, in three or four sentences, explain why the person is being let go. For instance, "Production in your area is down 4%, and we are continuing to have quality problems. We have talked about these problems several times in the past 3 months, and the solutions are not being followed through. We have to make a change."[84] Remember to describe the situation, rather than attacking the employee personally by saying things like "Your production is just not up to par." Also emphasize that the decision is final and irrevocable.

4. *Listen.* Continue the interview until the person appears to be talking freely and reasonably calmly about the reasons for his or her termination and the support package (including severance pay).

5. *Review all elements of the severance package.* Describe severance payments, benefits, access to office support people, and the way references will be handled. However, under no conditions should any promises or benefits beyond those already in the support package be implied.

6. *Identify the next step.* The terminated employee may be disoriented and unsure what to do next. Explain where the employee should go next, upon leaving the interview.

outplacement counseling

A systematic process by which a terminated person is trained and counseled in the techniques of self-appraisal and securing a new position.

OUTPLACEMENT COUNSELING[85]   **Outplacement counseling** is a systematic process by which a terminated person is trained and counseled in the techniques of conducting a self-appraisal and securing a new job that is appropriate to his or her needs and talents.[86] As the term is generally used, *outplacement* does not imply that the employer takes responsibility for placing the terminated person in a new job. Instead it is a counseling service whose purpose is to provide the person with advice, instructions, and a sounding board to help formulate career goals and successfully execute a job search. Outplacement counseling thus might more accurately (but more ponderously) be called "career counseling and job search skills for terminated employees." The outplacement counseling is considered part of the terminated employee's support or severance package.

Outplacement counseling is usually conducted by outplacement firms such as Drake Beam Moran, Inc., or Right Associates, Inc. Managers who are let go typically have office space and secretarial services they can use at local offices of such firms, in addition to the counseling services.

EXIT INTERVIEWS   Many employers conduct final exit interviews with employees who are leaving the firm. These are usually conducted by the HR department. They aim at eliciting information about the job or related matters that might give the employer a better insight into what is right—or wrong—about the company. The assumption, of course, is that because the employee is leaving, he or she will be candid.

Based on one survey, the quality of information you can expect from exit interviews is questionable. The researchers found that at the time of separation, 38% of those leaving blamed salary and benefits, and only 4% blamed supervision. Followed up 18 months later, however, 24% blamed supervision and only 12% blamed salary and benefits. Getting to the real problem during the exit interview may thus require some heavy digging.[87]

Layoffs and the Plant Closing Law

Nondisciplinary separations are a fact of life in organizations and can be initiated by either employer or employee. For the employer, reduced sales or profits may require layoffs or downsizings, for instance, while employees may terminate their own employment to retire or to seek better jobs.

plant closing law

The Worker Adjustment and Retraining Notification Act, which requires notifying employees in the event an employer decides to close its facility.

THE PLANT CLOSING LAW Until 1989 there were no federal laws requiring notification of employees when an employer decided to close its facility. However, in that year the Worker Adjustment and Retraining Notification Act (popularly known as the **plant closing law** became effective. The law requires employers of 100 or more employees to give 60 days' notice before closing a facility or starting a layoff *of 50 people or more.* The law does not prevent the employer from closing down, nor does it require saving jobs. The act simply gives employees time to seek other work or retraining by giving them advance notice of the shutdown).

Not all plant closings and layoffs are covered by the law, although many are. Employers are responsible for giving notice to employees who will (or who reasonably may be expected to) experience a covered "employment loss." Employment losses include terminations (other than discharges for cause, voluntary departures, or retirement), layoffs exceeding 6 months, and reductions of more than 50% in employees' work hours during each month of any 6-month period. Generally speaking, workers who are reassigned or transferred to certain employer-sponsored programs or who are given an opportunity to transfer or relocate to another employer location within a reasonable commuting distance need not be notified. While there are exceptions to the law, the penalty for failing to give notice is fairly severe: 1-day's pay and benefits to each employee for each day's notice that should have been given, up to 60 days.

The law is not entirely clear about how the notice to employees must be worded. However, if you write a letter to the individual employees to be laid off, a paragraph toward the end of the letter that might suit the purpose would be as follows:

Please consider this letter to be your official notice, as required by the federal plant closing law, that your current position with the company will end 60 days from today because of a (layoff or closing) that is now projected to take place on (date). After that day your employment with the company will be terminated, and you will no longer be carried on our payroll records or be covered by any company benefit programs. Any questions concerning the plant closing law or this notice will be answered in the HR office.[88]

layoff

A situation in which there is a temporary shortage of work and employees are told there is no work for them but that management intends to recall them when work is again available.

A **layoff**, in which workers are sent home for a time, is a situation in which three conditions are present: (1) there is no work available for the employees, (2) management expects the no-work situation to be temporary and probably short-term, and (3) management intends to recall the employees when work is again available.[89] A layoff is therefore not a termination, which is a permanent severing of the employment relationship. However, some employers use the term *layoff* as a euphemism for discharge or termination.

bumping/layoff procedures

Detailed procedures that determine who will be laid off if no work is available; generally allow employees to use their seniority to remain on the job.

BUMPING/LAYOFF PROCEDURES Employers who encounter frequent business slowdowns and layoffs often have detailed procedures that allow employees to use their seniority to remain on the job. Most such procedures have these features in common:[90]

1. For the most part, seniority is the ultimate determinant of who will work.
2. Seniority can give way to merit or ability, but usually only when none of the senior employees is qualified for a particular job.
3. Seniority is usually based on the date the employee joined the organization, not the date he or she took a particular job.
4. Because seniority is usually companywide, an employee in one job is usually allowed to bump or displace an employee on another job provided the more senior employee is able to do the job in question without further training.

ALTERNATIVES TO LAYOFFS Many employers today recognize the enormous investments they have in recruiting, screening, and training their employees and in winning their commitment and loyalty. As a result, many employers are more hesitant to lay off employees at the first signs of business decline.

voluntary reduction in pay plan

An alternative to layoffs in which all employees agree to reductions in pay to keep everyone working.

voluntary time off

An alternative to layoffs in which some employees agree to take time off to reduce the employer's payroll and avoid the need for a layoff.

rings of defense

An alternative layoff plan in which temporary supplemental employees are hired with the understanding that they may be laid off at any time.

downsizing

Refers to the process of reducing, usually dramatically, the number of people employed by the firm.

There are several alternatives to layoff. With the **voluntary reduction in pay plan,** all employees agree to reductions in pay in order to keep everyone working. Other employers arrange to have all or most of their employees accumulate their vacation time and to concentrate their vacations during slow periods. Temporary help thus does not have to be hired for vacationing employees during peak periods, and employment automatically falls off when business declines. Other employees agree to take **voluntary time off,** which again has the effect of reducing the employer's payroll and avoiding the need for a layoff. Control Data Corporation avoids layoffs with what it calls its **rings of defense** approach. Temporary supplemental employees are hired with the understanding that their work is of a temporary nature and they may be laid off at any time or fired. Then when layoffs come, the first ring of defense is the cadre of supplemental workers.[91]

Adjusting to Downsizings and Mergers

Downsizing—reducing, usually dramatically, the number of people employed by the firm—is being done by more and more employers.[92] Ironically, though, most firms find that their operating earnings don't improve after major staff cuts are made. In one survey, for instance, only 43% of the surveyed downsized firms saw operating earnings improve.[93]

Several things probably contribute to this anomaly. For one thing, many firms that downsize don't actually eliminate all the employees that they claim were let go; they instead retain them either as "consultants," or "temporary workers," or as "redeployees," who are shifted to other jobs with the firm.[94] For another, the remaining employees' morale may decline.

From a practical point of view, steps should be and often are taken to reduce the remaining employees' uncertainty and to address their concerns.[95] A postdownsizing program instituted at Duracell, Inc. illustrates the steps involved. These included a post-downsizing-announcement activities program, including a full staff meeting at the facility; immediate follow-up in which remaining employees were split into groups with senior managers to express their concerns and have their questions answered; and long-term support for the program, for instance by encouraging supervisors to meet with their employees frequently and informally to encourage an open-door atmosphere. Other companies, such as the Diners Club subsidiary of Citigroup, use attitude surveys to help management monitor how the postdownsizing efforts are progressing with the remaining employees.[96]

HANDLING THE MERGER/ACQUISITION   In terms of dismissals and downsizings, mergers or acquisitions are usually one-sided: In many mergers one company essentially acquires the other, and it is often the employees of the latter who find themselves out looking for new jobs.

In such a situation, the employees in the acquired firm will be hypersensitive to mistreatment of their colleagues. It thus behooves you to take care that those let go are treated fairly. Seeing your former colleagues fired is bad enough for morale. Seeing them fired under conditions that look like bullying rubs salt in the wound and poisons the relationship for years to come. As a rule, therefore,[97]

Avoid the appearance of power and domination.

Avoid win/lose behavior.

Remain businesslike and professional in all dealings.

Maintain as positive a feeling about the acquired company as possible.

Remember that the degree to which your organization treats the acquired group with care and dignity will affect the confidence, productivity, and commitment of those remaining.

Regardless of why you're downsizing, the process should be carefully thought out both to avoid unnecessary consequences and to ensure that the process is fair. Steps for implementing a reduction in force include:[98]

Identify objectives and constraints. For example, decide how many positions will be eliminated, which locations will be affected, and what criteria are to be used to identify the employees who will be offered voluntary exit incentives.

Form a downsizing team. This management team should, for example, prepare a communication strategy for explaining the downsizing, establish hiring and promotion levels, produce a downsizing schedule, and supervise the displaced employees' benefit programs.

Address legal layoff selection issues. You'll want to ensure that the downsizing isn't viewed as a mere subterfuge to lay off protected classes of employees. Therefore, review factors such as age, race, and gender before finalizing and communicating any dismissals.

Plan postimplementation actions. As noted above, downsizings can adversely affect the morale of the surviving employees, so that postimplementation activities such as surveys and explanatory meetings can help maintain morale. Similarly, some suggest a hiring freeze of at least 6 months after the layoffs have taken effect.[99]

Address security concerns. As with any large scale layoffs, it may be wise to have security personnel in place in case there's a problem from one or two employees.

Retirement

retirement

The point at which a person gives up one's work, usually between the ages of 60 to 65, but increasingly earlier today due to firms' early retirement incentive plans.

preretirement counseling

Counseling provided to employees who are about to retire, which covers matters such as benefits advice, second careers, and so on.

Retirement for many employees is bittersweet; the employee may be free of the daily requirements of his or her job, but at the same time be slightly adrift as a result of not having a job to go to. About 30% of the employers in one survey therefore said they offered formal **preretirement counseling** aimed at easing the passage of their employees into retirement. The most common preretirement practices were:

Explanation of Social Security benefits (reported by 97% of those with preretirement education programs)

Leisure time counseling (86%)

Financial and investment counseling (84%)

Health counseling (82%)

Psychological counseling (35%)

Counseling for second careers outside the company (31%)

Counseling for second careers inside the company (4%)

Among employers that did not have preretirement education programs, 64% believed that such programs were needed, and most of these said their firms had plans to develop them within 2 or 3 years.

Another important trend is granting part-time employment to employees as an alternative to outright retirement. Several surveys of blue- and white-collar employees showed that about half of all employees over age 55 would like to continue working part-time after they retire.[100]

We invite you to visit the Dessler page on the Prentice Hall Web site at **www.prenhall.com/dessler** for our on-line study guide, Internet exercises, current events, links to related Web sites, and more.

SUMMARY

1. The supervisor plays an important role in the career management process. Important guidelines include: Avoid reality shock, be demanding, provide realistic job previews, conduct career-oriented performance appraisals, and encourage job rotation.

2. In making promotion decisions, you have to decide between seniority and competence, a formal or informal system, and ways to measure competence.

3. More firms today engage in career development activities. Training and educational opportunities are examples. Many firms also institute comprehensive career management/promotion-from-within programs. Such programs can help foster employee commitment.

4. Career-oriented appraisals play a crucial role in managing careers. Here the supervisor and employee link the latter's past performance, career preferences, and developmental needs to develop an appropriate career plan.

5. Career records/job posting systems are also important. Maintaining career-related data on employees and then openly posting all jobs ensure that the career goals and skills of inside candidates are matched openly and fairly with promotional opportunities.

6. Firms give employees vehicles through which to express opinions and concerns. For example, Toyota's hot line provides employees with an anonymous channel through which they can express concerns to top management. Firms such as IBM and FedEx engage in periodic anonymous opinion surveys.

7. A fair and just discipline process is based on three prerequisites: rules and regulations, a system of progressive penalties, and an appeals process. A number of discipline guidelines are important, including that discipline should be in line with the way management usually responds to similar incidents; that management must adequately investigate the matter before administering discipline; and that managers should not rob a subordinate of his or her dignity.

8. The basic aim of discipline without punishment is to gain an employee's acceptance of the rules by reducing the punitive nature of the discipline itself. In particular, an employee is given a paid day off to consider his or her infraction before more punitive disciplinary steps are taken.

9. Managing dismissals is an important part of any supervisor's job. Among the reasons for dismissal are unsatisfactory performance, misconduct, lack of qualifications, changed job requirements, and insubordination. In dismissing one or more employees, however, remember that termination at will as a policy has been weakened by exceptions in many states. Furthermore, great care should be taken to avoid wrongful discharge suits.

10. In the termination interview, plan what you will say, get to the point, describe the situation, listen, review the benefits, and identify the next step.

KEY TERMS

career planning and development 363
reality shock 364
speak up! programs 374
opinion surveys 375
top-down programs 375
discipline 375
dismissal 378
terminate at will 378

insubordination 379
wrongful discharge 380
termination interview 382
outplacement counseling 383
plant closing law 384
layoff 384
bumping/layoff procedures 384

voluntary reduction in pay plan 385
voluntary time off 385
rings of defense 385
downsizing 385
retirement 386
preretirement counseling 386

1. Explain career-related factors to keep in mind when making the employee's first assignments.
2. Describe specific techniques you would use to foster top-down communication in an organization.
3. Describe the similarities and differences between discipline without punishment and a typical discipline procedure.
4. Explain how you would ensure fairness in disciplining, discussing particularly the prerequisites to disciplining, disciplining guidelines, and the discipline without punishment approach.

1. Develop a résumé for yourself, using the guidelines presented in this chapter. (See the Appendix).
2. Write a one-page essay stating, "Where I would like to be career-wise 10 years from today."
3. Working individually or in groups, choose three occupations (such as management consultant, HR manager, or salesperson) and make an assessment of the future demand for this occupation over the next 10 years or so. Does this seem like a good occupation to pursue? Why or why not?
4. Working individually or in groups, choose several occupations, such as programmer, lawyer, and accountant, and identify as many job openings for these occupations on the Internet as you can. Do you think the Internet is a valuable job search source for these occupations? Why or why not?
5. Working individually or in groups, obtain copies of the student handbook for your college and determine to what extent there is a formal career planning process through which students can discover more about their career options. Do you think the process should be an effective one? Based on your contacts with other students, has it been an effective process? Why or why not?
6. Working individually or in groups, determine the nature of the academic discipline process in your college. Do you think it is an effective one? Based on what you read in this chapter would you recommend any modification of the student discipline process?

EXPERIENTIAL EXERCISE

Purpose: The purpose of this exercise is to provide you with some experience in analyzing and handling a disciplinary situation.

Required Understanding: Students should be thoroughly familiar with the following case, titled "Botched Batch." However, *do not read the "Award" or*

"Discussion" sections until after the groups have completed their deliberations.

How to Set Up the Exercise/Instructions: Divide the class into groups of four or five students. The group should take the arbitrator's point of view and assume that they are to analyze the case and make the arbitrator's decision. Review the case again at this point, but please do not read the *"Award"* section.

Each group should answer the following questions:

1. What would your decision be if you were the arbitrator? Why?
2. Do you think the employer handled the disciplinary situation correctly? Why? What would you have done differently?

Botched Batch

Facts: A computer department employee made an entry error that botched an entire run of computer reports. Efforts to rectify the situation produced a second set of improperly run reports. As a result of the series of errors, the employer incurred extra costs of $2,400, plus a weekend of overtime work, by other computer department staffers. Management suspended the employee for 3 days for negligence, and also revoked a promotion for which the employee had previously been approved.

Protesting the discipline, the employee stressed that she had attempted to correct her error in the early stages of the run by notifying the manager of computer operations of her mistake. Maintaining that the resulting string of errors could have been avoided if the manager had followed up on her report and stopped the initial run, the employee argued that she had been treated unfairly because the manager had not been disciplined even though he compounded the problem, whereas she was severely punished. Moreover, citing her "impeccable" work record and management's acknowledgment that she had always been a

"model employee," the employee insisted that the denial of her previously approved promotion was "unconscionable."

(*Please do* not *read beyond this point until after you have completed the experiential exercise.*)

Award: The arbitrator upholds the 3 day suspension, but decides that the promotion should be restored.

Discussion: "There is no question," the arbitrator notes, that the employee's negligent act "set in motion the train of events that resulted in running two complete sets of reports reflecting improper information." Stressing that the employer incurred substantial cost because of the error, the arbitrator cites "unchallenged" testimony that management had commonly issued 3-day suspensions for similar infractions in the past. Thus, the arbitrator decides, the employer acted with just cause in meting out an "evenhanded" punishment for the negligence.

Turning to the denial of the already approved promotion, the arbitrator says that this action should be viewed "in the same light as a demotion for disciplinary reasons." In such cases, the arbitrator notes, management's decision normally is based on a pattern of unsatisfactory behavior, an employee's inability to perform, or similar grounds. Observing that management had never before reversed a promotion as part of a disciplinary action, the arbitrator says that by tacking on the denial of the promotion in this case, the employer substantially varied its disciplinary policy from its past practice. Because this action on management's part was not "evenhanded," the arbitrator rules, the promotion should be restored.

CASE INCIDENT   Job Insecurity at IBM

For more than 50 years IBM was known for its policy of job security. Throughout all those years, it had never laid off any employees, even as the company was going through wrenching changes. For example, in the late

1970s and 1980s, IBM had to close its punch card manufacturing plants and division, but the thousands of employees who worked in those plants were given an opportunity to move to comparable jobs in other IBM divisions.

Unfortunately, IBM's full-employment policy evaporated quickly when its computer industry market share dropped throughout the 1980s; both its sales revenue and profits began to erode. By 1991 it had become apparent that a drastic restructuring was needed. The firm therefore accelerated its downsizing efforts, instituting various early retirement and incentive plans aimed at getting employees to voluntarily leave IBM. Various imaginative schemes were introduced, including spinning off certain operations to groups of employees who then quit IBM while becoming independent consultants, doing tasks very similar to those they used to do while employees of IBM. By 1992, however, at least 40,000 more employees still had to be trimmed, and by 1993 it had become apparent that IBM's cherished full employment policy had to be discarded. For the first time, IBM began laying off employees, and eventually tens of thousands more employees were let go, beginning with about 300 employees of the firm's Armonk, New York, headquarters.

▓ QUESTIONS

1. What do you think accounts for the fact that a company like IBM can have high job security but still lose market share, sales, and profitability? In other words, why do you think job security did not translate into corporate success as well as it might have at IBM?

2. What sorts of steps do you think IBM could have taken in order to continue to avoid layoffs? If you don't think any such steps were feasible, explain why.

3. Given IBM's experience with its full employment policy, what do you think are the implications for other companies thinking of instituting full employment policies of their own?

Case Application

THE MENTOR RELATIONSHIP TURNS UPSIDE DOWN

"I wish I could talk this problem over with Walter," Carol Lee thought. Walter Lemaire had been her mentor for several years at Larchmont Consulting, yet now he was her problem.

Carol thought back to the beginning of her association with Larchmont and with Walter. She had joined the firm as a writer and editor; her job during those early years had been to revise and polish the consultants' business reports. The work brought her into frequent contact with Walter, who was a senior vice president at the time. Carol enjoyed discussing the consultants' work with him, and when she decided to try to join the consulting team she asked for his help. Walter became her mentor as well as her boss and guided her through her successful transition to consultant and eventually partner.

At each promotion along the way to partner, Carol cemented her relationship with her new subordinates and peers by acknowledging the inevitable initial awkwardness and by meeting with each person individually to forge a new working relationship. Her career prospered, and when Walter moved on to run a start-up software publishing venture for Larchmont, Carol was promoted to take his place. However, his new venture faltered, and the partners decided someone else would have to step in. Despite the fact that Carol was much younger than Walter and once had worked for him, she was given the assignment of rescuing the start-up operation.

Carol's discomfort over the assignment only grew as she began to review the history of the new venture. Her rescue mission was going to entail undoing much of what Walter had done, reversing his decisions about everything from product design to marketing and pricing. Carol was so reluctant to second-guess her old mentor and boss that she found herself all but unable to discuss any of her proposed solutions with him directly. She doubted that any of her past experience had prepared her to assume the role of Walter's boss, and in these difficult circumstances her need to turn the operation around would be, she felt, like "pouring salt on his wounds."

QUESTIONS

1. What is Carol's role in Walter's career development now? Should Larchmont have any such role? Why or why not?
2. What advice would you offer Carol for approaching Walter?

3. If Carol has to dismiss Walter, how specifically would you suggest she procede?
4. Assume Carol has heard a rumor that Walter has considered resigning. What should she do about it?

Note: The incident in this case is based on an event at an unidentified firm described in Jennifer Frey, "Pride and Your Promotion," *Working Woman*, October 1996.

NOTES

1. Sherry Sullivan, William Carden, and David Martin, "Careers in the Next Millennium: Directions for Future Research," *Human Resource Management Review*, Vol. 8, no. 2 (1998), p. 165.
2. Douglas Hall, "In Protean Careers of the 21st Century," *Academy of Management Executive*, Vol. 10, no. 4 (1996), p. 8.
3. Kenneth Brousseau, Michael Driver, Kristina Eneroth, and Rikerd Larsson, "Career Pandemonium: Realigning Organizations and Individuals," *Academy of Management Executive*, Vol. 10, no. 4 (1996), pp. 52–66; Brent Allred, Charles Snow, and Raymond Miles, "Characteristics of Managerial Careers in the 21st Century," *Academy of Management Executive*, Vol. 10, no. 4 (1996), pp. 17–27.
4. Sullivan, Carden, and Martin, "Careers in the Next Millenium," p. 165; see also Richard Koonce, "Plan on a Career That Bobs and Weaves," *Training and Development Journal*, Vol. 52, no. 4 (April 1998), pp. 14–16.
5. Ibid., p. 165.
6. Richard Bolles, *What Color is Your Parachute?* (Berkeley, CA: Ten Speed Press, 1976), p. 86.
7. The Guidance Information System, Time Share Corporation, 630 Oakwood Avenue, West Hartford, CT 06110, described in Andrew Dubrin, *Human Relations: A Job-Oriented Approach* (Reston, VA: Reston, 1982), p. 358.
8. Douglas Hall, *Careers in Organizations* (Pacific Palisades, Goodyear Publishing, 1976), p. 154.
9. Robert Jameson, *The Professional Job Changing System* (Verona, NJ: Performance Dimensions, 1975).
10. Richard Payne, *How to Get a Better Job Quicker* (New York: New American Library, 1987).
11. Personal Interview, March 1992.
12. Edward Schein, *Career Dynamics: Matching Individual and Organizational Needs* (Reading, MA: Addison-Wesley, 1978).
13. Richard Reilly, Mary Tenopyr, and Steven Sperling, "The Effects of Job Previews on Job Acceptance and Survival Rates of Telephone Operator Candidates," *Journal of Applied Psychology*, Vol. 64 (1979).
14. J. Sterling Livingston, "Pygmalion in Management," *Harvard Business Review*, Vol. 48 (July–August 1969), pp. 81–89.
15. Joel Ross, *Managing Productivity* (Reston, VA: Reston, 1979).
16. Douglas Hall and Francine Hall, "What's New in Career Management?" *Organizational Dynamics*, Vol. 4 (Summer 1976).
17. H. G. Kaufman, *Obsolescence and Professional Career Development* (New York: AMACOM, 1974).
18. Hall and Hall, "What's New in Career Management?" p. 350.
19. Schein, *Career Dynamics*, p. 19. See also Robin Jacobs and Robert Bolton, "Career Analysis: The Missing Link in Managerial Assessment and Development," *Human Resource Management Journal*, Vol. 3, no. 2 (1994), pp. 55–62.
20. Schein, op cit. p. 19.
21. Fred Otte and Peggy Hutcheson, *"Helping Employees Manage Careers,"* (Upper Saddle River, NJ: Prentice Hall, 1992), p. 143.
22. Timothy Newby and Ashlyn Heide, "The Value of Mentoring," *Performance Management Quarterly*, Vol. 5, no. 4 (1992), pp. 2–15; see also John Arnold and Karen Johnson, "Mentoring in Earl Career," *Human Resource Management*, Vol. 7, no. 4 (1997), pp. 61–70.
23. Belle Rose Ragins, "Diversified Mentoring Relationships in Organizations: A Power Perspective," *Academy of Management Review*, Vol. 22, no. 2 (1997), p. 513.
24. See for example, Daniel Quinn Mills, *Labor-Management Relations* (New York: McGraw-Hill, 1986), pp. 387–396.
25. Charles Halaby, "Bureaucratic Promotion Criteria," *Administrative Science Quarterly*, Vol. 23 (September 1978), pp. 466–484.
26. See, for example, Gary Powell and D. Anthony Butterfield, "Effect of Race on Promotions to Top Management in a Federal Department," *Academy of Management Journal*, Vol. 40, no. 1 (1997), pp. 112–128.
27. Ibid., p. 124.
28. Joseph Famularo, *Handbook of Modern Personnel Administration* (New York; McGraw-Hill, 1972).
29. Ibid.
30. Ibid., p. 17.

31. R. Tucker, M. Moravee, and K. Ideus, "Designing a Dual Career-Track System," *Training & Development*, Vol. 6 (1992), pp. 55–58; Schmidt, "The New Focus for Career Development," p. 26.

32. Susan Schmidt, "The New Focus for Career Development," *Journal of Employment Counseling*, Vol. 31, (March 1994), pp. 25–26.

33. Robert Marrujo and Brian Kleiner, "Why Women Fail to Get to the Top," *Equal Opportunities International*, Vol. 11, no. 4 (1992), pp. 1–5.

34. Unless otherwise noted, this is based on Ibid.

35. Ibid.

36. P. Watts, "Lending a Helping Hand," *Executive Female*, Vol. 12 (1989), pp. 38–40; quoted in Ibid., p. 1.

37. These are based on Marrujo and Kleiner, "Why Women Fail to Get to the Top," p. 3; and Ann Morrison, P. Whiate, and Ellen Van Velsor, *Breaking the Glass Ceiling* (Reading, MA: Addison-Wesley, 1987).

38. See also Ronald Burke and Carol McKeen, "Supporting the Career Aspirations of Managerial and Professional Women," *Business and the Contemporary World* (Summer 1993), pp. 69–80.

39. See, for example, Richard Chanick, "Career Growth for Baby Boomers," *Personnel Journal*, Vol. 71, no. 1 (January 1992), pp. 40–46.

40. Ibid.

41. Commerce Clearing House, "Top Executives are Growing Reluctant to Relocate," *Ideas and Trends*, December 10, 1982, p. 218.

42. Personal Interview, March 1992.

43. Personal Interview, March 1992.

44. Goldman Sachs, "Internal Placement Center: Guidelines for Managers."

45. Ibid., p. 1.

46. Ibid.

47. W. Chan Kim and Rene Maugorgne, "Fair Process: Managing in the Knowledge Economy," *Harvard Business Review* (July/August 1997), pp. 65–66.

48. Daniel Skarlicki and Gary Latham, "Increasing Citizenship Behavior Within a Labor Union: A Test of Organizational Justice Theory," *Journal of Applied Psychology*, Vol. 81, no. 2 (1996) pp. 161–169.

49. M. Audrey Korsgaard, Loriann Roberson, and R. Douglas Rymph, "What Motivates Fairness? The Role of Subordinate Assertive Behavior on Managers' Interactional Fairness," *Journal of Applied Psychology*, Vol. 83, no. 5 (1998), pp. 731–744.

50. Ibid., p. 735.

51. Kim and Mauborgne, "Fair Process: Managing in the Knowledge Economy," pp. 65–75.

52. Toyota Motor Manufacturing, USA, Inc., *Team Member Handbook*, February 1988, pp. 52–53.

53. Lester Bittel, *What Every Supervisor Should Know* (New York: McGraw-Hill, 1974), p. 308; see also Paul Falcone, "The Fundamentals of Progressive Discipline," *HRMagazine* (February 1997), pp. 90–92.

54. Based on George Odiorne, *How Managers Make Things Happen* (Upper Saddle River, NJ: Prentice Hall, 1961), pp. 132–143; see also Bittel, *What Every Manager Should Know*, pp. 285–298. See also Cynthia Fukami and David Hopkins, "The Role of Situational Factors in Disciplinary Judgments," *Journal of Organizational Behavior*, Vol. 14, no. 7 (December 1993), pp. 665–676.

55. Nonpunitive discipline discussions based on David Campbell et al., "Discipline Without Punishment—At Last," *Harvard Business Review* (July/August 1995), pp. 162–178; Gene Milbourne, Jr., "The Case Against Employee Punishment," *Management Solutions* (November 1986), pp. 40–45; Mark Sherman and Al Lucia, "Positive Discipline and Labor Arbitration," *Arbitration Journal* Vol. 47, no. 2 (June 1992), pp. 56–58; Michael Moore, Victor Nichol, and Patrick McHugh, "No-Fault Programs: A Way to Cut Absenteeism," *Employment Relations Today* (Winter 1992/1993), pp. 425–432; and "'Positive Discipline' Replaces Punishment," *BNA Bulletin to Management*, April 27, 1995, p. 136.

56. "Electronic Monitoring and Surveillance," *BNA Bulletin to Management*, June 9, 1997, pp. 196–197.

57. "Telephone and Electronic Monitoring: A Special Report on the Issues and the Law," *BNA Bulletin to Management*, April 3, 1997, p. 1.

58. Samuel Greengard, "Privacy: Entitlement or Illusion?" *Personnel Journal* (May 1996), p. 74.

59. Eryn Brown, "The Myth of e-mail Privacy," *Fortune*, February 3, 1997, p. 66.

60. "Surveillance of Employees," *BNA Bulletin to Management*, April 25, 1996, p. 136.

61. "Telephone and Electronic Monitoring: A Special Report on the Issues and the Law," p. 2.

62. "Curbing the Risks of E-mail Use," *BNA Bulletin to Management*, April 10, 1997, p. 120.

63. *Vega-Rodriguez v. Puerto Rico Telephone Company* CA1,#.962061,4/8/97, discussed in "Video Surveillance Withstands Privacy Challenge," *BNA Bulletin to Management*, April 17, 1997, p. 121.

64. "Secret Videotaping Leads to $200,000 Settlement," *BNA Bulletin to Management*, January 22, 1998, p. 17.

65. Joseph Famularo, *Handbook of Modern Personnel Administration* (New York: McGraw-Hill, 1982), pp. 65.3–65.5.

66. Ibid., p. 65.3.

67. Ibid., p. 65.4.

68. Ibid., pp. 65.4–65.5.

69. Brian Klaas and Gregory Dell'omo, "Managerial Use of Dismissal: Organizational-Level Determinants," *Personnel Psychology*, Vol. 50 (1997), pp. 927–953.

70. Ibid., p. 946.

71. Dina Mansour-Cole and Susanne Scott, "Hearing It Through the Grapevine: The Influence of Source, Leader-Relations, and Legitimacy on Survivors' Fairness Perceptions," *Personnel Psychology*, Vol. 51 (1998), pp. 25–54.

72. Ibid., p. 47.

73. "Fairness to Employees Can Stave Off Litigation," *BNA Bulletin to Management*, November 27, 1997, p. 377.

74. Bureau of National Affairs, *The Employment-at-Will Issue* (Washington, DC: BNA, 1982). See also Emily Joiner, "Erosion of the Employment at Will Doctrine," *Personnel*, Vol. 61, no. 5 (September–October 1984), pp. 12–18; Harvey Steinberg, "Where Law and Personnel Policies Collide: The At Will Employment Crossroad," *Personnel*, Vol. 62, no. 6 (June 1985), pp. 37–43.

75. See Teresa Brady, "Employee Handbooks: Contracts or Empty Promises?" *Management Review* (June 1993), pp. 33–35.

76. Ibid., p. 35.

77. Note, however, that under recent court rulings at least one U.S. Court of Appeals (for the Seventh Circuit) has held that employee handbooks distributed to long-term employees before employers began amending their handbooks to contain "no contract" and "at-will employment" disclaimers may still be viewed by the court as contracts with these employees. The case was *Robinson v. Ada S. McKinley Community Services, Inc.*, 19F.3d 359 (7th Cir. 1994); see Kenneth Jenero, "Employers Beware: You May Be Bound by the Terms of Your Old Employee Handbooks," *Employee Relations Law Journal*, Vol. 20, no. 2 (Autumn 1994), pp. 299–312.

78. Robert Paul and James Townsend, "Wrongful Termination: Balancing Employer and Employee Rights—A Summary with Recommendations," *Employee Responsibilities and Rights Journal*, Vol. 6, no. 1 (1993), pp. 69–82. Wrongful termination is particularly a problem when the employee is a "whistle-blower." See for example Rosalia Costa-Clarke, "The Cost Implications of Terminating Whistle-Blowers," *Employment Relations today*, Vol. 21, no. 4 (Winter 1994), pp. 447–454.

79. Ibid., p. 81.

80. Ibid.

81. Ibid., p. 74.

82. "One More Heart Risk: Firing Employees," *The Miami Herald*, March 20, 1998, pp. C1, C7.

83. Based on James Coil, III, and Charles Rise, "Three Steps to Creating Effective Employee Releases," *Employment Relations Today* (Spring 1994), pp. 91–94.

84. William J. Morin and Lyle York, *Outplacement Techniques* (New York: AMACOM, 1982), pp. 101–131; F. Leigh Branham, "How to Evaluate Executive Outplacement Services," *Personnel Journal*, Vol. 62 (April 1983), pp. 323–326; and Sylvia Milne, "The Terminational Interview," *Canadian Manager* (Spring 1994), pp. 15–16.

85. Morin and York, *Outplacement Techniques*, p. 117. See also Sonny Weide, "When You Terminate an Employee," *Employment Relations Today* (August 1994), pp. 287–293.

86. Commerce Clearing House, *Ideas and Trends in Personnel*, July 9, 1982, pp. 132–146.

87. Joseph Zarandona and Michael Camuso, "A Study of Exit Interviews: Does the Last Word Count?" *Personnel*, Vol. 62, no. 3 (March 1981), pp. 47–48.

88. Commerce Clearing House, *Ideas and Trends*, August 9, 1988, p. 133; see also Bureau of National Affairs, "Plant Closing Notification Rules: A Compliance Guide," *Bulletin to Management*, May 18, 1989. See also Nancy Ryan, "Complying with the Worker Adjustment and Retraining Notification Act (WARNACT)," *Employee Relations Law Journal*, Vol. 18, no. 1 (Summer 1993), pp. 169–176.

89. See, for example, "Mass Layoffs, Third Quarter, 1996," *BNA Bulletin to Management*, April 17, 1997, pp. 124–125.

90. Commerce Clearing House, *Personnel Practices/Communications* (Chicago: CCH, 1992), p. 1402.

91. Ibid., p. 1410.

92. See, for example, "Mass Layoffs, Third Quarter, 1996," *BNA Bulletin to Management*, April 17, 1997, pp. 124–125.

93. Ibid.

94. See, for example, "Downsizing: Working Through the Pain," *BNA Bulletin to Management*, June 6, 1996, p. 184; and Jennifer Laabs, "Create Job Orders, Not Pink Slips," *Personnel Journal*, June 1996, pp. 97–99.

95. See, for example, "Cushioning the Blow of Layoffs," *BNA Bulletin to Management*, July 3, 1997, p. 216; and "Levi Strauss Cushions Blow of Plant Closings," *BNA Bulletin to Management*, November 20, 1997, p. 370.

96. Les Feldman, "Duracell's First Aid for Downsizing Survivors," *Personnel Journal*, August 1987, p. 94; James Emshoff, "How to Increase Employee Loyalty While You Downsize," *Business Horizons* (March/April 1994), pp. 49–57. See also Shari Caudron, "Teach Downsizing Survivors How to Thrive," *Personnel Journal* (January 1996), pp. 38–48.

97. James Emshoff, "How To Increase Employee Loyalty While You Downsize." See also Robert Ford and Pamela Perrewé, "After the Layoff: Closing the Barn Door Before All the Horses Are Gone," *Business Horizons* (July–August 1993), pp. 34–40.

98. These are suggested by attorney Ethan Lipsig and discussed in "The Lowdown on Downsizing," *BNA Bulletin to Management*, January 9, 1997, p. 16.

99. See also "Firms Need Layoff Strategies, Not Hasty Evacuation Plans," *BNA Bulletin to Management*, December 3, 1998, p. 383.

100. "Preretirement Education Programs," *Personnel*, Vol. 59 (May/June 1982), p. 47. For a discussion of why it is important for retiring employees to promote aspects of their lives aside from their careers, see Daniel Halloran, "The Retirement Identity Crisis—and How to Beat It," *Personnel Journal*, Vol. 64 (May 1985), pp. 38–40. For an example of a program aimed at training preretirees to prepare for the financial aspects of their retirement, see, for example, Silvia Odenwald, "Pre-Retirement Training Gathers Steam," *Training & Development Journal*, Vol 40, no. 2 (February 1986), pp. 62–63; "Pay Policies," *BNA Bulletin to Management*, March 29, 1990, p. 103.

VIDEO CASE

PART III
APPRAISING PERFORMANCE

BECAUSE PERFORMANCE APPRAISALS ARE USUALLY CLOSELY TIED TO SALARY INCREASES AND CAREER ADVANCEMENT, THEY LOOM LARGE FOR MOST EMPLOYEES. APPRAISAL INTERVIEWS ARE OFTEN DIFFICULT FOR MANAGERS, TOO. WHILE REWARDING GOOD WORK AND MOTIVATING EMPLOYEES IS EASY AND ENJOYABLE, HELPING SOMEONE FACE UP TO POOR PERFORMANCE CAN BE A PAINFUL EXPERIENCE, EVEN IF THE INTENT IS TO FIND WAYS TO IMPROVE JOB SKILLS AND HELP BOTH THE FIRM AND THE EMPLOYEE IN THE LONG RUN. WHEN AN APPRAISAL INTERVIEW BECOMES CONFRONTATIONAL, NOT ONLY DO BOTH PARTIES SUFFER EMOTIONALLY, BUT AN OPPORTUNITY FOR COMMUNICATING WAYS TO IMPROVE JOB PERFORMANCE IS LOST.

For these reasons, as Chapter 10 explains, managers should have clear and objective standards that are applied uniformly across the organization. Of course, where more than one manager has input to an employee appraisal, such as is the case at Quicktakes, all those involved should share a clear understanding of what the standards are, what the criteria mean, and how these are to be applied. For all employees, whether they are performing well or poorly, the manager should keep careful written records of how their work meets, exceeds, or fails these standards. Further, the manager should be in frequent informal contact with each employee about his or her performance throughout the year, not just at evaluation time. It is sometimes said that the best appraisal systems are those that yield no surprises.

In Part 3 we see how Tom Bailey's appraisal is finalized by Hal Boylston and Janet Mason, post-production supervisor and Tom's immediate superior, after being drafted by a management committee that also makes salary recommendations. (You may recall one member of the committee, Quicktakes' co-owner and director of sales, Karen Jarvis.) Tom is a problem employee. His performance is erratic and his commitment to the job is in question. He is often late and his attitude is poor. Janet is clearly unhappy with him, and she is willing to let him know by giving him a poor evaluation.

Observe the process by which Hal and Janet come to a decision about Tom, and note whether there are any flaws in it. Do you think the process yields similar reactions from good or outstanding performers at Quicktakes as it does for Tom?

Janet bears the responsibility for conveying the details of his appraisal to Tom. As you view the second part of the video, you'll undoubtedly spot communication mistakes made by both parties. Perhaps these are inevitable, given Tom's negative feelings about his job and Janet's impatience with his poor attitude. Watch, however, for any point at which the conversation could have been turned around. Was there any possibility for a different outcome?

QUESTIONS

1. Janet and Hal both feel that the members of the salary review committee are less familiar with certain job requirements and the performance of individual employees than they themselves are. Is there any advantage in having such a committee? If so, how can Hal and Janet make better use of it? How can they address the potential flaws in Quicktakes' evaluation system?

2. Is Janet making any mistakes in forming her evaluation of Tom? What are they, and what can she do to prevent them?

3. Does Janet bear any responsibility for Tom's poor performance? If so, why?

4. Tom apparently sees money as a motivator, while Janet uses it as an after-the-fact reward. How does this difference in viewpoint add to the difficulty of determining Tom's raise?

5. What did Janet and Tom each do to contribute to the hostile nature of the appraisal meeting? What, specifically, could Janet have done to improve the tone of the meeting and its outcome?

ESTABLISHING PAY PLANS

When he became CEO of IBM, Louis Gerstner, Jr., knew he had to spark the firm out of its lethargy. For years employees worked in a sort of cocoon, insulated from the market, paid not on performance but primarily on seniority. One of Gerstner's first steps was to order a dramatic change in IBM's compensation plan, to emphasize performance and thereby stress the firm's new strategy of competing aggressively. ▲

Behavioral Objectives

When you finish studying this chapter, you should be able to:

▲ *Discuss* four basic factors determining pay rates.
▲ *Explain* in detail each of the five basic steps in establishing pay rates.
▲ *Present* the basic process of job evaluation.
▲ *Conduct* a salary survey.

Chapter Outline

▲ Basic Aspects of Compensation
▲ Basic Factors in Determining Pay Rates
▲ Establishing Pay Rates
▲ Current Trends in Compensation
▲ Pricing Managerial and Professional Jobs
▲ Current Issues in Compensation Management

BASIC ASPECTS OF COMPENSATION

employee compensation
All forms of pay or rewards going to employees and arising from their employment.

Compensation at Work

Employee compensation refers to all forms of pay or rewards going to employees and arising from their employment,[1] and it has two main components. There are *direct financial payments* in the form of wages, salaries, incentives, commissions, and bonuses, and there are *indirect payments* in the form of financial benefits like employer-paid insurance and vacations.

In turn, there are essentially two ways to make direct financial payments to employees: on increments of time and on performance. Most employees are still paid mostly based on the time they put in on the job. For example, blue-collar workers are usually paid hourly or daily *wages*; this is sometimes called *day work*. Other employees—especially managerial, professional, and often secretarial and clerical—are *salaried*. They are compensated on the basis of a longer period of time (like a week, month, or year), rather than hourly or daily.

The second option is to pay for performance. *Piecework* is an example; it ties compensation directly to the amount of production (or number of "pieces") the worker produces, and is popular as an incentive pay plan. For instance, a worker's hourly wage is divided by the standard number of units he or she is expected to produce in one hour. Then for each unit produced over and above this standard, the worker is paid an incentive. Salespeople's commissions are another example of compensation tied to production (in this case, sales).

In this chapter we explain how to formulate plans for paying employees a fixed wage or salary; succeeding chapters cover financial incentives and bonuses and employee benefits.

Psychologists know that people have many needs, only some of which can be satisfied directly with money. Other needs—for achievement, affiliation, security, or self-actualization, for instance—also motivate behavior, but can only be satisfied indirectly (if at all) by money. Yet even with all our modern motivation techniques (like job enrichment), there's no doubt that money is still the most important motivator. As two researchers put it:

> *Pay in one form or another is certainly one of the mainsprings of motivation in our society. . . . The most evangelical human relationist insists it is important, while protesting that other things are too (and are, perhaps, in his view, nobler). It would be unnecessary to belabor the point if it were not for a tendency for money drives to slip out of focus in a miasma of other values and other practices. As it is, it must be repeated: Pay is the most important single motivator used in our organized society.*[2]

BASIC FACTORS IN DETERMINING PAY RATES

Four basic factors influence the design of any pay plan: legal, union, policy, and equity factors.

Legal Considerations in Compensation

First, various laws stipulate what employers can or must pay in terms of minimum wages, overtime rates, and benefits. These laws include:[3]

Davis-Bacon Act
A law passed in 1931 that sets wage rates for laborers employed by contractors working for the federal government.

1931 DAVIS-BACON ACT The **Davis-Bacon Act** provides for the Secretary of Labor to set wage rates for laborers and mechanics employed by contractors working for the federal government. Amendments to the act provide for employee benefits and require contractors or subcontractors to make necessary payment for these benefits.

Walsh-Healey Public Contract Act

A law enacted in 1936 that requires minimum-wage and working conditions for employees working on any government contract amounting to more than $10,000.

Fair Labor Standards Act

Congress passed this act in 1938 to provide for minimum wages, maximum hours, overtime pay, and child labor protection. The law has been amended many times and covers most employees.

1936 WALSH-HEALEY PUBLIC CONTRACT ACT   The **Walsh-Healey Public Contract** Act sets basic labor standards for employees working on any government contract that amounts to more than $10,000. The law contains minimum wage, maximum hour, and safety and health provisions. Today it requires that time and a half be paid for work over 40 hours a week.

1938 FAIR LABOR STANDARDS ACT   The **Fair Labor Standards Act,** originally passed in 1938 and since amended many times, contains minimum wage, maximum hours, overtime pay, equal pay, record-keeping, and child labor provisions covering the majority of U.S. workers—virtually all those engaged in the production and/or sale of goods for interstate and foreign commerce. In addition, agricultural workers and those employed by certain larger retail and service companies are included.

One important provision governs overtime pay. It states that overtime must be paid at a rate of at least one and a half times normal pay for any hours worked over 40 in a workweek. Thus, if a worker covered by the act works 44 hours in one week, he or she must be paid for 4 of those hours at a rate equal to one and a half times the hourly or weekly base rate the person would have earned for 40 hours. For example, if the person earns $8 an hour (or $320 for a 40-hour week), he or she would be paid at the rate of $12 per hour (8 times 1.5) for each of the 4 overtime hours worked, or a total of $48 extra. If the employee instead receives time off for the overtime hours, the number of hours granted off must also be computed at the one and a half time rate. For example, a person working 4 hours overtime would be granted 6 hours off in lieu of overtime pay.

The act also sets a minimum wage. This wage not only sets a floor or base wage for employees covered by the act; it also serves as an index that usually leads to increased wages for practically all workers whenever the minimum wage is raised. (The minimum wage in 1999 was $5.15 for the majority of those covered by the act.) The act also contains child labor provisions. These prohibit employing minors between 16 and 18 years of age in hazardous occupations such as mining and carefully restricts employment of those under 16.

Certain categories of employees are exempt from the act or certain provisions of the act, and particularly from the act's overtime provisions. An employee's exemption depends on the responsibilities, duties, and salary of the job. However, bona fide executive, administrative, and professional employees (like architects) are generally exempt from the minimum wage and overtime requirements of the act.[4]

Violating provisions of this act can be problematical. For example, several years ago a federal judge ordered the owners of a Colorado beef processing plant to pay nearly $2 million in back wages to 5,071 employees because the firm violated the Fair Labor Standards Act by not paying those employees time and a half their regular rate of pay for hours worked in excess of 40 per week and for not keeping required records.[5] And trying to evade the letter of the law by claiming that the employees are not employees but "independent contractors" who are more like consultants than employees is similarly no solution, as we'll see.[6]

Equal Pay Act of 1963

An amendment to the Fair Labor Standards Act designed to require equal pay for women doing the same work as men.

1963 EQUAL PAY ACT   The **Equal Pay Act,** an amendment to the Fair Labor Standards Act, states that employees of one sex may not be paid wages at a rate lower than that paid to employees of the opposite sex for doing roughly equivalent work. Specifically, if the work requires equal skills, effort, and responsibility and is performed under similar working conditions, employees of both sexes must receive equal pay unless the differences in pay are based on a seniority system, a merit system, the quantity or quality of production, or "any factor other than sex." The act thus assumes that differences in pay may exist for men and women performing essentially the same jobs if those differences are based on such considerations as the quality or quantity of the person's work.

Yet even today the average woman who works can still expect to earn only about 72 cents for each $1 earned by the average man who is working in the same occupation.[7] While that's up from the approximately 60 cents for each dollar earned by a man that prevailed throughout much of the post-World War II period, such a gap is still unacceptable.[8] The slight narrowing of the gap probably reflects several things, including changing values as well as convergence in men and women's schooling and work experience and declining wages in blue-collar (traditionally "men's") work.[9]

Civil Rights Act

This law makes it illegal to discriminate in employment because of race, color, religion, sex, or national origin.

1964 CIVIL RIGHTS ACT   Title VII of the **Civil Rights Act** is known as the Equal Employment Opportunity Act of 1964. It established the Equal Opportunity Employment Commission (EEOC). Title VII makes it an unlawful employment practice for an employer to discriminate against any individual with respect to hiring, compensation, terms, conditions, or privileges of employment because of race, color, religion, sex, or national origin.

Employee Retirement Income Security Act (ERISA)

The law that provides government protection of pensions for all employees with company pension plans. It also regulates vesting rights (employees who leave before retirement may claim compensation from the pension plan).

1974 EMPLOYEE RETIREMENT INCOME SECURITY ACT (ERISA)   The **Employee Retirement Income Security Act (ERISA)** in effect renegotiated every pension contract in the country. It provides for the creation of government-run employer-financed corporations to protect employees against the failure of their employer's pension plan. In addition, it set regulations regarding vesting rights. (Vesting refers to the equity or ownership the employees build up in their pension plan should their employment be terminated before retirement.) It also covers portability rights (the transfer of an employee's vested rights from one organization to another) and contains fiduciary standards to prevent dishonesty in the funding of pension plans.

THE TAX REFORM ACT OF 1986   The Tax Reform Act of 1986 represented the most extensive overhaul of the tax code in over 40 years.[10] It affected employee compensation in two ways. First, it reduced the number of individual tax rates to just three brackets—15%, 28%, and (today) a third bracket of 31%. Second, the act increased benefits coverage for rank-and-file employees, while reducing tax-favored benefits that can be provided to highly paid employees.

OTHER LEGISLATION AFFECTING COMPENSATION   Various other discrimination laws have an important influence on compensation decisions. For example, the *Age Discrimination in Employment Act* prohibits age discrimination against employees who are 40 years of age and older in all aspects of employment, including compensation.[11] The *Americans with Disabilities Act* similarly prohibits discrimination against qualified persons with disabilities in all aspects of employment, including compensation. The *Family and Medical Leave Act* aims to entitle eligible employees, both men and women, to take up to 12 weeks of unpaid, job-protected leave for the birth of a child or for the care of a child, spouse, or parent. And employers that are federal government contractors or subcontractors are required by various executive orders not to discriminate and to take affirmative action in various areas of employment, including compensation.

Each of the 50 states has its own *workers' compensation laws,* which today cover over 85 million workers. Among other things, the aim of these laws is to provide a prompt, sure, and reasonable income to victims of work-related accidents. *The Social Security Act of 1935* has been amended several times. It is aimed at protecting U.S. workers from total economic destitution in the event of termination of employment beyond their control. Employers and employees contribute equally to the benefits provided by this act. This act also provided for unemployment compensation—jobless benefits—for workers unemployed through no fault of their own for up to 26 weeks. (Social Security payments—payments to those who are disabled or retired, for instance—are discussed in Chapter 12.) The *federal wage garnishment law* limits the amount of an employee's earnings that can be garnished in any one week and protects the worker from discharge due to garnishment.

Union Influences on Compensation Decisions

Unions and labor relations laws also influence how pay plans are designed. The National Labor Relations Act of 1935 (or Wagner Act) and associated legislation and court decisions legitimized the labor movement. It gave unions legal protection and granted employees the right to organize, to bargain collectively, and to engage in concerted activities for the purpose of collective bargaining or other mutual aid or protection. Historically, the wage rate has been the main issue in collective bargaining. However, other issues including time off with pay, income security (for those in industries with periodic layoffs), cost-of-living adjustment, and various benefits like health care are also important.[12]

The National Labor Relations Board (NLRB) is the group created by the National Labor Relations Act to oversee employer practices and to ensure that employees receive their rights. It has made a series of rulings that underscores the need to involve union officials in developing the compensation package. For example, the employee's union must be given a written explanation of an employer's "wage curves"—the graph that relates job to pay rate. The union is also entitled to know the salary of each employee it is representing.[13]

Compensation Policies

An employer's compensation policies also influence the wages and benefits it pays, since these policies provide important compensation guidelines. Such policies are usually written by the HR or compensation manager in conjunction with top management.[14]

One consideration is whether to be a leader or a follower regarding pay. For example, a hospital might have a policy of starting nurses at a wage of 20% above the prevailing market wage.

The assumption that paying low wage rates makes a firm more competitive may be a "dangerous myth."[15] It's a firm's overall labor costs that determine how competitive it will be, and such costs are driven not just by pay rates but by productivity as well. As one expert points out, "managers should remember that the issue is not just what you pay people, but also what they produce."

Other important policies include how to award salary increases and promotions, overtime pay policy, and policies regarding probationary pay and leaves for military service, jury duty, and holidays. From a practical point of view, geography plays a role in compensation policies, too. For example, a job that paid $50,000 annually in Seattle, San Diego, or Houston would pay about $57,000 in New York City and almost $60,000 in San Jose, California, because of geography-based pay differentials.[16]

Equity and Its Impact on Pay Rates

Finally, the need for equity is a critical factor in determining pay rates, specifically external equity and internal equity. Externally, pay must compare favorably with rates in other organizations, or an employer will find it hard to attract and retain qualified employees. Pay rates must also be equitable internally; each employee should view his or her pay as equitable given other pay rates in the organization. Some firms administer surveys to learn employees' perceptions and feelings about their compensation system. Questions typically addressed include "How satisfied are you with your pay?" "What criteria were used for your recent pay increase?" and "What factors do you believe are used when your pay is determined?"[17]

When employees become aware of inequities in the pay system, disappointment and often conflict can result. Some firms maintain strict secrecy over pay matters for this reason.

In practice, the process of establishing pay rates while ensuring external and internal equity takes five steps:

1. Conduct a *salary survey* of what other employers are paying for comparable jobs (to help ensure *external equity*).
2. Determine the worth of each job in your organization through *job evaluation* (to ensure *internal equity*).
3. Group similar jobs into *pay grades*.
4. Price each pay grade by using *wage curves*.
5. Fine-tune pay rates.

Each of these steps is explained in the next section.

ESTABLISHING PAY RATES

Step 1. Conduct the Salary Survey

INTRODUCTION   Compensation or **salary surveys** play a central role in pricing jobs. Virtually every employer therefore conducts at least an informal survey.[18]

Employers use salary surveys in three ways. First, survey data are used to price **benchmark jobs** that anchor the employer's pay scale and around which its other jobs are slotted, based on their relative worth to the firm. (*Job evaluation*, explained next, is the technique used to determine the relative worth of each job.) Second, 20% or more of an employer's positions are usually priced directly in the marketplace (rather than relative to the firm's benchmark jobs), based on a formal or informal survey of what comparable firms are paying for comparable jobs. Finally, surveys also collect data on *benefits* like in-

salary survey

A survey aimed at determining prevailing wage rates. A good salary survey provides specific wage rates for specific jobs. Formal written questionnaire surveys are the most comprehensive, but telephone surveys and newspaper ads are also sources of information.

benchmark job

A job that is used to anchor the employer's pay scale and around which other jobs are arranged in order of relative worth.

surance, sick leave, and vacation time to provide a basis for decisions regarding employee benefits.

Salary surveys can be formal or informal.[19] Informal telephone surveys are good for quickly checking on a relatively small number of easily identified and quickly recognized jobs, such as when a bank's HR director wants to confirm the salary at which to advertise a newly open cashier's job. Such informal techniques are also good for checking discrepancies, such as when the HR director wants to find out if some area banks are really paying tellers on some sort of incentive plan.

Perhaps 20% of large employers use their own formal questionnaires to collect compensation information from other employers. One page from such a survey is presented in Figure 11-1. This is part of a questionnaire that inquires about things like number of employees, overtime policies, starting salaries, and paid vacations. For a survey to be useful, it must be specific; most respondents in one study claimed the survey's job categories were too broad or imprecise, for instance.[20]

COMMERCIAL, PROFESSIONAL, AND GOVERNMENT SALARY SURVEYS   Many employers also rely on surveys published by various consulting firms, professional associations, or government agencies. For example, the Bureau of Labor Statistics (BLS) annually conducts three types of surveys: (1) area wage surveys; (2) industry wage surveys; and (3) professional, administrative, technical, and clerical (PATC) surveys, currently (through the year 2000) being conbined into a National Compensation Survey.

The BLS annually performs about 200 area wage surveys. These provide pay data for a variety of clerical and manual occupations. An employer could use this information to help price jobs ranging from secretary to messenger to office clerk. Area wage surveys also provide data on weekly work schedules, paid holidays and vacation practices, and health insurance pension plans, as well as on shift operations and differentials.

Industry wage surveys provide data similar to that in the area wage surveys, but by industry rather than geographic area. They thus provide national pay data for workers in selected jobs for industries like building, trucking, and printing.

PATC surveys collect pay data on 80 occupational levels in the fields of accounting, legal services, personnel management, engineering, chemistry, buying, clerical supervisory, drafting, and clerical. They provide information about straight-time earnings as well as production bonuses, commissions, and cost-of-living increases.

Private consulting and/or executive recruiting companies like Hay Associates, Heidrick and Struggles, and Hewitt Associates annually publish data covering the compensation of top and middle management and members of boards of directors. Professional organizations like the Society for Human Resource Management and the Financial Executives Institute publish surveys of compensation practices among members of their associations. Watson Wyatt Data Services of Rochelle Park, New Jersey, publishes various annual compensation surveys. For example, their top management compensation surveys cover dozens of top positions including chief executive officer, top real estate executive, top financial executive, top sales executive, and top claims executive, all categorized by function and industry. They also offer middle management compensation surveys, supervisory management compensation surveys, sales and marketing personnel surveys, professional and scientific personnel surveys, and surveys of technician and skilled trades, and office personnel, among others. The surveys generally cost about $500 to $700 each, but can be well worth the expense if they help you avoid the dual shoals of (1) paying too much, or (2) suffering turnover as a result of not paying competitively.[21]

USING THE INTERNET TO DO COMPENSATION SURVEYS   A rapidly expanding array of Internet-based options makes it fairly easy for anyone today (especially smaller firms) to access published compensation survey information.

FIGURE 11-1

Compensation Survey

Source: David Belcher and Thomas Atchison, *Compensation Administration* (Upper Saddle River, NJ: Prentice Hall, 1987), pp. 112–113.

Name of organization participating in the survey: _____
Address: _____   Industry: _____
Code No: _____   Date this form was completed: _____
Data furnished by: Name _____   Title _____

1. Briefly describe major products (or services) of your reporting unit: _____
_____
_____
_____
_____

2. Employment:
   Total number of employees in company, division, or plant for which survey data is reported:
   Hourly   _____
   Nonexempt salaried _____
   Exempt salaried   _____
   Total   _____

3. General increase and structure adjustments:
   a. During the past twelve months, has your firm granted a general increase to employees in the following classifications?
      Hourly   _____ No _____ Yes Amount or % _____ Date _____
      Nonexempt salaried _____ No _____ Yes Amount or % _____ Date _____
      Exempt salaried   _____ No _____ Yes Amount or % _____ Date _____
   b. During the same period, did you have a structure adjustment?
      Hourly   _____ No _____ Yes Amount or % _____ Date _____
      Nonexempt salaried _____ No _____ Yes Amount or % _____ Date _____
      Exempt salaried   _____ No _____ Yes Amount or % _____ Date _____

4. Merit increases:
   a. Does your firm maintain a merit increase budget for granting pay increases during a time period?
      Hourly   _____ No _____ Yes
      Nonexempt salaried _____ No _____ Yes
      Exempt salaried   _____ No _____ Yes
   b. If no, what was the approximate salary increase for the last period?
      Hourly $ _____
      Nonexempt salaried $ _____
      Exempt salaried $ _____
   c. If yes (if you have a merit increase budget), it is:

	Merit	Promotion	Total
Hourly	_____ . ___ %	_____ . ___ %	_____ . ___ %
Nonexempt salaried	_____ . ___ %	_____ . ___ %	_____ . ___ %
Exempt salaried	_____ . ___ %	_____ . ___ %	_____ . ___ %

   d. What are the dates of your current budget year?
      From _____ to _____, inclusive.

5. Union? _____ Yes _____ No
   If yes, list by name: _____
   _____
   _____

6. Cost of living:
   Do you grant a cost-of-living allowance? _____ No _____ Yes
   If yes, what is the current amount and group involved? _____
   _____

7. Are any employee groups on automatic progression? _____ No _____ Yes
   If yes, groups frequency, and amount: _____
   _____

8. Does your firm grant pay increases on an anniversary date or fixed calendar date(s)?

	Anniversary Date	Fixed Calendar	Date(s)
Hourly	_____	_____	_____
Nonexempt	_____	_____	_____
Exempt	_____	_____	_____

9. What is the frequency of your salary increases?

	Times per Year			
	1	2	3	Other
Hourly	___	___	___	_____
Nonexempt	___	___	___	_____
Exempt	___	___	___	_____

10. Any additional information that might help us interpret your pay data: _____
_____
_____
_____

Let's look at an example (this one is based on pricing a job in Miami, Florida, although the same process would apply for any city or state in which you're looking). Assume that your accounting clerk has just resigned; you are interested in advertising for a new employee, but first want to decide what a reasonable pay range would be. You've already spoken with a representative at your state's local "unemployment" office to get a preliminary picture, and perhaps to managers at one or two local personnel staffing firms with whom you've dealt in the past. You've also checked the classified ads. Now you want to go on the Internet to obtain additional information. How to do it?

In Florida, you might start by accessing the state's Florida Occupational Employment Wage Survey (ftp://lmi.floridajobs.org/library/OWS/msa5000.txt). Scanning down the list by metropolitan statistical area (MSA), you will be interested in the listing of jobs for the Miami MSA, starting with Accountants & Auditors and going down the list to "Bookkeeping, Accounting & Auditing Clerks." Here the most recent data would show an hourly pay rate of $8.44 to $12.71 per hour, with a mean of $10.93 and median of $10.61. Other similar State of Florida reports can be accessed by searching for Florida Occupational Wage Survey. The U.S. government's Bureau of Labor Statistics also publishes an Internet-based series that can be used for comparison purposes. Find them at http://stats.bls.gov/ocshome.htm.

Realistically, the data published by both the U.S. and local state governments sometimes tends to be somewhat out of date. Therefore, to get a real-time picture of what employers in your area are paying for accounting clerks, it's useful to access the on-line Internet sites of one or two of your local newspapers. In this case, for instance, the *Ft. Lauderdale News & Sun Sentinel* has a site called Career Path, which lists career opportunities—in other words, just about all the jobs listed in the newspaper by category (including accounting clerk) and, in many instances, wage rates (http://www.sun-sentinel.com/careerpath/cgi-bin-edgil/ftlemp.cgi). From this listing you'll find, for instance, jobs listed for "Accounts receivable clerks—$10.00 per hour," "Accounting clerk—$25k," "Accounting clerk—credit clerk, to $22k," and "Accounts payable clerk, $22–26k," among many others. Switching to *The Miami Herald*'s Herald on-line Web site (called HeraldLink) classifieds, you similarly find a list of several dozen related job listings. For example, there is a "Payroll clerk, Doral area, $25k," an "Accounting clerk—City of Hialeah starting at $594 biweekly," and "Accounting assistant—Miami Lakes area, to $29k." More Web sites for compensation purposes are available from consulting firms; others are listed in this textbook's Web site page for this chapter, and in the Technology box on page 415.

The Internet also provides numerous fee-based sources of international salary data. For example, William M. Mercer, Inc., an international consulting firm (http://www.mercer.com) publishes an annual global compensation planning report summarizing compensation trends for more than 40 countries plus representative pay data for four common benchmark jobs.[22] Accounting firm KPMG International (http://www.kpmg.com) includes reports from surveys compiled by KPMG's various international offices. Watson Wyatt Worldwide (http://www.watsonwyatt.com) publishes an annual global remuneration planning report on worldwide pay levels.

Some firms price all their jobs based on such surveys. However in most cases, surveys are used to price benchmark jobs, around which other jobs are then slotted based on the jobs relative worth. Determining the relative worth of a job is the purpose of job evaluation, which we'll address next.

Step 2. Determine the Worth of Each Job: Job Evaluation

job evaluation

A systematic comparison done in order to determine the worth of one job relative to another.

PURPOSE OF JOB EVALUATION   **Job evaluation** is aimed at determining a job's relative worth. It is a formal and systematic comparison of jobs to determine the worth of one job relative to another and eventually results in a wage or salary hierarchy. The basic procedure is to compare the *content of jobs* in relation to one another, for example, in terms of their effort, responsibility, and skills. Suppose you know (based on your salary survey and compensation policies) how to price key benchmark jobs, and can use job evaluation to determine the relative worth of all the other jobs in your firm relative to these key jobs. Then you are well on your way to being able to equitably price all the jobs in your organization.

COMPENSABLE FACTORS   There are two basic approaches you could use for comparing several jobs. First, you could take a more intuitive approach. You might decide that one job is "more important" than another and not dig any deeper into why in terms of specific job-related factors.

As an alternative, you could compare the jobs by focusing on certain basic factors they have in common. In compensation management, these basic factors are called **compensable factors**. They are the factors that determine your definition of job content, establish how the jobs compare to each other, and set the compensation paid for each job.

Some employers develop their own compensable factors. However, most use factors that have been popularized by packaged job evaluation systems or by federal legislation. For example, the Equal Pay Act focuses on four compensable factors—*skills, effort, responsibility*, and *working conditions*. As another example, the job evaluation method popularized by the Hay consulting firm focuses on three compensable factors: *know-how, problem solving*, and *accountability*.

The compensable factors you focus on depend on the job and the method of job evaluation to be used. For example, you might choose to include the compensable factor of decision making for a manager's job, which might be inappropriate for the job of assembler.

Identifying compensable factors plays a central role in job evaluation. In job evaluation, each job is usually compared with all comparable jobs using the same compensable factors. An employer thus evaluates the same elemental components for each job and is then better able to compare them—for example, in terms of the degree of skills, effort, responsibility, and working conditions present in each.[23]

PLANNING AND PREPARATION FOR THE JOB EVALUATION   Job evaluation is mostly a judgmental process, one demanding close cooperation between supervisors, personnel specialists, and the employees and their union representatives. The main steps involved include identifying the need for the program, getting cooperation, and then choosing an evaluation committee; the latter then carries out the actual job evaluation.[24]

Identifying the need for job evaluation should not be difficult. For example, dissatisfaction reflected in high turnover, work stoppages, or arguments may result from the inequities of paying employees different rates for similar jobs. Similarly, managers may express uneasiness with the current, informal way of assigning pay rates to jobs, accurately sensing that a more systematic means of assigning pay rates would be more equitable.

Next, since employees may fear that a systematic evaluation of their jobs may actually reduce their wage rates, getting employee cooperation for the evaluation is a second important step. You can tell employees that as a result of the impending job evaluation program, wage rate decisions will no longer be made just by management whim, that job evaluation will provide a mechanism for considering the complaints they have been expressing, and that no present employee's rate will be adversely affected as a result of the job evaluation.[25]

Next choose a job evaluation committee; there are two reasons for doing so. First, the committee should bring to bear the points of view of several people who are familiar with the jobs in question, each of whom may have a different perspective regarding the nature of the jobs. Second, if the committee is composed at least partly of employees, the committee approach can help ensure greater acceptance of the job evaluation results by employees.

---

compensable factor

A fundamental, compensable element of a job, such as skills, effort, responsibility, and working conditions.

The composition of the committee can be important. The group usually consists of about five members, most of whom are employees. While management has the right to serve on such committees, its presence can be viewed with suspicion by employees and "it is probably best not to have managerial representatives involved in committee evaluation of nonmanagerial jobs. . . ."[26] However, an HR specialist can usually be justified on the grounds that he or she has a more impartial image than line managers and can provide expert assistance in the job evaluation. One option is to have this person serve in a nonvoting capacity. Union representation is possible. In most cases, though, the union's position is that it is accepting job evaluation only as an initial decision technique and is reserving the right to appeal the actual job pricing decisions through grievances or bargaining channels.[27] Once appointed, each committee member should receive a manual explaining the job evaluation process, and special instructions that explain how to conduct a job evaluation.

The evaluation committee performs three main functions. First, it usually identifies 10 or 15 key benchmark jobs. These will be the first jobs to be evaluated and will serve as the anchors or benchmarks against which the relative importance or value of all other jobs can be compared. Next, the committee may select compensable factors (although the human resource department will usually choose these as part of the process of determining the specific job evaluation technique to be used). Finally, the committee turns to its most important function—actually evaluating the worth of each job. For this, the committee will probably use one of the following job evaluation methods: the ranking method, the job classification method, the point method, or the factor comparison method.

RANKING METHOD OF JOB EVALUATION   The simplest job evaluation method ranks each job relative to all other jobs, usually based on some overall factor like "job difficulty." There are several steps in the job **ranking method**.

ranking method

The simplest method of job evaluation that involves ranking each job relative to all other jobs, usually based on overall difficulty.

1. *Obtain job information.* Job analysis is the first step. Job descriptions for each job are prepared and are usually the basis on which the rankings are made. (Sometimes job specifications are also prepared, but the job ranking method usually ranks jobs according to "the whole job," rather than a number of compensable factors. Therefore, job specifications—which list the job's demands in terms of problem solving, decision making, and skills, for instance—are not quite as necessary with this method as they are for other job evaluation methods.)

2. *Select raters and jobs to be rated.* It is often not practical to make a single ranking of all jobs in an organization. The more usual procedure is to rank jobs by department or in "clusters" (such as factory workers or clerical workers). This eliminates the need to compare directly, say, factory jobs and clerical jobs.

3. *Select compensable factors.* In the ranking method, it is common to use just one factor (such as job difficulty) and to rank jobs on the basis of the whole job. Regardless of the number of factors you choose, it's advisable to explain the definition of the factor(s) to the evaluators carefully so that they evaluate the jobs consistently.

4. *Rank jobs.* Next the jobs are ranked. The simplest way is to give each rater a set of index cards, each of which contains a brief description of a job. These cards are then ranked from lowest to highest. Some managers use an "alternation ranking method" for making the procedure more accurate. Here you take the cards, first choosing the highest and the lowest, then the next highest and next lowest, and so forth until all the cards have been ranked. Because it is usually easier to choose extremes, this approach facilitates the ranking procedure. A job ranking is illustrated in Table 11-1. Jobs in this small health facility are ranked from maid up to office manager. The corresponding pay scales are shown on the right.

TABLE 11-1 Job Ranking by Olympia Health Care

RANKING ORDER	ANNUAL PAY SCALE
1. Office manager	$33,000
2. Chief nurse	32,500
3. Bookkeeper	24,000
4. Nurse	22,500
5. Cook	21,000
6. Nurse's aide	18,500
7. Maid	15,500

After ranking, it becomes possible to slot additional jobs between those already ranked and to assign an appropriate wage rate.

5. *Combine ratings.* Usually several raters rank the jobs independently. Then the rating committee (or employer) can simply average the rankings.

Pros and Cons This is the simplest job evaluation method, as well as the easiest to explain. And, it usually takes less time to accomplish than other methods.

Some of its drawbacks derive more from how it's used than from the method itself. For example, there's a tendency to rely too heavily on "guesstimates." Similarly, ranking provides no yardstick for measuring the value of one job relative to another. For example, job number 4 may in fact be five times "more valuable" than job number 5, but with the ranking system all you know is that one job ranks higher than the other. Ranking is usually more appropriate for small organizations that can't afford the time or expense of developing a more elaborate system.

---

classification (or grading) method

A method for categorizing jobs into groups.

classes

Dividing jobs into classes based on a set of rules for each class, such as amount of independent judgment, skill, physical effort, and so forth, required for each class of jobs. Classes usually contain similar jobs—such as all secretaries.

grades

A job classification system synonymous with class, although grades often contain dissimilar jobs, such as secretaries, mechanics, and firefighters. Grade descriptions are written based on compensable factors listed in classification systems, such as the federal classification system.

grade definition

Written descriptions of the level of, say, responsibility and knowledge required by jobs in each grade. Similar jobs can then be combined into grades or classes.

JOB CLASSIFICATION (OR GRADING) EVALUATION METHOD Job **classification** is a simple, widely used method in which jobs are categorized into groups. The groups are called **classes** if they contain similar jobs, or **grades** if they contain jobs that are similar in difficulty but otherwise different. Thus, in the federal government's pay grade system, a "press secretary" and a "fire chief" might both be graded "GS–10" (GS stands for General Schedule). On the other hand, in its job class system, the State of Florida might classify all "secretary II's" in one class, all "maintenance engineers" in another, and so forth.

There are several ways to categorize jobs. One is to draw up *class descriptions* (the analogs of job descriptions) and place jobs into classes based on their correspondence to these descriptions. Another is to draw up a set of classifying rules for each class (for instance, how much independent judgment, skill, physical effort, and so on, does the class of jobs require?). Then the jobs are categorized according to these rules.

The usual procedure is to choose compensable factors and then develop class or grade descriptions that describe each class in terms of amount or level of the compensable factor(s) in jobs. The federal classification system in the United States, for example, employs the following compensable factors: (1) difficulty and variety of work, (2) supervision received and exercised, (3) judgment exercised, (4) originality required, (5) nature and purpose of interpersonal work relationships, (6) responsibility, (7) experience, and (8) knowledge required. Based on these compensable factors, a **grade definition** like that in Figure 11-2 is written. Then the evaluation committee reviews all job descriptions and slots each job into its appropriate class or grade; in the federal government system, for instance, the positions of automotive mechanic, welder, electrician, and machinist are classified as being in grade GS–10.

The job classification method has several advantages. The main one is that most employers usually end up classifying jobs anyway, regardless of the job evaluation method

FIGURE 11-2

Examples of Grade-Level Definitions in the Federal Government

Source: Douglass Bartley, *Job Evaluation* (Reading, MA: Addison-Wesley Publishing Company, Inc., 1981), p. 36.

GRADE	DEFINITION
GS–1	Includes those classes of positions the duties of which are to perform, under immediate supervision, with little or no latitude for the exercise of independent judgment— (A) the simplest routine work in office, business, or fiscal operations: or (B) elementary work of a subordinate technical character in a professional, scientific, or technical field.
GS–2	Includes those classes of positions the duties of which are— (A) to perform, under immediate supervision, with limited latitude for the exercise of independent judgment, routine work in office, business, or fiscal operations, or comparable subordinate technical work of limited scope in a professional, scientific, or technical field, requiring some training or experience; or (B) to perform other work of equal importance, difficulty, and responsibility, and requiring comparable qualifications.
GS–3	Includes those classes of positions the duties of which are— (A) to perform, under immediate or general supervision, somewhat difficult and responsible work in office, business or fiscal operations, or comparable subordinate technical work of limited scope in a professional, scientific, or technical field, requiring in either case— (i) some training or experience; (ii) working knowledge of a special subject matter; or (iii) to some extent the exercise of independent judgment in accordance with well-established policies, procedures, and techniques; or (B) to perform other work of equal importance, difficulty, and responsibility, and requiring comparable qualifications.
GS–4	Includes those classes of positions the duties of which are— (A) to perform, under immediate or general supervision, moderately difficult and responsible work in office, business, or fiscal operations, or comparable subordinate technical work in a professional, scientific, or technical field, requiring in either case— (i) a moderate amount of training and minor supervisory or other experience;

they use. They do this to avoid having to work with and price an unmanageable number of jobs; with the job classification method all jobs are already grouped into classes. The disadvantages are that it is difficult to write the class or grade descriptions, and considerable judgment is required to apply them. Yet many employers (including the U.S. government) use this method with success. The government, in fact, has concluded that more quantitative methods (like the two explained next) would cost much more than their additional accuracy warrants.[28]

point method

The job evaluation method in which a number of compensable factors are identified and then the degree to which each of these factors is present on the job is determined.

factor comparison method

A widely used method of ranking jobs according to a variety of skill and difficulty factors, then adding up these rankings to arrive at an overall numerical rating for each given job.

POINT METHOD OF JOB EVALUATION   The **point method** is a more quantitative job evaluation technique. It involves identifying (1) several compensable factors, *each having several degrees*, as well as (2) the degree to which each of these factors is present in the job. Thus, assume that there are five degrees of responsibility an employer's job could contain. And further assume a different number of points is assigned to each degree of each factor. Then, once the evaluation committee determines the degree to which each compensable factor (like "responsibility") is present in the job, the corresponding points for each factor can be added to arrive at a total point value for the job. The result is thus a quantitative point rating for each job. The point method is apparently the most widely used job evaluation method and is explained in detail in the appendix to this chapter.

FACTOR COMPARISON JOB EVALUATION METHOD   The **factor comparison method** is also a quantitative technique and entails deciding which jobs have more of the chosen compensable factors. The method is actually a refinement of the ranking method. With the ranking method, you generally look at each job as an entity and rank the jobs on some overall factor like job difficulty. With the factor comparison method, you rank each job several times—once for each compensable factor you choose. For example, jobs might first be ranked in terms of the compensable factor "skill." Then they are ranked according to their "mental requirements," and so forth. These rankings are combined for each job into an overall numerical rating for the job. This too is a widely used method and is also explained in more detail in the appendix to this chapter.

COMPUTERIZED JOB EVALUATIONS As explained more fully in the appendix to this chapter, using a quantitative job evaluation method such as the point plan can be a fairly time consuming matter. This is so because accumulating the information about "how much" of each compensable factor the job contains has traditionally been done through an often tedious process in which evaluation committees debate the level of each compensable factor in a job. They then write down their consensus judgments and manually compute each job's point values.

According to one expert, CAJE—computer-aided job evaluation—can dramatically streamline this whole process.[29] Computer-aided job evaluation, she says, can simplify job analysis, help keep job descriptions up to date, increase evaluation objectivity, reduce the time spent in committee meetings, and ease the burden of system maintenance. CAJE "features electronic data entry, computerized checking of questionnaire responses and automated output—not only of job evaluations, but also of a variety of compensation reports."[30]

Most CAJE systems have two main components. There is, first, a structured questionnaire. This contains items such as "enter total number of employees who report functionally to this position." Second, all CAJE systems are built around statistical models that allow the computer program to price jobs more or less automatically based on inputted information on such things as number of employees reporting to the positions, prices of benchmark jobs, current pay, and current pay grade midpoints.

Step 3. Group Similar Jobs into Pay Grades

Once a job evaluation method has been used to determine the relative worth of each job, the committee can turn to the task of assigning pay rates to each job, but it will usually want to first group jobs into **pay grades**. If the committee used the ranking, point, or factor comparison methods, it could assign pay rates to each individual job.[31] But for a larger employer such a pay plan would be difficult to administer, since there might be different pay rates for hundreds or even thousands of jobs. And even in smaller organizations there's a tendency to try to simplify wage and salary structures as much as possible. Therefore, the committee will probably want to group similar jobs (in terms of their ranking or number of points, for instance) into grades for pay purposes. Instead of having to deal with hundreds of pay rates, it might only have to focus on, say, 10 or 12.[32]

A pay grade is comprised of jobs of approximately equal difficulty or importance as determined by job evaluation. If the point method was used, the pay grade consists of jobs falling within a range of points. If the ranking plan was used, the grade consists of all jobs that fall within two or three ranks. If the classification system was used, then the jobs are already categorized into classes or grades. If the factor comparison method is used, the grade will consist of a specified range of pay rates, as explained in the appendix to this chapter. Ten to 16 grades per "job cluster" (a cluster is a logical grouping such as factory jobs, clerical jobs, and so on) are common.

pay grade

A pay grade is comprised of jobs of approximately equal difficulty.

Step 4. Price Each Pay Grade—Wage Curves

The next step is to assign pay rates to your pay grades. (Of course, if you chose not to slot jobs into pay grades, individual pay rates would have to be assigned to each individual job.) Assigning pay rates to each pay grade (or to each job) is usually accomplished with a wage curve.

FIGURE 11-3

Plotting a Wage Curve

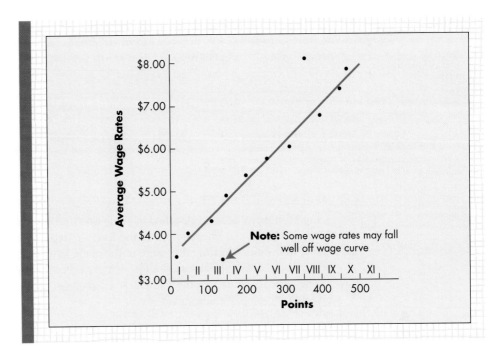

wage curve

Shows the relationship between the value of the job and the average wage paid for this job.

The **wage curve** depicts graphically the pay rates currently being paid for jobs in each pay grade, relative to the points or rankings assigned to each job or grade by the job evaluation. An example of a wage curve is presented in Figure 11-3. Note that pay rates are shown on the vertical axis, and the pay grades (in terms of points) are shown along the horizontal axis. The purpose of the wage curve is to show the relationship between (1) the value of the job as determined by one of the job evaluation methods and (2) the current average pay rates for your grades.

The pay rates on the graph are traditionally those now paid by the organization. If there is reason to believe that the present pay rates are substantially out of step with the prevailing market pay rates for these jobs, benchmark jobs within each pay grade are chosen and priced via a compensation survey. These new market-based pay rates are then plotted on the wage curve.

There are several steps in pricing jobs with a wage curve. First, *find the average pay for each pay grade*, since each of the pay grades consists of several jobs. Next *plot the pay rates* for each pay grade as was done in Figure 11-3. Then fit a line, called a *wage line* through the points just plotted. This can be done either freehand or by using a statistical method. Finally, *price jobs*. Wages along the wage line are the target wages or salary rates for the jobs in each pay grade. If the current rates being paid for any of your jobs or grades fall well above or below the wage line, that rate may be "out of line"; raises or a pay freeze for that job may be in order. Your next step, then, is to fine-tune your pay rates.

Step 5. Fine-Tune Pay Rates

Fine-tuning involves correcting out-of-line rates and (usually) developing rate ranges.

rate ranges

A series of steps or levels within a pay grade, usually based upon years of service.

DEVELOPING RATE RANGES   Most employers do not pay just one rate for all jobs in a particular pay grade. Instead, they develop **rate ranges** for each grade so that there might, for instance, be 10 levels or "steps" and 10 corresponding pay rates within each pay grade. This approach is illustrated in Table 11-2, which shows the pay rates and steps for some federal government pay grades. As of the time of this pay schedule, for instance, employ-

TABLE 11-2   Federal Government Pay Schedule: Grades GS 8–GS 10

GRADE	RATES AND STEPS WITHIN GRADE									
	1	2	3	4	5	6	7	8	9	10
GS–8	19,740	20,398	21,056	21,714	22,372	23,030	23,688	24,346	25,004	25,662
GS–9	21,804	22,531	23,258	23,985	24,712	25,439	26,166	26,893	27,620	28,347
GS–10	24,011	24,811	25,611	26,411	27,211	28,011	28,811	29,611	30,411	31,211

Note: Federal grades range from GS–1 to top grade of GS–18 (annual rate of $84,157).
Source: The U.S. Office of Personnel Management.

ees in positions that were classified in grade GS–10 could be paid annual salaries between
$24,011 and $31,211, depending on the level or step at which they were hired into the
grade, the amount of time they were in the grade, and their merit increases (if any). Another way to depict the rate ranges for each grade is with a *wage structure*, as in Figure 11-
4. The wage structure graphically depicts the range of pay rates (in this case, per hour) to
be paid for each pay grade.

FIGURE 11-4

Wage Structure

Note: This shows overlapping wage
classes and maximum–minimum
wage ranges.

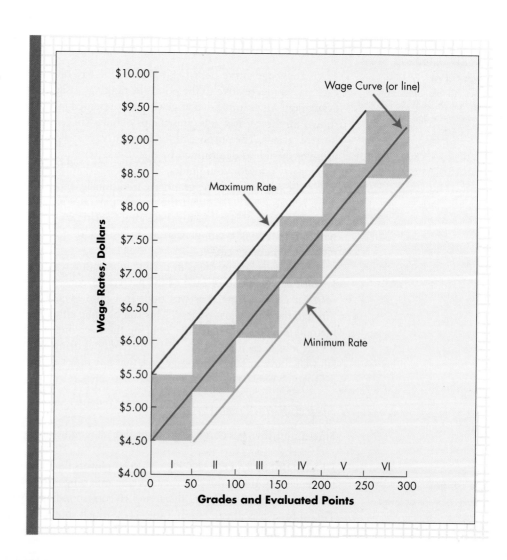

There are several benefits to using rate ranges for each pay grade. First, the employer can take a more flexible stance with respect to the labor market. For example, it makes it easier to attract experienced, higher-paid employees into a pay grade where the starting salary for the lowest step may be too low to attract such experienced personnel. Rate ranges also allow you to provide for performance differences between employees within the same grade or between those with different seniorities. As in Figure 11-4, most employers structure their rate ranges to overlap a bit, so that an employee with more experience or seniority may earn more than an entry-level position in the next higher pay grade.

The rate range is usually built around the wage line or curve. One alternative is to arbitrarily decide on a maximum and minimum rate for each grade, such as 15% above and below the wage line. As an alternative, some employers allow the rate range for each grade to become wider for the higher pay ranges, reflecting the greater demands and performance variability inherent in these more complex jobs.

CORRECTING OUT-OF-LINE RATES   The wage rate for a job may fall well off the wage line or well outside the rate range for its grade, as shown in Figure 11-3. This means that the average pay for that job is currently too high or too low, relative to other jobs in the firm. If a point falls well below the line, a pay raise for the job may be required. If the point falls well above the wage line, pay cuts or a pay freeze may be required.

Underpaid employees should have their wages raised to the minimum of the rate range for their pay grade, assuming you want to retain the employees and have the funds to do so. This can be done either immediately or in one or two steps.

Rates being paid to overpaid employees are often called *red circle, flagged,* or *over-rates,* and there are several ways to cope with this problem. One is to freeze the rate paid to employees in this grade until general salary increases bring the other jobs into line with it. A second alternative is to transfer or promote some or all of the employees involved to jobs for which they can legitimately be paid their current pay rates. The third alternative is to freeze the rate for 6 months, during which time you try to transfer or promote the overpaid employees. If you cannot, then the rate at which these employees are paid is cut to the maximum in the pay range for their pay grade.

CURRENT TRENDS IN COMPENSATION

Skill-Based Pay

With competency or skill-based pay, you are paid for the range, depth, and types of skills and knowledge you are capable of using rather than for the job you currently hold.[33] One expert defines competencies as "demonstrable characteristics of the person, including knowledge, skills, and behaviors, that enable performance."[34]

Why pay employees based on the skill levels they achieve, rather than based on the jobs they're assigned to? For example, why pay an Accounting Clerk II who has achieved a certain mastery of accounting techniques the same (or more than) someone who is an Accounting Clerk IV?

There are several possible reasons to do so. With more companies organizing around teams, "jobs" themselves are becoming something of an anachronism, because employees are often expected to easily rotate among jobs (and thus learn several skills). Indeed, "jobs" themselves are overlapping as individuals work on projects or processes together, as members of teams. Competency/skill-based pay can also help support an employer's new strategy. For example, Sony's strategic emphasis on miniaturization and precision manufacturing suggests that certain Sony employees should be rewarded—not just based on the jobs they're assigned to—but on their level of knowledge and accomplishment in these two strategically crucial areas. There are several key differences between skill-based pay (SBP) and job evaluation-driven job-based pay (JBP).[35]

1. *Competence testing.* With JBP, you receive the pay attached to your job regardless of whether or not you develop the competence needed to perform the job effectively. With SBP, your base pay is tied not to the job, but to your skills. You have to be certified as competent in the skills required by the job to get a pay increase.

2. *Effect of job change.* With JBP, your pay usually changes automatically when you switch jobs. With SBP that's not necessarily so. Before getting a pay raise, you must first demonstrate proficiency at the skills required by the new job.

3. *Seniority and other factors.* Pay in JBP systems is often tied to "time in grade" or seniority. In other words, the longer you're in the job, the more you get paid, regardless of how well you perform. SBP systems are based on skills, not seniority.

4. *Advancement opportunities.* Typically (but not always) there tend to be more opportunities for advancement with SBP plans than with JBP plans because of the companywide focus on skill building. A corollary to this is that SBP enhances organizational flexibility by making it easier for workers to move from job to job because their skills (and thus their pay) may be applicable to more jobs and thus more portable.

AN EXAMPLE   A skill-based pay plan was implemented at a General Mills manufacturing facility.[36] In this case, General Mills sought to boost the commitment and flexibility of its plant workers by implementing what it referred to as a high-involvement/high-performance work system, of which skill-based pay was one element. (Other elements included egalitarian management practices such as having no reserved parking spaces for management, and hiring employees whose values fit with the flexible, team-based organizational culture in the plant).

In this plant, the workers were paid based on their attained skill levels. There were basically four clusters (or "blocks") of jobs, corresponding to the four production areas: mixing, filling, packaging, and materials. Within each of these blocks, workers could attain three levels of skill. Level 1 indicates limited ability, such as knowledge of basic facts and ability to perform simple tasks without direction.[37] Level 2 means the employee attained partial proficiency and could, for instance, apply technical principles on the job. Attaining Level 3 means the employee is fully competent in the area and could, for example, analyze and solve production problems. Each production block had a different average wage rate. There were, therefore, 12 pay levels (four blocks with three pay levels each) in the plant.

Construction workers today are often compensated for their work through the method of skill-based pay, which originated with the craft guilds of the Middle Ages.

The actual pricing of the 12 skill levels was achieved in part by making the lowest of the 12 pay levels in each block equal to the average entry-level wage rate for similar jobs in the community. (Notice, therefore, that even with skill-based pay you still can't entirely escape evaluating jobs, market pricing them, and comparing them to one another in some fashion.)

A new employee could start in any block, but always at Level 1. If after several weeks the employee was able to complete certification at the next higher skill level, his or her salary was correspondingly raised. Furthermore, employees were continually rotated from production area (or block) to production area. To be rotatable into a block, however, the employee had to achieve Level 2 performance within their current block.

The system worked well. It encouraged learning new skills. It also fostered flexibility by encouraging workers to learn multiple skills and to willingly switch from block to block.

However, whether skill-based pay improves productivity is an open question. When used in conjunction with team-building and worker involvement and empowerment programs, it does appear to lead to higher quality as well as lower absenteeism rates and fewer accidents.[38] However, the findings in one firm, which are not conclusive, suggest that productivity was higher at its non-skill-based-pay facility.[39]

Basing pay on skills rather than on the job can be easier said than done.[40] However, it's still estimated that over 50% of *Fortune* 1,000 firms use some form of skill-based pay.[41] One major aerospace firm uses skill-based pay by having all exempt employees negotiate "learning contracts" with their supervisors. The employees then receive pay increases for meeting learning (skills-improvement) objectives.[42]

Broadbanding

Another trend today is for employers to reduce their salary grades and ranges from 10 or more down to 3 or 5, a process called *broadbanding*. Broadbanding means collapsing salary grades and ranges into just a few wide levels or "bands," each of which contains a relatively wide range of jobs and salary levels. Thus, instead of having, say, 10 salary grades each of which contains a salary range of, say, $15,000, the firm might collapse the 10 grades into 3 broad bands, each with a set of jobs such that the difference between the lowest- and highest-paid jobs might be $40,000 or more. One survey found that almost one-third of the 3,400 employers responding said they had adopted a broadbanding approach or were considering doing so.[43] Companies "broadband" for several reasons, most often to support overall organizational and strategic changes: For example, the broadbanding in one British company was aimed to support a new cost-cutting strategy and consequent flattening and downsizing of the organization.[44]

Broadbanding's basic advantage is that it injects greater flexibility into employee compensation.[45] Broadbanding is especially sensible where firms flatten their hierarchies and organize into self-managing teams. The new, broad salary bands can include both supervisors and subordinates and can also facilitate moving employees slightly up or down along the pay scale, without bumping the person into a new salary range (which might require accompanying promotional raises or demotional pay cuts). For example, "the employee who needs to spend time in a lower-level job to develop a certain skill set can receive higher-than-usual pay for the work, a circumstance considered impossible under traditional pay systems."[46]

Broadbanding also facilitates the sorts of less-specialized "boundaryless" jobs and organizations being embraced by many firms like General Electric. Less specialization and more participation in cross-departmental processes generally mean enlarged duties or capabilities and more possibilities for alternative career tracks; broader, more inclusive salary bands facilitate this. One expert argues that traditional quantitative evaluation plans actually reward *un*adaptability.[47] The argument here is that being slotted into a job that is

FIGURE 11-5

*Setting Salary Ranges
for Three Bands*

Source: David Hofrichter,
"Broadbanding: A 'Second
Generation' Approach,"
Compensation & Benefits Review,
Sept–Oct 1993, p. 56.

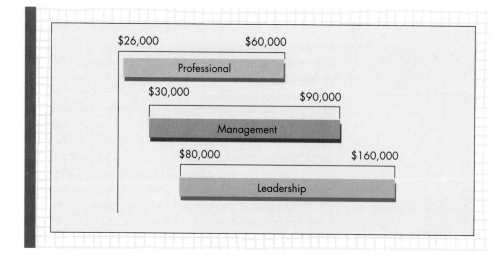

highly routine as defined by a compensable factor such as "know-how" is unlikely to encourage job incumbents to think independently or be flexible. Instead, the tendency may be for workers to concentrate on the specific, routine jobs to which they are assigned and for which they are rewarded.

Broadbanding a pay plan involves several steps. First, as illustrated in Figure 11-5, the number of bands is decided upon and each is assigned a salary range. The bands usually have wide salary ranges and also overlap substantially. As a result, there's much more flexibility to move employees from job to job within bands and less need to "promote" them to new grades just to get them higher salaries.

The bands are then typically subdivided into either specific jobs (see Figure 11-6) or skill levels (see Figure 11-7). For example, a band may consist of a number of jobs, each as-

FIGURE 11-6

*Assigning Market Values
to Jobs in a Band*

Source: David Hofrichter,
"Broadbanding: A 'Second
Generation' Approach,"
Compensation & Benefits Review,
Sept–Oct 1993, pp. 56–57.

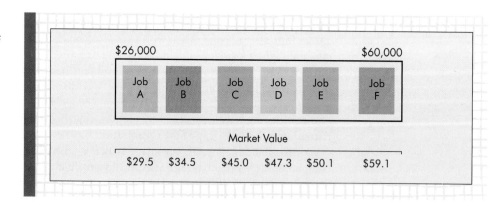

FIGURE 11-7

*Positioning Pay within
a Band Based on Skills*

Source: David Hofrichter,
"Broadbanding: A 'Second
Generation' Approach,"
Compensation & Benefits Review,
Sept–Oct 1993, pp. 56–57.

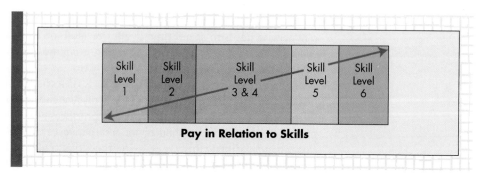

INFORMATION TECHNOLOGY AND HR

Web sites for Compensation Management

As mentioned earlier in this chapter, the explosion of Internet Web sites over the past few years includes hundreds—perhaps thousands—devoted specifically to compensation-related matters. Any short listing is bound to be incomplete, but it should at least give you the flavor of what's available out there. Here's a sampling.[48]

The Relocation Salary Calculator Site. Provided by the Center for Mobility Resources, this site computes salary differentials between cities all over the U.S. and abroad. Moving from New York to Paris? This is the site for you. Find it at http://www.homefair.com/homefair/cmr/salcalc.html.

AFL-CIO Executive Pay Watch. Users here can view CEO salaries, bonuses, and stock options for about 300 of the S&P 500 corporations and convert the amounts into the hours of work an average employee would have to perform to earn the same salary. Find it at http://www.aflcio.paywatch.org.

BLS Occupational Compensation Survey. This site leads to large files for the Bureau of Labor Statistics time series data, all of which can be downloaded. Find it at http://stats.bls.gov/ocshome.htm.

Industry/Occupation-Specific Sites. Interested in compensation information for specific industries and/or occupations? Try these sites:[49]

College and university faculty and staff salaries
   http://www.chronicle.merit.edu/almanac
Computer professionals
   http://techweb.cmp.com/mc/802/802f3.html
Engineering salaries
   http://www.proengineer.com/index.html
Accounting salaries
   http://www.acsysresources.com/acct.htm
Marketing salaries
   http://adage.com/cgi-bin/genDPcat.pl?cat+SALARY_SURVEY
MBAs
   http://www.usc.edu/dept/sba/career/emplorep.htm

signed a market value. More often, bands are subdivided into several skill levels. Recall that with this second approach, workers are not paid above market value just for doing a job well or for having seniority. Instead, they must increase their competencies such as skills, knowledge, and abilities.[50] The Technology box (above) shows some compensation Web sites.

Why Job Evaluation Plans Are Still Widely Used

With the trends toward skill-based pay and broadbanding, some question the continued need for quantitative job evaluation, yet systems such as the point and factor comparison plans are still used by 60% to 70% of U.S. firms.[51] There are several reasons for this. Proponents argue that individual differences in skill attainment *can* be taken into consideration even when point-type plans are used, since most firms do use salary ranges (not simply a target wage) for groups of similar jobs. More experienced (and skilled) people can therefore move up the range while keeping basically the job.[52] Job evaluation advocates also argue that a job description is not necessarily a job restriction; it's naive to "believe that employees automatically limit their behavior to what is written on a piece of paper."[53] They also say there's no reason why job evaluation needs to be limited to a narrow job. Instead, you could theoretically evaluate the "job" of doing a whole project and from that ascertain the problem solving, accountability, and knowledge that a worker would need to do all the jobs involved in that project. Furthermore, neither skill-based pay nor broadbanding entirely eliminates the need for evaluating the worth of one job relative to others. But in the final analysis, job evaluation's relative ease of use and familiarity are probably the major reasons for the continued use of quantitative plans.

THE HIGH-PERFORMANCE ORGANIZATION

Building Better, Faster, More Competitive Organizations Through HR: **Strategic Compensation Management**

▪ IBM

As most everyone knows by now, IBM represents a classic example of an organizational renewal for the 1990s. It dominated its industry in the 1970s and early 1980s. But by the late 1980s, missing out on exploiting new technologies and losing touch with customers were both parts of the problem that could be "linked to dysfunctional organizational dynamics and individual behavior patterns."[54] Transforming the early 1990s' IBM from a sluggish giant to a lean winner therefore required new CEO Louis Gerstner, Jr. to do more than just downsize and reorganize his firm; he had to transform IBM's culture—the shared values, attitudes, and behavior patterns that invisibly guided employees' behavior. The values Gerstner wanted to ingrain included: winning must be an obsession; execution, the cornerstone of winning, was built on speed and decisiveness; and teaming is something that a business like IBM must cultivate.

IBM's existing compensation plan was inconsistent with such performance-oriented values and culture. For example, prior to 1994, IBM had a single salary structure (for nonsales employees). Basically, everyone in this huge company's workforce was in a job whose relative worth was based on a decades-old point factor-based job evaluation.[55] What were some of the implications of this? For one thing, maintaining the point system for over a hundred thousand employees required "a massive and cumbersome" attention to point factor-manual spaced evaluations. This structure also cultivated an inward rather than an outward, market, focus on the employees part—and a corresponding preoccupation on internal equity rather than on market rates of pay.

Beginning in the mid 1990s, IBM took steps to change this situation, by making four major changes in its compensation plan:

1. The marketplace rules. In 1994–5 the company switched from its previous single salary structure (for nonsales employees) to different salary structures and merit budgets for different job families. This has enabled IBM to take different compensation actions for different job families (i.e., accountants vs. engineers vs. programmers, and so on) and has enabled IBM to concentrate on paying employees in different job families in a way that is more in keeping with the marketplace. The new approach thus sends the strong cultural signal that "a market-driven company must watch the market closely and act accordingly."[56]

2. Fewer jobs, evaluated differently, in broad bands. Second, IBM scrapped its point factor job evaluation system and its traditional salary grades. The new system (which is at heart basically a classification approach) has no points at all and is so remarkably simple that it can be adequately explained by a single chart as illustrated in Figure 11-8. The old system contained 10 different factors; the new one just 3 (skills, leadership requirements, and job scope).

   Changing the job evaluation method gave IBM an opportunity to review the number of its job titles. In the United States, the number of separate job titles was reduced from over 5,000 to fewer than 1,200.[57] This facilitated a shift from 24 salary grades to 10 broad bands. In turn, this shift communicated a new organizational model: IBM was to be a flatter organization that could "deliver goods and services to market faster."[58]

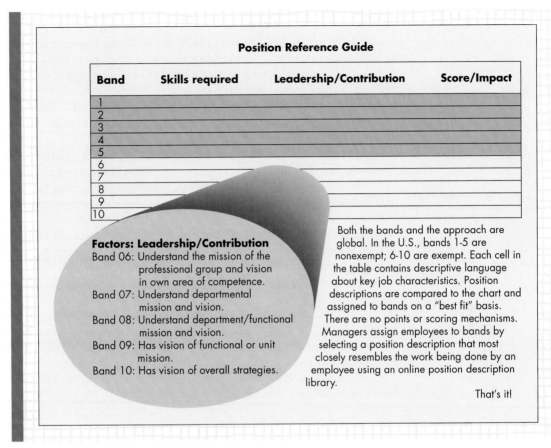

Position Reference Guide

Band	Skills required	Leadership/Contribution	Score/Impact
1			
2			
3			
4			
5			
6			
7			
8			
9			
10			

Factors: Leadership/Contribution

Band 06: Understand the mission of the professional group and vision in own area of competence.

Band 07: Understand departmental mission and vision.

Band 08: Understand department/functional mission and vision.

Band 09: Has vision of functional or unit mission.

Band 10: Has vision of overall strategies.

Both the bands and the approach are global. In the U.S., bands 1-5 are nonexempt; 6-10 are exempt. Each cell in the table contains descriptive language about key job characteristics. Position descriptions are compared to the chart and assigned to bands on a "best fit" basis. There are no points or scoring mechanisms. Managers assign employees to bands by selecting a position description that most closely resembles the work being done by an employee using an online position description library.

That's it!

FIGURE 11-8 *IBM'S New Pay Structure*

3. Managers manage. In the previous IBM compensation plan base salary increases were based on a complex comparison that linked performance appraisal scores to salary increases measured in tenths of a percent. The new system is very different. Managers get a budget and some coaching, the essence of which is: "Either differentiate the pay you give to stars versus acceptable performers or the stars won't be around too long."[59] The new approach basically lets managers rank employees on a variety of factors (such as critical skills, and results); which factors are used and what weights they're given is up to the manager.

4. Big stakes for stakeholders. As IBM was floundering in the late 1980s and early 90s, every nonexecutive employee's cash compensation (outside of sales) consisted of base salary (plus overtime, shift premiums, and some other adjustments). Pay for performance was a foreign concept.

   By 1997, most IBMers "around the world had 10% or more of their total cash compensation tied to performance."[60] In the new system there are only three performance appraisal ratings, "and a top-rated employee receives two-and-one-half times the award of an employee with the lowest ranking. (Awards are calibrated as percentages of pensionable earnings.)"[61]

The changes in IBM's compensation plan illustrate how compensation management can be used to support a company's strategic aims. In this case it helped change the company's culture to one that emphasizes being better, faster, and more competitive.

A Glimpse into the Future—The "New" Pay

The evolving practices in firms like IBM provide us with a glimpse into the future of compensation management, and that future is now, as far as many firms are concerned. Looking ahead a few years, experts see a continuation of intense global competition, an increasingly knowledge-based workforce (as exemplified, for instance, by those FedEx drivers with their hand-held computers), and an increasingly "virtual" workplace in which many (or all) of a firm's employees don't really work at "the firm" at all.[62] Here's what several compensation experts therefore say we can expect.

First, as at IBM, expect compensation to do more to contribute to the strategy of the company. The question managers will ask is, "What is the extent to which compensation program components, both separately and in combination, create value for the organization and its employees?"[63]

Second, with more emphasis on flexibility and on empowering employees, traditional job descriptions and hourly employee job classifications will be deemphasized.[64] Replacing them will be greater latitude for employees to evolve their responsibilities to meet customer needs as they see fit.

There will also be a related emphasis on paying employees for their competencies rather than just for the job's responsibilities and activities. Under the apprentice systems that started with the guilds of the Middle Ages, apprentices had to demonstrate competence at their trade before becoming journeymen, and then masters. So when firms like General Mills condense dozens or hundreds of jobs into a few broad bands and then base pay differentials on skill levels, we're really returning, to some extent, to the past.[65]

There will also be a growing emphasis on pay for improved results and on nontraditional pay (also called "alternative rewards"). As summarized in Figure 11-9, traditional

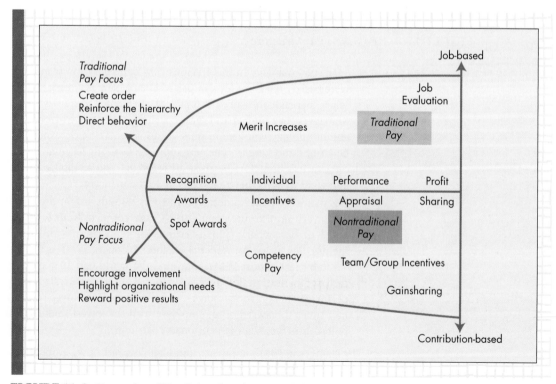

FIGURE 11-9 *Examples of Traditional and Nontraditional Pay*

Source: Sibson & Company, Inc. Reproduced in Charles Cumming, "Will Traditional Salary Administration Survive the Stampede to Alternative Rewards?" *Compensation & Benefits Review,* November–December 1992, p. 45.

pay plans based on job descriptions, job evaluations, and salary structures tend to focus, says this expert, on creating order, reinforcing the hierarchy, and directing behavior.[66] In the future (and, for many firms, now), the emphasis will shift from paying for the job to paying for the employee's contribution, encouraging involvement and commitment, and rewarding positive results. Nontraditional or alternative pay plans for doing this include competency or skill-based pay and the sorts of spot awards, team incentives, and gainsharing we'll discuss in chapter 12.

Given the increasing numbers of contingent workers and telecommuters, another expert predicts the need for "distinctly different" compensation arrangements for full-time core workers—those "whom the company must retain to maintain its core competencies—and temporary, part-time, consulting and other workers outside the organization."[67] Compensation for the core workers "will be designed to retain these vitally important assets and motivate them to improve their base of knowledge and productivity."[68] Skill-based pay, market-driven wages, and broad pay bands are some examples of the policies that will be used. Compensation for employees outside the core, on the other hand, "will be based on completion of work as jointly agreed upon. . . ."[69]

PRICING MANAGERIAL AND PROFESSIONAL JOBS

Developing a compensation plan to pay executive, managerial, and professional employees is similar in many respects to developing a plan for any employees.[70] The basic aims of the plan are the same in that the goal is to attract good employees and maintain their commitment. Furthermore, the basic methods of job evaluation—classifying jobs, ranking them, or assigning points to them, for instance—are about as applicable to managerial and professional jobs as to production and clerical ones.

Yet for managerial and professional jobs, job evaluation provides only a partial answer to the question of how to pay these employees. Such jobs tend to emphasize nonquantifiable factors like judgment and problem solving more than do production and clerical jobs. There is also a tendency to pay managers and professionals based on ability—based on their performance or on what they can do—rather than on the basis of static job demands like working conditions. Developing compensation plans for managers and professionals, therefore, tends to be relatively complex, and job evaluation, while still important, usually plays a secondary role to nonsalary issues like bonuses, incentives, and benefits.

Compensating Managers

BASIC COMPENSATION ELEMENTS   For a company's top executives, the compensation plan generally consists of four main components: base salary, short-term incentives, long-term incentives, and executive benefits and perks.[71] Base salary includes the obvious fixed compensation paid regularly as well as, often, guaranteed bonuses such as "10% of pay at the end of the fourth fiscal quarter, regardless of whether or not the company makes a profit." Short-term incentives are usually paid in cash or stock for achieving short-term goals, such as year-to-year increases in sales revenue. Long-term incentives include such things as stock options; these generally give the executive the right to purchase stock at a specific price for a specific period of time. They are aimed at encouraging the executive to take those actions that will drive up the value and price of the company's stock. Finally, special executive benefits and perks might include supplemental executive retirement plans, supplemental life insurance, and health insurance without a deductible or coinsurance. Executive compensation is obviously complicated by the variety of options and incentives it typically entails, and so that employers must be particularly aware of the tax and securities laws implications of their executive compensation decisions.[72]

The amount of salary managers are paid generally depends on the value of the person's work to the organization and how well the person is discharging his or her responsi-

The very high base salary of such executives as Mattel's CEO Jill Barad are usually an indication of their worth to the firm's stockholders. Barad reportedly earns about half her $2 million annual compensation in salary and the rest in incentives.

bilities. As with other jobs, the value of the person's work is usually determined through job analysis and salary surveys and the resulting fine-tuning of salary levels.

Salary is the cornerstone of executive compensation. It is on this element that the others are layered, with benefits, incentives, and perquisites normally awarded in some proportion to the manager's base pay. *Benefits* (including time off with pay, health care, employee services, survivor's protection, and retirement coverage) are discussed in Chapter 13. *Short-term incentives* are designed to reward managers for attaining short-term (normally yearly) goals. *Long-term incentives* are aimed at rewarding the person for long-term performance (in terms of increased market share and the like). Incentives are discussed in Chapter 12. *Perquisites* (perks for short) begin where benefits leave off and are usually given to only a select few executives based on organizational level and (possibly) past performance. Perks include use of company cars, yachts, and executive dining rooms. (These benefits are also covered in Chapter 13.) Executive compensation tends to emphasize performance incentives more than do other employees' pay plans, since organizational results are likely to reflect the contributions of executives more directly than those of lower-echelon employees. Incentives today equal 25% or more of a typical executive's base pay in many countries, including the United States, United Kingdom, France, and Germany.[73]

There is considerable disagreement regarding what determines executive pay and, therefore, whether top executives are worth what they are paid. The traditional wisdom is that a top manager's salary is closely tied to the size of the firm.[74] Yet two experts who tested this idea found this not to be the case.[74] Instead, say these experts, an executive's pay was mostly determined by the industry in which he or she worked, and the "corporate power structure," because executives who also serve on their firms' boards of directors can heavily influence how much they get paid. In another study the researchers basically argue that CEOs are paid for the level of complexity and unpredictability of the decisions they must make.[75] In this study, complexity was a function of such things as the number of businesses controlled by the CEO's firm, the number of corporate officers in each firm, and the level of R&D activity and capital investment activity.[76] The study concluded that regardless of performance, CEOs tended to be paid based on the complexity of the jobs they filled. In yet another study, the researcher found that four compensable factors—company size, profitability, number of employees, and experience—accounted for 83% of the difference in pay. It appears "that there are rational, acceptable, and abiding principles that govern the total cash compensation of top executives in manufacturing firms."[77]

Shareholder activism is combining with other changes to tighten the restrictions on what top executives are paid.[78] For example, the Securities and Exchange Commission voted in 1992 to approve final rules regarding executive compensation communications. The chief executive officer's pay is always to be disclosed as well as other officers' pay if their compensation (salary and bonus) exceeds $100,000. One result is that boards of directors must act responsibly in reviewing and setting executive pay. That, says one expert, includes determining the key performance requirements of the executive's job; assessing the appropriateness of the firm's current compensation practices; conducting a pay-for-performance survey; and testing shareholder acceptance of the board's pay proposals.[79]

The basic trend today is to reduce the relative importance of base salary and to boost the importance of incentives.[80] The main issue here is identifying the appropriate performance standards for each type of incentive and then determining how to link these to pay. Typical short-term measures of shareholder value include revenue growth and operating profit margin. Long-term shareholder value measures include rate of return above some predetermined base.

MANAGERIAL JOB EVALUATION   Despite questions regarding the rationality of executive pay, job evaluation is still important in pricing executive and managerial jobs in most firms. According to one expert, "the basic approach used by most large companies to ensure some degree of equity among various divisions and departments is to classify all executive and management positions into a series of grades, to which a series of salary ranges is attached."[81]

As with nonmanagerial jobs, one alternative is to rank the executive and management positions in relation to each other, grouping those of equal value. However, the job classification and point evaluation methods are also used, with compensable factors like position scope, complexity, difficulty, and creative demands.

Compensating Professional Employees

Compensating nonsupervisory professional employees like engineers and scientists presents unique problems.[82] Analytical jobs put a heavy premium on creativity and problem solving, compensable factors not easily compared or measured. Furthermore, the professional's economic impact on the firm is often related only indirectly to the person's actual efforts; for example, the success of an engineer's invention depends on many factors, like how well it is produced and marketed.

The job evaluation methods we explained previously can also be used for evaluating professional jobs.[83] The compensable factors here tend to focus on problem solving, creativity, job scope, and technical knowledge and expertise. Both the point method and factor comparison methods have been used, although the job classification method seems most popular. Here a series of grade descriptions are written, and each position is slotted into the grade having the most appropriate definition.

Yet, in practice, traditional methods of job evaluation are rarely used for professional jobs since "it is simply not possible to identify factors and degrees of factors which meaningfully differentiate among the values of professional work."[84] "Knowledge and the skill of applying it," as one expert noted, "are extremely difficult to quantify and measure."[85]

As a result, most employers use a market-pricing approach in evaluating professional jobs. They price professional jobs in the marketplace as best they can, to establish the values for benchmark jobs. These benchmark jobs and the employer's other professional jobs are then slotted into a salary structure. Specifically, each professional discipline (like mechanical engineering or electrical engineering) usually ends up having four to six grade levels, each of which requires a fairly broad salary range. This approach helps ensure that the employer remains competitive when bidding for professionals whose attainments vary widely and whose potential employers are literally found worldwide.[86]

CURRENT ISSUES IN COMPENSATION MANAGEMENT

comparable worth
The concept by which women who are usually paid less than men can claim that men in comparable rather than strictly equal jobs are paid more.

The Issue of Comparable Worth

THE ISSUE   Should women who are performing jobs *equal* to men's or just comparable to men's be paid the same as men? This is the basic issue in *comparable worth*.

Comparable worth refers to the requirement to pay equal wages for jobs of comparable (rather than strictly equal) value to the employer. In a limited sense, this means jobs that, while not equal, are at least quite similar, such as assemblers on one line versus assemblers on a different assembly line. In its broadest sense, though, comparable worth includes comparing quite dissimilar jobs, such as nurses to fire truck mechanics or secretaries to technicians.[87]

Equal pay legislation has a history of debate over whether "equal" or "comparable" should be the standard for comparison when comparing men's and women's jobs.[88] For years, "equal" was the standard in the United States, though "comparable" was and is used in Canada and many European countries.[89] As a result of court rulings, though, some experts now believe that comparable worth may become the standard in the United States.[90]

THE *GUNTHER* SUPREME COURT CASE   *Gunther v. County of Washington* was a pivotal case. It involved Washington County, Oregon, prison matrons who claimed sex discrimination. In this case, the county had evaluated nonequal, but comparable men's jobs as having 5% more "job content" (based on a point evaluation system) than the women's jobs, but paid the men 35% more.[91] After seesawing through the courts, Washington County finally agreed to pay 35,000 employees in female-dominated jobs almost $500 million in pay raises over 7 years in settlement of this suit.

COMPARABLE WORTH AND JOB EVALUATION   Some experts have argued that job evaluation procedures like the point method are inherently unfair to women because they ignore or underestimate the skills associated with the types of jobs often held by women.[92] For example, one expert argues that many of the skills associated with jobs like nursing and teaching go unrecognized because they "mirror traditional duties within the home"; they are ignored because it's assumed that they need not be learned on the job or are somehow less important than skills that are based on on-the-job training.[93]

By this line of reasoning job evaluation procedures like the point method may have an inherent bias against women, since they ignore the sorts of skills women may bring to the job, while crediting men for similar skills that must be learned on the job. For example, while men "typically receive points for dirt and grease that they encounter on the job under a factor designated 'working conditions,' nurses, who deal with [dirt and blood] on a daily basis, receive no such points."[94]

Therefore, the issue of comparable worth has important implications for an employer's job evaluation procedures. In virtually every comparable worth case that reached a court, the claim involved the use of the point method of job evaluation. Here each job is evaluated in terms of several factors (like effort, skill, and responsibility) and then assigned points based on the degree of each factor present in the job. Point plans therefore encourage comparable worth ratings of different jobs. For example, two positions such as Clerk-Typist IV and Junior Engineer might be evaluated as having the same number of points and, therefore, comparable worth. This would suggest that both jobs should be paid the same, although in practice market wage rates may be much higher for the male-dominated junior engineers than for the female-dominated clerk-typist mediating against any such change.[95]

As noted above, there is also the possibility of bias in the job evaluation plan itself. As noted, some traditional job evaluation point plans "tend to result in higher point totals for jobs traditionally held by males than for those traditionally held by females."[96] For example, the factor "supervisory responsibility" might heavily weigh chain-of-command factors such as number of employees supervised and downplay the importance of gaining the voluntary cooperation of other employees. One solution here is to rewrite the factor rules in job evaluation plans so as to give more weight to the sorts of activities that female-dominated positions frequently emphasize.[97]

IMPLICATIONS   Some argue that avoiding comparable worth problems doesn't require discarding point-type plans, just using them more wisely. For example, one suggestion is to stress prevailing market rates in pricing jobs, and then use an evaluation method (like the point method) only to slot in those jobs for which a market price is not readily available.[98] Another is for employers to price their jobs as they see fit (with or without point plans), but to ensure that women have equal access to all jobs; the idea here is to eliminate the wage discrimination issue by eliminating sex-segregated jobs.[99] To avoid comparable worth problems, ask questions like these:

> Are your job duties and responsibilities clearly documented either by a job analysis questionnaire or a job description? Are they reviewed and updated annually?
>
> When was your pay system last reviewed? If more than 3 years have passed, serious inequities could exist.
>
> Are there any circumstances where your pay plan indicates that jobs are comparable, even in the marketplace, but you are paying those jobs occupied by females or minorities less than predominantly male and/or white jobs?
>
> When was the last time you statistically checked the effect of your pay system on females and minorities? Could it be that you have discrimination in fact though not in intent?
>
> Is your pay system clearly documented in a salary administration manual? If not, the credibility and defensibility of your pay practices are ripe for challenge.[100]
>
> Are you complying with state comparable work laws? Many states have passed their own comparable work laws, and states tend to broadly interpret laws that mandate equal pay for comparable work.[101] In some states, workers may collect substantial back pay and other damages by showing a wage disparity, even when the comparable jobs seem substantially different on the surface.[102]

The Issue of Salary Compression

Salary Compression, a result of inflation, means that longer-term employees' salaries are lower than those for workers entering the firm today. Its symptoms include (1) high starting salaries compared to current employees' salaries; and/or (2) unionized hourly pay increases that overtake supervisory and nonunion hourly rates.

Dealing with salary compression is a tricky problem.[103] On the one hand, you don't want your long-termers to be treated unfairly or to become inordinately dissatisfied and possibly leave with their accumulated knowledge and expertise. On the other hand, mediocre performance or lack of assertiveness, rather than salary compression, may explain some low salaries.

In any case, there are several solutions.[104] As distasteful as it is to many employers to pay employees for seniority, you can pay raises based on longevity (or, preferably, on longevity plus skills). Second, a much more aggressive merit pay program can be installed. Third, supervisors can be authorized to recommend "equity" adjustments for selected incumbents who are both highly valued by the organization and also viewed as unfairly victimized by pay compression.

The Issue of Cost-of-Living Differentials

As mentioned earlier, cost-of-living differences between cities can cause serious compensation problems. For example, a family of four might live in Miami for just over $39,000 per year, while the same family's annual expenditures in Chicago or Los Angeles would be over $56,000.

Employers can use several methods to handle cost-of-living differentials. One is to give the transferred person a nonrecurring payment, usually in a lump sum or perhaps spread over 1 to 3 years.[105] Other employers pay a differential for ongoing costs in addition to a one-time allocation. For example, one employer pays a differential of $6,000 per year to people earning $35,000 to $45,000 who are transferred from Atlanta to Minneapolis.[106] Other companies simply increase the employee's base salary rate.

GLOBAL ISSUES IN HR

■ The Issue of Compensating Expatriate Employees

The question of cost-of-living differentials has particular relevance to multinational firms. The annual cost of sending a U.S. expatriate manager from the United States to Europe varies widely according to country. For example, it's estimated that the annual cost of keeping a U.S. expatriate in France might average $193,000, while in neighboring Germany the cost would be $246,000.[107]

Such wide discrepancies raise the issue of how multinational firms should compensate overseas employees. The issue is particularly important today, in part because of the growing need to staff overseas operations and in part because of the increasing frequency with which managers and professionals are moved from country to country.

Two basic international compensation policies are popular: home-based and host-based policies.[108]

Under a home-based salary policy, an international transferee's base salary reflects his or her home country's salary structure. Additional allowances are then tacked on for cost-of-living differences and housing and schooling costs, for instance. This is a reasonable approach for short-term assignments and avoids the problem of having to change the employee's base salary every time he or she moves. However, it can result in some difficulty at the host office if, say, employees from several different countries are all being paid different base salaries for performing essentially the same tasks.

In the host-based plan, the base salary for the international transferree is tied to the host country's salary structure. In other words, the manager from New York who is sent to France would have his or her base salary changed to the prevailing base salary for that position in France, rather than keep his or her New York base salary. Of course, cost-of-living, housing, schooling, and other allowances are tacked on here as well. However, this approach can cause some consternation to the New York manager who might, for instance, see his or her base salary plummet with a transfer to Bangladesh. And, he or she may face the problem of frequent salary fluctuations if he or she moves from country to country fairly often.

There's no one best way to deal with the international compensation problem. One compensation expert suggests a compromise of basing the person's new base salary on a percentage of home-country salary plus the higher of a percentage of (1) host-country salary or (2) the amount required in host-country currency to maintain a home-country standard of living in the host location.[109] A recent survey of multinational enterprises suggests that most set expatriates' salaries according to their home-country base pay.[110] (Thus, a French manager assigned to Kiev by a U.S. multinational will generally have a base salary that reflects the salary structure in the manager's home country, in this case France.) In addition, there will be various allowances including cost-of-living, relocation, housing, education, and hardship allowances (the latter for countries with relatively hard quality of life such as China). The multinational employer will also usually pay any extra tax burdens resulting from taxes the manager is liable for over and above those he or she would have to pay in the manager's home country. As in the United States, about one-third of the expatriates' compensation package consists of benefits. In time, the increasing globalization of business might lead to more global standardization of pay rates for most occupations around the world, according to two experts.[111]

SMALL BUSINESS APPLICATION

■ Developing a Pay Plan

Developing a pay plan that is internally and externally equitable is as important in a small firm as in a large one. Paying wage rates that are too high for the area may be unnecessarily expensive, and paying less may guarantee poor-quality help and high turnover. Similarly, wage rates that are internally inequitable will reduce morale and cause the president to be badgered mercilessly by employees demanding raises "the same as Joe down the hall." The president who wants to concentrate on major issues like sales would thus do well to institute a rational pay plan as soon as possible.

DEVELOPING A WORKABLE PAY PLAN

The first step should be to conduct a wage survey. The basic methods for doing so were described earlier in this chapter, but in a smaller business you'll generally depend on less-formal methods for collecting this information.

Four sources here can be especially useful. A careful perusal of the Sunday classified newspaper ads should yield useful information on wages offered for jobs similar to those you are trying to price. Second, your local Job Service office can be a wealth of information, as it compiles extensive information on pay ranges and averages for many of the jobs listed in the *Dictionary of Occupational Titles*. (This is another reason for using job titles that are consistent with those in the DOT.) The Job Service office can provide information on wages within the local area served by that office, as well as on the geographic region served by the group of Job Service offices of which your office is one member. Third, the Internet (as explained above) can yield a wealth of information on area pay rates. Finally, local employment agencies, always anxious to establish ties that could grow into business relationships, should be able to provide fairly good data regarding pay rates for different jobs.

Next, if you employ more than 20 employees or so, conduct at least a rudimentary job evaluation. For this, you will first require job descriptions, since these will be the source of data regarding the nature and worth of each job.

You will usually find it easier to split employees into three groups—managerial/professional, office/clerical, and plant personnel. For each of the three groups, determine the compensable factors to be evaluated and then rank or assign points to each job based on the job evaluation.

For each job or class of jobs (such as assemblers), you will want to create a pay range. The procedure for doing so was described earlier. However, in general, you should choose as the midpoint of your range the target salary as required by your job evaluation and then produce a range of about 30% around this average, broken into a total of five steps.

While it doesn't always work, you may find it useful to experiment with using the *Dictionary of Occupational Titles* data-people-things scores as a simple job evaluation method. As explained earlier (on pages 94–96) the experts at the Department of Labor have produced data-people-things scores for each job in the *Dictionary of Occupational Titles*.

There are many situations in which these scores can be used for job evaluation purposes, although they are not designed to be so used. Assigning job evaluation ratings to jobs based on the data-people-things scores seems to work best when you're dealing with jobs that are fairly similar in many respects. It often works well in evaluating all manufacturing jobs in a company's plant, for instance. Here you may have a range of jobs such as textile loom fixer; production supervisor; weaver; production crew member; and fabricator. Strictly speaking, the data-people-things scores for each job reflect the degree to which each of these three factors is present in each job (for instance, the degree to which the job requires manipulating data, dealing with people, or dealing with things). These scores are listed in the dictionary for each job title. Therefore, it is simple for you to, say, add up the D-P-T numerical score for each job to see whether it produces what appears to be a logical hierarchy of jobs (in terms of their value to the company). Again, this approach is not for everyone, but it is so simple that it is worth a try. A weighing scheme could be included if you believed that one factor should be weighing more heavily than the others.

COMPENSATION POLICIES

How small businesses set compensation policies is important, too. For example, you need to have a policy on when and how raises are computed. Many small-business owners make the mistake of appraising employees on their anniversary date, a year after they are hired. The problem here is that the raise for one employee then becomes the standard for the next, as employees have time to compare notes over the space of several weeks or months. This produces a never-ending cycle of appraisals and posturing for ever-higher raises.

The better alternative is to have a policy of once-a-year raises during a standard 1-week appraisal period, preferably about 4 weeks before the budget for next year must be produced. In this way, the administrative headache of conducting these appraisals and awarding raises is dealt with during a 1 (or 2) week period. Furthermore, the total required raise money (which of course has to be computed in advance by the company president) is known more precisely when next year's budget is compiled. Other required compensation policies include amount of holiday and vacation pay (as explained in Chapter 13), overtime pay policy, method of pay (weekly, biweekly, monthly), garnishments, and time card or sign-on sheet procedures. (For sources of sample policies, see the HR systems appendix at the end of this book, on pages 645–652.)

LEGAL ISSUES

This chapter outlined a number of federal, state, and local laws to which small and large employers must adhere. Local and state laws will often cover companies not covered by the Fair Labor Standards Act, but the latter is actually quite comprehensive. It covers most employees of enterprises engaged in activities affecting interstate or foreign commerce. Retail and service companies are covered if their annual gross volume of business is not less than $362,500 a year and any other type of business is covered if its volume is not less than $250,000 a year.[112]

Misclassification of exempt employees is probably the biggest mistake made by smaller firms. As noted earlier, some employees are exempt from the overtime and/or minimum wage requirements of the FLSA. A common small-business mistake is to assume that putting employees on a yearly salary exempts them from the overtime provisions of the act. You cannot make those workers exempt simply by paying them a yearly salary, nor can you make them exempt by claiming they are "managers" because they spend some of their time supervising other employees. Strictly speaking, employees have to spend at least 50% of their time actually supervising other employees to be classified as executive, managerial, or supervisory employees. It is not enough that they spend 80% of their time doing the same work as the people they supervise, and only 20% of their time actually supervising.[113] Employees in administrative jobs "directly related to management policies or general business operations" and who are salaried and earning at least $250 a week may also be exempt. These might include, for instance, executive and administrative assistants such as executive assistant to the president or executive secretary and staff members who act as advisory specialists such as HR directors, controllers, and credit managers.[114]

There are other common wage-hour traps to avoid.[115] With respect to meal and break periods, an employee must generally be paid for meal periods unless the period is at least 20 minutes long, the employee is completely relieved of duties, and the employee can leave his or her work post. Also beware of how you handle compensatory time off. Many smaller employers believe they can have an employee work, say, 45 hours in one week, pay the person for 40 hours and give them 5 hours compensatory time off in the following week. Doing so is illegal; if there is to be compensatory time off, the employer must provide 1½ hours off for each overtime hour worked. (Thus, if someone works 42 hours in one week, he or she should receive 3 hours of compensable time.) Furthermore, you cannot get around this by manipulating the pay period. For example, if your pay period ranges from Monday morning through Sunday night, you can't temporarily change the pay period to Saturday morning through Friday in order to accommodate the need to work extra hours on a weekend due to a rush job.[116]

Great care also must be taken when it comes to paying for time recorded. For example, suppose employees are required to clock in. They consistently clock in 15 minutes early or get into the habit of not clocking out for lunch. Here it is possible that a wage and hour inspector may conclude the employees were underpaid, since there is no record that they were clocked out for the period for which they were docked.

Also beware of how you use so-called independent contractors. Many small businesses hire, say, management consultants or part-time bookkeepers and then classify these people as independent contractors. Independent contractors are, as their name implies, not employed by the firm and are thus not eligible for unemployment compensation, worker's compensation, or any other benefits accruing to the firm's employees. At first glance, this seems like a cost-effective way to run a firm, and to some extent it can be. However, care must be taken not to call people who are legitimately employees "independent contractors" just to get around paying them benefits. There are many factors that determine whether a person is in fact an independent contractor. For example, a worker who is required to comply with another person's instructions about when, where, and how he or she is to work is ordinarily considered an employee, not an independent contractor.[117] Other important considerations include the extent to which the services rendered are an integral part of the employer's business; the permanency of the business relationship between the parties; the amount of individual investment in facilities and equipment by the workers; and the existence of the opportunity for profit and loss on the part of the worker.[118]

We invite you to visit the Dessler page on the Prentice Hall Web site at **www.prenhall.com/dessler** for our on-line study guide, Internet exercises, current events, links to related Web sites, and more.

SUMMARY

1. There are two bases on which to pay employees compensation—increments of time and volume of production. The former includes hourly or daily wages and salaries. Basing pay on volume of production ties compensation directly to the amount of production (or number of "pieces") the worker produces.

2. Establishing pay rates involves five steps: conduct salary survey, evaluate jobs, develop pay grades, use wage curves, and fine-tune pay rates.

3. Job evaluation is aimed at determining the relative worth of a job. It compares jobs to one another based on their content, which is usually defined in terms of compensable factors like skills, effort, responsibility, and working conditions.

4. The ranking method of job evaluation has five steps: (a) obtain job information, (b) select clusters of jobs to be rated, (c) select compensable factors, (d) rank jobs, and (e) combine ratings (of several raters). This is a simple method to use, but there is a tendency to rely too heavily on guesstimates. The classification (or grading) method is a second qualitative approach that categorizes jobs based on a class description or classification rules for each class.

5. The point method of job evaluation requires identifying a number of compensable factors and then determining the degree to which each of these factors is present in the job.

6. The factor comparison method, as explained in the appendix, is a quantitative job evaluation technique that entails deciding which jobs have more of certain compensable factors than others.

7. Most managers group similar jobs into wage or pay grades for pay purposes. These are comprised of jobs of approximately equal difficulty or importance as determined by job evaluation.

8. The wage curve (or line) shows the average target wage for each pay grade (or job). It can help show you what the average wage for each grade should be and whether any present wages or salaries are out of line. Developing a wage curve involves four steps: (1) find the average pay for each pay grade, (2) plot these wage rates for each pay grade, (3) draw the wage line, and (4) price jobs after plotting present wage rates.

9. Developing a compensation plan for executive, managerial, and professional personnel is complicated by the fact that factors like performance and creativity must take precedence over static factors like working conditions. Market rates, performance, and incentives and benefits thus play a much greater role than does job evaluation for these employees.

10. Broadbanding means collapsing salary grades and ranges into just a few wide levels or bands, each of which then contains a relatively wide range of jobs and salary levels.

11. Three main compensation issues discussed were comparable worth, salary compression, and cost-of-living differentials.

KEY TERMS

employee compensation 396
Davis-Bacon Act 396
Walsh-Healey Public Contract Act 397
Fair Labor Standards Act 397
Equal Pay Act of 1963 397
Civil Rights Act 398

Employee Retirement Income Security Act (ERISA) 398
salary surveys 400
benchmark job 401
job evaluation 403
compensable factors 404
ranking method 405
classification (or grading) method 406

classes 406
grades 406
grade definition 406
point method 407
factor comparison method 407
pay grade 408
wage curve 409
rate ranges 409
comparable worth 421

DISCUSSION
QUESTIONS

1. What is the difference between exempt and nonexempt jobs?
2. Should the job evaluation depend on an appraisal of the jobholder's performance? Why? Why not?
3. What is the relationship between compensable factors and job specifications?
4. What are the pros and cons of the following methods of job evaluation: ranking, classification, factor comparison, and point method?
5. In what respect is the factor comparison method similar to the ranking method? How do they differ?
6. What are the pros and cons of broadbanding, and would you recommend your current employer (or some other firm you're familiar with) use it? Why or why not?
7. It was recently reported in the news that the average pay for most university presidents ranged around $200,000 per year, but that a few earned closer to $500,000 per year. What would account for such a disparity in the pay of universities' chief executive officers?

INDIVIDUAL AND
GROUP ACTIVITIES

1. Working individually or in groups, conduct salary surveys for the following positions: entry-level accountant and entry-level chemical engineer. What sources did you use, and what conclusions did you reach? If you were the HR manager for a local engineering firm, what would you recommend that you pay for each job?
2. Working individually or in groups, use the BLS area wage surveys to determine local area earnings for the following positions: File Clerk I; Accounting Clerk II; Secretary V. How do the BLS figures compare with comparable jobs listed in your Sunday newspaper? What do you think accounts for any discrepancy?
3. Working individually or in groups, use the ranking method to evaluate the relative worth of the jobs listed in question 2, above. (You may use the *Dictionary of Occupational Titles* as an aid.) To what extent do the local area earnings for these jobs correspond to your evaluations of the jobs?

EXPERIENTIAL EXERCISE

Purpose: The purpose of this exercise is to give you experience in performing a job evaluation using the ranking method.

Required Understanding: You should be thoroughly familiar with the ranking method of job evaluation and try to obtain job descriptions for your college's dean, department chairperson, director of admissions, library director, registrar, and your professor.

How to Set Up the Exercise/Instructions: Divide the class into groups of four or five students. The groups

will perform a job evaluation of the positions of dean, department chairperson, and professor using the ranking method.

1. Perform a job evaluation by ranking the jobs. You may use one or more compensable factors.
2. If time permits, a spokesperson from each group can put his or her group's rankings on the board. Did the groups end up with about the same results? How did they differ? Why do you think they differed?

CASE INCIDENT

Salary Inequities at Acme Manufacturing

Joe Blackenship was trying to figure out what to do about a problem salary situation he had in his plant. Blackenship recently took over as president of Acme Manufacturing. The founder, Bill George, had been president for 35 years. The company was family owned and located in a small eastern Arkansas town. It had approximately 250 employees and was the largest employer in the community. Blackenship was a member of the family that owned Acme, but he had never worked for the company prior to becoming president. He had an M.B.A. and a law degree, plus 15 years of management experience with a large manufacturing organization, where he was senior vice president for human resources when he made his move to Acme.

A short time after joining Acme, Blackenship started to notice that there was considerable inequity in the pay structure for salaried employees. A discussion with the human resources director led him to believe that salaried employees' pay was very much a matter of individual bargaining with the past president. Hourly paid factory employees were not part of the problem because they were unionized and their wages were set by collective bargaining. An examination of the salaried payroll showed that there were 25 employees, ranging in pay from that of the president to that of the receptionist. A closer examination showed that 14 of the salaried employees were female. Three of these were front-line factory supervisors and 1 was the human resources director. The other 10 were nonmanagement.

This examination also showed that the human resources director appeared to be underpaid, and that the 3 female supervisors were paid somewhat less than any of the male supervisors. However, there were no similar supervisory jobs in which there were both male and female job incumbents. When asked, the HR director said she thought the female supervisors may have been paid at a lower rate mainly because they were women, and perhaps George did not think that women needed as much money because they had working husbands. However, she added the thought that they were paid less because they supervised less-skilled employees than did male supervisors. Blackenship was not sure that this was true.

The company from which Blackenship had moved had a good job-evaluation system. Although he was thoroughly familiar and capable with this compensation tool, Blackenship did not have time to make a job evaluation study at Acme. Therefore, he decided to hire a compensa-

tion consultant from a nearby university to help him. Together they decided that all 25 salaried jobs should be in the same job-evaluation cluster, that a modified ranking method of job evaluation should be used, and that the job descriptions recently completed by the HR director were current, accurate, and usable in the study.

The job evaluation showed that there was no evidence of serious inequities or discrimination in the non-management jobs, but that the HR director and the three female supervisors were being underpaid relative to comparable male salaried employees.

Blackenship was not sure what to do. He knew that if the underpaid female supervisors took the case to the local EEOC office, the company could be found guilty of sex discrimination and then have to pay considerable back wages. He was afraid that if he gave these women an immediate salary increase large enough to bring them up to where they should be, the male supervisors would be upset and the female supervisors might comprehend the total situation and want back pay. The HR director told Blackenship that the female supervisors had never complained about pay differences, and they probably did not know the law to any extent.

The HR director agreed to take a sizable salary increase with no back pay, so this part of the problem was solved. Blackenship believed he had four choices relative to the female supervisors:

1. To do nothing.
2. To gradually increase the female supervisors' salaries.
3. To increase their salaries immediately.
4. To call the three supervisors into his office, discuss the situation with them, and jointly decide what to do.

■ QUESTIONS

1. What would you do if you were Blackenship?
2. How do you think the company got into a situation like this in the first place?
3. Why would you suggest Blackenship pursue the alternative you suggested?

Source: This case was prepared by Professor James C. Hodgetts of the Fogelman College of Business and Economics of the University of Memphis. All names are disguised. Used by permission.

Case Application

SALARY ADMINISTRATION IN THE ENGINEERING DEPARTMENT

Introduction

Majestic Corporation was a major chemical company with many plant locations. The Rockville plant was one of the company's largest, and it produced a wide variety of chemical products. As part of its complex, the plant also housed Majestic's applied and developmental research laboratories and an engineering department.

The engineering department performed engineering services not only for Rockville but also for many other Majestic Corporation plant facilities. At this time, the department consisted of approximately one hundred personnel who were supervised by seven engineering supervisors reporting to the chief engineer. Engineers in the department were organized in functional groups such as mechanical design, instrument and electrical design, corrosion, pollution abatement and environmental quality, materials handling, and computer technology. Other engineers specialized in various production processes, performing chemical engineering work to improve existing processes and drawing upon functional groups as projects demanded. Approximately one-half of the engineers had less than five years' experience at Rockville; the other half had up to thirty-five years' experience with the company. Some seventy engineers performed professional engineering work in the department; the remainder were supervisors, computer specialists, technicians, secretaries, and word processors.

Salary Administration Policy

Majestic had a well-formulated salary administration plan. Each year, corporate headquarters allocated a "raise budget" to each plant, and the plant human resources department coordinated allocation of available raise funds. Each raise budget was expressed as a percentage of existing salaries, which was thus a constraint on the total amount of raises granted in one year. At the time of this case, company policy stated that any raise to be granted an engineering employee depended on the following factors:

1. *Present performance level.*
   a. Excellent—maximum of 10%.
   b. Above adequate plus—maximum of 8%.
   c. Above adequate—maximum of 7%.
   d. Above adequate minus—maximum of 6%.
   e. Adequate—maximum of 5%.
   f. Below adequate—no raise permitted.

2. *Employee's present salary in relation to the guide-rate for job level.* For engineering positions (for which progressive job titles existed, such as assistant engineer, engineer, senior engineer, etc.) there was a single curve as a guide-rate at each performance level relative to the number of years since the employee received the baccalaureate degree. The curves sloped upward from zero years' experience to twenty years' experience and then leveled out. (Figure 11-10 shows the salary curves for "engineers." Similar curves were developed for each of the other job categories in the company. These curves were periodically revised and updated to reflect current conditions.)

3. *Availability of raise budget.* This was expressed as a percentage of total plant salaries at the beginning of the year.

4. *Raise frequency.* Newly hired employees could be given a raise after six months with Majestic, and thereafter no more frequently than every eleven months. The policy guideline for raise frequency was:
   a. Excellent—eleven to twelve months.
   b. Above adequate plus—twelve to thirteen months.
   c. Above adequate—twelve to fourteen months.
   d. Above adequate minus—thirteen to fifteen months.
   e. Adequate—fifteen to eighteen months.

5. *Promotional adjustment.* On promotion to a higher-level job, a person could be given an additional raise of up to 15% if necessary to bring his or her salary in line with the higher-level salary curve. This was not usually applied to the promotion from assistant engineer to engineer or to senior engineer.

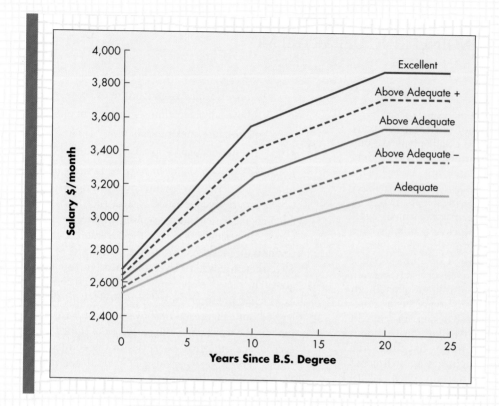

FIGURE 11-10
Salary Curves for Engineers

Deviation from these policy guidelines could be granted if a supervisor made a very strong case for doing so. Seldom, however, was permission granted by higher management for deviation from the guidelines.

In addition, each year supervisors had to furnish a "potential-for-promotion" rating to the HR department for each employee. The scale here was excellent, good, fair, and limited. These ratings were forwarded to the salary administrator in the HR department. However, according to policy, the potential-for-promotion rating was not supposed to influence salary administration. The potential ratings were supposedly used in organizational planning and for developing training programs.

Mechanics of Salary Administration

About March of each year, each engineering department supervisor prepared a salary raise plan for employees for the following year. Each individual plan was reviewed with the salary administrator in the human resources department who negotiated some adjustments in order to:

1. Ensure equity among various plant groups;
2. Ensure that planned increases were within the plant raise budget;
3. Ensure that no one was overlooked.

The engineering supervisors also reviewed their raise plans with the chief engineer to be sure that the department head concurred with their decisions. The salary administrator usually "kept" a small reserve of raise money to cover exceptional performance improvements and new employees not on the plan. There was seldom any major problem using up the entire plant raise budget. A few January raises could be moved up to December or vice versa to do the fine tuning.

The Situation

Tom Green, one of the engineering department supervisors, had just returned from a review of his next year's salary plan with the HR salary administrator. Green went into John Benson's office; Benson was a fellow engineering supervisor. Tom closed the door.

Tom: You know those personnel types are a real slippery bunch of so and so's.

John: Oh, what have they done now?

Tom: I've just returned from reviewing next year's salary plan with Fran Hays (the HR department salary administrator), and she wants to pass out the raises based on the ratings I assigned my engineers for potential rather than on the ratings I assigned them for present job performance.

John: Did Hays really say that?

Tom: No, I just concluded that from the adjustments she recommended. She was constantly pushing raises up for the new kids we've hired out of college the past few years whom we have rated excellent on potential but only so-so on present performance. Fran says we don't have to worry about our people getting too high on the salary curve because they mostly will be promoted to higher-level jobs in a few years anyway. Of course, this doesn't leave much raise budget for our real good performers that have reached their top level of advancement.

John: I know what you mean. Mike Jones just transferred into my group last year, and he is about $400 below where his excellent performance and thirty years' experience should put him. I don't know what we would do around here without engineers such as Mike. The sad part is that Mike will be retiring in about seven or eight years, and his pension will be based on his last five years' salary. I feel I've got to get his salary in line within a year or two.

Tom: Too bad his former bosses didn't go to bat for Mike.

John: I really think that the HR office is working pretty hard to do a good job of salary administration. Generally, I think they are fair. The trouble is that there is just not enough raise money to do everything we would like to do.

During their discussion, Tom Green and John Benson reached the conclusion that an employee's present performance was measured reasonably by the annual performance-appraisal system but that the potential rating was extremely subjective. HR staff had never really defined what it meant by "excellent potential" for advancement, and company policy was supposed to be that the potential ratings were not to influence salary administration anyway. The chief engineer had attempted to fill the definitional vacuum by providing the guidelines shown in Table 11-3 to the engineering supervisors.

Majestic Corporation had the dual-advancement route, whereby individuals could move up the managerial ladder, or advance by the technological route from "engineer" to "senior engineer" to "engineering specialist," "senior engineering specialist," "technologist," and "advanced technologist." Majestic tried to make pay and status for top technological jobs "equal" to top managerial jobs. The above criteria were applied to either managerial or technical advancement. Both Green and Benson concluded that the potential rating was still too highly subjective.

■ QUESTIONS

1. What do you think of Majestic's Salary Administration Policy? How would you change it?

2. Would you recommend broadbanding for engineer jobs at Majestic? Why or why not?

3. How would you proceed now if you were Tom Green?

Source: Raymond L. Hilgert, and Cyril C. Ling, *Cases and Experiential Exercises in Human Resource Management* (Upper Saddle River, NJ: Prentice Hall, 1996), pp. 216–220.

TABLE 11-3 Chief Engineer's Guidelines for Potential Rating

POTENTIAL RATING	CRITERIA
Excellent	Expect person to advance two job levels in five years
Good	Expect person to advance one level in five years
Fair	Person may or may not advance one level in the next five years
Limited	Expect person definitely will not move beyond present level

NOTES

1. Thomas Patten, Jr., *Pay: Employee Compensation and Incentive Plans* (New York: Free Press, 1977), p. 1. See also Jerry McAdams, "Why Reward Systems Fail," *Personnel Journal*, Vol. 67, no. 6 (June 1988), pp. 103–113; James Whitney, "Pay Concepts for the 1990s," Part I, *Compensation and Benefits Review*, Vol. 20, no. 2 (March–April 1988), pp. 33–34; and James Whitney, "Pay Concepts for the 1990s," Part II, *Compensation and Benefits Review*, Vol. 20, no. 3 (May–June 1988), pp. 45–50. See also "Aligning Work and Rewards: A Round Table Discussion," *Compensation and Benefits Review*, Vol. 26, no. 4 (July–August 1994), pp. 47–63 and Marlene Morganstern, "Compensation and the New Employment Relationship," *Compensation and Benefits Review*, Vol. 27, no. 2 (March 1995), pp. 37–44.

2. Orlando Behling and Chester Schriesheim, *Organizational Behavior* (Boston: Allyn and Bacon, 1976), p. 233.

3. Based partly on Richard Henderson, *Compensation Management* (Reston, VA: Reston, 1980).

4. A complete description of exemption requirements is found in U.S. Department of Labor, *Executive, Administrative, Professional & Outside Salesmen Exempted from the Fair Labor Standards Act* (Washington, DC: U.S. Government Printing Office, 1973).

5. "Employer Ordered to Pay $2 Million in Overtime," *BNA Bulletin to Management*, September 26, 1996, pp. 308–309.

6. Michael Wolfe, "That's Not an Employee, That's an Independent Contractor," *Compensation & Benefits Review* (July–August 1996), p. 61.

7. Earl Mellor, "Weekly Earnings in 1985: A Look at More than 200 Occupations," *Monthly Labor Review*, Vol. 109, no. 9 (September 1986), pp. 27–34; Bureau of National Affairs, *Fair Employment Practices* (1988), p. 27. See also John R. Hellenbeck et al., "Sex Differences in Occupational Choice, Pay, and Worth: A Supply-Side Approach to Understanding the Male-Female Wage Gap," *Personnel Psychology*, Vol. 40, no. 4 (Winter 1987), pp. 715–744.

8. Allison Wellington, "Changes in the Male/Female Wage Gap, 1976–1985," *The Journal of Human Resources*, Vol. 29, no. 2 (1989), pp. 383–411, and June O'Neill and Solomon Polachek, "Why the Gender Gap in Wages Narrowed in the 1980s," *Journal of Labor Economics*, Vol. 11, no. 1 (1993), pp. 205–228.

9. O'Neill and Polachek, "Why the Gender Gap in Wages Narrowed."

10. Commerce Clearing House, *Ideas and Trends in Personnel*, October 31, 1986, pp. 169–171.

11. Robert Nobile, "How Discrimination Laws Affect Compensation," *Compensation & Benefits Review* (July–August 1996), pp. 38–42.

12. Henderson, *Compensation Management*, pp. 101–127; see also Barry Hirsch and Edward Schumacher, "Unions, Wages, and Skills," *Journal of Human Resources*, Vol. 33, no. 1 (Winter 1998), pp. 201–219.

13. Ibid., p. 115.

14. Joseph Famularo, *Handbook of Modern Personnel Administration* (New York: McGraw-Hill, 1972), pp. 27–29. See also Bruce Ellig, "Strategic Pay Planning," *Compensation and Benefits Review*, Vol. 19, no. 4 (July–August 1987), pp. 28–43; Thomas Robertson, "Fundamental Strategies for Wage and Salary Administration," *Personnel Journal*, Vol. 65, no. 11 (November 1986), pp. 120–132. One expert cautions against conducting salary surveys based on job title alone. He recommends job-content salary surveys that examine the content of jobs according to the size of each job so that, for instance, the work of the president of IBM and that of a small clone manufacturer would not be inadvertently compared. See Robert Sahl, "Job Content Salary Surveys: Survey Design and Selection Features," *Compensation & Benefits Review* (May–June 1991), pp. 14–21.

15. Jeffrey Pfeffer, "Six Dangerous Myths About Pay," *Harvard Business Review* (May–June 1998), pp. 109–119.

16. "Locality Pay Differentials," *BNA Bulletin to Management*, April 25, 1996, pp. 132–133; and "Annual Pay Levels and Growth in Pay by State," *BNA Bulletin to Management*, October 30, 1997, pp. 348–350.

17. Vicki Kaman and Jodie Barr, "Employee Attitude Surveys for Strategic Compensation Management," *Compensation & Benefits Review* (January–February 1991), pp. 52–65.

18. "Use of Wage Surveys," *BNA Policy and Practice Series* (Washington, DC: Bureau of National Affairs, 1976), pp. 313–314. In a recent survey of compensation professionals, uses of salary survey data were reported. The surveys were used most often to adjust the salary structure and ranges. Other uses included determining the merit budget, adjusting individual job rates, and maintaining pay leadership. D. W. Belcher, N. Bruce Ferris, and John O'Neill, "How Wage Surveys Are Being Used," *Compensation & Benefits Review* (September–October 1985), pp. 34–51. For further discussion, see, for example, Kent Romanoff, Ken Boehm, and Edward Benson, "Pay Equity: Internal and External Considerations," *Compensation & Benefits Review*, Vol. 18, no. 3 (May–June 1986), pp. 17–25.

19. Henderson, *Compensation Management*, pp. 260–269.

20. Joan O'Brien and Robert Zawacki, "Salary Surveys: Are They Worth the Effort?" *Personnel*, Vol. 62, no. 10 (October 1985), pp. 70–74.

21. For more information on these surveys, see the company's brochure "Domestic Survey References," Watson Wyatt Data Services, 218 Route 17 North, Rochelle Park, NJ 07662, 1998.

22. "International Sources of Salary Data," *Compensation & Benefits Review* (May–June 1998), p. 23.

23. You may have noticed that job analysis as discussed in Chapter 3 can be a useful source of information on compensable factors, as well as on job descriptions and job specifications. For example, a quantitative job analysis technique like the position analysis questionnaire generates quantitative information on the degree to which the following five basic factors are present in each job: having decision making/communication/social responsibilities, performing skilled activities, being physically active, operating vehicles or equipment, and processing information. As a result, a job analysis technique like the PAQ is actually as (or some say, more) appropriate as a job evaluation technique in that jobs can be quantitatively compared to one another on those five dimensions and their relative worth thus ascertained. Another point worth noting is that

you may find that a single set of compensable factors is not adequate for describing all your jobs. Many managers, therefore, divide their jobs into job clusters. For example, you might have a separate job cluster for factory workers, for clerical workers, and for managerial personnel. Similarly, you would then probably have a somewhat different set of compensable factors for each job cluster.

24. A. N. Nash and F. J. Carroll, Jr., "Installation of a Job Evaluation Program," from *Management of Compensation* (Monterrey, CA: Brooks/Cole, 1975), reprinted in Craig Schneier and Richard Beatty, *Personnel Administration Today: Readings and Commentary* (Reading, MA: Addison-Wesley, 1978), pp. 417–425; and Henderson, *Compensation Management*, pp. 231–239. According to one survey, about equal percentages of employers use individual interviews, employee questionnaires, or observations by personnel representatives to obtain the actual job evaluation information. See Mary Ellen Lo Bosco, "Job Analysis, Job Evaluation, and Job Classification," *Personnel*, Vol. 62, no. 5 (May 1985), pp. 70–75. See also Howard Risher, "Job Evaluation: Validity and Reliability," *Compensation and Benefits Review*, Vol. 21, no. 1 (January–February 1989), pp. 22–36; and David Hahn and Robert Dipboye, "Effects of Training and Information on the Accuracy and Reliability of Job Evaluations," *Journal of Applied Psychology*, Vol. 73, no. 2 (May 1988), pp. 146–153.

25. As explained later, the practice of red circling is used to delay downward adjustments in pay rates that are presently too high given the newly evaluated jobs. See also E. James Brennan, "Everything You Need to Know About Salary Ranges," *Personnel Journal*, Vol. 63, no. 3 (March 1984), pp. 10–17.

26. Nash and Carroll, "Installation of a Job Evaluation," p. 419.

27. Ibid.

28. C. F. Lutz, "Quantitative Job Evaluation in Local Government in the United States," *International Labor Review* (June 1969), pp. 607–619.

29. Sondra O'Neal, "CAJE: Computer-Aided Job Evaluation for the 1990s," *Compensation & Benefits Review* (November–December 1990), pp. 14–19.

30. Ibid.

31. If you used the job classification method, then of course the jobs are already classified.

32. David Belcher, *Compensation Administration* (Upper Saddle River, NJ: Prentice Hall, 1973), pp. 257–276.

33. Gerald Ledford, Jr., "Three Case Studies on Skill-Based Pay: An Overview," *Compensation & Benefits Review* (March–April 1991), pp. 11–23.

34. Gerald Ledford, Jr., "Paying for the Skills, Knowledge, and Competencies of Knowledge Workers," *Compensation & Benefits Review* (July–August 1995), p. 56; see also Richard Sperling and Larry Hicks, "Trends in Compensation and Benefits Strategies," *Employment Relations Today*, Vol. 25, no. 2 (Summer 1998), pp. 85–99.

35. Gerald Ledford, Jr., "Three Case Studies on Skill-Based Pay: An Overview," p. 12. See also Kathryn Cofsky, "Critical Keys to Competency-Based Pay," *Compensation & Benefits Review* (November–December 1993), pp. 46–52.

36. Gerald Ledford, Jr., and Gary Bergel, "Skill-Based Pay Case Number 1: General Mills," *Compensation & Benefits Review* (March–April 1991), pp. 24–38; see also Gerald Barrett, "Comparison of Skill-Based Pay with Traditional Job Evaluation Techniques," *Human Resource Management Review*, Vol. 1, no. 2 (Summer 1991), pp. 97–105. See also Barbara Dewey, "Changing to Skill-Based Pay: Disarming the Transition Land Mines," *Compen-*

sation & Benefits Review, Vol. 26, no. 1 (January–February 1994), pp. 38–43.

37. This is based on Ledford and Bergel, "Skill-Based Pay Case Number 1," pp. 28–29.

38. Kevin Parent and Carline Weber, "Case Study: Does Paying for Knowledge Pay Off?" *Compensation & Benefits Review* (September–October 1994), pp. 44–50; and Edward Lawler, III, Gerald Ledford, Jr., and Lei Chang, "Who Uses Skill-Based Pay, and Why," *Compensation & Benefits Review* (March–April 1993), pp. 22–26.

39. Parent and Weber, "Case Study." For a good discussion of the conditions under which competency-based pay is more effective, see Edward Lawler, III, "Competencies: A Poor Foundation for the New Pay," *Compensation & Benefits Review* (November–December 1996), pp. 20–26.

40. Edward Lawler, III, "Competencies: A Poor Foundation for the New Pay," *Compensation & Benefits Review* (November–December 1996), pp. 20–22.

41. Ledford, "Paying for Skills, Knowledge, and Competencies of Knowledge Workers," p. 55.

42. Ibid., p. 58. See also Melvyn Stark, Warren Luther, and Steve Balvano, "Jaguar Cars Drives Toward Competency-Based Pay," *Compensation & Benefits Review* (November–December 1996), pp. 34–40.

43. "Broadbanding of Pay Structures Gains Prominence," BNA Policy and Practice Series, *Bulletin to Management*, January 20, 1994, p. 17.

44. Duncan Brown, "Broadbanding: A Study of Company Practices in the United Kingdom," *Compensation & Benefits Review* (November–December 1996), p. 43.

45. David Hofrichter, "Broadbanding: A 'Second Generation' Approach," *Compensation & Benefits Review* (September–October 1993), pp. 53–58. See also Gary Bergel, "Choosing the Right Pay Delivery System to Fit Banding," *Compensation & Benefits Review*, Vol. 26, no. 4 (July–August 1994), pp. 34–38.

46. Ibid., p. 55.

47. For example, see Sondra Emerson, "Job Evaluation: A Barrier to Excellence?" *Compensation & Benefits Review* (January–February 1991), pp. 39–51; Nan Weiner, "Job Evaluation Systems: A Critique," *Human Resource Management Review*, Vol. 1, no. 2 (Summer 1991), pp. 119–132.

48. Fay Hansen, "Where to Find Compensation and Benefits Sources on the Web?" *Compensation & Benefits Review* (July–August 1997), pp. 16–22.

49. "101 + Hot Web Sites for Compensation & Benefits Professionals," *American Management Association International*, New York, NY, 1998, pp. 7–8.

50. Ibid., pp. 53 and 57.

51. Emerson, "Job Evaluation," p. 39.

52. This is based on Laurent Dufetel, "Job Evaluation: Still at the Frontier," *Compensation & Benefits Review* (July–August 1991), pp. 53–67.

53. Ibid., p. 54.

54. Andrew Richter, "Paying the People in Black at Big Blue," *Compensation & Benefits Review* (May–June 1998), p. 51.

55. Ibid., pp. 53–54.

56. Ibid., p. 54.

57. Ibid.

58. Ibid.

59. See Ibid., p. 55.

60. Ibid., p. 56.

61. Ibid., p. 56.

62. Jude Rich, "Future Compensation Shock," *Compensation & Benefits Review* (November–December 1996), pp. 27–33; N. Fredric Crandall and Marc Wallace, Jr., "Inside the Virtual Workplace: Forging a New Deal for Work and Rewards," *Compensation & Benefits Review*, (January–February 1997), Vol. 29, no. 1, pp. 27–38.

63. Gerry Newman and Frank Krzystofiak, "Value-Chain Compensation," *Compensation & Benefits Review* (May/June 1998), p. 60.

64. Jude Rich, "Meeting the Global Challenge: A Measurement and Reward Program for the Future," *Compensation & Benefits Review* (July–August 1992), p. 27.

65. Ibid., p. 28.

66. Charles Cumming, "Will Traditional Salary Administration Survive the Stampede to Alternative Rewards," *Compensation & Benefits Review*, (November–December 1992), pp. 42–47.

67. Jude Rich, "Future Compensation Shock," *Compensation & Benefits Review*, (November–December 1996), p. 29.

68. Ibid., p. 29.

69. Ibid., p. 29. See also Crandall and Wallace, "Inside the Virtual Workplace" pp. 27–36.

70. Dale Yoder, *Personnel Management and Industrial Relations* (Upper Saddle River, NJ: Prentice Hall, 1970), pp. 643–645; Famularo, *Handbook of Modern Personnel Administration*, pp. 32.1–32.6 and 30.1–30.8.

71. Mark Meltzer and Howard Goldsmith, "Executive Compensation for Growth Companies," *Compensation & Benefits Review*, November–December 1997, pp. 41–50.

72. Douglas Tormey, "Executive Compensation: Creating 'Legal' Checklist," *Compensation & Benefits Review*, (July–August 1996), pp. 12–36.

73. "Executive Pay," The *Wall Street Journal*, April 11, 1996, pp. R16, R170.

74. Nardash Agarwal, "Determinants of Executive Compensation," *Industrial Relations*, Vol. 20, no. 1 (Winter 1981), pp. 36–45. See also John A. Fossum and Mary Fitch, "The Effects of Individual and Contextual Attributes on the Sizes of Recommended Salary Increases," *Personnel Psychology*, Vol. 38, no. 3 (Autumn 1985), pp. 587–602.

75. Andrew Henderson and James Fredrickson, "Information-Processing Demands as a Determinant of CEO Compensation," *Academy of Management Journal*, Vol. 39, no. 3 (1996), pp. 576–606.

76. Ibid., pp. 585–586.

77. Foster, " "Does Executive Pay Make Sense?" p. 50.

78. This is based on William White, "Managing the Board Review of Executive Pay," *Compensation & Benefits Review* (November–December 1992), pp. 35–41.

79. Ibid., pp. 38–40; see also H. Anthony Hampson, "Tying CEO Pay to Performance: Compensation Committees Must Do Better," *The Business Quarterly*, Vol. 55, no. 4 (Spring 1991), pp. 18–22.

80. William White and Raymond Fife, "New Challenges for Executive Compensation in the 1990s," *Compensation & Benefits Review* (January–February 1993), pp. 27–35.

81. Famularo, *Handbook of Modern Personnel Administration*, pp. 32.1–32.6. See also Peter D. Sherer, Donald Schwab, and Herbert Henneman, "Managerial Salary-Raise Decisions A Policy-Capturing Approach," *Personnel Journal*, Vol. 40, no. 1 (Spring 1987), pp. 27–38.

82. Famularo, *Handbook of Modern Personnel Administration*, pp. 30.1–30.1.5.

83. Ibid., pp. 30.1–30.5. See also Patric Moran, "Equitable Salary Administration in High-Tech Companies," *Compensation & Benefits Review*, Vol. 18, no. 5 (September–October 1986), pp. 31–40.

84. Robert Sibson, *Compensation* (New York: AMACOM, 1981), p. 194.

85. Helen Remick, "The Comparable Worth Controversy," *Public Personnel Management Journal* (Winter 1981), pp. 371–383.

86. See also Bernisha Bridges, "The Role of Rewards in Motivating Scientific and Technical Personnel: Experience at Egland AFB," *National Productivity Review* (Summer 1993), pp. 337–348.

87. Helen Remick, "The Comparable Worth Controversy," *Public Personnel Management Journal* (Winter 1981), p. 38; U.S. Department of Labor, *Perspectives on Working Women: A Data Book*, October 1980.

88. Helen Remick, "The Comparable Worth Controversy," *Public Personnel Management Journal* (Winter 1981), pp. 371–383.

89. *Ibid.*, p. 377

90. *Ibid*

91. *County of Washington v. Gunther*, U.S. Supreme Court No. 80–429, June 8, 1981.

92. Jennifer Quinn, "Visibility and Value: The Role of Job Evaluation in Assuring Equal Pay for Women," *Law and Policy in International Business*, Vol. 25, no. 4 (Summer 1994), pp. 1403–1444.

93. Ibid., p. 1411.

94. Ibid., p. 1411.

95. See David Thomsen, "Compensation and Benefits—More on Comparable Worth," *Personnel Journal*, Vol. 60 (May 1981) pp. 348–349; Marvin Levine, "Comparable Worth in the 1980s: Will Collective Bargaining Supplant Legislative and Judicial Interpretations?" *Labor Law Journal*, Vol. 38, no. 6 (June 1987), pp. 323–335; Peter Olney, Jr., "Meeting the Challenge of Comparable Worth," Part II, *Compensation & Benefits Review*, Vol. 19, no. 3 (May–June 1987), pp. 45–53; and Jennifer Quinn, "Visibility and Value: The Role of Job Evaluation in Assuring Equal Pay for Women," *Law and Public Policy in International Business*, Vol. 25, no. 4 (Summer 1994), pp. 1403–1444.

96. Mary Gray, "Pay Equity Through Job Evaluation: A Case Study," *Compensation & Benefits Review*, (July–August 1992), p. 46.

97. Ibid., pp. 46–51; see also Teresa Brady, "How Equal is Equal Pay?," *Management Review*, Vol. 87, no. 3 (March 1998), pp. 59–61.

98. Brinks, "The Comparable Worth Issue: A Salary Administration Bombshell," *Personnel Administration*, Vol. 26, no. 11, (November 1981), p. 40.

99. Michael Carter, "Comparable Worth: An Idea Whose Time Has Come?" *Personnel Journal*, Vol. 60 (October 1981), p. 794; and Peter Olney, Jr., "Meeting the Challenge of Comparable Worth," Part I, *Compensation & Benefits Review*, Vol. 19, no. 2 (March–April 1987), pp. 34–44. See also Mary Virginia Moore and Yohannan Abraham, "Comparable Worth: Is It A Moot Issue? Part II: The Legal and Juridical Posture," *Public Personnel Management*, Vol. 23, no. 2 (Summer 1994), pp. 263–286.

100. Brinks, "The Comparable Worth Issue," p. 40.

101. James Coil, III and Charles Rice, "State Comparable Work Laws: Equal Pay for Unequal Work," *Employment Relations Today* (Autumn 1993), p. 333.

102. Ibid., p. 333. See also Paul Greenlaw and Robert D. Lee, Jr., "Three Decades of Experience with the Equal Pay Act," *Review of Public Personnel Administration*, Vol. 13, no. 4 (1993), pp. 43–58.

103. Wendell C. Lawther, "Ways to Monitor (and Solve) the Pay Compression Problem," *Personnel* (March 1989), pp. 84–87.

104. Ibid., p. 87.

105. Rugus Runzheimer, Jr., "How Corporations are Handling Cost of Living Differentials," *Business Horizons*, Vol. 23 (August 1980), p. 39.

106. Ibid., p. 39.

107. Jack Anderson, "Compensating Your Overseas Executives, Part II: Europe in 1992," *Compensation & Benefits Review* (July–August 1990), p. 28.

108. This is based on Ibid., pp. 29–31.

109. Ibid., p. 31.

110. Richard Hodgetts and Fred Luthans, "U.S. Multinationals' Expatriates' Compensation Strategies," *Compensation & Benefits Review* (January–February 1993), pp. 57–62.

111. George Milkovich and Matt Bloom, "Rethinking International Compensation," *Compensation & Benefits Review*, Vol. 30, no. 1, (January–February 1998), pp. 15–24.

112. Wayne Outten and Noah Kinigstein, *The Rights of Employees* (New York: Bantam Books, 1983), pp. 201–202.

113. Commerce Clearing House, "How to Avoid the Ten Most Common Wage-Hour Traps," *Ideas and Trends*, March 10, 1989, p. 43.

114. Arthur Silbergeld and Mark Tuvim, "Recent Cases Narrowly Construe Exemption from Overtime Provisions of Fair Labor Standards Act," *Employment Relations Today* (Summer 1994), pp. 241–250; see also Charles Fine, "Exempt or Not? Classification Can Mean Big Dollars," *Management Review* (July 1993), pp. 58–60. Also see Matthew Smith and Steven Winterbauer, "Overtime Compensation Under the FLSA: Pay Them Now or Pay Them Later," *Employee Relations Labor Journal*, Vol. 19, no. 1 (Summer 1993), pp. 23–51.

115. Ibid.

116. With more companies, establishing all-salaried workforces, firms are seeking to erase, to as great an extent as possible, the distinction between exempt and nonexempt employees. As a result, there are some exceptions that permit fluctuating workweeks. See Christopher Martin and Jerry Newman, "The FLSA Overtime Provision: A New Controversy," *Compensation & Benefits Review* (July–August 1991), pp. 60–63.

117. For a full discussion, see Peter Gold and Michael Esposito, "The Right to Control: Are Your Workers Independent Contractors or Employees?" *Compensation & Benefits Review* (July–August 1992), pp. 30–37.

118. "Employee versus Independent Contractor," *BNA Bulletin to Management*, March 28, 1996, p. 104.

12

PAY-FOR-PERFORMANCE AND FINANCIAL INCENTIVES

Tampa, Florida-based AmeriSteel and its mini-steel mills faced a problem. Declining profits and sales meant its new strategy had to emphasize becoming more competitive—and fast. Yet for 20 years its employees had come to expect above-average raises, in good times and bad. To support its new cost-cutting strategy, a new incentive plan—a "gainsharing" plan—was installed. From now on, employees would be rewarded as if they were partners in the firm: sharing in the cost savings they produced, and taking home less in those years in which profits declined[1] ▲

MONEY AND MOTIVATION: BACKGROUND

The use of financial incentives—financial rewards paid to workers whose production exceeds some predetermined standard—was first popularized by Frederick Taylor in the late 1800s. As a supervisory employee of the Midvale Steel Company, Taylor had become concerned with what he called "systematic soldiering"—the tendency of employees to work at the slowest pace possible and to produce at the minimum acceptable level. What especially intrigued him was the fact that some of these same workers still had the energy to run home and work on their cabins, even after a hard 12-hour day. Taylor knew that if he could find some way to harness this energy during the workday, huge productivity gains would be achieved.

At this time, primitive piecework systems were already in use but were generally ineffective. Workers were paid a piece rate for each piece they produced, based on quotas arrived at informally. However, rate cutting by employers was flagrant, and the workers knew that if their earnings became excessive, their pay per piece would be cut. As a result, most workers produced just enough to earn a decent wage, but little enough so that their rate per piece would not be reduced.

One of Taylor's great insights was in seeing the need for a standardized, acceptable view of a **fair day's work.** As he saw it, this fair day's work should depend not on the vague estimates of supervisors but on a careful, formal, scientific process of inspection and observation. It was this need to evaluate each job scientifically that led to the **scientific management** movement. In turn, scientific management gave way in the Depression-plagued 1930s to the human relations movement and its focus on satisfying workers' social—not just financial—needs. For many years incentives declined in popularity.

fair day's work

Frederick Taylor's observation that haphazard setting of piecework requirements and wages by supervisors was not sufficient, and that careful study was needed to define acceptable production quotas for each job.

scientific management

The careful, scientific study of the job for the purpose of boosting productivity and job satisfaction.

Performance and Pay

Today's emphasis on shareholder-value is creating a renaissance for financial incentive or pay-for-performance plans. Indeed, intense competition and higher business risk seems to be a fertile environment in which pay-for-performance plans flourish. One study focused on 20 *Fortune* 500 companies ranging in size from 4,000 to 275,000 employees.[2] Data were obtained regarding the proportion of variable pay for managers in these companies, as well as on the degree of turbulence faced by their companies. (Turbulence was reflected by such events as reductions in force, sale or spinoff of assets or operations, leveraged buyouts, acquisition by another company, mergers, joint ventures, and attempted takeovers.) The researchers concluded that "our data showed that organizations in which turbulence was greater shifted the financial risk to their managers by paying proportionally higher levels of variable pay."[3]

Another study involved 34 stores of a large retailer, 15 of which implemented a new incentive plan. The researchers found that implementing the sales associatés' incentive plan "enables a store to capture more customers from its competitors when there is more intense competition."[4] In other words, the new sales-incentive plan was particularly effective in the stores facing the greatest competition.

This second study also highlights the relationship between strategy and incentives. In this case the purpose of the new sales incentive was to help implement the retail chain's new customer-focused service strategy, a strategy that basically required sales consultants to focus on identifying and satisfying the needs of individual customers. By paying the sales associates in part based on how they performed their customer-service duties, the retail chain was able to focus the associates' behavior on doing whatever was necessary to satisfy the customer, without a detailed set of instructions regarding how to do so; their own commitment and self-control then made sure they supported the company's new service strategy.

In 1998 the DuPont Company similarly implemented a performance-based plan for its 50,000 U.S.-based chemicals and specialties employees.[5] According to the president of

DuPont's U.S. region, "This is the first time in DuPont's history that the compensation of all U.S.C & S employees can be linked directly to their specific business's performance.... Our goal is to ensure that we provide shareholders with superior performance and value creation.... With employees focused on business performance and their specific role in the success of their business, we believe we will achieve this goal more quickly."[6]

Types of Incentive Plans

There are several types of incentive plans.[7] *Individual incentive programs* give income over and above base salary to individual employees who meet a specific individual performance standard.[8] **Spot bonuses** are awarded, generally to individual employees, for accomplishments that are not readily measured by a standard, such as "to recognize the long hours this employee put in last month," or "to recognize exemplary customer service this week."[9] *Group incentive programs* are like individual incentive plans but they give pay over and above base salary to all team members when the group or team collectively meets a specified standard for performance, productivity, or other work-related behavior.[10]

Profit-sharing plans are generally organizationwide incentive programs that provide employees with a share of the organization's profits in a specified period.[11] *Gainsharing programs* are organizationwide pay plans designed to reward employees for improvements in organizational productivity. As we'll see, gainsharing plans generally include employee suggestion systems and focus on reducing labor costs through employee suggestions and participation.[12]

Variable pay refers to any plan—usually a group plan—that ties pay to productivity or to some other measure of the firm's profitability. Variable pay is distinguished from plans like individual incentive programs or spot bonuses by the fact that variable pay always ties compensation to business outcomes, with cash payouts based on predetermined *measures of group performance.*[13] In other words, "a true variable pay plan must be group, team, or company oriented. . . ."[14] The family of variable pay plans thus generally does not include plans (like piecework) that simply reward individual efforts. On the other hand gainsharing plans (discussed below) and organizationwide profit sharing are variable pay plans.[15] Both individual plans (such as piecework) and variable plans are all considered

spot bonus

A spontaneous incentive awarded to individuals for accomplishments not readily measured by a standard.

variable pay

Any plan that ties pay to productivity or profitability, usually as one-time lump payments.

Incentive plans are among the benefits enjoyed by UPS drivers, who are measured by numerous standards such as packages delivered per hour.

pay-for-performance plans. However, the whole topic of variable pay is in a state of flux, and, confusing as it may be, some experts do include individual performance plans within the domain of variable pay.[16]

For simplicity we will discuss these incentive or pay-for-performance plans as follows: incentives for operations employees; incentives for managers and executives; incentives for salespeople; incentives for white-collar and professional employees (merit pay); and organizationwide incentive plans.

INCENTIVES FOR OPERATIONS EMPLOYEES

piecework

A system of pay based on the number of items processed by each individual worker in a unit of time, such as items per hour or items per day.

straight piecework plan

Under this pay system each worker receives a set payment for each piece produced or processed in a factory or shop.

guaranteed piecework plan

The minimum hourly wage plus an incentive for each piece produced above a set number of pieces per hour.

Piecework Plans

Several incentive plans are particularly well suited for use with operations employees, such as for those doing production work. **Piecework** is the oldest incentive plan and is still the most commonly used. Earnings are tied directly to what the worker produces; the person is paid a *piece rate* for each unit he or she produces. Thus, if Tom Smith gets $0.40 apiece for stamping out doorjambs, then he would make $40 for stamping out 100 a day and $80 for stamping out 200.

Developing a workable piece-rate plan requires both job evaluation and (usually) industrial engineering. Job evaluation enables you to assign an hourly wage rate to the job in question. But the crucial issue in piece-rate planning is the production standard, and this standard is usually developed by industrial engineers. Production standards are stated in terms of a standard number of minutes per unit or a standard number of units per hour. In Tom Smith's case, the job evaluation indicated that his doorjamb stamping job was worth $8 an hour. The industrial engineer determined that 20 jambs per hour was the standard production rate. Therefore, the piece rate (for each doorjamb) was $8.00 divided by 20 = $0.40 per doorjamb.

With a **straight piecework plan**, Tom Smith would be paid on the basis of the number of doorjambs he produced; there would be no guaranteed minimum wage. However, after passage of the Fair Labor Standards Act, it became necessary for most employers to guarantee their workers a minimum wage. With a **guaranteed piecework plan,** Tom Smith would be paid $5.15 per hour (the minimum wage) whether or not he stamped out 13 doorjambs per hour (at $0.40 each). But as an incentive he would also be paid at the piece rate of $0.40 for each unit he produced over 13.

Piecework generally implies straight piecework, a strict proportionality between results and rewards regardless of the level of output. Thus, in Smith's case, he continues to get $0.40 apiece for stamping out doorjambs, even if he stamps out many more than planned, say, 500 per day. On the other hand, some piecework plans call for a sharing of productivity gains between worker and employer, such that the worker "receives credit for only some of the above-normal production."[17]

ADVANTAGES AND DISADVANTAGES   Piecework incentive plans have their advantages. They are simple to calculate and easily understood by employees. Piece-rate plans appear equitable in principle, and their incentive value can be powerful because rewards are directly tied to performance.

Piecework also has disadvantages. One is its somewhat unsavory reputation among some employees, based on some employers' history of raising production standards when their workers' earnings became "excessive". Another disadvantage is more subtle; since the piece rate is quoted on a per-piece basis, in workers' minds production standards become tied inseparably to the amount of money earned. When an attempt is made to revise production standards, it meets considerable worker resistance, even if the change is fully justified.[18]

In fact, the industrial engineered specificity of piecework plans provides the seeds of piecework's biggest disadvantage these days. Piecework plans tend to be tailor-made for relatively specialized jobs in which employees do basically the same narrow tasks over and over again many times a day. This in turn fosters a certain rigidity; employees become pre-occupied with producing the number of units needed. They become less willing to concern themselves with meeting quality standards or switching from job to job (since doing so could reduce the person's productivity).[19] Similarly, attempts to introduce new technology or processes may incur more resistance, insofar as they require major adjustments to standards, and negotiations with employees. Equipment also tends not to be as well maintained, since employees are focusing on maximizing each machine's output. Options include team-based incentive plans and gainsharing-type programs, which we will discuss later in this chapter.

Standard Hour Plan

standard hour plan

A plan by which a worker is paid a basic hourly rate but is paid an extra percentage of his or her base rate for production exceeding the standard per hour or per day. Similar to piecework payment but based on a percent premium.

The **standard hour plan** is like the piece-rate plan, with one major difference. With a piece-rate plan the worker is paid a particular rate per each piece that he or she produces. With the standard hour plan the worker is rewarded by a *percent premium that equals the percent by which his or her performance exceeds the standard.* The plan assumes the worker has a guaranteed base rate.

As an example, suppose the base rate for Smith's job is $8 per hour. (The base rate may, but need not, equal the hourly rate determined by the job evaluation.) And again assume that the production standard for Smith's job is 20 units per hour, or 3 minutes per unit. Suppose that in one day (8 hours) Smith produces 200 doorjambs. According to the production standard, this should have taken Smith 10 hours (200 divided by 20 per hour); instead it took him 8 hours. He produced at a rate 25% (40 divided by 160) higher than the standard rate. The standard rate would be 8 hours times 20 (units per hour) = 160; Smith actually produced 40 more, or 200. He will, therefore, be paid at a rate 25% above his base rate for the day. His base rate was $8 per hour times 8 hours equals $64. So he'll be paid 1.25 times 64 or $80.00 for the day.

The standard hour plan has most of the advantages of the piecework plan and is fairly simple to compute and easy to understand. But the incentive is expressed in units of time instead of in monetary terms (as it is with the piece-rate system). Therefore, there is less tendency on the part of workers to link their production standard with their pay. Furthermore, the considerable clerical job of recomputing piece rates whenever hourly wage rates are reevaluated is avoided.[20]

Team or Group Variable Pay Incentive Plans

team or group incentive plan

A plan in which a production standard is set for a specific work group, and its members are paid incentives if the group exceeds the production standard.

As the name suggests, **team** or **group incentive plans** pay the incentive based on the team's results, rather than to individual employees based on their individual performances. This can be done in several ways.[21] One is to set work standards for each member of the group and to maintain a count of the output of each member. Members are then paid based on one of three formulas: (1) all members receive the pay earned by the highest producer, (2) all members receive the pay earned by the lowest producer, or (3) all members receive payment equal to the average pay earned by the group. A second approach is to set a production standard based on the final output of the group as a whole; all members then receive the same pay, based on the piece rate that exists for the group's job. The group incentive can be based on either the piece rate or standard hour plan, but the latter is somewhat more prevalent.

A third option is to choose a measurable definition of group performance or productivity that the group can control. You could, for instance, use broad criteria such as total labor hours per final product. Piecework's precisely engineered standards are thus not necessarily required here.[22]

A fourth and increasingly prevalent approach is to tie team performance to the company's strategic goals. One company, for instance, wanted to create a pay plan that was "driven by strategy," and to help do this by paying teams for results. To accomplish this, the company set up a pool of money—such that if the company reached 100% of its goal, the employees would share in about 5% of this. Basically, that 5% pool was then divided by the number of employees to arrive at the value of a "share." Each work team then received two goals, and if the team achieved both its goals, each employee would earn one share, in addition to his or her base pay. Employees on teams that reached only one goal would earn one-half share. Those on teams reaching neither goal earned no shares. The results of this new plan—in terms of changing employee attitudes and focusing teams on strategic goals—was or were reportedly "extraordinary."[23]

There are several reasons to use team incentive plans. Increasingly today, jobs are interrelated, as they are on project teams. Here one worker's performance reflects not just his or her own effort but that of coworkers as well, so team incentives make sense. Team plans also reinforce group planning and problem solving and help ensure collaboration.[24] In Japan, "the first rule is never reward only one individual." Instead, employees are rewarded as a group in order to reduce jealousy, to make group members indebted to one another (as they would be to the group), and to encourage a sense of cooperation.[25] There tends to be less bickering among group members over who has "tight" production standards and who has loose ones. Group incentive plans also facilitate on-the-job training, since each member of the group has an interest in getting new members trained as quickly as possible.[26]

A group incentive plan's chief disadvantage is that each worker's rewards are no longer based solely on his or her own efforts. In one study, however (in which the researchers arranged to pay the group based on the performance of its best member), the group incentive was as effective as an individual one in improving performance.[27] "Free riders"—team members who share in the team awards but don't put their hearts into the team's efforts—can be a problem. Some experts recommend having all team members commit to a shared set of values in the form of a written statement emphasizing putting the goals of the team before their own personal interests as well as basing part of each team member's pay on some measures of individual (not team) performance.[28]

INCENTIVES FOR MANAGERS AND EXECUTIVES

Most employers award their managers and executives short term bonuses and long term incentives because of the role managers play in determining divisional and corporate profitability.[29] Of those offering short-term incentive plans, virtually all—96%—provide those incentives in the form of cash payments; for those offering long-term incentive plans, about 48% offer stock options, which are intended to motivate and reward management for the corporation's long-term growth, prosperity, and shareholder value. For mature companies, base-salary, short term incentives, long term incentives, and benefits might be 60%, 15%, 15%, and 10% respectively for executives. For growth companies the corresponding figures would be 40%, 45%, 25%, and 10%.[30]

Short-Term Incentives: The Annual Bonus

annual bonus

Plans that are designed to motivate short-term performance of managers and are tied to company profitability.

Most firms have **annual bonus** plans aimed at motivating the short-term performance of their managers and executives. Unlike salaries, which rarely decline with reduced performance, short-term bonuses can easily result in plus or minus adjustments of 25% or more in total pay.

There are three basic issues to be considered when awarding short-term incentives: eligibility, fund-size, and individual awards. Bonus eligibility is usually broad, covering both top and lower level executives and is mainly decided in one of two ways. According to one 1997 survey, about 25% of companies decide based on job level or job title who will be eligible for a short term bonus. About 54% of employers decide eligibility on a combination of factors including job level/title, base salary level, and discretionary considerations (such as identifying key jobs that have a measurable impact on profitability). Base salary level alone is reportedly the sole determinant of eligibility in less then 3% of the companies polled.[31]

The size of the bonus is usually greater for top-level executives. Thus, an executive earning $150,000 in salary may be able to earn another 80% of his or her salary as a bonus, while a manager in the same firm earning $80,000 can earn only another 30%. Similarly, a supervisor might be able to earn up to 15% of his or her base salary in bonuses. Average bonuses range from a low of 10% to a high of 80% or more. A typical company might establish a plan whereby executives could earn 45% of base salary, managers 25%, and supervisory personnel 12%.

HOW MUCH TO PAY OUT (FUND SIZE)   Next, a decision must be made regarding fund size—the total amount of bonus money that will be available—and there are several ways to do this. Some companies use a *nondeductible formula*. Here a straight percentage (usually of the company's net income) is used to create the short-term incentive fund. Others use a *deductible formula* on the assumption that the short-term incentive fund should begin to accumulate only after the firm has met a specified level of earnings.

In practice, what proportion of profits is usually paid out as bonuses? There are no hard and fast rules, and some firms do not even have a formula for developing the bonus fund (they make that decision on a totally discretionary basis).[32] One alternative is to reserve a minimal amount of the profits, say, 10% for safeguarding stockholders' investments, and then to establish a fund for bonuses equal to, say, 20% of the corporate operating profit before taxes in excess of this base amount. Thus, if the operating profits were $100,000, then the management bonus fund might be 20% of $90,000 or $18,000.[33] Other illustrative formulas used for determining the executive bonus fund are as follows:

> Ten percent of net income after deducting 5% of average capital invested in business.
>
> Twelve and one-half percent of the amount by which net income exceeds 6% of stockholders' equity.
>
> Twelve percent of net earnings after deducting 6% of net capital.[34]

DECIDING INDIVIDUAL AWARDS   The third issue is deciding the *individual awards* to be paid. Typically a target bonus is set for each eligible position, and adjustments are then made for greater or less than targeted performance. A maximum amount, perhaps double the target bonus, may be set. Performance ratings are obtained for each manager, and preliminary bonus estimates are computed. Estimates for the total amount of money to be spent on short-term incentives are thereby made and compared with the bonus fund available. If necessary, the individual estimates are then adjusted.

A related question is whether managers will receive bonuses based on individual performance, corporate performance, or both. Keep in mind that there is a difference between a profit-sharing plan and a true, individual incentive bonus. In a profit-sharing plan, each person gets a bonus based on the company's results, regardless of the person's actual effort. With a true individual incentive, it is the manager's individual effort and performance that are rewarded with a bonus.

Here, again, there are no hard and fast rules. Top-level executive bonuses are generally tied to overall corporate results (or divisional results if the executive is, say, the vice president of a major division). The assumption is that corporate results reflect the person's individual performance. But as one moves further down the chain of command, corporate profits become a less-accurate gauge of a manager's contribution. For, say, supervisory personnel or the heads of functional departments, the person's performance is a more logical determinant of his or her bonus.

Many experts argue that in most organizations managerial and executive-level bonuses should be tied to both organizational and individual performance, and there are several ways to do this.[35] Perhaps the simplest is the *split-award method*, which breaks the bonus into two parts. Here the manager actually gets two separate bonuses, one based on his or her individual effort and one based on the organization's overall performance. Thus, a manager might be eligible for an individual performance bonus of up to $10,000, but receive an individual performance bonus of only $8,000 at the end of the year, based on his or her individual performance evaluation. In addition, though, the person might also receive a second bonus of $8,000 based on the company's profits for the year. Thus, even if there are no company profits, the high-performing manager would still get an individual performance bonus.

One drawback to this approach is that it pays too much to the marginal performer, who, even if his or her own performance is mediocre, at least gets that second, company-based bonus. One way to get around this is to use the *multiplier method*. For example, a manager whose individual performance was poor might not even receive a company-performance-based bonus, on the assumption that the bonus should be a *product* of individual *and* corporate performance. When either is very poor, the product is zero.

Whichever approach is used, outstanding performers should never be paid less than their normal reward, regardless of organizational performance, and they should get substantially larger awards than do other managers. They are people the company cannot afford to lose, and their performance should always be adequately rewarded by the organization's incentive system. Conversely, marginal or below-average performers should never receive awards that are normal or average, and poor performers should be awarded nothing. The money saved on those people should be given to above-average performers.[36]

Long-Term Incentives

Long-term incentives aim to motivate and reward managers for the firm's long-term growth and prosperity and to inject a long-term perspective into the executives' decisions. If only short-term criteria were used, a manager could, for instance, boost profitability by reducing plant maintenance; this tactic might, of course, catch up with the company over 2 or 3 years. Long-term incentives also are intended to encourage executives to stay with the company by giving them the opportunity to accumulate capital (like company stock) that can be "cashed in" after a number of years. Long-term incentives, or **capital accumulation programs**, are most often reserved for senior general and functional area executives.

In addition to stock options, there are four popular long-term incentives: cash, stock, stock appreciation rights, and phantom stock.[37] The popularity of these plans changes over time due to economic conditions and trends, internal company financial pressures, changing attitudes toward long-term incentives, and changes in tax law as well as other factors.[38,39]

capital accumulation programs

Long-term incentives most often reserved for senior executives. Six popular plans include stock options, stock appreciation rights, performance achievement plans, restricted stock plans, phantom stock plans, and book value plans.

stock option

The right to purchase a stated number of shares of a company stock at today's price at some time in the future.

STOCK OPTIONS   The **stock option** is the most popular long-term incentive. A stock option is the right to purchase a specific number of shares of company stock at a specific price during a period of time; the executive thus hopes to profit by exercising his or her option to buy the shares in the future but at today's price. The assumption is that the price of the stock will go up, rather than go down or stay the same. Unfortunately, this depends partly on considerations outside the executive's control, such as general economic conditions. Stock price is, of course, affected by the firm's profitability and growth, and to the extent the executive can affect these factors, the stock option can be an incentive. However, in one survey it was found that over half the executives saw little or no relationship between their performance and the value of their stock options.[40]

Nonqualified stock options (NSOs) are the most popular stock options. They are options to purchase stock at a stated price, usually the fair market value at the time of the grant.[41]

Several trends have increased the attractiveness of stock options as a long-term executive incentive. High share prices over the past few years have made stock options very attractive to managers and executives, of course, although that could be expected to change if and when the markets take a dramatic downturn. Stock options also help companies comply with a particular IRS regulation concerning shareholder approval of performance-based pay plans.[42] Furthermore, the strong emphasis in the past few years on corporate competitiveness and shareholder value creation as a performance indicator of corporate success has made more shareholders (and therefore boards of directors) interested in emphasizing executive stock options at the expense of alternatives such as cash incentives.[43]

One of the interesting trends in stock options as long-term incentives is that increasingly, they're not just for high-level managers and executives—or even just managers and executives—anymore. In 1998, for instance, IBM more than tripled the number of employees who get stock options, after doubling the number in 1997.[44] Experts today refer to such relatively wide dispersal of stock options as broad-based stock option plans. In turn, the trend toward broad-based stock option plans is aimed at providing support for the competitive strategies being pursued by many companies today. As two compensation experts recently put it, "Companies are asking more from employees than ever before. They have cut out layers of management, downsized, outsourced, empowered employees, [and so forth]."[45] But as a result, some employees are left with the feeling that they are corporate "partners" only in name, working harder but receiving little in return. As a result, say these experts,

> Companies are increasingly interested in drawing employees into the new deal by implementing broad-based stock option plans. By giving stock options to non-executives, companies make good the promise of letting employees share in the company's success.[46]

Of course, all stock option plans are not created equal. For example, stock option plans for key employees such as top executives will typically provide for a very significant upside in the value of stock the employee can receive but be limited to relatively few employees. On the other hand, more companies today are implementing what you might call non-key-employee stock option plans in which the potential appreciation is relatively modest but in which all or most employees can participate.

This idea is summarized in Figure 12-1. This figure illustrates four types of stock option plans, each generally aimed at satisfying a different set of purposes. For example, the key employee program may go to a handful of top executives but provide significant economic incentives both to motivate these people and to keep them on board. On the other hand, the "compensation program" (which is more like the one being put in place at IBM) offers a broad list of employees a highly competitive total compensation package to motivate them, to retain them, and to emphasize that the company intends to share its success with its employees.[47] In turn, Internet technologies can then help companies manage such broad-based plans by providing employees an easy way to check option status, place market orders, and receive updated information.[48]

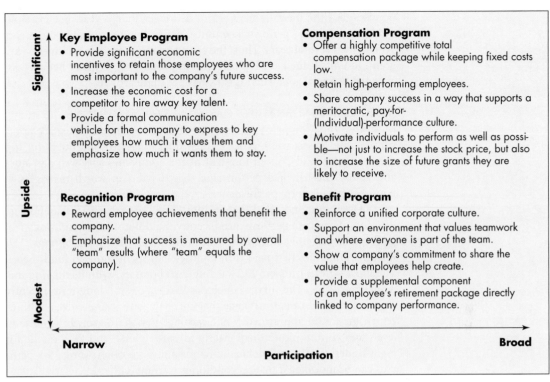

FIGURE 12-1 *Typical Business Purposes of Stock Option Plans*

Source: *Compensation & Benefits Review*, July–Aug. 1998, p. 25.

OTHER PLANS   There are several other popular long-term incentive plans. *Stock appreciation rights* (SARs) are usually attached to stock options; they permit the recipient either to exercise the option (by buying the stock) or to take any appreciation in the stock price in cash, stock, or some combination of these. A *performance achievement plan* awards shares of stock for the achievement of predetermined financial targets, such as profit or growth in earnings per share. With *restricted stock plans*, shares are usually awarded without cost to the executive: Thus, the employee can sell the stock (for which he or she paid nothing) but is restricted from doing so for, say, five years. Finally, under *phantom stock plans* executives receive not shares but "units" that are similar to shares of company stock. Then at some future time they receive value (usually in cash) equal to the appreciation of the "phantom" stock they own.[49]

Whichever long-term plan is used, a main concern is achieving a "better balance between the personal motives and financial incentives of executives and their fiduciary responsibility to shareholders."[50] The problem is that traditional executive incentives often don't build in any real risk for the executive, so the executives' and the shareholders' interests could diverge. Often, for instance, options can be exercised with little or no cash outlay by the executive who then turns around and quickly sells his or her stock. There is, therefore, a growing emphasis on building more executive risk into the long-term incentive formula.[51]

PERFORMANCE PLANS   Performance plans are one means for doing so. They "are plans whose payment or value is contingent on financial performance measured against objectives set at the start of a multi-year period."[52] These grants are similar to annual bonuses, but the measurement period is longer than a year. For example, the plan may award zero to 300 "performance units" depending on the company's earnings per share growth over several years. Thus, the executive might be able to achieve, say, a $50,000 cash grant, in units valued at $100 per unit, in proportion to his or her success in meeting the assigned financial goals such as earnings per share growth.

LONG-TERM INCENTIVES: CASH VS. STOCK OPTIONS   A study by consultants McKinsey and Company, Inc. suggests that giving managers stock options may be the simplest and wisest route as far as providing long-term incentives for top executives. In the McKinsey study, about one-half of the companies surveyed had stock options only, and about one-half had performance-based plans in which managers were given cash bonuses for long-term performance.

The results indicated that in most cases the return to shareholders of companies with long-term cash performance incentives did not differ significantly from that of companies that had only stock-based incentive plans (like stock options). This was so even though companies that paid cash bonuses had spent more to fund their incentive plans. The most serious problem in awarding cash bonuses lay in identifying the proper performance measures. The survey concludes that successful, long-term incentive plans should (1) use measures of performance that correlate with shareholder wealth creation (that is, return on equity and growth), not earnings-per-share growth; (2) establish valid target levels and communicate them clearly to participants; and (3) provide for target adjustment under certain well-defined circumstances (in other words, the performance standards can be modified if market conditions warrant it).[53]

LONG-TERM INCENTIVES FOR OVERSEAS EXECUTIVES   Developing long-term incentives for a firm's overseas operations presents some tricky problems, particularly with regard to taxation. For example, extending a U.S. stock option plan to local nationals in a firm's overseas operations could subject them to immediate taxation on the stocks, even though the shares could not be sold because of requirements built into the company's plan.[54]

The problem extends to U.S. executives stationed overseas. For example, it's not unusual for an executive to be taxed $40,000 on $140,000 of stock option income if he or she is based in the United States. However, if that person receives the same $140,000 stock option income while stationed overseas, he or she may be subject to both the $40,000 U.S. tax and a foreign income tax (depending on the country) of perhaps $94,000. Therefore, ignoring the overseas country's tax burden has the effect of either virtually eliminating the incentive value of the stock from the executive's point of view or dramatically boosting the cost of the stock to the company (assuming the company pays the foreign income tax). In any case, firms cannot assume that they can simply export their executives' incentive programs. Instead, they must consider various factors including tax treatment, the regulatory environment, and foreign exchange controls.[55]

RELATING STRATEGY TO EXECUTIVE COMPENSATION   Few HR practices have as profound or obvious a potential impact on strategy as does how the company crafts its long-term incentives. Whether expanding sales through joint ventures abroad, consolidating operations and downsizing the workforce, or some other, few strategies can be accomplished in just 1 or 2 years. As a result the long-term signals that you send to your executives regarding the results and activities that will (or will not) be rewarded can have a determining impact on whether or not the firm's strategy is implemented effectively. For example, a strategy to boost sales by expanding abroad might suggest linking incentives to increased sales abroad. A cost-reduction strategy might instead emphasize linking incentives to improved profit margins.

Compensation experts therefore suggest defining the strategic context for the executive compensation plan before creating the compensation package itself, as follows:

1. Define the strategic context for the executive compensation program, including the internal and external issues that face the company and its business objectives—boosting sales abroad, downsizing, and so on.

2. Based on your strategic aims, shape each component of the executive compensation package (base salary, short-term incentives, long-term incentives, and benefits and perquisites), and then group the components into a balanced whole.

3. Create a stock option plan to give the executive compensation package the special character it needs to meet the unique needs of the executives and the company.

4. Check the executive compensation plan for compliance with all legal and regulatory requirements and for tax effectiveness.

5. Install a process for reviewing and evaluating the executive compensation plan whenever a major business change occurs.

Strategic context elements to consider in creating the executive compensation plan include: What are the organization's long-term goals, and how can the compensation structure support them? What defines the organization's work culture—its basic values regarding what people should and should not do—and how will the compensation program mold that culture? What are the company's specific business objectives—for example, growth in market share or expansion abroad—and how can the compensation program help push the company in that direction? And, how will the executive compensation program fit into the organization's overall pay strategy?[56]

Shaping each executive component (salary, short-term incentives, long-term incentives, and benefits and perks) should be easier once the strategic framework is in place. One expert suggests tracing, in each business, the main financial factors that tend to drive a company's strategy.[57] Some of these are illustrated in Figure 12-2 on page 450. As this expert says, "In many companies, a careful analysis of historical financials shows that well over 90% of economic value change is driven by a few simple items that can be separated out. . . ."[58] Specifically, about 10 or 15 financial items—pricing, discounts, raw materials costs, and net sales, for instance—are generally the controllable factors that drive the improvements in the value of the company and the value of the shareholders' and owners' investment.[59] These are therefore the sorts of specific items executives financial incentives can be linked to.

INCENTIVES FOR SALESPEOPLE

Sales compensation plans have typically relied heavily on incentives (sales commissions), although this varies somewhat by industry. In the tobacco industry, for instance, salespeople are usually paid entirely via commissions, whereas in the transportation equipment industry salespeople tend to be paid a salary. However, the most prevalent approach is to use a combination of salary and commissions to compensate salespeople.[60]

The widespread use of incentives for salespeople is due to three factors: tradition, the unsupervised nature of most sales work, and the assumption that incentives are needed to motivate salespeople. The pros and cons of salary, commission, and combination plans follow.

Salary Plan

In a salary plan salespeople are paid a fixed salary, although there may be occasional incentives in the form of bonuses, sales contest prizes, and the like.[61]

There are several reasons to use straight salary. It works well when your main aim is

FIGURE 12-2

Link Incentives to the
Factors That Drive
Economic Value Added

Source: *Compensation v Benefits*
Review, July–Aug. 1998, p. 44.

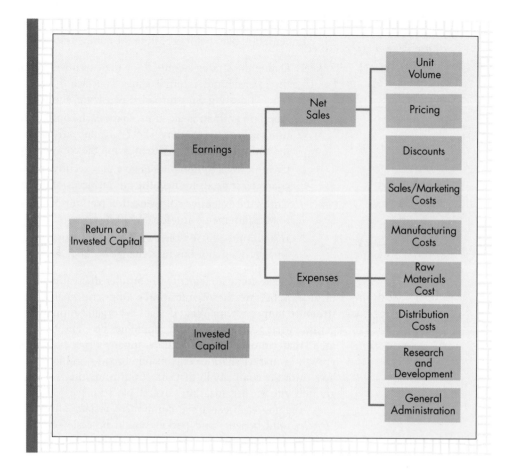

prospecting (finding new clients), or when the salesperson is mostly involved in account servicing, such as developing and executing product training programs for a distributor's sales force or participating in national and local trade shows.[62] Jobs like these are often found in industries that sell technical products. This is one reason why the aerospace and transportation equipment industries have a relatively heavy emphasis on salary plans for their salespeople.

There are advantages to paying salespeople on a straight salary basis. Salespeople know in advance what their income will be, and the employer also has fixed, predictable sales force expenses. Straight salary makes it simple to switch territories or quotas or to reassign salespeople, and it can develop a high degree of loyalty among the sales staff. Commissions tend to shift the salesperson's emphasis to making the sale rather than to prospecting and cultivating long-term customers. A long-term perspective is encouraged by straight salary compensation.

The main disadvantage is that salary plans don't depend on results.[63] In fact, salaries are often tied to seniority rather than to performance, which can be demotivating to potentially high-performing salespeople who see seniority—not performance—being rewarded.

Commission Plan

Commission plans pay salespeople in direct proportion to their sales; they pay for results, and only for results.

The commission plan has several advantages. Salespeople have the greatest possible incentive, and there is a tendency to attract high-performing salespeople who see that effort will clearly lead to rewards. Sales costs are proportional to sales rather than fixed, and the company's selling investment is reduced. The commission basis is also easy to understand and compute.

But the commission plan too has drawbacks. Salespeople focus on making a sale and on high-volume items; cultivating dedicated customers and working to push hard-to-sell items may be neglected. Wide variances in income between salespeople may occur; this can lead to a feeling that the plan is inequitable. More serious is the fact that salespeople are encouraged to neglect nonselling duties like servicing small accounts. In addition, pay is often excessive in boom times and very low in recessions.

RESEARCH INSIGHT   Recent research evidence presents further insights into the impact of sales commissions. One study addressed whether paying salespeople on commission influenced salesperson turnover. One potential drawback of paying salespeople only commission is that the stress of working "without a financial net" might induce more salespeople to leave. Specifically, when pay is 100% at risk, as one sales representative put it,

> *If I go on vacation, I lose money. If I'm sick, I lose money. If I'm not willing to drop everything on a moment's notice to close with a customer, I lose money. I can't see how anyone could stay in this job for long. It's like a trapeze act and I'm working without a net!*[64]

The participants in this study were 225 field sales representatives from a national home telecommunications company. About 85% were men, 65% were married, and their average age was 39, although their ages ranged from 22 to 62. Twenty-one percent had a bachelor's degree and 3% a master's degree. Median tenure was 6 months, which means half the employees left by the end of that period.

As it turns out, paying salespersons under maximally contingent reward conditions—in other words, where commissions accounted for 100% of pay—was the situation with by far the highest turnover of salespersons. On the other hand, turnover was much lower in the situation in which salespersons were paid a combination of a base pay plus commissions.[65] These findings suggest that 100% commissions can be a double-edged sword; it can drive higher sales by focusing the attention of strong-willed salespeople on maximizing sales. On the other hand, it can undermine the desire of salespeople to stay without the financial safety net.

To some extent, of course, the effects on the salesperson of a commission pay plan will depend a lot on that person's personality. A second study further illustrates that fact. In this study, 154 sales representatives were responsible for contacting and renewing existing members and identifying and adding new members.[66] A number of the sales reps in this study were more extroverted than were the others; in other words, they were more sociable, outgoing, talkative, aggressive, energetic, and enthusiastic.[67]

One might expect that extroverted salespeople will usually generate higher sales than less extroverted ones, but interestingly, this is not always the case. In this study, extroversion was positively associated with higher performance (in terms of percentage of existing members renewing their memberships, and the count of new members paying membership fees) *only when the salespeople were explicitly rewarded for accomplishing these tasks.* In this study, in other words, being extroverted didn't always lead to higher sales; extroverts only sold more than those less extroverted when their rewards were contingent on their performance.

Combination Plan

Most companies pay their salespeople a combination of salary and commissions, usually with a sizable salary component. Early studies suggested that the most popular salary/commission split was 80% base salary and 20% incentives, with 70/30 and 60/40 splits being the second and third most frequently reported arrangements.[68] These splits have not appeared to change dramatically over the years. For example, one compensation expert recently used a 70% base salary/30% incentive mix as an example; this both cushioned the downside risk from the salesperson's point of view, while limiting the risk that the upside rewards would get out of hand from the firm's point of view.[69]

Combination plans provide some of the advantages of both straight salary and straight commission plans and some of their disadvantages. Salespeople have a floor to their earnings. Furthermore, the company can direct its salespeople's activities by detailing what services the salary component is being paid for, while the commission component provides a built-in incentive for superior performance.

However, the salary component isn't tied to performance, so the employer is therefore trading away some incentive value. Combination plans also tend to become complicated, and misunderstandings can result. This might not be a problem with a simple "salary plus commission" plan, but most plans are not so simple. For example, there is a "commission plus drawing account" plan. Here a salesperson is paid basically on commissions but can draw on future earnings to get through low sales periods. Similarly, in the "commission plus bonus" plan, salespeople are again paid primarily on the basis of commissions. However, they are also given a small bonus for directed activities like selling slow-moving items.

An example can help illustrate the complexities of the typical combination plan. In one company the following three-step formula is applied:

Step 1: Sales volume up to $18,000 a month. Base salary plus 7% of gross profits plus 0.5% of gross sales.

Step 2: Sales volume from $18,000 to $25,000 a month. Base salary plus 9% of gross profits plus 0.5% of gross sales.

Step 3: Over $25,000 a month. Base salary plus 10% of gross profits plus 0.5% of gross sales.

In all cases, base salary is paid every 2 weeks, while the earned percentage of gross profits and gross sales is paid monthly.[70]

The sales force also may get various special awards.[71] At Oakite Company, for instance, several recognition awards are used to boost sales. For example, a President's Cup is awarded to the top division manager and there is a VIP Club for the top 105 of the sales force in total dollars sales. The VIP Club is well publicized within the firm and carries a lot of prestige. Other firms such as Airwick Industries award televisions and Lenox china as special sales awards.

INCENTIVES FOR OTHER PROFESSIONALS AND EMPLOYEES

merit pay (merit raise)
Any salary increase awarded to an employee based on his or her individual performance.

Merit Pay As an Incentive

Merit pay or a **merit raise** is any salary increase that is awarded to an employee based on his or her individual performance. It is different from a bonus in that it usually becomes part of the employee's base salary, whereas a bonus is a one-time payment. Although the term *merit pay* can apply to the incentive raises given to any employees—exempt or nonexempt, office or factory, management or nonmanagement—the term is more often used with respect to white-collar employees and particularly professional, office, and clerical employees. For the years 1993 to 1999, merit increases have generally averaged between 3.9% and 4.3% per year.[72]

Merit pay has both advocates and detractors and is the subject of much debate.[73] Advocates argue that only pay or other rewards tied directly to performance can motivate improved performance. They contend that the effect of awarding pay raises across the board (without regard to individual performance) may actually detract from performance by showing employees they'll be rewarded the same regardless of how they perform.

On the other hand, merit pay detractors present good reasons why merit pay can backfire. One is that the usefulness of the merit pay plan depends on the validity of the performance appraisal system, since if performance appraisals are viewed as unfair, so too will the merit pay that is based on them.[74] Similarly, supervisors often tend to minimize differences in employee performance when computing merit raises. They give most employees about the same raise, either because of a reluctance to alienate some employees or because of a desire to give everyone a raise that will at least help them stay even with the cost of living. A third problem is that almost every employee thinks he or she is an above-average performer; being paid a below-average merit increase can thus be demoralizing.[75] However, while problems like these can undermine a merit pay plan, there seems little doubt that merit pay can and does improve performance. But you must make sure that the performance appraisals are carried out effectively.[76]

MERIT PAY: TWO NEW OPTIONS   Traditional merit pay plans have two basic characteristics: (1) Merit increases are usually granted to employees at a designated time of the year in the form of a higher base salary (or *raise*), and (2) the merit raise is usually based exclusively on individual performance, although the overall level of company profits may affect the total sum available for merit raises.[77] Two adaptations of merit pay plans are becoming more popular today. One awards merit raises in one lump sum once a year (making them, in effect, short term bonuses for lower-level workers). The other new approach ties awards to both individual and organizational performance.

Lump-sum merit payments are attractive for several reasons. Traditional merit increases are cumulative, but some lump-sum merit raises are not. Since the employee's lump-sum merit raise (of, say 5% of his or her base salary) is awarded in one lump sum, the rise in payroll expenses can be significantly slowed. (Traditionally, someone with a salary of $20,000 per year might get a 5% increase. This moves the employee to a new base salary of $21,000. If the employee gets another 5% increase next year, then the new merit increase of 5% is tacked on not just to the $20,000 base salary but to the extra $1,000 the employee received last year.) Lump-sum merit raises can also help contain benefit costs, since the level of benefits is often tied to a person's current base pay. Lump-sum merit increases can also be more dramatic motivators than traditional merit pay raises. For example, a 5% lump-sum merit payment to our $20,000 employee is $1,000, as opposed to a traditional weekly increment of $19.25 for 52 weeks. Knowing that base salary levels are not being permanently affected by merit pay decisions can also give management more flexibility (say, in a particularly good year) to award somewhat higher lump-sum merit raises. However, before a firm surrenders the merit raise tool that's often used for raising base salaries, any substantial base salary inequities should be eliminated. That way, weaker performers' salaries will not be frozen above higher performers' salaries. The timing of the merit increases may also become more important, since you must now consider the impact of the lump-sum payments on your firm's cash flow.

Another merit pay option is to award lump-sum merit pay based on both individual and organizational performance. A sample matrix for doing so is presented in Table 12-1. In this example the company's performance might be measured by rate of return or sales divided by payroll costs. Company performance is then weighed equally with the employee's performance as measured by his or her performance appraisal. Thus, an outstanding performer would still receive a lump-sum award even if the organization's performance were marginal. However, employees with unacceptable performance would receive no lump-sum awards even for a year in which the organization's performance was outstanding. The advantage of this approach is that it forces employees to focus on organizational goals like profitability and improved productivity. The drawback is that it can

TABLE 12-1 Lump-Sum Award Determination Matrix (an example)

THE EMPLOYEE'S PERFORMANCE (WEIGHT = .50)	THE ORGANIZATION'S PERFORMANCE (WEIGHT = 0.50)				
	OUTSTANDING (1.00)	EXCELLENT (0.80)	COMMENDABLE (0.60)	MARGINAL OR ACCEPTABLE (0.40)	UNACCEPTABLE (0)
Outstanding (1.00)	1.00	0.90	0.80	0.70	0.00
Excellent (0.80)	0.90	0.80	0.70	0.60	0.00
Commendable (0.60)	0.80	0.70	0.60	0.50	0.00
Acceptable (0.00)	—	—	—	—	—
Unacceptable (0.00)	—	—	—	—	—

Source: John F. Sullivan, "The Future of Merit Pay Programs." *Compensation and Benefits Review* (May–June 1989), p. 29.
Instructions. To determine the dollar value of each employee's incentive award. (1) multiply the employee's annual, straight time wage or salary as of June 30 times his or her maximum incentive award and (2) multiply the resultant product times the appropriate percentage figure from this table. For example, if an employee had an annual salary of $20,000 on June 30 and a maximum incentive award of 7% and if her performance and the organization's performance were both "excellent," the employee's award would be $1,120: ($20,000 × 0.07 × 0.80 = $1,120).

reduce the motivational value of the reward by lowering the impact of the employee's own performance on the reward.[78]

Incentives for Professional Employees

Professional employees are those whose work involves the application of learned knowledge to the solution of the employer's problems. They include lawyers, doctors, economists, and engineers. Professionals almost always reach their positions through prolonged periods of formal study.[79]

Pay decisions regarding professional employees involve unique problems. One is that for most professionals money has historically been somewhat less important as an incentive than it has been for other employees. This is true partly because professionals tend to be paid well anyway, and partly because they are already driven—by the desire to produce high-caliber work and receive recognition from colleagues.

However, that's certainly not to say that professionals don't want financial incentives, particularly those in high-demand occupations like software and systems developers for information technology firms. For example, a recent survey of 300 IT departments found that 77% were paying bonuses and incentives including stock options and profit sharing to IT professionals.[80] Many are also offering benefits that are highly attractive to such professionals, including better vacations, more flexible work hours,[81] equipment for home offices[82], and improved pension plans.[83]

ORGANIZATION WIDE VARIABLE PAY PLANS

Many employers have incentive plans in which most or all employees can participate. These variable pay plans include profit-sharing, employee stock ownership (ESOP), and Scanlon/gainsharing plans.

Profit-Sharing Plans

profit-sharing plan

A plan whereby most employees share in the company's profits.

Profit sharing plans in which all or most employees receive a share of the company's annual profits—are popular today. American Airline's employees split $250 million in profit-sharing bonuses in 1998, for instance[84], Ford Motor Co. recently introduced a profit-sharing plan for salaried employees[85], and General Motors recently increased its profit-sharing payout because profits had improved.[86] Yet research on such plans effectiveness is sketchy. In one early survey, about half the employers believed their profit-sharing plans had been beneficial[87] but the benefits were not necessarily in terms of increased performance and motivation. Instead the plans may increase each worker's sense of commitment, participation, and partnership. They may also reduce turnover and encourage employee thrift. A recent study concludes that there is "ample" evidence that profit-sharing plans boost productivity, but that their effect on profits is insignificant, once the costs of the plans' payouts themselves are factored in.[88]

There are several types of profit-sharing plans. In cash plans, the most popular, a percentage of profits usually 15% to 20% is distributed as profit shares to employees at regular intervals. The Lincoln Incentive system is a more complex plan, first instituted at the Lincoln Electric Company of Ohio. In one version employees work on a guaranteed piecework basis, and total annual profits (less taxes, 6% dividends to stockholders, and a reserve for investment) are distributed each year among employees based on their merit rating.[89] The Lincoln plan also includes a suggestion system that pays individual workers rewards for savings resulting from their suggestions. The plan has been quite successful.

There are also *deferred profit-sharing plans*. Here a predetermined portion of profits is placed in each employee's account under the supervision of a trustee. There is a tax advantage to such plans, since income taxes are deferred, often until the employee retires and is taxed at a lower rate.

Employee Stock Ownership Plan (ESOP)

employee stock ownership plan (ESOP)

A corporation contributes shares of its own stock to a trust in which additional contributions are made annually. The trust distributes the stock to employees on retirement or separation from service.

Under the most basic form of **employee stock ownership plans (ESOP)**, a corporation contributes shares of its own stock—or cash to be used to purchase such stock—to a trust, one established to purchase shares of the firm's stock for employees.[90] These contributions are generally made annually in proportion to total employee compensation, with a limit of 15% of compensation. The trust holds the stock in individual employee accounts and distributes it to employees upon retirement or other separation from service assuming the employee has worked long enough to earn ownership of the stock. (Stock options, as discussed earlier in this chapter, go directly to the employees individually to be used as they see fit, rather than into a retirement-related trust.)

Employee stock ownership plans have several advantages. The corporation receives a tax deduction equal to the fair market value of the shares that are transferred to the

Employee stock ownership plans are increasingly popular compensation options and are one of the benefits of working at Hallmark Cards, Inc.

trustee. Corporations can also claim an income tax deduction for dividends paid on ESOP-owned stock.[91] Employees are not taxed until they receive a distribution from the trust, usually at retirement when their tax rate is reduced. The Employee Retirement Income Security Act (ERISA) allows a firm to borrow against employee stock held in trust and then repay the loan in pretax rather than after-tax dollars, another tax incentive for using such plans.[92] The Deficit Reduction Act of 1984 and the Tax Reform Act of 1986 both included substantial tax advantages for ESOP formation, and ESOPs thereafter became a common vehicle for financing acquisitions. The Revenue Reconciliation Act of 1989 reduced several of the ESOP tax benefits but the programs remain popular nevertheless. ESOPs can also help the shareholders of close corporations (in which, for instance, a small family owns virtually all the shares) to diversify their assets by placing some of their shares of the company's stock into the ESOP trust and purchasing other marketable securities for themselves in their place.[93]

Research suggests that ESOPs do encourage employees to develop a sense of ownership in and commitment to the firm.[94] They do so in part because they provide opportunities for increased financial incentives, create a new sense of ownership, and help to build teamwork.[95] The following High Performance box illustrates how one company "shares the wealth" through companywide bonuses and ESOP plans.

THE HIGH-PERFORMANCE ORGANIZATION

Building Better, Faster, More Competitive Organizations Through HR: Sharing the Wealth

■ Thermacore, Inc.—Lancaster, PA

According to management, Thermacore's employees represent the key to the company's performance and competitiveness, and its success in transforming from a low volume research and development enterprise to a high volume production facility and technology leader has mostly occurred because of its employees' dedication and commitment. To enable employees to participate in and benefit from the company's strong growth and performance in recent years, Thermacore has therefore developed various bonus and employee stock purchase programs, which it feels accounts in part for its success.

The annual employee bonus is a very effective way to let employees share in the wealth generated by operations during the year. All employees of Thermacore and its parent corporation, DTX, are eligible for the bonus program. The most unique aspect of the program is that all employees receive the same amount of bonus regardless of total compensation, seniority, or position in the company. Although Thermacore provides other methods for rewarding and recognizing performance, the bonus program affects all employees and has proven to be a very effective incentive.

The bonus pool is based on pre-federal income tax income minus a minimum, threshold guarantee to the stockholders. The threshold guarantee is typically 15% of equity at the beginning of the year. The income to be placed in the bonus pool is then determined by multiplying company income (less the 15 percent-of-equity guarantee) by an employee bonus pool rate determined by the Board of Directors and senior management. Last year, the bonus pool rate was 12%. Full-year, regular employees then receive a full share, and part-time employees receive a share based on the percentage of time worked compared to full-year, regular employees. Last year, the full bonus share was more than $1,300 per employee.

Thermacore also has a stock ownership plan open to all employees. Each year, the stockholders and the Board of Directors approve a gross dollar value to be offered to active employees of the company. For example, the Board may decide to increase the outstanding stock in the company by $100,000. A subscription period (normally one month) is announced for purchase of stock at a price per share set by the Board. No one employee may subscribe for more than $10,000 worth of stock. Thermacore is a private company so stock is only traded within the company. Shares are sold to the employees at a small discount, in consideration for the company receiving the right-of-first refusal should the employee wish to leave the company or sell stock. Payment may be made in cash at the closing of the subscription period or by payroll deduction.

Thermacore's programs provide effective ways to reward all employees for the growth and profitability of the company and to acquire equity. Management believes these programs are an effective incentive and means of sharing the wealth.

Source: Copyright 1998, Best Manufacturing Practices Center of Excellence.

Scanlon Plan

Few would argue with the fact that the most powerful way of ensuring commitment is to synchronize the organization's goals with those of its employees—to ensure in other words that the two sets of goals overlap, and that by pursuing his or her goals, the worker pursues the employer's goals as well. Many techniques have been proposed for obtaining this idyllic state, but few have been implemented as widely or successfully as the **Scanlon plan,** an incentive plan developed in 1937 by Joseph Scanlon, a United Steel Workers Union official.[96]

Scanlon plan

An incentive plan developed in 1937 by Joseph Scanlon and designed to encourage cooperation, involvement, and sharing of benefits.

The Scanlon plan is remarkably progressive, considering that it was developed some 60 years ago. As currently implemented, Scanlon plans have the following basic features.[97] The first is the *philosophy of cooperation* on which they are based. This philosophy assumes that managers and workers have to rid themselves of the "us" and "them" attitudes that normally inhibit employees from developing a sense of ownership in the company. It substitutes instead a climate in which everyone cooperates because he or she understands that economic rewards are contingent on honest cooperation. A pervasive philosophy of cooperation must therefore exist in the firm for the plan to succeed.[98]

A second feature of the plan is what its practitioners refer to as *identity*. This means that to focus employee involvement, the company's mission or purpose must be clearly articulated, and employees must fundamentally understand how the business operates in terms of customers, prices, and costs, for instance. *Competence* is a third basic feature. The program today, say three experts, "explicitly recognizes that a Scanlon plan demands a high level of competence from employees at all levels."[99] The plan therefore assumes that hourly employees can competently perform their jobs as well as identify and implement improvements, and that supervisors have leadership skills for the participative management that is crucial to a Scanlon plan.

The fourth feature of the plan is the *involvement system.*[100] This takes the form of two levels of committees—the departmental level and the executive level. Productivity-improving suggestions are presented by employees to the appropriate departmental-level committees, which transmit the valuable ones to the executive-level committee. The latter then decides whether to implement the suggestion.

The fifth element of the plan is the *sharing of benefits formula*. Basically, the Scanlon plan assumes that employees should share directly in any extra profits resulting from their cost-cutting suggestions. If a suggestion is implemented and successful, all employees usually share in 75% of the savings. For example, assume that the normal monthly ratio of payroll costs to sales is 50%. (Thus, if sales are $600,000, payroll costs should be $300,000.) Assume suggestions are implemented and result in payroll costs of $250,000 in a month when sales were $550,000 and payroll costs should have been $275,000 (50% of sales). The saving attributable to these suggestions is $25,000 ($275,000 minus $250,000). Workers would typically share in 75% of this ($18,750) while $6,250 would go to the firm. In practice, a portion, usually one-quarter of the $18,750, is set aside for the months in which labor costs exceed the standard.

The Scanlon plan has been quite successful at reducing costs and fostering a sense of sharing and cooperation among employees. In one study, labor costs were cut by 10% and grievances were cut in half after implementation of such a plan.[101]

There are several conditions required for their success. They are usually more effective when there is a relatively small number of participants, generally fewer than 1,000. They are more successful when there are stable product lines and costs, since it is important that the labor costs/sales ratio remain fairly stable. Good supervision and healthy labor relations seem essential. And, of course, it is crucial that there be strong commitment to the plan on the part of both workers and management, particularly during the confusing phase-in period.[102]

Gainsharing Plans

gainsharing plan

An incentive plan that engages employees in a common effort to achieve productivity objectives and share the gains.

The Scanlon plan is one early version of what today is known as a **gainsharing plan,** an incentive plan that engages many or all employees in a common effort to achieve a company's productivity objectives; any resulting incremental cost-savings gains are shared among employees and the company.[103] In addition to the Scanlon plan, other types of gainsharing plans include the Rucker and Improshare plans.

The basic difference among these plans is the formula used to determine employee bonuses.[104] For example, the Scanlon formula divides payroll expenses by total sales. The Rucker formula uses sales value minus materials and supplies, all divided into payroll expenses. In a survey of 223 companies with gainsharing plans, 95 had custom-designed plans, and the rest used standardized plans like Scanlon, Rucker, or Improshare.[105]

Workers at AmeriSteel boosted the firm's productivity after the introduction of a gainsharing incentive plan.

STEPS IN GAINSHARING PLANS   There are eight basic steps in implementing a gainsharing plan.[106] *First*, establish general plan objectives. These might include boosting productivity or reinforcing teamwork, for instance.

Second, define specific performance measures. These usually include productivity measures such as labor hours or cost per unit produced, loans processed per hour, or total cost per full-time employee. Possible financial measures include profits before interest and taxes and return on net assets. The *third* step is formulating the funding formula, such as "improvement in payroll expenses divided by total sales." This creates the pot of dollars that is shared among participants. (In one study, an average of 46.7% of incremental gains was provided to employees, with the remainder staying with the company.)[107] *Fourth*, determine a method for dividing and distributing the employees' share of the gains among the employees themselves. Typical methods include equal percentage of pay or equal shares, although some plans also try to modify awards to a limited degree based on individual performance. *Fifth*, make the size of the payment meaningful to get participants' attention and motivate their behavior. One expert suggests a potential of 4% to 5% of pay and a 70% to 80% chance of achieving the plan's performance objectives as an effective combination. The *sixth* component is to choose the form of payment, which is usually cash but occasionally is common stock or deferred cash. *Seventh*, decide how frequently bonuses are to be paid. This in turn depends on the performance measures used. Most financial performance measures tend to be computed annually, whereas labor productivity measures tend to be computed quarterly or monthly.

Eighth, develop the support or involvement system. The most commonly used systems for fostering a sense of employee involvement include steering committees, update meetings, suggestion systems, coordinators, problem-solving teams, department committees, training programs, newsletters, inside auditors, and outside auditors.

The financial formula can be quite straightforward.[108] Assume a supplier wants to boost quality. Doing so would translate into fewer customer returns, less scrap and rework, and therefore higher profits. Historically, $1 million in output results in $20,000 (2%) scrap, returns, and rework. The company tells its employees that if next month's production results in only 1% scrap, returns, and rework, the 1% saved would be a gain, to be split 50/50 with the workforce, less a small amount for reserve for months in which scrap exceeds 2%. Awards are posted monthly but allocated quarterly.[109]

MAKING THE PLAN WORK   Several factors contribute to a gainsharing plan's success. While you may focus on just one goal (like quality), many firms use a "family of measures." For example, one firm chose seven variables (productivity, cost performance, product damage, customer complaints, shipping errors, safety, and attendance) and set specific goals for each (such as zero lost-time accidents, for safety). The specific monthly bonuses were attached to each goal achieved.[110] Quality, customer service, productivity, and cost represent another familiar family of measures.[111]

Successful gainsharing programs have several other key ingredients, according to one expert.[112] Management must be committed to implementing and maintaining the gainsharing plan, since managers will have to set and maintain consistent team goals, foster an atmosphere conducive to team effort and cooperation, and reduce adversarial relationships between management and employees. The financial incentive component itself should be simple and should measure and reward performance with a specific set of measurable goals and a clear allocation formula. Employee involvement is required so that the employees who are actually doing the jobs are encouraged to suggest performance improvement ideas. And the partnership between management and employees, as they pursue common goals on which the gainsharing plan's success will depend, requires two-way communication rather than just goal setting and top-down directives.[113]

At-Risk Variable Pay Plans

A growing number of firms including Saturn Corp., and DuPont are implementing new organizationwide incentive plans. At-risk variable pay plans are essentially plans that put some portion of the employee's weekly pay at risk, subject to the firm's meeting its financial goals.

In the DuPont plan, for instance, the employee's at-risk pay is a maximum of 6%. This means each employee's base pay will be 94% of his or her counterpart's salary in other (non-at-risk) DuPont departments.[114] Employees can then match or exceed their counterparts' pay if their department reaches certain predetermined financial goals. At Saturn, the at-risk component was initially designed to be about 20%, but was recently cut back to 5%. The at-risk approach is aimed in part at paying employees like partners. It is actually similar to much more extensive programs in Japan in which the at-risk portion might be 50% to 60% of a person's yearly pay. To the extent that at-risk pay is part of a more comprehensive program aimed at turning employees into committed partners—a program stressing trust and respect, extensive communications, and participation and opportunities for advancement, for instance—at-risk programs should be successful.

DEVELOPING MORE EFFECTIVE INCENTIVE PLANS

What can you do to make your incentive plan more effective? We'll address that question next, focusing on two main issues: when to use such plans; and how to implement such plans.

When to Use Incentives

The first thing to keep in mind is that there are some common-sense conditions under which pay based on time—not on an incentive—just makes somewhat more sense:

1. When employees are unable to control quantity or output (such as on machine-paced assembly lines), pay based on time may be more appropriate.
2. When delays in the work are frequent and beyond employees' control, it is impractical to tie workers' pay to their output.
3. Most incentive plans tie pay to the quantity, rather than the quality, of output. When quality is a primary consideration, pay based on time is often (but not always) more appropriate.

Therefore, in general, it makes more sense to use an incentive plan when:

1. There is a clear relationship between employee effort and quantity or quality of output.
2. The job is standardized, the work flow is regular, and delays are few or consistent.
3. Quality is less important than quantity, or, if quality is important, it too is easily measured and controlled.[115]

How to Implement Incentive Plans

Second, how you implement the plan is important. Specifically,

1. *Link the incentive with your strategy.* Know how the incentive plan will contribute to implementing the company's strategy and achieving its business objectives. For example, on the production floor at Honeywell's Commercial Aviation Systems Division in Phoenix, assembly workers "can be heard discussing

such weighty matters as operating profit, economic value added, and working capital." They focus on these matters because a percentage of each employee's yearly pay is based on the achievement of annual company objectives. "If results fall short of expectations, so do employees' paychecks."[116]

2. *Ensure that effort and rewards are directly related.* The incentive plan should reward employees in direct proportion to their increased productivity or quality. Employees must also perceive that they can actually do the tasks required. Thus, the standard has to be attainable, and you have to provide the necessary tools, equipment, and training.[117]

3. *Make the plan understandable and easily calculable by the employees.* Employees should be able to calculate easily the rewards they will receive for various levels of effort.

4. *Set effective standards.* The standards should be viewed as fair by your subordinates. They should be set high but reasonable—there should be about a 60 to 70% chance of success. And the goal should be specific—this is much more effective than telling someone to "do your best."

5. *Guarantee your standards.* View the standard as a contract with your employees. Once the plan is operational, use great caution before decreasing the size of the incentive in any way.[118] Rate cuts have long been the nemesis of incentive plans.

6. *Guarantee an hourly base rate.* Particularly for plant personnel, it's usually advisable to guarantee employees' base rate.[119] They'll therefore know that no matter what happens they can at least earn a minimum guaranteed base rate.

7. *Get support for the plan.* Restrictions by members of the work group can undermine the plan; get the work group's support for the plan before starting it.

8. *Have good measurement systems.* For some types of incentives the measurement system is relatively clear and obvious, such as numbers of items produced or sold. However, for other incentive plans (and particularly merit pay plans) designing a good measurement system is as important as designing the incentive plan itself. In the case of merit pay, for instance, the performance appraisal form and the process used to appraise performance must be clear and fair if the merit plan is to be of any use.[120]

9. *Emphasize long-term as well as short-term success.*[121] For example, just paying assembly workers for quantity of items produced may be short-sighted: longer-term improvements such as those deriving from work-improvement suggestions are usually equally important in improving the value of the firm.

10. *Take the corporate culture into consideration.* Employees' behavior tends to reflect the values they believe their company adheres to, and these values are a big part of a company's culture. Compensation experts recommend that incentive plans be consistent with the desired culture of the company.[122] For example, a consulting firm was having trouble getting its geographical divisions to share information and refer new business leads to each other. The company implemented a cross-selling commission system so that employees in one division could earn additional commissions by referring new business to another division most suited for the client. "Over time, this was enough to change the thought process from 'me' to 'we.' . . ."[123]

Why Incentive Plans Don't Work

Some experts are very wary about all types of incentive and pay-for-performance plans. Their reasoning can be summarized by the following points:

Performance pay can't replace good management. Performance pay is supposed to motivate workers, but lack of motivation is not always the culprit. Ambiguous instructions, lack of clear goals, inadequate employee selection and training, unavailability of tools, and a hostile workforce (or management) are just a few of the factors that impede performance.

You get what you pay for. This fact cuts both ways. Psychologists are fond of saying that people often put their effort where they know they'll be rewarded; a well-designed incentive plan can therefore help to focus workers' attention on, say, cutting scrap or lowering costs. But this also can backfire. An incentive plan that rewards a group based on how many pieces they produce could lead to rushed production and lower quality. Similarly, awarding a plantwide incentive for reducing accidents may simply reduce the number of reported accidents.

"Pay is not a motivator."[124] Psychologist Frederick Herzberg makes the point that money only buys temporary compliance, and that as soon as the incentive is removed, the "motivation" disappears too. He argues that too little money can create an atmosphere in which motivation won't take place. However, he says that adding more money won't boost motivation. Instead, Herzberg says that employers should provide adequate financial rewards and then build other motivators like opportunities for achievement and psychological success into their jobs.

Rewards punish. Many view punishment and reward as two sides of the same coin. "Do this and you'll get that" is not really very different from "Do this or here's why you won't get that" in other words.[125]

Rewards rupture relationships. Incentive plans have the potential for reducing teamwork by encouraging individuals (or individual groups) to blindly pursue financial rewards for themselves. Some performance appraisal systems may then exacerbate the situation, for instance, by forcing employees or groups to be ranked.

Rewards can unduly restrict performance. One expert says that "Excellence pulls in one direction; rewards pull in another. Tell people that their income will depend on their productivity or performance rating, and they will focus on the numbers. Sometimes they will manipulate the schedule for completing tasks or even engage in patently unethical and illegal behavior."[126]

Rewards may undermine responsiveness. Since the employees' primary focus is on achieving some specific goal like cutting costs, any changes or extraneous distractions mean that achieving that goal will be harder. Incentive plans can therefore mediate against change and responsiveness.

Rewards undermine intrinsic motivation. There is considerable evidence that contingent financial rewards (incentives) may actually undermine the intrinsic motivation that often results in optimal performance.[127] Two psychologists note, "The research has consistently shown that any contingent payment system tends to undermine intrinsic motivation."[128] The argument is that financial incentives undermine the feeling that the person is doing a good job voluntarily.

People work for more than money. As one observer recently put it, "People do work for money—but they work even more for meaning in their lives. In fact, they work to have fun. Companies that ignore this fact are essentially bribing their employees and will pay the price in a lack of loyalty and commitment."[129]

COMMITMENT AND INCENTIVES.   Potential pitfalls like these don't mean that incentive plans cannot be useful or should not be used. However they do suggest that such plans are more effective when implemented as part of a comprehensive management program aimed at bringing out the best in workers by tapping their commitment, self-discipline, and desire to do their jobs well. Incentives, in other words, are probably best installed within a framework of HR-related practices that encourage employee commitment by making the company the sort of place in which the employee wants to work. What are the elements of such an approach? Activities that contribute to building commitment include: clarifying and communicating the goals and mission of the organization; guaranteeing organizational justice, for instance, by having a comprehensive grievance procedure and extensive two-way communications; creating a sense of community by emphasizing teamwork and encouraging employees to interact; supporting employee development, for instance, by emphasizing promotion from within, developmental activities, and career-enhancing activities; and generally committing to "people-first values," for instance by emphasizing by word and deed that employees are deeply respected by the company and its management.[130]

In summary, any incentive plan is more apt to succeed if implemented with management support, employee acceptance, and a supportive culture characterized by teamwork, trust, and involvement at all levels.[131] This probably helps to explain why some of the longest-lasting incentive plans, like the Lincoln, Scanlon, and Rucker plans, depend heavily on things like two-way communications and employee involvement in addition to incentive pay.

SMALL BUSINESS APPLICATIONS

Several other considerations are especially relevant for implementing incentive plans in a small business.

ADAPT INCENTIVES FOR NONEXEMPTS TO THE FAIR LABOR STANDARDS ACT (FLSA)

Smaller firms without HR groups may be unaware that under the FLSA, incentive payments usually must be included in overtime pay calculations.[132] Specifically, overtime rates must be paid to nonexempt employees based on their previous week's earnings, and unless the incentive bonuses are structured properly, the amount of the bonus itself becomes part of the week's wages. It must then be included in base pay when computing any overtime that week.

Certain bonuses are excludable from overtime pay calculations. For example, Christmas and gift bonuses that are not based on employees' hours worked, or are so substantial that employees don't consider them a part of their wages do not have to be included in overtime pay calculations. Similarly, purely discretionary bonuses in which the employer retains discretion over how much if anything will be paid are excludable.

The problem is that many other types of incentive pay definitely must be included in your calculations. Under the FLSA, bonuses to be included in overtime pay computations include those promised to newly hired employees, those provided in union contracts or other agreements, and those announced to induce employees to work more productively, steadily, rapidly, or efficiently or to induce them to remain with the company. Such bonuses would include individual and group production bonuses, bonuses for quality and accuracy of work, efficiency bonuses, attendance bonuses, length-of-service bonuses, and sales commissions.[133]

To see how incentive bonuses can affect overtime pay, consider the following example. Alison works 45 hours in a particular week at a straight-time rate of $6.00 an hour. In that week she also earns a production bonus of $18.00. Her new regular rate for that week becomes $45 \times \$6.00 = \$270.00 + \$18.00 = \$288.00$, and $288.00 divided by 45 = \$6.40 per hour. Her new hourly rate is therefore $6.40 per hour for that week. Additional half-time pay ($3.20 per hour) is due her for the 5 hours overtime she worked as part of her 45 hours. Her total weekly pay for that week is, therefore, $288.00 + (5 \times 3.20) = \$304.00$.

The computational problem can be even more complicated with gainsharing and other productivity-related bonuses, since these are usually paid over intervals longer than a single pay period. Here, determining the new regular rate for overtime pay calculations can be deferred until after the bonus is determined. However, at that point the bonus must be apportioned over the workweeks in which it was earned. This actually requires employers to go back and recalculate overtime rates for all those weeks retroactively. This can be very time consuming, as you can imagine.

CONSIDER THE COMPANY'S SITUATION

In designing the incentive plan, consider the firm's life-cycle situation.[134] Small firms experiencing rapid growth usually prefer a broader-based profit-sharing-type plan to the more complicated individual incentive- or gainsharing-type plans. For one thing, profit-sharing plans tend to be simpler and less expensive to implement, and require less planning and administrative paperwork. Furthermore, small firms' employees tend to feel more directly tied to the company's profitability than do those employed in very big firms. Similarly, companies in a survival or turnaround situation, or those threatened by takeover, might also opt for less-complicated profit-sharing plans. That way managers can focus all their energies on the crisis, rather than on the administrative effort required to design and implement more complicated incentive plans.

STRESS PRODUCTIVITY AND QUALITY MEASURES IF POSSIBLE

Remember that profitability is not always the same as productivity, and that it's usually productivity and quality for which employees should be held accountable, not profitability. The reason is that productivity and quality are controllable, whereas profitability can be influenced by things like competition and government regulations.

GET EMPLOYEE INPUT IN SYSTEM DESIGN

It's usually helpful to get input from your employees in the design of the plan, since this can help foster their commitment to the plan. Many employers therefore use a design team composed of selected employees and supervisors.

Incentive Plans in Practice

In practice, most companies utilize several incentive plans, including, for instance, individual performance awards, team awards, and gainsharing plans. The percentage of companies using each of several selected incentive plans is summarized in Figure 12-3. Based on this sample of 1,244 companies, about 41% have individual performance awards, 25% have team awards, and 19% have gainsharing plans. An example of a comprehensive compensation plan containing a variety of incentive awards is presented in the following High-Performance feature.

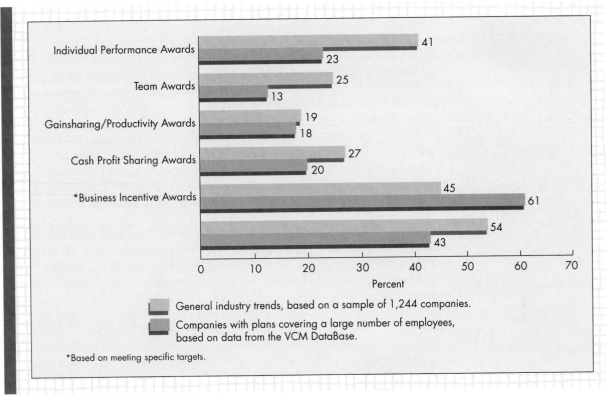

FIGURE 12-3 *What Kinds of Incentive Pay Are Companies Using?*

Source: Compensation & Benefits Review, July–Aug. 1998, p. 15.

THE HIGH-PERFORMANCE ORGANIZATION

Building Better, Faster, More Competitive Organizations Through HR: Incentive Plans

■ Example of a Total Compensation Program

Progressive firms like Federal Express aim to boost quality and productivity by using innovative incentive plans to help foster their employees' commitment.[135] At Federal Express, quarterly pay reviews and periodic national and local salary surveys are used to maintain highly competitive salary ranges and pay schedules. However, there is also a heavy emphasis on pay-for-performance. As one manager put it, "We are convinced people want to see a relationship between performance and reward. . . . I think people want to know that when they knock themselves out to reach their part of our 100% customer satisfaction goal, their efforts will not go unnoticed."[136] Federal Express pay-for-performance programs include the following.

Merit Program. All salaried employees receive merit salary increases based on their individual performance. Many hourly employees also now receive merit increases rather than automatic step progression increases to recognize individual performance.[137]

Pro Pay. Many hourly Federal Express employees can receive lump-sum merit bonuses once they reach the top of their pay range. Pro Pay is paid only if the employee has been at the top of his or her pay range for a specified period of time (normally 6 months) and only if he or she has had an above-average performance review.

Star/Superstar Program. Salaried employees with a specified performance rating may be nominated for a Star or Superstar lump-sum bonus. Stars represent up to the top 10% of performers in each division, whereas Superstars represent up to the top 1% of performers in each division.

Profit Sharing. Federal Express's profit-sharing plan distributes profits based on the overall profit levels of the corporation. The board of directors annually sets the amount paid, based on pretax profits. Payments to the plan can be in the form of stock, cash, or both and are usually made semiannually in June and December. The plan is designed to integrate with the firm's pension and savings plans to provide a comprehensive retirement program.

MBO/MIC and BO/PIC Programs. The management incentive compensation (MIC) and professional incentive compensation (PIC) programs generally reward managers and professionals for achievement of divisional and corporate profit goals.[138] The MBO (or PBO) bonuses are tied to individual manager's or professional's attainment of people, service, or profit-related goals. Thus, for a regional sales manager, a "people" goal could be an improvement in the person's leadership index score on the firm's annual feedback action survey.[139]

Bravo Zulu Voucher Program. The Bravo Zulu Voucher Program allows managers to provide immediate rewards to employees for outstanding performance above and beyond the normal requirements of the job. (Bravo Zulu is a title borrowed from the U.S. Navy's semaphore signal for "well done.") Bravo Zulu vouchers can be in the form of a check or some other form of reward (such as dinner vouchers or theater tickets). It's estimated that more than 150,000 times a year a Federal Express manager presents an employee with one of these awards, which average about $50.[140]

Golden Falcon Award. The Golden Falcon Award is given to permanent employees who demonstrate service to customers that is above and beyond the call of duty. Candidates are usually nominated based on solicited internal or external customer letters citing the candidate's outstanding performance. Nominated candidates are reviewed by the Golden Falcon committee, and the final selection is made by the chief operating officer. Winners are announced monthly through company publications and/or video programs. They receive a Golden Falcon lapel pin and shares of Federal Express common stock.

With the exception of the merit program, all of these pay-for-performance programs are forms of lump sum payments. In other words, Pro Pay, Star/Superstar, profit sharing, MBO/MIC, PBO/PIC, Bravo Zulu, and Golden Falcon awards are paid as one-time lump-sum awards, separate from base pay. They all let the company reward outstanding performance without permanently increasing its fixed payroll costs. The variability also reflects changes in business conditions and allows Federal Express to react to adverse economic conditions while maintaining its full employment policy.

We invite you to visit the Dessler page on the Prentice Hall Web site at **www.prenhall.com/dessler** for our on-line study guide, Internet exercises, current events, links to related Web sites, and more.

SUMMARY

1. The scientific use of financial incentives can be traced back to Frederick Taylor. Although such incentives became somewhat less popular during the human relations era, most writers today agree that they can be quite effective.

2. Piecework is the oldest type of incentive plan. Here a worker is paid a piece rate for each unit he or she produces. With a straight piecework plan, workers are paid on the basis of the number of units produced. With a guaranteed piecework plan, each worker receives his or her base rate (such as the minimum wage) regardless of how many units he or she produces.

3. Other useful incentive plans for plant personnel include the standard hour plan and group incentive plans. The former rewards workers by a percent premium that equals the percent by which their performance is above standard. Group incentive plans are useful where the workers' jobs are highly interrelated.

4. Most sales personnel are paid on some type of salary plus commission (incentive) basis. The trouble with straight commission is that there is a tendency to focus on "big-ticket" or "quick-sell" items and to disregard long-term customer building. Management employees are often paid according to a bonus formula that ties the bonus to, for example, increased sales. Stock options are one of the most popular executive incentive plans.

5. Profit sharing and the Scanlon plan are examples of organizationwide incentive plans. The problem with such plans is that the link between a person's efforts and rewards is sometimes unclear. On the other hand, such plans may contribute to developing a sense of commitment among employees. Gainsharing and merit plans are two other popular plans.

6. Experts list several objections to using incentive plans. These include: performance can't replace good management. You get what you pay for: "Pay is not a motivator", rewards punish; and rewards puncture relationships.

7. We suggest using incentive plans when units of output are easily measured, employees can control output, the effort-reward relationship is clear, work delays are under employees' control, quality is not paramount, and the organization must know precise labor costs anyway (to stay competitive).

KEY TERMS

DISCUSSION QUESTIONS

1. Compare and contrast six types of incentive plans.

2. Explain five reasons why incentive plans fail.

3. Describe the nature of some important management incentives.

4. When and why would you pay a salesperson a salary and commission combined?

5. What is merit pay? Do you think it's a good idea to award employees merit raises? Why or why not?

6. In this chapter we listed a number of reasons experts give for not instituting a pay-for-performance plan (such as "rewards punish"). Do you think these points (or any of them) are valid? Why or why not?

7. What is a Scanlon plan? Based on what you've read in this book so far, what features of a committee-building program does the Scanlon plan include?

8. Suppose your instructor decided to award final grades to teams of students in this class, instead of to individuals. What would be the pros and cons of such an approach? Would you like the idea?

INDIVIDUAL AND GROUP ACTIVITIES

1. Working individually or in groups, develop an incentive plan for the following positions: chemical engineer, plant manager, used-car salesperson. What factors did you have to consider in reaching your conclusions?

2. A state university system in the southeast recently instituted a "Teacher Incentive Program" (TIP) for its faculty. Basically, faculty committees within each university's colleges were told to award $5,000 raises (not bonuses) to about 40% of their faculty members based on how good a job they did teaching undergraduates, and how many they taught per year. What are the potential advantages and pitfalls of such an incentive program? How well do you think it was accepted by the faculty? Do you think it had the desired effect?

EXPERIENTIAL EXERCISE

Analyze a Compensation System

Express Automotive, an automobile mega-dealership with over 600 employees that represents 22 brands, has just received a very discouraging set of survey results. It seems their customer satisfaction scores have fallen for the ninth straight quarter. Customer complaints included:

> It was hard to get prompt feedback from mechanics by phone.
>
> Salespeople often did not return phone calls.
>
> The finance people seemed "pushy."
>
> New cars were often not properly cleaned or had minor items that needed immediate repair or adjustment.
>
> Cars often had to be returned to have repair work redone.

The following table describes Express Automotive's current compensation system.

Directions:
Divide the class into five groups. Assign one group to each of the five teams in column one. Each group should analyze the compensation package for their team. Each group should be able to identify the ways in which the current compensation plan (1) helps company performance and/or (2) impedes company performance. Once the groups have completed their analysis discuss the following questions as a class:

1. In what ways might your group's compensation plan contribute to the customer service problems?

2. Are there rewards that your department provides that impede the work of other departments?

3. What recommendations would you make to improve the compensation system in a way that would likely improve customer satisfaction.

Express Compensation System

TEAM	RESPONSIBILITY	CURRENT COMPENSATION METHOD
1. Sales force	Persuade buyer to purchase a car.	Very small salary (minimum wage) with commissions. Commission rate increases with every 20 cars sold per month.
2. Finance office	Help close the sale; persuade customer to use company finance plan.	Salary, plus bonus for each $10,000 financed with the company.
3. Detailing	Inspect cars delivered from factory, clean and make minor adjustments.	Piecework paid on the number of cars detailed per day.
4. Mechanics	Provide factory warranty service, maintenance and repair.	Small hourly wage, plus bonus based on 1) number of cars completed per day and 2) finishing each car faster than the standard estimated time to repair.
5. Receptionists/phone service personnel	Primary liaison between customer and sales force, finance, and mechanics.	Minimum wage.

CASE INCIDENT

"Distributing the Raise Pool"

John Jones, a department head at Southeast Banking, has been given a raise pool of 6%. He has considered two ways to distribute the pool:

PERFORMANCE GROUPS	METHOD 1 EQUALLY	METHOD 2 MERIT
Top ⅓ of performers	6%	12%
Average ⅓ of performers	6%	6%
Lower ⅓ of performers	6%	0%

■ QUESTIONS

1. What will be the motivational effects on each of the three groups under each method of distribution?

2. How would you distribute the pool? Why?

Source: Professor John E. Oliver, Valdosta State University, Valdosta, GA

Case Application

BRINGING THE TEAM CONCEPT INTO COMPENSATION—OR NOT

One of the first things Sandy Caldwell wanted to do in his new position at Hathaway Manufacturing was improve productivity through teamwork at every level of the firm. As the new Human Resource Manager for the suburban plant, Sandy set out to change the culture to accommodate the team-based approach he had become so enthusiastic about in his most recent position.

Sandy started by installing the concept of team management at the highest level, to oversee the operations of the entire plant. The new management team consisted of manufacturing, distribution, planning, technical, and human resource executives. Together they developed a new vision for the 500-employee facility, which they expressed in the simple phrase, "Excellence Together." They drafted a new mission statement for the firm that focused on becoming customer-driven and team-based, and that called upon employees to raise their level of commitment and begin acting as "owners" of the firm.

The next step was to convey the team message to employees throughout the company. The communication process went surprisingly well, and Sandy was happy to see his idea of a "workforce of owners" begin to take shape. Teams trained together, developed production plans together, and embraced the technique of 360-degree feedback, in which an employee's performance evaluation is obtained from supervisors, subordinates, peers, and internal or external customers. Performance and morale improved, and productivity began to tick upward. The company even sponsored occasional celebrations to reward team achievements, and the team structure seemed firmly in place.

Sandy decided to change one more thing. Hathaway's long-standing policy had been to give all employees the same annual pay increase. But Sandy felt that in the new team environment, outstanding performance should be the criterion for pay raises. After consulting with CEO Regina Cioffi, Sandy sent a memo to all employees announcing the change to team-based pay for performance.

The reaction was immediate and 100% negative. As Sandy later recalled, "All hell broke loose." None of the employees were happy with the change, and foremost among their complaints two stood out. First, because the 360-degree feedback system made everyone responsible in part for someone else's performance evaluation, no one was comfortable with the idea that pay raises would be linked to peer input. Second, there was a widespread perception that the way the change was decided upon, and the way it was announced, put the firm's commitment to team effort in doubt. Simply put, employees felt left out of the decision process.

Sandy and Regina arranged a meeting for early the next morning. Sitting in her office over their coffee, they began a painful debate. Should the new policy be retracted as quickly as it was adopted, or should it be allowed to stand?

■ QUESTIONS

1. Does the pay for performance plan seem like a good idea? Why or why not?

2. What advice would you give Regina and Sandy as they consider their decision?

3. What mistakes did they make in adopting and communicating the new salary plan? How might Sandy have approached this major compensation change a little differently?

4. Assuming the new pay plan were eventually accepted, how would you address the fact that in the new performance evaluation system, employees' input affects their peers' pay levels?

Note: The incident in this case is based on an actual event at Frito-Lay's Kirkwood, New York plant, as reported in C. James Novak, "Proceed with Caution When Paying Teams," *HR Magazine*, (April 1997), p. 73.

NOTES

1. Steven Gross and Dan Duncan, "Gainsharing Plan Spurs Record Productivity and Payouts at AmeriSteel" Compensation & Benefits Review, November/December 1998, pp 46–50.

2. Linda Stroh, Jeanne Brett, Joseph Baumann, and Anne Reilly, "Agency Theory and Variable Pay Compensation Strategies," *Academy of Management Journal*, Vol. 39, no. 3 (1996), pp. 751–767.

3. Ibid., p. 762.

4. Rajiv Banker, Seok-Young Lee, Gordon Potter, and Dhinu Srinivasan, "Contextual Analysis of Performance Impacts of Outcome-Based Incentive Competition," *Academy of Management Journal,* Vol. 39, no. 4 (1996), pp. 940–941.

5. "DuPont to Implement Performance-Based Pay," *BNA Bulletin to Management,* June 11, 1998, pp. 177, 182.

6. Ibid., p. 177.

7. Except as noted, this section is based on "Non-Traditional Incentive Pay Programs," *Personnel Policies Forum Survey,* No. 148 (May 1991), The Bureau of National Affairs, Inc., Washington, D.C.

8. Ibid., p. 3.

9. Ibid., p. 9.

10. Ibid., p. 13.

11. Ibid., p. 19.

12. Ibid., p. 24.

13. "Designing a Variable Pay Plan," *BNA Bulletin to Management,* (June 20, 1996), p. 200.

14. Ibid., p. 200.

15. "Employers Use Pay to Lever Performance," *BNA Bulletin to Management,* (August 21, 1997), p. 272.

16. See, for example, Kenan Abosch, "Variable Pay: Do We Have the Basics in Place?" *Compensation & Benefits Review* (July–August 1998), pp. 2–22.

17. Richard Henderson, *Compensation Management* (Reston, VA: Reston, 1979), p. 363. For a discussion of the increasing use of incentives for blue-collar employees, see, for example, Richard Henderson, "Contract Concessions: Is the Past Prologue?" *Compensation & Benefits Review,* Vol. 18, no. 5 (September–October 1986), pp. 17–30. See also A. J. Vogl, "Carrots, Sticks and Self-Deception," *Across-the-Board,* 3–1, no. 1 (January 1994), p. 314; see also Philip Lewis, "Managing Performance—Related Pay Based on Evidence from the Financial Services Sector," *Human Resource Management Journal,* Vol. 8, no. 2 (1998), pp. 66–77.

18. David Belcher, *Compensation Administration* (Upper Saddle River, NJ: Prentice Hall, 1973), p. 314.

19. For a discussion of these, see Thomas Wilson, "Is It Time to Eliminate the Piece Rate Incentive System?" *Compensation & Benefits Review* (March–April 1992), pp. 43–49.

20. Measured day work is a third type of individual incentive plan for production workers. See, for example, Mitchell Fein, "Let's Return to MDW for Incentives," *Industrial Engineering* (January 1979), pp. 34–37.

21. Henderson, *Compensation Management,* pp. 367–368. See also David Swinehart, "A Guide for More Productive Team Incentive Programs," *Personnel Journal,* Vol. 65, no. 7 (July 1986); Anne Saunier and Elizabeth Hawk, "Realizing the Potential of Teams through Team-based Rewards," *Compensation & Benefits Review* (July–August 1994), pp. 24–33; and Shari Caudron, "Tie Individual Pay to Team Success," *Personnel Journal,* Vol. 73, no. 10 (October 1994), pp. 40–46.

22. Another suggestion is as follows: equal payments to all members on the team; differential payments to team members based on their contributions to the team's performance; and differential payments determined by a ratio of each group member's base pay to the total base pay of the group. See Kathryn Bartol and Laura Hagmann, "Team-based Pay Plans: A Key to Effective Teamwork," *Compensation & Benefits Review* (November–December 1992), pp. 24–29.

23. Richard Seamn, "Rejuvenating an Organization with Team Pay," *Compensation & Benefits Review* (September–October 1997), pp. 25–30.

24. James Nickel and Sandra O'Neal, "Small Group Incentives: Gainsharing in the Microcosm," *Compensation & Benefits Review* (March–April 1990), p. 24. See also Jane Pickard, "How Incentives Can Drive Teamworking," *Personnel Management* (September 1993), pp. 26–32; and Shari Caudron, "Tie Individual Pay to Team Success," *Personnel Journal* (October 1994), pp. 40–46.

25. Jon P. Alston, "Awarding Bonuses the Japanese Way," *Business Horizons,* Vol. 25 (September–October 1982), pp. 6–8.

26. See, for example, Peter Daly, "Selecting and Assigning a Group Incentive Plan," *Management Review* (December 1975), pp. 33–45. For an explanation of how to develop a successful group incentive program, see K. Dow Scott and Timothy Cotter, "The Team That Works Together Earns Together," *Personnel Journal,* Vol. 63 (March 1984), pp. 59–67.

27. Manuel London and Greg Oldham, "A Comparison of Group and Individual Incentive Plans," *Academy of Management Journal,* Vol. 20, no. 1 (1977), pp. 34–41. Note that the study was carried out under controlled conditions in a laboratory setting. See also Thomas Rollins, "Productivity-Based Group Incentive Plans: Powerful, But Use with Caution," *Compensation & Benefits Review,* Vol. 21, no. 3 (May–June 1989), pp. 39–50; discusses several popular group incentive plans, including gainsharing and lists dos and don'ts for using them.

28. Robert Heneman and Courtney Von Hippel, "Balancing Group and Individual Rewards: Rewarding Individual Contributions to the Team," *Compensation & Benefits Review* (July–August 1995), pp. 63–68.

29. Mark Meltzer and Howard Goldsmith, "Executive Compensation for Growth Companies," *Compensation & Benefits Review* (November–December 1997), pp. 41–50.

30. Ibid.

31. Mark Meltzer and Howard Goldsmith, "Executive Compensation for Growth Companies", *Compensation $ Benefits Review,* Novemeber/December 1997, pp 44–45.

32. Ibid., p. 188. Meltzer and Goldsmith, "Executive Compensation for Growth Companies; p. 44.

33. See, for example, Ralph Bavier, "Managerial Bonuses," *Industrial Management* (March–April 1978), pp. 1–5. See also Charles Tharp, "Linking Annual Incentive Awards to Individual Performance," *Compensation & Benefits Review,* Vol. 17 (November–December 1985), pp. 18–43.

34. Ellig, *Executive Compensation,* p. 189.

35. F. Dean Hildebrand, Jr., "Individual Performance Incentives," *Compensation Review,* Vol. 10 (Third Quarter, 1978), p. 32.

36. Ibid., pp. 28–33.

37. The following is based on Edward Redling, "The 1981 Tax Act: Boom to Managerial Compensation," *Personnel,* Vol. 57 (March–April 1982), pp. 26–35, and on Meltzer and Goldsmith, "Executive Compensation for Growth Companies, pp. 45–47.

38. See both William M. Mercer Meidinger, Inc., "How Will Reform Tax Your Benefits?" *Personnel Journal,* Vol. 65, no. 12 (December 1986), pp. 49–63; and Jack H. Schechter, "The Tax Reform Act of 1986: Its Impact on Compensation and Benefits," *Compensation & Benefits Review,* Vol. 18, no. 6 (November–December 1986), pp. 11–24.

39. See also Paul Bradley, "Justify Executive Bonuses to the Board," *Personnel Journal* (September 1988), pp. 116–125, and his "Long-Term Incentives: International Executives Need Them Too," *Personnel* (August 1988)pp. 40–42.

40. Belcher, *Compensation Administration*, p. 548; Schechter, "The Tax Reform Act of 1986," p. 23. See also Rein Linney and Charles Marshall, "ISOs vs. NSOs: The Choice Still Exists," *Compensation & Benefits Review*, Vol. 19, no. 1 (January–February 1987), pp. 13–25.

41. Meltzer and Goldsmith, "Executive Compensation," pp. 47–48.

42. Pearl Meyer, "Stock is No Longer Optional," *Journal of Business Strategy*, Vol. 19, no. 2 (March–April 1998), pp. 28–31.

43. Christopher Young, "Trends in Executive Compensation," *Journal of Business Strategy*, Vol. 19, no. 2 (March–April 1998), pp. 21–25.

44. Ira Sager, "Stock Options: Lou Takes a Cue from Silicon Valley," *Business Week*, March 30, 1998, p. 34.

45. Jeff Staiman and Cary Thompson, "Designing and Implementing a Broad-Based Stock Option Plan," *Compensation & Benefits Review* (July–August 1998), p. 23.

46. Ibid., p. 23.

47. Ibid., p. 25.

48. David Jarcho, "How to Use Technology to Effectively Deliver Broad-Based Stock Option Plans," *Compensation & Benefits Review* (July–August 1998), pp. 87–90.

49. Ray Stata and Modesto Maidique, "Bonus System for Balanced Strategy," *Harvard Business Review*, Vol. 59 (November–December 1980), pp. 156–163; Alfred Rappaport, "Executive Incentives Versus Corporate Growth," *Harvard Business Review*, Vol. 57 (July–August 1978), pp. 81–88. See also Crystal Graef, "Rendering Long-Term Incentives Less Risky for Executives," *Personnel*, Vol. 65, no. 9 (September 1988), pp. 80–84.

50. Ira Kay, "Beyond Stock Options: Emerging Practices in Executive Incentive Programs," *Compensation & Benefits Review* (November–December 1991), p. 19.

51. For a discussion see Ibid., pp. 18–29.

52. Jeffrey Kanter and Matthew Ward, "Long-Term Incentives for Management, Part 4: Performance Plans," *Compensation & Benefits Review* (January–February 1990), p. 36. Meltzer and Goldsmith, "Executive Compensation for Growth Companies," 46–47.

53. Jude Rich and John Larson, "Why Some Long-Term Incentives Fail," *Compensation Review*, Vol. 16 (First Quarter 1984), pp. 26–37. See also Eric Marquardt, "Stock Option Grants: Is Timing Everything?" *Compensation & Benefits Review*, Vol. 20, no. 5 (September–October 1988), pp. 18–22.

54. Robert Klein, "Compensating Your Overseas Executives, Part 3: Exporting U.S. Stock Option Plans to Expatriates," *Compensation & Benefits Review* (January–February 1991), pp. 27–38.

55. For a discussion see Ibid.

56. This section is based on Meltzer and Goldsmith, "Executive Compensation for Growth Companies," pp. 41–50. See also James Nelson, "Linking Compensation to Business Strategy," *Journal of Business Strategy*, via, nd, pp. 25–28.

57. Richard Semler, "Developing Management Incentives That Drive Results," *Compensation & Benefits Review* (July–August 1998), pp. 41–48.

58. Ibid., p. 44.

59. Ibid., p. 47.

60. This section based primarily on John Steinbrink, "How to Pay Your Sales Force," *Harvard Business Review*, Vol. 57 (July–August 1978), pp. 111–122. See also John Tallitsch and John Moynahan, "Fine-Tuning Sales Compensation Programs," *Compensation & Benefits Review*, Vol. 26, no. 2 (March–April 1994), pp. 34–37.

61. Straight salary by itself is not, of course, an incentive compensation plan as we use the term in this chapter.

62. Steinbrink, "How to Pay," p. 112.

63. T. H. Patten, "Trends in Pay Practices for Salesmen," *Personnel*, Vol. 43 (January–February 1968), pp. 54–63. See also Catherine Romano, "Death of a Salesman," *Management Review*, Vol. 83, no. 9 (September 1994), pp. 10–16.

64. David Harrison, Meghna Virick, and Sonja William, "Working Without a Net: Time, Performance, and Turnover Under Maximally Contingent Rewards," *Journal of Applied Psychology*, Vol. 81, no. 4 (1996), p. 332.

65. Ibid., pp. 331–345.

66. Greg Stewart, "Reward Structure as a Moderator of the Relationship Between Extroversion and Sales Performance," *Journal of Applied Psychology*, Vol. 81, no. 6 (1996), pp. 619–627.

67. Ibid., p. 619.

68. Steinbrink, "How to Pay," p. 115.

69. Bill O'Connell, "Dead Solid Perfect: Achieving Sales Compensation Alignment," *Compensation & Benefits Review* (March–April 1996), pp. 46–47.

70. In the salary plus bonus plan, salespeople are paid a basic salary and are then paid a bonus for carrying out specified activities. For a discussion of how to develop a customer-focused sales compensation plan, see, for example, Mark Blessington, "Designing a Sales Strategy with the Customer in Mind," *Compensation & Benefits Review* (March–April 1992), pp. 30–41. See also Bill O'Connell, "Dead Solid Perfect: Achieving Sales Compensation Alignment," *Compensation & Benefits Review* (March–April 1996), pp. 41–48.

71. This is based on "Sales Incentives Get the Job Done," *Sales and Marketing Management*, September 14, 1981, pp. 67–120.

72. Joanne Sammer, "Merit Pay Remains One Step Ahead of Inflation," *Compensation & Benefits Review* (November–December 1996), pp. 14–15; Fay Hansen, "Currents in Compensation and Benefits," *Compensation & Benefits Review*, (November/December) 1998, p. 6.

73. See, for example, Herbert Meyer, "The Pay for Performance Dilemma," *Organizational Dynamics* (Winter 1975), pp. 39–50; Thomas Patten, Jr., "Pay for Performance or Placation?" *Personnel Administrator*, Vol. 24 (September 1977), pp. 26–29; William Kearney, "Pay for Performance? Not Always," *MSU Business Topics* (Spring 1979), pp. 5–16. See also Hoyt Doyel and Janet Johnson, "Pay Increase Guidelines with Merit," *Personnel Journal*, Vol. 64 (June 1985), pp. 46–50.

74. Nathan Winstanley, "Are Merit Increases Really Effective?" *Personnel Administrator*, Vol. 27 (April 1982), pp. 37–41. See also William Seithel and Jeff Emans, "Calculating Merit Increases: A Structured Approach," *Personnel*, Vol. 60, no. 5 (June 1985), pp. 56–68; Donald Campbell et al., "Merit Pay, Performance Appraisal, and Individual Motivation: An Analysis and Alternative," *Human Resource Management*, Vol. 37, no. 2 (Summer 1998), pp. 131–146.

75. James T. Brinks, "Is There Merit in Merit Increases?" *Personnel Administrator*, Vol. 25 (May 1980), p. 60. See also Dan Gilbert and Glenn Bassett, "Merit Pay Increases are a Mistake," *Compensation & Benefits Review*, Vol. 26, no. 2 (March–April 1994), pp. 20–25.

76. *Merit Pay: Fitting the Pieces Together* (Chicago: Commerce Clearing House, 1982).

77. Suzanne Minken,"Does Lump Sum Pay Merit Attention?" *Personnel Journal* (June 1988), pp. 77–83. See also Jerry Newman and Daniel Fisher, "Strategic Impact Merit Pay," *Compensation & Benefits Review* (July–August 1992), pp. 38–45.

78. John F. Sullivan, "The Future of Merit Pay Programs," *Compensation & Benefits Review* (May–June 1988), pp. 22–30.

79. This section is based primarily on Robert Gibson, Compensation (New York: AMACOM, 1981), pp. 189–207.

80. Esther Shein, "Team Spirit: IT is Getting Creative with Compensation to Foster Collaboration," PC Week, May 11, 1998, pp. 69–72.

81. Rose-Robin Pedone, "engineering the job market," LI Business News, July 27, 1998, p1B.

82. Julia King, "Name Yor Price; As Talent Plays Hardball with Software Firms," Computerworld (Sept. 16, 1996), p. 32.

83. Richard Arnold, "Catching a Star," CA Magazine, Oct 1998, p. S30–33.

84. "American Airlines' Profit Sharing Tops $250 Million," Knight-Ridder/Tribune Business News, (Feb 27, 1998), p. 227.

85. "Ford Motor Co. Profit-Sharing Plan," The Wall Street Journal, (Oct. 13, 1998), p. B5.

86. "Sharing the Wealth—GM", Ward's Auto World, (March 1998), p. 7.

87. Bert Metzger and Jerome Colletti, "Does Profit Sharing Pay?" (Evanston, IL: Profit Sharing Research Foundation, 1971), quoted in Belcher, *Compensation Administration*, p. 353. See also D. Keith Denton, "An Employee Ownership Program That Rebuilt Success," *Personnel Journal*, Vol. 66, no. 3 (March 1987), pp. 114–118; and Edward Shepart, "Profit Sharing and Productivity: Further Evidence from the Chemicals Industry," *Industrial Relations*, Vol. 33, no. 4 (October 1994), pp. 452–466.

88. Seongsu Kim, "Does Profit Sharing Increase Firms' Profits?", Journal of Labor Research, (Spring 1998), pp 351–371.

89. Belcher, *Compensation Administration*, p. 351.

90. Based on Randy Swad, "Stock Ownership Plans: A New Employee Benefit," *Personnel Journal*, Vol. 60 (June 1982), pp. 453–455.

91. See James Brockardt and Robert Reilly, "Employee Stock Ownership Plans After the 1989 Tax Law: Valuation Issues," *Compensation & Benefits Review* (September–October 1990), pp. 29–36.

92. Donald Sullivan, "ESOPs," *California Management Review*, Vol. 20, no. 1 (Fall 1977), pp. 55–56. For a discussion of the effects of employee stock ownership on employee attitudes, see Katherine Klein, "Employee-Stock Ownership and Employee Attitudes: A Test of Three Models," *Journal of Applied Psychology*, Vol. 72, no. 2 (May 1987), pp. 319–331; and John Gamble, "ESOPs: Financial Performance and Federal Tax Incentives," *Journal of Labor Research*, Vol. 19, no. 3 (Summer 1998), pp. 529–542.

93. Steven Etkind, "ESOPs Create Liquidity for Shareholders and Help Diversify Their Assets," *Estate Planning*, Vol. 24, no. 4 (May 1998), pp. 158–165.

94. Everett Allen, Jr., Joseph Melone, and Jerry Rosenbloom, *Pension Planning* Burr Ridge, IL: McGraw-Hill, 1981), p. 316. Note that the Tax Reduction Act of 1975 has also led to the creation of the so-called TRAFOP. This is a regular employee stock ownership plan except that a portion of the investment tax credit that employers receive for investing in capital equipment can be invested in the employee stock ownership plan.

95. William Smith, Harold Lazarus, and Harold Murray Kalkstein, "Employee Stock Ownership Plans: Motivation and Morale Issues," *Compensation & Benefits Review* (September–October 1990), pp. 37–46.

96. Brian Moore and Timothy Ross, *The Scanlon Way to Improved Productivity: A Practical Guide* (New York: Wiley, 1978), p. 2.

97. These are based in part on Steven Markham, K. Dow Scott, and Walter Cox, Jr., "The Evolutionary Development of a Scanlon Plan," *Compensation & Benefits Review* (March–April 1992), pp. 50–56.

98. J. Kenneth White, "The Scanlon Plan: Causes and Correlates of Success," *Academy of Management Journal*, Vol. 22 (June 1979), pp. 50–56.

99. Markham et al., "The Evolutionary Development of a Scanlon Plan," p. 51.

100. Moore and Ross, *The Scanlon Way*, pp. 1–2.

101. George Sherman, "The Scanlon Plan: Its Capabilities for Productive Improvement," *Personnel Administrator* (July 1976).

102. "The Effects of Improshare on Productivity," *Industrial and Labor Relations Review*, Vol. 45, no. 2 (1991), pp. 311–322.

103. Barry W. Thomas and Madeline Hess Olson, "Gainsharing: The Design Guarantees Success," *Personnel Journal* (May 1988), pp. 73–79. See also "Aligning Compensation with Quality," *Bulletin to Management*, BNA Policy and Practice Series, April 1, 1993, p. 97.

104. See Theresa A. Welbourne and Louis Gomez Mejia, "Gainsharing Revisited," *Compensation & Benefits Review* (July–August 1988), pp. 19–28.

105. Carla O'Dell and Jerry McAdams, *People, Performance, and Pay* (American Productivity Center and Carla O'Dell, 1987), p. 34.

106. Thomas and Olson, "Gainsharing," pp. 75–76. See also Thomas McGrath, "Gainsharing: Engineering the Human Factor of Productivity," *Industrial Engineering* (September 1993), pp. 61–63; and Paul Rossler and C. Patrick Koelling, "The Effect of Gainsharing on Business Performance at a Paper Mill," *National Productivity Review* (Summer 1993), pp. 365–382.

107. O'Dell and McAdams, *People, Performance, and Pay*, p. 42.

108. This is paraphrased from Woodruff Imberman, "Boosting Plant Performance with Gainsharing," *Business Horizons* (November–December 1992), p. 77.

109. For other examples, see Timothy Ross and Larry Hatcher, "Gainsharing Drives Quality Improvement," *Personnel Journal* (November 1992), pp. 81–89. See also Jerry McAdams, "Employee Involvement and Performance Reward Plans: Design, Implementation, and Results," *Compensation & Benefits Review*, Vol. 27, no. 2 (March 1995), pp. 45–55.

110. John Belcher, Jr., "Gainsharing and Variable Pay: The State of the Art," *Compensation & Benefits Review* (May–June 1994), pp. 50–60. See also Kevin Patton and Dennis Daley, "Gainsharing in Zebulon: What Do Workers Want?" *Public Personnel Management*, Spring 1998, U27, N1, pp. 117–132.

111. Robert Masternak, "Gainsharing Boosts Quality and Productivity at a B. F. Goodrich Plant," *National Productivity Review* (Spring 1993), pp. 225–238. See also Susan Hanlon, David Meyer, and Robert Taylor, "Consequences of Gainsharing: A Field Experiment Revisited," *Group & Organization Management*, Vol. 19, no. 1 (March 1994), pp. 87–111.

112. This is based on Thomas McGrath, "How Three Screw Machine Companies Are Tapping Human Productivity Through

Gainsharing," *Employment Relations Today* (Winter 1993/94), pp. 437–446.

113. See, for example, Moore and Ross, *The Scanlon Way to Improved Productivity*, pp. 157–164; Jeffrey Ewing, "Gainsharing Plans: Two Key Factors," *Compensation & Benefits Review*, Vol. 21, no. 1, Jan/Feb 1989, pp. 51–52. For a description of the implementation of a gainsharing plan in health care institutions, see Steven Markham et al., "Gainsharing Experiments in Health Care," *Compensation & Benefits Review* (March–April 1992), pp. 57–64. See also Dwight Willett, "Promoting Quality Through Compensation," *Business Quarterly*, Autumn 1993, pp. 107–111; and Robert Masternak, "Gainsharing: Overcoming Common Myths and Problems to Achieve Dramatic Results," *Employment Relations Today*, Winter 1993/94, pp. 425–436.

114. Robert McNutt, "Sharing Across the Board: DuPont's Achievement Sharing Program," *Compensation & Benefits Review* (July–August 1990), pp. 17–24.

115. Belcher, *Compensation Administration*, pp. 309–310.

116. Shari Caudron, "How Pay Launched Performance," *Personnel Journal* (September 1996), p. 70.

117. See, for example, James Gutherie and Edward Cunningham, "Pay for Performance: The Quaker Oats Alternative," *Compensation & Benefits Review*, Vol. 24, no. 2 (March–April 1992), pp. 18–23.

118. Gary Yukl and Gary Latham, "Consequences of Reinforcement Schedules and Incentives Magnitudes for Employee Performance: Problems Encountered in an Industrial Setting," *Journal of Applied Psychology*, Vol. 60 (June 1975).

119. J. Keith Louden and J. Wayne Deegan, *Wage Incentives* (New York: Wiley, 1959), p. 26.

120. Alfie Kohn, "Challenging Behaviorist Dogma: Myths About Money and Motivation," *Compensation & Benefits Review* (March–April 1998), pp. 27–32.

121. Ibid., pp. 30–31.

122. Francine McKenzie and Matthew Shilling, "Avoiding Performance Measurement Traps: Ensuring Effective Incentive Design and Implementation," *Compensation & Benefits Review* (July–August 1998), p. 64.

123. Ibid., p. 64.

124. The following five points are based on Alfie Kohn, "Why Incentive Plans Cannot Work," *Harvard Business Review* (September–October 1993), pp. 54–63.

125. Ibid., p. 58.

126. Ibid., p. 62.

127. Ibid.

128. Edward Deci and Richard Ryan, *Intrinsic Motivation and Self-Determination in Human Behavior* (New York: Plenum Press, 1985), quoted in Ibid., p. 62.

129. Pfeffer, "Six Dangerous Myths about Pay," *Harvard Business Review* (May–June 1998), p. 112.

130. Gary Dessler, "How to Win Your Employees' Commitment," Working Paper, September 1998.

131. Steven Gross and Jeffrey Bacher, "The New Variable Pay Programs: How Some Succeed, Why Some Don't," *Compensation & Benefits Review* (January–February 1993), pp. 55–56; see also George Milkovich and Carolyn Milkovich, "Strengthening the Pay-Performance Relationship: The Research," *Compensation & Benefits Review* (November–December 1992), pp. 53–62; and Jay Schuster and Patricia Zingheim, "The New Variable Pay: Key Design Issues," *Compensation & Benefits Review* (March–April 1993), pp. 27–34.

132. This is based on William E. Buhl, "Keeping Incentives Simple for Nonexempt Employees," *Compensation & Benefits Review* (March–April 1989), pp. 14–19.

133. Ibid., pp. 15–16.

134. The following are based on Michael J. Cissell, "Designing Effective Reward Systems," *Compensation & Benefits Review* (November–December 1987), pp. 49–56.

135. The following is based on Gary Dessler, *Winning Commitment* (New York: McGraw-Hill Book Company, 1993), Chapter 9.

136. *Blueprints for Service Quality: The Federal Express Approach* (New York: AMA Membership Publication Division, 1991), pp. 31–32.

137. "Compensation at Federal Express," company document, p. 8.

138. Unless otherwise indicated the section on pay-for-performance is based on "Compensation at Federal Express," pp. 8–9.

139. *Blueprints for Service Quality*, p. 32.

140. Ibid., pp. 34–35.

13

BENEFITS AND SERVICES

itney Bowes had a problem. Technological advances like the Internet were letting competitors make increased erosions into its core postage-meter business. The firm knew it had to make itself more competitive. One problem: Its employees had reportedly adopted an "entitlement mentality" when it came to benefits—the benefits were something they were "entitled to," pretty much regardless of performance. How could the firm change that mind-set in a way that underscored its new strategy of making itself, and its employees, more intensely competitive? Among other HR techniques, the firm could attach a price to each benefit and give employees a fixed amount of "flex dollars" to spend on their benefits.[1] ▲

THE BENEFITS PICTURE TODAY

benefits

Indirect financial payments given to employees. They may include health and life insurance, vacation, pension, education plans, and discounts on company products, for instance.

Benefits represent an important part of just about every employee's pay; they can be defined as all the indirect financial and nonfinancial payments an employee receives for continuing his or her employment with the company.[2] They include such things as time off with pay, health and life insurance, pensions, education plans, and child-care facilities.

Administering benefits today is an increasingly specialized task. It demands special expertise because workers are more financially sophisticated and demanding and because federal legislation concerning things like pregnancy benefits requires that benefit plans comply with new laws. In a 1997 decision, for instance, the U.S. Court of Appeals for the Ninth Circuit ordered Microsoft to offer the same retirement and stock purchase plan benefits it offered its regular employees to about 800 workers classified by Microsoft as temporary workers or independent contractors. The court found that Microsoft had incorrectly classified these workers as independent contractors when they were, in fact, employees.[3]

Benefits represent a major expense for most employers, but one that has stabilized in the past few years after peaking in 1995. For example, employer spending on benefits fell from $14,659 per employee in 1995 to $14,086 per employee in 1996, or from 42% of payroll to 41.3%.[4] As you can see summarized in Figure 13-1, payments for time not worked represent the biggest chunk of benefits payments, followed by legally required

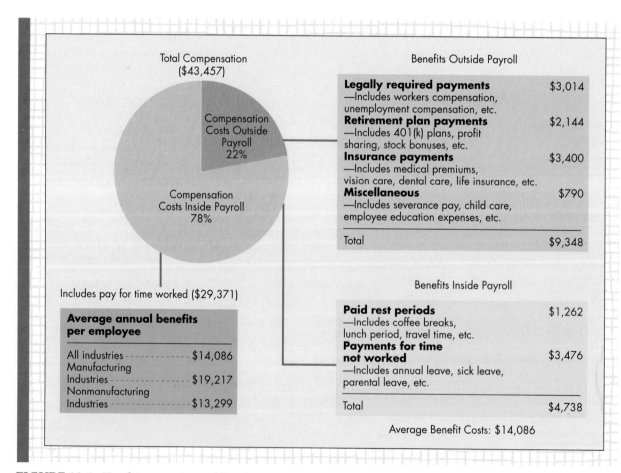

FIGURE 13-1 *Total Average Annual Employee Compensation, 1996 (Pay and Benefits)*

Source: BNA Bulletin to Management, January 29, 1998, p. 29.

Like Yahoo! founders, David Filo (left) and Jerry Yang, managers today realize the value of offering benefits such as paid tuition, on-site health clubs, and flexible hours in order to attract and retain employees.

payments, for unemployment compensation, retirement plan payments, insurance payments, and severance pay.[5]

The moderation in benefits costs (although they are still very high) can be attributed to several things. After rising at 10 to 12% per year in the early 1990s, health insurance premiums barely increased in 1996 and grew just 2.1% between 1996 and 1997.[6] The stock market's rise into 1998 may also have helped "firms to finance pension from appreciation rather than from increased contributions. . . ."[7] And downsizing-related benefits (such as for severance pay) declined as well. In any event, most employees don't realize the high cost to the employer of the benefits pay received, so it's advisable to list the benefits' true costs on each employee's pay stub as a reminder.

Most full-time employees in the United States do receive benefits.[8] For example, in one survey of about 33 million full-time employees, roughly 89% received paid holidays, 96% got paid vacations, and 77% received employer-provided medical coverage. Similarly, 80% of employees benefit from some type of employer-supported retirement plan, and about 87% receive life insurance benefits.

There are many benefits and various ways to classify each. For example, Social Security is both a legally required employer payment and a contribution toward most employees' future retirement income. In the remainder of this chapter we will classify benefits as (1) pay for time not worked, (2) insurance benefits, (3) retirement benefits, and (4) services.

PAY FOR TIME NOT WORKED

supplemental pay benefits

Benefits for time not worked such as unemployment insurance, vacation and holiday pay, and sick pay.

Supplemental pay benefits—in other words, pay for time not worked—are typically one of an employer's most expensive benefits because of the large amount of time off that many employees receive. Common time-off-with-pay periods include holidays, vacations, jury duty, funeral leave, military duty, sick leave, sabbatical leave, maternity leave, and unemployment insurance payments for laid-off or terminated employees. While some of these (such as unemployment insurance and maternity leave) can also be viewed as legally required benefits, the fact is that pay for time not worked is a substantial part of almost every employer's payroll bill. In this section we'll discuss some of the major time-off-with-pay elements, specifically: unemployment insurance (if the person is laid off); vacation and holiday pay; sick pay; severance pay (if the person is terminated); and supplemental unemployment benefits (which guarantee income if the plant is temporarily closed).

Unemployment Insurance

unemployment insurance

Provides weekly benefits if a person is unable to work through some fault other than his or her own.

All states have **unemployment insurance** or compensation acts. These provide for weekly benefits if a person is unable to work through some fault other than his or her own. The benefits derive from an unemployment tax on employers that can range from 0.1% to 5% of taxable payroll in most states. States each have their own unemployment laws, but these all follow federal guidelines. An employer's unemployment tax rate reflects its rate of personnel terminations.

Unemployment benefits are not meant for all dismissed employees—only those terminated through no fault of their own. Thus, strictly speaking, a worker fired for chronic lateness has no legitimate claim to benefits. But in practice many managers take a lackadaisical attitude toward protecting their employers against unwarranted claims. Therefore, employers spend thousands of dollars per year on unemployment taxes that would not be necessary if they protected themselves.

Carefully adhering to the procedures listed in Table 13-1 can therefore help protect your employer. Determine whether you could answer yes to questions such as, "Do you

TABLE 13-1 An Unemployment Insurance Cost Control Survey

CAUSE—DO YOU . . .	YES	NO	SOME-TIMES	CAUSE—DO YOU	YES	NO	SOME-TIMES
Lateness				3. Transfer employees to different departments	—	—	—
1. Tell employees whom to call when late	—	—	—	4. Have a flexible workweek that reflects high and low periods of productivity	—	—	—
2. Keep documented history of lateness and warning notices	—	—	—	5. Temporarily lay off employees for one week during slack periods	—	—	—
3. Suspend chronically late employees before discharging them	—	—	—	6. Attempt to find temporary or part-time jobs for laid-off employees	—	—	—
Absenteeism				*Job Refusal*			
1. Tell employees whom to call when absent	—	—	—	1. Issue a formal notice to employees collecting benefits to return to work	—	—	—
2. Rule that three days' absence without calling in is reason for automatic discharge	—	—	—	2. Require new employees to stipulate in writing their availability to work overtime, night shifts, etc.	—	—	—
3. Keep documented history of absence and warning notices	—	—	—	*Not Qualified*			
4. Request doctor's note on return to work	—	—	—	1. Set probationary periods to evaluate new employees	—	—	—
Illness				2. Conduct follow-up interviews one to two months after hire	—	—	—
1. Keep job open, if possible	—	—	—	*Deliberate Unsatisfactory Performance*			
2. Offer leave of absence	—	—	—	1. Document all instances, recording when and how employees did not meet job requirements	—	—	—
3. Request doctor's note on return to work	—	—	—	2. Require supervisors to document the steps taken to remedy the situation	—	—	—
Pregnancy				3. Require supervisors to document employee's refusal of advice and direction	—	—	—
1. Follow EEOC ruling, "no discharge"	—	—	—	*Violation of Company Rule*			
2. Request doctor's note indicating how long employee may work	—	—	—	1. Make sure all policies and rules of conduct are understood by all employees	—	—	—
3. Change jobs within company when practical	—	—	—	2. Require all employees to sign a statement acknowledging acceptance of these rules	—	—	—
4. Offer maternity leave	—	—	—	3. Meet with employee and fill out documented warning notice	—	—	—
Leave of Absence				4. Discharge at the time violation occurs, or suspend	—	—	—
1. Make written approval mandatory	—	—	—	*Wrong Benefit Charges*			
2. Stipulate date for return to work	—	—	—	1. Check state charge statement for			
3. Offer position at end of leave	—	—	—	(a) correct employee	—	—	—
Leave Job Voluntarily				(b) correct benefit amount	—	—	—
1. Conduct exit interview	—	—	—	(c) correct period of liability	—	—	—
2. Obtain a signed resignation statement	—	—	—				
3. Mail job abandonment letter	—	—	—				
4. Mail job review questionnaire three to six months after separation	—	—	—				
Layoff							
1. Hire employees with established "benefit year" if you anticipate layoffs	—	—	—				
2. Keep employees on when the cost to replace them would more than offset paying their salary	—	—	—				

CAUSE—DO YOU . . .	YES	NO	SOME-TIMES	CAUSE—DO YOU	YES	NO	SOME-TIMES
Claim Handling				4. Determine advantage of transfer of experience resulting from mergers, acquisition, or other corporate charges	—	—	—
1. Assign a claims supervisor or central office to process all separation information	—	—	—				
2. Respond to state claim forms on time	—	—	—	*Communication*			
3. Use proper terminology on claim form and attach documented evidence regarding separation	—	—	—	1. Hold periodic workshops with key personnel to review procedures and support effort to reduce turnover costs	—	—	—
4. Attend hearings and appeal unwarranted claims	—	—	—	2. Immediately investigate who or what is responsible for costly errors and why	—	—	—
5. Conduct availability checks and rehire employees collecting benefits	—	—	—	*Management Reports*			
Administration				1. Point to turnover problems as they occur by			
1. Have a staff member who knows unemployment insurance laws and who				(a) location	—	—	—
				(b) department	—	—	—
(a) works with the personnel department to establish proper use of policies and procedures	—	—	—	(c) classification of employee	—	—	—
(b) anticipates and reports costly turnover trends	—	—	—	2. Evaluate the effectiveness of current policies and procedures used to			
				(a) recruit	—	—	—
(c) successfully protests unwarranted claims and charges for unemployment benefits	—	—	—	(b) select	—	—	—
				(c) train	—	—	—
				(d) supervise	—	—	—
(d) recommends appropriate tax remedies:				(e) separate	—	—	—
				3. Help create policies and procedures for			
1. Verify the contribution rate assigned by the state	—	—	—	(a) less costly layoffs	—	—	—
2. Test for rate modification	—	—	—	(b) increased survival rate	—	—	—
3. Test for voluntary contribution and advisability of a joint account	—	—	—	(c) retention of employees	—	—	—

Explanation: Each "no" or "sometimes" answer represents an area where you lack control; each "yes" is a strong point that acts to save you money.

Source: Reprinted from the January 1976 issue of *Personnel Administrator.* Copyright 1976, the American Society for Personnel Administration.

tell employees whom to call when they're late?" or "Do you have a rule that 3 days' absence without calling is reason for automatic discharge?" By establishing policies and rules in these areas, you will be able to show that an employee's termination was a result of the person's inadequate performance (rather than lack of work or some other cause beyond his or her control). Some additional guidelines for cutting unemployment insurance costs include:

> *Understand the unemployment insurance code.* Many states annually publish updated employer's guides with names such as "Twenty-seven Ways to Avoid Losing Your Unemployment Appeal." You or someone on your staff should become an expert in understanding the unemployment insurance code in your state and how the system works.

Train managers and supervisors. Train managers and supervisors to use a checklist such as the one in Table 13-1. Don't let otherwise ineligible, dismissed employees successfully apply for unemployment compensation.

Conduct exit interviews. Routinely conducting exit interviews with everyone who leaves the organization can produce information useful for protesting unemployment claims.

Verify unemployment claims. Remember to check every unemployment claim against the individual's personnel file. Make sure to double-check the reasons the employee gives for why he or she left your employ.

File the protest against a former employee's claim on a timely basis. In most states you have 10 days in which to protest a claim.

Know your local unemployment insurance official. Most unemployment officers appreciate cooperative employers and are historically understaffed and overworked. Taking a hostile, adversarial position may undermine your ability to get the benefit of their doubt on a claim you might otherwise have won.

Audit the annual benefit charges statement. Once a year you will receive a benefit charges statement regarding the status of your unemployment compensation account. Thoroughly audit this, since errors such as inaccurate charges against your account may be included in it.[9]

Vacations and Holidays

The number of paid employee vacation days varies considerably from employer to employer. In the United States the average is about 10 days per year.[10] Even within the same employer, the number of vacation days will normally depend on how long the employee has worked at the firm. Thus, a typical vacation policy might call for:

1. One week after 6 months to 1 year of service;
2. Two weeks after 1 to 5 years of service;
3. Three weeks after 5 to 10 years of service;
4. Four weeks after 15 to 25 years of service; and
5. Five weeks after 25 years of service.[11]

The average number of annual vacation days is generally greater in industrialized countries outside the United States.[12] For example, compared with the average 10-day U.S. vacation, employees in Sweden and Austria can expect 30-day vacations; in France 25 days; and in the United Kingdom, Spain, Norway, Finland, and Belgium 20 to 25 days.

The number of paid holidays similarly varies considerably from employer to employer, from a minimum of about 5 to 13 or more. Common paid holidays include New Year's Day, Memorial Day, Independence Day, Labor Day, Thanksgiving Day, and Christmas Day. Other common holidays include Martin Luther King, Jr., Day; Good Friday; President's Day (third Monday in February); Veteran's Day; the Friday after Thanksgiving; the day before Christmas, and the day before New Year's.[13]

Several practical policy issues must be addressed. For example, will employees get their regular base rate of pay while on vacation, or vacation pay based on average earnings (which may include overtime)? And will employees get paid for accrued vacation time if they leave before taking their vacations?

Holiday pay policy issues must also be addressed. For example, many employers will not pay an employee for a holiday unless the employee has been at work the day before and the day after the holiday. Most employers also provide for some pay premium—such as time and a half—when employees must work on a holiday.

Sick Leave

Sick leave provides pay to an employee when he or she is out of work due to illness. Most sick leave policies grant full pay for a specified number of permissible sick days—usually up to about 12 per year. The sick days are often accumulated at the rate of, say, 1 day per month of service.

Sick leave pay causes consternation for many employers. The problem is that while many employees use their sick days only when they are legitimately sick, others simply use their sick leave as extensions to their vacations, whether they are sick or not. According to one recent survey, for instance, personal illnesses accounted for only about 45% of unscheduled sick leave absences. Family issues (27%), personal needs (13%), a mentality of "entitlement" (9%), and stress (6%), were other reasons cited.[14] While the figure varies considerably by size of firm, unscheduled absenteeism for all employers averages about 1.6% of all scheduled work hours. Thus a company with 10 employees and a 40-hour workweek might expect to have employees calling in with unscheduled absences at the rate of about .016 × 400 or 6.4 hours per week.[15]

Employers have tried several tactics to reduce the problem. Some now buy back unused sick leave at the end of the year by paying their employees a daily equivalent sum for each sick leave day not used. The drawback is that the policy can encourage legitimately sick employees to come to work despite their illness.[16] Others have experimented with holding monthly lotteries in which only employees with perfect monthly attendance are able to participate; those who participate are eligible to win a cash prize. Still others aggressively investigate all absences, for instance, by calling the absent employees at their homes when they are out sick. Marriott has a program called BeneTrade through which employees can trade the value of some sick days for other benefits.

A leave bank or paid time off (PTO) is another option today.[17] For example, one hospital previously granted new employees 25 days off per year (10 vacation days, 3 personal days, and 12 sick days). Employees used, on average, 5 of those 12 sick days (as well as all vacations and personal days).[18] The PTO allowed new employees to instead accrue 18 PTO days to be used as they see fit. ("Catastrophic leaves" defined as short-term illnesses causing absences for more than 5 consecutive work days, as well as special absences like jury duty and bereavement leave, were handled with separate accounts.) The new plan reportedly resulted in substantial cash savings including almost $400,000 over 3 years in lower overtime, and $350,000 saved in reduced temporary help.

PARENTAL LEAVE AND THE FAMILY AND MEDICAL LEAVE ACT OF 1993

Parental leave is a benefit whose time has come. About half of workers today are women, and 80% of them are expected to become pregnant at some time during their work lives.[19] Furthermore, many women and men today are heads of single-parent households. Partly as a response to this, the Family and Medical Leave Act of 1993 (FMLA) was signed into law by President Clinton. Among its provisions, which are summarized in Figure 13-2, the law stipulates that:

1. Private employers of 50 or more employees must provide eligible employees up to 12 weeks of unpaid leave for their own serious illness, the birth or adoption of a child, or the care of a seriously ill child, spouse, or parent.

2. Employers may require employees to take any unused paid sick leave or annual leave as part of the 12-week leave provided in the law.

3. Employees taking leave are entitled to receive health benefits while they are on unpaid leave, under the same terms and conditions as when they were on the job.

FIGURE 13-2

Family and Medical Leave Act Poster

> ### YOUR RIGHTS
> ### under the
> ### FAMILY AND MEDICAL LEAVE ACT OF 1993
>
> FMLA requires covered employers to provide up to 12 weeks of unpaid, job-protected leave to "eligible" employees for certain family and medical reasons. Employees are eligible if they have worked for a covered employer for at least one year, and for 1,250 hours over the previous 12 months, and if there are at least 50 employees within 75 miles.
>
> REASONS FOR TAKING LEAVE: Unpaid leave must be granted for *any* of the following reasons:
>
> • to care for the employee's child after birth, or placement for adoption or foster care;
> • to care for the employee's spouse, son or daughter, or parent, who has a serious health condition; or
> • for a serious health condition that makes the employee unable to perform the employee's job.
>
> At the employee's or employer's option, certain kinds of *paid* leave may be substituted for unpaid leave.
>
> ADVANCE NOTICE AND MEDICAL CERTIFICATION: The employee may be required to provide advance leave notice and medical certification. Taking of leave may be denied if requirements are not met.
>
> • The employee ordinarily must provide 30 days advance notice when the leave is "foreseeable."
> • An employer may require medical certification to support a request for leave because of a serious health condition, and may require second or third opinions (at the employer's expense) and a fitness for duty report to return to work.
>
> JOB BENEFITS AND PROTECTION:
>
> • For the duration of FMLA leave, the employer must maintain the employee's health coverage under any "group health plan."
> • Upon return from FMLA leave, most employees must be restored to their original or equivalent positions with equivalent pay, benefits, and other employment terms.
> • The use of FMLA leave cannot result in the loss of any employment benefit that accrued prior to the start of an employee's leave.
>
> UNLAWFUL ACTS BY EMPLOYERS: FMLA makes it unlawful for any employer to:
>
> • interfere with, restrain, or deny the exercise of any right provided under FMLA;
> • discharge or discriminate against any person for opposing any practice made unlawful by FMLA or for involvement in any proceeding under or relating to FMLA.
>
> ENFORCEMENT:
>
> • The U.S. Department of Labor is authorized to investigate and resolve complaints of violations.
> • An eligible employee may bring a civil action against an employer for violations.
>
> FMLA does not affect any Federal or State law prohibiting discrimination, or supersede any State or local law or collective bargaining agreement which provides greater family or medical leave rights.
>
> FOR ADDITIONAL INFORMATION: Contact the nearest office of the Wage and Hour Division, listed in most telephone directories under U.S. Government, Department of Labor.
>
> U.S. Department of Labor, Employment Standards Administration   WH Publication 1420
> Wage and Hour Division, Washington, D.C. 20210   June 1993

4. Employers must guarantee employees the right to return to their previous or equivalent position with no loss of benefits at the end of the leave; however, the law provides a limited exception from this provision to certain highly paid employees.

A number of employers have found complying with this act somewhat onerous. "We have found that basically any illness is now covered by the law . . ." said one benefits director; another contends that her company can no longer "impose any discipline—even the downgrading of attendance ratings—for absences due to any cause covered by the law."[20] Employees also seem to be surprisingly aware of their rights under the Family and Medical Leave Act, with over half the complaints filed with the Department of Labor's Wage and Hour Division in 1996 stemming from the Act.[21] And individual supervisors (not just employers) have been held liable under the act for improperly preventing workers from exercising their FMLA rights.[22]

While leaves awarded under the Family and Medical Leave Act are generally unpaid, they are not costless to the employer. For example, one study concluded that the costs associated with recruiting new temporary-replacement workers, training replacement workers, and compensating for the lower level of productivity of these workers could represent a substantial expense over and above what employers would normally pay their full-time employees.[23] Find out more about the FMLA at www.dol.gov/elaws.

Having a clear procedure for any leave of absence (including one awarded under the Family and Medical Leave Act) is therefore essential. A form such as in Figure 13-3 on page 484 should be the centerpiece of any such procedure. In general, no employee should be given a leave until it's clear what the leave is for. If the leave is for medical or family reasons, medical certification should be obtained from the attending physician or medical practitioner. A form like this also places on record the employee's expected return date and the fact that without an authorized extension his or her employment may be terminated. One employment lawyer suggests that employers should "kind of bend over backward" to determine if an employee is eligible for leave based on the employee's situation and not be too abrupt in turning the person down.[24]

Severance Pay

severance pay

A one-time payment some employers provide when terminating an employee.

Many employers provide **severance pay**—a one-time payment—when terminating an employee. The payment may range from 3 or 4 days' wages to 1 or more years' salary. Other firms provide "bridge" severance pay by keeping employees (especially managers) on the payroll for several months until they've found a new job.

Such payments make sense on several grounds. It is a humanitarian gesture as well as good public relations. In addition, most managers expect employees to give them at least one or two weeks' notice if they plan to quit; it therefore seems appropriate to provide at least one or two weeks' severance pay if an employee is being terminated. Avoiding litigation is another oft-mentioned reason for severance pay. And the Worker Adjustment and Retraining Notification ("plant closing") Act of 1989 requires covered employers to give employees 60 days' written notice of plant closures or mass layoffs.

For whatever reason, severance pay is increasingly common for workers who lose jobs. In one survey of 3,000 HR managers, 82% of responding organizations reported having a severance policy (ranging from 66% for very small firms to over 90% for larger firms).[25] The reason for the dismissal influences whether or not the employee gets severance pay; for example, about 95% of employees dismissed due to downsizings got severance pay, while only about a third of respondents offer severance in cases of termination for poor performance. Roughly half the employees receiving severance payments get lump sum amounts, and the other half receive salary continuation for a time. The average maximum severance is 39 weeks for executives and about 30 weeks for other downsized employees.[26] Severance pay at the rate of 1 week of severance pay for each year of service is the policy at about half the firms responding to another survey.[27]

Supplemental Unemployment Benefits

supplemental unemployment benefits

Provide for a "guaranteed annual income" in certain industries where employers must shut down to change machinery or due to reduced work. These benefits are paid by the company and supplement unemployment benefits.

In some industries (such as automaking), shutdowns to reduce inventories or change machinery are common, and in the past employees were laid off or furloughed and had to depend on unemployment insurance. **Supplemental unemployment benefits** are paid by

FIGURE 13-3

Sample Application for Leave of Absence

Source: BNA Bulletin to Management, September 30, 1993, p. 6.

Name _____   Date of Application _____

Location _____   Department _____

Type of Leave Requested (Check each that applies.)

[ ] Medical*   [ ] Educational
[ ] Family*   [ ] Other _____
[ ] Military

Start Date (first day of leave) _____   Return Date (date of return to work) _____

Absence is to be (check each that applies): [ ] unpaid
                                             [ ] fully paid
                                             [ ] partially paid (Please explain.)
                                             _____
                                             _____
                                             _____

Should vacation benefits be used?   [ ] No
                                       [ ] Yes (# of hours) _____

Reason for Requested Leave (Explain why leave is necessary.)

_____
_____
_____
_____
_____
_____
_____
_____

*A medical certification is required for medical/family leaves of absence. The health care provider's certification must include:
◇ The date the health condition began;
◇ The expected duration of the condition;
◇ Appropriate medical facts necessary to verify leave requests;
◇ An estimate of the amount of time required to be off work; and
◇ If for a family member's serious health condition, a statement that the employee is needed to care for that family member.
Refer to the Family Leave of Absence Policy for further certification and reporting requirements.

Employee's Signature   _____   Date _____

I understand that if I do not return from my leave of absence at the expiration of this leave, unless an extension has been approved in advance, my employment may be terminated.

Supervisor's Signature   _____   Date _____

the company and supplement unemployment benefits, thus enabling the workers to better maintain their standards of living. Supplemental benefits are becoming more prevalent in collective bargaining agreements. They provide benefits over and above state employment compensation for three contingencies: layoffs, reduced workweeks, and relocations. Such benefits are most popular in heavy manufacturing operations such as in the auto and steel industries. Here weekly or monthly plant shutdowns are normal, and some plan for guaranteeing minimum annual income is more appropriate.

INSURANCE BENEFITS

worker's compensation
Provides income and medical benefits to work-related accident victims or their dependents regardless of fault.

Worker's Compensation

Worker's compensation laws [28] are aimed at providing sure, prompt income and medical benefits to work-related accident victims or their dependents, regardless of fault.[29] Every state has its own worker's compensation law. However, there has been continuing congressional interest in establishing minimum national standards for state compensation laws.[30] Some states run their own insurance programs. However, most require employers to carry worker's compensation insurance with private state-approved insurance companies.

Worker's compensation benefits can be either monetary or medical. In the event of a worker's death or disablement, the person's dependents are paid a cash benefit based on prior earnings—usually one-half to two-thirds the worker's average weekly wage, per week of employment. In most states there is a set time limit—such as 500 weeks—for which benefits can be paid. If the injury causes a specific loss (such as an arm), the employee may receive additional benefits based on a statutory list of losses, even though he or she may return to work. In addition to these cash benefits, employers must furnish medical, surgical, and hospital services needed by the employee.

For an injury or illness to be covered by worker's compensation, one must only prove that it arose while the employee was on the job. It does not matter that the employee may have been at fault; if the person was on the job when the injury occurred, he or she is entitled to worker's compensation. For example, suppose all employees are instructed to wear safety goggles when working at their machines. One worker does not and is injured while on the job. The company must still provide worker's compensation benefits. The fact that the worker was at fault in no way waives his or her claim to benefits.

Worker's compensation is usually handled by state administrative commissions. However, neither the state nor the federal government contributes any funds for worker's compensation. Employers are responsible for insuring themselves or for arranging for the appropriate coverage through an insurance company.

The employment provisions of the Americans with Disabilities Act (ADA) influence how most employers handle worker's compensation cases. For one thing, ADA provisions generally prohibit employers from inquiring about an applicant's worker's compensation history, a practice that was widespread prior to the passage of the ADA. Furthermore, the ADA makes it more important that injured employees get back to work more quickly or be accommodated if their injury leads to a disability. Failing to let an employee return to work who is on worker's compensation because of an injury, or failing to accommodate him or her, could lead to litigation under ADA.[31]

CONTROLLING WORKER'S COMPENSATION COSTS   Minimizing the number of worker's compensation claims is an important goal for all employers. While the employer's insurance company usually pays the claims, the costs of the premiums depend on the number and dollar amount of claims. Minimizing such claims is thus important.

In practice, there are several ways to reduce such claims. First, you can screen out accident-prone workers and also reduce accident-causing conditions in your facilities. Second, you can reduce the accidents and health problems that trigger these claims, by, for instance, instituting effective safety and health programs and complying with government standards on these matters.

Third, you can institute rehabilitation programs for injured employees, since worker's compensation costs increase as long as an employee can't work. The objective is to institute corrective physical therapy programs (including exercise equipment; career counseling to guide injured employees into new, less strenuous jobs; and nursing assistance, for instance) so as to reintegrate recipients back into your workforce.[32]

Case management is an increasingly preferred option. It refers to "the treatment of injured workers on a case-by-case basis by an assigned manager, usually a registered nurse, who coordinates with the physician and health plan to determine which care settings are the most effective for quality care and cost."[33] Costs can reportedly be reduced considerably by assigning a professional to coordinate and oversee the worker's rehabilitation and gradual reassimilation into the firm's workforce. Safety/injury protection and case management programs were viewed by respondents in one survey as the most common workers' compensation cost containment measures. Other effective techniques included monitoring health care providers for compliance with their fee schedules, and auditing medical bills.[34] The following High-Performance feature illustrates one company's workers' compensation program.

THE HIGH-PERFORMANCE ORGANIZATION

Building Better, Faster, More Competitive
Organizations Through HR: Workers' Compensation

■ *Weirton Steel Corporation—Weirton, WV*

Workers' compensation benefits, paid to workers injured on the job, directly affect a company's cost of doing business. Because it adds no value to the product, it is in the best interest of Weirton and its employees to aggressively pursue the reduction of workers' compensation payouts through safety awareness and an effective workers' compensation program. In 1996, Weirton established a workers' compensation program to review, contain, and reduce the costs of workers' compensation. Injury claims are now thoroughly reviewed, payout periods are monitored, and recovery is assisted.

For example, the reporting process was modified to allow a more thorough review of the injuries by inclusion of independent medical examiners and third-party administrators. Accident reports are now submitted for a compensation claims ruling within 24 hours of filing, or within three days if questioned. Weekly management meetings are held to review each case. In cooperation with the Operations Department, an aggressive Modified Duty program was established to return employees to the workplace in an area that is amenable to their injuries. Unique to the program is the Options Rehab program where the patient agrees to follow rehabilitation treatment. Rehab protocol decrees that if surgery is required, it should be performed as soon as possible, followed by prescribed rehabilitation, and a proper transition back to work. The program is developing a treatment protocol for high occurrence injuries such as back strain, knee injuries, and shoulder injuries. Additionally, there is increased follow-up of patients off work through biweekly physician visits and calls from case managers.

The workers' compensation program provides an aggressive, proactive approach toward case reduction, which has reduced the number of cases and produced substantial cost savings. Since implementing these changes, the number of workers' compensation cases have dropped from 140 in July 1995 to 77 in July 1996. Payouts have dropped from $153 thousand per month in 1991 to $101 thousand per month in 1996.

Life Insurance

Most employers provide **group life insurance** plans for their employees. As a group, employees can obtain lower rates than if they buy such insurance as individuals. And group plans usually contain a provision for including all employees—including new ones—regardless of health or physical condition.

In many cases the employer pays 100% of the base premium, which usually provides life insurance equal to about two years' salary. The employee then pays for any additional life insurance coverage. In some cases the cost of even the base premium is split 50/50 or 80/20 between the employer and employee, respectively. In general, there are three key personnel policy areas to be addressed: the benefits-paid schedule (amount of life insurance benefits is usually tied to the annual earnings of the employee); supplemental benefits (continued life insurance coverage after retirement, and so on); and financing (the amount and percent that the employee contributes).[35]

Hospitalization, Medical, and Disability Insurance

Most employers—about 80% of medium and large firms and 69% of small firms—make available to their employees some type of hospitalization, medical, and disability insurance; along with life insurance, these benefits form the cornerstone of almost all benefits programs.[36] Hospitalization, health, and disability insurance is aimed at providing protection against hospitalization costs and loss of income arising from accidents or illness occurring from off-the-job causes. Many employers purchase such insurance from life insurance companies, casualty insurance companies, or Blue Cross (for hospital expenses) and Blue Shield (for physician expenses) organizations. Others contract directly with health maintenance organizations or preferred provider organizations, both of which are discussed later.

Most health insurance plans provide, at a minimum, basic hospitalization and surgical and medical insurance for all eligible employees as a group. As with life insurance, group rates are usually lower than individual rates and are generally available to all employees—including new ones—regardless of health or physical condition. Most basic plans pay for hospital room and board, surgery charges, and medical expenses (such as doctors' visits to the hospital). Some group plans also provide major medical coverage to meet high medical expenses that result from long-term or serious illnesses; with hospitalization costs rapidly rising this is an increasingly popular option. The employer's health and hospitalization plans must comply with the Americans with Disabilities Act.[37] For example, the employer's insurance policy shouldn't make distinctions on the basis of disability unless those distinctions are justified by recognized differences based on actuarial data or historic costs.[38]

Many employers are also sponsoring health-related insurance plans covering expenses like eye care and dental services. In fact, dental insurance plans have been one of the fastest-growing items, with the number of persons in the United States with dental coverage now over 100 million.[39] In most employer-sponsored dental plans, participants must pay a specified amount of deductible dental expenses (typically $25 or $50 each year) before the plan kicks in with benefits. In a majority of the cases the participants in such plans have premiums paid for entirely by their employers.[40]

Accidental death and dismemberment coverage is another option. This provides a fixed lump-sum benefit in addition to life insurance benefits when death is accidental. It also provides a range of benefits in case of accidental loss of limbs or sight. Other options provide payments for diagnostic visits to the doctor's office, vision care, hearing aid plans, payment for prescription drugs, and dental care plans. Employers must provide the same health care benefits to employees over the age of 65 that are provided to younger workers, even though the older workers are eligible for the federally funded Medicare health insurance plan.[41]

Disability insurance is aimed at providing income protection or compensation for loss of salary due to illness or accident. The disability payments usually begin when normal sick leave is used up and may continue to provide income to age 65 or beyond.[42] The disability benefits usually range from 50% to 75% of the employee's base pay if he or she is disabled.

health maintenance organization (HMO)

A prepaid health care system that generally provides routine round-the- clock medical services as well as preventive medicine in a clinic-type arrangement for employees, who pay a nominal fee in addition to the fixed annual fee the employer pays.

Preferred Provider Organizations (PPOs)

Groups of health care providers that contract with employers, insurance companies, or third-party payers to provide medical care services at a reduced fee.

Many employers offer membership in a **health maintenance organization (HMO)** as a hospital/medical option. The HMO itself is a medical organization consisting of several specialists (surgeons, psychiatrists, and so on) operating out of a community-based health care center. The HMO generally provides routine round-the-clock medical services at a specific site to employees who pay a nominal fee. The HMO also receives a fixed annual fee per employee from the employer (or employer and employee), regardless of whether any service actually is provided.[43]

Preferred provider organizations (PPOs) have been defined as a cross between HMOs and the traditional doctor/patient arrangement: They are "groups of health care providers that contract with employers, insurance companies, or third-party payers to provide medical care services at a reduced fee."[44] Unlike an HMO with its relatively limited list of health care providers often concentrated in one health care center, PPOs let employees select providers (such as participating doctors); they agree to provide price discounts and submit to certain utilization controls, such as on the number of diagnostic tests that can be ordered.[45] Employees may obtain increased health cost savings and a wider choice of doctors than are typically available with an HMO. The doctors themselves benefit from the increased number of patients. HMOs and PPOs are compared in Figure 13-4.

REDUCING HEALTH BENEFIT COSTS   The average cost per employee of health benefits has risen from about $1,700 in 1985 to about $3,700 in 1997 in some firms; giant firms like General Motors spend hundreds of millions of dollars per year just on health care

FIGURE 13-4

New Health Insurance Options Differ on Key Dimensions

Source: George Milkovich and Jerry Newman, *Compensation* (Burr Ridge, IL: McGraw-Hill, 1993), p. 444.

ISSUE	TRADITIONAL COVERAGE	HEALTH MAINTENANCE ORGANIZATION (HMO)	PREFERRED PROVIDER ORGANIZATION (PPO)
Who is eligible?	May live anywhere.	May be required to live in HMO–designated service area.	May live anywhere.
Who provides health care?	Doctor and health care facility of patient's choice.	Must use doctors and facilities designated by HMO.	May use doctors and facilities associated with PPO. If not, may pay additional copayment/deductible.
How much coverage on routine, preventative level?	Does not cover regular checkups and other preventative services. Diagnostic tests may be covered in part or full.	Covers regular checkups, diagnostic tests, other preventative services with low or no fee per visit.	Same as with HMO, if doctor and facility are on approved list. Copayments and deductibles are assessed at much higher rate for others not on list.
Hospital care.	Covers doctors and hospital bills.	Covers doctors and hospital bills if HMO–approved hospital.	Covers doctors and hospitals if PPO–approved.

benefits.[46] Caught between rising benefits costs and the belt-tightening occurring in firms today, many managers now find controlling and reducing health care costs topping their to-do lists. As a result, many employers have been changing their medical plans to do the following.

1. Move away from 100% medical cost payments. Over 70% of plans now include a deductible.

2. Increase annual deductibles. Today, almost 40% of firms use a deductible of $150 or more.

3. Limit the annual out-of-pocket medical expenses an employee pays. Interestingly, the number of plans with a "stop-loss" amount, which limits the out-of-pocket expense an employee would have to pay during a year, has increased from 80% to 89% recently. In other words, while employers are asking employees to pay higher deductibles, they are giving employees more protection against catastrophic medical expenses.

4. Require medical contributions. Most employers require employee contributions to their medical premiums.[47]

5. Use gatekeepers. A case management procedure—in which, for instance, a general practitioner serves as a gatekeeper and channels the patient to the appropriate specialist and/or hospital as needed—was cited as "very effective" by 69% of the employers in one survey.[48]

6. Focus on health promotion and preventive health care. According to one survey, 56% of the firms were sponsoring drug and alcohol abuse programs; 31% were offering stop-smoking sessions; 45% were providing physical fitness classes; and 18% had exercise facilities on company premises. Many employers (70%) were training employees in first aid and CPR. Most were also increasing their communication efforts; 69% explain the problem of rising health care costs to employees and 54% offer tips about how to use company health benefits wisely.[49]

   HealthTrust, Inc. has changed its health and hospitalization plan to include such things as a preventive-care program including mammograms, prostate exams, and well-baby care; a prenatal program called "Healthy Beginnings"; an employee assistance program for seeking help for emotional or substance abuse problems; and a higher deductible ($1,000) for individuals injured when engaged in high-risk activities such as not wearing seatbelts when driving.[50]

   Thirty-nine percent of respondents in one survey used financial incentives or disincentives to encourage good health (such as higher premiums for smokers).[51] *Health care initiatives* is the umbrella term used to describe efforts such as the use of training or education, newsletters, classes, workshops, and incentives or disincentives. The "vast majority" of employers use such health initiatives today, according to one survey.[52]

7. Form health care coalitions.[53] In Memphis, Tennessee, 11 self-insured employers including Federal Express and Holiday Inn formed a coalition to study health care costs, identify more efficient health care providers, and use their purchasing power to obtain discounts on health and hospital care prices.[54]

MANAGING HEALTH CARE COSTS: AIDS   By now, the fatal nature of AIDS—Acquired Immune Deficiency Syndrome—is unfortunately well known to everyone.[55] Several insurance companies have concluded that the best way to manage the cost of AIDS is to redesign benefits plans with an eye toward providing required care in the least costly way. This often means treating the AIDS sufferer in his or her home and allowing that cost to be paid under the benefits plan (as is not usually allowed now). Plus, the emphasis will increasingly be on individual case management (ICM). Here a special ICM nurse will be assigned to the patient and an alternative treatment plan will be designed. The plan will be individualized, taking into consideration the patient's ability to care for himself or herself, the availability of others who are able to help in the person's treatment, and the age and condition of the patient.

MENTAL HEALTH BENEFITS   It is estimated that employers spend just over 8% of their health plan dollars on mental health treatment.[56] These costs are rising quickly because of widespread drug and alcohol problems, an increase in the number of states that require employers to offer a minimum package of mental health benefits, and the fact that other health care claims are higher for employees with high mental health claims. The Mental Health Parity Act of 1996, implemented for most group health plan's for years beginning on or after January 1, 1998, sets minimum mental health care benefits at the national level.[57]

One step in slowing the rise in mental health benefits is for employers to tighten up the process. One New York financial services firm—faced with a big jump in mental health costs in one recent year—rejected the idea of placing across-the-board limits on mental health coverage. Instead it redesigned the mental health portion of its health plan. The plan now includes a utilization review to certify treatment, increased outpatient benefits, and a selected network of cost-efficient providers. The new program cut mental health benefit plan costs significantly while still providing needed benefits for company employees.[58]

Pregnancy Discrimination Act (PDA)

An amendment to Title VII of the Civil Rights Act that prohibits sex discrimination based on "pregnancy, childbirth, or related medical conditions." It requires employers to provide benefits—including sick leave and disability benefits and health and medical insurance—the same as for any employee not able to work because of disability.

THE PREGNANCY DISCRIMINATION ACT   The **Pregnancy Discrimination Act (PDA)** is aimed at prohibiting sex discrimination based on "pregnancy, childbirth, or related medical conditions."[59] Before enactment of this law in 1978, temporary disability benefits for pregnancies were generally paid in the form of either sick leave or disability insurance, if at all. However, while most employers provide temporary disability income to their employees for up to 26 weeks for most illnesses, those that provided benefits for pregnancy usually limited benefits to only 6 weeks for normal pregnancies. Many believed that the shorter duration of pregnancy benefits constituted discrimination based on sex; it was this issue that the PDA was aimed at settling.

Specifically, the act requires employers to treat women affected by pregnancy, childbirth, or related medical conditions the same as any employees not able to work, with respect to all benefits, including sick leave and disability benefits, and health and medical insurance. Thus, it is illegal for most employers to discriminate against women by providing benefits of lower amount or duration for pregnancy, childbirth, or related medical conditions. For example, if an employer provides up to 26 weeks of temporary disability income to employees for all illnesses, it is now required to provide up to 26 weeks for pregnancy and childbirth also, rather than the more typical 6 weeks that prevailed before the act.

COBRA REQUIREMENTS   The ominously titled COBRA—Comprehensive Omnibus Budget Reconciliation Act—requires most private employers to make continued health benefits available to terminated or retired employees and their families for a period of time, generally 18 months. The former employee must pay for this coverage, if desired, as well as a small fee for administrative costs.

Care must be taken in administering COBRA, especially with respect to informing employees of their COBRA rights. For one thing, you don't want a terminated or retired employee to get injured and then come back and claim that he or she didn't know that his or her insurance coverage could have been continued. Therefore, when a new employee first becomes eligible for your company's insurance plan, an explanation of COBRA rights should be received and acknowledged. More important, all employees separated from the company for any reason should sign a form acknowledging that they have received and understood information about their COBRA rights.

LONG-TERM CARE   Today, the oldest group of baby boomers is reaching age 50, and as a result, long-term care insurance—care to support people in their old age—is reportedly "emerging as the key new employee benefit."[60] The Health Insurance Portability and Accountability Act, enacted in 1996, lets employers and employees deduct the cost of long-term care insurance premiums from their annual income taxes, adding further attractiveness to this particular benefit.[61]

There are several types of long-term care for which employers can provide insurance benefits for their employees. For example, adult day care facilities offer structured programs including social and recreational activities. Assisted living facilities offer shared housing and supervision for those who cannot function independently. Custodial care is assistance given by people who have no medical skills to help individuals perform daily living activities such as bathing.

RETIREMENT BENEFITS

As the 77 million or so baby boomers born between 1946 and 1964 stampede into retirement, "employers are increasingly revising and improving their retirement benefits."[62] The first contingent of baby boomers will turn 65 in the year 2011, and many reportedly won't wait that long to retire; 38% of boomers aged 45 to 52 now want to retire by age 55, for instance.[63] As a result, employers are being much more aggressive about taking "various steps to enhance the retirement plans they offer and boost employee participation in those plans."[64]

Social Security

social security

Provides three types of benefits: retirement income at the age of 62 and thereafter; survivor's or death benefits payable to the employee's dependents regardless of age at time of death; and disability benefits payable to disabled employees and their dependents. These benefits are payable only if the employee is insured under the Social Security Act.

Many people assume that **social security** provides income only when they are old, but it actually provides three types of benefits. First are the familiar retirement benefits. These provide an income if you retire at age 62 or thereafter and are insured under the Social Security Act. Second, there are survivor's or death benefits. These provide monthly payments to your dependents regardless of your age at death, again assuming you were insured under the Social Security Act. Finally, there are disability payments. These provide monthly payments to you and your dependents if you become totally disabled for work and meet certain specified work requirements.[65] The Medicare program, which provides a wide range of health services to people 65 or over, is also administered through the Social Security system.

Social Security (technically, federal old age and survivor's insurance) is paid for by a tax on the employee's wages, shared equally by employees and employer. If you are self-employed, you pay the entire sum less 2% of your self-employment income. The figure rises fairly often; in 1999 employers and their employees each were paying a Social Security tax of 6.2% on the first $62,700 of the employee's earnings. Each also pay a Medicare tax of 1.45% of the employee's total earnings.[66]

Pension Plans

pension plans

Plans that provide a fixed sum when employees reach a predetermined retirement age or when they can no longer work due to disability.

defined benefit pension plan

A plan that contains a formula for determining retirement benefits.

There are many types of **pension plans**.[67] For example, there are defined benefit pension plans and defined contribution benefit plans.[68] A **defined benefit pension plan** contains a formula for determining retirement benefits so that the actual benefits to be received are defined ahead of time. For example, the plan might include a formula that specifies a dollar amount or a percentage of annual salary for predicting the individual's eventual pen-

defined contribution plan

A plan in which the employer's contribution to employees' retirement or savings funds is specified.

Employees today often look ahead to their retirement with specific financial goals in mind and evaluate their current job benefits in light of their future needs.

deferred profit-sharing plan

A plan in which a certain amount of profits is credited to each employee's account, payable at retirement, termination, or death.

vesting

Provision that money placed in a pension fund cannot be forfeited for any reason.

sion. A **defined contribution plan** specifies what contribution the employer will make to a retirement or savings fund set up for the employee. The defined contribution plan does not define the eventual benefit amount, only the periodic contribution to the plan. In a defined benefit plan, the employee knows ahead of time what his or her retirement benefits will be upon retirement. With a defined contribution plan, the employee cannot be sure of his or her retirement benefits. Those benefits depend on both the amounts contributed to the fund and the retirement fund's investment earnings.

Under a 401(k) plan, based on Section 401(k) of the Internal Revenue Code, employees can have a portion of their compensation, which would otherwise be paid in cash, put into a company profit-sharing or stock bonus plan by the employer. This results in a pretax reduction in salary, so the employee isn't taxed on those set-aside dollars until after he or she retires (or removes the money from the pension fund). Some employers also match a portion of what the employee contributes to the 401(k) plan. One attraction of 401(k) is that employees may have a range of investment options for their 401(k) funds, including mutual stock funds and bond funds. Employers usually choose 401(k) "providers" (such as investment firms) to set up and administer their 401(k) plans; such choices should be made with the utmost care, not only because of the employer's responsibility to its employees but also because changing 401(k) providers can be a "grueling venture."[69]

There are several types of defined contribution plans.[70] In a savings and thrift plan (a 401(k) is one example), employees contribute a portion of their earnings to a fund; this contribution is usually matched in whole or in part by the employer. In **deferred profit-sharing plan,** employers typically contribute a portion of their profits to the pension fund, regardless of the level of employee contribution. An employee stock ownership plan (ESOP) is a qualified, tax-deductible stock bonus plan in which employers contribute stock to a trust for eventual use by employees.

The entire area of pension planning is complicated, partly because of the many federal laws governing pensions. For example, companies want to ensure that their pension contributions are "qualified" or tax deductible; they must, therefore, adhere to the pertinent income tax codes. The Employee Retirement Income Security Act (ERISA) restricts what companies can, cannot, and must do in regard to pension plans (more on this in a moment). In unionized companies, the union must be allowed to participate in the administration of the pension plan under the Taft-Hartley Act.

While an employer usually must develop a pension plan to meet its own unique needs, there are several key policy issues to consider, including:[71]

Membership requirements. For example, what is the minimum age or minimum service at which employees become eligible for a pension?

Benefit formula. This usually ties the pension to the employee's final earnings, or an average of his or her last three or four years' earnings.

Plan-Funding. One issue here is whether the plan will be contributory or noncontributory. In the former, contributions to the pension funds are made by both employees and the employer. In a noncontributory fund—the prevailing type, by the way—only the employer contributes.

Vesting. *Vested funds* refers to the money that the employer and employee have placed in the latter's pension fund that cannot be forfeited for any reason. The employees' contributions are always theirs and cannot be forfeited. However, until the passage of the Employee Retirement Income Security Act, the employer's contribution was not necessarily vested. So, you could have worked for a company for 30 years and be left with no pension if the company went out of business 1 year before you were to retire. That generally can't happen today.[72]

On average, just over half of full-time workers participate in some type of pension plan, although the actual percentages depend on several things. For example, older workers tend to have higher participation rates, and employees of larger firms have participation rates as much as three times higher than those in very small firms.[73] Workers earning lower incomes (particularly under $25,000 per year) seem to be more at risk of receiving little or no pension income, because they contribute significantly less to pension plans than do workers earning more.[74]

Particularly given these variations in participation rates, employers are taking steps to encourage more employees to plan for their retirements and to contribute to a pension plan.

THE QUESTION OF PORTABILITY   Many employers today are redesigning their pension plans in order to make their pensions more "portable." For example, Duracel International, Inc. has redesigned and simplified its pension plan to make it easier for employees to take their retirement income when they leave and roll it over into a new employer's savings plan or IRA.[75] Doing so represents a dramatic shift in pension planning for most employers. Traditionally, one purpose of a pension was to "lock in" workers, to tie them to the company by giving them substantially smaller pensions should they leave before retirement age.

Today's needs for flexible staffing and the realities of ongoing corporate restructurings and downsizings are causing more employers to make their pension plans more portable. This is often facilitated by switching from defined benefit to defined contribution plans, since the former are more appropriate for employees who plan to stay with the firm until retirement. Another approach is to allow workers who leave the firm before retirement to receive initial benefits at a younger age.[76]

Pensions and the Law

Employee Retirement Income Security Act (ERISA)

Signed into law by President Ford in 1974 to require that pension rights be vested, and protected by a government agency, PBGC.

The **Employee Retirement Income Security Act (ERISA)** was signed into law in 1974.[77] ERISA was aimed at protecting the pensions of workers and stimulating the growth of pension plans.

Before enactment of ERISA, pension plans as noted above often failed to deliver expected benefits to employees. Any number of reasons, such as business failure and inadequate funding, could result in employees losing their expected pensions and facing the prospect of being unable to retire.

Today, under ERISA and the Tax Reform Act of 1986, participants in a pension plan must have a nonforfeitable right to 100% of their accrued benefits after 5 years of service. As an alternative, the employer may choose to phase in vesting over a period of 3 to 7 years. Under the Tax Reform Act of 1986, an employer can require that an employee complete a period of no more than 2 years' service to the company before becoming eligible to participate in the plan. However, if you require more than 1 year of service before eligibility, the plan must grant employees full and immediate vesting rights at the end of that period.[78]

Pension Benefits Guarantee Corporation (PBGC)

Established under ERISA to ensure that pensions meet vesting obligations; also insures pensions should a plan terminate without sufficient funds to meet its vested obligations.

Among other things, the **Pension Benefit Guarantee Corporation (PBGC)** was established under ERISA to ensure that pensions meet vesting obligations; the PBGC also insures pensions should a plan terminate without sufficient funds to meet its vested obligations.[79]

Several factors are making some experts uncomfortable about the security of employees' pensions despite the existence of the Pension Benefit Guarantee Corp.[80] For example, the PBGC guarantees only defined benefit plans, not defined contribution plans. Furthermore, PBGC payments are not unlimited: It will pay an individual a pension of up to about $27,000 per year, for instance. This may seem like a lot, but it might not be to, say, an airline pilot who retired expecting a pension of $70,000 per year.

Furthermore, according to the PBGC, more and more employers are terminating their defined benefit plans and replacing them with uninsured defined contribution plans. One reason for this is that the accounting profession's "Employers Accounting for Pensions," rule, commonly known as FASB 87, requires employers with defined benefits plans to estimate on their balance sheets the size of the employers' liability. FASB 87 does not apply to defined contribution plans. Unlike defined benefits plans, defined contribution plans do not guarantee how much an employee will receive on retirement, only what each party's contribution to the plan will be. Many defined plans remain underfunded.

Benefits Trends

golden offerings

Offers to current employees aimed at encouraging them to retire early, perhaps even with the same pensions they would expect if they retired at, say, age 65.

Retirement benefits are getting a new twist with so-called **golden offerings**—early retirement windows and other voluntary separation arrangements. These are aimed at avoiding dismissals by offering special retirement packages to long-term employees. According to one survey of a cross section of U.S. industries and locations, about one -third of companies offered such voluntary separation plans recently, while another 9% were considering an offering.

early retirement window

A type of golden offering by which employees are encouraged to retire early, the incentive being liberal pension benefits plus perhaps a cash payment.

EARLY RETIREMENT WINDOWS   Most of these plans take the form of **early retirement window** arrangements in which specific employees (often age 50+) are eligible to participate. The "window" means that the company opens up (for a limited time only) the chance for an employee to retire earlier than usual. The financial incentive is usually a combination of improved or liberalized pension benefits plus a cash payment. One expert concludes that early retirement has become the method of choice for reducing midmanagement and white-collar workforces, with about 13% of 362 employers surveyed providing such early retirement windows in 1 recent year.[81]

One recent study found, perhaps not surprisingly, that deteriorating financial conditions for the company often precede early retirement programs. In turn, announcements of early retirement programs tend to be followed by positive stock market reactions up to 2 years following such announcements, since investors "likely view declines in long-term head counts as more favorable than the initial short-term costs of funding the early retirement programs."[82]

Early retirement windows like these must be used with caution. Age discrimination is the fastest-growing type of discrimination claim today, and unless structured properly, early retirement programs can be challenged as de facto programs for forcing the discharge of older employees against their will.[83] While it is generally legal to use incentives like early retirement benefits to encourage individuals to choose early retirement, the employee's decision must be voluntary. In fact, in several cases individuals who were eligible for and elected early retirement later challenged their early retirement by claiming that their decision was not voluntary. In one case (*Paolillo* v. *Dresser Industries, Inc.*), employees were told on October 12 that they were eligible to retire under a "totally voluntary" early retirement program and must inform the company by October 18 of their decisions. However, they were not informed of the details of the program until October 15. The employees subsequently sued, claiming coercion. The U.S. Court of Appeals for the Second Circuit (New York) agreed with them, arguing that an employee's decision to retire must be voluntary and without undue strain.[84]

Employers must exercise caution in encouraging employees to take early retirement. The waivers of future claims that they sign should meet EEOC guidelines. In particular, it must be knowing and voluntary, not provide for the release of prospective rights or claims, and not be an exchange for consideration that included benefits to which the employee was already entitled. It should give the employee ample opportunity to think over the agreement and to seek advice from legal counsel.[85] The Older Workers' Benefit Protection Act (OWBPA), signed into law in 1990, imposes specific limitations on waivers that purport to release a terminating employee's potential claims against his or her employer based on age discrimination.[86]

EMPLOYEE SERVICES BENEFITS

While an employer's time off, insurance, and retirement benefits account for the main part of its benefits costs, most employers also provide various services including personal services (such as legal and personal counseling), job-related services (such as subsidized child-care facilities), educational subsidies, and executive perquisites (such as company cars and planes for its executives).

Companies today are also offering many more "convenient workplace" benefits aimed at "easing family conflicts and time pressures."[87] Among the staggering array of convenience benefits offered or under consideration at firms today are: flexible work hour scheduling; compressed workweeks; telecommuting; sabbatical leave; on-site fitness centers; employee discounts for health centers; athletic teams; discounts for social events; wellness programs; on-site ATM or check cashing; direct paycheck deposit; cafeteria on premises; on-site gift store; on-site dry cleaning; on-site postal service; on-site medical care; time off for children's school activities; child-care referral; elder care referral (for the employee's parents); paternity leaves; and espresso carts.[88] We'll look more closely at employee services benefits in the following sections.

Personal Services Benefits

First, many companies provide service benefits in the form of personal services that most employees need at one time or another. These include credit unions, legal services, counseling, and social and recreational opportunities.

CREDIT UNIONS   Credit unions are usually separate businesses established with the employer's assistance. Employees usually become members of a credit union by purchasing a share of the credit union's stock for $5 or $10. Members can then deposit savings that accrue interest at a rate determined by the credit union's board of directors. Perhaps more important to most employees, loan eligibility and the rate of interest paid on the loan are usually more favorable than those found in banks and finance companies.

COUNSELING SERVICES   Employers are also providing a wider range of counseling services to employees. These include financial counseling (for example, how to overcome existing indebtedness problems); family counseling (for marital problems and so on); career counseling (in terms of analyzing one's aptitudes and deciding on a career change); job placement counseling (for helping terminated or disenchanted employees find new jobs); and preretirement counseling (aimed at preparing retiring employees for what many find is the trauma of retiring). Many employers also make available to employees a full range of legal counseling through legal insurance plans.[89] For example, a referral-and-discount plan lets employees use an attorney who provides free or inexpensive consulting based on a fee schedule.

employee assistance program (EAP)

A formal employer program for providing employees with counseling and/or treatment programs for problems such as alcoholism, gambling, or stress.

EMPLOYEE ASSISTANCE PROGRAMS (EAPS)   An **employee assistance plan (EAP)** is a formal program for providing employees with counseling and/or treatment for problems such as alcoholism, gambling, or stress. Fifty to 75% of all employers with 3,000 or more employees offer EAPs,[90] and there are several models in use.[91] For example with the in-house model, the entire assistance staff is employed by the company. In the out-of-house model the company contracts a vendor to provide employee assistance staff and services in its own offices, the company's offices, or a combination of both. In the consortium model several companies pool their resources to develop a collaborative EAP program.

Overall, the trend today is toward consolidation of employee assistance program providers. Therefore more employers are offering EAP benefits that provide one-stop shopping from large off-site providers. These fulfill a variety of employee assistance needs, including, for instance, dealing with alcoholism, gambling, and stress.[92] Key steps for ensuring a successful EAP program include:[93]

Specify goals and philosophy. The short- and long-term goals expected to be achieved for both the employee and employer should be specified.

Develop a policy statement. This should define the purpose of the program, employee eligibility, the roles and responsibility of various personnel in the organization, and procedures for taking advantage of the plan.

Ensure professional staffing. Carefully consider the professional and state licensing requirements as they apply to the people staffing these facilities.

Maintain confidential record-keeping systems. Everyone involved with the EAP, including secretaries and support staff, must understand the importance of confidentiality. Furthermore, make sure files are locked, access is limited and monitored, and identifying information is kept to a minimum.

Provide supervisory training. Supervisors should understand the program's policies, procedures, and services, as well as the company's policies regarding confidentiality. Perhaps more important, all supervisors should be trained to recognize the outward symptoms of problems like alcoholism and to encourage employees to use the services of the EAP.

Be aware of legal issues. For example, in most states counselors must disclose suspicions of child abuse to an appropriate state agency: Your in-house counselors thus put your company in the legal position of having to comply in such an instance. Three ways to safeguard your legal interests include retaining legal advice on establishing your EAP, carefully screening the credentials of the staff you hire, and obtaining professional liability insurance for the EAP.

OTHER PERSONAL SERVICES   Some employers also provide various social and recreational personal services for their employees, including company-sponsored athletic events, dance clubs, annual summer picnics, craft activities, and parties.[94] In practice, the benefits offered are limited only by your creativity. Other examples of somewhat more innovative benefits include:

Lakefront vacations—one company owns lakeshore property and rents cottages and campsites to employees at low rates.

Weight loss program—several companies subsidize costs of weight loss workshops.

Cultural subsidy—the company will pay 33% of the cost of tickets to cultural activities such as theater, ballet, museum, and so on up to $100 per year per employee.

Lunch-and-learn program—interested employees can attend lunchtime talks on a variety of subjects, including stress management, weight control, computer literacy, fashion, and travel.[95]

Job-Related Services Benefits

Job-related services aim to help employees perform their jobs, and constitute a second category of services.

Subsidizing day care facilities for children of employees has many benefits for the employer, including lower employee absenteeism.

SUBSIDIZED CHILD CARE   Today over 50% of all U.S. women with children under six years old are in the workplace, and a Commerce Department survey recently reported there were almost 10 million children younger than age five requiring child care.[96] Subsidized day care is therefore an increasingly popular employee benefit.

Most employees still make provisions privately to take care of their children; for example, relatives accounted for 48% of all child-care providers in one study.[97] Organized day care centers of all types accounted for another 30% of the child-care arrangements, and nonrelatives accounted for most of the remaining child-care arrangements.

On the other hand, employers increasingly understand that with so many single-parent and dual-earner families, child care can be a very important benefit. Many employers simply investigate the day care facilities in their communities and recommend certain ones to interested employees. But more employers are setting up company-sponsored day care facilities themselves, both to attract young parents to the payroll and to reduce absenteeism. Often (as at the Wang Laboratories day care facility in Lowell, Massachusetts), the center is a private tax-exempt venture run separately from but subsidized by the firm. Employees are charged $30 a week for a child's care, and about 75 children from 2 to 4 years old are now enrolled. Where successful, the day care facility is usually close to the workplace (often in the same building), and the employer provides 50% to 75% of the operating costs.[98]

A survey found that employers can gain considerably by instituting subsidized day care centers: increased ability to attract employees, lower absenteeism, improved morale, favorable publicity, and lower turnover are some of the benefits attributed to day care programs.[99] To make sure the program is worthwhile and that its costs do not get out of hand, however, good planning is required. This often starts with a questionnaire to survey employees in order to answer such questions as, "What would you be willing to pay for care for one child in a child care center near work?" and "Have you missed work during the past 6 months because you needed to find new care arrangements?" The evidence regarding the actual effects of employer-sponsored child care on employee absenteeism and satisfaction are positive.[100]

ELDER CARE   With the average age of the U.S. population rising, elder care is increasingly a concern for many employers and individuals. Elder care is designed to help employees who must help elderly parents or relatives who are not fully able to care for themselves.[101]

From the employer's point of view, elder care benefits are important for much the same reasons as are child-care benefits; the responsibility for caring for an aging relative can affect the employee's performance at work.[102] A number of employers are, therefore, instituting elder care benefits, including flexible hours, long-term care insurance coverage, and company-sponsored elder care centers.

The elder care program instituted by one aerospace company helps to illustrate what a typical program involves. Utilizing a program kit made available by the American Association of Retired Persons (AARP), the company program had three parts.

1. A lunchtime elder care fair was held at which 31 community organizations involved with providing services to older people came to explain to employees the services that were available.
2. Next there were 10 lunchtime information sessions for employees aimed at explaining various aspects of elder care, such as independent versus dependent living and housing, the aging process, and legal concerns of elder care.
3. Finally, the company also distributed AARP's publication entitled "Care Management Guide." This lists potential problems associated with elder care in a question-and-answer format.[103]

SUBSIDIZED EMPLOYEE TRANSPORTATION   Some employers also provide subsidized employee transportation.[104] In one such program, Seattle First National Bank negotiated separate contracts with a transit system to provide free year-round transportation to more than 3,000 of the bank's employees. At the other extreme, some employers just facilitate employee car pooling, perhaps by acting as the central clearinghouse to identify employees from the same geographic areas who work the same hours.

FOOD SERVICES   Food services are provided in some form by many employers; they let employees purchase meals, snacks, or coffee, usually at relatively low prices. Most food operations are nonprofit, and, in fact, some firms provide food services below cost. The advantages to the employee are clear, and for the employer the service can ensure that employees do not drift away for long lunch hours. Even employers that do not provide full dining facilities generally make available food services such as coffee wagons or vending machines for the convenience of employees.

EDUCATIONAL SUBSIDIES   Educational subsidies such as tuition refunds have long been a popular benefit for employees seeking to continue or complete their educations. Payments range from all tuition and expenses to some percentage of expenses to a flat fee of several hundred dollars per year. Many more employers are experimenting with providing in-house college programs, such as Master of Business Administration programs, in which college faculty teach courses on the employer's premises. Other in-house educational programs include remedial work in basic literacy and training for improved supervisory skills.

As far as tuition reimbursement programs are concerned, one survey found that nearly all the 619 companies surveyed pay for courses directly related to an employee's present job. Most companies also reimburse non-job-related courses (such as a secretary taking an accounting class) that pertain to the company business. Some employers also pay for self-improvement classes, such as foreign language study, even though they are unrelated to company business or the employee's job.[105] Chrysler, Ford, and General Motors recently agreed to provide $1,000 annually to dependents of current or retired UAW members for tuition.[106]

FAMILY-FRIENDLY BENEFITS   The pressures of balancing work and family life have led many employers to bolster what they call their family-friendly benefits. While there's no single list of what does or does not constitute a "family-friendly benefit," they are generally those like child care, elder care, and flexible work hours that enable employees to better balance the demands of their family and work lives. Ninety percent of responding employees in one survey said work/life benefits were "important" or "very important" to them; relevant benefits here included on-site day care, flexible work schedules (discussed in Chapter 8), referral services for child care and elder care, long-term care insurance, and family leave.[107]

Many more employers added these kinds of benefits in the 1990's. For example, a survey by Hewitt Associates concluded that 85% of employers provided some type of child-care assistance in 1995, up from 64% in 1990. Similarly, flexible scheduling arrangements jumped to 67% from 54%; elder care benefits jumped to 26% from 12% and 77% of employers at least provided resource and referral services for elder care assistance.[108]

The family-friendly benefits at several companies are illustrative. Eddie Bauer, Inc. reportedly "believes its associates shouldn't confuse having a career with having a life."[109] Since 1994 Eddie Bauer has therefore introduced more than 20 new family-friendly type benefits ranging from on-site mammography to emergency child-care services. Also included in the firm's existing family-friendly benefits are a casual dress code, subsidies for liberal paid parental leave, alternative transportation options, and a compressed work-week and telecommuting.[110] At the First Tennessee Bank in Memphis, the family-friendly benefits program is called *Family Matters*. Here a main emphasis was on flexibility; for example, the previous bank policy forced employees to take vacations in 2 week blocks and required terminating any employee who missed more than 8 days in a 12-month period. Under the *Family Matters* plan, employees can now follow flextime schedules, scale back to working as few as 20 hours a week and still keep benefits, and schedule more hours of work early in the month to take time off late in the month if that's what they need to do.[111]

A main problem in implementing family-friendly benefits seems to be employees' reluctance to use them because of "perceptions that managers frown upon those who take advantage of work/life programs."[112] In one survey, many employees said their supervisors "send mixed signals if employees try to use the benefit . . ." and as a result many employees simply do not use them.[113] Establishing a management training program to "demonstrate work/life benefits' value in improving business productivity" is therefore not just prudent but, probably, mandatory.[114]

RESEARCH INSIGHT   Having family-friendly benefits assumes that work-family conflicts spill over to the employee's job and somehow undermine the person's job satisfaction and performance. A recent study suggests that this is, in fact, the case.[115] Two researchers reviewed two computer databases, to find all studies focusing on work and family conflict, job satisfaction, and life satisfaction. They were thereby able to review all the statistical relationships studied between, for instance, (1) work-life conflicts and (2) satisfaction with work.

What the researchers found was that "the relationship between job satisfaction and various [work-family] conflict measures is strong and negative across all samples; people with high levels of [work-family] conflict tend to be less satisfied with their jobs."[116] Similarly, there was a strong negative correlation between work-family conflict and measures of "life satisfaction," in other words, the extent to which the employees were satisfied with their lives in general. Managers should therefore understand that offering employees family-friendly benefits and letting them use them can apparently have very positive effects on the employees, one of which is making them more satisfied with their work and their jobs.

Executive Perquisites

Perquisites (perks, for short) are usually given to only a few top executives. Perks can range from the substantial to the almost insignificant. In addition to a $200,000 annual salary, for instance, the president of the United States has an expense account of $50,000 for household expenses and entertainment, $100,000 for travel, and free use of the White House and Camp David (not to mention a fleet of limousines, Air Force One, and various helicopters).[117] On the other hand, perks may entail little more than the right to use the executive washroom.

Many popular perks fall between these extremes. These include management loans (which typically enable senior officers to use their stock options); salary guarantees (also known as golden parachutes), to protect executives even if their firms are the targets of acquisitions or mergers; financial counseling (to handle top executives' investment programs); and relocation benefits, often including subsidized mortgages, purchase of the executive's current house, and payment for the actual move.[118] A potpourri of other executive perks includes time off with pay (including sabbaticals and severance pay), outplacement assistance, company cars, chauffeured limousines, security systems, company planes and yachts, executive dining rooms, physical fitness programs, legal services, tax assistance, liberal expense accounts, club memberships, season tickets, credit cards, and children's education. As you can see, employers have many ways of making their hardworking executives' lives as pleasant as possible!

Indeed, this tendency continues in the face of a decade of corporate downsizings, restructurings, and more restrictive tax laws.[119] Some of the most visible status perks such as executive apartments and suites are more rare, as are company planes and full-time chauffeurs. However, two-thirds of companies provide executives with personal or leased automobiles, over half provide supplemental life insurance, half set aside reserved parking spots, and half pay for executives' annual physical exams.[120] And more than 32% of surveyed companies cover their CEO's spouse's travel expenses.[121]

<table>
<tr><td>

FLEXIBLE BENEFITS PROGRAMS

---

flexible benefits program

Individualized plans allowed by employers to accommodate employee preferences for benefits.

</td><td>

"Variety is the spice of life," the saying goes. This applies very well to employee benefits, since the benefits that one worker finds attractive may be unattractive to another. As a result, there is a trend toward **flexible benefits programs** that permit employees to develop individualized benefits packages for themselves by choosing the benefits options they prefer.

Employee Preferences for Various Benefits

One classic study illustrates employees' preferences for various benefits.[122] Questionnaires were mailed listing seven possible benefit options to 400 employees of a midwestern public utility company. Completed questionnaires were received from 149 employees (about 38% of those surveyed). Overall, two extra weeks of vacation was clearly the most preferred benefit, while a pay increase was second. Overall, a shorter 7-hour 35-minute workday was the least-preferred benefit option.

But this is not the full story; the employee's age, marital status, and sex influenced his or her choice of benefits. For example, younger employees significantly favored the family dental plan. Younger employees also showed a greater preference for the 4-day workweek. As might be expected, preference for the pension option increased significantly with employee age. Married workers showed more preference for the pension increase and for the family dental plan than did single workers.

When given the opportunity to choose, employees do prefer flexibility in their benefits plans. In a recent survey of working couples, for instance, 83% took advantage of flexi-

</td></tr>
</table>

ble hours, 69% took advantage of the sorts of flexible-style benefits options packages we'll discuss next, and 75% said that flexible-style benefits plans are the sort of plans they would like to see their companies offer.[123]

The Cafeteria Approach

Because employees do have different preferences for benefits, more employers today let employees individualize their benefits plans. The "cafeteria" approach is the main way to do this.

The terms *flexible benefits plan* and *cafeteria benefits plan* are generally used synonymously. The idea is to give each employee a benefits fund budget, and to let the person spend that on whichever benefits he or she prefers, subject to two constraints. First, the employer must carefully limit total cost for each benefits package. Second, each benefit plan must include certain nonoptional items. These include, for example, Social Security, worker's compensation, and unemployment insurance.

The plan at Pitney Bowes provides an example; they called it Life Plan.[124] Pitney Bowes attaches a "price" to every benefit offered and allows employees to "shop" for the benefits they need each year. Each employee gets a certain number of "flex dollars" to spend each year on the benefits they prefer. Employees can "buy" whatever benefits they want up to the limit of their available flex dollars; they can even supplement that amount with their personal funds if they so choose.

The flex dollars themselves are awarded based on an employee's salary, length of service, age, and number of dependents covered by benefits.[125] In establishing the program, Pitney Bowes included numerous traditional benefits such as medical, dental, short-term disability, pension plans, and vacations. In addition, however, it expanded its benefits choices to include such things as group legal services, a loan broker to help employees shop for the best priced college financing, and unlimited personal financial planning (for a special fee of $175 per year).[126]

Pitney Bowes' flexible Life Plan benefit program has been successful. Employees get to choose the benefits they really want and need; the company has found that its benefits costs per employee dropped dramatically, in part because it isn't giving all employees with benefits which, it turned out, many don't need; and the program has helped to highlight for employees the considerable cost of each of their benefits, so they now better appreciate what the firm is spending on them.[127]

Advantages and disadvantages of flexible benefit programs are summarized in Figure 13-5.[128] The flexibility is of course the main advantage. One problem is that imple-

FIGURE 13-5

Advantages and Disadvantages of Flexible Benefits Programs

Source: Milkovich and Newman, *Compensation* (Burr Ridge, IL: McGraw-Hill, 1998), p. 405

ADVANTAGES

1. Employees choose packages that best satisfy their unique needs.
2. Flexible benefits help firms meet the *changing* needs of a *changing work force*.
3. Increased involvement of employees and families improves understanding of benefits.
4. Flexible plans make introduction of new benefits less costly. The new option is added merely as one among a wide variety of elements from which to choose.
5. Cost containment—the organization sets the dollar maximum. Employee chooses within that constraint.

DISADVANTAGES

1. Employees make bad choices and find themselves not covered for predictable emergencies.
2. Administrative burdens and expenses increase.
3. Adverse selection—employees pick only benefits they will use. The subsequent high benefit utilization increases its cost.
4. Subject to nondiscrimination requirements in Section 125 of the Internal Revenue Code.

menting a cafeteria plan can involve substantial clerical and administrative costs. Each employee's benefits have to be carefully priced and periodically updated, and even a medium-sized firm should computerize the administration of its plan.[129] Although most employees favor flexible benefits, many don't like to spend time choosing among available options, and many choose the wrong ones. Various firms have therefore developed computerized aids, as explained in the following Technology box. However, flexible benefits plans are increasingly popular, so we may assume that the pros outweigh the cons.

INFORMATION TECHNOLOGY AND HR

Computers and Benefits Administration

Whether it is a flexible benefits plan or some other, computers play an important role in benefits administration, and benefits-management technology is becoming increasingly sophisticated. Telephone-based interactive voice response systems allow employees to easily get updates on their benefits packages without dealing directly with HR specialists. Desktop PC-based systems let employees interactively update and manipulate their benefits packages, as do centralized computer kiosks (as explained just below). The Internet is used increasingly, for instance, to get employees medical information about hospitals and doctors and to do interactive financial planning and investment modeling.[130]

Computers are also being used to inform employees about their benefits and to answer routine questions that might otherwise go unasked or take up a human resource manager's time.[131] Such questions include: "In which option of the medical plan am I enrolled?" "Who are my designated beneficiaries for the life insurance plan?" "If I retire in two years, what will be my monthly retirement income?" and "What is the current balance in my company savings plan?"

At General Foods Corporation, employees use a computer system called Benefits Window, which lets them easily look up information about their benefits at centrally located interactive kiosks situated around the facilities. As illustrated in Figure 13-6, employees key in their Social Security numbers and then identify such basic plan items as their beneficiaries, the value of their thrift investment plan (TIP) accounts, the value of their contributory retirement accounts, and the value of their ESOP accounts.

FIGURE 13-6

Employee Benefits Menu

Source: Anthony J. Barra, "Employees Keep Informed with Interactive KIOSKS," *Personnel Journal*, October 1988), p. 46. Reprinted with permission.

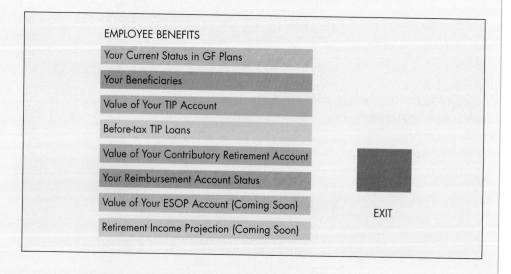

EMPLOYEE BENEFITS

Your Current Status in GF Plans

Your Beneficiaries

Value of Your TIP Account

Before-tax TIP Loans

Value of Your Contributory Retirement Account

Your Reimbursement Account Status

Value of Your ESOP Account (Coming Soon)

Retirement Income Projection (Coming Soon)

EXIT

RESEARCH INSIGHT   Computerized Decision Aids can make employees more satisfied with their benefits packages.[132] One study compared the effects of two computerized decision-making aids on employees' flexible benefits decisions. The first, a computerized decision aid called "Choice Maker," basically helps employees evaluate their flexible benefits options by simplifying the mathematical task of calculating the costs of their selections.[133] For example, if the employee asks Choice Maker how much it will cost to choose a particular medical care option plus a pension plan plus a long-term care option, Choice Maker calculates the costs; the employee can thereby test various options packages. The second computerized aid is called Personal Choice Expert. This is a computerized expert system. This means it is designed to help employees create a benefits package for themselves consistent with what benefits experts would have done for them based on the employees preferences as discussed in private counseling sessions. The employees using these decision aids made better benefits package choices and were more satisfied with their benefits than were those without access to these aids.

How Do Your Benefits Measure Up?

Figure 13-7 (pages 504–505) summarizes the benefits provided by several large companies including Sears Roebuck and NationsBank. How do your benefits stack up by comparison?[134]

SMALL BUSINESS APPLICATIONS

■ Benefits and Employee Leasing

Particularly for a business with few employees, employee leasing can facilitate benefits management. Leasing firms (also called "employee leasing," "staff leasing," or "professional employer" organizations) arrange to have all the employer's employees transferred to the employee leasing firm's payroll.[135] The employee leasing firm thus becomes the legal employer and usually handles all employee-related activities such as recruiting, hiring, and paying tax liabilities (Social Security payments, unemployment insurance, and so on).

However, it's for benefits management that employee leasing is often most advantageous. Getting insurance is the most serious personnel problem many smaller employers face. Even group rates for life or health insurance can still be quite high when only 20 or 30 employees are involved. This is where employee leasing comes in. Remember that the leasing firm is the legal employer of your employees. The employees therefore are absorbed into a much larger insurable group, along with other employers' former employees. As a result, the employee leasing company can often provide benefits smaller companies cannot obtain at anywhere near as favorable a cost, if at all. A small-business owner may thereby be able to get insurance for its people that it couldn't otherwise afford. The leasing firm's fee may even be outweighed by the reduced insurance costs, plus the savings gained by letting the leasing company handle your firm's HRM.[136]

Employee leasing may sound too good to be true, and it often is. Many employers are uncomfortable letting a third party become the legal employer of their employees (who literally have to be terminated by the employer and rehired by the leasing firm). And, some employee leasing firms have gone out of business after apparently growing successfully for several years. Such a business failure leaves the original employer having to hire back all its workers as "new" employees, and with the problem of finding new insur-

(continued on page 504)

FIGURE 13-7 *How Does Your Company Measure Up?*

Source: Kimberly Seals McDonald, "Your Benefits," *Fortune*, Vol. 134, no. 12, December 23, 1995, pp. 200–201.

Health Care	JOHNSON & JOHNSON New Brunswick, New Jersey U.S. employees: 35,000	SEARS ROEBUCK Hoffman Estates, Illinois U.S. employees: 300,000
Primary medical benefits Most popular plan Average monthly cost Other health plan options	POS[1] is the most popular plan. $14 single, $48 family of four 1 indemnity plan; 2 HMOs[3]	82% enrolled in one of 200 HMOs $46 single, $123 family of four 2 indemnity plans; 1 POS plan
Health perk Dental coverage Mental health Vision/eye care	No extra cost Up to 80% reimbursement; max 52 visits/year One eye exam each year	Coverage through HMO Three visits through EAP[4] Discount eye-care through Sears Optical
Special features	Flexible spending account (FSA) for health care	Flexible spending account for health care.
Our Grade	**A**	**B–**
Retirement and Savings		
Average yearly pension[5]	$18,050	$18,540
Early retirement perks and drags	Full pension for early retirees[6]	Full pension for early retirees[7]
401(k) options Number of options Company match policy	6 funds; J&J stock 75% of contribution up to 6% of pay; 1/3 matched in company stock	4 funds; Sears stock 70% of contribution up to 5% of pay, in company stock
Retiree health coverage (average monthly cost)[8]	Over 65: free[9] Under 65: $14	Over 65: $30 Under 65: $126
Special features	Executive stock options only	100% of salaried employees receive stock options. Pension offered in lump sum or yearly payments.
Our Grade	**A**	**B**
Lifestyle		
Vacation time After 1 year After 10 years	2 weeks 3 weeks	2 weeks 3 weeks
Flexibility benefits	Full range of flexibility benefits.[11] At HQ and other sites, employees can design flexible schedules. Compressed week in summer.	Full range of flexibility benefits.[11]
Child care	Full range of dependent-care benefits.[13] On-site I.M. Pei-designed center at HQ.	On-site care at HQ
Special features	Up to $3,000 of adoption expenses. Free fitness centers at numerous sites.	Concierge services at HQ.- Discounted health club memberships.[14]
Our Grade	**A**	**B+**
Final Grade[15]	**A**	**B**

N.A. Not available. [1]A point-of-service plan allows enrollee to use a network provider at a lower cost or go out of network and receive care at a higher cost. HMOs restrict or provide no benefits if enrollee goes outside of plan. [2]Cost varies by region. [3]Number of HMOs available varies by region. [4]Other coverage also available through employee assistance program (EAP). [5]Based on 65 year-old employee with 30 years of service and final pay of $75,000, with 6% less each ????. [6]Full pension possible at age 62. Minimum of five years in savings plan required. [7]Full pension available at age 63; partial pension at age 55 with 20 years of service. [8]Applies to individual coverage in a managed plan.

HEWLETT-PACKARD Palo Alto, California U.S. employees: 61,000	LANDS' END Dodgeville, Wisconsin U.S. employees: 6,000	NATIONSBANK Charlotte, North Carolina U.S. employees: 62,500
62% enrolled in one of 68 HMOs N.A. 1 indemnity plan; several preferred provider organizations (PPOs)	88% enrolled in indemnity plan $28 single, $78 family of four None	34% enrolled in HMO $38 single, $160 family of four[2] 1 indemnity plan; 1 POS; 1 PPO
First $2,500/year depending on plan. Three visits through EAP[4]	First $1,000/year $50,000 lifetime max One eye exam per year	Several different plans Five visits through EAP[4] Through HMO
Free long- or short-term disability. Flat $55,000 death benefit; dependent-child death benefit, $10,000.	No restrictions on doctor or hospital selection. Employee may contribute to flexible spending account.	Flexible spending account up to $5,000 or 10% of pay, whichever is greater
B	**A**	**C**
Retirement and Savings		
$15,800	None	N.A.
Reduced pension for early retirees	No early retirement	Reduced pension for early retirees
9 funds; HP stock 100% of contribution up to 3% of pay, 50% on next 2%	5 funds; Lands' End stock 50% of contribution up to 6% of pay	5 funds; NationsBank stock 75% of contribution up to 6% of pay, in company stock
Over 65: N.A. Under 65: N.A.	Over 65: none Under 65: $215	Over 65: N/A Under 65: N/A
Lump-sum pension option. Profit sharing paid twice/year. Stock match of 1 HP share for every 2 bought.	Immediate vesting in 401(k) plan. Profit-sharing plan pays a minimum bonus of 2% cash contribution.	All below the level of senior VP receive stock options (eligible part-timers, 100 shares; VP, 500).[10]
C	**D+**	**B**
Lifestyle		
3 weeks 4 weeks	2 weeks 4 weeks	2 weeks 3 weeks
Full range of flexibility benefits.[11] 5% of employees on flextime work schedules.	Job-sharing, flextime, and part-time options. Hourly employees can share up to five different jobs.	Variety of flexibility benefits.[12] Employees on family leave can return to work part-time.
Child care referral service	Subsidies and tuition. On-site child care, but only during gym workout.	Full range of dependent-care benefits[13]
Discounted on-site health clubs. New-mother facilities.[14] Up to $2,500 for adoption expenses.	Pays for stop-smoking programs. New-mother facilities.[14] On site health club for employees' families.	One week of paid paternity or adoption leave for each year of service, up to 6 weeks
B+	**B**	**C+**
B	**B−**	**C+**

[9]Applies only to employees who were 60 on 1/1/96. [10]Up to $25,000 of pension available in lump sum. [11]Full range includes job sharing, flextime, telecommuting, part-time, and compressed workweek. [12]Variety includes job sharing, flextime, part-time, and compressed workweek. [13]Full range of dependent care includes on-site, near-site, emergency backup and working-late child care, as well as dependent-care subsidies and tuition assistance. Options may not be available at all work sites. [14]Not available at all sites. [15]Final grade (40% health care, 40% retirement and savings, and 20% lifestyle) were determined by FORTUNE surveys and interviews with companies and benefits consultants.

ance carriers to take on the job of insuring them. The original insurance plan may have prevented the original insurer from cutting off services to the employer's employees. But if the health history of your employees has taken a turn for the worse, it may be hard to re-purchase insurance at any price.

If you decide to use a leasing firm, there are several commonsense guidelines to fol-low. Of course, check the prospective leasing firm with your local Better Business Bureau. Get a full list of local clients so you can completely verify the leasing firm's references. Fur-thermore.[137]

- Choose a financially stable and well-managed leasing firm. You should try to check the firm's capitalization and credit ratings. Also look at the number of years it has been in business.

- Look for a firm that provides benefits at least as good as or better than those you now offer.

- Make sure the firm pays its bills. If the leasing firm does not pay its insurance pre-miums on time, it could be a catastrophe for your firm. The leasing firm may be the legal entity responsible for the payments. However, from a practical point of view, it is your employees who will be left without insurance, and this will turn into a problem for your firm.

- Finally, review the firm's policies. Remember that most leasing firms will not just administer your own firm's personnel policies. Instead they will institute their own personnel policies (regarding, for instance, performance appraisals, periodic reviews for raises, and so on). It is therefore important to ensure their personnel policies are consistent with yours and that any inconsistencies are worked out be-fore the transition.

We invite you to visit the Dessler page on the Prentice Hall Web site at **www.prenhall.com/dessler** for our on-line study guide, Internet exercises, current events, links to related Web sites, and more.

SUMMARY

1. The financial incentives we discussed are usually paid to specific employees whose work is above standard. Employee benefits, on the other hand, are available to all em-ployees based on their membership in the organization. We discussed four types of benefit plans: pay supplements, insurance, retirement benefits, and services.

2. Supplemental pay benefits provide pay for time not worked. They include unemploy-ment insurance, vacation and holiday pay, severance pay, and supplemental unemploy-ment benefits.

3. Insurance benefits are another type of employee benefit. Worker's compensation, for example, is aimed at ensuring prompt income and medical benefits to work accident victims or their dependents regardless of fault. Most employers also provide group life insurance and group hospitalization, accident, and disability insurance.

4. Two types of retirement benefits were discussed: Social Security and pensions. Social Security does not just cover retirement benefits but survivor's and disability benefits as well. There are three basic types of pension plans: group, deferred profit sharing, and savings plans. One of the critical issues in pension planning is vesting, the money that employer and employee have placed in the latter's pension fund, which cannot be for-

feited for any reason. ERISA basically ensures that pension rights become vested and protected after a reasonable amount of time.

5. Most employers also provide benefits in the form of employee services. These include food services, recreational opportunities, legal advice, credit unions, and counseling.

6. Surveys suggest two conclusions regarding employees' preferences for benefits. First, time off (such as 2 extra weeks' vacation) seems to be the most preferred benefit. Second, the employee's age, marital status, and sex clearly influence his or her choice of benefits. (For example, younger employees were significantly more in favor of the family dental plan than were older employees). This suggests the need for individualizing the organization's benefit plans.

7. The cafeteria approach allows the employee to put together his or her own benefit plan, subject to total cost limits and the inclusion of certain nonoptional items. Many firms have installed cafeteria plans; they require considerable planning and computer assistance.

KEY TERMS

benefits   476
supplemental pay benefits   477
unemployment insurance   477
sick leave   481
severance pay   483
supplemental unemployment benefits   483
worker's compensation   485
group life insurance   487
health maintenance organization (HMO)   488

Preferred Provider Organizations (PPOs)   488
Pregnancy Discrimination Act (PDA)   490
social security   491
pension plans   491
defined benefit pension plan   491
defined contribution plan   492
deferred profit-sharing plan   492
vesting   492

Employee Retirement Income Security Act (ERISA)   493
Pension Benefits Guarantee Corporation (PBGC)   493
golden offerings   494
early retirement window   494
employee assistance plan (EAP)   495
flexible benefits programs   500

DISCUSSION QUESTIONS

1. You are applying for a job as a manager and are at the point of negotiating salary and benefits. What questions would you ask your prospective employer concerning benefits? Describe the benefits package you would try to negotiate for yourself.

2. Explain how you would go about minimizing your organization's unemployment insurance tax.

3. Explain how ERISA protects employees' pension rights.

4. In this chapter we presented findings concerning the preferences by age, marital status, and sex for various benefits. What are these findings and how would you make use of them if you were a human resource manager?

5. What is "portability"? Why do you think it is (or isn't) important to a recent college graduate?

INDIVIDUAL AND GROUP ACTIVITIES

1. Working individually or in groups, compile a list of the perks available to the following individuals: the head of your local airport; the president of your college or university; the president of a large company in your area. Do they have certain perks in common? What do you think accounts for any differences?

2. Working individually or in groups, contact insurance companies that offer workers' compensation insurance and compile a list of their suggestions for reducing workers' compensation costs. What seems to be their main recommendations?

3. You are the HR consultant to a small business with about 40 employees. At the present time the firm offers only 5 days vacation, 5 paid holidays, and legally mandated benefits such as unemployment insurance payments. Develop a list of other benefits you believe it should offer, along with your reasons for suggesting them.

EXPERIENTIAL EXERCISE

Purpose: The purpose of this exercise is to provide practice in developing a benefits package for a small business.

Required Understanding: Be very familiar with the material presented in this chapter. In addition, review chapter 11 to reacquaint yourself with sources of compensation survey information; and come to class prepared to share with your group the benefits package for the small business in which you work or in which someone with whom you're familiar works.

How to Set Up the Exercise/Instructions: Divide the class into groups of four or five students. Your assignment is as follows: Maria Cortes runs a small personnel recruiting office in Miami and has decided to start offering an expanded benefits package to her 25 employees. At the current time, the only benefits are 7 paid holidays per year and 5 sick days per year. In her company, there are 2 other managers, as well as 17 full-time recruiters and 5 secretarial staff members. In the time allotted, your group should create a benefits package in keeping with the size and requirements of this firm.

CASE INCIDENT

"Benefits? Who Needs Benefits?"

The fast-growing Fastonal company may be in a league of its own when it comes to benefits. The company's business is about as low tech as you can get—it sells nuts and bolts—almost 50,000 different kinds—through 620 company-owned stores. But while their products may be mundane, their financial performance is anything but: Profits have been rising at over 38% per year for five years, and the total return to shareholders of over 40% annually was higher than Coca-Cola's or GE's. Whatever accounts for that kind performance, it's certainly not the company's fringe benefits. When Bob Kierlan, the company's founder and president travels (or, often, his firm's other employees travel) he doesn't fly business class; in fact, he doesn't fly at all. On one recent trip, for instance, he drove 5,000 miles round trip in one of the company's vans. He and the company's chief financial officer dined on that trip at Burger King and Subway. And,

following company policy, they didn't get reimbursed for their road meals since "you've got to eat anyway." When they travel, employees stay at Days Inns types of establishments. Furthermore, the company provides no stock option, 401(k), or other pension plans. At Fastonal, the "benefits" are more often in terms of the wide range of decisions employees get to make and the opportunity to quickly move up and manage a company store, often after only six months at the company.

■ **QUESTIONS**

1. It would be an exaggeration, of course to imply that the company offers no benefits at all. What sort of benefits must a company like this absolutely provide in order to successfully recruit and retain high-quality employees? Why?

2. What are the advantages and disadvantages to Fastanol of offering a pension plan? Do you think they should implement one? Why or why not?

3. Some critics argue that the labor market is too tight for Fastonal to continue to grow as fast as it has in the past. Critics therefore suggest the company has a dilemma. Minimizing benefits is a good idea because it keeps costs down; however it may soon become less of a good idea if it makes it more difficult to hire good employees. What do you think the company should do? Why?

Source: Based on Richard Teitelbanm, "Who Is Bob Kierlan—and Why Is He So Successful?" *Fortune.* December 8, 1997, pp 24–248.

Case Application

FAMILY VALUES OR ABUSE OF BENEFITS?

Jim Colburn sat at his desk quietly staring at the phone. He could not believe what he had just heard. Sarah Conrad had just called to tell him that she would not be coming back to work. She was to have returned that morning from her six-week paid maternity leave. Jim was Sarah's supervisor at Birch & Green P.C., a small accounting partnership with a total of eight employees. Sarah had joined the firm three years ago as a staff accountant.

Birch & Green P.C. was formed five years ago by Mike Birch and Dale Green. The firm was located in a community of approximately fifty thousand people in the Midwest. Anticipating the growth of their clientele, Birch & Green hired Jim Colburn as a staff accountant/supervisor. Along with his accounting duties, Jim was responsible for the hiring, training, and supervising of all additional staff. Sarah was the first person that Jim hired after joining the firm.

Sarah Conrad had graduated with a 3.92 grade point average from a state university in December of 1994. The following May, Sarah took and passed all sections of the Uniform CPA Examination. That summer, she married a young man whom she had dated during her senior year at the university. Although Sarah was much sought after by several of the "Big Five" accounting firms, Sarah chose to accept the offer from Birch & Green. Sarah was impressed with the firm's vision for future growth as well as the personable atmosphere of the office and the "family orientation" of the partners and Jim Colburn. Jim had told her during the employment selection interview that the firm believed that "the family should come first, work second." Sarah also liked the idea of getting in on the "ground floor" of a growing firm. She believed that the opportunity to reach the level of partner would come more quickly at a small firm.

Sarah had been a model employee for the past three years. Jim could still remember how happy everyone in the office was when Sarah announced she was pregnant. Because the firm had never dealt with a maternity situation before, Jim met with the partners to discuss the firm's policies concerning maternity leave and benefits. The partners reviewed the requirements of the 1978 Pregnancy Discrimination Act and the Family and Medical Leave Act of 1993.

The 1978 Pregnancy Discrimination Act had amended Title VII of the Civil Rights Act of 1964. Under this Act, employers are not required to provide specific benefits to employees; however, if the employer does offer health insurance and temporary disability plans to employees, the employer cannot discriminate on the basis of pregnancy. Title VII of the Civil Rights Act of 1964, as amended, prohibits discrimination on the basis of race, color, religion, sex, or national origin with respect to compensation and terms, conditions or privileges of employment. Federal, state and local governments are covered by these statutes, as are private employers with fifteen or more employees.

The Family and Medical Leave Act of 1993 was the first federal mandate requiring employers to provide family benefits. This act mandates that employers with more than fifty employees provide up to twelve weeks of unpaid job-protected leave per year for the birth or adoption of a child or the serious illness of the employee

(continued)

or an immediate family member. The act also allows employers to recapture health insurance premiums paid during the leave if the employee does not return to work.

After reviewing the legislation on family benefits and maternity leave, the firm decided to offer Sarah a benefits package that would include six weeks of paid maternity leave, would allow her to take an additional six weeks of unpaid leave with continued health and medical insurance coverage, and would offer her the option to return as either a full- or part-time employee. The partners decided to offer these benefits despite the fact that they were exempt—because of size—from the Family and Medical Leave Act. Birch and Green firmly believed that "the family should come first," and they wanted to help their employees where possible. Jim Colburn also pointed out that the policy would help the firm to remain competitive in recruiting top accounting prospects.

Sarah Conrad was elated when Jim Colburn presented the benefits package to her. After discussing it with her husband, Sarah informed Jim that she planned to take the six weeks of paid leave and then return to work on a full-time basis. She had confirmed this decision several times during her pregnancy, including just before she left on maternity leave. This was the reason that Jim Colburn was so surprised when Sarah called to say that she would not be returning to work. Sarah had been in every other week, including last Friday, for the past six weeks to pick up her check, and she had never mentioned the possibility of not returning to work.

When Jim Colburn brought this news to Mike Birch and Dale Green, they all felt that Sarah Conrad had acted in bad faith. They discussed whether the company should pursue any legal or other efforts to demand that Sarah repay the income and health care premiums that she had received during the past six weeks.

■ QUESTIONS

1. Was the company legally required to offer the benefits package to Sarah? If not, what benefits were they required to offer, if any?

2. Was the package they offered Sarah discriminating in any way? How?

3. What would you do now if you were Jim, Mike, and Dale?

Source: This case was prepared by Charles St. Clair, Marketing and Management Instructor at Moberly (Missouri) Area Community College, and Ron Stephens, Professor of Management and Management Department Chair at Central Missouri State University at Warrensburg. Used by permission.

The names of the organization, individuals, and locations are disguised.

NOTES

1. David Hom, "How Pitney Bowes Broadens Benefit Choices With Value-Added Services," *Compensation & Benefits Review* (March/April 1996), pp. 60–66.

2. Based on Frederick Hills, Thomas Bergmann, and Vida Scarpello, *Compensation Decision Making* (Fort Worth: The Dryden Press, 1994), p. 424. See also L. Kate Beatty, "Pay and Benefits Break Away from Tradition," *HR Magazine*, Vol. 39, no. 11 (November 1994), pp. 63–68.

3. "Rehash of Microsoft Case Upholds Benefit Eligibility," *BNA Bulletin to Management*, July 31, 1997, p. 241.

4. "Employee Benefit Costs Declined in 1996, Survey Reveals," *BNA Bulletin to Management*, January 29, 1998, p. 29.

5. Ibid.

6. "Health Care Benefits," *BNA Bulletin to Management*, July 10, 1997, pp. 220–221.

7. "Employee Benefit Costs Declined in 1996, Survey Reveals," p. 29.

8. This is based on "Employee Benefits in Medium and Large Firms," *BNA Bulletin to Management*, September 4, 1997, pp. 284–285.

9. This is based on Bonnie De Clark, "Cutting Unemployment Insurance Costs," *Personnel Journal*, Vol. 62 (November 1983), pp. 868–870.

10. K. Matthes, "In Pursuit of Leisure: Employees Want More Time Off," *HR Focus*, No. 7 (1992).

11. Richard Henderson, *Compensation Management* (Upper Saddle River, NJ: Prentice Hall, 1994), p. 556.

12. Matthes, "In Pursuit of Leisure."

13. Henderson, *Compensation Management*, p. 555.

14. Ibid., p. 116.

15. "BNA's Quarterly Report on Job Absence and Turnover, Third Quarter 1997," *BNA Bulletin to Management*, December 11, 1997, pp. 1–4.

16. Miriam Rothman, "Can Alternatives to Sick Pay Plans Reduce Absenteeism?" *Personnel Journal*, Vol. 60 (October 1981), pp. 788–791; Richard Bunning, "A Prescription for Sick Leave," *Personnel Journal*, Vol. 67, no. 8 (August 1988), pp. 44–49.

17. This is based on M. Michael Markowich and Steve Eckberg, "Get Control of the Absentee-Minded," *Personnel Journal* (March 1996), pp. 115–120.

18. Ibid., p. 119.

19. This is based on Margaret Meiers, "Parental Leave and the Bottom Line," *Personnel Journal* (September 1988), pp. 108–115.

20. "Employers Complain About Leave Law and Absences," *BNA Bulletin to Management*, June 19, 1997, p. 193.

21. "Military Duty, Family Leave Laws Produce Complaints," *BNA Bulletin to Management*, June 13, 1996, p. 186.

22. "Individual Liability Under FMLA," *BNA Fair Employment Practices*, November 30, 1995, p. 139.

23. Dawn Gunch, "The Family Leave Act: A Financial Burden?" *Personnel Journal* (September 1993), p. 49.

24. Gillian Flynn, "Employers Need an FMLA Brush-Up," *Workforce* (April 1997), pp. 101–104.

25. "Severance Practices," *BNA Bulletin to Management*, January 11, 1996, pp. 12 and 13.

26. Ibid.

27. "Severance Pay Common for Workers Who Lose Jobs," *BNA Bulletin to Management*, August 31, 1995, p. 273.

28. Joseph Famularo, *Handbook of Modern Personnel Administration* (New York: McGraw-Hill, 1972), pp. 51–62; see also Glenn Whittington, "Workers' Compensation Legislation Enacted in 1997," *Monthly Labor Review*, Vol. 21, no. 1, pp. 23–28.

29. Richard Henderson, *Compensation Management* (Reston, VA: Reston, 1979), p. 250. For an explanation of how to reduce worker's compensation costs, see Betty Strigel Bialk, "Cutting Workers' Compensation Costs," *Personnel Journal*, Vol. 66, no. 7 (July 1987), pp. 95–97.

30. Henderson, *Compensation Management*, p. 90. Also see Bureau of National Affairs, "Workers' Compensation Total Disability Benefits by State," 1989, pp. 172–173, for a list showing worker's compensation by state.

31. "Worker's Compensation and ADA," *BNA Bulletin to Management*, August 6, 1992, p. 248.

32. See, for example, Bialk, "Cutting Workers' Compensation Costs," pp. 95–97.

33. "Using Case Management in Workers' Compensation," *BNA Bulletin to Management*, June 6, 1996, p. 181.

34. "Firms Cite Own Efforts as Key to Controlling Costs," *BNA Bulletin to Management*, March 21, 1996, p. 89. See also "Workers' Compensation Outlook: Cost Control Persists," *BNA Bulletin to Management*, January 30, 1997, pp. 33–44.

35. Robert E. Sibson, *Wages and Salaries: A Handbook for Line Managers* (New York: American Management Association, 1967), p. 235.

36. "Employee Benefits in Small Firms," *BNA Bulletin to Management*, June 27, 1991, pp. 196–197.

37. Richard Gisonny and Michael Langan, "EEOC Provides Guidance on Application of ADA on Health Plans," *Benefits Law Journal*, Vol. 6, no. 3 (Autumn 1993), pp. 461–467.

38. Johnathan Mook, "The ADA and Employee Benefits: A Regulatory and Litigation Update," *Benefits Law Journal*, Vol. 7, no. 4 (Winter 1994–95), pp. 407–429.

39. Rita Jain, "Employer-Sponsored Dental Insurance Eases the Pain," *Monthly Labor Review* (October 1988), p. 18. "Employee Benefits,"

40. Ibid., p. 23.

41. Bureau of National Affairs, *Bulletin to Management*, December 23, 1982, p. 1; "TEFRA—The Tax Equity and Fiscal Responsibility Act of 982," *Personnel*, Vol. 59 (November–December 1982), p. 43.

42. A. N. Nash and S. J. Carroll, Jr., "Supplemental Compensation," in *Perspectives on Personnel: Human Resource Management*, Herbert Heneman, III and Donald Schwab, eds. (Burr Ridge, IL: McGraw-Hill, 1978), p. 223.

43. Thomas Snodeker and Michael Kuhns, "HMOs: Regulations, Problems, and Outlook," *Personnel Journal*, Vol. 60 (August 1981), pp. 629–631.

44. Frederick Hills, Thomas Bergmann, and Vida Scarpello, *Compensation Decision Making* (Fort Worth: The Dryden Press, 1994), p. 137.

45. George Milkovich and Jerry Newman, *Compensation* (Burr Ridge, IL: McGraw-Hill, 1993), p. 445.

46. "Employee Benefits Costs," *BNA Bulletin to Management*, January 2, 1997 pp 4–5.

47. Hewitt Associates, "Health Care Costs Becoming Shared Responsibility," *News and Information*, June 21, 1984. See also, *Health Care Cost Containment* (New York: William Mercer-Meidinger, 1984), as discussed in *Compensation Review* (Fourth Quarter 1984), pp. 8–9; and Thomas Paine, "Outlook for Compensation and Benefits: 1986 and Beyond," Hewitt Associates, October 30, 1985. See also John Parkington, "The Trade-Off Approach to Benefits Cost Containment: A Strategy to Increase Employee Satisfaction," *Compensation and Benefits Review*, Vol. 19, no. 1 (January–February 1987), pp. 26–35; Hewitt Associates, "Employer-Sponsored Medical Plans Designed to Make Employees Better Health Care Consumers, Study Says," *News and Information*, July 28, 1989 (100 Half Day Road, Lincolnshire, IL 60015); Janet Norwood, "Measuring the Cost and Incidence of Employee Benefits," *Monthly Labor Review*, Vol. 11, no. 8 (August 1988), p. 368; Robert C. Penzkover, "Health Incentives at Quaker Oats," *Personnel Journal*, Vol. 68, no. 3 (March 1989), pp. 114–118; Anne Skagen, "Managing Health Care Costs," Part III, "Focus on Case Management," *Compensation and Benefits Review*, Vol 20, no. 6 (November–December 1988), pp. 56–63; Hewitt Associates, *News and Information*, February 6, 1990; "Health Care Cost Sharing: Coating the Pill," *BNA Bulletin to Management*, March 10, 1994, p. 73; and "Requiring Employers to Share Health Care Costs Results in Lower Use of All Health Care Services," *BNA Bulletin to Management*, March 10, 1994, p. 79.

48. "Managing Health Care Costs," *BNA Bulletin to Management*, August 27, 1992, p. 272.

49. Hewitt Associates, "Employers Trim Future Health Care Costs by Keeping Employees' Well,'" *News and Information*, June 7, 1984; Morton Grossman and Margaret Magnus, "The Boom in Benefits," *Personnel Journal* (November 1988), pp. 51–55; and "Employer Initiatives Help Cycle Health Care Costs," *BNA Bulletin to Management*, July 31, 1997, pp. 241–242.

50. Don Bohl, "Company Bets That Wellness Incentives Plus Preventive Care Will Contain Health Care Costs," *Compensation and Benefits Review* (July–August 1993), pp. 20–23.

51. "Employer Initiatives Help Curb Health Care Costs," *BNA Bulletin to Management*, July 31, 1997, pp. 241–242.

52. Ibid., p. 241.

Commerce Clearing House *Ideas and Trends in Personnel*, January 23, 1991, pp. 9–11.

53. Shari Caudron, "Teaming up to Cut Health-Care Costs," *Personnel Journal* (September 1993), p. 194. See also "Fraudulent Health Plans Targeted," *BNA Bulletin to Management*, April 14, 1994, p. 120.

54. Ibid., p. 107. See also Ann Knoll, "Top Ten Mistakes Made in Employee Health Benefit Plans," *Compensation and Benefits Review* (January–February 1994), pp. 54–58.

55. The following is based on Michael Gomez, "Managing Health Care Costs," Part I, "The Dilemma of AIDS," *Compensation and Benefits Review* (September–October 1988), pp. 23–31; and Nancy Breuer, "AIDS Issues Haven't Gone Away," *Personnel Journal*, Vol. 71, no. 1 (January 1992), pp. 47–49. See also Kato Keeton, "AIDS Related Attitudes Among Government Employees: Implications for Training Programs," *Review of Public Personnel Administration* (Spring 1993), pp. 65–90.

56. This is based on Thomas C. Billet, "Managing Health Care Cost," Part II, "Coping with Mental Health," *Compensation and Benefits Review* (September–October 1988), pp. 32–36; see also Nancy Jackson, "Health Care on the Home Front," *Workforce*, Vol. 77, no. 3 (March 1998), pp. 30ff.

57. Ronald Bachman, "Time for Another Look," *HRMagazine* (March 1997), pp. 93–96.

58. Ibid., pp. 35–36.

59. This is based on Paul Greenlaw and Diana Foderaro, "Some Practical Implications of the Pregnancy Discrimination Act," *Personnel Journal*, Vol. 58 (October 1979), pp. 677–681. See also Commerce Clearing House, "Supreme Court Says Giving Women Pregnancy Leave is Lawful Even in the Case Where Men Receive No Disability Leave Whatever," *Ideas and Trends in Personnel*, January 23, 1987, pp. 9–10.

60. James Weil, "Baby Boomer Needs Will Spur Growth of Long-Term Care Plans," *Compensation & Benefits Review* (March/April 1996), p. 49.

61. Carolyn Hirschman, "Will Employers Take the Lead in Long-Term Care?" *HRMagazine* (March 1997), pp. 59–66.

62. Geoffrey Coldin, "How to Beat the Boomer Rush," *Fortune*, August 18, 1997, pp. 59–63.

63. Brenda Paik Sunoo, "Millions May Retire," *Workforce* (December 1997), p. 48.

64. "Retirement Plans Getting A Boost, Surveys Find," *BNA Bulletin to Management*, November 7, 1996, p. 353.

65. Jerome B. Cohen and Arthur Hanson, *Personnel Finance* (Burr Ridge, IL: McGraw-Hill, 1964), pp. 312–320. See also BNA, January 14, 1988, pp. 12–13. This article explains changes in the Social Security law and presents an exhibit showing how to estimate your Social Security benefits.

66. "Social Security and Employees," *BNA Bulletin to Management*, February 1, 1996, pp. 36–37.

67. See, for example, Henderson, *Compensation Management*, pp. 289–290; Famularo, *Handbook*, pp. 37.1–37.9.

68. Avy Graham, "How Has Vesting Changed Since Passage of Employee Retirement Income Security Act?" *Monthly Labor Review* (August 1988), pp. 20–25.

69. Lindsay Wyatt, "401(k) Conversion: It's As Easy As Riding a Bike," *Workforce* (April 1997), p. 66.

70. Ibid., p. 20.

71. Sibson, *Wages and Salaries*, p. 234. For an explanation of how to minimize employee benefits litigation related to pension and health benefits claims, see Thomas Piskorski, "Minimizing Employee Benefits Litigation Through Effective Claims Administration Procedures," *Employee Relations Law Journal*, Vol. 20, no. 3 (Winter 1994/95), pp. 421–431.

72. See Irwin Tepper, "Risk vs. Return in Pension Fund Investment," *Harvard Business Review*, Vol. 56 (March–April 1977), pp. 100–107; and William Rupert, "ERISA: Compliance May Be Easier Than You Expect and Pay Unexpected Dividends," *Personnel Journal*, Vol. 55 (April 1976). For a discussion of a recent survey regarding retirement planning and the challenges that employees face in planning retirement policy for the year 2000, see Diane Filipowski, "Retirement Planning in the Year 2000," *Personnel Journal* (July 1993), p. 34.

73. "Pension Plan Coverage," *BNA Bulletin to Management*, April 4, 1996, pp. 108–109.

74. "Lower Income Workers Pensions at Risk, Report Finds," *BNA Bulletin to Management*, August 22, 1996, p. 271.

75. Kathleen Murray, "How HR is Making Pensions Portable," *Personnel Journal* (July 1993), pp. 36–46.

76. Murray, "How HR is Making Pensions Portable," p. 43.

77. Robert Paul, "The Impact of Pension Reform on American Business," *Sloan Management Review*, Vol. 18 (Fall 1976), pp. 59–71. See also John M. Walbridge, Jr., "The Next Hurdle for Benefits Manager: Section 89," *Compensation & Benefits Review*, Vol. 20, no. 6 (November–December 1988), pp. 22–35.

78. Bureau of National Affairs, "Tax Reform Act: Major Changes in Store for Compensation Programs," *Bulletin to Management*, October 9, 1986, p. 1.

79. In fact, unfunded pension liabilities of American firms have continued to grow. "Pension Survey: Unfunded Liabilities Continue to Grow," *Business Week*, August 25, 1980, pp. 94–97. See also James Benson and Barbara Suzaki, "After Tax Reform" Part III, "Planning Executive Benefits," *Compensation and Benefits Review*, Vol. 20, no. 2 (March–April 1988), pp. 45–57; and BNA, "Post-Retirement Benefits Impact of FASB New Accounting Rule," February 23, 1989, p. 57.

80. For a discussion see Milton Zall, "Understanding the Risks to Pension Benefits," *Personnel Journal* (January 1992), pp. 62–69.

81. "Trends," *BNA Bulletin to Management*, May 7, 1992, p. 143.

82. Wallace Davidson, III, Dan Worrell, and Jeremy Fox, "Early Retirement Programs and Firm Performance," *Academy of Management Journal*, Vol. 39, no. 4 (1996), p. 980.

83. Marco Colosi, Philip Rosen, and Sara Herrin, "Is Your Early Retirement Package Countring Disaster? *Personnel Journal* (August 1988), pp. 59–67; see also Jenny McCune, "The Future of Retirement," *Management Review*, Vol. 87, no. 4 (April 1998), pp. 10–16.

84. *Paolillo v. Dresser Industries*, 821F.2d81 (2d cir., 1987).

85. See also Eugene Seibert and Jo Anne Seibert, "Look Into Window Alternatives," *Personnel Journal* (May 1989), pp. 80–87.

86. Arthur Silbergeld, "Release Agreements Must Comply with the Older Workers' Benefit Protection Act," *Employment Relations Today* (Winter 1992/93), pp. 457–460.

87. Don Bohl, "Mini Survey: Companies That Tend to Create the 'Convenient Work Place,'" *Compensation & Benefits Review* (May/June 1996), pp. 23–26.

88. Ibid., pp. 24–25.

89. See Henderson, *Compensation Management*, pp. 336–339. See also Lewis Burger, "Group Legal Service Plans: A Benefit Whose Time

has Come," *Compensation & Benefits Review*, Vol. 18, no. 4 (July–August 1986), pp. 28–34; Gillian Flynn, "Legal Assistance Offers Prepaid Peace of Mind," *Personnel Journal* (October 1996), pp. 48–56.

90. Richard T. Hellan, "Employee Assistance: An EAP Update: A Perspective for the '80s," *Personnel Journal*, Vol. 65, no. 6 (1986), p. 51.

91. See Dale Masi and Seymour Friedland, "EAP Actions & Options," *Personnel Journal* (June 1988), pp. 61–67.

92. Michael Prince, "EAPs Becoming Part of Larger Programs," *Business Insurance*, Vol. 32, no. 24 (June 15, 1998), pp. 14–16.

93. Based on Masi and Friedland, "EAP Actions." See also Harry Turk, "Questions and Answers: Avoiding Liability for EAP Services," *Employment Relations Today* (Spring 1992), pp. 111–114.

94. "Employee Benefit Costs," *BNA Bulletin to Management*, January 16, 1992, pp. 12–14.

95. The Research Staff of Hewitt Associations, *Innovative Benefits*, Hewitt Associates.

96. "Child Care Options," *BNA Bulletin to Management*, July 4, 1996, p. 212.

97. Ibid.

98. This is based on Ibid., pp. 212–214.

99. "Employers and Child Care: Establishing Services Through the Workplace," Women's Bureau, U.S. Department of Labor, Washington, DC, 1982. See also BNA, "Special Survey on Child Care Assistance Programs," *Bulletin to Management*, March 26, 1987. Donald J. Peterson and Douglas Massengill, "Child Care Programs Benefit Employers, Too." *Personnel*, Vol. 65, no. 5 (May 1988), pp. 58–62; and Toni A. Campbell and David E. Campbell, "Employers and Child Care," *Personnel Journal*, Vol. 67, no. 4 (April 1988), pp. 84–87.

100. Lorri Johnson, "Effectiveness of an Employee-Sponsored Child Care Center," *Applied H.R.H. Research*, Vol. 2, no. 1 (Summer 1991), pp. 38–67.

101. Commerce Clearing House, "As the Population Ages, There is Growing Interest in Adding Elder Care to the Benefits Package," *Ideas and Trends*, August 21, 1987, pp. 129–131.

102. Kelli Earhart, R. Dennis Middlemist, and Willie Hopkins, "Elder Care: An Emerging Assistance Issue," *Employee Assistance Quarterly*, Vol. 8, no. 3 (1993), pp. 1–10.

103. For another example, see "Elder Care: A Maturing Benefit," *BNA Bulletin to Management*, February 20, 1992, pp. 50–55.

104. Mary Zippo, "Subsidized Employee Transportation: A Three Way Benefit," *Personnel*, Vol. 57 (May–June 1980), pp. 40–41.

105. Hewitt Associates, Survey of Educational Reimbursement Programs, 1984.

106. "Chrysler Benefit to Cover Tuition, Dependent Care," *BNA Bulletin to Management*, October 2, 1997, p. 313.

107. "Work/Life Perks Often Avoided by Workers, Poll Finds," *BNA Bulletin to Management*, March 19, 1998, p. 81.

108. "Family-Friendly Benefits Have Spread Greatly," *BNA Bulletin to Management*, March 7, 1996, p. 73.

109. Leslie Fraught, "At Eddie Bauer You Can Have Work and Have a Life," *Workforce* (April 1997), p. 84.

110. Ibid., p. 84.

111. Gillian Flynn, "Making a Business Case for Balance," *Workforce* (March 1997), pp. 68–74.

112. "Work/Life Perks Often Avoided by Workers, Poll Finds," *BNA Bulletin to Management*, March 19, 1998, p. 81.

113. Ibid., p. 81.

114. Ibid., p. 81.

115. Ellen Ernst Kossek and Cynthia Ozeki, "Work-Family Conflict, Policies, and the Job-Life Satisfaction Relationship: A Review and Direction for Organizational Behavior-Human Resources Research," *Journal of Applied Psychology*, Vol. 83, no. 2 (1998), pp. 139–149.

116. Ibid., pp. 143–144.

117. Bruce Ellig, *Executive Compensation: A Total Pay Perspective* (New York: McGraw-Hill, 1982), p. 141.

118. Lindroth, "Inflation, Taxes, and Perks," p. 939.

119. Matthew Budman, "The Persistence of Perks," *Across the Board* (February 1994), pp. 44–46.

120. Ibid., p. 44.

121. Ibid., p. 45.

122. J. Brad Chapman and Robert Ottermann, "Employee Preference for Various Compensation and Fringe Benefit Options," (Berea, OH: ASPA Foundation, 1975). See also, William White and James Becker, "Increasing the Motivational Impact of Employee Benefits," *Personnel* (January–February 1980), pp. 32–37; and Barney Olmsted and Suzanne Smith, "Flex for Success!" *Personnel*, Vol. 66, no. 6 (June 1989), pp. 50–55.

123. "Couples Want Flexible Leave, Benefits," *BNA Bulletin to Management*, February 19, 1998, p. 53.

124. David Hom, "How Pitney Bowes Broadens Benefit Choices with Value-Added Services," *Compensation & Benefits Review* (March–April 1996), pp. 60–66.

125. Ibid., p. 60.

126. Ibid., p. 62.

127. For further insights into the growth of flexible benefits plans see, "New Benefits Highlight Trends Toward Flexibility," *BNA Bulletin to Management*, April 16, 1998, p. 113.

128. George Milkovich and Jerry Newman, *Compensation* (Burr Ridge, IL: McGraw-Hill, 1993), p. 405.

129. See Caroline A. Baker, "Flex Your Benefits," *Personnel Journal*, Vol. 67, no. 5 (May 1988), pp. 54–58, for a discussion of the pros and cons of three basic approaches to flexible benefits; and Carol Woodley, "The Benefits of Flexibility," *Personnel Management* (May 1993), pp. 36–39.

130. "Technology Revolutionizes Administration," *BNA Bulletin to Management*, November 9, 1995; "Benefits Merge Onto Information Superhighway," *BNA Bulletin to Management*, February 29, 1996, p. 66; Miriam Scott, "Interactive Benefits Systems Save Time and Dollars for Employers, Employees," *Employee Benefit Plan Review* (February 1995), pp. 16–18.

131. This is based on Anthony Barra, "Employees Keep Informed with Interactive KIOSKs," *Personnel Journal* (October 1988), pp. 43–51.

132. This is based on Michael Sturman, John Hannon, and George Milkovich, "Computerized Decision Aids for Flexible Benefits Decisions: The Effect of an Expert System and Decision Support System on Employee Intentions and Satisfaction with Benefits," *Personnel Psychology*, Vol. 49 (1996), pp. 883–908.

133. Ibid., p. 889.

134. Based on Kimberly Seals McDonald, "Your Benefits," *Fortune* Vol. 134, no. 12, December 23, 1995, pp. 199–201.

135. Jennifer Laabs, "PEOs Make HR Easier With Staff Leasing," *Personnel Journal* (December 1996), pp. 64–72.

136. For a discussion see, for example, Marvin Selter, "On the Plus Side of Employee Leasing," *Personnel Journal* (April 1986), pp. 87–91; David Altaner, "Employees for Lease," *Weekly Business News/Sun Sentinel*, November 9, 1987, pp. 8–9.

137. John Naisbitt, "Employee Leasing Takes off," *Success!* (April 1986), p. 12. See also John Quesnel, "Who Pays the Pensions of Leased Employees?", *Pensions and Benefits*, Vol. 26, no. 14, July 13, 1998, p. 14.

VIDEO CASE

 SKILLS LIVE!

PART IV
ESTABLISHING PAY PLANS

A RECENT SURVEY OF NEARLY HALF A MILLION U.S. EMPLOYEES FOUND THAT FEWER FEEL THEY ARE PAID FAIRLY COMPARED TO COMPARABLE EMPLOYEES IN OTHER ORGANIZATIONS, AND MORE FEEL THEY ARE UNDERPAID FOR THE KIND OF WORK THEY DO THAN FELT THAT WAY A YEAR AGO (AS REPORTED IN "PAY GRIPES," *WALL STREET JOURNAL*, FEB. 23, 1999, P. B10). SO PERHAPS IT IS ONLY NATURAL FOR MOST OF US TO FEEL, AS DOES ONE OF THE CHARACTERS IN PART IV, THAT WE DESERVE MORE THAN WE ARE PAID. STILL, WHEN SUCH FEELINGS ACTUALLY REFLECT A LOOSELY ORGANIZED PAY PLAN, REAL PAY INEQUITY CAN RESULT, WITH RESULTING PROBLEMS FOR THE FIRM THAT FAR OUTWEIGH THE ORIGINAL EMPLOYEE'S DISSATISFACTION.

Equity is only one of four factors that influence the formulation of pay plans. The other three are legislation (such as the Fair Labor Standards Act, which sets the minimum wage), union agreements and contracts, and company compensation policies that govern everything from overtime policies to criteria for pay increases. Yet pay equity is the force behind the five-step process for establishing pay plans that is outlined in chapter 11. You will want to recall, as you prepare to watch this video, that those steps are:

1. Conduct a salary survey of what other employers are paying for comparable jobs (to help ensure external equity).
2. Determine the worth of each job in the organization through job evaluation (to ensure internal equity).
3. Group similar jobs into pay grades.
4. Price each pay grade by using wage curves.
5. Fine tune pay rates.

It is probably not necessary to go through such a formal process in the very smallest firms, but a company doesn't have to grow very large before it faces the problem of setting salary levels for comparable jobs, and paying for different skill levels in the same job. Whether the policy is "open pay" or pay secrecy, equity is still an important goal of any good pay plan. It is no defense of an inequitable pay plan to say that people can be paid unfairly because they're unaware they are.

Karen Jarvis, executive vice president and director of sales, and Hal Boylston, president, have responded to Kim's request for a meeting. (You may recall meeting Kim, one of Quicktakes' writers, in Part I.) Kim has been with the firm for a long time, and she has begun to feel underpaid as her own living expenses begin to climb. As you listen to her conversation with Hal and Karen, ask yourself the following questions:

QUESTIONS

1. Is Kim making a good business argument for the raise she demands?
2. Compare Hal's and Karen's responses in their private conversation after Kim leaves the room, with the salary review committee's reaction to Tom Barley in Part III. Are the two reactions based on the same kind of evidence?
3. What do you think they should do next?

14

LABOR RELATIONS AND COLLECTIVE BARGAINING

In 1998 the NBA basketball stars threatened a work stoppage. The NBA owners reacted by "locking out" the players, effectively closing down half of the 1998–1999 basketball season. While some pundits sarcastically referred to it as the strike of the billionaires versus the millionaires, there seemed little doubt that the ill will caused by the work stoppage would taint the game for years to come. The basic strategy of the owners was to place a cap on what the highest paid players could earn, in order to balance what the owners saw as their considerable costs of operations with the television and product endorsement revenues they could expect for the next few years. The agreement finally negotiated in January 1999, was a workable wage solution that fits in the framework of that strategy. ▲

Behavioral Objectives

When you finish studying this chapter, you should be able to:

▲ *Describe* the history of the labor movement and why workers unionize.

▲ *Discuss* in detail the nature of the major federal labor relations laws.

▲ *Describe* the process of a union drive and election.

▲ *Explain* to an HR manager how to avoid losing a unionization election.

▲ *Describe* the nature of the collective bargaining process.

▲ *List* important do's and don'ts for handling grievances.

Chapter Outline

▲ Introduction: The Labor Movement
▲ Unions and the Law
▲ The Union Drive and Election
▲ The Collective Bargaining Process
▲ Contract Administration: Grievances
▲ The Future of Unionism

**INTRODUCTION:
THE LABOR
MOVEMENT**

Today just over 16 million U.S. workers belong to unions—around 14.1% of the total number of men and women working in this country today.[1] Many are still traditional blue-collar workers, but unions increasingly appeal to white-collar workers, too. For instance, federal, state, and local governments employed almost 7 million union members in 1996, accounting for almost 38% of total government employees. And in some industries—including transportation and public utilities, where over 26% of employees are union members—it's still relatively difficult to get a job without joining a union.[2] Union membership in other countries is declining, but is still very high: 37% of employed workers in Canada, 43% in Mexico, 44% in Brazil, 44% in Italy, and 24% in Japan, for instance.[3] Why are unions important? How did they get that way? Why do workers join them? How are union agreements hammered out? These are some of the questions addressed in this chapter.

A Brief History of the American Union Movement

To understand what unions are and what they want, it is useful to understand "where they've been." Unions have a long history. As early as 1790, skilled craftsmen (shoemakers, tailors, printers, and so on) organized themselves into trade unions. They posted their "minimum wage" demands and had "tramping committees" go from shop to shop to ensure that no member accepted a lesser wage.

From these earliest unions to the present time, the history of the union movement has been one of alternate expansion and contraction. Union membership grew until a major depression around 1837 resulted in a membership decline. Membership then began increasing as the United States entered its industrial revolution. In 1869 a group of tailors met and formed the Knights of Labor; the Knights were interested in political reform and agitation and often sought political changes. By 1885 they had 100,000 members, which (as a result of winning a major strike against a railroad) exploded to 700,000 members the following year. Partly because of their focus on social reform, and partly due to a series of unsuccessful strikes, the Knights' membership dwindled rapidly thereafter. By 1893 when the Knights were dissolved, there were virtually no members.

In 1886 Samuel Gompers formed the American Federation of Labor. It consisted mostly of skilled workers and, unlike the Knights, eschewed social reform for practical bread-and-butter gains for its members. The Knights of Labor had engaged in a class struggle to alter the form of society, and thereby get a bigger chunk of benefits for its members. Gompers, on the other hand, aimed at raising day-to-day wages and improving the working conditions of his constituents. The AFL grew rapidly until after World War I, at which point its membership exceeded 5.5 million people.

The 1920s was a period of stagnation for the U.S. union movement, and by 1923 AFL membership had declined to about 3.5 million members. This decline and stagnation were a result of several things, including a postwar depression, manufacturers' renewed resistance to unions, the death of Samuel Gompers, and the apparent prosperity of the 1920s. By 1929, as a result of the Great Depression, millions of workers had lost their jobs, and by 1933 union membership was down to fewer than 3 million workers.

Membership began to increase in the mid-1930s. As part of his New Deal programs, President Roosevelt passed the National Industrial Recovery Act, which made it easier for labor to organize. Other federal laws as well as prosperity and World War II also contributed to the rapid increase in membership, which topped out at about 21 million workers in the 1970s. Then membership again began to decline, to about 16 million wage and salary workers today.[4]

Today the labor movement is undergoing dramatic changes. At the present time, organized labor's share of the workforce in the United States is about 14.1% and dropping.

Assuming this trend persists, by the year 2000 unions will represent only 13% of all non-farm workers, down from about 34% in 1955. The union membership proportion is dropping rapidly because the number of union members is falling while total employment is rising.[5]

Why Do Workers Organize?

Much time and money have been spent trying to discover why workers unionize, and many theories have been proposed. There is no simple answer to the question, partly because each worker probably joins for his or her own reasons.

It does seem clear that workers don't unionize just to get more pay or better working conditions, though these are important factors. In fact (for whatever reason), weekly earnings of union members are much higher than those of nonunion workers: about $50 a week more in service jobs, $60 in manufacturing, $130 in government, and as much as $300 a week more in construction jobs, for instance.[6] Similarly, there are significant differences in the benefits received by union and nonunion employees.[7] For example, union workers receive significantly more holidays, sick leave, unpaid leave, insurance plan benefits, long-term disability benefits, and various other benefits than do nonunion workers.[8]

Yet the urge to unionize more often seems to boil down to the belief on the part of workers that it is only through unity that they can get their fair share of the "pie" and also protect themselves from the arbitrary whims of management. (For example, in March 1998, angry FedEx pilots rejected for a time a proposed agreement backed by their own union heads, in part, said one pilot, because "there was a trust relationship that has deteriorated."[9]) In practice, therefore, low morale, fear of job loss, and poor communication help foster unionization. Yet in reality, unions can't always protect job security, as evidenced by the huge loss of union jobs in manufacturing industries and airlines over the past few years.[10]

RESEARCH INSIGHT   It is dissatisfaction with basic bread-and-butter issues like pay, rather than with noneconomic issues like type of work and supervision, that leads to prounion voting (although noneconomic issues are often somewhat important as well). This is illustrated in Table 14-1, which summarizes the correlation between job satisfac-

TABLE 14-1   Correlation Between Job Satisfaction and
Voting for Union Representation

ISSUE	CORRELATION WITH VOTE FOR UNION
Are you satisfied with the job security at this company?	-.42
Are you satisfied with your wages?	-.40
Taking everything into consideration, are you satisfied with this company as a place to work?	-.36
Do supervisors in this company treat all employees alike?	-.34
Are you satisfied with your fringe benefits?	-.31
Do your supervisors show appreciation when you do a good job?	-.30
Do you think there is a good chance for you to get promoted in this company?	-.30
Are you satisfied with the type of work you are doing?	-.14

Source: Adapted from Jeanne M. Brett, "Why Employees Want Unions," *Organizational Dynamics*, Spring 1980, p. 51.
Copyright 1980 by AMACOM, a division of American Management Associations.

tion and voting for union representation in one study. Notice that dissatisfaction with issues such as job security and wages was most strongly correlated with a vote for the union, while the employees' satisfaction with factors such as supervisor and type of work was less so.[11]

The author of this study contends that dissatisfaction alone will not automatically lead to unionization. Instead, she says dissatisfied employees must first believe they are without the ability to influence a change in the conditions causing the dissatisfaction. Then a large enough group of employees would have to believe it could improve things through collective action. Thus, dissatisfied employees who believe the union will be instrumental in achieving their goals present a potent combination.[12] Indeed, union instrumentality—the workers' belief that the union can successfully get the improvements the workers seeks—is consistently a predictor of prounion voting.[13]

In summary (as mentioned above), the urge to unionize often boils down to the belief that it is only through unity that the workers can get their fair share of the pie and also protect themselves from the arbitrary whims of management. Here is how one writer describes the motivation behind the early unionization of automobile workers:

> *In the years to come, economic issues would make the headlines when union and management met in negotiations. But in the early years the rate of pay was not the major complaint of the autoworkers . . . Specifically, the principal grievances of the autoworkers were the speed-up of production and the lack of any kind of job security. As production tapered off, the order in which workers were laid off was determined largely by the whim of foremen and other supervisors. . . . The worker had no way of knowing when he would be laid off, and had no assurance when, or whether, he would be recalled . . . Generally, what the workers revolted against was the lack of human dignity and individuality, and a working relationship that was massively impersonal, cold, and nonhuman. They wanted to be treated like human beings—not like faceless clockcard numbers.[14] (See Figure 14-1 for a picture of early auto plant working conditions).[15]*

FIGURE 14-1

Early Auto Plant Working Conditions

Source: Warner Pflug, *The UAW in Pictures* (Detroit: Wayne State University Press, 1971), p. 14.

Note: In addition to the backbreaking work required in the early auto plants, health hazards were an ever-present danger. Lighting was poor, dust often filled the air, and unguarded moving belts led to many injuries.

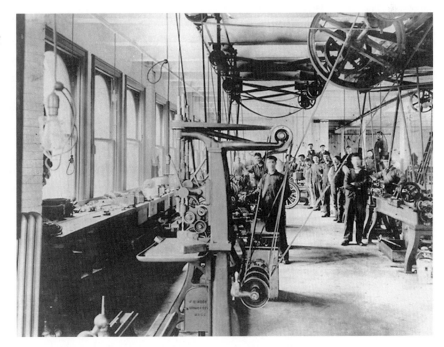

What Do Unions Want?

We can generalize by saying that unions have two sets of aims, one for union *security* and one for *improved wages, hours, working conditions*, and *benefits* for their members.

UNION SECURITY   First and probably foremost, unions seek security for themselves. They fight hard for the right to represent a firm's workers and to be the exclusive bargaining agent for all employees in the unit. (As such, they negotiate contracts for *all* employees, including those not members of the union.) Five types of union security are possible.

closed shop

A form of union security in which the company can hire only union members. This was outlawed in 1947 but still exists in some industries (such as printing).

union shop

A form of union security in which the company can hire nonunion people but they must join the union after a prescribed period of time and pay dues. (If they do not, they can be fired.)

agency shop

A form of union security in which employees who do not belong to the union must still pay union dues on the assumption that union efforts benefit all workers.

open shop

Perhaps the least attractive type of union security from the union's point of view, the workers decide whether or not to join the union; and those who join must pay dues.

1. **Closed shop**[16] The company can hire only union members. This was outlawed in 1947 but still exists in some industries (such as printing).
2. **Union shop** The company can hire nonunion people but they must join the union after a prescribed period of time and pay dues. (If not, they can be fired.)
3. **Agency shop** Employees who do not belong to the union still must pay union dues on the assumption that the union's efforts benefit all the workers.
4. **Open shop** It is up to the workers whether or not they join the union—those who do not, do not pay dues.
5. **Maintenance of membership arrangement** Employees do not have to belong to the union. However, *union members* employed by the firm must maintain membership in the union for the contract period.

IMPROVED WAGES, HOURS, AND BENEFITS FOR MEMBERS   Once their security is assured, unions fight to better the lot of their members—to improve their wages, hours, and working conditions, for example. The typical labor agreement also gives the union a role in other HR activities, including recruiting, selecting, compensating, promoting, training, and discharging employees.

The AFL-CIO

WHAT IT IS   The American Federation of Labor and Congress of Industrial Organizations (AFL-CIO) is a voluntary federation of about 100 national and international labor unions in the United States. It was formed by the merger of the AFL and CIO in 1955, with the AFL's George Meany as its first president. For many people in the U.S., it has become synonymous with the word *union*.

There are about 2.5 million workers who belong to unions that are not affiliated with the AFL-CIO. Of these workers, about half belong to the largest independent union, the United Auto Workers (about 1 million members).[17]

THE STRUCTURE OF THE AFL-CIO   There are three layers in the structure of the AFL-CIO (and other U.S. unions). First, there is the *local* union. This is the union the worker joins and to which he or she pays dues. It is also usually the local union that signs the collective bargaining agreement determining the wages and working conditions. The local is in turn a single chapter in the *national* union. For example, if you were a typesetter in Detroit, you would belong to the local union there, which is one of hundreds of local chapters of the International Typographical Union with headquarters in Colorado Springs.

The third layer in the structure is the *national federation*, in this case, the AFL-CIO. This federation is composed of about 100 national and international unions, which in turn are comprised of over 60,000 local unions.

Most people tend to think of the AFL-CIO as the most important part of the labor movement, but it is not. The AFL-CIO itself really has little power, except what it is allowed to exercise by its constituent national unions. Thus, the president of the teachers' union wields more power in that capacity than in his capacity as a vice president of the AFL-CIO. Yet as a practical matter, the AFL-CIO does act as a spokesperson for labor, and its president, John Sweeney, has accumulated political clout far in excess of a figurehead president.

UNIONS AND THE LAW

Background

Until about 1930 there were no special labor laws. Employers were not required to engage in collective bargaining with employees and were virtually unrestrained in their behavior toward unions; the use of spies, blacklists, and the firing of union agitators were widespread. "Yellow dog" contracts, whereby management could require nonunion membership as a condition for employment, were widely enforced. Most union weapons—even strikes—were illegal.

The one-sided situation lasted from the Revolution until the Great Depression (around 1930). Since then, in response to changing public attitudes, values, and economic conditions, labor law has gone through three clear changes: from "strong encouragement" of unions, to "modified encouragement coupled with regulation," and finally to "detailed regulation of internal union affairs."[18]

Period of Strong Encouragement: The Norris-LaGuardia Act (1932) and the National Labor Relations or Wagner Act (1935)

Norris-LaGuardia Act

This law marked the beginning of the era of strong encouragement of unions and guaranteed to each employee the right to bargain collectively "free from interference, restraint, or coercion."

The **Norris-LaGuardia Act** set the stage for a new era in which union activity was encouraged. It guaranteed to each employee the right to bargain collectively "free from interference, restraint, or coercion." It declared yellow dog contracts unenforceable. And it limited the courts' abilities to issue injunctions for activities such as peaceful picketing and payment of strike benefits.[19]

Yet this act did little to restrain employers from fighting labor organizations by whatever means they could muster. Therefore, the National Labor Relations (or Wagner) Act was passed in 1935 to add teeth to the Norris-LaGuardia Act. It did this by (1) banning certain unfair labor practices; (2) providing for secret-ballot elections and majority rule for determining whether a firm's employees were to unionize; and (3) creating the **National Labor Relations Board (NLRB)** for enforcing these two provisions.

National Labor Relations Board (NLRB)

The agency created by the Wagner Act to investigate unfair labor practice charges and to provide for secret-ballot elections and majority rule in determining whether or not a firm's employees want a union.

National Labor Relations (or Wagner) Act

This law banned certain types of unfair labor practices and provided for secret-ballot elections and majority rule for determining whether or not a firm's employees want to unionize.

UNFAIR EMPLOYER LABOR PRACTICES   The **Wagner Act** deemed "statutory wrongs" (but not crimes) five unfair labor practices used by employers:

1. It is unfair for employers to "interfere with, restrain, or coerce employees" in exercising their legally sanctioned right of self-organization.

2. It is an unfair practice for company representatives to dominate or interfere with either the formation or the administration of labor unions. Among other management actions found to be unfair under practices 1 and 2 are bribing employees, using company spy systems, moving a business to avoid unionization, and blacklisting union sympathizers.

3. Companies are prohibited from discriminating in any way against employees for their legal union activities.

4. Employers are forbidden to discharge or discriminate against employees simply because the latter file unfair practice charges against the company.

5. Finally, it is an unfair labor practice for employers to refuse to bargain collectively with their employees' duly chosen representatives.

An unfair labor practice charge is filed (see Figure 14-2) with the National Labor Relations Board. The board then investigates the charge and determines if formal action should be taken. Possible actions include dismissal of the complaint, request for an injunction against the employer, or an order that the employer cease and desist.

FROM 1935 TO 1947   Union membership increased quickly after passage of the Wagner Act in 1935. Other factors such as an improving economy and aggressive union leadership contributed to this rise as well. But by the mid-1940s the tide had begun to turn. Largely because of a series of massive postwar strikes, public policy began to shift against what many viewed as the union excesses of the times. The stage was set for passage of the Taft-Hartley Act of 1947.

Period of Modified Encouragement Coupled with Regulation: The Taft-Hartley Act (1947)

Taft-Hartley Act

Also known as the Labor Management Relations Act, this law prohibited union unfair labor practices and enumerated the rights of employees as union members. It also enumerated the rights of employers.

The **Taft-Hartley** (or Labor Management Relations) **Act** reflected the public's less enthusiastic attitudes toward unions. It amended the National Labor Relations (Wagner) Act with provisions aimed at limiting unions in four ways: (1) by prohibiting unfair union labor practices, (2) by enumerating the rights of employees as union members, (3) by enumerating the rights of employers, and (4) by allowing the president of the United States to temporarily bar national emergency strikes.

UNFAIR UNION LABOR PRACTICES   The Taft-Hartley Act enumerated several labor practices that unions were prohibited from engaging in:

1. First, unions were banned from restraining or coercing employees from exercising their guaranteed bargaining rights. For example, some specific union actions the courts have held illegal under this provision include stating to an antiunion employee that he or she will lose his or her job once the union gains recognition; issuing patently false statements during union organizing campaigns; and making threats of reprisal against employees subpoenaed to testify against the union at NLRB hearings.

2. It is also an unfair labor practice for a union to cause an employer to discriminate in any way against an employee in order to encourage or discourage his or her membership in a union. In other words, the union cannot try to force an employer to fire a worker because he or she doesn't attend union meetings, opposes union policies, or refuses to join a union. There is one exception to this. Where a closed or union shop prevails (and union membership is therefore a prerequisite to employment), the union may demand discharge for a worker who fails to pay his or her initiation fees and dues.

3. It is an unfair labor practice for a union to refuse to bargain in good faith with the employer about wages, hours, and other employment conditions. Certain strikes and boycotts are also considered unfair union labor practices.

4. It is an unfair labor practice for a union to engage in "featherbedding." (Here an employer is required to pay an employee for services not performed.)

RIGHTS OF EMPLOYEES   The Taft-Hartley Act also protected the rights of employees against their unions. For example, many people felt that compulsory unionism violated the basic U.S. right of freedom of association. New right-to-work laws sprang up in 19

FIGURE 14-2

NLRB Form 501: Filing an Unfair Labor Practice Charge

FORM NLRB 501
(2 81)

FORM EXEMPT UNDER
44 U.S.C. 3512

UNITED STATES OF AMERICA
NATIONAL LABOR RELATIONS BOARD
CHARGE AGAINST EMPLOYER

INSTRUCTIONS: File an original and 4 copies of this charge with NLRB Regional Director for the region in which the alleged unfair labor practice occurred or is occurring.	DO NOT WRITE IN THIS SPACE	
	CASE NO.	DATE FILE

1. EMPLOYER AGAINST WHOM CHARGE IS BROUGHT

a. NAME OF EMPLOYER	b. NUMBER OF WORKERS EMPLOYED	
c. ADDRESS OF ESTABLISHMENT *(street and number, city, State, and ZIP code)*	d. EMPLOYER REPRESEN-TATIVE TO CONTACT	e. PHONE NO.
f. TYPE OF ESTABLISHMENT *(factory, mine, wholesaler, etc.)*	g. IDENTIFY PRINCIPAL PRODUCT OR SERVICE	

h. THE ABOVE-NAMED EMPLOYER HAS ENGAGED IN AND IS ENGAGING IN UNFAIR LABOR PRACTICES WITHIN THE MEANING OF SECTION 8(a), SUBSECTIONS (1) AND _____ OF THE NATIONAL
(list subsections)
LABOR RELATIONS ACT, AND THESE UNFAIR LABOR PRACTICES ARE UNFAIR LABOR PRACTICES AFFECTING COMMERCE WITHIN THE MEANING OF THE ACT.

2. BASIS OF THE CHARGE *(be specific as to facts, names, addresses, plants involved, dates, places, etc.)*

BY THE ABOVE AND OTHER ACTS, THE ABOVE-NAMED EMPLOYER HAS INTERFERED WITH, RESTRAINED, AND COERCED EMPLOYEES IN THE EXERCISE OF THE RIGHTS GUARANTEED IN SECTION 7 OF THE ACT.

3. FULL NAME OF PARTY FILING CHARGE *(if labor organization, give full name, including local name and number)*

4a. ADDRESS *(street and number, city, State, and ZIP code)*	4b. TELEPHONE NO.

5. FULL NAME OF NATIONAL OR INTERNATIONAL LABOR ORGANIZATION OF WHICH IT IS AN AFFILIATE OR CONSTITUENT UNIT *(to be filled in when charge is filed by a labor organization)*

6. DECLARATION

I declare that I have read the above charge and that the statements therein are true to the best of my knowledge and belief.

By _____   _____
(signature of representative or person filing charge)   (title, if any)

Address _____   _____
                               (telephone number)   (date)

WILLFULLY FALSE STATEMENTS ON THIS CHARGE CAN BE PUNISHED BY FINE AND IMPRISONMENT
(U.S. CODE, TITLE 18, SECTION 1001)

states (mainly in the South and Southwest). These outlawed labor contracts that made union membership a condition for keeping one's job. In New York, for example, many printing firms have union shops. There you can't work as a press operator unless you belong to a printers' union. In Florida such union shops—except those covered by the Railway Labor Act—are illegal, and printing shops typically employ both union and nonunion press operators. Even today, union membership varies widely by state, from a high of 26.8% in New York to a low of 3.7% in South Carolina, for instance. (Other representative membership densities, as summarized in Figure 14-3, are: California, 16.5%; Florida, 7.4%; Texas, 6.5%; Michigan, 23.9%; Arizona, 5.8%; and Ohio, 19.4%).[20] This provision also allowed an employee to present grievances directly to the employer (without going through the union) and required the employee's authorization before union dues could be subtracted from his or her paycheck.

RIGHTS OF EMPLOYERS   The Taft-Hartley Act also explicitly gave employers certain rights. First, it gave them full freedom to express their views concerning union organization. For example, you as a manager can tell your employees that in your opinion unions are worthless, dangerous to the economy, and immoral. You can even, generally speaking, hint that unionization and subsequent high-wage demands might result in the permanent closing of the plant but not its relocation. Employers can set forth the union's record in regard to violence and corruption, if appropriate, and can play upon the racial prejudices of workers by describing the union's philosophy toward integration. In fact, your only major restraint is that you must avoid threats, promises, coercion, and direct interference with workers who are trying to reach a decision. There can be no threat of reprisal or force or promise of benefit.[21]

The employer (1) cannot meet with employees on company time within 24 hours of an election or (2) suggest to employees that they vote against the union while they are at home or in the employer's office, although he or she can do so while in their work area or where they normally gather.

national emergency strikes

Strikes that might "imperil the national health and safety."

NATIONAL EMERGENCY STRIKES   The Taft-Hartley Act also allows the U.S. president to intervene in **national emergency strikes.** These are strikes (for example, on the part of steel firm employees) that might "imperil the national health and safety." The president may appoint a board of inquiry and, based on its report, apply for an injunction restraining the strike for 60 days. If no settlement is reached during that time, the injunction can be extended for another 20 days. During this last period, employees are polled in a secret ballot to ascertain their willingness to accept the employer's last offer.

Period of Detailed Regulation of Internal Union Affairs: The Landrum-Griffin Act (1959)

Landrum-Griffin Act

The law aimed at protecting union members from possible wrongdoing on the part of their unions.

In the 1950s, Senate investigations revealed unsavory practices on the part of some unions, and the result was the **Landrum-Griffin Act** (officially, the Labor Management Reporting and Disclosure Act). An overriding aim of this act was to protect union members from possible wrongdoing on the part of their unions. It also was an amendment to the National Labor Relations (Wagner) Act.

First, this law contains a bill of rights for union members. Among other things, it provides for certain rights in the nomination of candidates for union office. It also affirms a member's right to sue his or her union and ensures that no member can be fined or suspended without due process, which includes a list of specific charges, time to prepare defense, and a fair hearing.

This act also laid out rules regarding union elections. For example, national and international unions must elect officers at least once every 5 years, using some type of secret-

FIGURE 14-3

Union Membership Density by State

Source: Union Membership and Earnings Data Book, The Bureau of National Affairs, Inc., from Compensation & Benefits Review, September/October 1997, p. 17.

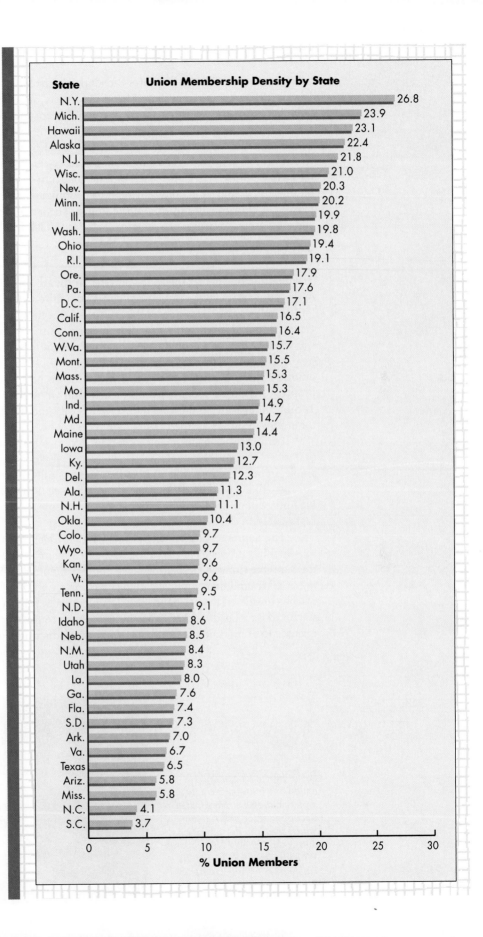

Union Membership Density by State

ballot mechanism. And it regulates the kind of person who can serve as a union officer. For example, persons convicted of felonies (bribery, murder, and so on) are barred from holding union officer positions for a period of 5 years after conviction.

The Senate investigators also discovered flagrant examples of employer wrongdoing. Union agents had been bribed, and so-called "labor relations consultants" had been used to buy off union officers, for example. Such bribery had been a federal crime starting with the passage of the Taft-Hartley Act. But the Landrum-Griffin Act greatly expanded the list of unlawful employer actions. For example, companies can no longer pay their own employees to entice them not to join the union. The act also requires reports from unions and employers, covering such practices as the use of labor relations consultants.

Labor Law Today

The question of whether the courts and the NLRB are contributing to a more encouraging or discouraging climate for unions today is not entirely clear.

On the one hand, some NLRB decisions favor unions. In one case known as the *Jean Country* case, a union and a shopping center took their case to the NLRB. The question was whether the union could picket a store (Jean Country) on private property in a shopping mall. Under the old rule that dated back to 1986, the NLRB would balance the union's right to engage in labor activity with the property owner's right to decide how the property should be used. It would then decide whose rights prevailed in that instance. Technicalities aside, in this case the NLRB basically modified its rule, thus making it easier for unions to show why their rights should prevail.[22]

On the other hand, many important recent NLRB and court decisions have gone against unions, and this could have the effect of weakening workers' union rights. For example, in one decision[23] the NLRB adopted a less tolerant stance in dealing with misconduct by striking workers. In another decision,[24] the NLRB held it would no longer evaluate the impact of misleading employer campaign statements on worker free choice in a union representation election.[25]

The Supreme Court's decision in *TWA v. Independent Federation of Flight Attendants* is an instance of a court's ruling strengthening management's hand. For the first time, the Supreme Court held that management can announce it will continue to operate during a strike, "and that employees in the bargaining unit who wish to work during the strike will be considered the permanent holders of any new jobs they fill, assuming they want to stay in those jobs."[26] Strikers who want to return to their previous jobs must wait for an opening to occur, said the Court. This may prove discouraging to union members consid-

Labor difficulties can affect almost any industry including professional sports. Here David Robinson (of the San Antonio Spurs) speaks to the media during the 1998–99 NBA lockout. With him are the NBA Players' Union director Billy Hunter and Players' Association president Patrick Ewing.

ering a walkout, given the employer's right to also bring in outside replacements. In another case reminiscent of the *Jean Country* case, the Supreme Court held that union organizers do not have the right to trespass on private property to get their message to employees. As long as the employees are not inaccessible—as they would be if they lived on company property, for instance—the court said nonemployee union organizers would have to stay off the employer's property.[27] This means, said one NLRB member, that in the future unions will have to show "extreme difficulty" in reaching employees in order to gain access to private property.[28] The pendulum today seems to have swung a bit more toward discouragement of union activities.

GLOBAL HRM

■ Unions Go Global

Any company that thinks it can avoid the pressures of unionization by sending manufacturing and jobs abroad is sorely mistaken.[29] Today, as we've seen, all businesses are becoming globalized, and regional trade treaties like NAFTA will increase even more the amount of business that firms do abroad. This fact is not lost on unions, some of which are already expanding their influence abroad.

Here are just two examples:

U.S. unions are helping Mexican unions to organize, especially in U.S.-owned factories. For example, the United Electrical Workers is subsidizing organizers at Mexican plants of the General Electric company.

When the Campbell Soup Company threatened to move some operations to Mexico, the Farm Labor Organizing Committee, a midwestern union, discouraged the move by helping its Mexican counterpart win a stronger contract, one that would have cost Campbell Soup higher wages if it made the move.

U.S. unions gain several things by forming such alliances. By helping workers, (for example, in Mexico) unionize, they help to raise the wages and living standards of local workers. In addition, that may in turn discourage corporate flight from the United States in search of low wages. Unions also help solidify their own positions in the U.S. with the added leverage they get from having unions abroad to help them fight their corporate campaigns.

THE UNION DRIVE AND ELECTION

It is through the union drive and election that a union tries to be recognized to represent employees.[30] This process has five basic steps as follows:

Step 1. Initial Contact

During the *initial contact* stage, the union determines the employees' interest in organizing, and an organizing committee is established.

The initiative for the first contact between the employees and the union may come from the employees, from a union already representing other employees of the firm, or from a union representing workers elsewhere. Sometimes a union effort starts with a disgruntled employee contacting the local union to learn how to organize his or her place of work. Sometimes, though, the campaign starts when a union decides it wants to expand to representing other employees in the firm or when the company looks like an easy one to organize. In any case, there is an initial contact between a union representative and a few employees.

Once an employer becomes a target, a union official usually assigns a representative to assess employee interest. The representative visits the firm to determine whether enough employees are interested to make a union campaign worthwhile. He or she also identifies employees who would make good leaders in the organizing campaign and calls them together to create an organizing committee. The objective here is to "educate the committee about the benefits of forming a union, the law and procedures involved in forming a local union, and the issues management is likely to raise during a campaign."[31]

The union must follow certain rules when it starts contacting employees. The law allows union organizers to solicit employees for membership as long as it doesn't endanger the performance or safety of the employees. Therefore, much of the contact often takes place off the job, for example, at home or at eating places near work. Organizers can also safely contact employees on company grounds during off hours (such as lunch or break time). Under some conditions, union representatives may solicit employees at their work stations, but this is rare. Yet, in practice, there will be much informal organizing going on at the workplace as employees debate the merits of organizing. In any case, this initial contact stage may be deceptively quiet. Sometimes the first inkling management has of the campaign is the distribution or posting of handbills soliciting union membership.

LABOR RELATIONS CONSULTANTS   Labor relations consultants are increasingly influencing the unionization process, with both management and unions now using such trained outside advisors. These advisors may be law firms, researchers, psychologists, labor relations specialists, or public relations firms. In any case, their role is to provide advice and related services not just when a vote is expected (although this is when most of them are used) but at other times as well. For the employer, the consultant's services may range from ensuring that the firm properly fills out routine forms, to managing the whole union campaign. Unions, on the other hand, may use public relations firms to improve their image or specialists to manage corporate campaigns aimed at pressuring the firm's shareholders and creditors into influencing management to agree to the union's demands.

The use by management of consultants (who are often referred to disparagingly by unions as "union busters") has apparently grown tremendously. A study by the AFL-CIO's Department of Organization and Field Services concluded, for example, that management consultants were involved in 85% of the elections they surveyed and that the consultant "ran the show" for the employers 72% of the time.[32] The widespread use of such consultants—only some of whom are actually lawyers—has raised the question of whether some have advised their clients to engage in activities that are illegal or questionable under various labor laws. One tactic, for instance, is to delay the union vote with lengthy hearings at the NLRB. The longer the delay in the vote, it is argued, the more time the employer has to drill antiunion propaganda into the employees. During these delays employees who are not antiunion can be eliminated, and the bargaining unit can be packed with promanagement employees.[33] Others accuse consultants of advising employers to lie to the NLRB, for example, by backdating memoranda in order to convince the board that the wage increase being offered was decided months before the union campaign ever began.[34] The ethics of the matter aside, any employers using such consultants are required to report their use.

Unions are not without their own creative ways to win elections, one of which is called union salting. **Union salting** refers to a union organizing tactic by which workers who are in fact employed full-time by a union as undercover union organizers are hired by

union salting

Refers to a union organizing tactic by which workers who are in fact employed full-time by a union as undercover organizers are hired by unwitting employers.

unwitting employers. A 1995 U.S. Supreme Court decision, in *NLRB v. Town and Country Electric*, held the tactic to be legal.[35]

Salting can be detrimental to employers in several ways, beyond the obvious chance that the employer is more likely to find itself organized. Rejecting job candidates because they belong to unions can result in a lawsuit; firing them when they initiate an organizing campaign can similarly backfire.

For the employer, the solution usually means concentrating on the basic blocking and tackling of effective HR management. For example: carefully check job references; don't hire applicants who aren't truthful on their job applications; enforce a no-solicitation policy; and require new employees to sign a statement that they will comply with company policies during their employment.[36]

Step 2. Obtaining Authorization Cards

authorization cards

In order to petition for a union election, the union must show that at least 30% of employees may be interested in being unionized. Employees indicate this interest by signing authorization cards.

For the union to petition the NLRB for the right to hold an election, it must show that a sizable number of employees may be interested in being organized. The next step is thus for union organizers to try to get the employees to sign **authorization cards**. (Among other things, these authorize the union to seek a representation election.) Thirty percent of the eligible employees in an appropriate bargaining unit must sign before an election can be petitioned.

During this stage, both union and management typically use various forms of propaganda. The union claims it can improve working conditions, raise wages, increase benefits, and generally get the workers better deals. Management need not be silent; it can attack the union on ethical and moral grounds and cite the cost of union membership, for example. Management can also explain its track record, express facts and opinions, and explain the law applicable to organizing campaigns and the meaning of the duty to bargain in good faith (if the union should win the election) to its employees. However, neither side can threaten, bribe, or coerce employees, and an employer may not make promises of benefit to employees or make unilateral changes in terms and conditions of employment that were not planned to be implemented prior to the onset of union organizing activity.

WHAT MANAGEMENT CAN DO   There are several steps management can take with respect to the authorization cards themselves. For example, the NLRB has ruled that "an employer may lawfully inform employees of their right to revoke their authorization cards, even when employees have not solicited such information." The employer can also distribute pamphlets that explain just how employees can revoke their cards.[37] However, management can go no further than explaining to employees the procedure for card revocation and furnishing resignation language. Any type of material assistance such as postage or stationery is prohibited. The employer also cannot check to determine which employees have actually revoked their authorization cards.

What can you do about educating employees who have not yet decided whether to sign their cards? Above all, it is an unfair labor practice to tell employees that they cannot sign a card or to give them the impression that it is against their best interests to do so. What you can do is prepare supervisors so they can explain what the card actually authorizes the union to do. For example, the authorization card in Figure 14-4 actually does three things: It lets the union seek a representation election (it can be used as evidence that 30% of your employees have an interest in organizing); it designates the union as a bargaining representative in all employment matters; and it states that the employee has applied for membership in the union and will be subject to union rules and bylaws. The latter is especially important; the union, for instance, may force the employee to picket and fine any member who does not comply with union instructions. Explaining the serious legal and practical implications of signing the card can thus be an effective management weapon.

FIGURE 14-4

Sample Authorization Card

Source: Reproduced with permission from *Human Resources Management Ideas and Trends Newsletter,* August 20, 1982, published and copyrighted by Commerce Clearing House, Inc., Chicago, IL 60646.

UNITED GLASS AND CERAMIC WORKERS OF NORTH AMERICA, AFL–CIO, CLC

OFFICIAL MEMBERSHIP APPLICATION AND AUTHORIZATION

I, hereby apply for membership in the United Glass and Ceramic Workers of North America, AFL–CIO, CLC. I hereby designate and authorize the United Glass and Ceramic Workers of North America, AFL–CIO, CLC, as my collective bargaining representative in all matters pertaining to wages, rates of pay and other conditions of employment. I also authorize the United Glass and Ceramic Workers of North America, AFL–CIO, CLC, to request recognition from my employer as my bargaining agent.

SIGNATURE OF APPLICANT _____

EMPLOYED BY _____

APPLICATION RECEIVED BY _____

DATE _____

One thing management should not do is look through signed authorization cards if confronted with them by union representatives. Doing so could be construed as an unfair labor practice by the NLRB, which could view it as spying on those who signed. It could also later form the basis of a charge alleging discrimination due to union activity if someone who signed a card is subsequently disciplined.

During this stage, unions can picket the company, subject to three constraints: (1) the union must file a petition for an election within 30 days after the start of picketing; (2) the firm cannot already be lawfully recognizing another union; and (3) there cannot already have been a valid NLRB election during the past 12 months.

Step 3. Hold a Hearing

Once the authorization cards have been collected, one of three things can occur. If the employer chooses not to contest union recognition, no hearing is needed and a "consent election" is held immediately. If the employer chooses not to contest the union's right to an election, and/or the scope of the bargaining unit, and/or which employees are eligible to vote in the election, no hearing is needed and the parties can stipulate an election. If an employer does wish to contest the union's right, it can insist on a hearing to determine those issues. An employer's decision about whether to insist on a hearing is a strategic one based on the facts of each case and whether it feels it needs additional time to develop a campaign to try to persuade a majority of its employees not to elect a union to represent them.

Most companies do contest the union's right to represent their employees, claiming that a significant number of them don't really want the union. It is at this point that the U.S. National Labor Relations Board gets involved. The NLRB is usually contacted by the union, which requests a hearing. Based on this, the regional director of the NLRB sends a hearing officer to investigate. The examiner sends both management and union a notice of representation hearing (NLRB Form 852, Figure 14-5). This states the time and place of the hearing.

Several issues are investigated in this hearing. First, does the record indicate there is enough evidence to hold an election? (For example, did 30% or more of the employees in an appropriate bargaining unit sign the authorization cards?) Second, the examiner must decide what will the bargaining unit be? The latter is a crucial matter for the union, for employees, and for the employer. The **bargaining unit** is the group of employees that the union will be authorized to represent and bargain for collectively. If the entire organization is viewed as a bargaining unit, the union will represent all nonsupervisory, nonman-

bargaining unit

The group of employees the union will be authorized to represent.

FIGURE 14-5

NLRB Form 852: Notice of Representation Hearing

FORM NLRB-852
(6-61)

**UNITED STATES OF AMERICA
BEFORE THE NATIONAL LABOR RELATIONS BOARD**

Case No.

NOTICE OF REPRESENTATION HEARING

The Petitioner, above named, having heretofore filed a Petition pursuant to Section 9 (c) of the National Labor Relations Act, as amended, 29 U.S.C. Sec 151 et seq., copy of which Petition is hereto attached, and it appearing that a question affecting commerce has arisen concerning the representation of employees described by such Petition.

YOU ARE HEREBY NOTIFIED that, pursuant to Section 3(b) and 9(c) of the Act, on the day of   , 19   , at

a hearing will be conducted before a hearing officer of the National Labor Relations Board upon the question of representation affecting commerce which has arisen, at which time and place the parties will have the right to appear in person or otherwise, and give testimony.

Signed at   on the   day of   , 19

Regional Director, Region
National Labor Relations Board

agerial, and nonconfidential employees, although it is oriented mostly toward blue-collar workers. However, professional and nonprofessional employees may be included in the same bargaining unit only if the professionals agree to it. If your firm disagrees with the examiner's decision regarding the bargaining unit, you can challenge the decision. This will require a separate step and NLRB ruling.

There are also other questions to be addressed in the NLRB hearing. These include: "Does the employer qualify for coverage by the NLRB?" "Is the union a labor organization within the meaning of the National Labor Relations Act?" "Do any existing collective bargaining agreements or prior elections bar the union from holding a representation election?"

Finally, if the results of the hearing are favorable for the union, the NLRB will direct that an election be held. It will issue a Notice of Election notice to that effect, and NLRB Form 707 (Figure 14-6) will be sent to the employer to post.

FIGURE 14-6

NLRB Form 707: Notice to Employees

UNITED STATES OF AMERICA ★ NATIONAL LABOR RELATIONS BOARD

NOTICE OF ELECTION

GENERAL

PURPOSE OF THIS ELECTION — This election is to determine the representative, if any, desired by the eligible Employees for purposes of collective bargaining with their Employer. (See VOTING UNIT in this Notice for a description of eligible employees.) A majority of the valid ballots cast will determine the results of the election.

SECRET BALLOT — The election will be by SECRET ballot under the supervision of the Regional Director of the National Labor Relations Board. Voters will be allowed to vote without interference, restraint, or coercion. Electioneering will not be permitted at or near the polling place. Violations of these rules should be reported immediately to the Regional Director or the agent in charge of the election. Your attention is called to Section 12 of the National Labor Relations Act:

ANY PERSON WHO SHALL WILLFULLY RESIST, PREVENT, IMPEDE, OR INTERFERE WITH ANY MEMBER OF THE BOARD OR ANY OF ITS AGENTS OR AGENCIES IN THE PERFORMANCE OF DUTIES PURSUANT TO THIS ACT SHALL BE PUNISHED BY A FINE OF NOT MORE THAN $5,000 OR BY IMPRISONMENT FOR NOT MORE THAN ONE YEAR, OR BOTH.

Upon arrival at the voting place, voters should proceed to the Board agent and identify themselves by stating their name. The Board agent will hand a ballot to each eligible voter. Voters will enter the voting booth and mark their ballot in secret. DO NOT SIGN YOUR BALLOT. Fold the ballot before leaving the voting booth, then personally deposit it in a ballot box under the supervision of the Board agent and leave the polling area.

A sample of the official ballot is shown at the center of this Notice.

ELIGIBILITY RULES — Employees eligible to vote are those described under VOTING UNIT in this Notice of Election, including employees who did not work during the designated payroll period because they were ill or on vacation or temporarily laid off, and also including employees in the military service of the United States who appear in person at the polls. Employees who have quit or been discharged for cause since the designated payroll period and who have not been rehired or reinstated prior to the date of this election are not eligible to vote.

SPECIAL ASSISTANCE — Any employee or other participant in this election who has a handicap, and who in order to participate in this election needs special assistance, such as a sign language interpreter, should notify the Regional Director as soon as possible and request the necessary assistance.

CHALLENGE OF VOTERS — If your eligibility to vote is challenged, you will be allowed to vote a challenged ballot. Although you may believe you are eligible to vote, the polling area is not the place to resolve the issue. Give the Board agent your name and any other information you are asked to provide. After you have received a ballot, proceed to the voting booth, mark your ballot and fold it so to keep the mark secret. DO NOT SIGN YOUR BALLOT. Return to the Board agent who will ask you to place your ballot in a challenged envelope, seal the envelope, place it in the ballot box, and leave the polling area. Your eligibility will be resolved later.

AUTHORIZED OBSERVERS — Each of the interested parties may designate an equal number of observers, this authorized to act as checkers at the voting place and at the counting of ballots; (b) assist in the identification of voters; (c) challenge voters and ballots; and (d) otherwise assist the Regional Director or agent.

INFORMATION CONCERNING ELECTION — The Act provides that only one valid representation election may be held in a 12-month period. Any employee who desires to obtain any further information concerning the terms and conditions under which this election is to be held, or who desires to raise any question concerning the holding of an election, the voting unit, or eligibility rules, may do so by communicating with the Regional Director or agent in charge of the election.

S A M P L E

RIGHTS OF EMPLOYEES

Under the National Labor Relations Act, employees have the right
- To self-organization
- To form, join, or assist labor organizations
- To bargain collectively through representatives of their own choosing
- To act together for the purpose of collective bargaining or other mutual aid or protection
- To refuse to do any or all of these things unless the Union and Employer, in a State where such agreements are permitted, enter into a lawful union-security agreement requiring employees to pay periodic dues and initiation fees. Nonmembers who inform the union that they object to the use of their payments for nonrepresentational purposes may be required to pay only their share of the union's costs of representational activities (such as collective bargaining, contract administration, and grievance adjustment).

It is the responsibility of the National Labor Relations Board to protect employees in the exercise of these rights.

The Board wants all eligible voters to be fully informed about their rights under Federal law and wants both Employers and Unions to know what is expected of them when it holds an election.

If agents of either Unions or Employer interfere with your right to a free, fair, and honest election, the election can be set aside by the Board. When appropriate, the Board provides other remedies, such as reinstatement for employees fired for exercising their rights, including backpay from the party responsible for their discharge.

The following are examples of conduct that interfere with the rights of employees and may result in the setting aside of the election:
- Threatening loss of jobs or benefits by an Employer or a Union
- Promising or granting promotions, pay raises, or other benefits to influence an employee's vote by a party capable of carrying out such promises
- An Employer firing employees to discourage or encourage union activity or a Union causing them to be fired to encourage union activity
- Making campaign speeches to assembled groups of employees on company time within the 24-hour period before the election
- Incitement by either an Employer or a Union of racial or religious prejudice by inflammatory appeals
- Threatening physical force or violence to employees by a Union or an Employer to influence their votes

The National Labor Relations Board protects your right to a free choice

Improper conduct will not be permitted. All parties are expected to cooperate fully with this Agency in maintaining basic principles of a fair election as required by law. The National Labor Relations Board as an agency of the United States Government does not endorse any choice in the election.

NATIONAL LABOR RELATIONS BOARD

an agency of the

UNITED STATES GOVERNMENT

GPO : 1987 O – 172-308

WARNING: THIS IS THE ONLY OFFICIAL NOTICE OF THIS ELECTION AND MUST NOT BE DEFACED BY ANYONE. ANY MARKINGS THAT YOU MAY SEE ON ANY SAMPLE BALLOT OR ANYWHERE ON THIS NOTICE HAVE BEEN MADE BY SOMEONE OTHER THAN THE NATIONAL LABOR RELATIONS BOARD, AND HAVE NOT BEEN PUT THERE BY THE NATIONAL LABOR RELATIONS BOARD. THE NATIONAL LABOR RELATIONS BOARD IS AN AGENCY OF THE UNITED STATES GOVERNMENT, AND DOES NOT ENDORSE ANY CHOICE IN THE ELECTION.

Step 4. The Campaign

During the campaign that precedes the election, both the union and the employer appeal to employees for their votes. The union emphasizes that it will prevent unfairness, set up a grievance/seniority system, and improve unsatisfactory wages. Union strength, they'll say, will give employees a voice in determining wages and working conditions. For its part, management will emphasize that improvements such as those the union promises don't require unionization, and that wages are equal to or better than they would be with a union contract. Management will also emphasize the financial cost of union dues; the fact that the union is an "outsider"; and that if the union wins, a strike may follow.[38] It can even attack the union on ethical and moral grounds, while insisting that employees will not be as well off and may lose freedom. But neither side can threaten, bribe, or coerce employees.

Step 5. The Election

Finally, the election can be held within 30 to 60 days after the NLRB issues its Decision and Direction of Election. The election is by secret ballot, and the NLRB provides the ballots (see Figure 14-7), voting booth, and ballot box and counts the votes and certifies the results of the election.

The union becomes the employees' representative if it wins the election, and winning means getting a majority of the votes cast, not a majority of the total workers in the bargaining unit. (Also keep in mind that if an employer commits an unfair labor practice, a "no union" election may be reversed. As representatives of their employer, supervisors must therefore be very careful not to commit such "unfair" practices.)

FIGURE 14-7
Sample NLRB Ballot

```
UNITED STATES OF AMERICA

National Labor Relations Board

OFFICIAL SECRET BALLOT
FOR CERTAIN EMPLOYEES OF

_____

Do you wish to be represented for purposes of collective bargaining by —




_____

MARK AN "S" IN THE SQUARE OF YOUR CHOICE


        YES                              NO
       ┌───┐                           ┌───┐
       │   │                           │   │
       └───┘                           └───┘


DO NOT SIGN THIS BALLOT. Fold and drop in ballot box.
If you spoil this ballot return it to the Board Agent for a new one.
```

How to Lose an NLRB Election

Of the 3,160 collective bargaining elections held in 1997, about 49% were lost by employers.[39] Yet according to a study by the University Research Center, many such elections need not have been lost. According to expert Matthew Goodfellow, there is no sure way an employer can win an election. However, there are five sure ways an employer could lose one.[40]

REASON 1. ASLEEP AT THE SWITCH   In 68% of the companies studied (those that lost to the union) executives were caught unaware, not having paid attention to symptoms of low employee morale. In these companies, turnover and absenteeism had increased, productivity was erratic, and safety was poor. Grievance procedures were rarely used. When the first reports of authorization cards being distributed began trickling back to top managers, they usually responded with a knee-jerk reaction.

A barrage of one-way communications ensued, in which top management bombarded workers with letters describing how the company was "one big family" and calling for a "team effort." As Goodfellow observes,[41]

> Yet the best strategy is to not be caught asleep in the first place: Overall, prudence dictates that management spend time and effort even when the atmosphere is calm testing the temperature of employee sentiments and finding ways to remove irritants. Doing that cuts down on the possibility that an election will ever take place. . . .

REASON 2. APPOINTING A COMMITTEE   Of the losing companies, 36% formed a committee to manage the campaign. According to the expert, there are three problems in doing so:

1. Promptness is of the essence in an election situation, and committees are notorious for slow deliberation.
2. Most of the members of such a committee are neophytes so far as an NLRB situation is concerned. Their views therefore are mostly reflections of wishful thinking rather than experience.
3. A committee's decision is usually a homogenized decision, with everyone seeking to compromise on differences. The result is often close to the most conservative opinion—but not necessarily the most knowledgeable or most effective one.

This expert suggests instead giving full responsibility to a single decisive executive. This person should in turn be assisted by a human resource director and a consultant/advisor with broad experience in labor relations.

REASON 3. CONCENTRATING ON MONEY AND BENEFITS   In 54% of the elections studied, the company lost because top management concentrated on the "wrong" issues: money and benefits. As this expert puts it:

> Employees may want more money, but quite often if they feel the company treats them fairly, decently, and honestly, they are satisfied with reasonable, competitive rates and benefits. It is only when they feel ignored, uncared for, and disregarded that money becomes a major issue to express their dissatisfaction.

REASON 4. INDUSTRY BLIND SPOTS   The researcher found that in some industries employees felt more ignored and disregarded than in others. For example, in industries that are highly automated (such as paper manufacturing and automotive), there was some tendency for executives to regard hourly employees as "just cogs in the machinery," although this is changing today as firms implement more quality-improvement programs. Here (as in reason 3) the solution is to begin paying more serious attention to the needs and attitudes of employees.

REASON 5. DELEGATING TOO MUCH TO DIVISIONS OR BRANCHES   For companies with plants scattered around the country, unionization of one or more plants tends to lead to unionization of others. Indeed, in the United States, United Kingdom, and some other countries, the tendency is for more decentralization of decision-making and there are "widespread reports of a shift to the plant level away from the company-wide agreements."[42] Organizing several of the plants then gives the union a wedge in the form of a contract that can be used to tempt other plants' workers.

Part of the solution here is to keep the first four "reasons" above in mind and thereby to keep those first few plants from being organized. Beyond that, firms with multi-plant operations should not abdicate all decisions concerning personnel and industrial relations to plant managers. Effectively dealing with unionization—taking the "pulse" of the workers' attitudes, knowing what is bothering them, reacting appropriately when the union first appears, and so on—generally requires strong centralized guidance from the main office and its human resource staff.

The Supervisor's Role

Supervisors must be knowledgeable about what they can and can't do to legally hamper organizing activities, lest they commit unfair labor practices. Such practices could (1) cause a new election to be held after your company has won a previous election, or (2) cause your company to forfeit the second election and go directly to contract negotiation.

In one case a plant superintendent reacted to a union's initial organizing attempt by prohibiting distribution of union literature in the plant's lunchroom. Since solicitation of off-duty workers in nonwork areas is generally legal, the company subsequently allowed the union to post union literature on the company's bulletin board and to distribute union literature in nonworking areas inside the plant. However, the NLRB still ruled that the initial act of prohibiting distribution of the literature was an unfair labor practice, one that was not "made right" by the company's subsequent efforts. The NLRB used the superintendent's action as one reason for invalidating an election that the company had won.[43] To avoid such problems, employers should have rules governing distribution of literature and solicitation of workers and train supervisors in how to apply them.[44]

Rules Regarding Literature and Solicitation

There are a number of steps an employer can take to legally restrict union organizing activity.[45]

> Nonemployees can always be barred from soliciting employees during their work time—that is, when the employee is on duty and not on a break. Thus, if the company cafeteria is open to whomever is on the premises, union organizers can solicit off-duty employees who are in the cafeteria but not the cafeteria workers (such as cooks) who are not on a break.
>
> Employers can usually stop employees from soliciting other employees for any purpose if one or both employees are on paid-duty time and not on a break.
>
> Most employers (not including retail stores, shopping centers, and certain other employers) can bar nonemployees from the building's interiors and work areas as a right of private property owners. In certain cases, nonemployees can also be barred

from exterior private property areas—such as parking lots—if there is a business reason (such as safety) and the reason is not just to interfere with union organizers.

Whether or not employers must give union representatives permission to organize on employer-owned property at shopping malls is a matter of legal debate. In 1992, the U.S. Supreme court ruled in *Lechmere, Inc. v. National Labor Relations Board* that nonemployees may be barred from an employer's property if they have reasonable alternative means of communicating their message to the intended audience. On the other hand, if the employer permits other organizations such as the Salvation Army to set up at their workplaces, discriminating against the union organizers may be viewed as an unfair labor practice.[46]

Employees can be denied access to interior or exterior areas only if the employer can show that the rule is required for reasons of production, safety, or discipline. (However, in general, off-duty employees cannot be considered to have the same status as nonemployees. Off-duty employees therefore cannot be prohibited from remaining on the premises or returning to the premises unless this prohibition is also required for reasons of production, safety, or discipline.)

Such restrictions are only valid if they are not imposed in a discriminatory manner. For example, if employees are permitted to collect money for wedding, shower, and baby gifts, to sell Avon products or Tupperware, or to engage in other solicitation during their working time, the employer will not be able to lawfully prohibit them from union soliciting during work time. To do so would discriminate on the basis of union activity, which is an unfair labor practice. Here are two examples of specific rules aimed at limiting union organizing activity:

"Solicitation of employees on company property during working time interferes with the efficient operation of our business. Nonemployees are not permitted to solicit employees on company property for any purpose. Except in break areas where both employees are on break or off the clock, no employee may solicit another employee during working time for any purpose."

"Distribution of literature on company property not only creates a litter problem but also distracts us from our work. Nonemployees are not allowed to distribute literature on company property. Except in the performance of his or her job, an employee may not distribute literature unless both the distributor and the recipient are off the clock or on authorized break in a break area or off company premises. Special exceptions to these rules may be made by the company for especially worthwhile causes such as United Way, but written permission must first be obtained and the solicitation will be permitted only during break periods."[47]

Finally, remember that there are many more ways to commit unfair labor practices than just keeping union organizers off your private property. For example, one employer decided to have a cookout and a paid day off 2 days before a union representation election. The NLRB held that this was too much of a coincidence and represented coercive conduct. The union had lost the first vote but won the second vote as a result.[48]

Guidelines for Employers Wishing to Stay Union-Free

In addition to establishing rules and training supervisors in their application, you can use several additional guidelines for preserving a union-free workplace including:

1. *Practice preventive employee relations.* Fair discipline policies, open worker-management communications, and fair salaries, wages, and benefits can contribute to preserving a union-free workplace.

2. *Recognize the importance of location.* Unions have traditionally been weaker in the South and Southwest than in the North, Northeast, or Far West, for instance.

3. *Seek early detection.* Detect union organizing activity as early as possible, and remember that your best source is probably first-line supervisors. They should be trained to look for changes in employee behavior. In addition, you should look for direct signs of union activity such as posters, buttons, and authorization cards.

4. *Do not volunteer.* Obviously, never voluntarily recognize a union without a secret election supervised by the NLRB.

5. *Beware of the authorization cards.* As previously explained, authorization cards must be handled correctly. When confronted by the union submitting authorization cards, get another manager in as a witness and do not touch the cards (or, worse, count or examine them in any way). When the organizer leaves, call your lawyer.

6. *Present your case.* Again, present your case to your employees forcefully and relentlessly. Executives' speeches to employees during working hours, informal meetings in the dining areas, and informational letters are all good tools.

7. *Postpone the election.* There may be an advantage in postponing the election as long as possible. This will give you more time to prepare and communicate your case and could wear down the union's resolve and majority.

8. *Pick your time carefully.* Within the guidelines set by the NLRB, you should carefully choose the time and date of the election. For example, you may find that employees are in a better frame of mind on Friday than on Monday and that pay day affords you an opportunity to get in the final word by stuffing some information in pay envelopes.[49]

9. *Consider your options.* Finally, consider the option of not staying union-free. Although we have emphasized staying union-free, some employers do opt to let the union in. Union membership may make health benefits available at group rates that many employers could not afford, and industrywide or associationwide wage agreements can remove the burden of having to negotiate salaries and raises with each of your employees. Some unions may be easier to get along with than others, if you have a choice. Therefore, consider your options.

Decertification Elections: When Employees Want to Oust Their Union

Winning an election and signing an agreement do not necessarily mean that the union is in the company to stay—quite the opposite. The same law that grants employees the right to unionize also gives them a way to legally terminate their union's right to represent them. The process is known as *decertification*. In the 1990's employees voted for decertification in about 78% of elections.[50] (Unions won about 49% of the original certification elections held in 1997.)[51]

Decertification campaigns don't differ much from certification campaigns (those leading up to the initial election).[52] The union organizes membership meetings and house-to-house visits, mails literature into the homes, and uses phone calls, NLRB appeals, and (sometimes) threats and harassment to win the election.[53] For its part, managers use meetings—including one-on-one meetings, small-group meetings, and meetings with entire units—as well as legal or expert assistance, letters, improved working conditions, and subtle or not-so-subtle threats to try to influence the vote. Employers are also increasingly turning to consultants. These consultants (who claim they act as "marriage brokers" between workers and management)[54] provide managers and supervisors with, among other things, detailed advice concerning how to behave during the preelection period.[55]

THE COLLECTIVE BARGAINING PROCESS	## What Is Collective Bargaining?

When and if the union is recognized as your employees' representative, a day is set for management and labor at the bargaining table to negotiate a labor agreement. This agreement will contain specific provisions covering wages, hours, and working conditions.

collective bargaining
The process through which representatives of management and the union meet to negotiate a labor agreement.

What exactly is **collective bargaining**? According to the National Labor Relations Act:

> *For the purpose of [this act] to bargain collectively is the performance of the mutual obligation of the employer and the representative of the employees to meet at reasonable times and confer in good faith with respect to wages, hours, and terms and conditions of employment, or the negotiation of an agreement, or any question arising thereunder, and the execution of a written contract incorporating any agreement reached if requested by either party, but such obligation does not compel either party to agree to a proposal or require the making of a concession.*

In plain language, this means that both management and labor are required by law to negotiate wages, hours, and terms and conditions of employment "in good faith." In a moment we will see that the specific terms that are negotiable (since wages, hours, and conditions of employment are too broad to be useful in practice) have been clarified by a series of court decisions.

What Is Good Faith?

good faith bargaining
A term that means both parties are communicating and negotiating and that proposals are being matched with counterproposals with both parties making every reasonable effort to arrive at agreements. It does not mean that either party is compelled to agree to a proposal.

Bargaining in **good faith** is the cornerstone of effective labor management relations. It means that both parties communicate and negotiate, that proposals are matched with counterproposals, and that both parties make every reasonable effort to arrive at an agreement.[56] It does not mean that either party is compelled to agree to a proposal. Nor does it require that either party make any specific concessions (although as a practical matter, some may be necessary).

WHEN IS BARGAINING NOT IN GOOD FAITH?   As interpreted by the NLRB and the courts, a violation of the requirement for good faith bargaining may include the following:

1. *Surface bargaining.* This involves merely going through the motions of bargaining without any real intention of completing a formal agreement.
2. *Inadequate concessions.* Although no one is required to make a concession, the courts' and NLRB's definitions of good faith suggest that a willingness to compromise is an essential ingredient in good faith bargaining.
3. *Inadequate proposals and demands.* The NLRB considers the advancement of proposals to be a positive factor in determining overall good faith.
4. *Dilatory tactics.* The law requires that the parties meet and "confer at reasonable times and intervals." Obviously, refusal to meet at all with the union does not satisfy the positive duty imposed on the employer.
5. *Imposing conditions.* Attempts to impose conditions that are so onerous or unreasonable as to indicate bad faith will be scrutinized by the board.
6. *Making unilateral changes in conditions.* This is viewed as a strong indication that the employer is not bargaining with the required intent of reaching an agreement.

Labor and management must both be prepared for the collective bargaining process, undertaken here by labor and management representatives of the New York City Department of Sanitation.

7. *Bypassing the representative.* An employer violates its duty to bargain when it refuses to negotiate with the union representative. The duty of management to bargain in good faith involves, at a minimum, recognition that this statutory representative is the one with whom the employer must deal in conducting bargaining negotiations.

8. *Committing unfair labor practices during negotiations.* Such practices may reflect poorly upon the good faith of the guilty party.

9. *Witholding information.* Information must be supplied to the union, upon request, to enable it to understand and intelligently discuss the issues raised in bargaining.

10. *Ignoring bargaining items.* Refusal to bargain on a *mandatory* item (one *must* bargain over these) or insistence on a *permissive* item (one *may* bargain over these) is usually viewed as bad faith bargaining.[57] (We will present these items in the following discussion.)

The Negotiating Team

Both union and management send a negotiating team to the bargaining table, and both teams usually go into the bargaining sessions having "done their homework." Union representatives have sounded out union members on their desires and conferred with the union representatives of related unions.

Management uses several techniques to prepare for bargaining. First, it prepares the data on which to build its bargaining position.[58] Pay and benefit data are compiled and include comparisons to local pay rates and to rates paid for similar jobs within the industry. Data on the distribution of the workforce (in terms of age, sex, and seniority, for instance) are also important, because these factors determine what you will actually pay out in benefits. Internal economic data regarding cost of benefits, overall earnings levels, and the amount and cost of overtime are important as well.

Management will also "cost" the current labor contract and determine the increased cost—total, per employee, and per hour—of the union's demands. And, it will try to identify probable union demands. Here it will use information from grievances and feedback from supervisors to determine what the union's demands might be, and thus prepare counteroffers and arguments ahead of time.[59] Other popular tactics are attitude surveys to test employee reactions to various sections of the contract that management may feel require change, and informal conferences with local union leaders to discuss the operational effectiveness of the contract and to send up trial balloons on management ideas for change.

Bargaining Items

Labor law sets out categories of items that are subject to bargaining: These are *mandatory, voluntary,* and *illegal items.*

Voluntary (or permissible) **bargaining items** are neither mandatory nor illegal; they become a part of negotiations only through the joint agreement of both management and union. Neither party can be compelled against its wishes to negotiate over voluntary items. You cannot hold up signing your contract because the other party refuses to bargain on a voluntary item.

Illegal bargaining items are forbidden by law. A clause agreeing to hire "union members exclusively" would be illegal in a right-to-work state, for example.

There are about 70 basic items over which bargaining is **mandatory** under the law, and some are presented in Figure 14-8. They include wages, hours, rest periods, layoffs, transfers, benefits, and severance pay. Others are added as the law evolves. For instance, drug testing evolved into a mandatory item as a result of court decisions in the 1980s.[60]

Bargaining Stages[61]

The actual bargaining typically goes through several stages of development.[62] First, each side presents its demands. At this stage both parties are usually quite far apart on some issues. Second, there is a reduction of demands. At this stage each side trades off some of its demands to gain others. Third comes the subcommittee studies; the parties form joint subcommittees to try to work out reasonable alternatives. Fourth, an informal settlement is reached and each group goes back to its sponsor. Union representatives check informally with their superiors and the union members; management representatives check with top management. Finally, once everything is in order, a formal agreement is fine-tuned and signed.

---

voluntary bargaining items

Items in collective bargaining over which bargaining is neither illegal nor mandatory—neither party can be compelled against its wishes to negotiate over those items.

illegal bargaining items

Items in collective bargaining that are forbidden by law; for example, the clause agreeing to hire "union members exclusively" would be illegal in a right-to-work state.

mandatory bargaining items

Items in collective bargaining that a party must bargain over if they are introduced by the other party—for example, pay.

FIGURE 14-8

Bargaining Items

Source: Michael B. Carrell and Christina Heavrin, *Collective Bargaining and Labor Relations: Cases, Practice, and Law* (New York: Macmillan Publishing Company, 1991), p. 127.

MANDATORY	PERMISSIBLE	ILLEGAL
Rates of pay	Indemnity bonds	Closed shop
Wages	Management rights as to union affairs	Separation of employees based on race
Hours of employment	Pension benefits of retired employees	Discriminatory treatment
Overtime pay	Scope of the bargaining unit	
Shift differentials	Including supervisors in the contract	
Holidays	Additional parties to the contract such as the international union	
Vacations		
Severance pay	Use of union label	
Pensions	Settlement of unfair labor changes	
Insurance benefits	Prices in cafeteria	
Profit-sharing plans	Continuance of past contract	
Christmas bonuses	Membership of bargaining team	
Company housing, meals, and discounts	Employment of strike breakers	
Employee security		
Job performance		
Union security		
Management-union relationship		
Drug testing of employees		

HINTS ON BARGAINING   Expert Reed Richardson has the following advice for bargainers:[63]

1. Be sure you have *set clear objectives* for every bargaining item and you understand on what grounds the objectives are established.
2. *Do not hurry.*
3. When in doubt, *caucus* with your associates.
4. Be *well prepared* with firm data supporting your position.
5. Always strive to keep some *flexibility* in your position. Don't get yourself out on a limb.
6. Don't just concern yourself with what the other party says and does; *find out why.* Remember that economic motivation is not the only explanation for the other party's conduct and actions.
7. Respect the importance of *face saving* for the other party.
8. Constantly be alert to the *real intentions* of the other party with respect not only to goals but also priorities.
9. Be a good *listener.*
10. Build a reputation for being *fair but firm.*
11. Learn to *control your emotions*; don't panic. Use emotions as a tool, not an obstacle.
12. Be sure as you make each bargaining move that you know its *relationship* to all other moves.
13. Measure each move against your *objectives.*
14. Pay close attention to the *wording* of every clause negotiated; words and phrases are often a source of grievances.
15. Remember that collective bargaining negotiations are, by their nature, part of a *compromise* process. There is no such thing as having all the pie.
16. Try to *understand* people and their personalities.
17. Consider the impact of present negotiations on those in *future years.*

There are also several things negotiators can do to foster the trust on which many successful negotiations are based. Trust, to paraphrase one expert, means that "I trust you when I expect you to cooperate and not exploit me."[64] Trust-building behaviors include:

Show willingness to trust. Give indications of your own growing propensity to trust by not exploiting any moves made by the other negotiator, and then by sending signals of your own intention to exhibit trustworthy behavior.

Check understanding. Check the understanding of the other negotiator that the trusting signals are being correctly interpreted.

Indicate the adverse consequences of a failure to respond. Finally, and only if all the previous moves have failed to generate a willingness to offer trust, send signals as to the adverse consequences of trust being offered and not reciprocated.[65]

Impasses, Mediation, and Strikes[66]

IMPASSE DEFINED   In collective bargaining, an impasse occurs when the parties are not able to move further toward settlement. An impasse usually occurs because one party is demanding more than the other will offer. Sometimes an impasse can be resolved through a third party—a disinterested person such as a mediator or arbitrator. If the impasse is not resolved in this way, a work stoppage, or *strike*, may be called by the union to bring pressure to bear on management.[67]

THIRD-PARTY INVOLVEMENT   Three types of third-party interventions are used to overcome an impasse: mediation, fact-finding, and arbitration. With **mediation** a neutral third party tries to assist the principals in reaching agreement. The mediator usually holds meetings with each party to determine where each stands regarding its position, and then this information is used to find common ground for further bargaining. The mediator is always a go-between. As such, he or she communicates assessments of the likelihood of a strike, the possible settlement packages available, and the like. The mediator does not have the authority to fix a position or make a concession.

In certain situations, as in a national emergency dispute where the president of the United States determines that it would be a national emergency for a strike to occur, a *fact finder* may be appointed. A fact finder is a neutral party who studies the issues in a dispute and makes a public recommendation of what a reasonable settlement ought to be.[68] For example, presidential emergency fact-finding boards have successfully resolved impasses in certain critical transportation disputes.

Arbitration is the most definitive type of third-party intervention, because the arbitrator often has the power to determine and dictate the settlement terms. Unlike mediation and fact-finding, arbitration can guarantee a solution to an impasse. With binding arbitration, both parties are committed to accepting the arbitrator's award. With nonbinding arbitration, they are not. Arbitration may also be voluntary or compulsory (in other words, imposed by a government agency). In the United States, voluntary binding arbitration is the most prevalent.

STRIKES   A strike is a withdrawal of labor, and there are four main types of strikes. An **economic strike** results from a failure to agree on the terms of a contract that involve wages, benefits, and other conditions of employment—from an impasse, in other words. **Unfair labor practice** strikes, on the other hand, are aimed at protesting illegal conduct by the employer. A **wildcat strike** is an unauthorized strike occurring during the term of a contract. A **sympathy strike** occurs when one union strikes in support of the strike of another union.[69] Picketing is one of the first activities occurring during a strike. The purpose of picketing is to inform the public about the existence of the labor dispute and often to encourage others to refrain from doing business with the struck employer.

Employers can make several responses when they become the object of a strike. One is to *shut down* the affected area and thus halt their operations until the strike is over. A second alternative is to *contract out* work during the duration of the strike in order to blunt the effects of the strike on the employer. A third alternative is for the employer to *continue operations*, perhaps using supervisors and other nonstriking workers to fill in for the striking workers. A fourth alternative is the *hiring of replacements* for the strikers. In an economic strike, such replacements can be deemed permanent and would not have to be let go to make room for strikers who decided to return to work. If the strike were an unfair labor practice strike, the strikers would be entitled to return to their jobs upon making an unconditional offer to do so. Major work stoppages involving a thousand or more workers have dropped significantly over the past 10 years or so, from about 140 in 1981 to about 40 in 1991, and 29 in 1997.[70]

PREPARING FOR THE STRIKE   When a strike is imminent, plans must be made to deal with it. For example, two experts say that when a strike is imminent or already under way, following these guidelines can minimize confusion.[71]

---

mediation

Intervention in which a neutral third party tries to assist the principals in reaching agreement.

arbitration

The most definitive type of third-party intervention, in which the arbitrator usually has the power to determine and dictate the settlement terms.

economic strike

A strike that results from a failure to agree on the terms of a contract that involve wages, benefits, and other conditions of employment.

unfair labor practice strike

A strike aimed at protesting illegal conduct by the employer.

wildcat strike

An unauthorized strike occurring during the term of a contract.

sympathy strike

A strike that takes place when one union strikes in support of the strike of another.

Pay all striking employees what they are owed on the first day of the strike.

Secure the facility. Supervisors should be on the alert for strangers on the property, and access should be controlled. The company should consider hiring guards to protect replacements coming to and from work and to watch and control the picketers, if necessary.

Notify all customers. You may decide not to notify customers but to respond to inquiries only. A standard official response to all customers should be prepared and should be merely informative.

Contact all suppliers and other persons with whom you do business who will have to cross the picket line. Establish alternative methods of obtaining supplies.

Make arrangements for overnight stays in the facility and for delivered meals in case the occasion warrants such action.

Notify the local unemployment office of your need for replacement workers.

Photograph the facility before, during, and after picketing. If necessary, install videotape equipment and a long-distance microphone to monitor picket line misconduct.

Record any and all facts concerning strikers' demeanor and activities and such incidents as violence, threats, mass pickets, property damage, or problems. Record police response to any request for assistance.

Gather the following evidence: number of pickets and their names; time, date, and location of picketing; wording on every sign carried by pickets; and descriptions of picket cars and license numbers.

corporate campaign

An organized effort by the union that exerts pressure on the corporation by pressuring the company's other unions shareholders, directors, customers, creditors, and government agencies, often directly.

boycott

The combined refusal by employees and other interested parties to buy or use the employer's products.

OTHER ALTERNATIVES   Management and labor each have other weapons they can use to try to break an impasse and achieve their aims. The union, for example, may resort to a **corporate campaign.** A corporate campaign is an organized effort by the union that exerts pressure on the corporation by pressuring the company's other unions, shareholders, directors, customers, creditors, and government agencies, often directly. Thus, individual members of the board of directors might be shocked by picketing of their homes, political figures might be pressured to agree to union demands, and the company's banks might become targets of a union member **boycott.**[72]

Inside games are another union tactic, one often used in conjunction with corporate campaigns. Inside games can be defined as union efforts to convince employees to impede or to disrupt production, for example, by slowing the work pace, refusing to work overtime, filing mass charges with government agencies, refusing to do work without receiving detailed instructions from supervisors or management even though such instruction has not previously been required, and engaging in other disruptive activities such as castigating management and staging sick-outs.[73] Inside games can be viewed as essentially de facto strikes—albeit "strikes" in which the employees are being supported by the company, which continues to pay them. Thus in one inside game at Caterpillar's Aurora, Illinois, plant, United Auto Workers' grievances in the final stage before arbitration rose from 22 to 336. The effect, of course, was to clog the grievance procedure and tie up workers and management in unproductive endeavors on company time.[74]

lockout

A refusal by the employer to provide opportunities to work.

For their part, employers can try to break an impasse with lockouts. A **lockout** is a refusal by the employer to provide opportunities to work. The employees are (sometimes literally) locked out and prohibited from doing their jobs (and thus from getting paid).

A lockout is not generally viewed as an unfair labor practice by the NLRB. For example, if your product is a perishable one (such as vegetables), then a lockout may be a legitimate tactic to neutralize or decrease union power. A lockout is viewed as an unfair labor practice by the NLRB only when the employer acts for a prohibited purpose. It is not a prohibited purpose to try to bring about a settlement of negotiations on terms favorable to the employer. Lockouts today are not widely used, though; employers are usually reluctant to cease operations when employees are willing to continue working (even though there may be an impasse at the bargaining table).[75] However, in 1998, basketball players threatened a strike and the owners then instituted a lockout.

Both employers and unions can seek injunctive relief if they believe the other side is taking actions that could cause irreparable harm to the other party. In the baseball strike of 1994, for instance, the National Labor Relations Board obtained a "Section 10(j)" injunction from a federal district court to force baseball owners back to the bargaining table. To obtain such relief, the NLRB must show the district court that an unfair labor practice—such as interfering with the union organizing campaign—if left unremedied, will irreparably harm the other party's statutory rights. (For example, if the employer is interfering with the union's organization campaign, or if the union is retaliating against employees for trying to gain access to the NLRB, the other side might press the NLRB for 10(j) injunctive relief.) Such relief is requested after the NLRB issues an unfair labor practices complaint. The injunctive relief itself is a court order compelling a party or parties either to resume or to desist a certain action.[76]

The Contract Agreement Itself

The actual contract agreement may be 20 or 30 pages long or longer. It may contain just general declarations of policy or a detailed specification of rules and procedures. The tendency today is toward the longer, more detailed contract. This is largely a result of the increased number of items the agreements have been covering.

The main sections of a typical contract cover subjects such as these:

> (1) management rights, (2) union security and automatic payroll dues deduction, (3) grievance procedures, (4) arbitration of grievances, (5) disciplinary procedures, (6) compensation rates, (7) hours of work and overtime, (8) benefits: vacations, holidays, insurance, pensions, (9) health and safety provisions, (10) employee security seniority provisions, and (11) contract expiration date.

Changes to Expect After Being Unionized

Unionization will have profound effects on the company. Professor Dale Beach says there are five basic areas in which the union's impact will be felt.[77] Unionization will restrict management's freedom of action; it will result in union pressure for uniformity of treatment of all employees; it will require improved human resources policies and practices; it will require one spokesperson to be used for the employees; and it will lead to centralization of labor relations decision making.

Perhaps the most obvious impact is that unionization restricts management's freedom of action. Decisions such as who gets laid off when business slows, who gets to work overtime, and who gets a raise will now be subject to a union challenge, for example.

Given the prospect of such challenges and the numerous written contract provisions regarding pay, benefits, promotion, and the like, unionization also generally results in the employer's HR policies, procedures, and rules becoming more systematized, centralized, and sophisticated. Standardized appraisal procedures may be introduced, for example.

<table>
<tr><td>

CONTRACT
ADMINISTRATION:
GRIEVANCES

</td></tr>
</table>

The Important Role of Contract Administration

Hammering out a labor agreement is not the last step in collective bargaining; in some respects, it is just the beginning. No labor contract can ever be so complete that it covers all contingencies and answers all questions. For example, suppose the contract says you can only discharge an employee for "just cause." You subsequently discharge someone for speaking back to you in harsh terms. Was it within your rights to discharge this person? Was speaking back to you harshly "just cause"?

grievance

Any factor involving wages, hours, or conditions of employment that is used as a complaint against the employer.

Problems like this are usually handled and settled through the labor contract's **grievance** procedure. This procedure provides an orderly system whereby both employer and union determine whether or not the contract has been violated.[78] It is the vehicle for administering the contract on a day-to-day basis. Through the grievance process, various clauses are interpreted and given meaning, and the contract is transformed into a "living organism." Remember, though, that this day-to-day collective bargaining involves interpretation only; it usually doesn't involve negotiating new terms or altering existing ones.[79]

What Are the Sources of Grievances?

From a practical point of view, it is probably easier to list those items that don't precipitate grievances than to list the ones that do. Just about any factor involving wages, hours, or conditions of employment has and will be used as the basis of a grievance.

However, certain grievances are more serious than others since they are usually more difficult to settle. Discipline cases and seniority problems including promotions, transfers, and layoffs would top this list. Others would include grievances growing out of job evaluations and work assignments, overtime, vacations, incentive plans, and holidays.[80] Here are five actual examples of grievances as presented by Reed Richardson:[81]

Absenteeism. An employer fired an employee for excessive absences. The employee filed a grievance stating that there had been no previous warnings or discipline related to excessive absences.

Insubordination. An employee on two occasions refused to obey a supervisor's order to meet with him unless a union representative was present at the meeting. As a result, the employee was discharged and subsequently filed a grievance protesting discharge.

Overtime. Sunday overtime work was discontinued after a department was split. Employees affected filed a grievance protesting loss of the overtime work.

Plant rules. The plant had a posted rule barring employees from eating or drinking during unscheduled breaks. The employees filed a grievance claiming the rule was arbitrary.

Seniority. A junior employee was hired to fill the position of a laid-off senior employee. The senior employee filed a grievance protesting the action.

ALWAYS ASK: WHAT IS THE REAL PROBLEM?   A grievance is often just a symptom of an underlying problem. For example, an employee's concern for his or her security may prompt a grievance over a transfer, work assignment, or promotion. Sometimes bad relationships between supervisors and subordinates are to blame: This is often the cause of grievances over "fair treatment," for instance. Organizational factors such as automated jobs or ambiguous job descriptions that frustrate or aggravate employees also cause grievances. Union activism is another cause; for example, the union may solicit grievances from workers to underscore ineffective supervision. Problem employees are yet another cause of grievances. These are individuals, who, by their nature, are negative, dissatisfied,

DIVERSITY COUNTS

Gender Differences in Disputes and Dispute Resolution

One reason for having a grievance process is that problems and disputes in the workplace are normal and probably unavoidable.[82] As explained elsewhere in this chapter, disputes commonly arise over issues such as work assignments, work schedules, and discipline; once such disputes arise, they should be addressed. They may be addressed formally (such as through union-negotiated grievance procedures) or informally, such as in face-to-face conversations.

Given the likelihood that you will find yourself engaged in some type of workplace dispute, the results of one recent study provide some food for thought. The study focused on disputes over tasks and interpersonal treatment, and involved 34 in-depth interviews with 23 women and 11 men clerical workers in both unionized and nonunionized firms.[83] The researchers draw three conclusions from their study.

First, there are gender differences in the origins of workplace problems and disputes. At least with these workers in these companies, "women workers displayed more sensitivity to problems associated with interpersonal relations in the workplace than men, more often voicing workplace disputes concerning personality conflicts."[84] On the other hand, the men clerical workers were relatively less likely to express concerns over personality conflicts in the workplace.[85]

Second, more women generally described how difficult it was to resolve personality conflicts through

and grievance prone.[88] *Disciplinary measures*—a major source of grievances—and *dismissal*—a frequent result of disciplinary measures—were explained in chapter 10.

The Grievance Procedure

Most collective bargaining contracts contain a very specific grievance procedure. This specifies the various steps in the procedure, time limits associated with each step, and specific rules such as "all charges of contract violation must be reduced to writing." Virtually every labor agreement signed today contains a grievance procedure clause. (Nonunionized employers need such procedures, too; we'll discuss this in the following chapter.)

Union grievance procedures differ from firm to firm. Some contain simple two-step procedures. Here the grievant, union representative, and company representative first meet to discuss the grievance. If a satisfactory solution is not found, the grievance is brought before an independent third-person arbitrator, who hears the case, writes it up, and makes a decision.

At the other extreme, the grievance procedure may contain six or more steps. The first step might be for the grievant and shop steward to meet informally with the grievant's supervisor to try to find a solution. If one is not found, a formal grievance is filed and a meeting scheduled among the employee, shop steward, and the supervisor's boss. The next steps involve the grievant and union representatives meeting with higher-and higher-level managers. Finally, if top management and the union can't reach agreement, the grievance may go to arbitration. (See the "Diversity Counts" box, above, for another perspective).

Guidelines for Handling Grievances

DEVELOPING THE PROPER ENVIRONMENT   The best way to handle a grievance is to develop a work environment in which grievances don't occur in the first place.[89] Constructive grievance handling depends first on your ability to recognize, diagnose, and cor-

formalized channels (including grievance procedures). The reason, apparently, is that the sorts of personality conflicts sensed by the female clerical workers rarely "escalate to a point that they can be labeled or proven as harassment."[86] Instead they were more subtle occurrences that "eat away at women workers" to use the researchers phrase.[87] As a result, women were much less likely to use formal dispute resolution procedures for eliminating interpersonal conflicts. Instead they were much more likely to request lateral transfers to solve problems in the workplace. In turn such lateral transfers may reduce a woman's likelihood of receiving a raise or getting more training, since her average tenure on a job will tend to be lower than a man's (who either discounts the interpersonal conflict or tries to solve it through some formal or informal procedure).

A third conclusion is that, given the above, workplace dispute resolution procedures may actually constrain women's abilities to succeed at work. For example suppose it is true that formal dispute resolution procedures such as grievance processes are unlikely to be useful forums for addressing simple interpersonal conflicts. Then women may be at a disadvantage when it comes to solving an interpersonal conflict that they may be relatively attuned to. One implication is that more formal and informal procedures should be built into an employer's dispute resolution processes in order to give both women and men a better opportunity to air interpersonal disputes and get on with their work.

rect the causes of potential employee dissatisfaction (causes such as unfair appraisals, inequitable wages, or poor communications) before they become formal grievances.

SOME GUIDELINES: DO'S AND DON'TS[90]   As a manager, your behavior in handling grievances is crucial. You are on the firing line and must, therefore, steer a course between treating employees fairly and maintaining management's rights and prerogatives. One expert has developed a list of do's and don'ts as useful guides in handling grievances.[91] Some of the most critical ones are presented next:

Do

- Investigate and handle each and every case as though it may eventually result in an arbitration hearing.
- Talk with the employee about his or her grievance; give the person a good and full hearing.
- Require the union to identify specific contractual provisions allegedly violated.
- Comply with the contractual time limits of the company for handling the grievance.
- Visit the work area of the grievance.
- Determine whether there were any witnesses.
- Examine the grievant's personnel record.
- Fully examine prior grievance records.
- Treat the union representative as your equal.
- Hold your grievance discussions privately.
- Fully inform your own supervisor of grievance matters.

Don't

- Discuss the case with the union steward alone—the grievant should definitely be there.
- Make arrangements with individual employees that are inconsistent with the labor agreement.
- Hold back the remedy if the company is wrong.
- Admit to the binding effect of a past practice.
- Relinquish to the union your rights as a manager.
- Settle grievances on the basis of what is "fair." Instead, stick to the labor agreement, which should be your only standard.
- Bargain over items not covered by the contract.
- Treat as subject to arbitration claims demanding the discipline or discharge of managers.
- Give long written grievance answers.
- Trade a grievance settlement for a grievance withdrawal (or try to make up for a bad decision in one grievance by bending over backward in another).
- Deny grievances on the premise that your "hands have been tied by management."
- Agree to informal amendments in the contract.

THE FUTURE OF UNIONISM

Unions Fall on Hard Times

The 1970s and 1980s were hard times for unions, and during those years their rolls dropped steeply. About 22% of the nonfarm U.S. workforce belonged to unions in 1975. By 1998 that figure had dropped to about 14.1%. This slide actually began in the early 1950s. By then most easily organized workers in industries like mining, transportation, and manufacturing had been unionized.

Several factors contributed to the decline in union membership. Traditionally, unions have appealed mostly to blue-collar workers, and the proportion of blue-collar jobs has been decreasing as service-sector and white-collar service jobs have increased. Furthermore, several economic factors, including intense international competition, outdated equipment and factories, mismanagement, new technology, and government regulation, have hit those industries (like mining and manufacturing) that have traditionally been unionized. The effect of all this has been the permanent layoff of hundreds of thousands of union members, the permanent closing of company plants, the relocation of companies to nonunion settings (either in the United States or overseas), and mergers and acquisitions that have eliminated union jobs and affected collective bargaining agreements. Other changes, including the deregulation of trucking, airlines, and communications, have helped to erode union membership as well.[92]

Furthermore, the various EEO, safety, and similar laws described elsewhere in this book now provide the sort of protection that up to a few years ago only unions could provide. Foremost on this list are those court decisions that erode the employment-at-will doctrine, making it harder for employers in many states to fire employees without just cause. On this and many other fronts, employee rights regarding job security, privacy, occupational safety, equal employment opportunities, pension vesting, and pay policies are now provided by law. To that extent, the role formerly played by unions has been reduced.[93]

Double-breasting is another way that companies are putting unions under more pressure. This term refers to a tactic whereby employers avoid their obligations under union contracts by establishing and running nonunion companies to which they may transfer union work. The NLRB permits this under certain circumstances. It is, for instance, a common practice in the construction industry.

Technology will also impact unionization. Computer systems and other modern technologies may reduce labor demand, for instance. Electronic work (like processing credit card claims) is highly portable compared with factory work. Modern office work—and its workers—can thus be shifted almost literally at the touch of a button from one state to another, and even overseas.[94]

What's Next for Unions?

Does all this mean we no longer need unions? Probably not. But it does mean a change in the way unions operate and in the role they see for themselves.

First, unions are increasingly going after a "piece of the pie" in terms of ownership and control of corporations. As a United Steelworkers Union president put it, "We are not going to sit around and allow management to louse things up like they did in the past."[95] Today, for instance, over eight million workers own a piece of their employers—from United Airlines to smaller firms like Foldcraft Co.—through employee stock ownership plans.[96] (Recall that these ESOPs are basically pension plans through which a company's employees accumulate shares of their company's stock.) As a result, nonmanagement employees now sit on boards of directors at more than 300 firms in their role as representatives of the firm's employee stock ownership plans.

Second, unions are becoming both more aggressive and more sophisticated in how they present themselves to the public. The AFL-CIO has a program to train a thousand unionists in the fundamentals of how to come across well on television, for instance. Unions are also entering into more cooperative pacts with employers, such as working with them in developing team-based employee participation programs.

During the last 10 years or so, the major union effort has been aimed at organizing white-collar workers. Service-oriented industries such as insurance, banking, retail trade, and government are now being organized by unions. More than 10% of white-collar workers have already become unionized. The number is increasing rapidly, particularly among professionals, many of whom work in the public sector.[97] And the AFL-CIO promises much more aggressive organizing efforts. President John Sweeney's "Formula for a Turnaround" is summarized in Figure 14-9.

FIGURE 14-9

Union's Formula for a Turnaround

Among the campaign proposals of the AFL–CIO ticket led by John Sweeney:

- **ORGANIZING:** Create a separate AFL–CIO organizing department.
- **POLITICS:** Create a training center to develop campaign organizers, campaign managers, and candidates. Create a policy center to develop new approaches to economic and public policy.
- **CORPORATE CAMPAIGNS:** Create a Strategic Campaign Fund that could provide grants to unions 'in important and difficult contract fights.'
- **STRIKES:** Create a support team to help in long-running strikes.
- **PENSIONS:** Create a clearinghouse to manage a database of union pension-fund investments to support unions in corporate-governance campaigns.
- **OTHER:** Expand AFL–CIO Executive Council from 33 to 45 vice presidents and bar individuals over 70 from running for top AFL–CIO offices.

Unions and Employee Participation Programs

The quality circles and total quality management programs discussed elsewhere in this book are a two-edged sword as far as unions are concerned. On the one hand, they can be the basis for building better communications and for boosting union management harmony. On the other, they may undercut union security by building relationships between workers and management that make unions obsolete. Unions are therefore somewhat schizophrenic about the subject of commitment-building participation programs.

Based on the research, at least, worker participation programs don't seem to be the threat union leaders fear they may be. One study, for instance, found few differences between how quality programs' participants and nonparticipants viewed the performance of their unions.[98] Another researcher found that quality program participants were actually more involved in and satisfied with the union than were nonparticipants.[99]

The critical issue seems to be whether or not the union is asked to help develop and implement the total quality program. For example, one study concluded that union officers were much less likely to view the quality program negatively when they were involved in its design and implementation.[100] Similarly, in another study, the researchers found that "union members who participated in [such] programs were less likely than nonparticipants to view [them] as a threat to the union, and also remained more loyal to the union."[101]

THE HIGH-PERFORMANCE ORGANIZATION

Building Better, Faster, More Competitive Organizations Through HR: Union-Management Relations

■ **Department of Energy, Oak Ridge Operations, Oak Ridge, TN**

Department of Energy, Oak Ridge Operations provides a good example of the impact of successful employee-participation-based labor-management relations. Several years ago, Total Quality (TQ) efforts were begun with joint-training retreats, where labor and management assembled to determine differences and similarities and how to apply new solutions to continuing problems. These small groups from both sides began to work as teams. (Other actions, such as those related to production floor statistical process control and concurrent engineering, had been in place for years, but had not been applied to the human resources area.) Next, the unions began participating on benchmarking teams, to illustrate to them the potential applicability of this TQ continuous improvement tool.

The current TQ focus reportedly remains a driving force behind union-management relations, and has been accepted by union leaders and most members. The 18 different unions spearheaded by the Atomic Trades and Labor Council are thus working with management to use TQ to not only work "smarter," but also to continuously improve health and safety and community outreach at Oak Ridge.

The Oak Ridge Health and Safety Tripartite Program of DOE/Union/Management has become the National Labor Relations Board model for all other DOE facilities, as well as other companies having numerous on-site unions.

Source: Copyright 1998, Best Manufacturing Practices Center of Excellence.

Are Employee Participation Programs Unfair Labor Practices?

The proliferation of employee participation programs—quality circles, quality improvement programs, quality of work life teams, and so on—has added urgency to a question that's been debated in labor relations circles for over 50 years: Are employee participation programs like these "sham unions" and therefore illegal under the National Labor Relations Act? At the present time, they are "subject to serious legal challenge under the National Labor Relations Act (NLRA)"[102] as unfair labor practices. For example, a program giving employees more input into how they perform their jobs at United Parcel Service recently faced strong opposition from the Teamsters union. Under this program, hourly employees work together in self-directed teams establishing priority on how work is to be done. UPS argues that the program recognizes that such employee involvement and teamwork can translate into higher productivity. For its part, the Teamsters union (which represents the company's drivers and other hourly workers) is suspicious that the program is merely a tactic for subverting the union's influence on its members.[103]

To understand the problem, it's useful to know that a principal goal of the National Labor Relations (or Wagner) Act was to outlaw so-called sham unions. Two years before passage of the NLRA, the National Recovery Act of 1933 tried to give employees the right to organize and to bargain collectively. This in turn triggered an enormous increase in sham unions that were actually company-supported organizations aimed at keeping legitimate unions out. This helped to lead to passage of the National Labor Relations Act.

The problem is that, because of the way the NLRA is written and frequently interpreted, participative programs such as quality circles and quality-improvement teams could be viewed as sham unions. In part, this is so because the NLRA defines a *labor organization* as

> *Any organization of any kind, or any agency or employee representation committee or plan, in which employees participate and which exists for the purpose, in whole or in part, of dealing with employers concerning grievances, labor disputes, wages, rates of pay, hours of employment, or conditions of work.[104]*

Whether or not an employer's participation program will be viewed as an impermissible labor organization revolves around two main criteria. One is dominance. For example, if the employer formulates the idea for the committees, creates them, controls the development of their constitution or governing rules, or maintains control over the committees' functions, they could be viewed as impermissibly dominated by the employer.[105]

The participation committee's actual role is the second consideration. If the committees focus exclusively on issues such as quality and productivity improvement, they may be more likely to be viewed by the courts as outside the purview of the National Labor Relations Act. On the other hand, if the committees become involved in union-type matters such as wages, working conditions, and hours of work, they may be more likely to be viewed as basically unions. Thus, in the Electromation Corp. case decided in 1992 by the NLRB, the firm set up action committees to advise management regarding matters such as absenteeism/infractions, pay progression, and the attendance bonus plan. When a Teamsters local lost a certification election at this firm, the union filed an unfair labor practice suit with the NLRB. It claimed, in part, that the action committees were unlawfully dominated labor organizations. The NLRB decided in favor of the union but did not really clarify when and under what conditions participation programs might be acceptable. The issue continues to move through the NLRB and courts.

TOWARD "SAFE" PARTICIPATION PROGRAMS   For now, two experts urge employers to take these prudent steps to avoid having their employee participation programs viewed as sham unions:[106]

1. If you want to establish participation programs, involve employees in the formation of these programs to the greatest extent practical.

2. Continually emphasize to employees that the committees exist for the *exclusive purpose* of addressing such issues as quality and productivity. Stress that they are not intended to be vehicles for dealing with management on items that are generally viewed as mandatory bargaining items between unions and management, such as pay and working conditions.

3. Of course, make sure you don't try to set up such committees at the same time union organizing activities are beginning in your facility.

4. Fill the committees with volunteers rather than elected employee representatives. Also rotate membership frequently to ensure broad employee participation.

5. Participate in the day-to-day activities of the committees as little as possible. Avoid even the suspicion of unlawful interference or, worse, the perception of domination.

At Corning the union plays a major role in its team-based production program's success. Union and management signed a joint philosophical statement that they called "a partnership in the workplace." It articulates six "essential values" including "recognition of the rights of workers to participate in decisions that affect their working lives."[107] As part of its new role, the union has a hand in the content and administration of all the firm's training programs, and work redesign committees (which include shop floor workers) work on restructuring their jobs. What we may be moving toward, proposes one expert, is an era in which union-management relations are more similar to what they've traditionally been in countries like Germany and Japan, where both the workers and their unions have considerable input in how their firms are run.[108]

At other firms, new types of labor contracts, called modern operating agreements (MOA), are being signed to formalize these new, more cooperative union management arrangements. Unlike traditional union agreements, MOAs "are designed to give hourly workers a greater say in how their jobs are performed. The agreements establish work teams, decentralize decision making, include union representatives on key plant operating committees, reduce the number of job classifications, and use a pay-for-knowledge system that links employees' wage rates to the number of different operations they can perform."[109] Increasingly, in other words, the labor agreements of tomorrow will probably reflect employers' growing awareness of the need to do what it takes to win their employees' commitment.

We invite you to visit the Dessler page on the Prentice Hall Web site at **www.prenhall.com/dessler** for our on-line study guide, Internet exercises, current events, links to related Web sites, and more.

SUMMARY

1. Union membership has been alternately growing and shrinking since as early as 1790. A major milestone was the creation in 1886 of the American Federation of Labor by Samuel Gompers. Most recently the trend in unionization has been toward organizing white-collar workers, particularly since the proportion of blue-collar workers has

been declining. In any case, we saw that while wages and benefits are important factors in unionization, workers are also seeking fair, humane, and equitable treatment.

2. In addition to improved wages and working conditions, unions seek security when organizing. We discussed five possible arrangements, including the closed shop, the union shop, the agency shop, the open shop, and maintenance of membership.

3. The AFL-CIO is a national federation comprised of 109 national and international unions. It can exercise only that power it is allowed to exercise by its constituent national unions.

4. During the period of strong encouragement of unions, the Norris-LaGuardia Act and the Wagner Act were passed; these marked a shift in labor law from repression to strong encouragement of union activity. They did this by banning certain types of unfair labor practices, by providing for secret-ballot elections, and by creating the National Labor Relations Board.

5. The Taft-Hartley Act reflected the period of modified encouragement coupled with regulation. It enumerated the rights of employees with respect to their unions, enumerated the rights of employers, and allowed the U.S. president to temporarily bar national emergency strikes. Among other things, it also enumerated certain union unfair labor practices. For example, it banned unions from restraining or coercing employees from exercising their guaranteed bargaining rights. And employers were explicitly given the right to express their views concerning union organization.

6. The Landrum-Griffin Act reflected the period of detailed regulation of internal union affairs. It grew out of discoveries of wrongdoing on the part of both management and union leadership and contained a bill of rights for union members. (For example, it affirms a member's right to sue his or her union.)

7. There are five steps in a union drive and election: the initial contact, obtaining authorization cards, holding a hearing with the NLRB, the campaign, and the election itself. Remember that the union need only win a majority of the votes cast, not a majority of the workers in the bargaining unit eligible to vote.

8. There are five surefire ways to lose an NLRB election: be caught sleeping at the switch, form a committee, emphasize money and benefits, have an industry blind spot, and delegate too much to divisions. Supervisors should be trained regarding how to administer the employer's union literature and solicitation rules.

9. Bargaining collectively in good faith is the next step if and when the union wins the election. Good faith means that both parties communicate and negotiate, and that proposals are matched with counterproposals. The negotiating team is composed of union and management representatives who have prepared by researching the issues. Bargaining items are categorized as mandatory, voluntary, or illegal. The bargaining sessions go through several stages. Some hints on bargaining include do not hurry, be prepared, find out why, and be a good listener.

10. An impasse occurs when the parties aren't able to move further toward settlement. Third-party involvement—namely, arbitration, fact-finding, or mediation—is one alternative. Sometimes, though, a strike occurs. Preparing for the strike involves such steps as securing the facility, notifying all customers, and photographing the facility. Boycotts and lockouts are two other anti-impasse weapons sometimes used by labor and management.

11. Grievance handling has been called day-to-day collective bargaining. It involves the continuing interpretation of the collective bargaining agreement but usually not its renegotiation.

12. While just about any management action might lead to a grievance, the most serious actions involve discipline cases, seniority problems, actions growing out of a job eval-

uation and work assignments, and overtime and benefits. But remember that a grievance is often just a symptom; always try to find the underlying problem.

13. Most agreements contain a carefully worded grievance procedure. It may be a two-step procedure or (at the other extreme) involve six or more steps. In any case, the steps usually involve meetings between higher- and higher-echelon managers until (if agreement isn't reached) the grievance goes to arbitration. Grievance handling is as important in nonunion organizations as in those that are unionized.

KEY TERMS

closed shop   520
union shop   520
agency shop   520
open shop   520
Norris-LaGuardia Act   521
National Labor Relations Board (NLRB)   521
Wagner Act   521
Taft-Hartley Act   522
national emergency strikes   524

Landrum-Griffin Act   524
union salting   528
authorization cards   529
bargaining unit   530
collective bargaining   538
good faith bargaining   538
voluntary bargaining items   540
illegal bargaining items   540
mandatory bargaining items   540

mediation   542
arbitration   542
economic strike   542
unfair labor practice strike   542
wildcat strike   542
sympathy strike   542
corporate campaign   543
boycott   543
lockout   543
grievance   545

DISCUSSION QUESTIONS

1. Explain the structure and purpose of the AFL-CIO.
2. Discuss five sure ways to lose an NLRB election.
3. Describe important tactics you would expect the union to use during the union drive and election.
4. Briefly explain why labor law has gone through a cycle of repression and encouragement.
5. Explain in detail each step in a union drive and election.
6. What is meant by good faith bargaining? When is bargaining not in good faith?
7. Define impasse, mediation, and strike, and explain the techniques that are used to overcome an impasse.

INDIVIDUAL AND GROUP ACTIVITIES

1. You are a supervisor in a small manufacturing plant. The union contract covering most of your employees is about to expire. Working individually or in groups, discuss how to prepare for union contract negotiations.
2. You are the president of a small firm of 30 employees. Although you are not unionized, you would like to have an appeals process that would serve a purpose similar to that of a grievance procedure. Working individually or in groups, prepare a presentation describing what this appeals process might entail.

EXPERIENTIAL EXERCISE

Purpose: The purpose of this exercise is to give you practice in dealing with some of the elements of a union organizing campaign.

Required Understanding: You should be familiar with the material covered in this chapter, as well as the following incident, "An Organizing Question on Campus."

How to Set Up the Exercise/Assignments: Divide the class into groups of four or five students. Assume that you are labor relations consultants retained by the college to identify the problems and issues involved and to advise Art Tipton about what to do next. Each group will spend about 45 minutes discussing the issues and outlining those issues as well as an action plan for Tipton.

If time permits, a spokesperson from each group should list on the board the issues involved and the group's recommendations.

■ AN ORGANIZING QUESTION ON CAMPUS

Art Tipton is a human resources director of Pierce University, a private university located in a large urban city. Ruth Ann Zimmer, a supervisor in the maintenance and housekeeping services division of the university, has just come into Art's office to discuss her situation. Zimmer's division of the university is responsible for maintaining and cleaning physical facilities of the university. Zimmer is one of the department supervisors who supervises employees who maintain and clean on-campus dormitories.

In the next several minutes, Zimmer proceeds to express her concerns about a union-organizing campaign that has begun among her employees. According to Zimmer, a representative of the Service Workers Union has met with a number of the employees, urging them to sign union authorization cards. She has observed several of her employees "cornering" other employees to talk to them about joining the union and to urge them to sign union authorization (or representation) cards. Zimmer even observed this during the working hours as employees were going about their normal duties in the dormitories. Zimmer reports that a number of her employees have come to her asking for her opinions about the union. They reported to her that several other supervisors in the department had told their employees not to sign any union authorization cards and not to talk about the union at any time while they were on campus. Zimmer also reports that one of her fellow supervisors told his employees in a meeting that anyone who was caught talking about the union or signing a union authorization card would be disciplined and perhaps terminated.

Zimmer says that the employees are very dissatisfied with their wages and many of the conditions that they have endured from students, supervisors, and other staff people. She says that several employees told her that they had signed union cards because they believed that the only way university administration would pay attention to their concerns was if the employees had a union to represent them. Zimmer says that she made a list of employees whom she felt had joined or were interested in the union, and she could share these with Tipton if he wanted to deal with them personally. Zimmer closes her presentation with the comment that she and other department supervisors need to know what they should do in order to stomp out the threat of unionization in their department.

CASE INCIDENT   Disciplinary Action

FACTS   The employee, a union shop steward, was on her regularly scheduled day off at home. She was called by her supervisor and told to talk to three union members and instruct them to attend a work function called a "Quest for Quality Interaction Committee" meeting. The Quest for Quality program was a high priority with the employer for improving patient care at the facility and was part of a corporate program. The union had objected to the implementation of the Quest for Quality program and had taken the position that employees could attend the program if their jobs were threatened, but they should do so under protest and then file a grievance afterward.

On the day in question, the union shop steward, in a conference call with the three employees, told them

(continued)

that she would not order them to attend the Quest for Quality meeting, although she had been asked by her supervisor to instruct them to go to the meeting. The supervisor who had called the union shop steward had herself refused to order the employees to attend the meeting, but relied on the union shop steward to issue the order to the employees. When the union shop steward failed to order the employees to attend the meeting, the employer suspended the union shop steward for two weeks. She grieved the two-week suspension.

The union position was that the company had no authority to discipline the union shop steward on her day off for failure to give what it termed a management direction to perform the specific job function of attending a mandatory corporate meeting. The union pointed out that it was unfair that the employer refused to order the employees directly to attend the meeting but then expected the union shop steward to do so. The union argued that while it is not unusual to call a union shop steward for assistance in problem solving, the company had no right to demand that he or she replace supervisors or management in giving orders and then discipline the union official for refusing to do so.

The company position was that the opposition of the union to the Quest for Quality meetings put the employees in a position of being unable to attend the meetings without direction from the union shop steward; that the union shop steward was given a job assignment of directing the employees to attend the meeting; and

that failure to follow that job assignment was insubordination and just cause for her suspension.

Nonetheless, the union contended that the arbitrator must examine the nature of the order when deciding whether the insubordination was grounds for discipline. As to the nature of the order in this case, the employer had to demonstrate that the order was directly related to the job classification and work assignment of the employee disciplined. The refusal to obey such an order must be shown to pose a real challenge to supervisory authority. The employee did not dispute the fact that she failed to follow the orders given to her by her supervisor, but pointed out that she was not on duty at the time and that the task being given to her was not because of her job with the company but because of her status as a union shop steward.

■ QUESTIONS

1. As the arbitrator, do you think the employer had just cause to discipline the employee? Why or why not?

2. If the union's opposition to the Quest for Quality program encouraged the employees not to participate, why shouldn't the union be held responsible for directing the employees to attend?

Source: Adapted from Cheltenham Nursing and Rehabilitation Center, 89 LA 361 (1987); in Michael Carrell and Christina Heavrin, *Labor Relations and Collective Bargaining* (Upper Saddle River, NJ: Prentice Hall, 1995), pp. 100–101.

Case Application

EMPOWERMENT THROUGH ASSIGNMENT FLEXIBILITY

Paper Corporation of America (PCA) and the two unions in their mill, the International Brotherhood of Electrical Workers (IBEW) and the United Paperworkers International Union (UPI) have just negotiated a labor agreement in which the company will offer gainsharing in return for assignment flexibility. The gainsharing program will allow workers to receive quarterly payments when there are increases in productivity. A portion of any productivity gain will automatically go to the workers. It is anticipated that each worker might receive several hundred dollars annually as a result of the gainsharing program.

Assignment Flexibility (AF) means that workers who are members of one union may be asked to perform work that traditionally has been performed by a different union's members. In other words, members of the IBEW may be asked to perform tasks that have been performed only by UPI members in the past and vice versa. Assignment flexibility is controversial among union members because, in the past, unions guarded "their work" in order to insure job security. Historically, it was not acceptable for members of one union to perform the work of another. It was also not acceptable for managers to perform productive work that could be performed by a union member. The purpose of Assignment Flexibility is to make labor more productive by having available idle workers perform tasks that need to be done, but which are not being done because the workers who usually perform the tasks are otherwise employed. For example, if a machine breaks down and the operator is idle, the operator may be assigned to routine maintenance work that is usually done by the mechanic who is working on the inoperative machine. Or, the operator might be assigned to help the mechanic work on the machine, thereby freeing a second mechanic or helper for other tasks. The productivity that would have been lost due to the idle time of the operator is regained, and the gain is shared by the company and, through gainsharing, the workers.

PCA hired a facilitator and trainer to help them implement AF in their mill. A Flexibility Committee of four top managers and four union local presidents worked out a program for implementing AF, and all mill personnel received training in how to implement assignment flexibility safely and effectively.

During the training, a participative process was taught. The process empowered workers to participate in the decision to perform or not to perform AF assignments by requiring that the supervisor and the worker agree on the answer to five questions. The five questions were as follows:

1. Can the worker perform the task safely?
2. Does the worker have the knowledge, skills, and abilities to do the job?
3. Are the tools and time available?
4. Is the assignment consistent with contract language?
5. Does it make sense?

Before implementing the assignment, the supervisor and the worker had to agree that the answers to all five questions were yes. Every person in the mill was given a laminated plastic card with the questions and the directions listed. They were instructed to keep the cards with them at all times while in the mill and to refer to the card when an AF decision was to be made.

An interesting incident occurred the very first weekend that AF was officially implemented. A set-up supervisor, who was a senior operator filling in for an absent supervisor, asked two members of the shipping department to unload a truckload of materials. The job was usually done by members of the service crew, a group of unskilled laborers who did various unskilled jobs around the mill. The two shipping department employees refused to do the job because they said they

didn't feel safe doing it. In fact, according to members of the Flexibility Committee, there was nothing unsafe about the task, and the two workers had actually performed the task in the past. It was just hard work that was normally done by the unskilled service crew.

The set-up supervisor discussed the AF criteria with the two shipping department workers. He was shocked when they said they couldn't perform the job safely, but he did as he had learned in the AF training program, and did not force the two to do the job since they said they couldn't do it safely. The truck was eventually unloaded by members of the service crew.

When the regular supervisor and the department head returned to work on Monday, the set-up supervisor informed them of the incident. The department head wrote disciplinary, reprimand memoranda to both the employees saying the following:

> "This weekend you refused to carry out an assignment given by your supervisor. In particular, you refused to unload a truckload of core buggies.
>
> As you know, an employee does have the right, in fact an obligation, to refuse an assignment where he feels that he can not do the work in a safe manner. However, refusal to carry out an assignment, any assignment, regardless of the reason for refusal, is a serious matter and will be treated as such.
>
> In general, employees who refuse an assignment are to be sent home and appropriate disciplinary action taken.
>
> In this particular instance, the set-up supervisor did not make it clear that you must either do the work or go home.
>
> Therefore, the purpose of this letter is to give you written warning that a future refusal to perform any assigned work will result in your being sent home and that appropriate disciplinary action will be taken."

In addition to the reprimands, the department head sent a memorandum to the shop steward of the union of which the two shipping department workers were members. The memo stated the following:

> "This weekend we had an incident where two employees refused to carry out an assignment given by the supervisor. In particular, they refused to unload a truckload of core buggies.

(continued)

The purpose of this letter is to notify you that failure to carry out an assignment, *any assignment,* is a serious offense and will be treated as such. Employees who refuse an assignment will be sent home and appropriate disciplinary action will be taken.

In this particular instance, the set-up supervisor did not make it clear that they must either do the work or go home. Both employees have received a written warning that a future refusal to perform *any* assignment will result in being sent home and appropriate disciplinary action will be taken.

As you know, an employee does have the right, in fact an obligation, to refuse an assignment where he feels that he can not do the work in safe manner. However, whether he refuses the work *for safety reason or any other reason,* he will be sent home and appropriate disciplinary action will be taken.

Please let me know if you have any questions."

■ QUESTIONS

The Flexibility Committee was asked by both management and the union to render an opinion on the inci-dent. If you were a member of the committee, how would you answer the following questions?

1. Were the actions of the set-up supervisor correct? Why or why not?

2. Were the actions of the two shipping department workers correct? Why or why not?

3. Were the actions of the department head correct? Why or why not?

4. What would have been the correct way for each of the above parties to act?

5. Do you think this incident will affect the successful use of AF in the mill? Why or why not?

6. What effects do you think successful use of allowing workers to participate in decision making will have on empowerment and the organizational culture of PCA in the long term?

7. What does this case tell us about implementing change, particularly empowerment, in organizations?

Source: Adapted from John E. Oliver, Valdosta State University, Valdosta, GA.

NOTES

1. "Union Membership Fell Again in 1997," *BNA Bulletin to Management,* February 26, 1998, p. 60.

2. Ibid.

3. "Union Membership Around the World," *BNA Bulletin to Management,* November 13, 1997, pp. 364–365.

4. "Union Membership Fell Again in 1997," *BNA Bulletin to Management,* op. cit, p. 60.

5. "Beyond Unions: A Revolution in Employee Rights is in the Making," *Business Week,* July 8, 1985, p. 72; Bureau of National Affairs, "Union Membership in 1988," *Bulletin to Management,* April 13, 1989. See also Timothy Koeller, "Union Activity and the Decline in American Trade Union Membership," *Journal of Labor Research,* Vol. 15, no. 1 (Winter 1994), pp. 19–32.

6. "Union Membership and Earnings," *BNA Bulletin to Management,* February 13, 1997, pp. 52–53; "Union Membership Fell Again in 1997," *BNA Bulletin to Management,* February 26, 1998, p. 60.

7. William Wiatrowski, "Employee Benefits for Union and Nonunion Workers," *Monthly Labor Review* (February 1994), pp. 34–36.

8. Ibid., p. 35.

9. Nicole Harris, "Flying into a Rage?" *Business Week,* April 27, 1998, p. 119.

10. W. Clay Hammer and Frank Schmidt, "Work Attitude as Predictors of Unionization Activity," *Journal of Applied Psychology,* Vol. 63, no. 4 (1978), pp. 415–421. See also Amos Okafor, "White Collar Unionization: Why and What to Do," *Personnel,* Vol. 62, no. 8 (August 1985), pp. 17–20. See also Michael E. Gordon and Angelo DiNisi, "A Re-Examination of the Relationship Between Union Membership and Job Satisfaction," *Industrial and Labor Relations Review,* Vol. 48, no. 2 (January 1995), pp. 222–236.

11. Jeanne Brett, "Why Employees Want Unions," *Organizational Dynamics* (Spring 1980); and John Fossum, *Labor Relations* (Dallas, TX: Business Publications, 1982), p. 4.

12. Clive Fullager and Julian Barling, "A Longitudinal Test of a Model of the Antecedents and Consequences of Union Loyalty," *Journal of Applied Psychology,* Vol. 74, no. 2 (April 1989), pp. 213–227. Adrienne Eaton, Michael Gordon and Jeffrey Keefe, "The Impact

of Quality of Work Life Programs and Grievance Systems Effectiveness on Union Commitment," *Industrial and Labor Relations Review*, Vol. 45, no. 3 (April 1992), pp. 591–604.

13. See, for example, Satish Deshpande, "A Meta-Analysis of Some Determinants of Union Voting Intent," *Relations Industrielles*, Vol. 47, no. 2 (1992), pp. 334–341; and Hugh Hindman and Charles Smith, "Correlates of Union Membership and Joining Intentions in a Unit of Federal Employees," *Journal of Labor Research*, Vol. 14, no. 4 (Fall 1993), pp. 439–454. See also Lee Graf et al., "Profiles of Those Who Support Collective Bargaining in Institutions of Higher Learning and Why: An Empirical Examination," *Journal of Collective Negotiations*, Vol. 23, no. 2 (1994), pp. 151–162.

14. Warner Pflug, *The UAW in Pictures* (Detroit: Wayne State University Press, 1971), pp. 11–12.

15. See also M. Gordon and others, "Commitment to the Union: Development of a Measure and an Examination of Its Correlates," *Journal of Applied Psychology* (August 1980), pp. 474–499. For an interesting discussion of this, see Bert Klandermans, "Perceived Costs and Benefits of Participation in Union Action," *Personnel Psychology*, Vol. 39, no. 2 (Summer 1986), pp. 379–398.

16. These are based on Richard Hodgetts, *Introduction to Business* (Reading, MA: Addison-Wesley, 1977), pp. 213–214.

17. "Boardroom Reports," The Conference Board, New York, December 15, 1976, p. 6. See also "Perspectives on Employment," Research Bulletin 194, 1986, The Conference Board, 845 Third Avenue, New York, NY 10020.

18. The following material is based on Arthur Sloane and Fred Witney, *Labor Relations* (Upper Saddle River, NJ: Prentice Hall, 1977), p. 137.

19. Ibid., p. 106.

20. "Union Membership by State and Industry," *BNA Bulletin to Management*, May 29, 1997, pp. 172–173.

21. Sloane and Witney, *Labor Relations*, p. 121.

22. Commerce Clearing House. This is based on "NLRB Announces New Rule on When Unions Can Picket Stores in Malls," *Ideas and Trends*, November 2, 1988, pp. 181–184. Jean Country and Brook Shopping Centers, Inc., as nominee for Dollar Land Syndicate (Retail and Wholesale Employees Union, Local 305, AFL-CIO), 291 NLRB No. 4, Sept. 27, 1988. It should be noted that the NLRB held that in balancing the interests involved, it was essential to consider whether those seeking to exercise the right to organize on private property had reasonable alternative means of doing so without trespassing on the owner's property. Previously, the NLRB had held it must sometimes refrain from considering that issue in determining whether such organizational rights could be exercised under a balancing test. In a 1992 case, *Lechmere, Inc. v. NLRB*, "the court has been asked to decide whether an operator of a chain of New England retail stores committed an unfair labor practice when it prevented non-employee union organizers from distributing union literature on a company property." The issue again raises the question—first raised by the Supreme Court 35 years ago in *NLRB v. Babcock & Wilcox*—as to whether union organizers can be banned from company premises when they can easily contact employees "through the usual channels" of communication. On January 27, 1992, the Supreme Court decided in favor of the employer in this case. For a discussion of this, see Craig Hukill, "Labor and the Supreme Court: Significant Issues of 1991–92," *Monthly Labor Review* (January 1992), p. 35.

23. Cora Koch, "Clear Pine Mouldings: The NLRB Adopts a Stricter Standard for Strike Misconduct," *Employee Relations Law Journal*, Vol. 11, no. 3, Winter 1985/86, pp. 493–507.

24. Midland National Life Insurance Company.

25. This is based on "Taft Act Losing Teeth," a summary of a speech by Professor Charles Craver of the George Washington University, National Law Center, in Bureau of National Affairs, *Bulletin to Management*, March 16, 1989, p. 88.

26. Commerce Clearing House, "Supreme Court Ruling Gives Management Greater Power to Fill Jobs During a Strike," *Ideas and Trends*, March 23, 1989, p. 46.

27. *Lechmere Inc. v. National Labor Relations Board*, U.S. S. Ct., No. 90–970, 1/27/92.

28. "Difficulties Foreseen for Union Organizing Efforts," *BNA Bulletin to Management*, February 13, 1992, p. 42.

29. This is based on David Moberg, "Like Business, Unions Must Go Global," The *New York Times*, December 19, 1993, p. 13.

30. See William J. Glueck, "Labor Relations and the Supervisor," in M. Jean Newport, *Supervisory Management: Tools and Techniques* (St. Paul, MN: West, 1976), pp. 207–234. See also "Big Labor Tries the Soft Sell," *Business Week*, October 13, 1986, p. 126.

31. William Fulmer, "Step by Step Through a Union Election," *Harvard Business Review*, Vol. 60 (July–August 1981), pp. 94–102. For an interesting description of contract negotiations see Peter Dramton and Joseph Tracy, "The Determinants of U.S. Labor Disputes," *Journal of Labor Economics*, Vol. 12, no. 2 (April 1994) pp. 180–209.

32. *Labor Relations Consultants: Issues, Trends, Controversies* (Rockville, MD: Bureau of National Affairs, 1985), p. 7.

33. Ibid., p. 71.

34. Ibid., p. 72.

35. For a discussion, see Cory Fine, "Beware the Trojan Horse," *Workforce* (May 1998), pp. 45–51.

36. Ibid., p. 46.

37. Commerce Clearing House, "More on Management's Pre-election Campaign Strategy," *Ideas and Trends in Personnel*, August 20, 1982, pp. 158–159.

38. Fulmer, "Step by Step," p. 94. See also "An Employer May Rebut Union Misrepresentations," *BNA Bulletin to Management*, January 16, 1986, p. 17.

39. "Unions Won More Representation Elections Than They Lost in 1997," *BNA Bulletin to Management*, June 4, 1998, p. 173.

40. This section is based on Matthew Goodfellow, "How to Lose an NLRB Election," *Personnel Administrator*, Vol. 23 (September 1976), pp. 40–44. See also Mark Spagnardi, "Conducting a Successful Union-free Campaign: a Primer (Part I)," *Employee Relations Law Journal*, Vol. 24, no. 2, Fall 1998, pp. 35–51.

41. Ibid.

42. Harry Katz, "The Decentralization of Collective Bargaining: A Literature Review and Comparative Analysis," *Industrial and Labor Relations Review*, Vol. 47, no. 1 (October 1993), p. 11.

43. Frederick Sullivan, "Limiting Union Organizing Activity Through Supervisors," *Personnel*, Vol. 55 (July–August 1978), pp. 55–65. Richard Peterson, Thomas Lee, and Barbara Finnegan, "Strategies and Tactics in Union Organizing Campaigns," *Industrial Relations*, Vol. 31, no. 2 (Spring 1992), pp. 370–381. See also Alan Story, "Employer Speech, Union Representation Elections, and the First Amendment," *Berkeley Journal of Employment and Labor Law*, Vol. 16, no. 2 (1995), pp. 356–457.

44. Sullivan, "Limiting Union Organizing Activity," p. 60. See also Jonathon Segal, "Unshackle Your Supervisors to Stay Union Free," *HR Magazine*, Vol. 43, no. 7, June 1998, p. 177.

45. Ibid., pp. 62–65.

46. "Union Access to Employer's Customers Restricted," *BNA Bulletin to Management*, February 15, 1996, p. 49; "Workplace Access for Unions Hinges on Legal Issues," *BNA Bulletin to Management*, April 11, 1996, p. 113.

47. Ibid., pp. 4–65. The appropriateness of these sample rules may be affected by factors unique to an employer's operation, and they should therefore be reviewed by the employer's attorney before implementation.

48. B&D Plastics Inc., 302 NLRB No. 33, 1991, 137 LRRM 1039; discussed in "No Such Things as a Quote Free Lunch," *BNA Bulletin to Management*, May 23, 1991, pp. 153–154.

49. Charles Wentz, Jr., "Preserving a Union-Free Workplace," *Personnel*, October 1987, pp. 68–72.

50. Francis T. Coleman, "Once a Union, Not Always a Union," *Personnel Journal*, Vol. 64, no. 3 (March 1985), p. 42. See total article, pp. 42–45, for an excellent discussion of the benefits of decertification for both employers and workers. See also "Decertification: Fulfilling Unions' Destiny?" *Personnel Journal*, Vol. 66 (June 1987), pp. 144–148; "Union Election Win Rate Decreases," *BNA Bulletin to Management*, November 10, 1994, pp. 356–357.

51. "Unions Won More Representation Elections Than They Lost in 1997," *BNA Bulletin to Management*, June 4, 1998, p. 173.

52. William Fulmer, "When Employees Want to Oust Their Union," *Harvard Business Review*, Vol. 56 (March–April 1978), pp. 163–170; Coleman, "Once a Union, Not Always a Union," pp. 42–45. See also "Decertification: Fulfilling Unions' Destiny?" pp. 144–148.

53. Fulmer, "When Employees Want to Oust Their Union," p. 167. See also David Meyer and Trevor Bain, "Union Decertification Election Outcomes: Bargaining Unit Characteristics and Union Resources," *Journal of Labor Research*, Vol. 15, no. 2 (Spring 1994), pp. 117–136.

54. *The Economist*, November 17, 1979, p. 50.

55. See also William Fulmer and Tamara Gilman, "Why Do Workers Vote for Union Decertification?" *Personnel*, Vol. 58 (March–April 1981), pp. 28–35; and Shane Premeaux et al., "Managing Tomorrow's Unionized Workers," *Personnel* (July 1989), pp. 61–64, for a discussion of some important differences (in preferred management styles) between unionized and nonunionized employees.

56. Dale Yoder, *Personnel Management* (Upper Saddle River, NJ: Prentice Hall, 1972), p. 486. See also Michael Ballot, *Labor-Management Relations in a Changing Environment* (New York: John Wiley and Sons, 1992), pp. 169–425.

57. Quoted in Reed Richardson, *Collective Bargaining by Objectives* (Upper Saddle River, NJ: Prentice Hall, 1977), p. 150; adapted from Charles Morris, ed., *The Developing Labor Law* (Washington, DC: Bureau of National Affairs, 1971), pp. 271–310.

58. John Fossum, *Labor Relations*, pp. 246–250.

59. Boulwareism is the name given to a strategy, now generally held in disfavor, by which the company, based on an exhaustive study of what it thought its employees wanted, made but one offer at the bargaining table and then refused to bargain any further unless convinced by the union on the basis of new facts that its original position was wrong. The NLRB subsequently found that the practice of offering the same settlement to all units, insisting that certain parts of the package could not differ among agreements and communicating to the employees about how negotiations were going amounted to an illegal pattern. Fossum, *Labor Relations*, p. 267. See also William Cooke, Aneil Mishra, Gretchen Spreitzer,

and Mary Tschirhart, "The Determinants of NLRB Decision-Making Revisited," *Industrial and Labor Relations Review*, Vol. 48, no. 2 (January 1995), pp. 237–257.

60. Commerce Clearing House, "Drug Testing/Court Rulings," *Ideas and Trends*, January 25, 1988, p. 16.

61. Bargaining items based on Richardson, *Collective Bargaining*, pp. 113–115; bargaining stages based on William Glueck, "Labor Relations and the Supervisor," in M. Gene Newport, *Supervisory Management* (St. Paul, MN: West, 1976), pp. 207–234.

62. See also Yoder, *Personnel Management*, pp. 517–518.

63. Richardson, *Collective Bargaining*, p. 150.

64. R. E. Fells, "Developing Trust in Negotiation," *Employee Relations*, Vol. 15, no. 1 (1993), p. 35.

65. Ibid., pp. 40–41.

66. Fossum, *Labor Relations*, pp. 298–322.

67. Although considerable research has been done on the subject, it's not clear what sorts of situations precipitate impasses. At times, however, it seems that the prospect of having the impasse taken to an arbitrator actually "chills" the negotiation process. Specifically, if neither the union nor the management negotiators want to make the tough political decision to make the tough choices, they might consciously or unconsciously opt to declare an impasse knowing that the arbitrator will then have to take the heat. See Linda Babcock and Craig Olson, "The Causes of Impasses in Labor Disputes," *Industrial Relations*, Vol. 31, no. 2 (Spring 1992), pp. 348–360.

68. Fossum, *Labor Relations*, p. 312. See also Thomas Watkins, "Assessing Arbitrator Competence," *Arbitration Journal*, Vol. 47, no. 2 (June 1992), pp. 43–48.

69. Ibid., p. 317.

70. "Number of Major Strikes and Lockouts Hit New Low in 1997," *BNA Bulletin to Management*, March 12, 1998, p. 77.

71. Stephen Cabot and Gerald Cuerton, "Labor Disputes and Strikes: Be Prepared," *Personnel Journal*, Vol. 60 (February 1981), pp. 121–126. See also Brenda Sunoo, "Managing Strikes, Minimizing Loss," *Personnel Journal*, Vol. 74, no. 1 (January 1995), pp. 50ff.

72. For a discussion see Herbert Northrup, "Union Corporate Campaigns and Inside Games as a Strike Form," *Employee Relations Law Journal*, Vol. 19, no. 4 (Spring 1994), pp. 507–549.

73. Ibid., 513.

74. Ibid., p. 518.

75. For a discussion of the cost of a strike, see Woodruff Inberman, "Strikes Cost More Than You Think," *Harvard Business Review*, Vol. 57 (May–June 1979), pp. 133–138. The NLRB held in 1986 in Harter Equipment, Inc., 280 NLRB No. 71, that an employer could lawfully hire temporary replacements during the course of a lockout, in the absence of proof of specific antiunion motivation, in order to bring economic pressure to bear upon a union to support a legitimate bargaining position.

76. Clifford Koen, Jr., Sondra Hartmen, and Dinah Payne, "The NLRB Wields a Rejuvenated Weapon," *Personnel Journal* (December 1996), pp. 85–87.

77. Dale Beach, *Personnel* (New York: Macmillan, 1975), pp. 117–119.

78. Arthur A. Sloane and Fred Witney, *Labor Relations*, 5th edition (Upper Saddle River, NJ: Prentice Hall, 1977), pp. 229–231.

79. Richardson, *Collective Bargaining*, p. 184.

80. Lester Bittel, *What Every Supervisor Should Know* (New York: McGraw-Hill, 1974), p. 308, based on a study of 1,000 grievances made by the American Arbitration Association.

81. Richardson, *Collective Bargaining*.

82. This feature is based on Patricia Gwartney-Gibbs and Denise Lach, "Gender Differences in Clerical Workers' Disputes over Tasks, Interpersonal Treatment, and Emotion," *Human Relations*, Vol. 46, no. 6 (1994), pp. 611–639.

83. Ibid., p. 615.

84. Ibid., p. 633.

85. Ibid., p. 634.

86. Ibid., p. 634.

87. Ibid., p. 634.

88. J. Brad Chapman, "Constructive Grievance Handling," in M. Gene Newport, *Supervisory Management* (St. Paul, MN: West Publishing Co., 1976), pp. 253–274. For a discussion of the impact of supervisory behavior on grievance initiation, see Brian Bemmels, "The Determinants of Grievance Initiation," *Industrial and Labor Relations Review*, Vol. 47, no. 2 (January 1994), pp. 285–301.

89. See, for example, Clyde Summers, "Protecting All Employees Against Unjust Dismissal," *Harvard Business Review*, Vol. 58 (January–February 1980) pp. 132–139; and George Bohlander and Harold White, "Building Bridges: Non-Union Employee Grievance Systems," *Personnel* (July 1988), pp. 62–66.

90. See Newport, *Supervisory Management*, p. 273, for an excellent checklist.

91. For a full discussion of these and others, see Walter Baer, *Grievance Handling: 101 Guides for Supervisors* (New York: American Management Association, 1970). For an interesting discussion of major league baseball's grievance arbitration system, see Glenn Wong, "Major League Baseball's Grievance Arbitration System: A Comparison with Non-sport Industry," *Labor Law Journal*, Vol. 38, no. 2 (February 1987), pp. 84–99.

92. "AFL-CIO Launching New Strategy to Win Over Nonunion Workers," *Compensation and Benefits Review*, Vol. 18, no. 5 (September–October 1986), p. 8; Shane R. Premeaux, R. Wayne Moody, and Art Bethke, "Decertification: Fulfilling Unions' Destiny?" *Personnel Journal*, Vol. 66, no. 6 (June 1987), p. 144; and Peter A. Susser, "The Labor Impact of Deregulation," *Employment Relations Today*, Vol. 13, no. 2 (Summer 1986), pp. 117–123 and William Moore, "The Determinants and Effects of Right to Work Laws: A Review of the Recent Literature," *Journal of Labor Research*, Vol. 19, no. 3, Summer 1998, pp. 445–469.

93. "Beyond Unions," pp. 72–77.

94. Dennis Chamot, "Unions Need to Confront the Results of New Technology," *Monthly Labor Review* (August 1987), p. 45.

95. "The Battle for Corporate Control," *Business Week*, May 18, 1987, p. 107.

96. See, for example, Dominic Bencivenga, "Employee-Owners Help Bolster the Bottom Line," *HRMagazine* (February 1997), pp. 79–83.

97. Sar Levitan and Frank Gallo, "Collective Bargaining and Private Sector Employment," *Monthly Labor Review* (September 1989), pp. 24–33; Charles Craver, "The American Labor Movement in the Year 2000," *Business Horizons*, November–December 1993,

pp. 64–69; and Barbara Ettorre, "Will Unions Survive?" *Management Review* (August 1993), pp. 9–15.

98. Thomas Kochan, Harry Katz, and Nancy Mower, *Worker Participation and American Unions: Threat or Opportunity* (Kalamazoo, MI: W. E. Upjohn, 1984). See also Lowell Turner, "Participation, Democracy, and Efficiency in the U.S. Workplace," *Industrial Relations Journal*, Vol. 28, no. 4, December 1997, pp. 309–313.

99. Nil Verma, "Employee Involvement Programs: Do They Alter Worker Affinity Towards Unions?" Proceedings of the 39th Annual Meetings, New Orleans, December 1986 (Madison, WI: Industrial Relations Research Association, 1987), pp. 306–312.

100. Adrienne Eaton, "The Extent and Determinants of Local Union Control of Participative Programs," *Industrial and Labor Relations Review*, Vol. 43, no. 5 (1990), pp. 604–620.

101. Adrienne Eaton, Michael Gordon, and Jeffrey Keefe, "The Impact of Quality of Work Life Programs and Grievance System Effectiveness on Union Commitment," *Industrial and Labor Relations Review*, Vol. 45, no. 3 (April 1992), p. 591. See also Keith Knauss and Michael Matuszak, "An Anti-Union Corporate Culture and Quality Improvement Programs," *Labor Studies Journal*, Vol. 19, no. 3 (Fall 1994), pp. 21–39.

102. This is based on Kenneth Jenero and Christopher Lyons, "Employee Participation Programs: Prudent or Prohibited?" *Employee Relations Law Journal*, Vol. 17, no. 4 (Spring 1992), pp. 535–566. See also Edward Cohen-Rosenthal and Cynthia Burton, "Improving Organizational Quality by Forging the Best Union-Management Relationship," *National Productivity Review*, Vol. 13, no. 2 (Spring 1994), pp. 215–231.

103. "Union Fights Team Program at UPS," *BNA Bulletin to Management*, March 14, 1996, p. 88.

104. Jenero and Lyons, "Employee Participation Programs," p. 539.

105. See Ibid., p. 551, and Mary Pivec and Howard Robbins, "Employee Involvement Remains Controversial," *HR Magazine*, Vol. 41, no. 11, November 1996, pp. 145–150.

106. These are based on Ibid., pp. 564–565. See also "Fallout from Electromation," *BNA Bulletin to Management*, March 4, 1993, p. 65; and Bob Smith, "Employee Committee or Labor Union," *Management Review*.

107. For a discussion of this, see John Hoerr, "What Should Unions Do?" *Harvard Business Review* (May–June 1991), pp. 30–45. See also Roy Marshall, "The Future Role of Government in Industrial Relations," *Industrial Relations*, Vol. 31, no. 1 (Winter 1992), pp. 31–49.

108. Ibid., pp. 42–43; for an additional view on this topic, see David Blanchflower and Richard Freeman, "Unionism in the United States and Other Advanced OECD Countries," *Industrial Relations*, Vol. 31, no. 1 (Winter 1992), pp. 56–79.

109. "New Agreements Improve Labor Relations," *Bulletin to Management*, September 5, 1991, p. 279; and Joseph D. Reid, "Future Unions," *Industrial Relations*, Vol. 31, no. 1 (Winter 1992), pp. 122–136. For another view see George Bohlander and Marshall Campbell, "Forging a Labor-Management Partnership: The Magna Copper Experience," *Labor Studies Journal*, Vol. 18, no. 4 (Winter 1994), pp. 3–20.

15

EMPLOYEE SAFETY AND HEALTH

Weirton Steel Corporation (Weirton, W. Va.) competes in an ever-changing industrial environment and devotes a great deal of time and study to protect its employees. The company's commitment to safety reflects its broad strategy to minimize accidents and injuries in all aspects of its operations. Weirton has fully integrated safety into its overall HR process to reduce incidents as well as to lower workers compensation costs. It is the company's goal to incorporate safety into the everyday routines of its employees—not only at work, but also at home. ▲

Behavioral Objectives

When you finish studying this chapter, you should be able to:

▲ *Discuss* OSHA and how it operates.
▲ *Describe* the supervisor's role in safety.
▲ *Conduct* a safety survey.
▲ *Explain* in detail how to prevent accidents at work.
▲ *Discuss* major health problems at work and how to remedy them.

Chapter Outline

▲ Why Employee Safety and Health Are Important
▲ Basic Facts About Occupational Safety Law
▲ The role of management commitment to safety
▲ What Causes Accidents?
▲ How to Prevent Accidents
▲ Employee Health: Problems and Remedies

<table>
<tr><td>

WHY EMPLOYEE SAFETY AND HEALTH ARE IMPORTANT

</td><td>

Safety and accident prevention concerns managers for several reasons, one of which is the staggering number of work-related accidents. For example, a total of 6,218 U.S. workers recently died in workplace incidents, and there were over 6.2 million nonfatal injuries and illnesses resulting from accidents at work—roughly 8.4 cases per 100 full-time workers in the United States per year.[1] And, many safety experts believe such figures actually underestimate the true numbers. One study, published in the Journal of the American Medical Association in 1998, said workers actually suffer an estimated 13.2 million nonfatal injuries, and 862,200 illnesses annually, for a total cost of $171 billion each year.[2] Many injuries and accidents, the theory goes, just go unreported.

But even figures like these don't tell the whole story. They don't reflect the human suffering incurred by the injured workers and their families or the economic costs incurred by employers—costs that averaged over $23,000 per serious accident.[3] Nor do they reflect the legal implications. The owners of a Hamlet, North Carolina, food processing plant were sued and imprisoned because exit doors were bolted when a tragic fire occurred a few years ago; in another case a federal jury found a construction contractor criminally guilty for violating OSHA regulations after three of his employees were killed in a sewage tunnel explosion.[4] And one company president, charged with making false statements to OSHA, got a sentence of 8 to 14 months in jail.[5]

</td></tr>
</table>

<table>
<tr><td>

BASIC FACTS ABOUT OCCUPATIONAL SAFETY LAW

Occupational Safety and Health Act

The law passed by Congress in 1970 "to assure so far as possible every working man and woman in the nation safe and healthful working conditions and to preserve our human resources."

Occupational Safety and Health Administration (OSHA)

The agency created within the Department of Labor to set safety and health standards for almost all workers in the United States.

</td><td>

Purpose

The **Occupational Safety and Health Act**[6] was passed by Congress in 1970 "to assure so far as possible every working man and woman in the nation safe and healthful working conditions and to preserve our human resources." The only employers not covered by the act are self-employed persons, farms in which only immediate members of the employer's family are employed, and certain workplaces that are already protected by other federal agencies or under other statutes. Federal agencies are covered by the act, although provisions of the act usually don't apply to state and local governments in their role as employers.

Under the act's provisions, the **Occupational Safety and Health Administration (OSHA)** was created within the Department of Labor. OSHA's basic purpose is to administer the act and to set and enforce the safety and health standards that apply to almost all workers in the United States. The standards are enforced through the Department of Labor; OSHA has inspectors working out of branch offices throughout the country to ensure compliance.

OSHA Standards

OSHA operates under the "general" standard that each employer:

shall furnish to each of his [or her] employees employment and a place of employment which are free from recognized hazards that are causing or are likely to cause death or serious physical harm to his [or her] employees.

To carry out this basic mission, OSHA is responsible for promulgating legally enforceable standards. These are contained in five volumes covering general industry standards, maritime standards, construction standards, other regulations and procedures, and a field operations manual.

The standards are very complete and seem to cover just about every conceivable hazard in great detail. For example, a small part of the standard governing handrails for scaffolds is presented in Figure 15-1. OSHA regulations list not just standards but also hazard communication and training. For example, OSHA's new standard on respiratory protection—published in the *Federal Register*, January 8, 1998—includes requirements for

</td></tr>
</table>

> Guardrails not less than 2" × 4" or the equivalent and not less than 360 or more than 420 high, with a midrail, when required, of a 1" × 4" lumber or equivalent, and toeboards, shall be installed at all open sides on all scaffolds more than 10 feet above the ground or floor. Toeboards shall be a minimum of 4" in height. Wire mesh shall be installed in accordance with paragraph (a) (17) of this section.

FIGURE 15-1 *OSHA Standards Example*

Source: General Industry Standards and Interpretations, U.S. Department of Labor, OSHA (Volume 1: Revised 1989, Section 1910.28(b) (15)), p. 67.

program administration; worksite-specific procedures; requirements regarding the selection, use, cleaning, maintenance, and repair of respirators; employee training; respirator fit tests; and medical evaluations of the employees who would use the respirators.[7]

OSHA Recordkeeping Procedures

Under OSHA, employers with 11 or more employees must maintain records of occupational injuries and illnesses. Both occupational injuries and occupational illnesses must be reported. An occupational illness is any abnormal condition or disorder caused by exposure to environmental factors associated with employment. Included here are acute and chronic illnesses that may be caused by inhalation, absorption, ingestion, or direct contact with toxic substances or harmful agents. As summarized in Figure 15-2, all occupational illnesses must be reported.[8] Similarly, most occupational injuries also must be reported, specifically those injuries that result in medical treatment (other than first aid), loss of consciousness, restriction of work (one or more lost workdays), restriction of motion, or transfer to another job.[9] If an on-the-job accident occurs that results in the death of an employee or in the hospitalization of five or more employees, all employers, regardless of size, must report the accident in detail to the nearest OSHA office. A form used to report occupational injuries or illness is shown in Figure 15-3.

OSHA's recordkeeping requirements are broader than you might think because of the breadth of its definition of occupational injuries and illnesses.[10] Examples of recordable conditions include: food poisoning suffered by an employee after eating in the employer's cafeteria; colds compounded by drafty work areas; and ankle sprains that occur during voluntary participation in a company softball game at a picnic the employee was required to attend.[11] OSHA pursues recordkeeping violations during investigations, so it behooves employers to fastidiously record injuries or illnesses incurred at work.

Inspections and Citations

OSHA standards are enforced through inspections and (if necessary) citations. Today OSHA may not conduct warrantless inspections without an employer's consent. It may, however, inspect after acquiring a judicially authorized search warrant or its equivalent.[12]

INSPECTION PRIORITIES   OSHA has a list of inspection priorities. Imminent danger situations get top priority. These are conditions in which it is likely that a danger exists that can immediately cause death or serious physical harm. Second priority is given to catastrophes, fatalities, and accidents that have already occurred. (Such situations must be reported to OSHA within 48 hours.) Third priority is given to valid employee complaints of alleged violation of standards. Next in priority are periodic special-emphasis inspections aimed at high-hazard industries, occupations, or substances. Finally, random inspections and reinspections generally have last priority. Most inspections result from employee complaints.

Safety should be a foremost consideration in the workplace. One motivational device to enhance safety training and procedures is the sense of pride such "accident free" tallies signs like this can inspire.

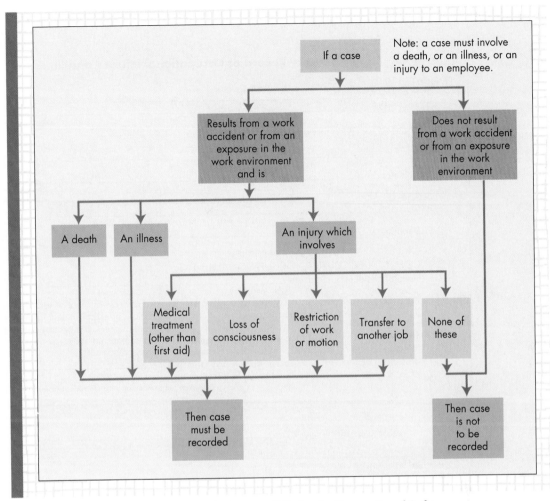

FIGURE 15-2 *What Accidents Must be Reported Under the Occupational Safety and Health Act (OSHA)*

OSHA no longer follows up every employee complaint with an inspection. The focus now is on high-priority problems.[13] Under its priority system, OSHA conducts an inspection within 24 hours when a complaint indicates an immediate danger, and within 3 working days when a serious hazard exists. For a "nonserious" complaint filed in writing by a worker or a union, OSHA will respond within 20 working days. Other nonserious complaints are handled by writing to the employer and requesting corrective action.

THE INSPECTION ITSELF The inspection itself begins when the OSHA officer arrives at the workplace.[14] He or she displays official credentials and asks to meet an employer representative. (You should always insist on seeing the officer's credentials, which include photograph and serial number.) The officer explains the visit's purpose, the scope of the inspection, and the standards that apply. An authorized employee representative is given an opportunity to accompany the officer during the inspection. Other employees will also be consulted during the inspection, and the inspector can stop and question workers (in private if necessary) about safety and health conditions. Each employee is protected under the act from discrimination for exercising his or her disclosure rights.

OSHA No. 101
Case or File No.

Form approved
OMB No. 44R 1453

Supplementary Record of Occupational Injuries and Illnesses

EMPLOYER
1. Name _____
2. Mail address _____
   (No. and street)   (City or town)   (State)
3. Location, If different from mail address _____

INJURED OR ILL EMPLOYEE
4. NAME _____ Social Security No. _____
   (First name)   (Middle name)   (Last name)
5. Home address _____
   (No. and street)   (City or town)   (State)
6. Age _____   7. Sex: Male _____ Female _____ (Check one)
8. Occupation _____
   (Enter regular job title, *not* the specific activity he/she was performing at time of injury.)
9. Department _____
   (Enter name of department or division in which the injured person is regularly employed, even
   though he/she may have been temporarily working in another department at the time of injury.)

THE ACCIDENT OR EXPOSURE TO OCCUPATIONAL ILLNESS
10. Place of accident or exposure _____
    (No. and street)   (City or town)   (State)
    If accident or exposure occurred on employer's premises, give address of plant or establishment in which
    it occurred. Do not indicate department of division within the plant or establishment. If accident occurred
    outside employer's premises at an identifiable address, give that address. If it occurred on a public
    highway or at any other place which cannot be identified by number and street, please provide place
    references locating the place of injury as accurately as possible.
11. Was place of accident or exposure on employer's premises? _____ (Yes or No)
12. What was the employee doing when injured? _____
    (Be specific. If he/she was using tools or equipment or handling.
    _____
    material, name them and tell what he/she was doing with them.)
    _____
13. How did the accident occur? _____
    (Describe fully the events which resulted in the injury or occupational illness. Tell what
    happened and how it happened. Name any objects or substances involved and tell how they were involved. Give
    full details on all factors which led or contributed to the accident. Use separate sheet for additional space.)

OCCUPATIONAL INJURY OR OCCUPATIONAL ILLNESS
14. Describe the injury or illness in detail and indicate the part of body affected. _____
    (e.g.: amputation of right index finger
    _____
    at second joint; fracture of ribs; lead poisoning; dermatitis of left hand, etc.)
15. Name the object or substance which directly injured the employee. (For example, the machine or thing
    he/she struck against or which struck him/her; the vapor or poison inhaled or swallowed; the chemical or
    radiation which irritated the skin; or in cases of strains, hernias, etc., the thing he/she was lifting, pulling,
    etc.)
    _____
    _____
16. Date of injury or initial diagnosis of occupational illness _____
                                                                    (Date)
17. Did employee die? _____ (Yes or No)
OTHER
18. Name and address of physician _____
19. If hospitalized, name and address of hospital _____

Date of report _____   Prepared by _____
Official position _____

FIGURE 15-3 *Form Used to Record Occupational Injuries and Illnesses*

Finally, after checking the premises and employer's records, the inspector holds a closing conference with the employer's representative. Here the inspector discusses what has been found in terms of apparent violations for which a citation and penalty may be issued or recommended. At this point the employer can produce records to show compliance efforts.

citations

Summons informing employers and employees of the regulations and standards that have been violated in the workplace.

CITATIONS AND PENALTIES   After the inspection report has been submitted to the OSHA office, the area director determines what citations, if any, will be issued. The **citations** inform the employer and employees of the regulations and standards that have been violated and of the time limit set for rectifying the problem. These citations must be posted at or near the place where the violation occurred. Under some circumstances, the inspector can post a citation immediately to ensure that employees receive protection in the shortest possible time.

OSHA can also impose penalties. With changes mandated by the Omnibus Budget Reconciliation Act of 1990, penalties generally range from $5,000 up to $70,000 for willful or repeat serious violations, although in practice the penalties can be far higher. For example, in a negotiated settlement, Penzoil Products agreed to pay a $1.5 million penalty to settle citations received after an explosion at its Rouseville, Pennsylvania, refinery where five employees were killed.[15] And, in fact, many cases with OSHA are settled before litigation in what attorneys call "pre-citation settlements": here the citation and agreed-on penalties are issued simultaneously, after the employers initiate negotiation settlements with OSHA.[16] There is also a maximum of $7,000 a day in penalties for failure to rectify a violation.

All told, OSHA has recently averaged about 42,000 inspections per year, cited 150,000 violations, and issued more than $98 million in proposed penalties per year.[17] OSHA's standard regarding the employer's responsibility to communicate health hazards (such as carcinogens) at work recently resulted in the highest number of citations; for instance, OSHA cited over 2,900 violations of its requirement for having a written hazard communication plan.[18]

In general, OSHA calculates penalties based on the gravity of a particular violation and usually takes into consideration such factors as the size of the business, the firm's compliance history, and the employer's good faith. In practice, OSHA must have a final order from the independent Occupational Safety and Health Review Commission (OSHRC) to enforce a penalty. While that appeals process has been speeded up of late, an employer who files a notice of contest can still drag out an appeal for years.[19]

Indeed, many employers do appeal their citations, at least to the OSHA district office, in part (reportedly) because small-business people in particular feel that OSHA may be "investing too much time and energy looking for little ways to trip up honest, safety-conscious employers and not enough going after companies that might knowingly be exposing their workers to great danger."[20]

What do experts suggest managers do when OSHA inspectors unexpectedly show up? Suggestions include:[21]

- Don't overreact—instead, be professional and do not behave in either a cavalier or unnecessarily obstructionist manner. Also remember that almost every violation is considered "serious" unless it only involves paperwork (such as record keeping).
- Don't say "take a look around": instead, the OSHA inspector should always be accompanied by a person from management.
- Be cautious about what you say: "A lot of times [the inspector] will just suggest what an employee should say [about a potential hazard]. Don't admit to anything. If you admit a violation, you're dead."[22]

- Present a positive but honest image: emphasize that you have a safety program in place, and that you do care.

- Don't argue with the OSHA inspector: answer all questions in a courteous and respectful manner.

- Appeal on time: if you plan to appeal you must do so in writing within 15 working days after receiving the citation, or you must at least file a notice that you will contest within those 15 working days. In the meantime, you can try to reach a settlement within that period.

Responsibilities and Rights of Employers and Employees

Both employers and employees have responsibilities and rights under the Occupational Safety and Health Act. Employers, for example, are responsible for meeting their duty to provide "a workplace free from recognized hazards," for being familiar with mandatory OSHA standards, and for examining workplace conditions to make sure they conform to applicable standards. Employers have the right to: seek advice and off-site consultation from OSHA; request and to receive proper identification of the OSHA compliance officer before inspection, and to be advised by the compliance officer of the reason for an inspection.

Employees also have rights and responsibilities but cannot be cited for violations of their responsibilities. They are responsible, for example, for complying with all applicable OSHA standards, for following all employer safety and health rules and regulations, and for reporting hazardous conditions to the supervisor. Employees have a right to demand safety and health on the job without fear of punishment. Employers are forbidden to punish or discriminate against workers who complain to OSHA about job safety and health hazards.

DEALING WITH EMPLOYEE RESISTANCE While employees have a responsibility to comply with OSHA standards, the fact is they often resist complying, and in most such cases the employer remains liable for any penalties.[23] This problem is typified by the

Dangerous conditions should be spotted and corrected at once to abide by OSHA requirements and to protect workers' health and safety. This woman's loose hair obviously violates safety requirements for use of the band saw.

refusal of some workers to wear hard hats as mandated by the OSHA requirements. Employers have attempted to defend themselves against penalties for such noncompliance by citing worker intransigence and their own fear of wildcat strikes and walkouts. Yet in most cases courts have held employers liable for safety violations at the workplace regardless of the fact that the violations were due to employee resistance.[24] The result is that an employer is in a difficult position. On the one hand, the courts and OSHA claim that employers must obtain employee compliance; on the other hand, doing so is often all but impossible.

Yet it is possible for employers to reduce their liability, since "courts have recognized that it is impossible to totally eliminate all hazardous conduct by employees."[25] In the event of a problem the courts may take into consideration issues such as whether the employer's safety procedures were adequate; whether the training really gave employees the understanding, knowledge, and skills required to perform their duties safely; and whether the employer really required employees to follow the procedures. However, the only surefire way to totally eliminate liability is to ensure that no safety violations occur.

There are several other tactics you can use to overcome the liability problem.[26] First, the courts have held that an employer can bargain in good faith with its union for the right to discharge or discipline any employee who disobeys an OSHA standard. Yet most unions refuse to bargain over hard hats (and many other OSHA issues) because they oppose having penalties assessed against their members. As a second alternative, one expert suggests greater use of safety disputes arbitration. The use of a formal arbitration process by aggrieved employers could provide a relatively quick and inexpensive method for resolving an OSHA-related dispute. Other employers have turned to positive reinforcement and training for gaining employee compliance; more on this shortly.

The Changing Nature of OSHA

The Occupational Safety and Health Act and Administration both have been criticized on many grounds.[27] Critics have argued, for example, that too many OSHA rules are nit-picking, and that OSHA has had an overly adverse effect on small businesses.

In response, OSHA has made several changes in its policies and procedures. Small businesses with 10 or fewer employees no longer have to file accident reports or undergo routine inspections, and the accident report itself has been simplified and condensed.[28] As mentioned, OSHA inspectors must also now obtain warrants before entering an employer's premises.[29]

Similarly, on July 16, 1998, President Clinton signed two OSHA reform bills. The overall aim is to help OSHA focus on achieving its aims through cooperation rather than through confrontation. One bill requires OSHA to focus on criteria such as reduced injuries and illnesses as indicators of OSHA compliance, rather than on such measures as numbers of inspections, or citations and fines. The other bill authorizes OSHA to fund state-administered programs to help employers identify and correct violations.[30]

On the whole, OSHA in fact seems to be moving toward achieving its aims through cooperation. One example is its Cooperative Compliance program,[31] implemented in 1998 and aimed at getting employers to voluntarily provide safe workplaces.[32]

To the chagrin of some employers, OSHA is also becoming more technologically advanced in reporting its inspection results. For example, you can find on OSHA's Worldwide Web site (www.osha.gov) easy access to your company's (or your competitor's) OSHA enforcement history. All the details are there, ranging from the results of the inspections conducted at small firms such as ABC Plumbing Company in North Carolina to those at large firms such as Capital City's ABC (part of Disney), the media giant.[33]

SMALL BUSINESS APPLICATIONS

■ OSHA and the Small Business

The OSHA inspection process in large firms differs from that in small ones in several important aspects.[34] The actual inspection time on-site is understandably much longer in larger firms, about 147 hours versus about 70 hours in smaller firms. Violations uncovered per employee are also about twice as high in large firms, 1.70 for large firms versus 0.84 for small firms. And, interestingly, once a financial penalty has been recommended by OSHA, large firms negotiated an average reduction of 4.46% while small firms negotiated an average 1.97% reduction.

Why do smaller firms manage to obtain such relatively small reductions in their fines? One likely explanation is that smaller firms believe they haven't the bargaining power required to work with OSHA inspectors and administrators to resolve violations stemming from complaints. Consequently, the results of one study show that small firms were more likely than their large-firm counterparts to cave in and just resolve violations through an informal agreement process.[35]

However, small-business owners should remember that they are actually in a good position to bargain with OSHA. While they may not have the financial clout of larger firms, they do have fewer violations per employee and lower injury rates than larger firms, and inspectors spend much less time on-site in smaller firms. Lower accident and injury rates and less time inspecting the plant should conceivably translate into lower penalties.[36]

THE ROLE OF MANAGEMENT COMMITMENT TO SAFETY

As a safety-minded manager, you must aim to instill in your workers the desire to work safely. Minimizing hazards (by ensuring that spills are wiped up, machine guards are adequate, and so forth) is important, but no matter how safe the workplace is, accidents will occur unless workers want to and do act safely. Of course, you could try closely watching each subordinate, but most managers know this won't work. In the final analysis, your best (and perhaps only) alternative is to get workers to want to work safely.[37]

Top Management Commitment

Most safety experts agree that safety commitment begins with top management. Historically, for instance, DuPont's accident rate has been much lower than that of the chemical industry as a whole. If DuPont's record had been average, it would have spent an additional $26 million in compensation and other costs, or 3.6% of its profits. To recover the difference, DuPont would have had to boost sales by about $500 million, given the company's 5.5% net return on sales.[38] This good safety record is probably partly due to an organizational commitment to safety, which is evident in the following description:

> *One of the best examples I know of in setting the highest possible priority for safety takes place at a DuPont Plant in Germany. Each morning at the DuPont Polyester and Nylon Plant the director and his assistants meet at 8:45 to review the past 24 hours. The first matter they discuss is not production, but safety. Only after they have examined reports of accidents and near misses and satisfied themselves that corrective action has been taken do they move on to look at output, quality, and cost matters.*[39]

In summary, without the full commitment of all levels of management, attempts to reduce unsafe acts by workers will meet with little success. The first-line supervisor is a critical link in the chain. If the supervisor does not take safety seriously, it's unlikely that those under him or her will either.

<table>
<tr><td>

WHAT CAUSES ACCIDENTS?

</td><td>

The Three Basic Causes of Accidents

</td></tr>
</table>

There are three basic causes of workplace accidents: chance occurrences, unsafe conditions, and unsafe acts on the part of employees. Chance occurrences (such as walking past a plate glass window just as someone hits a ball through it) contribute to accidents but are more or less beyond management's control. We will therefore focus on unsafe conditions and unsafe acts.

Unsafe Conditions and Other Work-Related Accident-Causing Factors

unsafe conditions

The mechanical and physical conditions that cause accidents.

Unsafe conditions are one main cause of accidents. They include such factors as:

- Improperly guarded equipment
- Defective equipment
- Hazardous procedures in, on, or around machines or equipment
- Unsafe storage—congestion, overloading
- Improper illumination—glare, insufficient light
- Improper ventilation—insufficient air change, impure air source[40]

The basic remedy here is to eliminate or minimize the unsafe conditions. OSHA standards address the mechanical and physical conditions that cause accidents. Furthermore, a checklist of unsafe conditions can be useful for spotting problems. One such checklist is presented in Figure 15-4; another can be found in the appendix to this chapter.

While accidents can happen anywhere, there are some high-danger zones. About one-third of industrial accidents occur around forklift trucks, wheelbarrows, and other handling and lifting areas, for example. The most serious accidents usually occur near metal and woodworking machines and saws, or around transmission machinery like gears, pulleys, and flywheels.[41] Falls on stairs, ladders, walkways, and scaffolds are the third most common cause of industrial accidents. Hand tools (like chisels and screwdrivers) and electrical equipment (extension cords, electric droplights, and so on) are other big causes of accidents.[42]

THREE OTHER WORK-RELATED ACCIDENT FACTORS   In addition to unsafe conditions, three other work-related factors contribute to accidents: the *job itself*, the *work schedule*, and the *psychological climate* of the workplace.

Certain jobs are inherently more dangerous than others. For example, the job of crane operator results in about three times more accident-related hospital visits than does the job of supervisor. Similarly, some departments' work is inherently safer than others'. A bookkeeping department usually has fewer accidents than a shipping department.

Work schedules and fatigue also affect accident rates. Accident rates usually don't increase too noticeably during the first 5 or 6 hours of the workday. But after that, the accident rate increases faster than the increase in the number of hours worked. This is due partly to fatigue and partly to the fact that accidents occur more often during night shifts.

Unfortunately, some of the most important working condition-related causes of accidents are not as obvious as these, because they involve workplace psychology. For exam-

I. GENERAL HOUSEKEEPING

Adequate and wide aisles—no materials protruding into aisles

Parts and tools stored safely after use—not left in hazardous positions that could cause them to fall

Even and solid flooring—no defective floors or ramps that could cause falling or tripping accidents

Waste cans and sand pails—safely located and properly used

Material piled in safe manner—not too high or too close to sprinkler heads

Floors—clean and dry

Firefighting equipment—unobstructed

Work benches orderly

Stockcarts and skids safely located, not left in aisles or passageways

Aisles kept clear and properly marked; no air lines or electric cords across aisles

II. MATERIAL HANDLING EQUIPMENT AND CONVEYANCES

On all conveyances, electric or hand, check to see that the following items are all in sound working conditions:

Brakes—properly adjusted

Not too much play in steering wheel

Warning device—in place and working

Wheels—securely in place; properly inflated

Fuel and oil—enough and right kind

No loose parts

Cables, hooks or chains—not worn or otherwise defective

Suspended chains or hooks conspicuous

Safely loaded

Properly stored

III. LADDERS, SCAFFOLD, BENCHES, STAIRWAYS, ETC.

The following items of major interest to be checked:

Safety feet on straight ladders

Guardrails or handrails

Treads, not slippery

No splinted, cracked, or rickety

Properly stored

Extension ladder ropes in good condition

Toeboards

IV. POWER TOOLS (STATIONARY)

Point of operation guarded

Guards in proper adjustment

Gears, belts, shafting, counterweights guarded

Foot pedals guarded

Brushes provided for cleaning machines

Adequate lighting

Properly grounded

Tool or material rests properly adjusted

Adequate work space around machines

Control switch easily accessible

Safety glasses worn

Gloves worn by persons handling rough or sharp materials

No gloves or loose clothing worn by persons operating machines

V. HAND TOOLS AND MISCELLANEOUS

In good condition—not cracked, worn, or otherwise defective

Properly stored

Correct for job

Goggles, respirators, and other personal protective equipment worn where necessary

VI. WELDING

Arc shielded

Fire hazards controlled

Operator using suitable protective equipment

Adequate ventilation

Cylinder secured

Valves closed when not in use

VII. SPRAY PAINTING

Explosion-proof electrical equipment

Proper storage of paints and thinners in approved metal cabinets

Fire extinguishers adequate and suitable; readily accessible

Minimum storage in work area

VIII. FIRE EXTINGUISHERS

Properly serviced and tagged

Readily accessible

Adequate and suitable for operations involved

FIGURE 15-4 *Checklist of Mechanical or Physical Accident-Causing Conditions*

Source: Courtesy of the American Insurance Association. From "A Safety Committee Man's Guide," 1–64.

ple, one researcher watched the official hearings regarding fatal accidents suffered by off-shore oil workers in the British sector of the North Sea.[43] From this and similar studies, it's apparent that several basically psychological aspects of the work environment can set the stage for subsequent unsafe acts. For example, a strong pressure within the organization to complete the work as quickly as possible, employees who are under a great deal of stress, and a poor safety climate—for instance, supervisors who never mention safety—are a few of the less obvious working conditions that can set the stage for accidents. Similarly, accidents occur more frequently in plants with a high seasonal layoff rate and where there is hostility among employees, many garnished wages, and blighted living conditions. Temporary stress factors such as high workplace temperature, poor illumination, and a congested workplace are also related to accident rates.[44]

What Causes Unsafe Acts (A Second Basic Cause of Accidents)

unsafe acts

Behavior tendencies and undesirable attitudes that cause accidents.

Most safety experts and managers know that it's impossible to eliminate accidents just by reducing unsafe conditions. People cause accidents, and no one has found a surefire way to eliminate **unsafe** employee **acts** such as:

- Throwing materials
- Operating or working at unsafe speeds—either too fast or too slow
- Making safety devices inoperative by removing, adjusting, or disconnecting them
- Using unsafe procedures in loading, placing, mixing, or combining
- Lifting improperly
- Distracting, teasing, abusing, startling, quarreling, and horseplay

Unsafe acts such as these can undermine even the best attempts on your part to minimize unsafe conditions. We should, therefore, discuss the causes of unsafe acts.[45]

PERSONAL CHARACTERISTICS AND ACCIDENTS   A model summarizing how personal characteristics are linked to accidents is presented in Figure 15-5. Psychologists

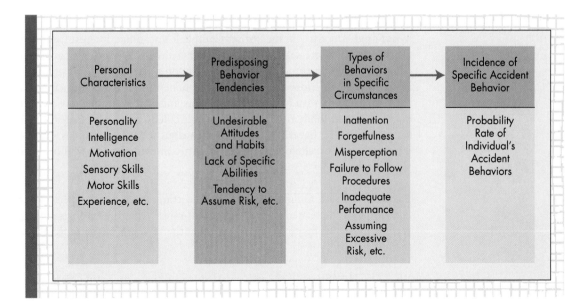

FIGURE 15-5 *How Personal Factors May Influence Employee Accident Behavior*

Ernest McCormick and Joseph Tiffin say that personal characteristics (personality, motivation, and so on) serve as the basis for certain "behavior tendencies," such as the tendency to take risks, and undesirable attitudes. These behavior tendencies in turn result in unsafe acts, such as inattention and failure to follow procedures. In turn, such unsafe acts increase the probability of someone's having an accident.

WHAT TRAITS CHARACTERIZE "ACCIDENT-PRONE" PEOPLE?   Psychologists have tried for years to determine what package of traits distinguishes those who are accident prone from those who are not.[46]

While some believe that most accident-prone people are impulsive, most experts today doubt that accident proneness is universal—that some people will have more accidents no matter what situation they are put in. Instead the consensus is that the person who is accident prone on one job may not be on a different job—that accident proneness is situational. For example, personality traits (such as emotional stability) may distinguish accident-prone workers on jobs involving risk, and lack of motor skills may distinguish accident-prone workers on jobs involving coordination. In fact, many human traits have been found to be related to accident repetition in specific situations, as the following discussion illustrates.[47]

Vision   Vision is related to accident frequency for many jobs. For example, passenger car drivers, intercity bus drivers, and machine operators who have high visual skills have fewer injuries than those who do not.[48]

Age   We also know that accidents are generally most frequent between the ages of 17 and 28, declining thereafter to reach a low in the late 50s and 60s.[49] While different patterns might be found with different jobs, this age factor seems to be a fairly general one.

Perceptual Versus Motor Skills   One researcher concludes that "where [a worker's] perceptual skill is equal to, or higher than, his motor skill, the employee is a relatively safe worker. But where the perception level is lower than the motor level, the employee is accident prone and his accident proneness becomes greater as this difference increases."[50] This theory seems to be a twist on the "look before you leap" theme; a worker who reacts more quickly than he or she can perceive is more likely to have accidents.

Vocational Interests   In the Strong-Campbell Vocational Interest Inventory (discussed in chapter 5), there are scales for, among other things, aviator and banker. One researcher equated "adventuresomeness" with the aviator scale and "cautiousness" with the banker scale. He then developed an "accident-proneness" index by subtracting the second from the first. Then in a study of both hazardous and nonhazardous jobs in a food-processing plant, he found that employees with high accident-proneness scores had higher accident rates on both the hazardous and nonhazardous jobs. The findings suggest that it seems possible to use psychological tests to identify individuals who will be accident prone on specific jobs.

Summary   These findings don't provide a complete list of the personal traits that have been found to be related to higher accident rates. What the findings do suggest is that for specific jobs it seems to be possible to identify accident-prone individuals and to screen them out.

RESEARCH INSIGHT   As you can deduce from the preceding discussions, there is usually no one single cause—whether acts or conditions—of workplace injuries; instead, accident causes tend to be multifaceted.

This is illustrated by a recent study of employed adolescents.[51] Participants were 319 adolescents recruited by the researcher through advertisements at three colleges and 37 high schools in New York state. To be eligible, the student had to be between 16 and 19 years old, currently working for pay in a formal organization at least 5 hours per week, and a full-time student. The students were asked to complete detailed questionnaires. These questionnaires measured both possible predictors of workplace injuries (such as gender) as well as the number and nature of any job injuries actually suffered.

It was clear that there were several factors or predictors related to the number of workplace injuries these adolescents suffered. For example, gender was important; adolescent boys reported more work injuries than did adolescent girls (perhaps because they also reported greater exposure to physical hazards on the job). Personality was important; for example, "negative affectivity"—the extent to which individuals experience negative moods and emotional reactivity, as measured by items such as "Often I get irritated at little annoyances"—was positively related to work injuries. Other predictors related to work injuries included: job tenure (the longer on the job, the more injuries, perhaps because more experienced workers got the jobs involving higher skill levels and greater exposure to risks); exposure to physical hazards; excessive workloads; job boredom; poor physical health; and on-the-job substance abuse.

The results of a study focusing on adolescents don't necessarily apply to working adults. However, one apparent implication of this study is that employers need comprehensive safety programs—they can't just rely on a single "magic bullet" such as trying to screen out high-risk individuals, since accidents seem to have multiple causes. With that in mind, let's turn to a discussion of how to prevent accidents.

HOW TO PREVENT ACCIDENTS

In practice, accident prevention boils down to two basic activities: (1) reducing unsafe conditions and (2) reducing unsafe acts through various means.

Reducing Unsafe Conditions

Reducing unsafe conditions is an employer's first line of defense. Safety engineers should design jobs to remove or reduce physical hazards. In addition, supervisors and managers play a role in reducing unsafe conditions. Use a checklist like the one in Figure 15-4 (page 572) or the self-inspection checklist in the appendix of this chapter to identify and remove potential hazards.

Sometimes the solution for eliminating an unsafe condition is obvious, and sometimes it's more subtle. For example, slips and falls at work are often the result of debris or a slippery substance on the floor.[52] Relatively simple remedies for problems like these include slip-reducing floor coatings, floor mats, increased lightbulb wattage, and a system to quickly block off spills. But special safety gear can also reduce the problems associated with otherwise unsafe conditions. For example, slip-resistant footwear with gridded or grooved soles can reduce slips and falls. Some other new safety and health products are presented in Figure 15-6.

Reducing Unsafe Acts Through Selection and Placement

Reducing unsafe acts is the second basic approach, and one way to do this is to screen out those who might be accident prone before they are hired. The basic technique is to identify the human trait (such as visual skill) that might be related to accidents on the specific job in question. Then determine whether scores on this trait are in fact related to accidents on the job.[53] For example:

NEW Products

Edited by Virginia Sutcliffe

New safety and health products to help you run your business more effectively.

Dual-Purpose Lenses

Dalloz Safety's Willson I/O Indoor/Outdoor lenses are designed for people who frequently move from one lighting environment to another. Wilson I/O lenses are

made of impact-resistant optical grade polycarbonate, provide 100 percent UV protection, and meet all U.S. and Canadian safety standards. I/O lenses are available in various Dalloz frames, such as Prevail, Eclipse and Santa Cruz. *Dalloz Safety, Reading, Pa.* **Circle 250**

Overboots

Fully waterproof, Norcross Safety Products' Servus SF Super-Fit overboots protect hard-to-fit work boots. Their button-and-loop closures and ex-

tra-large kick-off lugs make them easy to pull on and off, yet they fit comfortably and snugly over boots. Reinforced heels and toes, a slip-resistant outsole, a reinforced upper, and seamless molded construction offer protection and durability. Low-cut and 12 inch models are offered in sizes six to 15. *Norcross Safety Products, Rock Island, Ill.* **Circle 251**

Disposable Waste

Sharps Disposal by Mail System provides a convenient, environmentally sound disposal service for small generators of medical waste or used biohazard clean up materials. The system consists of a sharps container,

pick-up cones, a protective bag liner, pre-paid postage return box and wall mounting brackets. Available in three container sizes ranging from one to three gallons. *Sharps Compliance Inc., Houston, Texas* **Circle 252**

Washable Gloves

Valeo Inc. has developed a fully washable line of anti-vibration and material handling gloves. Several models are available in synthetic leather or neo-

prene, full- or half-fingered, wrist wrap or standard. All gloves feature sure-grip palms. *Valeo Inc., Waukesha, Wis.* **Circle 253**

Respirators

MSA is offering a free, easy-to-understand selection guide to MSA Air-Purifying Respirators. It is divided into two parts: by hazard category, by the appropriate family

of respirators and by a table of listings by industry. All MSA respirators are certified by NIOSH and comply with OSHA's revised respiratory protection standard, 29 CFR Part 1910.134. *MSA, Pittsburgh, Pa.* **Circle 254**

Safe Lifting

The Drum Gripper from T & S Equipment Co. enables the user to safely lift 30 or 55 gallon steel drums with a

fork truck. Available as a single- or double-drum gripper with capacities to 1,500 pounds. Fork pockets are 20-1/2 inches high by 7-1/2 inches wide on 13-1/2-inch centers. *T & S Equipment, Angola, Ind.* **Circle 255**

Workwear

Carhartt's Flame-Resistant workwear is made from 100 percent Nomex IIIA fiber, which becomes thicker

when near heat. Garment features include Velcro closures and zippers on bibs and overalls, a knitted headband on hood and front hand-warmer pockets. All garments meet OSHA and ASTM guidelines for flame resistance. *Carhartt Inc., Dearborn, Mich.* **Circle 256**

Vibration Reminder

Innovative Tracking Solutions Corp.'s Private Practice Vibration Reminder Disk prompts workers throughout the day to take 30-second breaks to perform conditioning exercises at their workstations to help reduce the chance of developing repetitive stress injuries. The disk can be kept in a pocket, clipped under clothes or kept inside a special skin pouch-patch. Choose reminder intervals of 60, 45,

www.ohinteractive.com

December 1998 / **Occupational Hazards** 57

FIGURE 15-6 *New Safety and Health Products to Help You Run Your Business More Effectively*

Source: Occupational Hazards, December 1998, p. 57.

Emotional stability and personality tests. Psychological tests—especially tests of emotional stability—have been used to screen out accident-prone taxicab drivers. Here the test was especially effective when administered under disturbing and distracting conditions. In this case, researchers found that taxi drivers who made five or more errors on such tests averaged 3 accidents, while those who made fewer than five errors averaged only 1.3 accidents.[54]

Measures of muscular coordination. We also know that coordination is a predictor of safety for certain jobs. In one study, more than 600 employees were divided into two groups according to test scores on coordination tests. Here it was found that the poorest quarter had 51% more accidents than those in the better three quarters.[55]

Tests of visual skills. Good vision plays a part in preventing accidents in many occupations, including driving and operating machines. In a study in a paper mill, 52 accident-free employees were compared with 52 accident-prone employees. Here the researcher found that 63% of the no-accident group passed a vision test, while only 33% of the accident group passed it.[56]

Employee reliability tests. Several studies suggest that a test such as the Employee Reliability Inventory (ERI) can help employers reduce unsafe acts at work. The ERI purportedly measures reliability dimensions such as emotional maturity, conscientiousness, safe job performance, and courteous job performance.[57] The ERI is intended to be used as a preinterview questionnaire, in other words, one used to develop follow-up questions that can be asked during interviews and reference checks.[58] While the findings of at least one study were not definitive, the addition of the inventory to the selection process did seem to be associated with reductions in work-related accidents.[59]

SUMMARY   In summary, Professor Norman Maier concludes that:

> *Of great practical importance is the fact that there is a definite relationship between these accident-proneness tests and proficiency on the job. By selecting employees who do well— that is, score low—on accident-proneness tests, managers can reduce accidents and improve the caliber of the employees at the same time.*[60]

THE ADA AND SAFETY   The Americans with Disabilities Act has particular relevance for safety-related screening decisions. For example, many employers used to inquire about applicants' worker's compensation history prior to hiring, in part to avoid both habitual worker's compensation claimants and hiring accident-prone individuals. Under the ADA it is unlawful to inquire (prior to hiring) about an applicant's worker's compensation injuries and claims. Similarly, you cannot ask applicants whether they have a disability nor require applicants to take tests that tend to screen out those with disabilities. However, you can usually ask whether an applicant has the ability to perform a job and even ask, "Do you know of any reason why you would not be able to perform the various functions of the job you are seeking?"[61]

Reducing Unsafe Acts Through Posters and Other Propaganda

Propaganda such as safety posters can help reduce unsafe acts. In one study, for example, their use apparently increased safe behavior by more than 20%.[62] On the other hand, posters are no substitute for a comprehensive safety program; instead, they should be combined with other techniques like screening and training to reduce unsafe conditions and acts. The posters should also be changed often.[63]

Reducing Unsafe Acts Through Training

Safety training can also reduce accidents. Such training is especially appropriate for new employees. You should instruct them in safe practices and procedures, warn them of potential hazards, and work on developing their predisposition toward safety. OSHA has published two booklets, "Training Requirements Under OSHA" and "Teaching Safety and Health in the Workplace," that are useful in this regard. The Suburu-Isuzu automotive plant in Lafayette, Indiana, has employees engage in a series of exercises before starting work, including touching their toes, twisting their torsos, swinging their arms, and performing other stretching exercises, to help minimize work-related injuries.[64]

Reducing Unsafe Acts Through Incentive Programs and Positive Reinforcement

While you might not expect that people need incentives to work safely (given that they are the ones who are liable to be hurt), incentive and positive reinforcement programs have been successful at reducing workplace injuries. For example, UPS has been giving its drivers safety awards since 1993.[65] At the manufacturing facilities of Clariant Corp., managers and employees are evaluated annually on meeting goals in four key areas including safety performance; their bonuses (up to 8% of gross pay) therefore depend on their safety records.[66] On the other hand, one expert warns that eliminating unsafe conditions is, first, managers' responsibility; incentives "attack unsafe acts and employee behaviors," but can't substitute for good job design and engineering controls.[67]

Positive reinforcement programs can also improve safety at work.[68] One program was instituted in a wholesale bakery that bakes, wraps, and transports pastry products to retail outlets nationwide.[69] An analysis of the safety-related conditions existing in the plant before the study suggested a number of areas that needed improvement. For example, new hires received no formal safety training, and safety was rarely mentioned on a day-to-day basis. Commercial safety posters were placed at the entrance to the work area and on a bulletin board in the dining room but often were not updated for 6 months. No single person was responsible for safety. Similarly, employees received little or no positive reinforcement for performing safely. Managers said little or nothing to employees who took the time to act safely. Although the accident rate had been climbing, many employees had yet to experience an injury from unsafe performance, so this "punishment" was also missing.

THE NEW SAFETY PROGRAM   The new safety program stressed positive reinforcement and training. A reasonable goal (in terms of observed incidents performed safely) was set and communicated to workers to ensure that they knew what was expected of them in terms of good performance.

Next came a training phase. Here employees were presented with safety information during a 30-minute training session. Employees were shown pairs of slides depicting scenes that were staged in the plant. In one transparency, for example, the wrapping supervisor was shown climbing over a conveyor; the parallel slide illustrated the supervisor walking around the conveyor. After viewing an unsafe act, employees were asked to describe what was wrong ("What's unsafe here?"). Then, once the problem had been aired, the same incident was again shown performed in a safe manner, and the safe-conduct rule was explicitly stated ("Go around, not over or under, conveyors").

At the conclusion of the training phase, the employees were shown a graph with their pretraining safety record (in terms of observed incidents performed safely) plotted.

They were encouraged to consider increasing their performance to the new safety goal for the following reasons: for their own protection; to decrease costs for the company; and to help the plant get out of last place in the safety ranking of the parent company. Then the graph and a list of safety rules (do's and don'ts) were posted in a conspicuous place in the work area.

REINFORCEMENT AND SAFETY   The graph played a central role in the study's final, "positive reinforcement" phase. Whenever observers walked through the plant collecting safety data, they posted on the graph the percentage of incidents they had seen performed safely by the group as a whole, thus providing the workers with feedback on their safety performance. Workers could then compare their current safety performance with both their previous performance and their assigned goal. In addition, supervisors praised workers when they performed selected incidents safely. Safety in the plant subsequently improved markedly.[70]

Reducing Unsafe Acts Through Top-Management Commitment

One of the most consistent research findings is that successful safety programs require a strong management commitment to safety.[71] This commitment manifests itself in top management's being personally involved in safety activities on a routine basis; giving safety matters high priority in meetings and production scheduling; giving the company safety officer high rank and status; and including safety training in new workers' training.

Reducing Unsafe Acts by Emphasizing Safety

It's the safety-minded supervisor's job to set the tone so his or her subordinates want to work safely. This involves more than talking-up safety, ensuring that spills are wiped up, or enforcing safety rules, although such things are important.[72] As important or more than what you say is what you do, so (like the DuPont manager quoted earlier), it's crucial to show by both word and deed that safety is crucial. For example,[73]

- praise employees when they choose safe behaviors; listen when employees offer suggestions, concerns, or complaints;
- be a good example, for instance, by following every safety rule and procedure;
- continuously improve and simplify plant safety, for instance by removing hazards where possible;
- visit plant areas regularly;
- maintain open safety communications, for instance by telling employees as much as possible about safety activities such as testing alarms and changing safety equipment or procedures; and
- link managers' bonuses to safety improvements. For example, Georgia-Pacific reduced its workers' compensation costs with an HR policy that forces managers to halve accidents or forfeit 30% of their bonuses.[74]

Reducing Unsafe Acts by Establishing a Safety Policy

Your safety policy should emphasize that the firm will do everything practical to eliminate or reduce accidents and injuries. It should also emphasize that accident and injury prevention are not just important but of the utmost importance at your firm.

Reducing Unsafe Acts by Setting Specific Loss Control Goals

Analyze the number of accidents and safety incidents and then set specific safety goals to be achieved. For example, safety goals can be set in terms of frequency of lost-time injuries per number of full-time employees.[75]

Reducing Unsafe Acts by Conducting Safety and Health Inspections

This means routinely inspecting all premises for possible safety and health problems, using checklists as aids. Also investigate all accidents and "near misses," and have a system in place for letting employees notify management about hazardous conditions.[76]

Reducing Unsafe Acts by Monitoring Work Overload and Stress

In one recent study "role overload" (formally defined as the degree to which the employee's performance was seen as being affected by inadequate time, training, and resources) was significantly associated with unsafe behaviors.[77] Similarly, other researchers have suggested that as work overload increases, workers are more likely to adopt more risky work methods. Given this, employers and their supervisors should monitor employees (and particularly those in relatively hazardous jobs) for signs of stress and overload.

In summary, steps to take in reducing workplace accidents include:

- Reduce unsafe conditions.
- Reduce unsafe acts through selection and other means.
- Use posters and other propaganda.
- Provide safety training.
- Use positive reinforcement.
- Emphasize top-management commitment.
- Emphasize safety.
- Establish a safety policy.
- Set specific loss control goals.
- Conduct safety and health inspections regularly.
- Monitor work overload and stress.

Safety Beyond the Plant Gate

While most employers necessarily focus on improving safety behavior and conditions at work, more and more employers find that off-work safety programs are important too. It's been estimated, for instance, that U.S. businesses pay about $400 per employee yearly to cover the health care costs and related expenses resulting from off-the-job injuries to employees and their families, and that about six million people "suffered temporary or permanent disabling injuries from off-the-job accidents in 1997."[78]

Chemical manufacturer Rohm & Haas implemented such an off-the-job safety program at all its sites in the United States. At its Deerpark, Texas, facility an off-the-job safety team, composed of 10 volunteer employees, organized a series of surveys and programs with the aim of reducing off-the-job injuries. For example, one month the safety team conducted a seatbelt check: "If employees had their seatbelts on when they drove up to the plant, they received a scratch-off lottery ticket and information on seatbelt safety."[79]

The following Global HRM feature illustrates the fact that safety management is a high priority for companies around the world.

Long drives pose their own particular dangers for truck drivers, especially at night. Hours on the road are usually regulated.

GLOBAL HRM

Safety at Saudi Petrol Chemical

Abdullah Al-Sekhan, the industrial safety and security manager for the Saudi Petrol Chemical Co. in Jubail City, Saudi Arabia, says that his company's excellent safety record is a result of the fact that "our employees are champions of safety . . ."[80]

At Mr. Al-Sekhan's company (nicknamed "Sadaf," which means seashell in Arabic) employees are involved in every part of the safety process. They serve on safety committees, develop and lead daily and monthly safety meetings, and conduct job safety analyses, for instance.

At Sadaf, safety begins with the company's top management team. Senior management representatives serve on the company's Management Health and Safety Committee. Among other things, this committee meets once a month to review incident reports, establish health and safety goals, review safety statistics, and endorse and sponsor safety programs. At the departmental level, employee volunteers serve on department health and safety committees where they similarly monitor safety performance and review departmental safety statistics.

Sadaf's "safety-first" culture is cultivated almost from the day the new employee arrives at work. For example, new employees are encouraged to participate in the safety process during their new employee orientation. Then (about 6 weeks later) they attend a 1-day orientation where company officials explain and emphasize the importance of the company's health, safety, and environmental policies and programs. Employees also participate in monthly departmental training sessions to discuss departmental safety issues and to discuss safety suggestions. The firm's employees also work with their departmental committees to conduct monthly safety audits, to review and document departmental job safety and to submit safety suggestions (about 60 suggestions are submitted per month). Employees are actually required to report every incident and near miss of a safety nature, and as a result more than 600 reports are submitted each year. The information is used to track incident trends and to enable management and departmental employees to develop safety recommendations.

Controlling Worker's Compensation Costs

Worker's compensation costs have soared.[81] While these costs are generally paid by the employer's insurance carrier, the insurance premiums themselves are proportional to the firm's worker's compensation experience rate. Thus, the more worker's compensation claims a firm has, the more the firm will pay in insurance premiums.

There are several factors in reducing worker's compensation claims:

Before the accident. The appropriate time to begin "controlling" worker's compensation claims is before the accident happens, not after. This involves taking all the steps summarized above. For example, remove unsafe conditions, and screen out employees who might be accident prone for the job in question.

After the accident. The occupational injury or illness can obviously be a traumatic event for the employee, and the way the employer handles it is important. The employee will have specific questions, such as where to go for medical help and whether he or she will be paid for any time off. It is also usually at this point that the employee decides whether to retain a worker's compensation attorney to plead his or her case. Employers should therefore provide first aid, and make sure the worker gets quick medical attention; make it clear that you are interested in the injured worker and his or her fears and questions; document the accident; file required accident reports; and encourage a speedy return to work.[82]

Facilitate the employee's return to work. In managing worker's compensation costs,

> Perhaps the most important and effective thing an employer can do to reduce costs is to develop an aggressive return-to-work program, including making light-duty work available. Surely the best solution to the current workers' compensation crisis, for both the employer and the employee, is for the worker to become a productive member of the company again instead of a helpless victim living on benefits.[83]

The following "High-Performance Organization" feature illustrates how well-designed safety programs can improve a company's performance.

THE HIGH-PERFORMANCE ORGANIZATION

Building Better, Faster, More Competitive Organizations Through HR: Safety Programs

■ Dayton Parts, Inc.—Harrisburg, PA

Prior to the 1990s, Dayton Parts, Inc. (DPI) had no worker safety program, and injuries were viewed as a natural part of manufacturing. In the early 1990s, new DPI management and high worker's compensation costs prompted DPI to aggressively pursue and manage worker safety.

The primary goal of the safety program is to increase safety awareness at DPI. The following initiatives, designed to help DPI meet its goal, are supported by a strong company commitment to safety, and an executive safety committee that meets quarterly to address current safety issues and make plans for the future.

■ An employee safety committee has been established with representatives from across the company. This group tours the plant, lists safety problems, and works with maintenance personnel to have those problems repaired.

- A "stretching" program is required for all manufacturing, distribution and service employees prior to starting production work each day, to help avoid work-related injuries.

- A "Working Safe" Incentive Program rewards safe workers. After one year without a lost-time accident, workers become eligible to win a "Safety Day" off from work in a monthly lottery, or a $100 bonus at the end of the year.

- A housekeeping committee monitors the cleanliness of the manufacturing plant. This program has evolved into a competition for the cleanest department in the plant.

- A formal safety training program includes monthly meetings where short safety videos are shown and safety issues are discussed. Longer training classes have been established for topics such as forklift operation, personal protective equipment, and back injury avoidance.

- When injuries occur, DPI now works closely with the injured employee to be sure he or she receives the necessary medical attention and returns to work when able. A case manager ensures that the injured employee sees a doctor on the approved list and accompanies the employee to the doctor's office. DPI makes weekly phone contact with the employee when the employee is not able to work. In addition, light duty jobs are created to provide productive work while employees are under injury restrictions.

In 1988, DPI had 1,000 days of lost work due to injuries. After the safety program took effect, the number of lost days dropped substantially to 91 days in 1993 and 69 days in 1994.

Source: Copyright 1998, Best Manufacturing Practices Center of Excellence.

EMPLOYEE HEALTH: PROBLEMS AND REMEDIES[84]

A number of health-related substances and problems can undermine employee performance at work. These include alcoholism, stress, asbestos, video displays, AIDS, and workplace violence.

Alcoholism and Substance Abuse

Alcoholism and substance abuse are serious and widespread problems at work.[85] While the percentage of full-time U.S. workers engaging in illegal drug use has reportedly dropped by more than half since 1985, about 15% of workers still report having used illicit drugs in the past year, 7.3% report currently using elicit drugs, and 7.4% report continued heavy alcohol use.[86] Fifty percent of alcoholics are women, 25% are white-collar workers, 45% are professional/managerial personnel, 37% are high school graduates, and 50% have completed or attended college.

Some experts estimate that as many as 50% of all "problem employees" in industry are actually alcoholics. In one auto assembly plant, 48.6% of the grievances filed over the course of 1 year were alcohol related.[87] In the United States alone, substance abusers cost employers about $30 billion annually in lost production and account for 40% of all industrial fatalities.

The effects of alcoholism on the worker and the work are severe.[88] Both the quality and quantity of the work decline sharply, and a form of "on-the-job absenteeism" occurs as efficiency declines. The alcoholic's on-the-job accidents usually don't increase significantly, apparently because he or she becomes much more cautious (but his or her effectiveness suffers as well). However, the off-the-job accident rate is three to four times higher than for nonalcoholics. Morale of other workers is affected as they have to shoulder the work of their alcoholic peer.

Recognizing the alcoholic on the job is another problem. Early symptoms such as tardiness can be similar to those of other problems and thus hard to classify. The supervisor is not a psychiatrist, and without specialized training, identifying—and dealing with—the alcoholic is difficult.

A chart showing observable behavior patterns that indicate alcohol-related problems is presented in Table 15-1. As you can see, alcohol-related problems range from tardiness in the earliest stages of alcohol abuse to prolonged unpredictable absences in its later stages.[89]

VARIOUS TECHNIQUES USED TO DEAL WITH THESE PROBLEMS For many employers, dealing with alcohol and substance abuse begins with substance abuse testing. For example, more than one-third of businesses recently reported testing applicants and/or employees for alcohol.[90] Of those administering such tests, about three-fourths of the employers test if there's reasonable cause and following an accident. About 48% of those test-

TABLE 15-1 Observable Behavior Patterns Indicating Possible Alcohol-Related Problems

STAGE	ABSENTEEISM	GENERAL BEHAVIOR	JOB PERFORMANCE
I Early	Tardiness Quits early Absence from work situations ("I drink to relieve tension")	Complaints from fellow employees for not doing his or her share Overreaction Complaints of not "feeling well" Makes untrue statements	Misses deadlines Commits errors (frequently) Lower job efficiency Criticism from the boss
II Middle	Frequent days off for vague or implausible reasons ("I feel guilty about sneaking drinks"; "I have tremors")	Marked changes Undependable statements Avoids fellow employees Borrows money from fellow employees Exaggerates work accomplishments Frequent hospitalization Minor injuries on the job (repeatedly)	General deterioration Cannot concentrate Occasional lapse of memory Warning from boss
III Late Middlle	Frequent days off; several days at a time Does not return from lunch ("I don't feel like eating"; "I don't want to talk about it"; "I like to drink alone")	Aggressive and belligerent behavior Domestic problems interfere with work Financial difficulties (garnishments, and so on) More frequent hospitalization Resignation: does not want to discuss problems Problems with the laws in the community	Far below expectation Punitive disciplinary action
IV Approaching Terminal Stage	Prolonged unpredictable absences ("My job interferes with my drinking")	Drinking on the job (probably) Completely undependable Repeated hospitalization Serious financial problems Serious family problems: divorce	Uneven Generally incompetent Faces termination or hospitalization

Note: Based on content analysis of files of recovering alcoholics in five organizations. From *Managing and Employing the Handicapped: The Untapped Potential,* by Gopal C. Pati and John I. Adkins, Jr., with Glenn Morrison (Lake Forest, IL: Brace-Park, Human Resource Press, 1981).

Source: Gopal C. Pati and John I. Adkins, Jr., "The Employer's Role in Alcoholism Assistance," Vol. 62, no. 7 (July 1983), p. 570.

ing also have random testing programs, and about 12% do regular, periodic alcohol testing of their employees.[91]

However, the real question is, what to do when an employee tests positive for alcohol or drugs? Disciplining, discharge, in-house counseling, and referral to an outside agency are the four traditional prescriptions. Traditionally, discipline short of discharge is used more often with alcoholics than for dealing with drug problems.[92]

In-house counseling, one example of an employee assistance program, is used more often in dealing with alcoholics and those with emotional disorders. In most cases the counseling is offered by the HR department or the employer's medical staff. Immediate supervisors with special training also provide counseling in many instances.

Many companies use outside agencies such as Alcoholics Anonymous, psychiatrists, and clinics to deal with the problems of alcoholism and emotional illness. Outside agencies are used less often in the case of drug problems.

In practice, of course, each employer tends to develop its own approach to dealing with substance abuse problems. For example, one HR director says, "We present the employee with the option of a mandatory professional assessment (which may result in rehab and/or counseling depending on the results of the assessment). If the employee refuses the professional assessment, employment is terminated."[93] Another, perhaps summarizing well the current thinking among employers, describes her company's policy this way:

> *Some employers have zero tolerance and terminate immediately. Some employers don't have a choice (pharmaceutical labs, for example). Others are lenient. Our policy is a three-strikes-and-you're-out process. The first step is a warning notification and permission given to us to test the employee at any time we want—for a period of five years. The second step is a mandatory substance abuse rehabilitation program at the employee's own expense . . . the third step is immediate termination for cause.[94]*

Other popular actions involve supervisory training or company policy.[95] Trice says supervisors should be trained to identify the alcoholic and the problem he or she creates. Employers should also establish a company policy. This policy should state management's position on alcohol and drug abuse and on the use and possession of illegal drugs on company premises. It should also list the methods (such as urinalysis) that might be used to determine the causes of poor performance and state the company's views on rehabilitation, including workplace counseling. Specific penalties for policy violations should be noted. This policy should then be communicated to all employees.

Supervisors should be the company's first line of defense in combating drug abuse in the workplace, but they should not try to be company detectives or medical diagnosticians. Guidelines supervisors should follow include these:

If an employee appears to be under the influence of drugs or alcohol, ask how the employee feels and look for signs of impairment such as slurred speech. An employee judged to be unfit for duty may be sent home. (See Table 15-1.)

Make a written record of your observations and follow up each incident. In addition to issuing a written reprimand, managers should inform workers of the number of warnings the company will tolerate before requiring termination.

Troubled employees should be referred to the company's employee assistance program.

Additional steps employers reportedly take to combat substance abuse on the job include *conducting workplace inspections* (searching employees for illegal substances), and *using undercover agents* (only as a last resort, according to one expert).[96]

WORKPLACE SUBSTANCE ABUSE AND THE LAW Because of the seriousness of the problem and the existence of federal law, most employers are taking additional steps to deal with alcohol and substance abuse on the job. The federal Drug-Free Workplace Act of 1988 requires employers with federal government contracts or grants to ensure a drug-free workplace by taking (and certifying that they have taken) a number of steps. For example, to be eligible for contract awards or grants, employers must agree to:

> Publish a policy prohibiting the unlawful manufacture, distribution, dispensing, possession, or use of controlled substances in the workplace.

> Establish a drug-free awareness program that informs employees about the dangers of workplace drug abuse.

> Inform employees that they are required, as a condition of employment, not only to abide by the employer's policy but also to report any criminal convictions for drug-related activities in the workplace.[97]

New U.S. Department of Transportation rules expanding drug testing in the transportation industry went into effect in 1995.[98] These rules require random breath alcohol tests as well as preemployment, postaccident, reasonable suspicion, and return to duty testing for workers in safety-sensitive jobs in transportation industries including aviation, interstate motor carrier, railroad, pipeline, and commercial marine.

Dealing with alcoholism and drugs at work does entail legal risks: Employees have sued for invasion of privacy, wrongful discharge, defamation, and illegal searches. Therefore, before implementing any drug control program, ask:

> *How will you inform workers about your substance abuse policy?* Providing employees with adequate notice of rules and procedures for handling drug-related problems is critical to avoiding wrongful discharge allegations. Use employee handbooks, bulletin board postings, pay inserts, and the like to publicize your substance abuse plans.

> *What testing, such as urinalysis, will be required of prospective and current employees?* If you decide to implement drug-screening programs, you must choose appropriate tests that include reliable procedures for analysis, verification, and retesting. The conditions under which testing may occur and the procedures for handling employees who refuse to be tested should be explained.

> *What accommodations would you make for employees who voluntarily seek treatment for drug or alcohol problems?* Since substance abuse is considered a physical handicap under federal and some state laws, you may be required to make reasonable accommodations for employees who enter alcohol or drug treatment programs.

Other factors must be considered. For example, searches on company property even without prior notice may be legal if they are conducted in a reasonable manner and avoid violating employees' privacy expectations. Similarly, conducting internal undercover investigations may be legal and even advised if there are repeated reports of employees using or selling drugs on the job. However, any such activities may trigger employee lawsuits and should be conducted only after a thorough review of their legal implications.[99]

The Problems of Job Stress and Burnout

Problems such as alcoholism and drug abuse sometimes result from stress, especially *job stress*. Here job-related factors such as overwork, relocation, and problems with customers eventually put the person under such stress that a pathological reaction such as drug abuse occurs.

There are two main sources of job stress—environmental and personal.[100] First, a variety of external, *environmental factors* can lead to job stress. These include work schedule, pace of work, job security, route to and from work, and the number and nature of customers or clients. Even noise, including people talking and telephones ringing, contributes to stress, with 54% of office workers in one recent survey reporting they were bothered often by such noise.[101]

However, no two people react to the same job in the very same way, because personal factors also influence stress. For example, Type A personalities—people who are workaholics and who feel driven to always be on time and meet deadlines—normally place themselves under greater stress than do others. Similarly, your tolerance for ambiguity, patience, self-esteem, health and exercise, and work and sleep patterns can also affect how you react to stress. Add to job stress the stress caused by nonjob problems like divorce and, as you might imagine, many workers are problems waiting to happen.

Job stress has serious consequences for both employer and employee. The human consequences of job stress include anxiety, depression, anger, and various physical consequences, such as cardiovascular disease, headaches, and accidents. For the organization, consequences include reductions in the quantity and quality of job performance, increased absenteeism and turnover, and increased grievances, and health care costs.[102] A study of 46,000 employees concluded that stress and depression may cause employees to seek medical care for vague physical and psychological problems and can in fact lead to more serious health conditions. The health care costs of the high-stress workers was 46% higher than those of their less-stressed coworkers.[103]

Yet stress is not necessarily dysfunctional. Some people, for example, work well only when under a little stress and find they are more productive as a deadline approaches. Others find that stress may result in a search that leads to a better job or to a career that makes more sense, given their aptitudes. A modest level of stress may even lead to more creativity if a competitive situation results in new ideas being generated.[104] As a rule, however, employers don't worry about the sorts of modest stress that lead to such positive consequences. Instead, and for obvious reasons, they focus on dysfunctional stress and its negative consequences.

REDUCING JOB STRESS   There are a number of things you can do to alleviate stress, ranging from commonsense remedies such as getting more sleep and eating better to more exotic remedies such as biofeedback and meditation. Finding a more suitable job, getting counseling, and planning and organizing each day's activities are other sensible responses.[105] In his book *Stress and the Manager*, Dr. Karl Albrecht suggests the following ways to reduce job stress.[106]

> Build rewarding, pleasant, cooperative relationships with as many of your colleagues and employees as you can.
>
> Don't bite off more than you can chew.
>
> Build an especially effective and supportive relationship with your boss.
>
> Understand the boss's problems and help him or her to understand yours.
>
> Negotiate with your boss for realistic deadlines on important projects. Be prepared to propose deadlines yourself, instead of having them imposed on you.
>
> Study the future. Learn as much as you can about likely coming events and get as much lead time as you can to prepare for them.
>
> Find time every day for detachment and relaxation.
>
> Take a walk around the office now and then to keep your body refreshed and alert.
>
> Make a noise survey of your office area and find ways to reduce unnecessary noise.
>
> Get away from your office from time to time for a change of scene and a change of mind.
>
> Reduce the amount of trivia to which you give your attention. Delegate routine paperwork to others whenever possible.

Limit interruptions. Try to schedule certain periods of "uninterruptibility" each day and conserve other periods for your own purposes.

Don't put off dealing with distasteful problems.

Make a constructive "worry list." Write down the problems that concern you and beside each write down what you're going to do about it, so that none of the problems will be hovering around the edges of your consciousness.

One expert recommends this three-step stress-reduction technique:[107]

- Develop awareness: "The first thing a person needs to do is take some time to ask: What's happening in my life? Am I showing signs of stress? Where's the pressure coming from?"[108]
- Adjust attitudes: Because stress reflects how someone reacts to events, "Attitude basically means recognizing that you have a choice."
- Take action: Actions to alleviate stress include those listed previously, for instance: undertaking physical activities such as exercise; using time management techniques to fight stress caused by letting tasks build up; and setting priorities.[109]

The employer and its HR specialists and supervisors can also play a role in identifying and reducing job stress. Based on a survey of 1,299 employers by one insurance company, the researchers suggest the following steps employers can take to reduce workplace stress:

Allow employees to talk freely with one another and to consult with colleagues about work issues.

Reduce personal conflicts on the job.

Ensure adequate staffing and expense budgets.

Have open communication between management and employees.

Support employee's efforts, for instance, by regularly asking how they are doing.

Provide competitive personal leave and vacation benefits.

Maintain current levels of employee benefits, since reduced benefits lead to stress.

Reduce the amount of red tape for employees.

Recognize and reward employees for their accomplishments and contributions.

Ensure effective job fit, since stress overload can result when workers are mismatched with jobs.[110] Similarly, giving employees more control over their jobs can also mediate the effects of job stress.[111]

Provide employee assistance programs including professional counseling help.[112]

Burnout

burnout

The total depletion of physical and mental resources caused by excessive striving to reach an unrealistic work-related goal.

Burnout is a phenomenon closely associated with job stress. **Burnout** has been defined as the total depletion of physical and mental resources caused by excessive striving to reach an unrealistic work-related goal.[113] Signs of impending burnout include:[114]

You are unable to relax.

You identify so closely with your activities that when they fall apart you do too.

The positions you worked so hard to attain often seem meaningless now.

You would describe yourself as a workaholic and constantly strive to obtain your work-related goals to the exclusion of almost all outside interest.

What can a burnout candidate do? Here are some suggestions:

Break your patterns. First, survey how you spend your time. Are you doing a variety of things or the same one over and over? The more well rounded your life is, the better protected you are against burnout.

Get away from it all periodically. Schedule occasional periods of introspection during which you can get away from your usual routine, perhaps alone, to seek a perspective on where you are and where you are going.

Reassess your goals in terms of their intrinsic worth. Are the goals you've set for yourself attainable? Are they really worth the sacrifices you'll have to make?

Think about your work. Could you do as good a job without being so intense or by also pursuing outside interests?

RESEARCH INSIGHT   If you're thinking of taking off on a vacation in order to eliminate your burnout, you might as well save your money, according to a recent study.[115] In this study, 76 clerks in an administrative department in the headquarters of an electronics firm in central Israel completed questionnaires measuring job stress and burnout twice before a vacation, once during the vacation, and twice after the vacation.

The clerks' burnout certainly did decline during the vacation. The problem was the burnout quickly returned to prevacation levels by the time of the second postvacation survey. At least for these 76 clerks, burnout returned partway toward its prevacation level by 3 days after the vacation, and all the way by 3 weeks after they returned to work.[116]

The good news, of course, is that burnout can apparently be reduced by removing the stressors that caused the burnout in the first place, such as by sending the employee off on a vacation. The bad news is that (without other changes) the burnout will quickly return once the vacation is over. One implication, as these researchers point out, is that minivacations during the workday—"such as time off for physical exercise, meditation, power naps, and reflective thinking"—might have a constructive effect on reducing stress and burnout.[117]

Asbestos Exposure at Work

There are four major sources of occupational respiratory diseases: asbestos, silica, lead, and carbon dioxide. Of these, asbestos has become a major concern, in part because of publicity surrounding asbestos in buildings such as schools constructed before the mid-1970s. Major efforts are now underway to rid these buildings of the cancer-causing asbestos.

OSHA standards require several actions with respect to asbestos. Companies must monitor the air whenever an employer expects the level of asbestos to rise to one-half the allowable limit. (You would therefore have to monitor if you expected asbestos levels of 0.1 fibers per cubic centimeters.) Engineering controls—walls, special filters, and so forth—are required to maintain an asbestos level that complies with OSHA standards. Respirators can only be used if additional efforts are still required to achieve compliance.

Video Display Health Problems and How to Avoid Them

The fact that many workers today must spend hours each day working with video display terminals (VDTs) is creating health problems at work. Short-term eye problems like burning, itching, and tearing as well as eyestrain and eye soreness are common complaints among video display operators. Surveys have found that 47% to 76% of operators complain of such problems, and while no permanent vision problems have surfaced yet, long-term studies are underway.

Studies by NIOSH-The National Institute for Occupational Safety and Health have addressed the possible radiation, muscular, and stress problems of working at a video display. With respect to radiation, researchers conclude that "the VDT does not present a radiation hazard to the employees working at or near a terminal."[118] Another NIOSH study concluded that pregnant women who use computer monitors don't run any greater risk of having miscarriages than do women who are not exposed to VDTs.[119]

Backaches and neckaches are widespread among display users. These often occur because employees try to compensate for display problems like glare by maneuvering into awkward body positions. Researchers also found that employees who used VDTs and had heavy workloads were prone to psychological distress like anxiety, irritability, and fatigue. There may also be a tendency for computer users to suffer from cumulative motion disorders, such as carpel tunnel syndrome, caused by repetitive use of the hands and arms at uncomfortable angles.[120]

NIOSH has therefore provided general recommendations regarding the use of VDTs. These can be summarized as follows:

1. Give employees rest breaks. The Institute recommends a 15-minute rest break after 2 hours of continuous VDT work for operators under moderate workloads and 15-minute breaks every hour for those with heavy workloads.
2. Design maximum flexibility into the work station so that it can be adapted to the individual operator. For example, use movable keyboards, adjustable chairs with midback supports, and a video display in which screen height and position are independently adjustable.
3. Reduce glare with devices such as shades over windows, terminal screen hoods properly positioned, and recessed or indirect lighting.
4. Give VDT workers a complete preplacement vision exam to ensure properly corrected vision for reduced visual strain.
5. Place the keyboard in front of the employee, tilted away with the rear portion lower than the front.
6. Place the computer mouse and mousepad as close to the user as possible, and ensure there are no obstructions on the desk that impede mouse movement.[121]
7. The height of the table or chair should allow wrists to be positioned at the same level as the elbow.
8. The monitor and typing material should be at or just below eye level, and the monitor should be a distance of 18 to 30 inches from the eyes.
9. The wrists should be able to rest lightly on a pad for support.
10. The feet should be flat on the floor, or on a footrest.[122]

Many VDT vision problems can be reduced by using the right equipment and a little common sense. As Figure 15-7 illustrates, adjustable stands, partitions, and screen filters can help minimize VDT-caused problems.[123]

AIDS and the Workplace

AIDS (Acquired Immune Deficiency Syndrome) is a disease that undermines the body's immune system, leaving the victim susceptible to a wide range of serious and fatal diseases. Starting in February 1997, government officials began announcing drops in AIDS deaths nationwide for the first time since the disease was discovered. Many AIDS patients have reportedly seen their symptoms dramatically reduced or eliminated, largely because of recently approved protease inhibitor drugs. As a result, many more people with AIDS are now contemplating a return to work.[124]

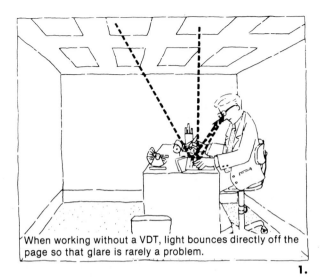

When working without a VDT, light bounces directly off the page so that glare is rarely a problem.

1.

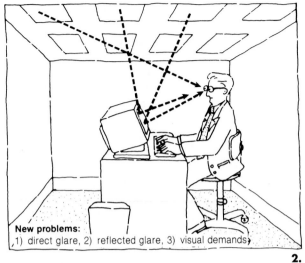

New problems:
1) direct glare, 2) reflected glare, 3) visual demands

2.

The fixed position of the VDT on the left causes light from an overhead light source to reflect off the task surface and into the operator's eyes. By installing an adjustable stand, as shown on the right, the VDT can be repositioned so reflected light misses the operator's eyes.

3.

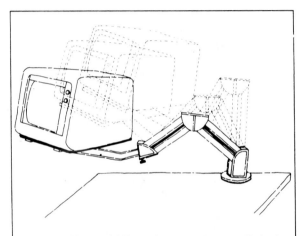

The most effective VDT stands permit almost unlimited adjustment of task position.

4.

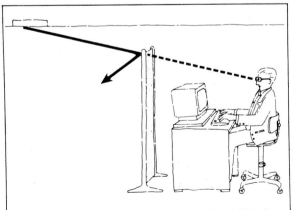

Floor-mounted partitions can be used to block light from light sources, but other corrective measures usually produce more effective results.

5.

FIGURE 15-7 *Simple Techniques for Reducing VDT Vision Problems*

Source: BNA, "Solutions to VDT Viewing Problems," *Datagraph*, November 5, 1987, pp. 356, 357.

Some of employers' most crucial AIDS-related questions concern their legal responsibilities in dealing with AIDS sufferers. While case law is still evolving on this issue, several conclusions are warranted. First, you cannot single out an employee to be tested for AIDS, because to do so would be to subject the person to discriminatory treatment under the ADA. Similarly, while you can probably require a physical exam that includes an AIDS test as a condition of employment, refusing to hire the person because of positive test results could put you at risk of a handicap discrimination suit. Mandatory leave cannot be required of a person with AIDS unless work performance has deteriorated, and preemployment inquiries about AIDS (such as inquiries about any other illnesses or disabilities) would not be advisable given the prohibitions of the Americans with Disabilities Act.

Providing sympathy and support and making reasonable accommodations to persons with AIDS, and using education and counseling to deal with the fears of the person's coworkers, are some of the concrete prescriptions for dealing with the concerns this disease will elicit at work.[125]

From a practical point of view, there are several legal issues employers must keep in mind. For one thing, all employees (including managers) should be very familiar with their obligations under the Americans with Disabilities Act and the Family and Medical Leave Acts. For example, reasonable accommodations such as providing refrigerator access for storage of medicines, and allowing medical breaks should be communicated to all supervisors and managers.[126]

From a practical point of view, your procedure for dealing with AIDS will usually begin with a statement of your firm's AIDS policy. The policy's purpose is twofold: to reassure employees regarding the impossibility of spreading AIDS through casual contact, and to lay out the legal rights of employees who are diagnosed with an AIDS-related condition. The policy, therefore, usually contains a medical overview of what we know about AIDS and lists a number of supervisors' responsibilities such as maintaining confidentiality of all medical conditions and records.[127] Points to be covered in an AIDS policy (a sample AIDS policy can be found at http://www.shrm.org/docs/whitepapers/wp3.html) might include:

Discrimination or harassment will not be tolerated.

The company will attempt to reasonably accommodate employees.

Medical information will remain confidential.

HIV-positive employees (HIV is the precursor to AIDS) should be allowed to continue working as long as they can safely and effectively perform the essential functions of their jobs.

There is no medical basis for employees to refuse to work with fellow employees or customers who are HIV-positive.

The concerns of employees who fear HIV-positive coworkers and customers should be taken seriously and should be addressed with appropriate information and counseling.[128]

Workplace Smoking

THE NATURE OF THE PROBLEM   Smoking is a serious problem for both employees and employers. The Congressional Office of Technology Assessment estimates that each employee-smoker costs an employer between $2,000 and $5,000 yearly, for instance.[129] These costs derive from higher health and fire insurance, as well as increased absenteeism and reduced productivity (which occurs when, for instance, a smoker takes a 10-minute break to finish a cigarette down the hall). Studies even show that for some reason smokers have a significantly greater risk of occupational accidents than do nonsmokers, as well as much higher absenteeism rates. In a study of Boston postal workers, this was so even when other factors were controlled such as drug use, age, exercise habits, and race.[130] In general, "smoking employees are less healthy than non-smokers, are absent more, make more and more expensive claims for health and disability benefits, and endanger coworkers who breathe smokey air."[131] Employers today are also being sued by nonsmoking employees who are (perhaps rightfully) concerned with inhaling secondhand smoke.

WHAT YOU CAN AND CANNOT DO   Suppose you want to institute a smoking ban, or a policy against hiring any smokers in the future: What are your legal rights? The answer depends on several things, including the state in which you are located, whether or not your firm is unionized, and the details of the situation. Fourteen states regulate smoking in the private-sector workplace, and in them your position would be stronger if you decided to impose a smoking ban. (States restricting private worksite smoking are Arkansas, Connecticut, Florida, Missouri, Minnesota, Montana, Nebraska, Nevada, New Jersey, New York, Utah, Vermont, Washington, and West Virginia.)[132]

There are no hard and fast rules, though. For example, instituting a smoking ban for unionized employees who formerly were allowed to smoke means altering conditions of work. It is therefore subject to collective bargaining.

In general, you can deny a job to a smoker as long as you don't use smoking as a surrogate for some other kind of discrimination.[133] A "no-smokers hired" policy does not, according to one expert, violate the Americans with Disabilities Act (since smoking is not considered a disability), and in general "employers' adoption of a no-smokers-hired" policy is not illegal under federal law. . . ."[134]

The problem arises, of course, when you try to implement smoking restrictions in a facility where you already have smokers. Here the best advice seems to be to proceed with aid of counsel or one step at a time, starting with restrictions that are not too confining.

SMOKING POLICIES   Employer smoking bans are on the rise, because of either health concerns, economic concerns, or the fear that nonsmoking employees will themselves sue for a workplace free of secondhand smoke. In one survey of 283 employers, one-quarter of the organizations polled prohibited smoking anywhere on company premises—up from 14% the previous year. (More than four out of five insurance companies and utilities banned smoking in the workplace.) Beyond that, the number of companies with some type of smoking policies has also shot up to over 60%.[135]

From a practical point of view, most employers probably should be considering some smoking restrictions. As summarized in Figure 15-8, policies can range from total prohibitions to "Smokers and nonsmokers should courteously work out a compromise among themselves."

Dealing with Violence at Work

THE NATURE OF THE PROBLEM   Violence against employees has become an enormous problem at work. Homicide is the second leading cause of job-related deaths, accounting for about 17% of fatal injuries to workers.[136] While robbery was the primary motive for homicide at work, roughly one of seven workplace homicide victims was killed by a coworker or personal associate.[137] And these numbers are just the tip of the iceberg. For example, 29 U.S. Postal Service supervisors and colleagues were slain by disgruntled postal workers in the last 10 years, but there were also 350 assaults by postal workers in one year alone.[138]

As noted, employees are not always the perpetrators. In a survey of nearly 600 full-time workers nationwide, 68% of violent attacks were attributed to clients, patients, and other strangers.[139] Coworkers accounted for about 20% of the attacks, and an employer or boss about 7%.

FIGURE 15-8

Degrees of Restrictions on Employee Smoking— A Scale

Source: J. Carroll Swart, "Corporate Smoking Policies: Today and Tomorrow," *Personnel*, August 1988, p. 62.

POLICY A

It is the policy of the company to hire nonsmokers only. Smoking is prohibited off the job, and smoking is prohibited on the job.

POLICY B

Smoking is prohibited in all areas on company premises.

POLICY C

Smoking is prohibited in all areas in company buildings.

POLICY D

Smoking is prohibited in all areas in company buildings, with few exceptions. Smoking is permitted in the smoking section of the cafeteria (or room with a similar function in your company, if there is no cafeteria); in specially designated smoking rooms (smoking lounges); and in private offices, which may be designated "smoking permitted" or "no smoking" by the occupant.

POLICY E

Smoking is prohibited in all common areas except those designated "smoking permitted." Smoking is permitted in specially designated smoking rooms (smoking lounges). In open offices and in shared workspace areas where smokers and nonsmokers work together, where smokers' and nonsmokers' preferences are in conflict, employees and management will endeavor to find a satisfactory compromise. On failure to find a compromise, the preferences of the nonsmoker will prevail.

Private offices may be designated "smoking permitted" or "no smoking" by the occupant.

POLICY F

It is the policy of the company to respect the preferences of both smokers and nonsmokers in company buildings. Where smokers' and nonsmokers' preferences are in conflict, employees and management will endeavor to find a satisfactory compromise. On failure to reach a compromise, the preferences of the nonsmoker will prevail.

POLICY G

The company places no restrictions on employee smoking (the company does not have a smoking policy).

"Smoking Permitted" is synonymous with "Designated Smoking Area." The latter term is increasing in usage.

A basic assumption is that all companies have policies prohibiting smoking in areas where there are safety and fire hazards and where sensitive equipment may be damaged. In reference to the scale above, the term "smoking policy" refers to a written statement or statements that place restrictions on smoking and intend to accommodate health concerns.

Employers should eliminate such violence on humanitarian grounds, but there are legal reasons for doing so as well. For example, an employer may be sued by the employee's victim, on the theory that the employer negligently hired or retained someone who the employer should reasonably have known could act violently. And even if the employee was not negligently hired or retained, employers may still in general be liable for employees' violent acts when the employees' actions were performed within the scope of employment.[140]

REDUCING INCIDENTS OF WORKPLACE VIOLENCE   There are several concrete steps employers can take to reduce workplace violence. These include instituting heightened security arrangements, improving employee screening, training for violence reduction, and paying more attention to retaining potentially violent employees.

HEIGHTENED SECURITY MEASURES   Heightened security measures are an employer's first line of defense against workplace violence, whether that violence comes from coworkers, customers, or outsiders. NIOSH suggests these sensible precautions for reducing the risk of workplace violence:[141] improve external lighting; use drop safes to minimize cash on hand, and post signs noting that only a limited amount of cash is on hand; install silent alarms and surveillance cameras; increase the number of staff on duty; provide staff training in conflict resolution and nonviolent response; and close establishments during high-risk hours late at night and early in the morning.[142] Employers can also issue a weapons policy that states, for instance, that regardless of their legality, firearms and other dangerous or deadly weapons cannot be brought onto the facility either openly or concealed.[143]

Because about half of workplace homicides occur in the retail industry, OSHA recently issued voluntary recommendations aimed at reducing homicides and injuries in such establishments. Particularly for late night or early morning retail workers, OSHA's suggestions include: install mirrors and improved lighting; provide silent and personal alarms; reduce store hours during high-risk periods; install drop safes and signs that indicate little cash is kept on hand; erect bullet-resistance enclosures; and increase staffing during high-risk hours.[144] Security is further discussed in the "Diversity Counts" box.

IMPROVED EMPLOYEE SCREENING   Screening out potentially explosive employees and applicants is the employer's next line of defense. At a minimum this means instituting a sound preemployment investigation. Obtain a detailed employment application and solicit an applicant's employment history, educational background, and references.[145] A personal interview, personnel testing, and a review and verification of all information provided should also be included. Sample interview questions to ask might include, for instance, "What frustrates you?" and "Who was your worst supervisor and why?"[146]

Certain background circumstances should provide a red flag indicating the need for a more in-depth background investigation of the applicant. This investigation should help screen out potentially violent employees and provide a record that everything that could have been done was done to screen out the violent employee. Red flags include:[147]

> An unexplained gap in employment
>
> Incomplete or false information on the resume or application
>
> A negative, unfavorable, or false reference
>
> Prior insubordinate or violent behavior on the job
>
> A criminal history involving harassing or violent behavior
>
> A prior termination for cause with a suspicious (or no) explanation
>
> A history of depression or significant psychiatric problems
>
> A history of drug or alcohol abuse
>
> Strong indications of instability in the individual's work or personal life as indicated, for example, by frequent job changes or geographic moves
>
> Lost licenses or accreditations[148]

WORKPLACE VIOLENCE TRAINING   Enhanced security and screening should be supplemented with workplace violence training. Several firms offer video training programs that explain what workplace violence is, identify its causes and signs, and offer tips on how to prevent it and what to do when it occurs.[149] Supervisors can also be trained to identify the clues that typically precede violent incidents. These include:[150]

> *Verbal threats.* Individuals often talk about what they may do. An employee might say, "Bad things are going to happen to so-and-so," or "That propane tank in the back could blow up easily."

DIVERSITY COUNTS

In Occupational Safety and Health

While men have more fatal occupational injuries than do women, the proportion of women who are victims of assault is much higher. Of all women who die on the job, 39% are the victims of assault, for instance, whereas only 18% of males who died at work were murdered. Violence against women in the workplace is therefore a particularly serious problem.[151]

Fatal workplace violence against women has three main sources. Over three-fourths of all females who were murdered at work were victims of random criminal violence carried out by an assailant unknown to the victim, as might occur during a robbery. The remaining criminal acts were carried out either by coworkers, family members, or previous friends or acquaintances.

There's nothing "typical" about workplace violence, but research sheds some light on the typical female victim. She is a white female (79%), in her early thirties (mean age approximately 31), working as a salesperson (31%) in a convenience store (46%) and is shot by an unknown assailant (88%) about 11:00 p.m.[152]

Workplace violence data are tragic under any circumstances, but these "typical" figures are particularly disconcerting. As one expert notes, jobs that involve serving the public, such as convenience-store employee, fast-food server, or retail store cashier are exactly the sorts of jobs that are easily filled by women, since they offer flexible hours, require minimal training, and allow women to raise children and work their way through school.[153] It is therefore particularly "shocking to think that women carry the horrible risk of being murdered while working at the very job they need to survive."[154]

Concrete security improvements including better lighting, cash drop-boxes, and similar steps are especially pertinent if such violent acts against women are to be reduced. Some firms, such as Abbott Laboratories in the Chicago area, have taken additional steps including implementing a task force on workplace violence, training supervisors to identify which employees may be violent, and establishing an employee assistance program to which a new workplace violence prevention team refers potentially violent employees.[155]

Physical actions. Troubled employees may try to intimidate others, gain access to places where they do not belong, or flash a concealed weapon in the workplace to test reactions.

Frustration. Most cases do not involve a panicked individual; a more likely scenario would involve an employee who has a frustrated sense of entitlement to a promotion, for example.

Obsession. An employee may hold a grudge against a coworker or supervisor, and some cases stem from romantic interest.[156]

A related step to take is to create a workplace culture emphasizing mutual respect and civility. The company should emphasize in word and deed that it believes deeply in these values.[157]

One opportunity to do so occurs during terminations and downsizings. As one writer puts it, "as difficult as downsizings and layoffs are, they're often made worse because they're handled insensitively—marginalizing everyone in the workplace . . . [many have been] marched into a large hall and fired. The message is that everyone is disposable." The remedy is to treat everyone with courtesy, civility, and respect—including those who are being forced to leave the organization.[158]

ENHANCED ATTENTION TO RETAINING EMPLOYEES   Employers can also enhance their procedures for evaluating which employees should or should not be retained. Particularly given the potential liability of retaining employees who subsequently commit violent acts, circumstances to beware of in deciding whether or not to retain employees include:[159]

> An act of violence on or off the job
>
> Erratic behavior evidencing a loss of perception or awareness of actions
>
> Overly defensive, obsessive, or paranoid tendencies
>
> Overly confrontational or antisocial behavior
>
> Sexually aggressive behavior
>
> Isolationist or loner tendencies
>
> Insubordinate behavior with a suggestion of violence
>
> Tendency to overreact to criticism
>
> Exaggerated interest in war, guns, violence, mass murders, catastrophes, and so on
>
> The commission of a serious breach of security
>
> Possession of weapons, guns, knives, or like items at the workplace
>
> Violation of privacy rights of others such as searching desks or stalking
>
> Chronic complaining and the raising of frequent, unreasonable grievances
>
> A retributory or get-even attitude

Use caution when firing or disciplining potentially violent employees. One expert suggests that you not make it sound as if you're accusing the employee, but instead say that according to company policy you're required to take action. Also try to emphasize something good about the employee—that he or she is loyal or puts in a lot of time at the company, for instance. Providing job counseling for terminated employees may also help get the employee over the traumatic adjustment he or she may have to make in leaving the firm.[160]

Other recommendations on how to terminate potentially violent employees, from a clinical psychologist who specializes in threat management, are summarized in Figure 15-9.

DEALING WITH ANGRY EMPLOYEES   What do you do when confronted by an angry, potentially explosive employee? Here are some suggestions:[161]

> Make eye contact.
>
> Stop what you are doing and give your full attention.
>
> Speak in a calm voice and create a relaxed environment.
>
> Be open and honest.
>
> Let the person have his or her say.
>
> Ask for specific examples of what the person is upset about.
>
> Be careful to define the problem.
>
> Ask open-ended questions and explore all sides of the issue.
>
> Listen: As one expert says, "Often, angry people simply want to be listened to. They need a supportive, empathic ear from someone they can trust."[162]

LEGAL CONSTRAINTS ON REDUCING WORKPLACE VIOLENCE   As sensible as it is to try to screen out potentially violent employees, doing so incurs the risk of liability and

FIGURE 15-9

How to Terminate Potentially Violent Employees—and Live

Source: *Workforce*, August 1998, p. 50.

1. Conduct a threat assessment to determine exactly what kind of aggressive behavior to expect. Is this person a gun enthusiast or a physically abusive person? Knowing what behavior to expect will help you plan the right security measures.
2. Carry out surveillance activities. If, after conducting your threat assessment, you know the employee is prone to violent outbursts, psychologist Manny Tau suggests putting a surveillance team on the employee up to and immediately following the termination. Thanks to surveillance at several companies, Tau has been able to stop people with guns and baseball bats from ever reaching the HR office.
3. Don't conduct the termination alone. Rather, bring in a security guard or a workplace violence expert like Tau. "Be sure to get someone who understands workplace violence," he says. "It takes less than a second to take a gun away from unskilled security personnel." Ideally, the security guard should be in plain clothes. "You don't want to escalate the situation."
4. Use an office near an exit to the building. Don't box yourself into a situation in which there's no way out.
5. Minimize the amount of furniture and things that can be thrown around. This means removing all pens, pencils, clocks and heavy books from the desk. Also, make sure you are closest to the door. Too often, HR managers sit behind their desks on the far side of the office, making it impossible to escape if something goes awry.
6. Don't wear loose clothing. This includes ID badges around the neck.
7. Treat employees with a great deal of respect. Do whatever you can to build the person's dignity. Avoid raising your voice, arguing, questioning their integrity, staring and talking in condescending tones.
8. Terminate employees on Monday morning. Conventional wisdom has it that Friday afternoon is the best time for termination. "This is the worst day of the week because the employee's anger has a chance to fester all weekend," Tau says. It's much better to terminate employees on Monday because this gives them plenty of time during the week to search for other opportunities and get on with their lives.

lawsuits. Most states have policies that encourage the employment and rehabilitation of ex-offenders; some states therefore limit the use of criminal records in hiring decisions.[163] For example, except in certain limited instances, Article 23-A of the New York Corrections Law makes it unlawful to discriminate against job applicants on the basis of their prior criminal convictions. Similarly, Title VII of the Civil Rights Act of 1964 has been interpreted by the courts as restricting employers from making employment decisions based on arrest records, since doing so may unfairly discriminate against minority groups. Aside from federal law, most states prohibit discrimination based on arrest records under any circumstances, and on prior convictions unless a direct relationship exists between the prior conviction and the job, or the employment of the individual presents an unreasonable risk to people or property.[164] And developing a "violent employee" test trait profile could end up merely describing a mental impairment and thus run afoul of the Americans with Disabilities Act.[165] Eliminating workplace violence while safely navigating the legal shoals is, therefore, a tricky business.

We invite you to visit the Dessler page on the Prentice Hall Web site at **www.prenhall.com/dessler** for our on-line study guide, Internet exercises, current events, links to related Web sites, and more.

SUMMARY

1. The area of safety and accident prevention is of concern to managers at least partly because of the staggering number of deaths and accidents occurring at work. There are also legal and economic reasons for safety programs.

2. The purpose of OSHA is to ensure every working person a safe and healthful workplace. OSHA standards are very complete and detailed and are enforced through a system of workplace inspections. OSHA inspectors can issue citations and recommend penalties to their area directors.

3. Supervisors play a key role in monitoring workers for safety. Workers in turn have a responsibility to act safely. A commitment to safety on the part of top management that is filtered down through the management ranks is an important aspect of any safety program.

4. There are three basic causes of accidents: chance occurrences, unsafe conditions, and unsafe acts on the part of employees. In addition, three other work-related factors (the job itself, the work schedule, and the psychological climate) also contribute to accidents.

5. Unsafe acts on the part of employees as a cause of accidents are to some extent the result of certain behavior tendencies on the part of employees, and these tendencies are possibly the result of certain personal characteristics.

6. Most experts doubt that there are accident-prone people who have accidents regardless of the job. Instead the consensus seems to be that the person who is accident prone in one job may not be on a different job. For example, vision is related to accident frequency for drivers and machine operators but might not be for other workers, such as accountants.

7. There are several approaches to preventing accidents. One is to reduce unsafe conditions. The other approach is to reduce unsafe acts—for example, through selection and placement, training, positive reinforcement, propaganda, and top-management commitment.

8. Alcoholism, drug addiction, stress, and emotional illness are four important and growing health problems among employees. Alcoholism is a particularly serious problem and one that can drastically lower the effectiveness of your organization. Techniques including disciplining, discharge, in-house counseling, and referrals to an outside agency are used to deal with these problems.

9. Stress and burnout are other potential health problems at work. You can reduce job stress by getting away from work for a while each day, delegating, and developing a "worry list."

10. Asbestos, video display health problems, AIDS, and workplace smoking are other employee health problems discussed in this chapter.

11. Violence against employees is an enormous problem at work. Steps that can reduce workplace violence include improved security arrangements, better employee screening, and violence-reduction training.

KEY TERMS

Occupational Safety and Health Act   563

Occupational Safety and Health Administration (OSHA)   563

citations   567

unsafe conditions   571

unsafe acts   573

burnout   588

DISCUSSION QUESTIONS

1. How would you go about providing a safer environment for your employees to work in?

2. Discuss how to minimize the occurrence of unsafe acts on the part of your employees.

3. Discuss the basic facts about OSHA—its purpose, standards, inspection, and rights and responsibilities.

4. Explain the supervisor's role in safety.

5. Explain what causes unsafe acts.

6. Describe at least five techniques for reducing accidents.

7. Analyze the legal and safety issues concerning AIDS.

8. Explain how you would reduce stress at work.

1. Working individually or in groups, answer the question, "Is there such a thing as an accident-prone person?"

2. Working individually or in groups, use the checklists in this chapter to identify safety hazards in your college or university.

EXPERIENTIAL EXERCISE

Purpose: The purpose of this exercise is to give you practice in identifying unsafe conditions.

Required Understanding: You should be familiar with material covered in this chapter, particularly that on unsafe conditions and that in Figure 15-4 and the appendix.

How to Set Up the Exercise/Instructions: Divide the class into groups of four or five students.

Assume that you are a safety committee retained by the school to identify and report on any possible unsafe conditions in and around the school building.

Each group will spend about 45 minutes in and around the building you are now in for the purpose of identifying and listing possible unsafe conditions. (Make use of the checklists in Figure 15-4 or the appendix.)

Return to the class in about 45 minutes, and a spokesperson for each group should list on the board the unsafe conditions you think you have identified. How many were there? Do you think these also violate OSHA standards? How would you go about checking?

CASE INCIDENT

The New Safety Program

Employees' safety and health are very important matters in the laundry and cleaning business. Each facility is a small production plant in which machines, powered by high-pressure steam and compressed air, work at high temperatures washing, cleaning, and pressing garments often under very hot, slippery conditions. Chemical vapors are continually produced, and caustic chemicals are used in the cleaning process. High-temperature stills are almost continually "cooking down" cleaning sol-

vents in order to remove impurities so that the solvents can be reused. If a mistake is made in this process—such as injecting too much steam into the still—a boilover occurs, in which boiling chemical solvent erupts out of the still, onto the floor, and onto anyone who happens to be standing in its way.

As a result of these hazards and the fact that chemically hazardous waste is continually produced in these stores, several government agencies (including

OSHA and the Environmental Protection Agency) have instituted strict guidelines regarding the management of these plants. For example, posters have to be placed in each store notifying employees of their right to be told what hazardous chemicals they are dealing with and what is the proper method for handling each chemical. Special waste-management firms must be used to pick up and properly dispose of the hazardous waste.

A chronic problem the owners have is the unwillingness on the part of the cleaning-spotting workers to wear safety goggles. Not all the chemicals they use require safety goggles, but some—like the hydrofluorous acid used to remove rust stains from garments—are very dangerous. The latter is kept in special plastic containers because it dissolves glass. Some of the employees feel that wearing safety goggles can be troublesome; they

are somewhat uncomfortable, and they also become smudged easily and thus cut down on visibility. As a result, it is sometimes almost impossible to get employees to wear their goggles.

■ QUESTIONS

1. How should a laundry go about identifying hazardous conditions that should be rectified?

2. Would it be advisable for a firm to set up a procedure for screening out accident-prone individuals?

3. How would you suggest that owners get all employees to behave more safely at work? Also, how would you advise them to get those who should be wearing goggles to do so?

Case Application

INTRODUCING ERGONOMICS: WHAT WENT WRONG?

Human resource manager Roger Scanlon was flipping through a business magazine on the train home one night when he read that the U.S. Postal Service had recently saved more than $10 million with a new ergonomics program in its automated mail sorting system. Roger was impressed, and the next morning he began putting together a plan for research and training in ergonomics at his own firm, Harbor Office Supply. He told his boss he was sure Harbor could realize financial savings and a reduction in absenteeism and turnover if the workplace could be made more ergonomically designed.

Roger knew that Harbor relied heavily on its many data entry clerks, particularly since several of the firm's major corporate customers had adopted stockless purchasing operations and now placed their office supply orders directly with Harbor's clerks. Over the last few years, as business increased, absenteeism has risen as well, and various work-related health complaints seemed to be on the rise. Despite brighter lighting and posters reminding employees to take frequent short breaks, the clerks often reported headaches, backaches, eyestrain, and even some cases of carpal tunnel syndrome.

Roger began by surveying the data entry supervisors to learn their observations of worker behavior. Were people wringing their wrists, stretching their necks and backs, bringing pillows and backrests from home in their attempt to make their workstations more comfortable? He asked the supervisors to question employees about the kinds of problems they were experiencing, and to give him a tally of reported problems. Next he researched the injury and illness records, looking for reasons for absenteeism and sick leave, and even for transfer requests and employee turnover.

It seemed to Roger that Harbor's records and the supervisors' reports indicated there were several ways to improve the firm's ergonomic profile and achieve the promised improvements in cost and performance. He decided to implement a two-step program that would consist of training and some office renovation. With management's approval, he developed a 2-hour training program for the entire staff that focused on showing employees how to correct their posture at their workstations, how to adjust the lighting around their computer screens, how to schedule regular breaks in their work,

(continued)

and how to use stretching and mild exercise to prevent stiffness and strain. Supervisors were given an extra training session on spotting potential health problems in their workers that could be caused by excessively repetitive work, poor posture, and inadequate light and ventilation.

The second part of the program was to include training in ergonomic principles for the purchasing staff, and the purchase and installation of new ergonomic workstations, adjustable chairs, and accessories like slanted keyboards and screen filters. Roger had even arranged for the clerks' work areas to be redesigned to put more clerks near the windows. But before this part of the plan could be put into action, Roger discovered that instead of the decrease in complaints he expected, the first few weeks after the training session had actually brought an increase in the rate of illness and injury the clerks were reporting. Roger's boss told him the CEO was now questioning whether to spend the money on the renovation and new equipment. She asked him to attend a meeting of the three of them to discuss what had gone wrong.

■ QUESTIONS

1. Did anything go wrong? If so, what?
2. What elements of Roger's plan could be improved?
3. What do you think accounts for the increase in reported illness and injury?
4. Given your answer to question 3, do you think Harbor should go ahead with the renovation?

APPENDIX 15-1

■ Self-Inspection Safety and Health Checklist

GENERAL

		ACTION
	OK	**NEEDED**

1. Is the required OSHA workplace poster displayed in your place of business as required where all employees are likely to see it? ☐ ☐
2. Are you aware of the requirement to report all workplace fatalities and any serious accidents (where 5 or more are hospitalized) to a federal or state OSHA office within 48 hours? ☐ ☐
3. Are workplace injury and illness records being kept as required by OSHA? ☐
4. Are you aware that the OSHA annual summary of workplace injuries and illnesses must be posted by February 1 and must remain posted until March 1? ☐ ☐
5. Are you aware that employers with 10 or fewer employees are exempt from the OSHA record-keeping requirements, unless they are part of an official BLS or state survey and have received specific instructions to keep records? ☐ ☐
6. Have you demonstrated an active interest in safety and health matters by defining a policy for your business and communicating it to all employees? ☐ ☐
7. Do you have a safety committee or group that allows participation of employees in safety and health activities? ☐ ☐
8. Does the safety committee or group meet regularly and report, in writing, its activities? ☐ ☐
9. Do you provide safety and health training for all employees requiring such training, and is it documented? ☐ ☐
10. Is one person clearly in charge of safety and health activities? ☐ ☐
11. Do all employees know what to do in emergencies? ☐ ☐
12. Are emergency telephone numbers posted? ☐ ☐
13. Do you have a procedure for handling employee complaints regarding safety and health? ☐ ☐

WORKPLACE

		ACTION
ELECTRICAL WIRING, FIXTURES AND CONTROLS	**OK**	**NEEDED**

1. Are your workplace electricians familiar with the requirements of the National Electrical Code (NEC)? ☐ ☐
2. Do you specify compliance with the NEC for all contract electrical work? ☐ ☐
3. If you have electrical installations in hazardous dust or vapor areas, do they meet the NEC for hazardous locations? ☐ ☐
4. Are all electrical cords strung so they do not hang on pipes, nails, hooks, etc.? ☐ ☐
5. Is all conduit, BX cable, etc., properly attached to all supports and tightly connected to junction and outlet boxes? ☐ ☐
6. Is there no evidence of fraying on any electrical cords? ☐ ☐
7. Are rubber cords kept free of grease, oil, and chemicals? ☐ ☐
8. Are metallic cable and conduit systems properly grounded? ☐ ☐
9. Are portable electric tools and appliances grounded or double insulated? ☐ ☐

Develop Your Own Checklist.

10. Are all ground connections clean and tight? ☐ ☐
11. Are fuses and circuit breakers the right type and size for the load on each circuit? ☐ ☐
12. Are all fuses free of "jumping" with pennies or metal strips? ☐ ☐

These Are Only Sample Questions.

13. Do switches show evidence of overheating? ☐ ☐
14. Are switches mounted in clean, tightly closed metal boxes? ☐ ☐
15. Are all electrical switches marked to show their purpose? ☐ ☐
16. Are motors clean and kept free of excessive grease and oil? ☐ ☐
17. Are motors properly maintained and provided with adequate overcurrent protection? ☐ ☐
18. Are bearings in good condition? ☐ ☐
19. Are portable lights equipped with proper guards? ☐ ☐
20. Are all lamps kept free of combustible material? ☐ ☐
21. Is your electrical system checked periodically by someone competent in the NEC? ☐ ☐

EXITS AND ACCESS

	OK	ACTION NEEDED

1. Are all exits visible and unobstructed? ☐ ☐
2. Are all exits marked with a readily visible sign that is properly illuminated? ☐ ☐
3. Are there sufficient exits to ensure prompt escape in case of emergency? ☐ ☐
4. Are areas with limited occupancy posted and is access/egress controlled to persons specifically authorized to be in those areas? ☐ ☐
5. Do you take special precautions to protect employees during construction and repair operations? ☐ ☐

Develop Your Own Checklist.

These Are Only Sample Questions.

FIRE PROTECTION

	OK	ACTION NEEDED

1. Are portable fire extinguishers provided in adequate number and type? ☐ ☐
2. Are fire extinguishers inspected monthly for general condition and operability and noted on the inspection tag? ☐ ☐
3. Are fire extinguishers recharged regularly and properly noted on the inspection tag? ☐ ☐
4. Are fire extinguishers mounted in readily accessible locations? ☐ ☐
5. If you have interior standpipes and valves, are these inspected regularly? ☐ ☐
6. If you have a fire alarm system, is it tested at least annually? ☐ ☐
7. Are plant employees periodically instructed in the use of extinguishers and fire protection procedures? ☐ ☐
8. If you have outside private fire hydrants, were they flushed within the last year and placed on a regular maintenance schedule? ☐ ☐
9. Are fire doors and shutters in good operating condition? ☐ ☐
   Are they unobstructed and protected against obstruction? ☐ ☐
10. Are fusible links in place? ☐ ☐
11. Is your local fire department well acquainted with your plant, location and specific hazards? ☐ ☐
12. Automatic Sprinklers:
    Are water control valves, air and water pressures checked weekly? ☐ ☐
    Are control valves locked open? ☐ ☐
    Is maintenance of the system assigned to responsible persons or a sprinkler contractor? ☐ ☐
    Are sprinkler heads protected by metal guards where exposed to mechanical damage? ☐ ☐
    Is proper minimum clearance maintained around sprinkler heads? ☐ ☐

HOUSEKEEPING AND GENERAL WORK ENVIRONMENT

	OK	ACTION NEEDED

1. Is smoking permitted in designated "safe areas" only? ☐ ☐
2. Are NO SMOKING signs prominently posted in areas containing combustibles and flammables? ☐ ☐
3. Are covered metal waste cans used for oily and paint soaked waste? ☐ ☐
   Are they emptied at least daily? ☐ ☐
4. Are paint spray booths, dip tanks, etc., and their exhaust ducts cleaned regularly? ☐ ☐
5. Are stand mats, platforms or similar protection provided to protect employees from wet floors in wet processes? ☐ ☐
6. Are waste receptacles provided, and are they emptied regularly? ☐ ☐
7. Do your toilet facilities meet the requirements of applicable sanitary codes? ☐ ☐
8. Are washing facilities provided? ☐ ☐
9. Are all areas of your business adequately illuminated? ☐ ☐
10. Are floor load capacities posted in second floors, lofts, storage areas, etc.? ☐ ☐
11. Are floor openings provided with toe boards and railings on a floor hole cover? ☐ ☐
12. Are stairways in good condition with standard railings provided for every flight having four or more risers? ☐ ☐

13. Are portable wood ladders and metal ladders adequate for their purpose, in good condition and provided with secure footing? OK ☐ ACTION NEEDED ☐

14. If you have fixed ladders, are they adequate, and are they in good condition and equipped with side rails or cages or special safety climbing devices, if required? ☐ ☐

15. For Loading Docks:

Are dockplates kept in serviceable condition and secured to prevent slipping? ☐ ☐

Do you have means to prevent car or truck movement when dockplates are in place? ☐ ☐

MACHINES AND EQUIPMENT

ACTION NEEDED

1. Are all machines or operations that expose operators or other employees to rotating parts, pinch points, flying chips, particles or sparks adequately guarded? OK ☐ ☐
2. Are mechanical power transmission belts and pinch points guarded? ☐ ☐
3. Is exposed power shafting less than 7 feet from the floor guarded? ☐ ☐
4. Are hand tools and other equipment regularly inspected for safe condition? ☐ ☐
5. Is compressed air used for cleaning reduced to less than 30 psi? ☐ ☐
6. Are power saws and similar equipment provided with safety guards? ☐ ☐
7. Are grinding wheel tool rests set to within $1/8$ inch or less of the wheel? ☐ ☐
8. Is there any system for inspecting small hand tools for burred ends, cracked handles, etc.? ☐ ☐
9. Are compressed gas cylinders examined regularly for obvious signs of defects, deep rusting or leakage? ☐ ☐
10. Is care used in handling and storing cylinders and valves to prevent damage? ☐ ☐
11. Are all air receivers periodically examined, including the safety valves? ☐ ☐
12. Are safety valves tested regularly and frequently? ☐ ☐
13. Is there sufficient clearances from stoves, furnaces, etc., for stock, woodwork, or other combustible materials? ☐ ☐
14. Is there clearance of at least 4 feet in front of heating equipment involving open flames, such as gas radiant heaters, and fronts of firing doors of stoves, furnaces, etc.? ☐ ☐
15. Are all oil and gas fired devices equipped with flame failure controls that will prevent flow of fuel if pilots or main burners are not working? ☐ ☐
16. Is there at least a 2-inch clearance between chimney brickwork and all woodwork or other combustible materials? ☐ ☐
17. For Welding or Flame Cutting Operations:

Are only authorized, trained personnel permitted to use such equipment? ☐ ☐

Have operators been given a copy of operating instructions and asked to follow them? ☐ ☐

Are welding gas cylinders stored so they are not subjected to damage? ☐ ☐

Are valve protection caps in place on all cylinders not connected for use? ☐ ☐

Are all combustible materials near the operator covered with protective shields or otherwise protected? ☐ ☐

Is a fire extinguisher provided at the welding site? ☐ ☐

Do operators have the proper protective clothing and equipment? ☐ ☐

Develop Your Own Checklist.

These Are Only Sample Questions.

MATERIALS

ACTION NEEDED

1. Are approved safety cans or other acceptable containers used for handling and dispensing flammable liquids? OK ☐ ☐
2. Are all flammable liquids that are kept inside buildings stored in proper storage containers or cabinets? ☐ ☐
3. Do you meet OSHA standards for all spray painting or dip tank operations using combustible liquids? ☐ ☐
4. Are oxidizing chemicals stored in areas separate from all organic material except shipping bags? ☐ ☐
5. Do you have an enforced NO SMOKING rule in areas for storage and use of hazardous materials? ☐ ☐
6. Are NO SMOKING signs posted where needed? ☐ ☐

	OK	ACTION NEEDED
7. Is ventilation equipment provided for removal of air contaminants from operations such as production grinding, buffing, spray painting and/or vapor degreasing, and is it operating properly?	☐	☐
8. Are protective measures in effect for operations involved with X-rays or other radiation?	☐	☐
9. For Lift Truck Operations:		
Are only trained personnel allowed to operate forklift trucks?	☐	☐
Is overhead protection provided on high lift rider trucks?	☐	☐
10. For Toxic Materials:		
Are all materials used in your plant checked for toxic qualities?	☐	☐
Have appropriate control procedures such as ventilation systems, enclosed operations, safe handling practices, proper personal protective equipment (e.g., respirators, glasses or goggles, gloves, etc.) been instituted for toxic materials?	☐	☐

EMPLOYEE PROTECTION

	OK	ACTION NEEDED
1. Is there a hospital, clinic or infirmary for medical care near your business?	☐	☐
2. If medical and first-aid facilities are not nearby, do you have one or more employees trained in first aid?	☐	☐
3. Are your first-aid supplies adequate for the type of potential injuries in your workplace?	☐	☐
4. Are there quick water flush facilities available where employees are exposed to corrosive materials?	☐	☐
5. Are hard hats provided and worn where any danger of falling objects exists?	☐	☐
6. Are protective goggles or glasses provided and worn where there is any danger of flying particles or splashing of corrosive materials?	☐	☐
7. Are protective gloves, aprons, shields or other means provided for protection from sharp, hot or corrosive materials?	☐	☐
8. Are approved respirators provided for regular or emergency use where needed?	☐	☐
9. Is all protective equipment maintained in a sanitary condition and readily available for use?	☐	☐
10. Where special equipment is needed for electrical workers, is it available?	☐	☐
11. When lunches are eaten on the premises, are they eaten in areas where there is no exposure to toxic materials, and not in toilet facility areas?	☐	☐
12. Is protection against the effect of occupational noise exposure provided when the sound levels exceed those shown in Table G-16 of the OSHA noise standard?	☐	☐

Develop Your Own Checklist.

These Are Only Sample Questions.

Source: OSHA Handbook for Small Business.

NOTES

1. "Occupational Injuries and Illnesses," *BNA Bulletin to Management*, January 18, 1996, pp. 20–21; "Workplace Fatalities—1997," *BNA Bulletin to Management*, August 28, 1997, pp. 276–277; "Occupational Injuries and Illnesses," *BNA Bulletin to Management*, January 15, 1998, p. 13; "Workplace Deaths Unchanged: Homicides at Six Year Low," *BNA Bulletin to Management*, August 27, 1998, p. 269.

2. "Workplace Injuries Cost $171 Billion, Cause 66,500 Deaths, Study Says," *BNAC Communicator* (Winter 1998), p. 9.

3. *Workers' Compensation Manual for Managers and Supervisors* (Chicago: Commerce Clearing House, Inc., 1992), p. 12. See also Guy Toxcano and Janice Windau, "The Changing Character of Fatal Work Injuries," *Monthly Labor Review*, Vol. 117, no. 10 (October 1994), pp. 17–28.

4. *U.S. v. S.A. Healy Company*, DC E Wis, No. 90-CR-123, 2/20/91.

5. *US. v. Mickey*, DC N Ohio, 1-92-CR-0380, 12/4/92. Note that under a recent decision of the U.S. Court of Appeals for the Seventh Circuit, employers must have actual knowledge that an un-

safe condition exists and that it violates federal standards for them to be found guilty of criminal violations of the Occupational Safety and Health Act; "Criminal Violation Depends on Knowledge," *BNA Bulletin to Management*, March 5, 1998, p. 68.

6. Much of this is based on "All About OSHA," (revised), U.S. Department of Labor, Occupational Safety and Health Administration (Washington, DC).

7. "Safety Rule on Respiratory Protection Issues," *BNA Bulletin to Management*, January 8, 1998, p. 1.

8. "OSHA Hazard Communication Standard Enforcement," *BNA Bulletin to Management*, February 23, 1989, p. 13.

9. "What Every Employer Needs to Know About OSHA Record Keeping," U.S. Department of Labor, Bureau of Labor Statistics (Washington, DC), report 412-3, p. 3.

10. Brian Jackson and Jeffrey Myers, "Just When You Thought You Were Safe: OSHA Record-Keeping Violations," *Management Review*, May 1994, pp. 62–63.

11. Ibid., p. 62.

12. "Supreme Court Says OSHA Inspectors Need Warrants," *Engineering News Record*, June 1, 1978, pp. 9–10. W. Scott Railton, "OSHA Gets Tough on Business," *Management Review*, Vol. 80, no. 12 (December 1991), pp. 28–29.

13. Michael Verespej, "OSHA Revamps Its Inspection Policies," *Industry Week*, September 17, 1979, pp. 19–20. See also Horace E. Johns, "OSHA's Impact," *Personnel Journal*, Vol. 67, no. 11 (November 1988), pp. 102–107.

14. This section is based on "All About OSHA," pp. 23–25. See also Robert Sand, "OSHA Access to Privileged Materials: Criminal Prosecutions; Damages for Fear of Cancer," *Employee Relations Law Journal*, Vol. 19, no. 1 (Summer 1993), pp. 151–157.

15. "Employers Hit with Megafines for OSHA Violations," *BNA Bulletin to Management*, May 9, 1996, p. 146.

16. "Settling Safety Violations Has Benefits," *BNA Bulletin to Management*, July 31, 1997, p. 248.

17. "Enforcement Activity Increased in 1997," *BNA Bulletin to Management*, January 29, 1998, p. 28.

18. Ibid., p. 28.

19. "OSHA Instruction on Penalties," *BNA Bulletin to Management*, February 7, 1991, p. 33; Commerce Clearing House, "OSHA Will Begin Higher Fines March 1st," *Ideas and Trends in Personnel*, January 23, 1991, p. 14; John Bruening, OSHRC on the Comeback Trail," *Occupational Hazards* (January 1991), pp. 33–36. OSHA is also stressing record-keeping violations. See for example, Brian Jackson and Jeffrey Myers, "Just When You Thought You Were Safe: OSHA Record-Keeping Violations," *Management Review*, Vol. 83, no. 5 (May 1994), pp. 62–63.

20. Steve Bates, "When OSHA Calls," *Nation's Business*, Vol. 86, no. 9 (September 1998), pp. 14–22.

21. Ibid., pp. 21–22.

22. Ibid., pp. 21–22.

23. Roger Jacobs, "Employee Resistance to OSHA Standards: Toward a More Reasonable Approach," *Labor Law Journal* (April 1979), pp. 219–230. See also Charles Chadd, "Managing OSHA Compliance: The Human Resources Issues," *Employee Relations Law Journal*, Vol. 20, no. 1 (Summer 1994), pp. 101–113.

24. Ibid., p. 220.

25. Charles Chadd, "Managing OSHA Compliance: The Human Resources Issues," *Employee Relations Law Journal*, no. 4 (Summer 1994), p. 106.

26. These are based on Jacobs, "Employee Resistance to OSHA Standards," pp. 227–230.

27. Michael Verespej, "Has OSHA Improved?" *Industry Week*, August 4, 1989, p. 50.

28. "What Every Employer Needs to Know About OSHA Record Keeping."

29. Willie Hammer, *Occupational Safety Management and Engineering*, 3rd ed. (Upper Saddle River, NJ: Prentice Hall, 1985), pp. 62–63.

30. "Initial OSHA Reform Bills Become Law," *BNA Bulletin to Management*, July 30, 1998, p. 236.

31. "OSHA Seeks 'Cooperative Compliance'," *BNA Bulletin to Management*, September 4, 1997, p. 288; "OSHA's Cooperative Program Shoves Off," *BNA Bulletin to Management*, December 25, 1997, p. 416.

32. Lisa Finnegan, "Is 1999 OSHA's Year?" *Occupational Hazards*, December 1998, p. 28.

33. Gregg LaBar, "Your OSHA Compliance Record: Online," *Occupational Hazards*, Vol. 59, no. 8 (August 1997), p. 10.

34. This is based on Robert Scherer, Daniel Kaufman, and M. Fall Anina, "Complaint Resolution by OSHA in Small and Large Manufacturing Firms," *Journal of Small Business Management* (January 1993), pp. 73–83. See also Robert Sand, "Pragmatic Suggestions for Negotiating Reductions in OSHA Citations," *Employee Relations Law Journal*, Vol. 20, no. 1 (Summer 1994), pp. 153–159.

35. Ibid, p. 79.

36. Ibid. Note that although penalty reductions were about twice as large in large firms, the amount of total penalties paid by large and small firms differed as well, amounting to $566 for small firms, and $1,209 for large firms.

37. Lester Bittel, *What Every Supervisor Should Know* (New York: McGraw-Hill, 1974), p. 25. For an example of an effective safety training program, see Michael Pennacchia, "Interactive Training Sets the Pace," *Safety and Health*, Vol. 135, no. 1 (January 1987), pp. 24–27; and Philip Poynter and David Stevens, "How to Secure an Effective Health and Safety Program at Work," *Professional Safety*, Vol. 32, no. 1 (January 1987), pp. 32–41. Appointing a safety committee can also be useful. See for example, Neville Tompkins, "Getting the Best Help From Your Safety Committee," *HRMagazine*, Vol. 40, no. 4 (April 1995), p. 76.

38. David S. Thelan, Donna Ledgerwood, and Charles F. Walters, "Health and Safety in the Workplace: A New Challenge for Business Schools," *Personnel Administrator*, Vol. 30, no. 10 (October 1985), p. 44.

39. Hammer, *Occupational Safety Management and Engineering*.

40. "A Safety Committee Man's Guide," Aetna Life and Casualty Insurance Company, Catalog 872684.

41. "Workplace Fatalities," *BNA Bulletin to Management*, August 28, 1997, pp. 276–277.

42. "A Safety Committee Man's Guide," pp. 17–21. OSHA has identified 10 major causes of accidents: inadequate training, inability to do the job, lack of job understanding, improper tools and equipment, poor-quality materials, poor maintenance, poor work environment, incorrect shop maintenance, tight work schedules, and overly tight schedules. See Myron Peskin and Frances McGrath, "Industrial Safety: Who is Responsible and Who Benefits?" *Business Horizons*, Vol. 35, no. 3 (May–June 1992), pp. 66–70. See also Daniel Webb, "Why Safety Programs Fail," *People Management*, Vol. 1, no. 2 (January 1995), pp. 38–39.

43. For a discussion of this see David Hofmann and Adam Stetzer, "A Cross-Level Investigation of Factors Influencing Unsafe Behaviors and Accidents," *Personnel Psychology*, Vol. 49 (1996), pp. 307–308.

44. Willard Kerr, "Complementary Theories of Safety Psychology," in Edwin Fleishman and Alan Bass, *Industrial Psychology* (Burr Ridge, IL; McGraw-Hill, 1974), pp. 493–500. See also Alan Fowler, "How to Make the Workplace Safer," *People Management*, Vol. 1, no. 2 (January 1995), pp. 38–39.

45. List of unsafe acts from "A Safety Committee Man's Guide," Aetna Life and Casualty Insurance Company.

46. A. G. Arbous and J. E. Kerrich, "The Phenomenon of Accident Proneness," *Industrial Medicine and Surgery*, Vol. 22 (1953), pp. 141–148, reprinted in Fleishman and Bass, *Industrial Psychology*, p. 485.

47. Ernest McCormick and Joseph Tiffin, *Industrial Psychology* (Upper Saddle River, NJ: Prentice Hall, 1974), pp. 522–523; Norman Maier, *Psychology and Industrial Organization* (Boston: Houghton Mifflin, 1965), pp. 458–462; Milton Blum and James Nayler, *Industrial Psychology* (New York: Harper & Row, 1968), pp. 519–531. For example, David DeJoy, "Attributional Processes and Hazard Control Management in Industry," *Journal of Safety Research*, Vol. 16 (Summer 1985), pp. 61–71. Miner and Brewer, "Management of Ineffective Performance, in Dunnette, ed., *Handbook of Industrial and Organizational Psychology*, pp. 1004–1005.

48. McCormick and Tiffin, *Industrial Psychology* p. 523.

49. John Miner and J. Frank Brewer, "Management of Ineffective Performance," in Marvin Dunnette, ed., *Handbook of Industrial and Organizational Psychology* (Chicago: Rand McNally, 1976), pp. 995–1031; McCormick and Tiffin, *Industrial Psychology*, pp. 24–525. Younger employees probably have more accidents also, at least in part because they fail to perceive specific situations as being as risky as do older employees. See, for example, Peter Finn and Barry Bragg, "Perceptions of the Risk of an Accident by Young and Older Drivers," *Accident Analysis and Prevention*, Vol. 18, no. 4 (August 1986). See also Olivia Mitchell, "The Relation of Age to Workplace Injuries," *Monthly Labor Review*, Vol. 111, no. 7 (July 1988), pp. 8–13.

50. Blum and Nayler, *Industrial Psychology*, p. 522.

51. Michael Frone, "Predictors of Work Injuries Among Employed Adolescents," *Journal of Applied Psychology*, Vol. 83, no. 4 (1998), pp. 565–576.

52. Susannah Figura, "Don't Slip Up on Safety," *Occupational Hazards*, Vol. 58, no. 11 (November 1996), pp. 29–31.

53. Maier, *Psychology and Industrial Organization*, pp. 463–467; McCormick and Tiffin, *Industrial Psychology*, pp. 533–536; and Blum and Nayler, *Industrial Psychology*, pp. 525–527.

54. D. Wechsler, "Test for Taxicab Drivers," *Journal of Personnel Research*, Vol. 5 (1926), pp. 24–30, quoted in Maier, *Psychology and Industrial Organization*, p. 64. See also Leo DeBobes, "Psychological Factors in Accident Prevention," *Personnel Journal*, Vol. 65 (January 1986); Curtiss Hansen, "A Causal Model of the Relationship Among Accidents, Biodata Personality, and Cognitive Factors," *Journal of Applied Psychology*, Vol. 74, no. 1 (February 1989), pp. 81–90.

55. Maier, *Psychology and Industrial Organization*, p. 463.

56. S. E. Wirt and H. E. Leedkee, "Skillful Eyes Prevent Accidents," Annual Newsletter, National Safety Council, Industrial Nursing Section (November 1945), pp. 10–12, quoted in Maier, *Psychology and Industrial Organization*, p. 466.

57. Gerald Borofsky, Michelle Bielema, and James Hoffman, "Accidents, Turnover, and Use of a Pre-employment Screening Interview," *Psychological Reports* (1993), pp. 1067–1076.

58. Ibid., p. 1069.

59. Ibid., p. 1072.

60. Maier, *Psychology and Industrial Organization*, p. 464.

61. *Workers' Compensation Manual for Managers and Supervisors*, pp. 22–23.

62. S. Laner and R. J. Sell, "An Experiment on the Effect of Specially Designed Safety Posters," *Organizational Psychology*, Vol. 34 (1960), pp. 153–169, in McCormick and Tiffin, *Industrial Psychology*, p. 536.

63. McCormick and Tiffin, *Industrial Psychology*, p. 537. A group of international experts met in Belgium in 1986 and concluded that a successful safety poster must be simple and specific and reinforce safe behavior rather than negative behavior. See, "What Makes an Effective Safety Poster," *National Safety and Health News*, Vol. 134, no. 6 (December 1986), pp. 32–34.

64. David Gunsch, "Employees Exercise to Prevent Injuries," *Personnel Journal* (July 1993), pp. 58–62.

65. Jennifer Laabs, "Cashing in on Safety," *Workforce* (August 1997), p. 57.

66. Gregg LaBar, "Awards and Incentives in Action," *Occupational Hazards*, Vol. 59, no. 1 (January 1997), pp. 91–92.

67. Gregg LeBar, "Putting Incentives to Work," *Occupational Hazards*, Vol. 59, no. 6 (June 1997), pp. 59–62.

68. OSHA has published two useful training manuals: *Training Requirements of OSHA Standards*, February 1976 and *Teaching Safety and Health in the Work Place*, U.S. Department of Labor, Occupational Safety and Health Administration, 1976; J. Surry, "Industrial Accident Research: Human Engineering Approach" (Toronto: University of Toronto, Department of Industrial Engineering), June 1968, Chapter 4, quoted in McCormick and Tiffin, *Industrial Psychology*, p. 534. For an example of a very successful incentive program aimed at boosting safety at Campbell Soup Company, see Frederick Wahl, Jr., "Soups on for Safety," *National Safety and Health News*, Vol. 134, no. 6 (December 1986), pp. 49–53. For a discussion of how employee involvement can impact job re-design and employee safety, see Douglas May and Catherine Schwoerer, "Employee Health by Design: Using Employee Involvement Teams in Ergonomics Job Redesign," *Personnel Psychology*, Vol. 47, no. 4 (Winter 1994), pp. 861–876.

69. Judi Komaki, Kenneth Barwick, and Lawrence Scott, "A Behavioral Approach to Occupational Safety: Pinpointing and Reinforcing Safe Performance in a Food Manufacturing Plant," *Journal of Applied Psychology*, Vol. 63 (August 1978), pp. 434–445. See also Robert Reber, Jerry Wallin, and David Duhon, "Preventing Occupational Injuries Through Performance Management," *Public Personnel Management*, Vol. 22, no. 2 (Summer 1993), pp. 301–311; Anat Arkin, "Incentives to Work Safely," *Personnel Management*, Vol. 26, no. 9 (September 1994), pp. 48–52; and Peter Making and Valerie Sutherland, "Reducing Accidents Using a Behavioral Approach," *Leadership & Organizational Development Journal*, Vol. 15, no. 5 (1994), pp. 5–10.

70. Judi Komaki, Arlene Heinzmann, and Lorealie Lawson, "Effect of Training and Feedback: Component Analysis of A Behavioral Safety Program," *Journal of Applied Psychology*, Vol. 65 (June 1980), pp. 261–270. See also Jorma Sari, "When Does Behavior Modification Prevent Accidents?" *Leadership & Organizational Development Journal*, Vol. 15, no. 5 (1994), pp. 11–15.

71. Dove Zohar, "Safety Climate in Industrial Organization; Theoretical and Implied Implications," *Journal of Applied Psychology*, Vol. 65 (February 1980), p. 97. For a discussion of the importance of getting employees involved in managing their own safety program, see John Lutness, "Self-managed Safety Program Gets Workers Involved," *Safety and Health*, Vol. 135, no. 4 (April 1987), pp. 42–45. See also Frederick Streff, Michael Kalsher, and E. Scott Geller, "Developing Efficient Workplace Safety Programs: Observations of Response Co-Variations," *Journal of Organizational Behavior Management*, Vol. 13, no. 2 (1993), pp. 3–14.

72. Michael Pennacchia, "Interactive Training Sets the Pace"; and Philip Poynter and David Stevens, "How to Secure an Effective Health and Safety Program at Work."

73. William Kincaid, "10 Habits of Effective Safety Managers," *Occupational Hazards*, Vol. 58, no. 11 (November 1996), pp. 41–43.

74. "With Pay on the Line, Managers Improve Safety," *BNA Bulletin to Management*, March 20, 1997, p. 89.

75. *Workers' Compensation Manual for Managers and Supervisors*, p. 24. James Frierson, "An Analysis of ADA Provisions on Denying Employment Because of a Risk of Future Injury," *Employee Relations Law Journal*, Vol. 13, no. 2 (1993), pp. 3–14.

76. "Workplace Safety: Improving Management Practices," *BNA Bulletin to Management*, February 9, 1989, pp. 42 and 47; see also Marlene Morgenstern, "Workers' Compensation: Managing Costs," *Compensation & Benefits Review* (September–October 1992), pp. 30–38. See also Linda Johnson, "Preventing Injuries: The Big Payoff," *Personnel Journal* (April 1994), pp. 61–64; and David Webb, "The Bathtub Effect: Why Safety Programs Fail," *Management Review* (February 1994), pp. 51–54.

77. David Hofmann and Adam Stetzer, "A Cross-Level Investigation of Factors Influencing Unsafe Behaviors and Accidents," *Personnel Psychology*, Vol. 49 (1996), p. 329.

78. Virginia Sutcliffe, "Employee Safety: Beyond the Plant Gate," *Occupational Hazards* (December 1998), pp. 41–42.

79. Ibid., p. 42.

80. S. L. Smith, "Sadaf Drives for Safety Excellence," *Occupational Hazards* (November 1998), p. 41.

81. *Workers' Compensation Manual for Managers and Supervisors*, p. 10.

82. See, for example, Ibid., pp. 36–39.

83. Ibid., p. 51.

84. This section is based largely on Miner and Brewer, "Management of Ineffective Performance," pp. 1005–1023.

85. James Schreir, "Survey Supports Perceptions: Work-site Drug Use Is on the Rise," *Personnel Journal* (October 1987), pp. 114–118. Pallassana Balgopal, "Combating Alcoholism in Industries: Implications for Occupational Social Work," *Management and Labor Studies*, Vol. 17, no. 1 (January 1992), pp. 33–42. For a review of the background factors possibly leading to drug abuse, see for example, Richard Clayton et al., "Risk and Protective Factors: A Brief Review," *Drugs & Society, A Journal of Contemporary Issues*, Vol. 8, no. 3–4 (1995), pp. 7–14.

86. "Drug Use Among Workers," *BNA Bulletin to Management*, May 2, 1996, pp. 140–141.

87. Gopal Pati and John Adkins, Jr., "The Employer's Role in Alcoholism Assistance," *Personnel Journal*, Vol. 62, no. 7 (July 1983), pp. 568–572. For a discussion of how the work environment can encourage drug dealing, see Richard Lyles, "Should the Next Drug Bust Be in Your company?" *Personnel Journal*, Vol. 63 (October 1994), pp. 46–49.

88. Harrison Trice, "Alcoholism and the Work World," *Sloan Management Review*, No. 2 (Fall 1970), pp. 67–75, reprinted in W. Clay Hamner and Frank Schmidt, *Contemporary Problems in Personnel*, rev. ed. (Chicago: St. Clair Press, 1977), pp. 496–502. Note also that dependence on ordinary substances can be as devastating as hard drug problems. See, for example, Peter Minetos, "Are You Addicted to Legal Drugs?" *Safety and Health*, Vol. 136, no. 2 (August 1987), pp. 46–49. For a discussion of substance abuse in the small business see, for example, Harry Lasher and John Grashof, "Substance Abuse in Small Business: Business Owner Perceptions and Reactions," *Journal of Small Business Management* (January 1993), pp. 63–72.

89. Pati and Adkins, "Employer's Role in Alcoholism Assistance." See also Commerce Clearing House, "How Should Employers Respond to Indications an Employee May Have an Alcohol or Drug Problem?" *Ideas and Trends*, April 6, 1989, pp. 53–57.

90. "Employee Alcohol Testing on the Rise," *BNA Bulletin to Management*, August 20, 1998, p. 261.

91. Ibid., p. 261.

92. Based on Miner and Brewer, "Management of Ineffective Performance." The survey was conducted jointly by the American Society for Personnel Administration and the Bureau of National Affairs. The results were based on an analysis of the questionnaire data made by Professors Miner and Brewer, who acknowledge the assistance of John B. Schappi, associate editor of the Bureau of National Affairs, and Mary Green Miner, director of *BNA Surveys*, in making this information available.

93. Brenda Sunoo, "Positive Drug Tests Results: Terminate or Rehabilitate?" *Personnel Journal* (December 1996), p. 94.

94. Ibid., p. 94.

95. Trice, "Alcoholism and the Work World." See also Larry A. Pace and Stanley J. Smits, "Substance Abuse: A Proactive Approach," *Personnel Journal*, Vol. 68, no. 4 (April 1989), pp. 84–90; and Commerce Clearing House, "Typical Behavior Changes in an Employee with a Drinking Problem," *Ideas and Trends*, April 6, 1989, p. 56.

96. From Henry Alevic, "Drug Abuse in the Workplace" (Personnel Services, Inc., 2303 W. Meadowview Road, Greensboro, NC 27407), reprinted in *BNA Bulletin to Management*, August 29, 1985, p. 72. Stanley Smits and Larry Pace, "Workplace Substance Abuse: Establish Policies," *Personnel Journal* (May 1989), pp. 88–93.

97. This is quoted from "Drug-Free Workplace: New Federal Requirements," *BNA Bulletin to Management*, February 9, 1989, pp. 1–4. Note that the Drug-Free Workplace Act does not mandate or mention testing employees for illegal drug use.

98. January 1, 1995 for employers with 50 or more safety sensitive workers; January 1, 1996 for smaller employers. "Alcohol Misuse Prevention Programs: Department of Transportation Final Rules," *BNA Bulletin to Management*, March 24, 1994, pp. 1–8.

99. *BNA Bulletin to Management*, December 19, 1985, p. 200. Based on a speech by San Francisco attorneys Victor Schacter and Robert Kristoff. See also Alfred Klein, "Employees Under the Influence—Outside the Law?" *Personnel Journal*, Vol. 65, no. 9 (September 1986), pp. 56–58; Martin Aron, "Drug Testing: The Employer's Dilemma," *Labor Law Journal*, Vol. 38, no. 3 (March 1987), pp. 157–165; "Drug Testing 'To Do' List," *BNA Bulletin to Management*, August 10, 1989, p. 250.

100. This is based on Terry Beehr and John Newman, "Organizational Stress, Employer Health, and Organizational Effectiveness: A

Factor Analysis, Model, and Literature Review," *Personnel Psychology* Vol. 31 (Winter 1978), pp. 665–699. See also Stephan Motowizio, John Packard, and Michael Manning, "Occupational Stress: Its Causes and Consequences for Job Performance," *Journal of Applied Psychology*, Vol. 71, no. 4 (November 1986), pp. 618–629.

101. Eric Sundstrom, et al., "Office Noise, Satisfaction, and Performance," *Environment and Behavior*, Vol. 26, no. 2 (March 1994), pp. 195–222.

102. Michael Manning, Conrad Jackson, and Marceline Fusilier, "Occupational Stress, Social Support, and the Costs of Health Care," *Academy of Management Journal*, Vol. 39, no. 3 (1996), pp. 738–750.

103. "Stress, Depression Cost Employers," *Occupational Hazards* (December 1998), p. 24.

104. Andre DuBrin, *Human Relations: A Job Oriented Approach* (Reston, VA: Reston, 1978), pp. 66–67.

105. John Newman and Terry Beehr, "Personnel and Organizational Strategies for Handling Job Stress: A Review of Research and Opinion," *Personnel Psychology* (Spring 1979), pp. 1–43. See also "Work Place Stress: How to Curb Claims," *BNA Bulletin to Management*, April 14, 1988, p. 120.

106. Karl Albrecht, *Stress and the Manager* (Englewood Cliffs, NJ: Spectrum, 1979). For a discussion of the related symptoms of depression see James Krohe, Jr., "An Epidemic of Depression?" *Across-the-Board* (September 1994), pp. 23–27.

107. John Kelly, "Get a Grip on Stress," *HRMagazine* (February 1997), pp. 51–54.

108. Ibid., p. 51.

109. Ibid., p. 53.

110. "Solutions to Workplace Stress," *BNA Bulletin to Management*, February 11, 1993, p. 48. See also Christopher Bachler, "Workers Take Leave of Job Stress," *Personnel Journal*, Vol. 74, no. 1 (January 1995), p. 38.

111. Pascale Carayon, "Stressful Jobs and Non-Stressful Jobs: A Cluster Analysis of Office Jobs," *Ergonomics*, Vol. 37, no. 2 (1994), pp. 311–323.

112. "Managing Stress in the Workplace," *BNA Bulletin to Management*, January 18, 1996, p. 24.

113. Herbert Freudenberger, *Burn-Out* (Toronto: Bantam Books, 1980). See also Susan Jackson, Richard Schwab, and Randall Schuler, "Toward an Understanding of the Burnout Phenomenon," *Journal of Applied Psychology*, Vol. 71, no. 4 (November 1986), pp. 630–640; and James R. Redeker and Jonathan Seagal, "Profits Low? Your Employees May Be High!" *Personnel*, Vol. 66, no. 6 (June 1989), pp. 72–76. See also Cary Cherniss, "Long Term Consequences of Burnout: An Exploratory Study," *Journal of Organizational Behavior*, Vol. 13, no. 1 (January 1992), pp. 1–11; and Raymond Lee and Blake Ashforth, "A Further Examination of Managerial Burnout: Toward an Integrated Model," *Journal of Organizational Behavior*, Vol. 14 (1993), pp. 3–20.

114. Freudenberger, *Burn-Out.*

115. Mina Westman and Dov Eden, "Effects of a Respite from Workout on Burnout: Vacation Relief and Fade-Out," *Journal of Applied Psychology*, Vol. 82, no. 4 (1997), pp. 516–527.

116. Ibid., p. 516.

117. Ibid., p. 526.

118. See, for example, Michael Smith and others, "An Investigation of Health Complaints and Job Stress in Video Display Operations,"

Human Factors (August 1981), pp. 387–400; see also "How to Protect Workers from Reproductive Hazards," *BNA Fair Employment Practices*, July 23, 1987, pp. 89–90. See also Commerce Clearing House, "Suffolk County New York Passes Law Covering Employers with Twenty Terminals or More Regarding VDT Regulation," *Ideas and Trends* (1988), p. 48.

119. "Fear of Birth Risks from VDTs Dispelled," *BNA Bulletin to Management*, January 22, 1998, p. 20.

120. J. A. Savage, "Are Computer Terminals Zapping Workers' Health?" *Business and Society Review* (1994); "Carpel Tunnel Claims Up, But Cost Per Claim Down," *BNA Bulletin to Management*, July 25, 1996, p. 233.

121. These are based on "Inexpensive Ergonomic Innovations," *BNA Bulletin to Management*, February 1, 1996, p. 40.

122. Sondra Lotz Fisher, "Are Your Employees Working Ergosmart?" *Personnel Journal* (December 1996), pp. 91–92.

123. "Solutions to VDT Viewing Problems," *BNA Bulletin to Management*, November 5, 1987, pp. 356–357.

124. Maureen Minehan, "New AIDS Survival Rates Mean Patients Returning to Work," *HRMagazine*, Vol. 42, no. 10 (October 1997), p. 208.

125. "AIDS and the Workplace: Issues, Advice, and Answers," *BNA Bulletin to Management*, November 14, 1985, pp. 1–6. See also David Ritter and Ronald Turner, "AIDS: Employer Concerns and Options," *Labor Law Journal*, Vol. 38, no. 2 (February 1987), pp. 67–83; and "How Employers Are Responding to AIDS in the Workplace," *BNA Fair Employment Practices*, February 18, 1988, pp. 21–22. For a complete guide to services and information regarding "The Work Place and AIDS," see *Personnel Journal*, Vol. 60, no. 10 (October 1987), pp. 65–80. See also William H. Wager, "AIDS: Setting Policy, Educating Employees at Bank of America," *Personnel*, Vol. 65, no. 8 (August 1988), pp. 4–10. See also Margaret Magnus, "AIDS: Fear and Ignorance," *Personnel Journal*, Vol. 67, no. 2 (February 1988), pp. 28–32, for poll regarding major workplace comments associated with AIDS. See also "AIDS/HIV in the Workplace: A Fact Sheet for Employees," *BNA Bulletin to Management*, October 6, 1994.

126. Ibid., p. 208.

127. Commerce Clearing House, "The Wells Fargo AIDS Policy," *Ideas and Trends*, April 5, 1988, pp. 52–53.

128. Quoted or paraphrased from Michael Esposito and Jeffrey Myers, "Managing AIDS in the Workplace," *Employee Relations Law Journal*, Vol. 19, no. 1 (Summer 1993), p. 68.

129. Marco Colossi, "Do Employees Have the Right to Smoke?" *Personnel Journal* (April 1988), pp. 72–79.

130. "Where's There's Smoke There's Risk," *BNA Bulletin to Management*, January 30, 1992, pp. 26 and 31.

131. Daniel Warner, "We Do Not Hire Smokers: May Employers Discriminate Against Smokers?" *Employee Responsibilities and Rights Journal*, Vol. 7, no. 2 (1994), p. 129.

132. Commerce Clearing House, "State Laws Regulating Smoking," *Ideas and Trends*, January 9, 1987, pp. 4–5.

133. Jim Collison, "Workplace Smoking Policies: Sixteen Questions and Answers," *Personnel Journal* (April 1988), p. 81. See also Daniel Warner, "We Do Not Hire Smokers," pp. 129–140.

134. Warner, Ibid., p. 138.

135. "Smoking Bans on the Rise," *BNA Bulletin to Management*, March 16, 1989, p. 82.

136. Gus Toscano and Janaice Windau, "The Changing Character of Fatal Work Injuries," *Monthly Labor Review* (October 1994), pp. 17–28. See also "Workplace Violence," *BNA Bulletin to Management*, October 31, 1996, pp. 348–349.

137. Toscano and Windau, Ibid., p. 17.

138. Based on Louis DiLorenzo and Darren Carroll, "The Growing Menace: Violence in the Workplace," *New York State Bar Journal* (January 1995), p. 24.

139. "Workplace Violence: Sources and Solutions," *BNA Bulletin to Management*, November 4, 1993, p. 345.

140. Alfred Feliu, "Workplace Violence and the Duty of Care: The Scope of an Employer's Obligation to Protect Against the Violent Employee,"*Employee Relations Law Journal*, Vol. 20, no. 3 (Winter 1994/95), pp. 381–406.

141. "Workplace Violence: Sources and Solutions," *BNA Bulletin to Management*, November 4, 1993, p. 345.

142. Ibid.

143. "Weapons in the Workplace: A Review of Employer Policies," *BNA Bulletin to Management*, June 5, 1996, pp. 1–7; Lloyd Nigro and William Waugh, Jr., "Violence in the American Workplace: Challenges to the Public Employer," *Public Administration Review* (July/August 1996), pp. 326–333.

144. "OSHA Addresses Top Homicide Risk," *BNA Bulletin to Management*, May 14, 1998, p. 148.

145. Feliu, "Workplace Violence and the Duty of Care," p. 395.

146. Dawn Anfuso, "Workplace Violence," *Personnel Journal* (October 1994), pp. 66–77.

147. Feliu, "Workplace Violence and the Duty of Care," p. 395.

148. Quoted from Feliu, Ibid., p. 395.

149. Anfuso, "Workplace Violence," p. 71. Excellence in Training Corp. is in Des Moines, Iowa.

150. "Preventing Workplace Violence," *BNA Bulletin to Management*, June 10, 1993, p. 177. See also Jenny McCune, "Companies Grapple with Workplace Violence," *Management Review*, Vol. 83, no. 3 (March 1994), pp. 52–57.

151. This is based on Beverly Younger, "Violence Against Women in the Workplace," *Employee Assistance Quarterly*, Vol. 9, no. 3/4 (1994), pp. 113–133.

152. Ibid., p. 120.

153. Ibid., p. 121.

154. Ibid.

155. Ibid., pp. 129–130.

156. Quoted or paraphrased from Ibid., p. 177 and based on recommendations from Chris Hatcher.

157. Shari Caudron,"Target: HR," *Workforce* (August 1998), p. 48.

158. Helen Frank Bensimon, "What To Do About Anger in the Workplace," *Training & Development*, Vol. 51, no. 9 (September 1997), pp. 28–32.

159. Feliu, "Workplace Violence," pp. 401–402.

160. Shari Caudron, "Target: HR," *Workforce* (August 1998), pp. 44–52.

161. Donna Rosato, "New Industry Helps Managers Fight Violence," *USA Today*, August 8, 1995, p. 1.

162. Helen Frank Bensimon, "What To Do About Anger in the Workplace," *Training & Development*, Vol. 51, no. 9 (September 1997), pp. 28–32.

163. Louis DiLorenzo and Darren Carroll, "The Growing Menace: Violence in the Workplace," *New York State Bar Journal* (January 1995), p. 25.

164. Quoted from Feliu, "Workplace Violence," p. 393.

165. DiLorenzo and Carroll, "The Growing Menace," p. 27.

VIDEO CASE

PART V
LABOR RELATIONS

LIKE MANY WORKERS IN
SPECIALIZED OCCUPATIONS, THE
ACTORS WE MEET IN THIS VIDEO
ARE UNION MEMBERS. AS YOU'VE
LEARNED FROM CHAPTER 14,
LABOR UNIONS IN THE UNITED
STATES HAVE EXPERIENCED
PERIODS OF EXPANSION AND
CONTRACTION THROUGHOUT
THEIR HISTORY.

Some managers fear any kind of interaction with labor unions. The threat of strikes, slowdowns, and job actions becomes very real when contract negotiations are strained or bogged down. While they are infrequent and represent the extreme of poor labor-management relations, these are still viewed as powerful negotiating strategies and often prove detrimental to the firm's morale, public image, and bottom line. But management often can contribute a great deal to creating a positive relationship with labor, and there are many specific actions, some outlined in Chapter 14, that managers can take to prevent minor disagreements from reaching the status of a grievance.

The first of these is to develop a work environment in which grievances simply don't need to occur. (Recall that a grievance is an employee's filing of a statement that the union contract or company policy has been violated by management. That initiates a formal procedure for determining whether a violation in fact took place.) From what you'll see of Quicktakes' oil-company video operation in Part 5, you may be able to form an opinion about whether such a healthy environment exists there.

You may also want to keep in mind the do's and don'ts for handling grievance procedures that are outlined in the chapter, since they are useful strategies for many kinds of interaction with unions. Some recommended actions include giving the employee a fair hearing and holding grievance discussions in private. Actions to avoid include making arrangements inconsistent with the contract and refusing to admit it if the company is wrong. It will probably be clear to you from this video segment that acting hastily is also to be avoided.

The reason for guidelines like these is to protect the manager (and the firm) from making errors that could result in unfairness and an escalation of the disagreement. It is thus important for managers to have a good understanding of any union contracts that are in effect and to master the skills of working successfully with union employees and their representatives.

Disciplinary measures and dismissal are major sources of grievances. Perhaps if Hal were aware of this, he might react differently in the situation you are about to see.

QUESTIONS

1. Chapter 14 makes the point that grievances are often merely a symptom of an underlying problem. Do you think this is the case here? If so, why? What do you think Jim's real problem is? What should he do about it?

2. Do you think Hal is doing everything he can to maintain a good relationship with the actors' union? Why or why not? If not, what more could he do, or what could he do differently?

3. Is Hal using good management techniques in dealing with Jim? Is Jim a problem employee, as defined in the chapter? What might Hal do differently in managing Jim?

4. What unintended effect will Hal's suspension of Jim have on Caitlin? Is there a possibility of another grievance arising from this incident? If you think so, what should Hal do about it?

5. Does Jim have good grounds for a grievance? Assuming he does, what actions should Hal take immediately, and what other, more extensive, preparations should he make?

16

MANAGING HUMAN RESOURCES IN AN INTERNATIONAL BUSINESS

ord Motor Company is driving hard to finish implementing its "Ford 2000" strategy. This strategy aims to dramatically reduce all Ford car design and manufacturing costs by making the firm a truly global competitor; this means that activities like car design will no longer be done regionally, but on an integrated global scale. But implementing that strategy means Ford must be able to assign its employees anyplace around the globe where they fit best. Implementing Ford 2000, in other words, depends very heavily on human resource management. ▲

Behavioral Objectives

When you finish studying this chapter, you should be able to:

▲ *Explain* how to improve international assignments through employee selection.

▲ *Answer* the question, "What sort of special training do overseas candidates need?"

▲ *Discuss* the major considerations in formulating a compensation plan for overseas employees.

▲ *Describe* the main considerations in repatriating employees from abroad.

▲ *Explain* how building employee commitment can be a cornerstone of an employer's HR philosophy.

Chapter Outline

<table>
<tr><td>

THE INTER-
NATIONALIZATION
OF BUSINESS

</td><td>

The Growth of International Business

You don't have to look very far to see how important international business is to companies here and abroad. In the United States, exports rose over 74% during the 1990s, a rate of growth that's over twice that of any other component of the gross national product.[1]

</td></tr>
</table>

This rapid export growth reflects the fact that more U.S.-based companies are focusing their marketing efforts not just in the U.S. but also abroad. Huge global companies like Procter & Gamble, IBM, and Citibank have long had extensive overseas operations, of course. But with the European Market unification, the introduction of the euro currency in 1999, the opening of Eastern Europe, and the rapid development of demand in other areas of the world, more and more companies are finding their success depends on their ability to market and manage overseas. And, of course, to companies like Toyota and Royal Dutch Shell, the United States is "overseas," and tens of thousands of firms from abroad already have thriving operations on (and beyond) U.S. shores.

As a result of this internationalization, companies must increasingly be managed globally, but this confronts managers with several challenges. Market, product, and production plans must be coordinated on a worldwide basis, for instance, and organization structures capable of balancing centralized home-office control with adequate local autonomy must be created.

For example, Ford Motor Company today is managed as a global business. Activities such as product development and vehicle design are conducted on a worldwide basis, rather than in regional development centers. Manufacturing and purchasing are also handled globally.[2] Ford approaches HR on the same global basis, "moving employees from anywhere to anywhere if they're the best ones to do the job."[3] At Ford and at other global companies, this kind of global HR perspective "requires understanding different cultures, what motivates people from different societies, and how that's reflected in the structure of international assignments."[4] As a result, as we'll see in this chapter, some of the most pressing challenges companies face concern the impact of "going global" on the employers' human resource management systems. This is because all those HR activities we've touched on in this book (such as recruiting, selecting, training, and compensating employees) are complicated by the sorts of cultural and political differences that characterize different countries around the world.

HR and the International Business Challenge

As companies have gone global, the number of their employees abroad has increased. In terms of employees overseas, for instance, a recent survey of 351 companies found that virtually every firm had at least one employee on international assignment; about 67% of the firms had between 1 and 40 employees abroad, while the remaining firms have 41 or more employees on international assignment. About 20% of the assignments were short term, up to 1 year, while 50% were for up to 3 years, and about 30% were for up to 5 years or more.[5]

With more employees abroad, HR departments have had to tackle new global challenges. For example, senior international HR managers in eight large companies were recently asked questions such as, "What are the key global pressures affecting human resource management practices in your firm currently and for the projected future?"[6] The three broad global HR challenges that emerged were as follows:

- Deployment: Easily getting the right skills to where they are needed in the organization regardless of geographical location;

- Knowledge and innovation dissemination: Spreading state-of-the art knowledge and practices throughout the organization regardless of where they originate; and

- Identifying and developing talent on a global basis: Identifying who has the ability to function effectively in a global organization and developing these abilities.[7]

Dealing with such challenges means most employers have had to scramble to develop HR policies and procedures just for handling global assignments. This process itself can be very complex: For example, consider some of the factors you'd need to address just in deciding who to deploy to an overseas assignment and how to pay that person. From a practical point of view, you'd have to address issues such as:[8]

1. Candidate identification, assessment, and selection. In addition to the required technical and business skills, key traits to consider for global assignments include, for instance: cultural sensitivity, interpersonal skills, and flexibility.

2. Cost projections. The average cost of sending an employee and family on an overseas assignment is reportedly between three and five times the employee's predeparture salary; as a result, quantifying total costs for a global assignment and deciding whether to use an expatriate or a local employee are essential in the budgeting process.

3. Assignment letters. The assignee's specific job requirements and associated pay will have to be documented and formally communicated in an assignment letter.

4. Compensation, benefits, and tax programs. We'll see in this chapter that there are many ways to compensate employees who are transferred abroad, given the vast differences in living expenses around the world. Some common approaches to international pay include home-based plus a supplement and destination-based pay.

5. Relocation assistance. The assignee will probably have to be assisted with such matters as maintenance of the person's home and automobiles, shipment and storage of household goods, and so forth.

6. Family support. Cultural orientation, language training, education assistance, and emergency provisions are just some of the matters to be addressed here before the family is shipped abroad.[9]

And that's just the tip of the iceberg. Cross-cultural, technical, and language training programs will probably be required. The complex and differentiated tapestry of labor laws and rules from country to country and provisions for reassimilating the expatriate when he or she returns home are some of the other issues you'll have to address.

RESEARCH INSIGHT   The need to take local customs and laws into consideration is illustrated by a recent study of the Dundee, Scotland, facility of NCR Corporation. The researcher collected information on several HRM activities at Dundee including the strategic role of HRM, recruitment, employee training and development, compensation, industrial relations, and flexible working patterns.[10] The findings suggested that any attempt to simply transfer home-office HR best practices to a host country facility without accommodating cultural and other differences would be futile. For example, although in many respects Dundee HR "follows the parent company's overall policies . . . to a fair extent senior managers in Dundee do things as they choose to do."[11] "Almost all, some 95% of the education and training policies and specific programs implemented in Dundee are defined here."[12] On the other hand, compensation and benefits tend to "follow the parent company's policies, and the system is fairly centralized with this respect" although there are instances where "these policies are translated into practices and procedures in a manner which are specific to NCR Dundee."[13]

New Destinations

Sending employees abroad and managing HR globally is complicated by the nature of the countries into which many firms are expanding. Employers today are not just transferring employees into the relatively lush surroundings of industrialized countries. For example, Figure 16-1 on pages 618–619 identifies 7 of the 15 countries chosen most often by 192 HR managers "as among the three countries they see emerging as assignment locations for their organizations."[14] The list ranges from the People's Republic of China (increasingly the most likely destination for a foreign assignment) down through India, Brazil, the Russian Federation, and finally Australia.

Notice the range of HR-related challenges an employer can expect when assigning employees in some of these countries. In China, for instance, special insurance should cover emergency evacuations for serious health problems; telephone communication can be a "severe handicap" in Russia; medical facilities in Russia may not meet international standards; and the compensation plan for employees in Mexico may have to deal with an inflation rate that approaches 52% per year.[15]

How Intercountry Differences Affect HRM

To a large extent, companies operating only within the borders of the United States have the luxury of dealing with a relatively limited set of economic, cultural, and legal variables. Notwithstanding the range from liberal to conservative, for instance, the United States is basically a capitalist competitive society. And while a multitude of cultural and ethnic backgrounds are represented in the U.S. workforce, various shared values (such as an appreciation for democracy) help to blur the otherwise sharp cultural differences. While the different states and municipalities certainly have their own laws affecting HRM, a basic federal law framework also helps produce a fairly predictable set of legal guidelines regarding matters such as employment discrimination, labor relations, and safety and health.

A company operating multiple units abroad is generally not blessed with such relative homogeneity. For example, minimum legally mandated holidays may range from none in the United Kingdom to 5 weeks per year in Luxembourg. And while there are no formal requirements for employee participation in Italy, employee representatives on boards of directors are required in Denmark for companies with more than 30 employees. The point is that the management of the HR function in multinational companies is complicated enormously by the need to adapt personnel policies and procedures to the differences among countries in which each subsidiary is based. The following are some intercountry differences that demand such adaptation.[16]

CULTURAL FACTORS   Wide-ranging cultural differences from country to country require corresponding differences in HR practices among a company's foreign subsidiaries. For instance, incentive plans in Japan still tend to focus on the work group, while in the West the more usual prescription is still to focus on individual worker incentives.[17] Similarly, in a study of about 330 managers from Hong Kong, the People's Republic of China, and the United States, U.S. managers tended to be most concerned with getting the job done while Chinese managers were most concerned with maintaining a harmonious environment; Hong Kong managers fell between these two extremes.[18]

A study by Professor Geert Hofstede identified other international cultural differences. For example, Hofstede says societies differ in *power distance,* in other words, the extent to which the less powerful members of institutions accept and expect that power will be distributed unequally.[19] He concluded that such an inequality was higher in some countries (such as Mexico) than in others (such as Sweden). *Masculinity versus femininity* refers, said Hofstede, to the extent to which society values assertiveness ("masculinity") versus caring (what he called "femininity"). Japan and Austria ranked high in masculinity; Denmark and Chile ranked low.

Studies show how such cultural differences can influence HR policies.[20] For example, compared to employees in the United States, "Mexican workers expect managers to keep their distance rather than to be close, and to be formal rather than informal." Similarly, compared to the United States, in Mexican organizations "formal rules and regulations are not adhered to unless someone of authority is present."[21] In Mexico, individualism is not valued as highly as it is in the United States. As a result, workers don't place as much importance on self-determination as do those in the United States, and tend to expect to receive a wider range of services and benefits (such as food baskets and medical attention for themselves and their families).[22]

In fact, the list of cultural differences from country to country is almost endless. In Germany, for instance, you should never arrive even a few minutes late and should always address senior people formally, with their titles.[23] Such cultural differences are a two-way street, and employees from abroad similarly need to be oriented to avoid the culture shock of coming to work in the United States.[24] For example, in the Intel booklet "Things You Need to Know About Working in the U.S.A." topics covered include sexual harassment, recognition of gay and lesbian rights, and Intel's expectations about behavior.[25]

ECONOMIC FACTORS   Differences in economic systems among countries also translate into intercountry differences in HR practices. In free enterprise systems, for instance, the need for efficiency tends to favor HR policies that value productivity, efficient workers, and staff cutting where market forces dictate. Moving along the scale toward more socialist systems, HR practices tend to shift toward preventing unemployment, even at the expense of sacrificing efficiency.

LABOR COST FACTORS   Intercountry differences in labor costs are substantial. Hourly compensation costs in U.S. dollars for production workers recently ranged from $1.51 in Mexico to $5.82 in Taiwan, $13.77 in the United Kingdom, $17.20 in the United States, and $31.88 in Germany, for instance.[26]

There are other comparative labor costs to consider. For example, wide gaps exist in hours worked. Portuguese workers average about 1,980 hours of work annually, while German workers average 1,648 hours. Several European countries including the United Kingdom and Germany require substantial severance pay to departing employees, usually equal to at least 2 year's service in the United Kingdom and 1 year in Germany.[27] And if it's vacation you want, abroad is often the place to be. Compared to the usual 2 or 3 weeks of U.S. vacation, workers in France can expect 2½ days of paid holiday per full month of service per year, Italians usually get between 4 and 6 weeks off per year, and Germans get 18 working days per year after 6 months of service, for instance.[28]

INDUSTRIAL RELATIONS FACTORS   Industrial relations, and specifically the relationship between the worker, the union, and the employer, vary dramatically from country to country. In Germany, for instance, *codetermination* is the rule. Here employees have the legal right to a voice in setting company policies. In this and several other countries, workers elect their own representatives to the supervisory board of the employer, and there is also a vice president for labor at the top-management level.[29]

In many other countries the state interferes little in the relations between employers and unions. In the United States, for instance, HR policies on most matters such as wages and benefits are set not by the state but by the employer, or by the employer in negotiations with its labor unions. In Germany, on the other hand, the various laws on codetermination, including the Works Constitution Act (1972), largely determine the nature of HR policies in many German firms.

Country or Region	Type of Government	GDP Per Capita (US$)	Inflation Rate	Native Languages	Travel Per Diem (US$)	Entry Requirements	Standard Workweek	Labor Law Snapshot
People's Republic of China (PRC) (*Zhonghua Renmin Gongheguo*)	Communist state	$2,900	10.1%	Standard Chinese or Mandarin, Yue (Cantonese), Wu, Minbei, Minnan, Xiang, Gan, Hakka dialects, minority languages.	Range: $119–226	U.S. citizens must have a passport and visa. Most business visitors on initial visits enter on tourist visas, which don't require a letter of invitation.	Mon. through Fri., 08:00–noon and 13:00 (or 14:00)–17:00	Rules for hiring Chinese nationals depend on the type of establishment: wholly–owned, joint venture or representative office.
Republic of India	Federal republic	$1,500	9%	English is important for national, political and commercial communication. Hindi is the primary tongue of 30% of the people.	Range: $186–306	A passport and a visa are required. Also: evidence of yellow fever immunization if the traveler is arriving from an infected area.	Most offices: Mon. through Fri., Some offices: Mon. through Sat.	Less than 2% of the total workforce is unionized. Worker days lost to strikes and lockouts have declined since 1991.
Federative Republic of Brazil (*Rebublica Federativa do Brasil*)	Federal republic	$6,100	23%	Official language: Portuguese. Also Spanish, English and French.	Range: $56–252	Travelers must have a temporary business visa (valid for 90 days) if they plan to transact business.	Mon. through Fri., 08:30 or 09:00–17:30 or 18:00 with a one- to two-hour lunch. Some factories: half-days on Sat.	Labor unions, especially in the most skilled sectors, tend to be well-organized and aggressive in defending wages and conditions.
Russian Federation (*Rossiyskaya Federatsiya*)	Federation	$5,300	7%	Primary language: Russian.	Range: $191–319	U.S. citizens must have a passport and visa. Visas are issued based on support from a sponsor: a Russian individual or organization.	40 hours per week.	Local labor mobility within Russia is limited by housing shortages and difficulties in obtaining government-required residence permits.
United Mexican States (*Estados Unidos Mexicanos*)	Federal republic operating under a centralized government	$7,700	52%	Spanish and various Mayan dialects.	Range: $61–255	U.S. citizens can apply for a business visa for up to 30 days on arrival in Mexico. Longer stays require a FM-3 visa.	48 hours including one paid day of rest.	For overtime, workers must be paid twice their normal rate—and three times their hourly rate when more than nine hours per week of overtime.
Republic of Singapore	Republic within a common-wealth	$22,900	1.7%	National language: Malay. Other languages: Chinese, Tamil and English.	$211	Passports are required. Visas aren't necessary for U.S.-based travelers.	44 hours: Mon. through Fri., 08:30–17:30 and Sat., 08:30–13:00.	The government places a ceiling on the % of foreign workers various industries may employ and a monthly levy for each foreign worker.
Hong Kong	Territory of China as of July 1997	$27,500	8.4%	Chinese (Cantonese) and English.	$344	Visas allowing residence and local employment for expats are granted on the basis of simple procedures.	Mon. through Fri., 09:00–17:00. Sat. was traditionally a half-day, but many companies now advertise 5-day workweeks.	Minimal labor relations difficulties. The average number of days lost due to industrial conflicts is one of the lowest in the world.

FIGURE 16-1 *Emerging Destinations for Foreign Assignments*

Source: Global Workforce, January 1998, pp. 18–21.

Labor Force	Unemployment Rate	Literacy Rate	Telephone System	Health & Medical Care	International Schools	Hardship Premium	Direct Investment (US$)	U.S. Companies	Embassy Information
583.6 million (1991)	5.2% (1995)	81.5% (1995)	Domestic and international services are increasingly available for private use. Unevenly distributed system.	Co. insurance should cover emergency evacuations. Serious cases are often handled in Hong Kong.	9 schools in 6 cities	15–25%	Foreign investment including (U.S.): $38 billion in 1995.	Information not available.	**Embassy of the PRC** 2300 Connecticut Ave. NW Washington, D.C. 20008 Tel: 202 / 328-2500 E-mail: webmaster@china-embassy.org URL: www.china-embassy.org/
314.751 million (1990)	Info not available.	52% (1995)	Probably the least adequate system of the industrializing countries. Slows industrial and commericial growth.	Adequate care is available in population centers. Doctors and hospitals often expect payment in cash.	6 schools in 6 cities	10–20%	U.S. investment: $192 million in 1995.	CMS Generation Coca-Cola General Motors Guardian J. Makowski Williams Corp.	**Embassy of India** 2107 Massachusetts Ave. NW Washington, D.C. 20008 Tel: 202 / 939-7000 URL: www.indiaserver.com/embusa/
57 million (1989)	5% (1995)	83.3% (1995)	Good working system.	Information not available.	12 schools in 10 cities	0–10%	U.S. Investment: $23.6 billion by end of 1995.	Alcoa Caterpillar Dow Chemical Ford IBM Xerox.	**Embassy of Brazil** 3006 Massachusetts Ave. NW Washington, D.C. 20008 Tel: 202 / 745-2700 E-mail: scitech@brasil.emb.nw.dc.us URL: www.brasil.emb.nw.dc.us/
85 million (1993)	8.2% (1995)	98% (1995)	Enlisting foreign help to speed up modernization. A severe handicap to the economy.	Far below Western standards with severe shortages of basic supplies.	3 schools in 3 cities.	10–25%	Foreign investment (including U.S.): $2.1 billion in 1996.	Information not available.	**Embassy of the Russian Federation** 2650 Wisconsin Ave. NW Washington, D.C. 20007 Tel: 202 / 298-5700 URL: www.russianembassy.org
33.6 million (1994)	10% (1995)	89.6% (1995)	Adequate domestic service for business and gov't, but the public is poorly served.	Dependable in the principal cities. Most private doctors have U.S. training.	15 schools in 10 cities	0–5%	Information not available.	Information not available.	**Embassy of Mexico** 1911 Pennsylvania Ave. NW Washington, D.C. 20006 Tel: 202 / 728-1600
1.649 million (1994)	2.6% (1995)	91.1% (1995)	Good domestic facilities and international service.	Information not available.	7 schools in a small country (3X the size of Wash., D.C.)	0%	Foreign investment (including U.S.) in manufacturing: $4.1 billion in 1996	Approximately 1,300 U.S.-based firms.	**Embassy of the Republic of Singapore** 1824 R St. NW Washington, D.C. 20009 Tel: 202 / 537-3100
2.915 million (1994)	3.5% (1995)	92.2% (Age 15+ had some school; 1995)	Modern facilities provide excellent domestic and international service.	Information not available.	11 schools in a small region (6X the size of Wash., D.C.)	0%	U.S. Investment: $13.8 billion by the end of 1995.	More than 1,100 U.S.-based businesses.	**Embassy of the PRC** 2300 Connecticut Ave. NW Washington, D.C. 20008 Tel: 202 / 328-2500 E-mail: webmaster@china-embassy.org URL: www.china-embassy.org/

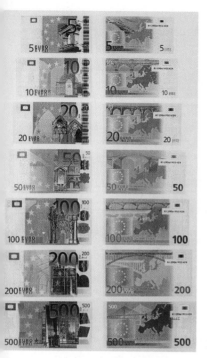

Among the many changes taking place in the international business arena is the introduction of the euro, the new single currency to be used by member nations of the European Union beginning in 1999.

THE EUROPEAN COMMUNITY (EC)[30]   In 1992 the 12 separate countries of the European community (EC) were unified into a common market for goods, services, capital, and even labor. Generally speaking, tariffs for goods moving across borders from one EC country to another disappeared, and employees (with some exceptions) now find it easier to move freely between jobs in the EC countries. The 1999 introduction of single currency—the euro—further blurred many of these differences.

However, differences remain. Many countries have minimum wages while others do not, and hours permitted in the workday and workweek vary from no maximum in the U.K. to 48 per week in Greece and Italy. Other differences exist in matters like minimum number of annual holidays, and minimum notice of termination to be given by employers.

Employment contracts represent another big HR difference between the United States and Europe. For most U.S. positions, for instance, written correspondence is normally limited to a short offer letter listing the date, job title, and initial compensation for the new hire.[31] In most European countries, on the other hand, employers are usually required to provide a detailed statement of the job. The European Union, for instance, has a directive requiring employers to provide such written proof (including details of terms and conditions of work) within 2 months of the employee's starting work.[32] Even within the EU, requirements vary. In England, a detailed written statement is required including rate of pay, date employment began, hours of work, vacation entitlement, place of work, disciplinary rules, and grievance procedure, for instance. While Germany doesn't require a written contract, it's still customary to have one specifying most particulars about the job and conditions of work. In Italy, as in Germany, written agreements aren't legally required but "even more so than in Germany, prudence dictates that written particulars are desirable in the complex, and at times confusing, legal structure in Italy."[33]

It's true the European Unions impact will be to gradually reduce these sorts of differences. However, cultural differences will still undoubtedly lead to differences in HR practices from country to country. Into the near future, in other words, and even just within Europe, managing human resources multinationally will entail tricky problems for HR managers.

In summary, intercountry differences in cultures, economic systems, labor costs, and legal and industrial relations systems complicate the task of selecting, training, and managing employees abroad. Such differences translate into corresponding differences in management styles and practices from country to country, and such differences "may strain relations between headquarters and subsidiary personnel or make a manager less effective when working abroad than at home."[34] International assignments thus run a relatively high risk of failing unless special steps are taken to select, train, and compensate international assignees.

IMPROVING INTERNATIONAL ASSIGNMENTS THROUGH SELECTION

Why International Assignments Fail

International assignments are the heart of international HR, and it's therefore somewhat disconcerting to see how often such assignments fail. For example, the number of U.S. expatriate assignments that end early reportedly ranges from 16% to 50%, and the direct costs of each such failure probably reach several hundreds of thousands of dollars.[35]

Another survey of U.S., European, and Japanese multinationals concluded that three-quarters of U.S. multinational companies experience expatriate assignment failure rates of 10% or more.[36] European and Japanese multinationals reported lower failure rates, with only about one-sixth of Japanese multinationals and 3% of European multinationals reporting more than a 10% expatriate recall rate.

The exact number of failures is understandably hard to quantify, in part because "failure" means different things to different people. Early return rates for the person sent abroad is perhaps the most obvious indicator. However, some expats may fail because they prove to be technically inept, while others simply withdraw psychologically, quietly running up the hidden costs of reduced productivity and poisoned customer and staff relations.[37]

Discovering why such assignments fail is therefore an important research task, and considerable progress has been made. In the study mentioned previously, the reasons reported for the expatriate failures differed between the U.S., European, and Japanese managers.[38] For U.S. firms, the reasons in descending order of importance were: inability of spouse to adjust; managers' inability to adjust; other family problems; managers' personal or emotional immaturity; and inability to cope with larger overseas responsibility. Managers of European firms emphasized only the inability of the manager's spouse to adjust as an explanation for the expatriate's failed assignment. Japanese firms emphasized (in descending order): inability to cope with larger overseas responsibility; difficulties with new assignment; personal or emotional problems; lack of technical competence; and finally, inability of spouse to adjust. Other studies similarly emphasize the often devastating affects that dissatisfied spouses can have on the international assignment.[39]

These findings underscore a truism regarding international assignment selection, namely, that it's usually not inadequate technical competence but family and personal problems that undermine the international assignee. As one expert puts it:

> *The selection process is fundamentally flawed. . . . Expatriate assignments rarely fail because the person cannot accommodate to the technical demands of the job. The expatriate selections are made by line managers based on technical competence. They fail because of family and personal issues and lack of cultural skills that haven't been part of the process.*[40]

International Staffing: Sources of Managers

Multinationals utilize several types of international managers. *Locals* are citizens of the countries where they are working. *Expatriates* are noncitizens of the countries in which they are working.[41] *Home-country nationals* are the citizens of the country in which the multinatioanal company's headquarters is based.[42] *Third-country nationals* are citizens of a country other than the parent or the host country—for example, a British executive working in a Tokyo subsidiary of a U.S. multinational bank.[43]

Expatriates still represent a minority of multinationals' managers. Thus, "most managerial positions are filled by locals rather than expatriates in both headquarters or foreign subsidiary operations."[44]

There are several reasons to rely on local, host-country management talent for filling the foreign subsidiary's management ranks. Many people simply prefer not to work in a foreign country, and in general the cost of using expatriates is far greater than the cost of using local workers.[45] The MNC may be viewed locally as a "better citizen" if it uses local management talent, and indeed some governments actually press for the "nativization" of local management.[46] There may also be a fear that expatriates, knowing they're posted to the foreign subsidiary for only a few years, may overemphasize short-term projects rather than focus on more necessary long-term tasks.[47]

Yet, there are also several reasons for using expatriates—either home-country or third-country nationals—for staffing subsidiaries. The major reason is reportedly technical competence: In other words, employers often can't find local candidates with the required technical qualifications.[48] Multinationals also increasingly view a successful stint abroad as a required step in developing top managers. (For instance, after a term abroad, the head of General Electric's Asia-Pacific region was transferred back to a top executive position as vice chairman at GE in 1995.) Control is another important reason to use an expat. The assumption is that home-office managers are already steeped in the firm's policies and culture, and thus more likely to implement headquarters' instructions and ways of doing things.

One potential pitfall in hiring employees from abroad—bogus credentials—doesn't seem to be a widespread problem, but prudence still suggests taking some special precautions. For one thing, a "4-year college degree" from institutions of higher learning abroad doesn't necessarily mean the same as it might, say, from a U.S. school: in some countries those 4 years include part of what Americans usually call high school. And from a practical point of view, the distances involved and the fact that you are probably unfamiliar with the college abroad make it easier to be misled by bogus credentials. Some suggestions:[49]

Don't rush into accepting a credential if you have reservations;

If you have any questions about a document, try to get the original;

Confirm the existence of the institution through references such as the "International Handbook of Universities," or the "Commonwealth Universities Handbook." You can also call the appropriate foreign consulate or embassy in New York or Washington;

Write or fax the institution named and enclose a copy of the document submitted for verification;

If you must accept documents from countries not diplomatically related to the U.S. (such as Iran), have the applicant sign a form declaring that the document's information is true and have his or her signature notarized;

Verify the applicant's foreign credentials even if the person is now transferring from a school in your country, such as a U.S. school;

Beware of telltale signs that may indicate fraudulent credentials: poor copies, stains over key information, type erasures, evidence of substituted names, credentials received too late to make proper verification possible, or typed material that's added on at an angle, for instance.[50]

International Staffing Policy

Multinational firms' top executives are often classified as either ethnocentric, polycentric, or geocentric, and these values translate into corresponding corporate policies.[51] In an ethnocentric corporation, "the prevailing attitude is that home country attitudes, management style, knowledge, evaluation criteria, and managers are superior to anything the host country might have to offer."[52] In the polycentric corporation, "there is a conscious belief that only host country managers can ever really understand the culture and behavior of the host country market; therefore, the foreign subsidiary should be managed by local people."[53] Geocentrism assumes that management candidates must be searched for on a global basis, on the assumption that the best manager for any specific position anywhere on the globe may be found in any of the countries in which the firm operates.

These three sets of multinational values translate into three broad international staffing policies. With an ethnocentric staffing policy all key management positions are filled by parent-country nationals.[54] At Royal Dutch Shell, for instance, virtually all financial controllers around the world are Dutch nationals. Reasons given for ethnocentric staffing policies include lack of qualified host-country senior management talent, a desire to maintain a unified corporate culture and tighter control, and the desire to transfer the parent firm's core competencies (for instance, a specialized manufacturing skill) to a foreign subsidiary more expeditiously.[55]

A polycentric-oriented firm would staff foreign subsidiaries with host-country nationals and its home-office headquarters with parent-country nationals. This may reduce the local cultural misunderstandings that might occur when expatriate managers are used. It will also almost undoubtedly be less expensive. One expert estimates that an expatriate executive can cost a firm up to three times as much as a domestic executive because of transfer expenses and other expenses such as schooling for children, annual home leave, and the need to pay income taxes in two countries.[56]

A geocentric staffing policy "seeks the best people for key jobs throughout the organization, regardless of nationality,"—similar to what Ford Motor Company is doing today.[57] This may let the global firm use its human resources more efficiently by transferring the best person to the open job, wherever he or she may be. It can also help build a stronger and more consistent culture and set of values among the entire global management team. Team members here are always interacting, networking, and building bonds with each other, as they move from assignment to assignment around the globe and participate in global development activities.

Selecting International Managers

There are common traits that managers to be assigned domestically and overseas will obviously share. Wherever a person is to be posted, he or she will need the technical knowledge and skills to do the job and the intelligence and people skills to be a successful manager, for instance.[58]

However, as mentioned earlier in this chapter, foreign assignments are different. There is the need to cope with a workforce and management colleagues whose cultural inclinations may be drastically different from one's own, and the stress that being alone in a foreign land can bring to bear on the single manager. And, of course, if spouse and children will share the assignment, there are the complexities and pressures that the family will have to confront, from learning a new language, to shopping in strange surroundings, to finding new friends and attending new schools.

RESEARCH INSIGHT   Selecting managers for expatriate assignments therefore means screening them for traits that predict success in adapting to what may be dramatically new environments, and here the research suggests several things to look for.

One recent study identified five factors perceived by international assignees to contribute to success in a foreign assignment. They were *job knowledge and motivation, relational skills, flexibility/adaptability, extracultural openness,* and *family situation.* (Some of the specific items, that constitute each of these five factors are presented in Figure 16-2).[59] In this study 338 international assignees from many countries and organizations completed questionnaires; they were asked to indicate which of various listed managerial traits were important for the success of managers on foreign assignment. Various reported items (including managerial ability, organizational ability, administrative skills, and creativity) were then statistically combined into a single "job knowledge and motivation" factor. Respect, courtesy and tact, display of respect, and kindness were some of the items comprising the "relational skills" factor. "Flexibility/adaptability" included such items as resourcefulness, ability to deal with stress, flexibility, and emotional stability. "Extracultural openness" included variety of outside interests, interest in foreign countries, and openness. Finally, several items including adaptability of spouse and family, spouse's positive opinion, willingness of spouse to live abroad, and stable marriage comprise the "family situation" factor.[60]

The five factors were not equally important in the foreign assignee's success, according to the responding managers. As the researchers conclude, "Family situation was generally found to be the most important factor, a finding consistent with other research on international assignments and transfers."[61] So, while all five factors were seen as important to the expatriate's success, the company that ignores the candidate's family situation does so at its peril.

A recent study by researchers of the University of Southern California provides an additional perspective. In this case 838 managers from six international firms and 21

Orientation and training for international assignments can help employees and their families avoid culture shock and better adjust to their new surroundings. Lack of such training is often the cause of employee failure in overseas postings.

FIGURE 16-2

Five Factors Important in International Assignee Importance Factors' Components

Source: Adapted from Arthur Winfred, Jr., and Winston Bennett, Jr., "The International Assignee: The Relative Importance of Factors Perceived to Contribute to Success," *Personnel Psychology*, Vol. 48 (1995), pp. 106–107.

I) Job Knowledge and Motivation
Managerial ability
Organizational ability
Imagination
Creativity
Administrative skills
Alertness
Responsibility
Industriousness
Initiative & energy
High motivation
Frankness
Belief in mission & job
Perservance

II) Relational Skills
Respect
Courtesy & tact
Display of respect
Kindness
Empathy
Nonjudgmentalness
Integrity
Confidence

III) Flexibility/Adaptability
Resourcefulness
Ability to deal with stress
Flexibility
Emotional stability
Willingness to change
Tolerance for ambiguity
Adaptability
Independence
Dependability
Political sensitivity
Positive self-image

IV) Extra-Cultural Openness
Variety of outside interests
Interest in foreign cultures
Openness
Knowledge of local language(s)
Outgoingness & extraversion
Overseas experience

V) Family Situation
Adaptability of spouse & family
Spouse's positive opinion
Willingness of spouse to live abroad
Stable marriage

countries were evaluated.[62] The researchers specifically studied the extent to which personal characteristics (such as "sensitivity to cultural differences") could be used to distinguish between managers who had high potential as international executives and those whose potential was not as high.

As summarized in Figure 16-3, 14 personal characteristics successfully distinguished the managers identified by their companies as "high potential." Consistent with results such as those mentioned previously, the characteristics—such as sensitive to cultural differences, business knowledge, brings out the best in people, takes risks, and is open to criticism—reflect a blend of technical expertise, openness and flexibility in dealing with people and getting things done.

ADAPTABILITY SCREENING   Given such findings, *adaptability screening* is often recommended as part of the expatriate screening process. Generally conducted by a professional psychologist or psychiatrist, adaptability screening aims to assess the family's probable success in handling the foreign transfer, and to alert the couple to personal issues (such as the impact on children) the foreign move may involve.[63]

Past experience is often the best predictor of future success. Companies like Colgate-Palmolive therefore look for overseas candidates whose work and nonwork experience, education, and language skills already demonstrate a commitment to and facility in living and working with different cultures.[64] Even several successful summers spent traveling overseas or participating in foreign student programs would seem to provide some concrete basis for believing that the potential transferee can accomplish the required adaptation when he or she arrives overseas.

Both the potential assignee and his or her family also require realistic previews about the problems to expect in the new job (such as mandatory private schooling for the children) as well as about the cultural benefits, problems, and idiosyncrasies of the country in question. Indeed, international HR managers speak of using realistic previews to avoid culture shock in much the same way as we discussed using them to avoid reality

FIGURE 16-3

Traits Distinguishing Successful International Executives

Source: Gretchen Spreitzer, Morgan McCall, Jr., and Joan Mahoney, "Early Identification of International Executives," *Journal of Applied Psychology*, Vol. 82, no. 1 (1997), pp. 6–29.

SCALE	SAMPLE ITEM
Sensitive to Cultural Differences	When working with people from other cultures, works hard to understand their perspectives.
Business Knowledge	Has a solid understanding of our products and services.
Courage to Take a Stand	Is willing to take a stand on issues.
Brings Out the Best in People	Has a special talent for dealing with people.
Acts with Integrity	Can be depended on to tell the truth regardless of circumstances.
Is Insightful	Is good at identifying the most important part of a complex problem or issue.
Is Committed to Success	Clearly demonstrates commitment to seeing the organization succeed.
Takes Risks	Takes personal as well as business risks.
Uses Feedback	Has changed as a result of feedback.
Is Culturally Adventurous	Enjoys the challenge of working in countries other than his/her own.
Seeks Opportunities to Learn	Takes advantage of opportunities to do new things.
Is Open to Criticism	Appears brittle—as if criticism might cause him/her to break.*
Seeks Feedback	Pursues feedback even when others are reluctant to give in.
Is Flexible	Doesn't get so invested in things that she/he cannot change when something doesn't work.
*Reverse scored	

shock among new employees. In any case, the rule should be to "spell it all out" ahead of time, as many world-class firms do for their international transferees.[65]

There are also paper-and-pencil tests that can be used to help select employees for overseas assignments. The Overseas Assignment Inventory is one such assessment tool. Based on 12 years of research with more than 7,000 candidates, the test reportedly identifies in candidates the characteristics and attitudes international candidates should have.[66]

INTERNATIONAL SELECTION IN PRACTICE   The importance of factors such as "adaptability" notwithstanding, job skills or competencies are still the major factor in selecting employees for international assignments. For example, in one worldwide survey of 323 companies, 70% of respondents listed "skills or competencies" as the most important selection criteria when choosing candidates for such assignments. "Job performance" ranked second. The presumed ability to adapt to new cultural situations—as measured by factors such as "prior international living experience or assignment," and "familiarity with assignment country"—were rarely ranked as most important or second most important by employers.[67] One can only wonder whether this helps explain the high failure rate of foreign assignees. The Diversity Counts box provides another perspective.

DIVERSITY COUNTS

Sending Women Managers Abroad

While the number and proportion of women managers working domestically has climbed fairly quickly in the past few years, the same can't be said about women managers assigned abroad. Women filled only about 6% of the overseas international management positions at major companies, according to one estimate, compared with about 37% of domestic U.S. management positions. Women comprise only about 14% of the total expatriate population, according to another survey.[68]

This raises the question why more firms don't send more women managers abroad, and the answer seems to come down to several erroneous assumptions firms make. One myth is that women are reluctant to transfer overseas and/or don't want to be

international managers. International management expert Nancy Adler says this myth seems to be based in part on research that has shown that when men are assigned overseas and are accompanied by their nonworking wives, the wife's inability to adjust is a major reason that the assignments fail. However, findings like these certainly don't necessarily extend to career women. For example, surveys of more than a thousand MBAs revealed no significant difference between female and male MBAs in pursuing international careers. In fact, "more than 4 out of 5 MBAs—both women and men—wanted international assignment at some time during their career."[69] Yet the erroneous myth remains a problem: In one study most women said that it had

---

TRAINING AND MAINTAINING INTERNATIONAL EMPLOYEES

Careful screening is just the first step in ensuring the foreign assignee's success. The employee may then require special training, and international HR policies must be formulated for compensating the firm's overseas managers and maintaining healthy labor relations.

Orienting and Training Employees for International Assignments

When it comes to providing the orientation and training required for success overseas, the practices of most U.S. firms reflect more form than substance. One consultant says that despite many companies' claims, there is generally little or no systematic selection and training for assignments overseas. In one survey, a sample of company executives agreed that international business required employees be firmly grounded in the economics and practices of foreign countries. However, few of their companies actually provided such overseas-oriented training to their employees.[75] A recent survey of U.S. companies that assign employees abroad found that only 42% have a "formal program for briefing employees regarding conditions in the host country."[76]

What sort of special training do overseas candidates need? One firm specializing in such programs prescribes a four-step approach.[77] Level 1 training focuses on the impact of cultural differences, and on raising trainees' awareness of such differences and their impact on business outcomes. Level 2 aims at getting participants to understand how attitudes (both negative and positive) are formed and how they influence behavior. (For example, unfavorable stereotypes may subconsciously influence how a new manager responds to and treats his or her new foreign subordinates.) Level 3 training provides factual knowledge about the target country, while Level 4 provides skill building in areas like language and adjustment and adaptation skills.

never occurred to their employers to consider women for overseas posts.[70]

The fact that dual-career marriages make sending female managers abroad impractical is a second erroneous myth. For example, in one survey more than three-fourths of HR executives cited dual-career marriages as a reason for not sending women managers abroad; yet responses of women international managers in separate interviews showed that dual-career couples' career problems can indeed be ironed out.[71]

Perhaps the most persistant myth is the assumption that women would face so much foreign prejudice that they could not succeed if sent abroad. The assumption here is that foreigners in general (and foreign men in particular) are so unduly prejudiced

against women managers that the latter could not perform effectively. Yet here also, the evidence belies the myth: In one survey, all the women managers (97%) reported that their international assignments were successful.[72] Even in a historically patriarchal society like Hong Kong's, another study found that "problems associated with their gender in conjunction with that specific cultural environment did not materialize and did not engender any significant impediment to [the women managers'] effective managerial performance in ways that might have been anticipated."[73] So here, too, "the excuse used by some companies for not sending women on overseas assignments—that local values are antithetical to such female participation—appeared to be unfounded."[74]

Beyond these special training practices there is also the need for more traditional training and development of overseas employees. At IBM, for instance, such development includes a series of rotating assignments that permits overseas IBM managers to grow professionally. IBM and other firms have also established management development centers around the world where executives can hone their skills. Beyond that, classroom programs (such as those at the London Business School, or at INSEAD in Fountainebleu, France) provide overseas executives the sorts of opportunities to hone their functional skills that similar stateside programs do for their U.S.-based colleagues.

In addition to honing functional skills, international management development also fosters improved control of global operations by building a unifying corporate culture. The assumption here is that the firm should bring together managers from its far-flung subsidiaries and steep them for a week or two in the firm's cherished values and current strategy and policies. The managers should then be more likely to adhere to these values, policies, and aims once they return to their assignments abroad.

International Compensation

The whole area of international compensation management presents some tricky problems. On the one hand, there is a certain logic in maintaining companywide pay scales and policies so that, for instance, divisional marketing directors throughout the world are all paid within the same narrow range. This reduces the risk of perceived inequities and dramatically simplifies the job of keeping track of disparate country-by-country wage rates.

Yet not adapting pay scales to local markets can present the HR manager with more problems than it solves. The fact is that it can be enormously more expensive to live in some countries (like Japan) than others (like Greece); if these cost-of-living differences aren't considered, it may be almost impossible to get managers to take "high-cost" assignments.

However, the answer is usually not just to pay, say, marketing directors more in one country than in another. For one thing, you could thereby elicit resistance when telling a marketing director in Tokyo who's earning $3,000 per week to move to your division in Spain, where his or her pay for the same job will drop by half (cost of living notwithstanding). One way to handle the problem is to pay a similar base salary companywide and then add on various allowances according to individual market conditions.[78]

Determining equitable wage rates in many countries is no simple matter. We've seen that there is a wealth of "packaged" compensation survey data already available in the United States, but such data are not so easy to come by overseas. As a result, "one of the greatest difficulties in managing total compensation on a multinational level is establishing a consistent compensation measure between countries that builds credibility both at home and abroad."[79]

Some multinational companies deal with this problem by conducting their own local annual compensation surveys. For example, Kraft conducts an annual study of total compensation in Belgium, Germany, Italy, Spain, and the United Kingdom. Kraft tries to maintain a fairly constant sample group of study participants (companies) in its survey. It then focuses on the total compensation paid to each of 10 senior management positions held by local nationals in these firms. The survey covers all forms of compensation including cash, short- and long-term incentives, retirement plans, medical benefits, and perquisites.[80] Kraft then uses these data to establish a competitive value for each element of pay. This information in turn becomes the input for annual salary increases and proposed changes in the benefit package.

THE BALANCE SHEET APPROACH   The most common approach to formulating expatriate pay is to equalize purchasing power across countries, a technique known as the balance sheet approach.[81] The basic idea is that each expatriate should enjoy the same standard of living he or she would have had at home. With the balance sheet approach, four main home-country groups of expenses—income taxes, housing, goods and services, and reserve—are the focus of attention. The employer estimates what each of these four expenses is for the expatriate's home country and also what each is expected to be in the expatriate's host country. Any differences—such as additional income taxes or housing expenses—are then paid by the employer.

In practice this usually boils down to building the expatriate's total compensation around five or six separate components. For example, base salary will normally be in the same range as the manager's home-country salary. In addition, however, there might be an overseas or foreign service premium. This is paid as a percentage of the executive's base salary,[82] in part to compensate the manager for the cultural and physical adjustments he or she will have to make. There may also be several allowances, including a housing allowance and an education allowance for the expatriate's children. Income taxes represent another area of concern. In many cases a U.S. manager posted abroad must pay not just U.S. taxes but also income taxes in the country to which he or she is posted.

INCENTIVES   One trend today is to award long-term incentive pay to overseas managers. While it may not seem particularly logical, many U.S. multinationals only permitted the top managers at corporate headquarters to participate in long-term incentive programs like stock option plans.[83] Equally problematical was the fact that many of the multinationals that did offer overseas managers long-term incentives (80% in one survey) used only overall corporate performance criteria when awarding incentive pay. Since the performance of the company's stock on a U.S. stock market may have little relevance to, say, a manager in a German subsidiary, the incentive value of such a reward was highly suspect.

This is particularly so in that, as one expert writes, "regardless of size, a foreign subsidiary's influence on its parent company's stock price (in U.S. dollars) is more likely to result from exchange rate movements than from management action."[84]

The answer here, more multinationals are finding, is to formulate new long-term incentives specifically for overseas executives. More and more U.S. multinationals are thus devising performance-based long-term incentive plans that are tied more closely to performance at the subsidiary level. These can help build a sense of ownership among key local managers while providing the financial incentives needed to attract and keep the people you need overseas.

BEYOND COMPENSATION   Particularly for employees in less-industrialized countries, HR managers should take nonmonetary factors. For example, a Johnson & Johnson HR manager points out that after losing professional talent at a rate of over 25% per year, "I talked to lots of our people and people in other companies and I found that most of them joined a multinational to enhance their career through training and development. If they didn't get that, they left."[85] As a result, many companies including ABB, P&G, and Siemens have established corporate-style campus training centers to provide local employees with state-of-the-art training and development programs.[86]

Performance Appraisal of International Managers

Several things complicate the task of appraising an expatriate's performance.[87] For one thing, the question of who actually appraises the expatriate is crucial. Obviously local management must have some input, but the appraisals may then be distorted by cultural differences. Thus, a U.S. expatriate manager in India may be evaluated somewhat negatively by his host-country bosses who find his use of participative decision making inappropriate in their culture. On the other hand, home-office managers may be so out of touch that they can't provide valid appraisals because they're not fully aware of the situation the manager faces. Similarly, the expatriate may be measured by objective criteria such as profits and market share, but local events (such as political instability) may affect the manager's performance while remaining "invisible" to home-office staff.[88]

Two experts make these five suggestions for improving the expatriate appraisal process:

1. Stipulate the assignment's difficulty level. For example, being an expatriate manager in China is generally considered more difficult than working in England, and the appraisal should take such difficulty-level differences into account.

2. Weigh the evaluation more toward the on-site manager's appraisal than toward the home-site manager's distant perceptions of the employee's performance.

3. If, however (as is usually the case), the home-site manager does the actual written appraisal, have him or her use a former expatriate from the same overseas location to provide background advice during the appraisal process. This can help ensure that unique local issues are considered during the appraisal process.

4. Modify the normal performance criteria used for that particular position to fit the overseas position and characteristics of that particular locale. For example, "maintaining positive labor relations" might be more important in Chile, where labor instability is more common, than it would be in the United States.

5. Attempt to give the expatriate manager credit for his or her insights into the functioning of the operation and specifically the interdependencies of the domestic and foreign operations. In other words, don't just appraise the expatriate manager in terms of quantifiable criteria like profits or market share. His

or her recommendations regarding how home office/foreign subsidiary communications might be enhanced and similar insights should affect the appraisal, too.

International Labor Relations

Firms opening subsidiaries abroad will find substantial differences in labor relations practices among the world's countries and regions. This is important; remember that while union membership is dropping in most countries around the world, as a percentage of wage and salary earners it is still relatively high in most countries compared with the United States' 14%: for example, Brazil, 44%; Argentina, 39%; Germany, 29%; Denmark, 80%; Japan, 24%; Egypt, 39%; and Israel, 23%. Any firm going abroad therefore must pay particular attention to its labor relations plans.[89]

The following synopsis illustrates some of these labor relations differences by focusing on Europe. However, keep in mind that similarly significant differences would exist as we move, say, to South and Central America, and to Asia. Some important differences between labor relations practices in Europe and the United States include:[90]

Centralization. In general, collective bargaining in Western Europe is likely to be industrywide or regionally oriented, whereas U.S. collective bargaining generally occurs at the enterprise or plant level.

Union structure. Because collective bargaining is relatively centralized in most European countries, local unions in Europe tend to have much less autonomy and decision-making power than in the United States, and they basically concentrate on administrative and service functions.

Employer organization. Due to the prevalence of industrywide bargaining, the employer's collective bargaining role tends to be performed primarily by employer associations in Europe; individual employers in the United States generally (but not always) represent their own interests when bargaining collectively with unions.

Union recognition. Union recognition for collective bargaining in Western Europe is much less formal than in the United States. For example, in Europe there is no legal mechanism requiring an employer to recognize a particular union; even if a union claims to represent 80% of an employer's workers, another union can try to organize and bargain for the other 20%.

Union security. Union security in the form of formal closed-shop agreements is largely absent in continental Western Europe.

Labor-management contracts. As in the United States, most European labor-management agreements are legally binding documents, except in Great Britain, where such collective agreements are viewed as "gentlemen's agreements" existing outside the law.

Content and scope of bargaining. U.S. labor-management agreements tend to focus on wages, hours, and working conditions. European agreements, on the other hand, tend to be brief and simple and to specify minimum wages and employment conditions, with employers free to institute more generous terms. The relative brevity of the European agreements is a function of two things: Industrywide bargaining makes it difficult to write detailed contracts applicable to individual enterprises, and in Europe the government is much more heavily involved in setting terms of employment such as vacations and working conditions.

Grievance handling. In Western Europe, grievances occur much less often than in the U.S.; when raised, they are usually handled by a legislated machinery outside the union's formal control.

Strikes. Strikes generally occur less frequently in Europe. This is probably due to industrywide bargaining, which generally elicits less management resistance than in the United States, where union demands "cut deeper into the individual enterprise's revenues."[91]

Worker participation. Worker participation has a long history in Western Europe, where it tends to go far beyond matters such as pay and working conditions. The aim is to create a system by which workers can participate in a meaningful way in the direct management of the enterprise. Determining wages, hours, and working conditions is not enough; employees should participate in formulating all management decisions. In many countries in Western Europe, works councils are required. A *works council* is a committee in which plant workers consult with management about certain issues or share in the governance of the workplace.[92] *Codetermination* is a second form of European worker participation. Codetermination means that there is mandatory worker representation on an enterprise's board of directors. It is especially prevalent in Germany.

Safety and Fair Treatment Abroad

Making provisions to ensure employee safety and fair treatment doesn't stop at a country's borders. While the U.S. has often taken the lead with respect to matters such as occupational safety, other countries are also quickly adopting such laws, and, in any event, it's hard to make a legitimate case for being less safety conscious or fair with workers abroad than you are with those at home.

Having employees abroad does raise some unique safety and fair treatment issues, however. For example, "kidnapping has become a way of life" in some countries south of the U.S. border, and in many places—"Brazil, Nigeria, the Philippines, Russia and New Guinea, to name a few—street crime is epidemic, although tourists and business people are rarely kidnapped or assassinated."[93] As one security executive at an oil company put it, "It's crucial for a company to understand the local environment, local conditions and what threat exists."[94] Keeping business travelers out of crime's way is a specialty all its own, but suggestions here include:[95]

> Provide expatriates with general training about traveling, living abroad, and the place they're going to, so they're more oriented when they get there;
>
> Tell them not to draw attention to the fact they're Americans by wearing flag emblems or t-shirts with American names, or by using American cars, for instance;
>
> Have travelers arrive at airports as close to departure time as possible and wait in areas away from the main flow of traffic where they're not as easily observed;
>
> Equip the expat's car and home with adequate security systems;
>
> Tell employees to vary their departure and arrival times and take different routes to and from work;
>
> Keep employees current on crime and other problems by regularly checking, for example, the State Department's travel advisory service and consular information sheets. These provide up-to-date information on possible threats in almost every country of the world;
>
> Advise employees to remain confident at all times: body language can attract perpetrators, and those who look like victims often become victimized.[96]

Wages paid to foreign non-management workers abroad are a well-publicized aspect of employee fair treatment today. For example, high-profile companies including Nike, Inc. have recently received bad publicity for the working conditions, long hours, and low pay rates for factory workers in countries such as Indonesia.[97]

Many companies, including Nike, have therefore taken steps to lift wages and improve the foreign workers' lot. Also currently under discussion is a plan to create the Fair Labor Association. This would be a private entity controlled by both corporate and human rights or labor representatives, with a mandate to take steps such as accrediting auditors to certify whether or not companies comply with their code of conduct.[98]

Repatriation: Problems and Solutions

Repatriation, the process of moving back to the parent company and country from the foreign assignment, is often a bittersweet experience for the returning expatriate. It means returning one's family to familiar surroundings and old friends.[99] But the returning employee all too often learns that in many respects his or her employer has ignored the manager's career and personal needs.

Several repatriation problems are quite common. One is the expatriate's fear that he or she has been "out of sight, out of mind" during an extended foreign stay and thus has lost touch with the parent firm's culture, top executives, and those responsible for the firm's promotion processes. Indeed, such fears can be well founded. Many repatriates are temporarily placed in mediocre or makeshift jobs.[100] Many are shocked to find that the executive trappings of the overseas job (private schools for the children and a company car and driver, for instance) are lost upon return, and that the executive again is just a small fish in a big pond. Perhaps more exasperating is discovering that some of the expatriate's former colleagues have been more rapidly promoted while he or she was overseas. Even the expatriate's family may undergo a sort of reverse culture shock, as spouse and children face the often daunting task of picking up old friendships and habits or starting new schools upon their return.

Progressive multinationals anticipate and avoid these problems by taking several sensible steps. They can be summarized as follows:[101]

Write repatriation agreements. Many firms including Dow Chemical and Union Carbide use repatriation agreements. These guarantee in writing that the international assignee will not be kept abroad longer than some period (such as 5 years), and that on return he or she will be given a mutually acceptable job.

Assign a sponsor. The employee should be assigned a sponsor (such as a senior manager at the parent firm's home office). This person's role is to look after the expatriate while he or she is away. This includes keeping the person apprised of significant company events and changes back home, monitoring his or her career interests, and putting the person's name into consideration for key openings when the expatriate is ready to come home.

Provide career counseling. Provide formal career counseling sessions to ensure that the repatriate's job assignments upon return meet his or her needs.[102]

Keep communications open. Keep the expatriate "plugged in" to home-office business affairs by providing management meetings around the world, frequent home leave combined with stays at headquarters to work on specific projects, and regularly scheduled meetings at headquarters.[103]

Offer financial support. Many firms such as Alcoa pay real estate and legal fees and help the expatriate to rent or in some other way maintain his or her residence, so that the repatriate and his or her family can literally return "home."

Develop reorientation programs. Provide the repatriate and his or her family with a reorientation program to facilitate their adjustment back into the home culture.

Build in return trips. One study concluded that particularly when expatriates come from a more homogeneous culture (in this case Finland) and are sent to a more "novel" culture, they can benefit by more frequent trips back to the home country "to ensure that expatriates stay in touch with home-country norms and changes during their international assignment."[104]

We invite you to visit the Dessler page on the Prentice Hall Web site at **www.prenhall.com/dessler** for our on-line study guide, Internet exercises, current events, links to related Web sites, and more.

SUMMARY

1. International business is important to almost every business today, and so firms must increasingly be managed globally. This confronts managers with many new challenges, including coordinating production, sales, and financial operations on a world-wide basis. As a result, companies today have pressing international HR needs, for instance with respect to selecting, training, paying, and repatriating its global employees.

2. Few firms today are immune from the need to manage employees abroad. One recent survey of 351 companies found that virtually all had at least one or more employees on foreign assignment.

3. Intercountry differences impact a company's HR management processes. Cultural factors such as Hofstede's power distance, individualism versus collectivism, and masculinity versus femininity suggest differences in values, attitudes, and therefore behaviors and reactions of people from country to country. Economic factors and labor cost factors help determine whether HR's emphasis should be on efficiency, commitment building, or some other approach. Industrial relations and specifically the relationship between the worker, the union, and the employer manifest themselves in concepts such as Germany's codetermination; these in turn influence the nature of a company's specific HR policies from country to country. Even within the relatively unified European Community, substantial differences in matters like minimum wage laws and length of workday exist between member countries.

4. A large percentage of expatriate assignments fail, but the batting average can be improved through careful international assignee selection. First, there are various sources HR can use to staff its domestic and foreign subsidiaries. Most managerial positions are filled by locals rather than expatriates. This is not always the case, though. In the ethnocentric corporation the prevailing attitude is that home-country managers are superior; in polycentric firms, host-country managers predominate; and in geocentric firms the best manager for any specific position is chosen from among the firm's global workforce.

5. Selecting managers for expatriate assignments means screening them for traits that predict success in adapting to dramatically new environments. Such expatriate traits include adaptability and flexibility, cultural toughness, self-orientation, job knowledge and motivation, relational skills, extracultural openness, and family situation. Adaptability screening focusing on the family's probable success in handling the foreign transfer can be an especially important step in the expatriate selection process.

6. Prior to assignment, training for overseas managers typically focuses on cultural differences, on how attitudes influence behavior, and on factual knowledge about the target country. The most common approach to formulating expatriate pay is to equalize purchasing power across countries, a technique known as the balance sheet approach. With this approach the employer estimates expenses for income taxes, housing, goods and services, and reserve, and pays supplements to the expatriate in such away as to maintain the same standard of living he or she would have had at home.

7. The expatriate appraisal process can be complicated by the need to have both local and home-office supervisors provide input into the expatriate's performance review. Suggestions for improving the expatriate appraisal process include stipulating difficulty level, weighing the on-site manager's appraisal more heavily, and having the home-site manager get background advice from managers familiar with the location abroad before completing the expatriate's appraisal.

8. Firms opening subsidiaries abroad find substantial differences in labor relations practices among the world's countries and regions. For example, even within Europe differences exist with respect to centralization of collective bargaining, local union autonomy, use of employer associations, procedures for gaining union recognition, and grievance handling.

9. Repatriation problems are very common but can be minimized. They include the often well-founded fear that the expatriate is "out of sight, out of mind" and difficulties in reassimilating the expatriate's family back into the home-country culture. Suggestions for avoiding these problems include using repatriation agreements, assigning a sponsor, offering career counseling, keeping the expatriate plugged in to home-office business, providing financial support to maintain the expatriate's home-country residence, and offering reorientation programs to the expatriate and his or her family.

DISCUSSION QUESTIONS

1. You are the president of a small business. What are some of the ways you expect being involved internationally will affect your business?

2. What are some of the specific uniquely international activities an international HR manager typically engages in?

3. What intercountry differences affect HRM? Give several examples of how each may specifically affect HRM.

4. You are the HR manager of a firm that is about to send its first employees overseas to staff a new subsidiary. Your boss, the president, asks you why such assignments fail, and what you plan to do to avoid such failures. How do you respond?

5. What special training do overseas candidates need? In what ways is such training similar to and different from traditional diversity training?

6. How does appraising an expatriate's performance differ from appraising that of a home-office manager? How would you avoid some of the unique problems of appraising the expatriate's performance?

7. What do you think accounts for the fact that worker participation has a long and relatively extensive history in Europe? How do you think this relatively extensive participation affects the labor relations process?

8. As an HR manager, what program would you establish to reduce repatriation problems of returning expatriates?

INDIVIDUAL AND GROUP ACTIVITIES

1. Give three specific examples of multinational corporations in your area. Check in the library or Internet or with each firm to determine in what countries these firms have operations, and explain the nature of some of their operations, and whatever you can find out about their international HR policies.

2. Choose three traits useful for selecting international assignees, and create a straightforward test (not pencil and paper) to screen candidates for these traits.

3. Describe the most common approach to formulating expatriate pay. Use a library or Internet source to determine the relative cost of living in five countries as of this year, and explain the implications of such differences for drafting a pay plan for managers being sent to each country.

EXPERIENTIAL EXERCISE

Compensation Incentives for Expatriate Employees

It is not uncommon for companies to offer financial supplements for executives living abroad. The international operations division has asked the HR department to develop a standard compensation plan for expatriate employees. They have provided you with a list of issues that seem to make a foreign assignment more difficult than a domestic one. You have been asked to decide which of these issues are most important and to specify the effect each should have on compensation.

YOUR RANKING	ISSUES	DESCRIPTION	EFFECT ON COMPENSATION
	Health care	Physicians and hospital do not meet Western standards.	Make contingency money available to fly expatriate to closest country with Western-style health care. (Example)
	Family life	There are no English language schools for children—children of expatriates will need to attend private boarding schools.	
	Inflation	Target country currency is unstable. Currency may inflate by as much as 20% per month.	
	Infrastructure	The expatriate will not be able to have his or her own phone or TV.	
	Political risk	Assigned country faces the risk of political upheaval.	

■ **DIRECTIONS**

Divide the class into small teams. Ask each team to perform the following tasks:

1. Rank order the issues from one to five (number one being the most important).
2. Assume that each employee has a base salary equal to their U.S. compensation. You may add from 0 to 50% to that as a supplement for each item on the list.

Answer the following discussion questions as a team:

1. What will be the effort of each on compensation?
2. How much did you need to increase compensation overall to satisfy the expected needs of your expatriate workers?
3. What problems might this level of compensation create?

CASE INCIDENT

"Boss, I Think We Have a Problem"

Central Steel Door Corp. has been in business for about 20 years, successfully selling a line of steel industrial grade doors, as well as the hardware and fittings required for them. Focusing mostly in the United States and Canada, the company had gradually increased its presence from the New York City area, first into New England and then down the Atlantic Coast, then through the Midwest and West, and finally into Canada. The company's basic expansion strategy was always the same: choose an area, open a distribution center; hire a regional sales manager; then let that regional sales manager help staff the distribution center and higher local sales reps.

Unfortunately, the company's traditional success in finding sales help has not extended to its overseas operations. With the introduction of the new European currency, Mel Fisher, president of Central Steel Door, decided to expand his company abroad, into Europe. However, the expansion has not gone smoothly at all. He tried for 3 weeks to find a sales manager by advertising in the *International Herald Tribune*, which is read by businesspeople in Europe and by American expatriates living and working in Europe. Although the ads placed in the *Tribune* also run for about a month in the *Tribune's* Internet Web site, Mr. Fisher so far has received only five applications. One came from a possibly viable candidate, whereas four came from candidates who Mr. Fisher refers to as "lost souls," people who seem to have spent most of their time traveling restlessly from country to country sipping espresso in sidewalk cafes. When asked what he had done for the last 3 years, one told Mr. Fisher he'd been on a "walkabout."

Other aspects of his international HR activities have been equally problematical. Fisher alienated two of his U.S. sales managers by sending them to Europe to temporarily run the European operations, but neglecting to work out a compensation package that would cover their relatively high living expenses in Germany and Belgium. One ended up staying the better part of the year, and Mr. Fisher was rudely surprised to be informed by the Belgian government that his sales manager owed thousands of dollars in local taxes. The managers had hired about 10 local people to staff each of the two distribution centers. However, without full-time local European sales managers, the level of sales was disappointing, so Fisher decided to fire about half the distribution center employees. That's when he got an emergency phone call from his temporary sales manager in Germany: "I've just been told that all these employees should have had written employment agreements and that in any case we can't fire anyone without at least 1 year's notice, and the local authorities here are really up in arms. Boss, I think we have a problem."

■ QUESTIONS

1. Based on the chapter and the case incident, compile a list of 10 international HR mistakes Mr. Fisher has made so far.

2. How would you have gone about hiring a European sales manager? Why?

3. What would you do now if you were Mr. Fisher?

Case Application

TAKING A FAST BOAT TO NOWHERE

Two years after sending an ambitious and highly regarded executive to Hong Kong to oversee a major expansion into Asia, the U.S. firm Bandag Inc. closed its Chinese office and laid the executive off. "I was a star 18 months ago," said Gerald Borenstein. "Now they have no use for me."

After his careful analysis inspired Bandag, a leading producer of retread tires, to make the move into Asia, Borenstein appeared to have fallen victim to the economic downturn that ended the prosperous 1990s in the East. "Three years ago, going overseas seemed like a pretty safe bet for people positioning themselves to come back in a higher position," says a Motorola executive who left Asia just before the economy went sour. "Now you're looking at what could be a career-shattering situation," But was the economic crisis the only factor in Borenstein's fall?

From its headquarters in Muscatine, Iowa, 3½ hours from Des Moines, Bandag throws a wide international net. It has factories and dealers from Brazil to Europe to Indonesia, and in 1997 about a third of its $822 million revenue came from overseas. The vast Chinese market was a logical next step, and Borenstein's analysis of its potential encouraged management to send him there to reconnoiter. "The company had strategies to become more aggressive, take more risks, become more entrepreneurial and find business outside U.S. markets," Borenstein recalls. "That was music to my ears."

The decision to open a Hong Kong office was made in 1997. Henry Li, an Eastman Kodak executive based in Hong Kong, was recruited to head the operation, and Borenstein was named his deputy. He was told there were no guarantees what his next position in the company would be, although he and Bandag both expected that if he did well, another overseas posting would follow. He knew the risks and figured he would beat the odds.

The move to Hong Kong offered Borenstein a higher profile, greater responsibilities, and perks typical for an expatriate executive. He and his family moved to a 3-bedroom apartment overlooking the city and were allowed a full-time housekeeper and private schooling for their two children, adding considerable value to Borenstein's salary, which remained in the low six figures.

For the first several months things went even better than planned. Sales surpassed expectations, and Borenstein and Li hired more staff, rented spacious offices, and prepared for further expansion. Bandag's CEO took notice, traveling to Hong Kong to be briefed by Borenstein and inviting him back to Muscatine for further conferences. Contact with headquarters was frequent and positive.

The economic downturn began in the summer of 1997. Thailand's and Indonesia's currencies collapsed, and Bandag saw its prospects for quick Asian profits evaporating. Stiffer competition at home brought pressure to cut costs in the Hong Kong operation, which Borenstein and Li were reluctant to do. Believing sales would still take off, the two paid salary and expenses for four engineers although they had work for only one and maintained expensive office space for 20 employees in Beijing even though they had only 16. "We didn't react quickly enough that sales weren't coming in," Borenstein now recalls. He even regrets entertaining visiting Bandag executives at his Hong Kong home. "They said we lived in a palace," he remembers. "I got a lot of flak over that."

Then the executive who sent Borenstein to China retired, and several of Borenstein's other contacts were reassigned. He began to skip headquarters meetings, believing the 18 hours travel time weren't worth the few hours of home-office contact he would get. His e-mail slowed to a trickle, and the phone calls from Iowa gradually stopped. He found himself increasingly taking Li's side in disagreements with the home office.

Finally, in July, Borenstein and Li flew to headquarters to make a major presentation about Bandag's options in dealing with the Asian crisis. Once there, they found the morning session cut short and the afternoon canceled. Instead, in a confrontation with top executives, they learned that Bandag had decided it just wasn't the right time to expand in China. Ten days later, Li resigned and Borenstein was told there was no longer any job for him, in Asia *or* the United States. He and his family eventually returned to California, and he still hopes to find another job overseas.

■ **QUESTIONS**

1. What uncontrollable factors contributed to the crisis in Borenstein's career? Over which factors did he have control?

2. Whether you think they would have changed the eventual outcome or not, how might Borenstein have handled the controllable factors differently?

3. How did Bandag handle the HR aspects of staffing and managing the new Hong Kong facility? What improvements would you suggest? Why?

4. What, if anything, could Bandag have done differently to minimize the impact of the economic downturn on Borenstein and his family?

Source: Jonathan Kaufman, "An American Expatriate Finds Hong Kong Post a Fast Boat to Nowhere," *Wall Street Journal*, Jan. 21, 1999, pp. A1 and A8.

APPENDIX 16-1

■ Toward an HR Philosophy and Auditing The HRM Function

TOWARD A PHILOSOPHY OF HR MANAGEMENT

The Need for a Philosophy

People's actions are always based in part on the assumptions they make, and this is especially true in regard to human resource management. The basic assumptions you make about people—Can they be trusted? Do they dislike work? Can they be creative? Why do they act as they do?—comprise your philosophy of HR. And the people you hire, the training you provide, and your leadership style all reflect (for better or worse) this basic philosophy.

Yet throughout this book we have emphasized the "nuts and bolts" of HR management by focusing on the concepts and techniques all managers need to carry out their personnel-related tasks. It's therefore easy to lose sight of the fact that these techniques, while important, can't be administered effectively without a unifying philosophy. To repeat, it is this philosophy or framework that provides direction with respect to the people you hire, the training you provide, and how you motivate employees.

For more and more employers, the essence of the difference between personnel management and human resource management is indeed a philosophical one; it revolves around the latter's emphasis on earning the employees' commitment, which means creating an environment that makes the employees identify with the company and its objectives and to treat them as if they're their own. In practice, creating this environment means providing employees with fair and equitable treatment, an opportunity for each employee to use his or her skills to the utmost and to self-actualize, open and trusting communications, adequate and fair compensation, and a safe and healthy work environment.

Every personnel action you take, in other words, affects your employees' commitment, and your actions will in turn reflect your basic values and assumptions about people. It is when your personnel actions are geared not just toward satisfying your organization's staffing needs but also toward satisfying your employees' needs to grow and to self-actualize that your personnel management system can be properly referred to as a human resource management system.

BUILDING EMPLOYEE COMMITMENT

A Recap

Many employers translate such an HRM philosophy into practices that win their employees' commitment. HRM practices described in this book that can help build commitment include the following:

- *Establish people-first values.* As one manager said, "You start the process of boosting employee commitment by making sure you know how you and your top managers really feel about people." In other words, you must be willing to commit to the idea that your employees are your most important assets and that they can be trusted, treated with respect, involved in making on-the-job decisions, and encouraged to grow and reach their full potential. Then put those values in writing, hire and promote into management those people who have people-first values, and translate your people-first values into actions every day.

- *Guarantee fair treatment.* Establish a super grievance procedure that guarantees fair treatment of all employees in all grievance and disciplinary matters. Boost upward and downward communications with Speak Up! or similar programs. Institute multiple, formal, easy-to-use channels that employees can use to express concerns and gripes and to get answers to matters that concern them. Also use periodic opinion surveys such as survey-feedback-action, and use every opportunity to tell employees what's going on in your organization.

- *Use value-based hiring.* The time to start building commitment is before—not after—employees are hired. High-commitment firms are thus very careful about whom they hire. Start by clarifying your firm's own values and ideology so they can be part of the screening process. Then make your screening process exhaustive, for instance, by designing screening tools like structured interviews to help select applicants based partly on their values. Recruit actively, so those hired see that many were rejected and that they are part of an elite. Go on to provide candid, realistic previews of what working at your firm will be like. Self-selection is important for building commitment—for instance, use long probationary periods or a long, exhaustive screening process that requires some "sacrifice" on the part of employees.

- *Provide for employee security.* Practice lifetime employment without guarantees. While specifying that all employment relationships will be employment-at-will arrangements, emphasize your commitment to lifetime employment without guarantees, with statements such as: "Stable employment and continual improvement of the well-being of our team members are essential and can be obtained through the smooth, steady growth of our company." Company practices that facilitate employee security include using a compensation plan that places much of each employee's salary at risk, hiring large numbers of temporary or part-time employees, and cross-training employees to wear "several hats."

- *Assess the rewards package.* Build a pay plan that encourages employees to think of themselves as partners. This means employees should have a healthy share of the profits in good years and share in the downturn during bad times. Therefore, put a significant portion of pay at risk. Institute stock ownership plans that encourage employees to see they have a significant investment in your firm. Emphasize self-reporting of hours worked rather than devices like time clocks.

- *Actualize employees.* High-commitment firms engage in actualizing practices that aim to ensure that all employees have every opportunity to use all their skills and gifts at work and become all they can be. Commit to actualizing, front-load new employees' jobs with challenge, enrich workers' jobs and empower them, and institute comprehensive promotion-from-within/career progress programs.

Practices like these can help an employer win its employees' commitment, by creating a situation in which the employees' and employer's goals become one. Then (it is hoped), employees do their jobs not just because they must but because they want to—they work as if they own the company. And in an era that requires high levels of worker flexibility, creativity, quality, and initiative, committed employees are a firm's best competitive edge.[105]

THE HIGH-PERFORMANCE ORGANIZATION: BUILDING BETTER, FASTER, MORE COMPETITIVE ORGANIZATIONS THROUGH HR

Globalized competition, deregulation, and technological advances require all companies today to be better, faster, and more competitive. The mergers and downsizings of the 1990's are perhaps the most obvious manifestation of this drive toward competitiveness. Less obvious but perhaps no less important has been HR's emerging new role in making companies better, faster, and more competitive, both directly (as we've seen in the special boxed features in this book describing, for instance, how testing programs can boost productivity) as well as more subtly by creating committed employees willing to respond to the challenges of heightened competition.

Indeed, the need for companies today to be better, faster, and more competitive lends a special urgency to having committed employees, ones who do their jobs as if they own the company. With fewer supervisors in the now downsized organizations, and with more emphasis on teamwork and innovation and with even factory jobs today more high-tech, it's usually committed and highly trained employees—not just machines—that give firms their competitive advantage.

HR plays a central role in this process, and the process can be summarized as follows: HR activities (such as value-based hiring, and employee-development) →competent, committed employees→Better, faster, more competitive organizations. Today it has become commonplace to say that HR is and should be a partner in developing and implementing a company's strategy. HR's role in creating employee commitment is a good example of HR's potential strategic role: By creating committed employees HR can help create the competitive advantage for the firm, and thereby have a determining effect on whether or not the company is good enough, fast enough, and competitive enough to survive and to thrive.

AUDITING THE HR FUNCTION

Designing an HR system is not enough. Effectively implementing it is another. Several suggestions have been made for ways to assess how a firm's HR department is actually doing. One approach is to use accounting and statistical techniques to calculate the cost of human resources, such as the dollar investment in human assets resulting from training. In this way the bottom-line contribution of HR can be quantitatively assessed.[106] For an employer with the wherewithal to conduct such a program, it may well be worth considering. A second, less rigorous, but still effective approach follows.

THE HR REVIEW At a minimum, an HR review should be conducted, aimed at tapping top managers' opinions regarding how effective HR has been. Such a review should contain two parts: what should be, and what is.[107]

The question "what should be" refers to the HRM department's broad aims and involves two things. It should start, first, with a very broad philosophy or vision statement. This might envision HR as being "recognized as an excellent resource rather than a bureaucratic entity, a business-oriented function, and the conscience of the company," for example. This vision might also enumerate the characteristics of the HR staff, for instance, as "being experts in their areas of responsibility, demonstrating a commitment to excellence, and being creative, analytical problem solvers." The vision statement should thus set the tone for HR.

Second, this broad vision gets more focus with an HRM mission statement. This describes what the mission of the department should be, for instance, "to contribute to the achievement of the company's business objectives by assisting the organization in making effective and efficient use of employee resources and, at the same time, assisting employees at all levels in creating for themselves satisfying and rewarding work lives."[108]

Next, the HR review's focus shifts to an evaluation of "what is." This part of the evaluation consists of six steps and requires input from the corporate HR staff, division heads, divisional HR heads, and those other experts (like the benefits administrator) who report directly to the head of corporate HR. The issues to be addressed are as follows:

1. *What are the HR functions?* Here those providing input (division heads and so forth) give their opinions about what they think HR's functions should be. The list can be extensive, ranging from EEO enforcement and health benefits management to employee relations management, recruitment and selection, training, and even community relations management. The important point here is to crystallize what HR and its main "clients" believe HR's functions should be.

2. *How important are these functions?* The participants then rate each of these functions on a 10-point scale of importance, ranging from low (1–3) to medium (4–7) to high (8–10). This provides an estimate of how important each of the 15 or 20 identified HRM functions are in the views of HRM executives and of their clients (like division managers).

3. *How well is each of the functions performed?* Next have the same participants evaluate how well each of these HR functions is actually being performed. You may find, for example, that four functions— say, employee benefits, compensation, employee relations, and recruiting—receive "high" ratings from more than half the raters. Other functions may get "medium" or "low" ratings.

4. *What needs improvement?* The next step is to determine which of the functions rated most important are not being well performed. Functions (like "labor relations") that are assessed as highly important but evaluated as low in terms of performance will require the quickest attention. To formalize the comparison of importance and performance ratings, have the participants compare the median importance and performance ratings for each of the 15 to 20 functions identified in step 1.

   The discussions at this stage will help identify the HR functions in which the department has to improve its performance. They should help to pinpoint specific problems that contributed to the low performance ratings and help provide recommendations for improving performance.

5. *How effectively does the corporate HR function use resources?* This next step consists of checks to determine whether the HR budget is being allocated and spent in a way that's consistent with the functions HR should be stressing. First, make an estimate of where the HR dollars are being spent—for instance, on recruiting, EEO compliance, compensation management, and so on. Questions to ask here are: "Is expense allocation consistent with the perceived importance and performance of each of the HR functions?" and "Should any dollars be diverted to low-performing functions to improve their effectiveness?"

6. *How can HR become most effective?* This final step is aimed at allowing you one last, broader view of the areas that need improvement and how they should be improved. For example, at this step it may be apparent that a large divisionally organized company needs to strengthen divisional and on-site HRM staffs so that responsibilities for certain HR functions can be moved closer to the user.

NOTES

1. "The Gross National Product," *Occupational Outlook Quarterly* (Fall 1989), U.S. Department of Labor; Ellen Brandt, "Global HR," *Personnel Journal* (March 1991), pp. 38–44; Charlene Marmer Solomon, "HR Heads into the Global Age," *Personnel Journal*, October 1993, pp. 76–77; and Rachel Moskowitz and Drew Warnick, "The Job Outlook in Brief," *Occupational Outlook Quarterly*, Spring 1996, pp. 3–43.

2. Charlene Solomon, "Today's Global Mobility," *Global Workforce* (July 1998), p. 16.

3. Ibid., p. 16.

4. Ibid., p. 16.

5. "International Assignments," *BNA Bulletin to Management*, February 8, 1996, pp. 44–45; "International Assignment Policies and Practices," *BNA Bulletin to Management*, May 1, 1997, pp. 140–141.

6. Keren Roberts, Ellen Kossek, and Cynthia Ozeki, "Managing the Global Workforce: Challenges and Strategies," *Academy of Management Executive*, Vol. 12, no. 4 (1998), pp. 93–106.

7. Ibid., p. 94.

8. This is based on John Fadel and Mark Petti, "International HR Policy Basics," *Global Workforce* (April 1997), pp. 29–30.

9. Paraphrased or quoted from Ibid., pp. 29–30.

10. Monir Tayeb, "Transfer of HRM Practices Across Cultures. An American Company in Scotland," *The International Journal of Human Resource Management*, Vol. 9, no. 2 (April 1998), pp. 332–358.

11. Ibid., p. 342.

12. Ibid., p. 344.

13. Ibid., p. 345.

14. "Fifteen Top Emerging Markets," *Global Workforce* (January 1998), pp. 18–21.

15. Ibid.

16. Thee are based on Eduard Gaugler, "HR Management: An International Comparison," *Personnel* (August 1988), pp. 24–30. See also Yasuol Kuwahara. "New Developments in Human Resource Management in Japan," *Asia Pacific Journal of Human Resources*, Vol. 31, no. 2 (1993), p. 3–11; and Charlene Marmer Solomon, "How Does Your Global Talent Measure Up?" *Personnel Journal* (October 1994), pp. 96–108.

17. For a discussion of this, see Gaugler Ibid., p. 26; see also George Palmer, "Transferred to Tokyo—A Guide to Etiquette in the Land of the Rising Sun," *Multinational Business*, No. 4 (1990–1991), pp. 36–44.

18. David Ralston, Priscilla Elsass, David Gustafson, Fannie Cheung, and Robert Terpstra, "Eastern Values: A Comparison of Managers in the United States, Hong Kong, and the People's Republic of China," *Journal of Applied Psychology*, Vol. 71, no. 5 (1992), pp. 664–671.

19. Geert Hofstede, "Cultural Dimensions in People Management," in Vladimir Pucik, Noel Tishy, and Carole Barnett (Eds.), *Globalizing Management* (New York: John Wiley & Sons, Inc., 1992), p. 143.

20. Randall Schuler, Susan Jackson, Ellen Jackofsky, and John Slocum, Jr., "Managing Human Resources in Mexico: A Cultural Understanding," *Business Horizons* (May/June 1996), pp. 55–61.

21. Ibid.

22. Ibid.

23. Valerie Frazee, "Establishing Relations in Germany," *Global Workforce* (April 1997), p. 17.

24. Charlene Solomon, "Destination U.S.A.," *Global Workforce* (April 1997), pp. 19–23.

25. Ibid., p. 21.

26. "Labor Costs in Manufacturing by Nation," *BNA Bulletin to Management*, April 10, 1997, pp. 116–117.

27. "Comparing Employment Practices," *BNA Bulletin to Management*, April 22, 1993, p. 1.

28. "Vacation Policies Around the Globe," *Global Workforce* (October 1996), p. 9.

29. This is discussed in Gaugler, "HR Management," p. 28.

30. This is based on Rae Sedel "Europe 1992: HR Implications of the European Unification," *Personnel* (October 1989), pp. 19–24. See also Chris Brewster and Ariane Hegewish, "A Continent of Diversity," *Personnel Management* (January 1993), pp. 36–39.

31. Alan Chesters, "Employment Contracts—In Writing or Not?" *Global Workforce* (April 1997), p. 12.

32. Ibid., p. 12.

33. Ibid., p. 13.

34. Daniels and Radebaugh, *International Business*, p. 764.

35. For a discussion see Margaret Shaffer and David Harrison, "Expatriates Psychological Withdrawal from International Assignments: Work, Nonwork, and Family Influences," *Personnel Psychology*, Vol. 51 (1998), pp. 87–118.

36. R. L. Tung, "Selection and Training Procedures of U.S., European, and Japanese Multinationals," *California Management Review*, Vol. 25 (1982), pp. 51–71; see also Jennifer Laabs, "Like Finding a Needle in a Haystack: Recruiting in the Global Village," *Workforce*, Vol. 77, no. 4 (April 1998), pp. 30–33.

37. Ibid., p. 88.

38. Discussed in Charles Hill, *International Business*, pp. 511–515.

39. Charlene Solomon, "One Assignment, Two Lives," *Personnel Journal* (May 1996), pp. 36–47; and Michael Harvey, "Dual-Career Couples During International Relocation: The Trailing Spouse," *The International Journal of Human Resource Management*, Vol. 9, no. 2 (April 1998), pp. 309–330.

40. Michael Schell, quoted in Charlene Marmer Solomon, "Success Abroad Depends on More than Job Skills," p. 52.

41. Daniels and Radebaugh, *International Business*, p. 767.

42. Arvind Phatak, *International Dimensions of Management* (Boston: PWS Kent, 1989), pp. 106–107.

43. Ibid., p. 106.

44. Daniels and Radebaugh, *International Business*, p. 767.

45. Ibid., p. 769; Phatak, *International Dimensions of Management*, p. 106.

46. Phatak, *International Dimensions of Management*, p. 108.

47. Daniels and Radebaugh, *International Business*, p. 769.

48. Ibid., p. 769; Phatak, *International Dimensions of Management*, p. 106.

49. Christopher Bachler, "Global Impats—Don't Let Them Surprise You," *Personnel Journal* (June 1996), p. 60.

50. Ibid., p. 60.

51. Howard Perlmutter, "The Torturous Evolution of the Multinational Corporation," *Columbia Journal of World Business*, Vol. 3, no. 1 (January–February 1969), pp. 11–14, discussed in Phatak, *International Dimensions of Management*, p. 129.

52. Phatak, *International Dimensions of Management*, p. 129.

53. Ibid.

54. Hill, *International Business*, p. 507.

55. Ibid., pp. 507–510.

56. Ibid., p. 509.

57. Ibid.

58. Phatak, *International Dimensions of Management*, p. 113; and Charlene Marmer Solomon, "Staff Selection Impacts Global Success," *Personnel Journal* (January 1994), pp. 88–101. For another view, see Anne Harzing, "The Persistent Myth of High Expatriate Failure Rates," *International Journal of Human Resource Management*, Vol. 6, no. 2 (May 1995), pp. 457–474.

59. Winfred Arthur, Jr., and Winston Bennett, Jr., "The International Assignee: The Relative Importance of Factors Perceived to Contribute to Success," *Personnel Psychology*, Vol. 48 (1995), pp. 99–114.; table on pp. 106–107. See also Davison and Betty Punnett, "International Assignments: Is There a Role for Gender and Race in Decisions?" *International Journal of Human Resource Management*, Vol. 6, no. 2 (May 1995), pp. 411–441.

60. Arthur and Bennett Ibid., pp. 105–108

61. Ibid., p. 110.

62. Gretchen Spreitzer, Morgan McCall, Jr., and Joan Mahoney, "Early Identification of International Executive Potential," *Journal of Applied Psychology*, Vol. 82, no. 1 (1997), pp. 6–29.

63. Phatak, *International Dimensions of Management*, p. 119.

64. See, for example, Blocklyn, "Developing the International Executive," p. 45.

65. Ibid., p. 45.

66. Discussed in Madelyn Callahan, "Preparing the New Global Manager," *Training and Development Journal* (March 1989), p. 30. The publisher of the inventory is the New York consulting firm Moran, Stahl & Boyer; see also Jennifer Laabs, "The Global Talent Search," *Personnel Journal* (August 1991), pp. 38–44 for a discussion of how firms such as Coca-Cola recruit and develop international managers; and T. S. Chan, "Developing International Managers: A Partnership Approach," *Journal of Management Development*, Vol. 13, no. 3 (1994), pp. 38–46.

67. "International Assignment Policies and Practices," *BNA Bulletin to Management*, May 1, 1997, pp. 140–141, based on a survey by Organization Resources Counselors, Inc., New York City.

68. Nancy Adler, "Women Managers in a Global Economy," *Training & Development* (April 1994), p. 31; and Charlene Solomon, "Women Expats: Shattering the Myths," *Global Workforce* (May 1998), p. 12.

69. Nancy Adler, "Women Managers in a Global Economy," *Training and Development* (April 1994), p. 31; Solomon, "Women Expats," pp. 12–13.

70. Adler, Ibid., p. 32.

71. Ibid.

72. Ibid., pp. 32–33.

73. R. I. Westwood and S. M. Leung, "International Studies of Management & Organization," Vol. 24, no. 3, p. 81.

74. Ibid., p. 81.

75. Callahan, "Preparing the New Global Manager," p. 29–30. See also Charlene Marmer Solomon, "Global Operations Demand that HR Rethink Diversity," *Personnel Journal* (July 1994), pp. 40–50.

76. Valerie Frazee, "Expats are Expected to Dive Right In," *Personnel Journal*, December 1996, p. 31.

77. This is based on Ibid., p. 30. See also Daniel Feldman, "Repatriate Moves as Career Transitions," *Human Resource Management Review*, Vol. 1, no. 3 (Fall 1991), pp. 163–178; and John Yanouzas and Sotos Boukis, "Transporting Management Training into Poland: Some Surprises and Disappointments," *Journal of Management Development*, Vol. 12, no. 1 (1993), pp. 64–71; Jennifer Laabs, "How Gillette Grooms Global Talent," *Personnel Journal* (August 1993), pp. 64–76; and Charlene Marmer Solomon, "Transplanting Corporate Cultures Globally," *Personnel Journal* (October 1993), pp. 78–88. Information for setting up a language training program can be found in the "Standard Guide for Use-Oriented Foreign Language Instruction," issued for about $18.00 from the American Society for Testing and Materials, 610.832.9585, as explained in Stephen Dolainski, "Are Expats Getting Lost in the Translation," *Workforce*, p. 34.

78. James Stoner and R. Edward Freeman, *Management*, 4th ed. (Upper Saddle River, NJ: Prentice Hall, 1989), p. 783. See also John Cartland, "Reward Policies in a Global Corporation," *Business Quarterly* (Autumn 1993), pp. 93–96; and Laura Mazur, "Europay," *Across-the-Board* (January 1995), pp. 40–43.

79. Hewitt Associates, "On Compensation," (May 1989), p. 1 (Hewitt Associates, 86–87 East Via De Ventura, Scottsdale, Arizona 85258).

80. Hewitt Associates, Ibid., p. 2.

81. Hill, *International Business*, pp. 519–520; Valerie Frazee, "Is the Balance Sheet Right for Your Expats?" *Global Workforce* (September 1998), pp. 19–26.

82. Phatak, *International Dimensions of Management*, p. 134.

83. This is based on Brian Brooks, "Long-Term Incentives: International Executives Need Them, Too," *Personnel* (August 1988), pp. 40–42. See also James Ward and Mark Blumenthal, "Localization: A Study in Cost Containment," *Innovations in International Compensation*, Vol. 17, no. 4 (November 1991), pp. 3–4; and Laura Mazur, "Europay," pp. 40–43.

84. Brooks, "Long-Term Incentives," p. 41.

85. Mike Johnson, "Beyond Pay: What Rewards Work Best When Doing Business in China," *Compensation & Benefits Review* (November/December 1998), p. 53.

86. Ibid., p. 53.

87. Except as noted, this is based on Gary Addou and Mark Mendenhall, "Expatriate Performance Appraisal: Problems and Solutions," in Mark Mendenhall and Gary Addou, *International Human Resource Management* (Boston: PWS Kent Publishing Co., 1991), pp. 364–374.

88. Ibid., p. 366. See also Maddy Janssens, "Evaluating International Managers' Performance: Parent Company Standards as Control Mechanism," *The International Journal of Human Resource Management*, Vol. 5, no. 4 (December 1994), pp. 853–873.

89. "Union Membership Around the World," *BNA Bulletin to Management*, November 13, 1997, pp. 364–365.

90. Robert Sauer and Keith Voelker, *Labor Relations: Structure and Process* (New York: Macmillan, 1993), pp. 510–525.

91. Ibid., p. 516. See also Marino Regini, "Human Resource Management and Industrial Relations in European Companies," *The International Journal of Human Resource Management*, Vol. 4, no. 3 (September 1993), pp. 555–568.

92. Quoted from Ibid., p. 519.

93. Samuel Greengard, "Mission Possible: Protecting Employees Abroad," *Workforce* (August 1997), pp. 30–32.

94. Ibid., p. 32.

95. These are based on or quoted from Ibid., p. 32.

96. Ibid., p. 32.

97. Erin Bernstein, "A Floor Under Foreign Factories?" *Business Week*, November 2, 1998, pp. 126–128.

98. Ibid., p. 126.

99. Definition based on Dennis Briscoe, *International Human Resource Management*, p. 65. See also Linda Stroh, "Predicting Turnover Among Repatriates: Can Organizations Affect Retention Rates?" *International Journal of Human Resource Management*, Vol. 6, no. 2 (May 1995), pp. 443–456.

100. Phatak, *International Dimensions of Management*, p. 124. See also Reyer Swaak, "Today's Expatriate Families: Dual Careers and Other Obstacles," *Compensation and Benefits Review*, Vol. 27, no. 3 (May 1995), pp. 21–26.

101. These are based on Briscoe, *International Human Resource Management*, p. 66; Phatak, *International Dimensions of Management*, p. 124; Daniels and Radebaugh, *International Business*, p. 772; and Valerie Frazee, "Welcome Your Repatriates Home," *Global Workforce* (April 1997), pp. 24–28.

102. Briscoe, *International Human Resource Management*, p. 66.

103. Phatak, *International Dimensions of Management*, p. 126.

104. Hal Gregersen and Linda Stroh, "Coming Home to the Arctic Cold: Antecedents to Finnish Expatriate and Spouse Repatriation Adjustment," *Personnel Psychology*, Vol. 50 (1997), p. 651.

105. For a discussion of employees as a competitive advantage see, for example, Peg Anthony and Lincoln Norton, "Link HR to Corporate Strategy," *Personnel Journal* (April 1991), pp. 75–86. Jeffrey Arthur, "The Link Between Business Strategy and Industrial Relations Systems," *Industrial and Labor Relations Review*, Vol. 45, no. 3 (April 1992), pp. 488–506. Michael Donahue, "Do Your Human Resources Add Value?", *Management Accounting*, June 1996, pp. 47–48; Gary Dessler, "How to Earn Your Employees' Commitment," *The Academy of Management Executive*, May 1999, pp. 56–68.

106. For a recent discussion along these lines, see Joel Lapoint and Jo Ann Verdin, "How to Calculate the Cost of Human Resources," *Personnel Journal* (January 1988), pp. 34–45.

107. This is based on Bruce R. Ellig, "Improving Effectiveness Through an HR Review," *Personnel* (June 1989), pp. 56–64.

108. Ibid., p. 57.

VIDEO CASE

PART VI
MANAGING HUMAN RESOURCES IN AN INTERNATIONAL BUSINESS

LIVING AND WORKING ABROAD HAVE A GREAT DEAL OF APPEAL FOR MANY AMERICANS, WHO ENVISION THEMSELVES LEADING GLAMOROUS LIVES ON EXPENSE ACCOUNTS IN FOREIGN CAPITALS. YET BEING AN EXPATRIATE EMPLOYEE IS NOT THE SAME AS BEING ON VACATION ABROAD. WORK IS STILL WORK, FOR ONE THING. HOME OFFICE EXPECTATIONS MAY RUN HIGH, AND THE STRESS OF ADJUSTING TO THEIR NEW ENVIRONMENT OFTEN PROVES AN INSURMOUNTABLE DIFFICULTY FOR TRANSPLANTED EMPLOYEES AND THEIR FAMILIES. SOME FIRMS WITH INTERNATIONAL OPERATIONS THEREFORE CHOOSE TO HIRE LOCALLY, TO AVOID THE PROBLEMS INHERENT IN TRAINING, MAINTAINING, AND REPATRIATING THEIR U.S. WORKERS.

Whether hiring locally or not, all international firms face problems of compensating employees fairly when, due to location, some have higher living expenses than others. The cost of living in cities like London, New York, and Tokyo is notoriously high; employees of international firms who transfer there face even greater adjustment problems then usual if their salaries do not meet the expense of their new environments, and their families' standard of living begins to drop.

Sometimes employees transfer to locales where living is far cheaper than at home, and the firm faces a different but equally difficult choice—should salary be adjusted downward during the employee's tenure abroad, to prevent pay inequities from arising in the overseas office?

Cultural differences, such as varying expectations for vacations and holidays and different labor practices must also be acknowledged and dealt with fairly, as Hal is about to find out.

In this segment we meet the lone member of Quicktakes' London operation, and he is British. It would appear, then, that Quicktakes has solved one major problem that firms face when first expanding their operations overseas. Tim has no difficulty adjusting to working in Europe, he is multilingual, and he has no disenchanted family members wishing to return home to the United States.

In fact, all the problems between Tim and Quicktakes seem to flow the other way. It is the video producer's U.S. employees who are having trouble with Tim. His free spending on meals and amenities and his generous holiday allowance are well known. If that were not enough to cause dissatisfaction, Tim's sales are down. Now he appears at headquarters to ask Hal for a raise, and Hal must decide what to do.

QUESTIONS

1. Are Tim's vacation time and expense account privileges inequitable? Why or why not? Justify your answer.

2. Is Tim justified in asking for a salary increase? Why or why not? If you answered no, would you allow him the time off instead? Why or why not?

3. Who do you think has the upper hand in the conversation between Tim and Hal? Why? Is this ideal for management?

4. Why do you think Tim came to see Hal before going to Eddie?

5. Do you think Tim's threat to quit is sincere? What do you think he is really trying to accomplish by it?

6. What do you think of Hal's proposal that Tim become a freelancer and work for Quicktakes in that capacity? Discuss the advantages and disadvantages for Quicktakes of this proposal. Does it offer Tim anything?

APPENDIX A
Establishing and Computerizing Human Resource Systems

INTRODUCTION

Consider the paperwork required to manage a company's HR system. Just to start with, for example, recruiting and hiring an employee might require a Notice of Available Position, a Help Wanted Advertising Listing, an Employment Application, an Interviewing Checklist, various verifications—of education, and immigration status, for instance—and a Telephone Reference Checklist. You'd then need an Employment Agreement, Confidentiality and Noncompete Agreements, and an Employer Indemnity Agreement. To process that new employee you might need a Hiring Authorization Form, an Employee Background Verification, a New Employee Checklist, and various forms for withholding tax and to obtain new employee data. And to keep track of the employee once on board, you'd need—just to start—an Employee Changes Form, Personnel Data Sheet, Daily and Weekly Time Records, an Hourly Employee's Weekly Time Sheet, an Overtime Permit, an Expense Report, a Vacation Request, an Absence Request, an Affirmative Action Summary, and an EEO Policy Statement and Analysis of Promotions. Then come the performance appraisal forms, a Critical Incidents Report, Notice of Probation, First (or Second) Warning Notice Form, a Disciplinary Notice, a New Employee Evaluation, a Performance Evaluation, and a Letter of Commendation, and (eventually) a Retirement Checklist, Notice of Dismissal, Reduction in Workforce Notice, Employee Check-out Record, Separation Notice, and Employment Reference Response.

In this Appendix, we'll see that the preceding list barely scratches the surface of the paperwork you'll need to run the HR part of your business. This has several implications. First, you obviously can't wing it. Perhaps with just one or two employees you could keep track of everything in your head, or just write a separate memo for each HR action, and place it in a manilla folder for each worker. But with more than a few employees you'll need to create a human resource system comprised of standardized forms.

Very small firms can handle all or most of this sort of HR recordkeeping through manual paper and pencil forms and systems. But as the company grows, various parts of the HR system—payroll, or appraising, for instance—will have to be computerized if the firm is to remain competitive. (After all, you don't want to spend twice as much time on HR as do your competitors.) We'll cover manual and computerized HR systems in this Appendix.

BASIC COMPONENTS OF MANUAL HR SYSTEMS

Very small employers (say, with 10 employees or less) will probably start with a manual HR system. From a practical point of view, this generally means obtaining and organizing a set of standardized personnel forms covering each important aspect of the HR—recruitment, selection, training, appraisal, compensation, safety process—as well as some means for organizing all this information for each of your employees.

As noted above, the number of forms you could conceivably need even for a small firm is quite large. This is illustrated from the menu of forms shown in Table A-1, which is adapted from the Table of Contents of a compilation of HR agreements and forms.[1] A reasonable way to obtain the basic component forms of a manual HR system is to start with a compilation of forms book like that one. Another example is James Jenks, *The Hiring, Firing (and Everything in Between) Personnel Forms Book* (Richfield, CT: Roundlake Publishing, 1996). The forms you want can then be adapted from these sources for your particular situation. Office supply stores (such as Office Depot and Office Max) also sell packages of personnel forms. For example, Office Depot sells packages of individual personnel forms including an Application for Employment, Performance Evaluation, Record of Employee Earnings, Weekly Expense Report, and Health Insurance Claim Form as well as a "Human Resource Kit" containing 10 copies of each of the following: Application, Employment Interview, Reference Check, Employee Record, Performance Evaluation, Warning Notice, Exit Interview, and Vacation Request, plus a Lawsuit-Prevention Guide.[2] Also available (and highly recommended) is a package of Employee Record Folders. The folders can be used to maintain a file on each individual employee; on the outside of the pocket is printed a form for recording information such as name, start date, company benefits, and so on.

Several direct mail catalog companies similarly offer a variety of HR materials. For example, HRdirect (100 Enterprise Place, Dover, DE, 19901, phone: 1-800-346-1231) offers packages of personnel forms including ones to be used for: Short- and Long-Form Employee Applications, Applicant Interviews, Mail Reference Checking, Employee Performance Reviews, Job Descriptions, Exit Interviews, Absentee Calendars and Reports, and Sexual Harassment Charge Investigation forms. Various legal-compliance forms including standardized No Weapons Policy, Harassment Policy, FMLA Notice forms, as well as posters (for instance covering legally re-

TABLE A-1   Personnel Forms

SECTION 1 Recruiting and Selecting		
Notice of Available Position	Verification of Licensure	Non-Compete Agreement (Accounts)
Help Wanted Advertising Listing	Verification of Military Status	Non-Compete Agreement (Area)
Bonus for Employee Referral	Unsuccessful Candidate Letter	Non-Disclosure of Trade Secrets
Employee Referral Request	Applicant Rejection Letter 1	Acknowledgement of Temporary
Prospective Employee Referral	Applicant Rejection Letter 2	Employment
Applicant Referral Program	Applicant Notification	Employer Indemnity Agreement
Job Bid	Applicant Reply	Employee Indemnity Agreement
Resume Acknowledgement	No Decision on Hiring	Waiver of Liability
Applicant Acknowledgement	Employment Confirmation	
Acknowledgement of Reference		**SECTION 3**
Applicant Interview Confirmation	**SECTION 2**	**Processing New Employees**
Preliminary Employment Application	**Employment Agreements**	
Veteran/Handicapped Status		Rehire Form
Employment Application	Independent Contractor's Agreement	Hiring Authorization
Employment Application Disclaimer	Employment Agreement	Relocation Expense Approval
and Acknowledgement	Addendum to Employment Agreement	Letter to New Employee 1
Applicant Waiver	Agreement with Sales Representative	Letter to New Employee 2
Authorization to Release Information	Letter Extending Sales Representative	Letter to New Employee 3
Medical Testing Authorization	Agreement	Letter to New Employee 4
Applicant Interview Schedule	Change in Terms of Sales	New Employee Announcement
Rescheduled Appointment	Representative Agreement	Employee Background Verification
Interviewing Checklist	Conflict of Interest Declaration	New Employee Orientation Checklist
Applicant Rating	Consent for Drug/Alcohol Screen	New Employee Checklist
Clerical Applicant Rating	Testing	New Personnel Checklist
Applicant Interview Summary	Polygraph Examination Consent Form	Employee Agreement and Handbook
Applicant Comparison Summary	Agreement to Accept Night Work	Acknowledgement
Telephone Reference Checklist	Expense Recovery Agreement	Job Description
Medical Records Request	Agreement on Inventions and Patents	Emergency Procedures
Request for Reference	Agreement on Proprietary Rights	Summary of Employment Terms
Request for Transcript	Employees Agreement on	Payroll Deduction Authorization
Verification of Education	Confidentiality Data	Payroll Deduction Direct Deposit
Verification of Employment	Confidentiality Agreement	Authorization
	Employee's Covenants	Direct Deposit Authorization
	Employee Secrecy Agreement	Withholding Tax Information
	General Non-Compete Agreement	Employee File

New Employee Data
Emergency Phone Numbers
Established Workday and Workweek
    Schedules and Policies
Consent for Drug/Alcohol Screening
Receipt for Company Property
Samples and Documents Receipt
EEO Analysis of New Hires

SECTION 4
Personnel Management

Employment Record
Personnel Data Change
Employee Information Update
Employee Salary Record
Employment Changes
Personnel Data Sheet
Personnel File Access Log
Request to Inspect Personnel File
Consent to Release Information
Telephone Reference Record
Personnel Activity Report
Personnel Requirement Projections
Temporary Employment Requisition
Temporary Personnel Requisition
Employee Flextime Schedule
Weekly Work Schedule
Daily Time Record
Employee Daily Time Record
Weekly Time Record
Hourly Employees' Weekly Time Sheet
Department Overtime Request
Overtime Permit
Overtime Authorization
Overtime Report
Department Overtime Report
Department Payroll
Expense Report
Mileage Reimbursement Report
Payroll Change Notice
Pay Advice
Payroll Summary
Vacation Request Memo
Vacation Request
Employee Health Record
Accident Report
Illness Report
Injury Report
Disability Certificate
Physician's Report
Employee Sympathy Letter 1
Employee Sympathy Letter 2
Employee Sympathy Letter 3
Employee Sympathy Letter 4
Absence Request
Funeral Leave Request
Leave Request/Return from Leave
Military Duty Absence
Late Report
Employee Absence Report
Absence Report

Department Absence Report
Annual Attendance Record
Employee Suggestion
Suggestion Plan 1
Suggestion Plan 2
Suggestion Plan 3
Memo Regarding Drug Testing
Test Notice—Polygraph
Information Notice—Polygraph
Notice of Affirmative Action Policy
Affirmative Action Notice to Suppliers
Affirmative Action Self-Identification
Affirmative Action Supplier's
    Compliance Certificate
Affirmative Action Summary
Equal Employment Opportunity Policy
Current EEO Workforce Analysis
EEO Analysis of Promotions
Employee Transfer Request
Off-Duty Employment Request
Grievance Form

SECTION 5
Performance Evaluation

Employee Consultation
Employee Counseling Activity Sheet
Critical Incidents Report
Incident Report
Notice of Ongoing Investigation—
    Polygraph
Notice of 30-Day Evaluation
Notice of Probation
Notice of Extended Probation
Excessive Absenteeism Warning
First Warning Notice
Second Warning Notice
Disciplinary Notice
Disciplinary Warning
Disciplinary Report
Suspension Without Pay Notice
Employee Self-Evaluation
Performance Analysis Employee
    Worksheet
Employee Performance Checklist
New Employee Evaluation
Managerial Evaluation
Performance Evaluation
Production Personnel Evaluation
Sales Personnel Evaluation
Standard Evaluation
Temporary Employee Evaluation
Employee Performance Review
Performance Appraisal Interview
    Report
Employee Rating Response
Performance Objectives
Coaching Form
Employee Performance Improvement
    Plan
Letter of Commendation
Salary Change Request

SECTION 6
Benefits

Accrued Benefits Statements
Employee Benefits Analysis
Benefits Planning Checklist
Employee Benefits Survey
Employee Benefits List
Combined Resolution—Incentive
    Stock Option Plan
Resolution—Signing Bonus
Resolution—Paid-Up Annuity Plan
Resolution—Relocation Allowance
Resolution—Performance Bonus
Resolution—Low-Interest Loan
Resolution—Company Car
Resolution—Club Membership
Resolution—At-Home Entertainment
    Allowance
Resolution—Tuition Benefit
Resolution—Scholarship Aid Program
Resolution—Financial Counseling Plan
Resolution—Sabbatical Leave
Resolution—Child Care Plan
Resolution—Wage Continuation Plan
Resolution—Merchandise Discount
    Program

SECTION 7
Termination/Separation

Retirement Checklist
Resignation
Termination Checklist
Notice of Dismissal
Notice of Termination Due to Absence
Notice of Termination Due to Work
    Rules Violation
Reduction in Workforce Notice
Termination Letter for Excessive
    Absenteeism
Termination Letter for Lack of Work
Termination Letter for Intoxication on
    the Job
Letter Terminating Sales Representative
Employee Checkout Record
General Release
Mutual Release
Employee Release
Employee Exit Interview
Separation Notice
Personnel Separation Report
Employee Separation Report
Unemployment Compensation Record
EEO Analysis of Terminations
Reference Report
Employment Reference Response
Refusal to Grant References
Notice of Confidentiality Agreement
COBRA Letter to Terminating Employee
COBRA Employee Information Letter
COBRA Compliance

Source: Mario German, Personnel Director (Deerfield Beach, FL: EZ Legal Books, 1994), pp. vi, vii, and viii.

quired postings for matters such as the Americans with Disabilities Act and Occupational Safety and Health Act) are similarly available.

G. Neil Company of Sunrise, Florida (phone: 1-800-999-9111), is another direct mail catalog personnel materials source. In addition to a complete line of personnel forms, documents, and posters, it also offers manual paper-based systems for keeping track of matters such as attendance history, conducting job analyses, and for tracking vacation requests and safety records. A complete HR "start-up" kit is available containing 25 copies of each of the following basic components of a manual HR system: Long Form Application for Employment; Attendance History; Performance Appraisal; Payroll/Status Change Notice; Absence Report; Vacation Request & Approval; W-4 Form; I-9 Form; New Employee Data Records; Separation Notice; Interview Evaluation; Self-Appraisal; Weekly Time Sheets; Accident/Illness Report; Exit Interview; Pre-Employment Phone Reference Check; Employee Warning Notice; Performance Appraisal-Exempt Positions; and tabbed dividers, all organized in a file box.

AUTOMATING INDIVIDUAL HR TASKS

As your company grows, it becomes increasingly unwieldy and uncompetitive to rely exclusively on manual HR systems. For example, conducting performance appraisals for a few employees and keeping track of the results may not be much of a problem, but for a company with 40 or 50 employees or more the amount of management time devoted to conducting appraisals can multiply into weeks. It is therefore at about this stage that most small- to medium-size firms begin computerizing individual HR tasks.

Here again there are a variety of sources available. For example, at the Web site for the International Association for Human Resource Information Management (http://www.ihrim.org/marketplace/buyers_guide/buyers_guide_cat.html) you'll find a categorical buyers' guide listing software vendors. These firms provide software solutions for virtually all personnel tasks, ranging from benefits management to compensation, compliance, employee relations, outsourcing, payroll, and time and attendance systems. To choose just one of a multitude of examples, for instance, click on the company name Again Technologies. Inc. under the category Compensation, and you'll find the following description:

Need help administering your incentive plans? Let Comp$ense make your life easier. We deliver customized business solutions to administer any type of variable pay incentive compensation plans.

Off-the-shelf software is available elsewhere, too. For example, the G. Neil Companies (mentioned previously) sells off-the-shelf software packages for controlling attendance, employee recordkeeping, writing job descriptions, writing employee policies handbooks, and conducting computerized employee appraisals. HRdirect (also mentioned previously) offers software for writing employee policy manuals, writing performance reviews, creating job descriptions, tracking attendance and hours worked for each employee, employee scheduling, writing organizational charts, managing payroll, conducting employee surveys, scheduling and tracking employee training activities, and managing OSHA compliance. A program called People Manager maintains employee records on items such as marital status, number of dependents, emergency contact and phone numbers, hire date, and job history. It also enables employers to quickly produce 30 standard reports on matters such as attendance, benefits, and ethnic information.

ESTABLISHING HUMAN RESOURCE INFORMATION SYSTEMS (HRIS)

Why an HRIS?

Larger companies are integrating their separate HR systems into integrated human resource information systems (HRIS). An HRIS may be defined as interrelated components working together to collect, process, store, and disseminate information to support decision making, coordination, control, analysis, and visualization of an organization's human resource management activities.[3]

There are at least three reasons for installing such a system. First is competitiveness; an HRIS can significantly improve the efficiency of the HR operation and therefore a company's bottom line. For example W. H. Brady Company, a Milwaukee-based manufacturer of identification products such as labels, reportedly cut several hundred thousand dollars a year from its HR budget through the use of HRIS.[4] Software producer PeopleSoft reportedly has a ratio of one HR staffer to each 110 employees, a savings of millions of dollars a year in payroll savings when compared with the traditional ratio of one HR staffer per 50 employees, and it credits that to its HRIS. And sometime during the year 2000 the company expects the HR to employee ratio to shrink to $1:500$.[5]

The HRIS can also bump the firm up to a new plateau in terms of the number and variety of HR-related reports it can produce. Citibank, for instance (now part of Citigroup), has a global database of information on all employees including their compensation, a skills inventory bank of more than 10,000 of its managers, and a compensation and benefits practices database for each of the 98 countries in which the company has employees.[6]

Finally, the HRIS can also help shift HR's attention from transactions-processing to strategic HRM. As the HRIS takes over tasks such as updating employee information and electronically reviewing résumés, the types of HR staff needed and their jobs tend to change. There is less need for entry-level HR data processors, for instance, and more for analysts capable of reviewing HR activities in relation to the company's plans and engaging in activities such as management development. Let's look more closely at how these advantages come about.

HRIS in Action

How exactly can an HRIS achieve these kinds of performance improvements? At some point the employer will outgrow the separate (manual or computerized) component approach to managing HR. Some estimate that firms with fewer than 150 employees can efficiently use computerized component systems, each separately handling tasks such as attendance, and benefits and payroll management. However beyond that point larger firms should turn to either off-the-shelf or customizable HRIS packages.[7] The advantages of moving from component systems to integrated human resource information systems arise from the following.

IMPROVED TRANSACTION PROCESSING   It's been said that "the bread and butter of HRIS is still basic transaction processing."[8] One study—conducted at pharmaceuticals company Warner-Lambert just before they implemented an HRIS—found that 71% of HR employees' time was devoted to transactional and administrative tasks, for instance. In other words, an enormous amount of time was devoted to tasks like checking leave balances, maintaining address records, and monitoring employee benefits distributions.[9] HRIS packages are intended to be comprehensive. They therefore generally provide relatively powerful computerized processing of a wider range of the firm's HR transactions than would be possible if individual systems for each HR task had to be used.

ON-LINE PROCESSING   Many HR information systems make it possible (or easier) to make the company's employees themselves literally part of the HRIS. For example, Merck installed an employee kiosk at which employees can verify and correct their home address and work location. Estimated savings reportedly approach $640,000 for the maintenance of that data alone, and many companies report similar savings. One shipping company estimates they'll reduce transaction processing

and related paperwork from $50 down to $30 or less per employee using direct-access kiosks and integrative voice response (IVR) phone scripts.[10] But using kiosks, IVR, or (increasingly) the employee's own desktop PC systems not only move the burden of the recordkeeping from HR to the employees' themselves. It also should "support employees' quest for 'what if' information relating to, for example, the impact on their take-home pay of various benefits options, W-4 changes, insurance coverage, retirement planning and more."[11]

IMPROVED REPORTING CAPABILITY   Because the HRIS is comprehensive with respect to the number of HR tasks it handles the installation of such a system significantly improves HR's reporting capabilities.

For most of these systems, the number and variety of reports possible is limited only by the manager's imagination. For a start, reports might be available, for instance (companywide and by department) for: health care cost per employee, pay and benefits as a percent of operating expense, cost per hire, report on training, volunteer turnover rates, turnover costs, time to fill jobs, and return on human capital invested (in terms of training and education fees, for instance).[12] Similarly, you might want to calculate and review: human resource cost information by business unit; personal and performance information on candidates for global assignments; demographics of the candidate pool to meet diversity reporting requirements; benefit plan funding requirements and controls; union membership information; information required for HR if a merger, acquisition or divestiture is expected; and data on your global executive-level population for development, promotion, and transfer purposes.[13]

HR SYSTEM INTEGRATION   Because its software components (recordkeeping, payroll, appraisal, and so forth) are integrated, a true HRIS enables an employer to dramatically reengineer its entire HR function by having the information system itself take over and integrate many of the tasks formerly carried out by HR employees.

The system installed at PeopleSoft (mentioned above) provides a good example of this:

> *Sophisticated workflow technology routes promotions, salary increases, transfers and other forms through the organization to the proper managers for approval. As one person signs off, it's routed to the next. If anyone forgets to process a document, a smart agent issues reminders until the task is completed. Training materials—including video—are almost entirely on-line, and all payroll checks are distributed electronically.*
>
> *But the company's hiring process may be the most futuristic aspect of all. Applications sent via the*

World Wide Web or fax are automatically deposited into a database; those submitted on paper are scanned into the computer and plugged into the same database. Once a hiring manager has selected an applicant for an interview, the system phones that person and asks him or her to select an interview time by punching buttons on a touchtone phone. At the end of the call, the client/server database notifies the interviewers of the appointment, and even offers a reminder the day of the interview. It's all handled without human interaction. And an orientation program for new hires works much the same way.[14]

HRIS APPLICATIONS   Because of such capabilities, even many mid-size firms are installing HR information systems today. For example, Grand Casinos, Inc. installed an HRIS called the Human Resource Manager, a package from PDS, Inc. to help with the hiring of several thousand new casino employees. "This system consolidates the human resources operations of Grand Casinos' nine separate properties, and lets these operations share resumes and other applicant information."[15] State Capital Credit Union in Madison, Wisconsin, with 105 employees, uses a desktop version of an HRIS called Spectrum HR/1200. This system, "tracks applicant history and status, salary and staffing changes across departments, benefits plan participation, pension plan contributions, employee training, and turnover. It maintains compliance statistics, . . . and wage and hour information."[16] State Capital's system also performs other HR tasks including internal job postings, benefits billing, payroll reconciliation, and personalized letters and labels for applicant and employee correspondence.[17]

HRIS IMPLEMENTATION PITFALLS   As most everyone knows by now, implementing a sophisticated information system is often more of a challenge than the client expects, and several potential pitfalls account for this. Cost is one problem; for example, a representative from Allstate Insurance Company recently reported that the costs of moving to a new HRIS had increased 10% per year for 5 years and that additional investment would be required to make the transition.[18] Other systems run into management resistance. At Warner-Lambert, for instance, the new HRIS requires line managers to input some information (such as on performance appraisals) into the HR system, and some object to doing tasks previously performed by HR.[19] Others trigger resistance by including inconvenient or unworkable user interfaces for the employees to use; still others are installed without enough thought being given to whether or not the new HRIS will be compatible with the firm's existing HR information systems. Inadequate documentation or training can undermine the system's utility, and increase the resistance to the system of exactly those employees and managers who are supposed to aid in its use.[20]

Actually installing the HRIS therefore needs to be viewed as a whole but also as a process composed of separate projects, each of which must be planned and realistically scheduled.[21] Given these sorts of hurdles a careful needs assessment obviously needs to be done prior to adopting an HRIS. Particularly for firms with less than 150 employees consideration should be given to depending more on individual software packages for managing separate tasks such as attendance, benefits and payroll, and OSHA compliance.[22]

HRIS Vendors

Many firms today offer HRIS packages. At the Website for the International Association for Human Resource Information Management (mentioned above), for instance, Automatic Data Processing, Inc., Business Information Technology, Inc., Human Resource Microsystems, Lawson Software, Oracle Corporation, PeopleSoft, Inc., Restrac Web Hire, SAP America, Inc., and about 25 other firms are listed as HRIS vendors. As another example, Best Software Limited, a Canadian software publisher, offers a line of ABRA HR for windows products for firms ranging in size from 20 to 10,000 employees. One of their products, Best! Imperativ HRMS, reportedly "doesn't replicate everything" a major HRIS system does but offers much of it at a relatively low price.[23] For example, you can use a special Website to click on employee, then benefits, then benefit enrollment; a box then pops up, in which you can enter the name of an employee and then his or her benefits enrollment. Similarly, you can point and click to find a list of employees reporting to a particular supervisor, and print over a hundred reports such as salary lists, employee profiles, and EEO reports.[24]

INTERNETS, INTRANETS, AND HRM

HR and the Internet

As we've seen throughout this book there is a wealth of information available on the Internet that employers and employees can use to help them carry out their HR tasks. For example under Human Resources & Benefits topics, the Infoseek Web browser lists over 300 HR-related sites including the American Society for Training and Development (www.astd.org/), BenefitsLink (www.benefitslink.com/), the Social Security Administration On-line (www.ssa.gov/), the American Compensation Association (www.ahrm.org/aca/aca.htm), and American Safety & Health Training (www.safety-training.com/).

Many employees find that the Internet is especially useful for searching for and finding jobs. For example, the Website www.100hot.com/jobs/lists career-job search related Websites including Career Mosaic, JobTrak, Careers at IBM, www.jobcenter.com, www.careermart.com, telecommuting jobs, the virtual job fair, and Singapore job openings. Indeed, as *Fortune* magazine recently noted, "The Internet is a far more powerful job-search tool than it was just months ago. Now you can't ignore it."[25] Dozens and dozens of companies from high-tech start-ups to firms such as Fidelity Investments and GE are now posting job openings on the Internet and conducting searches through the Web. (Five "best search sites" are summarized in Figure A-1.

Firms are reporting extraordinary results with their recruitment Websites. For example, since opening its Internet site several years ago Silicon Graphics has collected 4,000 to 12,000 resumes per month and about a fourth of its new hires now come to the firm through the Web.[26] Many sites including Career Mosaic (www.career-mosaic.com), and Monster Board (www.monster.com) provide quick ways for employers to get job postings on the Web. And of course once the resumes are electronically submitted, programs such as *Resumix* or *Restrac* allows the employer to quickly screen applicants based on criteria such as education or skill sets.[27] Synchronous and Asynchronous Internet-based training are just two other examples of how firms make the Internet part of their HR systems today.[28]

HR and Intranets

Employers are also creating internal company internets or "intranets" as part of their HR information systems. For example, LG&E Energy Corporation uses their intranet for benefits communication.[29] Employees can access the benefits homepage and (among other things) review the company's 401(k) plan investment options, get answers to frequently asked questions about the company's medical and dental plans, and report changes in family status (such as marriage) that may impact the employee's benefits.

A list of other HR-related ways in which employers use the intranet include: create an electronic employee directory; automate job postings and applicant tracking; set up training registration; provide electronic pay stubs; publish an electronic employee handbook; offer more enticing employee communications and newsletters; let employees update their personal profiles and access their accounts, such as 401(k)s; conduct open benefits enrollments; provide leave status information; conduct performance and peer reviews; manage succession planning (in part by locating employees with the right skill set to fill openings); and create discussion groups or forums.[30]

Several companies provide assistance in building the databases needed to create intranets. For example the WorkWise HR Web Builder from Paradigm Software Development, Inc. in Seattle, Washington, helps employers create HR-oriented Web pages. The package basically in-

FIGURE A-1

Best Search Sites

Source: Fortune, March 2, 1998, p. 206.

careermosaic.com	This so-called big board typically has 70,000 jobs listed. Its services are free to job seekers. You can scan the listings and even post your resume for potential employers to see.
careerpath.com	Roughly 250,000 jobs here, culled from the help-wanted sections of 53 major papers including the *Washington Post* and *Chicago Tribune*. You can do a focused search by region or industry.
hoovers.com	First rate research site. Offers profiles and financial data on more than 12,000 public and private companies worldwide. Provides links to other free sites where you can dig still further.
nationjob.com	Perfect for passive job seekers. Develop a profile for your ideal job—location, industry, salary. Provide your E-mail address. Then sit back and wait as appropriate listings get sent to you.
netshare.com	One of the few viable sites where it's the job seeker who pays. What you get for $125 a quarter, $325 a year; access to exclusive listings of executive jobs that pay $70,000 and up.

cludes the Web page templates into which the employer then has to insert the necessary information.[31]

In summary, firms are increasingly moving beyond manual HR systems today, by computerizing individual HR tasks, installing HR Information Systems, and using the Internet and Intranets. In so doing HR managers are able to reengineer the way that HR does its job, accomplish those "bread and butter" transactional HR job's cost-competitively, and increasingly turn its attention to truly being a strategic partner with the firm's other top executives.

NOTES

1. Mario German, *Personnel Director* (Deerfield Beach, FL: E-Z Legal Books, 1994), pp. vi, vii, and viii.

2. Office Depot, Winter 1998 Catalog (Delray Beach, FL: Office Depot, 1998), p. 430.

3. Adapted from Kenneth Laudon and Jane Laudon, *Management Information Systems: New Approaches to Organization and Technology* (Upper Saddle River, NJ: Prentice Hall, 1998), p. G7.

4. Samuel Greengard, "Finding Time to be Strategic," *Personnel Journal* (October 1996), pp. 84–89.

5. Samuel Greengard, "Client/Server: HR's Helping Hand?" *Personnel Journal* (May 1996), p. 92.

6. Linda Stroh, "Integrated HR Systems Help Develop Global Leaders," *HRMagazine*, Vol. 43, no. 5 (April 1998), pp. 14–18.

7. Tony Berardine, "Human Resource Information Systems Improve Management Decision-Making," *Canadian Manager*, Vol. 22, no. 5 (Winter 1997), pp. 17–18.

8. Gerald Groe, "Information Technology and HR," *Human Resource Planning*, Vol. 19, no. 1 (March 1996), pp. 56–62.

9. "HR Execs Trade Notes on Human Resource Information Systems," *BNA Bulletin to Management*, December 3, 1998, p. 1.

10. Marc Miller, "Great Expectations: Is Your HRIS Meeting Them?" *HR Focus*, Vol. 75, no. 4 (April 1998), pp. 1–3.

11. Ibid., p. 2.

12. Jac Fitz-enz, "Top Ten Calculations for Your HRIS," *HR Focus*, Vol. 75, no. 4 (April 1998), p. 3.

13. Linda Stroh, "Integrated HR Systems," p. 16.

14. Samuel Greengard, "Client/Server: HR's Helping Hand?" *Personnel Journal* (May 1996), p. 92.

15. Stephanie Wilkinson, "Hire and Higher: Client/Server and Web-Based Systems Raise the Stakes for Solving HR Headaches," *PC Week*, Vol. 13, no. 27 (July 8, 1996), pp. 45–47.

16. Mary Mink, "Software Eases HR Tasks," *Credit Union Executive*, Vol. 36, no. 6 (November–December 1996), p. 35.

17. Ibid.

18. "HR Execs Trade Notes on Human Resource Information Systems," *BNA Bulletin to Management*, December 3, 1998, p. 2.

19. "HR Execs Trade Notes on Human Resource Information Systems," p. 1.

20. Victor Haines and Andre Petit, "Conditions for Successful Human Resource Information Systems," *Human Resource Management*, Vol. 36, no. 2 (Summer 1997), pp. 261–276.

21. James Schultz, "Avoid the DDTs of HRIS Implementation," *HR Magazine*, Vol. 42, no. 5 (May 1997), pp. 37–41. See also Bill Roberts, "The New HR Is: Good Deal on $6 Million Paperweight?" *HR Magazine*, Vol 43, no. 3, Feb 1998, p. 40.

22. Tony Berardine, "Human Resource Information Systems Improve Management Decision Making," *Canadian Manager*, Vol. 22, no. 4 (Winter 1997), pp. 17–19.

23. Jim Meade, "Below Cost Alternative to the Traditional HRIS: Best! Imperative HRMS Offers Great Value," *HRMagazine*, Vol. 43, no. 9 (August 1998), pp. 37–40.

24. Ibid. Note that increasing numbers of HRIS depend on so-called client/server systems. For more information see, for instance, Eric Baker, "Do You Need a Client/Server System?" *HRMagazine* (February 1997), pp. 37–43.

25. Justin Martin, "Changing Jobs? Try the Net." See also Jennifer Laabs, "Career Help on the Internet," *Global Workforce*, Vol. 3, no. 2, March 1998, pp. 21–22.

26. "Use the Web to Automate Recruiting," *Workforce* (March 1997), p. 78.

27. Ibid., p. 78.

28. "Drive Change with Long Distance Learning," *Workforce* (March 1997), pp. 81–82.

29. Frank Kuzmits, "Communicating Benefits: A Double-Click Away," *Compensation and Benefits Review*, (September/October 1998), pp. 60–64.

30. Samuel Greengard, "Increase the Value of Your Intranet," *Workforce*, (March 1997), pp. 88–94; Samuel Greengard, "Achieving Greater Intranet Efficiency," *Workforce*, (September 1998), pp. 71–77.

31. Roderick Munn, "Software Review," *HR Magazine*, (March 1997), pp. 43–46.

APPENDIX B
Managing Your Career

FACTORS THAT AFFECT CAREER CHOICES

Managing your career has never been as important as it is today.[1] As mentioned earlier, the paternalistic career management systems that characterized many firms in the past are disappearing.[2] Today, instead, the individual must be responsible for creating and managing his or her own career. In today's job marketplace, as one writer puts it, "employee ability replaces security."[3] As a result, "self-determination is the underlying principal governing the organization, and in this spirit individuals manage their own careers."

The first step in planning a career for yourself or someone else is to learn as much as possible about your interests, aptitudes, and skills.

Identify Occupational Orientation

Career-counseling expert John Holland says that a person's personality (including values, motives, and needs) is one career choice determinant. For example, a person with a strong social orientation might be attracted to careers that entail interpersonal rather than intellectual or physical activities and to occupations such as social work. Based on research with his Vocational Preference Test (VPT), Holland found six basic personality types or orientations.[4]

1. *Realistic orientation.* These people are attracted to occupations that involve physical activities re-

quiring skill, strength, and coordination. Examples include forestry, farming, and agriculture.

2. *Investigative orientation.* Investigative people are attracted to careers that involve cognitive activities (thinking, organizing, understanding) rather than affective activities (feeling, acting, or interpersonal and emotional tasks). Examples include biologist, chemist, and college professor.

3. *Social orientation.* These people are attracted to careers that involve interpersonal rather than intellectual or physical activities. Examples include clinical psychology, foreign service, and social work.

4. *Conventional orientation.* A conventional orientation favors careers that involve structured, rule-regulated activities, as well as careers in which it is expected that the employee subordinate his or her personal needs to those of the organization. Examples include accountants and bankers.

5. *Enterprising orientation.* Verbal activities aimed at influencing others characterize enterprising personalities. Examples include managers, lawyers, and public relations executives.

6. *Artistic orientation.* People here are attracted to careers that involve self-expression, artistic creation, expression of emotions, and individualistic activities. Examples include artists, advertising executives, and musicians.

Most people have more than one **occupational orientation** (they might be social, realistic, and investigative, for example), and Holland believes that the more similar or compatible these orientations are, the less internal conflict or indecision a person will face in making a career choice. To help illustrate this, Holland suggests placing each orientation in one corner of a hexagon, as in Figure B-1. As you can see, the model has six corners, each of which represents one personal orientation (for example, enterprising). According to Holland's research, the closer two orientations are in this figure, the more compatible they are. Holland believes that if your number one and number two orientations fall side by side, you will have an easier time choosing a career. However, if your orientations turn out to be opposite (such as realistic and social), you may experience more indecision in making a career choice because your interests are driving you toward very different types of careers. In Table B-1, we have summarized some of the occupations that have been found to be the best match for each of these six personal occupational orientations.

Identify Career Directions

MBA students at the Harvard Business School take a quiz to help them identify career directions and make career choices in which they'll be happy.[5] To take a short-form version of this quiz, you'll need three types of information. First (see Figure B-2) this approach assumes that all executive work is based on one or more of eight core activities such as "quantitative analysis," and "managing people." Begin by reading each of those activities.

Next (see Figure B-3) quickly go through each of the second figure's pairs of statements and indicate which one is more interesting to you. Then add the bold letters for your total score on each core function and record that score in the second figure.

Then, use Figure B-4 to see what kind of successful businesspeople share your career direction's interests. For example, if you scored high (in Figure B-3) on "Enterprise Control" and "Managing People," then CEOs, Presidents, Division Managers, and General Managers are the sorts of people whose career interest directions are most similar to yours.

Identify Skills

Successful performance depends not just on motivation but also on ability. You may have a conventional orientation, but whether you have *the skills* to be an accountant, banker, or credit manager will largely determine which specific occupation you ultimately choose. Therefore, you have to identify your skills—or those of your employees.

AN EXERCISE One useful exercise for identifying **occupational skills** is to take a blank piece of paper and head it "The Most Enjoyable Occupational Tasks I Have Had." Then write a short essay that describes the tasks. Make sure to go into as much detail as you can about your duties and responsibilities and what it was about each task that you found enjoyable. (In writing your essay, by the way, notice that it's not necessarily the most enjoyable *job* you've had, but the most enjoyable *task* you've had to perform; you may have had jobs that you

FIGURE B-1

Choosing an Occupational Orientation

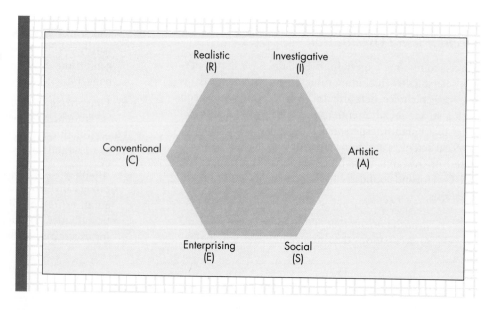

TABLE B-1 Occupations Scoring High on Each Occupational Orientation Theme

REALISTIC	INVESTIGATIVE	ARTISTIC	SOCIAL	ENTERPRISING	CONVENTIONAL
Consider these occupations if you score *high* here:					
Agribusiness managers	Biologists	Advertising executives	Auto sales dealers	Agribusiness managers	Accountants
Carpenters	Chemists	Art teachers	Guidance counselors	Auto sales dealers	Auto sales dealers
Electricians	Engineers	Artists	Home economics teachers	Business education teachers	Bankers
Engineers	Geologists	Broadcasters	Mental health workers	Buyers	Bookkeepers
Farmers	Mathematicians	English teachers	Ministers	Chamber of Commerce executives	Business education teachers
Foresters	Medical technologists	Interior decorators	Physical education teachers	Funeral directors	Credit managers
Highway patrol officers	Physicians	Medical illustrators	Recreation leaders	Life insurance agents	Executive housekeepers
Horticultural workers	Physicists	Ministers	School administrators	Purchasing agents	Food service managers
Industrial arts teachers	Psychologists	Musicians	Social science teachers	Realtors	IRS agents
Military enlisted personnel	Research and development managers	Photographers	Social workers	Restaurant managers	Mathematics teachers
Military officers	Science teachers	Public relations directors	Special education teachers	Retail clerks	Military enlisted personnel
Vocational agricultural teachers	Sociologists	Reporters	YMCA/YWCA directors	Store managers	Secretaries

Note: for example, if you score high on "realistic," consider a career as a carpenter, engineer, farmer, and so on.

Source: Reproduced by special permission of the publisher, Consulting Psychologists Press, Inc., Palo Alto, CA 94306, from *Manual for the SVIV-SCII*, Fourth Edition, by Jo-Ida C. Hansen and David P. Campbell, copyright 1985 by the Board of Trustees of Leland Stanford Junior University.

Business Career Interest Inventory (BC II)

Part 1: *All executive work is based on one or more of the following eight core activities. Read them.*

Application of Technology: Taking an engineering-like approach to business problems and using technology to solve them (operations process analysis, process redesign, production planning).

Quantitative Analysis: Problem-solving that relies on mathematical and financial analysis (determining the most advantageous debt/equity structure, analyzing market research).

Theory Development and Conceptual Thinking: Taking a broadly conceptual, quasi-academic approach to business problems (developing a new general economic theory or model of market behavior).

Creative Production: Highly creative activities (the generation of new business ideas such as line extensions or additional markets, the development of new marketing concepts).

Counseling and Mentoring: Developing a variety of personal relationships in the workplace and helping others in their careers (human-resources coaching, training, and mentoring).

Managing People: Accomplishing business goals through working directly with people (particularly as a frontline manager, team leader, director, or direct supervisor).

Enterprise Control: Having ultimate strategy and decision-making authority as well as resource control for an operation (as a division manager, president, CEO, partner in a professional firm, or entrepreneur).

Influence Through Language and Ideas: Exercising influence through the skillful use of persuasion (negotiating, dealmaking, sales functions, and relationship development).

FIGURE B-2 *Finding the Job You Should Want (Part 1)*

Source: James Waldroop and Timothy Butler, "Finding the Job You *Should* Want," *Fortune*, March 2, 1998, p. 211.

PART 2: *Reread the brief descriptions of the eight sets of activities on the previous page, then quickly go through each of the following pairs and indicate which one is more interesting to you by placing the bold letter for that choice in the box to the left. Don't leave any out and don't record any ties. Mark your first intuitive response.*

☐ 1. Creative **P**roduction *or* **I**nfluence Through Language and Ideas

☐ 2. **M**anaging People *or* Creative **P**roduction

☐ 3. **E**nterprise Control *or* **A**pplication of Technology

☐ 4. **T**heory Development *or* Creative **P**roduction

☐ 5. **M**anaging People *or* **C**ounseling and Mentoring

☐ 6. **Q**uantitative Analysis *or* **T**heory Development

☐ 7. **I**nfluence Through Language and Ideas *or* **E**nterprise Control

☐ 8. **Q**uantitative Analysis *or* **E**nterprise Control

☐ 9. **A**pplication of Technology *or* **I**nfluence Through Language and Ideas

☐ 10. **I**nfluence Through Language and Ideas *or* **Q**uantitative Analysis

☐ 11. **T**heory Development *or* **C**ounseling and Mentoring

☐ 12. **A**pplication of Technology *or* Creative **P**roduction

☐ 13. **A**pplication of Technology *or* **M**anaging People

☐ 14. **T**heory Development *or* **I**nfluence Through Language and Ideas

☐ 15. Creative **P**roduction *or* **C**ounseling and Mentoring

☐ 16. **C**ounseling and Mentoring *or* **Q**uantitative Analysis

☐ 17. **T**heory Development *or* **E**nterprise Control

☐ 18. **E**nterprise Control *or* Creative **P**roduction

☐ 19. **M**anaging People *or* **T**heory Development

☐ 20. **A**pplication of Technology *or* **T**heory Development

☐ 21. **E**nterprise Control *or* **C**ounseling and Mentoring

☐ 22. Creative **P**roduction *or* **Q**uantitative Analysis

☐ 23. **C**ounseling and Mentoring *or* **I**nfluence Through Language and Ideas

☐ 24. **Q**uantitative Analysis *or* **M**anaging People

☐ 25. **E**nterprise Control *or* **M**anaging People

☐ 26. **A**pplication of Technology *or* **C**ounseling and Mentoring

☐ 27. **M**anaging People *or* **I**nfluence Through Language and Ideas

☐ 28. **A**pplication of Technology *or* **Q**uantitative Analysis

Add the bold letters for your total score on each core function and record that score below:

☐ **A**pplication of Technology

☐ **C**ounseling and Mentoring

☐ **Q**uantitative Analysis

☐ **M**anaging People

☐ **T**heory Development and Conceptual Thinking

☐ **E**nterprise Control

☐ Creative **P**roduction

☐ **I**nfluence Through Language and Ideas

Based on the scores above, identify your most significant interests. Most people will find one to three clear leaders. What does it all mean? Turn the page to find out.

FIGURE B-3 *Finding the Job You Should Want (Part 2)*

Source: James Waldroop and Timothy Butler, "Finding the Job You *Should* Want," *Fortune*, March 2, 1998, p. 212.

really didn't like except for one of the specific duties or tasks in the job, which you really enjoyed.) Next. on other sheets of paper, do the same thing for two other tasks you have had. Now go through your three essays and underline the skills that you mentioned the most often. For ex-

ample, did you enjoy putting together and coordinating the school play when you worked in the principal's office one year? Did you especially enjoy the hours you spent in the library doing research for your boss when you worked one summer as an office clerk?[6]

FIGURE B-4

*Finding the Job You
Should Want (Part 3)*

Source: James Waldroop and Timothy
Butler, "Finding the Job You *Should
Want*," *Fortune,* March 2, 1998,
p. 214.

PART 3: *Now that you know which activity combinations you prefer, see what kind of successful business people share your interests.*

ENTERPRISE CONTROL and MANAGING PEOPLE: CEOs, presidents, division
managers, and general managers who enjoy both strategy and the operational aspects of the
position—the CEO who enjoys playing the COO role as well.

ENTERPRISE CONTROL and QUANTITATIVE ANALYSIS: Investment bankers, other financial professionals who enjoy dealmaking, partners in Big Six firms, top-level executives in commercial and investment banks, investment managers.

APPLICATION OF TECHNOLOGY and QUANTITATIVE ANALYSIS: Individual contributors who have a strong interest in engineering analysis (systems analysts, tech consultants,
process consultants); production and operations managers.

CREATIVE PRODUCTION and INFLUENCE THROUGH LANGUAGE AND IDEAS: Advertising executives, brand managers, corporate trainers, salespeople, public relations specialists; people in the fashion, entertainment, and media industries.

COUNSELING AND MENTORING and MANAGING PEOPLE: Human-resources managers, managers who enjoy coaching and developing the people reporting to them, managers
in nonprofit organizations with an altruistic mission.

ENTERPRISE CONTROL and INFLUENCE THROUGH LANGUAGE AND IDEAS: Execu-
tives (CEOs, presidents, general managers) whose leadership style relies on persuasion and consensus building; marketing managers, salespeople.

APPLICATION OF TECHNOLOGY and ENTERPRISE CONTROL: Managers and senior executives in high technology, telecommunications, biotech, information systems (internally or consulting), and other engineering-related fields.

THEORY DEVELOPMENT and QUANTITATIVE ANALYSIS: Economic-model builders,
quantitative analysts, "knowledge base" consultants, market forecasters, business professors.

CREATIVE PRODUCTION and ENTERPRISE CONTROL: Solo entrepreneurs, senior executives in industries where the product or service is of a creative nature (fashion, entertainment, advertising, media).

CREATIVE PRODUCTION: Entrepreneurs who partner with a professional manager, short-term
project managers, new-product developers, advertising "creatives"; individual contributors in
fashion, entertainment, and media.

APTITUDES AND SPECIAL TALENTS For career
planning purposes, a person's **aptitudes** are usually measured with a test battery such as the general aptitude test
battery (GATB). This instrument measures various aptitudes including intelligence and mathematical ability.
Considerable work has been done to relate aptitudes,
such as those measured by the GATB, to specific occupations. For example, the U.S. Department of Labor's *Dictionary of Occupational Titles* lists the nature and titles of
hundreds of occupations, along with the aptitudes required for success in these occupations.[7]

Identify Career Anchors

Edgar Schein says that career planning is a continuing
process of discovery—one in which a person slowly develops a clearer occupational self-concept in terms of
what his or her talents, abilities, motives, needs, attitudes,
and values are. Schein also says that as you learn more
about yourself, it becomes apparent that you have a dom-
inant career anchor, *a concern or value that you will not
give up if a choice has to be made.*

Career anchors, as their name implies, are the piv-
ots around which a person's career swings; a person becomes conscious of them as a result of learning about his
or her talents and abilities, motives and needs, and attitudes and values. Based on his research at the Massachusetts Institute of Technology, Schein believes that career
anchors are difficult to predict ahead of time because they
are evolutionary and a product of a process of discovery.
Some people may never find out what their career anchors are until they have to make a major choice—such as
whether to take the promotion to the headquarters staff
or strike out on their own by starting a business. It is at

this point that all the person's past work experiences, interests, aptitudes, and orientations converge into a meaningful pattern (or career anchor) that helps show what is the most important factor in driving the person's career choices.

Based on his study of MIT graduates, Schein identified five career anchors.[8]

TECHNICAL/FUNCTIONAL CAREER ANCHOR

People who had a strong technical/functional career anchor tended to avoid decisions that would drive them toward general management. Instead they made decisions that would enable them to remain and grow in their chosen technical or functional fields.

MANAGERIAL COMPETENCE AS A CAREER ANCHOR

Other people show a strong motivation to become managers and their career experience enabled them to believe that they had the skills and values required to rise to such general management positions. A management position of high responsibility is their ultimate goal. When pressed to explain why they believed they had the skills necessary to gain such positions, many in Schein's research sample answered that they were qualified for these jobs because of what they saw as their competencies in a combination of three areas: (1) analytical competence (ability to identify, analyze, and solve problems under conditions of incomplete information and uncertainty); (2) interpersonal competence (ability to influence, supervise, lead, manipulate, and control people at all levels); and (3) emotional competence (the capacity to be stimulated by emotional and interpersonal crises rather than exhausted or debilitated by them, and the capacity to bear high levels of responsibility without becoming paralyzed).

CREATIVITY AS A CAREER ANCHOR

Some of the graduates had gone on to become successful entrepreneurs. To Schein these people seemed to have a need "to build or create something that was entirely their own product—a product or process that bears their name, a company of their own, or a personal fortune that reflects their accomplishments." For example, one graduate had become a successful purchaser, restorer, and renter of townhouses in a large city; another had built a successful consulting firm.

AUTONOMY AND INDEPENDENCE AS CAREER ANCHORS

Some seemed driven by the need to be on their own, free of the dependence that can arise when a person elects to work in a large organization where promotions, transfers, and salary decisions make them subordinate to others. Many of these graduates also had a strong techni-cal/functional orientation. However, instead of pursuing this orientation in an organization, they had decided to become consultants, working either alone or as part of a relatively small firm. Others had become professors of business, freelance writers, and proprietors of a small retail business.

SECURITY AS A CAREER ANCHOR

A few of the graduates were mostly concerned with long-run career stability and job security. They seemed willing to do what was required to maintain job security, a decent income, and a stable future in the form of a good retirement program and benefits.

For those interested in *geographic security*, maintaining a stable, secure career in familiar surroundings was generally more important than pursuing superior career choices, if choosing the latter meant injecting instability or insecurity into their lives by forcing them to pull up roots and move to another city. For others, security meant *organizational security*. They might today opt for government jobs, where tenure still tends to be a way of life. They were much more willing to let their employers decide what their careers should be.

ASSESSING CAREER ANCHORS

To help you identify career anchors, take a few sheets of blank paper and write out your answers to the following questions:[9]

1. What was your major area of concentration (if any) in high school? Why did you choose that area? How did you feel about it?

2. What is (or was) your major area of concentration in college? Why did you choose that area? How did you feel about it?

3. What was your first job after school? (Include military if relevant.) What were you looking for in your first job?

4. What were your ambitions or long-range goals when you started your career? Have they changed? When? Why?

5. What was your first major change of job or company? What were you looking for in your next job?

6. What was your next major change of job, company, or career? Why did you initiate or accept it? What were you looking for? (Do this for each of your major changes of job, company, or career.)

7. As you look back over your career, identify some times you have especially enjoyed. What was it about those times that you enjoyed?

8. As you look back, identify some times you have not especially enjoyed. What was it about those times you did not enjoy?

9. Have you ever refused a job move or promotion? Why?

10. Now review all your answers carefully, as well as the descriptions for the five career anchors (managerial competence, technical/functional, security, creativity, autonomy). Based on your answers to the questions, rate each of the anchors from 1 to 5; 1 equals low importance, 5 equals high importance.

Managerial competence _____

Technical/functional competence _____

Security _____

Creativity _____

Autonomy _____

What Do You Want to Do?

We have explained occupational orientations, skills, and career anchors and the role these play in choosing a career. But there is at least one more exercise you should try that can prove enlightening. Answer the question: "If you could have any kind of job, what would it be?" Invent your own job if need be, and don't worry about what you can do—just what you want to do.[10]

Identify High-Potential Occupations

Learning about yourself is only half the job of choosing an occupation. You also have to identify those occupations that are right (given your occupational orientations, skills, career anchors, and occupational preferences) as well as those that will be in high demand in the years to come.

FIND OUT ABOUT OCCUPATIONS AND CAREERS

Investigating occupations can take hours (or perhaps days or weeks) of library and Internet research. The *Dictionary of Occupational Titles* is the bible of the vocational field and lists detailed job descriptions for more than 20,000 occupations. It provides a listing of the responsibilities, duties, and procedures for each job in the manual. Also listed for each job are the physical demands of the job, as well as individual working conditions, and (based on the judgment of experts) the interests, aptitudes, educational requirements, and vocational preparation required of those seeking each job. ⟨For a new downloadable version called O*NET98 go to www.doleta.gov/programs/onet/⟩

The *Occupational Outlook Handbook* gives an outline for about 700 occupations, including the prospects for the occupation and the major work, required training, earnings, and working conditions. There is also an *Occupational Outlook Handbook for College Graduates*, and the U.S. Employment Service publishes *Occupations in Demand*, a comprehensive listing of jobs most frequently requested of 2,500 job service offices around the country. *Occupations in Demand* provides information on local areas having large numbers of openings, industries requesting workers, pay ranges, and average number of openings available. It also lists jobs not requiring previous work experience.

Occupational Outlook Quarterly is published every 3 months and provides information about occupations that are most in demand. As an example, Figure B-5 shows the 10 fastest growing occupations requiring a Bachelor's degree as projected for the 10 years 1996 to 2006. Note that computer-related occupations (database administrators, computer engineers, and systems analysts) head the list.[11] Another source is the *Encyclopedia of Careers and Vocational Guidance*, which provides descriptions of over 650 occupations. For information about federal jobs and filling out applications, try the U.S. Office of Personnel Management's *Handbook X118*, which gives detailed job descriptions for hundreds of government positions. The U.S. Office of Education, in conjunction with Harvard University, has developed a computerized career information system called the Guidance Information System (GIS). Using this computerized system, you provide input on your occupational preferences and skills. The system then suggests one or more feasible matching occupations.

The government can also help. The U.S. federal government is increasingly providing a range of even more useful services.

They offer, first, what they call "America's Career Kit." This is actually a set of Internet sites through which individuals can access three important career-related databases. The first is America's Job Bank [www.ajb.dni.us]. This is a national database of job listings that recently listed more than 800,000 jobs a day. It's run by the U.S. Department of Labor's Employment and Training Administration in collaboration with state employment agencies and is free to jobseekers.[12] America's Talent Bank is related to America's Job Bank. The former is a national database of résumés posted by jobseekers; when the computer matches an employer's listing and a jobseeker's résumé, it notifies both parties.[13] America's Career Infonet also links through America's Job Bank and is a source you can use for information on career exploration. For example, "if you need help deciding which career to pursue or want more information on a field that

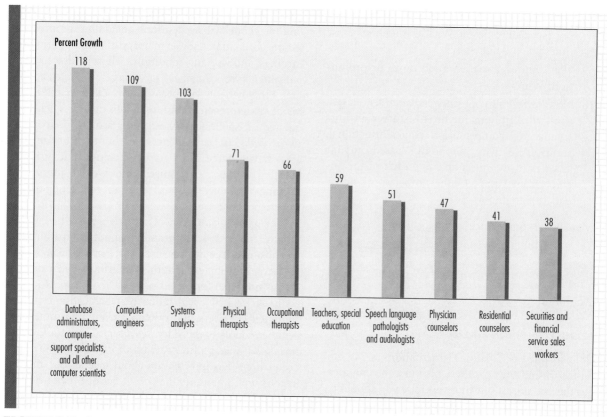

FIGURE B-5 *"Ten Fastest Growing Occupations Requiring a Bachelor's Degree"*

Source: "Ten Fastest Growing Occupations Requiring a Bachelor's Degree," *Occupational Outlook Quarterly,* Summer 1998, p. 52.

interests you, America's Career Infonet is a good place to start. You can begin by doing a search of an occupation to learn about job duties, earnings, training, and employment outlook."[14]

Related to these initiatives, the U.S. Government's One-Stop Career Centers have been called "the new malls of American labor."[15] In many cases these one-stop career centers have blossomed out of the familiar state employment offices. In them, jobseekers can now apply for unemployment benefits, register with the state job service, talk to career counselors, use computers to write résumés and access the Internet, and use career libraries, which offer books and videos on various employment topics. In some centers job hunters can even make use of free telephones, fax machines, and photocopiers to facilitate their job searches.[16]

By the way, don't underestimate the advantages of seeking employment at small, fast-growth start-ups. For example a recent *Fortune* magazine article entitled "Is It Time to Bail From Big-Company Life?" describes how

more and more executives are leaving their big company pay and perks behind for what *Fortune* calls the "risky world of start-ups."[17] One happy former mega-company president, for instance, is now CEO of a small San Francisco area Internet information services company. He's reportedly earning about 30% of his former salary but has stock options that could make him a multimillionaire someday. As he says, "no one knows where the Internet will go. I thought this would be fun."[18]

FINDING THE RIGHT JOB

Helping You Get the Right Job

You have identified your occupational orientation, skills, and career anchors and have picked out the occupation you want and made plans for a career. And (if necessary) you have embarked on the required training. Your next step is to find a job that you want in the company and locale in which you want to work. Following are techniques for doing so.

Job Search Techniques

DO YOUR OWN RESEARCH   Perhaps the most direct way of unearthing the job you want, where you want it, is to pick out the geographic area in which you want to work and find out all you can about the companies in that area that appeal to you and the people you have to contact in those companies to get the job you want. Most public libraries have local directories. For example, the reference librarian in one Fairfax County, Virginia, library suggested the following sources for patrons seeking information about local businesses:

> *Industrial Directory of Virginia*
> *Industrial Directory of Fairfax County*
> *Principal Employers of the Washington Metro Area*
> *The Business Review of Washington*

Other general reference material you can use include *Who's Who in Commerce and Industry, Who's Who in America, Who's Who in the East,* and *Poor's Register.* Using these guides, you can find the person in each organization who is ultimately responsible for hiring people in the position you seek. As explained elsewhere in this Appendix, the Internet has, of course, caused an explosion of expert career advice. Another excellent source you can use here is the *Wall Street Journal's* interactive edition, which you can find at http://careers.wsj.com.

PERSONAL CONTACTS   According to one survey, the most popular way to seek job interviews is to rely on personal contacts such as friends and relatives.[19] For example, one Department of Labor study indicates that about 19% of managers got their jobs through friends and about 6% got them through relatives. Let as many responsible people as you can know that you are in the market for a job and specifically what kind of job you want. (Beware, though, if you are currently employed and don't want your job search getting back to your current boss; if that is the case, better just pick out two or three very close friends and tell them it is absolutely essential that they be discreet in seeking a job for you.)

No matter how close your friends or relatives are to you, by the way, you don't want to impose too much on them by shifting the burden of your job search to them. It is sometimes best to ask them for the name of someone they think you should talk to in the kind of firm in which you'd like to work, and then do the digging yourself.

ANSWERING ADVERTISEMENTS   Most experts agree that answering ads is a low-probability way to get a job,

and it becomes increasingly less likely that you will get a job this way as the level of job increases. Answering ads, in other words, is fine for jobs that pay under $20,000 per year, but it's highly unlikely that as you move up in management you are going to get your job by simply answering classified ads. Nevertheless, good sources of classified ads for professionals and managers include the *New York Times,* the *Wall Street Journal,* and a separate *Wall Street Journal* listing of job openings.

In responding to ads, be sure to create the right impression with the materials you submit; check the typing, style, grammar, neatness, and so forth, and check your résumé to make sure it is geared to the job for which you are applying. In your cover letter, be sure to have a paragraph or so in which you specifically address why your background and accomplishments are appropriate to the job being advertised; you must respond clearly to the company's identified needs.[20]

Be very careful in replying to blind ads, however (those with just a post office box). Some executive search firms and companies will run ads even when no position exists just to gauge the market, and there is always the chance that you can be trapped into responding to your own firm.

EMPLOYMENT AGENCIES   Agencies are especially good at placing people in jobs paying up to about $30,000, but they can be useful for higher-paying jobs as well. Their fees for professional and management jobs are usually paid by the employer. Assuming you know the job you want, review eight or so back issues of the Sunday classified ads in your library to identify the agencies that consistently handle the positions you want. Approach three or four initially, preferably in response to specific ads, and avoid signing any contract that gives an agency the exclusive right to place you.

EXECUTIVE RECRUITERS   Executive recruiters are retained by employers to seek out top talent for their clients, and their fees are always paid by the employer. They do not do career counseling, but if you know the job you want, it pays to contact a few. Send your résumé and a cover letter summarizing your job objective in precise terms, including job title and the size of company you want, work-related accomplishments, current salary, and salary requirements. Firms are usually listed in the Yellow Pages under "Executive Search Consultants." However, beware, because some firms today call themselves executive search or career consultants but do no searches: They just charge a (often hefty) fee to help you manage your search. Remember that with a search firm you never pay a fee. A list of executive recruiters is also available from the Management Information Service of the American Management Association, 135 West 50th Street, New York, New York 11020.

What sorts of things will the headhunter look for? Ten important items include:[21] you have demonstrated the ability to get results; you come well recommended by your peers and competitors; you understand who the search consultant works for and what he is trying to do; you are likeable and presentable, and your ego is in check; you can think strategically and understand how to institute change in an organized direction; you have achieved the results you have because of the way you treat others; not in spite of it; you can sell yourself concisely; you have at least some of the key specific experiences that the job entails; you are honest, fair, and a good source and even take the time when somebody calls you as a source to give them other sources that you believe are high potential; and you know who you are and what you want.[22]

CAREER COUNSELORS   Career counselors will not help you find a job per se; rather, they specialize in aptitude testing and career counseling. They are listed in the Yellow Pages under "Career Counseling" or "Vocational Guidance." Their services usually cost $300 or so and include psychological testing and interviews with an experienced career counselor. Check the firm's services, prices, and history as well as the credentials of the person you will be dealing with.

EXECUTIVE MARKETING CONSULTANTS   Executive marketing consultants manage your job-hunting campaign. They generally are not recruiters and do not have jobs to fill. Depending on the services you choose, your cost will range from $400 to $5,000 or more. The process may involve months of weekly meetings. Services include résumé and letter writing, interview skill building, and developing a full job-hunting campaign. Before approaching a consultant, though, you should definitely do in-depth self-appraisal (as explained in this chapter) and read books like Richard Bolles's *The Quick Job Hunting Map* and *What Color Is Your Parachute?*

Then check out three or four of these firms (they are listed in the Yellow Pages under "Executive Search Consultants") by visiting each and asking: What exactly is your program? How much does each service cost? Are there any extra costs, such as charges for printing and mailing résumés? What does the contract say? After what point will you get no rebate if you're unhappy with the services? Then review your notes, check the

Better Business Bureau, and decide which of these firms (if any) is for you.

Finding a Job on the Internet

With more and more companies listing job openings on the Internet, just about any serious job hunter should be using this valuable source.[23]

Here's just a sampling of how you can use the Internet to help you find a job. The On-Line Career Center, a not-for-profit employer association located in Ann Arbor, Michigan, lets job hunters submit their résumés at no charge, and your résumé will remain on the system for 90 days. All expenses are paid by On-Line Career Center member employers, who are companies that pay an annual fee to post their job openings on the Center's Internet service. Corporate recruiters have desktop Internet access with on-line software specifically designed for recruiting and employment; individuals may conduct employment searches and make their résumé available to all recruiters searching for applicants on the Internet.[24]

The Yahoo list at Stanford University is another way to discover job openings on the Internet. The Yahoo list at Stanford is a "list of lists" that helps you zero in on the Internet site that is of most use to you. In this case, you can click on "business" and then on "employment." If you do, you'll see a screen like the one in Figure B-6. Following your search to other submenus might take you to a screen like the one in Figure B-7, which shows career opportunities at Fidelity Investments.

Preparing your résumé for distribution on the Internet requires some special preparation, and you'll probably need a separate electronic version of your résumé. For one thing you'll probably need to save your electronic résumé "as a plain, pure, nondocument mode, 7-bit ASCII text file."[25] You'll also have to set your left margin at zero but keep your right margin at 65. Also—unlike the typical paper résumé—you may want to start your electronic résumé with a list of key words; thus a freshly minted law school graduate interested in a particular specialty might list "international intellectual property China" as key words, if that's the special area of expertise he or she wants to pursue.

Writing Your Résumé

Your résumé is probably your most important selling document, one that can determine whether you "make the cut" and get offered a job interview. Here are some résumé pointers, as offered by employment counselor Richard Payne and other experts.[26] An example of a good résumé is presented in Figure B-8.

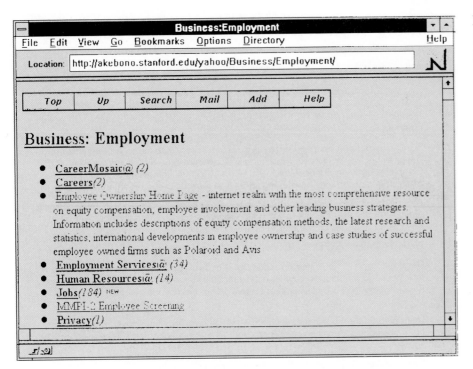

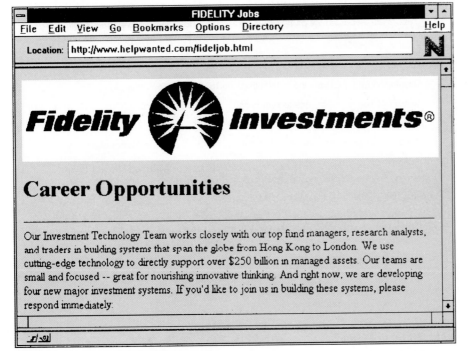

CONRAD D. STAPLETON
77 Pleasantapple Way
Coltsville, NY 10176
(914) 747-1012

CONFIDENTIAL

JOB OBJECTIVE

Senior Production Manager in a situation requiring extensive advertising and promotion experience.

PRESENT POSITION

VALUE-PLUS DIVISION, INTERCONTINENTAL CORPORATION

1994–Present

Product Manager, NEW PRODUCTS, LAUDRYON SOAP and CARBOLENE CLEANER, reporting to Group Product Manager.

Recommended and obtained test market authorization, then managed all phases of development of THREE test brands, scheduled for introduction during Fall/Winter 1993. Combined first year national volume projects to $20 million, with advertising budget of $6 million. Concurrently developing several new products for 1994 test marketing.

Also responsible for two established brands: LAUNDRYON SOAP, a $7 million brand, and CARBOLENE CLEANER, a $4 million regional brand. Currently work with three advertising agencies on test and established brands.

1991–1993

Product Manager, WEEKENDER PAINTS, a $6 million brand.

Developed and implemented a repositioning of this brand (including new copy and new package graphics) to counter a 10-year sales downtrend averaging 10% a year. Repositioning increased test market volume 16%, and national volume 8% the following year.

Later initiated development of new, more competitive copy than advertising used during repositioning. Test area sales increased 35%. National airing is scheduled for Fall 1991.

Developed plastic packaging that increased test market volume 10%.

Also developed and implemented profit improvement projects which increased net profit 33%.

1990

Product Manager, SHINEZY CAR WASH, a $4 million brand.

Initiated and test marketed an improved aerosol formula and a liquid refill. Both were subsequently expanded nationally and increased brand volume 26%.

RICHARDS-DONALDS COMPANY

1989–1990

Assistant Product Manager, reporting to Product Manager.

Concurrent responsibility on PAR and SHIPSHAPE detergents. Developed locally tailored annual promotion plans. These resulted in 30% sales increase on PAR and stabilization of SHIPSHAPE volume.

1988–1989

Product Merchandising Assistant

Developed and implemented SUNSHINE SUDS annual promotion plan.

1987–1988

Academic Leave of Absence to obtain MBA. See EDUCATION.

1985–1987

Account Manager, Field Sales.

Account Manager for Shopper's Pal, the most difficult chain in Metropolitan Westchester. Achieved sales increase of 10% and distribution of all Lever products, introduced while I was on territory. Based on this performance was awarded Food'N Things Cooperatives, the second most difficult account, and achieved similar results.

EDUCATION

READING SCHOOL, University of Maryland

MBA in Marketing Management. Average grade 3.5 out of 4.0 Thesis: "The Distribution of Pet Supplies through Supermarkets," graded 4.0 out of 4.0. Courses included quantitative methods, finance, accounting and international business.

ELTON COLLEGE, Kansas City, Missouri

BA in Liberal Arts. Was one of 33, out of freshman class of 110, who completed four years of this academically rigorous program. Theses required each year. Judge in Student Court during senior year.

FIGURE B-8 *Example of a Good Résumé*

Source: Richard Payne, *How to Get a Better Job Quicker* (New York: Signet, 1988), pp. 80–81.

INTRODUCTORY INFORMATION   Start your résumé with your name, address, and telephone number. Using your office phone number, by the way, can indicate either that (1) your employer knows you are leaving or (2) you don't care whether he or she finds out. You're usually better off using your home phone number.

JOB OBJECTIVE   State your job objective next. This should summarize in one sentence the specific position you want, where you want to do it (type and size of company), and a special reason an employer might have for wanting you to fill the job. For example, "Production manager in a medium-size manufacturing company in a situation in which strong production scheduling and control experience would be valuable." Always try to put down the most senior title you know you can expect to secure, keeping in mind the specific job for which you are applying.

JOB SCOPE   Indicate the scope of your responsibility in each of your previous jobs, starting with your most recent position. For each of your previous jobs, write a paragraph that shows job title, whom you reported to directly and indirectly, who reported to you, how many people reported to you, the operational and human resource budgets you controlled, and what your job entailed (in one sentence).

YOUR ACCOMPLISHMENTS   Next (and this is very important) indicate your "worth" in each of the positions you held. This is the heart of your résumé. It shows for each of your previous jobs: (1) the concrete action you took and why you took it and (2) the specific result of your action—the "payoff." For example, "As production supervisor, I introduced a new process to replace costly hand soldering of component parts. The new process reduced assembly time per unit from 30 to 10 minutes and reduced labor costs by over 60%." Use several of these worth statements for each job.

LENGTH   Keep your résumé to two pages or less, and list education, military service (if any), and personal background (hobbies, interests, associations) on the last page.

PERSONAL DATA   Do not put personal data regarding age, marital status, or dependents on top of page one. If you must include it, do so at the end of the résumé, where it will be read after the employer has already formed an opinion of you.

Finally, two last points. First, do not produce a slipshod résumé: Avoid overcrowded pages, difficult-to-read copies, typographical errors, and other problems of this sort. Second, do not use a make-do résumé—one from 10 years ago. Produce a new résumé for each job you are applying for, gearing your job objective and worth statements to the job you want.

MAKE YOUR RÉSUMÉ SCANNABLE   For many job applications it's important to write a scannable résumé, in other words, one that is electronically readable by a computer system. Many medium- and larger-size firms that do extensive recruiting and hiring now use software to quickly and automatically review large numbers of résumés, screening out those that don't seem to match (often based on the absence of certain key words that the employer is looking for).

There are several guidelines to keep in mind for writing scannable résumés.[27] These can be summarized as follows:

Use type no smaller than 10 points and no larger than 14 points.

Do not use italicized type, and do not underline words.

Use type styles that work well for résumés and can be scanned as well as read, such as Helvetica, Futura, Optima, Times Roman, New Century Schoolbook, Courier, Univers, and Bookman.

Submit only high-resolution documents. Documents produced on a laser printer work best. Many photocopies and faxes are not clean enough for scanning.

Make sure to present your qualifications using powerful key words appropriate to the job or jobs for which you are applying. For example, trainers might use key words and phrases such as: computer-based training, interactive video, and group facilitator.

Handling the Interview

You have done all your homework and now the big day is almost here; you have an interview next week with the person who is responsible for hiring for the job you want. What must you do to excel in the interview? Here are some suggestions. (Also review interviewing in chapter 6 at this point.)

PREPARE, PREPARE, PREPARE   First, remember that preparation is essential. Before the interview, learn all you can about the employer, the job, and the people doing the recruiting. At the library, look through business periodicals to find out what is happening in the employer's field. Who is the competition? How are they doing?

UNCOVER THE INTERVIEWER'S NEEDS Spend as little time as possible answering your interviewer's first questions and as much time as possible getting the person to describe his or her needs—what the person is looking to get accomplished and the type of person needed. Use open-ended questions, such as "Could you tell me more about that?"

RELATE YOURSELF TO THE PERSON'S NEEDS Once you have a handle on the type of person your interviewer is looking for and the sorts of problems he or she wants solved, you are in a good position to describe your own accomplishments in terms of the interviewer's needs. Start by saying something like, "One of the problem areas you've indicated is important to you is similar to a problem I once faced." Then state the problem, describe your solution, and reveal the results.

THINK BEFORE ANSWERING Answering a question should be a three-step process: pause, think, speak. Pause to make sure you understand what the interviewer is driving at, think about how to structure your answer, and then speak. In your answer, try to emphasize how hiring you will help the interviewer solve his or her problem.

MAKE A GOOD APPEARANCE AND SHOW ENTHUSIASM Appropriate clothing, good grooming, a firm handshake, and the appearance of controlled energy are important.

FIRST IMPRESSIONS COUNT Studies of interviews show that in almost 80% of the cases, interviewers make up their minds about the applicant during the first few minutes of the interview. A good first impression may turn to bad during the interview, but it is unlikely. Bad first impressions are almost impossible to overcome.

NOTES

1. Sullivan, Carden, and Martin, "Careers in the Next Millenium," p. 178.
2. For example, see Nigel Nicholson, "Career Systems in Crisis: Change and Opportunity in the Information Age," *Academy of Management Executive*, Vol. 10, no. 4 (1996), p. 41.
3. Ibid., p. 41.
4. John Holland, *Making Vocational Choices: A Theory of Careers* (Upper Saddle River, NJ: Prentice Hall, 1973).
5. This is based on James Waldroop and Timothy Butler, "Finding the Job You *Should* Want," *Fortune*, March 2, 1998, p. 211–214.
6. Richard Bolles, *The Quick Job Hunting Map* (Berkeley, CA: Ten Speed Press, 1979), pp. 5–6.
7. Ibid., p. 5.
8. Schein, *Career Dynamics*, pp. 128–129; and Edgar Schein, "Career Anchors Revisited: Implications for Career Development in the 21st Century," *Academy of Management Executive*, Vol. 10, no. 4 (1996), pp. 80–88.
9. Ibid., pp. 257–262.
10. This example is based on Richard Bolles, *The Three Boxes of Life* (Berkeley, CA: Ten Speed Press, 1976).
11. "Ten Fastest Growing Occupations Requiring a Bachelor's Degree," *Occupational Outlook Quarterly* (Summer 1998), p. 52.
12. Megan Barkume, "Career Guidance from the Federal Government: Helping Workers Help Themselves," *Occupational Outlook Quarterly* (Winter 1998–99), pp. 8–11.
13. Ibid., p. 10.
14. Ibid., p. 10.
15. Matthew Mariani, "One-Stop Career Centers: All in One Place and Everyplace," *Occupational Outlook Quarterly* (Fall 1997), pp. 3–15.
16. Ibid., pp. 3–15; Barkume, "Career Guidance," p. 9.
17. Eileen Gunn, "Is It Time to Bail from Big-Company Life?" *Fortune*, March 2, 1998, pp. 217–218.
18. Ibid., p. 217.
19. Robert Jameson, *The Professional Job Changing System* (Verona, NJ: Performance Dynamics, 1975). See also Kenneth McRae, "Career-Management Planning: A Boon to Managers and Employees," *Personnel*, Vol. 62, no. 5 (May 1985), pp. 56–60. See also John Wareham, "How to Make a Headhunter Call You," *Across-the-Board*, Vol. 32, no. 1 (January 1995), pp. 49–50.
20. The percentage of job seekers who look for work by placing or answering ads has almost doubled since 1970, according to data compiled by the Bureau of Labor Statistics. See Michelle Harrison Ports, "Trends in Job Search Methods, 1970–92," *Monthly Labor Review*, October 1993, pp. 63–67.
21. John Rau, "And the Winner Is . . . ," *Across-the-Board*, Vol. 54, no. 10 (November/December 1997), pp. 38–42.
22. Based on Ibid., pp. 32–42.
23. Except as noted, this section is based on Alfred Glossbrenner and Emily Glossbrenner, *Finding a Job on the Internet* (NY: McGraw-Hill, 1995).
24. Ibid., pp. 104–105.
25. Ibid., p. 194.
26. Payne, *How to Get a Better Job Quicker*. See also Larry Salters, "Résumé Writing for the 1990s," *Business and Economics Review*, Vol. 40, no. 3 (April 1994), pp. 11–18.
27. This is based on Erica Gordon Sorohan, "Electrifying a Job Search," *Training & Development* (October 1994), pp. 7–9.

APPENDIX C
Quantitative Job Evaluation Methods

THE FACTOR COMPARISON JOB EVALUATION METHOD

The factor comparison technique is a *quantitative* job evaluation method. It has many variations and appears to be the most accurate, the most complex, and one of the most widely used job evaluation methods.

It is actually a refinement of the ranking method and entails deciding which jobs have more of certain compensable factors than others. With the ranking method you generally look at each job as an entity and rank the jobs. With the factor comparison method you rank each job *several times—once for each compensable factor you choose*. For example, jobs might be ranked first in terms of the factor "skill." Then they are ranked according to their "mental requirements." Next they are ranked according to their "responsibility," and so forth. Then these rankings are combined for each job into an overall numerical rating for the job. Here are the required steps.

STEP 1. OBTAIN JOB INFORMATION This method requires a careful, complete job analysis. First, job descriptions are written. Then job specifications are developed, preferably in terms of the compensable factors the job evaluation committee has decided to use. For the factor comparison method, these compensable factors are usually (1) mental requirements, (2) physical requirements, (3) skill requirements, (4) responsibility, and (5) working conditions. Typical definitions of each of these five factors are presented in Figure C-1.

STEP 2. SELECT KEY BENCHMARK JOBS Next, 15 to 25 key jobs are selected by the job evaluation committee. These jobs will have to be representative benchmark jobs, acceptable reference points that represent the full range of jobs to be evaluated.

STEP 3. RANK KEY JOBS BY FACTOR Here evaluators are asked to rank the key jobs on each of the five factors (mental requirements, physical requirements, skill requirements, responsibility, and working conditions). This ranking procedure is based on job descriptions and job specifications. Each committee member usually makes this ranking individually, and then a meeting is held to develop a consensus on each job. The result of this process is a table, as in Table C-1. This shows how each key job ranks on each of the five compensable factors.

STEP 4. DISTRIBUTE WAGE RATES BY FACTORS This is where the factor comparison method gets a bit more complicated. In this step the committee members have to divide up the present wage now being paid for each key job, distributing it among the five compensable factors. They do this is accordance with their judgments about the importance to the job of each factor. For example, if the present wage for the job of common laborer is

667

FIGURE C-1

Sample Definitions of Five Factors Typically Used in Factor Comparison Method

Source: Jay L. Otis and Richard H. Leukart, *Job Evaluation: A Basis for Sound Wage Administration*, p. 181. © 1954, revised 1983. Reprinted by permission of Prentice Hall, Upper Saddle River, NJ.

1. Mental Requirements
Either the possession of and/or the active application of the following:
A. (inherent) Mental traits, such an intelligence, memory, reasoning, facility in verbal expression, ability to get along with people and imagination.
B. (acquired) General education, such as grammar and arithmetic; or general information as to sports, world events, etc.
C. (acquired) Specialized knowledge such as chemistry, engineering, accounting, advertising, etc.

2. Skill
A. (acquired) Facility in muscular coordination, as in operating machines, repetitive movements, careful coordinations, dexterity, assembling, sorting, etc.
B. (acquired) Specific job knowledge necessary to the muscular coordination only; acquired by performance of the work and not to be confused with general education or specialized knowledge. It is very largely training in the interpretation of sensory impressions.
  Examples
  (1) In operating an adding machine, the knowledge of *which* key to depress for a sub-total would be skill.
  (2) In automobile repair, the ability to determine the significance of a certain knock in the motor would be skill.
  (3) In hand-firing a boiler, the ability to determine from the appearance of the firebed how coal should be shoveled over the surface would be skill.

3. Physical Requirements
A. Physical effort, as sitting, standing, walking, climbing, pulling, lifting, etc.; both the amount exercised and the degree of the continuity should be taken into account.
B. Physical status, as age, height, weight, sex, strength and eyesight.

4. Responsibilities
A. For raw materials, processed materials, tools, equipment and property.
B. For money or negotiable securities.
C. For profits or loss, savings or methods' improvement.
D. For public contact.
E. For records.
F. For supervision.
  (1) Primarily the complexity of supervision *given* to subordinates; the number of subordinates is a secondary feature. Planning, direction, coordination, instruction, control and approval characterize this kind of supervision.
  (2) Also, the degree of supervision *received*. If Jobs A and B gave no supervision to subordinates, but A received much closer immediate supervision than B, then B would be entitled to a higher rating than A in the supervision factor.
    To summarize the four degrees of supervision:
    Highest degree—gives much—gets little
    High degree—gives much—gets much
    Low degree—gives none—gets little
    Lowest degree—gives none—gets much

5. Working Conditions
A. Environmental influences such as atmosphere, ventilation, illumination, noise, congestion, fellow workers, etc.
B. Hazards—from the work or its surroundings.
C. Hours.

TABLE C-1 Ranking Key Jobs by Factors[1]

	MENTAL REQUIREMENTS	PHYSICAL REQUIREMENTS	SKILL REQUIREMENTS	RESPONSIBILITY	WORKING CONDITIONS
Welder	1	4	1	1	2
Crane operator	3	1	3	4	4
Punch press operator	2	3	2	2	3
Security guard	4	2	4	3	1

[1] 1 is high, 4 is low.

TABLE C-2 Ranking Key Jobs by Wage Rates[1]

	HOURLY WAGE	MENTAL REQUIRE-MENTS	PHYSICAL REQUIRE-MENTS	SKILL REQUIRE-MENTS	RESPONSIBILITY	WORKING CONDITIONS
Welder	$9.80	4.00(1)	0.40(4)	3.00(1)	2.00(1)	0.40(2)
Crane operator	5.60	1.40(3)	2.00(1)	1.80(3)	0.20(4)	0.20(4)
Punch press operator	6.00	1.60(2)	1.30(3)	2.00(2)	0.80(2)	0.30(3)
Security guard	4.00	1.20(4)	1.40(2)	0.40(4)	0.40(3)	0.60(1)

[1] 1 is high, 4 is low.

$4.26, our evaluators might distribute this wage as follows:

Mental requirements	$0.36
Physical requirements	$2.20
Skill requirements	$0.42
Responsibility	$0.28
Working conditions	$1.00
Total	$4.26

You make such a distribution for all key jobs.

STEP 5. RANK KEY JOBS ACCORDING TO WAGES ASSIGNED TO EACH FACTOR
Here you again rank each job, factor by factor, but the ranking is based on the wages assigned to each factor. As shown in Table C-2, for example, for the "mental requirements" factor, the welder job ranks first, whereas the security guard job ranks last.

Each member of the committee first makes this distribution working independently. Then the committee meets and arrives at a consensus concerning the money to be assigned to each factor for each key job.

STEP 6. COMPARE THE TWO SETS OF RANKINGS TO SCREEN OUT UNUSABLE KEY JOBS
You now have two sets of rankings for each key job. One was your original ranking (from step 3). This shows how each job ranks on each of the five compensable factors. The second ranking reflects for each job the wages assigned to each factor. You can now draw up a table like the one in Table C-3.

For each factor, this shows both rankings for each key job. On the left is the ranking from step 3. On the right is the ranking based on wages paid. For each factor, the ranking based on the amount of the factor (from step 3) should be about the same as the ranking based on the wages assigned to the job (step 5). (In this case they are). If there's much of a discrepancy, it suggests that the key job might be a fluke, and from this point on, such jobs are no longer used as key jobs. (Many managers don't bother to screen out unusable key jobs. To simplify things, they skip over our steps 5 and 6, going instead from step 4 to step 7; this is an acceptable alternative.)

STEP 7. CONSTRUCT THE JOB-COMPARISON SCALE
Once you've identified the usable, true key jobs, the next step is to set up the job-comparison scale (Table C-4). (Note that there's a separate column for each of the five comparable factors.) To develop it, you'll need the assigned wage table from step 4.

For each of the factors for all key jobs, you write the job next to the appropriate wage rate. Thus, in the assigned wage rate table (Table C-2), the welder job has $4.00 assigned to the factor "mental requirements." Therefore,

TABLE C-3 Comparison of Factor and Wage Rankings

	MENTAL REQUIREMENTS		PHYSICAL REQUIREMENTS		SKILL REQUIREMENTS		RESPONSIBILITY		WORKING CONDITIONS	
	A[1]	$[2]	A[1]	$[2]	A[1]	$[2]	A[1]	$[2]	A[1]	$[2]
Welder	1	1	4	4	1	1	1	1	2	2
Crane operator	3	3	1	1	3	3	4	4	4	4
Punch press operator	2	2	3	3	2	2	2	2	3	3
Security guard	4	4	2	2	4	4	3	3	1	1

[1] Amount of each factor based on step 3.
[2] Ratings based on distribution of wages to each factor from step 4.

TABLE C-4 Job- (Factor) Comparison Scale

	MENTAL REQUIREMENTS	PHYSICAL REQUIREMENTS	SKILL REQUIREMENTS	RESPONSIBILITY	WORKING CONDITIONS
.20	....	....	....	Crane Operator	Crane Operator
.30	....	....	....	....	Punch Press Operator
.40	....	Welder	Sec. Guard	Sec. Guard	Welder
.50					
.60	....	....	....	....	Sec. Guard
.70					
.80				Punch Press Operator	
.90					
1.00				(Plater)	
1.10					
1.20	Sec. Guard				
1.30	....	Punch Press Operator			
1.40	Crane Operator	Sec. Guard	(Inspector)	(Plater)	
1.50	....	(Inspector)	....	....	(Inspector)
1.60	Punch Press Operator				
1.70	(Plater)				
1.80	....	....	Crane Operator	(Inspector)	
1.90					
2.00	....	Crane Operator	Punch Press Operator	Welder	
2.20	....	(Plater)			
2.40	(Inspector)	....	....	....	(Plater)
2.60					
2.80					
3.00	....	....	Welder		
3.20					
3.40					
3.60					
3.80					
4.00	Welder				
4.20					
4.40					
4.60					
4.80					

on the job-comparison scale (Table C-4) write "welder" in the "mental requirements" factor column, next to the "$4.00" row. Do the same for all factors for all key jobs.

STEP 8. USE THE JOB-COMPARISON SCALE Now all the other jobs to be evaluated can be slotted, factor by factor, into the job-comparison scale. For example, suppose you have a job of plater that you want to slot in. You decide where the "mental requirements" of the plater job would fit as compared with the "mental requirements" of all the other jobs listed. It might, for example, fit between punch press operator and inspector. Similarly, you would ask where the "physical requirements" of the plater's job fit as compared with the other jobs listed. Here you might find that it fits just below crane operator. You would do the same for each of the remaining three factors.

AN EXAMPLE Let us work through an example to clarify the factor comparison method. We'll just use four key jobs to simplify the presentation—you'd usually start with 15 to 25 key jobs.

Step 1. First, we do a job analysis.

Step 2. Here we select our four key jobs: welder, crane operator, punch press operator, and security guard.

Step 3. Based on the job descriptions and specifications, here we rank key jobs by factor, as in Table C-1.

Step 4. Here we distribute wage rates by factor, as in Table C-2.

Step 5. Then we rank our key jobs according to wage rates assigned to each key factor. These rankings are shown in parentheses in Table C-2.

Step 6. Next compare your two sets of rankings. In each left-hand column (marked A) is the job's ranking from step 3 based on the amount of the compensable factor. In each right-hand column (marked $) is the job's ranking from step 5 based on the wage assigned to that factor, as in Table C-3.

In this case, there are no differences between any of the pairs of A (amount) and $ (wage) rankings, so all our key jobs are usable. If there had been any differences (for example, between the A and $ rankings for the welder job's "mental requirements" factor) we would have dropped that job as a key job.

Step 7. Now we construct our job-comparison scale as in Table C-4. For this, we use the wage distributions from step 4. For example, let us say that in steps 4 and 5 we assigned $4.00 to the "mental requirements" factor of the welder's job. Therefore, we now write "welder" on the $4.00 row under the "mental requirements" column as in Table C-4.

Step 8. Now all our other jobs can be slotted, factor by factor, into our job-comparison scale. We do not distribute wages to each of the factors for our other jobs to do this. We just decide where, factor by factor, each of our other jobs should be slotted. We've done this for two other jobs in the factor comparison scale: They're shown in parentheses. Now we also know what the wages for these two jobs should be, and we can also do the same for all our jobs.

A VARIATION   There are several variations to this basic factor comparison method. One converts the dollar values on the factor comparison chart (Table C-4) to points. (You can do this by multiplying each of the dollar values by 100, for example.) The main advantage in making this change is that your system would no longer be "locked in" to your present wage rates. Instead, each of your jobs would be compared with one another, factor by factor, in terms of a more constant point system.

PROS AND CONS   We've presented the factor comparison method at some length because it is (in one form or another) a very widely used job evaluation method. Its wide use derives from several advantages: First, it is an accurate, systematic, quantifiable method for which detailed step-by-step instructions are available. Second, jobs are compared to other jobs to determine a relative value. Thus, in the job-comparison scale you not only see that a welder requires more mental ability that a plater; you also can determine about how much more mental ability is required—apparently about twice as much ($4.00 versus $1.70). (This type of calibration is not possible with the ranking or classification methods.) Third, this is also a fairly easy job evaluation system to explain to employees.

Complexity is probably the most serious disadvantage of the factor comparison method. Although it is fairly easy to explain the factor comparison scale and its rationale to employees, it is difficult to show them how to build one. In addition, the use of the five factors is an outgrowth of the technique developed by its originators. However, using the same five factors for all organizations and for all jobs in an organization may not always be appropriate.

The Point Method of Job Evaluation

The point method is widely used. It requires identifying several compensable factors (like skills and responsibility), each with several degrees, and also the degree to which each of these factors is present in the job. A different number of points is usually assigned for each degree of each factor. So once you determine the degree to which each factor is present in the job, you need only add up the corresponding number of points for each factor and arrive at an overall point value for the job.[1] Here are the steps:

STEP 1. DETERMINE CLUSTERS OF JOBS TO BE EVALUATED   Because jobs vary widely by department, you usually will not use one point-rating plan for all jobs in the organization. Therefore, the first step is usually to cluster jobs, for example, into shop jobs, clerical jobs, sales jobs, and so forth. Then the committee will generally develop a point plan for one group or cluster at a time.

STEP 2. COLLECT JOB INFORMATION   This means performing a job analysis and writing job descriptions and job specifications.

STEP 3. SELECT COMPENSABLE FACTORS   Here select compensable factors, like education, physical requirements, or skills. Often each cluster of jobs may require its own compensable factors.

STEP 4. DEFINE COMPENSABLE FACTORS   Next carefully define each compensable factor. This is done to ensure that the evaluation committee members will each apply the factors with consistency. Examples of definitions are presented in Figure C-2. The definitions are often drawn up or obtained by the human resource specialist.

STEP 5. DEFINE FACTOR DEGREES   Next define each of several degrees for each factor so that raters may judge the amount or degree of a factor existing in a job. Thus, for the factor "complexity" you might choose to have six degrees, ranging from "job is repetitive" through "requires initiative." (Definitions for each degree are shown in Figure C-2.) The number of degrees usually does not exceed five or six, and the actual number de-

pends mostly on judgment. Thus, if all employees either work in a quiet, air-conditioned office or in a noisy, hot factory, then two degrees would probably suffice for the factor "working conditions." You need not have the same number of degrees for each factor, and you should limit degrees to the number necessary to distinguish among jobs.

STEP 6. DETERMINE RELATIVE VALUES OF FACTORS   The next step is to decide how much weight (or how many total points) to assign to each factor. This is important because for each cluster of jobs some factors are bound to be more important than others. Thus, for executives the "mental requirements" factor would carry far more weight than would "physical requirements." The opposite might be true of factory jobs.

The process of determining the relative values or weights that should be assigned to each of the factors is generally done by the evaluation committee. The committee members carefully study factor and degree definitions and then determine the relative value of the factors

FIGURE C-2

Example of One Factor in a Point Factor System

Source: Richard W. Beatty and James R. Beatty, "Job Evaluation," Ronald A. Berk (Ed.), *Performance Assessment: Methods and Applications* (Baltimore: Johns Hopkins University Press, 1986), p. 322.

Example of One Factor in a Point Factor System (Complexity/Problem Solving)

The mental capacity required to perform the given job as expressed in resourcefulness in dealing with unfamiliar problems, interpretation of data, initiation of new ideas, complex data analysis, creative or developmental work.

Level	Point Value	Description of Characteristics and Measures
0	0	Seldom confronts problems not covered by job routine or organizational policy; analysis of data is negligible. *Benchmark:* General secretary, switchboard/receptionist.
1	40	Follows clearly prescribed standard practice and demonstrates straightforward application of readily understood rules and procedures. Analyzes noncomplicated data by established routine. *Benchmark:* Statistical clerk, billing clerk.
2	80	Frequently confronts problems not covered by job routine. Independent judgment exercised in making minor decisions where alternatives are limited and standard policies established. Analysis of standardized data for information of or use by others. *Benchmark:* Social worker, executive secretary.
3	120	Exercises independent judgment in making decisions involving nonroutine problems with general guidance only from higher supervision. Analyzes and evaluates data pertaining to nonroutine problems for solution in conjunction with others. *Benchmark:* Nurse, accountant, team leader.
4	160	Uses independent judgment in making decisions that are subject to review in the final stages only. Analyzes and solves nonroutine problems involving evaluation of a wide variety of data as a regular part of job duties. Makes decision involving procedures. *Benchmark:* Associate director, business manager, park services director.
5	200	Uses independent judgment in making decisions that are not subject to review. Regularly exercises developmental or creative abilities in policy development. *Benchmark:* Executive director.

for the cluster of jobs under consideration. Here is one method for doing this:

First, assign a value of 100% to the highest-ranking factor. Then assign a value to the next highest factor as a percentage of its importance to the first factor, and so forth. For example,

Decision making	100%
Problem solving	85%
Knowledge	60%

Next, sum up the total percentage (in this case 100% + 85% + 60% = 245%). Then convert this 245% to a 100% system as follows:

Decision making:	100 ÷ 245 = 40.82 =	40.8%
Problem solving:	85 ÷ 245 = 34.69 =	34.7%
Knowledge:	60 ÷ 245 = 24.49 =	24.5%
Totals		100.0%

STEP 7. ASSIGN POINT VALUES TO FACTORS AND DEGREES

In step 6 total weights were developed for each factor in percentage terms. Now assign points to each factor as in Table C-5. For example, suppose it is decided to use a total number of 500 points in the point plan. Because the factor "decision making" had a weight of 40.8%, it would be assigned a total of 40.8% × 500 = 204 points.

Thus, it was decided to assign 204 points to the decision-making factor. This automatically means that the highest degree for the decision-making factor would also carry 204 points. Then assign points to the other degrees for this factor, usually in equal amounts from the lowest to the highest degree. For example, divide 204 by the number of degrees (say, 5); this equals 40.8. Then the lowest degree here would carry about 41 points. The second degree would carry 41 plus 41, or 82 points. The third degree would carry 123 points. The fourth degree would carry 164 points. Finally, the fifth and highest degree would carry 204 points. Do this for each factor (as in Table C-5).

STEP 8. WRITE THE JOB EVALUATION MANUAL

Developing a point plan like this usually culminates in a *point manual* or *job evaluation manual.* This simply consolidates the factor and degree definitions and point values into one convenient manual.

STEP 9. RATE THE JOBS

Once the manual is complete, the actual evaluations can begin. Raters (usually the committee) use the manual to evaluate jobs. Each job based on its job description and job specification is evaluated factor by factor to determine the number of points that should be assigned to it. First, committee members determine the degree (first degree, second degree, and so on) to which each factor is present in the job. Then they note the corresponding points (see Table C-5) that were previously assigned to each of these degrees (in step 7). Finally, they add up the points for all factors, arriving at a total point value for the job. Raters generally start with rating key jobs and obtain consensus on these. Then they rate the rest of the jobs in the cluster.

"PACKAGED" POINT PLANS

Developing a point plan of one's own can obviously be a time-consuming process. For this reason a number of groups (such as the National Electrical Manufacturer's Association and the National Trade Association) have developed standardized point plans. These have been used or adapted by thousands of organizations. They contain ready-made factor and degree definitions and point assessments for a wide range of jobs and can often be used with little or no modification. One survey of U.S. companies found that 93% of those using a ready-made plan rated it successful.

PROS AND CONS

Point systems have their advantages, as their wide use suggests. This is a quantitative technique that is easily explained to and used by employees. On the other hand, it can be difficult to develop a point plan, and this is one reason many organizations have opted for ready-made plans. In fact, the availability of a number of ready-made plans probably accounts in part for the wide use of point plans in job evaluation.

TABLE C-5 Evaluation Points Assigned to Factors and Degrees

	FIRST-DEGREE POINTS	SECOND-DEGREE POINTS	THIRD-DEGREE POINTS	FOURTH-DEGREE POINTS	FIFTH-DEGREE POINTS
Decision making	41	82	123	164	204
Problem solving	35	70	105	140	174
Knowledge	24	48	72	96	123

NOTES

1. For a discussion, see, for example, Roger Plachy, "The Point Factor Job Evaluation System: A Step-by-Step Guide, Part I," *Compensation & Benefits Review*, Vol. 19, no. 4 (July–August 1987), pp. 12–27; Roger Plachy, "The Case for Effective Point-Factor Job Evaluation, Viewpoint I," *Compensation & Benefits Review*, Vol. 19, no. 2 (March–April 1987), pp. 45–48; Roger Plachy, "The Point-Factor Job Evaluation System: A Step-by-Step Guide, Part II," *Compensation & Benefits Review*, Vol. 19, no. 5 (September–October 1987), pp. 9–24; and Alfred Candrilli and Ronald Armagast, "The Case for Effective Point-Factor Job Evaluation, Viewpoint II," *Compensation & Benefits Review*, Vol. 19, no. 2 (March–April 1987), pp. 49–54. See also Robert J. Sahl, "How to Install a Point-Factor Job Evaluation System," *Personnel*, Vol. 66, no. 3 (March 1989), pp. 38–42.

GLOSSARY

A

action learning A training technique by which management trainees are allowed to work full time analyzing and solving problems in other departments.

adverse impact The overall impact of employer practices that result in significantly higher percentages of members of minorities and other protected groups being rejected for employment, placement, or promotion.

affirmative action Steps that are taken for the purpose of eliminating the present effects of past discrimination.

Age Discrimination in Employment Act of 1967 The act prohibiting arbitrary age discrimination and specifically protecting individuals over 40 years old.

agency shop A form of union security in which employees who do not belong to the union must still pay union dues on the assumption that union efforts benefit all workers.

Albemarle Paper Company v. Moody Supreme Court case in which it was ruled that the validity of job tests must be documented and that employee performance standards must be unambiguous.

alternation ranking method Ranking employees from best to worst on a particular trait.

Americans with Disabilities Act (ADA) The act requiring employers to make reasonable accommodations for disabled employees, it prohibits discrimination against disabled persons.

annual bonus Plans that are designed to motivate short-term performance of managers and are tied to company profitability

application form The form that provides information on education, prior work record, and skills.

appraisal interview A discussion following a performance appraisal in which supervisor and employee discuss the employee's rating and possible remedial actions.

appraisal interview An interview in which the supervisor and subordinate review the appraisal and make plans to remedy deficiencies and reinforce strengths.

arbitration The most definitive type of third-party intervention, in which the arbitrator usually has the power to determine and dictate the settlement terms.

authority The right to make decisions, direct others' work, and give orders.

authorization cards In order to petition for a union election, the union must show that at least 30% of employees may be interested in being unionized. Employees indicate this interest by signing authorization cards.

B

bargaining unit The group of employees the union will be authorized to represent.

behavior modeling A training technique in which trainees are first shown good management techniques in a film, are then asked to play roles in a simulated situation, and are then given feedback and praise by their supervisor.

behaviorally anchored rating scale (BARS) An appraisal method that aims at combining the benefits of narrative critical incidents and quantified ratings by anchoring a quantified scale with specific narrative examples of good and poor performance.

benchmark job A job that is used to anchor the employer's pay scale and around which other jobs are arranged in order of relative worth.

benefits Indirect financial payments given to employees. They may include health and life insurance, vacation, pension, education plans, and discounts on company products, for instance.

bias The tendency to allow individual differences such as age, race, and sex to

675

affect the appraisal rates these employees receive.

bona fide occupational qualification (BFOQ) Requirement that an employee be of a certain religion, sex, or national origin where that is reasonably necessary to the organization's normal operation. Specified by the 1964 Civil Rights Act.

boycott The combined refusal by employees and other interested parties to buy or use the employer's products.

bumping/layoff procedures Detailed procedures that determine who will be laid off if no work is available; generally allow employees to use their seniority to remain on the job.

burnout The total depletion of physical and mental resources caused by excessive striving to reach an unrealistic work-related goal.

business necessity Justification for an otherwise discriminatory employment practice, provided there is an overriding legitimate business purpose.

business process reengineering (BPR) The redesign of business processes to achieve improvements in such measures of performance as cost, quality, service, and speed.

C

candidate-order error An error of judgment on the part of the interviewer due to interviewing one or more very good or very bad candidates just before the interview in question.

capital accumulation programs Long-term incentives most often reserved for senior executives. Six popular plans include stock options, stock appreciation rights, performance achievement plans, restricted stock plans, phantom stock plans, and book value plans.

career planning and development The deliberate process through which a person becomes aware of personal career-related attributes and the lifelong series of stages that contribute to his or her career fulfillment.

case study method A development method in which the manager is presented with a written description of an organizational problem to diagnose and solve.

central tendency A tendency to rate all employees the same way, such as rating them all average.

citations Summons informing employers and employees of the regulations and standards that have been violated in the workplace.

Civil Rights Act of 1991 (CRA 1991) It places burden of proof back on employers and permits compensatory and punitive damages.

Civil Rights Act This law makes it illegal to discriminate in employment because of race, color, religion, sex, or national origin.

classes Dividing jobs into classes based on a set of rules for each class, such as amount of independent judgment, skill, physical effort, and so forth, required for each class of jobs. Classes usually contain similar jobs—such as all secretaries.

classification (or grading) method A method for categorizing jobs into groups.

closed shop A form of union security in which the company can hire only union members. This was outlawed in 1947 but still exists in some industries (such as printing).

collective bargaining The process through which representatives of management and the union meet to negotiate a labor agreement.

comparable worth The concept by which women who are usually paid less than men can claim that men in comparable rather than strictly equal jobs are paid more.

compensable factor A fundamental, compensable element of a job, such as skills, effort, responsibility, and working conditions.

competitive advantage Any factors that allow an organization to differentiate its product or service from those of its competitors to increase market share.

computerized forecast The determination of future staff needs by projecting a firm's sales, volume of production, and personnel required to maintain this volume of output, using computers and software packages.

confrontation meetings A method for clarifying and bringing into the open intergroup misconceptions and problems so that they can be resolved.

content validity A test that is *content valid* is one in which the test contains a fair sample of the tasks and skills actually needed for the job in question.

corporate campaign An organized effort by the union that exerts pressure on the corporation by pressuring the company's other unions shareholders, directors, customers, creditors, and government agencies, often directly.

cost leadership The enterprise aims to become the low-cost leader in an industry.

criterion validity A type of validity based on showing that scores on the test are related to job performance.

critical incident method Keeping a record of uncommonly good or undesirable examples of an employee's work-related behavior and reviewing it with the employee at predetermined times.

cross-functional team A quality improvement team formed to address problems that cut across organizational boundaries.

cultural change A change in a company's shared values and aims.

D

Davis-Bacon Act A law passed in 1931 that sets wage rates for laborers employed by contractors working for the federal government.

deferred profit-sharing plan A plan in which a certain amount of profits is credited to each employee's account, payable at retirement, termination, or death.

defined benefit pension plan A plan that contains a formula for determining retirement benefits.

defined contribution plan A plan in which the employer's contribution to employees' retirement or savings funds is specified.

Department of Labor–job analysis Standardized method for rating, classifying, and comparing virtually every kind of job based on data, people, and things.

diary/logs Daily listings made by workers of every activity in which they engage along with the time each activity takes.

differentiation A firm seeks to be unique in its industry along dimensions that are widely valued by buyers.

directive interview An interview following a set sequence of questions.

discipline A procedure that corrects or punishes a subordinate because a rule or procedure has been violated.

dismissal Involuntary termination of an employee's employment with the firm.

disparate rejection rates One test for adverse impact in which it can be demonstrated that there is a discrepancy between rates of rejection of members of a protected group and of others.

downsizing Refers to the process of reducing, usually dramatically, the number of people employed by the firm.

E

early retirement window A type of golden offering by which employees are encouraged to retire early, the incentive being liberal pension benefits plus perhaps a cash payment.

economic strike A strike that results from a failure to agree on the terms of a contract that involve wages, benefits, and other conditions of employment.

employee advocacy HR must take responsibility for clearly defining how management should be treating employees, make sure employees have the mechanisms required to contest unfair practices, and represent the interests of employees within the framework of its primary obligation to senior management.

employee assistance program (EAP) A formal employer program for providing employees with counseling and/or treatment programs for problems such as alcoholism, gambling, or stress.

employee compensation All forms of pay or rewards going to employees and arising from their employment.

employee orientation A procedure for providing new employees with basic background information about the firm.

Employee Retirement Income Security Act (ERISA) Signed into law by President Ford in 1974 to require that pension rights be vested, and protected by a government agency, PBGC.

Employee Retirement Income Security Act (ERISA) The law that provides government protection of pensions for all employees with company pension plans. It also regulates vesting rights (employees who leave before retirement may claim compensation from the pension plan).

employee stock ownership plan (ESOP) A corporation contributes shares of its own stock to a trust in which additional contributions are made annually. The trust distributes the stock to employees on retirement or separation from service.

Equal Employment Opportunity Commission (EEOC) The commission, created by Title VII, is empowered to investigate job discrimination complaints and sue on behalf of complainants.

Equal Pay Act of 1963 An amendment to the Fair Labor Standards Act designed to require equal pay for women doing the same work as men.

Equal Pay Act of 1963 The act requiring equal pay for equal work, regardless of sex.

expectancy chart A graph showing the relationship between test scores and job performance for a large group of people.

F

factor comparison method A widely used method of ranking jobs according to a variety of skill and difficulty factors, then adding up these rankings to arrive at an overall numerical rating for each given job.

fair day's work Frederick Taylor's observation that haphazard setting of piecework requirements and wages by supervisors was not sufficient, and that careful study was needed to define acceptable production quotas for each job.

Fair Labor Standards Act Congress passed this act in 1936 to provide for minimum wages, maximum hours, overtime pay, and child labor protection. The law has been amended many times and covers most employees.

federal agency guidelines Guidelines issued by federal agencies charged with ensuring compliance with equal employment federal legislation explaining recommended employer procedures in detail.

flexible benefits program Individualized plans allowed by employers to accommodate employee preferences for benefits.

flextime A plan whereby employees build their workday around a core of midday hours.

Flexyears A work arrangement under which employees can choose (at six-month intervals) the number of hours they want to work each month over the next year.

forced distribution method Similar to grading on a curve; predetermined percentages of ratees are placed in various performance categories.

four-day workweek An arrangement that allows employees to work four ten-hour days instead of the more usual five eight-hour days.

functional control The authority exerted by an HR manager as coordinator of personnel activities.

functional job analysis A method for classifying jobs similar to the Department of Labor job analysis but additionally taking into account the extent to which instructions, reasoning, judgment, and verbal facility are necessary for performing job tasks.

functional team A quality improvement team composed of volunteers who typically work together as natural work units.

G

gainsharing plan An incentive plan that engages employees in a common effort to achieve productivity objectives and share the gains.

globalization The tendency of firms to extend their sales or manufacturing to new markets abroad.

golden offerings Offers to current employees aimed at encouraging them to retire early, perhaps even with the same pensions they would expect if they retired at, say, age 65.

good faith bargaining A term that means both parties are communicating and negotiating and that proposals are being matched with counterproposals with both parties making every reasonable effort to arrive at agreements. It does not mean that either party is compelled to agree to a proposal.

good faith effort strategy Employment strategy aimed at changing practices that have contributed in the past to excluding or underutilizing protected groups.

grade definition Written descriptions of the level of, say, responsibility and knowledge required by jobs in each grade. Similar jobs can then be combined into grades or classes.

grades A job classification system synonymous with class, although grades often contain dissimilar jobs, such as secretaries, mechanics, and firefighters. Grade descriptions are written based on compensable factors listed in classification systems, such as the federal classification system.

graphic rating scale A scale that lists a number of traits and a range of performance for each. The employee is then rated by identifying the score that best describes his or her level of performance for each trait.

grievance Any factor involving wages, hours, or conditions of employment that is used as a complaint against the employer.

Griggs v. The Duke Power Company Case heard by the Supreme Court in which the plaintiff argued that his employer's requirement that coal handlers be high school graduates was unfairly discriminatory. In finding for the plaintiff, the Court ruled that discrimination need not be overt to be illegal, that employment practices must be related to job performance, and that the burden of proof is on the employer to show that hiring standards are job related.

group life insurance Provides lower rates for the employer or employee and includes all employees, including new employees, regardless of health or physical condition.

guaranteed piecework plan The minimum hourly wage plus an incentive for each piece produced above a set number of pieces per hour.

H

halo effect In performance appraisal, the problem that occurs when a supervisor's rating of a subordinate on one trait biases the rating of that person on other traits.

health maintenance organization (HMO) A prepaid health care system that generally provides routine round-the- clock medical services as well as preventive medicine in a clinic-type arrangement for employees, who pay a nominal fee in addition to the fixed annual fee the employer pays.

human resource management The policies and practices one needs to carry out the "people" or human resource aspects of a management position, including recruiting, screening, training, rewarding, and appraising.

I

illegal bargaining items Items in collective bargaining that are forbidden by law; for example, the clause agreeing to hire "union members exclusively" would be illegal in a right-to-work state.

implied authority The authority exerted by a personnel manager by virtue of others' knowledge that he or she has access to top management (in areas like testing and affirmative action).

in-house development centers A company-based method for exposing prospective managers to realistic exercises to develop improved management skills.

insubordination Willful disregard or disobedience of the boss's authority or legitimate orders; criticizing the boss in public.

ISO 9000 The written standards for quality management and assurance of the International Organization for Standardization.

J

job analysis The procedure for determining the duties and skill requirements of a job and the kind of person who should be hired for it.

job description A list of a job's duties, responsibilities, reporting relationships, working conditions, and supervisory responsibilities—one product of a job analysis.

job evaluation A systematic comparison done in order to determine the worth of one job relative to another.

job instruction training (JIT) Listing of each job's basic tasks, along with key points in order to provide step-by-step training for employees.

job posting Publicizing an open job to employees (often by literally posting it on bulletin boards) and listing its attributes, like qualifications, supervisor, working schedule and pay rate.

job rotation A management training technique that involves moving a trainee from department to department to broaden his or her experience and identify strong and weak points.

job sharing A concept that allows two or more people to share a single full-time job.

job specification A list of a job's "human requirements," that is, the requisite education, skills, personality, and so on—another product of a job analysis.

job-related interview A series of job-related questions which focuses on relevant past job-related behaviors.

L

Landrum-Griffin Act The law aimed at protecting union members from possible wrongdoing on the part of their unions.

layoff A situation in which there is a temporary shortage of work and employees are told there is no work for them but that management intends to recall them when work is again available.

lead team A quality improvement team headed by a vice president or other manager that serves as a steering committee for all the teams that operate in its area.

line authority The authority exerted by a personnel manager by directing the activities of the people in his or her own department and in service areas (llike the plant cafeteria).

line manager A manager who is authorized to direct the work of subordinates and responsible for accomplishing the organization's goals.

lockout A refusal by the employer to provide opportunities to work.

M

Malcolm Baldridge Award An award created by the U.S. Department of Commerce to recognize quality efforts of U.S. companies.

management assessment centers A situation in which management candidates are asked to make decisions in hypothetical situations and are scored on their performance. It usually also involves testing and the use of management games.

management by objectives (MBO) Involves setting specific measurable goals with each employee and then periodically reviewing the progress made.

management development Any attempt to improve current or future management performance by imparting knowledge, changing attitudes, or increasing skills.

management game A development technique in which teams of managers compete with one another by making computerized decisions regarding realistic but simulated companies.

management process The five basic functions of planning, organizing, staffing, leading, and controlling.

mandatory bargaining items Items in collective bargaining that a party must bargain over if they are introduced by the other party—for example, pay.

mediation Intervention in which a neutral third party tries to assist the principals in reaching agreement.

merit pay (merit raise) Any salary increase awarded to an employee based on his or her individual performance.

Meritor Savings Bank, FSB v. Vinson U.S. Supreme Court's first decision on sexual harassment holding that existence of a hostile environment even without economic hardship is sufficient to prove harassment, even if participation was voluntary.

N

national emergency strikes Strikes that might "imperil the national health and safety."

National Labor Relations (or Wagner) Act This law banned certain types of unfair labor practices and provided for secret-ballot elections and majority rule for determining whether or not a firm's employees want to unionize

National Labor Relations Board (NLRB) The agency created by the Wagner Act to investigate unfair labor practice charges and to provide for secret-ballot elections and majority rule in determining whether or not a firm's employees want a union.

nondirective interview An unstructured conversational-style interview. The interviewer pursues points of interest as they come up in response to questions.

Norris-LaGuardia Act This law marked the beginning of the era of strong encouragement of unions and guaranteed to each employee the right to bargain collectively "free from interference, restraint, or coercion."

O

occupational market conditions The Bureau of Labor Statistics of the U.S. Department of Labor publishes projections of labor supply and demand for various occupations, as do other agencies.

Occupational Safety and Health Act The law passed by Congress in 1970 "to assure so far as possible every working man and woman in the nation safe and healthful working conditions and to preserve our human resources."

Occupational Safety and Health Administration (OSHA) The agency created within the Department of Labor to set safety and health standards for almost all workers in the United States.

Office of Federal Contract Compliance Programs (OFCCP) This office is responsible for implementing the executive orders and ensuring compliance of federal contractors.

on-the-job training (OJT) Training a person to learn a job while working at it.

open shop Perhaps the least attractive type of union security from the union's point of view, the workers decide whether or not to join the union; and those who join must pay dues.

opinion surveys Communication devices that use questionnaires to regularly ask employees their opinions about the company, management, and work life.

organizational development (OD) A method aimed at changing the attitudes, values, and beliefs of employees so that employees can improve the organization.

organizational development interventions HR-based techniques aimed at changing employees' attitudes, values, and behavior.

outplacement counseling A systematic process by which a terminated person is trained and counseled in the techniques of self-appraisal and securing a new position.

P

paired comparison method Ranking employees by making a chart of all possible pairs of the employees for each trait and indicating which is the better employee of the pair.

panel interview An interview in which a group of interviewers questions the applicant.

pay grade A pay grade is comprised of jobs of approximately equal difficulty.

Pension Benefits Guarantee Corporation (PBGC) Established under ERISA to ensure that pensions meet vesting obligations; also insures pensions should a plan terminate without sufficient funds to meet its vested obligations.

pension plans Plans that provide a fixed sum when employees reach a predetermined retirement age or when they can no longer work due to disability.

performance analysis Verifying that there is a performance deficiency and determining whether that deficiency should be rectified through training or through some other means (such as transferring the employee).

personnel replacement charts Company records showing present performance and promotability of inside candidates for the most important positions.

piecework A system of pay based on the number of items processed by each individual worker in a unit of time, such as items per hour or items per day.

plant closing law The Worker Adjustment and Retraining Notification Act, which requires notifying employees in the event an employer decides to close its facility.

point method The job evaluation method in which a number of compensable factors are identified and then the degree to which each of these factors is present on the job is determined.

position analysis questionnaire (PAQ) A questionnaire used to collect quantifiable data concerning the duties and responsibilities of various jobs.

position replacement card A card prepared for each position in a company to show possible replacement candidates and their qualifications.

Preferred Provider Organizations (PPOs) Groups of health care providers that contract with employers, insurance companies, or third-party payers to provide medical care services at a reduced fee.

Pregnancy Discrimination Act (PDA) An amendment to Title VII of the Civil Rights Act that prohibits sex discrimination based on "pregnancy, childbirth, or related medical conditions."

Pregnancy Discrimination Act (PDA) An amendment to Title VII of the Civil Rights Act that prohibits sex discrimination based on "pregnancy, childbirth, or related medical conditions." It requires employers to provide benefits—including sick leave and disability benefits and health and medical insurance—the same as for any employee not able to work because of disability.

preretirement counseling Counseling provided to employees who are about to retire, which covers matters such as benefits advice, second careers, and so on.

profit-sharing plan A plan whereby most employees share in the company's profits.

programmed learning A systematic method for teaching job skills involving presenting questions or facts, allowing the person to respond, and giving the learner immediate feedback on the accuracy of his or her answers.

protected class Persons such as minorities and women protected by equal opportunity laws including Title VII.

Q

qualifications inventories Manual or computerized systematic records listing employees' education, career and development interests, languages, special skills, and so on to be used in forecasting inside candidates for promotion.

quota strategy Employment strategy aimed at mandating the same results as the good faith effort strategy through specific hiring and promotion restrictions.

R

ranking method The simplest method of job evaluation that involves ranking each job relative to all other jobs, usually based on overall difficulty.

rate ranges A series of steps or levels within a pay grade, usually based upon years of service.

ratio analysis A forecasting technique for determining future staff needs by using ratios between sales volume and number of employees needed.

reality shock Results of a period that may occur at the initial career entry when the new employee's high job expectations confront the reality of a boring, unchallenging job.

reliability The characteristic that refers to the consistency of scores obtained by the same person when retested with the identical or equivalent tests.

restricted policy Another test for adverse impact, involving demonstration that an employer's hiring practices exclude a protected group, whether intentionally or not.

retirement The point at which a person gives up one's work, usually between the ages of 60 to 65, but increasingly earlier today due to firms' early retirement incentive plans.

reverse discrimination Claim that due to affirmative action quota systems, white males are discriminated against.

rings of defense An alternative layoff plan in which temporary supplemental employees are hired with the understanding that they may be laid off at any time.

role playing A training technique in which trainees act out the parts of people in a realistic management situation.

S

salary survey A survey aimed at determining prevailing wage rates. A good salary survey provides specific wage rates for specific jobs. Formal written questionnaire surveys are the most comprehensive, but telephone surveys and newspaper ads are also sources of information.

Scanlon plan An incentive plan developed in 1937 by Joseph Scanlon and designed to encourage cooperation, involvement, and sharing of benefits.

scatter plot A graphical method used to help identify the relationship between two variables.

scientific management The careful, scientific study of the job for the purpose of boosting productivity and job satisfaction.

self-directed team A work team that uses consensus decision making to choose its own team members, solve job-related problems, design its own jobs, and schedule its own break time.

sensitivity training A method for increasing employees' insights into their own behavior by candid discussions in groups led by special trainers.

severance pay A one-time payment some employers provide when terminating an employee.

sexual harassment Harassment on the basis of sex that has the purpose or effect of substantially interfering with a person's work performance or creating an intimidating, hostile, or offensive work environment.

sick leave Provides pay to an employee when he or she is out of work because of illness.

situational interview A series of job-related questions which focuses on how the candidate would behave in a given situation.

social security Provides three types of benefits: retirement income at the age of 62 and thereafter; survivor's or death benefits payable to the employee's dependents regardless of age at time of death; and disability benefits payable to disabled employees and their dependents. These benefits are payable only if the employee is insured under the Social Security Act.

speak up! programs Communications programs that allow employees to register questions, concerns, and complaints about work-related matters.

spot bonus A spontaneous incentive awarded to individuals for accomplishments not readily measured by a standard.

staff manager A manager who assists and advises line managers.

standard hour plan A plan by which a worker is paid a basic hourly rate but is paid an extra percentage of his or her base rate for production exceeding the standard per hour or per day. Similar to piecework payment but based on a percent premium.

stock option The right to purchase a stated number of shares of a company stock at today's price at some time in the future.

straight piecework plan Under this pay system each worker receives a set payment for each piece produced or processed in a factory or shop.

strategic change A change in a company's strategy, mission, and vision.

stress interview An interview in which the applicant is made uncomfortable by a series of often rude questions. This technique helps identify hypersensitive applicants and those with low or high stress tolerance.

strictness/leniency The problem that occurs when a supervisor has a tendency to rate all subordinates either high or low.

structural change The reorganizing-redesigning of an organization's departmentalization, coordination, span of control, reporting relationships, or centralization of decision making.

structured sequential interview An interview in which the applicant is interviewed sequentially by several persons and each rates the applicant on a standard form.

succession planning A process through which senior-level openings are planned for and eventually filled.

supplemental pay benefits Benefits for time not worked such as unemployment insurance, vacation and holiday pay, and sick pay.

supplemental unemployment benefits Provide for a "guaranteed annual income" in certain industries where employers must shut down to change machinery or due to reduced work. These benefits are paid by the company and supplement unemployment benefits.

survey research A method that involves surveying employees' attitudes and providing feedback to the work groups as a basis for problem analysis and action planning.

sympathy strike A strike that takes place when one union strikes in support of the strike of another.

T

Taft-Hartley Act Also known as the Labor Management Relations Act, this law prohibited union unfair labor practices and enumerated the rights of employees as union members. It also enumerated the rights of employers.

task analysis A detailed study of a job to identify the skills required so that an appropriate training program may be instituted.

team building Improving the effectiveness of teams such as corporate officers and division directors through use of consultants, interviews, and team-building meetings.

team or group incentive plan A plan in which a production standard is set for a specific work group, and its members are paid incentives if the group exceeds the production standard.

technological change Modifications to the work methods an organization uses to accomplish its tasks.

Telecommuting A work arrangement in which employees work at remote locations, usually at home, using video displays, computers, and other telecommunications equipment to carry out their responsibilities.

termination at will The idea, based in law, that the employment relationship can be terminated at will by either the employer or the employee for any reason.

termination interview The interview in which an employee is informed of the fact that he or she has been dismissed.

test validity The accuracy with which a test, interview, and so on measures what it purports to measure or fulfills the function it was designed to fill.

Title VII of the 1964 Civil Rights Act The section of the act that says an employer cannot discriminate on the basis of race, color, religion, sex, or national origin with respect to employment.

top-down programs Communications activities including in-house television centers, frequent roundtable discussions, and in-house newsletters that provide continuing opportunities for the firm to let all employees be updated on important matters regarding the firm.

total quality management (TQM) A type of program aimed at maximizing customer satisfaction through continuous improvements.

training The process of teaching new employees the basic skills they need to perform their jobs.

trend analysis Study of a firm's past employment needs over a period of years to predict future needs.

U

unclear performance standards An appraisal scale that is too open to interpretation; instead include descriptive phrases that define each trait and what is meant by standards like "good" or "unsatisfactory."

unemployment insurance Provides weekly benefits if a person is unable to work through some fault other than his or her own.

unfair labor practice strike A strike aimed at protesting illegal conduct by the employer.

union salting Refers to a union organizing tactic by which workers who are in fact employed full-time by a union as undercover organizers are hired by unwitting employers.

union shop A form of union security in which the company can hire nonunion people but they must join the union after a prescribed period of time and pay dues. (If they do not, they can be fired.)

unsafe acts Behavior tendencies and undesirable attitudes that cause accidents.

unsafe conditions The mechanical and physical conditions that cause accidents.

V

variable pay Any plan (but usually a group plan) that ties pay to productivity or profitability, usually as one-time lump payments.

vestibule simulated training Training employees on special off-the-job equipment, as in airplane pilot training, whereby training costs and hazards can be reduced.

vesting Provision that money placed in a pension fund cannot be forfeited for any reason.

Vietnam Era Veterans' Readjustment Act of 1974 An act requiring that employers with government contracts take affirmative action to hire disabled veterans.

Vocational Rehabilitation Act of 1973 The act requiring certain federal contractors to take affirmative action for disabled persons.

voluntary bargaining items Items in collective bargaining over which bargaining is neither illegal nor mandatory—neither party can be compelled against its wishes to negotiate over those items.

voluntary reduction in pay plan An alternative to layoffs in which all employees agree to reductions in pay to keep everyone working.

voluntary time off An alternative to layoffs in which some employees agree to take time off to reduce the employer's payroll and avoid the need for a layoff.

W

wage curve Shows the relationship between the value of the job and the average wage paid for this job.

Walsh-Healey Public Contract Act A law enacted in 1936 that requires minimum-wage and working conditions for employees working on any government contract amounting to more than $10,000.

Wards Cove v. Atonio U.S. Supreme Court decision that makes it difficult to prove a case of unlawful discrimination against an employer.

wildcat strike An unauthorized strike occurring during the term of a contract.

work samples Actual job tasks used in testing applicants' performance.

work sampling technique A testing method based on measuring performance on actual basic job tasks.

worker's compensation Provides income and medical benefits to work-related accident victims or their dependents regardless of fault.

wrongful discharge An employee dismissal that does not comply with the law or does not comply with the contractual arrangement stated or implied by the firm via its employment application forms, employee manuals, or other promises.

PHOTO CREDITS

NAME AND ORGANIZATION INDEX

SUBJECT INDEX

www.prenhall.com/dessler www.prenhall.com/dessler
www.prenhall.com/dessler www.prenhall.com/dessler
www.prenhall.com/dessler www.prenhall.com/dessler
www.prenhall.com/dessler www.prenhall.com/dessler
www.prenhall.com/dessler www.prenhall.com/dessler
www.prenhall.com/dessler www.prenhall.com/dessler
www.prenhall.com/dessler www.prenhall.com/dessler
www.prenhall.com/dessler www.prenhall.com/dessler
www.prenhall.com/dessler www.prenhall.com/dessler
www.prenhall.com/dessler www.prenhall.com/dessler
www.prenhall.com/dessler www.prenhall.com/dessler
www.prenhall.com/dessler www.prenhall.com/dessler
www.prenhall.com/dessler www.prenhall.com/dessler
www.prenhall.com/dessler www.prenhall.com/dessler
www.prenhall.com/dessler www.prenhall.com/dessler
www.prenhall.com/dessler www.prenhall.com/dessler
www.prenhall.com/dessler www.prenhall.com/dessler
www.prenhall.com/dessler www.prenhall.com/dessler
www.prenhall.com/dessler www.prenhall.com/dessler
www.prenhall.com/dessler www.prenhall.com/dessler
www.prenhall.com/dessler www.prenhall.com/dessler
www.prenhall.com/dessler www.prenhall.com/dessler
www.prenhall.com/dessler www.prenhall.com/dessler